P9-CCA-564

ELEMENTS OF WRITING

JAMES L. KINNEAVY
JOHN E. WARRINER

First Course

Holt, Rinehart and Winston
Harcourt Brace Jovanovich

Austin • Orlando • San Diego • Chicago • Dallas • Toronto

Critical Readers

Grateful acknowledgment is made to the following critical readers who reviewed pre-publication materials for this book:

John Algeo
University of Georgia
Athens, Georgia

Alice Bartley
Byrd Middle School
Henrico County, Virginia

Elaine A. Espindle
Peabody Veterans Memorial High School
Peabody, Massachusetts

Merry Anne Hilty
Heskett Middle School
Bedford, Ohio

Janet Hoeltzel
Union Seventh Grade Center
Broken Arrow, Oklahoma

Carolyn Kavanagh
East Flagstaff Junior High School
Flagstaff, Arizona

Rebecca Hight Miller
Westridge Middle School
Orlando, Florida

Patty Sais
Truman Middle School
Albuquerque, New Mexico

Martha Teague Weaver
Cullman Middle School
Cullman, Alabama

Acknowledgments: See pages 935–940, which are an extension of the copyright page.

Printed in the United States of America

ISBN 0-03-047142-7

6 7 8 9 045 95

Authors

James L. Kinneavy, the Jane and Roland Blumberg Centennial Professor of English at The University of Texas at Austin, directed the development and writing of the composition strand in the program. He is the author of *A Theory of Discourse* and coauthor of *Writing in the Liberal Arts Tradition*. Professor Kinneavy is a leader in the field of rhetoric and composition and a respected educator whose teaching experience spans all levels—elementary, secondary, and college. He has continually been concerned with teaching writing to high school students.

John E. Warriner developed the organizational structure for the Handbook of Grammar, Usage, and Mechanics in the book. He coauthored the *English Workshop* series, was general editor of the *Composition: Models and Exercises* series, and editor of *Short Stories: Characters in Conflict*. He taught English for thirty-two years in junior and senior high school and college.

Writers and Editors

Ellen Ashdown has a Ph.D. in English from the University of Florida. She has taught composition and literature at the college level. She is a professional writer of educational materials and has published articles and reviews on education and art.

Norbert Elliot has a Ph.D in English from the University of Tennessee. A director of the writing program at New Jersey Institute of Technology, he is a specialist in test development and writing assessment.

Mary Hix has an M.A. in English from Wake Forest University. She has taught freshman composition courses. She is a professional writer and editor of educational materials in language arts.

Madeline Travers-Hovland has a Master of Arts in Teaching from Harvard University. She has taught English in elementary and secondary school and has been an elementary school librarian. She is a professional writer of educational materials in literature and composition.

Alice M. Sohn has a Ph.D. in English Education from Florida State University. She has taught English in middle school, secondary school, and college. She has been a writer and editor of educational materials in language arts for twelve years.

Patricia Street was an honor's major in English Expression at Brown University. A professional writer for twenty-five years and a writer/editor of educational materials in language arts for five years, she is currently compiling a reference book for writers.

Acknowledgments

We wish to thank the following teachers who participated in field testing of pre-publication materials for this series:

Susan Almand-Myers
Meadow Park Intermediate School
Beaverton, Oregon

Theresa L. Bagwell
Naylor Middle School
Tucson, Arizona

Ruth Bird
Freeport High School
Sarver, Pennsylvania

Joan M. Brooks
Central Junior High School
Guymon, Oklahoma

Candice C. Bush
J. D. Smith Junior High School
N. Las Vegas, Nevada

Mary Jane Childs
Moore West Junior High School
Oklahoma City, Oklahoma

Brian Christensen
Valley High School
West Des Moines, Iowa

Lenise Christopher
Western High School
Las Vegas, Nevada

Mary Ann Crawford
Ruskin Senior High School
Kansas City, Missouri

Linda Dancy
Greenwood Lakes Middle School
Lake Mary, Florida

Elaine A. Espindle
Peabody Veterans Memorial High School
Peabody, Massachusetts

Joan Justice
North Middle School
O'Fallon, Missouri

Beverly Kahwaty
Pueblo High School
Tucson, Arizona

Lamont Leon
Van Buren Junior High School
Tampa, Florida

Susan Lusch
Fort Zumwalt South High School
St. Peters, Missouri

Michele K. Lyall
Rhodes Junior High School
Mesa, Arizona

Belinda Manard
McKinley Senior High School
Canton, Ohio

Nathan Masterson
Peabody Veterans Memorial High School
Peabody, Massachusetts

Marianne Mayer
Swope Middle School
Reno, Nevada

Penne Parker
Greenwood Lakes Middle School
Lake Mary, Florida

Amy Ribble
Gretna Junior-Senior High School
Gretna, Nebraska

Kathleen R. St. Clair
Western High School
Las Vegas, Nevada

Carla Sankovich
Billinghurst Middle School
Reno, Nevada

Sheila Shaffer
Cholla Middle School
Phoenix, Arizona

Joann Smith
Lehman Junior High School
Canton, Ohio

Margie Stevens
Raytown Middle School
Raytown, Missouri

Mary Webster
Central Junior High School
Guymon, Oklahoma

Susan M. Yentz
Oviedo High School
Oviedo, Florida

Contents in Brief

Table of Contents

PART ONE WRITING

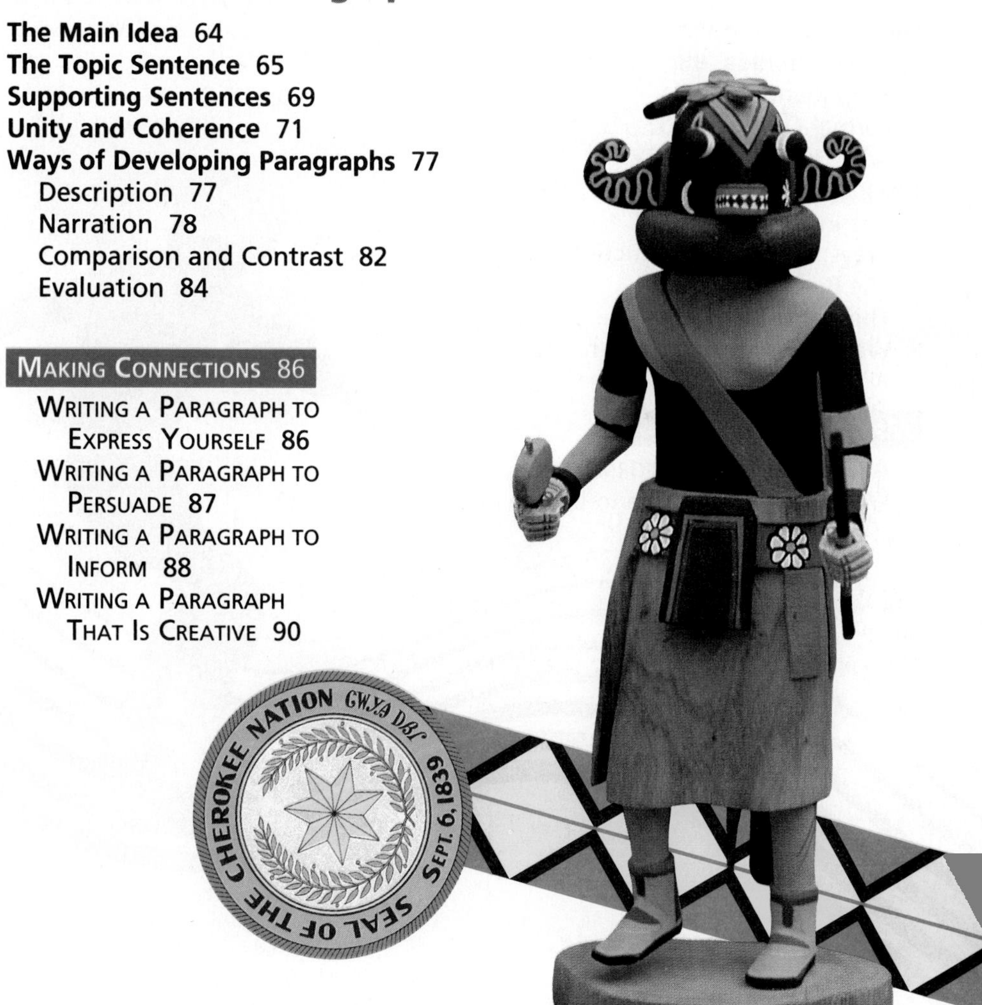
CHEROKEE NATION GWYA DBP
SEPT. 6, 1839
SEAL OF THE

CHAPTER 4 EXPRESSIVE WRITING 114

NASA

CHAPTER 8 WRITING TO PERSUADE 242

CHAPTER 11 WRITING EFFECTIVE SENTENCES 354

CHAPTER 12 ENGLISH: ORIGINS AND USES 379

PART TWO HANDBOOK

Roberto Clemente
Pittsburgh Pirates

CHAPTER 15 THE PARTS OF SPEECH 443

CHAPTER 16 COMPLEMENTS 472

CHAPTER 17 THE PHRASE 489

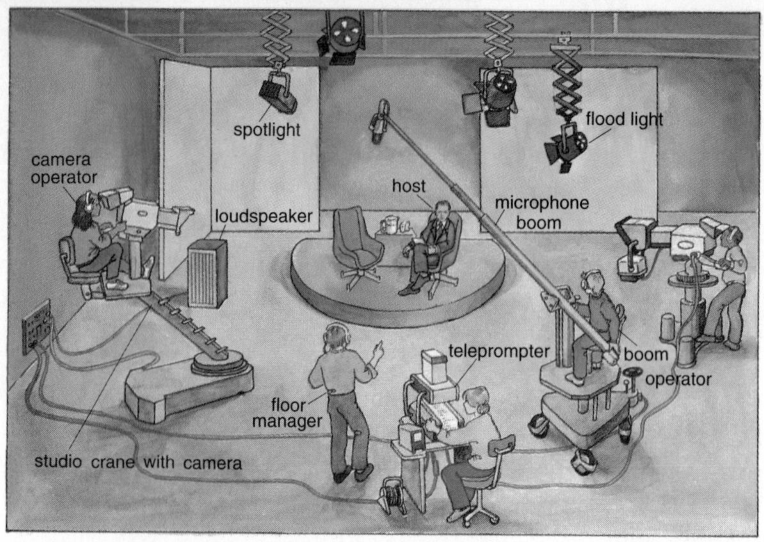
spotlight
flood light
camera operator
host
loudspeaker
microphone boom
teleprompter
boom operator
floor manager
studio crane with camera

HARDWARE
FLOWERS
BRANCH LIBRARY
MUSIC
FRUITS VEGETABLES
DELI
CLEA
FRESH PRODUCE
AMBULANCE
HOT DOGS
SUBWAY

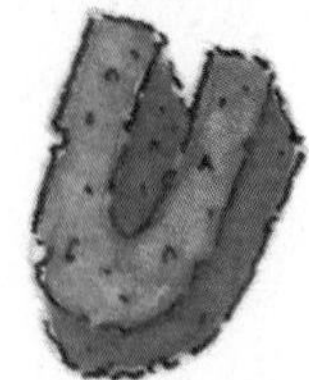

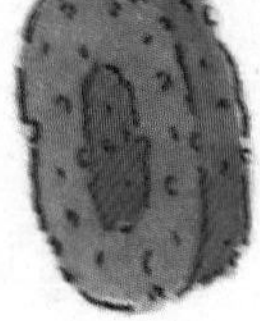

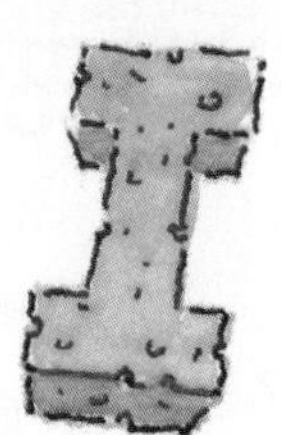

Improving Your Spelling

PART THREE RESOURCES

CHAPTER 30 LISTENING 808

Strategies for Active Listening

throw in
offside
free kick
corner kick

Models

Fiction

Arna Bontemps, *Chariot in the Sky: A Story of the Jubilee Singers*
Mona Gardner, "The Dinner Party"
Virginia Hamilton, *A White Romance, Willie Bea and the Time the Martians Landed*
Rudyard Kipling, "Rikki-tikki-tavi"
Barry Lopez, "Coyote Places the Stars"
Gary Paulsen, *Hatchet*
Marjorie Kinnan Rawlings, *The Yearling*
Mari Sandoz, "Winter Thunder"
George Shannon, "A Drink for Crow," *Stories to Solve*
Virginia Driving Hawk Sneve, "The Medicine Bag"
Gary Soto, "The Jacket," "The Marble Champ"
Mildred Taylor, *Roll of Thunder, Hear My Cry*
Yoshiko Uchida, *A Jar of Dreams*

Nonfiction

"A Doll Made to Order," *Newsweek*
"Ubuhlali and Umnaka—Beaded Necklaces and Bangles," *African Crafts*
Dan Carlinsky, "Kites"
Michael DiLeo, "Dream of the Blue Dolphins," *American Way*
Lonnie Dyer, "Kachinas: Sacred Drama of the Hopis"
Wallace H. Black Elk and William S. Lyon, *Black Elk: The Sacred Ways of a Lakota*
Delia Ephron, "How to Eat Like a Child"
Anthony Glass, *Journal of an Indian Trader*
Whitney Hair, "Cures from the Jungle," *Ranger Rick*
Fred Johnson, *Meet-a-Cheetah*
Gary Johnson, "A Son's Challenge"
Marjorie Lamb, "One Day a Month, Go Without Meat," *2 Minutes a Day for a Greener Planet*
Gary Larson, *The PreHistory of the Far Side*
John G. Neihardt, *Black Elk Speaks*
Dudley Randall, "Questions and Answers"
Sally Ride with Susan Okie, "Weightless in Space," *To Space and Back*
Carson I. A. Ritchie, *Insects, The Creeping Conquerors and Human History*
Louise L. Sherman, "A Review of Lois Lowry's *Number the Stars*"
Monica Sone, *Nisei Daughter*
James P. Terzian and Kathryn Cramer, *Mighty Hard Road*
Greg Walz-Chojnacki, "The Spaceport Mermaids," *Odyssey*
Eudora Welty, *One Writer's Beginnings*
Eliot Wigginton, *I Wish I Could Give My Son a Wild Raccoon*
Elizabeth Yates, *My Diary—My World*

Poetry

Matsuo Basho, *Haiku*
Robert Frost, "Stopping by Woods on a Snowy Evening"
Ted Hughes, "My Aunt"

PART ONE

WRITING

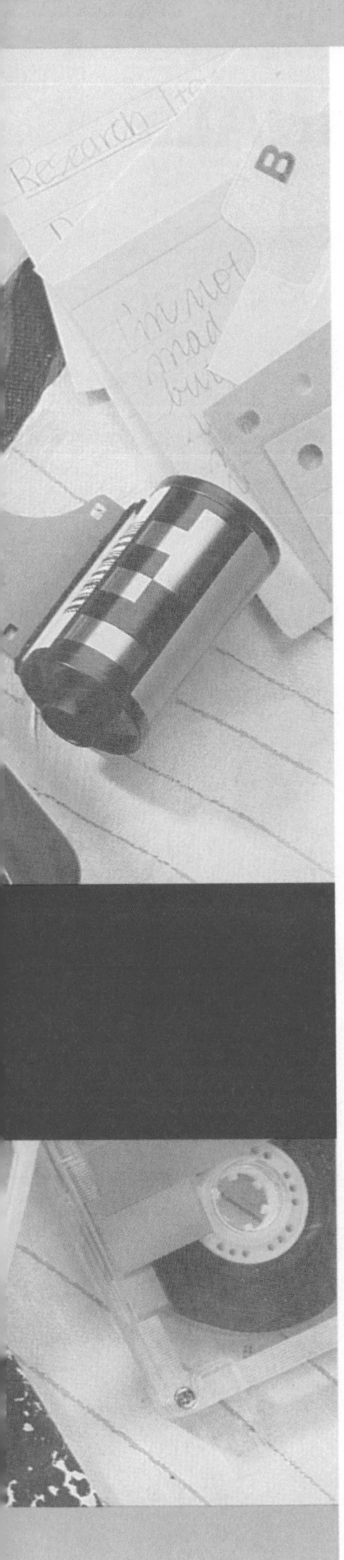

Introduction To Writing

Calling the Signals

Process and Structure

1 Writing and Thinking
2 Learning About Paragraphs
3 Learning About Compositions

Aims For Writing

4 Expressive Writing
5 Using Description
6 Creative Writing
7 Writing to Inform
8 Writing to Persuade
9 Writing About Literature
10 Writing a Report

Language and Style

11 Writing Effective Sentences
12 English: Origins and Uses

INTRODUCTION TO WRITING

CALLING THE SIGNALS

James L. Kinneavy

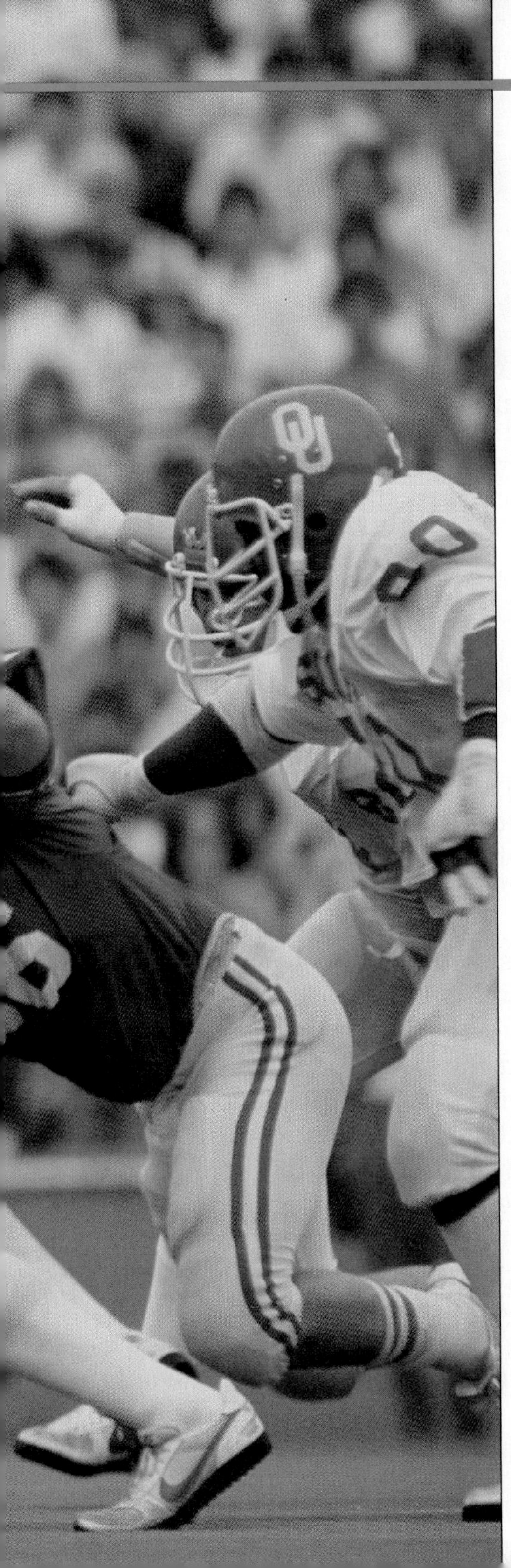

The quarterback looks up at the game clock. Nine seconds to go. An anxious buzz fills the stands as the fans desperately hope for a last-minute miracle. "22!" the quarterback calls out, quickly glancing around to make sure that the team is in place. "Red—44—Hup!" The defensive line digs in, pawing the ground like a herd of raging bulls. A running back moves quickly across the field behind the line. "Hup! Hup!" the quarterback yells. He takes the ball from the center. Helmets and pads crash as both teams struggle for precious ground.

The quarterback set the play in motion. But he was just the instrument. Where did it all really begin? Who was really **calling the signals**?

The Signal Callers

Long before football season opened, players and coaches labored over the hundreds of pages that make up the team's playbook. The big play didn't begin on the field. Someone planned it. Someone wrote it down. And then—at long last—the players put all that writing into action on the playing field.

It's this way with almost everything that happens in life—from the very simplest things to the most complicated. Writers call many of the signals.

Movie actors and TV stars act out what someone else has first written. Singers sing notes and lyrics that are scored on paper. Scientists record the results of their experiments on paper. Politicians are elected because they make convincing speeches—speeches that are often written by someone else. And the laws they help pass after they're elected are all written down. Even most of the world's religions are based on the written word.

Is writing calling your signals? Probably. Have you ever bought anything after seeing it advertised? Somebody wrote the words that persuaded you. How did you learn that new computer game? Did you read the instructions? Somebody wrote them. Have you ever tried out for a sport? Somebody wrote the announcement about the time and place of the tryouts. Somebody wrote the words you're reading now!

Writers are people with power. They call the signals.

What's the Power?

All *writers* share the same power—the power of communication. They all have something to say (a ***subject***), someone to say it to (an ***audience***), and a way to say it (a ***language***). You can have this power of communication, too. Try to think of communication as a triangle. Language—both written and spoken—is at the center.

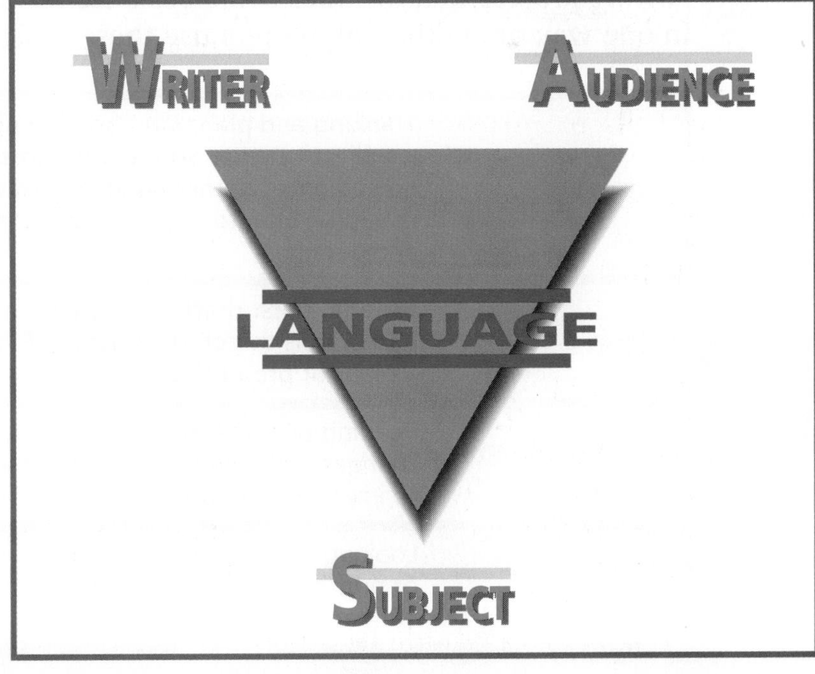

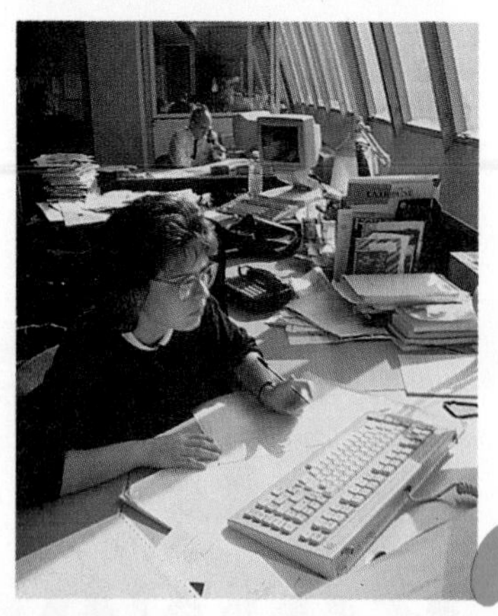

How Do Writers Communicate?

The Writing Process

Powerful communicators know that planning is the key to good writing. Planning helps writers develop their ideas and then communicate them in a way that readers will understand and enjoy. Planning is an important part of a ***writing process*** that includes some basic steps, or stages. In one way or another, all writers use these basic steps.

Prewriting	Thinking and planning—coming up with a subject to write about, a purpose, and an audience; gathering ideas and details, making a plan for presenting ideas and details
Writing	Writing a first draft—using sentences and paragraphs to get ideas across; following a plan for presenting ideas
Evaluating and Revising	Reading over the draft to see what changes are needed; making changes to improve the draft
Proofreading and Publishing	Looking for and fixing mistakes; writing or printing out a final copy; sharing it with an audience

Why Do Writers Write?

The Aims of Writing

Writers almost always have some purpose in mind for writing. They know what they want to accomplish before they start. All writing has one or more of four basic ***aims***, or purposes. These are to inform, to persuade, to express yourself, and to be creative.

To Inform	Writers may give facts and other kinds of information, or they may explain something.
To Persuade	Writers sometimes try to persuade other people. They want readers to think about something differently or to take action.
To Express Themselves	Often, writers write just to express their own feelings and thoughts.
To Be Creative	Writers may also write to be creative. They create stories, poems, songs, and plays.

On the next few pages are four models. Each one is about a girl named Lupe. However, the models are all different because each has a different aim. Notice how the aim shapes what the writers say and how they say it.

PERSUASIVE WRITING

Dear Lupe,

What's this I hear about your being down in the dumps because you think you're no good at sports? If you want to be a sports champion, moping won't get you there. But I can tell you what will.

First of all, think what you do best. What are your strong points? Find a sport that'll let you use your talents. You're intelligent. You think out your problems and overcome them. You've got a lot of determination. And, you've never minded competing. These are all talents that make you a winner.

Remember, Lupe, champions aren't all muscle and sweat. There are sports that need smart, spirited people like you. Look around. Find one that suits your talents. Then everyone will know what I know. Lupe's a winner!

Keep me posted. There's a sport out there that's just right for you. Use your talents. Go for it.

Love,
Grandpa

Reader's Response

1. Do you think that anyone can become good in at least one sport by trying hard enough? Why or why not?
2. What reasons does Grandpa use to convince Lupe she can be good at a sport? Do his reasons convince you?

EXPRESSIVE WRITING

I did it! I won! I'm the new playground marble champion. My back's killing me and my thumb's so sore I can hardly write, but I guess I've found my sport.

I felt pretty good in all the matches except the last girls' match. The girl looked really tough to beat. She was. I'm not sure how I did it. Then I had to face the boys' winner.

Was I ever scared! It wasn't as bad as I thought it would be, though.

I got two big trophies. A guy from the newspaper took my picture and wrote down some things about me. It's supposed to be in the paper tomorrow. I can't wait. Grandpa'll be so proud. People kept congratulating me, even when we went out for pizza to celebrate. It was kind of embarrassing to get so much attention, but it was fun.

It was a great day. I won two sports trophies and met some nice people and even made new friends. Everybody was super nice to me. It was one of the best days ever.

Reader's Response

1. How would you feel if you won a tournament, as Lupe did?
2. Who is writing this journal entry? What are Lupe's thoughts and feelings about her victory?

Local girl wins marble tournament

Twelve-year-old Lupe Medrano of 127 Broad Street is this year's winner of the annual Playground Marble Tournament. The tournament, sponsored by the Fresno Marble Association, was held yesterday at the city playground.

Lupe, a seventh-grade student at Central Middle School, first defeated a long series of opponents to win the girls' division. She then played and defeated the winner of the boys' division to win the championship.

Lupe admitted she had never played marbles until two weeks ago. She said she trained by doing fingertip push-ups to strengthen her wrists, and by squeezing an eraser to strengthen her thumb. "I also practiced for hours every day," she said.

The head referee and the president of the Fresno Marble Association presented Lupe with her two trophies.

Reader's Response

1. Have you ever been in any kind of tournament? Can you tell your classmates something about tournaments that this article doesn't tell?
2. Does this article mostly give facts about Lupe and the tournament, or does it express the writer's feelings? How can you recognize the writer's aim?

CREATIVE WRITING

The Marble Champ

by Gary Soto

Lupe Medrano, a shy girl who spoke in whispers, was the school's spelling bee champion, winner of the reading contest at the public library three summers in a row, blue ribbon awardee in the science fair, the top student at her piano recital, and the playground grand champion in chess. She was a straight-A student and—not counting kindergarten, when she had been stung by a wasp—never missed one day of elementary school. She had received a small trophy for this honor and had been congratulated by the mayor.

But though Lupe had a razor-sharp mind, she could not make her body, no matter how much she tried, run as fast as the other girls'. She begged her body to move faster, but could never beat anyone in the fifty-yard dash.

The truth was that Lupe was no good in sports. She could not catch a pop-up or figure out in which direction to kick the soccer ball. One time she kicked the ball at her own goal and scored a point for the other team. She was no good at baseball or basketball either, and even had a hard time making a hula hoop stay on her hips.

It wasn't until last year, when she was eleven years old, that she learned how to ride a bike. And even then she had to use training wheels. She could walk in the swimming pool but couldn't swim, and chanced roller skating only when her father held her hand.

"I'll never to be good at sports," she fumed one rainy day as she lay on her bed gazing at the shelf her father had made to hold her awards. "I wish I could win something, anything, even marbles."

At the word "marbles," she sat up. "That's it. Maybe I could be good at playing marbles." She hopped out of bed and rummaged through the closet until she found a can full of her brother's marbles. She poured the rich glass treasure on her bed and picked five of the most beautiful marbles.

She smoothed her bedspread and practiced shooting, softly at first so that her aim would be accurate. The marble rolled from her thumb and clicked against the targeted marble. But the target wouldn't budge. She tried again and again. Her aim became accurate, but the power from her thumb made the marble move only an inch or two. Then she realized that the bedspread was slowing the marbles. She also had to admit that her thumb was weaker than the neck of a newborn chick.

She looked out the window. The rain was letting up, but the ground was too muddy to play. She sat cross-legged on the bed, rolling her five marbles between her palms. Yes, she thought, I could play marbles, and marbles is a sport. At that moment she realized that she had only two weeks to practice. The playground championship, the same one her brother had entered the previous year, was coming up. She had a lot to do.

To strengthen her wrists, she decided to do twenty push-ups on her fingertips, five at a time. "One, two, three . . ." she groaned. By the end of the first set she was breathing hard, and her muscles burned from exhaustion. She did one more set and decided that was enough push-ups for the first day.

She squeezed a rubber eraser one hundred times, hoping it would strengthen her thumb. This seemed to work because the next day her thumb was sore. She could hardly hold a marble in her hand, let alone send it flying with power. So Lupe rested that day and listened to her brother, who gave her tips on how to shoot: get low, aim with one eye, and place one knuckle on the ground.

"Think 'eye and thumb'—and let it rip!" he said.

After school the next day she left her homework in her backpack and practiced three hours straight, taking time only to eat a candy bar for energy. With a popsicle stick, she drew an odd-shaped circle and tossed in four marbles. She used her shooter, a milky agate with hypnotic swirls, to blast them. Her thumb *had* become stronger.

After practice, she squeezed the eraser for an hour. She ate dinner with her left hand to spare her shooting hand and said nothing to her parents about her dreams of athletic glory.

Practice, practice, practice. Squeeze, squeeze, squeeze. Lupe got better and beat her brother and Alfonso, a neighbor kid who was supposed to be a champ.

"Man, she's bad!" Alfonso said. "She can beat the other girls for sure. I think."

The weeks passed quickly. Lupe worked so hard that one day, while she was drying dishes, her mother asked why her thumb was swollen.

"It's muscle," Lupe explained. "I've been practicing for the marbles championship."

"You, honey?" Her mother knew Lupe was no good at sports.

"Yeah. I beat Alfonso, and he's pretty good."

That night, over dinner, Mrs. Medrano said, "Honey, you should see Lupe's thumb."

"Huh?" Mr. Medrano said, wiping his mouth and looking at his daughter.

"Show your father."

"Do I have to?" an embarrassed Lupe asked.

"Go on, show your father."

Reluctantly, Lupe raised her hand and flexed her thumb. You could see the muscle.

The father put down his fork and asked, "What happened?"

"Dad, I've been working out. I've been squeezing an eraser."

"Why?"

"I'm going to enter the marbles championship."

Her father looked at her mother and then back at his daughter. "When is it, honey?"

"This Saturday. Can you come?"

The father had been planning to play racquetball with a friend Saturday, but he said he would be there. He knew his daughter thought she was no good at sports and he wanted to encourage her. He even rigged some lights in the backyard so she could practice after dark. He squatted with one knee on the ground, entranced by the sight of his daughter easily beating her brother.

The day of the championship began with a cold blustery sky. The sun was a silvery light behind slate clouds.

"I hope it clears up," her father said, rubbing his hands together as he returned from getting the newspaper. They ate breakfast, paced nervously around the house waiting for 10:00 to arrive, and walked the two blocks to the playground (though Mr. Medrano wanted to drive so Lupe wouldn't get tired). She signed up and was assigned her first match on baseball diamond number three.

Lupe, walking between her brother and her father, shook from the cold, not nerves. She took off her mittens, and everyone stared at her thumb. Someone asked, "How can you play with a broken thumb?" Lupe smiled and said nothing.

She beat her first opponent easily, and felt sorry for the girl because she didn't have anyone to cheer for her. Except for her sack of marbles, she was all alone. Lupe invited the girl, whose name was Rachel, to stay with them. She smiled and said, "OK." The four of them walked to a card table in the middle of the outfield, where Lupe was assigned another opponent.

She also beat this girl, a fifth-grader named Yolanda, and asked her to join their group. They proceeded to more matches and more wins, and soon there was a crowd of people following Lupe to the finals to play a girl in a baseball cap. This girl seemed dead serious. She never even looked at Lupe.

"I don't know, Dad, she looks tough."

Rachel hugged Lupe and said, "Go get her."

"You can do it," her father encouraged. "Just think of the marbles, not the girl, and let your thumb do the work."

The other girl broke first and earned one marble. She missed her next shot, and Lupe, one eye closed, her thumb quivering with energy, blasted two marbles out of the circle but missed her next shot. Her opponent earned two more before missing. She stamped her foot and said "Shoot!" The score was three to two in favor of Miss Baseball Cap.

The referee stopped the game. "Back up, please, give them room," he shouted. Onlookers had gathered too tightly around the players.

Lupe then earned three marbles and was set to get her fourth when a gust of wind blew dust in her eyes and she missed badly. Her opponent quickly scored two marbles, tying the game, and moved ahead six to five on a lucky shot. Then she missed, and Lupe, whose eyes felt scratchy when she blinked, relied on instinct and thumb muscle to score the tying point. It was now six to six, with only three marbles left. Lupe blew her nose and studied the angles. She dropped to one knee, steadied her hand, and shot so hard she cracked two marbles from the circle. She was the winner!

"I did it!" Lupe said under her breath. She rose from her knees, which hurt from bending all day, and hugged her father. He hugged her back and smiled.

Everyone clapped, except Miss Baseball Cap, who made a face and stared at the ground. Lupe told her she was a great player, and they shook hands. A newspaper photographer took pictures of the two girls standing shoulder-to-shoulder, with Lupe holding the bigger trophy.

Lupe then played the winner of the boys' division, and after a poor start beat him eleven to four. She blasted the marbles, shattering one into sparkling slivers of glass. Her opponent looked on glumly as Lupe did what she did best—win!

The head referee and the President of the Fresno Marble Association stood with Lupe as she displayed her trophies for the newspaper photographer. Lupe shook hands with everyone, including a dog who had come over to see what the commotion was all about.

That night, the family went out for pizza and set the two trophies on the table for everyone in the restaurant to see. People came up to congratulate Lupe, and she felt a little embarrassed, but her father said the trophies belonged there.

Back home, in the privacy of her bedroom, she placed the trophies on her shelf and was happy. She had always earned honors because of her brains, but winning in sports was a new experience. She thanked her tired thumb. "You did it, thumb. You made me champion." As its reward, Lupe went to the bathroom, filled the bathroom sink with warm water, and let her thumb swim and splash as it pleased. Then she climbed into bed and drifted into a hard-won sleep.

Reader's Response

1. How do you think this story might have ended if Lupe had lost the marble tournament?
2. Most people like to read short stories like this. Do you? Why or why not? What do you like best about this story?

Writing and Thinking Activities

1. Get together with two or three other students. Then discuss these questions about the four models you've just read.
   a. Which model mostly tells the writer's thoughts and feelings?
   b. Which one tries to convince its reader to do something? What does the writer want the reader to do?
   c. Which one mostly tells readers facts and details about the event?
   d. Which model makes you feel that you're actually at the event? How has the writer been creative?
2. When you communicate with other people, what are your aims? During two hours of a typical day, keep track of each time you use language. Think about the times you write, read, speak, and listen. How often is your aim to inform? to persuade? to express yourself? to be creative? Share what you found out with two or three classmates. What aims do each of you most often have?
3. Which type of writing do you think is used most often? Is it informative, persuasive, self-expressive, or creative? Pick out a magazine or newspaper to bring to class. Work with some other students to find examples of all four types of writing. Then decide which one is used most. Do some publications have just one type of writing?
4. What is creative writing? To be creative is the main purpose of writing that creates literature, such as novels, short stories, poems, and plays. But isn't all writing creative in some way? What about letters, book reports, and newspaper articles? Would you call them creative? Find some examples of writing that is creative, even though the basic purpose or aim is informative, persuasive, or self-expressive.

1 WRITING AND THINKING

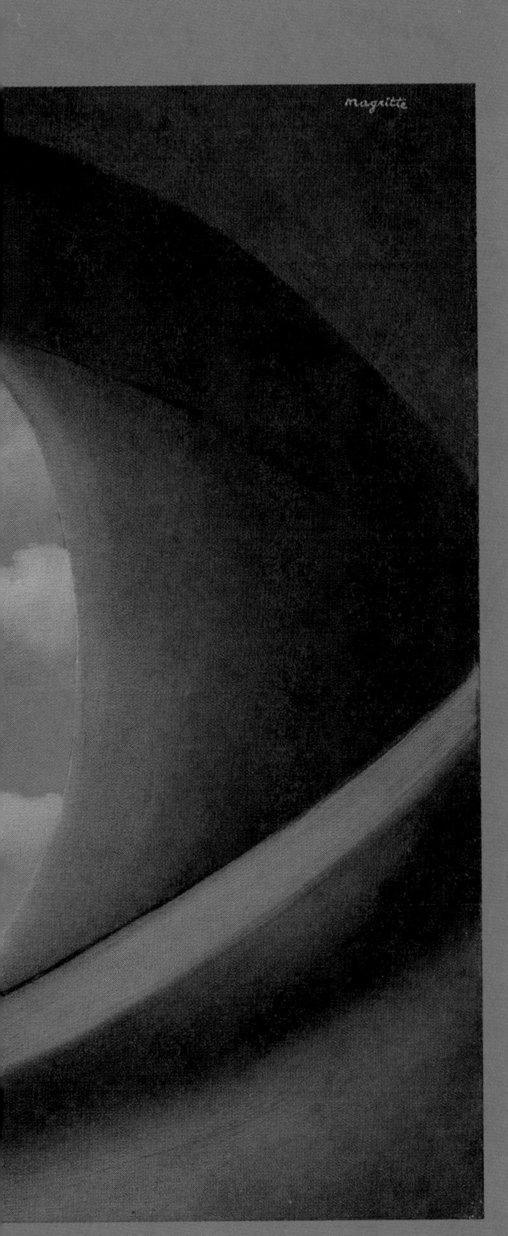

Looking at the Process

Did you ever stop and think about what happens when you write? You actually go through an amazing **process.** It begins with thoughts and feelings that grow in your brain until they finally flow out as written words on paper.

Writing and You. Do you find that it's sometimes easy to write, but at other times the words just won't cooperate? Is your brain brimming with ideas? Or is it often hard to think of something to write about? Professional writers have the same problems. Sometimes they can't come up with a good idea. The words just won't come out right. What is the hardest part of writing for you?

As You Read. As you read what editor Dudley Randall says about writing poetry, see if you think his advice applies to other kinds of writing besides poetry.

The False Mirror, Rene Magritte (1928). Oil on canvas, $21\frac{3}{4} \times 31\frac{7}{8}$". Collection, The Museum of Modern Art, New York. Purchase. © 1992 C. Herscovici/ARS, N.Y. Photograph © 1992 The Museum of Modern Art, New York.

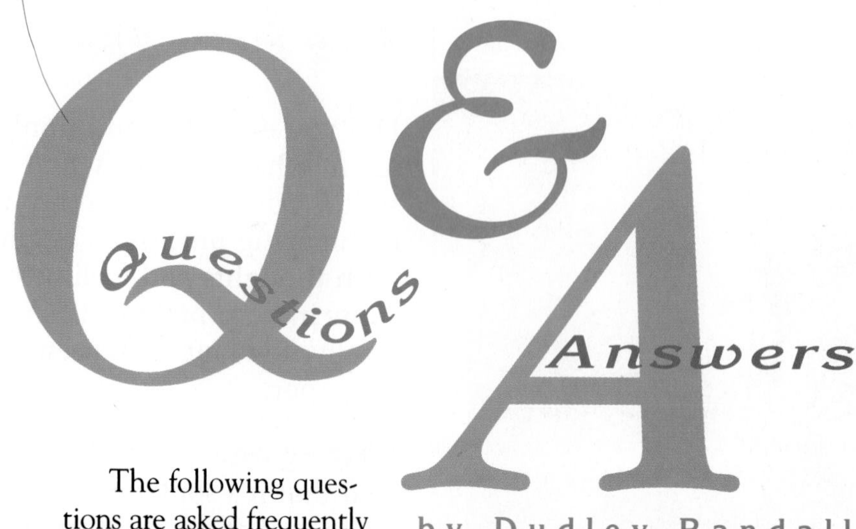

Questions & Answers

by Dudley Randall

The following questions are asked frequently in letters from beginning poets to Broadside Press. The answers are by Dudley Randall, Broadside Press editor.

1Q. I am a fifteen year old high school student and have been writing poetry for one year. How do I go about having a book published?

A. How fortunate that you became a poet so early! You have many years of writing ahead of you, so it's not necessary to rush into the permanence of book format. Some poets, Robert Hayden among them, published books very young, and now they don't want their juvenile publications to be seen. I asked Hayden for permission to reprint a poem from his first book, *Heartshape in the Dust,* and he said, "No, *no,* No, NO, *NO!* I wrote those poems in my apprentice years, when I was learning to write, and I don't want any of them reprinted."

This period of learning how to write, discovering new poets, experimenting with new forms, can be one of your most enjoyable. Don't terminate it prematurely. Read, read, read. And write, write, write.

Don't try for book publication until you have published extensively in magazines and newspapers. Mari Evans was well-known for her contributions to magazines and anthologies before she published her first book. Such publication will be an indication that many different editors have found your work acceptable. Then publishers, perhaps, will have seen your poems somewhere, and will be more willing to risk from \$500 to \$10,000 on a first book by you, than on a book by an unknown poet.

All the poems you sent me were in rimed couplets, which are only one of many forms and which have their limitations. Master the scores of other forms which you will find in Karl Shapiro's *A Prosody Handbook* or in any handbook on writing poetry. Also, learn correct spelling and grammar. When you have learned the rules, you can break them, if you have good reasons to.

After you have done these things, you can start sending your poems to magazines. Choose publications where the competition is not too tough, like your local newspaper, your school newspaper or yearbook, literary magazine, or your church bulletin. After mastering spelling, grammar, and forms, you will be ready to be published, but try ephemeral publications first, not the permanence of books, which you may regret later. Have fun!

"This period of learning how to write, discovering new poets, experimenting with new forms, can be one of your most enjoyable."

2

Q. I have a teacher who reads and criticizes my poems. He says they are full of clichés. What can I do?

A. One of the best ways to learn to write is to have your work read and criticized by a competent person. You must develop a thick skin to criticism, and the ability to evaluate it objectively and apply it to your work to make it better. Praise only flatters your ego, but searching criticism exposes your flaws and points out what you must do to write better.

Clichés are expressions which have been worked to death and have lost their freshness, surprise, and power, like "right on," "pigs," "Queen of the Nile," "Amerikkka," "sweet as a rose." Perhaps the reason you use clichés is that you have not read enough to observe their repetition. Read more widely and develop the knack of spotting over-used expressions and eliminate them from your writing.

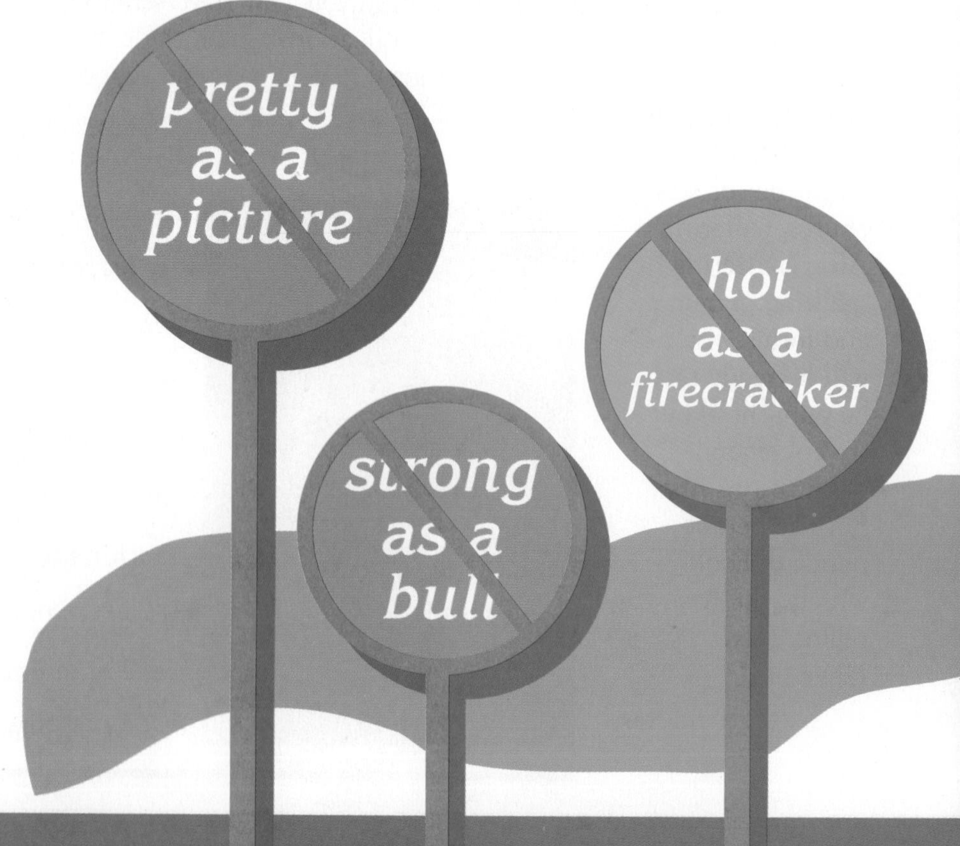

Reader's Response

1. In his first answer, Randall advises the fifteen year old poet, "Read, read, read. And write, write, write." How much reading do you do? What kinds of reading do you enjoy most?
2. Randall says that criticism helps you learn to write better. How do you feel when someone criticizes your writing? How do you think you can learn to be a better writer?
3. Clichés are hard to overcome. List some familiar clichés ("tough as nails," "fresh as a daisy," and so on). Then see if you can think of a fresh way to express each idea. You can work with a partner or several classmates.

Looking Ahead

In this chapter you'll practice a general approach or process that applies to all types of writing. As you work through the chapter, remember that

- careful thinking is part of writing
- the planning that you do before you write is crucial
- the writing process can be adapted to fit your own writing style

Aim—The "Why" of Writing

People write because they have something to say, someone to say it to, and a purpose for saying it. That's the general *why* for communicating. But what are the specific purposes people have for writing?

Maybe you think there are many, many purposes for writing. But there are really only a few.

WHY PEOPLE WRITE	
To express themselves	To get to know themselves better; to find meaning in their lives
To share information	To give information other people need or want; to share special knowledge
To persuade	To convince other people to do something or believe something
To create literature	To be creative; to say something in a unique way

Everything people write has one of these four purposes—sometimes more than one at the same time. For example, a writer may want to share information *and* to persuade, to express himself or herself *and* to create literature.

Like all the other writers in the world, you'll be writing for at least one of these four purposes.

Process—The "How" of Writing

Writing is a skill that improves with practice. It's also part of a *process*, a series of steps that lead to an end result. The following diagram shows the steps that usually take place in the writing process. But every writer is different. You may spend less time prewriting than the person sitting next to you. And that person may spend much more time revising than you do. As you review the writing process, notice how every stage requires thinking. Writing and thinking happen together whenever you write.

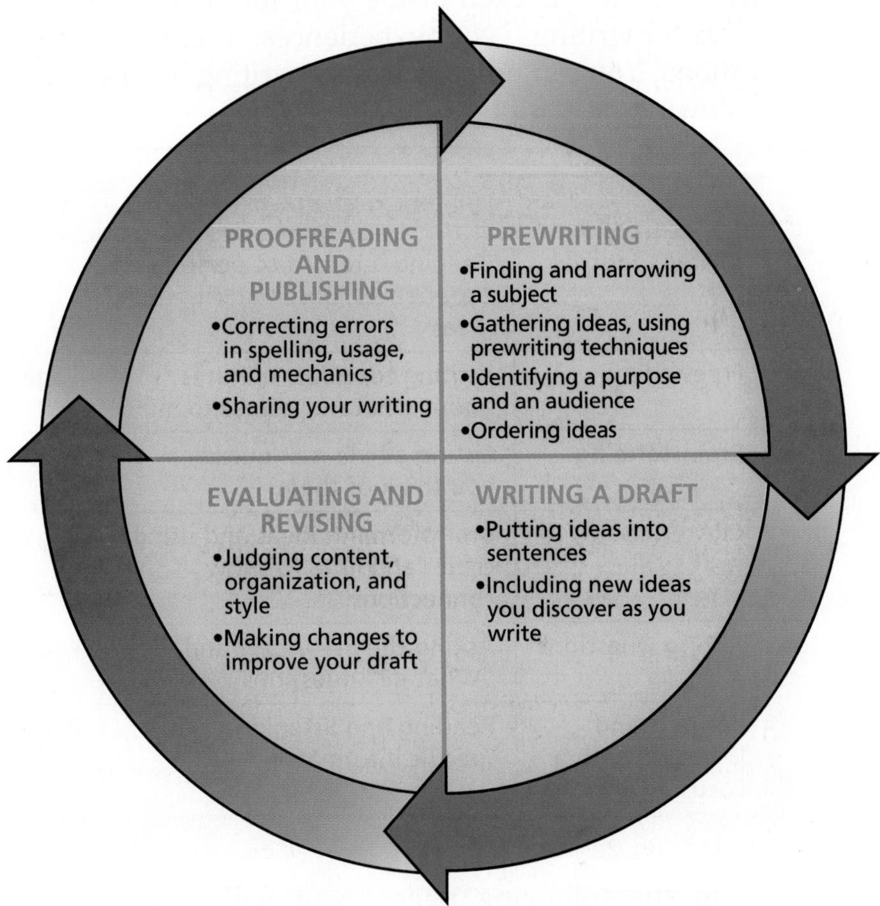

PROOFREADING AND PUBLISHING
•Correcting errors in spelling, usage, and mechanics
•Sharing your writing
PREWRITING
•Finding and narrowing a subject
•Gathering ideas, using prewriting techniques
•Identifying a purpose and an audience
•Ordering ideas
EVALUATING AND REVISING
•Judging content, organization, and style
•Making changes to improve your draft
WRITING A DRAFT
•Putting ideas into sentences
•Including new ideas you discover as you write

Unlike a chiseler working in stone, you can make changes easily when you write. At any point in the writing process, you can go back to an earlier stage or even start all over again. Suppose you're writing a committee report about a food drive your scout troop will sponsor. As you write your first draft, you may realize you don't know enough about the kinds of food you need to collect. So you go back to prewriting to gather more information.

Finding Ideas for Writing

Have you ever complained, "I can't think of anything to write about"? Locked inside your mind are thousands of ideas for writing—your experiences, interests, and observations. You can unlock ideas for writing by practicing the following prewriting techniques.

PREWRITING TECHNIQUES		
Writer's Journal	Keeping a record of personal experiences, observations, and ideas	Page 27
Freewriting	Writing for a few minutes about whatever comes to mind	Page 28
Brainstorming	Listing all ideas as quickly as you think of them	Page 29
Clustering	Brainstorming ideas and using circles and lines to show connections	Page 31
Asking Questions	Asking the *5W–How?* and "What if?" questions	Page 33
Reading and Listening with a Focus	Reading and listening to find specific information	Page 35

In the following pages, you will experiment with different prewriting techniques. Some will probably feel more comfortable and work better for you than others. And often you'll use more than one prewriting technique at a time. For example, you might browse through your writer's journal and decide to write about being in an emergency room after breaking your wrist. Then you might brainstorm to recall specific details about this experience.

Writer's Journal

In your ***writer's journal*** you'll write about things that happen and things that interest you. Journal entries can be very short or go on for several pages. You can include "Things I Like"—a special section of quotations, articles, and cartoons. Soon your journal will become a good sourcebook for writing ideas.

- For your writer's journal, use a special notebook or folder. Set aside a time to write every day.
- Forget about grammar, spelling, and punctuation at this stage. Just get your thoughts down on paper.
- Encourage your imagination. Write about dreams and daydreams. Try creating songs, poems, or stories. If you enjoy drawing, include pictures and cartoons.

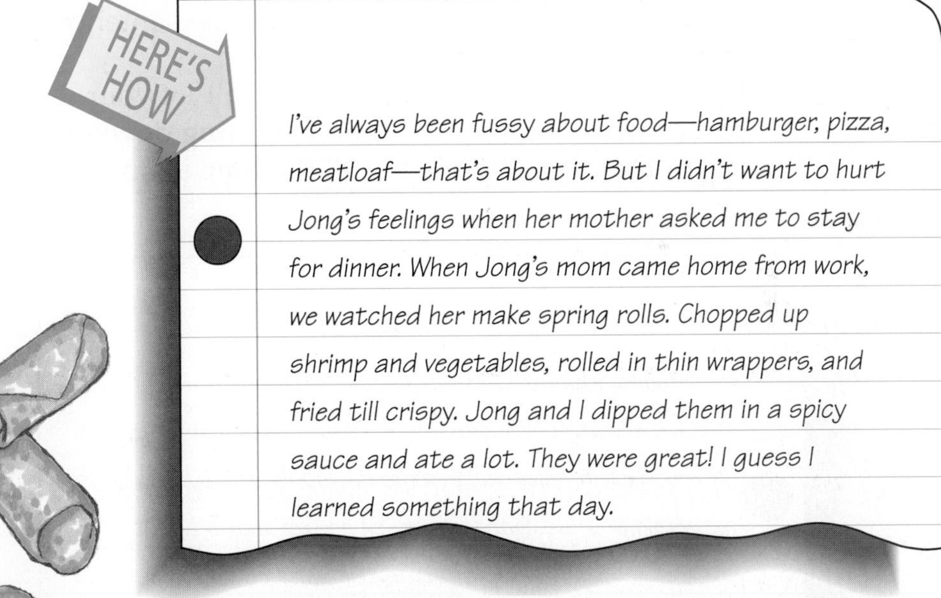

HERE'S HOW
I've always been fussy about food—hamburger, pizza, meatloaf—that's about it. But I didn't want to hurt Jong's feelings when her mother asked me to stay for dinner. When Jong's mom came home from work, we watched her make spring rolls. Chopped up shrimp and vegetables, rolled in thin wrappers, and fried till crispy. Jong and I dipped them in a spicy sauce and ate a lot. They were great! I guess I learned something that day.

EXERCISE 1 **Keeping a Writer's Journal**

Ten years from now, what will you remember about your life? Your ideas, feelings, and experiences are worth recording. Write a journal entry that you can share with your classmates. Write about something important that happened yesterday or something you're looking forward to.

Freewriting

Freewriting is writing down whatever ideas pop into your head about a subject. Set a time limit of three to five minutes, and go!

- Write about something that's important to you.
- Write whatever your subject makes you think of or remember. Don't worry about complete sentences, spelling, or punctuation.
- If you get stuck, write anything. Don't let your pen or pencil stop, just continue writing down all your ideas. Keep writing until the time is up.

HERE'S HOW

Whales, whales. Largest animal. Different kinds. Live in water. Not fish. Mammals, nurse their young. Studied in science. Breathe air. Sounds they make, whale sounds. Songs, even. Star Trek movie about whales. Moby Dick. What do killer whales kill? Hunting whales with harpoons. Little boats vs. big, scary whales. Blubber used for oil—something else for perfume. Will there be whales 100 years from now?

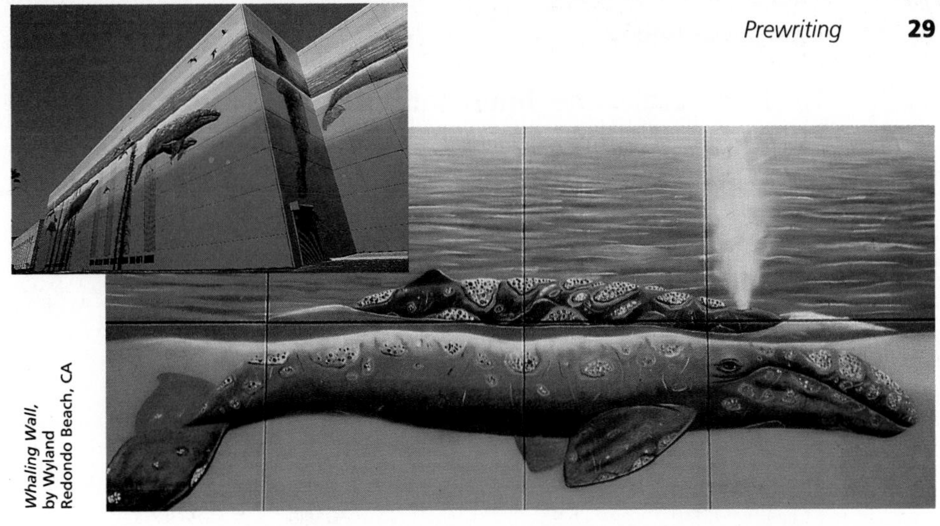

Whaling Wall, by Wyland Redondo Beach, CA

Focused freewriting, or ***looping,*** helps you narrow your topic and gather details. Choose a word or phrase from freewriting you've already done. (You might choose "hunting whales," for example.) Then freewrite for several minutes on this limited topic.

EXERCISE 2 **Using Freewriting**

Where do you go to have fun? Where do you go when you want to think? Where do you feel most at home? Think of a place that's special to you. How would you describe the place and your feelings about it? Freewrite in your journal for three minutes about the place. Or freewrite about another topic that's important to you.

Brainstorming

You can ***brainstorm*** alone, but it's more fun with a partner or a group. Then you can bounce ideas off each other.

- Write a subject—any subject—at the top of a piece of paper or on a chalkboard.
- Write down every single thought about the subject that comes to mind. Don't stop to judge ideas. (You can do that later.)
- Keep going until you run out of ideas.

Here are some brainstorming notes on the subject "shopping mall." Notice that the list includes some silly ideas that will be thrown out later.

Shopping Mall

place to meet friends
spend most of Saturday there
people watching, make up stories
shopping mall on Mars?
underwater shopping mall?
saw a movie star at the mall
non-shopping mall, don't shop much
walk around—talk
record stores, video games
some adults grouchy with us
everyone who's anyone
great food—yogurt bar, potato bar

EXERCISE 3 Using Brainstorming

Brainstorming is more fun in a group. Team up with two or three classmates for a brainstorming session on one of the following subjects or on one of your own. Brainstorm as long a list of ideas as you can.

1. UFOs
2. fears
3. rock groups
4. video games
5. community problems
6. heroes

Clustering

Clustering is sometimes called ***webbing*** or may be called ***making connections.*** When you make a cluster diagram, you break a topic into its smaller parts.

- Write your subject in the center of your paper and circle it.
- Around the subject, write related ideas as you think of them. Circle these ideas, and draw lines to connect them with the subject.
- An idea may make you think of other ideas. Connect these with circles and lines, too.

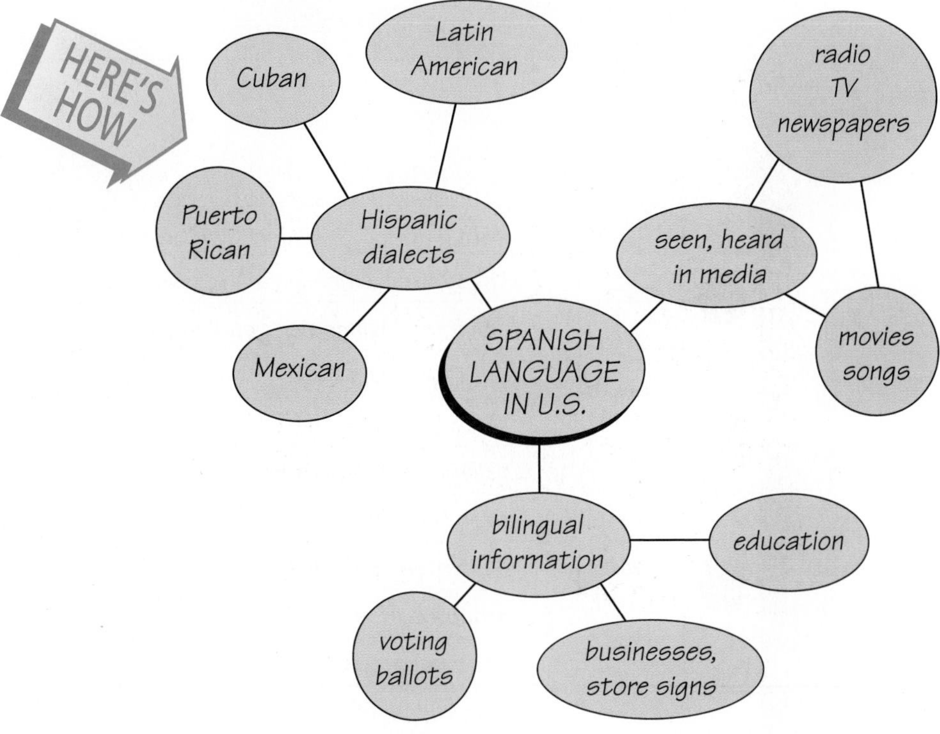

EXERCISE 4 **Using Clustering**

Make a cluster diagram for a subject you didn't use from Exercise 3 (page 30), or pick a subject of your own. Use circles and lines to show how ideas are connected.

CRITICAL THINKING

Observing with Your Five Senses

While you're awake, you receive steady input from each of your five senses (sight, sound, smell, taste, touch). Most of the time you ignore these ***sensory details.*** But as a writer you need to *observe* the world around you with all five senses alert and ready to receive information.

Here are a writer's notes on a Cuban American New Year's Eve celebration.

HERE'S HOW

SIGHT:	*dark night; brightly lit house; about thirty family members and friends; children playing; men tending the back-yard barbecue*
SOUND:	*record player; singing; people talking, telling jokes, laughter; children's shouts; TV in living room*
SMELL:	*slow-roasting pig; spicy smells; freshly ground coffee*
TASTE:	*crisp barbecued pork; black beans and rice; yucca; fried plantains; guava pastries; bitter orange*
TOUCH:	*warm night; breezes through open win-dows; embroidered tablecloth; paper plates and plastic forks and knives*

CRITICAL THINKING EXERCISE:
Observing Sensory Details

Imagine yourself as a supercomputer designed to record every sensory detail. You're collecting details for a description that will go into a time capsule to be opened in the year 3000. Collect details for all five senses as you observe one of the following.

1. a basketball or football game
2. a pizza parlor or other restaurant
3. the school cafeteria
4. a dance
5. a birthday party
6. a city street or highway

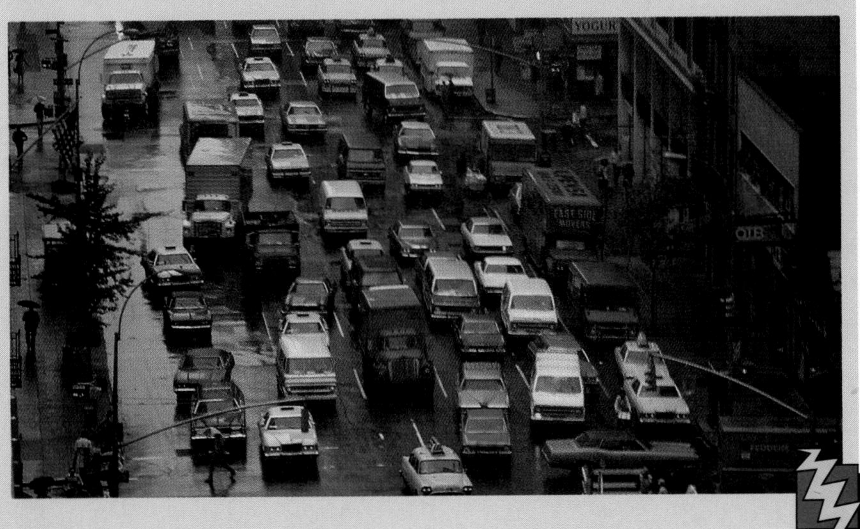

Asking Questions

Practice asking yourself two different kinds of questions. One kind helps you find facts. The other kind exercises your imagination.

5W-How?* Questions.** News reporters track down information by asking the ***5W-How? questions: *Who? What? Where? When? Why?* and *How?* For some topics, some question words won't apply. And with other topics, you may think of several good questions for a question word.

Here are some questions one writer asked when preparing to write a school newspaper article about new automobile designs.

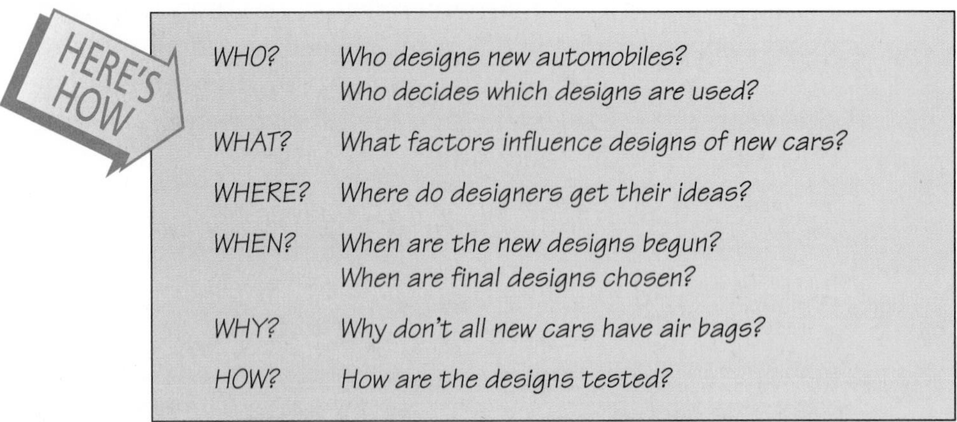

WHO?	*Who designs new automobiles?* *Who decides which designs are used?*
WHAT?	*What factors influence designs of new cars?*
WHERE?	*Where do designers get their ideas?*
WHEN?	*When are the new designs begun?* *When are final designs chosen?*
WHY?	*Why don't all new cars have air bags?*
HOW?	*How are the designs tested?*

"What if?" Questions. What if you could become invisible? What if you could fly? ***"What if?" questions*** will help you find ideas for creative writing. The following are some "What if?" questions you might ask to spark your imagination.

- *What if I could change one thing in my life?* (What if I were a genius? What if I lived on a ranch?)
- *What if some common thing did not exist?* (What if there were no telephones? What if Earth had no water?)
- *What if one situation in the world could be changed?* (What if everyone lived forever? What if everyone spoke the same language?)

EXERCISE 5 **Asking the *5W-How?* Questions**

As a reporter for your local newspaper, you have been assigned to write an article about a popular music group that's coming to town. Choose a real group, and make a list of *5W-How?* questions that you'd like to ask the musicians.

EXERCISE 6 **Asking "What if?" Questions**

You and a partner are planning a short story for your class magazine. Brainstorm as many "What if?" questions as you can. (This is the way movie producers get their ideas: What if a family went on a vacation and left their son home alone?) Then write a brief plot outline for your story.

EXAMPLES What if the person on TV could hear what you say?
What if two of your classmates were actually aliens from another planet?

Reading and Listening with a Focus

Suppose you're writing about what America was like before Columbus arrived in the New World. How can you find out? For a topic you can't observe directly, find information by reading and listening with a focus—with something specific in mind.

Reading. Reading sources include such items as books, magazines, newspapers, and pamphlets. Here are some techniques you can use to find specific information.

- Check a book's table of contents and index. Go directly to the pages on your topic.
- Don't read everything. Skim the text quickly. Look only for information on your topic. Don't forget to check photos and captions, too.
- When you find information on your topic, read carefully. Take notes on main ideas and important details.

REFERENCE NOTE: For more information on reading, see page 846 and pages 848–853.

Listening. Some people learn better by listening than by reading. You can gather information on a specific topic by listening to speeches, interviews, radio and TV programs, audiotapes, and videotapes. You can use the following techniques whenever you listen for information.

- Get ready ahead of time by thinking of questions on your topic.
- Listen for main ideas and important details. Take notes to help you remember.

REFERENCE NOTE: For more information on listening, see pages 808–813.

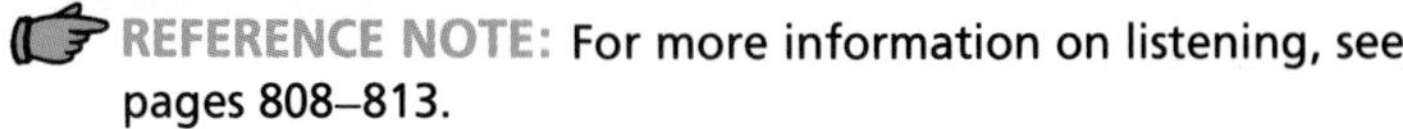

EXERCISE 7 Practicing Reading and Listening

Look through a TV program listing for this week (most newspapers publish a daily guide) and make a list of all the programs you can find about nature. (Nature programs include such areas as plants, animals, weather, astronomy, earth sciences, oceanography, and geology.) Choose one program on your list, and watch it. Jot down at least five facts you learned from watching the program.

Thinking About Purpose and Audience

Purpose. Before you write, always ask yourself, "*Why* am I writing?" This chart shows the basic *purposes* for writing and some forms you might use for each purpose.

MAIN PURPOSE	FORMS OF WRITING
To express your feelings	Journal entry, letter, personal essay
To explain or inform	Science or history report, news story, biography, autobiography, travel essay
To persuade	Persuasive essay, letter to the editor, advertisement, political speech
To be creative	Short story, poem, play

Audience. You also need to identify your *audience,* or readers. Think about how you'll adapt your writing to a specific audience. Ask yourself these questions:

- What do my readers already know about my topic?
- What will I need to explain? What will they find most interesting?
- What kinds of words and sentences (simple or more difficult and complex) should I use?

Perhaps your hobby is collecting arrowheads. If you're writing a letter to a relative in Juneau, Alaska, your cousin may have no idea what arrowheads are. You'll need to explain what they look like, how they're made, and where they're found. You'll probably use the kind of vocabulary

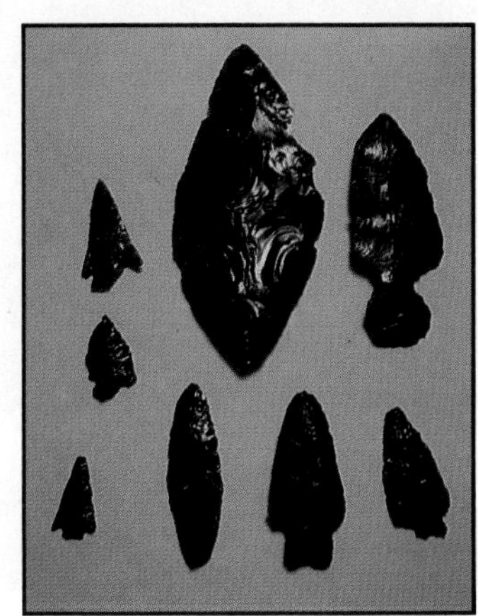

and language that you would use if you were speaking directly to your cousin.

But suppose you're writing a report on arrowheads for your history class. You may still need to supply some background information, but your report will sound more formal than the language you use when writing a letter to someone you know well.

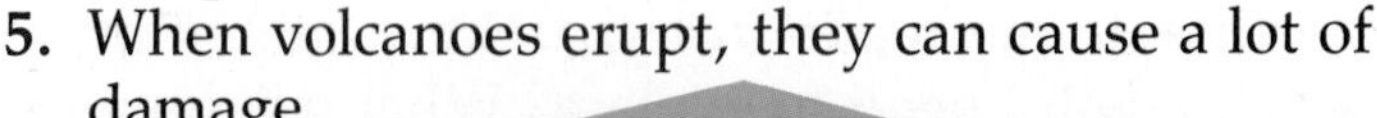

EXERCISE 8 **Thinking About Purpose and Audience**

You're writing a science report about active volcanoes in Hawaii. Your purpose is to inform, and your readers are your classmates. Which of these statements belong in your report? Which ones don't?

1. Two active volcanoes in Hawaii Volcanoes National Park are Mauna Loa and Kilauea.
2. The town of Volcano, Hawaii, where many scientists live, is built right next to an active volcano.
3. I'm really afraid to even think about volcanoes ever since I saw a late-night movie about a killer volcano.
4. Mount Vesuvius in Italy is a steep-sided, symmetrical composite volcano.
5. When volcanoes erupt, they can cause a lot of damage.

Arranging Ideas

How you present your ideas is just as important as what you have to say. So after you find a topic and gather information about it, you need to plan the order of ideas. This chart shows four common ways of ordering, or arranging, information.

WAYS TO ORGANIZE IDEAS

TYPE OF ORDER	DEFINITION	EXAMPLES
Chronological	Describe events in the order they happen.	Story, narrative poem, explanation of a process, history, biography, play
Spatial	Describe objects according to location (near to far, left to right, and so on).	Description, directions, explanation
Importance	Give details from least to most important or the reverse.	Persuasive writing, description, explanation, evaluative writing
Logical	Group related details together.	Definition, classification

 **REFERENCE NOTE:** For more information on arranging ideas, see pages 74–75.

CRITICAL THINKING
Arranging Ideas

Your topic, purpose, and details will give you a clue about which order to use. For example, you're writing a description of Skylab, the U.S. space station launched in 1973. Your purpose is to inform; your audience is your classmates. You've collected information about each room. So you decide to use spatial order, moving from one end of the space station to the other end.

In the following story of a mongoose fighting a cobra named Nagaina, a natural order is chronological. What happens first? What happens last?

> Rikki-tikki was bounding all round Nagaina, keeping just out of reach of her stroke, his little eyes like hot coals. Nagaina gathered herself together, and flung out at him. Rikki-tikki jumped up and backward. Again and again and again she struck, and each time her head came with a whack on the matting of the veranda and she gathered herself together like a watch spring. Then Rikki-tikki danced in a circle to get behind her, and Nagaina spun around to keep her head to his head, so that the rustle of her tail on the matting sounded like dry leaves blown along by the wind.
>
> Rudyard Kipling, "Rikki-tikki-tavi"

CRITICAL THINKING EXERCISE:
Choosing an Order for Ideas

For each of the following writing situations, think about the kinds of details you would use. Then choose an appropriate order for those details. Look at the chart on page 39, Ways to Organize Ideas, for a description of each of the types of order.

1. In a letter to a pen pal, you describe what your room looks like.
2. You are writing a letter to the editor of the local newspaper. To persuade readers to approve a new park tax, you give three reasons why your town needs more parks.
3. You enjoy creative writing. For your little sister's birthday present, you plan to write an adventure story about dragons.
4. For an English assignment, you are going to review a new book that you have just read, telling whether you think it's worth recommending to your classmates.

Using Visuals to Organize Ideas

Visuals—such as charts, graphs, maps, sequence chains, time lines, drawings, or diagrams—can turn messy, disorganized prewriting notes into neat packages of ideas and details. Charts and sequence chains can help you organize your ideas.

Charts. Think about the details you have gathered, and look for ways to group ideas. Then decide on the headings that will cover most of your information. Write your details under those headings. In the following chart, for example, one writer gives three types of information about the Ojibwas and the Seminoles.

HERE'S HOW

	OJIBWAS 1600s	SEMINOLES 1700s
WHERE THEY LIVED	Around the Great Lakes	Florida
KIND OF HOUSE	Wigwam	Open-sided houses on stilts
SOURCES OF FOOD	Hunted, fished, farmed, and gathered wild plants	Hunted, fished, and farmed

Sequence Chains. A ***sequence chain*** organizes events in chronological order. You can use a sequence chain to show the main events in a story or the steps in a process. The following is a sequence chain for a short story.

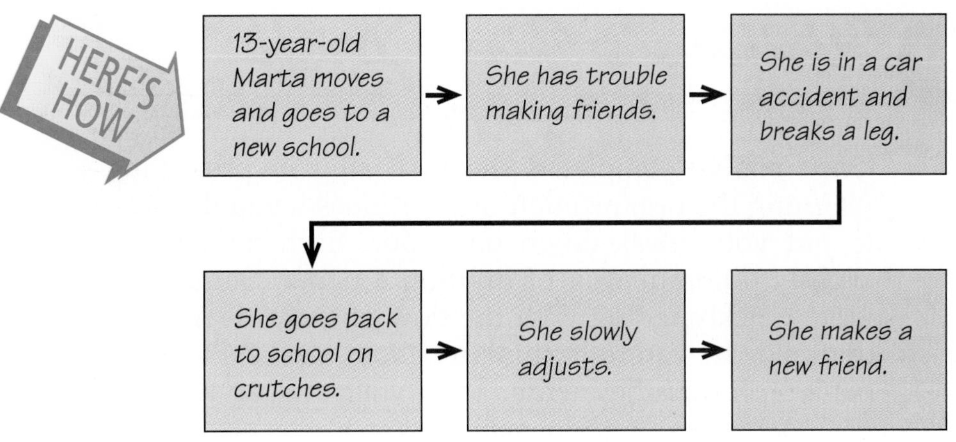

EXERCISE 9 Making a Chart

How can you show a comparison of two countries? Make a chart to organize the following notes about the United States and China. What headings will you use?

The United States has a total area of 3,600,000 square miles.
It has more than 250,000,000 people.
Its form of government is a republic.
China has a population of more than 1,100,000,000 people.
It is governed by a communist regime.
It has a total area of more than 3,690,000 square miles.

EXERCISE 10 Making a Sequence Chain

Create a sequence chain for one of these assignments. (Do one or the other, not both.)

1. Show the main events in a story. You can create a plot for a short story, or show the events in a story that you have read or in a movie or TV show that you have seen.
2. Show the stages in the writing process. Use the information in the pie-shaped diagram on page 25.

Writing a First Draft

Once you've completed the final step in prewriting—planning the organization of your ideas—you'll be ready to put your ideas down on paper. Each person has a slightly different way of drafting a paper. Some people write quickly, going with the flow of their ideas. Others draft slowly, carefully thinking about each sentence and paragraph that they write. Trust your own style, and do whatever works best for you.

- Use your prewriting plans to guide you as you write your first draft.
- As you write, you may come up with new ideas. Include these ideas in your draft.
- Don't worry about spelling and grammar errors. You can correct them later.

In writing, ***voice*** is the way the words sound. As you put your ideas into sentences and paragraphs, try to express your ideas simply and naturally. Don't use words just because they sound "important." Your writing should have your own voice—and sound like you.

On page 45 is the first draft of a paragraph about Mary McLeod Bethune, an African American educator from South Carolina who lived from 1875 to 1955. Notice the writer's questions that appear in brackets. These show that the writer will later return to the prewriting stage to find more information before writing the final draft. Notice, also, that the writing in this draft does not sound as polished as the final draft will. In this first draft there are problems with both content and organization that the writer will fix later.

Mary McLeod Bethune was the first in her family to go to school. She started when she was eleven. [Twelve? Check this.] The school was a mission school for black children. [Where? Go back for details.] Mary was a fast learner. She had to walk a long way to and from school. Mary's family sacrificed to let her attend school. When she was in school, she couldn't help with all the chores on the family farm. Mary liked to plow. When she started her third year, she helped the teacher. She also began teaching her brothers and sisters at home to read. Mary was good at math. She helped people with their accounts so the big planters couldn't cheat them.

EXERCISE 11 **Writing a First Draft**

Many children and adults in the world today don't know how to read any language. Imagine that you were never taught to read. What would you miss? How would it change your life? Get ready to write a draft of a paragraph telling how you'd feel if you couldn't read. Use one or more of the prewriting techniques on pages 26–36 to explore your thoughts on this topic. Arrange your ideas in a way that makes sense. For this topic, logical order or order of importance might work well. Draft your paragraph and share it with your classmates.

Evaluating and Revising

You can't fix a TV set—or anything else—until you figure out what's wrong with it. In the same way, after you've finished your first draft and are looking over what you've written, you'll need to figure out what parts aren't working so that you can fix them. *Evaluating* and *revising* are really two separate steps in the writing process, but most people do them together.

Evaluating

When you ***evaluate*** your writing, you judge what's good about it and what needs to be improved. You evaluate writing more often than you realize. Each time you decide whether you like a book or magazine, you're evaluating.

Self-Evaluation. It's often harder to judge your own writing than someone else's. Use these tips to evaluate your own writing.

- Put your draft aside for awhile. Rest your brain.
- Read your paper carefully at least three times. Each time focus on something different. For example, you might ask yourself questions like these:
  Are the ideas clear?
  Are the ideas in the most effective order?
  Are sentences well worded and smoothly connected to each other?
- Read your paper aloud to yourself. Listen for awkward or unclear spots.

Peer Evaluation. You can get some feedback on your writing from a partner or several classmates. (A peer is someone who is your equal—in this case, your classmate.) When you use peer evaluation, get ready to play two roles: (1) a writer whose work is being evaluated, and (2) a reader who is evaluating a classmate's writing.

GUIDELINES FOR PEER EVALUATION

Tips for the Writer

1. Make a list of questions for the reader. Ask what the reader thinks about parts of your paper you're not sure about.
2. Keep an open mind. Take all of the comments that your reader makes seriously, and don't be offended by any criticism. Even professional writers get suggestions for improvement from their editors.

Tips for the Reader

1. Always tell the writer something good about the paper.
2. Focus on content and organization. Don't point out spelling and grammar errors.
3. Put your suggestions into helpful questions: "Can you say this in easier words?" or "Can you add some specific details?"
4. Suggest something specific the writer can do to improve the paper.

CRITICAL THINKING

Evaluating Writing

Whenever you evaluate, you judge something by measuring it against established standards. Here are some basic standards for judging good writing. (See page 51 for a more detailed list of standards.)

1. The writing is interesting. It grabs and holds your attention.
2. The writing has a clear main idea.
3. The main idea is supported with enough details.
4. The ideas are presented in a clear and reasonable order.

CRITICAL THINKING EXERCISE:

Evaluating a Paragraph

If you think octopuses are scary, wait till you meet the giant squid. With one or two classmates, evaluate the following paragraph. Use the standards for good writing given on page 47. Write at least one comment on what's good about the paragraph. Then write at least one comment on what needs to be improved.

> A strange sea creature that people rarely see because it lives in deep waters is the giant squid. Giant squids can grow up to sixty feet long. There are old sea stories about giant squids attacking boats. They wrap their tentacles around them. Rows of sucking disks line the arms. The giant squid's eyes are huge, up to 15 inches wide. Boy, I wouldn't want to meet one, would you? Old sailors called giant squids sea monsters.

Revising

When you *revise,* you make changes to improve your writing. You can make your changes by hand or on a typewriter or word processor. Whatever you use as your writing tool, to revise your writing you'll use just four basic revision techniques: ***adding, cutting, replacing,*** and ***reordering.*** (To understand the examples, see the chart of symbols on page 55.)

REVISION TECHNIQUES	
TECHNIQUE	EXAMPLE
1. **Add.** Add new information and details. Add words, sentences, or paragraphs.	The book *Lovey: A Very Special Child* is written by a woman who teaches children with severe emotional problems.
2. **Cut.** Take out repeated, unnecessary, or related ideas.	~~The children have serious problems.~~ One of the children, Hannah, hides in a closet at first.
3. **Replace.** Replace weak or awkward wording with precise words or details.	Hannah doesn't talk to the teacher or other kids, but she ~~acts up~~ cries and screams when she's upset.
4. **Reorder.** Move information, sentences, and paragraphs for clear order.	In time, Hannah joins the class and begins to talk and learn. The teacher patiently works with Hannah.

In the following revised paragraph (you read it earlier as a first draft, page 45), the writer has used these four revision techniques. Do you think the changes improve the paragraph? How?

Mary McLeod Bethune was the first in
her family to go to school. She started
when she was eleven. ~~[Twelve? Check~~
~~this.]~~ The ^Presbyterian school was a mission school for — cut/add
black children ^in Mayesville, South Carolina. ~~[Where? Go back for~~ — add/cut
~~details.]~~ Mary was a fast learner. She had — cut/reorder
to walk ~~a long way~~ ^three miles to and from school. — replace
Mary's family sacrificed to let her attend
school. When she was in school, she
couldn't help with all the chores on the
family farm. ~~Mary liked to plow.~~ When she — cut
started her third year, she helped the
teacher. She also began teaching her
brothers and sisters at home to read. Mary
was good at math. She helped ~~people~~ ^both black and white neighbors with — replace
their accounts so the big planters couldn't
cheat them.

Mary McLeod Bethune at the college she founded in 1904 in Daytona Beach, Florida.

GUIDELINES FOR EVALUATING AND REVISING

	EVALUATION GUIDE	REVISION TECHNIQUE
	CONTENT	
1	Is the writing interesting?	**Add** specific examples, a brief story, dialogue, or details. **Cut** repeated or boring details.
2	Are there enough details?	**Add** details, facts, statistics, or examples to support the main idea.
3	Is the main idea clear?	**Add** a sentence that clearly states your main idea.
4	Are there unrelated ideas?	**Cut** the ideas that are not related to your topic.
	ORGANIZATION	
5	Are ideas and details arranged in a clear order?	**Reorder** ideas and details to make the meaning more easily understood.
6	Are the connections between ideas and sentences clear?	**Add** transitional words and phrases, such as *first*, *next*, *finally*, *similarly*, *because*, *for example*, and so on. (See pages 74–75.)
	STYLE	
7	Does the language fit the audience and purpose?	**Replace** slang and contractions in formal writing. Use *I* and *me* when you need to create a relaxed feeling.
8	Do sentences read smoothly?	**Reorder** words to vary sentence beginnings. Reword to vary sentence structure.

EXERCISE 12 Evaluating and Revising a Paragraph

With a partner, evaluate the following first draft. Then, revise the paragraph. Use the Guidelines for Evaluating and Revising on page 51. You may add, cut, reorder, or replace words and details.

Many Arab Americans live in the United States. Syrians arrived first in the late nineteenth century. They taught their heritage to their American-born children. Syrian American-born children learn to read and write the Arabic language. In Detroit, there is a large Arab American population. In Detroit, the people hold an Arab World Festival every year. They dance traditional dances like the debke, eat traditional foods, sell traditional Old World crafts. Doug Flutie, an Arab American, won the Heisman Trophy in 1984. There are many Arabic-language newspapers and journals in the United States. Many people from Egypt, Lebanon, and Jordan came to the United States after World War II.

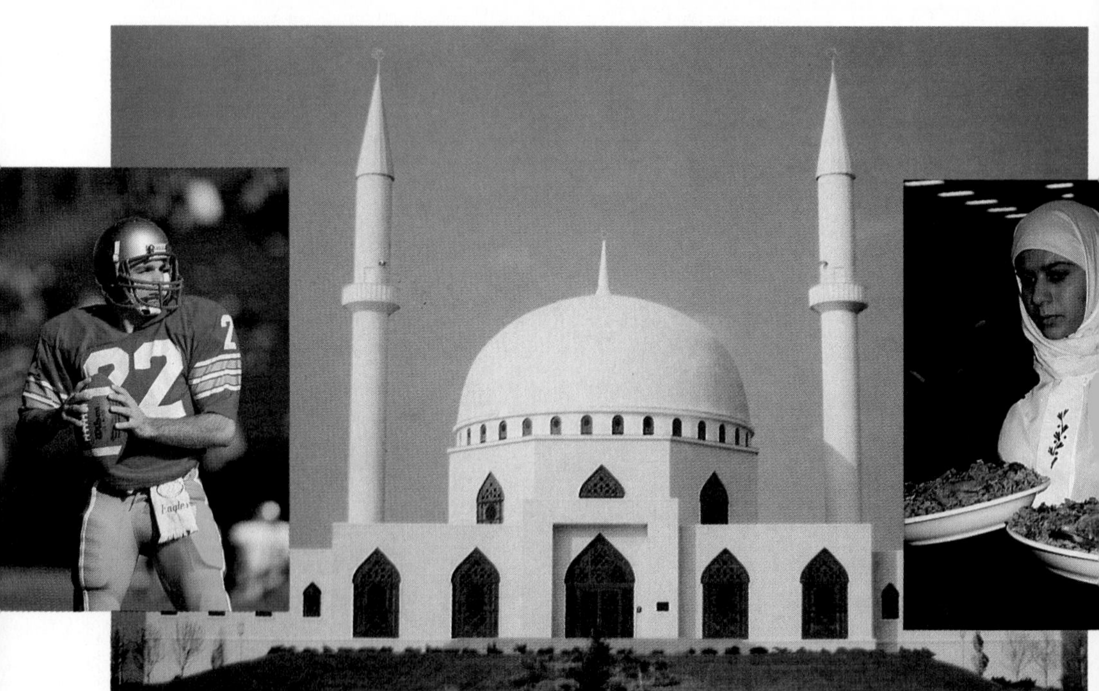

Islamic Center of Greater Toledo, Ohio

Proofreading and Publishing

One last step to finish your writing, then you'll need to find a way to share what you've written with an audience.

Proofreading

Remember puzzle pictures that asked, "What's wrong with this picture?" You had to search carefully to find mistakes—a cat wearing one plaid sock, a man writing with a fish, a woman wearing a reversed coat. Think of ***proofreading*** as solving a puzzle—searching out and fixing all the mistakes in grammar, spelling, capitalization, and punctuation.

Be sure to allow enough time to put your paper aside for awhile. It's easier to find mistakes when you've had a break. Try peer proofreading, too. Exchange papers with a partner and see if you can find errors in each other's papers.

GUIDELINES FOR PROOFREADING

1. Is every sentence a complete sentence, not a fragment or run-on? (See pages 354–360.)
2. Does every sentence begin with a capital letter? Does every sentence end with the correct punctuation mark? Are punctuation marks used correctly within sentences? (See pages 675–676 and pages 701–761.)
3. Do plural subjects have plural verbs? And do singular subjects have singular verbs? (See pages 551–569.)
4. Are verb forms and verb tenses used correctly? (See pages 580–598.)
5. Are adjective and adverb forms used correctly in comparisons? (See pages 629–636.)
6. Are the forms of personal pronouns used correctly? (See pages 606–621.)
7. Does every pronoun agree with its antecedent (the word it refers to) in number and gender? Are pronoun references clear? (See pages 572–574.)
8. Is every word spelled correctly? (See pages 764–793.)

EXERCISE 13 **Proofreading a Paragraph**

Can you find and correct the mistakes in this paragraph? (You should find six.) You can use a dictionary and the **Handbook** on pages 394–793.

When she heard the words tropical rain forest, Janet always thinked of a jungle. She was surprized to learn that few bushes grow in most parts of a tropical rain forest. The crowns of trees blocks the sunlight from the ground, so you can easy walk through most areas of a rain forest. Only where enough sunlight hits the ground do you find jungles. Thick, tangled masses of plants. Grow by rivers and in places where the land was once cleared.

Publishing

After proofreading your paper, find yourself a reader—or a listener. Remember that the purpose of most writing is to communicate with a reader. You may want to try one of the following ideas.

- Submit your writing to the school newspaper, yearbook, or magazine. Your local newspaper might publish a letter to the editor.
- Read aloud what you've written to your classmates or family or friends.
- Post book and movie reviews. You could use your class bulletin board, or you could use a library bulletin board for reviews that are written by the whole school.
- Make a class booklet. Each student should submit one piece of writing. You can also include original drawings and cartoons. Lend your booklet to other classes and to the school library.
- Keep a folder that contains your best writing. Share it with your family and friends or a trusted adult.

Follow the guidelines on the next page when making the final copy of your paper.

GUIDELINES FOR THE FORM OF A PAPER

1. Use only one side of a sheet of paper.
2. Write in blue or black ink, type, or use a word processor.
3. Leave margins of about one inch at the top, sides, and bottom of each page.
4. Follow your teacher's instructions for placing your name, the date, your class, and the title on your paper.
5. Double-space if you type. Don't skip lines if you write.
6. Indent the first line of each paragraph.
7. Keep your paper neat and clean.

EXERCISE 14 Identifying Ways to Publish

What are other ways to publish your writing? Think about all the types of writing (stories, poems, letters, essays, and reports) that can be shared in different ways. Brainstorm with your classmates to list other publishing ideas.

SYMBOLS FOR REVISING AND PROOFREADING

SYMBOL	EXAMPLE	MEANING OF SYMBOL
≡	San juan	Capitalize a lowercase letter.
/	Ruth's Father	Lowercase a capital letter.
∧	the name of school (the)	Insert a missing word, letter, or punctuation mark.
℘	Take it it back.	Leave out a word, letter, or punctuation mark.
∿	beleif	Change the order of letters or words.
¶	¶ "Help!" he called.	Begin a new paragraph.
⊙	Dr Chiang Woo	Add a period.
∧,	Oh I don't know.	Add a comma.

MAKING CONNECTIONS

A Writer's Revisions

Here's a chance to peek over the shoulder of Robert Frost, one of America's best-known poets. You can watch as he hesitates, changes his mind, scratches an idea out, starts over, gets a line just right. On the left is Frost's poem "Stopping by Woods on a Snowy Evening." Read the poem, then compare it with Frost's original handwritten version. It shows the changes he made in his first draft. What changes did Frost make?

Stopping by Woods on a Snowy Evening

by Robert Frost

Whose woods these are I think I know.
His house is in the village, though;
He will not see me stopping here
To watch his woods fill up with snow.

My little horse must think it queer
To stop without a farmhouse near
Between the woods and frozen lake
The darkest evening of the year.

He gives his harness bells a shake
To ask if there is some mistake.
The only other sound's the sweep
Of easy wind and downy flake.

The woods are lovely, dark, and deep,
But I have promises to keep,
And miles to go before I sleep,
And miles to go before I sleep.

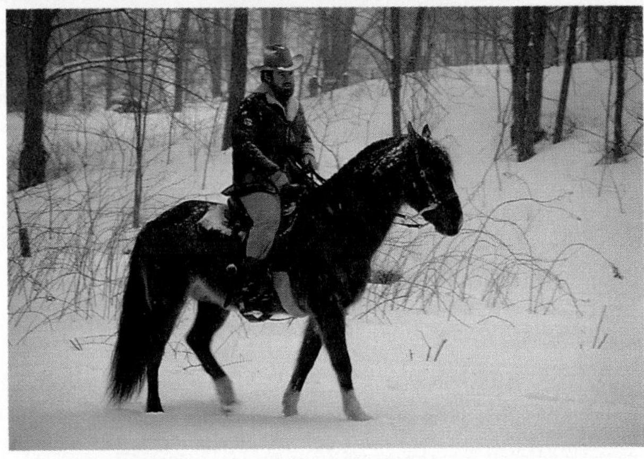

Do you think the horse is better as a he or a she? Frost seems to have changed his mind at least twice. Which lines in the poem seem to have given him the most trouble? Originally (in Stanza 2), Frost wrote "Between a forest and a lake." Why do you suppose he changed those words to "Between the woods and frozen lake" in the final version of the poem?

Write a journal entry about how you revise. Describe what you do when you revise and how you feel about revising. Do you spend a great deal of time revising, or a little? Can you remember a time when you made some great improvements as you revised?

Reflecting on the Writing Process

If writing is a "basic skill for getting through life," in what ways do you use writing in your daily life? For two or three days, keep a record in your journal listing each time you write and the reason you write. For example, you might jot down a class assignment, write a note to a friend, make a list of things you must do after school, or take a phone message. Record each and every time you write and the reason.

You may be surprised at the many ways you and your classmates use writing! Share examples from your writing record with the rest of the class.

2 Learning About Paragraphs

Looking at the Parts

Have you ever thought about the **parts** of a bicycle? A bike has handlebars, wheels, and a seat, but not all bikes are alike. Some are bigger than others; some have more parts than others.

You can think of paragraphs that way, too. They all have words, and they all say something. But some are bigger than others and some have more parts than others.

Writing and You. Some paragraphs stand alone, but most of them work together like links in a chain. Have you ever noticed that paragraphs can be very short—even a single word or sentence, and that other paragraphs go on and on?

As You Read. The following paragraphs are from a book about the life of a Native American, Black Elk. What do you notice about the sizes of the paragraphs?

Senegalese Fishing Village, Frank Frazier (1989), Visions in Black Gallery.

"They put us in some of those shining wagons and took us to a very beautiful place..."

FROM

Black Elk Speaks

as told through

JOHN G. NEIHARDT

(Flaming Rainbow)

Black Elk (at left) and his friend, Elk, participating in Buffalo Bill's Wild West Show, touring England.

One day we were told that Majesty was coming. I did not know what that was at first, but I learned afterward. It was Grandmother England (Queen Victoria), who owned Grandmother's Land [Canada] where we lived awhile after the Wasichus murdered Crazy Horse.

She came to the show in a big shining wagon, and there were soldiers on both sides of her, and many other shining wagons came too. That day other people could not come to the show—just Grandmother England and some people who came with her.

Sometimes we had to shoot in the show, but this time we did not shoot at all. We danced and sang, and I was one of the dancers chosen to do this for the Grandmother, because I was young and limber then and could dance many ways. We stood right in front of Grandmother England. She was little but fat and we liked her, because she was good to us. After we had danced, she spoke to us. She said something like this: "I am sixty-seven years old. All over the world I have seen all kinds of people; but today I have seen the best-looking people I know. If you belonged to me, I would not let them take you around in a show like this." She said other good things too, and then she said we must come to see her, because she had come to see us. She shook hands with all of us. Her hand was very little and soft. We gave a big cheer for her, and then the shining wagons came in and she got into one of them and they all went away.

In about a half-moon after that we went to see the Grandmother. They put us in some of those shining wagons and took us to a very beautiful place where there was a very big house with sharp, pointed towers on it. There were many seats built high in a circle, and these were just full of Wasichus who were all pounding their heels and yelling: "Jubilee! Jubilee! Jubilee!" I never heard what this meant.

They put us together in a certain place at the bottom of the seats. First there appeared a beautiful black wagon with two

black horses, and it went all around the show place. I heard that the Grandmother's grandson, a little boy, was in that wagon. Next came a beautiful black wagon with four gray horses. On each of the two right hand horses there was a rider, and a man walked, holding the front left hand horse. I heard that some of Grandmother's relatives were in this wagon. Next came eight buckskin horses, two by two, pulling a shining black wagon. There was a rider on each right hand horse and a man walked, holding the front left hand horse. There were soldiers, with bayonets, facing outward all around this wagon. Now all the people in the seats were roaring and yelling "Jubilee!" and "Victoria!" Then we saw Grandmother England again. She was sitting in the back of the wagon and two women sat in the front, facing her. Her dress was all shining and her hat was all shining and her wagon was all shining and so were the horses. She looked like a fire coming.

Afterward I heard that there was yellow and white metal all over the horses and the wagon.

When she came to where we were, her wagon stopped and she stood up. Then all those people stood up and roared and bowed to her; but she bowed to us. We sent up a great cry and our women made the tremolo. The people in the crowd were so excited that we heard some of them got sick and fell over. Then when it was quiet, we sang a song to the Grandmother.

That was a very happy time.

We liked Grandmother England, because we could see that she was a fine woman, and she was good to us. Maybe if she had been our Grandmother, it would have been better for our people.

Reader's Response

1. Why did Black Elk like "Grandmother" England?
2. Have you ever met anyone you liked as much as Black Elk liked the Queen of England, someone who was very different from you? Write a brief journal entry about the experience.

Writer's Craft

3. There are two very long paragraphs in this passage. Each one has at least eighteen lines. What is the first of these long paragraphs about? the second?
4. Neihardt uses two very short paragraphs here. Which of these paragraphs do you think moves the reader from one idea to another? Which makes an idea stand out?

LOOKING AHEAD

In this chapter, you'll study the form and structure of paragraphs. Even though most paragraphs are a part of a longer piece of writing, keep in mind that

- most paragraphs have a central, or main, idea
- sensory details, facts, and examples may be used to support the main idea
- description, narration, comparison and contrast, and evaluation are four ways of developing paragraphs

The Parts of a Paragraph

The Main Idea

Paragraphs that stand alone almost always have a main idea. So do paragraphs that are part of a longer piece of writing. The ***main idea*** is the big idea in the paragraph. In the following paragraph, you will find the main idea in the first sentence. It tells you that this paragraph is about how Hopis use Kachina dolls.

> Because Hopis have no written language, Kachina dolls are used to pass tribal lore and religion down through generations. Given to the young during special dances, Kachina dolls are then hung in the home as constant reminders of Hopi ancestry and heritage. Though too young to understand their meaning, infants are given Kachina paddle dolls as toys, so that from birth they are familiar with Hopi custom.
>
> Lonnie Dyer,
> "Kachinas: Sacred Drama of the Hopis"

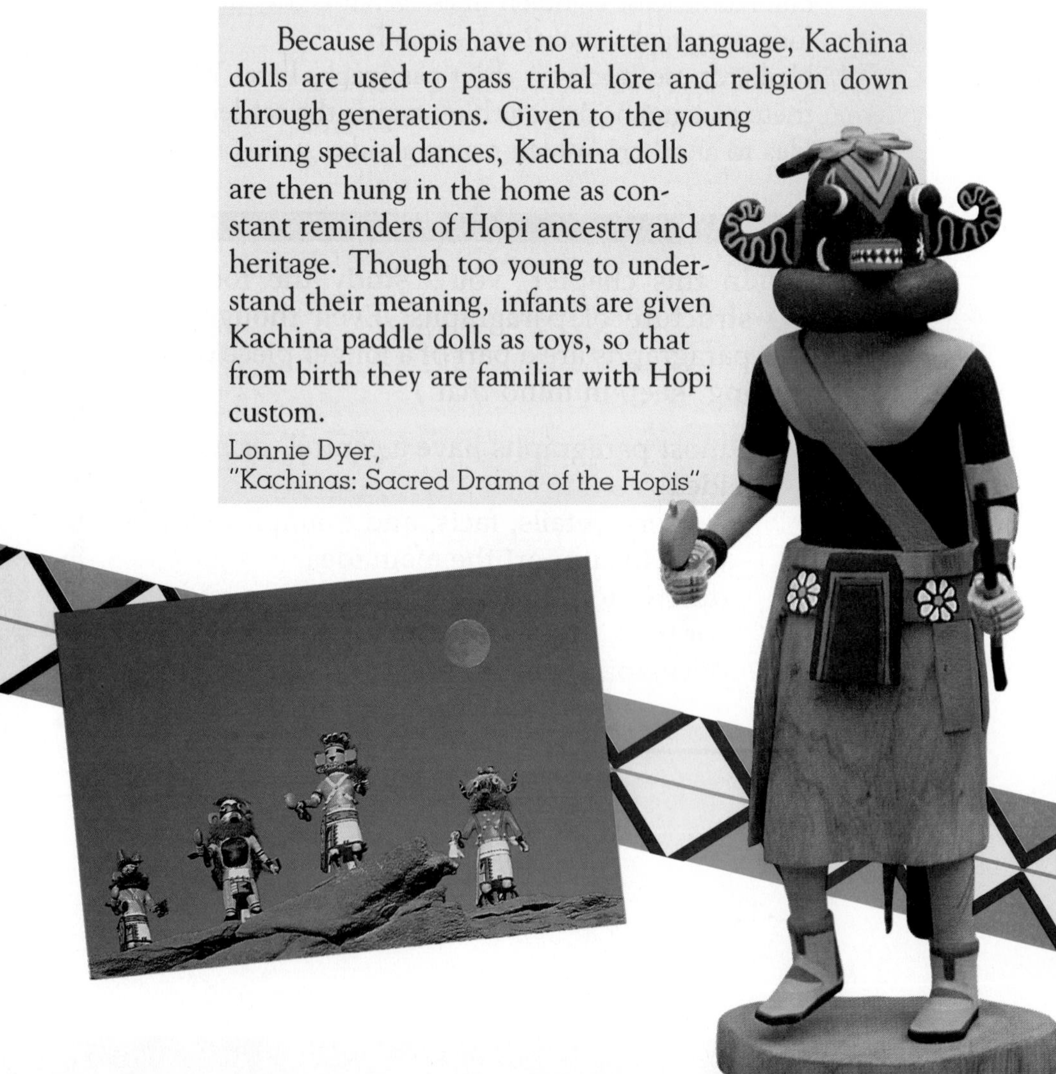

The Topic Sentence

Location of the Topic Sentence. The ***topic sentence*** states the main idea of the paragraph. You may find it at the beginning of the paragraph, in the middle, or even at the end. Then it's like a surprise ending. In the paragraph on page 64, the topic sentence is the first sentence of the paragraph: *Because Hopis have no written language, Kachina dolls are used to pass tribal lore and religion down through generations.*

In the paragraph below, the topic sentence is last. This sentence makes clear that the villagers are preparing for a battle. The other sentences lead up to that point.

> Quickly, quickly we gathered the sheep into the pens. Children rushed through the village gathering firewood to pile inside the homes. Men and women scooped up pots and pots of water, filling cisterns and containers as rapidly as possible. People pulled the last ears of corn from the fields and turned their backs on the dry stalks. Finally, we all stood together in the plaza in the center of the village for just a moment before the fighters went to stand near the walls and the wide-eyed children were coaxed inside the houses. And so we prepared for the coming battle.

Importance of a Topic Sentence. Paragraphs that relate a series of events or that tell a story often don't have a topic sentence. Read the following paragraph. It doesn't have a topic sentence. But all the sentences are about one main idea—the runner's plans for a race.

> She dug her running shoe into the cracked sidewalk in front of her. She pictured the broken sidewalk along a fairly empty thoroughfare where she must run. That highway snaking through the city was wide and black. If anyone was going to block her path, try to mug her, it would happen there. Out there, the sky above her would look gray-purple. And by the time she got there, it would most likely start to rain. She could *perform* in rain. She ran almost truer when it rained. Maybe it was that she was more conscious of slippery surfaces and compensated.
>
> Virginia Hamilton, *A White Romance*

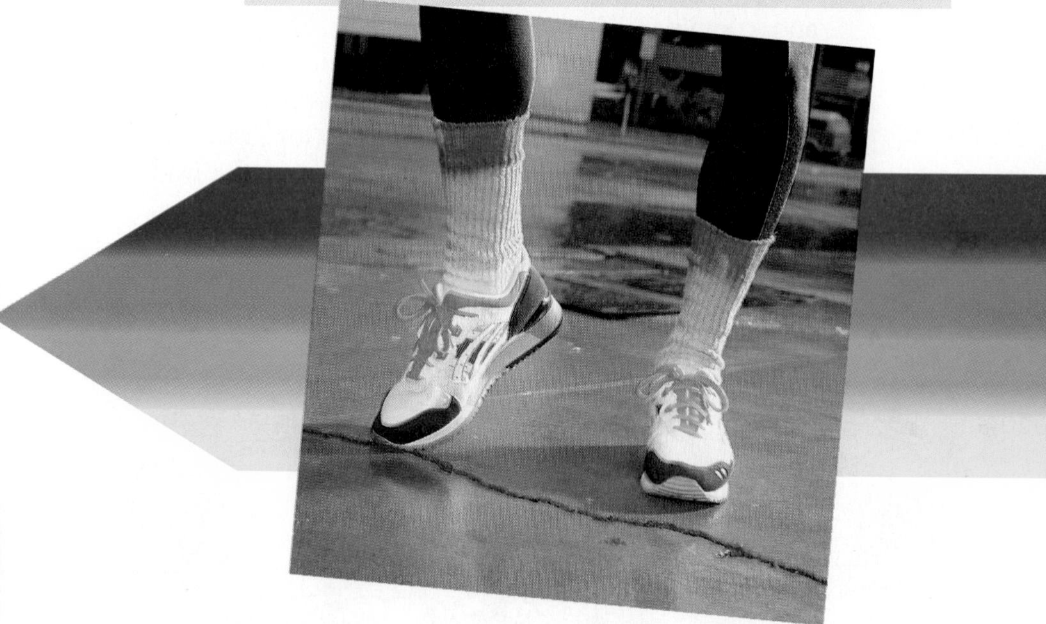

Although all paragraphs don't have to have topic sentences, it is helpful to use them when you are writing. They may help you focus on your main idea. They also help the reader find the main idea.

In a longer piece of writing, start a new paragraph when you change ideas. Also, if you are writing dialogue (the actual words of people), start a new paragraph when you change speakers.

EXERCISE 1 Identifying Main Ideas and Topic Sentences

Finding a main idea is like detective work. In each of the following paragraphs search out the main idea. If there's a topic sentence, identify it. If there is no topic sentence, look at all the details in the paragraph and tell in your own words the main idea of the paragraph.

1. He turned and looked back at the stand of raspberries. The bear was gone, the birds were singing, he saw nothing that could hurt him. There was no danger here that he could sense, could feel. In the city, at night, there was sometimes danger. You could not be in the park at night, after dark, because of the danger. But here, the bear had looked at him and had moved on and—this filled his thoughts—the berries were so good.

Gary Paulsen, from *Hatchet*

2. Like lots of other kids her age, eight-year-old Auralea Moore plays baseball, swims and skis. She also has a favorite plaything: a 19-inch doll named Susan, who was handcrafted to look like her. Auralea was born with spina bifida, a birth defect that has left her paralyzed from the waist down. Her look-alike doll, equipped with a pair of blue and silver "designer" braces, helps her remember that although she may be handicapped, she is definitely not out of the action.

"A Doll Made to Order," *Newsweek*

3. Personally, I thought Maxwell was just about the homeliest dog I'd ever seen in my entire life. He looked like a little old man draped in a piece of brown velvet that was too long, with the leftover cloth hanging in thick folds under his chin. Not only that, his long droopy ears dragged on the ground, he had sad wet eyes and huge thick paws with splayed toes. I mean, who could love a dog like that, except my brother Joji, aged nine, who is a bit on the homely side himself.

Yoshiko Uchida, *A Jar of Dreams*

Supporting Sentences

Supporting sentences give details that explain or prove the main idea. These sentences are called ***supporting sentences*** because they contain *sensory details, facts,* or *examples* that support the main idea of the paragraph.

Sensory details are words that describe one of the five senses—sight, sound, touch, taste, and smell. ***Facts*** give information that can be proved true in a concrete way. For instance, it's a fact that sea gulls drop clams on rocks to break them open. It's also a fact that great herds of buffalo once roamed the western plains. ***Examples*** give typical instances of an idea. A manatee is an example of a mammal that lives in the water. A chameleon is a lizard whose changes in coloring are an example of protective coloration. This chart shows the kinds of details you can use to support the main idea of the paragraph.

SUPPORTING SENTENCES	
Sensory Details	Examples
Sight	The bright sun glared off the front windshield of the car.
Sound	Thunder boomed down the canyon, echoing off the walls.
Touch	My hands felt frozen to the cold, steel handlebars.
Taste	Thirstily, she gulped down the sweet orange juice.
Smell	The sharp, unpleasant odor of fresh asphalt met his nose.
Facts	In 1961, Roger Maris slammed sixty-one home runs to break the old record of sixty held by Babe Ruth.
Examples	Fierce windstorms occur throughout the world. In the central United States, tornadoes have wind speeds over two hundred miles per hour.

EXERCISE 2 **Collecting Supporting Details**

When you write paragraphs, you have to collect (find or think up) details of support. You can practice with the following topic sentences. For each, one kind of supporting detail is suggested—sensory details, facts, or examples. List at least two details to support each topic sentence.

EXAMPLE **1. The appliance that toasts our bread has changed over the years. (facts)**

1. *Details: It originated in the early 1900s. It consisted of bare wires with no thermostat. The first pop-up toaster appeared in 1926.*

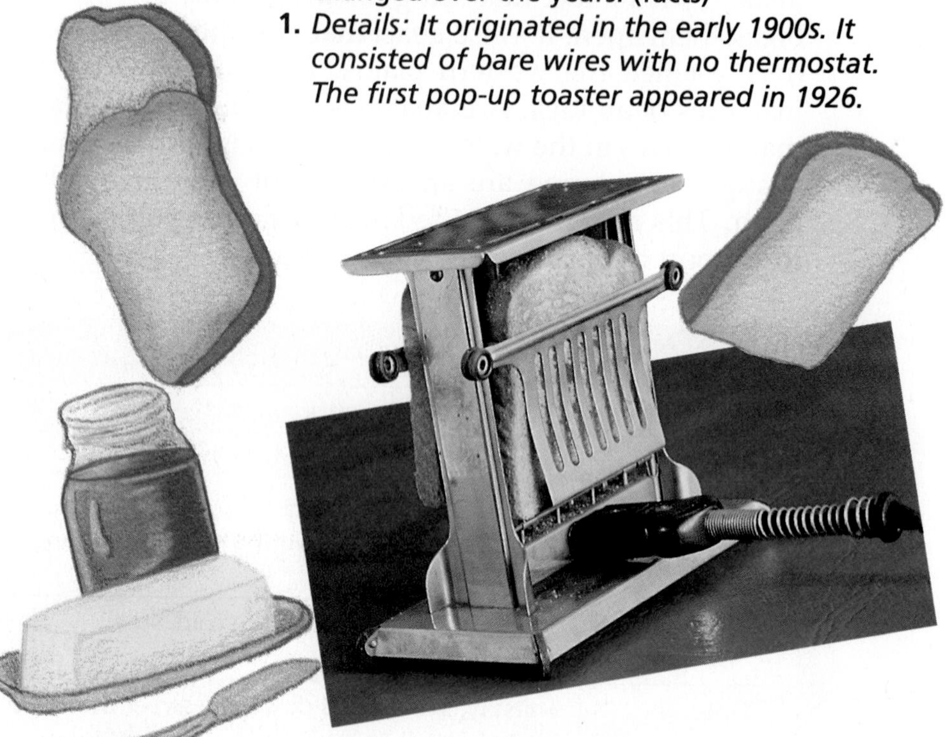

1. The time I spend getting ready for school in the mornings is not my favorite part of the day. (sensory details)
2. My dream is to spend two days in a shopping mall. (examples)
3. One person's actions can make a difference in the lives of others. (facts)
4. When I'm hungry, I can just imagine my favorite meal. (sensory details)

Unity and Coherence

A paragraph is a little like a car. It has to have *unity*—you don't want one blue fender on a red car. And it has to have *coherence*—the back of the car has to be connected to the front.

Unity

A paragraph has ***unity*** when all the sentences support, or tell something about, one main idea. A paragraph that doesn't have unity may confuse your readers. For example, in a paragraph about Bonnie St. John, you might tell how she became a skiing champion despite losing a leg. But if you mentioned a friend who is also a skier, you would destroy the unity. That information wouldn't be related to your main idea.

In the paragraph on the following page, the first sentence states the main idea. Notice how all the other sentences tell something more about the heavy snow.

The snow began quietly this time, like an afterthought to the gray Sunday night. The moon almost broke through once, but toward daylight, a little wind came up and started white curls, thin and lonesome, running over the old drifts left from the New Year storm. Gradually the snow thickened, until around eight-thirty the two ruts of the winding trails were covered and undisturbed, except down in the Lone Tree district, where an old, yellow bus crawled heavily along, feeling out the ruts between the choppy sand hills.

Mari Sandoz, "Winter Thunder"

EXERCISE 3 **Identifying Sentences That Destroy Unity**

Each of the following paragraphs has one sentence that destroys the unity. Try your skill at finding the sentences that don't belong. [Hint: First, decide what the main idea is. Next, decide whether each supporting sentence is closely connected to the main idea.]

1. It felt like an oven to Tamara as she walked up the street toward the park. It was a hot day for baseball practice. She wondered if the Cardinals game would be on television that evening. Tamara told herself she couldn't let the heat slow her down, though. The coach would be deciding today who would start in the season's first game. And she wanted to be playing third.

2. Canoes are made for many different purposes. White-water canoes are for use in fast, rock-filled streams. They're made to turn quickly to avoid obstacles. Other canoes are made for lakes and quiet rivers. They don't turn too quickly, so they won't be your first choice for use on a river with lots of rapids. On the other hand, they're easy to paddle in a straight line. The white-water canoe can't be paddled in a perfectly straight line no matter what you do. You can also find canoes that are made to carry either one or two people. Before choosing a canoe, think about what kind of water you'll be using it in.

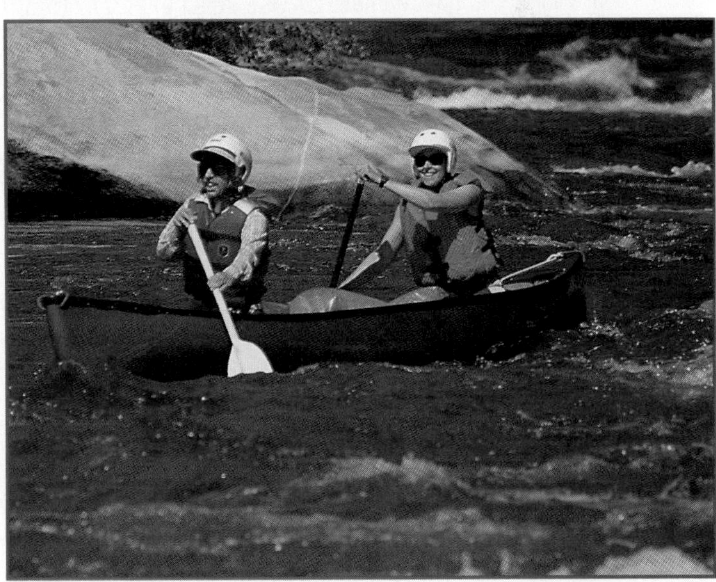

Coherence

A paragraph has ***coherence*** when readers can tell how and why ideas are connected.

To create coherence you can do two things. First, you can arrange your details in an *order* that makes sense to the reader. In the section Ways of Developing Paragraphs (page 77), you'll learn more about how to organize details.

The second way of creating coherence in paragraphs is to use *transitional words* or *phrases* to connect ideas. These are words and phrases like *for example, mainly,* and *in addition.* They not only connect ideas, but also tell why and how they're related.

The following chart shows examples of some of the common words and phrases used for transitions that help to create coherence.

TRANSITIONAL WORDS AND PHRASES		
COMPARING AND CONTRASTING IDEAS		
also	another	similarly
although	but	too
and	however	yet
SHOWING CAUSE AND EFFECT / NARRATION		
as a result	for	so that
because	since	therefore
SHOWING TIME / NARRATION		
after	first, second, etc.	then
before	next	until
finally	often	when
SHOWING PLACE / DESCRIPTION		
above	down	next
around	here	over
before	in	there
beside	into	under

The following paragraph tells how Native Americans are recognized everywhere. The writer uses transitional words to show how ideas are connected. Notice, for example, how the writer says that at "first" kids pretend they don't see him. "Then" they turn and look.

> When I go someplace, most of the time those little people see me. At first they'll pretend not to see me. They go past me a little ways, and then they will turn back and look at me. Then they'll nudge their mama or daddy or grandma or grandpa, and I'll hear them say, "There's an Indian back there." So the Indians are still here. We never phased away. We didn't just blend into society and vanish. In fact, we're appearing more and more and more. We get around more now, too. Indians are not just confined only to the United States or one state or one county or one city or one house. They know us all over this Earth.
>
> Wallace H. Black Elk and William S. Lyon, *Black Elk: The Sacred Ways of a Lakota*

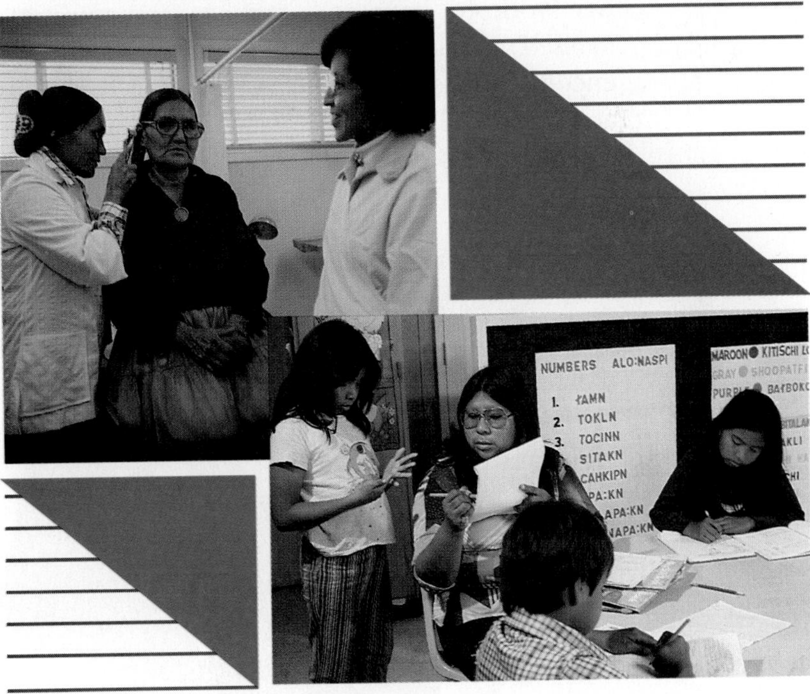

EXERCISE 4 Identifying Transitional Words and Phrases

Identifying transitional words and phrases can help you see how they work when they are used in paragraphs. Using the chart on page 74 as a guide, make a list of all the transitional words and phrases in the following paragraph.

When she was elected to be chief of the Cherokee Nation in 1987, Wilma Mankiller took on a huge job. But she was used to challenges. In 1976, she had developed many needed projects for Cherokees in rural Oklahoma. First, she taught people how to build their own homes. Next, she installed new water supply lines. Finally, she started new rural health clinics. Then she had to overcome serious injuries she suffered in an auto accident in late 1979. So while others were impressed with the new chief's dedication, no one who really knew her well found her leadership ability surprising. Once elected as chief, Mankiller continued her work to improve Cherokee communities. She focused on housing and education needs, and she encouraged her people to be proud of their language and culture. Then, in 1991, Wilma Mankiller was re-elected for a second term as chief.

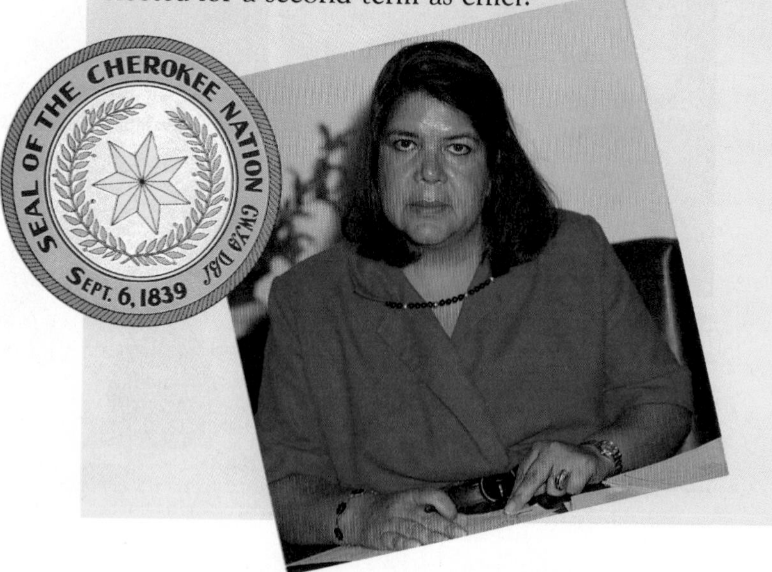

Ways of Developing Paragraphs

What you're writing about, your subject or topic, usually determines the way you develop it. Here are four ways of writing a paragraph.

WAYS OF DEVELOPING PARAGRAPHS	
Description	Looking at parts of a person, place, or thing
Narration	Looking at changes in a person, place, or thing over time
Comparison and Contrast	Finding likenesses and differences between people, places, or things
Evaluation	Judging the person, place, or thing's value or worth

Description

How would you describe your favorite hangout to one of your friends? What does the Ninja Turtle Michelangelo look like?

In answering either of these questions, you're ***describing*** something. That means you're picking out specific details, or features, to tell about that will help someone else recognize it.

In describing something, you often use ***spatial order.*** Spatial order organizes details according to their location. In the following paragraph, notice how the writer uses sensory details and spatial order to describe her father's farm.

> The farm my father grew up on, where Grandpa Welty and Grandma lived, was in southern Ohio in the rolling hills of Hocking County, near the small town of Logan. It was one of the neat, narrow-porched, two-story farmhouses, painted white, of the Pennsylvania-German country. Across its front grew feathery cosmos and barrel-sized peony bushes with stripy heavy-scented blooms pushing out of the leaves. There was a springhouse to one side, down a little

walk only one brick in width, and an old apple orchard in front, the barn and the pasture and fields of corn and wheat behind. Periodically there came sounds from the barn, and you could hear the crows, but everything else was still.

Eudora Welty, *One Writer's Beginnings*

EXERCISE 5 **Collecting Descriptive Details**

How would you describe an insect, a rock star, or a movie set? Work in a group of two or three classmates. Choose one of the subjects below and list sensory details that describe it. Then, arrange them in spatial order.

1. the creepiest animal you've ever seen
2. your favorite car
3. the best setting for a science fiction movie
4. your classroom, moments before a holiday break
5. your favorite season

Narration

What happened when a character lost in the frigid arctic wilderness couldn't build a fire? How is soccer played? What caused the ocean liner *Titanic* to sink?

When you answer any of these questions, you are ***narrating.*** That means you are telling about an event or an action as it changes over time. Because narrating tells about changes in time, you usually use ***chronological,*** or time, ***order.***

You can use narration to tell a story (what happened to the character in the Arctic), to explain a process (how to play soccer), or to explain causes and effects (what caused the *Titanic* to sink).

Telling a Story. Everybody loves a good story. You've probably listened to one or told one today. It may have been made up, or it may have been about something that really happened.

The following is a story slaves told many years ago about some strange escapes from slavery.

Uncle Mingo's forehead wrinkled like a mask in the moonlight. "Don't make light of what old folks tell you, son," he warned. "If the old folks say they seen slaves pick up and fly back to Africa, like birds, just don't you dispute them. If they tell you about a slave preacher what led his whole flock to the beach and sat down on the sand with them, looking across the ocean toward home, don't ask no questions. Next morning nobody could find trace of that preacher or his people. And no boat had been there neither. One day when I was chopping cotton in the field, I looked up and the old fellow working in the row next to mine was gone. He was too feeble to run away, and I couldn't see no place for him to hide. None of the others in the field saw him leave either, but later on an old woman drinking water at a well, told us she noticed something pass in front of the sun about that time, like a hawk or a buzzard maybe, but she didn't pay it much mind."

Arna Bontemps, *Chariot In the Sky: A Story of the Jubilee Singers*

Explaining a Process. When you tell how to do something or how something works, you're ***explaining a process.*** Often, this means telling how to do something step by step—what is done first, then next, and so on. This is chronological order.

The following paragraph tells how kites may have been developed.

Like a lot of very old activities, no one is quite sure how kite flying started. Perhaps an ancient Chinese first noticed big leaves of certain plants fluttering at the end of long vines. Then, after watching "leaf-kites" for a while, he tied his straw hat to a string just for fun and happily found that the wind kept it flying. Later, he may have stretched a piece of animal skin over a bamboo frame and flown that from the end of a line.

Dan Carlinsky, "Kites"

Explaining Causes and Effects. Narrating is also used to ***explain causes and effects.*** In other words, narrating can be used to tell how one event is a result of an earlier event.

The following paragraph tells what causes crickets to stop chirping. It also tells one helpful effect of their sudden silence.

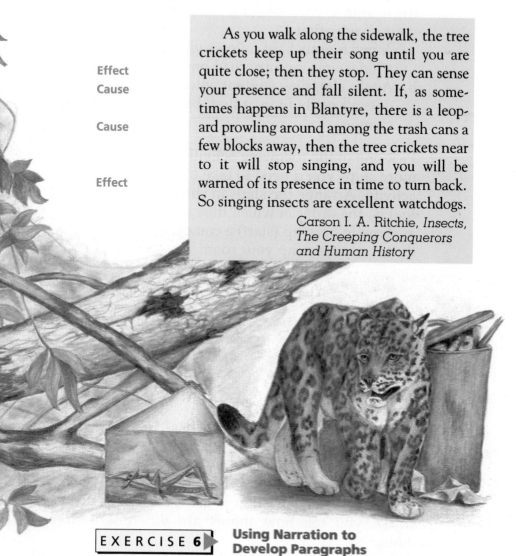

> As you walk along the sidewalk, the tree crickets keep up their song until you are quite close; then they stop. They can sense your presence and fall silent. If, as sometimes happens in Blantyre, there is a leopard prowling around among the trash cans a few blocks away, then the tree crickets near to it will stop singing, and you will be warned of its presence in time to turn back. So singing insects are excellent watchdogs.
>
> Carson I. A. Ritchie, *Insects, The Creeping Conquerors and Human History*

Effect (quite close; then they stop)
Cause (They can sense your presence)
Cause (leopard prowling around)
Effect (you will be warned of its presence)

EXERCISE 6 **Using Narration to Develop Paragraphs**

Can you tell a story about the time you were most frightened? Can you explain how to tie your shoes? Can you tell the causes and effects of not cleaning up your room for a month? The following exercises will give you some practice in telling about events in the order in which they happen. Follow the directions for each item.

1. Each of the topics below could be the subject of a story. Select one of these topics and make up three or more events that might be in the story. Arrange all of the events in chronological order. Don't forget to use your imagination.
   a. A mysterious light follows your family's car down a lonesome, country road one night.
   b. A tall, shy, new student enters your school. He doesn't really fit in at first, but soon the situation changes.

2. Pick one of the following activities. Then list three or more steps you'd need to take in order to perform this activity. Arrange the steps in chronological order—that is, the order in which they should happen.
   c. how to boot up (start) a computer
   d. how to clean up your room

3. Choose one of the following. Give at least three possible causes or three possible effects.
   e. missing the school bus (give causes)
   f. a water shortage in your town or region (give effects)

Comparison and Contrast

How are ice skates like roller blades? In what ways are they different?

If you can answer these questions, you can compare and contrast ice skates and roller blades. Whenever you ***compare,*** you tell how things are alike. Whenever you ***contrast,*** you tell how things are different from one another.

When you compare and contrast, you can use ***logical order.*** Something that is logical is something that makes sense. When you compare and contrast, it is logical to group related ideas together.

Read the following paragraph. The writer compares and contrasts her two sisters. How are the sisters alike? How are they different?

> My sisters may be twins, but they are very different. Sara and Sally look exactly alike. They both have long, braided black hair and big black eyes with eyelashes out to there. But the resemblance stops with looks. If they just stand still, they can pretend to be each other. If they talk or move, the joke is over. Sara talks all the time and bounces just like Winnie the Pooh's friend Tigger. Sally never says anything except "Pass the peanut butter," and she moves like a sick snail. How can they be twins?

Comparison

Contrast

EXERCISE 7 **Speaking and Listening: Comparison and Contrast**

Remember the ice skates and roller blades? Now it's your turn to think about two subjects that are enough alike to be compared and different enough to be interesting. Write one statement that tells how these subjects are alike and one statement that tells how they are different. Share your statements with a small group. With the help of the group, think of some other similarities and differences.

You might compare and contrast the following items:

1. being a child and being a teenager
2. good horror movies and bad horror movies
3. living in a large city and living in a small community

Evaluation

Do you like broccoli? Did you enjoy Robert M. Service's poem "The Cremation of Sam McGee"?

Whenever you answer questions like these, you're ***evaluating.*** In other words, you're telling whether you think broccoli and the poem are good or bad. You'd want to give reasons for your answer. For example, you might say you gagged on cooked broccoli, but you love raw broccoli with cheese dip. You might say you enjoyed the poem because of its rhyme or because of its humor.

When writing an evaluation, you will probably organize it by ***order of importance.*** For example, you might place your most important information first. Then you'd put your next most important information, and so on. Or, you might arrange your most important information last, so that you gradually lead up to your biggest point.

The following paragraph was written to persuade people not to build more buildings in Yellowstone National Park. Notice the reasons the writer gives for the evaluation.

I don't think that more hotels, campgrounds, and restaurants should be built in Yellowstone National Park. The park is set aside to protect the animals and plants that live there and to allow people to experience the wilderness. When more buildings go up, more people crowd into the park. **Reason** And the more people there are, the less room there is for wildlife and for wilderness. **Reason** People don't just take up space. They also scare the animals and keep them from living as they would naturally live in the wild. In Yellowstone National Park, I think **Evaluation** the most important thing is to protect the animals and the natural wilderness. If this means putting a stop to more building, then the building should be stopped.

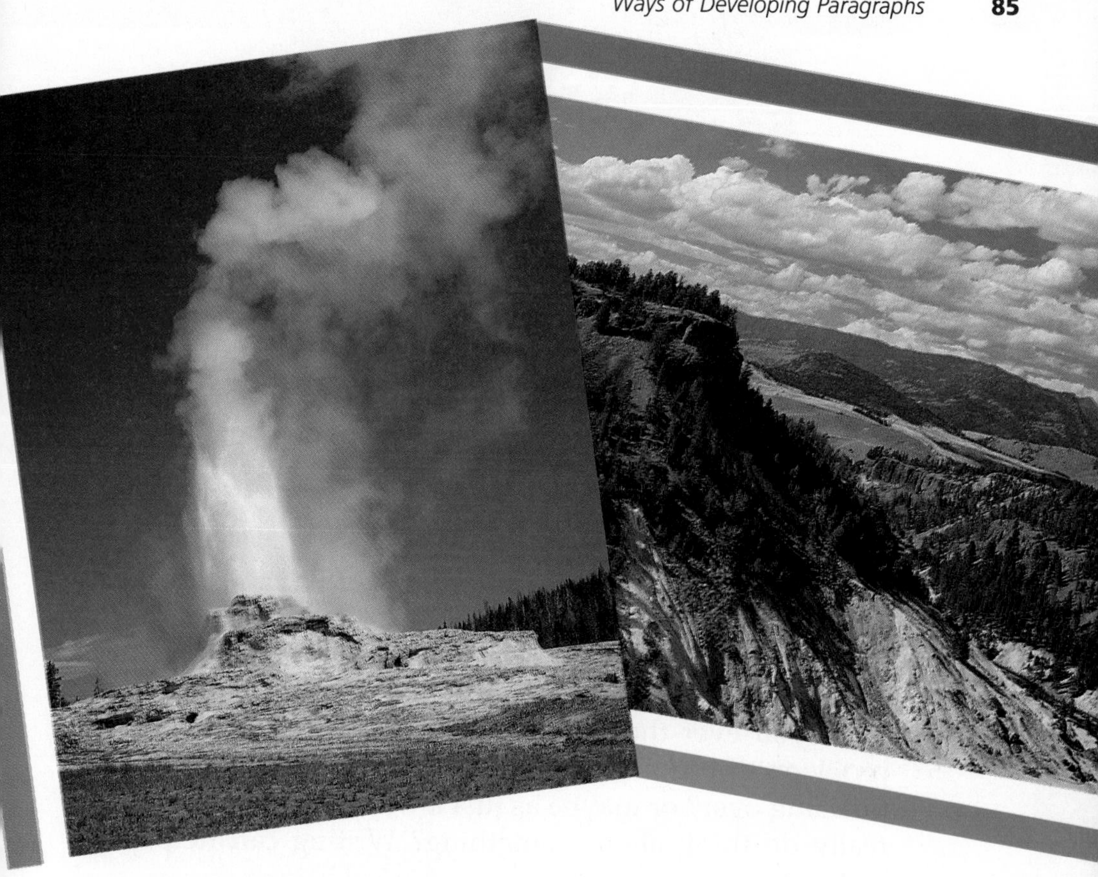

EXERCISE 8 **Developing an Evaluation**

What's your evaluation? Why do you think so? Choose one of the following subjects and write your evaluation of it. Give at least two reasons for your opinion. List first the reason you think is more important.

EXAMPLE **1.** our school's basketball team

1. *Evaluation:* *It's a very good team.*
Reasons: *(1) Our center is five foot ten.*
(2) Our guards are very quick.
(3) Players who are not even starting are also good shooters.

1. the street you live on
2. a book you've read lately or movie you've seen recently
3. the newest fad in clothes

MAKING CONNECTIONS

Now that you know the form and structure of paragraphs, how do you use your knowledge? Try applying what you've learned as you write paragraphs for different purposes. Remember that the basic purposes of writing are self-expression, information, persuasion, and creativity.

WRITING PARAGRAPHS FOR DIFFERENT PURPOSES

Writing a Paragraph to Express Yourself

Have you ever thought about writing as a way to think problems through? as a way to explore an idea you're puzzling over? or maybe as just a way to decide what you really do think about something? Writing can help you sort out your thoughts.

On a separate sheet of paper—or in your journal or diary if you keep one—write an expressive paragraph. Use one of the following sentences to get started. See where it leads you.

1. My closest friend means so much to me because ____.
2. I'm happiest when I'm ____ because ____.
3. One thing I'd like to change about myself is ____.
4. I get sad when I think about ____.
5. Something I'd really like to do within the next year is ____.

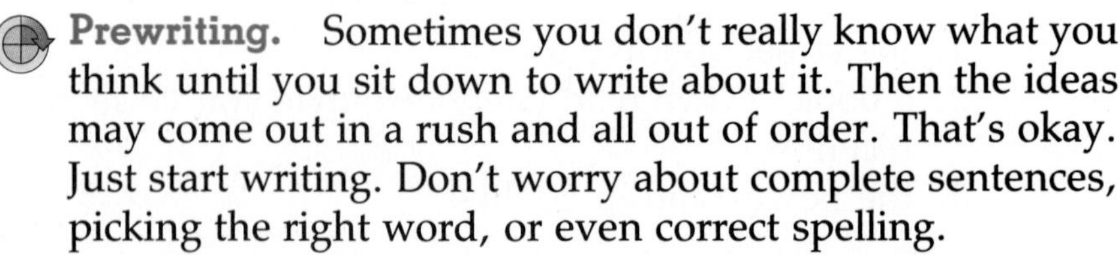

Prewriting. Sometimes you don't really know what you think until you sit down to write about it. Then the ideas may come out in a rush and all out of order. That's okay. Just start writing. Don't worry about complete sentences, picking the right word, or even correct spelling.

Writing, Evaluating, and Revising. Expressive writing is often a very personal kind of writing. You may not want to share this writing with others. In that case, just write a draft. You may not need to revise it. If you want to share it with others, though, you should reread it. Check it for unity and coherence. Are the sentences organized so the ideas are clear?

Proofreading and Publishing. If you have decided to share your writing with others, be sure that you proofread it carefully. Check your usage and mechanics. You may want to make a clean copy for others to read.

Writing a Paragraph to Persuade

One of the earliest skills you learned was persuasion. You may have used it to get your mom or dad to buy a certain cereal in the supermarket. Sometimes parents are easy to persuade. Sometimes they aren't. Convincing other people can be just as hard or harder. You need to have reasons that support the point you want to make.

Look at the photographs. One shows an abandoned railroad track. The other shows a bike path that was built along a strip of land that was once a railroad. Imagine that a railroad that runs through your county has been abandoned. The railroad company is willing to give it to the county, but the county doesn't know what to do with it.

Some people want to turn it into a bikeway, like the one in the photograph. But many people, especially people who own land along the railway, oppose the bikeway. They are afraid that they'd lose their privacy and that the county can't afford to build and maintain the bikeway.

Write a paragraph in which you try to persuade county leaders either to support the bikeway or to oppose it. Think about the advantages and disadvantages of your proposal and organize your reasons carefully. You may want to review the section on Evaluating (page 84) before you begin writing.

Prewriting. You may want to begin by listing your reasons for supporting or opposing the bikeway. Choose the best two or three reasons for your paragraph.

Writing, Evaluating, and Revising. You'll want to begin your paragraph with a clear topic sentence that states your opinion. You can use one of these topic sentences or make up your own.

> The county government should support making a bikeway where the railroad used to run.
>
> The county government should oppose making a bikeway where the railroad used to run.

After completing your draft, review it carefully. Do you have two or three reasons? Do they support your topic sentence? Have you arranged them in the best order? Revise your paragraph to make it more convincing.

Proofreading and Publishing. Proofread your final draft and correct any errors in usage and mechanics. Then share your paragraph with classmates, your parents, or neighbors. Ask them if it persuaded them.

Writing a Paragraph to Inform

In school and out, you'll be asked to write paragraphs that inform. Your teachers want to see what you have learned in class. A friend may want your recipe for making a pizza. A relative in another state may want to know what you did on vacation.

The chart below gives information about the 1989 San Francisco earthquake. Use the information to write an informative paragraph. Here's a topic sentence to get you started.

> Topic Sentence: The 1989 San Francisco earthquake caused a great deal of damage.

THE SAN FRANCISCO EARTHQUAKE OF 1989
Occurred October 17, 1989, with many aftershocks
Measured 7.1 on the Richter scale
Collapsed $1\frac{1}{4}$-mile section of double-decker Nimitz Freeway (I-880)
Caused delay of third game of World Series
Hundreds of buildings destroyed; thousands damaged
Damage of approximately six billion dollars
Official death toll of 63
More than 3,000 injured

Prewriting. Use notes from the chart to develop your paragraph. Before you begin, however, you might look for ways to organize them.

Writing, Evaluating, and Revising. Begin with your topic sentence. Then write two or three additional sentences, using information from the chart. You can add more information, if you like, from your own research. Evaluate your paragraph. Does it make sense? Do your facts support the topic sentence? Can the paragraph be reorganized so the information is clearer to readers?

Proofreading and Publishing. Reread your paragraph, looking carefully for errors in usage or mechanics. Make any needed corrections. Then share your paragraph with a friend.

Writing a Paragraph That Is Creative

Try to visualize this scene. It's a dark, moonless night. You've been walking along a sandy beach for more than an hour. You're all alone, and this part of the beach is isolated. There are no lights anywhere to be seen. The wind is getting stronger and stronger. Waves are crashing against the beach. Suddenly, you hear the sound of horse hooves pounding into the sand. Then you hear a dog barking. You turn and look toward the sounds. You can't

see anything at first. But then, the sounds draw closer. You can just make out the dark shape of a rider and horse coming toward you. A large dog races alongside, occasionally barking.

What happens next? Make it up. Write a paragraph that tells about the next event. Your paragraph doesn't have to tell the rest of the story. Just add some information about what occurs next. Use the following questions to help you write the paragraph.

- Is the rider a stranger or a friend?
- Is the dog chasing the horse and rider or running along with them?
- Do you feel threatened or relieved that the rider has come?
- Does the rider stop in front of you or go on past? If the rider stops, what do you say first?

Prewriting. Think about possible answers to the questions. You might try freewriting about the situation for a few minutes. Just let your ideas develop as you go. See where they lead you.

When you finish, read what you've written. Pick out one or two ideas and use them to develop your paragraph.

Writing, Evaluating, and Revising. Using the ideas from freewriting, write three or four sentences that tell what happens next. Remember, your paragraph doesn't have to complete the story. It only needs to tell the next part.

When you've finished your paragraph, review it. Does it leave the reader wanting to know more? Revise your paragraph to improve any weaknesses you've noticed.

Proofreading and Publishing. Read your final draft again and correct any errors in usage or mechanics. Then share your paragraph with a group of classmates. Discuss your ideas about how the story ends.

3 Learning About Compositions

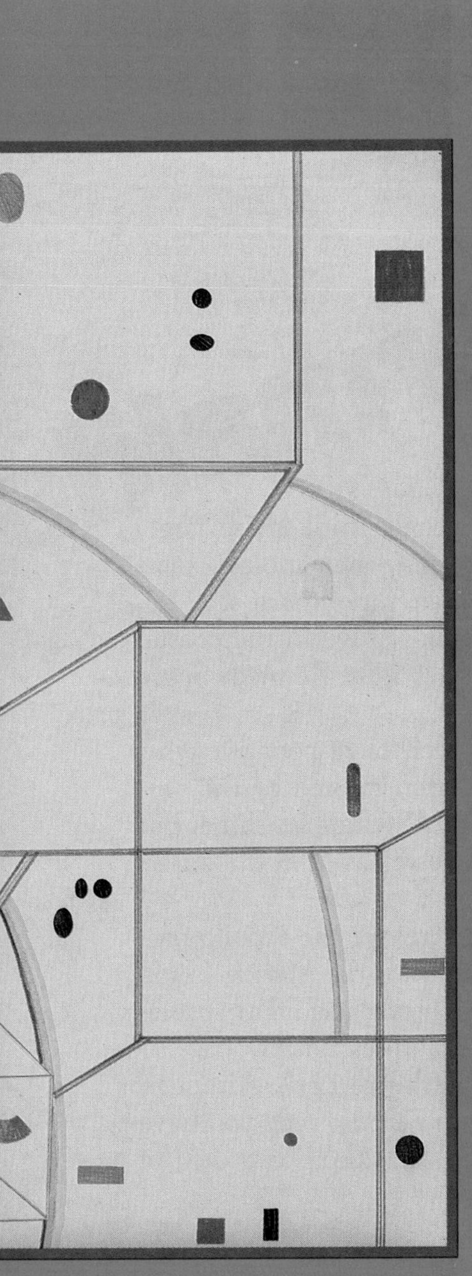

Looking at the Whole

When you think about the volleyball team, do you think about the individual players? *Daniel has a strong serve, but Sarah is more accurate.* Or do you think about the whole team? *Our seventh-grade team is going to win the tournament.* In writing, you can think of words, sentences, or paragraphs as parts. A composition is a **whole** piece of writing.

Writing and You. A magazine article tells about a baseball superstar. A newspaper report tells about a teenager doing volunteer work. A student's history paper explains how the Civil War started. Each of these is a whole piece of writing, a kind of composition. Why do you think the composition form is used so often?

As You Read. On the next pages is a magazine article about manatees. What can you tell about composition form from reading this article?

76 C-7, Al Held (1976). Colored pencil, graphite, crayon and felt-tip on paper. Sheet and image: 27 × 39 $\frac{15}{16}$ inches. Collection of Whitney Museum of American Art. Purchase with funds from the Drawing Committee. 86.2

"For centuries, sailors have told of the legendary mermaid which appeared to lonely mariners during their long sea voyages. Nowadays, astronauts, too, have the chance to see mermaids—at Kennedy Space Center in Florida."

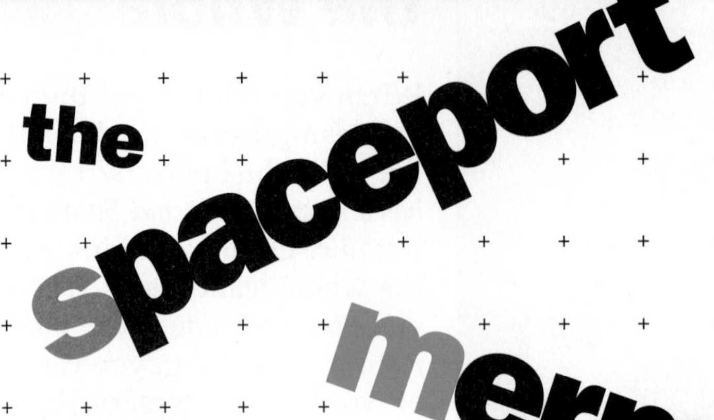

the spaceport mermaids

by Greg Walz-Chojnacki

Mermaids?

Well, manatees, actually. Some people think these large, flippered creatures may have looked like humanoids—mermaids—to bored, superstitious seamen after months at sea.

Thousands of these gentle sea mammals live in the coastal waters of Florida, including the waterways of the Kennedy Space Center.

Unfortunately, these creatures, which have poor eyesight, are an endangered species. They are often injured by the propellers of power boats that cruise under the Florida sunshine. But the playful animals have been finding a safe haven in the waters surrounding the space center.

When NASA purchased 188,000 acres for the Apollo program, it set aside a large part of the land for the Merritt Island Wildlife Refuge. NASA has a policy of protecting many species there, including bald eagles, alligators, and sea turtles.

NASA has been protecting manatees since 1977. Although manatee deaths have been increasing in Florida, only two have died in space center waters since 1984, and those two died of natural causes.

NASA, in cooperation with state and federal wildlife agencies, has attached space-age radio monitors to some manatees to identify and protect their habitats. NASA also gives special training to space center personnel who operate boats, so they can avoid harming the creatures.

Even the boats used to recover the Shuttle's solid rocket boosters have been built with the manatees in mind. When retrieving the boosters in the Atlantic Ocean, the ships use ordinary propellers. But the ships are powered by water jets when they reach the waters inhabited by manatees.

The manatees seem to know a safe place when they find one. Their numbers have been increasing at the space center since 1984.

NASA's manatee protection policy has been a real success. Kennedy Space Center employees have many opportunities to see these fascinating creatures in the waterways of America's spaceport.

Now, if astronauts start seeing mermaids in orbit, that will be a completely different kind of problem!

"Some people think these large, flippered creatures may have looked like humanoids—mermaids—to bored, superstitious seamen after months at sea."

Reader's Response

1. If you have ever seen a manatee or a dolphin, tell about your experience with the animal. Why do you think people like these animals so much?
2. When you think of NASA and the Kennedy Space Center, what usually comes to your mind? Do you think of manatees?

Writer's Craft

3. How do you know that the main idea of the article is about NASA protecting the manatee?
4. The first paragraph talks about astronauts seeing mermaids. You know that mermaids don't exist. Why do you think the author begins the article this way?
5. How does the ending relate to the first paragraph?

Looking Ahead

In this chapter, you'll learn about the parts of a composition. You'll find that most compositions are alike in certain ways. Most of them

- have one main idea
- have three main parts—an introduction, a body, and a conclusion
- have several paragraphs that work together to support the main idea

What Makes a Composition

Writing compositions probably isn't your favorite activity. Sometimes it's hard to think of something to write about. And then it may be hard to think of how to begin or end your composition.

In this chapter, you'll learn about composition form—how the different parts work together to create a whole piece of writing. Then you'll be able to use that form in other chapters to explain a process, to persuade, to write about literature, and to write a research report.

PEANUTS, reprinted by permission of UFS, Inc.

The Composition Plan

What are you doing this weekend? Will you work, play a sport, or take music lessons? You've probably already made some plans for this weekend and maybe for future ones. Compositions, like weekends, usually turn out much better when they are planned.

The Main Idea

When you have a topic for your composition, think what you want to say about it. What is most important and interesting? What you want to say about your topic is your ***main idea.***

One writer wanted to write about competing in a skateboarding contest. He thought about the days of practicing, the new tricks, and the excitement. He finally decided to focus on how much fun the contest was. "Skateboard contests are fun" became his main idea.

EXERCISE 1 **Writing the Main Idea**

Are you throwing away things that could be recycled instead? The writer who took the following notes became interested in recycling after hearing about the problems of too much trash. Read over the notes and decide on a main idea for a composition on recycling. Write down the main idea and then get together with two or three other students. Compare your ideas. Are they the same?

You can set up a recycling center in your home or school.
Try not to buy items in jars or boxes that can't be recycled.
Find out how to get a community recycling program started.
Don't accept food that's in plastic containers at fast-food restaurants.
Separate your trash, and throw away only what can't be recycled.
Don't waste paper—use both sides of your notebook and other writing paper.
Don't wrap your lunch in plastic.
Buy or make canvas or nylon grocery bags and lunch sacks that you can use again.
Don't buy things you don't really want or need.

You can always change your main idea for your composition. As you find ideas and think about your topic, you may decide that you want to say something different. Then you can just rewrite your main idea.

Early Plans

An ***early plan,*** sometimes called an ***informal outline,*** is a way to organize your ideas. First, put your ideas into related groups. Then, arrange the groups in an order that makes sense to readers.

Grouping. Look at the information you have. Which details belong together? Do you have several notes about one part of your topic? Follow these steps to group ideas.

1. Group notes that have something in common.
2. Write a heading for each group of notes.
3. Put the heading with that group of notes. (This will make it easier to organize your writing later.)
4. If you have notes that don't seem to fit, set them aside. Later, you may find a place to use them.

Ordering. The order you use depends partly on your information. What should come first? What last? If your composition tells about how to perform skateboarding tricks, you're writing about a step-by-step process. Then it's natural to use ***chronological*** (time) ***order.*** Is your composition about a trip to see the giant redwoods? You might use ***spatial order*** and describe the trees in the order you see them.

The important thing is to arrange your ideas in an order that makes sense to readers. The writer of the composition on pet pigs (page 102) uses ***logical order.*** The writer tells first about the benefits of having a pet pig and then tells about the drawbacks. In logical order, related ideas are grouped together. This early plan shows how the writer grouped related ideas for the essay.

TOPIC: PET PIGS	
BENEFITS	DRAWBACKS
clean easier than some other animals to housebreak don't shed or get fleas can communicate easy to train will play and do tricks easy to feed	can get very large can be lazy can be too playful not a good watch animal

EXERCISE 2 **Making an Early Plan**

Working with a partner, make an early plan for a composition based on the notes on recycling in Exercise 1. What will be the best order for the composition? After you decide, group the notes in that order. Then arrange the notes within the groups in a way that makes sense.

REFERENCE NOTE: For more help in arranging ideas, see pages 77–84.

Formal Outlines

A *formal outline* is more structured than an early plan. It uses letters and numbers to label main headings and ideas that belong below those headings. A formal outline can have either topics (single words or phrases) or complete sentences.

Here's a topic outline for the essay on pet pigs. Compare it to the finished composition, below. Notice that the introduction and conclusion aren't a part of the outline.

Title: The Patter of Little Hooves
Main Idea: Pigs make great pets.

I. Benefits
  A. Characteristics
    1. Cleanliness
    2. Ease of housebreaking
    3. Lack of fur and fleas
    4. Friendliness
  B. Enjoyment of games
    1. Fetching
    2. Swimming
    3. Rolling over
    4. Climbing stairs
II. Drawbacks
  A. Playfulness
  B. Inability to protect

REFERENCE NOTE: For more information about formal outlines, see pages 333–334.

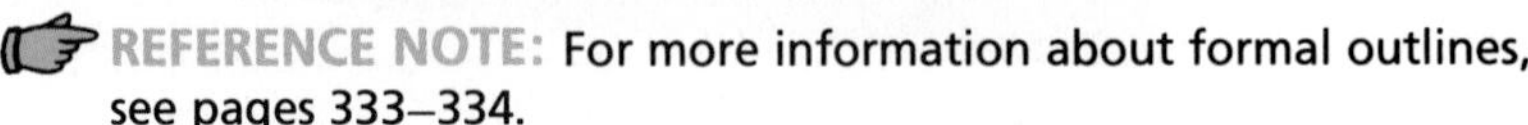

A WRITER'S MODEL

Here's the composition on pet pigs. See how the paragraphs are based on the parts of the outline? Does every paragraph support the idea that pigs make great pets?

The Patter of Little Hooves

INTRODUCTION

Main idea

What comes to mind when you think about pigs? Many people think of words like <u>dirty, smelly, unfriendly</u>, and even <u>stupid</u>. It may surprise you, but these words don't describe pigs at all. You may be even more surprised that many people think that pigs make great pets.

BODY

Main topic: Characteristics

As a matter of fact, pig lovers will tell you that pigs are very pleasant. Many people say that pigs are much better pets than cats or dogs. They point out that pigs are really very clean and are more easily housebroken than most other pets. Pigs don't shed or get fleas. And they are friendly companions. They are happy to sit quietly and watch TV with you and never complain about your choice of programs.

Main topic: Enjoyment of games

Pigs learn quickly and enjoy playing games. They will happily fetch sticks that are thrown for them. They can also be taught to swim, roll over, climb stairs, or do just about any other pet trick.

Main topic: Playfulness and inability to protect

On the other hand, pet pigs have their drawbacks. For one thing, they can be too playful. One pig owner found that nothing could stop her pet pig from taking the phone off the hook. He liked to hear the dial tone! Also, they won't protect you. They're more likely to smile at a burglar than to run the criminal off.

CONCLUSION

Pigs have possibly been around for about six million years. Yet it's only recently that people have begun to use words like <u>cuddly, sweet</u>, and <u>smart</u> to describe them. The day of the pig has finally arrived. Who knows? Maybe someday you'll hear the patter of little hooves around your house.

The Parts of a Composition

A composition may have several paragraphs, but it has three basic parts. The first part is the *introduction*. It's a little bit like the topic sentence in a paragraph. The second part may be much longer. It's called the *body*. The last part is the *conclusion*. It ends the composition.

The Introduction

Does the first paragraph of a book or an article sometimes capture your interest immediately? Do you keep reading to find out more?

Capturing the Reader's Interest. A good ***introduction*** grabs the reader's attention. It makes the reader want to read the rest of the composition. For example, the writer of the composition about pet pigs asks a question and follows it with a surprising statement. Just when the reader begins thinking about the usual bad words used to describe pigs, the writer says that pigs are not at all like most people think. Most readers will want to keep reading to find out why this is so.

Stating the Main Idea. A good introduction also states the main idea. This tells the reader what the composition will be about.

Ways to Write Introductions

You can use several different ways to make an introduction interesting. The following numbered examples show a few techniques you might try.

1. **Ask a question.** You've seen how a question works in the introduction to the composition on pigs. Here's another example. The writer asks a question and then immediately answers it.

> What's a top-notch sport that's rolling its way from coast to coast? In-line skating!

2. **Tell an anecdote.** An ***anecdote*** (a short, interesting, or even humorous story or incident) adds drama to your composition. Your reader will be caught by the humor or the human interest. Anecdotes add intriguing details to an introduction. This anecdote is from the introduction to a dramatic article about the son of a woman with multiple sclerosis.

> One Saturday afternoon in January 1989, Suzan Sharp, 43, and her eight-year-old son, David, were trudging across a snowy parking lot in Chippawa Falls, Wis., when Suzan's cane slid on an ice patch. She tumbled face-first into the slush. David rushed to his mother's side. "Are you all right, Mom?"
>
> Gary Johnson, "A Son's Challenge"

3. **State an interesting or startling fact.** Curiosity also makes a reader want to read on. An exciting statement of fact creates curiosity.

> Most people know about the huge Saint Bernards who save travelers lost in the mountains, but a tiny canary once saved its owner's life. As its elderly owner lay unconscious on the floor, the bird flew to a niece's house and got attention by tapping again and again on the window. It seems that pets of all kinds have saved human lives.

EXERCISE 3 Identifying Types of Introductions

Can you recognize the three ways of writing introductions? Working with two or three classmates, try to identify the technique used in each of these introductions.

1. There's a mystery in the sky. Centuries ago, ancient astronomers wrote about it. But when later astronomers looked for it, most of them thought the ancient astronomers were wrong. The mystery in the sky is whether there is a tenth planet, out beyond Neptune and Pluto. Many scientists believe Planet X is lurking out there waiting to be rediscovered!

2. *Do, re, mi, fa, sol, la, ti, do.* Did you ever wonder where in the world such words came from? An Italian monk named Guido d'Arezzo used the first syllable of each line of a Latin hymn to represent the music scale. Guido taught music in the monasteries, and the musical note system he developed made his work easier. Many people believe he is the inventor of written music.

3. Susanne woke up early on the morning of her thirteenth birthday. Someone had tied a string to the foot of her bed. On the string was a note that said, "Follow me." She put her hand on the string and started walking. The string led first to her brother's room, where he and their parents were waiting to go with her while she followed the string. It was the beginning of the most exciting birthday Susanne ever had.

The Body

The ***body*** of a composition usually contains several paragraphs, and every paragraph helps to support the main idea by developing a part of it.

All these paragraphs somehow have to stick together, too. Have you noticed that you lose interest if what you're reading never makes a point or connects ideas? Compositions that bore you probably don't have *unity* and *coherence*.

Unity. ***Unity*** means that the paragraphs in the body of your paper all work together to support your main idea. Look at the model composition on pigs (page 102). Notice how each of the paragraphs has its own main idea (topic). Now look at each of the paragraph topics again. Notice how each of these paragraph topics ties in with the main idea of the whole composition—"Pigs make great pets."

In addition, as you read each paragraph, you'll see that the details in it tie directly to the paragraph topic. So every sentence in every paragraph leads back to the main idea of the composition.

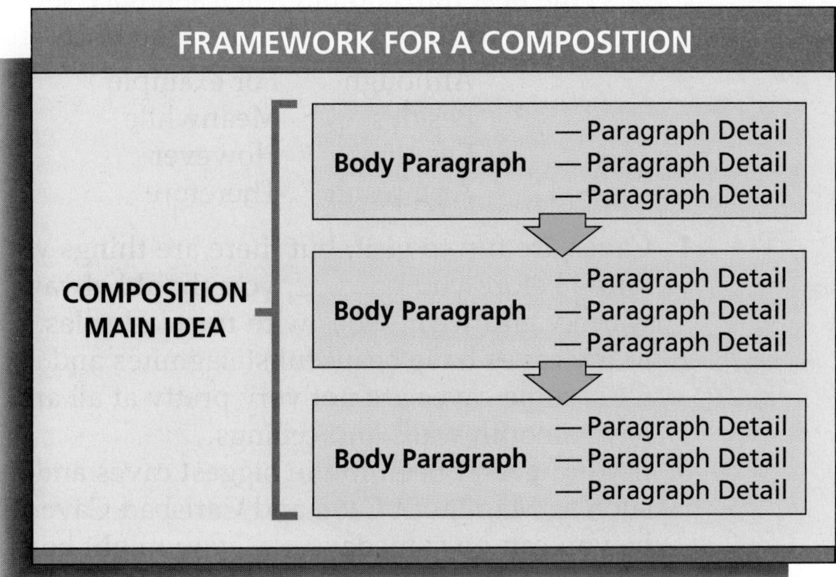

Coherence. Have you ever noticed how some things you read are easier to follow than others? One sentence leads easily into another, and one paragraph to the next. This type of writing has ***coherence.***

You can do two things to make sure your composition has coherence. First, arrange your ideas in an order that makes sense. Second, make sure it's obvious to your readers how your ideas are connected. For example, you can let your readers know how your ideas are connected by using ***transitional words and phrases*** such as *for example, first, then, next,* and *finally.* In the composition on pigs, words and phrases such as *for one thing, on the other hand,* and *as a matter of fact* help the reader see the connections the writer is making.

REFERENCE NOTE: See pages 74–75 for more information on transitional words and phrases.

EXERCISE 4 Using Transitions

Some transitional words and phrases are listed below. They are followed by some sentence sets that need them. Choose the best transition for each sentence set, but don't use the same word or phrase more than once.

Although	For example
Besides	Meanwhile
Eventually	However
As a result	Therefore

1. Caves are fun to visit, but there are things you should know before you go. ____, you should always dress warmly and wear shoes with nonskid soles.
2. Many caves have beautiful stalagmites and stalactites. ____, some caves are not very pretty at all and just have smooth walls and ceilings.
3. If you haven't been to the biggest caves and caverns, such as Mammoth Cave and Carlsbad Caverns, maybe you can go someday. ____, you might be able to visit a smaller cave close to where you live.

4. Caves are usually formed by water that flows underground and wears away rock over millions of years. ____, the water can form enormous rooms underground.
5. When caves are formed in limestone, dripping water dissolves the rock. Over time, the drips harden into crystal formations. ____, limestone caves often have beautiful sparkling shapes in them.

The Conclusion

Your ***conclusion*** should let your readers feel that your composition is complete. It shouldn't stop suddenly so that they feel let down. Your conclusion needs to tie the ideas together and flow once again into your main idea.

Ways to Write Conclusions

1. **Refer to your introduction.** In the model composition on pigs (pages 102–103), the writer brings readers back to the idea of "words used to describe pigs."

> **Introduction:** Many people think of words like *dirty, smelly, unfriendly,* and even *stupid.*
>
> **Conclusion:** Yet it's only recently that people have begun to use words like *cuddly, sweet,* and *smart* to describe them.

2. **Close with an interesting comment.** Another way to end your composition is to leave your readers with an interesting statement that clearly signals "the end."

> In-line skating may not replace bicycling as a way to travel, but for some people, it's the only way to roll!

3. **Restate your main idea.** One direct way to wrap up a composition is to restate your main idea *in different words*. This conclusion restates the idea that there is a mysterious planet somewhere out in space.

> Are some modern astronomers right about a tenth planet? Is it orbiting far beyond Pluto and Neptune, waiting for astronomers to find it? Maybe someday soon there will be a tenth planet to learn about: the mysterious Planet X.

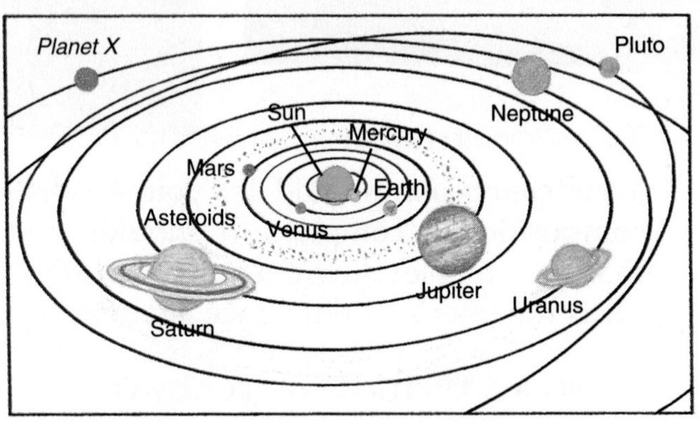

EXERCISE 5 **Writing a Conclusion**

The two models in this chapter—about manatees (page 94) and about pigs (page 102)—both use the same way of ending the composition. They both refer to the introduction. Write a new conclusion for one of these two models, using a different technique (pages 109–110). Then get together with two or three classmates and compare your conclusions.

MAKING CONNECTIONS

A Composition to Inform

You write for different purposes. You write to express your feelings, to tell a story, to persuade, or to inform. You can use the composition form you learned in this chapter for all these purposes.

Here are some notes about Saint Augustine, Florida, one of the oldest cities in the United States. To help you get started, the information has been organized into three groups. Study the notes until you're familiar with the information. Then write a short composition to *inform* your readers about this historic city. You may not want to use all the information.

SAINT AUGUSTINE, FLORIDA
HISTORY
1. Ponce de León landed near the area in 1513, looking for the fountain of youth. 2. He claimed the land for Spain. 3. The settlement of Saint Augustine was established in 1565 by Pedro Menéndez de Avilés. 4. Saint Augustine is the oldest continuously settled site (by Europeans) in the United States. 5. It was nearly destroyed by Sir Francis Drake and his English forces in 1586. 6. Spain transferred Florida to the United States in 1821.

SAINT AUGUSTINE, FLORIDA *(continued)*
LOCATION
1. Saint Augustine is located in northeastern Florida. 2. It is on a narrow peninsula formed by the Matanzas and San Sebastian rivers. 3. It is one-half mile from the Atlantic Ocean.
POINTS OF INTEREST
1. The Spanish fortress of Castillo de San Marcos was built in 1672 of coquina, a local shellrock. This is the oldest masonry fort in the United States. 2. The Cathedral of Saint Augustine was built in 1790. This is the seat of the oldest Catholic parish in the United States. 3. The Spanish Quarter is an area of reconstructed and restored buildings.

Writing a Composition to Inform

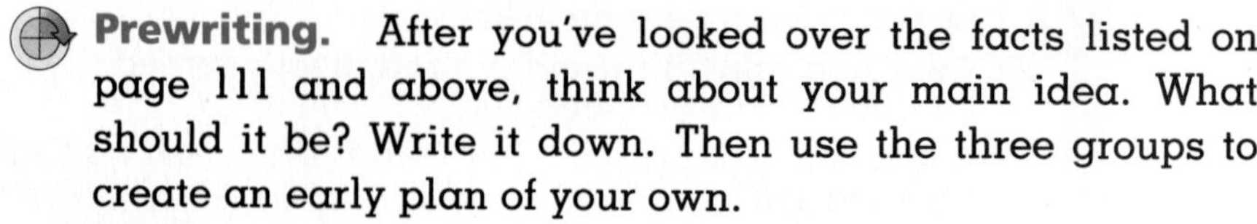

Prewriting. After you've looked over the facts listed on page 111 and above, think about your main idea. What should it be? Write it down. Then use the three groups to create an early plan of your own.

Writing, Evaluating, and Revising. Think about some way to capture your reader's attention, and write your introduction.

Next, draft the body paragraphs of your composition. Remember that each paragraph must have a topic that ties into your main idea. Then write a conclusion that ties your information together and ends your composition in a satisfactory way.

When you have finished, look over your first draft, and see what can be done to improve it. You might trade papers with a classmate and evaluate each other's writing. Ask these questions about your paper:

1. Does the introduction grab the reader's attention?
2. Is the main idea stated clearly?
3. Does each body paragraph connect to the main idea?
4. Do the details in each paragraph connect to the paragraph topic?
5. Does the conclusion tie the composition together and make it seem complete?

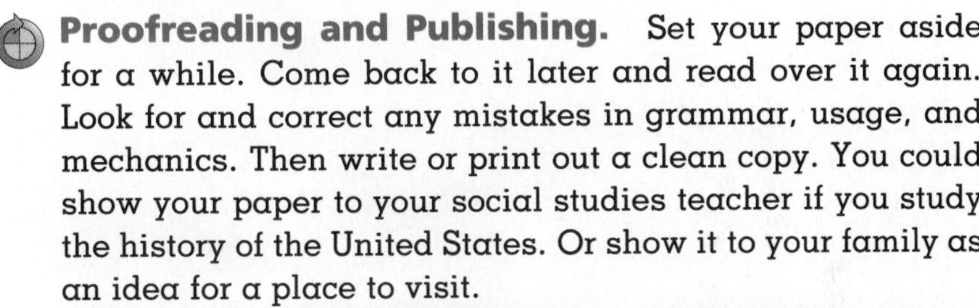

Proofreading and Publishing. Set your paper aside for a while. Come back to it later and read over it again. Look for and correct any mistakes in grammar, usage, and mechanics. Then write or print out a clean copy. You could show your paper to your social studies teacher if you study the history of the United States. Or show it to your family as an idea for a place to visit.

4 Expressive Writing

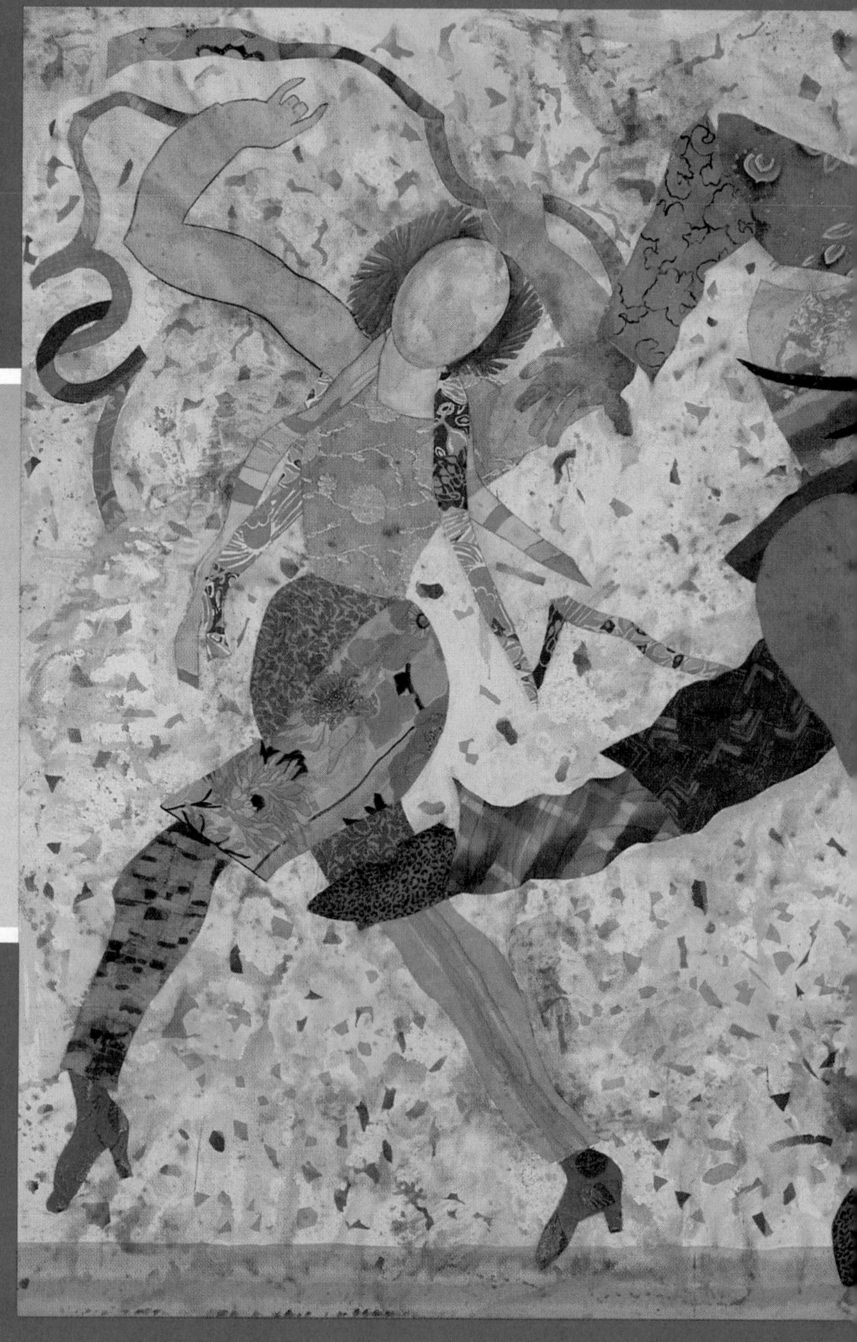

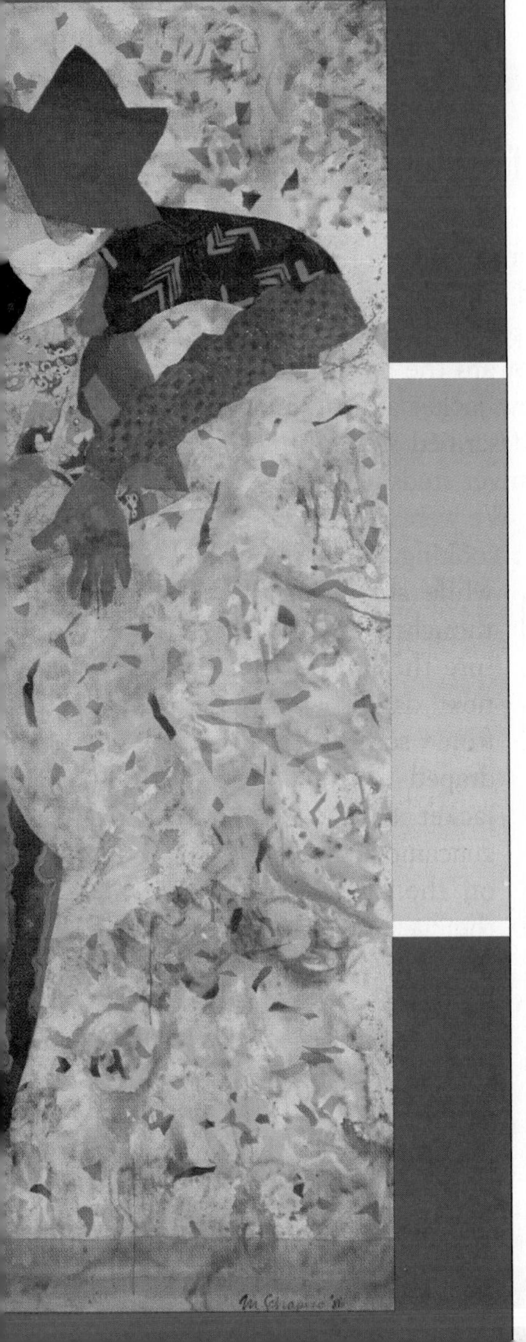

Discovering Yourself

You've already discovered many things about yourself. You hate math, but not English. You like to sit in your room and listen to all kinds of music. But you hate green peas and liver. Yet there is still more you can **discover about yourself,** through expressive writing.

Writing and You. A teenager writes to his cousin about how excited he is to be going away to basketball camp this summer. A famous actress writes a book telling her life story. A young girl tells her diary how much she likes her new bike. When have you expressed your personal feelings in writing?

As You Read. Here's a narrative in which a man expresses his feelings about a jacket he had to wear as a boy. What are his feelings?

Pas de Deux, Miriam Schapiro (1986). Acrylic and fabric on canvas. 90″ × 96″. Collection of Dr. & Mrs. Acinapura. Courtesy Bernice Steinbaum Gallery, NYC.

THE JACKET

by Gary Soto

My clothes have failed me. I remember the green coat that I wore in fifth and sixth grades when you either danced like a champ or pressed yourself against a greasy wall, bitter as a penny toward the happy couples.

When I needed a new jacket and my mother asked what kind I wanted, I described something like bikers wear: black leather and silver studs with enough belts to hold down a small town. We were in the kitchen, steam on the windows from her cooking. She listened so long while stirring dinner that I thought she understood for sure the kind I wanted. The next day when I got home from school, I discovered draped on my bedpost a jacket the color of day-old guacamole. I threw my books on the bed and approached the jacket slowly, as if it were a stranger whose hand I had to shake. I touched the vinyl sleeve, the collar, and peeked at the mustard-colored lining.

From the kitchen mother yelled that my jacket was in the closet. I closed the door

"From my bed, I stared at the jacket. I wanted to cry because it was so ugly and so big that I knew I'd have to wear it a long time."

to her voice and pulled at the rack of clothes in the closet, hoping the jacket on the bedpost wasn't for me but my mean brother. No luck. I gave up. From my bed, I stared at the jacket. I wanted to cry because it was so ugly and so big that I knew I'd have to wear it a long time. I was a small kid, thin as a young tree, and it would be years before I'd have a new one. I stared at the jacket, like an enemy, thinking bad things before I took off my old jacket whose sleeves climbed halfway to my elbow.

I put the big jacket on. I zipped it up and down several times, and rolled the cuffs up so they didn't cover my hands. I put my hands in the pockets and flapped the jacket like a bird's wings. I stood in front of the mirror, full face, then profile, and then looked over my shoulder as if someone had called me. I sat on the bed, stood against the bed, and combed my hair to see what I would look like doing something natural. I looked ugly. I threw it on my brother's bed and looked at it for a long time before I slipped it on and went out to the backyard, smiling a "thank you" to my mom as I passed her in the kitchen. With my hands in my pockets I kicked a ball against the fence, and then climbed it to sit looking into the alley. I hurled orange peels at the mouth of an open garbage can and when the peels were gone I watched the white puffs of my breath thin to nothing.

I jumped down, hands in my pockets, and in the backyard on my knees I teased my dog, Brownie, by swooping my arms while making bird calls. He jumped at me and missed. He jumped again and again, until a tooth sunk deep, ripping an L-shaped tear on my left sleeve. I pushed Brownie away to study the tear as I would a cut on my arm. There was no blood, only a few loose pieces of fuzz. Damn dog, I thought, and pushed him away hard when he tried to bite again. I got up from my knees and went to my bedroom to sit with my jacket on my lap, with the lights out.

That was the first afternoon with my new jacket. The next day I wore it to sixth grade and got a D on a math quiz. During the morning recess Frankie T., the playground terrorist, pushed me to the ground and told me to stay there until recess was over. My best friend, Steve Negrete, ate an apple while looking at me, and the girls turned away to whisper on the monkey bars. The teachers were no help: they looked my way and talked about how foolish I looked in my new jacket. I saw their heads bob with laughter, their hands half-covering their mouths.

Even though it was cold, I took off the jacket during lunch and played kickball in a thin shirt, my arms feeling like braille from goose bumps. But when I returned to class I slipped the jacket on and shivered until I was warm. I sat on my hands, heating them up, while my teeth chattered like a cup of crooked dice. Finally warm, I slid out of the jacket but a few minutes later put it back on when the fire bell rang. We paraded out into the yard where we, the sixth graders, walked past all the other grades to stand against the back fence. Everybody saw me. Although they didn't say out loud, "Man, that's ugly," I heard the buzz-buzz of gossip and even laughter that I knew was meant for me.

And so I went, in my guacamole jacket. So embarrassed, so

hurt, I couldn't even do my homework. I received Cs on quizzes, and forgot the state capitals and the rivers of South America, our friendly neighbor. Even the girls who had been friendly blew away like loose flowers to follow the boys in neat jackets.

I wore that thing for three years until the sleeves grew short and my forearms stuck out like the necks of turtles. All during that time no love came to me—no little dark girl in a Sunday dress she wore on Monday. At lunchtime I stayed with the ugly boys who leaned against the chainlink fence and looked around with propellers of grass spinning in our mouths. We saw girls walk by alone, saw couples, hand in hand, their heads like bookends pressing air together. We saw them and spun our propellers so fast our faces were blurs.

I blame that jacket for those bad years. I blame my mother for her bad taste and her cheap ways. It was a sad time for the heart. With a friend I spent my sixth-grade year in a tree in the alley waiting for something good to happen to me in that jacket, which had become the ugly brother who tagged along wherever I went. And it was about that time that I began to grow. My chest puffed up with muscle and, strangely, a few more ribs. Even my hands, those fleshy hammers, showed bravely through

the cuffs, the fingers already hardening for the coming fights. But that L-shaped rip on the left sleeve got bigger; bits of stuffing coughed out from its wound after a hard day of play. I finally scotch-taped it closed, but in rain or cold weather the tape peeled off like a scab and more stuffing fell out until that sleeve shriveled into a palsied arm. That winter the elbows began to crack and whole chunks of green began to fall off. I showed the cracks to my mother, who always seemed to be at the stove with steamed-up glasses, and she said that there were children in Mexico who would love that jacket. I told her that this was America and yelled that Debbie, my sister, didn't have a jacket like mine. I ran outside, ready to cry, and climbed the tree by the alley to think bad thoughts and watch my breath puff white and disappear.

But whole pieces still casually flew off my jacket when I played hard, read quietly, or took vicious spelling tests at school. When it became so spotted that my brother began to call me "camouflage," I flung it over the fence into the alley. Later, however, I swiped the jacket off the ground and went inside to drape it across my lap and mope.

I was called to dinner: steam silvered my mother's glasses as she said grace; my brother and sister with their heads bowed made ugly faces at their glasses of powdered milk. I gagged too, but eagerly ate big rips of buttered tortilla that held scooped up beans. Finished, I went outside with my jacket across my arm. It was a cold sky. The faces of clouds were piled up, hurting. I climbed the fence, jumping down with a grunt. I started up the alley and soon slipped into my jacket, that green ugly brother who breathed over my shoulder that day and ever since.

Reader's Response

1. The narrator blames his ugly jacket for the bad things that happen to him for three years while he wears it. Do you agree with this way of looking at things? How could a piece of clothing be responsible?
2. Have you ever had to wear a piece of clothing that you thought was ugly? In a short journal entry, write about how the experience made you feel.

Writer's Craft

3. Writers of personal narratives use sensory details—details of sight, sound, taste, touch, and smell—to make experiences seem real. What details of sight does the narrator use to make the jacket seem real to readers?
4. Personal narratives are about experiences that the writers think are important. Where does Gary Soto reveal that this experience was important to him? What do you think he discovered about himself?

Ways to Express Yourself

You'll find expressive writing all around you. You'll read it in magazines and newspapers and write it in journals and letters. Your writing is expressive when the focus is on you—what you experience, think, and feel. Here are some ways that you can develop expressive writing.

Narration: writing in your journal about an event that happened to you because you're in a wheelchair; writing the story of your childhood for the school's time capsule.

Description: describing your grandparents' house to show how you feel about it; writing a funny description of the broccoli served in the lunchroom.

Classification: in a letter to your cousin, comparing your two best friends; in your journal, exploring which you enjoy more, tennis or basketball.

Evaluation: writing an essay about the water quality in the park's drinking fountains; explaining to your friend why the Miami Dolphins are the best NFL team.

LOOKING AHEAD

In the main assignment in this chapter, you'll use the strategy of narration to write about a personal experience. As you work through the chapter, keep in mind that a good personal narrative

- tells about the events in the order that they happened
- gives details about the events
- explains the meaning of the experience to the writer

Writing a Personal Narrative

Prewriting

Choosing an Experience to Write About

A personal narrative is a true story about yourself. You often tell your good friends about your experiences. How do you decide which experiences are worth telling?

Start by thinking about events that meant something special to you: they touched your feelings. Your narrative could be about an experience that was funny, sad, amazing, or scary. Even a painful experience can make a good personal narrative. Did you ever break your leg? How did it happen? What did it feel like? A good friend would be eager to know. So would the audience for your narrative.

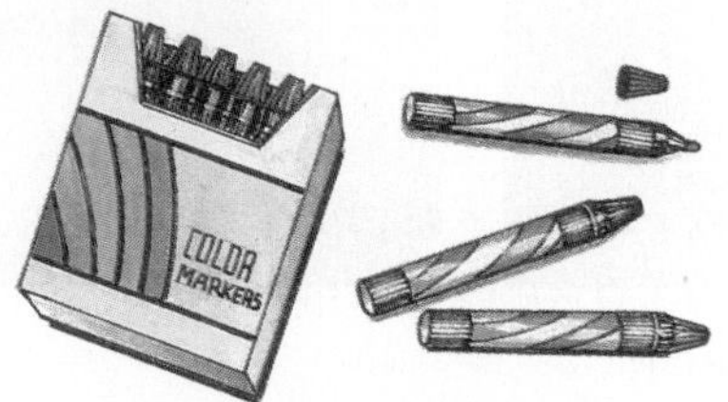

Keep these points in mind when you choose a topic for a personal narrative.

- *Write about something you remember well.* You want to *tell* about and *show* your experience to readers. You can't if you don't remember details about it.
- *Write about an experience that was important to you.* It doesn't have to be a big adventure, but it should have meaning for you.

- *Write about an experience you're willing to share.* You want to be comfortable sharing the experience with others.

EXERCISE 1 Speaking and Listening: Exploring Topics for Personal Narratives

Get together with a partner or a few classmates and read the statements below. Can you remember an experience that fits each description? Tell each other the best stories you remember. Discuss what makes them interesting as stories.

1. You and a friend disagreed.
2. Something happened that was embarrassing (at the time) but funny (later).
3. An event made strangers notice or hear about you.
4. You won a contest or some other honor.
5. You spent a frightening night, perhaps when the lights went out after a storm.

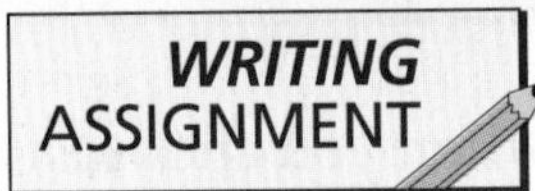

PART 1:
Choosing a Topic for a Personal Narrative

What experiences have you had that you want to explore in your writing? Choose one of those experiences to write about. Try looking through the list you made with your classmates for Exercise 1. If you find no ideas there, look through your journals, talk to your friends, or do a little private brainstorming.

Gathering and Organizing Your Ideas

In talking with friends, you often just start a story and hope to remember it as you go along. You write better, however, when you plan what to say and how to say it.

Thinking About Purpose and Audience

The *purpose* for writing a personal narrative is to discover your own thoughts and feelings and to learn a little about yourself. You also write to share the experience, and what it meant to you, with others.

Your *audience* is probably made up of your classmates and teacher and perhaps other adults you trust. Try to make your narrative interesting for them. Remember to give them the background information they may need to understand your narrative. Did you take a trip to the Grand Canyon? Explain its awesome beauty to them. Ask yourself what your audience will need to know in order to "be there" with you.

Recalling Details

A personal narrative is different from many other types of writing. That's because many of the details and events are stored inside your memory. You'll need to recall these details to make your experiences seem real for readers. Did you win a kite-designing contest? What sights and sounds will help you *tell* the experience so that readers can share it? What did people say and do? How did you feel?

As you plan your narrative, try to remember the following kinds of details.

1. **Events.** What happened? Make notes about all the little individual events that made up the whole event. You were chased by a huge dog! *The dog came bounding down the stairs; I turned; it took off from the bottom step . . .* and so on.

2. **Sensory details.** What did you hear, see, feel, and maybe even smell and taste? *That scratchy growl; that red glint in the dog's eye; the hot, moist smell of its breath . . .*

3. **Characters and places.** Were other people involved in your experience? What places were important? *Matt chased the dog down the stairs of the apartment building. Then I saw the dog dart between cars, cross the street, and run into Mr. Chang's market.*

4. **Dialogue and quotations.** Did you and others say anything interesting during the experience? *"Help! Somebody! Stop that dog!" "Aw, he won't bite—least, I've never known him to . . ."*
5. **Thoughts and feelings.** How did you think and feel? *I was terrified that the dog would bite me; I could feel the tingle of fear rushing up my back.*

A personal narrative is a first-person story, so the words *I* and *me* play an important part. Even though others shared the experience, you're writing from your point of view. As you jot down details, stress what *you* saw and heard and felt, what *you* did, what *you* thought, and what the event meant to *you.*

CRITICAL THINKING

Visualizing Sensory Details

Collecting sensory details is easy when you can observe the subject. In a personal narrative, however, your subject is an event in the past. Instead of observing it, you have to rely on memory. You have to ***visualize*** (see) the event in your mind before you can collect sensory details.

For example, you're trying to remember details about a lightning storm. Pick a specific moment during the storm and picture the moment in your mind. Then, note what you observe with all your senses, not just your eyes. What do you see? What sounds are present? What do you feel, both in your skin and in your emotions? Does anything have a taste or smell?

Don't give up too quickly. Collecting details by visualizing is like the poem about shaking the ketchup bottle—none'll come and then a lot'll, but you have to keep at it.

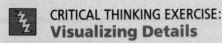

CRITICAL THINKING EXERCISE:
Visualizing Details

Think of an event or occasion that was special to you. Maybe you spent a perfect day with friends at the beach last summer. Maybe you made your first A on a test. Close your eyes and visualize until you get a mental picture of the experience. Then, list as many details as you can for each sense. If possible, compare your notes with those of another person who experienced the event with you.

Arranging Details

The next step in planning your personal narrative is to arrange the details you've recalled. You need to put them in an order that will make sense to your readers. Many writers begin with background information and then use chronological order for the other details. Using ***chronological order*** (time order) means telling events in the order they happened. You begin with the event that happened first, then go on to the second, and so on.

REFERENCE NOTE: For more information on chronological order, see pages 39, 79, and 100.

As you arrange your details, list them in a chart. On the next page you can see how one writer organized details for a personal narrative.

HERE'S HOW

The Moose and Me	
BACKGROUND:	Where: Grizzly State Park—my first camping trip When: last summer, first night of trip Who: Uncle Miguel, my cousin Ana, me
EVENTS	DETAILS
Arrived at campground.	Smell: fresh air Feeling: tired but excited
Family ate dinner.	Smell: smoke from campfire
I washed dishes in river.	Sight: soft evening light of sunset Touch: cool water Sound: river roaring, sound of birds Smell: sage and juniper
Felt neck prickling.	Quotation: "I'm being watched."
We see moose.	Sight: flat, gray antlers Sight: hugeness (antlers at least 5 to 6 feet wide); looked to weigh over 1,200 pounds
Moose drinks from river.	Sound: lap, lap Sight: Slowly surveys the scene and then strolls away Feeling: I'm small and he's huge.

PART 2:
Gathering and Organizing Ideas

You chose an experience to write about in Writing Assignment, Part 1. Now, make a chart like the one above and list each event in the order it happened. Then, jot down details about each event, including sensory details, dialogue, and thoughts or feelings. Save your work.

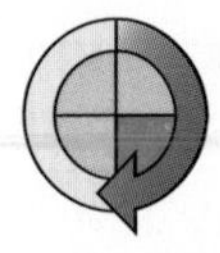

Writing Your First Draft

The Parts of a Personal Narrative

No two personal narratives are just alike, but they all have three basic parts.

- a *beginning* that grabs the reader's interest; sometimes gives background information and a hint about the importance of the experience
- a *middle* that tells about important events, describes people and places, and tells the writer's thoughts and feelings
- an *ending* in which the writer explains the outcome and shows the meaning of the experience

Here's how one professional writer, Michael DiLeo, uses these parts to create a personal narrative. Notice how he uses background information, dialogue, and sensory details to tell readers about his experience.

A MAGAZINE ARTICLE

Dream of the Blue Dolphins

by Michael DiLeo

BEGINNING
Attention grabber
Hint of meaning

In our dreams, there are certain just-out-of-reach experiences—like flying with eagles or running with wild horses—that promise to take us beyond the physical limitations of our bodies, to give us a glimpse of the full breadth of creation. Ten years ago, I was given the opportunity to make such a dream come true.

Background information

It all began at a party in San Francisco for the famed neurobiologist John Lilly. . . . At the time, Lilly was working with two dolphins, named Joe and Rosie, at a California oceanarium. In the middle of our conversation, Lilly said, "Would you like to swim with Joe and Rosie?" I quickly said yes.

Quotation

MIDDLE

Event 1

Sensory details

Sensory details

Thoughts and feelings

The back tank at Marine World where Lilly kept Joe and Rosie was small and circular, perhaps fifteen yards across. As I slipped into the cool water, Joe, the male, swam up, his dorsal fin slicing the surface, while Rosie kept her distance. He was a sleek, silver-gray bullet, whose size and fluid quickness were breathtaking. I felt an odd push-pull: I was drawn to him, and yet there was in my mouth a taste of fear, bitter as the chlorine in the pool, the pure anxiety of feeling completely out of my league. As instructed by Lilly, I took hold of Joe's dorsal fin with one hand. Instantly, I was swept under the water.

Quotation

Event 2

"He'll test you to see if you're a good swimmer," Lilly had told me, "and if he decides you are, you'll get a great ride." I must have passed, for Joe took me on a series of shallow, stone-skip soundings, then

Sensory details

dove straight down. Just before we reached the bottom, he turned and shot for the surface. As my lungs tightened and my arm felt like giving way, we exploded out of the water together in an astonishing leap. I was riding a dolphin in midair.

Event 3

Sensory details

ENDING

Outcome—meaning of experience

I caught my breath just before Joe performed another dive and jump. And another. His strength and control were beyond my comprehension. The line between air and water blurred as Joe kept up his crash course in the dolphin way of living in two worlds. He circled the tank, corkscrewing through the water, testing my grip and my supply of air at every turn. Variations on this repertoire continued for some time, until suddenly Joe did a quick flip and left me bobbing in the water, my heart pounding with excitement. It was years before it occurred to me to wonder whether Joe was expressing, not his excitement at interspecies contact, but simply the frustration of total confinement.

American Way

EXERCISE 2 **Analyzing the Organization of a Personal Narrative**

Read and think about the article "Dream of the Blue Dolphins." Then, meet with two or three classmates to discuss the following questions.

1. Does the first sentence grab your attention? Explain why or why not.
2. What background information do you get in the introduction? Do you need this information to understand the narrative? Why?
3. In what order are the events organized?
4. What are some sensory details that DiLeo uses to describe his experience with Joe?
5. How does DiLeo let his readers know what he felt about the experience? the meaning he thought it had?

A Writer's Model for You

Michael DiLeo has written narratives for many years. He has a few fancy writing techniques, but he starts with a basic framework. The model below follows that basic framework, without some of the fancy techniques. You may want to use it as a model for your own personal narrative.

A WRITER'S MODEL

The Moose and Me

BEGINNING
Attention grabber
Background information
Hint of importance

What would you do if you came face to face with one of the biggest animals in the United States? I'm a city kid, but last summer Uncle Miguel and my cousin Ana took me camping in the woods for a whole week in Montana's Grizzly State Park. My best memory comes from the first night we were there.

MIDDLE
Event 1
Sensory details

We had just eaten supper, and I was alone down at the river, washing dishes. The sun was setting, and its soft evening light was streaming through the trees. The only sounds were those of the birds and the roar of the river.

Thoughts and feelings
Event 2
Sensory details
Quotation
Feelings

Suddenly my neck began to prickle. I had a strange feeling I was being watched. I looked up and—wow! Right across the river, twenty feet away, stood a moose. You wouldn't believe his size! He had flat, gray and brown antlers that would have scraped a ceiling. I wasn't scared, though—in fact, I said to him, "Hey, moose, what's going on?" It was just as if I were talking to someone. That's the way I felt just then, a part of nature. The moose just looked at me, dipped his head, took a drink, looked around, and then walked off, calm as you please.

ENDING
Outcome—meaning of experience

I'm still a city kid, but I'll tell you one thing. I have a new respect for nature. That moose was so big and I'm so small. Yet I felt I could talk to him.

If you decide to model your personal narrative after the one you've just read about the moose, you can use the following framework.

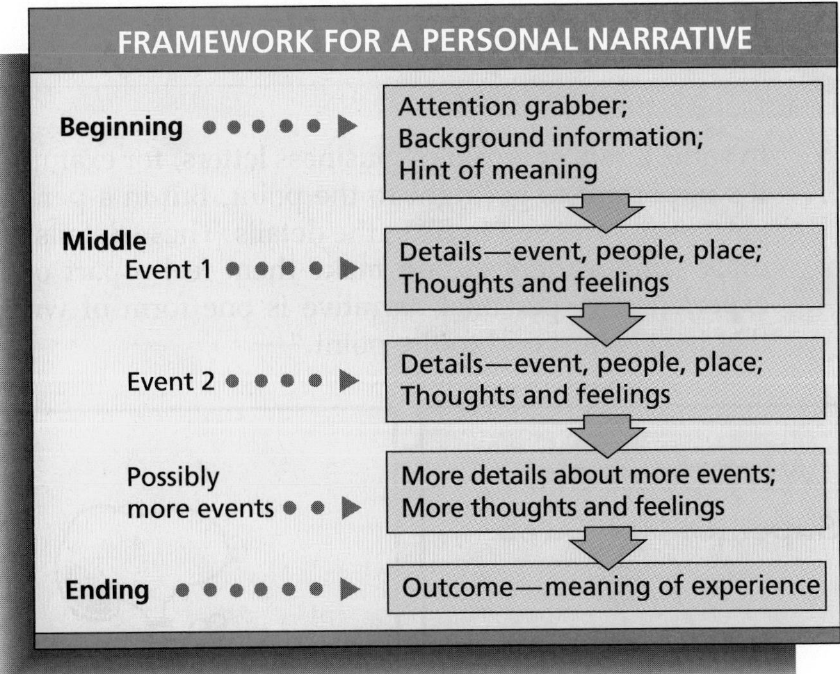

FRAMEWORK FOR A PERSONAL NARRATIVE
Beginning
Attention grabber; Background information; Hint of meaning
Middle
Event 1
Details—event, people, place; Thoughts and feelings
Event 2
Details—event, people, place; Thoughts and feelings
Possibly more events
More details about more events; More thoughts and feelings
Ending
Outcome—meaning of experience

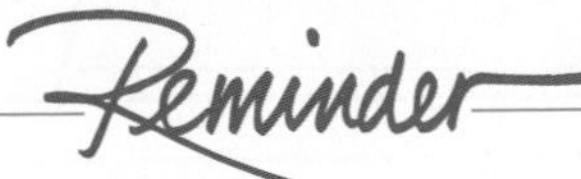

As you write your personal narrative

- arrange details about the events in chronological order
- include sensory details about each event
- include dialogue, thoughts, and feelings to make the experience come alive
- help your readers see the meaning of the experience

PART 3:
Writing a Draft of Your Personal Narrative

Now it's time to write. Use the chart you developed in Writing Assignment, Part 2 (page 129). Then just write the whole story as if you were telling it to a friend. Don't forget to end your narrative by telling its outcome and showing what the experience meant to you.

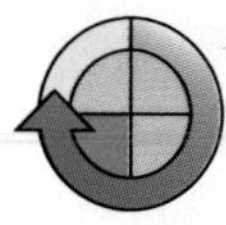

Evaluating and Revising

In some kinds of writing—business letters, for example—it's important to get right to the point. But in a personal narrative, you need to fill in the details. These details help draw your readers in and make them feel a part of the experience. A personal narrative is one form of writing that isn't "short and to the point."

Why dogs are superior to cats.

They just are, and that's all there is to it!

SHORT AND TO THE POINT!
SCHULZ

Use the chart on the next page to help you evaluate and revise your writing. First, ask yourself a question in the left-hand column. Then, if you find a weakness in your narrative, use the revision technique suggested in the right-hand column.

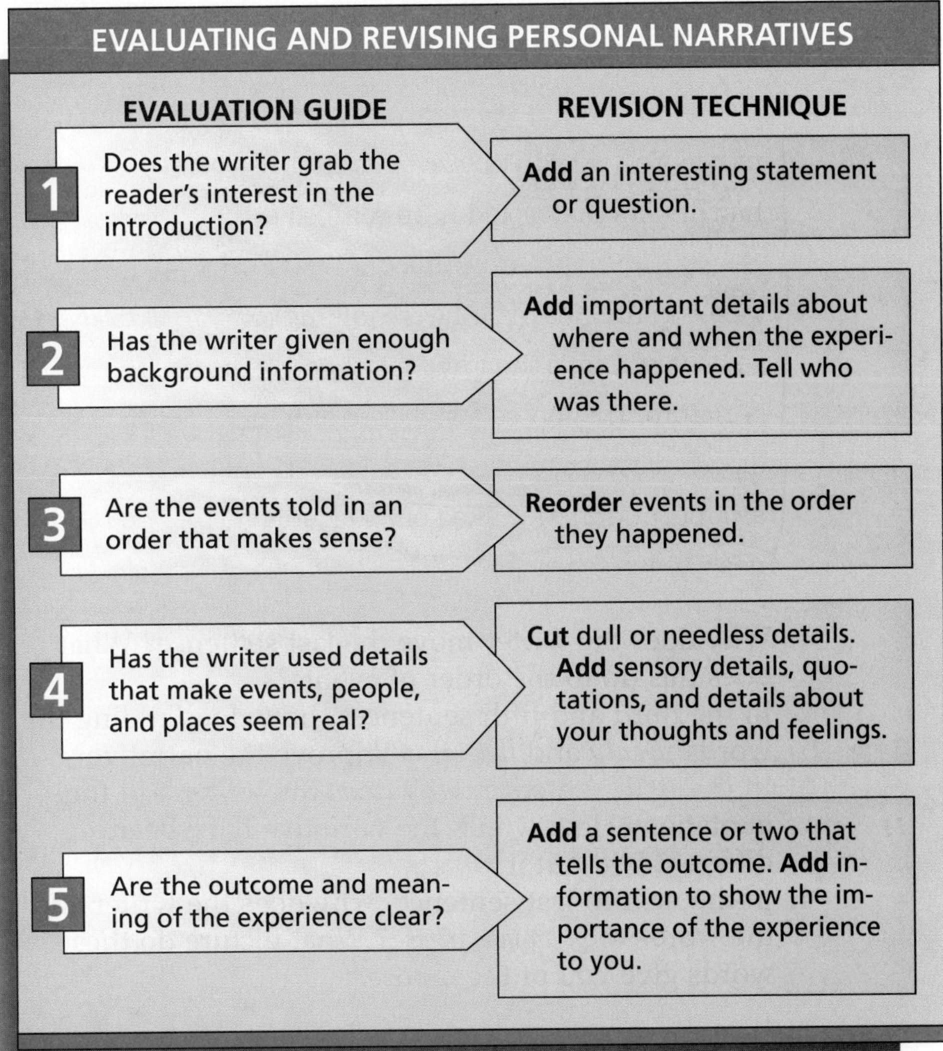

EVALUATING AND REVISING PERSONAL NARRATIVES

	EVALUATION GUIDE	REVISION TECHNIQUE
1	Does the writer grab the reader's interest in the introduction?	**Add** an interesting statement or question.
2	Has the writer given enough background information?	**Add** important details about where and when the experience happened. Tell who was there.
3	Are the events told in an order that makes sense?	**Reorder** events in the order they happened.
4	Has the writer used details that make events, people, and places seem real?	**Cut** dull or needless details. **Add** sensory details, quotations, and details about your thoughts and feelings.
5	Are the outcome and meaning of the experience clear?	**Add** a sentence or two that tells the outcome. **Add** information to show the importance of the experience to you.

EXERCISE 3 **Analyzing a Writer's Revisions**

Now's your chance to see inside an editor's mind. Working with a partner or a small group, study these revisions from the third paragraph of the writer's model on pages 133–134, and then answer the questions that follow. Get together with another group to compare your answers.

I had a strange feeling I was being watched. I looked up and—wow! Right across the river, ~~a few~~ twenty feet away, stood a moose. You wouldn't believe his size! He had flat, gray and brown antlers that would have scraped a ceiling. I wasn't scared, though—in fact, I ~~talked~~ said to him, "Hey, moose, what's going on?" It was just as if I were talking to ~~some guy~~ someone. That's the way I felt just then, a part of nature. The moose just looked at me, dipped his head, took a drink, looked around, and then walked off, calm as you please. Suddenly my neck began to prickle.

replace

add

replace/add

replace/add

add

reorder

1. Why does the writer move the last sentence? What does this do to the order of events?
2. In the third and fifth sentences, how does adding the words *twenty* and *flat, gray* improve the narrative?
3. In the sixth sentence, why does the writer add the quotation? How would the narrative have been different without it?
4. In the next-to-last sentence, why does the writer add the words *calm as you please*? What picture do these words give you of the moose?

Dialogue—words people actually say—can bring a personal narrative to life. For example, read the following two passages. Both express the same information. Isn't the second one much livelier?

1. Mario had called the National Weather Service and learned from a man there that it was snowing in the pass. Carmen thought we should go anyway and asked for my opinion. I agreed that we should try.

2. "I just called the National Weather Service," Mario announced. "The guy says it's snowing in the pass."

"Oh, let's go anyway," said Carmen. "We can make it. What do you think, Ginny?"

"I'm game," I replied.

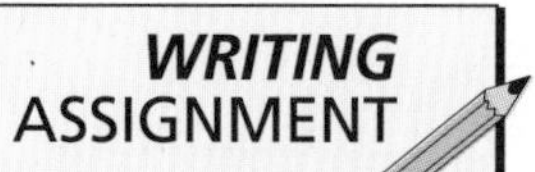

PART 4:

Evaluating and Revising Your Personal Narrative

You've seen how someone else improved a narrative. Now it's time to decide how to evaluate and improve your own narrative. Read your personal narrative with a partner and evaluate each other's work. As you work, use the evaluating and revising chart on page 137. (You might also want to use the peer-evaluation guidelines on page 47.) When you get your paper back, think about your partner's suggestions. Then, revise your narrative.

Proofreading and Publishing

Proofreading. Even simple mistakes in usage or mechanics can make your personal narrative hard to understand. It's important to proofread carefully and correct any mistakes you find.

MECHANICS HINT

Using Dialogue

You may often use dialogue in your narrative. The correct punctuation of dialogue is important so that readers know who is talking. In the first sentence below, you can't be sure who has called the National Weather Service. In the second sentence, punctuation makes the point clear.

EXAMPLES **Henry said I called the National Weather Service.**
Henry said, "I called the National Weather Service."

REFERENCE NOTE: For more help on punctuating dialogue, see pages 737–742.

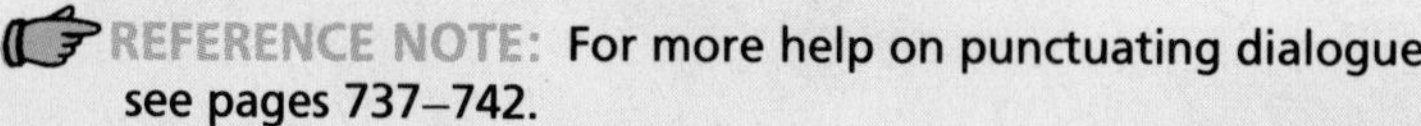

Publishing. Once you have revised, proofread, and made corrections, make a clean copy. An audience always finds a clean, neat paper more interesting than a messy, difficult-to-read one. Here are two ways you can publish your narrative.

- One audience for your narrative may be your own future self. Start a scrapbook of memories, beginning with this narrative. Years from now, you may be surprised at the picture you get of yourself.

- Make an anthology of personal narratives with your classmates. Create groupings of narratives on similar topics: outdoor adventures, conflicts with friends or family, school experiences, and so forth.

PART 5:
Proofreading and Publishing Your Personal Narrative

You've done a great deal of work, so reward yourself now with your best effort. Proofread your personal narrative carefully and correct the errors. (See page 53 for more help with proofreading.) Then publish your clean, corrected work. Try one of the suggestions above or any other way you'd like to share your narrative.

"Wait! Wait! . . . Cancel that, I guess it says 'helf.'"

WRITING WORKSHOP

A Journal Entry

Some types of expressive writing, like the personal narrative, are meant to be shared. But other types of expressive writing are just for the writer.

A journal is a place where you can write just for yourself. You can write freely about events, reveal your thoughts, and express your anger and emotions.

Here, for once, you don't have to stick to one subject or plan what you think before you write. It's fine to let your words wander and see where they go. That's because a journal is not just a record of events; it's a tool for exploring what you think and feel.

Of course, every time you write something down, there's a chance someone else will read it. It's not unusual for people's journals and diaries to be published after they die!

The excerpt on the next page is from the diary of an author named Elizabeth Yates. This passage about her sister Jinny was written in 1918 when Elizabeth was in the sixth grade. As you read this entry, think about the value such writing may have had for Yates at the time and later in her life.

from My Diary—My World

by Elizabeth Yates

Jinny is seven years older than me. She's beautiful and brilliant. Her hair is long and fair, and now that she is doing it up in a knot, she looks more than ever like one of the Greek goddesses in my mythology book. She can do everything well, even to tying the tie of her Peter Thomson suit, which I can never do with mine. And she doesn't get into trouble, which I do all the time. She writes not only the plays but other things, like a song for the Jugs and wonderful letters. She will be a very great writer someday, I know. I would do anything for her, and yet I can't seem to tell her, the way I can tell Brier, my secrets or my dream of being a writer.

Thinking It Over

1. What do you see in this little passage that you probably wouldn't see in a formal biography of Jinny?
2. What impression do you get of Jinny? of Elizabeth's feelings about her?
3. What does Elizabeth "tell" her journal here that she probably didn't tell Jinny?

Writing a Journal Entry

Prewriting. You can write about any subject in your journal. Elizabeth Yates wrote about her sister Jinny. You might write your journal entry about someone interesting or important in your life. Maybe you'd like to write about a family member or a friend. Don't worry about coming up with something polished that you can show the world. Just write to explore what you think and remember.

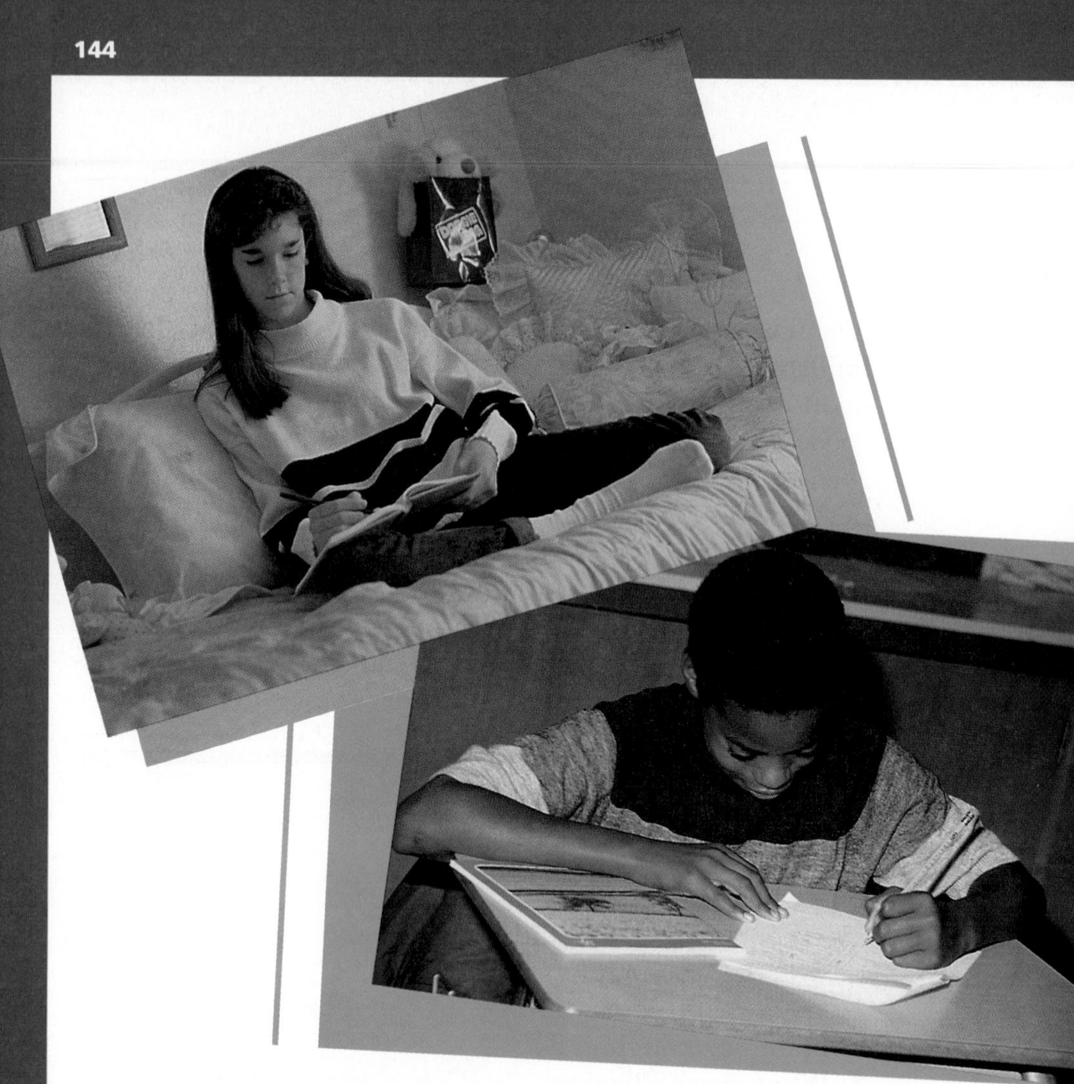

Writing. Write your journal entry. Then, reread it and think about what you've written. Is there anything else you want to say or explore? Don't forget that your only purpose in this kind of writing is to please yourself.

Publishing. After you've finished writing, go back and look at your entry. Did you discover anything new about yourself or your subject? Did you write anything you might use in another, more formal piece of writing, such as a personal narrative or a short story? Remember that you don't need to share your journal with anyone. However, saving what you've written to read again when you're older can be very interesting.

MAKING CONNECTIONS

WRITING ACROSS THE CURRICULUM

Expressive Writing and History

Historians learn about the past from public documents, such as newspapers and treaties, as well as from private documents, such as letters and journals. In the following journal entry, a trader describes a meeting with a group of Native Americans in Texas in 1808. As you read the entry, look for details about the events, people, and places that were part of the trader's experience. Remember that the time is 1808. Some of the spelling and capitalization will seem strange to you.

August 11th

The Messenger we sent to the Village returned early this Morning accompanied by six Indians and we were met by fifty men on Horseback, who Escorted us into the Village   when in sight of the town we hoisted our flag and they immediately hoisted a similar one which they had received of Dr. Sibly of Nacki-tosh. a man met us with an Invitation to the Chief's house. But we preferred encamping near the great spring and were conducted thither where I pitched my tent and hoisted my flag in front of it, about fifty yards from the Chiefs house.—a band of Women came immediately [and] pulled up and cleared away the grass and weeds from about the camp and also cleared a path down to the spring. I then waited on the Great Chief and was received with every token of Friendship I informed him I would wait on him again the next day & inform[ed] him for what purpose we had come to his

> Country & returned to my tent   we found our Camp filled with a quantity of green Corn, Beans, Water and Mus Melons.
>
> Anthony Glass, *Journal of an Indian Trader*

A personal narrative you write might one day become an important document about life today. Choose an event you remember—perhaps a hurricane or special trip—that might tell people a hundred years from now about life today. Write a personal narrative about your experience of the event. Include details that would help explain the experience to someone from a later time.

EXPRESSIVE WRITING AND PERSONAL LETTERS

Personal letters may be informative. For example, you might write to your aunt to tell her when you're arriving to visit. They also may be persuasive. You might write to a friend who moved away, trying to persuade him to come visit you in the summer. But often personal letters are expressive. We sometimes want to share our personal thoughts and feelings with good friends and close relatives, and a letter is one way to do that. In the following personal letter, a girl shares her feelings about her grandparents with a friend who lives some distance away.

December 2, 1993

Dear Joanna,

Thanks for the letter. It seems funny to think about you playing in the sun in Florida when it's already snowing here in Chicago. We got up early this morning to listen to the weather report. We were hoping the snow would be heavy enough that we wouldn't have to go to school. No such luck!

We had a great Thanksgiving. My grandparents cooked the meal, and we had Chinese food instead of turkey and dressing. While we were eating, they told me some stories about their life in China that I'd never heard before. It was kind of strange. I'd never thought much about China before. You know what I mean. The fact that my grandparents came from there didn't mean much to me.

Now I feel different. They made China sound so beautiful and so interesting. My grandfather says that Kweilin, where they lived, has lots of hills and rivers. I'd like to go there to visit when I get older. Want to go along?

Tell everybody I said hello, and tell your parents to let you come stay when school is out. You'll like Chicago, especially in the summer.

Your friend,
Amy

In this letter, Amy shares her thoughts and feelings about her experience with her grandparents. Do you have any thoughts or feelings you'd like to share with someone? Instead of calling, try writing a letter.

5 Using Description

Creating Pictures and Images

Words are a writer's paintbrush. With words, a writer can create a **picture** so funny, so sad, or so frightening, that you feel like laughing, crying, or shuddering in fright at the "sight" of it.

Writing and You. A science fiction writer describes how the sun looks when it becomes a nova. A newspaper reporter describes the terrible damage left by a killer hurricane. With their vivid words, writers make you feel as though you were there—hearing, seeing, feeling, smelling, or tasting what they are writing about. Have you ever described something in writing?

As You Read. Here's an excerpt from a short story that describes a Japanese meal. As you read, look for words that make the meal seem real to you. Can you see or taste it?

Doubled Back, Bev Doolittle (1988) © The Greenwich Workshop, Inc., Trumbull, CT 06611

FROM NISEI DAUGHTER

ニセイ

BY MONICA SONE

While the Matsuis and our parents reminisced about the good old days, we thumbed through the worn photograph albums and old Japanese tourist magazines. Finally Mrs. Matsui excused herself and bustled feverishly around the dining room. Then she invited us in. "*Sah,* I have nothing much to offer you, but please eat your fill."

"*Mah, mah,* such a wonderful assortment of *ogochi-soh,*" Mother bubbled.

Balding Mr. Matsui snorted deprecatingly. Mrs. Matsui walked around the table with an enormous platter of *osushi,* rice cakes rolled in seaweed. We each took one and nibbled at it daintily, sipping tea. Presently she sailed out of the kitchen bearing a magnificent black and silver lacquered tray loaded with carmine lacquer bowls filled with fragrant *nishime.* In pearly iridescent china bowls, Mrs. Matsui served us hot chocolatey *oshiruko,* a sweetened bean soup dotted with tender white *mochi,* puffed up like oversized marshmallows.

Father and Mother murmured over the superb flavoring of each dish, while Mr. Matsui guffawed politely, "*Nani,* this woman isn't much of a cook at all."

I was fascinated with the *yakizakana,* barbecued perch, which, its head and tail raised saucily, looked as if it were about to flip out of the oval platter. Surrounding this centerpiece were lacquer boxes of desserts, neatly lined rows of red and green oblong slices of sweet bean cakes, a mound of crushed lima beans, tinted red and green, called *kinton.* There was a vegetable dish called *kimpira* which looked like a mass of brown twigs. It turned out to be burdock, hotly seasoned with red pepper.

Reader's Response

1. Have you ever eaten a meal cooked by someone from a culture or country different than your own? Describe the meal for your classmates.
2. Imagine a meal in an unusual place. For example, perhaps you have lunch on Mount Everest or breakfast on the ocean floor. Write a short journal entry about the meal.

Writer's Craft

3. In this description, Monica Sone uses words like *enormous platter* and *magnificent black and silver lacquered tray* to create a picture of a Japanese meal. What are some other words she uses to paint a picture of the meal for you?
4. When they describe, writers often use *sensory details,* words that describe sights, sounds, tastes, textures, and smells. For example, "an enormous platter of *osushi*" helps you see the dish. What are some texture, or touch, words that Monica Sone uses? What are some taste words she uses?

"IN THE CHILDHOOD MEMORIES OF EVERY GOOD COOK, THERE'S A LARGE KITCHEN, A WARM STOVE, A SIMMERING POT AND A MOM."

BARBARA COSTIKYAN

Uses of Description

Writers of description always want to create a picture with words. But they don't always have the same purpose when they write. Here are four purposes the writers might have.

▶ **To Express Yourself:** in your journal, describing the emptiness in your old room as you pack and move to a new house; in a letter to a friend, describing the frightening characters in a horror movie.

To Persuade: describing the colorful, prize-filled piñata at a friend's birthday party so that your parents will let you have one at yours; describing the pitiful little puppy at the door to convince a friend to adopt it.

To Inform: describing your clothes so that an exchange student will recognize you at the train station; describing a missing bicycle so that a friend can help you look for it.

▶ **To Be Creative:** in a short story, describing the little alien from Mars who is the main character; in a school play, describing the horrible spider that falls from the ceiling.

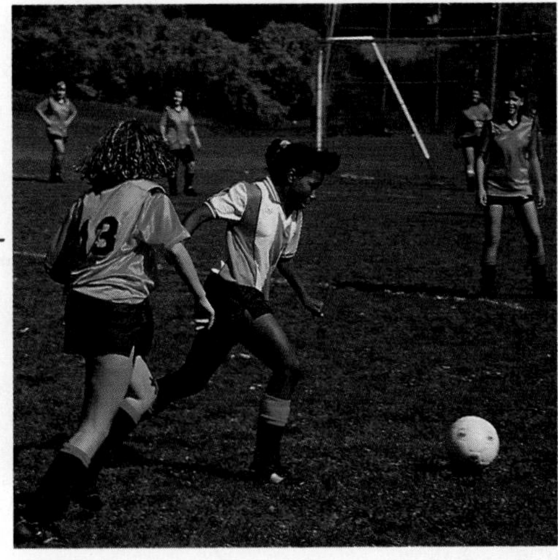

If you stop at a tourist-information station on the interstate highway, you'll find descriptions of that state's special attractions. When you read your newspaper, you'll read descriptions of soccer or football games. Descriptions are also in ads on the veterinarian's bulletin board and in information pamphlets about computers in the computer store. And you can relax and enjoy description in stories, novels, poems, and plays. The purpose of the descriptions may be different, but they're all alike in one way. All the writers want you to form a picture or image of their subjects.

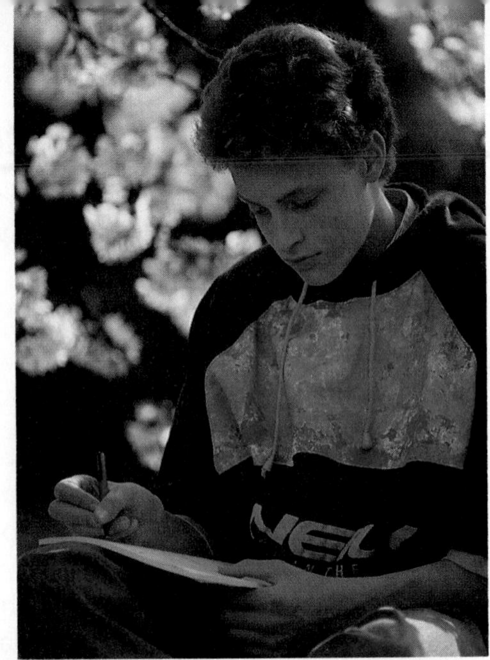

LOOKING AHEAD

In the main assignment in this chapter, you'll write a description. Your basic purpose will be to express yourself or to be creative. As you work through this chapter, keep in mind that an expressive or creative description

- is filled with details that create a picture or image of the subject
- uses sensory details, exact words, and figures of speech
- is clearly organized and easy to follow

Writing a Description

Planning a Description

A good description doesn't just come out of thin air. It's the result of thinking and planning.

Thinking About Subject, Purpose, and Audience

A Subject. You usually don't have to look around for a *subject* to describe. The subject is already there. For example, you need to describe a new jacket you want for your birthday. Or you need to describe your state capitol building in your history report. If you do have to think of a subject to write about, it helps to choose something you know well. You might think of an object in your own home or a place you know very well. If you don't know the subject well, you may have to use your imagination.

A Purpose. Your *purpose* for writing can take you in two different directions. The first direction is to describe something *exactly as it is.* For example, if you've lost your pet dog, Flash, you need to describe his exact color, size, and markings. Otherwise you might get the wrong dog back.

The second direction is the one you take in expressive or creative descriptions. You describe something in a way that will *create a feeling or mood.* You may want to describe your day at the beach to make your readers feel how exciting it was. You could show that excitement by describing how it felt to surf in on a big wave or to catch and reel in a fifty-pound shark or to watch the volleyball soar across the net.

An Audience. Your *audience* will also make a difference in your description. Your best friend would remember that Flash was brown and white, but she might not remember the black spot on his ear. Always ask yourself what your audience will need to know to clearly see what you describe.

When you want to show readers how you feel about a subject, put yourself into the picture. Use words like *I, me, my,* and *mine* when you talk about yourself. However, when you write a description for a formal report—like a science report—it may not be appropriate to use these words or to include your thoughts and feelings. You will have to decide which of these types of description—one that includes your feelings or one that is more focused on facts—better suits your purpose.

PART 1:

Beginning Your Description

In this chapter, you'll be writing a description of an object that expresses your feeling about it. First, you'll have to decide what you want to describe. You will be trying to create a feeling or mood, so you might want to choose something you have a specific feeling about. Also, make sure it's something you know well. Remember that your audience will include your teacher and classmates.

After you've finished doing all this thinking, write down the name of your subject. Then write two or three sentences that tell how you feel about it or how you want your readers to feel about it.

Collecting Details

Now that you have an interesting subject, how do you describe it? Where do you get the details to make it clear? You can observe, recall, or imagine it.

Observing. ***Observing*** a subject means paying close attention to it. It also means using all your senses. What do you see and hear? What do you feel, taste, and touch?

Recalling. Sometimes you can't observe a subject, but you can *recall* certain memories of it. You remember a pizza place because you had a good time there. Close your eyes and think about your subject. What do you see? What foods do you smell? What noises or music do you hear?

Imagining. You can *imagine* details about a subject you've never seen. This is especially important if you want to be creative. What's it like on the planet Saturn or inside a race car? What do you imagine you'd see? hear? smell? Or think about an alien from space. How does it look? walk? talk?

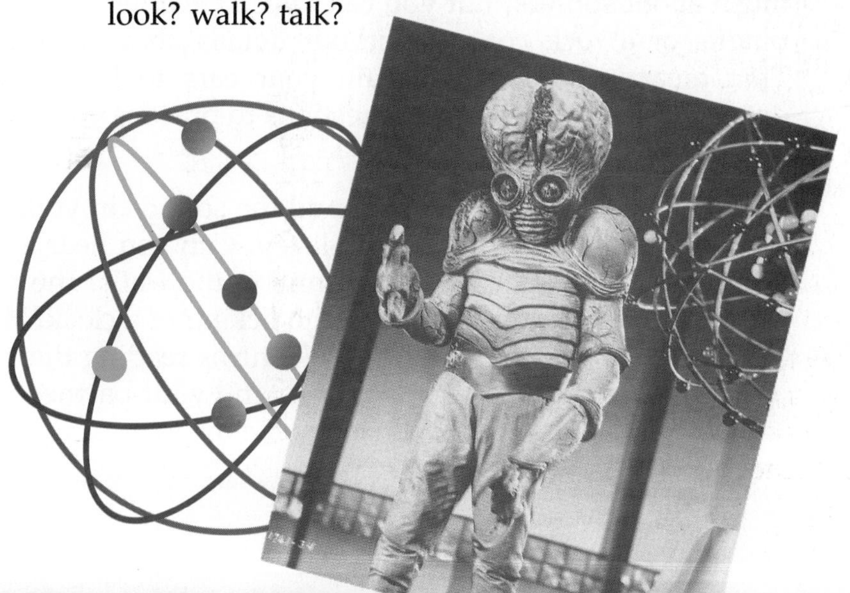

Here are one writer's notes to describe the dark, scary experience she had the time she crawled under a house. Notice that the writer used two of the three ways of collecting details (page 157).

HERE'S HOW

What I observe: darkness under house; muffled sounds; rays of light from house; damp smell; rough ground

What I recall: trash; sweating; imagining spiders and snakes; spider webs in my mouth; seeing my brother and his friend running toward house; hands and knees hurting

EXERCISE 1 **Speaking and Listening: Collecting Details**

If you're describing a book, you don't have to worry too much about sounds. But you can't describe a herd of elephants or a rock concert without details about sound. That means you need to train your ears to listen for details. Use the following suggestions to practice your listening skills.

1. Take five minutes to listen for all the sounds in your home. Jot down notes as you listen. Can you hear a car motor outside? a creaky sound in the walls? the humming of the refrigerator? the ticking of a clock?
2. Get together with a partner. Take turns reading the list of sounds you heard. Did you and your partner hear similar sounds? What are some differences in your lists?

CRITICAL THINKING

Observing Details

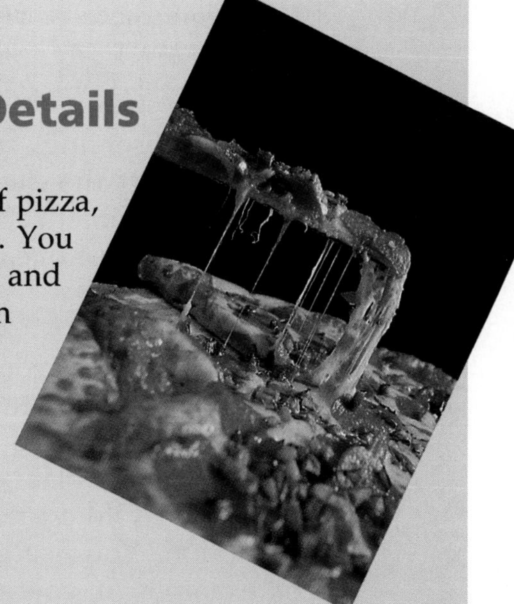

You're eating a big slice of pizza, piled with melting cheese. You smell the spicy pepperoni and see the bright bits of green pepper. Vivid details like these make your readers experience what you describe.

You don't observe details with just your eyes. You also observe them by hearing, tasting, touching, and smelling. Make yourself aware of even the smallest details. Sit on a park bench. What strikes you first? Is the bench wooden or concrete? Are there names or initials carved or drawn on the bench? Can you smell flowers nearby or the fumes of traffic? What do you hear?

CRITICAL THINKING EXERCISE:

Observing Details

Practice your observing skills. Choose something you can observe directly, like the subjects listed below. Use all your senses to observe the subject. Make a list of as many details about it as you can. Compare with classmates who chose similar subjects. What details are different?

1. your bedroom closet
2. your back yard late at night or early in the morning
3. an aquarium
4. your favorite food
5. the refrigerator in your house

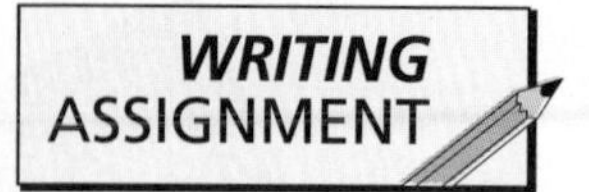

PART 2:
Collecting Details

Put your observing, recalling, and imagining skills into action! Collect the details for the subject you chose for Writing Assignment, Part 1 (page 156). Write your details in a chart like the one on page 158.

Selecting and Organizing Details

Sometimes, when you're going out, you choose everything you wear just to create a certain effect. You decide between a T-shirt and a shirt with buttons, or between a flashy belt and a plain one. You do the same kind of thing when you try to create a particular feeling or mood in a description. You use some details and leave out others. For example, if you want to show that the park was gloomy and depressing, you probably won't include details about the beautiful rose garden.

After you've chosen your details, you need to think about how to put them together. Here are two of the many ways you can arrange descriptive details.

spatial order: arrange details by location—good for describing places and objects

- from top to bottom or bottom to top
- from near to far or far to near
- from left to right or right to left

order of importance: arrange details by the importance you want to give them—good for describing people and animals

- from least to most important
- from most to least important

You don't have to use one of these organizations. Sometimes a description just won't work that way. However, it is important that you create a clear picture for your readers.

REFERENCE NOTE: For more help on arranging information, see pages 39–42 and 77–84.

When you plan a description

- collect details by observing, recalling, or imagining
- select the details that will help you create a special feeling
- decide the best way to organize the details

EXERCISE 2 **Selecting and Organizing Details**

Write a description of the house pictured here to create a feeling of mystery and suspense. Make a list of all the details from the picture that would help create that feeling. Think how to arrange the details. Which would be better—spatial order or order of importance? Arrange your details in the order you've chosen. Next, work with two or three classmates to compare details and the order you used. Try to decide which details and which order work the best.

PART 3:
Selecting and Organizing Details

Look over the details in the chart you made for Writing Assignment, Part 2 (page 160). Think about the feeling you want to create. Choose details and an order you think are best. Then list your details in that order.

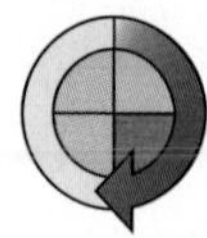

Writing Your First Draft

An artist paints a picture with brushes and paint. These are the artist's tools. When you write a description, you're painting a picture, too. Your tools are words.

The Basic Elements of Description

Sensory details. Sensory details come from using your senses—sight, touch, hearing, smell, and taste. In this paragraph, many sensory details help create a strong picture of hard work.

> It was hot work, dusty work. Chemicals used for spraying the vines smelled bad and choked him. Spider webs got in his face. Broken vines scratched his arms. Grapes stained his hands. Sweat poured into his eyes, in spite of the handkerchief wrapped around his forehead.
>
> James P. Terzian and Kathryn Cramer, *Mighty Hard Road*

Here's the beginning of a ***word bank*** for sensory details. You might start your own word bank in your journal. That way, you can add new words as you learn them.

A WORD BANK			
Sight	shiny faded broad	copper tall silvery	spotted rosy round
Touch	fuzzy scratchy	slippery cool	bumpy damp
Sound	screech mutter	murmur rumble	whisper roar
Smell	smoky rotten	fresh stale	spicy perfumy
Taste	warm sour	salty fresh	bitter sweet

Exact Words. Exact words make your description sharp. For example, an exact word for the color of your favorite sweater might be *turquoise* or *navy,* not *blue.* A duck doesn't *walk,* it *waddles.* In the following paragraph, a young boy finds a fawn, or young deer, that he has been looking for. As you read, notice how the writer uses exact words such as *startled, fawn,* and *stare.*

Movement directly in front of him startled him so that he tumbled backward. The fawn lifted its face to his. It turned its head with a wide, wondering motion and shook him through with the stare of its liquid eyes. It was quivering. It made no effort to rise or run. Jody could not trust himself to move.

Marjorie Kinnan Rawlings, *The Yearling*

Figures of speech. ***Figures of speech*** compare two things that are very different. When you use a figure of speech, you don't mean exactly what you say. "This room is a pig pen" doesn't *really* mean that pigs live in the room. It just means the room is messy. *Similes* and *metaphors* are two figures of speech that are easy to use.

A ***simile*** compares two things using the word *like* or *as.*

Little Man turned around and watched saucer-eyed as a bus bore down on him spewing clouds of red dust *like a huge yellow dragon breathing fire.*

Mildred Taylor, *Roll of Thunder, Hear My Cry*

A ***metaphor*** compares two things directly. It doesn't use *like* or *as*.

During the storm, the *sky was a cloudy sea.*

MECHANICS HINT

Noun Plurals

The exact words that you use in your descriptions are often nouns. Remember that nouns form their plurals in different ways.

Form the plural of many nouns by adding *s*.

EXAMPLES Little *rays* of light helped me see.

I imagined hairy *spiders* and coiled *snakes* in the darkness.

Add *es* to nouns ending in *s, x, z, ch,* or *sh*.

EXAMPLE In the dim light, I saw two small *foxes* hiding in the *bushes.*

Other nouns form their plurals in different ways. Use your dictionary to find the correct noun plurals.

REFERENCE NOTE: For more about noun plurals, see pages 773–776.

Maybe you've seen someone for the first time who stood out in your mind. Could you describe that person vividly? Read the following description of an old doctor. As you read, look for details and words that make the doctor seem real.

A PASSAGE FROM A NOVEL

from Willie Bea and the Time the Martians Landed

by Virginia Hamilton

Simile

Sensory details

Exact words

Dr. Taylor came in and he was old. To Willie Bea, he looked just like Moses on her Sunday School cards, but without a long beard. Wonderful white hair and sparkling eyes. Tall. Tall enough for heaven. Folks said he was eighty-seven, but to Willie Bea he looked closer to one hundred. His baby-fine snow-white hair reached to his shoulders. His black greatcoat came almost down to his ankles. He had on a green woolen scarf and he wore a black Homburg down low over his forehead. He wore old-fashioned leather spats that covered his feet from instep to

Exact words

ankle. He came in and bowed in greeting and for Marva to take his Homburg hat. He had his black bag in one hand and his cane in the other, so he couldn't very well take off the hat himself.

EXERCISE 3 **Analyzing a Description**

After reading the description, can you see Dr. Taylor in your mind? Discuss the following questions about him with your class or small group.

1. What feeling do you get about Dr. Taylor from the passage? Think of a word that describes the feeling.
2. What simile does the writer use to describe him?
3. What are three sensory details the writer uses to describe the doctor's hair and coat? What are the exact words she uses about his spats and hat?
4. The writer seems to use both spatial order and order of importance. Where does she use spatial order? Where does she seem to use order of importance?

A Writer's Model for You

Virginia Hamilton is a skilled professional writer. If it makes you nervous to try to match her skill, look at the following paragraph. It is a little less complicated than the description of Dr. Taylor.

A WRITER'S MODEL

Simile

Exact words

Last summer I discovered a different world when I crawled under the house to look for a lost baseball. The crawl space was like a secret cave. Mostly it was dark, but little rays of light from the house above helped me see. The ground smelled musty and damp, and it was rough on my hands and knees. Above me I could just barely hear music from the radio. Sticky cobwebs got in my mouth. It was cool, but I began to sweat. I imagined hairy spiders and coiled snakes in the darkness. I crawled quickly back to the front and poked my head out of the opening. Bright sunlight blinded my eyes. I felt like a bear coming out of its cave after a long winter's nap.

Sensory details

Writer's feelings

Simile

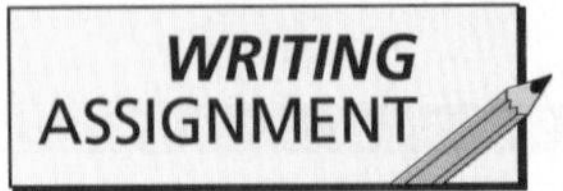

PART 4:
Writing a Draft of Your Description

Are you ready to paint a picture with words? Using the details that you've collected, write the first draft of your description. As you write, focus on the feeling you want to create about your subject. Remember to use sensory details, exact words, and figures of speech so that your description will seem real to your readers.

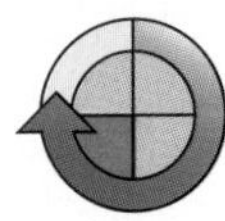

Evaluating and Revising

On page 156 you saw how Calvin's mother helped him evaluate his description. Next, he must revise his work. This same process of evaluating and revising will help you improve your first draft. Use the following chart and ask yourself each question in the left-hand column. If you find a problem, use the ideas in the right-hand column to solve it.

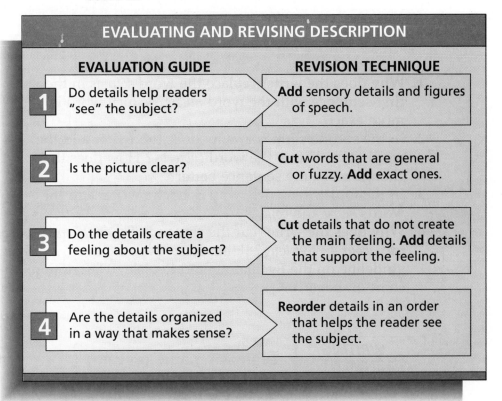

EVALUATING AND REVISING DESCRIPTION

	EVALUATION GUIDE	REVISION TECHNIQUE
1	Do details help readers "see" the subject?	**Add** sensory details and figures of speech.
2	Is the picture clear?	**Cut** words that are general or fuzzy. **Add** exact ones.
3	Do the details create a feeling about the subject?	**Cut** details that do not create the main feeling. **Add** details that support the feeling.
4	Are the details organized in a way that makes sense?	**Reorder** details in an order that helps the reader see the subject.

EXERCISE 4 **Analyzing a Writer's Revisions**

On the following page is part of the description you read on page 168. As you read, think about the changes the writer made during revision. With your class or in a small group, answer the questions that follow.

Above me I could just barely hear ~~sounds~~ music from the radio. Sticky ~~C~~cobwebs got in my mouth. It was cool, but I began to sweat. I imagined hairy spiders and coiled snakes in the darkness. I crawled quickly back to the front and poked my head out of the opening. ~~The crawl space was about 4 1/2 feet long.~~ Bright sunlight blinded my eyes. I felt like a bear coming out of its cave after a long winter's nap.

replace/add

add

cut

1. Why does the writer replace the word *sounds* in the first sentence with the word *music*? Which word is more exact?
2. In the second sentence, why does the writer add the word *Sticky* before the word *cobwebs*? How does this change make the sentence better?
3. In the fourth sentence, why does the writer add the words *hairy* and *coiled*?
4. Why does the writer cut the sentence *The crawl space was about 4 $\frac{1}{2}$ feet long*? [Hint: Read over the third guideline on the Evaluating and Revising Description chart on page 169.]

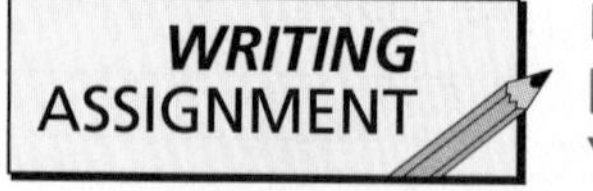

PART 5:

Evaluating and Revising Your Description

It's a good idea to take advantage of other people's evaluations of your writing. Exchange papers with a partner or with a small group of classmates, and comment on each other's descriptions. (Don't forget to use the peer-evaluation guidelines on page 47.) Think about your own evaluations and your classmates' or partner's. Then revise your first draft.

Proofreading and Publishing

In proofreading, you add the finishing touches to your description. Now you can catch and correct errors in grammar, usage, and mechanics. When your description is as good as you can make it, share it with others. Here are two ideas:

- Make a classroom display of the places and objects everyone described. Draw, find, or create pictures, cartoons, or photos to go along with the descriptions.
- Play a guessing game with a small group of classmates. Read your description aloud. Then ask your classmates to identify the main feeling they get from the description. Is the feeling the same as or different from the one you wanted to create?

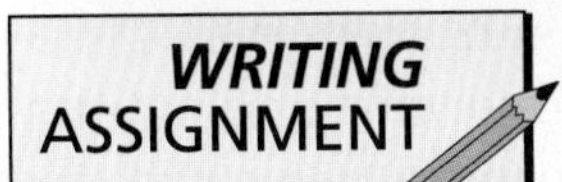

PART 6:
Proofreading and Publishing Your Description

You've worked hard to create a clear picture with your description. Now get your picture ready for viewing by proofreading and correcting it carefully. Exchange papers with a partner. See if your partner can catch errors you missed. Then publish or share your description.

A STUDENT MODEL

In the following paper, Matt Harris—a student at the University Laboratory School in Baton Rouge, Louisiana—writes about his dog, Sherman. Matt says it was hardest to "find the right words to describe Sherman, for he is difficult to describe." Even so, you'll probably notice that Matt finds just the right words to create a clear picture of Sherman.

No-Tail Sherman
by Matt Harris

Every time someone sees him, they ask what he is. We always tell them that Sherman is his name, and he is a Schipperke. He is a black, small, compact dog that is half fur. He has a fox- or wolf-like face, short fox ears, and no tail. Sherman weighs seventeen pounds and is a sweet, affectionate dog, although he is hyper and jumps up on everyone he sees. He doesn't smell bad too often; but when he does smell, he smells like a rotten onion just found on the bottom of an old grocery sack. Unfortunately, his bark can often be heard with a yip-brop-rorp and a bu-ru-ru-ru that is sharper than a razor blade. He prances lightly and with a bouncing motion, like a cat with springs on his feet. When he wants to go out, he whines like a hungry seal. If he gets the chance, he will get into the refrigerator and eat the peanut butter if the jar is left open. Sherman has a different attitude from most dogs. Most dogs lick the garbage can and attack the postman. Sherman licks the postman and attacks the garbage can.

Sherman is the most unusual dog I have ever known. I guess that is why I love him so much.

WRITING WORKSHOP

A Descriptive Poem

In this chapter, you've learned how to create a word-picture with sensory details, exact words, and figures of speech. You can use these same skills to write poetry. A kind of poetry that creates very small word-pictures is *haiku*.

Haiku is a Japanese form of poetry that describes one moment in nature. It has three lines with a certain number of syllables arranged in a pattern. As you read the following poems, notice how the writer captures a very simple but vivid scene in just three lines.

The lightning flashes!
And slashing through the darkness,
A night-heron's screech.

Matsuo Bashō, *translated by Earl Minor*

An old silent pond . . .
A frog jumps into the pond,
splash! Silence again.

Matsuo Bashō, *translated by Harry Behn*

Thinking It Over

1. Which haiku do you like more? Why?
2. What details of sight does the poet use in each haiku?
3. What details of sound or touch do the poems include?

Writing a Descriptive Poem

Prewriting. Choose a scene in nature that you can observe, recall, or imagine clearly. You might choose the sun rising over the ocean, fireworks in a dark sky, a dog shaking off water after a swim. Visualize the subject, and jot down sensory details that describe it. Can you think of comparisons that might help you?

Writing, Evaluating, and Revising. As you write your haiku, listen to the sounds of words as well as to their meaning. In the first haiku, the word *screech* has a sharp sound. That kind of sound fits with the word *slashing*. Play with words to try out different sounds. Read your haiku to some classmates. Ask them if your description captures the feeling you want to give.

Proofreading and Publishing. Check spelling, punctuation, and capitalization before you write a final copy. Then decide how to arrange your poem on a page. Leave white space around it to draw attention to how brief it is. Sign your poem, and if you wish, illustrate it with a drawing or decoration.

MAKING CONNECTIONS

MASS MEDIA AND DESCRIPTION

A Classified Ad

Classified ads are another form of description. They are called *classified* because they are arranged in categories, such as "Jobs," "Cars," or "Yard Sales."

Classified ads are usually short, because newspapers charge by the word or line. Within a short space, the writer must make the item sound better than other, similar items. As you read this type of ad, look for words that might make you want to buy the item. Ads often use abbreviations such as *w/* for *with* and *inc.* for *includes*.

Men's 10-speed bike. Black w/silver pinstripe. Excellent condition, new tires; inc. pump, water bottle, wrench. $70. Call Ed. 555–1685.

Cute, friendly gerbils. Clean, fun, easy to keep. No smells, little work. $5 each with week's food. Call Marin 555–5984.

Now try writing your own classified ad. Think of an object or pet you might sell someday and the way you would describe it. Then write a three- or four-line ad, making each line forty characters. (Each letter, number, space, and punctuation mark counts as a character.) Use abbreviations whenever possible. Later, exchange ads with your classmates.

DESCRIPTION AND LITERATURE

A Poem in Two Languages

Poets rely on the sounds of words as well as the meanings. Sometimes a word sounds very different in another language. Does a *perro* sound nicer than a *dog*? Does *agudo* sound as pointed as *sharp*?

Try writing a brief poem describing a scene in nature. Use any form you like. But don't write the whole poem in English. Instead, use some of the Spanish words in the following charts. If possible, have the words read aloud by someone who knows Spanish. Let your ear enjoy the sounds of these words.

The Spanish words that you can choose to use in your poem are shown in the two following charts. A collection of Spanish nouns is shown in the left-hand column of each chart, and a variety of Spanish adjectives is shown in the right-hand columns. You may use any of the nouns or any of the adjectives in your poem, or you can use noun and adjective combinations. However, there are a few important points to keep in mind when you use the words from these charts.

First, note that in Spanish, an adjective usually follows the noun it describes. For example, in English you would say "white flower," but in Spanish you would say *flor blanca*. Second, Spanish has a more complicated system than English for matching adjectives to the nouns they modify. For the purposes of this exercise, if you want to use a Spanish adjective to modify a Spanish noun, be sure to select the noun and adjective from the same numbered chart.

CHART #1	
NOUNS	ADJECTIVES
tree—*árbol*	dark—*oscuro*
sun—*sol*	cool—*fresco*
sky—*cielo*	blue—*azul*
day—*día*	red—*rojo*
water—*agua*	quiet—*tranquilo*

CHART #2	
NOUNS	ADJECTIVES
grass—*hierba*	cool—*fresca*
leaf—*hoja*	green—*verde*
flower—*flor*	black—*negra*
star—*estrella*	yellow—*amarilla*
night—*noche*	white—*blanca*

6 Creative Writing

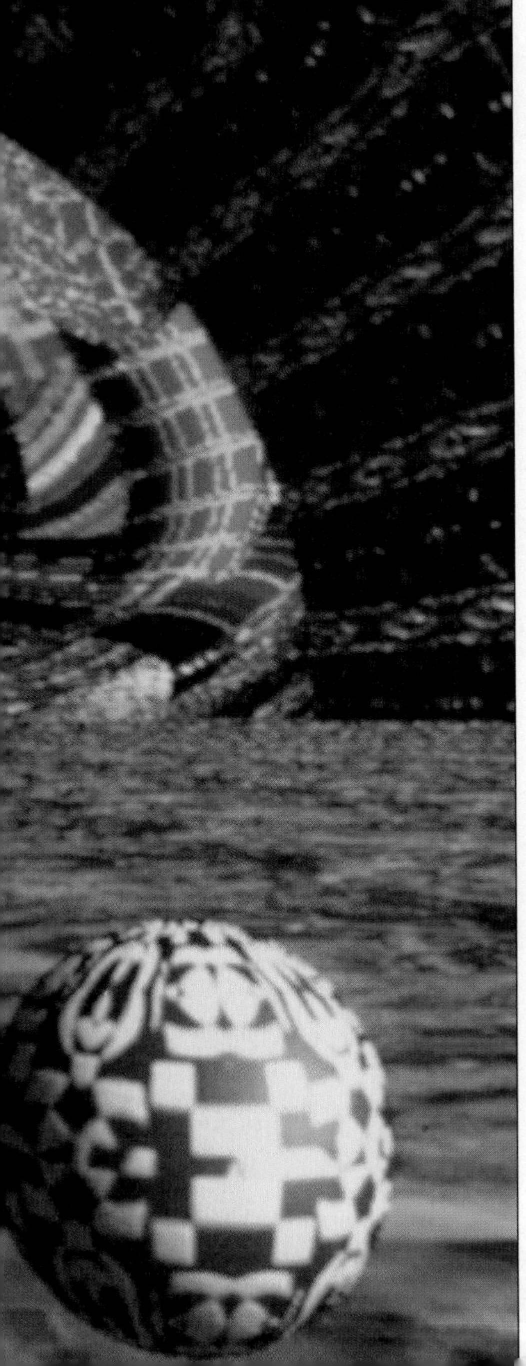

Imagining Other Worlds

You probably like to go to the movies. Most people do. It's a chance to escape—for just a little while—to **other worlds.** Movies allow our **imaginations** to run wild. Anything can happen. And, best of all, things usually come out okay in the end.

Writing and You. Writers use their imagination to write movie scripts, novels, stories, plays, poems, and even comic strips. They tickle our own imagination by creating, and having us believe in, people and places that never were and never will be. They make us burst with excitement, fear, unreal expectations, and fun. Have you ever used your imagination to make up a story for a little child?

As You Read. As you read the following folk tale, you'll see how people can also use imagination to explain the world around them.

Persepol, 1980, © David Em/represented by Roberta Spieckerman Associates, San Francisco.

Coyote Places the Stars

By Barry Lopez

One time there were five wolves, all brothers, who traveled together. Whatever meat they got when they were hunting they would share with Coyote. One evening Coyote saw the wolves looking up at the sky.

"What are you looking at up there, my brothers?" asked Coyote.

"Oh, nothing," said the oldest wolf.

Next evening Coyote saw they were all looking up in the sky at something. He asked the next oldest wolf what they were looking at, but he wouldn't say. It went on like this for three or four nights. No one wanted to tell Coyote what they were looking at because they thought he would want to interfere. One night Coyote asked the youngest wolf brother to tell him and the youngest wolf said to the other wolves, "Let's tell Coyote what we see up there. He won't do anything."

So they told him. "We see two animals up there. Way up there, where we cannot get to them."

"Let's go up and see them," said Coyote.

"Well, how can we do that?"

"Oh, I can do that easy," said Coyote. "I can show you how to get up there without any trouble at all."

Coyote gathered a great number of arrows and then began shooting them into the sky. The first arrow stuck in the sky and the second arrow stuck in the first. Each arrow stuck in the end of the one before it like that until there was a ladder reaching down to the earth.

"We can climb up now," said Coyote. The oldest wolf took his dog with him, and then the other four wolf brothers came, and then Coyote. They climbed all day and into the night. All the next day they climbed. For many days and nights they climbed until finally they reached the sky. They stood in the sky and looked over at the two animals the wolves had seen from down below. They were two grizzly bears.

"Don't go near them," said Coyote. "They will tear you apart." But the two youngest wolves were already headed over. And the next two youngest wolves followed them. Only the oldest wolf held back. When the wolves got near the grizzlies nothing happened. The wolves sat down and looked at the bears, and the bears sat there looking at the wolves. The oldest wolf, when he saw it was safe, came over with his dog and sat down with them.

Coyote wouldn't come over. He didn't trust the bears. "That makes a nice picture, though," thought Coyote. "They all look pretty good sitting there like that. I think I'll leave it that way for everyone to see. Then when people look at them in the sky they will say, 'There's a story about that picture,' and they will tell a story about me."

So Coyote left it that way. He took out the arrows as he descended so there was no way for anyone to get back. From down on the earth Coyote admired the arrangement he had left up there. Today they still look the same. They call those stars Big Dipper now. If you look up there you'll see three wolves make up the handle and the oldest wolf, the one in the middle, still has his dog with him. The two youngest wolves make up the part of the bowl under the handle and the two grizzlies make up the other side, the one that points toward the North Star.

When Coyote saw how they looked he wanted to put up a lot of stars. He arranged stars all over the sky in pictures and then made the Big Road across the sky with the stars he had left over.

When Coyote was finished he called Meadowlark over. "My brother," he said, "When I am gone, tell everyone that when they look up into the sky and see the stars arranged this way, that I was the one who did that. That is my work."

Now Meadowlark tells that story. About Coyote.

Reader's Response

1. Would you want Coyote for a friend? In a few words, describe his qualities—good and bad.
2. Were there places in the story where what happened was not what you expected? (What about those grizzlies?) In your journal, rewrite the story. Keep the same characters, but change the events of the story any way you want.

Writer's Craft

3. Item 1 above asked you to describe Coyote. What details in the story helped you know him?
4. Stories get set in motion because characters have problems and need to solve them. Who has a problem in this story? What is the problem? How is it solved?
5. How did the person who created this story use his imagination to explain a part of the world?

"We are a part of the earth and it is part of us."

Chief Seattle

Ways to Write Creatively

In this chapter you'll write a story and a poem, two types of creative writing. Other types are movie and play scripts, words for songs, children's books, and novels. Creative writing starts in the writer's imagination. Just as an artist uses paint, a writer uses words to create something special. Here are some ways of writing creatively.

Narration: in a television script, telling the story of a child genius and her longing for a normal life; telling a story about a Seminole boy who saves a panther cub in the Florida Everglades.

Description: in a song, describing a girl's hair and eyes; in a story about time travel, describing New York City in the year 4000.

Classification: in a poem, comparing envy to a wasp's sting; in a novel, contrasting a big-city girl with a boy from a small town.

Evaluation: in a poem, judging highways and billboards that interrupt and hide nature; in a play, showing how too much pride can drive away good friends.

LOOKING AHEAD

In this chapter, you'll use the strategy of narration to write a story. Keep in mind that an effective story

- entertains the reader
- solves a conflict, or problem
- holds the reader's attention with lifelike characters, an interesting plot, and a specific setting

Writing a Story

Finding a Story Idea

Here's the big question: Where do you find a story idea? Here's the answer: Anywhere and everywhere. You might get an idea from a magazine or a photograph, from another story or a cartoon, or from a daydream or a nightmare.

As you look and listen around you, you can also play the "What if?" game: imagining any change or new thing that comes into your head. This is a way writers get some great ideas: *What if* a father shrank his kids? *What if* a man could strap a rocket to his back?

Thinking About Purpose and Audience

In writing a story, the one *purpose* you have is to entertain your readers. You may do it by making them laugh over the mistakes of a silly character. Or you may do it by involving them in a deep mystery. Just give your *audience* something that keeps them turning the pages.

Starting with Characters and Situations

What keeps a reader turning pages? Almost always it's an interesting main ***character*** faced with a ***conflict***—a situation that holds a problem or challenge. How will the brave princess rescue the prince from the tower? How will the class clown ever get the honor roll student to take her seriously?

Character. You can begin your story idea by thinking of a character. Suppose your little sister has a girlfriend who's very, very, *very* shy but amazingly sharp when you get her to talk. Or pretend that you see a newspaper photo of a ninety-year-old man from Jamaica. These people stick in your mind somehow—perhaps the girl has unusual eyes or the man has an interesting face. Could you put one in a situation with conflict? Of course you don't have to start with a real person. What kind of story could you build around a shy mouse from Jamaica?

Situation. Or you could begin in the opposite way. Think of an interesting situation or problem. It may be something you've seen on television, heard about from a friend, or actually experienced.

Maybe you know of someone hiding a cat in an apartment where animals are forbidden. Or you've always wondered what it would be like to be lost in a large city where you don't speak the language. From there, you can build a conflict and a story.

Here are just a few examples of how you might start with a character or a situation to build a story idea. A million other ideas are possible. Just feel free to let your imagination run wild!

STORY IDEAS

Character: Ninety-year-old man, born in Jamaica. Has lived almost all his life in New York City.

Situation: *What if* . . . he took his Social Security check, ran away from his niece's apartment, and stowed away on a cruise ship bound for Jamaica.

Situation: Someone who can't speak English or Spanish is lost in Houston, Texas.
Character: *What if . . .* the person is a young boy who speaks Mayan, is visiting with a group of musicians, and has with him a wooden flute that he can play beautifully.

When you're looking for story ideas, remember

- ideas can come from anywhere: your own experience, TV, newspapers, photographs, songs, and more
- your story needs a main character and a conflict
- try starting with a character or situation and asking "What if?" to build a story idea

EXERCISE 1 **Building Story Ideas**

Now try your hand (and imagination) at using the following characters and situations to come up with story ideas. Work with a small group, and brainstorm as many ideas as you want. [Remember: Your situations must hold a *conflict*, or *problem.*]

1. **Character**: A young girl is extremely clever, but she's also painfully shy, always staying in the background.
   Situation: *What if* ______________________

2. **Character:** Ahmed Mostafa, with his elderly grandfather, takes care of dozens of homing pigeons on the roof of his building.
   Situation: *What if* ______________________

3. **Situation:** Someone is hiding a cat in an apartment where animals aren't allowed.
   Character: *What if* ______________________

4. **Situation:** All of the bicycles, roller skates, and skateboards disappear from a town.
   Character: *What if* ______________________

PART 1:
Finding a Story Idea

You may have gotten a great idea from the group brainstorming in Exercise 1. But if not, now you know how to go about getting one. Remember that you can use anything around you—from everyday experiences to space monsters on TV—to come up with characters and situations. Decide on your final story idea and write it down.

Planning Your Story

Professional writers plan their stories before they begin. Of course, that doesn't mean they don't make some changes along the way. Writers often surprise themselves!

Imagining Characters. If you want readers to pay attention to your story, your main character (and other important characters) should seem *alive.* The best way to get life into your characters is with specific, sharp *details.*

You can make up details: a lavender kitten with one orange eye and one purple eye. Or you can borrow details from real people: a Civil War general who has your own grandfather's twinkling green eyes. These questions will help you imagine your characters—make them solid.

- *What does the character look like?*
- *What is the character's name?*
- *How would you describe the character's personality?*
- *What does the character love and hate?*
- *What does the character sound like?*

One way to make notes on your characters is to keep the questions in mind and then freewrite a description.

HERE'S HOW

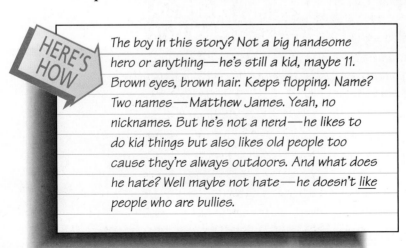

The boy in this story? Not a big handsome hero or anything—he's still a kid, maybe 11. Brown eyes, brown hair. Keeps flopping. Name? Two names—Matthew James. Yeah, no nicknames. But he's not a nerd—he likes to do kid things but also likes old people too cause they're always outdoors. And what does he hate? Well maybe not hate—he doesn't like people who are bullies.

Describing Setting. The ***setting*** is where and when the story takes place. A setting can be the corner of a room at night or a football stadium on Sunday afternoon. It can be the present or the age of dinosaurs.

The setting can give information about characters. A clean room, for example, shows readers that a character likes order and neatness. The setting can also create a mood. An abandoned house and a howling wind will make sure a scary story is scary.

Sometimes setting even creates a conflict. If you set your story in Alaska during a blizzard, your character might be trapped in the snow.

Here are some questions to help you plan your setting.

- *Where and when will my story take place?*
- *What places, weather, things, or times of day could be important in my story?*
- *What sensory details (smells, sights, sounds) can I use to describe these important parts of setting?*

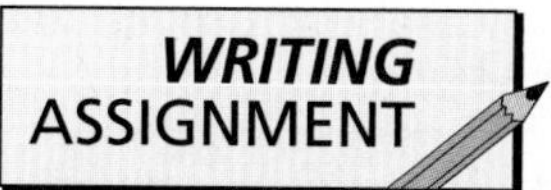

PART 2:
Planning Characters and Setting

To get a clearer picture of your characters and setting, use the questions on pages 189 and 190. You can jot down your responses, freewrite, or even use clustering. Write freely and let your ideas flow.

Planning Your Plot. Suppose you have an interesting character, a girl named Tuyet Nguyen, and a good solid setting for her, an old two-story house in Myer's Cove, where she lives with her parents and grandmother. Now you need a ***plot***, or series of events, for the story. While a plot is "what happens," it has these special parts:

- **A conflict:** As you've already learned, the main character must face some problem. *Tuyet wants piano lessons, but her family can't afford to pay for them.*
- **A series of events:** Your story must have action. The events must move forward as the character works on the conflict. *Tuyet may run errands to earn money, count her earnings daily, and dream of the lessons.*
- **A high point:** Your story also needs a moment, the high point, when the problem is going to be *settled* —one way or another. Readers' curiosity or suspense is at a high point. *Perhaps Tuyet's grandmother gets very sick. Will Tuyet have to sacrifice her piano lessons for her grandmother's medicine?*
- **An outcome:** The outcome shows how the problem is solved and what happens when it is. *Tuyet gives her savings to her parents and says she will forget the lessons. Her grandmother sees how much music means to her and promises to help Tuyet earn money when she is better.*

Creating a Story Map. When you plan your plot, you can put it into a story map that outlines your character, setting, and plot all at once. The following example shows how one writer mapped her story about Matthew James and the gang.

HERE'S HOW

A STORY MAP	
CHARACTERS:	Matthew James, the gang (Chief, Corker, Dunce), Ms. Paglia
SETTING:	Woods, neighborhood, and park—summertime
PLOT:	Conflict: Matthew James wants to stop the gang from chopping down the roses. Events: (1) Matthew James hears gang's plan. (2) Matthew worries about how to stop them. On a walk, he sees sprinklers: Idea! (3) The neighborhood goes to the picnic. High point: (4) The gang sneaks to the roses. (5) Matthew soaks them with the sprinklers. Outcome: (6) Ms. Paglia thinks the gang watered her roses and gives the boys flowers.

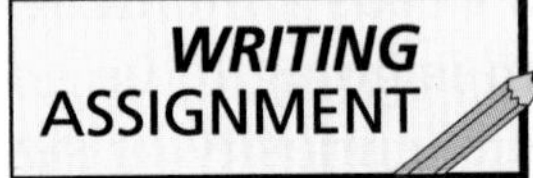

PART 3:

Creating a Story Map

Now it is time for the last stage of your planning. Exactly what will *happen* in your story? Remember that your plot needs certain elements: conflict, events, high point, and outcome. When you decide on the parts, put them into a story map like the one in the Here's How on this page. Don't forget to include characters and settings.

Writing Your First Draft

Combining the Basic Elements of a Story

A map to a place isn't the place. And your story map isn't a story—yet. How do you turn the map into a bursting-with-life tale? Here are some tips.

Making the Plot Move Along. A good *beginning* for a story hooks the reader's attention right away. You might start in the middle of an action—a burglar coming through the window, for example. Or you might describe the dark night and lonely street to set the mood.

In the *middle* of the story, keep your audience guessing. Make every event open up a possibility, create a surprise, or lead to the high point. What happens when Jowela sees the burglar? Don't let her stop to play a video game!

After your strong high point, make sure the *ending* is satisfying. Solve the problem but also tie up any loose ends. If Jowela traps the burglar and the police come, the conflict is over. But don't leave the burglar trapped in the shower stall. Get her out before Jowela and the police say good night.

Making Your Characters Seem Real. You've learned that specific details make lifeless characters into lively ones. Here are three good ways to use details.

- Give clear descriptions of *appearance*. Don't say *She dressed oddly* when you can say *She wore purple felt overalls, green high-heeled sneakers, and a bright red cape.* (For more help with descriptions, see Chapter 5.)

- Make *actions* specific. You could say *He sat down in the chair.* But readers would know this character much better if *He plopped down in the big recliner, dangling his legs over the arm.*
- Use *dialogue.* A summary of speech like *He refused to do it* will move action along. But ***dialogue***—a character's own words—can also reveal emotion and personality. Use fragments, contractions, and slang if they're right for the character. *"No way! Are you nuts? I wouldn't call her if she was Queen of the World."*

EXERCISE 2 **Speaking and Listening: Creating Dialogue**

With a partner, create dialogues for the characters in the following situations. Try to make the dialogue natural—like real speech. Present your dialogues to another partner group. Then ask for feedback about whether you sound real—and why or why not.

1. An elderly woman calls the police to report that her cat is up in a tree. The police officer tries to convince her that the cat will be okay.
2. Two teenage boys try to decide how to spend the afternoon. Should they go to the mall or to the ice skating rink?

Looking at a Short Story

Every story is different. Writers combine plot, characters, and setting in different ways. The writer of the following short story makes sure you're aware of setting at the start. As you read, see if you can guess the surprise ending.

A SHORT STORY

The Dinner Party

by Mona Gardner

BEGINNING
Setting

The country is India. A colonial official and his wife are giving a large dinner party. They are seated with their guests—

Situation and characters

army officers and government attachés and their wives, and a visiting American naturalist—in their spacious dining room, which has a bare marble floor, open rafters, and wide glass doors opening onto a veranda.

Event 1

A spirited discussion springs up between a young girl who insists that women have outgrown the jumping-on-a-chair-at-the-sight-of-a-mouse era and a colonel who says that they haven't.

Dialogue

"A woman's unfailing reaction in any crisis," the colonel says, "is to scream. And while a man may feel like it, he has that ounce more of nerve control than a woman has. And that last ounce is what counts."

MIDDLE
Event 2
Hint of conflict—suspense
Specific action

The American does not join in the argument but watches the other guests. As he looks, he sees a strange expression come over the face of the hostess. She is staring straight ahead, her muscles contracting slightly. With a slight gesture she summons the native boy standing behind her chair and whispers to him. The boy's eyes widen: He quickly leaves the room.

Event 3

Of the guests, none except the American notices this or sees the boy place a bowl of milk on the veranda just outside the open doors.

Suspense
Character
Setting

The American comes to with a start. In India, milk in a bowl means only one thing—bait for a snake. He realizes there must be a cobra in the room. He looks up at the rafters—the likeliest place—but they are bare. Three corners of the room are empty, and in the fourth the servants are waiting to serve the next course. There is only one place left—under the table.

Event 4

His first impulse is to jump back and warn the others, but he knows the commotion would frighten the cobra into striking. He speaks quickly, the tone of his voice so arresting that it sobers everyone.

Dialogue

"I want to know just what control everyone at this table has. I will count to three hundred—that's five minutes—and not one of you is to move a muscle. Those who move will forfeit fifty rupees. Ready!"

Suspense
Specific action
High point

The twenty people sit like stone images while he counts. He is saying " . . . two hundred and eighty . . ." when, out of the corner of his eye, he sees the cobra emerge and make for the bowl of milk. Screams ring out as he jumps to slam the veranda doors safely shut.

ENDING **Dialogue**	"You were right, Colonel!" the host exclaims. "A man has just shown us an example of perfect control."
Outcome	"Just a minute," the American says, turning to his hostess. "Mrs. Wynnes, how did you know that cobra was in the room?"
Surprise ending	A faint smile lights up the woman's face as she replies: "Because it was crawling across my foot."

EXERCISE 3 **Analyzing the Elements of a Short Story**

Think about the basic elements of "The Dinner Party." With a partner discuss the following questions.

1. Did you enjoy the story? How do you think you would have reacted if you'd been the American naturalist? or Mrs. Wynnes, the hostess?
2. How important is the story's setting? Could this story happen in your home? in some other setting in India?
3. How did the writer create suspense in the story?
4. Do you think the story has a message—an important idea? What is it?
5. Were you surprised by the story's ending? What clues does the writer give?

Using a Story Framework

"The Dinner Party" has vivid descriptions, great suspense, and a surprise ending. It even has a serious message about mistaken ideas about women. It's polished and professional. But even if your story doesn't have all these elements (plus a high point with a cobra!), it can be just as entertaining.

Notice how the following writer starts with action and gets quickly to characters and conflict. You might want to follow this model for your story.

A WRITER'S MODEL

The Gang's Surprise

BEGINNING
Main character/ Setting
Situation

Matthew James scrambled over the wall and dashed to his hideout under the ivy. He hastily brushed his dark hair from his forehead. His brown eyes were sharp as he watched the gang sneak through the woods and meet under the big willow tree. Chief, the gang leader, gave the orders.

Dialogue
Event 1

"Tomorrow while everyone's at the cookout, we'll chop off all of old lady Paglia's roses," he said.

Corker gave an approving whistle. Dunce nodded enthusiastically.

Dialogue
Specific action

"Then we'll put the dumb roses on Mr. O'Brian's front steps, and it will look like he picked them," Chief added. The gang hollered and hooted. Chief and the gang had disliked the two elderly people ever since the day they made the boys pick up trash they'd thrown on the neighborhood lawns.

Conflict

Matthew James heard every word the gang said. He knew he had to stop them. He also knew

it wouldn't be easy. He sure couldn't fight them.
MIDDLE The next day was sunny and bright.
Butterflies flitted and birds sang. But Matthew
Character James was in a lousy mood. Time was running
out, and he still had no plan.
Event 2 He walked down the street and watched Ms.
Paglia smell her roses. Her brown eyes twinkled
Specific action with delight. He watched Ms. Dent pull out
dandelions from her flower bed. Her brow was
creased but she was singing. Then Mr. Mason
Suspense hooked up his sprinkler system. There was a
sudden shower. Matthew James had a
brainstorm!

Event 3 At 5:00, the neighbors went to the park. At
5:45, the gang sneaked across the green back
yards. "Okay, make it fast," said Chief. The boys
took off at top speed toward Ms. Paglia's garden.
Event 4 They reached the yellow rose bushes. They
High point crouched down and pulled out pen knives. Then
Matthew James turned the faucet behind Mr.
Mason's garage. Water sprayed everywhere. The
gang screamed and tried to run for cover, but
there wasn't a dry spot anywhere. Matthew
James had hooked up every sprinkler on the
Specific action block. Water was shooting in all directions.

Event 5 Luckily, Matthew James turned off the sprinklers just in time. Ms. Paglia suddenly **Dialogue** appeared walking down the street. "I do believe I smell rain. Did it rain while I was in the park?" she asked herself. Then she noticed that her rose bushes were wet. "Well, my saints! Someone watered my roses," she said aloud. Suddenly, Ms. **Suspense** Paglia saw the gang huddled under a tree.

Appearance details "Come here!" she shouted. The gang looked like drowned rats—*frightened* drowned rats—but **ENDING** they obeyed. Ms. Paglia patted each boy on the head and invited them all to the cookout for dessert.

Matthew James took a secret path and arrived at the park just as Ms. Paglia was telling everyone what happened. "These dear boys watered all our flowers and yards—as a surprise!" she exclaimed. The gang looked very confused. **Outcome** Matthew James smiled.

"Good work," he said to himself and watched Ms. Paglia hand each soggy boy a yellow rose.

USAGE HINT

Using Verb Tenses

Story events are usually told in chronological order, using the past tense: *The villain **grasped** the prune. He **thrust** it fiercely toward my mouth.* To explain actions that happened before other past actions, use the past perfect tense.

EXAMPLE **I had seen** [past perfect] an escape route before the villain grasped [past] the prune.

REFERENCE NOTE: For more information on verb tenses, see pages 592–594.

PART 4:
Writing Your First Draft

Now it's time to begin your story. Go over the character and setting descriptions you wrote. Reread your story map, but remember that it's only a guide. You don't have to follow it exactly. Part of the fun of writing stories can be discovering new ideas. Begin writing and see what happens.

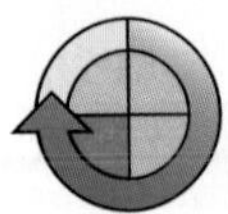

Evaluating and Revising

If you're like most writers, you feel a sense of accomplishment after you finish a draft. Part of you would like to quit. After all—you've written a story. But part of you knows the story could be better. And you want to make it as good as possible.

You need to read your story as a critic. Better yet, read it as a reader who wants to be entertained. To evaluate your story, use the guidelines on page 204 to find its strengths and weaknesses. If the answer to any question on the left-hand side of the chart is no, use the techniques on the right-hand side to make revisions.

The first thing readers see when they pick up a story is the title. Sometimes a title even *makes* them pick it up. Of course, not all titles are that exciting. But a good title isn't dull. Titles can come from an important character in the story, a significant plot event, or even the setting. What would be the best title for your story?

CRITICAL THINKING

Analyzing the Elements of a Story

All good writers *analyze* when they evaluate their writing. They examine their stories with a magnifying glass. They look at all the elements and how they fit together. When the writer of "The Gang's Surprise" analyzed her first paragraph, she made the following changes.

~~It was a June day in Burnside, before the neighborhood was going to have a big picnic with lots of food. A boy named~~ — cut

Matthew James ~~went~~ scrambled over the wall and dashed to his — replace/add

hideout under the ivy. (He hastily brushed his dark hair from his forehead.) His brown eyes — add

were sharp as he watched the gang sneak through the woods and meet under the big willow tree. Chief, the gang leader, gave the orders~~ to meet during the cookout and cut Ms. Paglia's roses.~~ ¶ "Tomorrow while everyone's at the cookout, we'll chop off all of old lady Paglia's roses," he said. — replace

CRITICAL THINKING EXERCISE:

Analyzing a Writer's Revisions

Work with a partner to analyze the revisions in the paragraph above. Use the following questions to guide your analysis. Also refer to the chart on page 204. It shows you the important elements of a short story.

1. Why did the writer cut so much from the beginning?
2. Why did the writer decide to use *scrambled* and *dashed* in the second sentence?
3. What's the reason for adding a whole sentence?
4. Do you think the replacement in the last sentence is a good revision? Why or why not?

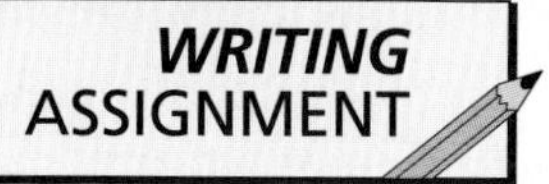

PART 5:

Evaluating and Revising Your Story

Use the chart on page 204 to help evaluate and revise your first draft. When you finish revising, swap stories with a classmate for feedback and suggestions.

EVALUATING AND REVISING SHORT STORIES

	EVALUATION GUIDE	REVISION TECHNIQUE
1	Does the beginning catch readers' interest?	**Add** (or **replace** other) sentences with vivid details of character, action, or setting.
2	Is the conflict clear early in the story?	**Add** or **reorder** sentences in which the main character faces a problem.
3	Do events create suspense or curiosity for readers?	**Cut** events that slow down action. **Add** events that keep readers wondering.
4	Does the plot have a strong high point and a satisfying outcome?	**Add** a tense scene that solves a conflict. **Add** details that explain how everything works out.
5	Are the characters lifelike and believable?	**Add** details about the characters' looks, actions, and thoughts. **Add** dialogue that sounds natural.
6	Is the setting clear? If possible, does it help set a mood?	**Add** specific details of time and place. **Add** vivid sensory details.

"Everyone you meet has a story."

Madeleine L'Engle

Proofreading and Publishing

Proofreading. Now it's time to polish your story. To make it shine, double-check carefully to find and correct any errors in spelling, usage, and mechanics.

Publishing. Don't be shy with your story. People *want* to be entertained. Let them see your special imagination. Here are two possibilities for publishing.

- Ask your principal if you may read some of the stories over the intercom during homeroom.
- Create giant comic-book murals of your stories and use them to decorate your classroom and the halls of your school.

PART 6:
Proofreading and Publishing Your Story

Make a neat, final copy of your story. Be sure to give that final copy one last good proofreading—and then share your story with an audience.

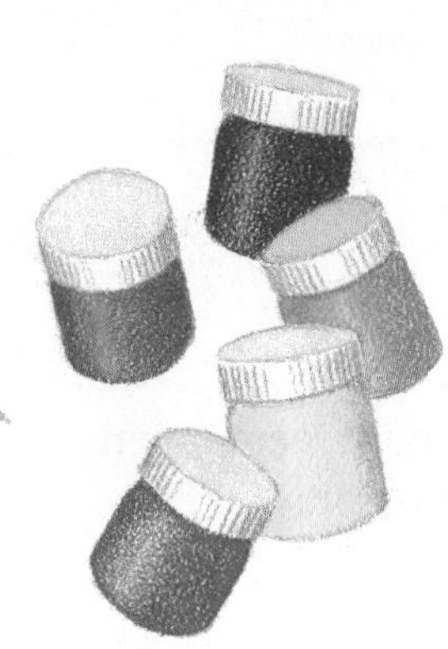

WRITING WORKSHOP

A Narrative Poem

A poem that tells a story is called a ***narrative poem.*** A narrative poem is much like the story you just wrote. It has characters, plot, setting, and sometimes even dialogue.

But poetry adds other elements to storytelling—especially sounds and images. To create musical sounds, poets use rhythm, rhyme, and repeated sounds. The ***rhythm*** is created by the beats—the syllables that are stressed. The beat may be regular or it may be uneven and loose.

Rhyme is a regular pattern of similar vowel sounds (like *pop* and *top*). Rhyming words are often, but not always, at the end of the lines. Poets also create musical sounds by repeating the first letters of words ("*l*ovely *l*aughing *l*adies").

Poets create ***images,*** or word pictures, with words that appeal to the senses. For example, you might look for words that will help your readers see, or hear, or even feel what you are describing.

The following poem has rhythm, rhyme, great word pictures, and a hungry weed. Hungry? See for yourself.

My Aunt
by Ted Hughes

You've heard how a green thumb
Makes flowers come
Quite without toil
Out of any old soil.

Well, my Aunt's thumbs were green.
At a touch, she had blooms
Of prize Chrysanthemums—
The grandest ever seen.

People from miles around
Came to see those flowers
And were truly astounded
By her unusual powers.

One day a little weed
Pushed up to drink and feed
Among the pampered flowers
At her water-can showers.

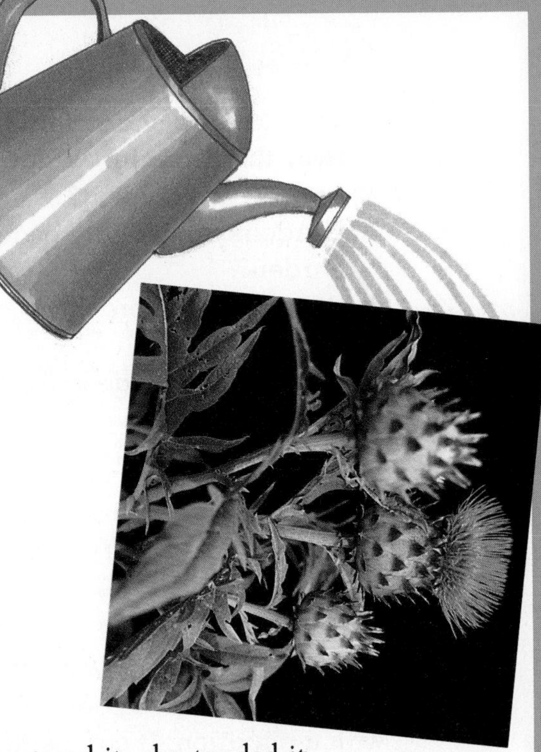

Day by day it grew
With ragged leaves and bristles
Till it was tall as me or you—
It was a King of Thistles

"Prizes for flowers are easy,"
My aunt said in her pride.
"But was there ever such a weed
The whole world wide?"

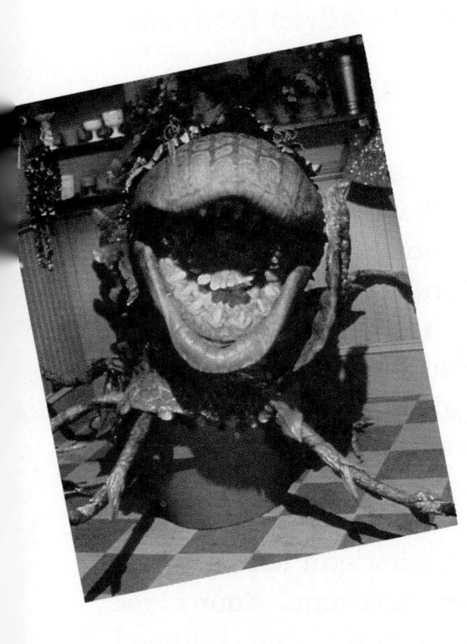

She watered it, she tended it,
It grew alarmingly.
As if I had offended it,
It bristled over me.

"Oh Aunt!" I cried. "Beware of that!
I saw it eat a bird."
She went on polishing its points
As if she hadn't heard.

"Oh Aunt!" I cried. "It has a flower
Like a lion's beard—"
Too late! It was devouring her
Just as I had feared.

Her feet were waving in the air—
But I shall not proceed.
Here ends the story of my Aunt
And her ungrateful weed.

Thinking It Over

1. Who are the characters in this poem? (If you name only two, think again.) What can you tell about them—and how do you know it?
2. Gardens are usually peaceful settings. Is that true of this garden?
3. Do you see more than one problem or conflict in the poem? Explain.
4. How would you describe the beat of the poem? What syllables are stressed?
5. What examples of sounds and images do you hear and see?

Writing a Narrative Poem

Prewriting. Apply what you know about writing stories to writing a narrative poem. Try beginning with a character or with a situation. It can be fantastic (like "My Aunt") or realistic. After you've jotted down a few ideas, share them with a few classmates. Then choose an idea that you really like.

Writing, Evaluating, and Revising. Whether you rhyme the ends of lines is up to you. Experiment with a few lines to decide. And listen for rhythm with your ear. Notice where the beats, or stresses, are. Even if they aren't regular, the rhythm should be pleasing, not annoying. You can break your poem into lines and stanzas that seem natural to you. And don't forget other tools of the poet—repeated sounds and sensory images. (For more on sensory images, see Chapter 4.) After you've finished writing, read your poem aloud to hear how it sounds. Exchange poems with a classmate for feedback.

Proofreading and Publishing. Make a clean copy of your poem and proofread it carefully one last time. Your class might create a poem clothesline to hang your finished poems on, or you might perform some of your poems at the next parent-teacher organization meeting or Parent's Day.

MAKING CONNECTIONS

MYTHS

Writing a Myth

Myths are stories that people have told and passed down to others through the ages. Very often they try to explain something about the natural world. For example, the sun is a god's chariot driven across the sky, or the stars are the result of Coyote's magic handiwork, as in "Coyote Places the Stars" on pages 180–182.

People everywhere tell myths—in the Northern African desert, in the Central American jungle, and on the Canadian Plains. You can, too. Why is the sea salty? Why do people sneeze? Make up a myth to explain anything you like. Or, if you know a myth from your culture, retell it in your own words. That's how myths stay alive.

CREATIVE WRITING AND LITERATURE

Writing a New Ending for a Story

Sometimes when you read a story, it doesn't end quite like you imagine it will. Sometimes you want a different ending, the *right* one—yours. Here's your chance to step into the author's shoes. Pick one of the stories in this chapter—"Coyote Places the Stars," "The Dinner Party," or "The Gang's Surprise." Try your hand at writing a new ending for it. Begin at the story's high point.

7 Writing to Inform

Working and Playing

Have dinosaur skeletons been found in the U.S.? How do you do an axel in ice skating? Where is the closest national park? Who wants to know? Someone somewhere does. We spend most hours **working or playing,** so the information we want is often about *processes:* how to do something or how something works.

Writing and You. You'd be surprised how much writing explains a process. A detective story explains how the murder weapon disappeared: it was an icicle. An article in *WaterSki* magazine gives tips for using a kneeboard. What process could you write about?

As You Read. Writers sometimes explain a special way of doing a familiar process. Do you think you know how to eat? Maybe not. As you read the following "how-to," notice the steps even a child could follow.

The Making of a Fresco Showing the Building of a City, Diego Rivera (1931), San Francisco Art Institute. Photo by Don Beatty © 1984.

How to EAT Like a Child

by Delia Ephron

Peas: Mash and flatten into thin sheet on plate. Press the back of the fork into the peas. Hold fork vertically, prongs up, and lick off peas.

Mashed potatoes: Pat mashed potatoes flat on top. Dig several little depressions. Think of them as ponds or pools. Fill the pools with gravy. With your fork, sculpt rivers between pools and watch the gravy flow between them. Decorate with peas. Do not eat.

Alternative method: Make a large hole in center of mashed potatoes. Pour in ketchup. Stir until potatoes turn pink. Eat as you would peas.

Animal crackers: Eat each in this order—legs, head, body.

Sandwich: Leave the crusts. If your mother says you have to eat them because that's the best part, stuff the crusts into your pants pocket or between the cushions of the couch.

Spaghetti: Wind too many strands on the fork and make sure at least two strands dangle down. Open your mouth wide and stuff in spaghetti; suck noisily to inhale the dangling strands. Clean plate, ask for seconds, and eat only half. When carrying your plate to the kitchen, hold it tilted so that the remaining spaghetti slides off and onto the floor.

Ice-cream cone: Ask for a double scoop. Knock the top scoop off while walking out the door of the ice-cream parlor. Cry. Lick the remaining scoop slowly so that ice cream melts down the outside of the cone and over your hand. Stop licking when the ice cream is even with the top of the cone. Be sure it is absolutely even. Eat a hole in the bottom of the cone and suck the rest of the ice cream out the bottom. When only the cone remains with ice cream coating the inside, leave on car dashboard.

Ice cream in bowl: Grip spoon upright in fist. Stir ice cream vigorously to make soup. Take a large helping on a spoon, place spoon in mouth, and slowly pull it out, sucking only the top layer of ice cream off. Wave spoon in air. Lick its back. Put in mouth again and suck off some more. Repeat until all ice cream is off spoon and begin again.

Cooked carrots: On way to mouth, drop in lap. Smuggle to garbage in napkin.

Spinach: Divide into little piles. Rearrange into new piles. After five or six maneuvers, sit back and say you are full.

Chocolate-chip cookies: Half-sit, half-lie on the bed, propped up by a pillow. Read a book. Place cookies next to you on the sheet so that crumbs get in the bed. As you eat the cookies, remove each chocolate chip and place it on your stomach. When all the cookies are consumed, eat the chips one by one, allowing two per page.

Milk shake: Bite off one end of the paper covering the straw. Blow through straw to shoot paper across table. Place straw in shake and suck. When the shake just reaches your mouth, place a finger over the top of the straw—the pressure will keep the shake in the straw. Lift straw out of shake, put bottom end in mouth, release finger, and swallow.

Do this until the straw is squished so that you can't suck through it. Ask for another. Open it the same way, but this time shoot the paper at the waitress when she isn't looking. Sip your shake casually—you are just minding your own business—until there is about an inch of shake remaining. Then blow through the straw until bubbles rise to the top of the glass. When your father says he's had just about enough, get a stomachache.

Chewing gum: Remove from mouth and stretch into spaghetti-like strand. Swing like a lasso. Put back in mouth. Pulling out one end and gripping the other end between teeth, have your gum meet your friend's gum and press them together. Think that you have just done something really disgusting.

Baked apple: With your fingers, peel skin off baked apple. Tell your mother you changed your mind, you don't want it. Later, when she is harassed and not paying attention to what she is doing, pick up the naked baked apple and hand it to her.

French fries: Wave one French fry in air for emphasis while you talk. Pretend to conduct orchestra. Then place four fries in your mouth at once and chew. Turn to your sister, open your mouth, and stick out your tongue coated with potatoes. Close mouth and swallow. Smile.

Reader's Response

1. You no doubt used a few of Delia Ephron's funny eating techniques when you were younger. Which one in her list was your specialty?
2. Now for the sequel: "How to Eat Like a Child II." Can you give special instructions for eating broccoli, cereal, two foods that no adult would combine, or something else? Share your technique.

Writer's Craft

3. The information you give in a "how-to" paper, even one about eating, usually includes equipment. Where does Ephron tell about equipment and how to use it?
4. Is Ephron writing for young children or for other readers? Is her article a real "how-to" paper or actually a "how-it-happens" paper? Does she want you to take her seriously? Give reasons for your answers.

Ways to Inform

You can share information in writing in four basic ways, or strategies. Which strategy do you use for explaining a process? It's the first one in the list below: *narration*—like narrating or telling a story. In a "how-to" process paper, for example, you're telling a step-by-step story of how to do something. Here are some specific examples of sharing information through the four basic writing strategies.

Narration: telling a friend how you make tempura; explaining in a paper how a wooden drum makes sounds of different pitches.

Description: in a letter to your grandfather, describing the set you helped paint for a play; describing a hummingbird's nest to your class.

Classification: in science, explaining what the parts of a plant are for; telling your parents the differences between two bikes that you like.

Evaluation: in a report on a movie, telling whether the plot was interesting and logical; explaining how well a new "instant" camera works.

LOOKING AHEAD

In your main assignment in this chapter, you'll be writing a process paper explaining how to do something. Your purpose will be to give information. As you work through the exercises and the writing assignment, keep in mind that a "how-to" paper

- includes all necessary materials and steps
- presents the steps of the process in the order they're done

Writing a "How-to" Paper

Choosing a Process to Explain

You can do many things that someone else might want to learn. Do you know how to keep your cat from getting fleas? Can you explain how to run a baby sitters' club? Are you good at racing dirt bikes? One way to look for a topic is to brainstorm a list of things you do well. Then, to narrow down the list, ask yourself these questions:

- What do I most like to spend time doing?
- What can I do best?

Thinking About Interest. To pick a topic, focus on interest—in two ways. Think about what interests you *and* what will interest your *audience.* A paper on how to get ready for school will bore an audience of teenagers—unless you make it funny! And most of your classmates already know how to heat up a pizza. But they might want to find out how to make a special food that you have at home, Navajo bread, for instance, or Japanese sushi. Or, you can write your paper for younger children. Just be sure that your topic and your audience match.

Thinking About Skill. The purpose of a "how-to" paper is to share information about a process so that your readers can do it themselves. This means you have to pick something you're good at. Writing about how to dance a hula might be a good idea. However, you have to be able to dance the hula well enough to explain it. Basically, the test of your explanation will be, "Does it work?" If your readers follow your directions on how to make a boomerang, the boomerangs they make should fly back.

To choose a "how-to" topic

- brainstorm a list of things you do well
- pick something that you really like to do
- pick a process that will interest your audience

EXERCISE 1 **Exploring Possible Topics**

Meet with a few classmates to discuss possible topics for a "how-to" paper. You might brainstorm from broad areas like "the outdoors," "crafts," and "what I do on Saturday." As you come up with ideas, give each other feedback. Would you like to learn the process? Can an idea be covered in a paragraph or two?

PART 1:
Choosing a Process to Explain

You can pick a topic from your work in Exercise 1 or a topic of your own. Are you known for how well you can lip-sync the words to your favorite song? Can you explain how to do it? Will you write about how to twirl a baton? Would you like to tell younger children how to draw monsters? When you've decided on your topic, write one sentence telling what it is and who your audience will be.

Gathering and Organizing Your Information

Planning your paper before you write will save time and make the writing easier. Since you know how to do the process, you probably have all the information you need. But if you have any questions, look for information in books, articles, or videotapes about the topic.

Listing Steps and Materials. Your readers need two kinds of information: (1) what steps to do and (2) what materials to use.

Here's a good technique for gathering information. Imagine yourself doing the process on a video screen. What steps do you see yourself going through? As you watch each step on your mental TV, think about the tools and materials you're using.

You can use a chart to organize your notes about steps and materials. Here's a chart one writer made for a "how-to" paper.

HERE'S HOW

How to Do a Magic Trick: Ballooney-Baloney	
Steps	Materials
1. Blow up some balloons.	Three or four balloons of ordinary colors (pink, blue, yellow). One balloon of unusual color (purple).
2. Stick two pieces of tape on one side of unusual balloon.	See-through tape, scissors.
3. Ask someone to stick pin into ordinary balloons.	Pins
4. Stick pin through center of tape on taped balloon.	

WRITING NOTE As you take notes, jot down any terms that your readers might not know. This is especially important if you're writing for an audience younger than yourself. It's also important if you're writing about an unusual process. Your notes on terms like *karate chop, cakewalk,* and *D & D module* will remind you to define them in the paper.

EXERCISE 2 **Listing Steps and Materials**

Many processes you do every day have become almost as easy for you as breathing. Do you think you can break them into clear and separate steps? Get together with a group of classmates and divide each of the following processes into steps. Also, list materials you would need.

1. washing your hair
2. fixing your breakfast
3. doing the dishes
4. sharpening a pencil

Organizing Your Information. On the next page are one writer's directions for making a Huichol yarn painting. Can you follow them?

You put a little liquid glue along the outline of your design. Add more glue inside the design and press yarn into it. The Huichols use traditional designs, and they use beeswax, not glue. They live in a part of Mexico where there are mountains. Cut the yarn for the inside of the design in small pieces. Put the pieces of yarn as close together as possible. You put the long yarn on the outline first. The design should be drawn on cardboard.

Suppose you tried to follow these directions the way they were written. Before you got to the end, you'd have to start over. And you would probably like to get your hands on the writer!

To make your process easy for readers to follow, first tell what materials are needed. Then give the steps in ***chronological order,*** the order that you'd do them.

As you're writing, many details may come into your mind. It's good to include details that relate directly to the process and help explain it. But don't use details that just get in the way (like the mountains in Mexico) or confuse your readers (like the beeswax).

To plan a "how-to" paper

- list the steps that you want readers to follow
- note the materials needed for each step
- be sure the steps are in chronological order
- use only details that will help readers do the process

CRITICAL THINKING

Arranging Steps in Chronological Order

Has this ever happened to you?

You ask an expert a simple question. The expert gives you a long and complicated answer. By the end you've forgotten what your question was! You're also more confused than you were before you asked the question.

That's one way an explanation can be confusing. Another way is to have an explanation move back and forth in time—jumping from what to do first to what to do last to everything in between! This is especially frustrating in a "how-to" paper. You want to go straight forward in time, or *chronologically:* what comes first, second, and so on.

CRITICAL THINKING EXERCISE:

Arranging Steps in Chronological Order

On the next page are out-of-order directions for making a kite into a "fighting kite" and for fighting other kites. Working with one or two classmates, put the steps into chronological order so that they're easy to follow. (You and your classmates might even enjoy actually following these directions.)

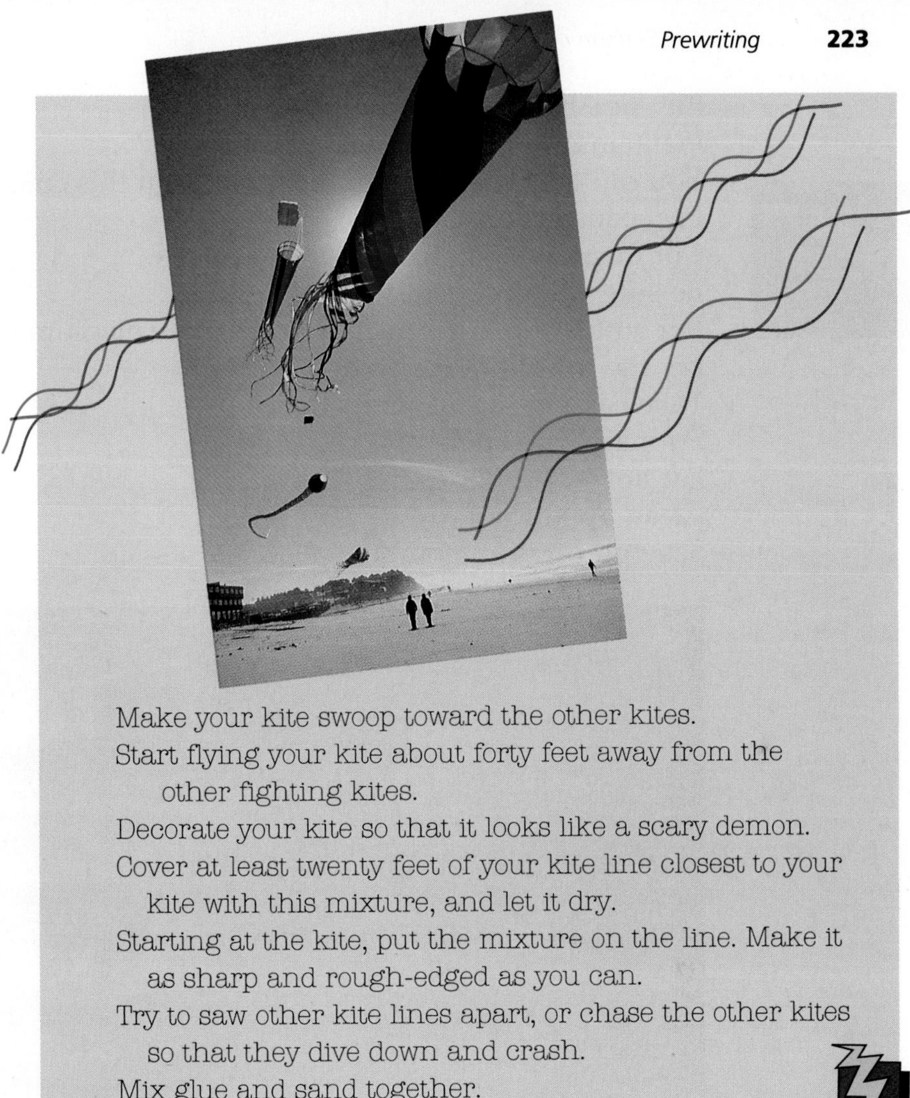

Make your kite swoop toward the other kites.
Start flying your kite about forty feet away from the other fighting kites.
Decorate your kite so that it looks like a scary demon.
Cover at least twenty feet of your kite line closest to your kite with this mixture, and let it dry.
Starting at the kite, put the mixture on the line. Make it as sharp and rough-edged as you can.
Try to saw other kite lines apart, or chase the other kites so that they dive down and crash.
Mix glue and sand together.

EXERCISE 3 Evaluating Details

All of the details in your "how-to" paper should help readers do the process. If a detail doesn't help, take it out. Ask yourself *Could readers make a mistake if I leave this detail out? Is this detail something my audience already knows?* On the next page are some notes for a paper about making fried plantains or bananas. The audience is a class of seventh-graders. Which information would you cross out?

Buy ripe bananas or plantains.
Plantains are not as sweet as bananas.
You can't get plantains in most places in this country.
Peel bananas or plantains.
Cut them in half lengthwise and across.
Be sure you don't cut yourself.
Put butter or margarine in frying pan on medium heat.
Fry the fruit until it's golden brown.
Take bananas or plantains out of pan.
Sprinkle with sugar and cinnamon.
Eat now.
Clean up kitchen.
Save peelings for compost pile.

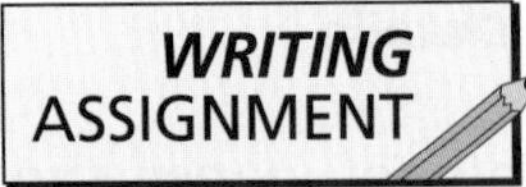

PART 2:

Gathering and Organizing Information

Fighting kites and fried bananas: That's enough practice. Now plan *your* "how-to" paper. Begin with a chart like the one on page 219. Be sure to list your steps in chronological order and jot down all materials. [Remember: You could find some terms to define.]

Writing Your First Draft

Putting Your Ideas on Paper

Thinking and planning are important, but you've probably done enough for now. It's time to get down to the business of writing.

Introduction. The introduction of a "how-to" paper can be just two or three sentences. As usual, you want to begin by catching your readers' interest. One way to do this is by giving the reader a reason for learning the process. Show that it's fun, challenging, or useful.

Body. Begin the body of your paper by listing the materials. Then, give the steps in chronological order. You can explain steps when needed and give helpful tips, but include only information that's directly related to the process. Also use transitional words like *first, now,* and *after this* to make the steps clear and easy to follow.

REFERENCE NOTE: For more information on transitional words and phrases, see pages 74–75.

Conclusion. Your conclusion should be brief. Probably one or two sentences will do. You might repeat why learning the process is a good idea, give another reason, or end with a final tip.

In the following explanation, the writer tells you how to make beads the way young people in southern Africa do it. As you read, ask yourself if you could follow her directions.

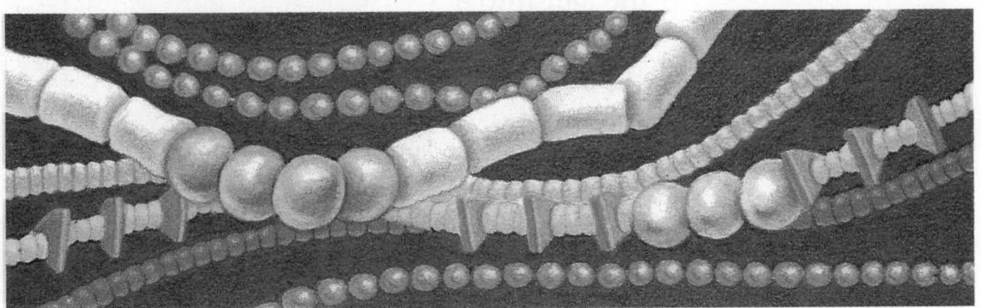

A PASSAGE FROM A BOOK

from Ubuhlali and Umnaka – Beaded Necklaces and Bangles

INTRODUCTION
Attention grabber
Reason for learning process

In the old days men and women as well as children wore beads; they were not simply decorations. In southern Africa, it was traditional to give beaded articles with special messages woven into them to loved ones and friends. . . .

The meanings of certain patterns and colors varied from place to place in southern Africa. Yellow usually symbolized wealth, and pink indicated poverty. Red showed anger and blue meant departure. White usually signified love. . . .

Process to be explained

Young people begin to learn beadwork by making simple necklaces of seeds and homemade beads. You can make your own beads as they were made long ago.

BODY
Step 1

For paste beads: Heat 3/4 cup of fine salt in a dry pan for a few minutes until

Step 2

it pops. Pour the salt into a bowl with 1/2 cup of flour.

Step 3
Explanation

Add 1/2 cup of water to which you have added a few drops of food coloring if you want tinted beads. Knead this mixture thoroughly.

Step 4
Step 5

Roll out a snake of the paste and cut into equal pieces. Roll each of the pieces into a smooth round ball.

Step 6

To make flat beads, roll the paste out with a jar or rolling pin and cut beads into the desired shape.

Step 7
Helpful hint

Pierce each ball with a round toothpick. Stick toothpicks into a ball of soft clay or grapefruit rind to dry. Turn the beads periodically to prevent them from sticking to the toothpicks and allow them to dry thoroughly.

Step 8
Helpful hint

If you have not already tinted the paste, paint your beads with poster paint and cover with clear nail polish. For silver and gold beads use metallic nail polish.

from *African Crafts*

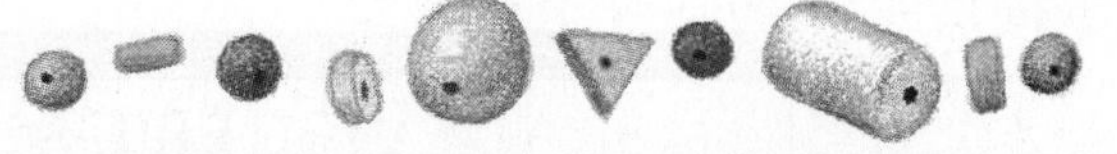

EXERCISE 4 Analyzing a "How-to" Explanation

Did you realize you could make beads using just salt, flour, and water? Take a closer look at this process by discussing the following questions with two or three classmates.

1. This passage is part of a chapter about African beadwork. How does the beginning introduce the topic? Do the first sentences grab your attention? Explain why or why not.
2. What are the basic steps in making both round and flat beads? What steps are different for round beads and flat beads?

3. The writer doesn't list all materials before giving the steps. Do you think she should have? Explain.
4. Are the steps in chronological order? Would you change the order of any information to make the process easier to follow? If so, what and why?
5. Because this chapter goes on, the model does not have a conclusion. Make up one or two sentences that give the passage a good ending.

Following a Basic Framework for a "How-to" Paper

The explanation you've just read about making beads is part of a whole book about African crafts, so it isn't exactly like the paper you'll write. Your readers will want to know right away what materials they will need, and they may need more explanation of steps—not just a recipe approach. The following writer's model is an example of the kind of paper you'll write.

A WRITER'S MODEL

INTRODUCTION
Attention grabber
Reasons for learning process

Magic tricks are fun to do. This one will wake up anyone in your audience who's decided to take a little nap. It's sure to surprise your friends. To make sure it doesn't surprise you, practice before you do it for a real audience.

BODY
List of materials
Helpful hints

You need to buy three or four balloons that are ordinary in color and one balloon that's an unusual color. Pink, blue, or yellow will do for the ordinary balloons. Try to get purple or black for the unusual one—your magic balloon. You also need a roll of tape, two or three long pins, and a pair of scissors. (Be sure that you get see-through tape.)

Step 1

Before you do the trick for your audience, you have to prepare. First, blow up the balloons. Next,

Step 2 cut two one-inch pieces of tape and stick them on
Explanation the "magic" balloon. It's important that both pieces be on one side of the balloon, so that you can turn that side away from the audience. Also
Helpful hint make sure the tape is perfectly smooth.

Now you're ready to show your trick. Ask
Step 3 volunteers from the audience to pop the ordinary
Explanation balloons. Give each volunteer a pin and cover your ears for the big bang. Then, tell the
Step 4 audience you have a magic balloon. Say some "magic" words like "Fiddle-faddle,
Helpful hint Ballooney-baloney" while you carefully stick a pin
Step 5 through the center of each tape. The tape keeps
Explanation the "magic" balloon from popping.

CONCLUSION After you've amazed your friends, you might
Final hints want to show them how it's done. Otherwise, keep this trick a secret and add it to other tricks you can do.

WRITING NOTE

You may want to add drawings or diagrams to your paper. Pictures often help explain a process. A diagram showing foot patterns, for instance, might help you tell how to do a Native American ceremonial dance. (Remember, in some cases one picture is worth a thousand words.)

It's often helpful to have a pattern to follow when you write. You may want to model your "how-to" paper on the one you've just read about the magic trick. Here is the framework it follows:

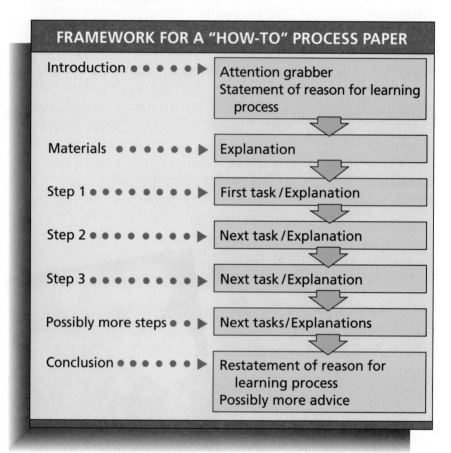

FRAMEWORK FOR A "HOW-TO" PROCESS PAPER

Introduction	Attention grabber Statement of reason for learning process
Materials	Explanation
Step 1	First task / Explanation
Step 2	Next task / Explanation
Step 3	Next task / Explanation
Possibly more steps	Next tasks/Explanations
Conclusion	Restatement of reason for learning process Possibly more advice

PART 3:
Writing Your First Draft

Now you're ready to put your process on paper from beginning to end. Be sure to use the chart of steps and materials you created in Writing Assignment, Part 2 (page 224). Whenever you have a question about what to do, look back at the basic framework above.

Evaluating and Revising

Don't be surprised when you find rough spots in your first draft. After all, *rough draft* is just another name for *first draft*!

For a "how-to" paper, evaluating with a partner is a big help. You know how to do your process, but someone who *doesn't* can see more quickly what's missing or confused. First, use Exercise 5 as a "test run" of your "how-to" paper with a partner.

Then, you can use the chart on the next page to take a closer look at your paper, find problems, and fix them. If your honest answer to a question in the left-hand column is *no*, use the revision technique in the right-hand column.

EXERCISE 5 Speaking and Listening: Explaining and Following a Process

Now you're going to read your draft out loud while a partner "acts out" the process. You'll need some imagination, but you have plenty—and this is a good test! First, read out your list of materials. Have your partner write each of the materials on a slip of paper. Then, read out the steps. Have your partner "use" the slips while pretending to do each step. Your partner can stop you and ask questions whenever something isn't clear. And *you* can call "Wait!" if there's a big mess. Make notes about problems right on your draft. Then, change roles.

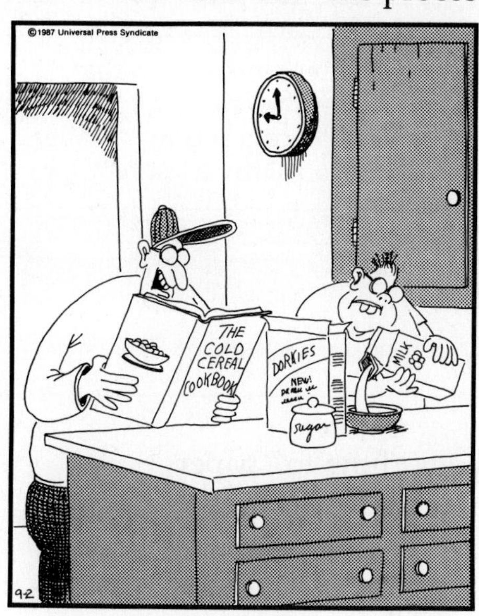

"Oh, wait! Wait, Cory! ... Add the cereal *first* and *then* the milk!"

EVALUATING AND REVISING PROCESS ESSAYS

	EVALUATION GUIDE	REVISION TECHNIQUE
1	Does the introduction grab the reader's attention and give reasons for learning the process?	**Add** interesting details to the beginning. **Add** a sentence that gives a reason for learning the process.
2	Does the paper list the materials before explaining the first step?	**Add** a list of all the materials needed before giving the first step.
3	Are the steps in chronological order? Are all the details necessary to explain the process?	**Reorder** the steps to put them in the order they must be done. **Cut** unnecessary details. **Add** any necessary details.
4	Do transitions help the reader follow the steps?	**Add** words like *first, then, before*, and *after*.
5	Does the paper end with a clear conclusion?	**Add** a sentence or two that restates the reason for learning the process or gives another reason. Offer a last hint.

As you evaluate and revise your "how-to" paper

- use specific words so your readers won't become confused by vague language
- vary sentence beginnings to keep your readers interested
- ask yourself if any part of your paper sounds complicated

USAGE HINT

Using Specific Adjectives and Nouns

It's especially important to use specific, exact adjectives and nouns in "how-to" papers. Specific adjectives and nouns answer the questions "How many?" or "What kind?" or "How much?" These kinds of words will make your paper more accurate and precise.

EXAMPLES *Vague Adjectives and Nouns*:
Heat **some** salt in a **container.**

Specific Adjectives and Nouns:
Heat **3/4 cup** of **fine** salt in a **dry pan.**

REFERENCE NOTE: For more information on specific adjectives and nouns, see pages 434–437 and 423–426.

EXERCISE 6 **Analyzing a Writer's Revisions**

Here's the way the writer revised the third paragraph in the model on pages 228–229. Study the changes. Then answer the questions that follow the paragraph.

Before you do the trick for your audience, you have to prepare. ~~Your audience may be made up of friends, relatives, or neighbors.~~ *Next,* Cut two *one-inch* pieces of tape and stick them on the "magic" balloon. But first blow up the balloons. It's important that both pieces be on one side of the balloon *so that you can turn that side away from the audience.* Also make sure the tape is perfectly smooth.

cut

add

reorder/cut/add

add

1. Why did the writer cut the second sentence?
2. What is the reason for moving the sentence about blowing up the balloons?
3. In the third sentence, why are *Next* and *one-inch* good additions?
4. How does the addition in the next-to-last sentence make the directions clearer for the reader?

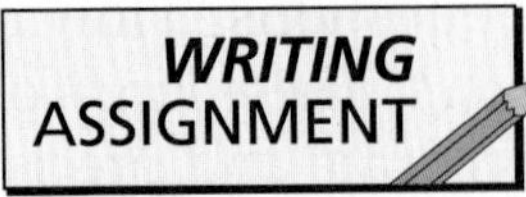

PART 4:
Evaluating and Revising Your Paper

Now it's time to use the chart on page 232 to evaluate and revise your paper. You can use it for a peer evaluation first. Then you can evaluate your own paper. When you're ready to make changes, look at what other students say about your paper. Which suggestions will you take? It's your paper, so the decision is up to you.

Proofreading and Publishing

Proofreading. Every detail is important in a "how-to" paper. That's why you need to proofread carefully. Some mistakes, like writing "pain" instead of "pin" may just puzzle readers and make them laugh. But other proofreading errors can cause trouble. If you're telling how to make beads and write "1/4 cup salt" instead of "3/4 cup salt," your readers won't end up with beads. One last check can help you catch this kind of mistake.

Publishing. Who was the audience you had in mind when you wrote your paper? Now you need to find a way to reach those readers. Here are three ways:

- Work with several classmates to produce a calendar. For each month, feature one "how-to" paper. Each paper might relate in some way to the weather or holidays in that month. Classmates who like to draw could do a diagram or picture to go with each process.
- If your paper is about a craft, give a copy to a store that sells craft supplies. The store could post your paper for its customers to read.
- Stage a class demonstration day. Some of your classmates can demonstrate how to do the processes they wrote about. Other classmates can pick a topic that sounds interesting and can follow the "how-to" paper's directions to do the process.

PART 5:
Proofreading and Publishing Your Paper

Proofread your "how-to" paper. Then, correct any mistakes you find in it. When your paper is as good as you can make it, find a way to share it. You may use one of the suggestions above or one of your own.

WRITING WORKSHOP

The Cause-and-Effect Paper

The "how-to" paper you just wrote gives information. It answers the question *How do you do that?* Another kind of paper that informs is a cause-and-effect paper. It answers the question *Why does that happen?* or *What is the result?* When you write a cause-and-effect paper, you start with an event or situation. Then you explain the causes for it (*Why?*) or its effects (*What's the result?*).

Here's an example. Teenagers often have messy rooms. You could explore the causes of this situation: Teenagers are too busy to keep their rooms looking neat. Or, you could write about the effects of teenagers' messy rooms: Homework—and many other things—get lost forever in them.

Causes and effects are sometimes obvious. But usually you do some thinking—exploring—to discover them. In this passage, astronaut Sally Ride writes about the effects of weightlessness that she discovered in space. Would you have guessed that these effects would happen?

Weightless in Space

by Sally Ride with Susan Okie

The best part of being in space is being weightless. It feels wonderful to be able to float without effort; to slither up, down, and around the inside of the shuttle just like a seal; to be upside down as often as I'm right side up and have it make no difference. On Earth being upside down feels different because gravity is pulling the blood toward my head. In space I feel exactly the same whether my head is toward the floor or toward the ceiling.

When I'm weightless, some things don't change. My heart beats at about the same rate as it does on Earth. I can still

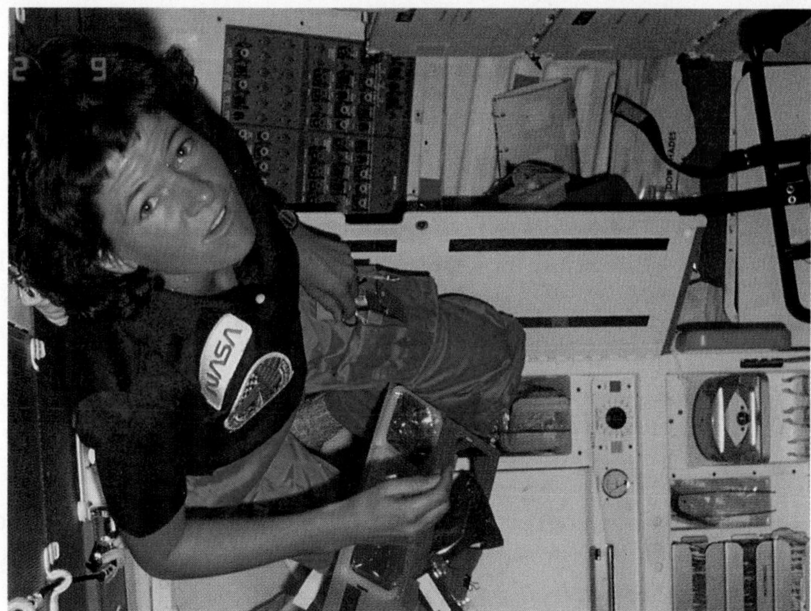

swallow and digest food. My eyes, ears, nose, and taste buds work fine; I see, hear, smell, and taste things just as I do at home.

I *look* a little different, though—all astronauts do. Since the fluid in our bodies is not pulled toward our feet as it is on Earth, more of this fluid stays in our faces and upper bodies. This makes our faces a little fatter and gives us puffy-looking cheeks. We are also about an inch taller while in orbit because in weightlessness our spines are not compressed. Unfortunately (for me, anyway), we shrink back to normal height when we return to Earth. . . .

In weightlessness the slightest touch can start an astronaut's body floating across the room or drifting over in a slow-motion somersault. The only way to stop moving is to take hold of something that's anchored in place. . . .

Some astronauts are uncomfortable while their bodies are adjusting to weightlessness. Almost half of all shuttle crew members are sick for the first day or two. . . .

By the third day of a week-long shuttle flight, though, all the astronauts are feeling fine. Weightlessness is pure fun, once everyone gets the hang of it.

from *To Space & Back*

Thinking It Over

1. What three effects of weightlessness does Sally Ride mention in the first paragraph?
2. Ride doesn't just list effects. She also explains them for readers. Find details that explain these effects: feeling the same whether upside down or right side up, the changed look of astronauts' faces, and being taller.
3. If you were in orbit, which effect would you like best?

Writing a Cause-and-Effect Paper

Prewriting. Like Sally Ride, you will write about effects in this paper. So think about something that makes you want to ask *What's the result of that?* Use one of the following ideas or think of one of your own. Just choose a situation you really want to explore, and then brainstorm all the effects you can.

- the effects of being an only child
- the effects of having a disability
- the effects of a hurricane on your town
- the effects of a school volunteer project

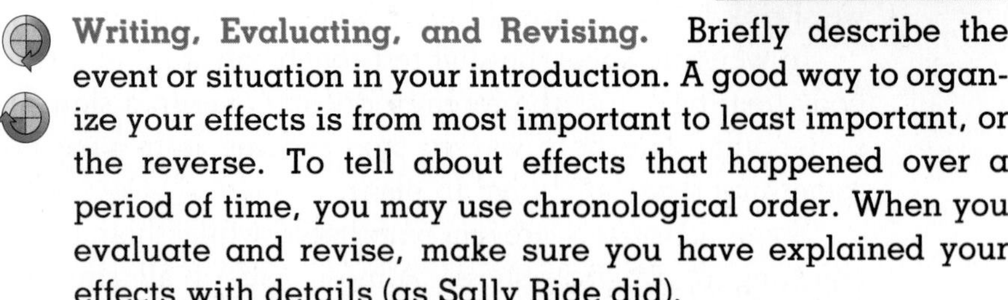

Writing, Evaluating, and Revising. Briefly describe the event or situation in your introduction. A good way to organize your effects is from most important to least important, or the reverse. To tell about effects that happened over a period of time, you may use chronological order. When you evaluate and revise, make sure you have explained your effects with details (as Sally Ride did).

Proofreading and Publishing. Before you share your paper, check your capitalization, spelling, and punctuation. Think about these possible audiences for your cause-and-effect essay: your family, an older friend, and the school or local newspaper.

MAKING CONNECTIONS

PROCESS ACROSS THE CURRICULUM

Folk Tales, Riddles, and Brainteasers

Here's a brainteaser in the form of an old folk tale. It's about a crow who has an idea for a process that will let him get a drink of water. Exactly what does the crow do? Can you figure out his process?

A Drink for Crow

told by George Shannon

Once there was a crow who had grown so thirsty he could barely caw. He flew down to a big pitcher where he had gotten a drink of water the day before, but there was only a little bit of water remaining at the bottom. He tried and tried to reach it with his beak, but the pitcher was too deep and his beak was too short. But just as he was about to give up, he knew what to do. He flew back and forth from the garden to the pitcher until he was able to drink easily from the pitcher while sitting on its edge.

What did the crow do?

Answer: The crow dropped pebbles in the pitcher, and the water level rose.

Make up or find other riddles or brainteasers that involve figuring out a process. (Remember *What am I?* riddles? They sometimes describe a process.) Ask your parents and relatives, too. They may know other folk-tale riddles. Then try to stump your classmates.

SPEAKING AND LISTENING

Process in Social Studies: Mapping and Directions

Giving clear directions is important. Here's a way to practice this skill by making a treasure map.

First, you need to decide what you're going to use for your "treasure." The value of the treasure doesn't matter, because the fun comes from looking for it. Your treasure can be anything small that's easily hidden. It could be a plastic figure or a key ring. Hide the treasure somewhere in your neighborhood.

Next, draw a map of the neighborhood. You can put real names of things on your map (pine tree, garbage cans, Fourth Street). Or you can pretend that the neighborhood is an imaginary place. Then you'd give imaginary names to real things. The pine tree might become "Giant's Tower," the garbage cans "Smelly Swamp," and Fourth Street, "Dragon's Lair." Use an arrow to mark a starting point. Use an ***X*** to mark the spot where the treasure is. Then, figure out five or six directions that would lead someone to the treasure and write them down.

Give your map to a friend who's going to hunt for the treasure. Then, go together to the starting point. Read your first direction—for instance, "Walk straight ahead to Smelly Swamp, turn left, and stop at the blinking light." Then, give the next direction. Read each one *only once.* (You can try to trick your friend a little, but make the directions accurate.) When your friend finds the treasure (or gets lost), talk about what was good and bad about the map. It might be the directions or your friend's listening powers.

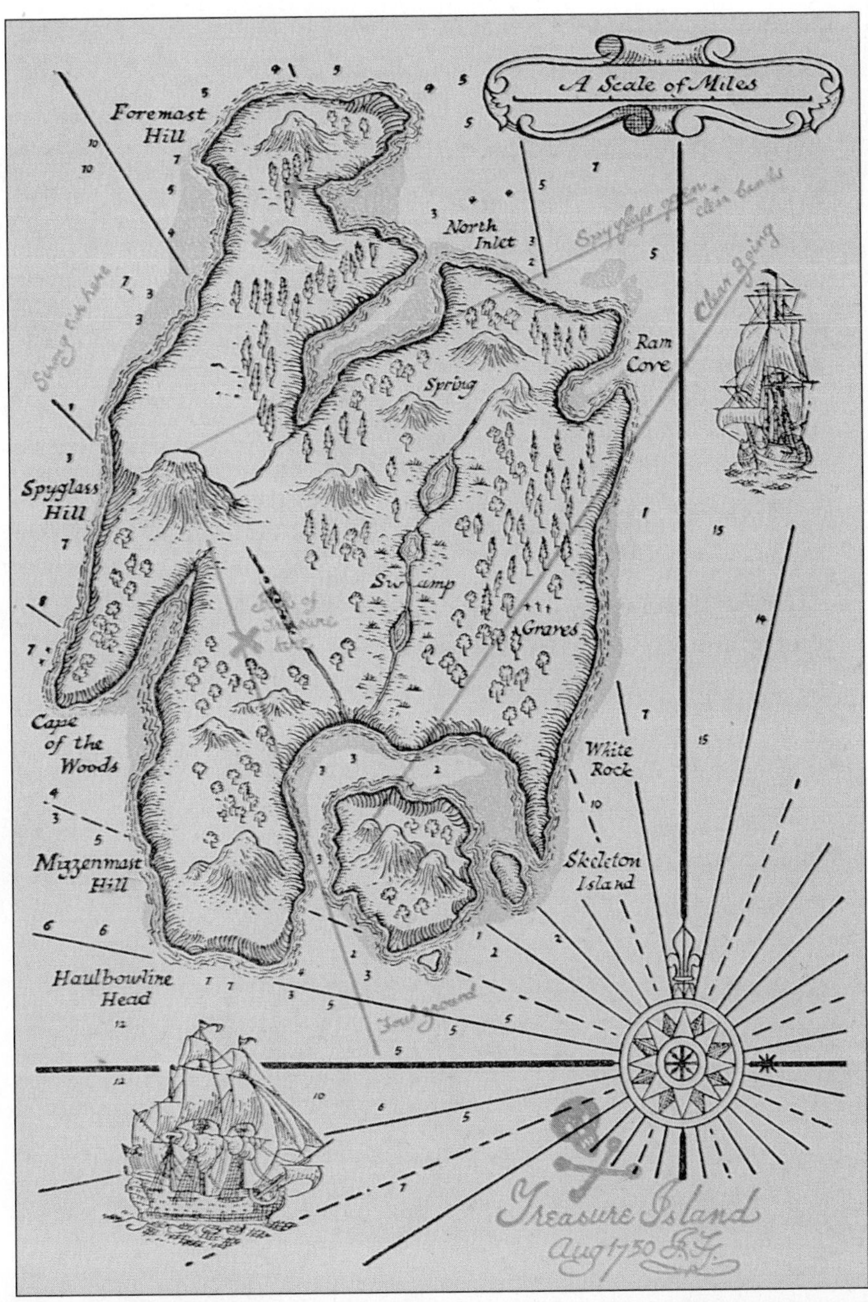

8 Writing to Persuade

Taking a Stand

When John Parker's Minutemen stood facing the advancing British troops at Lexington in 1775, Parker said, "Stand your ground." And they did. It's often important to **take a stand**—to have a belief you're willing to argue and defend. Doing so won't usually result in a revolution. But you may be able to persuade others that you're right.

Writing and You. Persuasion comes into every part of your life. You might try to talk your classmates into having a class picnic. You might write a speech persuading others how to vote in a school election. You might convince your big brother to lend you his radical shirt. Have you tried to persuade someone lately? Did it work?

As You Read. Advertisers often try to persuade us. Look at the ad on the next page. What is its purpose? Who is it trying to convince? Why?

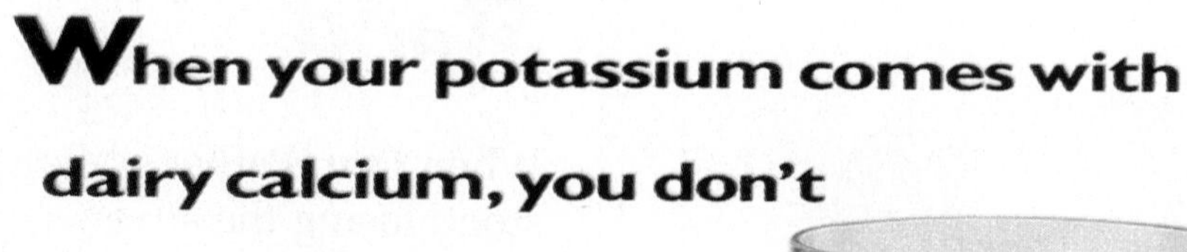

When your potassium comes with
dairy calcium, you don't
need a bunch.

An 8-ounce glass of milk has about as much potassium as the average banana. And an 8-ounce cup of yogurt has even more. Dairy foods can be an excellent source of potassium. And many other essential nutrients as well. Including, of course, calcium.

Milk and yogurt, like all dairy foods, also come in a variety of lower fat alternatives. So build your family's diet on a firm foundation of dairy foods. It's the perfect way to avoid nutritional slip-ups.

REAL®

Dairy Foods. The Basics of Good Nutrition.

©1990 N.D.B.
National Dairy Board
America's Dairy Farmers

Reader's Response

1. Does this ad persuade you that milk and other dairy foods are "the perfect way to avoid nutritional slip-ups"? Why or why not?
2. Which part of the ad did you look at first? What part of the ad do you find the most convincing? Why?
3. What's your favorite food? Is it as good as ads for it say it is? In your journal, brainstorm some vivid words to describe it. Create your own ad slogan; for instance, "Scrumptious Smithers' soup—steaming, zesty, robust."

Writer's Craft

4. Who is the audience for the ad for dairy foods? How can you tell? What kind of magazine do you think it appeared in?
5. What advantages does the ad writer claim for milk and other dairy products?
6. Milk has many nutrients, not just potassium. Why would the Dairy Board compare milk with bananas? [Hint: Have you seen any banana ads?]
7. What does the ad try to get the reader to do?

"Advertising is what you do when you can't go see somebody. That's all it is."

Fairfax Cone

Ways to Persuade

Persuasive writing tries to convince you to *do* something or *believe* something. Advertising comes in many forms—radio, television, newspapers, and billboards. And there are many kinds of persuasion besides advertising—editorials, speeches, sermons, and even songs. Here are some forms that persuasion can take.

Narration: telling what happened to a homeless family to convince classmates they should volunteer at a shelter; trying to convince your parents that a trip to the lake will result in a better grade on your paper about turtles.

Description: describing your school's gymnasium to persuade the school board to buy new bleachers; describing your cat's new kittens to convince a friend to take one.

Classification: comparing two television shows to convince your brother that yours is more entertaining; defining *sacrifice* to convince your sister to loan you her new sweater.

▶ **Evaluation:** deciding that a new local band is great and getting your friends to go hear them at the art festival; forming an opinion about safe bicycling and writing a letter to the editor, calling for adding bike lanes to streets.

LOOKING AHEAD

In the main assignment in this chapter, you'll be writing a persuasive paper. In your paper you will use the strategy of evaluation. As you work, keep in mind that an effective persuasive paper

- states the writer's opinion about the issue
- provides information to support the opinion
- may appeal to the reader's emotions

Writing a Persuasive Paper

Choosing a Topic

You may not realize how often you use persuasion. Think about it. Have you ever tried to convince your parents to increase your allowance? Have you ever tried to get a friend to try out for a team? Have you ever tried to persuade someone to go to a movie with you? All these situations involve persuasion. And just think—the more persuasive you are, the better your chances of having things go your way.

In this chapter, you'll get to practice your powers of persuasion. You'll be writing about an ***issue,*** a topic or idea that people have different opinions about.

Finding an Issue That Matters. It's important to choose an issue that matters to you. It should also be one that people around you think is important. Why try to convince people of something that neither you nor they have any interest in? Look for things that are happening in your school or neighborhood that you feel strongly about. For example, is your school setting up a new dress code you dislike? Should your community build a hockey rink? Does air pollution upset you? Is there too much violence in movies? Any one of these would be a good issue for persuasive writing. Just be sure it really matters to you.

Identifying Your Opinion. Your *opinion* is something you believe. It isn't something that can be proven true. For example, it's your opinion that Nolan Ryan is the greatest baseball pitcher of all time. You believe it, but others may disagree. A *fact,* on the other hand, can be proven true. It's a fact that Nolan Ryan pitched seven no-hit games. No one can deny it. As the famous baseball manager Casey Stengel used to say, "You could look it up."

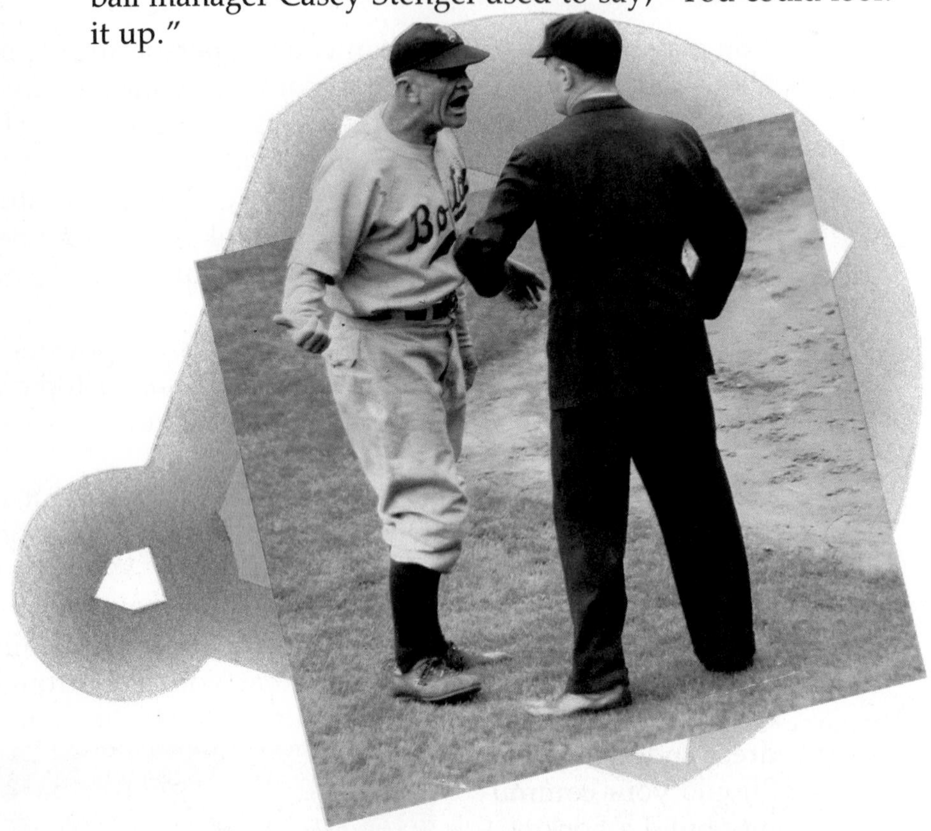

Putting your opinion down in black and white is the first step in writing a persuasive paper. You can do this by writing a ***statement of opinion*** that tells your topic and what you believe about it. Here are some examples of statements of opinion:

Driving a motorboat should require a license.
The city schools should set up tutoring classes for students who don't speak English.
Too many movies today use violence as entertainment.

When choosing a topic for persuasive writing

- brainstorm, listen to television and radio, and look through newspapers and magazines to find an issue you care about
- write a sentence identifying your issue and telling your opinion about it

EXERCISE 1 **Distinguishing Fact from Opinion**

With a small group, decide which of the following statements is a *fact* and which is an *opinion*. Keep in mind that a fact can be proven true while an opinion is a belief. Be ready to explain your reasoning about each statement.

1. Our school really should celebrate Harriet Tubman's birthday.
2. Some of the largest cities in the United States have Spanish names.
3. New York City is the largest city in the United States.
4. I. M. Pei, the architect, is the greatest American of Chinese descent.

EXERCISE 2 Exploring Possible Topics

With a small group of classmates, brainstorm possible topics for persuasive writing. Talk about what's going on at school. Think about issues you have heard about on television or radio. Look through copies of magazines such as *Sports Illustrated* or *Time* in your library. Make a list of at least five issues.

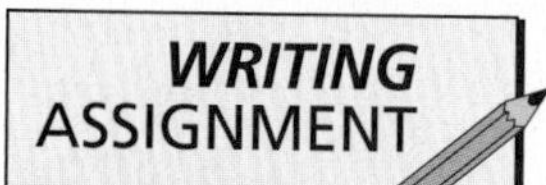

PART 1:
Choosing an Issue to Write About

Pick an issue for persuasive writing. Perhaps you'll stay with one you came up with in Exercise 2. Or you may want to take a stand on something else. Should we have a new national anthem because "The Star-Spangled Banner" is too hard to sing? Should all experiments on animals be outlawed? When you've decided what you want to write about, write a sentence that names the issue and states your opinion about it.

Planning Your Paper

Have you ever set out to get something you wanted—and succeeded? Then you probably gave your "plan of action" some careful thought. Persuading on paper takes the same planning.

Thinking About Purpose and Audience

Your *purpose* in persuasive writing is to make readers think a certain way or act a certain way. You can't do that without paying pretty close attention to *them*—to your *audience*. On your issue, what will be their interests and concerns? How can you appeal to your readers?

Suppose you want your classmates to support a city hockey rink. They'll be interested in being able to watch good teams play. Suppose you want to convince the city council. They'll worry about building costs. So to have the right appeal and answers, think ahead about audience.

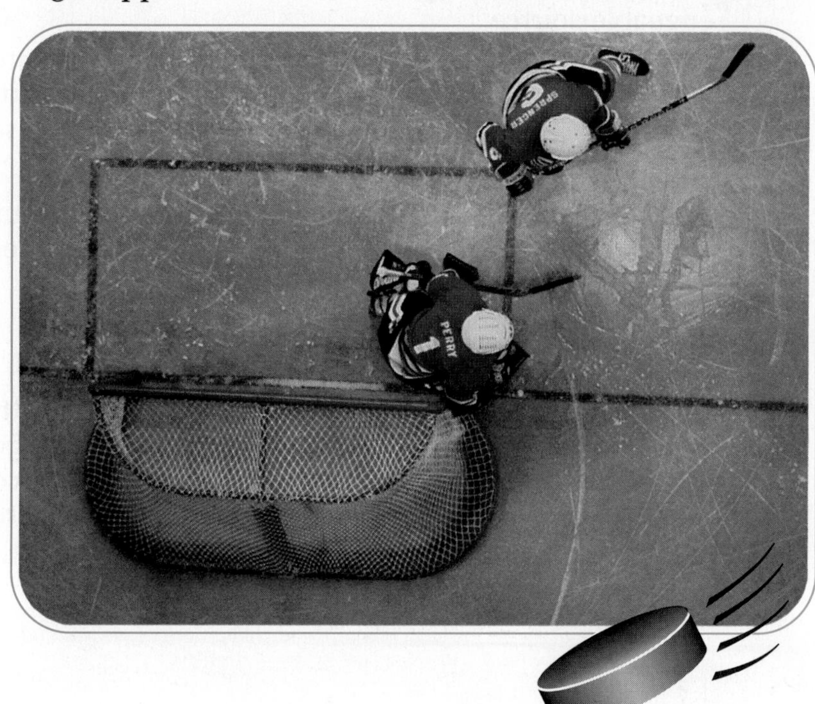

Supporting Your Opinion

Do you always accept what other people say just because they seem to believe their own words? Probably not. You have opinions of your own that may be completely different from theirs. How, then, do you go about changing other people's opinions? It *can* be done. You just have to give convincing ***support,*** or proof, for what you believe.

Finding Information to Support Your Opinion. There are several ways to find support for your opinions. Here are three.

1. Talk to friends and others interested in the issue.
2. Talk to experts—people who are knowledgeable about the issue.
3. Look in books, magazines, and newspapers.

As you use these methods, look for *reasons, facts,* or *opinions* from knowledgeable sources. The more support you find, the more likely you are to sway your readers. For example, one writer needed to support his opinion that everyone in Fresno, California, should be required to ration water. He found facts and the opinion of a knowledgeable source.

> Support/Opinion of an expert: According to Water Commissioner Carol Main, "Some people are cutting their water use, but not enough are doing it to save the amount of water we need."
>
> Support/Fact: In Fresno, people were asked to cut their water use voluntarily by 25 percent. They cut their use by 17.7 percent.

As you talk to people and read about the issue, you may find your opinion changing. That's okay. It simply means you've become better informed and better able to explain and defend your true point of view.

Using Appeals to the Emotions. Not all the support in good persuasive writing is factual. Some is emotional. You want to appeal to people's hearts as well as to their minds.

An organization is raising money to save California's redwood trees. You've been asked to write the appeal for donations. Will you just tell them how many trees will be saved? No. You'll describe a family enjoying a hike through a redwood forest. Then you'll say that a forest just like this one is being logged less than a hundred miles away. You'll describe the ugly, treeless landscape after the logging.

As you write, you'll consider how *you* feel about the issue. Do you feel fear? concern? hope? anger? Then you'll try to create the same emotions in your audience. Draw vivid word pictures. Use a powerful quotation. Tell about a sad incident. Make the audience feel the rightness of your cause.

Emotional appeals alone aren't enough, though. The best persuasion has a base of solid information. Then you can add feelings.

When you're gathering support, you can use a chart like the one in the Here's How on page 254.

OPINION:	*Athletes shouldn't charge for autographs.*
AUDIENCE:	*Junior high school students*
SUPPORT:	*1. The most popular players already earn millions.* *2. Fans will think less of their favorite players if they have to pay for autographs.* *3. Players in the past didn't ask fans to pay for autographs. Today's players should be more like them.*

CRITICAL THINKING

Evaluating Reasoning

Sometimes what seems like support for an opinion isn't support at all. Some reasons aren't really reasonable (logical), and some emotional appeals are tricks, not truth. Unsuspecting readers and listeners can be fooled by these "statements masquerading as reasons."

So be careful. If you use misleading support, some readers will spot it. Those who do won't be convinced.

STATEMENTS MASQUERADING AS REASONS

TECHNIQUE	STRATEGY	EXAMPLE
False Cause and Effect	Assumes that one event caused another just because one came before the other	"Not sending the band to out-of-town games put the team on a losing streak."
Attacking the Person	Ignores the issue by attacking the person instead of the person's view on the topic	"Supporters of this leash law are cat haters at heart."
Bandwagon	Asks you to believe or do something because many other people do	"Don't be the only family in your neighborhood without a Pereira tape deck."

CRITICAL THINKING EXERCISE:
Evaluating Persuasive Statements

With a small group, study each statement below. Why is the statement misleading? Which technique from page 254 is being used? Be prepared to explain.

1. Everyone is buying Bright-O toothpaste. The stores can hardly keep it on the shelves. Buy yours today!
2. After the principal shortened the homeroom period, many students got poorer grades.
3. Since he is an active deer hunter, it's no wonder that Bob says hunting helps conserve deer.
4. The kids at Del Rio Middle School who started skateboarding lost their A and B averages. Skateboarding definitely eats up study time.

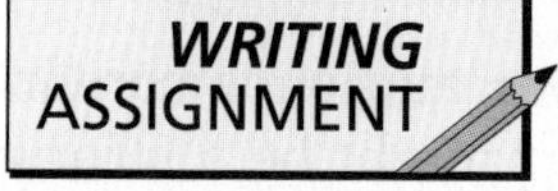

PART 2:
Finding Support for Your Opinion

You'll need information and perhaps emotional appeals to support the opinion statement you wrote for your paper. Use a chart like the one on page 254, and start backing up your belief. What reasons or facts can you think of? Whose expert opinion can you quote? What feelings can you tap—and how? Line up some strong support.

Writing Your First Draft

Combining the Elements of Persuasion

You've seen that the basic elements of persuasive writing are (1) a clear statement of your opinion and (2) support for that opinion. Now that you have both, you need to put them together in a way that's really convincing—in a way that gets your audience to think or to act as you'd like.

A Good Beginning. You need to try to grab your readers' attention from the start. You could begin with a question that creates strong feelings: "Would you want a nuclear waste dump across the street from your house?" Or you might begin with an interesting ***anecdote*** (little story): "Yesterday I walked out of a movie and asked for my money back. I got it." Once you have everyone's attention, you can state your opinion. With a good beginning, you've made the first step toward convincing your readers.

Clearly Organized Support. One way to organize support in persuasion is ***order of importance.*** Go from your most important reason to your least important, or the opposite. In other words, you try to capture your readers' sympathy at the start, or you build up to a powerful punch at the end. Either way can work. Just be sure to decide what's most important to *your readers,* not only to you.

A Good Ending. Leave your audience convinced that you're right. Your best ending might be a strong restatement of your opinion. Or it might be a ***call to action,*** a specific suggestion about something the audience can do.

The writer of the following chapter from a book wants readers to go without meat one day a month. Notice how she uses both information and emotion to support her opinion. Does she put it all together in a strong, persuasive package?

A CHAPTER FROM A BOOK

Title/Call to action

One Day a Month, Go Without Meat

by Marjorie Lamb

BEGINNING

Statement of opinion

SUPPORT

Expert opinion

Reason

Many North Americans are eating less meat than we used to, partly for our health, and partly out of the knowledge that meat consumption wastes our planet's resources. Frances Moore Lappé, in her wonderful book, *Diet For a Small Planet* (Ballantine Books), documents the hideous waste of protein fed to livestock compared to the minuscule amount of protein we receive from livestock in return. We could easily supply the human population of the Earth with enough protein if we stopped feeding it to our livestock. Cattle consume more than 15 pounds of grains for every pound of beef they give us in return.

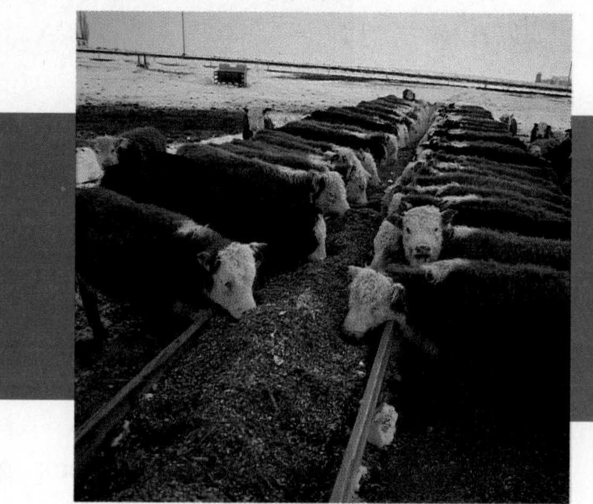

Reason

Facts

The demand for beef also means the clearing of vast tracts of tropical rainforest for cattle grazing. The land rapidly deteriorates, the soil erodes and becomes infertile.

Then more acreage must be cleared for cattle grazing. Land which once supported farmers in tropical countries now grows soya—not to feed the people, but for export as livestock feed. Some fast food chains get their beef from tropical lands such as Costa Rica. Ask your fast food outlet where their beef comes from.

Emotional appeal

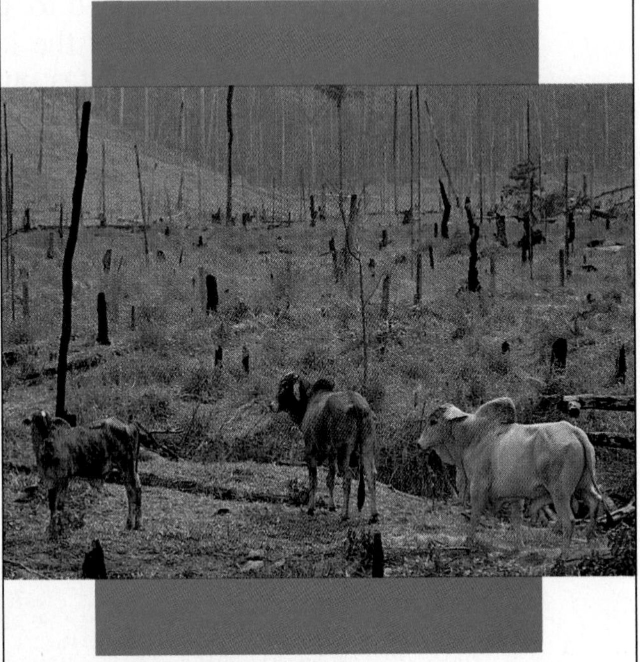

Facts

Reason

As cattle digest, they give off methane, a greenhouse gas. The world's cattle population, along with large areas of rice paddies, account for nearly half the global release of methane. More beef means more global warming.

Reason

Finally, livestock grazing requires tremendous amounts of water to irrigate pasture land. California alone uses enough water to meet the domestic needs of 22 million people, just to turn the desert into grassland for cattle and sheep grazing.

Fact and emotional appeal

ENDING
Summary of reasons

Emotional appeal

If we all reduced our meat consumption, we'd make a significant impact on the protein available for the rest of the world, save water for more reasonable uses and help preserve our tropical rainforests, which we desperately need for the health and survival of the planet.

from *2 Minutes a Day for a Greener Planet*

EXERCISE 3 **Analyzing Persuasive Writing**

After you read the excerpt from *2 Minutes a Day for a Greener Planet,* discuss it with some classmates. Use these questions to guide your analysis.

1. Many people who read Marjorie Lamb's book already believe we need a "greener planet." If her readers *did not,* do you think her opening sentence would be different? What opening would you write?
2. What words and phrases make the expert opinion of Frances Moore Lappé also an emotional appeal?
3. How much information does Lamb give compared to her emotional appeals? Do you think the balance is good?
4. Lamb's title contains her call to action because each chapter of her book gives a "quick and simple" act to save the earth. How does she conclude her chapter?
5. Does Lamb convince you of her opinion? Will you do what she asks? Why or why not?

Using a Basic Framework

The excerpt from Lamb's book shows you effective persuasion in action, but it's different from the composition you'll write. You'll probably be writing a simpler paper, with less extensive support—and of course you're not writing a whole book! On page 261 is a framework you can use when you're learning to write persuasion.

A WRITER'S MODEL

BEGINNING
Attention grabber—anecdote

Last week at a baseball card show, I asked a well-known baseball player for his autograph. Imagine my surprise when a man standing next to him said I would have to pay fourteen dollars before the player would sign his name!

Opinion
SUPPORT
Fact
Emotional appeals

Athletes shouldn't charge fans for autographs. The fans help many athletes get huge salaries in the first place. The most popular players—the ones fans ask for autographs most often—already earn millions of dollars. They don't really need this extra money. And how can you have respect for a player who won't even take a minute to sign his name for you? Babe Ruth was flattered just to have kids look up to him. He wouldn't have dreamed of asking people to pay for his autograph.

ENDING
Call to action
Restatement of opinion

Don't cave in and pay for an autograph. Players should see that an autograph is a way of saying "thank you" to loyal fans, and they shouldn't charge money.

You can use the following framework as a guide. The paper about athletes' autographs uses this framework.

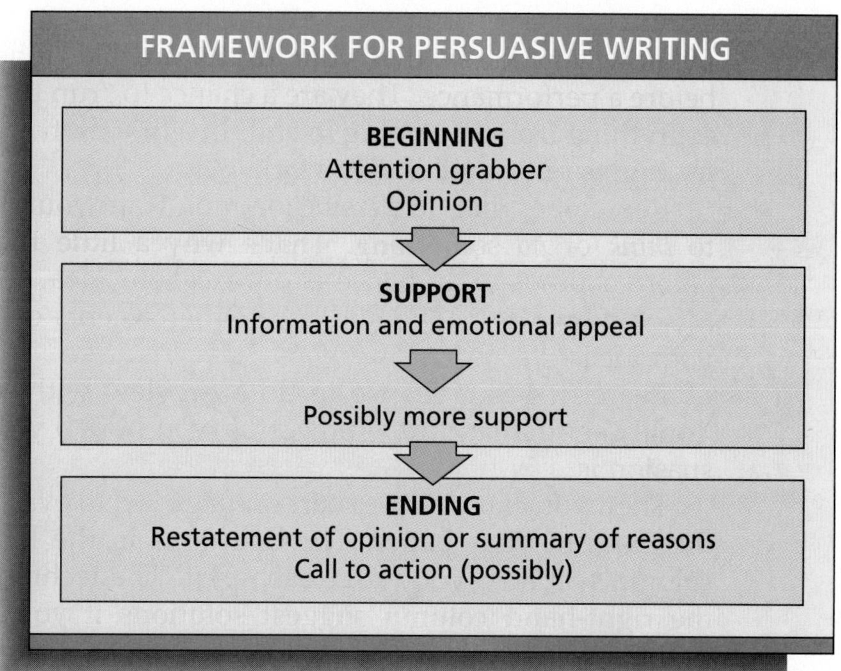

FRAMEWORK FOR PERSUASIVE WRITING
BEGINNING
Attention grabber
Opinion
SUPPORT
Information and emotional appeal
Possibly more support
ENDING
Restatement of opinion or summary of reasons
Call to action (possibly)

As you write the draft of your paper, remember to grab your audience's attention. When you're trying to persuade, you may be able to get their attention just by stating your opinion: "I think seventh-grade students should have a class party." But most of the time you'll need to do something special to make your audience want to read on.

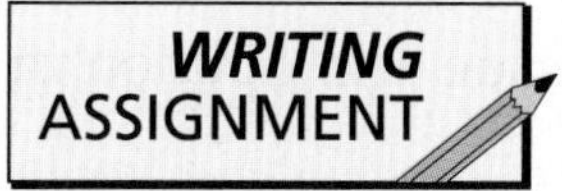

PART 3:
Writing Your First Draft

It's time to start writing. Look back at your statement of opinion and your chart of supporting information. Use the framework as a guide, and don't forget your audience.

Evaluating and Revising

By now you know that your drafts are like rehearsals before a performance. They are a chance to "run through" everything from beginning to end. In a first draft, you can try things out to see if they work.

Remember that, in persuasion, you want your readers to *think* or *do* something. That's why a little rehearsal before a preview audience is an excellent idea. You get to see how a real, live audience either accepts or rejects your ideas.

Exercise 4 is a chance to do a preview with a peer. You'll see firsthand how powerful (you hope!) your persuasion is.

Then you can use the chart on page 263 to evaluate all the parts of your paper. The questions in the left-hand column will help you judge each part. The techniques in the right-hand column suggest solutions if you find a problem.

EXERCISE 4 Speaking and Listening: Responding to an Argument

Try out your draft—out loud—with a partner. The listener will use the questions below to take notes as you speak. You can read your draft twice so your partner has a chance to catch everything. After you finish, look at your partner's responses to the questions. Jot down anything you want to keep in mind for your revising. Then change roles. You might even want to get another partner and repeat the process.

1. Can I state the speaker's issue and opinion in my own words?
2. Did the speaker grab my attention right from the start?
3. What supporting point really stood out for me?
4. Did my opinion change by the end? Why or why not?
5. What helpful suggestions can I give the speaker?

EVALUATING AND REVISING PERSUASIVE WRITING

	EVALUATION GUIDE	REVISION TECHNIQUE
1	Does the beginning grab the reader's attention?	**Add** an interesting question or brief story.
2	Is the writer's opinion clearly stated early in the paper?	**Add** a sentence giving your opinion, or **replace** the statement of opinion with a clearer one.
3	Is there enough support to convince the audience?	**Add** reasons, facts, or opinions from experts. **Add** a sentence that will appeal to your reader's feelings.
4	Does the writer include any incorrect or misleading statements?	**Cut** statements that depend on false cause and effect, attacking the person, or bandwagon.
5	Is the ending strong?	**Add** a sentence that restates your opinion or calls your reader to action.

"Just get it down on paper, and then we'll see what to do with it."

Maxwell Perkins

EXERCISE 5 Analyzing a Writer's Revisions

Study the writer's revisions of the middle paragraph of the composition on page 260. Then answer the questions that follow.

Athletes shouldn't charge fans for
(The fans help many athletes get huge salaries in the first place.)
autographs. The most popular players— **add**
the ones fans ask for autographs most
often—already earn millions of dollars.
They don't really need this extra money.
And how can you have respect for a
(take a minute to)
player who won't even sign his name for **add**
Babe Ruth
you? ~~A good player in the past~~ was **replace**
flattered just to have kids look up to him.
He wouldn't have dreamed of asking
people to pay for his autograph. ~~Anyone~~ **cut**
~~who pays for an autograph is pretty dumb.~~

1. What's the writer's reason for adding a new sentence after the first sentence?
2. What do you think the phrase *take a minute to* adds to the fourth sentence?
3. Why does the writer replace *A good player in the past* with *Babe Ruth*?
4. Do you see a good reason to cut the last sentence?

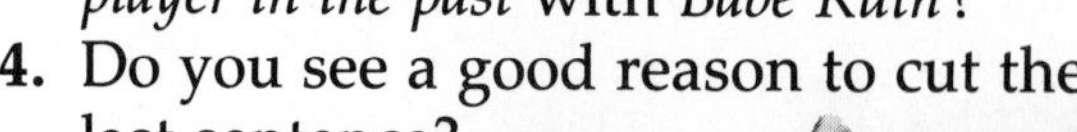

GRAMMAR HINT

Using Comparatives

In writing persuasion, you will sometimes want to compare one person or thing to another. You may want to show that your candidate for class president is *more experienced* than the other candidate. You may want to say that one brand of sneaker feels *better* than another. Be sure not to use the word *more* if the modifier is already in the comparative form (*longer*).

INCORRECT Powermax batteries last more longer than batteries from other manufacturers.
CORRECT Powermax batteries last **longer** than batteries from other manufacturers.

INCORRECT Super Crunchies cereal will make your breakfast more better every day!
CORRECT Super Crunchies cereal will make your breakfast **better** every day!

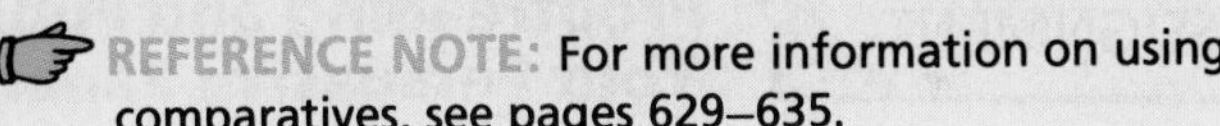

REFERENCE NOTE: For more information on using comparatives, see pages 629–635.

WRITING ASSIGNMENT

PART 4:
Evaluating and Revising Your Persuasive Paper

Do you have your notes from the "peer listening" in Exercise 4? Keep them in mind as you use the chart on page 263 to evaluate your paper. Start by exchanging papers with another student. Using the questions, write an evaluation of each other's work. Then evaluate your essay yourself. Revise it to correct any problems you or your partner has found.

Proofreading and Publishing

Proofreading. Proofreading is the last step before you share your work with others. And it's an important one. You need to find and correct any mistakes in spelling, capitalization, punctuation, or usage. If your readers see such mistakes, they may suspect you've made errors in your thinking, too.

Publishing. Here are two ways you can publish your writing.

- Join with three of your classmates to make an attractive bulletin-board display with your four papers. Use photographs and drawings to illustrate your papers.
- Find someone in class who disagrees with your opinion. Present the ideas from your persuasive paper as part of a debate.

PART 5:
Proofreading and Publishing Your Persuasive Paper

Proofread your writing carefully. Correct any errors you find. Then publish or share your work with others.

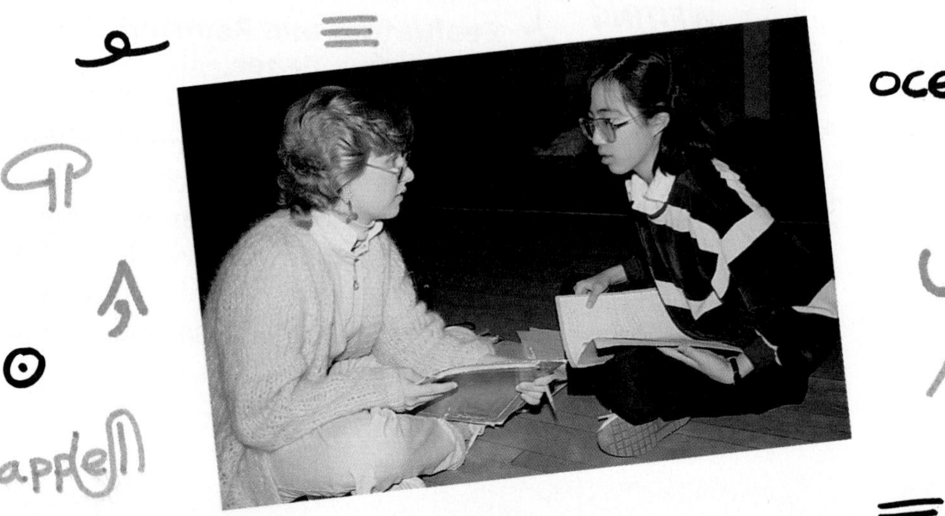

A STUDENT MODEL

Kathy Bobek attends Henry David Thoreau Intermediate School in Vienna, Virginia. She says the hardest thing about writing her persuasive paper was "trying to find words, strong ones, to express my thoughts." As you read her paper, you'll probably agree that she did find strong words to express herself. Does she convince you of her opinion on school dances?

School Dances
by Kathy Bobek

I feel that our school should let the seventh- and eighth-grade classes have their own dances. Wouldn't you and your friends love to have dances with just your friends and peers of only your grade? I'm sure most people want to socialize with friends who are in the same grade. They would want to do this and not have to worry about being made fun of by people of a higher or lower grade. The dances wouldn't have mixed grades, so more people would come to the dances, which would bring in more money. I also think there would be fewer people at each individual dance, which would also bring more order. Last but not least, I feel that the dances would be decorated more to the liking of the students. Each grade could have different people from their grade decorate each dance. What one grade might think is stupid or baby-ish, another might like. For these reasons, I think that having individual school dances for each grade would be a very good idea.

WRITING WORKSHOP

A Newspaper or Magazine Ad

Advertising is everywhere. Television and radio ads bombard your eyes and ears. Magazine and newspaper ads draw you in with pictures and bold words. All these ads have one aim—to grab your attention and convince you to buy or do something.

How do ads do it? They use certain techniques that have proved successful. Here are four.

1. *"We're the best."* The ad claims its product or service is better than that of its competitors. The ad may give facts to support the claim.
2. *"You'll feel or look better."* The ad promises you health, comfort, or beauty.
3. *"We'll solve your problem."* The ad suggests a problem (maybe one you never thought of) and offers to solve it.
4. *"A star athlete says . . ."* The ad quotes a famous person who uses or recommends the product or service.

"Do you know me? I have to deal with lions, wolves, and saber-toothed tigers . . . That's why I carry one of THESE."

These techniques aren't always so obvious in an ad. Advertisers can use them in very clever ways. But if you look closely, you can usually figure out which techniques are being used. What does this cereal ad promise you?

Every round a winner...
and every triangle, too!
Spelling bee champion
Pia Sanchez says,
"I start every day with Double Oats. They're simply supercalifragilistic-expialidocious."
38
Introducing
Double Oats
Who says a health-packed cereal can't be a taste sensation? Try this great new treat—toasty oat triangles and hearty oat puffs. With twelve essential vitamins and minerals. Extra low in sugar. Extra high in crunchy goodness.
TOASTED
DOUBLE
OATS
Crisp, Wholesome, Delicious!
New Nifty Shapes!
Ideal Source of Oat Bran

Thinking It Over

1. Which of the four techniques does the ad use to make you want to try Double Oats? (More than one is possible.) Does the ad persuade you?
2. How does the ad's headline connect the spelling bee with Double Oats?
3. Does the ad use any facts to support the claim that Double Oats is "a winner"? If so, identify them.
4. Why do you think the illustration includes the spelling-bee scene? Why wouldn't a picture of the cereal box be enough? Explain.

Writing an Ad

Prewriting. You're going to create an ad of your own. What will you sell? A new shampoo? A bicycle? Sneakers? List some possible products for your ad and choose one. Give it a good name. To plan your ad, think about the four advertising techniques. Which will you use? Jot down ideas for words and pictures. Also decide what audience you'll be trying to persuade.

Writing, Evaluating, and Revising. All three parts of an ad must work together—the headline, the information (a short paragraph), and the illustration. Keeping that in mind, write your headline. Make it short, direct, and catchy. Think about the ad techniques as you write your paragraph. What will appeal to your audience? Why will they want to buy the product? You can sketch your illustration, or clip it from a magazine. Arrange your ad on a sheet of paper. Then look it over carefully with a partner. Would you stop to read it in a magazine? Could you make it stronger?

Proofreading and Publishing. Since ads are brief and eye-catching, any mistakes in spelling, capitalization, or punctuation jump out at readers. Errors will take away from your message. Proofread carefully. Consider publishing your ad as part of a bulletin-board display or class album. Or put together a class magazine. Your persuasion papers from this chapter can be the articles. Ads can then be placed throughout the magazine. You may also want to include other writing—stories and poems, for instance.

MAKING CONNECTIONS

SPEAKING AND LISTENING

Comparing Persuasion in Different Forms

Join with two or three classmates in an ad hunt. Find one product that is advertised in two or more forms.

- Some *products* to consider are toothpaste, soap, cereal, shoes, clothing, cameras, and watches.
- Some *forms of advertising* to consider are television, magazines, newspapers, radio, and direct mail (ads that come in the mail).

WIN! WIN! WIN!
SALE
NEW
The Pierce Arrow
LUXURY in a car is as much a matter of engine building as it is of upholstery. Luxury as expressed in a Pierce-Arrow means efficiency first, attractive design second, a perfectly appointed car, built around a thoroughly tried-out machine.
THE PIERCE-ARROW MOTOR CAR COMPANY, BUFFALO, N. Y.
Licensed under Selden Patent

You may want to divide the forms among yourselves. That way, everybody won't be searching in the same places. Try to find your product advertised in as many different forms as possible. (You probably won't find it in all forms.) Cut out or record the ads if possible. Otherwise, take notes.

When the group gets together, ask yourselves:

1. How are the ads alike, and how are they different? Describe the ads. [Hint: What do you notice about words, pictures, color, sound, and motion?]
2. Which ad in which form is the most convincing to you? Why?

Report your findings to the class. Use the ads you've collected in your report.

PERSUASION IN ACTION

Letters to the Editor

Almost all newspapers and magazines have a "Letters to the Editor" section. It gives readers a chance to say what's on their minds. They may respond to a news item or an editorial. Or they may bring up a whole new issue.

The audience is really all the newspaper or magazine's readers, not just the editor. And the purpose often is to persuade. Here's a letter from a writer who wants readers to be aware that wild plants can be useful.

> CURES FROM THE JUNGLE
>
> I really enjoyed reading "In Search of Jungle Secrets" in the February 1990 issue of *Ranger Rick.* When I was nine years old, I got a very rare type of blood cancer. One of the drugs that was used to cure me came from the *rosy periwinkle.* This flower grows in Madagascar, an island off the African coast.

I am 15 years old now and very happy to be alive. I'm thankful for tropical plants that can be used to make medicines like the one that cured me.

Please tell everyone how important it is to save wild plants and other living things. Not only are they beautiful, but they also might contain some "secret" medicines that can save other people's lives too.

Whitney Hair, Cary, NC
Ranger Rick

Read a few more letters to the editor, and write one of your own. Think of an issue that concerns you, and choose a specific magazine or newspaper to write to.

Use the elements you've learned in this chapter: opinion statement, supporting information, emotional appeal (not overexcited, though), and perhaps a call to action. But be very brief. Editors often shorten long letters.

Then mail your letter. If it's published, bring the clipping to class.

9 Writing About Literature

Reading and Responding

Every day you spend time **reading and responding.** You read your favorite comic strips and laugh. You put a book down because it's so boring you can't stay awake. You have feelings and thoughts about almost everything you read.

Writing and You. People often put their responses in writing. Newspaper and TV critics respond to movies, books, and TV shows. Your friend may write in her journal about a movie she liked. Your teacher may ask you to respond in writing to a poem you read. Or you may be asked to write an in-depth book report. Did you realize that all these were responses?

As You Read. Following is a response about a book you may have read—*Number the Stars,* by Lois Lowry. As you read, think about the reviewer's opinion. Does she like the book? If so, why does she?

Book Objects, Steven Cortright (1986), courtesy Santa Barbara Museum of Art.

A Review of Lois Lowry's

UMBER THE STARS

by Louise L. Sherman

Annemarie's life in occupied Copenhagen in 1943 seemingly is not much changed by the war—until the Nazi persecution of Danish Jews begins. Annemarie's family becomes involved in the Resistance effort, helping a Jewish friend by having her pose as Annemarie's dead sister Lise. When an important packet must be taken to the captain of one of the ships smuggling Jews to neutral Sweden, Annemarie finds the courage needed to deliver it despite grave danger to herself. Later her Uncle Henrik tells her that *brave* means "not thinking about the dangers. Just thinking about what you must do." Lowry's story is not just of Annemarie; it is also of Denmark and the Danish people, whose Resistance was so effective in saving their Jews. Annemarie is not just a symbol, however. She is a very real child who is equally involved in playing with a new kitten and running races at school as in the dangers of the occupation. *Number the Stars* brings the war to a child's level of understanding, suggesting but not detailing its horrors. It is well plotted, and period and place are convincingly recreated. An afterword answers the questions that readers will have and reiterates the inspirational idealism of the young people whose courage helped win the war.

"...brave

means 'not thinking about the dangers.

Just thinking about what you must do.'"

Reader's Response

1. Does *Number the Stars* seem like a book you'd want to read? Explain why or why not.
2. If you've read this book, tell why you think it is or is not a good story.

Writer's Craft

3. What is the reviewer's opinion of *Number the Stars*? Does she like or dislike it? What sentences tell you this?
4. The reviewer uses details from the book to support her opinion about it. What does she say about why she likes or dislikes *Number the Stars*?

"She is a very real child who is equally involved in playing with a new kitten and running races at school as in the dangers of the occupation."

Purposes for Writing About Literature

The purpose of a review, like the one about *Number the Stars,* is to tell whether or not others should read a story, poem, or book. You might also write about literature in your journal or in a letter to friends, or make a poster showing your responses to a book. Then your purpose for writing about literature might be different—just to give your own feelings, or to persuade someone else to read something. When you write about literature, you usually have one of these four purposes.

Self-Expressive: writing in your journal about a short story character that seems just like you; writing to a friend about your favorite TV show.

Persuasive: in a note, writing about a movie to persuade your parents to let you see it; on a poster, writing about a book to persuade other students to read it.

Informative: telling a pen pal in Mexico about a film you saw about that country; explaining in a letter to a friend what happens in a movie your friend missed.

Creative: writing a journal entry as though you were a character in a story; imagining what happens to the character ten years after the story ends.

In the main assignment in this chapter, your purpose for writing about literature will be informative. You'll be analyzing a character in a story and telling about him or her. Keep in mind that a good character analysis

- tells about two or three character traits
- gives story details to support the analysis

Writing a Character Analysis

Reading and Responding to Stories

Before you can write about literature, you have to read it, respond to it, and think about it. You start with the story or poem itself and your reactions to it. Then you try to understand it.

Starting with a Personal Response

A personal response usually happens automatically. You know right away whether you like a movie or not. You walk out of the theater saying, "Those battle scenes were great!" or "What a boring movie!" You respond to literature—a poem, a novel, or a story—in the same way.

There is no right or wrong way to respond to literature. That's why it's called a "personal" response.

The following story is about a young boy who is embarrassed about the way his great-grandfather looks and acts. As you read, think about your personal response. Can you understand how the boy feels?

A SHORT STORY

The Medicine Bag

by Virginia Driving Hawk Sneve

My kid sister Cheryl and I always bragged about our Sioux grandpa, Joe Iron Shell. Our friends, who had always lived in the city and only knew about Indians from movies and TV, were impressed by our stories. Maybe we exaggerated and made

Grandpa and the reservation sound glamorous, but when we'd return home to Iowa after our yearly summer visit to Grandpa we always had some exciting tale to tell.

We always had some authentic Sioux article to show our listeners. One year Cheryl had new moccasins that Grandpa had made. On another visit he gave me a small, round, flat, rawhide drum which was decorated with a painting of a warrior riding a horse. He taught me a real Sioux chant to sing while I beat the drum with a leather-covered stick that had a feather on the end. Man, that really made an impression.

We never showed our friends Grandpa's picture. Not that we were ashamed of him, but because we knew that the glamorous tales we told didn't go with the real thing. Our friends would have laughed at the picture, because Grandpa wasn't tall and stately like TV Indians. His hair wasn't in braids, but hung in stringy, gray strands on his neck and he was old. He was our great-grandfather, and he didn't live in a tepee, but all by himself in a part log, part tar-paper shack on the Rosebud Reservation in South Dakota. So when Grandpa came to visit us, I was so ashamed and embarrassed I could've died.

There are a lot of yippy poodles and other fancy little dogs in our neighborhood, but they usually barked singly at the mailman from the safety of their own yards. Now it sounded as if a whole pack of mutts were barking together in one place.

I got up and walked to the curb to see what the commotion was. About a block away I saw a crowd of little kids yelling, with the dogs yipping and growling around someone who was walking down the middle of the street.

I watched the group as it slowly came closer and saw that in the center of the strange procession was a man wearing a tall black hat. He'd pause now and then to peer at something in his hand and then at the houses on either side of the street. I felt cold and hot at the same time as I recognized the man. "Oh, no!" I whispered. "It's Grandpa!"

I stood on the curb, unable to move even though I wanted to run and hide. Then I got mad when I saw how the yippy dogs were growling and nipping at the old man's baggy pant legs and how wearily he poked them away with his cane. "Stupid mutts," I said as I ran to rescue Grandpa.

When I kicked and hollered at the dogs to get away, they put their tails between their legs and scattered. The kids ran to the curb where they watched me and the old man.

"Grandpa," I said and felt pretty dumb when my voice cracked. I reached for his beat-up old tin suitcase, which was tied shut with a rope. But he set it down right in the street and shook my hand.

"*Hau, Takoza,* Grandchild," he greeted me formally in Sioux.

All I could do was stand there with the whole neighborhood watching and shake the hand of the leather-brown old man. I saw how his gray hair straggled from under his big black hat, which had a drooping feather in its crown. His rumpled black suit hung like a sack over his stooped frame. As he shook my hand, his coat fell open to expose a bright-red, satin shirt with a beaded bolo tie under the collar. His get-up wasn't out of place on the reservation, but it sure was here, and I wanted to sink right through the pavement.

"Hi," I muttered with my head down. I tried to pull my hand away when I felt his bony hand trembling, and looked up to see fatigue in his face. I felt like crying. I couldn't think of anything to say so I picked up Grandpa's suitcase, took his arm, and guided him up the driveway to our house.

Mom was standing on the steps. I don't know how long she'd been watching, but her hand was over her mouth and she looked as if she couldn't believe what she saw. Then she ran to us.

"Grandpa," she gasped. "How in the world did you get here?"

She checked her move to embrace Grandpa and I remembered that such a display of affection is unseemly to the Sioux and would embarrass him.

"*Hau,* Marie," he said as he shook Mom's hand. She smiled and took his other arm.

As we supported him up the steps the door banged open and Cheryl came bursting out of the house. She was all smiles and was so obviously glad to see Grandpa that I was ashamed of how I felt.

"Grandpa!" she yelled happily. "You came to see us!"

Grandpa smiled and Mom and I let go of him as he stretched out his arms to my ten-year-old sister, who was still young enough to be hugged.

"*Wicincala,* little girl," he greeted her and then collapsed.

He had fainted. Mom and I carried him into her sewing room, where we had a spare bed.

After we had Grandpa on the bed Mom stood there helplessly patting his shoulder.

"Shouldn't we call the doctor, Mom?" I suggested, since she didn't seem to know what to do.

"Yes," she agreed with a sigh. "You make Grandpa comfortable, Martin."

I reluctantly moved to the bed. I knew Grandpa wouldn't want to have Mom undress him, but I didn't want to, either. He was so skinny and frail that his coat slipped off easily. When I loosened his tie and opened his shirt collar, I felt a small leather pouch that hung from a thong around his neck. I left it alone and moved to remove his boots. The scuffed old cowboy boots were tight and he moaned as I put pressure on his legs to jerk them off.

I put the boots on the floor and saw why they fit so tight. Each one was stuffed with money. I looked at the bills that lined the boots and started to ask about them, but Grandpa's eyes were closed again.

Mom came back with a basin of water. "The doctor thinks Grandpa is suffering from heat exhaustion," she explained as she bathed Grandpa's face. Mom gave a big sigh, "*Oh hinh,* Martin. How do you suppose he got here?"

We found out after the doctor's visit. Grandpa was angrily sitting up in bed while Mom tried to feed him some soup.

"Tonight you let Marie feed you, Grandpa," spoke my dad, who had gotten home from work just as the doctor was leaving. "You're not really sick," he said as he gently pushed Grandpa back against the pillows. "The doctor said you just got too tired and hot after your long trip."

Grandpa relaxed, and between sips of soup he told us of his journey. Soon after our visit to him Grandpa decided that he would like to see where his only living descendants lived and what our home was like. Besides, he admitted sheepishly, he was lonesome after we left.

I knew everybody felt as guilty as I did—especially Mom. Mom was all Grandpa had left. So even after she married my dad, who's a white man and teaches in the college in our city, and after Cheryl and I were born, Mom made sure that every summer we spent a week with Grandpa.

I never thought that Grandpa would be lonely after our visits, and none of us noticed how old and weak he had become. But Grandpa knew and so he came to us. He had ridden on buses for two and a half days. When he arrived in the city, tired and stiff from sitting for so long, he set out, walking, to find us.

He had stopped to rest on the steps of some building downtown and a policeman found him. The cop, according to Grandpa, was a good man who took him to the bus stop and waited until the bus came and told the driver to let Grandpa out at Bell View Drive. After Grandpa got off the bus, he started walking again. But he couldn't see the house numbers on the other side when he walked on the sidewalk so he walked in the middle of the street. That's when all the little kids and dogs followed him.

I knew everybody felt as bad as I did. Yet I was proud of this eighty-six-year-old man, who had never been away from the reservation, having the courage to travel so far alone.

"You found the money in my boots?" he asked Mom.

"Martin did," she answered, and roused herself to scold. "Grandpa, you shouldn't have carried so much money. What if someone had stolen it from you?"

Grandpa laughed. "I would've known if anyone tried to take the boots off my feet. The money is what I've saved for a long time—a hundred dollars—for my funeral. But you take it now to buy groceries so that I won't be a burden to you while I am here."

"That won't be necessary, Grandpa," Dad said. "We are honored to have you with us and you will never be a burden. I am only sorry that we never thought to bring you home with us this summer and spare you the discomfort of a long trip."

Grandpa was pleased. "Thank you," he answered. "But do not feel bad that you didn't bring me with you, for I would not have come then. It was not time." He said this in such a way that no one could argue with him. To Grandpa and the Sioux, he once told me, a thing would be done when it was the right time to do it and that's the way it was.

"Also," Grandpa went on, looking at me, "I have come because it is soon time for Martin to have the medicine bag."

We all knew what that meant. Grandpa thought he was going to die and he had to follow the tradition of his family to pass the medicine bag, along with its history, to the oldest male child.

"Even though the boy," he said still looking at me, "bears a white man's name, the medicine bag will be his."

I didn't know what to say. I had the same hot and cold feeling that I had when I first saw Grandpa in the street. The medicine bag was the dirty leather pouch I had found around his neck. "I could never wear such a thing," I almost said aloud. I thought of having my friends see it in gym class, at the swimming pool, and could imagine the smart things they would say. But I just swallowed hard and took a step toward the bed. I knew I would have to take it.

But Grandpa was tired. "Not now, Martin," he said, waving his hand in dismissal, "it is not time. Now I will sleep."

So that's how Grandpa came to be with us for two months. My friends kept asking to come see the old man, but I put them off. I told myself that I didn't want them laughing at Grandpa. But even as I made excuses I knew it wasn't Grandpa that I was afraid they'd laugh at.

Nothing bothered Cheryl about bringing her friends to see Grandpa. Every day after school started there'd be a crew of giggling little girls or round-eyed little boys crowded around the old man on the patio, where he'd gotten in the habit of sitting every afternoon.

Grandpa would smile in his gentle way and patiently answer their questions, or he'd tell them stories of brave warriors, ghosts, animals, and the kids listened in awed silence. Those little guys thought Grandpa was great.

Finally, one day after school, my friends came home with me because nothing I said stopped them. "We're going to see the great Indian of Bell View Drive," said Hank, who was supposed to be my best friend. "My brother has seen him three times so he oughta be well enough to see us."

When we got to my house Grandpa was sitting on the patio. He had on his red shirt, but today he also wore a fringed leather vest that was decorated with beads. Instead of his usual cowboy boots he had solidly beaded moccasins on his feet that stuck out of his black trousers. Of course, he had his old black hat on—he was seldom without it. But it had been brushed and the feather in the beaded headband was proudly erect, its tip a brighter white. His hair lay in silver strands over the red shirt collar.

I started just as my friends did and I heard one of them murmur, "Wow!"

Grandpa looked up and when his eyes met mine they twinkled as if he were laughing inside. He nodded to me and my face got all hot. I could tell that he had known all along I was afraid he'd embarrass me in front of my friends.

"Hau, hoksilas, boys," he greeted and held out his hand.

My buddies passed in a single file and shook his hand as I introduced them. They were so polite I almost laughed. "How, there, Grandpa," and even a "How-do-you-do, sir."

"You look fine, Grandpa," I said as the guys sat on the lawn chairs or on the patio floor.

"Hanh, yes," he agreed. "When I woke up this morning it seemed the right time to dress in the good clothes. I knew that my grandson would be bringing his friends."

"You guys want some lemonade or something?" I offered. No one answered. They were listening to Grandpa as he started telling how he'd killed the deer from which his vest was made.

Grandpa did most of the talking while my friends were there. I was so proud of him and amazed at how respectfully quiet my buddies were. Mom had to chase them home at suppertime. As they left they shook Grandpa's hand again and said to me:

"Martin, he's really great!"

"Yeah, man! Don't blame you for keeping him to yourself."

"Can we come back?"

But after they left, Mom said, "No more visitors for a while, Martin. Grandpa won't admit it, but his strength hasn't returned. He likes having company, but it tires him."

That evening Grandpa called me to his room before he went to sleep. "Tomorrow," he said, "when you come home, it will be time to give you the medicine bag."

I felt a hard squeeze from where my heart is supposed to be and was scared, but I answered, "OK, Grandpa."

All night I had weird dreams about thunder and lightning on a high hill. From a distance I heard the slow beat of a drum. When I woke up in the morning I felt as if I hadn't slept at all. At school it seemed as if the day would never end and, when it finally did, I ran home.

Grandpa was in his room, sitting on the bed. The shades were down and the place was dim and cool. I sat on the floor in front of Grandpa, but he didn't even look at me. After what seemed a long time he spoke.

"I sent your mother and sister away. What you will hear today is only for a man's ears. What you will receive is only for a man's hands." He fell silent and I felt shivers down my back.

"My father in his early manhood," Grandpa began, "made a vision quest to find a spirit guide for his life. You cannot understand how it was in that time, when the great Teton Sioux were first made to stay on the reservation. There was a strong need for guidance from *Wakantanka,* the Great Spirit. But too many of the young men were filled with despair and hatred. They thought it was hopeless to search for a vision when the glorious life was gone and only the hated confines of a reservation lay ahead. But my father held to the old ways.

"He carefully prepared for his quest with a purifying sweat bath and then he went alone to a high butte top to fast and pray. After three days he received his sacred dream—in which he found, after long searching, the white man's iron. He did not understand his vision of finding something belonging to the white people, for in that time they were the enemy. When he came down from the butte to cleanse himself at the stream below, he found the remains of a campfire and the broken shell of an iron kettle. This was a sign which reinforced his dream. He took a piece of the iron for his medicine bag, which he had made of elk skin years before, to prepare for his quest.

"He returned to his village, where he told his dream to the wise old men of the tribe. They gave him the name Iron Shell, but neither did they understand the meaning of the dream. This first Iron Shell kept the piece of iron with him at all times and believed it gave him protection from the evils of those unhappy days.

"Then a terrible thing happened to Iron Shell. He and several other young men were taken from their homes by the soldiers and sent far away to a white man's boarding school. He was angry and lonesome for his parents and the young girl he had wed before he was taken away. At first Iron Shell resisted the teachers' attempts to change him and he did not try to learn. One day it was his turn to work in the school's blacksmith shop. As he walked into the place he knew that his medicine had brought him there to learn and work with the white man's iron.

"Iron Shell became a blacksmith and worked at the trade when he returned to the reservation. All of his life he treasured the medicine bag. When he was old, and I was a man, he gave it to me, for no one made the vision quest anymore."

Grandpa quit talking and I stared in disbelief as he covered his face with his hands. His shoulders were shaking with quiet sobs and I looked away until he began to speak again.

"I kept the bag until my son, your mother's father, was a man and had to leave us to fight in the war across the ocean. I gave him the bag, for I believed it would protect him in battle, but he did not take it with him. He was afraid that he would lose it. He died in a faraway place."

Again Grandpa was still and I felt his grief around me.

"My son," he went on after clearing his throat, "had only a daughter and it is not proper for her to know of these things."

He unbuttoned his shirt, pulled out the leather pouch, and lifted it over his head. He held it in his hand, turning it over and over as if memorizing how it looked.

"In the bag," he said as he opened it and removed two objects, "is the broken shell of the iron kettle, a pebble from the butte, and a piece of the sacred sage." He held the pouch upside down and dust drifted down.

"After the bag is yours you must put a piece of prairie sage within and never open it again until you pass it on to your son." He replaced the pebble and the piece of iron, and tied the bag.

I stood up, somehow knowing I should. Grandpa slowly rose from the bed and stood upright in front of me, holding the bag before my face. I closed my eyes and waited for him to slip it over my head. But he spoke.

"No, you need not wear it." He placed the soft leather bag in my right hand and closed my other hand over it. "It would not be right to wear it in this time and place where no one will understand. Put it safely away until you are again on the reservation. Wear it then, when you replace the sacred sage."

Grandpa turned and sat again on the bed. Wearily he leaned his head against the pillow. "Go," he said, "I will sleep now."

"Thank you, Grandpa," I said softly and left with the bag in my hands.

That night Mom and Dad took Grandpa to the hospital. Two weeks later I stood alone on the lonely prairie of the reservation and put the sacred sage in my medicine bag.

EXERCISE 1 Responding to a Story

What's your personal response to "The Medicine Bag"? How many stars would you give it? (Use four stars as the highest rating and one star as the lowest.) Draw the number of stars in your journal. Then write two or three sentences in your journal about your personal response to the characters and story events. Did you like Martin? How did you feel about the way he treated his great-grandfather? Did events in the story keep your interest? Would you like to read another story like this one?

Reading for Understanding

After reading some stories, you may stop at your personal response. But sometimes you need to go beyond it. For instance, you may want to explain to a friend why you want him or her to read a story. Or, you may have a school assignment to read a story and analyze it. Then you'll need to have some understanding of the basic parts, or elements, of a story. These are the characters, the plot, the setting, and the meaning.

BASIC ELEMENTS OF STORIES
CHARACTERS. The ***characters*** of a story are its actors—the people, animals, or creatures who play parts. You get to know characters in a story the same way you get to know people in real life. You observe what they say, what they think, and what they do. You also notice how they look and how other people respond to them.
PLOT. ***Plot*** is what happens in the story—the events that unfold from the beginning to the end. The plot almost always presents a ***conflict,*** or problem, that the main character has to overcome.
SETTING. Where and when a story's events occur make up its ***setting.*** In some stories, the setting causes things to happen. In others, the events might happen anywhere.
MEANING. The ***meaning,*** or main idea, of a story is what it tells you about people or life. The meaning of a story about a village hit by an earthquake could be "Hard times can bring out the best in people."

EXERCISE 2 Analyzing the Elements of a Story

How well do you understand the basic parts of a story? Read back over "The Medicine Bag" on pages 280–291. Then, with two or three classmates, answer the following questions.

1. Who are the two main characters? Imagine telling a friend about them. What word or two would you use to describe each one?
2. What conflict, or problem, does Martin face?
3. Briefly describe what happens at the most exciting point (the climax) in the story.
4. What is the setting? Why does this setting cause events in the story to happen?
5. The meaning of this story focuses on the way a boy reacts to his great-grandfather. Tell the meaning of the story in your own words.

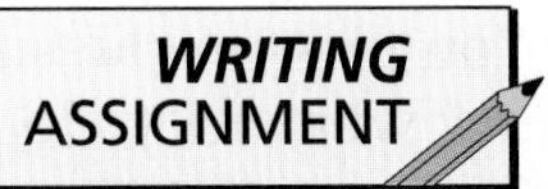

PART 1:

Reading and Responding to a Story

Choose a story, either one that you would like to read or one your teacher suggests. First, read it and check your own response. How do you feel about this story? Then, look at it more closely. Use the questions in Exercise 2 to analyze the story's basic elements.

Planning a Character Analysis

In a literature class, you are often asked to analyze a story or some part of it. A ***character analysis*** is one type of story analysis.

Studying a Character

When you analyze a character in a story, you try to find out what makes that character "tick." In your everyday life, you do this all the time. You pick up clues about the people around you by noticing what they do and say. To pick up clues about a character in a story, you do the same thing. These are the things you should especially watch for.

- Notice how the character **looks.** Does his or her appearance affect what happens?
- Watch how the character **behaves.** Does he or she take action to face the conflict? What do the character's actions show about what the character feels inside? Are the character's actions and feelings related in any way?
- Listen to what the character **says.** Does the character say how he or she feels? What kind of language does the character use?
- Notice the character's **thoughts.** What goes on in the character's mind? What does that tell you about him or her? Do any thoughts keep popping up over and over again?

As you read a story closely, take notes. Write down details that show how a character feels or thinks. Beside each note, write your own reaction or evaluation (for example: "he's embarrassed"; "cares what his friends think"; "shows honesty"; "proud"). On the next page are some notes one writer made about Martin.

HERE'S HOW

MARTIN

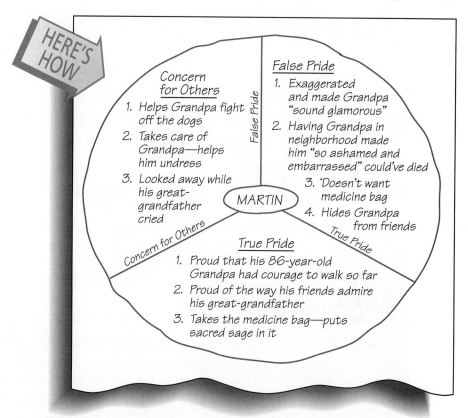

Concern for Others

1. Helps Grandpa fight off the dogs
2. Takes care of Grandpa—helps him undress
3. Looked away while his great-grandfather cried

False Pride

1. Exaggerated and made Grandpa "sound glamorous"
2. Having Grandpa in neighborhood made him "so ashamed and embarrassed" could've died
3. Doesn't want medicine bag
4. Hides Grandpa from friends

True Pride

1. Proud that his 86-year-old Grandpa had courage to walk so far
2. Proud of the way his friends admire his great-grandfather
3. Takes the medicine bag—puts sacred sage in it

CRITICAL THINKING

Analyzing a Character

When you ***analyze*** something, you look at its parts. This analysis helps you understand something better. When you analyze a character, you think about what the character says, does, thinks, and so on.

One way to analyze a character is to create a character wheel. To make one, first think about the character overall. What are his or her *major traits,* or characteristics? Choose two or three traits that you think are the most important. Then, look back through the story to find details that show those traits.

The Here's How above is an example of an analysis using a character wheel. Here are the parts of the wheel.

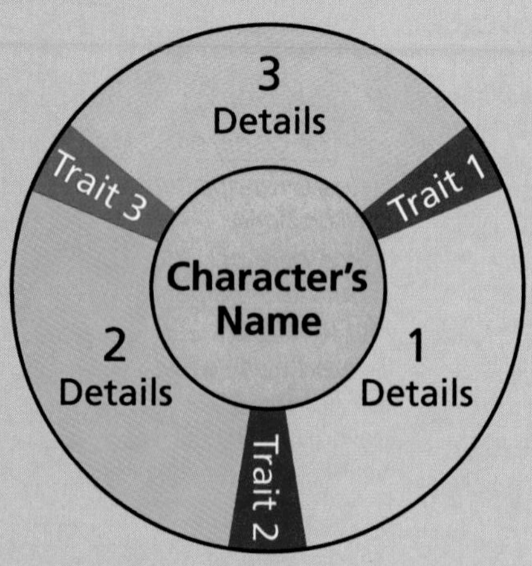

CRITICAL THINKING EXERCISE:
Analyzing a Character

Work with some classmates to analyze a character—perhaps Grandpa in "The Medicine Bag," a character in another story, or a character from one of your favorite TV shows. Work together to make a character wheel. Identify two or three character traits. Then have one person draw the wheel and write the traits on the spokes. As the group identifies details to go with each trait, one person can write them in the wheel between the spokes. What kind of person is this character? Can you write one or two sentences to summarize what you think?

EXERCISE 3 **Speaking and Listening: Creating and Analyzing a Character**

Make up your own character. Then tell a small group of classmates about your character. What does your character look like? How does he or she speak? walk? dress? Suppose the character takes your place at school today. How does he or she behave? Do your classmates like the character? Tell why. Now, listen to your classmates speak. What do you learn about their characters?

PART 2:
Choosing a Character to Analyze

Choose a character from the story you read for Writing Assignment, Part 1 (page 293). The character should be one you either liked or disliked very much. Next, make a character wheel like the one on page 295. Find two or three traits for your character to put on the wheel. Between the spokes, write details that support those traits.

Developing a Writing Plan

Thinking About Purpose and Audience. The *purpose* of a character analysis is to find out what kind of person a story character is. You do this so that you and your readers can understand a character better. When you know a story character in this way, you can often understand yourself or others better. The *audience* for the analysis is usually your teacher and classmates. You may also want to share your analysis with a friend or family member.

Stating Your Main Idea. Think about how you describe someone new in school to friends who have never met him or her. Usually, you describe a few major traits of that person. You may say, for example, that the person seems lonely or cheerful or very shy. In a character analysis, these traits become your *main idea.*

For your character analysis, choose one or two, perhaps three, major traits about your character. (It's better to look at fewer traits and explain them clearly.) Then write a sentence about them. That sentence is your ***main idea statement.*** If your character changes, you may need two or more sentences to express your main idea. Here's the main idea statement for the character wheel on page 295. The writer uses only two of the traits on his wheel.

EXAMPLE At first, Martin feels false pride. However, it becomes a true pride after he learns more about his great-grandfather and his heritage.

Organizing Your Information. One way to organize a character analysis is to decide which trait is most important and start or end with it. Another way is to treat the traits chronologically, in the order in which they appear in the story. Just be sure that you don't mix the details that support one trait with the details for another trait.

To develop a plan for your character analysis

- think about your purpose and audience
- identify some traits of the character
- look for details from the story to explain the traits
- decide what traits you will discuss in your paper
- write a main idea statement about those traits

PART 3:
Developing a Writing Plan

Think about the character you chose for Writing Assignment, Part 2 (page 297). Review the traits on your character wheel and choose one or two that you think are very important. Write a main idea statement about them. Then decide how you will organize your analysis. List the traits and supporting details in the order you will use them.

Writing Your First Draft

The Parts of a Character Analysis

Now it's time to write your character analysis and turn your notes into sentences and paragraphs. Your paper should be four or five paragraphs long. It will be organized like a composition.

- First paragraph: Name the title and author of the story and tell what character you're analyzing. State your main idea in one or two sentences.
- Middle (or body) paragraphs: In each paragraph, write about one trait and the details that explain it. Start a new paragraph for each trait.
- Last paragraph: Sum up the main points of your paper and restate your main idea.

REFERENCE NOTE: For more information on the parts of a composition, see pages 104–110.

Here's a model character analysis of Martin, the main character of "The Medicine Bag." It tells about two of Martin's character traits. As you read, notice how each trait has details to support it.

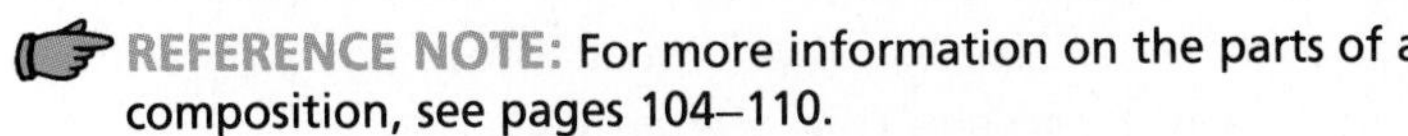

A WRITER'S MODEL

The Discovery of True Pride

INTRODUCTION
Author/Title
Character
Main idea

The main character in Virginia Driving Hawk Sneve's "The Medicine Bag" is a young boy named Martin. One of the strongest traits of this character is his pride. At the beginning of the story it is a false, bragging kind of pride. But at the end of the story it is a true pride—in his heritage.

BODY

First trait

Details—Martin's actions

At the beginning of the story, Martin admitted that he and his sister had always bragged about their Sioux "grandpa," who was actually their great-grandfather. For Martin, though, this pride in a way wasn't sincere. He exaggerated and made his great-grandfather sound like Indians in the movies and on TV.

Details—Martin's words and actions

When Grandpa actually walked into his neighborhood, Martin was embarrassed. He said that he felt hot and cold all over and was "so ashamed and embarrassed" he could have died. When Martin held his head down and pulled his hand away, he showed how his pride in his great-grandfather was not real. He was proud only of his pretend "grandpa," not the real one.

Details—Martin's thoughts

How Martin felt about the medicine bag also showed his false pride. His great-grandfather had come to give the medicine bag to Martin. But Martin didn't want it. He didn't want his friends to see him wearing it.

Details—Martin's actions

He didn't even want them to see his great-grandfather. They asked to, but Martin wouldn't let them. But one day they went right into

Second trait

Details—Martin's thoughts

Martin's house anyway. Grandpa seemed to have known they were coming. He had put on his best clothes, and he was impressive in his beaded vest and moccasins. When Martin saw that his friends thought Grandpa was great, he began to feel a true pride.

Details—Martin's thoughts and actions

The next day, Grandpa told Martin about the medicine bag. He explained how his father had passed it on to him. Then he asked Martin to find a piece of sacred sage to add to the medicine bag and save it for his own son. As Martin listened to the story, he began to understand his heritage and be proud of it. Soon after that Grandpa died. At the end of the story, Martin stood alone on the prairie and put the sacred sage in his medicine bag. He was now proud of the medicine bag and what it meant to his family.

CONCLUSION
Main idea in different words

Martin always had pride. But as he came to know his great-grandfather, that pride changed. It went from a false pride to a sincere pride and feeling of honor in his heritage.

Use details from the story to support the traits of your character. But don't just tell your readers what happens in the story. Many of your readers may already know the story, and it's boring to read something you already know.

A Framework for a Character Analysis

On the following page is a framework for a character analysis like the one about Martin. You may want to use this framework when you write your own analysis.

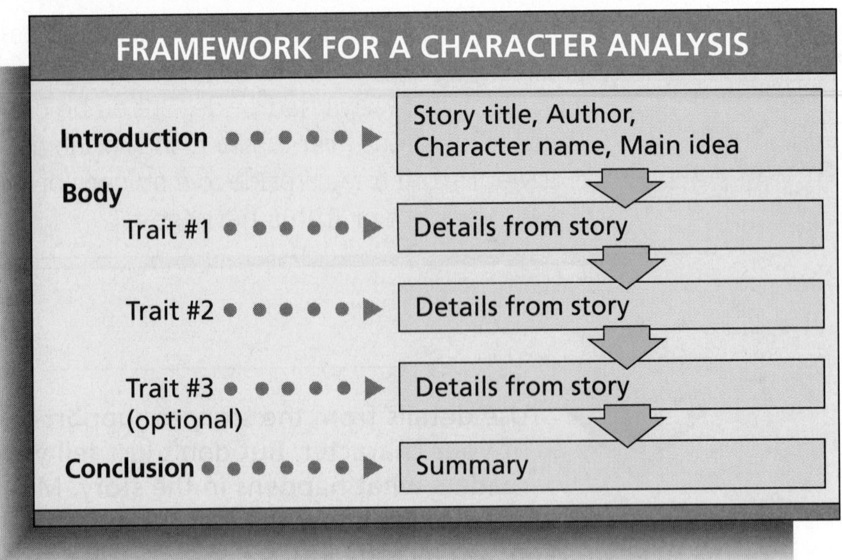

FRAMEWORK FOR A CHARACTER ANALYSIS
Introduction
Story title, Author, Character name, Main idea
Body
Trait #1
Details from story
Trait #2
Details from story
Trait #3 (optional)
Details from story
Conclusion
Summary

PART 4:
Writing Your First Draft

You've already done most of the work for your analysis. Now, use your main idea statement and the details on your character wheel to write a rough draft of a character analysis. Remember that you'll have a chance to make changes in your analysis later. It doesn't have to be perfect on the first try.

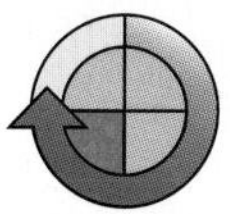

Evaluating and Revising

To evaluate your analysis, use the following guide. Ask yourself each question in the left-hand column. If you find a problem, use the ideas in the right-hand column to fix it.

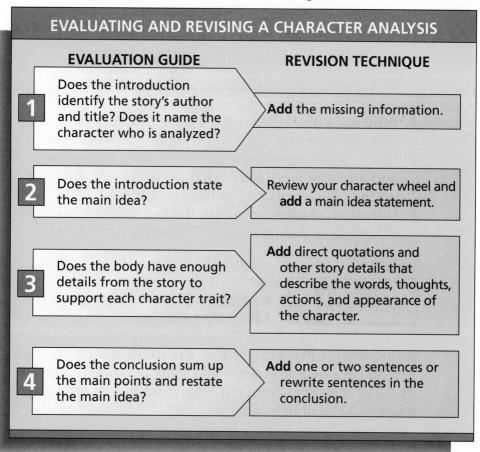

EVALUATING AND REVISING A CHARACTER ANALYSIS

	EVALUATION GUIDE	REVISION TECHNIQUE
1	Does the introduction identify the story's author and title? Does it name the character who is analyzed?	**Add** the missing information.
2	Does the introduction state the main idea?	Review your character wheel and **add** a main idea statement.
3	Does the body have enough details from the story to support each character trait?	**Add** direct quotations and other story details that describe the words, thoughts, actions, and appearance of the character.
4	Does the conclusion sum up the main points and restate the main idea?	**Add** one or two sentences or rewrite sentences in the conclusion.

EXERCISE 4 **Analyzing a Writer's Revisions**

On the next page is a first draft of the first paragraph of the analysis of Martin. With two or three classmates, figure out why the writer made the changes. Then answer the questions that follow.

The main character in Virginia Driving Hawk Sneve's ~~story~~ "The Medicine Bag" is a young boy named Martin. One of the strongest traits of this character is his pride. At the beginning of the story it is a false, bragging kind of pride. But at the end of the story it is a true pride—in his heritage. ~~That's because he'd gotten to know his great-grandfather and learned about the medicine bag.~~

replace

add

cut

1. Why does the writer replace the word *story* with *"The Medicine Bag"*?
2. In the same sentence, what words does the writer add after the word *boy*? What important information do the new words add to the paragraph?
3. Why does the writer cut out the last sentence? [Hint: Where does this information belong?]

PART 5:

Evaluating and Revising Your Character Analysis

A first draft is like a caterpillar; a revision is the butterfly. Reread your own first draft, and think of ways to "make it fly." The questions from the evaluating and revising chart on page 303 will help you.

Proofreading and Publishing

Proofreading. You've "given wings" to your paper. Now it's time to take care of the finishing details. Read carefully over your paper at least twice to check for mistakes.

MECHANICS HINT

Using Quotation Marks

Use quotation marks around the title of the story. And when you quote directly from a story, put quotation marks around the words. Do this even when a character isn't speaking.

EXAMPLES The main character in Virginia Driving Hawk Sneve's "The Medicine Bag" is a young boy named Martin.
He said that he felt hot and cold all over and was "so ashamed and embarrassed" he could have died.

REFERENCE NOTE: For more information on quotation marks, see pages 737–744.

Publishing. With your teacher's help, plan some special ways to share your papers. Here are two ideas:

- Create a "movie poster" to go with your paper, spotlighting the most exciting point of the story. Place the posters around the room.
- Find a "friend" for your character. Get together with three or four classmates and share your papers. Decide

which of your classmates' characters would make the best friend for your character. Write a short dialogue between the two characters.

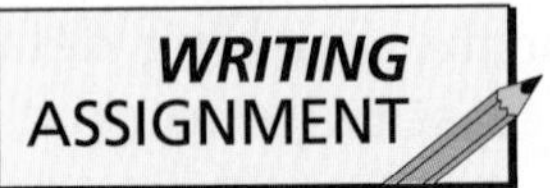

PART 6:
Proofreading and Publishing Your Character Analysis

You're at the finish line. Proofread your paper and make sure it has no errors and is clear to your readers. Use one of the ideas on page 305 and above, or another idea of your own, to share your paper with others.

A STUDENT MODEL

David Street, a student at West Ridge Middle School in Austin, Texas, writes about a well-known short story in his paper. David recommends "asking yourself questions about the story" and "working through many drafts before the final copy." As you read his paper, ask yourself if David makes you want to read O. Henry's story, "After Twenty Years."

Evaluation of "After Twenty Years"
by David Street

I enjoyed reading the story "After Twenty Years" by O. Henry because of the surprising twist at the end. My attention was quickly absorbed when the policeman, Jimmy Wells, noticed his old friend Bob and started carrying on a conversation with him. Bob's quick talking in the beginning of the conversation caught my attention, and his unusual and suspicious story kept me listening. O. Henry set up the meeting with an appropriate setting, which helped to attract my attention. He described the weather as "chilly gusts of wind with a taste of rain in them," and he made the streets nearly vacant. This scenery gave an eerie feeling to help elaborate on the mystery. The characters were described enough to set up the reader but not too much. He described Bob as having "a pale, square-jawed face with keen eyes, and a little white scar near his right eyebrow." Then he told how his "scarfpin was a large diamond, oddly set." These details give the reader a subtle clue that Bob might be some sort of a gangster. The plot was well thought out and fairly easy to follow. It gave the reader many clues that led up to the surprise ending. Overall, I enjoyed "After Twenty Years" because of the suspense and the ending. I would recommend it to anyone who enjoys unexpected twists in stories.

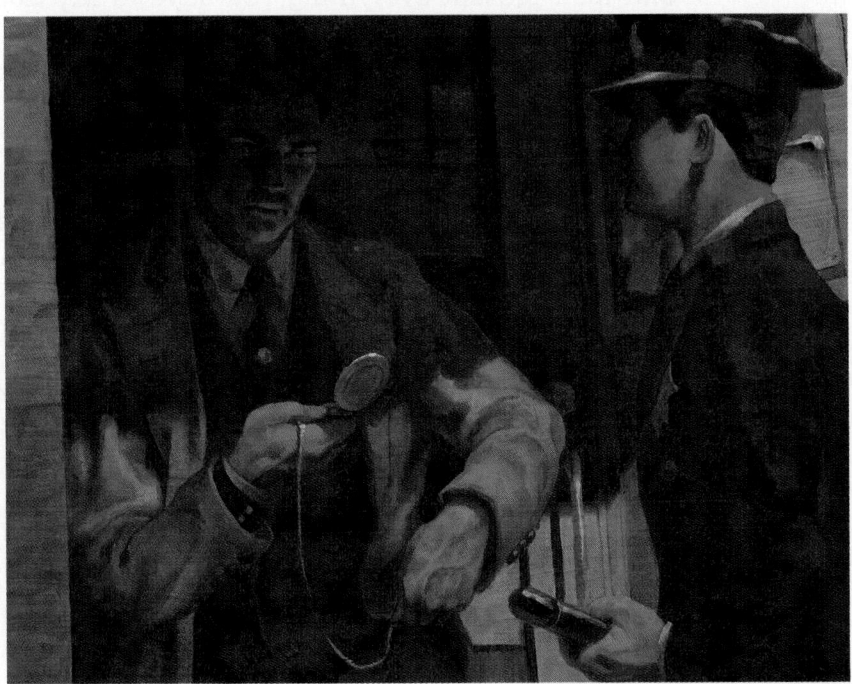

WRITING WORKSHOP

A Comparison of Two Characters

Sometimes you write an analysis of one character. But many times you can understand one character better by comparing him or her to another character.

When you compare two characters, you start by looking at their similarities. How are they alike? Sometimes you may also contrast them. How are they different?

When you write a paper or paragraph comparing two characters, you can organize it in one of two ways.

1. Present everything you have to say about one character, and then present everything you have to say about the other character, or
2. Present one detail about both characters, then a second detail about both characters, then a third detail about both characters, and so on.

Here's a writer's model comparing Martin in "The Medicine Bag" with the main character in "The All-American Slurp."

> Martin, a young boy whose ancestry is part Native American, is the main character in Virginia Driving Hawk Sneve's "The Medicine Bag." At the beginning of the story, he is embarrassed by his family background. Because his great-grandfather, called "Grandpa," doesn't look like the Indians in the movies, Martin is afraid his friends will laugh at him. The Chinese American girl in Lensey Namioka's "The All-American Slurp" is also embarrassed by her family background. At the beginning of the story she and her family are invited out to their first dinner in America. She feels her family has "disgraced" themselves because they don't know how to eat American food.

Both Martin and the Chinese American girl learn to be proud of their own families and heritage. Martin discovers that his friends really think Grandpa is great. He also listens to Grandpa tell about the medicine bag and begins to understand his heritage. The Chinese American girl learns that their American friends have as much trouble with chopsticks as her family had with the celery. She even discovers that the embarrassing sounds her family make when they eat soup, "Shloop, shloop," aren't so unusual. Her friend Meg makes the same sound when she drinks a milkshake. The Chinese American girl, like Martin, is no longer embarrassed by her heritage.

Thinking It Over

1. **In what ways are Martin and the Chinese American girl alike?**

2. **When you compare two things, you sometimes contrast (show differences) as well. Does this paper show any differences between the two characters? Can you think of any obvious differences?**

3. **How is this comparison paper organized? Did the writer use the first method or the second one (page 298)?**

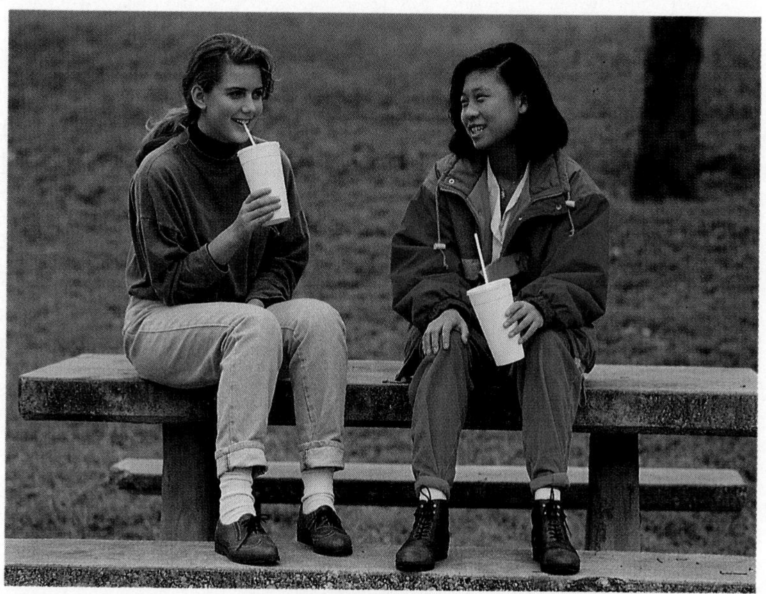

Writing a Comparison of Two Characters

Prewriting. Choose a character from another story to compare with the character in your analysis. The two characters should have something in common. They may face a similar conflict or be about the same age. For example, in the writer's model, both characters learn to be proud of their heritage.

Develop a chart like the one below. List the main traits the characters have in common. If there are important differences between them, list those too.

Martin	Chinese American girl
1. embarrassed by great-grandfather (false pride)	1. embarrassed by family
2. accepted his heritage (sincere pride)	2. accepted her heritage

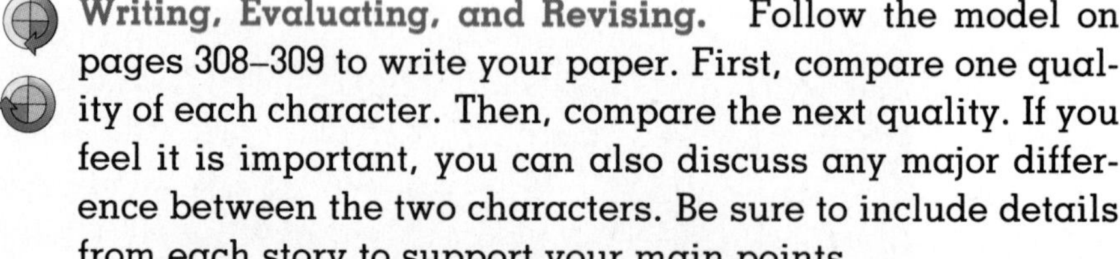

Writing, Evaluating, and Revising. Follow the model on pages 308–309 to write your paper. First, compare one quality of each character. Then, compare the next quality. If you feel it is important, you can also discuss any major difference between the two characters. Be sure to include details from each story to support your main points.

When you finish your draft, ask a classmate to read it. Have your reader tell you in his or her own words how your two characters are alike. Listen carefully. Take notes about anything your reader seems confused about. Then, make changes in your paper to help readers understand those points.

Proofreading and Publishing. Correct any mistakes in your paper, and then share it with your classmates. Did anyone else write about either of your characters?

MAKING CONNECTIONS

INFORMING THROUGH EVALUATION

Writing a Review

You have learned to analyze a story character by looking closely at his or her actions and words. People who write reviews of movies, books, or restaurants use similar methods. For example, a restaurant reviewer analyzes the quality of the food and service and makes an evaluation.

McHenry's Steak House

Subject Detail 1 Main idea	When you enter McHenry's Steak House, you're greeted warmly. The hosts make you feel as though you're a friend who has come to eat in their home. It's obvious from the start: This restaurant delivers more than just excellent food.
Detail 2	And the food *is* excellent. Especially good are the fresh swordfish and thick, juicy burgers. They are seasoned well and served with a big tossed salad and fresh vegetable. And if you aren't in the mood for these, try McHenry's special pizza for one. It's delicious!
Detail 3 Summing up	Prices at McHenry's are low. My meal came to only $8.95. This is a restaurant that you'll return to again and again. The people at McHenry's serve great food in a friendly way, without taking a big bite out of your budget.

Now, try your hand at writing a restaurant review. Pick a restaurant that you know well. It doesn't have to be a fancy one. You might write about a fast-food restaurant or even the school cafeteria!

Think of details to support your opinions. Be specific about the food, the service, the prices, and the appearance of the restaurant itself. Your audience will be your classmates. Give them a good "picture" of the restaurant. Through your writing, persuade them either to go to this restaurant or to avoid it!

WRITING ACROSS THE CURRICULUM

Analyzing Great Characters in History

You can use what you have learned about analyzing characters in literature to learn more about real people in history. You usually don't have any way of finding out what historical figures were thinking because you can't read their minds. But you can find out some of the things they said and did, as well as what other people said or wrote about them.

Pick some historical figure you have always been interested in—Abraham Lincoln, Pocahantas, Cleopatra, Martin Luther King, Jr. It's your decision. Then use your history book, encyclopedia articles, and biographies to catch up on the figure's personality. Was honesty really one of Lincoln's important character traits? Was Cleopatra a strong leader? Was Eleanor Roosevelt (pictured below) really one of the most active first ladies of all time? Decide which character trait seems to stand out or be most interesting in the figure you've chosen. Then choose one of the following ways to illustrate that trait:

1. Draw a picture showing the historical figure doing something that shows the trait.
2. Pretend you are the historical figure and write an entry in your diary. Use the figure's thoughts to show his or her character trait.
3. Write a dialogue between the historical figure you've chosen and someone else. Have your figure say something that shows the character trait.
4. Write a paragraph identifying the trait and telling about something the historical figure did that illustrates the trait.

10 WRITING A REPORT

Exploring Your World

The **world** around you is full of things to **explore** and learn about. Many of these wonders you'll be able to explore for yourself. Others you'll explore through the eyes of someone who wrote about them.

Writing and You. Reports are written summaries of someone's experience or knowledge. They allow scientists to tell us what they know about animals and the environment. Travel writers share their knowledge about distant lands in written reports. And we learn about the most distant planets in what is written about them. Reports are everywhere—in books, magazines, newspapers. What is the last thing you read a report about?

As You Read. Reports are based on fact. As you read the following report about the cheetah, look for the facts that help you learn more about this great animal.

Detail of poster commissioned for the National Forum on BioDiversity, Robert Goldstrom (1986).

from MEET-A-

Cheetah

BY FRED JOHNSON

All members of the cat family can move fast when they really want to. But there is one who can easily leave all the others far behind. In fact, he can leave any animal far behind. Nothing can outrun a cheetah (CHEE-tuh).

Cheetahs are found in Africa, in India, Afghanistan, and Arabia. Some scientists think that the cheetah is between the cat and dog families. They have the body build of dogs rather than cats.

Their claws, like dogs', are dull. And they cannot be pulled back into the paw. Their claws are of little use in fighting or killing. But like all cats, cheetahs have one claw that is very sharp and dangerous. This is a claw on the inside of the foreleg, something like your thumb. It can be pulled into the paw.

The cheetah's sense of smell is poor, but its eyesight is keen. Its fur is brownish-yellow with black or brown "polka dots." A clear black line runs from the inside corner of each eye down the side of the nose. A full-grown cheetah may measure as much as 7 feet long with his tail outstretched. How tall is the door to your room? A cheetah may be as long as your door is tall.

One surprising fact about the cheetah is that it can be tamed easily. Once it has become used to people, it seems to enjoy being a member of a human family.

The cheetah is also one of the few big cats which purrs when happy, just as a pet cat does. However, its purr is far louder and sounds more like an engine.

But the most amazing thing about cheetahs is their speed. They have been timed at speeds up to 80 miles an hour! Daniel P. Mannix is an animal owner and trainer. He tells of a cheetah which saw a man going down the road on a motorcycle. The cheetah went out to look at this strange, noisy animal. The man speeded up to 60 miles an hour—and the cheetah ran along beside him!

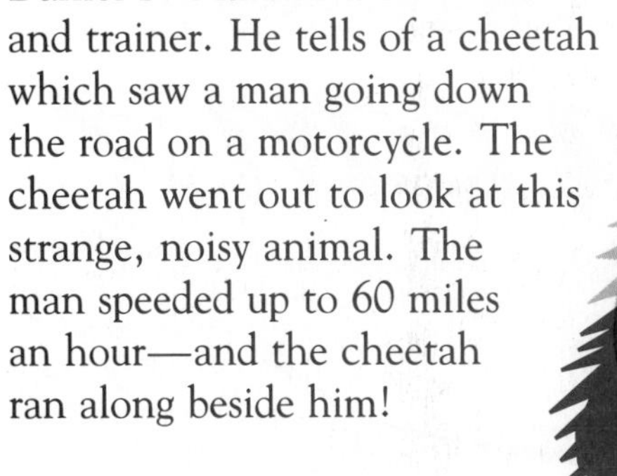

Reader's Response

1. What facts about the cheetah seem unusual or surprising to you? Would you like to read more about the animal? Why?
2. A *fact* can be something you observe directly—for example, that your cat has gray fur and likes milk. In your journal jot down some facts you know about a cat, dog, or some other pet.
3. Would you like to have a cheetah for a pet? Why?

Writer's Craft

4. What facts did you learn about the cheetah's length? about its speed?
5. One source for this report is an animal expert named Daniel P. Mannix. What information does he give about the cheetah?

"Nothing can outrun a cheetah"

Ways to Develop a Report

Reports come in many forms. You will read them in magazines and newspapers. You'll see them when you watch a television news show or a science program like *NOVA.* And you can even get them by telephone if you call for a weather report. All these kinds of reports give you information, developed in different ways. Here are some ways to develop a report.

Narration: telling about how the Spanish settled Saint Augustine; telling about the life of a civil rights leader.

Description: describing the Anasazi cliff dwellings; describing how the ruby-throated hummingbird looks.

Classification: comparing cheetahs with house cats; reporting on a member of the skink (a type of lizard) family.

Evaluation: reporting on the quality of various brands of portable radios; reporting on a series of tests about the durability of certain bicycles.

In this chapter, you'll learn how to gather information about a subject. Tons of information—much more than a human brain can hold—are stored away every week in sources like books and tapes. Writing a report lets you use those storehouses of information.

LOOKING AHEAD

In the main assignment in this chapter, you will write a short, informative report. You'll use the strategy of narration or classification. Remember that a report

- gives information about a subject
- uses a variety of sources
- lists the sources of the information

Writing a Report

Choosing and Narrowing a Subject

What causes earthquakes? Do vampire bats really exist? When did dogs first become pets? Who invented tab-top cans for carbonated soda? Writing a report is your chance to learn about an interesting subject.

Choosing Your Subject

To choose a subject, think about your interests. What kinds of books or magazines do you like to read? What kinds of subjects do you like hearing about on television programs like *NOVA* or *National Geographic World*? Do you have special collections of things like stamps or insects? What subjects do you enjoy talking, thinking, and wondering about?

Here are some ideas for general subjects. Try to think of three or four other subjects you'd like to learn more about.

dinosaurs	ancient kingdoms
pyramids	bats
early explorers of the United States	Native Americans
	the Old West
the Civil War	exploring space

Narrowing Your Subject

You probably realize that there's a great deal of information about a broad subject like dinosaurs—hundreds of books, articles, and TV programs. That's way too much information to try to sift through and include in a short report. You need to narrow broad subjects by focusing on just one part. The subjects you've just read include many smaller *topics*. On the next page you'll find some of them.

why dinosaurs disappeared
the pyramids of Egypt
the Spanish explorer Ponce de León
photography in the Civil War
the ancient kingdom of Kush
vampire bats
the Cherokee "Trail of Tears"
African American cowboys in the Old West
the first moon landing

As you narrow your subject, remember that any broad subject includes many smaller topics. For example, the subject "dinosaurs" also includes these topics: renaming the brontosaurus, famous dinosaur discoveries, and forms of protection against enemies.

Not all topics work equally well for a report. Here are some questions that will help you figure out if your topic will work for a report.

- Can you find facts about your topic? (*Facts* are information that experts have checked and believe is true.)
- Can you find enough information about your topic? (If your topic is *too* narrow, you may not find enough information.)
- Will you have enough time to find the information you need? (If you write a letter to get information, how long will it take to get an answer?)
- Is your topic interesting enough to hold your attention? (You'll put a great deal of time and effort into your report. If you like your topic, you'll be more willing to put the time and effort into it.)

EXERCISE 1 Choosing Topics for a Report

What's a good topic? Here are some topics for a report. Get together with one or two classmates and discuss each topic. Try to decide which topics are suitable for a short report. Can you find facts about the topic from sources like books or videotapes? Is it narrow enough? Is it appropriate for a report?

1. robots for surgery
2. why I like soccer
3. space—the final frontier
4. Egyptian mummies
5. Sarah Winnemucca, a Native American hero
6. the history of horses
7. Mexican birthday customs
8. my most exciting birthday
9. the killer fish—the piranha
10. schools in Japan

WRITING ASSIGNMENT

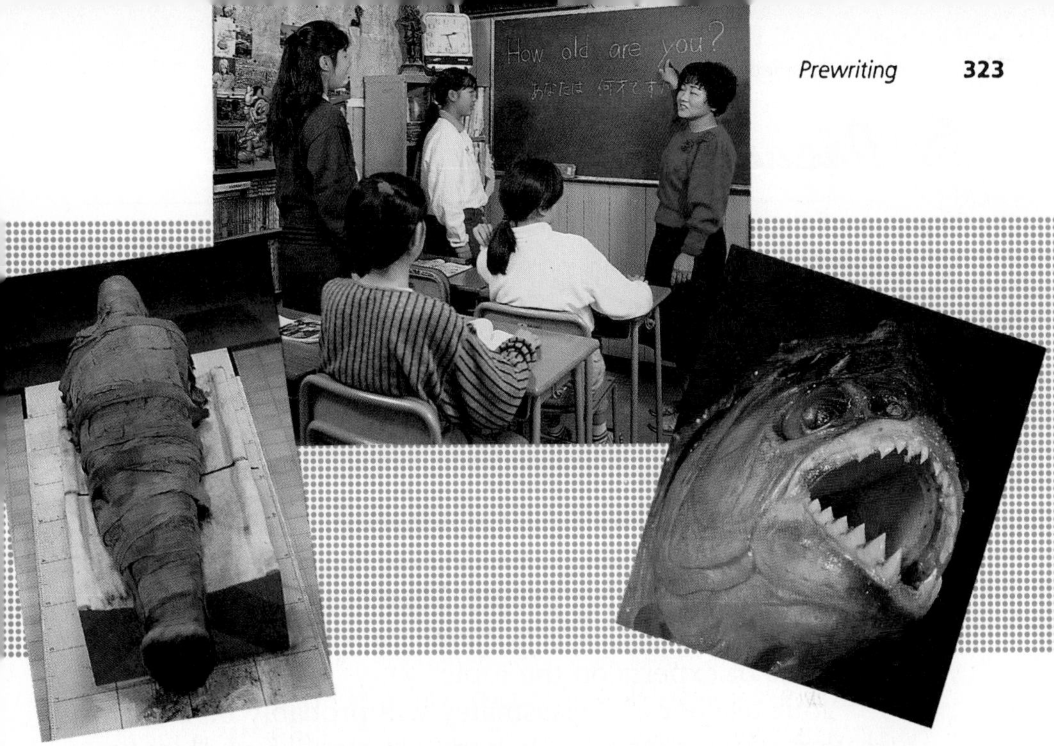

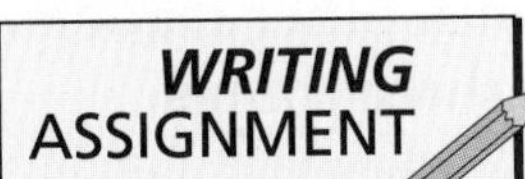

PART 1:
Choosing a Topic for Your Report

What would you like to know more about? Think of a subject you're interested in. Then narrow it to a topic for your report. Check your library to be sure it's a topic you can find facts about.

WRITING NOTE

Writing a report takes more time than one or two days. Don't try to do most of your report in one weekend. To do a good job in the time you have, make a schedule now. Then, stick to it. In your schedule, allow time to do five things:

1. Find information about your topic.
2. Take notes about the information.
3. Write your first draft.
4. Evaluate and revise your draft.
5. Proofread and publish your report.

Planning Your Report

When is the last time you planned a surprise for someone? You probably planned it carefully ahead of time so that it would work out just right. If you plan your report ahead, it should work out right, too.

Thinking About Audience and Purpose

The purpose for writing a report is to discover information and share it with other people. Most of the information in a report is made up of facts. Some information may be the opinions of experts on the topic.

Your teacher and classmates will probably be the first readers of your report. (On page 346, you'll find ideas you can use to share your report with other readers.) As you write your report, think about three things.

1. What information will interest your readers?
2. What do your readers already know?
3. What information do your readers need?

Reports are boring to readers if they already know all the facts you give, so look for new or unusual information about your topic. Try to give your readers all the information they need to understand the topic. If you think they may not know a word, tell them what it means. If they may not understand how something works, explain it to them.

EXERCISE 2 **Deciding About Audience and Purpose**

On the next page is some information you might put in a report on giant snakes. You are writing this report to give both your teacher and classmates facts about the snakes. Which information would you put in your report? Why wouldn't you include the other information?

1. *Giant* means "big."
2. One giant snake, the anaconda, can be as long as thirty feet.
3. I hate snakes.
4. Boa constrictor babies are born live; python babies are hatched from eggs.
5. There are many kinds of snakes.

▲ **boa constrictor** babies are born live

python babies are hatched from eggs ▼

Asking Questions

What would you like to know about your topic? What would your readers like to know? Make a list of questions that will help you find this information. First try the *5W-How?* questions—*Who? What? When? Where? Why? How?* Which questions you ask will depend on your topic. For a report on Africanized honeybees, also called "killer" bees, you might ask these questions.

What are Africanized honeybees?
When will they come here?
Where do they come from?
Why are they called "killer" bees?
How are they different from native bees?
How can they be stopped?

If you don't know much about your topic, you may want to get some general information about it first. You can read one or two encyclopedia articles about your topic, or you can watch a videotape about it. You might also talk to other people who know about the topic. Then make your list of questions.

PART 2:
Asking Questions About Your Topic

What do you want to know about your topic? What do you think your readers will want to know? Make a list of *5W-How?* questions that you'll answer in your report.

Finding Sources

Reading and Viewing. It's generally a good idea to have at least three sources of information for your report. If you use only one or two sources, you'll only be repeating what someone else has already said. When you use more sources, you can combine facts and opinions in new ways.

The library is a good place to start your hunt for information. It's full of ***print sources*** like encyclopedias, books, magazines and newspapers, and pamphlets. And don't forget about ***nonprint sources*** like videotapes, audiotapes, slides, and even CDs. (For help in finding and using library sources, see pages 816–822.)

Other places to look for information depend on your topic. You might check radio and TV guides for programs that will give you some information. You can also find videotapes about many science and history topics in local video stores. Here are some ideas for other places to look for sources.

museums	hospitals	bookstores
government offices	planetariums	zoos

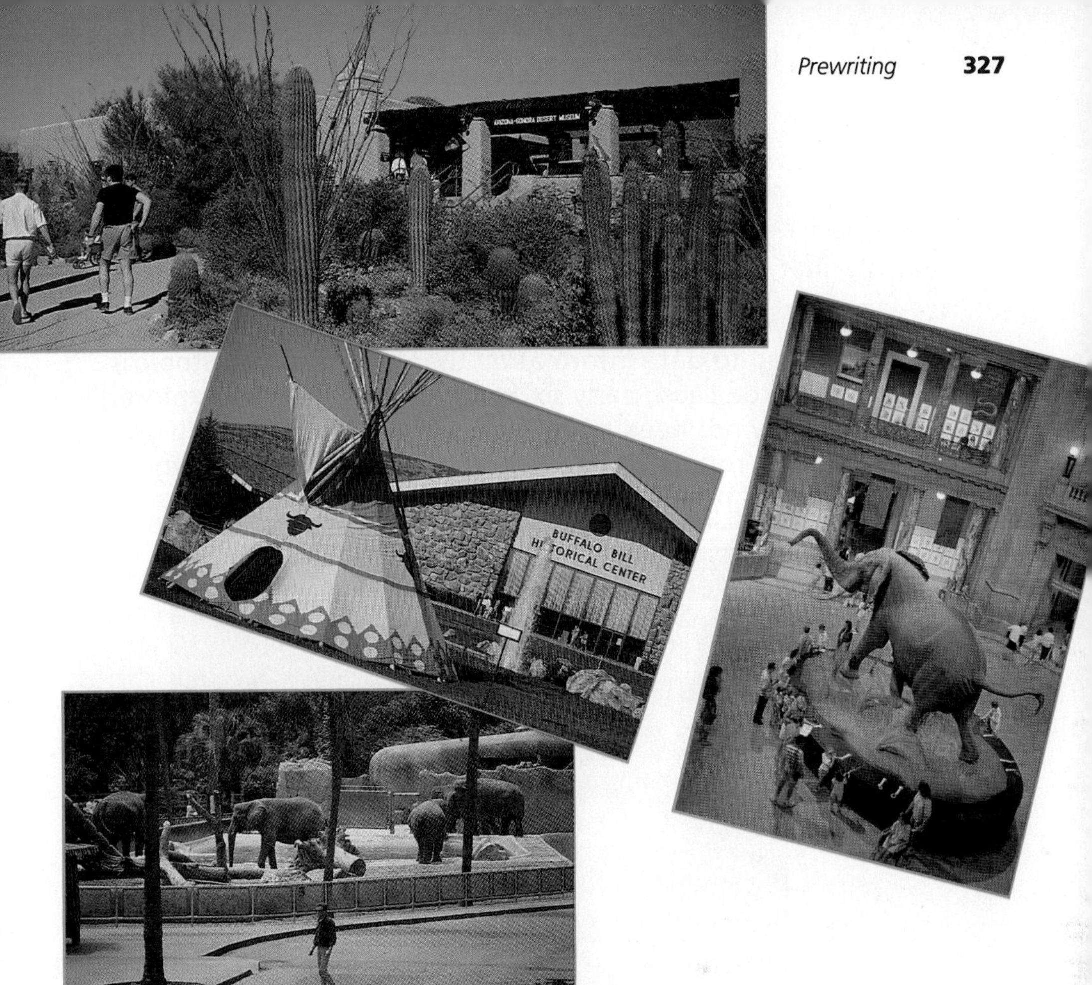

Interviewing. Here's an idea for a nonprint source. Interview someone who's an expert on your topic, perhaps a teacher, someone at a zoo or museum, or even a parent or high school student. It's only important that this person know a great deal about your topic. Suppose your topic is "mountain bikes." Your expert might be a bike store owner or a high school student who has taken trips on a mountain bike.

Before the interview do some reading about your topic. Make a list of questions to ask. Write each question at the top of a sheet of paper. To avoid *yes* or *no* answers, ask questions that begin with *Who, What, When, Where, Why,* and *How.* (For more information about interviewing, see page 811.)

Not all sources will be helpful to you. To judge how useful a source is, ask yourself these questions about it.

- *Is the information up-to-date?* Some topics simply need more up-to-date information than others. If your topic is "Ponce de León, early sixteenth-century Spanish explorer," you may not need many recent books and articles. If your topic is "robots and people who have disabilities," you will need new information.

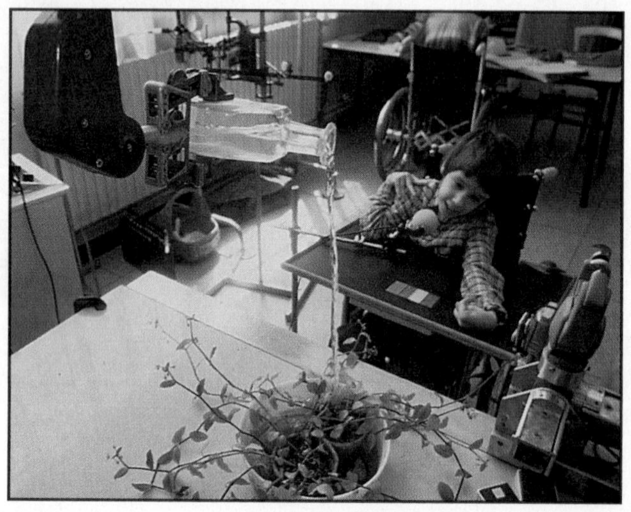

- *Can you trust the information?* Some sources give a truer picture of the facts than others. You can usually trust reference books more than the magazines you buy at the grocery store checkout stand. Can you tell why?

EXERCISE 3 **Speaking and Listening: Interviewing**

Practice your interviewing skills with a classmate. Ask a classmate to name a special interest, such as soccer, collecting stamps, or horror movies. Make out a list of *5W-How?* questions about the topic. Then interview your classmate about that topic. When you finish, change places and let your classmate interview you.

Listing Sources

The next step is to list each of your sources. Then, give each source a number. You'll use these *source numbers* later when you take notes. There are several different ways to list sources. The following chart shows the way the Modern Language Association recommends.

MLA GUIDE FOR LISTING SOURCES

Books. Give this information: author, title, city of publication, publisher, and copyright year.

Pringle, Laurence. Here Come the Killer Bees. New York: William Morrow, 1986.

Magazines and Newspapers. Give this information: author, title of article, name of magazine or newspaper, date, and page numbers.

Alper, Joseph. "The Big Sting." Health Apr. 1989: 53–54.

Sidener, Jonathan. " 'Killer Bees' May Reach Arizona Within a Year." The Arizona Republic 25 Oct. 1990: A1.

Encyclopedia Articles. Give this information: author, title of article, name of encyclopedia, year and edition (ed.).

Heinrich, Bernd. "Bee." The World Book Encyclopedia. 1990 ed.

Interviews. Give this information: expert's name, the words *Personal interview* or *Telephone interview,* and date.

Hardy, Ann. Telephone interview. 12 Dec. 1990.

Television or Radio Programs. Give this information: the title of the program, the producer or director if available, the network, the local station call letters and city, and the date of broadcast.

Living with Killer Bees. Prod. Tony Burden. PBS. KUHT, Houston. 24 Nov. 1991.

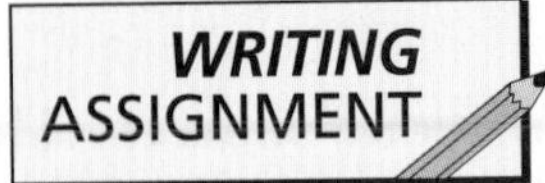

PART 3:
Finding and Listing Sources for Your Report

Where can you find information? What books and articles does your library have? Can you find a videotape about your topic? Do you know someone you can interview? Find three or four different sources of information about your topic. Then use the forms you've just read about on page 329 to list them.

Taking Notes

Now you're ready to start gathering information from your sources. Be sure to keep your list of questions in mind as you work. Your questions will help keep you focused on gathering the information you need to write about your topic. Here are some other tips for taking good notes.

- Write your notes on 4″ × 6″ cards or on sheets of paper.
- Use abbreviations and short phrases. You can also make lists of details and ideas. You don't have to write complete sentences.
- Use your own words unless the exact words in the source are especially interesting.
- Put quotation marks around an author's or interviewee's exact words. (Not using quotation marks around someone else's words is called ***plagiarism.*** Plagiarizing is not identifying the source of ideas and words that are not your own.)
- Write the source number you're using at the top of the note card or piece of paper. You'll use that number later when you try to recall where you got your information.
- Give each note a short label telling what the note is about. Write each label at the top of each card or piece of paper.
- At the bottom of the card, write the page number(s) where you found the information.

These two examples show you how to take notes.

How Different 2

Africanized bees chase 1/2 mi.
Native bees lose interest
after a few yds.

p. 54

label/source number

note written in your own words

page number(s)

This note is from the second source (see page 329), a magazine article titled "The Big Sting," by Joseph Alper. Notice how the card includes a label, a source number, and a page number. This information will come in handy later when the writer is planning and writing the report.

Where They'll Go 1

Where there are mild winters:
Fla., Ga., Miss., La., Tex., Ariz.,
Calif., Va., N.C., S.C.

p. 35

label/source number

note written in your own words

page number(s)

This note is from the first source (see page 329), a book titled *Here Come the Killer Bees,* by Laurence Pringle. Notice how the writer uses abbreviations. This simplifies note taking. (Just be sure you understand the abbreviations you use!)

To keep from getting confused

- don't put notes from different sources on the same card or sheet of paper
- don't place notes in your own words and quotations on the same card or sheet of paper
- do use a new card or sheet of paper whenever you write a new label

REFERENCE NOTE: For more help with taking notes, see pages 854–855.

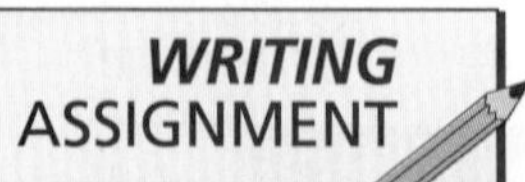

PART 4:
Taking Notes for Your Report

What interesting information can you gather about your topic? Take notes from the sources you listed for Writing Assignment, Part 3 (page 330). Use half-sheets of paper if you don't have note cards. Save your notes to use in writing your report.

Organizing and Outlining Your Information

By now you've found most of the information you will use in your report. The next step is to organize your notes into groups, like an *early plan* (see pages 100–101), and to make an *outline.* First, sort through your note cards or sheets of paper. (You want to figure out what note cards deal with the same or similar information.) Make several stacks. In each stack put notes that have the same or similar labels. Then, decide on a heading for each stack.

The headings of your stacks are the main ideas for your report. Decide how you will arrange these ideas in your report. Which ones will come first? last? What order of ideas will help your readers understand your topic? The writer of the killer bee report arranged headings this way, making an ***early plan*** for the report.

Nature of the bees
History of the bees
Africanized bees in the United States
Attempts to stop the bees
Ways to protect people

Next, make an ***outline*** for your report. You already have the main headings. These directions can help you with the rest of the outline.

1. Go through each stack of notes. Take out notes that aren't about the heading.
2. Put the rest of the notes in the order you'll discuss them in your report.
3. Use these notes to make subheadings for your outline.

The example on the next page shows how you might write your outline.

The Invasion of the Killer Bees

I. Nature of the bees
  A. Behavior of United States bees and killer bees
    1. Gentleness of United States bees
    2. Fierceness of Africanized bees
  B. Danger of United States bees and killer bees
    1. Little danger of United States bees
    2. Great danger of Africanized bees

II. History of Africanized bees
  A. Import of African bees to Brazil in 1956
  B. Escape of queen bees
  C. Spread of bees

III. Africanized bees in the United States
  A. Movement to western and southern states
  B. Effects on honey industry
  C. Effects on agriculture

IV. Attempts to stop Africanized bees
  A. Attempts to crossbreed bees
  B. Attempts to kill bees

V. Ways to protect people
  A. Knowledge about bees
  B. Advice from beekeeper

REFERENCE NOTE: For more help with making an early plan and outlining, see pages 100–102.

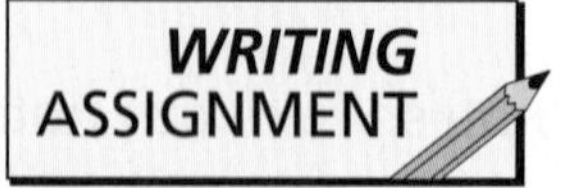

PART 5:
Writing an Outline for Your Report

You probably have many pieces of information for your report. Now you need to organize these pieces into groups and put them in order by writing an outline. You don't need to include everything in your outline. Just use headings and subheadings that will guide you when you write.

Writing Your First Draft

In one way, a report is not very different from other compositions you write. Like them, it has an introduction, a body, and a conclusion. The difference is that you use information from outside sources in your report. At the end of the report, you write a list of your sources to show readers where you found the information. That way, interested readers can look up your sources if they want to.

Understanding the Parts of a Report

Title Page. A report printed in a newspaper or magazine doesn't need a title page; it just needs a title. But reports that stand alone, like a school report or a business report, often need a cover page. On the cover page you put your name, the title of your report, the date, and any other information your teacher recommends.

Introduction. The ***introduction*** of the report isn't in your outline. It's a short opening paragraph where you do two things:

- catch your reader's attention
- tell what the report is about

Notice the introduction in the sample report on page 338. The writer first catches the reader's attention with a vivid example of attacking bees. At the same time, she introduces the topic of her report—Africanized honeybees, also known as "killer" bees.

Body. The ***body*** of the report contains paragraphs that discuss the information on your note cards and outline. The body of the sample report on pages 338–341 has nine paragraphs. Your own report may be shorter. Each paragraph should have enough information to inform readers about the main idea of each paragraph.

Conclusion. The *conclusion* is the final paragraph of your report, where you sum up your ideas. You may want to state the main idea of your report in a new way. Without writing the words *The End,* make sure your readers know your report is finished.

REFERENCE NOTE: For more information on how to write the introduction, body, and conclusion, look at Chapter 3, "Learning About Compositions," pages 104–110.

List of Sources. What if your readers want to know where they can find out more about your topic? They can turn to your *list of sources,* the place where you list the information about the sources you've used. After your conclusion, begin a new page. At the top of the paper, write the words *Works Cited.* (Some people use the word *Bibliography,* but it refers only to print sources like books.) List your sources in alphabetical order by the author's last name. If there is no author, alphabetize by the first word in the title.

List your sources in the way described on page 329. The Works Cited page of the sample report on page 341 shows you how to do this.

CRITICAL THINKING

Synthesizing Information

To *synthesize* means "to combine different things in a new way." A green plant synthesizes light, water, carbon dioxide, and certain minerals to make food. A music video synthesizes music, dance, and special effects to make a "mini-movie." When you write a report, you synthesize the information in your notes. You use other people's ideas, but you put them together in a new way.

On the next page there are some notes for the report on killer bees.

Bees in the United States 1

Where they'll go depends on mild winters.
Could live year-round in parts of the U.S.: as far north as San Francisco and S. Maryland, all Ala., Miss., La., Tex., Ariz., Va., N.C. & S.C.

pp. 34-35

This paragraph from the sample report on page 340 shows how this information is put into the writer's own words. This is a synthesis of the information.

Killer bees can live where the winters are mild. They will be year-round residents as far north as San Francisco and southern Maryland. They will also live all year in southern Texas and in Arizona, Alabama, Mississippi, Louisiana, Virginia, North Carolina, and South Carolina. In the summer, killer bees will live even in the northern states. They will die off there when it gets cold.

CRITICAL THINKING EXERCISE: Synthesizing Your Notes

Go over your notes under one heading of your outline. Try out different ways of putting the notes into your own words. Make up sentences that include the information you found. Next, get together with a partner and read your paragraph aloud as he or she listens and makes suggestions for changes. Then, exchange places with your partner and do the same with your partner's notes.

Writing Your Report

Use your outline as a guide while you write. You may want to turn each of the main headings in your outline into a topic sentence for a paragraph. (Be sure that each sentence has a subject and a verb.) The subheadings can become the details for each paragraph.

You can use the following sample report as a model for your own. Remember that your report doesn't have to be this long. Writing a good, short report can teach you just as much as writing a longer one.

A WRITER'S MODEL

The Invasion of the Killer Bees

INTRODUCTION
Main idea
Attention grabber

Very soon, much of the United States may be invaded by fierce Africanized honeybees from Brazil called "killer" bees. The invasion seems like a horror movie. In such a movie, millions of bees are attacking the people. They try to run, but there are so many bees that they can't see. They are stung over and over and over!

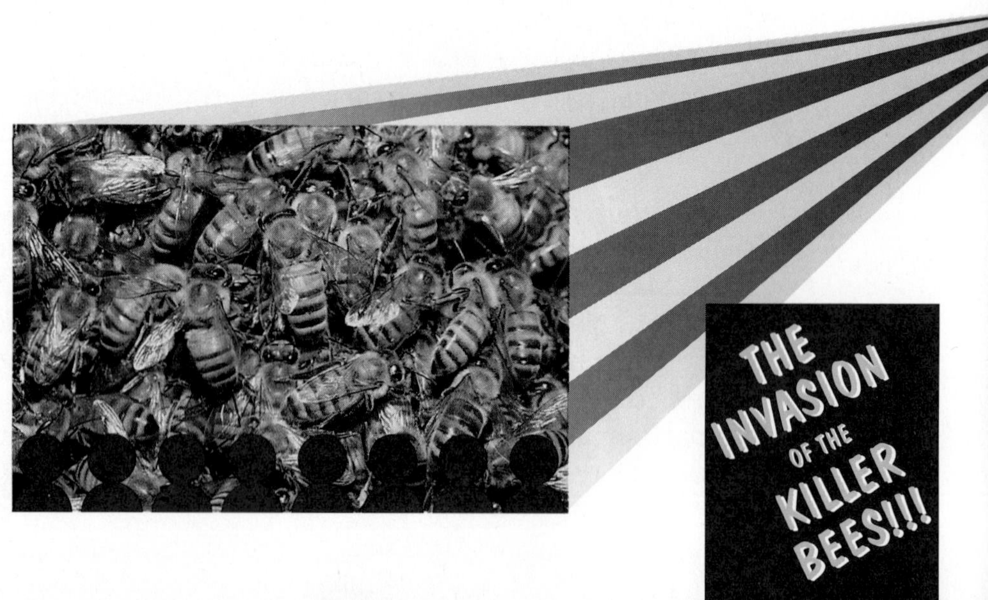
THE
INVASION
OF THE
KILLER
BEES!!!

BODY
Nature of the bees

The Africanized bees are very different from native bees that live in the United States. These bees, which first came from Europe, live mostly in hives and hollow trees. They have few enemies and are usually gentle. In Africa, honeybees build their nests in the open because the weather is so warm. To protect their nests, they have become very fierce.

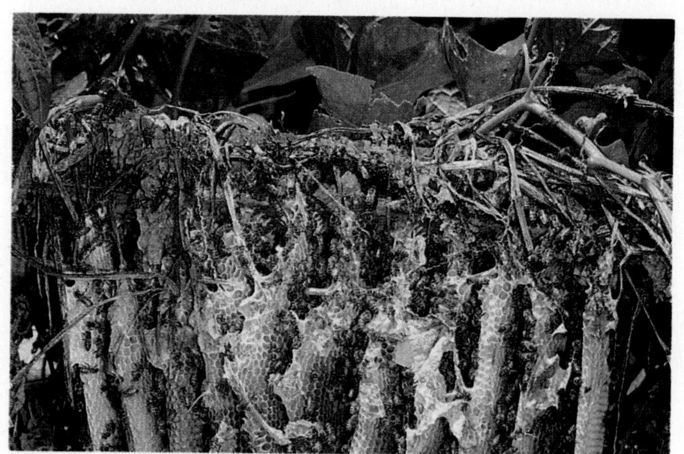

Killer bees are extremely nervous, and they are also fighters. Native bees chase people for a yard or so when they are bothered. Africanized bees, however, will chase for more than half a mile. Their poison is not different from the poison of ordinary bees, but they come after people in a big swarm. No one can survive a hundred or more stings. Dr. Kenneth Schuberth of the Johns Hopkins Medical Institutions says, "When you get that much venom in your system at once, it's like receiving a giant snake bite."

History of killer bees

The invasion of the killer bees began in 1956. In that year a scientist in Brazil imported seventy-five fierce queen bees from Africa. He wanted to crossbreed them with peaceful European bees. Twenty-six of these African bees accidentally escaped in 1957. They began attacking and killing animals and people.

The descendants of the African bees are the killer bees. They spread all over South America, flying more than five thousand miles in thirty years. Some of them have already crossed the United States' border. Many more of them will be here by the mid-1990s.

Killer bees in the United States

Killer bees can live where the winters are mild. They will be year-round residents as far north as San Francisco and southern Maryland. They will also live all year in southern Texas and in Arizona, Alabama, Mississippi, Louisiana, Virginia, North Carolina, and South Carolina. In the summer killer bees will live even in the northern states. They will die off there when it gets cold.

The invasion of the killer bees is serious. They kill people and animals, and they could ruin the honey industry. This industry is worth 150 million dollars a year. Wherever killer bees have gone, many beekeepers have changed jobs. Also, many crops cannot be grown without the pollinating that native bees do. After killer bees get here, fruits and vegetables may become much more expensive.

Attempts to stop the bees

Scientists have tried to tame the killer bees. The United States Department of Agriculture has tried to mate them with the European bees, which are much more peaceful. The results have not been too good because the resulting bees are still very fierce. There has also been an attempt to kill the bees. So far, the USDA has trapped and destroyed 13,700 swarms of killer bees in Mexico.

Ways to protect people

There is some hope. Most deaths from killer bees happen in the first four years after they come to a new place. Then people learn how to avoid them. Also, killer bees may become more peaceful in cool weather.

In an interview, a beekeeper had some advice about preparing for killer bees. She pointed out that people who live in South America have learned how to deal with African bees. Only strangers to these bees and their ways get killed.

According to the beekeeper, here's what to do once the killer bees get here. She said, "When you see a bee, run as far and as fast as you can. Run behind things that block the bee's vision. Run to a house. Then call the fire department."

CONCLUSION
Restatement of main idea

The fierce killer bees are on their way through the United States. If people are not ready for them, they can cause great harm to the honey industry and to agriculture. Killer bees can seriously hurt or even kill people. Will this country be ready for them?

Works Cited

Alper, Joseph. "The Big Sting." Health Apr. 1989: 53–54.

Hardy, Ann. Telephone interview. 12 Dec. 1990.

Kerby, Mona. Friendly Bees, Ferocious Bees. New York: Franklin Watts, 1987.

Patoski, Joe Nick. "Killer Buzz." Texas Monthly Dec. 1990: 104.

Pringle, Laurence. Here Come the Killer Bees. New York: William Morrow, 1986.

MECHANICS HINT

Punctuating Titles

In a printed book or magazine, italics are used to identify titles of books and magazines. In a handwritten or typewritten report, underlining does the same thing. In your report or list of sources, underline the title of each book, magazine, or encyclopedia. Notice this, however: don't underline the title of your own report or the titles of articles. Put quotation marks around the titles of articles in magazines or encyclopedias.

EXAMPLES **Book:**

Pringle, Laurence. Here Come the Killer Bees. New York: William Morrow, 1986.

Magazine:

Alper, Joseph. "The Big Sting." Health Apr. 1989: 53–54.

Encyclopedia:

Heinrich, Bernd. "Bee." The World Book Encyclopedia. 1990 ed.

REFERENCE NOTE: For more help with punctuating titles, see pages 735–736 and 743–744.

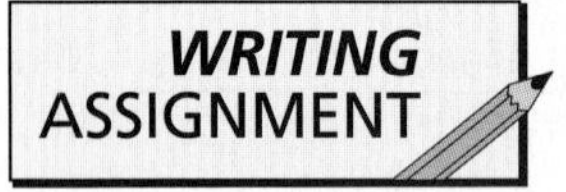

PART 6:

Writing Your First Draft

Using your notes and outline as a guide, write your first draft. Remember that it doesn't have to be as long as the sample report. At the end of your report, list your sources on a Works Cited page.

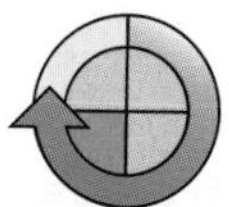

Evaluating and Revising

After you've written your first draft, put it away for a day. Then use the chart below to evaluate and improve it. Ask yourself each question at the left. Whenever you answer a question no, use the technique in the right-hand column to revise your report.

EVALUATING AND REVISING REPORTS

	EVALUATION GUIDE	REVISION TECHNIQUE
1	Does the report use at least three different sources?	**Add** sources. Try to use at least one nonprint source.
2	Does the report have enough information?	**Add** facts or the ideas of an expert.
3	Does the report give credit to an author's words?	**Add** quotation marks where you use someone's words.
4	Is information in the report clearly organized?	**Reorder** paragraphs so that the order of ideas is clear.
5	Does an interesting intro-duction give the report's topic?	**Add** (or rewrite) a sentence that tells your main idea.
6	Does a conclusion let readers know the report is over?	**Add** eye-catching details. **Add** a paragraph that summarizes or restates the main idea.
7	Does a list of sources in the correct form end the report?	**Add** a list of your sources. Use the form on page 341.

EXERCISE 4 Analyzing a Writer's Revisions

Before you revise your own draft, look at the changes another writer made. Working with a partner, study the writer's changes to one paragraph in the report on killer bees. Then answer the questions that follow. You and your partner might compare your answers to another pair's answers. Do your answers agree?

No one can survive a hundred or more stings. Killer bees are extremely nervous, and they are also fighters. Native bees chase people (for a yard or so) when they are bothered. Africanized bees, however, will chase for more than half a mile. Their poison is not different from the poison of ordinary bees, but they come after people in a big swarm. ~~I wouldn't want them chasing after me!~~ Dr. Kenneth Schuberth of the Johns Hopkins Medical Institutions says, "When you get that much venom in your system at once, it's like receiving a giant snake bite."

reorder | add | cut | add | add

1. Why did the writer move the first sentence to a new place in the paragraph? Where does it make more sense?
2. Why did the writer add the words *for a yard or so* to the third sentence? [Hint: Does the reader need this information?]
3. Why did the writer cut the sentence *I wouldn't want them chasing after me!*? [Hint: Does this sentence give a fact or an expert's ideas? How does this sentence change the way the paragraph sounds?]
4. Why did the writer add quotation marks to the last sentence?

EXERCISE 5 Evaluating a Report

Have you ever heard the song "Swing Low, Sweet Chariot"? It's a spiritual, a song first sung by slaves. Here's a paragraph from a report on spirituals. Get together with one or two classmates, and evaluate the paragraph. What are its weaknesses? What changes should be made? Use the evaluating and revising chart on page 343 to decide.

Spirituals were sung by slaves on southern plantations. Frederick Douglass, a former slave, said, Slaves are generally expected to sing as well as to work. Most of the songs were very sorrowful. Many of these spirituals are still sung today. They were often about a better life to come. Some of the spirituals had codes in them.

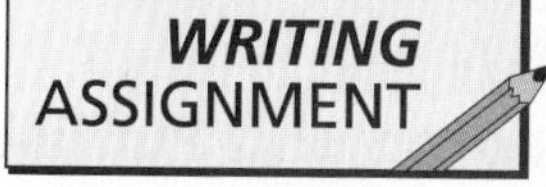

PART 7:

Evaluating and Revising Your Report

What changes will you make in your first draft to improve it? Read your report to a small group of classmates. Listen carefully to their suggestions. You might even want to take notes on what they like and dislike about your report. Then use the chart on page 343 to evaluate and revise the draft by yourself.

Proofreading and Publishing

Read your report carefully to make sure it has no mistakes in spelling, capitalization, usage, and punctuation. Then, think of a way to share your report. Here are two ideas.

- Bind all the reports in your class on similar subjects (such as animals or ancient cultures) into a book. (You can use staples or different kinds of report binders.) Number the pages in order from first to last page in the book. Make up a table of contents page and add it to the binder. Then decide on a title for the book of reports. Give a copy of the book to your school library.
- If your topic is about science or history, volunteer to give an oral report in your science or history class. Use the information in your report to prepare your talk.

PART 8:
Proofreading and Publishing Your Report

Now you're ready for the final touches. Make a clean copy of your report and proofread it carefully. Then use one of the ideas above or one of your own to share your report. Give a copy of your report to anyone you interviewed for information. (It's the courteous thing to do.)

WRITING WORKSHOP

A Book Report

You and your friends probably talk about the movies you've seen. When you do, you usually say whether the movie is worth seeing. What you're doing is giving a movie review. One kind of book report is like a movie review. It evaluates (judges) the book and tells whether the writer thinks the book is worth reading.

How do you evaluate a book? You can start with whether or not you liked it. But most readers want a little more information. Here are some questions you can ask yourself to evaluate a book.

1. *Do the characters seem like real people?*
2. *Do they change or grow in some way?*
3. *Why do events in the novel happen? Is there a reason, or do they happen by accident?*
4. *What's the novel's main idea, or theme? Does it apply to real life?*
5. *Does the book have suspense? Did it keep my interest?*

If you answer most of these questions yes, the book is probably very good. It's worth reading. If you answer most of them no, you probably shouldn't recommend the book to others.

Now back to your book report. How do you put it together? First, you have to get your readers' attention. Then, you have to let them know what book you are writing about. (Tell them the book's author and title.) After that you can begin to let them know your recommendation as you tell a little about the plot and characters. Don't tell too much, though. You don't want to spoil the suspense for someone who might read the book.

A sample book report appears on the next page. As you read it, look for the writer's recommendation.

Carlota, a Woman of Courage

Have you ever dived for sunken treasure? Ridden in a horse race? Faced a hostile army? The main character of Carlota, by Scott O'Dell, does all these things and more. Carlota is a good, exciting novel that readers will enjoy.

Carlota is about a young woman named Carlota de Zubarán, who lives with her grandmother and her father in California. The novel takes place in the last part of the 1848 war between the United States and Mexico. At that time, California was still a part of Mexico. Carlota's family, whose Spanish ancestors settled Mexico, is on the side of Mexico.

In many ways Carlota is like my friends and me. Sometimes she does not get along with the adults around her. For example, Carlota enjoys riding her horse out on the ranch with her father. This bothers her grandmother who wants her to dress and behave like a young woman. Later, in a serious incident, Carlota stands up to her father. Not knowing the war is over, some American soldiers are making their way to California. Carlota's father and some other ranchers track the soldiers and attack them. Carlota wounds one of the soldiers with her lance and then insists on taking care of him. This makes her father very angry.

The main idea of this novel is that sometimes courage means standing up for what you believe. This is harder to do when other people do not feel the same way you do. At first, Carlota hates the Americans because her father does. Then she realizes that the American she has wounded is also a human being, and she takes care of him. To do this, she must show courage and stand up against her father. As Carlota says, "I was ashamed, now, of what I had tried to do. The shame gave me courage" (125). In real life, there are many times when you must show this kind of courage.

Carlota is very suspenseful; it holds the reader's interest. Carlota has many adventures and many close calls. One of these adventures is the horse race at her sister's wedding. She has a dangerous fall from her horse, but she goes on to win a close and exciting victory. To share in these adventures and to enjoy a good book, read Carlota.

Thinking It Over

1. In the first two paragraphs, what information do you learn about the novel *Carlota*?
2. Does the writer think *Carlota* is a good or bad novel?
3. Give two reasons why the writer feels this way about *Carlota*.

Writing a Book Report

Prewriting. For your report choose a novel that you feel strongly about. It may be one that you think is very good—or one that you think is very bad. After you've read the book, take notes on it. To evaluate the book, answer the questions on page 347.

Writing, Evaluating, and Revising. In the first part of your report, use some interesting details to get your readers' interest. Give the title and author of the book. Then, tell briefly what the novel is about and when and where it takes place. Give your evaluation of the novel. Is it good or bad? When you revise, make sure you've given examples from the book. If you like, include a quotation from the book. Just be sure to give the author's exact words in quotation marks and the page number for the quotation in parentheses.

Proofreading and Publishing. Proofread your book report and correct any errors. Be sure that you've underlined the name of the book whenever it appears. Don't underline your own title for the report. Put a copy of your report into a file with other students' reports. You may even want to illustrate your report with drawings of events or people from the novel. Your teacher may keep the file for other students to use when they select books.

MAKING CONNECTIONS

RESEARCH ACROSS THE CURRICULUM

History

Do you ever wonder what your city (or a nearby city) looked like many years ago? What the place looked like even before a city was there? You can find out by doing some research, perhaps about the following things.

1. What's the history of the city? How old is it? Who first settled it? Why was a city started here? Who were some of the first families? What's the oldest building?
2. What was here two hundred years ago? Did Native Americans live here? Who were they, and how did they live? What happened to them?
3. Who is the oldest living resident of the city? Could you interview this person? In what ways has the town changed since this person was a child?

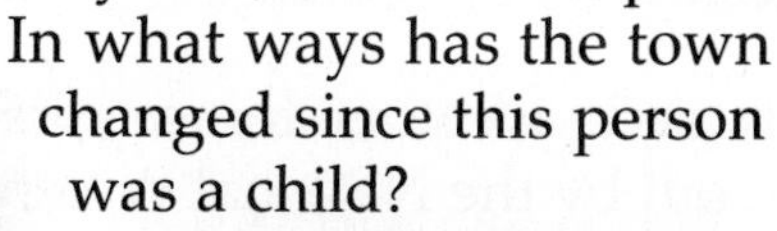

4. What natural resources made the area a good place to live? What are the native plants and animals? How might this place have looked before people arrived?
5. What ethnic groups from other countries settled in the city? When did they arrive? What part of the city did they settle in?
6. How do people earn their living in your city? Have the jobs changed since the city was started?

Get together with several of your classmates and find out about the history of the place where you live. Divide the questions, and decide on a research job for each classmate. The library is a good place to start your research. Other sources might be your local newspaper or a historical society or museum.

Take careful notes from your sources. Then, prepare a group report on the history of your city. Include drawings of important events, or of buildings, plants, and animals that have made your city an interesting place to live.

SPEAKING AND LISTENING

Reporting on the Weather

You've probably seen weather forecasters on TV. Some read reports put out by the National Weather Service. But others are *meteorologists,* highly trained scientists who study weather and report on it. They base their reports on facts collected from a vast network of weather stations. They also check records of weather patterns from earlier years. Then they make a forecast, a prediction of future weather.

Here's your chance to gather weather information and present a weather report to your class. You may want to do this activity with a partner.

First, listen to the TV or radio meteorologist on at least two stations. Notice the kind of information they report. Also pay attention to how they present the information they've gathered.

Next, take notes on the weather information that has been in your local paper for the past week. At the library, find last year's newspapers for that week. Read what the weather was like at this time last year. What, if anything, do you find is unusual about this year's rainfall, wind, or temperature?

Now gather information on this year's weather. Keep a record of your town's weather for at least three days. To collect your own data, record the temperature three times each day. Note the amount of precipitation (rain or snow). Describe the type and quantity of clouds. If you prefer, you can get this information from the National Weather Service. The closest airport will also have it.

Finally, make some weather charts:

- one chart comparing the weather last week to the weather at the same time last year
- one chart showing what the weather has been like for the past three days
- one chart showing what the weather will be like tomorrow

Then, make notes on the information you want to present along with your charts. Practice your weather report out loud until you can present your report in an interesting way.

11 Writing Effective Sentences

LOOKING AHEAD

In this chapter, you will learn how to make your sentences clearer and more interesting by

- writing complete sentences
- combining sentences
- improving your sentence style

Writing Clear Sentences

One of the best ways to make your writing clear is to use ***complete sentences.*** A complete sentence

- has a subject
- has a verb
- expresses a complete thought

EXAMPLES Some birds can imitate human speech.
Parrots and myna birds are great mimics.
Listen to that bird talk!

Each of the example word groups expresses a complete thought. Each has a verb. The last example may not appear to have a subject in it, but it actually has the unstated subject *you:* (You) Listen to that bird talk!

There are two common errors that get in the way of writing complete sentences: *sentence fragments* and *run-on sentences*. Once you learn how to recognize fragments and run-ons in your writing, you can revise them to form clear, complete sentences.

Sentence Fragments

A ***sentence fragment*** is a part of a sentence that has been punctuated as if it were a complete sentence. Because it is incomplete, a sentence fragment sends a confusing message.

FRAGMENT Was the first African American man to win the Wimbledon tennis championship. [The subject is missing. *Who* was the first African American man to win Wimbledon?]

SENTENCE Arthur Ashe was the first African American man to win the Wimbledon tennis championship.

FRAGMENT **Ashe the Wimbledon singles title in 1975.** [The verb is missing. What's the connection between Ashe and the singles title?]

SENTENCE **Ashe won the Wimbledon singles title in 1975.**

FRAGMENT **While he was a student at the University of California.** [This has a subject and a verb, but it doesn't express a complete thought. *What happened* while Ashe was a student?]

SENTENCE **Ashe also won several championships in college tennis while he was a student at the University of California.**

As you can see from the first two examples, you can correct some sentence fragments by adding a subject or verb. Other times a sentence fragment just needs to be attached to the sentence next to it. You may have accidentally separated it from the sentence it belongs with by putting in a period and a capital letter too soon.

FRAGMENT The crowd cheered wildly. **When Leon scored the winning touchdown.**

SENTENCE The crowd cheered wildly when Leon scored the winning touchdown.

GRAMMAR HINT

Identifying Fragments

Some words look like verbs but really aren't. These "fake" verbs can fool you into thinking a group of words is a sentence when it is really a fragment. A word that ends in *–ing* can't stand as a verb unless it has a helping verb (such as *is, are, were*) with it.

FRAGMENT The children playing on the swings. [Without the helping verb, this isn't a complete thought.]

SENTENCE The children **were playing** on the swings.

EXERCISE 1 Identifying Sentence Fragments

Decide which of the following groups of words are sentence fragments and which are complete sentences. This simple three-part test will help you.

1. Does the group of words have a subject?
2. Does it have a verb?
3. Does it express a complete thought?

If you answer *no* to any of the questions, write *F* to show that the group of words is a fragment. If the group of words is a complete sentence, write *S*. (Remember, the subject "you" isn't always stated directly in a sentence.)

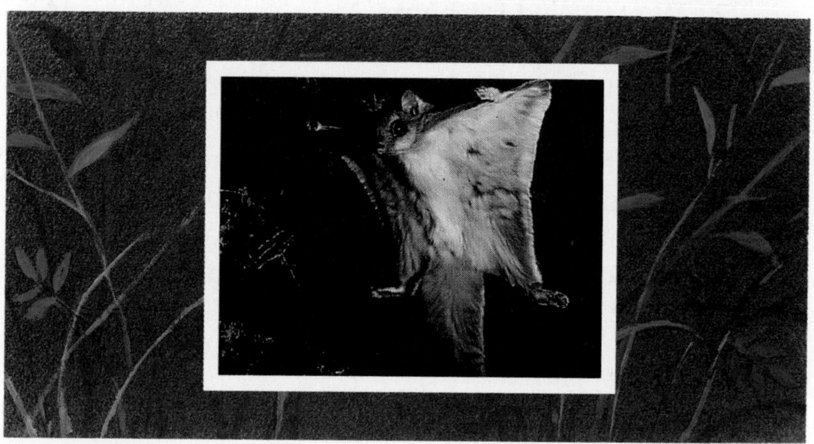

1. A flying squirrel a squirrel that can glide through the air.
2. Some Asian flying squirrels three feet long.
3. Leaps from one tree to another.
4. The squirrel glides downward, then straight, and finally upward.
5. Some flying squirrels more than fifty feet.
6. If they use a higher starting point.
7. Flying squirrels live in the forests of Asia, Europe, and North America.
8. Eat berries, birds' eggs, insects, and nuts.
9. Nest in the hollows of trees.
10. Notice how this squirrel stretches out its legs to help it glide.

EXERCISE 2 **Finding and Revising Fragments**

Some of the following groups of words are sentence fragments. Revise each fragment by (1) adding a subject, (2) adding a verb, or (3) attaching the fragment to a complete sentence. You may need to change the punctuation and capitalization, too. If the word group is already a complete sentence, write *S*.

EXAMPLE **1.** As soon as we finished eating breakfast.
1. *We left for our camping trip as soon as we finished eating breakfast.*

1. The whole family into the car.
2. We traveled for hours.
3. When we arrived at the campground.
4. My sister and I down to the river.
5. Took our fishing gear with us.
6. We cast our lines the way our aunt had taught us.
7. Because we didn't have the best bait.
8. We headed back to the campsite at sunset.
9. Dad cooking bean soup over the fire.
10. Mom and my sister the tent.

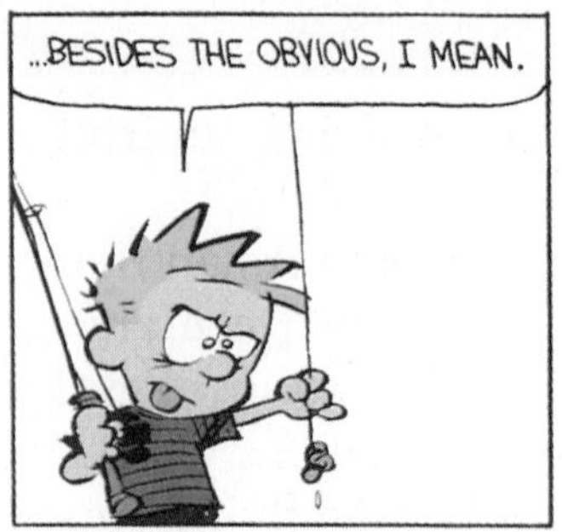

Run-on Sentences

A ***run-on sentence*** is actually two complete sentences punctuated like one sentence. In a run-on, the thoughts just run into each other. The reader can't tell where one idea ends and another one begins.

RUN-ON Edna Ferber was a novelist and playwright she wrote about American life in the 1800s.

CORRECT Edna Ferber was a novelist and playwright**.** **S**he wrote about American life in the 1800s.

RUN-ON Ferber's novel *Show Boat* was made into a musical play, some of her other novels were made into movies.

CORRECT Ferber's novel *Show Boat* was made into a musical play**.** **S**ome of her other novels were made into movies.

To spot run-ons, try reading your writing aloud. As you read, you will usually pause where one thought ends and another begins. If you pause at a place where you don't have any end punctuation, you may have a run-on sentence.

MECHANICS HINT

Using Commas Correctly

A comma does mark a brief pause in a sentence, but it doesn't show the end of a sentence. If you use just a comma between two sentences, you create a run-on sentence.

RUN-ON Clogging is a lively kind of dancing, the dancers wear special shoes to tap out the rhythm.

CORRECT Clogging is a lively kind of dancing**.** **T**he dancers wear special shoes to tap out the rhythm.

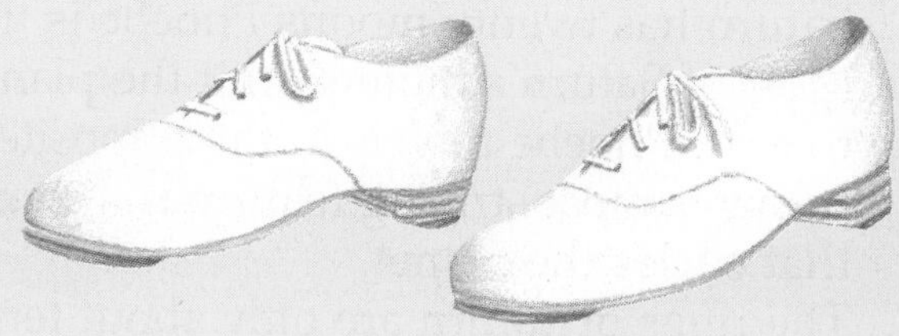

Revising Run-on Sentences

There are several ways you can revise run-on sentences. Here are two of them.

1. You can make two sentences.

   RUN-ON Asteroids are tiny planets they are sometimes called planetoids.

   CORRECT Asteroids are tiny planets**.** **T**hey are sometimes called planetoids.

2. You can use a comma and the coordinating conjunction *and, but,* or *or.*

   RUN-ON Some asteroids shine with a steady light, others keep changing in brightness.

   CORRECT Some asteroids shine with a steady light**, but** others keep changing in brightness.

EXERCISE 3 Identifying and Revising Run-ons

Decide which of the following groups of words are run-ons. Then revise each run-on by (1) making it into two separate sentences or (2) using a comma and a coordinating conjunction. If the group of words is already correct, write C.

1. Saturn is a huge planet it is more than nine times larger than Earth.
2. Saturn is covered by clouds, it is circled by bands of color.
3. The clouds at the equator are yellow, the clouds at the poles are green.
4. Saturn has twenty moons Phoebe is the smallest.
5. Most of Saturn's moons orbit the planet from west to east, Phoebe travels in the opposite direction.
6. Saturn's most striking feature is a group of rings that circles the planet.
7. The rings of Saturn are only about ten miles thick, they spread out from the planet for a great distance.

8. The rings are made up of billions of tiny particles.
9. Some of the rings are dark, but others are brighter.
10. Saturn is a beautiful planet you need a telescope to see it.

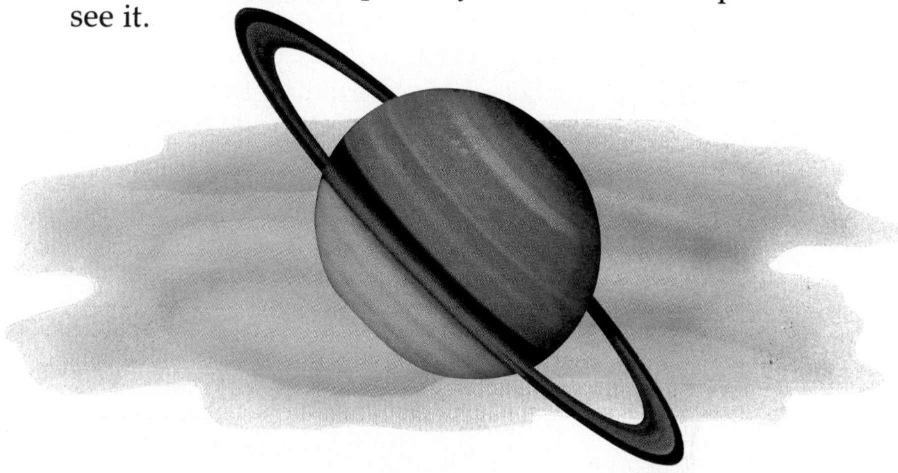

REVIEW A

The following paragraph is confusing because it contains some fragments and run-ons. First, identify the fragments and run-ons. Then, revise each fragment and run-on to make the paragraph clearer.

Many deserts have no plant life, some desert regions have a variety of plants. Many plants can survive. Where the climate is hot and dry. Cacti, Joshua trees, palm trees, and wildflowers grow in deserts. These plants. Do not grow close together. Are spread out, each plant gets water and minerals from a large area.

Combining Sentences

Short sentences can sometimes express your ideas well. But if you use only short sentences, your writing will sound choppy and dull. For example, read the following paragraph, which has only short sentences.

Thomas Edison invented the phonograph. He also experimented with robots. A lot of people don't know this. Edison created a talking doll. He created the talking doll in 1894. The doll would recite a nursery rhyme or poem. It said the words when a crank in its back was turned. The talking doll was very popular. Edison opened a factory. The factory made five hundred of the dolls every day.

Now read the revised paragraph. Notice how the writer has combined some of the short sentences to make longer, smoother sentences.

Thomas Edison invented the phonograph. A lot of people don't know that he also experimented with robots. Edison created a talking doll in 1894. When a crank in its back was turned, the doll would recite a nursery rhyme or poem. The talking doll was very popular, and Edison opened a factory that made five hundred of the dolls every day.

As you can see from the revision, sentence combining has also helped to reduce the number of repeated words and ideas. The revised paragraph is clearer, shorter, and more interesting to read.

Combining Sentences by Inserting Words

One way to combine short sentences is to take a key word from one sentence and insert it into the other sentence.

ORIGINAL The Easter lily is a flower. It is a white flower.
COMBINED The Easter lily is a **white** flower.

Sometimes you'll need to change the form of the key word before you can insert it. You can change the forms of some words by adding an ending such as *–ed, –ing, –ful,* or *–ly.* In its new form, the key word can be used to describe another word in the sentence.

ORIGINAL Easter lily plants have leaves. The leaves have points.

COMBINED Easter lily plants have **pointed** leaves.

EXERCISE 4 Combining Sentences by Inserting Words

Each of the following items contains two sentences. To combine the two sentences, take the italicized key word from the second sentence and insert it into the first sentence. The directions in parentheses will tell you how to change the form of the key word if you need to do so.

EXAMPLE **1.** Peanuts are the tiny fruit of the peanut plant. They have a good *taste.* (Change *taste* to *tasty.*)

1. *Peanuts are the tiny, tasty fruit of the peanut plant.*

1. This picture shows peanuts underground. They *grow* underground. (Add *–ing.*)
2. Peanuts are a crop of many warm regions. They are a *major* crop.
3. Peanuts are a food for snacking. Peanuts are good for your *health.* (Add *–ful.*)
4. The oil from peanuts is used in many dressings. The dressings are for *salad.*
5. Grades of peanut oil are used to make soap and shampoo. The *low* grades are used for these products.

Combining Sentences by Inserting Phrases

A *phrase* is a group of words that doesn't have a subject and a verb. You can combine sentences by taking a phrase from one sentence and inserting it into the other sentence.

ORIGINAL Arachne is a famous figure. She is a figure in Greek mythology.
COMBINED Arachne is a famous figure **in Greek mythology.**

MECHANICS HINT

Using Commas with Phrases

Some phrases need to be set off by commas. Before you insert a phrase into a sentence, ask yourself whether the phrase renames or explains a noun or pronoun. If it does, set it off with a comma (or two commas if the phrase is in the middle of the sentence).

ORIGINAL Arachne challenged Athena to a weaving contest. Athena was the goddess of wisdom.
COMBINED Arachne challenged Athena**, the goddess of wisdom,** to a weaving contest.

REFERENCE NOTE: For more information about phrases that need to be set off by commas, see pages 712–719.

Sometimes you can change the verb in a sentence to make a phrase. Just add *–ing* or *–ed* to the verb or put the word *to* in front of it. You can then use the phrase to describe a noun or pronoun in a related sentence. Be sure to place the phrase near the word(s) it modifies.

ORIGINAL The name *Eskimo* refers to several groups of people. These people live in and near the Arctic.
COMBINED The name *Eskimo* refers to several groups of people **living in and near the Arctic.**

ORIGINAL Early Eskimos had to follow a special way of life. They had to do this so they could survive in a harsh environment.

COMBINED **To survive in a harsh environment,** early Eskimos had to follow a special way of life.

REFERENCE NOTE: For more information about verb forms using *–ing, –ed,* or *to,* see pages 502–507.

EXERCISE 5 **Combining Sentences by Inserting Phrases**

Each of the following items contains two sentences. Combine the two sentences by taking the italicized word group from the second sentence and inserting it into the first sentence. The hints in parentheses tell you when and how to change the forms of words. Remember to insert commas where they are needed.

EXAMPLE **1.** Eskimo peoples followed their traditional way of life. They followed this way of life *for thousands of years.*

1. *Eskimo peoples followed their traditional way of life for thousands of years.*

1. Eskimos could build winter shelters in a few hours. They *stacked blocks of snow.* (Change *stacked* to *stacking.*)
2. They used harpoons. This is how they *hunted seals.* (Change *hunted* to *to hunt.*)

3. Eskimos also hunted and ate caribou. Caribou are *a type of deer*.
4. Whalers and fur traders came to the region and affected the Eskimo way of life. They arrived in the region *in the 1800s*.
5. Most Eskimos today follow a modern way of life. They are *like these Canadian Eskimos*.

Combining Sentences by Using *And, But,* or *Or*

You can also use the conjunctions *and, but,* and *or* to combine sentences. With these connecting words, you can make a *compound subject,* a *compound verb,* or a *compound sentence.*

Compound Subjects and Verbs

Sometimes two sentences have the same verb with different subjects. You can combine the sentences by linking the two subjects with *and* or *or*. You will end up with a ***compound subject.***

ORIGINAL Dolphins look a little like fish. Porpoises look a little like fish.

COMBINED **Dolphins and porpoises** look a little like fish.

Two sentences can also have the same subject with different verbs. You can use *and, but,* or *or* to connect the two verbs. The result is a ***compound verb.***

ORIGINAL Dolphins swim like fish. They breathe like other mammals.

COMBINED Dolphins **swim** like fish **but breathe** like other mammals.

GRAMMAR HINT

Checking for Subject–Verb Agreement

When you use the conjunction *and* to link two subjects, your new compound subject will be a plural subject. Don't forget to make the verb agree with the subject in number.

ORIGINAL Harry likes visiting the sea mammals at the aquarium. Dorothy likes visiting the sea mammals at the aquarium.

REVISED **Harry and Dorothy like** visiting the sea mammals at the aquarium. [The plural subject *Harry and Dorothy* takes the verb *like.*]

REFERENCE NOTE: For more information about agreement of subjects and verbs, see pages 551–569.

EXERCISE 6 **Combining Sentences by Creating Compound Subjects and Verbs**

Combine each of the following pairs of short, choppy sentences by using *and, but,* or *or.* If the two sentences have the same verb, make a compound subject. If they have the same subject, make a compound verb. Remember to check your combined sentences for subject–verb agreement.

1. Dolphins can't smell things as people do. They can't taste things as people do.
2. Dolphins hunt fish. Dolphins eat fish.

3. Baby dolphins catch waves near the beach. Baby dolphins ride waves near the beach.
4. Sharks sometimes attack porpoises. Sharks sometimes kill porpoises.
5. A porpoise could outswim most sharks. A tuna could outswim most sharks.

Compound Sentences

Sometimes you will want to combine two sentences that express equally important ideas. You can connect two closely related, equally important sentences by using a comma plus the coordinating conjunction *and, but,* or *or.* This creates a ***compound sentence.***

ORIGINAL My brother entered the Annual Chili Cook-off. His chili won a prize.
COMBINED My brother entered the Annual Chili Cook-off**,** **and** his chili won a prize.

ORIGINAL I didn't help him cook the chili. I helped him clean up the kitchen.
COMBINED I didn't help him cook the chili**,** **but** I helped him clean up the kitchen.

ORIGINAL We can help cook the meal. We can help wash the dishes.
COMBINED We can help cook the meal**,** **or** we can help wash the dishes.

A compound sentence tells the reader that the two ideas are closely related. If you combine two short sentences that are not closely related, you will confuse your reader.

UNRELATED Fernando mowed the grass, and I brought a broom.
RELATED Fernando mowed the grass, and I swept the sidewalk.

EXERCISE 7 **Combining Sentences by Forming a Compound Sentence**

Each of the following pairs of sentences is closely related. Make each pair into a compound sentence by adding a comma and a coordinating conjunction (*and, but,* or *or*).

EXAMPLE **1.** The Pueblos have lived in the same location for a long time. They have strong ties to their homeland.

1. *The Pueblos have lived in the same location for a long time, and they have strong ties to their homeland.*

1. Some Pueblos built villages in the valleys. Others settled in desert and mountain areas.
2. Desert surrounded many of the valleys. The people could grow crops with the help of irrigation systems.
3. Women gathered berries and other foods. Men hunted game.
4. Their adobe homes had several stories. The people used ladders to reach the upper levels.
5. Today, each Pueblo village has its own government. The Pueblo people still share many customs.

Combining Sentences by Using a Subordinate Clause

A *clause* is a group of words that contains a subject and verb. Some clauses can stand alone as a sentence. We call them ***independent.*** Other clauses can't stand alone as a sentence because they don't express a complete thought. We call them ***subordinate.***

INDEPENDENT CLAUSE	**Gertrude Ederle swam the English Channel.** [can stand alone]
SUBORDINATE CLAUSE	**when she was nineteen years old** [can't stand alone]

If two sentences are closely related, you can combine them by using a subordinate clause. Just turn one of the sentences into a subordinate clause and attach it to the other sentence (the independent clause). The subordinate clause will give information about a word or idea in the independent clause.

TWO SENTENCES	Gertrude Ederle swam the English Channel. She was nineteen years old at the time.
ONE SENTENCE	Gertrude Ederle swam the English Channel **when she was nineteen years old.**

Clauses Beginning with *Who, Which,* or *That*

You can make a short sentence into a subordinate clause by inserting *who, which,* or *that* in place of the subject.

ORIGINAL	The Everglades is an area of swamps. It covers the southern part of Florida.
COMBINED	The Everglades is an area of swamps **that covers the southern part of Florida.**

Clauses Beginning with Words of Time or Place

Another way to turn a sentence into a subordinate clause is to add a word that tells time or place at the beginning. Some words that can begin this type of clause are *after, before, where, wherever, when, whenever,* and *while.* You may also need to delete some words before you can insert the clause into another sentence.

ORIGINAL	No humans lived in the Everglades until 1842. In 1842, Seminoles fled to the area.
COMBINED	No humans lived in the Everglades until 1842, **when Seminoles fled to the area.**

MECHANICS HINT

Using Commas with Introductory Clauses

If you put your time or place clause at the beginning of the sentence, use a comma after the clause.

ORIGINAL People began draining the swamps to make farmland. The Everglades was in danger.

COMBINED **When people began draining the swamps to make farmland,** the Everglades was in danger.

REFERENCE NOTE: For more about the use of commas with subordinate clauses, see pages 713 and 720.

EXERCISE 8 **Combining Sentences by Using a Subordinate Clause**

Combine each sentence pair by making the second sentence into a subordinate clause and attaching it to the first sentence. The hints in parentheses tell you how to begin the subordinate clause. You may need to delete a word or two from the second sentence.

1. The pearl is a gem. It is made by certain kinds of oysters and clams. (Use *that.*)
2. Beautiful pearls are found in tropical seas. The best pearl oysters live there. (Use a comma and *where.*)
3. A valuable pearl has a shine. The shine comes from below its surface. (Use *that.*)
4. A pearl becomes round. It is formed in the soft part of the oyster. (Use *when.*)
5. Pearls should be wiped clean with a soft cloth. They are worn as jewelry. (Use *after.*)

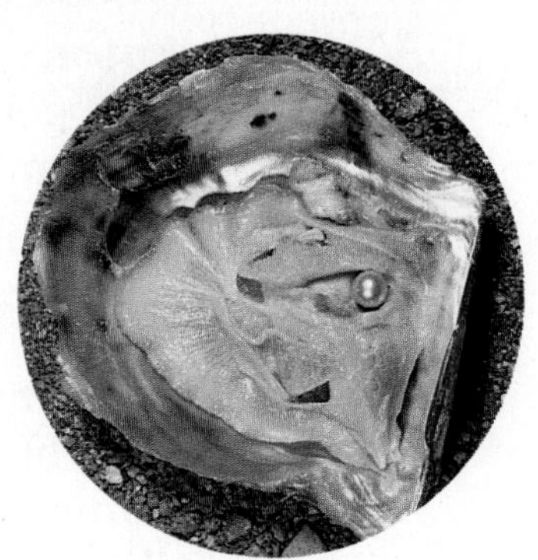

REVIEW B **Revising a Paragraph by Combining Sentences**

These paragraphs sound choppy because they have too many short sentences. Use the methods you've learned in this section to combine sentences in the paragraphs. The revised paragraphs should sound much better.

Pegasus is a winged horse. He is a beautiful horse. He is a horse from Greek mythology. Pegasus was created by Poseidon. Poseidon was the god of the sea. He was a Greek god. Athena caught Pegasus. Athena tamed Pegasus. Athena was the goddess of wisdom.

A hero could ride Pegasus. A true poet could ride Pegasus. These were the only kinds of people who could ride him. The first person to ride the winged horse was a Greek youth. The youth was sent by a king to kill a monster. The youth destroyed the monster. He became a hero.

Improving Sentence Style

When you combine short, choppy sentences, your writing is easier and more interesting to read. You can also make your writing more effective by avoiding *stringy* and *wordy sentences.* You can revise stringy and wordy sentences to make them shorter and clearer.

Revising Stringy Sentences

A ***stringy sentence*** is made up of several independent clauses strung together with words like *and* or *but*. Stringy sentences just ramble on and on. They don't give the reader a chance to pause before each new idea.

To fix a stringy sentence, you can

- break the sentence into two or more sentences
- turn some of the independent clauses into phrases or subordinate clauses

STRINGY Martina climbed the stairs of the haunted house and she knocked on the door several times but no one answered and she braced herself and then she opened the door.

REVISED Martina climbed the stairs of the haunted house. She knocked on the door several times, but no one answered. Bracing herself, she opened the door.

MECHANICS HINT

Punctuating Compound Sentences

When you revise a stringy sentence, you may decide to keep *and* or *but* between two closely related independent clauses. If you do this, remember to add a comma before the *and* or *but*.

ORIGINAL She knocked on the door several times but no one answered.

REVISED She knocked on the door several times**,** but no one answered.

REFERENCE NOTE: For more about compound sentences, see pages 536–538.

EXERCISE 9 **Revising Stringy Sentences**

Some of the following sentences are stringy and need to be improved. First, identify the stringy sentences. Then, revise them by (1) breaking each sentence into two or more sentences or (2) turning some of the independent clauses into phrases or subordinate clauses. If the sentence is effective and doesn't need to be improved, write *C*.

1. Mercedes O. Cubría was born in Cuba, but her mother died, and she moved to the United States, and she moved with her two sisters.

2. She worked as a nurse, and then she joined the Women's Army Corps, and she soon became an officer in the army.
3. Cubría was the first Cuban-born woman to become an officer in the U.S. Army.
4. Her job during World War II was to put important government papers into a secret code.
5. The war ended, and she was promoted to captain, and later her official rank rose to major.
6. Then there was the Korean War, and she worked as an intelligence officer, and she studied information about the enemy.
7. Cubría retired from the army in 1953 but was called to duty again in 1962.
8. After the Castro revolution, thousands of Cubans fled to the United States, and Cubría interviewed many of these refugees, and she also prepared reports on Cuba.
9. In her spare time, she helped people from Cuba find jobs and housing.
10. She retired again in 1973, and she settled in Miami, Florida, and she was surrounded by friends and family there.

Revising Wordy Sentences

Sometimes you may use more words in a sentence than you really need. Extra words don't make writing sound better or more impressive. They just get in the reader's way. You can revise ***wordy sentences*** in three different ways.

1. Replace a phrase with one word.

WORDY In the event that we win this game, our team will go to the playoffs.
REVISED **If** we win this game, our team will go to the playoffs.

WORDY In a state of exhaustion, Tony slumped across the bus seat and fell asleep.
REVISED **Exhausted,** Tony slumped across the bus seat and fell asleep.

2. Take out *who is* or *which is.*

LENGTHY Yesterday I went for a hike with Sonya, who is my best friend.
REVISED Yesterday I went for a hike with Sonya, **my best friend.**

LENGTHY Afterward, we drank some apple juice, which is a good thirst quencher.
REVISED Afterward, we drank some apple juice, **a good thirst quencher.**

3. Take out a whole group of unnecessary words.

WORDY What I mean to say is that I am going to work on my model airplane tonight.
REVISED I am going to work on my model airplane tonight.

WORDY I spend a lot of time building model airplanes because it is my favorite hobby, and I like model building better than any other hobby I've tried.
REVISED I spend a lot of time building model airplanes because it is my favorite hobby.

Here is a list of some common wordy phrases and their shorter, simpler replacements. Be on the lookout for these wordy phrases as you revise your writing.

WORDY	SIMPLER
at the point at which	when
by means of	by
due to the fact that	because, since
in spite of the fact that	although
in the event that	if
the fact is that	actually

EXERCISE 10 **Revising Wordy Sentences**

Some of the following sentences are wordy and need improving. Decide which of the sentences are wordy; then, revise them. You can (1) replace a phrase with one word, (2) take out *who is* or *which is,* or (3) take out a whole group of unnecessary words. If a sentence is effective as it is, write *C*.

1. Our science class has been learning about the starfish, which is a strange and beautiful fish.
2. What I want to say is that starfish are fascinating creatures.
3. A starfish has little feet tipped with suction cups that have suction power.
4. At the end of each arm is a sensitive "eyespot."
5. In spite of the fact that the eyespot cannot really see things, it can tell light from dark.
6. The starfish's mouth is in the middle of its body.
7. When it uses its arms, it can pull at the shells of clams.
8. At the point at which the clam's shell opens, the starfish can feed on the clam.
9. Starfish come in a variety of colors, shapes, and sizes, and some are bigger than others.

10. This photograph shows a candy cane starfish holding onto a soft coral by holding it with its suction cups.

REVIEW C

The following paragraph is hard to read because it contains stringy and wordy sentences. First, identify the stringy and wordy sentences. Then, revise them by using the methods you've learned. Notice how your revisions improve the style of the paragraph.

The movie *The Dark Crystal* features a lot of strange characters, and the characters are actually puppets, and they were designed by Jim Henson, and he was the man who created the Muppets. The puppets used in *The Dark Crystal* were different from the original Muppets, having things about them that were different. One thing is that they weren't as brightly colored as the TV Muppets. They also had legs and could move through a scene with their whole bodies showing. Some of the *Dark Crystal* characters were radio-controlled, and others were operated by puppeteers, and the puppeteers were hidden under the movie set.

Fill in the Missing Pieces

You are fishing in a bay when you suddenly spot a corked bottle bobbing in the water near the pier. You guess that the bottle has floated over from the summer camp across the bay. You pull the bottle out of the water and take out the cork. Inside is a piece of paper with a mysterious message. But some water has leaked into the bottle, and parts of the sentences have been washed away. Try to reconstruct the message by adding the missing words.

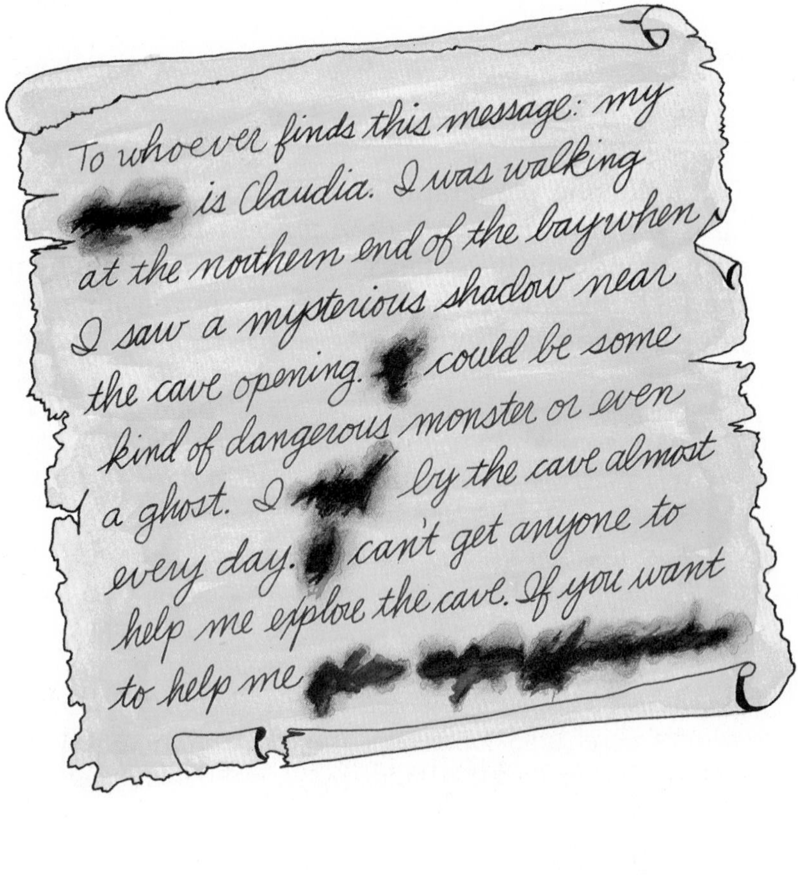

To whoever finds this message: my
[illegible] is Claudia. I was walking
at the northern end of the bay when
I saw a mysterious shadow near
the cave opening. [illegible] could be some
kind of dangerous monster or even
a ghost. I [illegible] by the cave almost
every day. [illegible] can't get anyone to
help me explore the cave. If you want
to help me [illegible]

12 English: Origins and Uses

LOOKING AHEAD

In this chapter, you will take a close look at the English language—where it comes from, how it has grown, and how it is used today. You will also examine your own use of language with an eye for style, learning

- what kinds of language are appropriate for particular situations
- how to improve your writing by choosing clearer, more effective words

A Changing Language

Languages have ancestors just as people do. English and dozens of other languages come from a single early language that was spoken thousands of years ago on the other side of the globe.

Although each language is unique, you can still see the family resemblance among words with the same meaning in related languages.

ENGLISH	GERMAN	FRENCH	SPANISH
new	neu	nouveau	nuevo
nose	Nase	nez	nariz
salt	Salz	sel	sal
young	jung	jeune	joven

No one knows exactly when English branched off as a separate language. However, we do know that a form of English was being spoken by tribes of people in the fifth century. These tribes migrated to the island of Britain and conquered the area that is now England. Their language is the ancestor of modern-day English.

The earliest known English writings date back about 1,300 years. This early form of English is so different from our English that it looks like a foreign language to us.

He þæt ful geþeáh
wæl-reow wíga, æt Wealhþeówe,
and þá gyddode, gúðe gefýsed.
Beowulf maðelode, bearn Ecgþeówes:

from *Beowulf*

The Growth of English

English didn't grow up all at once. If you had a time machine, you could stop off in England every few hundred years and witness gradual changes taking place in people's language. You would hear and see new pronunciations, forms, and meanings of words. You would also notice many new words being added to the language. By about 1500, you would probably be able to understand the English of the time. However, it would still sound strange to you.

How Do You Spell It?

Some English words have traveled through the centuries with only small changes in spelling. Others have undergone greater change. Here are some examples of present-day English words and their original forms.

PRESENT-DAY	**red**	**three**	**summer**	**sheep**	**fish**
ORIGINAL	**read**	**threo**	**sumor**	**sceap**	**fisc**

Even today, the spellings of words vary. Different spellings of a word can be standard in different places. For example, compare standard American and standard British spellings of some everyday words.

AMERICAN	**color**	**flavor**	**theater**	**tire**
BRITISH	**colour**	**flavour**	**theatre**	**tyre**

How Do You Say It?

By the 1300s, written English looked similar to the English we use. But English-speaking people of that time still pronounced words differently from the way we do. For example, they pronounced *meek* like *make, boot* like *boat*, and *mouse* like *moose.*

Changes in pronunciations help account for many of the English words that aren't spelled like they sound. For example, the word *knight* used to be pronounced with a strong *k* sound at the beginning. The letter remained part of the spelling even though the *k* sound was eventually dropped.

EXERCISE 1 Giving Present-Day Forms of Words

Here are five sets of English words written with their original spellings. See if you can figure out what the words are in present-day English.

1. bryht, deorc
2. sealt, mete
3. muth, lippa
4. docga, hors
5. plante, saed

What Does It Mean?

Read the following sentence:

> Without reply, the typewriter rose and withdrew, thrusting her pencil into the coil of her hair. . . .
>
> Frank Norris, *The Octopus*

When people read Frank Norris's sentence in the early 1900s, they didn't see anything strange about it. In those days, it wasn't unusual for a typewriter to get up and walk out of a room. The word *typewriter* could mean "typist" as well as "typewriting machine."

The meaning of *typewriter* has changed only slightly. But some words have ended up with meanings entirely different from their original ones. Nine hundred years ago, *awful* meant "awe-inspiring, very impressive." Today, it usually means "terrifying" or "very bad." Another good example is the word *nice*. In the 1300s, *nice* didn't mean "pleasant"; it meant "lazy" or "foolish."

The meanings of words are still changing today. For example, the word *bad* can now mean "good" in informal English. And *bonnet* means only "a hat" in the United States but also "the hood of a car" in Great Britain.

EXERCISE 2 **Answering Word-Origin Riddles**

See if you can answer each of the following riddles. First, look up the italicized word in a dictionary that gives word origins. (*Webster's New World Dictionary* is one.) The earliest meaning listed for the word will be your clue to the riddle. Give this meaning along with your answer.

EXAMPLE **1.** Where should a *villain* work?
1. *on a farm* (villain *meant "farm tenant")*

1. Why do *silly* people smile all the time?
2. What should you do with a *brat*?
3. Why do *comets* need shampoo?
4. Why is cheese a good food for your *muscles*?
5. What should you buy with your *salary*?

Where Does It Come From?

Have you ever *munched* a *burrito* or *feasted* on *chop suey?* If so, then you haven't just eaten foods from different cultures. You've also used words from different languages.

About 15 percent of the words we use are native to English. The rest have been borrowed or adapted from other languages. Many nonnative words were borrowed as English people came into contact with people from other cultures and lands. Here are a few examples of words that have been borrowed in the past one thousand years.

NORSE	leg, fellow, get
LATIN	area, candle, decorate, joke
FRENCH	beauty, dance, study
SPANISH	chili, hurricane, mustang
NATIVE AMERICAN LANGUAGES	bayou, chipmunk, squash
AFRICAN LANGUAGES	jazz, okra, gumbo

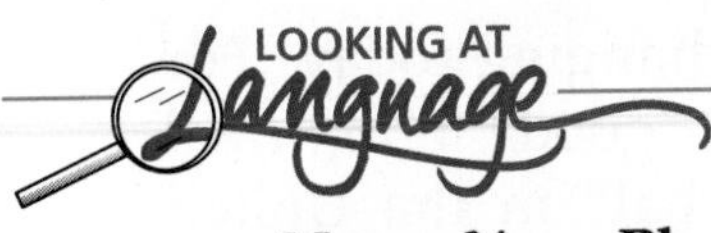

Name Your Phobia

Can you catch *brontophobia* from a brontosaurus? Has someone with *anthophobia* been bitten by ants? Neither of these words means what it sounds like. For each, the key to the meaning is the ending *–phobia,* which comes from the Greek word *phobos,* "fear."

The ending *–phobia* is added to Greek and Latin root words to describe all kinds of fears. *Brontophobia,* from *bronte,* "thunder," means "fear of thunder." *Anthophobia,* from *anthos,* "flower," means "fear of flowers." Some better-known phobias include *claustrophobia,* "fear of closed-in spaces," and *arachnophobia,* "fear of spiders."

See how Gary Larson came up with the *–phobia* word that he used in the following cartoon. Why would his made-up word look familiar to an *ornithologist,* someone who studies birds?

Anatidaephobia: The fear that somewhere, somehow, a duck is watching you.

> In coming up with the name for the phobia, I played around with words like "quackaphobia" and "duckalookaphobia" and so on. But then I got the bright idea to look up the scientific name for ducks, and discovered their family name is *Anatidae.* And so, I ended up coining a word that twelve ornithologists understood and everyone else probably went, "Say what?"
>
> Gary Larson,
> *The Prehistory of the Far Side*

EXERCISE 3 Researching Word Origins

Each of the following words came into English from another language. Using a dictionary that gives word origins, find out what language each word was borrowed from. Give a date for the word's entry into English if your dictionary lists one.

1. tea
2. sketch
3. shawl
4. parade
5. census
6. same
7. school
8. command
9. salsa
10. skunk

Dialects of American English

You probably know people whose English is different from yours. Maybe they pronounce words strangely, or maybe they use words in unfamiliar ways. Your English probably sounds as "funny" to them as theirs sounds to you.

Because ways of speaking vary so widely, the English of one group of people is bound to sound "funny" to another group. There are many different forms of English, and no form is better or worse than another. The variety of English used by a particular group of people is called a ***dialect.*** In this section, you'll learn about two types of American English dialects, *regional dialects* and *ethnic dialects.*

Regional Dialects

Do you carry a *pail* or a *bucket*? Do you *wash* (or *warsh*) the *car* (or *cah*)? Do you stand *on* line or *in* line? Where you come from can help determine what words you use, how you pronounce words, and how you put words together. A dialect shared by people from the same area of the United States is called a ***regional dialect.***

Not everyone who lives in a region uses that region's dialect. Someone from Alabama or Georgia won't necessarily say *y'all,* and someone from Boston may not pronounce *farm* like *fahm.* When people move from place to place, they often lose some of their old dialect and learn a new one.

Ethnic Dialects

People who share the same cultural heritage may share a dialect of English, too. The English used by a particular cultural group is called an ***ethnic dialect.*** Widely used American ethnic dialects include the Black English of many African Americans and the Spanish-influenced English of many people whose families come from Mexico, Central America, Cuba, and Puerto Rico.

Many words that are now part of general English usage originally came from ethnic dialects. For example, the words *afro, jazz,* and *jukebox* were originally Black English dialect words, and *arroyo, mesa,* and *taco* were originally from Hispanic English.

EXERCISE 4 Reading a Dialect

In the following excerpt, the speaker, Stanley Hicks, is describing some happy memories from his childhood. He is from Sugar Grove, North Carolina, and speaks Appalachian dialect. Read the passage aloud to hear the sounds of Hicks's dialect. Try to pronounce the words as the writer has spelled them. Is Stanley Hicks's dialect different from yours? If it is, tell how you would say the same things in your own words.

> And we used to play fox and goose. You've got two red foxes—you know, red grains of corn—and the rest of them is white. Play on a board like a checkerboard. And then the geese tries to hem these foxes up. Dad'd get 'em hemmed up and he'd say, "Que-e-e-e-e-e-e-e! Listen to her wheeze!" He'd say, "Watch her wiggle her tail, boys! She's a-dying!" It'd made us so cussed mad, you know. He was good on it. And then every time he'd jump one of our geese, he'd go "Quack!" Make like a goose a-hollering, you know.
>
> Eliot Wigginton,
> *I Wish I Could Give My Son a Wild Raccoon*

Standard American English

Every variety of English has its own set of rules and guidelines. No variety is the best or the most correct. However, one kind of English is more widely used and accepted than others in the United States. This variety is called ***standard American English.***

Standard American English is the one variety that belongs to all of us. Because it's commonly understood, it allows people from many different regions and cultures to communicate with one another clearly. It is the variety of English used most often in books and magazines, on radio and television. It is the variety people are expected to use in most school and business situations.

The **Handbook** in this textbook gives you some of the rules and guidelines for using standard American English. To identify the differences between standard American English and other varieties of English, the **Handbook** uses the labels *standard* and *nonstandard*. *Nonstandard* doesn't mean wrong language. It means language that is inappropriate in situations where standard English is expected.

REFERENCE NOTE: For more about standard English, see page 653.

Calvin & Hobbes, copyright 1987 Universal Press Syndicate.

Choosing Your Words

Because English offers you many different ways to say the same thing, you have to make decisions every time you speak and write. Sometimes you make these choices naturally. For example, you probably don't think much about word choice when you're talking with a friend. But at other times, especially when you write, you need to give some thought to the words you use. You need to make sure your words are clear, effective, and appropriate.

Formal and Informal English

Read the following sentences:

> I really enjoyed that story about the men who climbed Mount Everest.
> I really got into that story about the guys who climbed Mount Everest.

Just a few words have been changed from the first sentence to the second, but the effect of each sentence is different. One is written in ***formal English*** and the other in ***informal English.***

Different levels of formality in language are appropriate for different situations. You might use the more formal language of the first example sentence if you were telling a teacher how you liked a story. But if you were talking about the story to a classmate, you might use informal expressions like *got into* and *guys.*

Uses of Informal English

There are two kinds of informal English that you should be familiar with: *colloquialisms* and *slang.*

Colloquialisms are the casual, colorful expressions that we use in everyday conversation. Many colloquialisms aren't meant to be taken literally. They have understood meanings that are different from the basic meanings of the words.

EXAMPLES The band **brought down the house** with the last number.
The plot of that movie was **hard to swallow.**
We'll order some sandwiches **to go.**

Slang consists of made-up words or old words used in new ways. Slang words are usually the special language of a particular group of people, such as teenagers or musicians. You and your friends probably use slang that's unique to your generation.

Although slang words seem up-to-date when they're first used, they tend to fall out of style very quickly. Some of the slang words in the following sentences probably seem dated to you.

EXAMPLES That's a **cool** set of **wheels, dude.**
That last scene really **broke me up.**
Where did you get those **neat** shoes?
Tim just got a **rad** new haircut.

Don't use slang in essays, test answers, or reports. If you use slang in a formal speaking or writing situation, your audience may think you are not serious about your subject. However, you may want to use slang in short stories. For example, if one of your characters is a teenager, slang will help make the character's dialogue seem realistic.

EXERCISE 5 **Writing Letters in Formal or Informal English**

You've just returned from visiting a friend in another state. You want to write letters to your friend and your friend's parents telling them what a good time you had.

Write the thank-you note you would send to your friend's parents and the letter you would send to your friend. In each letter, mention some parts of your visit that you especially enjoyed—for example, a sightseeing trip, a day at an amusement park, or a family barbecue. Use the formal or informal English that you think is appropriate for each letter.

Denotation and Connotation

Suppose you heard someone say, "Cara is beautiful and scrawny." You'd probably wonder whether the person meant to compliment or insult Cara. *Scrawny* is another way of saying "thin." That is the word's basic meaning, or ***denotation.*** But *scrawny* and *thin* create very different pictures of a person. *Scrawny* suggests that Cara is bony and looks underfed. This is the emotional association, or ***connotation,*** of the word.

It's important to think about the connotations of the words you use. If you use a word without knowing its connotations, you may send the wrong message to your audience.

EXERCISE 6 **Responding to Connotations**

Which of the words in each pair would you prefer if someone were describing you? Why?

1. stubborn, determined
2. serious, grim
3. eccentric, weird
4. wishy-washy, undecided
5. sensitive, touchy

Tired Words and Expressions

A tired word is a dull, worn-out word. It has been used so often and so carelessly that it has become almost meaningless. Tired words like *nice, fine, great,* and *wonderful* are common in everyday conversation, but they are too dull and vague to be effective in writing.

Tired expressions are often called ***clichés.*** Many clichés were striking and vivid the first time they were used. But after a while, they lost their originality and their expressiveness. Here are some examples of clichés; you can probably think of many more.

break the ice	easier said than done
busy as a bee	eat like a horse
the crack of dawn	on top of the world
clear as a bell	sadder but wiser

Most writers have a few favorite words that they tend to overuse. If a word appears too often in your writing, find *synonyms* for it—words that have a similar meaning. You can look up synonyms in a *thesaurus,* a dictionary of synonyms. Here are just a few of the words that *Roget's International Thesaurus* lists as synonyms for *interesting: appealing, captivating, intriguing, thought-provoking.*

Keep in mind, though, that no two words have exactly the same meaning. Before you use a synonym, look up the word in a dictionary to make sure it has the meaning you intend.

EXERCISE 7 **Identifying Tired Words and Clichés**

Make a list of all the tired words and expressions you can think of. You may want to spend a few days watching and listening for them, jotting down words and expressions as you hear them. Then compare your list with those of your classmates. By combining lists, you'll have a handy collection of words and expressions to avoid when you write.

Jargon

Jargon is special language that is used by a particular group of people, such as people who share the same profession, occupation, sport, or hobby. For example, the word *set* is used as theater jargon for "the props and scenery arranged on a stage" or "the act of arranging scenery on a stage." The same word is also printer's jargon for "put a piece of writing into print." Like *set*, many jargon words are ordinary words that have been given special meanings.

Jargon can be practical and effective because it reduces many words to just one or two. However, don't use jargon when you are writing or speaking for a general audience who may not be familiar with the terms.

REFERENCE NOTE: For an example of how dictionaries label special uses of words, see page 826.

EXERCISE 8 **Translating Jargon**

Look up each of the following words in a dictionary to find out what the word means for the group indicated. For help with looking up special uses of words, see page 826.

1. *taw*—marble players
2. *strike*—baseball players
3. *pan*—filmmakers
4. *lock*—wrestlers
5. *proof*—photographers

Identify Dated Language

When you watch reruns of old television shows, you probably notice that the people's clothes and cars seem out of style. But have you ever noticed that their way of talking seems dated, too? By watching a television show from twenty years ago, you can get a good sense of how people's everyday language has changed over time.

Watch at least one rerun of a situation comedy from the 1970s. Listen to the characters' language—especially that of teenage characters. Jot down any words and expressions that seem dated or unfamiliar to you.

Which of the words and expressions on your list are colloquialisms or slang? What words and expressions do you and your friends use today to mean the same things?

PART TWO

HANDBOOK

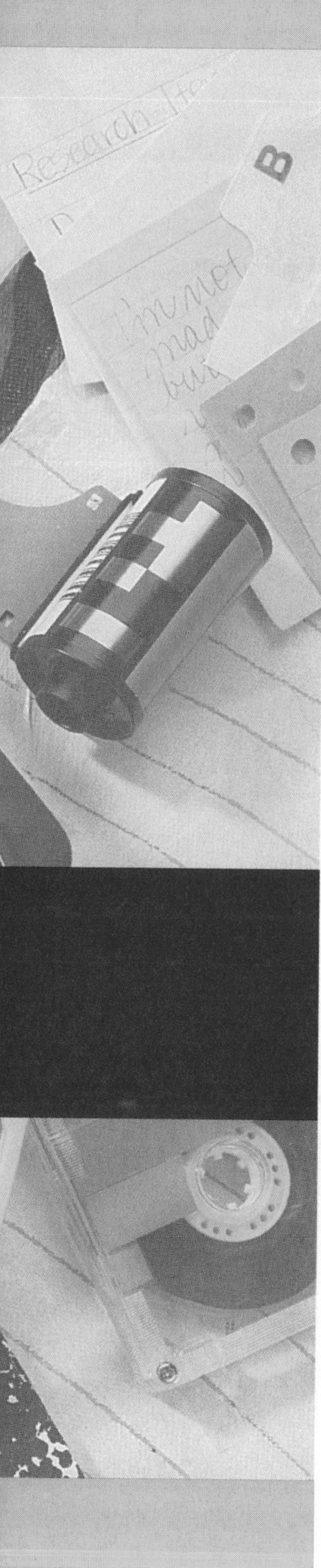

GRAMMAR

USAGE

MECHANICS

13 The Sentence

Subject and Predicate, Kinds of Sentences

Diagnostic Test

A. Identifying Sentences

Some of the following groups of words are sentences; others are not. If a group of words is a sentence, add a capital letter at the beginning and an appropriate punctuation mark at the end. If a group of words is not a sentence, write *sentence fragment*.

EXAMPLES
1. revised the paper and then proofread it
1. *sentence fragment*

2. we can meet you at the bus stop after school
2. *We can meet you at the bus stop after school.*

1. one day this week or maybe next week
2. will you lend me that book
3. on her vacation she met her pen pal for the first time
4. his favorite meal, cheese enchiladas with refried beans
5. lock the door on your way out

B. Identifying Simple Subjects and Simple Predicates

Identify each *simple subject* and *simple predicate* in the following sentences. [Hint: Be on the alert for compound subjects, compound verbs, and verb phrases.]

EXAMPLE 1. Foods and beverages with large amounts of sugar can contribute to tooth decay.
1. *Foods, beverages—simple subject; can contribute—simple predicate*

6. The lava from a volcano can be very dangerous.
7. The earthquake survivors camped on blankets in the streets.
8. In Beijing, cyclists pedal on the sidewalks and weave expertly through the busy streets.
9. Between 1896 and 1899, gold prospectors rushed to Alaska.
10. The weather during an Alaskan summer can be very hot.
11. Have you read this collection of Claude McKay's poems?
12. In the center of the table was a huge bowl of fruit.
13. Linked forever in legend are Paul Bunyan and Babe the Blue Ox.
14. Many famous racehorses have been raised or trained in Kentucky.
15. The bright lights and the tall buildings amaze and delight most visitors to New York City.

C. Classifying and Punctuating Sentences

For each of the following sentences, add the correct end mark of punctuation. Then label each sentence *declarative, interrogative, imperative,* or *exclamatory*.

EXAMPLE 1. Has anyone guessed the right number
1. *Has anyone guessed the right number?—interrogative*

16. We celebrate our parents' anniversary every year
17. Don't tell them about our surprise
18. Our cousins are coming all the way from Hawaii
19. Who is in charge of decorations
20. What a beautiful Navajo blanket that is

Sentence Sense

13a. A ***sentence*** is a group of words that expresses a complete thought.

A sentence begins with a capital letter and ends with a period, a question mark, or an exclamation point.

EXAMPLES **Alice Walker won a prize for her book.**
Please fasten your seat belt.
Why did you stop running?
Watch out for the car!

When a group of words looks like a sentence but does not express a complete thought, it is a ***sentence fragment.***

SENTENCE FRAGMENT **After they pitched the tent.** [This is not a complete thought. What happened after they pitched the tent?]
SENTENCE **After they pitched the tent, they built a campfire.**

SENTENCE FRAGMENT **Sailing around the world.** [The thought is not complete. Who is sailing around the world?]
SENTENCE **Some marine biologists are sailing around the world.**

SENTENCE FRAGMENT **Her hike through the Grand Canyon.** [The thought is not complete. What about her hike?]
SENTENCE **Sheila enjoyed her hike through the Grand Canyon.**

EXERCISE 1 Identifying Sentences

Tell whether each of the following groups of words is a *sentence* or a *sentence fragment*. If a group of words is a sentence, use a capital letter at the beginning and add a mark of punctuation at the end.

EXAMPLES [1] during her vacation last summer
1. *sentence fragment*

[2] my friend Michelle visited Colorado
2. *sentence—My friend Michelle visited Colorado.*

[1] she took an exciting boat trip on the Colorado River [2] running the rapids [3] at first her boat drifted calmly through the Grand Canyon [4] then the river dropped suddenly [5] and became foaming rapids full of dangerous boulders [6] which can break a boat [7] Michelle's boat was small, like the one in this picture [8] with one guide and four passengers [9] some people prefer large inflatable boats with outboard motors [10] that can carry eighteen passengers

The Subject and the Predicate

Every sentence has two parts: a *subject* and a *predicate.*

The Subject

13b. The ***subject*** tells whom or what the sentence is about.

EXAMPLES **Nicholasa Mohr** is a writer and an artist.
The girls on the team were all good students.

To find the subject, ask *who* or *what* is doing something, or *whom* or *what* is being talked about. The subject may come at the beginning, middle, or end of a sentence.

EXAMPLES **The pitcher** struck Felicia out. [*Who* struck Felicia out? *The pitcher* did.]
After practicing for hours, **Timmy** bowled two strikes. [*Who* bowled two strikes? *Timmy* did.]
Hiding in the tall grass was **a baby rabbit.** [*What* was hiding? *A baby rabbit* was.]

EXERCISE 2 **Identifying Subjects**

Identify the subject of each of the following sentences.

EXAMPLE **1.** Have you read a book by N. Scott Momaday?
1. *you*

1. Born in 1934 in Oklahoma, Momaday lived on Navajo and Apache reservations in the Southwest.
2. Momaday's father was a Kiowa.
3. As a young man, Momaday attended the University of New Mexico and Stanford University.
4. In *The Way to Rainy Mountain,* Momaday tells about the myths and history of the Kiowa people.
5. The book includes poems, an essay, and stories about the Kiowa people.
6. *The Way to Rainy Mountain* was published in 1969.

7. After Momaday's book came other works by Native American writers.
8. William Least Heat-Moon traveled in a van across the United States and wrote about his journey.
9. Was he inspired to write by his travels?
10. Readers of this Osage writer enjoy his beautiful descriptions of nature.

EXERCISE 3 Writing Subjects and Punctuating Sentences

Add subjects to fill in the blanks in the following sentences. Begin each sentence with a capital letter, and end it with a mark of punctuation.

EXAMPLE **1.** ___ is very heavy
1. *This bag of cement is very heavy.*

1. ___ is a difficult game to play
2. ___ works in the post office
3. Luckily for me, ___ was easy to read
4. Tied to the end of the rope was ___
5. Did ___ help you

Complete Subject and Simple Subject

The ***complete subject*** consists of all the words needed to tell *whom* or *what* a sentence is about.

13c. The ***simple subject*** is the main word or words in the complete subject.

EXAMPLES **The four new students** arrived early.
Complete subject The four new students
Simple subject students

A round walnut table with five legs stood in the middle of the dining room.
Complete subject A round walnut table with five legs
Simple subject table

GRAMMAR

If you leave out the simple subject, a sentence does not make sense.

EXAMPLES The four new . . . arrived early.
A round walnut . . . with five legs stood in the middle of the dining room.

A simple subject may consist of one word or several words.

EXAMPLES **Jets** break the sound barrier. [one word]
Does **Aunt Carmen** own a grocery store? [two words]
On the library shelf was ***The Island of the Blue Dolphins.*** [six words]

NOTE: In this book, the term *subject* refers to the simple subject unless otherwise indicated.

EXERCISE 4 Identifying Complete Subjects and Simple Subjects

Identify the complete subject in each of the following sentences. Then, underline the simple subject.

EXAMPLES
1. Stories about time travel make exciting reading.
1. *Stories about time travel*
2. Samuel Delany writes great science fiction.
2. *Samuel Delany*

1. Ray Bradbury is also a writer of science fiction.
2. *The Golden Apples of the Sun* is a collection of his short stories.
3. My favorite story in that book is "A Sound of Thunder."
4. The main character in the story is called Mr. Eckels.
5. For ten thousand dollars, Mr. Eckels joins Time Safari, Inc.
6. He is looking for the dinosaur *Tyrannosaurus rex.*
7. With four other men, Bradbury's hero travels over sixty million years back in time.
8. On the safari, trouble develops.

9. Because of one mistake, the past is changed.
10. The results of that mistake affect the future.

The Predicate

13d. The ***predicate*** of a sentence is the part that says something about the subject.

EXAMPLES Old Faithful **is a giant geyser in Yellowstone National Park.**
Jade Snow Wong **wrote about growing up in San Francisco's Chinatown.**

Like the subject, the predicate may be found anywhere in a sentence.

EXAMPLES **Outside the tent was** a baby bear.
Late in the night we **heard a noise.**

EXERCISE 5 Identifying Predicates

Identify the predicate in each of the sentences in the following paragraph.

EXAMPLE [1] My favorite sports poster is this one of Roberto Clemente.
1. *is this one of Roberto Clemente*

[1] Also among my treasures is a book about Clemente. [2] Clemente played right field for the Pittsburgh Pirates. [3] During his career, he won four National League batting titles. [4] In 1966, he was named the league's Most Valuable Player. [5] Twice Clemente helped lead the Pirates to World Series victories. [6] In fourteen World Series games, Clemente

never went without a hit. [7] Roberto Clemente died in a plane crash off the coast of his homeland, Puerto Rico. [8] The crash occurred on a flight to Nicaragua to aid earthquake victims. [9] After his death, Clemente was elected to the National Baseball Hall of Fame. [10] In New York, a park has been named for this beloved ballplayer.

EXERCISE 6 **Writing Predicates**

Make a sentence out of each of the following groups of words by adding a predicate to fill the blank or blanks.

EXAMPLES **1.** A flock of geese ____.
1. *A flock of geese flew high overhead.*
2. ____ a poster of Nelson Mandela.
2. *Over Kim's desk hung a poster of Nelson Mandela.*

1. My favorite food ____.
2. A course in first aid ____.
3. ____ our car ____.
4. Rock climbing ____.
5. Spanish explorers in the Americas ____.
6. Several computers ____.
7. ____ a new pair of roller skates.
8. The skyscrapers of New York City ____.
9. Some dogs ____.
10. ____ my family ____.

Complete Predicate and Simple Predicate

The ***complete predicate*** consists of all the words that say something about the subject.

13e. The ***simple predicate,*** or ***verb,*** is the main word or group of words in the complete predicate.

EXAMPLES The pilot broke the sound barrier.
Complete predicate broke the sound barrier.
Simple predicate (verb) broke

We should have visited the diamond field in Arkansas.

Complete predicate should have visited the diamond field in Arkansas.

Simple predicate (verb) should have visited

NOTE: In this book, the simple predicate is usually referred to as the *verb.*

EXERCISE 7 Identifying Complete Predicates and Verbs

Identify the complete predicate of each of the following sentences. Then, underline the verb.

EXAMPLE **1.** Nobody knows the creator of the U.S. flag.
1. *knows the creator of the U.S. flag*

1. Scholars are unsure about the history of the Stars and Stripes.
2. The Continental Congress approved a design for the flag.
3. The design included thirteen red stripes and thirteen white stripes.
4. The top inner quarter of the flag was a blue field with thirteen white stars.
5. The name of the designer remains a mystery.
6. During the American Revolution, the colonists needed a symbol of their independence.
7. George Washington wanted flags for the army.
8. Unfortunately, the flags did not arrive until after the Revolutionary War.
9. According to legend, Betsy Ross made the first flag.
10. Historians doubt the Betsy Ross story.

The Verb Phrase

Some verbs consist of more than one word. Such a verb is called a ***verb phrase.***

EXAMPLES Kathy **is riding** the Ferris wheel.
The carnival **has been** in town for two weeks.
Bernice **should have been** here sooner.

NOTE: The words *not* and *never* are not verbs. They are never part of a verb or verb phrase.

EXAMPLES She **has** not **written** to me recently.
I **will** never **forget** her.

EXERCISE 8 Identifying Verbs and Verb Phrases

Identify the verb or verb phrase in each of the following sentences.

EXAMPLES
1. Look at these beautiful pictures of Hawaii.
1. *Look*

2. They were taken by our science teacher.
2. *were taken*

1. Hawaii is called the Aloha State.
2. It was settled by Polynesians around the year 750.
3. The musical heritage and rich culture of the original Hawaiians have contributed much to the islands' popularity.
4. Hawaii has the largest, most active volcanoes in the world.
5. These volcanoes may be viewed by tourists in Hawaii Volcanoes National Park.

GRAMMAR

Finding the Subject

Sometimes it's difficult to locate the subject of a sentence. In such cases, it can help to find the verb first and then to ask yourself *whom* or *what* the verb is referring to.

EXAMPLES **In high school we will have more homework.** [The verb is *will have. Who* will have? *We* will have. *We* is the subject of the sentence.]

Can you untie this knot? [*Can untie* is the verb. *Who* can untie? *You* can untie. *You* is the subject of the sentence.]

The peak of Mount Everest was first reached by Sir Edmund Hillary and Tenzing Norgay. [The verb is *was reached. What* was reached? The answer is *peak. Peak* is the subject of the sentence.]

Ahead of the explorers lay a vast wilderness. [The verb is *lay.* What *lay?* The answer is *wilderness. Wilderness* is the subject of the sentence.]

NOTE: The subject of a sentence is never part of a prepositional phrase.

EXAMPLE **The papayas on the table look tasty.** [*What* look tasty? *Papayas.* To say *table look tasty* doesn't make sense.]

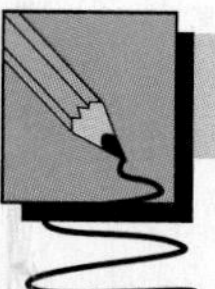

WRITING APPLICATION

Using Complete Sentences in a Letter

Sometimes a thought or an impression is so clear in your mind that you forget that others do not see it as clearly. Where you express such thoughts and expressions, you may be tempted to use a single word or phrase rather than a complete statement.

SENTENCE FRAGMENTS	What a great birthday party! All my friends. Good eats—popcorn, roasted peanuts, lots of goodies. Playing games. Music. Dancing.
COMPLETE SENTENCES	I had a great birthday party. All my friends were there. My mom and I made popcorn, roasted peanuts, and made lots of other goodies. Everybody had fun playing games, listening to music, and dancing.

To make sure that others can clearly understand you, use complete sentences.

WRITING ACTIVITY

Yesterday, you went to a birthday party. Write a letter to a friend or relative who lives far away. In your letter, describe where the party was held, how long it lasted, and what refreshments were served. Also include details about the activities you enjoyed and about the other people who were there. Use complete sentences to make sure your thoughts are clear.

Prewriting Make a list of the details that you'd like to include in your letter. At this stage, you don't have to use complete sentences—just jot down your thoughts as they come to you.

Writing Use your prewriting list of details as you write your rough draft. Choose details that would be interesting to your friend or relative. You might organize your letter chronologically (telling about events in the order they occurred). Or you might want to tell about one or two important events.

Evaluating and Revising Read your letter aloud. As you read, mark any parts of the letter that seem unclear. Add, cut, or rearrange details to make your letter clear and interesting to your reader. (See pages 361–371 for information on combining sentences.) Check your work once again to make sure you have used only complete sentences.

Proofreading Read over your letter for errors in spelling and punctuation. Be sure that you have capitalized the first word of each sentence and have ended each sentence with correct punctuation.

Compound Subjects and Compound Verbs

Compound Subjects

13f. A ***compound subject*** consists of two or more connected subjects that have the same verb. The usual connecting word is *and* or *or.*

EXAMPLES **Paris** and **London** remain favorite tourist attractions. [The two parts of the compound subject have the same verb, *remain.*]

Nelson Mandela or **Bishop Desmond Tutu** will speak at the conference. [The two parts of the compound subject have the same verb phrase, *will speak.*]

Among my hobbies are **reading, snorkeling,** and **painting.** [The three parts of the compound subject have the same verb, *are.*]

EXERCISE 9 **Identifying Compound Subjects**

Identify the compound subject in each of the following sentences.

EXAMPLE **1.** The shapes and sizes of sand dunes are determined by the wind.

1. *shapes, sizes*

1. The national parks and monuments of the United States include many of the world's most spectacular landforms.

2. The Grand Canyon and the waterfalls of Yosemite are examples of landforms shaped by erosion.
3. Water and other natural forces are continuing the age-old erosion of landforms.
4. On the Colorado Plateau, for example, natural bridges and arches like the ones shown below have been produced by erosion.
5. Likewise, Skyline Arch and Landscape Arch in Utah are two natural arches formed by erosion.
6. Underground, caves and immense caverns are created by rushing streams and waterfalls.
7. Stalagmites and stalactites such as the ones in the photo on the right are formed by lime deposits from drops of water seeping into these caverns.
8. In river systems throughout the world, canyons and gorges are cut into the earth by erosion.
9. Many rapids and waterfalls have also originated through erosion.
10. Do steep areas with heavy rainfall or dry regions with few trees suffer more from erosion?

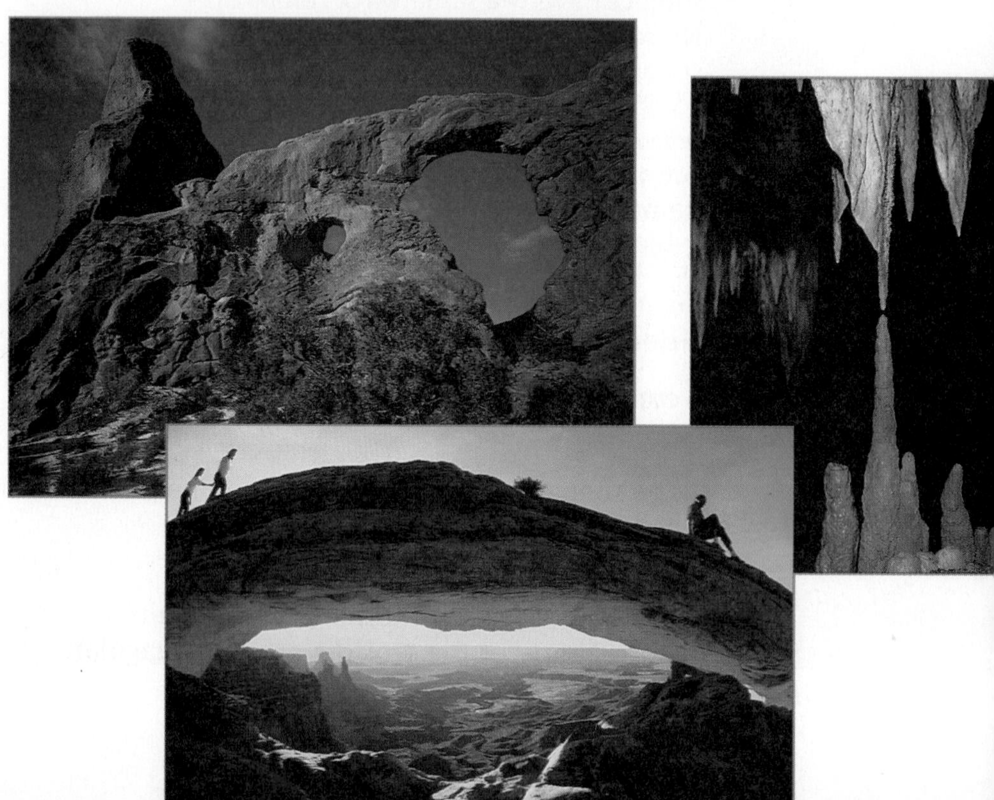

EXERCISE 10 Writing Compound Subjects

Add a compound subject to each of the following predicates. Use *and* or *or* to join the parts of your compound subjects.

EXAMPLE 1. ___ were at the bottom of my locker.
1. *My bus pass and a pair of gym socks were at the bottom of my locker.*

1. Yesterday ___ arrived in the mail.
2. ___ make loyal pets.
3. On the beach ___ spotted a dolphin.
4. ___ will present their report on Álvar Núñez Cabeza de Vaca.
5. In the attic were piled ___.

Compound Verbs

13g. A ***compound verb*** consists of two or more connected verbs that have the same subject. A connecting word—usually *and, or,* or *but*—is used to join the verbs.

EXAMPLES The basketball team **played** well but **lost** the game anyway.
The rain **has fallen** for days and **is** still **falling** in some areas.

A sentence may have both a *compound subject* and a *compound verb*. Notice in the following example that both subjects carry out the action of both verbs.

EXAMPLE A few **vegetables** and many **flowers sprouted** and **grew** in the rich soil. [The vegetables sprouted and grew, and the flowers sprouted and grew.]

EXERCISE 11 Identifying Compound Verbs

Identify each compound verb or verb phrase in the following sentences.

EXAMPLE 1. Just like children today, children in ancient Egypt played games and enjoyed toys.
1. *played, enjoyed*

1. Have you heard of the game Serpent or learned the game Senet?
2. For the Egyptian board game Serpent, players found or carved a serpent-shaped stone.
3. Players placed the serpent in the center of the board and then began the game.
4. They used place markers and threw bones or sticks as dice.
5. The players took turns and competed with one another in a race to the center.
6. Senet was another ancient Egyptian board game and was played by children and adults alike.
7. Senet looked like an easy game but was actually quite difficult.
8. Players moved their playing pieces toward the ends of three rows of squares but sometimes were stopped by their opponents.
9. Senet boards were complex and had certain squares for good luck and bad luck.
10. These squares could help players or could block their playing pieces.

EXERCISE 12 **Writing Appropriate Compound Verbs**

Where in the solar system are you? That's what you—the captain of this spaceship—want to find out. To do so, you've called up on your viewing screen the map shown on the next page. Look at the map and find your spaceship among the planets. Then use the map and the accompanying notes you've made in your log to write your official report for the last three days of June. (Be as imaginative as you want.) Use at least five sentences that have compound verbs.

EXAMPLE *We then landed on Jobel's Dark Spot and captured Shelzan, king of the Noidles.*

LOG NOTES

FRIDAY JUNE 28

rough trip through Banzoi Asteroid Belt contacted Intergalactic Command for instructions Dark Spot on Jobel captured Shelzan—king of the Noidles

SATURDAY JUNE 29

surveyed Prog strange light spotted ancient satellite Voyager I lost gravity field crater creature

SUNDAY JUNE 30

ship's fuel low sighted Bittzer's Comet landing on Grepinak took on supplies frozen fog plan next course

MONDAY JULY

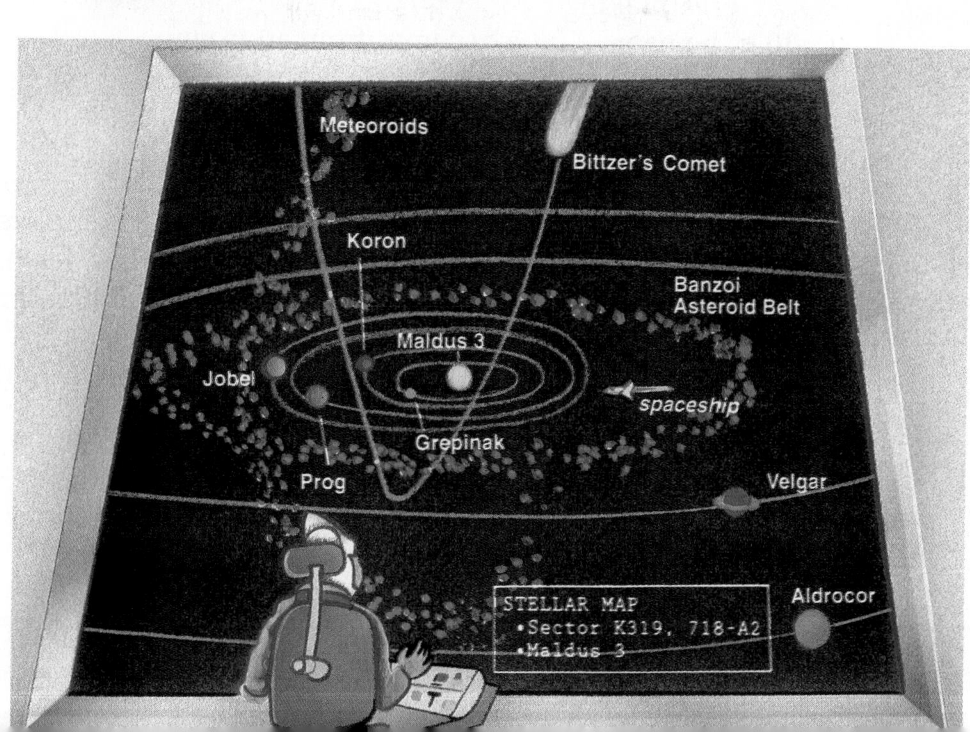

GRAMMAR

EXERCISE 13 Identifying Subjects and Verbs

Identify the subject and verb in each of the following sentences. Some of the subjects and verbs are compound.

EXAMPLE 1. American pioneers left their homes and traveled to the West.
1. *pioneers—subject; left, traveled—verbs*

1. Settlers faced and overcame many dangers.
2. Mount McKinley and Mount Whitney are two very high mountains.
3. Sacagawea of the Shoshones helped open the West.
4. Every winter many skiers rush to the Grand Tetons.
5. Few Hollywood stars have been both born and raised in California.
6. Broad valleys and dense forests cool and refresh travelers through the Appalachian Mountains.
7. On Beartooth Highway in Montana, excellent campgrounds and scenic overlooks provide many views of distant glaciers.
8. Mount Evans is west of Denver and can be reached by the highest paved road in America.
9. The view from the top slopes of Mount Evans is breathtaking.
10. The name *Kentucky* comes from an Iroquois word and means "meadowland."

REVIEW A Identifying Subjects and Predicates

Write the following sentences. Underline the complete subjects once and the complete predicates twice. Then, circle each simple subject and each verb or verb phrase.

EXAMPLE 1. The seven continents are divisions of the earth's land.
1. *The seven continents are divisions of the earth's land.*

1. The entire continent of Australia is occupied by a single nation.
2. Can you name the capital of Australia?

3. Australia is a federation of six states and two territories.
4. The continent was claimed for Britain by Captain James Cook.
5. The native people of Australia live mainly in the desert regions and have a very close bond to their environment.
6. British colonists settled in cities on the coast.
7. Many ranchers raise sheep and export wool.
8. In addition, large quantities of gold and uranium are mined in Australia.
9. The country is also highly industrialized and produces a variety of goods, ranging from shoes to airplanes.
10. Among Australia's unusual animals are the platypus and the anteater.

Kinds of Sentences

13h. A ***declarative sentence*** makes a statement. It is always followed by a period.

EXAMPLES Amy Tan was born in San Francisco**.**
I couldn't hear what Jason said**.**

13i. An ***imperative sentence*** gives a command or makes a request. It is usually followed by a period. A strong command is followed by an exclamation point.

EXAMPLES Be quiet during the play**.**
Please give me another piece of melon**.**
Stop**!**

The subject of a command or a request is always *you*, although *you* doesn't appear in the sentence. In such cases, *you* is called the ***understood subject.***

GRAMMAR

EXAMPLES (You) Be quiet during the play.
(You) Please give me another piece of melon.
(You) Stop!

The word *you* is the understood subject even when the person spoken to is addressed by name.

EXAMPLE Miguel, (you) please answer the door.

13j. An ***interrogative sentence*** asks a question. It is followed by a question mark.

EXAMPLES When did Thurgood Marshall retire from the Supreme Court**?**
Did the surfboard cost much**?**

13k. An ***exclamatory sentence*** shows excitement or expresses strong feeling. It is followed by an exclamation point.

EXAMPLES Gabriella won the match**!**
How terrifying that movie was**!**

PICTURE THIS

The time is the 1960s. The young men on stage are the Beatles. You are a reporter for *Rock Roots,* a music databank that is popular in the twenty-third century. You've been transported back in time to write a short review of this Beatles' concert. You find the Beatles' hair styles and clothes most unusual, and you're amazed at the number of police on the scene to protect the group from the crowd. As you watch the concert, you compare it with rock concerts of the twenty-third century. Because space is limited on the databank, your review must be no longer than ten sentences. In your review, use at least one example of each of the four kinds of sentences (declarative, imperative, interrogative, and exclamatory).

Subject: Beatles concert
Audience: users of music history databank *Rock Roots*
Purpose: to inform

EXERCISE 14 Classifying Sentences by Purpose

Label each of the following quotations as *declarative*, *imperative*, *interrogative*, or *exclamatory*.

EXAMPLE **1. Lead me from darkness to light!**

Brihadaranyaka Upanishad

1. ***exclamatory***

1. The only thing we have to fear is fear itself.
   Franklin Delano Roosevelt, 1933 Inaugural Address
2. Push yourself.
   from an interview with Nikki Giovanni
3. Do any human beings ever realize life while they live it?
   Thornton Wilder, *Our Town*
4. I am beginning, just beginning, to find out who I am.
   Gloria Steinem, "Sisterhood"
5. I have yet to meet a man who, on observing his own faults, blamed himself!
   Confucius, *The Sayings of Confucius*

GRAMMAR

REVIEW B Classifying and Punctuating Sentences

Add the correct end mark of punctuation to each of the following sentences. Then, label each sentence as *declarative, imperative, interrogative,* or *exclamatory.*

EXAMPLE **1. Are prairie dogs social creatures**
1. ***Are prairie dogs social creatures?—interrogative***

1. Many of these small mammals live together in underground "towns" like the one shown below
2. As you can see, American prairie dogs dig family burrows
3. These burrows sometimes cover several acres
4. Have you ever seen a prairie dog
5. These creatures can usually be seen at night or in the early morning
6. What alert animals prairie dogs are
7. At least one prairie dog always keeps a constant lookout for threats to the community
8. Look at how it sits up to see better
9. It will make a shrill whistle of alarm at the first sign of danger
10. It then dives headfirst into the burrow and alerts the entire colony

Review: Posttest 1

A. Identifying Sentences

Label each of the following groups of words as a *sentence* or a *sentence fragment*. Write each sentence, using a capital letter at the beginning and an end mark of punctuation.

EXAMPLES **1. having forgotten their homework**
1. *sentence fragment*

2. how strong the wind is
2. *sentence—How strong the wind is!*

1. after we visit the library and gather information for the report
2. are you ready for the big game next week
3. listen closely to our guest speaker
4. have read the first draft of my paper
5. an excellent short story, "The Medicine Bag," is in that book

B. Identifying Simple Subjects and Verbs

Identify the simple subject and the verb in each of the following sentences.

EXAMPLE **1. A computer can be a wonderful tool for people with disabilities.**
1. *computer—simple subject; can be—verb*

6. Specially designed machines have been developed in recent years.
7. Have you ever seen a talking computer?
8. It is used by both visually impaired people and sighted people.
9. Its electronic voice speaks the words typed into the machine.
10. Most computers show their writing on a screen.

GRAMMAR

11. However, these special models can give information by voice.
12. Close-captioned television is another interesting invention.
13. Subtitles appear on the television screens of hearing-impaired viewers.
14. These viewers can read the subtitles and enjoy their favorite shows.
15. Many new inventions make life easier and more enjoyable nowadays.

C. Classifying and Punctuating Sentences

Add the correct end mark of punctuation after the last word in each of the following sentences. Then, label each sentence *declarative, interrogative, imperative,* or *exclamatory*.

EXAMPLE **1. Flowers and insects depend on one another for life**
1. *life.—declarative*

16. Have you ever watched a bee in a garden
17. The bee flies busily from one flower to another
18. Notice the pollen on the legs and body of the bee
19. The bee is carrying pollen from flower to flower
20. What a remarkable insect the bee is

Review: Posttest 2

Writing Sentences

Identify each of the following sentence parts as a *complete subject* or a *complete predicate*. Then, use each sentence part in a sentence. Begin each sentence with a capital letter and end it with the correct mark of punctuation.

EXAMPLE **1. the tides of the oceans**
1. ***complete subject***
Are the tides of the oceans influenced by the moon?

1. the path through the woods
2. the city of San Juan
3. found a four-leaf clover
4. my favorite television show
5. can call a meeting and take a vote on the matter
6. splashed happily in the shallow water
7. one of the nurses
8. our broken VCR
9. will represent us at the meeting
10. mentioned rain and high winds

14 The Parts of Speech

Noun, Pronoun, Adjective

Diagnostic Test

Identifying Nouns, Pronouns, and Adjectives

Identify each italicized word in the following paragraph as a *noun*, a *pronoun*, or an *adjective*.

EXAMPLE The mangrove [1] *tree* grows in [2] *coastal* areas, and [3] *it* sends down roots from its branches.
1. *noun*
2. *adjective*
3. *pronoun*

In [1] *this* country [2] *mangroves* grow along the coasts of [3] *Florida*. [4] *They* form a [5] *wonderland* where land, water, and [6] *sky* blend. [7] *The* lush, green [8] *mangrove* islands and [9] *shoreline* are both beautiful and valuable. Mangroves are [10] *important* to [11] *our* [12] *environment*. They produce [13] *tons* of valuable [14] *vegetable* matter and are an essential part of [15] *tropical* biology. So far as [16] *we* know, the

[17] *first* reference to mangroves dates back to [18] *Egyptian* times. A [19] *South African* expert has also discovered evidence of mangrove islands along the [20] *Red Sea*.

The Eight Parts of Speech

noun	adjective	adverb	conjunction
pronoun	verb	preposition	interjection

The Noun

14a. A ***noun*** is a word that names a person, place, thing, or idea.

PERSONS	Jessye Norman, teacher, Dr. Ling, first baseman
PLACES	Grand Canyon, city, Nigeria, kitchen
THINGS	lamp, canary, Nobel Prize, Empire State Building
IDEAS	happiness, self-control, democracy, bravery

Notice that some nouns are made up of more than one word. Such nouns are called ***compound nouns.*** They may be written as one word, as a hyphenated word, or as two or more words.

ONE WORD	grandmother
HYPHENATED WORD	great-grandmother
TWO WORDS	grand piano

EXERCISE 1 **Identifying Nouns**

Identify the twenty-five nouns in the following paragraph. Some nouns will be used more than once.

EXAMPLE [1] We have been reading about patriotic heroines in our textbook.

1. *heroines, textbook*

[1] Rebecca Motte was a great patriot. [2] During the Revolutionary War, British soldiers seized her mansion in South Carolina. [3] General Harry Lee told Motte that the Americans would have to burn her home to smoke out the enemy. [4] Motte supported the plan and was glad to help her country. [5] She even supplied fire arrows and a bow for the attack. [6] But the enemy raised the white flag of surrender, and the house was saved. [7] Afterward, Motte invited soldiers from both sides to dinner.

Proper Nouns and Common Nouns

A ***proper noun*** names a particular person, place, thing, or idea. It always begins with a capital letter. A ***common noun*** names any one of a group of persons, places, or things. It is not capitalized.

COMMON NOUNS	PROPER NOUNS
girl	Kay O'Neill
writer	Octavio Paz
country	Panama
monument	Eiffel Tower
team	Atlanta Braves
book	*Tiger Eyes*
religion	Buddhism

EXERCISE 2 Identifying Common and Proper Nouns

Identify the nouns in the following paragraph as *common* or *proper*. [Note: Some nouns are used more than once.]

EXAMPLE [1] Mark visited an interesting museum in Colorado last month.

1. *Mark—proper; museum—common; Colorado—proper; month—common*

[1] Mark and his parents went to the Black American West Museum and Heritage Center in Denver. [2] The

museum displays many items that cowboys used. [3] These items are from the collection of Paul Stewart, the man who founded the museum. [4] Mark saw saddles, knives, hats, and lariats. [5] He also saw many pictures of African American cowboys. [6] The museum is located in an old house that is listed in the National Register of Historic Places. [7] The house once belonged to Dr. Justina L. Ford. [8] She was the first black woman physician in Colorado. [9] Mark was amazed by all of the old medical instruments in one display. [10] He said he was glad doctors don't use equipment like that any more.

EXERCISE 3 Revising Sentences by Using Proper Nouns

Revise the following sentences by substituting a proper noun for each common noun. You may need to change some other words in each sentence. You may also make up proper names to use.

EXAMPLE **1. An ambassador visited a local school and spoke about his country.**
1. ***Ambassador Rios visited Jackson High School and spoke about Brazil.***

1. That painting is in a famous museum.
2. The police officer directed us to the building on that street.
3. My relatives, who are from a small town, now live in a large city.
4. The librarian asked my classmate to return the book.
5. That newspaper is published daily; this magazine is published weekly.
6. The girl read a poem for the teacher.
7. That state borders on the ocean.
8. The owner of that store visited two countries during a spring month.
9. A man flew to a northern city one day.
10. The mayor visited our school and talked about our city.

GRAMMAR

Concrete Nouns and Abstract Nouns

A ***concrete noun*** names a person, place, or thing that can be perceived by one or more of the senses (sight, sound, taste, touch, smell). An ***abstract noun*** names an idea, a feeling, a quality, or a characteristic.

CONCRETE NOUNS	poster, music, beans, heat, Florida
ABSTRACT NOUNS	love, fun, freedom, pride, beauty

EXERCISE 4 **Writing Sentences with Concrete and Abstract Nouns**

Identify each noun in the following list as *concrete* or *abstract*. Then, use each noun in an original sentence.

EXAMPLE **1.** truth
1. *abstract—My mother said I should always tell the truth.*

1. soy sauce
2. brotherhood
3. laughter
4. ice
5. excitement

REVIEW A **Identifying and Classifying Nouns**

Identify the twenty nouns in the following paragraph. Then tell whether each noun is a *common noun* or a *proper noun.* Be sure to capitalize all proper nouns.

EXAMPLE [1] Lillian evanti sang operas in europe, latin america, and africa.
1. *Lillian Evanti—proper noun; operas—common noun; Europe—proper noun; Latin America—proper noun; Africa—proper noun*

[1] Evanti was the first African American woman to sing opera anywhere in the world. [2] Her talent was recognized early, when at the age of four, she gave a solo concert in washington, d.c. [3] As an adult, she performed in a special concert at the white house for president franklin roosevelt and his wife. [4] Evanti also composed a

musical piece titled *"Himno Panamericano,"* which was a great success. [5] Her career inspired many other African American singers.

REVIEW B Using the Different Kinds of Nouns

Complete the following poem based on this picture. Add common, proper, concrete, or abstract nouns as directed. Choose nouns that you think will help describe or explain the picture. For proper nouns, you'll need to make up names of people and places.

Jacob Lawrence, *Strong Man*, gouache on paper, 22 × 17", photo by Chris Eden, Francine Seders Gallery

Hanging Around

Meet my [1] ___*(common)*___, the really amazing,
Truly tremendous [2] ___*(proper)*___, that's who.
You can see what [3] ___*(abstract)*___ he gives
His fans who hang on him like glue.

The walls of his [4] ___*(concrete)*___ on [5] ___*(proper)*___
Are covered with [6] ___*(concrete)*___ that show
The muscled, tussled [7] ___*(common)*___ aplenty,
Who work out there, come rain or come snow.

Eduardo, [8] ___*(proper)*___, and I really enjoy
The [9] ___*(abstract)*___ of hanging on tight
Way above the [10] ___*(concrete)*___ and swinging,
Held up by the muscle man's might.

The Pronoun

GRAMMAR

14b. A ***pronoun*** is a word used in place of a noun or more than one noun.

EXAMPLES After Lois borrowed the book, Lois lost the book.
After Lois borrowed the book, **she** lost **it.**

Ask Dan if Dan has done Dan's homework.
Ask Dan if **he** has done **his** homework.

The word that a pronoun stands for (or refers to) is called its ***antecedent.***

EXAMPLE **Frederick,** [antecedent] have **you** [pronoun] turned in **your** [pronoun] report?

Sometimes the antecedent is not stated.

EXAMPLE **It** [pronoun] was hot outside today.

Personal Pronouns

A ***personal pronoun*** refers to the one speaking (*first person*), the one spoken to (*second person*), or the one spoken about (*third person*).

PERSONAL PRONOUNS		
	SINGULAR	PLURAL
First person	I, me, my, mine	we, us, our, ours
Second person	you, your, yours	you, your, yours
Third person	he, him, his, she, her, hers, it, its	they, them, their, theirs

NOTE: Some teachers prefer to call possessive pronouns (such as *my, your,* and *their*) possessive adjectives. Follow your teacher's directions in labeling these words.

Reflexive and Intensive Pronouns

A ***reflexive pronoun*** refers to the subject and directs the action of the verb back to the subject. An ***intensive pronoun*** emphasizes a noun or another pronoun.

REFLEXIVE AND INTENSIVE PRONOUNS	
FIRST PERSON	myself, ourselves
SECOND PERSON	yourself, yourselves
THIRD PERSON	himself, herself, itself, themselves

REFLEXIVE Tara enjoyed **herself** at the party.
The band members prided **themselves** on their performance.

INTENSIVE I **myself** cooked that delicious dinner.
Did you redecorate the room **yourself?**

NOTE: If you are not sure whether a pronoun is reflexive or intensive, use this test. Read the sentence aloud, omitting the pronoun. If the meaning of the sentence stays the same, the pronoun is intensive. If the meaning changes, the pronoun is reflexive.

EXAMPLES The children enjoyed **themselves** all morning. [Without *themselves,* the sentence doesn't make sense. The pronoun is reflexive.]
Mark repaired the car **himself.** [Without *himself,* the meaning stays the same. The pronoun is intensive.]

Demonstrative Pronouns

A ***demonstrative pronoun*** points out a person, a place, a thing, or an idea.

Demonstrative Pronouns			
this	that	these	those

EXAMPLES **This** is the book I told you about.
Are **these** the kinds of plants that bloom at night?

NOTE: Demonstrative pronouns can also be used as adjectives. When they are used in this way, they are called *demonstrative adjectives.*

DEMONSTRATIVE PRONOUN **Those** are very sturdy shoes.
DEMONSTRATIVE ADJECTIVE **Those** shoes are very sturdy.

Interrogative Pronouns

An ***interrogative pronoun*** introduces a question.

Interrogative Pronouns				
what	which	who	whom	whose

EXAMPLES **What** is the best brand of frozen yogurt?
Who wrote *Barrio Boy*?

Indefinite Pronouns

An ***indefinite pronoun*** does not refer to a definite person, place, thing, or idea.

Common Indefinite Pronouns				
all	both	few	nobody	other
any	either	more	none	several
anyone	everything	much	no one	some

EXAMPLES **Both** of the girls forgot their lines.
I would like **some** of that chow mein.

NOTE: Indefinite pronouns can also be used as adjectives.

PRONOUN **Some** are bored by this movie.
ADJECTIVE **Some** people are bored by this movie.

Relative Pronouns

A ***relative pronoun*** introduces a subordinate clause.

Relative Pronouns				
that	which	who	whom	whose

EXAMPLES Thomas Jefferson, **who** wrote the Declaration of Independence, was our country's third president.

Exercise is one of several methods **that** people use to control their weight.

REFERENCE NOTE: For more information about subordinate clauses, see pages 516–525.

EXERCISE 5 **Identifying Pronouns**

Identify each pronoun and its antecedent in the following sentences. [Note: A sentence may have more than one pronoun.]

EXAMPLE **1.** The drama coach said he would postpone the rehearsal.

1. *he—coach*

1. "I want you to study," Ms. Gaines said to the class.
2. The firefighter carefully adjusted her oxygen mask.
3. The children made lunch themselves.
4. Jenny and Rosa decided they would get popcorn, but Amy didn't want any.
5. Dad said to let him know when Tamisha came home.

EXERCISE 6 **Writing Appropriate Pronouns**

Rewrite each sentence, replacing the repeated nouns with pronouns.

1. Put the flowers in water before the flowers' petals droop.
2. The canoe capsized as the canoe neared the shore.

3. The players convinced the players that the players would win the game.
4. Lorraine oiled the bicycle before Lorraine put the bicycle in the garage.
5. Tim said, "Tim answered all six questions on the quiz."

EXERCISE 7 **Writing Sentences with Pronouns and Antecedents**

Your pen pal in another country has written you to ask about the American pastimes of roller-skating and in-line skating. In your next letter, you send this photograph along with a written description of these types of skating. In your letter, use at least five pronouns. Underline each pronoun and draw an arrow to its antecedent.

EXAMPLE *The skater slowly increases his speed.*

WRITING APPLICATION

Using Pronouns Clearly

When you write about people, you nearly always use pronouns for variety. Sometimes, though, pronouns can be confusing.

CONFUSING Joel wrote to Mark while he was on vacation. [Who was on vacation, Joel or Mark?]

CLEAR While Joel was on vacation, **he** wrote to Mark.

or

CLEAR While Mark was on vacation, Joel wrote to **him.**

When you use a pronoun, make sure that it refers clearly to its antecedent. If the pronoun reference is not clear, change the order of the sentence or reword parts of the sentence.

WRITING ACTIVITY

Your class is creating a bulletin board display for the school's Special People Day. For the display, write a brief report about someone you think is special. Tell why you think so. Be sure that the pronouns you use refer clearly to their antecedents.

Prewriting First, you'll need to select your subject. Someone special—perhaps a friend, a neighbor, or a relative—may come to mind immediately. If not, make a list of the different people you know. Which of these people really stands out? After you choose a subject, freewrite about that person. What makes this person special? Tell what that person has done to earn your respect and admiration.

Writing As you write your first draft, refer to your freewriting notes. In your first paragraph, catch the reader's attention and identify your subject. Your thesis statement should briefly state what is special about your subject. In the rest of your paragraphs, give specific examples that illustrate why the person is special.

GRAMMAR

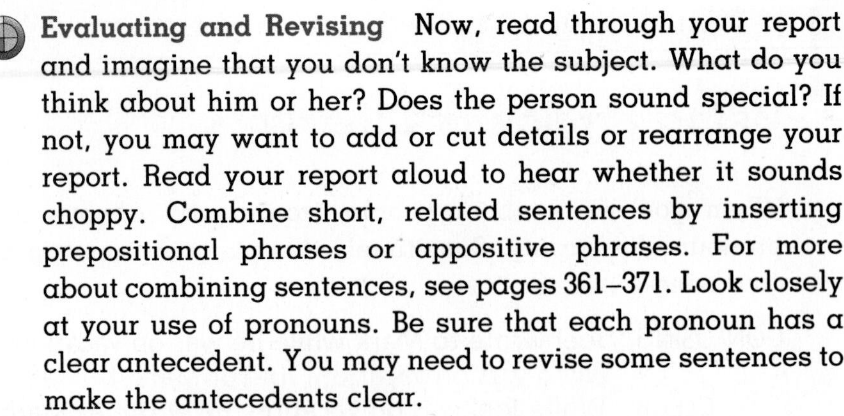

Evaluating and Revising Now, read through your report and imagine that you don't know the subject. What do you think about him or her? Does the person sound special? If not, you may want to add or cut details or rearrange your report. Read your report aloud to hear whether it sounds choppy. Combine short, related sentences by inserting prepositional phrases or appositive phrases. For more about combining sentences, see pages 361–371. Look closely at your use of pronouns. Be sure that each pronoun has a clear antecedent. You may need to revise some sentences to make the antecedents clear.

Proofreading and Publishing Check to see that you have spelled and capitalized all proper names correctly. You and your classmates may want to use your reports to make a classroom bulletin board display. If possible, include pictures or drawings of your subjects. You may also wish to send a copy of your report to the person you wrote about.

The Adjective

14c. An ***adjective*** is a word that modifies a noun or a pronoun.

To *modify* a word means to describe the word or to make its meaning more definite. An adjective modifies a noun or a pronoun by telling *what kind, which one, how much,* or *how many.*

WHAT KIND?	WHICH ONE OR ONES?	HOW MANY OR HOW MUCH?
happy children	seventh grade	full tank
busy dentist	these countries	five dollars
sunny day	any book	no marbles

Sometimes an adjective may come after the word that it modifies.

EXAMPLES **The box is empty.** [The adjective *empty* modifies *box.*]

A woman, kind and helpful, gave us directions. [The adjectives *kind* and *helpful* modify *woman*.]

Articles

The most commonly used adjectives are *a, an,* and *the.* These adjectives are called ***articles.*** *A* and *an* are called ***indefinite articles*** because they refer to someone or something in general. *The* is called a ***definite article*** because it refers to someone or something in particular.

Nouns Used as Adjectives

When a noun modifies another noun or a pronoun, it is considered an adjective.

NOUNS	NOUNS USED AS ADJECTIVES
bean	**bean** soup
spring	**spring** weather
gold	**gold** coin
football	**football** game

Demonstrative Adjectives

This, that, these, and *those* can be used both as adjectives and as pronouns. When they modify a noun, they are called ***demonstrative adjectives.*** When they are used alone, they are called ***demonstrative pronouns.***

DEMONSTRATIVE ADJECTIVES Did Jennifer draw **this** picture or **that** one?
Let's take **these** sandwiches and **those** apples on our picnic.

DEMONSTRATIVE PRONOUNS **This** is mine and **that** is his.
These are much more expensive than **those** are.

REFERENCE NOTE: For more information about demonstrative pronouns, see pages 429–430.

EXERCISE 8 Identifying Adjectives

Identify the twenty adjectives in the following paragraph and give the noun or pronoun each modifies. Do not include the articles *a, an,* and *the.*

EXAMPLE [1] Why don't you take the local bus on cold days?
1. *local—bus; cold—days*

[1] On winter afternoons, I sometimes walk home after basketball practice rather than ride on a crowded, noisy bus. [2] I hardly notice the heavy traffic that streams past me. [3] The wet sidewalk glistens in the bright lights from the windows of stores. [4] The stoplights throw green, yellow, and red splashes on the pavement. [5] After I turn the corner away from the busy avenue, I am on a quiet street, where a jolly snowman often stands next to one of the neighborhood houses. [6] At last, I reach my peaceful home. [7] There I am often greeted by my brother and sister. [8] I know they are glad to see me. [9] Delicious smells come from the kitchen. [10] This walk home always makes me feel tired but happy.

GRAMMAR

EXERCISE 9 Writing Appropriate Adjectives

Complete the following story by writing an appropriate adjective to fill each blank.

EXAMPLE [1] ____ parks have [2] ____ trails for hikers.
1. *National*
2. *many*

The hikers went exploring in the [1] ____ woods. Sometimes they had difficulty getting through the [2] ____ undergrowth. On [3] ____ occasions they almost turned back. Yet they kept going and were rewarded for their [4] ____ effort. During the [5] ____ hike through the woods, they discovered [6] ____ kinds of [7] ____ animals. In the afternoon the [8] ____ hikers pitched camp in a [9] ____ clearing. They were [10] ____ for supper and rest.

Proper Adjectives

A ***proper adjective*** is formed from a proper noun.

PROPER NOUNS	PROPER ADJECTIVES
Thanksgiving	**Thanksgiving** dinner
Catholicism	**Catholic** priest
Middle East	**Middle Eastern** country
Africa	**African** continent

Notice that a proper adjective, like a proper noun, always begins with a capital letter.

EXERCISE 10 Identifying Common and Proper Adjectives

Identify the ten adjectives in the following paragraph. Then tell whether each is a *common* or a *proper* adjective. Do not include the articles *a, an,* and *the.*

EXAMPLE [1] **We have been studying how various animals protect themselves.**

1. *various—common*

[1] Many small animals defend themselves in clever ways. [2] For example, South American armadillos wear suits of armor that consist of small, bony scales. [3] As you can see from the photograph, armadillos seem delicate, with their narrow faces. [4] However, their tough armor protects them well. [5] Likewise, the Asian anteater has scales that overlap like the shingles on a roof.

EXERCISE 11 **Using Proper Adjectives in Sentences**

Change the following proper nouns into proper adjectives. Then use each proper adjective in a sentence. Use a dictionary to help you spell the adjectives.

EXAMPLE **1. Spain**

1. *Spanish—Those Peace Corps volunteers take Spanish lessons every Tuesday.*

1. Mexico
2. Hawaii
3. Memorial Day
4. Korea
5. Congress

PICTURE THIS

GRAMMAR

You're a mobile reporter for a radio station, and you travel around looking for interesting stories. You just received a call about something strange happening at the beach. When you arrive, this is the amazing scene you see! Of course, you immediately call the station and start a live broadcast from the beach. Write at least five sentences that you would use in your broadcast. In your sentences, use a variety of adjectives that appeal to the senses. Remember, your radio listeners have only your words to help them visualize this scene.

Subject: unusual beach scene
Audience: radio listeners
Purpose: to inform

Kenny Scharf, *Feliz a Praia*, 1983–84, Acrylic and Spraypaint on Canvas, 6′10½″ × 12′2″, Collection: Mr. Tony Shafrazi, NY, Photo: Ivan Dalla Tana

GRAMMAR

Changing Parts of Speech

The way that a word is used in a sentence determines what part of speech it is. Some words may be used as nouns or as adjectives.

NOUN The helmet is made of **steel.**
ADJECTIVE It is a **steel** helmet.

Some words may be used as pronouns or as adjectives.

PRONOUN **That** is a surprise.
ADJECTIVE **That** problem is difficult.

REVIEW C Identifying Nouns, Pronouns, and Adjectives

Identify all of the nouns, pronouns, and adjectives in the following paragraph. Do not include the articles *a, an,* and *the.*

EXAMPLE **1. We walked along the empty beach at sundown.**
1. *We—pronoun; empty—adjective; beach—noun; sundown—noun*

[1] When the tide comes in, it brings a variety of interesting items from the sea. [2] When it ebbs, it leaves behind wonderful treasures for the watchful beachcombers. [3] Few creatures live here, but you almost certainly will find several animals if you try. [4] Some live in shallow burrows under the wet sand and emerge in the cool evening to dine on bits of plants and other matter. [5] A number of different species of beetle like this part of the beach. [6] Around them you can find bristly flies and tiny worms. [7] You might also come across old pieces of wood with round holes and tunnels in them. [8] These holes are produced by shipworms. [9] If you watch the shoreline carefully, you will see many signs of life that casual strollers miss. [10] Low tide is a marvelous time to search along the shore.

"Now! ... *That* should clear up a few things around here!"

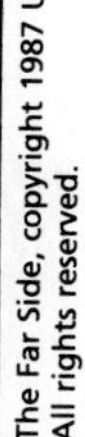

Review: Posttest 1

Identifying Nouns, Pronouns, and Adjectives

Identify each italicized word in the following paragraphs as a *noun*, a *pronoun*, or an *adjective*.

EXAMPLE The [1] *achievements* of the [2] *native* peoples of North America have sometimes been overlooked.
1. *noun*
2. *adjective*

Recent [1] *studies* show that the Winnebago people developed a [2] *calendar* based on careful observation of the [3] *heavens*.

An [4] *archaeologist* has found that the markings on an old [5] *calendar* stick are the precise records of a [6] *lunar* year and a solar year. These records are remarkably accurate, considering that at the time the [7] *Winnebagos* had neither a [8] *written* language nor a [9] *mathematical* system.

GRAMMAR

[10] *The* calendar stick is a carved [11] *hickory* branch with [12] *four* sides. [13] *It* is worn along the [14] *edges* and shows other signs of frequent use. A [15] *similar* stick appears in a portrait of an early chief of the Winnebagos. In it, the chief holds a calendar stick in [16] *his* right hand. [17] *Our* current theory is that the chief went out at [18] *sunrise* and sunset to observe the sun and the moon. [19] *He* then marked on the stick what he saw. According to one researcher, this is the [20] *first* indication that native North American peoples recorded the year day by day.

Review: Posttest 2

Using Words as Different Parts of Speech

Write ten sentences using each of the following words first as a noun or pronoun and then as an adjective. Underline the word and give its part of speech after the sentence.

EXAMPLES **1.** silk

1. *Leonie's scarf is made of silk.—noun*
May I borrow your silk scarf?—adjective

2. that

2. *That is a silly idea!—pronoun*
That idea is very silly!—adjective

1. this **2.** radio **3.** few **4.** light **5.** April

GRAMMAR

15 The Parts of Speech

Verb, Adverb, Preposition, Conjunction, Interjection

Diagnostic Test

Identifying Verbs, Adverbs, Prepositions, Conjunctions, and Interjections

Identify each numbered, italicized word or word group in the following paragraphs as a *verb,* an *adverb,* a *preposition,* a *conjunction,* or an *interjection.*

EXAMPLES [1] *Tomorrow,* we [2] *will order* equipment [3] *for* our summer camping trip.

1. *adverb*
2. *verb*
3. *preposition*

Have you ever [1] *hiked* into the wilderness [2] *with* a pack on your back and [3] *camped* under the stars? Backpacking [4] *was* once popular mainly with hardy mountaineers, [5] *but* now almost anyone who loves the outdoors [6] *can become* a backpacker.

First, however, you [7] *must be* able to carry a heavy pack long distances [8] *over* mountain trails. To get in shape, start with short walks and [9] *gradually* increase them to several miles. Doing leg exercises [10] *and* going on organized hikes can [11] *further* help build your strength. [12] *After* a few hikes, you [13] *should be* ready.

[14] *Oh,* you [15] *may be thinking,* what equipment and food should I take? Write [16] *to* the International Backpackers Association [17] *for* a checklist. The first item on the list will [18] *usually* be shoes with rubber [19] *or* synthetic soles. The second will [20] *certainly* be a sturdy backpack.

The Verb

15a. A ***verb*** is a word that expresses an action or a state of being.

EXAMPLES We **celebrated** the Chinese New Year yesterday.
The holiday **is** usually in February.

Action Verbs

(1) An ***action verb*** is a verb that expresses physical or mental action.

EXAMPLES The owls **hooted** all night.
Gloria **plays** with the children.
She **thought** about the problem.
I **believe** you.
Finish your work by three o'clock, please.

EXERCISE 1 **Identifying Action Verbs**

Identify the action verb in each of the following sentences.

EXAMPLE **1.** I saw that movie last week.
1. *saw*

1. For a science project, Elena built a sundial.
2. Mr. Santos carefully explained the problem again.
3. I enjoy soccer more than any other sport.
4. This waterfall drops two hundred feet.
5. Mike's bicycle skidded on the pavement.
6. Mrs. Karras showed us how to make stuffed grape leaves.
7. Mix the ingredients slowly.
8. The heavy traffic delayed us.
9. For the Jewish holiday of Purim, Rachel gave a costume party.
10. The early Aztecs worshiped the sun.

EXERCISE 2 **Writing Action Verbs**

Your pen pal in another country wants to know what students at your school do at school dances. To explain, you send this photograph to your pen pal. In addition, you write a letter describing the things that people do at school dances. In your letter, use at least ten action verbs. Include at least three verbs that express actions that can't be seen. Then underline the action verbs in your letter.

EXAMPLES
1. *Everyone dances to the fast songs.*
2. *Darnell and I sometimes invite the chaperone to dance.*

Transitive and Intransitive Verbs

(2) A ***transitive verb*** is an action verb that expresses an action directed toward a person or thing.

EXAMPLES Derrick **greeted** the visitors. [The action of *greeted* is directed toward *visitors.*]
Felicia **painted** her room. [The action of *painted* is directed toward *room.*]

With transitive verbs, the action passes from the doer—the subject—to the receiver of the action. Words that receive the action of a transitive verb are called ***objects.***

REFERENCE NOTE: For more information about objects and their uses in sentences, see pages 474–477.

An ***intransitive verb*** expresses action (or tells something about the subject) without passing the action to a receiver.

EXAMPLES The train **stopped.**
Last night we **ate** on the patio.

A verb may be transitive in one sentence and intransitive in another.

EXAMPLES The children **play** checkers. [transitive]
The children **play** quietly. [intransitive]

Mr. Lopez **is baking** bread. [transitive]
Mr. Lopez **is baking** this afternoon. [intransitive]

EXERCISE 3 Identifying Transitive and Intransitive Verbs

In each of the following sentences, identify the italicized action verb as *transitive* or *intransitive.*

EXAMPLE **1.** She *runs* early in the morning.
1. *intransitive*

1. If you do different kinds of exercises, you *are exercising* in the correct way.

2. When you exercise to improve endurance, flexibility, and strength, your body *develops.*
3. Aerobic exercise *builds* endurance.
4. When you *walk* quickly, you do aerobic exercise.
5. Many people *attend* classes in aerobic dancing.
6. They *enjoy* the fun of exercising to music.
7. Exercises that *improve* flexibility require you to bend and stretch.
8. *Perform* these exercises slowly for maximum benefit.
9. Through isometric and isotonic exercises, your muscle strength *increases.*
10. These exercises *contract* your muscles.

EXERCISE 4 **Writing Sentences with Transitive and Intransitive Verbs**

For each verb given below, write two sentences. In one sentence, use the verb as a *transitive* verb and underline its object. In the other, use the verb as an *intransitive* verb. You may use different tenses of the verb.

EXAMPLE **1.** write
1. *Alex is writing a research report. (transitive)*
Alex writes in his journal every day. (intransitive)

1. fly **2.** leave **3.** return **4.** draw **5.** drive

Linking Verbs

(3) A ***linking verb*** is a verb that expresses a state of being. A linking verb connects the subject of a sentence with a word in the predicate that explains or describes the subject.

EXAMPLES Howard Rollins **is** an actor. [The verb *is* connects *actor* with the subject *Howard Rollins.*]
The children **remained** quiet during the puppet show. [The verb *remained* links *quiet* with the subject *children.*]

Linking Verbs Formed from the Verb *Be*

am	has been	may be
is	have been	might be
are	had been	can be
was	will be	should be
were	shall be	would have been

Other Linking Verbs

appear	grow	seem	stay
become	look	smell	taste
feel	remain	sound	turn

Some words may be either action verbs or linking verbs, depending on how they are used.

ACTION Amy **looked** through the telescope.
LINKING Amy **looked** pale. [The verb links *pale* with the subject *Amy.*]

ACTION **Remain** in your seats until the bell rings.
LINKING **Remain** quiet. [The verb links *quiet* with the understood subject *you.*]

REFERENCE NOTE: For more about understood subjects in imperative sentences, see pages 415–416.

EXERCISE 5 **Identifying Linking Verbs**

Identify the linking verb in each sentence in the following paragraphs.

EXAMPLE [1] A radio station can be the voice of a community.
1. *can be*

[1] "Good morning, listeners! This is Roberto Martínez, your weather forecaster. [2] Unfortunately, the forecast looks bad today. [3] Outside the window here at Station

WOLF, the skies appear cloudy. [4] It certainly felt rainy earlier this morning. [5] And, according to the latest information, it should be a damp, drizzly day with an 85 percent chance of rainfall. [6] Now, for the latest scores, our sportscaster this morning is Marta Segal."

[7] "Well, Roberto, things have been quiet here around Arlington for the past few days. [8] But stay alert for sports action tonight. [9] It should be a great game between our own Arlington Angels and the visiting Jackson City Dodgers. [10] The team looked great at practice today, and I predict a hometown victory."

EXERCISE 6 Identifying Action Verbs and Linking Verbs

Identify the verb in each of the following sentences. Then label each verb as either an *action verb* or a *linking verb.* If the verb is a linking verb, give the two words that it connects.

EXAMPLES **1. We sent our dog to obedience school.**
1. *sent—action verb*

2. Some breeds are extremely nervous.
2. *are—linking verb; breeds, nervous*

1. Everyone felt sorry about the misunderstanding.
2. In daylight, this sweater looks blue.
3. The temperature plunged to almost ten degrees below zero.
4. The museum exhibited Inuit sculptures of whales and seals.
5. Loretta felt her way carefully through the dark, quiet room.
6. The city almost always smells musty after a heavy summer storm.
7. Dakar is the capital of Senegal.
8. The firefighter cautiously smelled the burned rags.
9. Antonia Novello is the Surgeon General of the United States.
10. They looked handsome in their party clothes.

 EXERCISE 7

Identifying Action Verbs and Linking Verbs

GRAMMAR

Identify the twenty verbs in the following paragraphs. Then label each verb as either an *action verb* or a *linking verb*.

EXAMPLE [1] **I always enjoy field trips.**
1. *enjoy—action verb*

[1] Last spring, our class visited the Hayden Planetarium. [2] It is a wonderful place, full of amazing sights. [3] We wandered through the various displays and saw a collection of fascinating exhibits. [4] One showed a space vehicle. [5] Another displayed a thirty-four-ton meteorite. [6] When this meteorite fell to earth many years ago, it made a huge crater.

[7] After lunch, we went to the show in the observatory. [8] As the room became darker, the picture of a galaxy appeared on the dome above us. [9] The lecturer said that the galaxy is so far away from here that its light reaches us centuries after its first appearance. [10] When we look at such stars, we actually see the ancient past! [11] I still feel a little strange when I think about the galaxy and its history. [12] We really live in a universe that is full of wonders.

 EXERCISE 8

Writing Sentences with Action Verbs and Linking Verbs

The circus is in town! Unfortunately, your best friend is sick and can't go. So that your friend won't miss out entirely, you take some photographs. Using the pictures on the next page and your imagination, write ten sentences describing the circus to your friend. In five of the sentences, use action verbs. In the other five, use linking verbs. Underline each verb that you use.

EXAMPLES **1.** *The trapeze artist leaps from the trapeze into the air.*
2. *He probably feels nervous, but he certainly looks brave!*

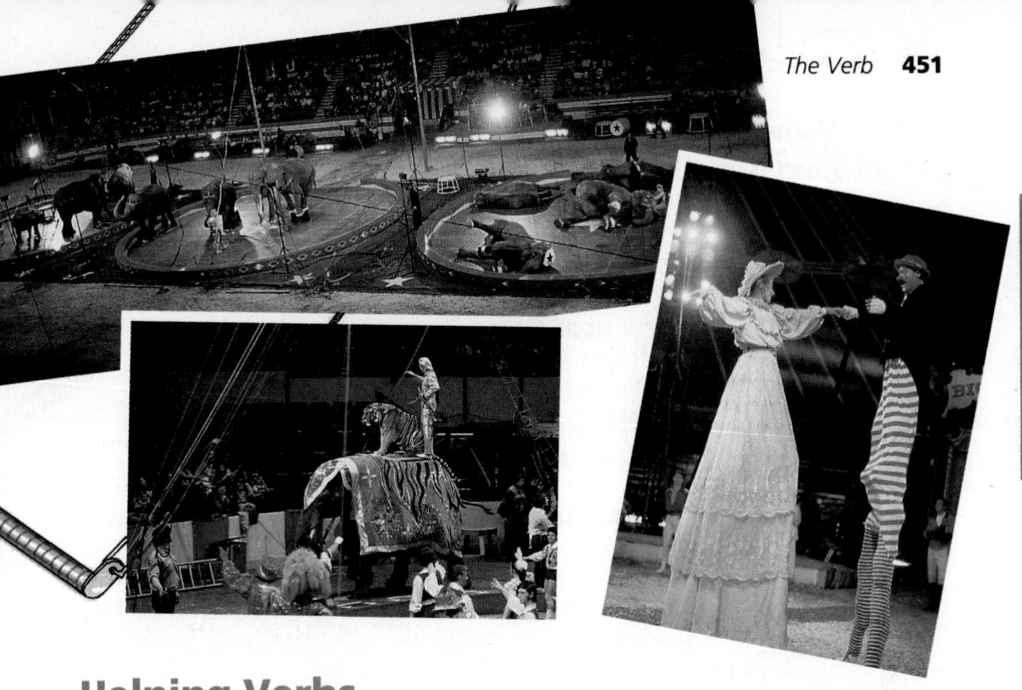

GRAMMAR

Helping Verbs

A ***verb phrase*** contains one main verb and one or more helping verbs.

EXAMPLES Many people in Africa **can speak** more than one language.
Kansas **has been named** the Sunflower State.
The ball **should have been caught** by the nearest player.

(4) A ***helping verb*** helps the main verb to express action or a state of being.

EXAMPLES **can** speak
has been named
should have been caught

Helping Verbs

am	be	do	might	shall
is	been	does	must	should
are	has	did	can	will
was	have	may	could	would
were	had			

Sometimes a verb phrase is interrupted by another part of speech, such as an adverb or a pronoun.

EXAMPLES Ken **does** not **have** a new desk.
Our school **has** always **held** a victory celebration.
Did you **hear** Cesar Chavez's speech?

EXERCISE 9 Identifying Verb Phrases and Helping Verbs

Identify the verb phrases in the following paragraphs. Underline the helping verbs.

EXAMPLE [1] You can recognize redwoods and sequoias by their bark.
1. *can recognize*

[1] Have you ever visited Redwood National Park? [2] The giant trees there can be an awesome sight. [3] For centuries, these trees have been an important part of the environment of the northwest United States. [4] Surely, these rare trees must be saved for future generations.

[5] More than 85 percent of the original redwood forest has been destroyed. [6] Because of this destruction, the survival of the forest is being threatened. [7] With proper planning years ago, more of the forest might already have been saved. [8] Unfortunately, redwood forests are still shrinking rapidly. [9] According to some scientists, redwood forests outside the park will have disappeared before the year 2000. [10] However, according to other experts, the redwood forests can still be saved!

EXERCISE 10 Writing Sentences with Verb Phrases

You are a member of the city planning board. Your job is to figure out what kind of traffic control is needed at the busy street corner shown on the next page. Does the intersection require stoplights, stop signs, or a traffic police officer? After you investigate the street corner, you will make your recommendation to the rest of the planning board. Using this photograph, make some notes about what is happening at the intersection. Write at least five sentences containing verb phrases. Then, underline each verb phrase and circle the helping verb.

EXAMPLE **1.** ***The number of crosswalks can confuse people.***

REVIEW A **Identifying Action Verbs and Linking Verbs**

Identify the verbs in the following paragraphs. Then, label each verb as an *action verb* or a *linking verb.* [Note: A sentence may contain more than one verb.]

EXAMPLE **[1] Have you ever seen a play in Spanish?**
1. ***Have seen—action verb***

[1] The Puerto Rican Traveling Theatre presents plays about Hispanic life in the United States. [2] Over the past twenty years, this group has become a leader in Hispanic theater. [3] Sometimes, a production has two casts—one that performs in English and one that speaks in Spanish. [4] In this way, speakers of both languages can enjoy the play.

[5] In recent years many young Hispanic playwrights, directors, and actors have begun their careers at the Traveling Theatre. [6] Some became well-known at the Puerto Rican Traveling Theatre and then moved on to

Broadway or Hollywood. [7] Others remain happy at the Traveling Theatre, where they enjoy the warm, supportive atmosphere.

[8] Each production by the Traveling Theatre has its own style. [9] Some shows are musicals, full of song and dance, while other plays seem more serious. [10] Light or serious, Puerto Rican Traveling Theatre productions present a lively picture of Hispanic life today.

The Adverb

15b. An ***adverb*** is a word that modifies a verb, an adjective, or another adverb.

An adverb answers the following questions:

Where?	How often?	To what extent?
When?	*or*	*or*
How?	How long?	How much?

EXAMPLES The sprinter ran **swiftly.** [*Swiftly* is an adverb modifying the verb *ran;* it tells *how.*]

Jolene was comforting a **very** small child. [*Very* is an adverb modifying the adjective *small;* it tells *to what extent.*]

The fire blazed **too wildly** for anyone to enter. [*Too* is an adverb modifying the adverb *wildly;* it tells *to what extent. Wildly* is an adverb modifying the verb *blazed;* it tells *how.*]

Dad **often** quotes from Archbishop Desmond Tutu's speech. [*Often* is an adverb modifying the verb *quotes;* it tells *how often.*]

Put the apples **there,** and we'll eat them **later.** [*There* is an adverb modifying the verb *put;* it tells *where. Later* is an adverb modifying the verb *eat;* it tells *when.*]

WORDS OFTEN USED AS ADVERBS	
Where?	away, here, inside, there, up
When?	ago, later, now, soon, then
How?	clearly, easily, quietly, slowly
How often? or *How long?*	always, usually, continuously, never, forever, briefly
To what extent? or *How much?*	almost, so, too, more, least, extremely, quite

NOTE: The word *not* is nearly always used as an adverb to modify a verb. When *not* is part of a contraction, as in *hadn't, aren't,* and *didn't,* the *–n't* is still an adverb and is not part of the verb.

Adverbs and Adjectives

Many adverbs end in *–ly*. These adverbs are formed by adding *–ly* to adjectives.

Adjective	**+ –*ly***	**= Adverb**
clear	+ –ly	= clearly
quiet	+ –ly	= quietly

However, some words ending in *–ly* are used as adjectives.

Adjectives Ending in –*ly*		
daily	friendly	lonely
early	kindly	timely

If you aren't sure whether a word is an adjective or an adverb, ask yourself what it modifies. If a word modifies a noun or a pronoun, it is an adjective.

EXAMPLES She gave us a **friendly** hello. [*Friendly* modifies the noun *hello,* so it is an adjective.]

Were you **lonely** yesterday? [The word *lonely* modifies the pronoun *you,* so it is an adjective.]

REFERENCE NOTE: For more about adjectives, see pages 434–437.

If a word modifies a verb, an adjective, or an adverb, then it's an adverb.

EXAMPLES People from many nations have come to the United States **recently.** [The adverb *recently* modifies the verb *have come.*]

English can be a **fairly** difficult language to learn. [The adverb *fairly* modifies the adjective *difficult.*]

Newcomers study **incredibly** hard to learn the language. [The adverb *incredibly* modifies the adverb *hard.*]

NOTE: The adverb *very* is overused. In your writing, try to use adverbs other than *very* to modify adjectives.

EXAMPLE Arnold Schwarzenegger is very strong.
Arnold Schwarzenegger is **amazingly** strong.

EXERCISE 11 Identifying Adverbs

Identify the adverb and the word or words it modifies in each sentence in the following sentences.

EXAMPLE **1.** Many Cherokees still live in the mountains of North Carolina.
1. *still—live*

1. Today, many Cherokee people make their homes in Oklahoma.
2. This area was not the Cherokees' original home.
3. These people once lived in Georgia, North Carolina, Alabama, and Tennessee.
4. In 1829, people hurried excitedly to northern Georgia for the first gold rush in the United States.
5. Many white settlers of the region fought greedily for the gold.

6. These settlers totally ignored the Cherokees' right to the land.
7. Feeling threatened by the settlers, the Cherokees largely supported the British.
8. Later, the Cherokees were forced by the United States government to leave their land.
9. The people were hardly given a chance to collect their belongings.
10. Many Cherokees will never forget the "Trail of Tears" that led their ancestors to Oklahoma.

The Position of Adverbs

One of the characteristics of adverbs is that they may appear at various places in a sentence. Adverbs may come before, after, or between the words they modify.

EXAMPLES We **often** study together.
We study together **often.**
Often we study together.

When an adverb modifies a verb phrase, it frequently comes in the middle of the phrase.

EXAMPLE We have **often** studied together.

An adverb that introduces a question, however, must be placed at the beginning of a sentence.

EXAMPLES **When** does your school start? [The adverb *when* modifies the verb phrase *does start.*]
How did you spend your vacation? [The adverb *how* modifies the verb phrase *did spend.*]

EXERCISE 12 **Identifying Adverbs**

Identify the twenty adverbs and the words they modify in the following paragraphs.

EXAMPLE [1] "To Build a Fire" is a dramatically suspenseful short story.
1. *dramatically—suspenseful*

GRAMMAR

[1] "To Build a Fire" is probably one of Jack London's best stories. [2] In this story, a nameless character goes outdoors on a terribly cold day in the Yukon. [3] Except for a dog, he is traveling completely alone to a mining camp. [4] Foolishly confident of his ability to survive the unusually harsh cold, he does not understand the dangers of the northern wilderness.

[5] The dog knows instinctively that they are certainly in a bad situation. [6] It slinks fearfully along at the man's heels and seems to question his every movement. [7] Soon both the dog's muzzle and the man's beard are frosted with ice.

[8] Along the way, the man accidentally falls into a hidden stream. [9] Desperately, he builds a fire under a tree to avoid frostbite. [10] The flames slowly grow stronger. [11] Unfortunately, he has built his fire in the wrong place. [12] A pile of snow suddenly falls from a tree limb and kills the fire. [13] Unable to relight the fire, the man again finds himself in serious trouble. [14] Based on what you now know about the story, what kind of ending would you write for "To Build a Fire"?

EXERCISE 13 **Writing Adverbs**

Supply ten different adverbs to fill the blanks in the following paragraph.

EXAMPLE [1] I have ____ been a real music lover.
1. *always*

Every Friday I [1] ____ go to the record store. I can [2] ____ wait to see what new cassettes and CDs have arrived. As soon as school is out, I bicycle [3] ____ to the store and join other [4] ____ enthusiastic customers. [5] ____ I stroll through the aisles and [6] ____ study the selections. I listen [7] ____ as the loudspeaker announces the day's specials. When I have decided what I want, I [8] ____ figure out which items I can afford. Then I walk [9] ____ to the cash register. I grin [10] ____ as I think of how much I will enjoy the music.

PICTURE THIS

GRAMMAR

You are part of an important deep-sea expedition. Your job is to record what you see down in the ocean. The other members of your team lower your diving bell into the water. The diving bell is a heavy steel cabin with thick windows. When you reach the right depth, you switch on the outside light. Through the window in front of you, you see this scene. Write a brief report describing your observations. In your report, use at least five adverbs. Underline each adverb that you use.

Subject: underwater observations
Audience: scientists and others interested in undersea exploration
Purpose: to inform

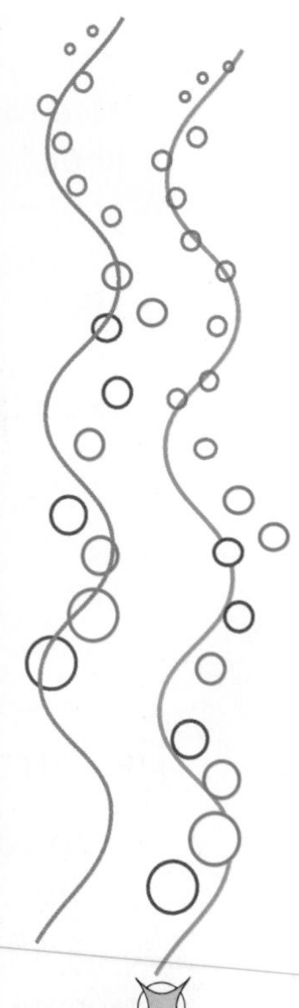

GRAMMAR

The Preposition

15c. A ***preposition*** is a word that shows the relationship between a noun or pronoun and another word in the sentence.

Notice how changing the preposition in these sentences changes the relationship of *cat* to *door* and *kite* to *tree.*

The cat walked **through** the door.
The cat walked **toward** the door.
The cat walked **past** the door.

The kite **in** the tree is mine.
The kite **beside** the tree is mine.
The kite **next to** the tree is mine. [Notice that a preposition may be made up of more than one word.]

Commonly Used Prepositions

aboard	before	for	off	toward
about	behind	from	on	under
above	below	in	out	underneath
across	beneath	in front of	out of	unlike
after	beside	inside	over	until
against	between	instead of	past	up
along	beyond	into	since	up to
among	by	like	through	upon
around	down	near	throughout	with
as	during	next to	till	within
at	except	of	to	without

EXERCISE 14 **Writing Prepositions**

In each of the following sentences, a preposition is missing. Choose two prepositions that would make sense in each sentence.

EXAMPLE **1.** The car raced ____ the highway.
1. *along, across*

1. We watched television ____ dinner.
2. She ran ____ the park.
3. A boat sailed ____ the river.
4. The dog crawled ____ the fence.
5. The runner jogged ____ the gym.

The Prepositional Phrase

A preposition is always followed by at least one noun or pronoun. This noun or pronoun is called the ***object of the preposition.*** The preposition, its object, and the object's modifiers make up a ***prepositional phrase.***

EXAMPLES You can press those leaves **under glass.** [The preposition *under* relates its object, *glass,* to *can press.*]
The books **in my pack** are heavy. [The preposition *in* relates its object, *pack,* to *books.*]

A preposition may have more than one object.

EXAMPLE Thelma's telegram **to Nina and Ralph** contained good news. [The preposition *to* relates its objects, *Nina* and *Ralph,* to *telegram.*]

The objects of prepositions may have modifiers.

EXAMPLE It happened **during the last examination.** [*The* and *last* are adjectives modifying *examination,* which is the object of the preposition *during.*]

NOTE: Be careful not to confuse a prepositional phrase beginning with *to* (*to the park, to him*) with a verb form beginning with *to* (*to sing, to be heard*). Remember that a prepositional phrase always ends with a noun or a pronoun.

EXERCISE 15 Identifying Prepositional Phrases

Identify the prepositional phrases in the following paragraphs. Underline the preposition once and its object twice. [Note: A sentence may contain more than one prepositional phrase.]

GRAMMAR

EXAMPLE [1] Lieutenant Robert Peary and Matthew Henson reached the North Pole in 1909.

1. *in 1909*

[1] Lieutenant Peary looked for the North Pole for many years. [2] Matthew Henson traveled with him on every expedition except the first one. [3] However, for a long time, Henson received no credit for his role.

[4] Peary had hired Henson as his servant on a trip to Nicaragua. [5] There, Peary discovered that Henson had sailing experience and could also chart a path through the jungle. [6] As a result, Peary asked Henson to join his Arctic expedition. [7] The two explorers became friends during their travels in the North. [8] On the final push to the North Pole, Henson was the only person who went with Peary.

[9] Yet because Peary was leader of the expedition, he received all the credit for the discovery. [10] Finally, after many years, Henson was honored by Congress, Maryland's state government, and two U.S. presidents.

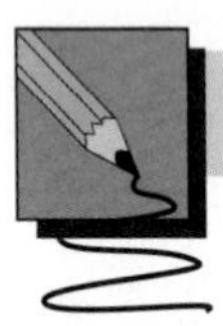

WRITING APPLICATION

Using Prepositional Phrases to Write Directions

You have probably given directions many times. They may have been directions telling how to get somewhere or how to do something. Using prepositional phrases can help you give directions that are clear and complete.

INCOMPLETE Walk straight ahead a little bit. Then turn and keep going. You will see the house.

COMPLETE Walk straight ahead *for four blocks, to the first stoplight.* Turn *to the right at that corner* and go *for two more blocks.* The house is *at the end of the driveway with the mailbox with flowers on it.*

GRAMMAR

WRITING ACTIVITY

Your class has decided to provide a "how-to" manual for seventh-graders. The manual will have chapters on crafts and hobbies, personal skills, school skills, and other topics. Write an entry for the manual, telling someone how to do a particular activity. You may use one of the following ideas or one of your own. In your entry, be sure to use prepositional phrases to make your directions clear and complete. Underline the prepositional phrases that you use.

1. how to keep a bicycle in good condition
2. how to care for houseplants
3. how to study for an essay test
4. how to bathe a cat or a dog
5. how to make friends at a new school
6. how to amuse a younger child

Prewriting First, picture yourself doing the activity you are describing. As you imagine doing the activity, jot down each thing that you do. Then put each step in the order that you do it. If necessary, change the order or add steps to make your directions clear and complete.

Writing Refer to your prewriting notes as you write your first draft. You may find it necessary to add or rearrange steps to make your directions clear and complete.

Evaluating and Revising Ask a friend or a classmate to read your paragraph. Then have your reader repeat the directions in his or her own words. If any part of the directions is unclear, revise your work.

Proofreading and Publishing Read over your entry again to check your spelling, grammar, and punctuation. Make sure you have used prepositional phrases correctly. (See pages 640–643 for more about the correct placement of phrase modifiers.) You and your classmates may wish to photocopy your manual entries or input them on a computer. You could then share your how-to hints with other students.

GRAMMAR

Prepositions and Adverbs

Some words may be used as prepositions or as adverbs. Remember that a preposition always has an object. An adverb never does. If you can't tell whether a word is used as an adverb or a preposition, look for an object.

ADVERB I haven't seen him **since.**

PREPOSITION I haven't seen him **since** Thursday. [*Thursday* is the object of the preposition *since.*]

ADVERBS The bear walked **around** and then went **inside.**

PREPOSITIONS The bear walked **around** the yard and then went **inside** the cabin. [*Yard* is the object of the preposition *around. Cabin* is the object of *inside.*]

EXERCISE 16 **Identifying Adverbs and Prepositions**

Identify the italicized word in each sentence in the following paragraphs as either an *adverb* or a *preposition.*

EXAMPLE [1] He watches uneasily as the hunter brings the pistol *up.*

1. *up—adverb*

[1] "The Most Dangerous Game" is the story of Rainsford, a famous hunter who falls *off* a boat and swims to a strange island. [2] Rainsford knows that this island is feared by every sailor who passes *by.* [3] In fact, *among* sailors, the place is known as "Ship-Trap Island."

[4] After looking *around* for several hours, Rainsford can't understand why the island is considered so dangerous. [5] Finally, he discovers a big house *on* a high bluff. [6] A man with a pistol *in* his hand answers the door. [7] Putting his pistol *down,* the man introduces Rainsford to the famous hunter General Zaroff. [8] Zaroff invites Rainsford *inside.* [9] Soon, however, Rainsford wishes he could get *out* and never see Zaroff again. [10] Rainsford has finally discovered the secret *about* the island—Zaroff likes to hunt human beings!

The Conjunction

15d. A ***conjunction*** is a word that joins words or groups of words.

Coordinating conjunctions connect words or groups of words used in the same way.

Coordinating Conjunctions						
and	but	for	nor	or	so	yet

EXAMPLES Jill **or** Anna [two nouns]
strict **but** fair [two adjectives]
over the river **and** through the woods [two prepositional phrases]
Alice Walker wrote the book, **yet** she did not write the movie script. [two complete ideas]

The word *for* may be used either as a conjunction or as a preposition. When *for* joins groups of words that are independent clauses or sentences, it is used as a conjunction. Otherwise, it is used as a preposition.

CONJUNCTION He waited patiently, **for** he knew his ride would be along soon.
PREPOSITION He waited patiently **for** his ride.

NOTE: When *for* is used as a conjunction, there should always be a comma in front of it.

EXAMPLE I'll be home late**,** **for** I have basketball practice today.

Correlative conjunctions are pairs of conjunctions that connect words or groups of words used in the same way.

Correlative Conjunctions	
both . . . . . . and	not only . . . . but also
either . . . . or	whether . . . . or
neither . . . . . nor	

EXAMPLES **Both** Bill Russell **and** Larry Byrd have played for the Celtics. [two nouns]

She looked **neither** to the left **nor** to the right. [two prepositional phrases]

Not only did Wilma Rudolph overcome her illness, **but** she **also** became an Olympic athlete. [two complete ideas]

EXERCISE 17 **Identifying Conjunctions**

Identify the conjunction in each of the following sentences. Be prepared to tell what words or groups of words each conjunction joins.

EXAMPLE **1. Both she and her mother enjoy sailing.**
1. *Both . . . and*

1. I wanted to see Los Lobos in concert, but I didn't have the money.
2. Our class is recycling not only newspapers but also aluminum cans.
3. He set the table with chopsticks and rice bowls.
4. Have you seen either Whitney Houston or Janet Jackson in person?
5. We learned to use neither too many adjectives nor too few.
6. That diet is dangerous, for it does not meet the body's needs.
7. Both the Mohawk and the Oneida are part of the Iroquois Confederacy.
8. It rained all day, yet we enjoyed the trip.
9. Shall we walk home or take the bus?
10. Revise your paper and proofread it carefully.

EXERCISE 18 Writing Conjunctions

For each blank in the following sentences, choose an appropriate conjunction.

EXAMPLE **1. ____ solve the problem yourself ____ ask your teacher for help.**
1. *Either—or*

1. We will visit ____ the Johnson Space Center ____ AstroWorld.
2. Alaska ____ Hawaii were the last two states admitted to the Union.
3. Those two students are twins, ____ they do not dress alike.
4. They were ____ hungry ____ thirsty.
5. ____ turn that radio down ____ take it into your room.

EXERCISE 19 Writing Sentences with Conjunctions

Follow the directions given below to write sentences using conjunctions.

EXAMPLE **1. Use *and* to join two verbs.**
1. *Jessye Norman smiled at the audience and bowed.*

1. Use *and* to join two adverbs.
2. Use *or* to join two prepositional phrases.
3. Use *for* to join groups of words that are sentences.
4. Use *but* to join two linking verbs.
5. Use *either . . . or* in an imperative sentence.

The Interjection

15e. An ***interjection*** is a word that expresses strong emotion.

An interjection has no grammatical relationship to the rest of the sentence. Usually an interjection is followed by an exclamation point.

EXAMPLES **Ouch!** That hurts!
Goodness! What a haircut!
Aha! I know the answer.

Sometimes an interjection is set off by a comma.

Oh, I wish it were Friday.
Well, what have you been doing?

GRAMMAR

EXERCISE 20 Writing Interjections

The people at this video arcade need your help. To express their excitement, they want to use some interjections—but they don't know any. Write five sentences that might be spoken by these people. In each sentence, use a different interjection from the list below. Underline the interjections you use. (Remember that an interjection may be followed by either an exclamation point or a comma.)

gee	yay	oh	wow
darn	no	oops	yes

EXAMPLE *Wow! That's the highest score ever!*

REVIEW B Identifying Parts of Speech

For the following sentences, identify the part of speech of each italicized word as a *verb,* an *adverb,* a *preposition,* a *conjunction,* or an *interjection.*

EXAMPLE **1.** ***Both*** **otters** ***and*** **owls hunt** ***from*** **dusk to dawn.**
1. ***both . . . and—conjunction; from—preposition***

1. *Oh!* I *just* spilled soup on the new white tablecloth!
2. Luis Alvarez *closely* studied atomic particles *for* many years.
3. *Did* Toni Morrison *or* Toni Cade Bambara *write* that book?
4. The Inuit hunters *ate* their meal *inside* the igloo.
5. They were tired, *yet* they did *not* quit working.

GRAMMAR

Determining Parts of Speech

Remember that you can't tell what part of speech a word is until you know how it is used in a particular sentence. A word may be used in different ways.

NOUN	The **play** had a happy ending.
VERB	The actors **play** their roles.
NOUN	The **outside** of the house needs paint.
ADVERB	Let's go **outside** for a while.
PREPOSITION	I saw the birds' nest **outside** my window.

REVIEW C **Writing Sentences**

Write ten sentences that meet the requirements in the following directions. Underline the given word in each sentence, and identify how it is used.

EXAMPLE **1.** Use *yet* as an adverb and as a conjunction.
1. *Are we there yet?—adverb*
The sky grew brighter, yet the rain continued falling.—conjunction

1. Use *walk* as a verb and a noun.
2. Use *like* as a preposition and a verb.
3. Use *well* as an interjection and an adverb.
4. Use *inside* as an adverb and a preposition.
5. Use *fast* as an adjective and an adverb.

GRAMMAR

Review: Posttest

A. Identifying Verbs, Adverbs, Prepositions, Conjunctions, and Interjections

Identify the part of speech of each italicized word in the following paragraphs.

EXAMPLES Some [1] *very* unusual words [2] *are used* [3] *in* crossword puzzles.
1. *adverb*
2. *verb*
3. *preposition*

The first crossword puzzle was published [1] *in* 1913. It [2] *appeared* on the Fun Page [3] *of* a New York City newspaper, [4] *and* readers [5] *immediately* [6] *asked* the editors [7] *for* more. [8] *Almost* every newspaper in the United States [9] *now* publishes a daily crossword puzzle.

Every day millions of Americans [10] *faithfully* work crossword puzzles. Many people take their puzzles [11] *quite* seriously. For many, solving puzzles [12] *is* a competitive game.

I [13] *do* puzzles [14] *strictly* for fun. Best of all, I can work on them [15] *by* myself. That way, no one knows whether I succeed [16] *or* fail. I [17] *occasionally* [18] *brag* about my successes. [19] "*Aha!*" I exclaim. "That was a tough one, [20] *but* I filled in every space."

B. Writing Sentences Using Words as Different Parts of Speech

Write ten sentences, using each of the following words first as an adverb and then as a preposition. Underline the word, and give its part of speech after the sentence.

EXAMPLE 1. around
1. *We walked* <u>*around*</u>*.—adverb*
We walked <u>*around*</u> *the mall.—preposition*

1. up **2.** near **3.** over **4.** through **5.** by

SUMMARY OF PARTS OF SPEECH

Rule	Part of Speech	Use	Examples
14a	noun	names	**Marie** had a good **idea.**
14b	pronoun	takes the place of a noun	Bill had an idea, but **he** would't tell **it** to **anyone.**
14c	adjective	modifies a noun or pronoun	I have **two Mexican** bowls, and both are **large** and **heavy.**
15a	verb	shows action or a state of being	Ada **has met** you, but she **is** not sure where.
15b	adverb	modifies a verb, an adjective, or another adverb	We left **early** when the sky was **almost completely** dark.
15c	preposition	relates a noun or a pronoun to another word	We looked **for** you **next to** the gate **at** the game.
15d	conjunction	joins words or groups of words	Bill **or** she will call us later **and** give us directions.
15e	interjection	shows strong feeling	**Ouch!** My arm is caught.

16 Complements

Direct and Indirect Objects, Subject Complements

Diagnostic Test

Identifying Complements

Identify the complement or complements in each of the following sentences. Then, label each complement as a *direct object*, an *indirect object*, a *predicate nominative*, or a *predicate adjective*.

EXAMPLE **1.** My mother bought us some tamales.
1. *us—indirect object; tamales—direct object*

1. Native American peoples taught the English colonists many useful skills for survival.
2. Rhode Island is the smallest state in the United States.
3. A hurricane of immense power lashed the Florida coast.

4. They became very anxious during the final minutes of the game.
5. This winter was colder and drier than normal.
6. My aunt showed us pictures of her new puppy.
7. The new homeowners found some rare photographs in the attic.
8. Although many eggshells are white, others are brown, and still others are bluish green.
9. Some consumers prefer eggs with brown shells.
10. During this entire month, Mars is too close to the sun to be seen easily from Earth.
11. Congress gave the president its support on the bill.
12. The movers carried the heavy sofa up the stairs.
13. I found a dollar in the pocket of my jeans.
14. That gigantic reflector is the world's most powerful telescope.
15. Did Henry Cisneros lead the state delegation at the convention last month?
16. *A Raisin in the Sun* was Lorraine Hansberry's most successful play.
17. Why do animals seem nervous during a storm?
18. The manager will pay all of the ushers an extra five dollars this week.
19. Luis Alvarez won a Nobel Prize for his research into nuclear power.
20. Our neighbor has offered my mother a good price for her car.

Recognizing Complements

16a. A ***complement*** is a word or a group of words that completes the meaning of a verb.

Every sentence has a subject and a verb. In addition, the verb often needs a complement to complete its meaning.

INCOMPLETE Dr. Charles Drew researched [*what?*] (S: Dr. Charles Drew; V: researched)

COMPLETE Dr. Charles Drew researched blood **plasma.** (S: Dr. Charles Drew; V: researched; C: plasma)

INCOMPLETE Medical societies honored [*whom?*] (S: societies; V: honored)

COMPLETE Medical societies honored **him.** (S: societies; V: honored; C: him)

INCOMPLETE Dr. Drew's research was [*what?*] (S: research; V: was)

COMPLETE Dr. Drew's research was **important.** (S: research; V: was; C: important)

Direct Objects

The ***direct object*** is one type of complement. It completes the meaning of a transitive verb.

REFERENCE NOTE: Transitive verbs are discussed on page 446.

16b. A ***direct object*** is a noun or a pronoun that receives the action of the verb or shows the result of that action. A direct object answers the question *Whom?* or *What?* after a transitive verb.

EXAMPLES Today, I met **Dr. Mason.** [*Dr. Mason* receives the action of the verb *met* and tells *whom* I met.]
That shop makes small **parts** for jet engines. [*Parts* tells *what* results from the action of the verb *makes.*]

A direct object can never follow a linking verb because a linking verb does not express action. Also, a direct object is never in a prepositional phrase.

LINKING VERB Augusta Savage **was** a sculptor during the Harlem Renaissance. [The verb *was* does not express action; therefore, it has no direct object.]

PREPOSITIONAL PHRASE **She worked with clay.** [*Clay* is not the direct object of the verb *worked;* it is the object in the prepositional phrase *with clay.*]

REFERENCE NOTE: For more about linking verbs, see pages 447–448. For more about prepositional phrases, see pages 491–497.

A direct object may be a compound of two or more objects.

EXAMPLE We bought **ribbon, wrapping paper,** and **tape.** [The compound direct object of the verb *bought* is *ribbon, wrapping paper,* and *tape.*]

EXERCISE 1 Identifying Direct Objects

Identify the direct object in each of the following sentences. [Remember: A direct object may be compound.]

EXAMPLE **1.** Many sports test an athlete's speed and agility.
1. *speed, agility*

1. However, long-distance, or marathon, swimming requires strength and endurance from an athlete.
2. A swimmer in training may swim five or six miles every day.
3. Marathon swimmers smear grease on their legs and arms for protection against the cold water.
4. During a marathon, some swimmers may lose seventeen pounds.
5. Fatigue, pain, and huge waves challenge marathon swimmers.
6. As they swim, they endure extreme isolation from the rest of the world.
7. Toward the end of the marathon, swimmers hear the loud applause and shouts of encouragement from their fans.
8. Spectators can watch only the finish of a marathon.
9. Nevertheless, they know the long distance that the athletes have traveled.
10. Emerging from the water, exhausted swimmers have successfully completed another marathon.

GRAMMAR

EXERCISE 2 **Identifying Direct Objects**

Identify the ten direct objects in the following paragraph. If a sentence does not contain a direct object, write *no direct object*. [Remember: Objects follow action verbs only.]

EXAMPLES [1] Have you ever flown a hang glider?

1. *hang glider*

[2] Hang gliding has become a popular sport.

2. *no direct object*

[1] Many adventurous people enjoy the thrill of gliding through the air. [2] As you can see, a hang glider can carry a full-grown person in its harness. [3] The hang glider has a lightweight sail with a triangular control bar underneath. [4] At takeoff, the pilot lifts the glider shoulder-high and runs hard down a slope into the wind. [5] The wind lifts the glider and carries the pilot off the ground. [6] Because of the wind currents, takeoffs from a hilltop or a cliff are the easiest. [7] Once airborne, the pilot directs the path of flight. [8] He or she also controls the glider's speed by pushing or pulling on the control bar. [9] For example, a gentle pull increases speed. [10] To land, the pilot stalls the glider near the ground and drops lightly to his or her feet.

Indirect Objects

The ***indirect object*** is another type of complement. Like a direct object, an indirect object helps to complete the meaning of a transitive verb. If a sentence has an indirect object, it always has a direct object also.

16c. An ***indirect object*** is a noun or pronoun that comes between the verb and the direct object. It tells *to whom* or *to what,* or *for whom* or *for what,* the action of the verb is done.

EXAMPLES **The waiter gave her a smile.** [The pronoun *her* is the indirect object of the verb *gave.* It answers the question "*To whom* did the waiter give a smile?"]

Pam left the waiter a tip. [The noun *waiter* is the indirect object of the verb *left.* It answers the question "*For whom* did she leave a tip?"]

NOTE: Linking verbs do not have indirect objects, because they do not show action. Also, an indirect object is never in a prepositional phrase.

INDIRECT OBJECT	Vinnie made **us** some lasagna.
PREPOSITIONAL PHRASE	Vinnie made some lasagna **for us.**

Like a direct object, an indirect object can be a compound of two or more objects.

EXAMPLE **Felicia threw Jane and Paula slow curve balls until they had warmed up.** [*Jane* and *Paula* are the indirect objects of the verb *threw.* They answer the question "*To whom* did Felicia throw curve balls?"]

EXERCISE 3 Identifying Direct Objects and Indirect Objects

Identify the direct object and the indirect object in each of the following sentences.

EXAMPLE **1. Did you buy Mom a calculator for her birthday?**
1. ***Mom—indirect object; calculator—direct object***

1. The usher found us seats near the stage.
2. I'll gladly lend you my typewriter.
3. The Nobel Committee gave Octavio Paz the Nobel Prize for literature.
4. Please show me your beaded moccasins.
5. Mai told the children stories about her family's escape from Vietnam.
6. Our teacher taught us some English words of Native American origin.
7. I fed the horse some hay.
8. My secret pal sent me a birthday card.
9. They owe you an apology.
10. Will you please save Ricardo a seat?

EXERCISE 4 **Identifying Objects of Verbs**

All of the following sentences contain direct objects. Some sentences contain indirect objects, too. Identify the object or objects in each sentence.

EXAMPLE **1. My parents gave me a choice of places to go on our camping vacation.**
1. ***me—indirect object; choice—direct object***

1. I told them my answer quickly.
2. I had recently read a magazine article about the Flathead Reservation in Montana.
3. We spent five days of our vacation there.
4. We liked the friendly people and the rugged land.
5. A Salishan tribe known as the Flatheads governs the huge reservation.
6. I especially liked the beautiful mountains and twenty-eight-mile-long Flathead Lake.
7. My parents assigned me the job of putting up our tent beside the lake.

8. Someone gave my father directions to the National Bison Range, and we went there one day.
9. We also attended the Standing Arrow Pow-Wow, which was the highlight of our stay.
10. The performers showed visitors traditional Flathead dances and games.

PICTURE THIS

The year is 1924, and you're a customer in this toy store. You are looking for gifts for your friends, but your attention soon turns to the conversations at the counter. The two salesmen seem to be having some trouble with their customers. As you watch and listen, you decide to write a story about this amusing incident. In your writing, use at least three direct objects and two indirect objects.

Wyndam Payne, Illustration from *The Mysterious Toyshop, A Fairy Tale*, by Cyril W. Beaumont, Published in London, 1924. Commercial color relief process, 6 × 9 inches. Copyright 1984 By The Metropolitan Museum of Art, Rogers Fund, 1970. (1970.544.1)

Subject: customers in a toy store
Audience: friends
Purpose: to entertain

Subject Complements

GRAMMAR

16d. A ***subject complement*** completes the meaning of a linking verb and identifies or describes the subject.

EXAMPLES Julio has been **president** of his class since October. [*President* identifies the subject *Julio.*]
Was it **you**? [*You* identifies the subject *it.*]
Barbara looks **sleepy** this morning. [*Sleepy* describes the subject *Barbara.*]

REFERENCE NOTE: For more information about linking verbs, see pages 447–448.

There are two kinds of subject complements—the *predicate nominative* and the *predicate adjective.*

Predicate Nominatives

16e. A ***predicate nominative*** is a noun or pronoun that follows a linking verb and explains or identifies the subject of the sentence.

EXAMPLES A good dictionary is a valuable **tool.** [*Tool* is a predicate nominative following the linking verb *is.* It explains the subject *dictionary.*]
This piece of flint may be an old **arrowhead.** [*Arrowhead* is a predicate nominative following the linking verb *may be.* It identifies the subject *piece.*]
The winner of the race was **she.** [*She* is a predicate nominative following the linking verb *was.* It identifies the subject *winner.*]

NOTE: Expressions such as *It is I* and *That was he* sound awkward even though they are correct. In conversation, you would probably say *It's me* and *That was him.* Such nonstandard expressions may one day become acceptable in writing as well as in speech. For now, however, it is best to follow the rules of standard English in your writing.

Like other sentence complements, a predicate nominative may be compound.

EXAMPLE The discoverers of radium were **Pierre Curie** and **Marie Sklodowska Curie.**

Be careful not to confuse a predicate nominative with a direct object. A predicate nominative always follows a linking verb. A direct object always follows an action verb.

PREDICATE NOMINATIVE We are the **delegates** from our school.
DIRECT OBJECT We elected the **delegates** from our school.

The predicate nominative is never part of a prepositional phrase.

PREDICATE NOMINATIVE Bill Russell became a famous basketball **coach.**
PREPOSITIONAL PHRASE Bill Russell became famous **as coach** of the Boston Celtics.

EXERCISE 5 Identifying Predicate Nominatives

Identify the linking verb and the predicate nominative in each of the following sentences.

EXAMPLE 1. Are whales mammals?
1. *Are—mammals*

1. Mount Kilimanjaro is the tallest mountain in Africa.
2. The kingdom of Siam became modern-day Thailand.
3. Dandelions can be a problem.
4. Sue Mishima is a lawyer.
5. When will a woman be president of the United States?
6. Reuben has become a fine pianist.
7. Variety is the spice of life.
8. At the moment, she remains our choice for mayor.
9. Alaska is the largest state in the United States.
10. *Philately* is another name for stamp collecting.

Predicate Adjectives

16f. A ***predicate adjective*** is an adjective that follows a linking verb and describes the subject of the sentence.

EXAMPLES Cold milk tastes **good** on a hot day. [*Good* is a predicate adjective that describes the subject *milk.*]

The pita bread was **light** and **delicious.** [*Light* and *delicious* form a compound predicate adjective that describes the subject *bread.*]

GRAMMAR

EXERCISE 6 **Identifying Predicate Adjectives**

Identify the linking verb and the predicate adjective in each of the following sentences.

EXAMPLE 1. The crowd became restless.
1. *became—restless*

1. Everyone felt good about the decision.
2. That container of milk smells sour.
3. Don't the Cuban black beans mixed with rice and onions taste delicious?
4. The situation appears complicated.
5. Everyone remained calm during the emergency.
6. Why does the water in that pond look green?
7. During Barbara Jordan's speech, the audience grew thoughtful and then enthusiastic.
8. Jan stays cheerful most of the time.
9. She must be happy with the results.
10. From here, the drums sound too loud.

EXERCISE 7 **Using Predicate Adjectives and Predicate Nominatives**

You want to write an adventure story, but you aren't sure how to begin. You remember reading about a professional writer who gets ideas from watching people and making up interesting identities for them. You decide to try this method of writing while you are sitting in this waiting room. Write a brief description of the other patients in the waiting room. Imagine the patients' jobs, families, backgrounds, and personalities. In your description, use five predicate adjectives and five predicate nominatives. Underline each predicate adjective once. Underline each predicate nominative twice. You may want to use your description to write the whole adventure story.

EXAMPLES *The woman next to the coats is Julia Johnson.*

She looks friendly, but she is really an international spy.

REVIEW A **Identifying Complements**

Identify the complement or complements in each of the following sentences. Then, label each complement as a *direct object*, an *indirect object*, a *predicate nominative*, or a *predicate adjective*.

EXAMPLES
1. Our teacher read us stories from the Leatherstocking Tales.
1. *us—indirect object; stories—direct object*
2. James Fenimore Cooper is the author of these tales.
2. *author—predicate nominative*

1. Leatherstocking was a fictional scout in Cooper's Leatherstocking Tales.
2. He was also a woodcrafter and a trapper.
3. He could not read, but he understood the lore of the woods.
4. To generations of readers, this character has become a hero.
5. He could face any emergency.
6. He always remained faithful and fearless.
7. Leatherstocking loved the forest and the open country.
8. In later years he grew miserable.
9. The destruction of the wilderness by settlers and others greatly disturbed him.
10. He told no one his views and retreated from civilization.

WRITING APPLICATION

Using Subject Complements to Write Riddles

Popcorn pops, flashlights light, and linking verbs link. Like popcorn and flashlights, linking verbs do just what their name suggests. They link subjects with subject complements, which identify or describe the subject. Notice how the subject complements in the following riddle give clues to the identity of the subject *I*.

RIDDLE I feel **smooth** to the touch.
I can be **white** or **brown.**
I am a **box** without a lid.
Inside me, you'll find gold.
What am I?

ANSWER an egg

WRITING ACTIVITY

A magazine for young people is sponsoring a riddle-writing contest. Whoever writes the best riddle will win the most advanced video game system on the market. You are determined to write the best riddle and win. Write two riddles to enter in the contest. In each one, use at least two subject complements.

Prewriting The best way to make up a riddle is to begin with the answer. List some animals, places, and things that suggest funny or hidden meanings. For instance, the example riddle plays on the idea that an egg is like a box of treasure. For each animal, place, or thing, jot down a description based on a funny or hidden meaning. Then choose the four animals, places, or things that you think will make the best riddles.

Writing Use your prewriting notes as you write your first draft. In each riddle, make sure that your clues will help your audience guess the answer. Be sure that you use a subject complement (a predicate nominative or a predicate adjective) in the riddle.

Evaluating and Revising Ask a friend to read your riddles. If the riddles are too difficult or too simple, revise them. You may want to add details that appeal to the senses. Linking verbs such as *appear, feel, smell, sound,* and *taste* can help you add such details. (For a longer list of linking verbs, see page 448.)

Proofreading and Publishing Read through your riddles again to check for errors in spelling, punctuation, and capitalization. Pay special attention to the capitalization of proper nouns. You and your classmates may want to publish a book of riddles. Collect your riddles and draw or cut out pictures as illustrations. Make photocopies for all the members of the class.

GRAMMAR

REVIEW B **Identifying Complements**

Identify the complement or complements in each sentence in the following paragraphs. Then label each complement as a *direct object,* an *indirect object,* a *predicate nominative,* or a *predicate adjective.* [Remember: A complement may be compound.]

EXAMPLE [1] Sean, my brother, won three medals at the Special Olympic games.
1. *medals—direct object*

[1] Sean was one of more than one hundred special-education students who competed in the regional Special Olympics last month. [2] The games brought students from many schools to our city. [3] The highlights of the games included track events such as sprints and relay races. [4] These were the closest contests. [5] Sean's excellent performance in the relays gave him confidence. [6] The softball throw and high jump were especially challenging events. [7] Sean looked relaxed but determined as he prepared for the high jump. [8] He certainly felt great after making the best jump.

[9] The Special Olympics are exciting and inspiring. [10] Many of the contestants have physical impairments; some cannot walk or see. [11] Teachers and volunteers train contestants in the different events. [12] However, the young athletes themselves are the force behind the program. [13] The pictures on the next page give you a glimpse of the excitement at the Special Olympics. [14] The two smiling girls on the left are winners of a sprint. [15] On the right, this determined boy gains the lead in the wheelchair race.

[16] Mrs. Duffy, one of the coaches, told us the history of the Special Olympics. [17] Eunice Kennedy Shriver founded the program in 1961. [18] To begin with, the program was a five-week camp. [19] Several years later, however, the camp became an international sports event with contestants from twenty-six states and Canada. [20] Today, the organizers of the Special Olympics sponsor regional and international games.

GRAMMAR

Review: Posttest 1

Identifying Complements

Identify the complement or complements in each of the following sentences. Label each complement as a *direct object*, an *indirect object*, a *predicate nominative*, or a *predicate adjective*.

EXAMPLE **1.** A respirator pumps oxygen into the lungs.
1. *oxygen—direct object*

1. Our cat avoids skunks and raccoons.
2. Jim Thorpe was a famous Native American athlete.
3. The teacher showed us a film about drug abuse.
4. The television commercials for that new product sound silly.
5. Who put the roses in that vase?
6. I sent my grandparents a card for their anniversary.
7. During her interview on television, Zina Garrison appeared relaxed and confident.
8. At first the colt seemed frightened.
9. Mrs. Karas offered us olives and stuffed grape leaves.

10. The DJ played songs by Freddie Jackson, Gloria Estefan, and Paula Abdul.
11. The newspaper story prompted an investigation by the mayor's office.
12. My sister has become a computer repair technician.
13. Write your name and address on the envelope.
14. The weather forecasters haven't issued a tornado warning.
15. Before long, the mistake became obvious to nearly everyone.
16. The sky looked gray and stormy.
17. The Egyptian writer Naguib Mahfouz won the Nobel Prize for literature in 1988.
18. The consumer group wrote the senator a letter.
19. *Barrio Boy* is the autobiography of Ernesto Galarza.
20. The candidate seems ambitious but sincere.

Review: Posttest 2

Writing Sentences with Complements

Write two sentences for each of the following kinds of complements. Underline each complement.

EXAMPLE 1. a direct object
1. *We heard the president's speech.*
Both of my parents enjoy novels set in ancient Rome.

1. a compound direct object
2. an indirect object followed by a direct object
3. a predicate nominative after a form of *be*
4. a predicate adjective after a form of *become* or *seem*
5. a compound predicate adjective after a linking verb other than *be, become,* or *seem*

17 THE PHRASE

Prepositional and Verbal Phrases

Diagnostic Test

A. Identifying Phrases

Identify the phrase in each of the following sentences.

EXAMPLES
1. Payat drew a picture of his adobe house.
1. *of his adobe house*
2. Returning her library books, Janelle chose two more.
2. *Returning her library books*

1. Organized in 1884, the first black professional baseball team was the Cuban Giants.
2. The jacket with a blue collar is mine.
3. My goal is to become a forest ranger.
4. On the sidelines, the coach paced nervously.
5. The student, frowning slightly, erased the title.
6. Guillermo hopes to visit us soon.
7. The charity received donations for the hungry.
8. Immediately after school, we left.

9. I practice my Japanese calligraphy on Mondays, Wednesdays, and Saturdays.
10. Several of my friends are absent today.

B. Identifying and Classifying Prepositional Phrases

Identify the prepositional phrase in each sentence, and classify the phrase as an *adjective phrase* or an *adverb phrase*. Then, give the word or words that the phrase modifies.

EXAMPLE 1. Harvest festivals are celebrated throughout the world.
1. *throughout the world—adverb phrase; are celebrated*

11. The view from Mount Fuji is spectacular.
12. Has the search party returned to the campsite yet?
13. After the game, we got something to eat.
14. We heard stories about our Cherokee ancestors.
15. An umbrella tent has supports on the outside.
16. The second-longest river in Africa is the Congo.
17. Jody was late for the party.
18. Boulder Dam was the original name of Hoover Dam.
19. The Hudson River was once the chief trading route for the western frontier.
20. Hearing a loud noise, Mr. Cárdenas stopped his car, got out, and looked underneath it.

17a. A ***phrase*** is a group of related words that is used as a single part of speech and does not contain both a subject and a verb.

EXAMPLES in the kitchen [phrase; no subject or verb]
played the guitar [phrase; no subject]

REFERENCE NOTE: If a group of words has both a subject and a verb, it is called a *clause*. See Chapter 18 for more about clauses.

EXERCISE 1 Identifying Phrases

Identify each of the following groups of words as a *phrase* or *not a phrase.*

EXAMPLES **1.** on the paper
1. *phrase*
2. after we eat
2. *not a phrase*

1. when you know
2. as they walked in
3. in the garden
4. is sleeping
5. remembered suddenly
6. smiling brightly
7. to the supermarket
8. with a warm smile
9. to laugh at myself
10. if he says so

Prepositional Phrases

17b. A ***prepositional phrase*** is a phrase that begins with a preposition and ends with a noun or a pronoun.

EXAMPLES under the umbrella
among good friends
for ourselves

Notice that an article or another modifier may appear in a prepositional phrase. The first example contains the article *the.* In the second example, *good* modifies *friends.*

REFERENCE NOTE: See page 460 for a list of commonly used prepositions.

The noun or pronoun that ends a prepositional phrase is called the ***object of the preposition.***

EXAMPLES Linh Phan has the lead in the school **play.** [The noun *play* is the object of the preposition *in.*]
They divided the prize between **them.** [The pronoun *them* is the object of the preposition *between.*]

EXERCISE 2 **Identifying Prepositional Phrases**

Identify each prepositional phrase in the following sentences. [Note: A sentence may contain more than one prepositional phrase.]

EXAMPLE [1] Many soldiers fought bravely during the Vietnam War.
1. *during the Vietnam War*

[1] One of these soldiers was Jan C. Scruggs. [2] When the war was over, he and other veterans wondered why there was no national memorial honoring those who had served in Vietnam. [3] Scruggs decided he would raise funds for a Vietnam Veterans Memorial. [4] The memorial would include the names of all American soldiers who had died or were missing in action. [5] Organizing the project took years of great effort. [6] Many different people contributed their talents to the project. [7] Maya Ying Lin, a college student, designed the memorial that now stands in Washington, D.C. [8] This picture shows the V-shaped, black granite wall that was built from Lin's design. [9] A glass company from Memphis, Tennessee, stenciled each name on the shiny granite. [10] Now, the men and women who fought and died in Vietnam will never be forgotten by the American people.

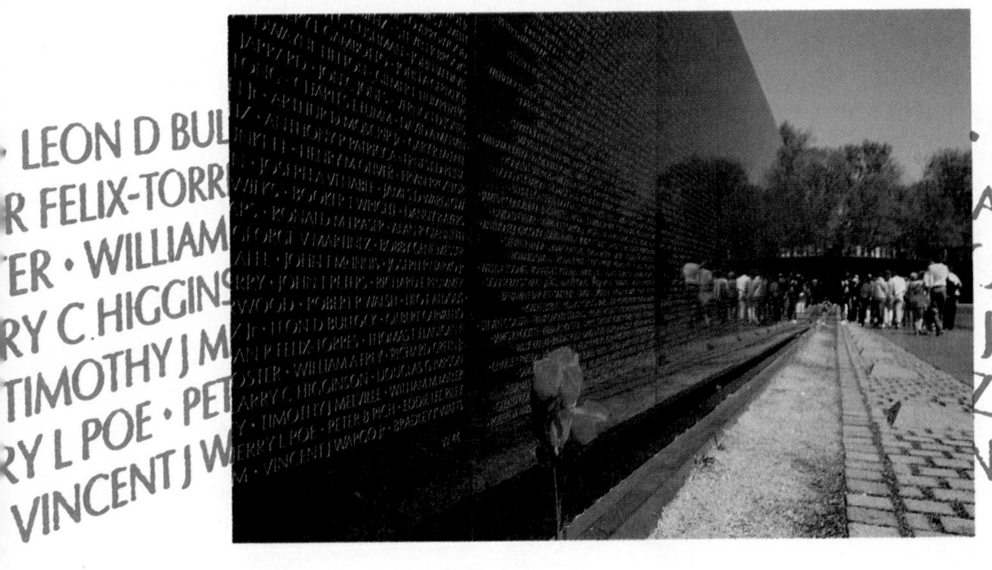

Adjective Phrases

A prepositional phrase used as an adjective is called an ***adjective phrase.***

ADJECTIVE Rosa chose the **blue** one.

ADJECTIVE PHRASE Rosa chose the one **with blue stripes.**

17c. An ***adjective phrase*** modifies a noun or a pronoun.

Adjective phrases answer the same questions that single-word adjectives answer.

What kind?	*Which one?*
How many?	*How much?*

EXAMPLES **The music store is the one with the neon sign.** [The prepositional phrase *with the neon sign* is used as an adjective modifying the pronoun *one.* The phrase answers the question *Which one?*]

We bought a tape by Janet Jackson. [*By Janet Jackson* is used as an adjective modifying the noun *tape.* The phrase answers the question *What kind?*]

EXERCISE 3 Identifying Adjective Phrases

Identify the adjective phrase in each of the following sentences, and give the word that each phrase modifies.

EXAMPLE 1. Marie Sklodowska Curie, a scientist from Poland, was awarded the Nobel Prize.
1. *from Poland—scientist*

1. While still a student, Marie became friends with Pierre Curie.
2. Pierre had already gained fame as a scientist.
3. Paris, France, was where the two of them met.

4. Their enthusiasm for science brought them together.
5. The marriage between the two scientists was a true partnership.
6. The year after their marriage another scientist discovered natural radioactivity.
7. The Curies began researching the radiation in certain substances.
8. Their theories about a new element were proved to be true.
9. Their research on the mineral pitchblende uncovered a new radioactive element, radium.
10. The Curies won a Nobel Prize for their discovery.

More than one adjective phrase may modify the same noun or pronoun.

EXAMPLE The sign **with neon letters near my house** flashes on and off all night long. [The two phrases, *with neon letters* and *near my house,* both modify the noun *sign.*]

An adjective phrase may also modify the object in another adjective phrase.

EXAMPLE A majority **of the mammals in the world** sleep during the day. [The adjective phrase *of the mammals* modifies the noun *majority.* The adjective phrase *in the world* modifies the noun *mammals,* which is the object of the preposition in the first phrase.]

EXERCISE 4 **Identifying Adjective Phrases**

Each numbered sentence in the following paragraph contains at least one adjective phrase. Identify each phrase and give the word that it modifies.

EXAMPLE [1] R.I.C.E. is the recommended treatment for minor sports injuries.

1. *for minor sports injuries—treatment*

[1] The first letters of the words *Rest, Ice, Compression,* and *Elevation* form the abbreviation *R.I.C.E.* [2] Total rest is

not necessary, just rest for the injured part of the body. [3] Ice helps because it deadens pain and slows the loss of blood. [4] Ice also reduces swelling in the injured area. [5] Compression with a tight bandage of elastic cloth prevents further strain on the injury. [6] This photograph shows a compression bandage treating the pulled hamstring of Carl Lewis. [7] The last step in the treatment is elevation of the injury. [8] The effect of gravity helps fluid drain away. [9] If pain continues, someone with medical training should be called. [10] Even injuries of a minor nature need proper attention.

EXERCISE 5 Using Adjective Phrases

In the following sentences, insert an adjective phrase for each blank. Then, give the word that the phrase modifies. Remember that an adjective phrase must modify a noun or a pronoun.

EXAMPLE **1.** A flock ___ flew overhead.
1. *A flock of small gray birds flew overhead.—flock*

1. The sound ___ suddenly filled the air.
2. The theater ___ often shows kung-fu movies.
3. May I have some more ___?
4. Our vacation ___ was relaxing.
5. Her photograph ___ looks like a prizewinner.
6. Baki found the answer ___.
7. He put the flowers in a vase ___.
8. A boy ___ hung a piñata in the tree.
9. The nest is in the top branch ___.
10. Someone ___ shouted for quiet.

GRAMMAR

Adverb Phrases

A prepositional phrase used as an adverb is called an ***adverb phrase.***

ADVERB The cavalry **soon** reached the fort.

ADVERB PHRASE **By noon** the cavalry reached the fort.

17d. An ***adverb phrase*** modifies a verb, an adjective, or another adverb.

Adverb phrases answer the same questions that single-word adverbs answer.

When?	*Why?*
Where?	*How often?*
How?	*To what extent?*

EXAMPLES We got our new puppy **at the animal shelter.** [The adverb phrase *at the animal shelter* modifies the verb *got,* telling *where.*]

A puppy is always ready **for a game.** [The adverb phrase *for a game* modifies the adjective *ready,* telling *how.*]

He barks loudly **for a puppy.** [The adverb phrase *for a puppy* modifies the adverb *loudly,* telling *to what extent.*]

Unlike adjective phrases, which usually follow the word or words they modify, adverb phrases may appear at various places in sentences.

EXAMPLES We planted elm seedlings **along the driveway.**

Along the driveway we planted elm seedlings.

At our house we have dinner early.

We have dinner early **at our house.**

GRAMMAR

EXERCISE 6 Identifying Adverb Phrases

Identify the adverb phrase in each of the following sentences, and give the word that each phrase modifies. [Note: Do not list adjective phrases.]

EXAMPLE **1. Pecos Bill will live forever in the many legends about him.**
1. *in the many legends—will live*

1. When he was only a baby, Pecos Bill fell into the Pecos River.
2. His parents searched for him but couldn't find him.
3. He was saved by coyotes, who raised him.
4. He thought for many years that he was a coyote.
5. After a long argument a cowboy convinced him that he was not a coyote.
6. During a drought he dug the bed of the Rio Grande.
7. On one occasion Bill rode a cyclone.
8. A mountain lion once leaped from a ledge above Bill's head.
9. Bill was ready for trouble and soon had the mountain lion tamed.
10. Stories like these about Pecos Bill are common in the West.

Like adjective phrases, more than one adverb phrase may modify the same word.

EXAMPLES She drove **for hours through the storm.** [Both adverb phrases, *for hours* and *through the storm,* modify the verb *drove.*]

The library is open **during the day on weekends.** [Both adverb phrases, *during the day* and *on weekends,* modify the adjective *open.*]

NOTE: An adverb phrase may be followed by an adjective phrase that modifies the object in the adverb phrase.

EXAMPLE The boat landed **on an island near the coast.** [The adverb phrase *on an island* modifies the verb *landed.* The adjective phrase *near the coast* modifies the noun *island.*]

EXERCISE 7 Identifying Adverb Phrases

Identify the ten adverb phrases in the following paragraph. Then, give the word or words that each phrase modifies. [Note: Do not list adjective phrases.]

GRAMMAR

EXAMPLE **[1] Never before had a blizzard struck the coastal area with such force.**

1. *with such force—had struck*

[1] The raging wind blew eleven-year-old Andrea over a sea wall near her home and trapped her in a deep snowdrift. [2] No one could hear her shouts over the howling wind.

[3] Suddenly, Andrea's dog charged through the snow toward the beach. [4] He plunged into the snow around Andrea and licked her face, warming the skin. [5] Then the huge dog walked around Andrea until the snow was packed down. [6] The dog pulled her to an open area on the beach. [7] With great effort, Andrea and her dog made their way home. [8] Grateful to their dog, Andrea's family served him a special steak dinner.

EXERCISE 8 Writing a Paragraph Using Adjective and Adverb Phrases

You are working with a park ranger for the summer. Together you are writing a safety pamphlet for campers. One part of the pamphlet will explain how to avoid coming into contact with poison ivy and poison oak. Using these drawings the ranger has given you and the notes on the next page, write a paragraph informing campers about these plants. Use at least two adjective phrases and three adverb phrases in your paragraph.

Notes

poison ivy and poison oak—plants can cause an allergic reaction when touched

some people react worse than others—some not at all

reaction includes itching and blistering of the skin

best method to deal with these plants—learn to recognize and avoid them

poison ivy—leaf made up of three leaflets that are glossy green, oval-shaped, and smoothly textured

poison oak—similar to poison ivy, but leaflets are thicker and smaller, and the ends are rounded rather than pointed

first aid—wash the area thoroughly with soap and water; visit a doctor if itching, swelling, and redness develop

REVIEW A Identifying and Classifying Prepositional Phrases

In the following sentences, identify each prepositional phrase and classify it as an *adjective phrase* or an *adverb phrase.* Then, give the word or words the phrase modifies.

EXAMPLE **1. Here is some information about sharks.**
1. *about sharks—adjective phrase; information*

1. Did you know that there are hundreds of types?
2. Scientists group these different types into twenty-eight large families.
3. Sharks within the same family share many traits.
4. The body shape, tail shape, and teeth determine the differences among families.

GRAMMAR

5. Sharks are found throughout the world's oceans.
6. As the chart shows, some sharks prefer cold waters, and others live mostly in warm tropical oceans.
7. Only thirty kinds of sharks are dangerous.
8. The huge whale shark, however, falls under the "not dangerous" category.
9. Divers can even hitch a ride on its fins.
10. Beautiful yet frightening to most people, sharks are perhaps the world's most awesome creatures.

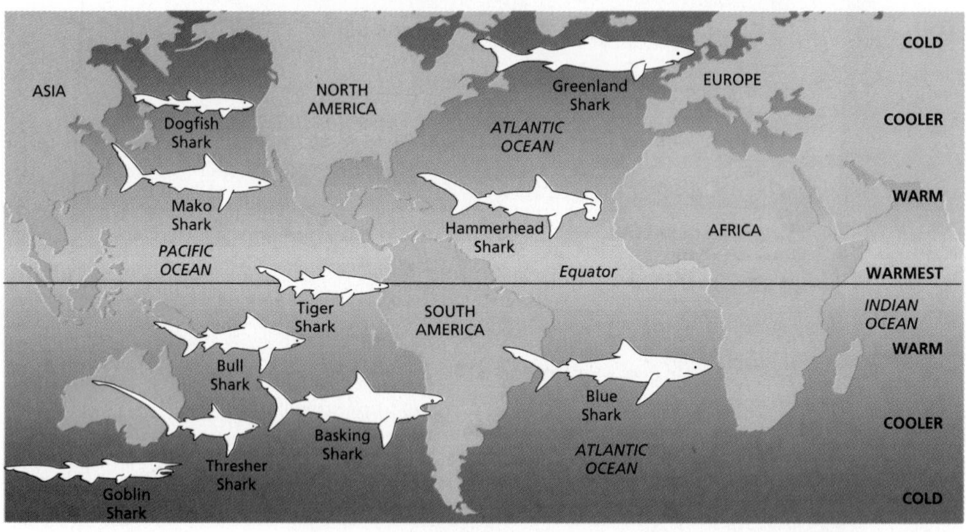

REVIEW B

Writing Sentences with Prepositional Phrases

Write five sentences of your own. In each sentence, use a different prepositional phrase from the following list. After each sentence, label the phrase as an *adjective phrase* or an *adverb phrase.*

EXAMPLE **1.** through the toll booth
1. *A car passed through the toll booth.—adverb phrase*

1. in the movie theater
2. for the Cinco de Mayo party
3. along the water's edge
4. about General Colin Powell
5. into the crowded department store

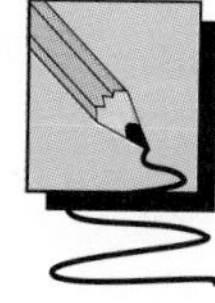

WRITING APPLICATION

Using Prepositional Phrases to Add Detail to Your Writing

GRAMMAR

Prepositional phrases add information to a sentence. Adjective phrases give details about *what kind, which one,* and *how many*. Adverb phrases tell details about *when, where, how, why, how much,* and *to what extent*.

WITHOUT PHRASES We fed the cat.
WITH PHRASES In the morning we fed the cat from the blue box of dry Kitty Bits.

WRITING ACTIVITY

You are writing a note to a friend explaining how to care for your pet while you are away on vacation. In your note, use a combined total of at least ten adjective phrases and adverb phrases to give detailed instructions to your friend.

Prewriting Begin by thinking about a pet you have or would like to have. Then, make a chart or list of the pet's needs. If you need more information about a particular pet, ask a friend or someone else who owns such a pet.

Writing As you write your first draft, focus on giving information about each of your pet's needs. Tell your friend everything he or she needs to know to care for your pet properly.

Evaluating and Revising Ask a family member or friend to read your note. Add any missing information and take out any unnecessary instructions. Be sure that you have used both adjective phrases and adverb phrases and that you have used a total of at least ten phrases.

Proofreading Read over your note again to check the grammar, punctuation, and spelling. Be sure that your prepositional phrases are properly placed. Remember that an adjective phrase follows the noun or pronoun it modifies. An adverb phrase may occur at various places in a sentence. (See page 720 for information on when to use commas with introductory prepositional phrases.)

Verbals and Verbal Phrases

A ***verbal*** is a word that is formed from a verb but is used as a noun, an adjective, or an adverb.

The Participle

17e. A ***participle*** is a verb form that can be used as an adjective.

There are two kinds of participles: *present participles* and *past participles.*

(1) ***Present participles*** end in *–ing.*

EXAMPLES Mr. Sanchez rescued three people from the **burning** building. [*Burning* is the present participle of the verb *burn.* The participle modifies the noun *building.*]

Chasing the cat, the dog ran down the street. [*Chasing* is the present participle of the verb *chase.* The participle acts as an adjective modifying the noun *dog.*]

(2) ***Past participles*** usually end in *–d* or *–ed.* Some past participles are irregularly formed.

EXAMPLES Well **trained** in gunnery, the soldier successfully carried out her mission. [The past participle *trained* modifies the noun *soldier.*]

We skated on the **frozen** pond. [The irregular past participle *frozen* modifies the noun *pond.*]

REFERENCE NOTE: For a list of irregular past participles, see pages 583–586.

NOTE: Be careful not to confuse participles used as adjectives with participles used in verb phrases. Remember that the participle in a verb phrase is part of the verb.

PARTICIPLE **Discouraged,** the fans went home.
VERB PHRASE The fans **were discouraged** and went home.

PARTICIPLE **Singing** cheerfully, the birds perched in the trees.
VERB PHRASE The birds **were singing** cheerfully in the trees.

EXERCISE 9 Identifying Participles and the Nouns They Modify

Identify the participles used as adjectives in the following sentences. After each participle, give the noun that the participle modifies.

EXAMPLE **1.** The deserted cities of the Anasazi are found in the Four Corners area of the United States.
1. *deserted—cities*

1. Utah, Colorado, New Mexico, and Arizona are the bordering states that make up the Four Corners.
2. Because of its natural beauty, Chaco Canyon is one of the most visited sights in this region of the Southwest.
3. Among the remaining ruins in Chaco Canyon are the houses, public buildings, and plazas of the Anasazi.
4. What alarming event may have caused these people to leave their valley?
5. Historians are studying the scattered remains of the Anasazi culture to learn more about these mysterious people.

EXERCISE 10 Identifying Participles and the Nouns or Pronouns They Modify

Identify the participles used as adjectives in the following sentences. Then, give the noun or pronoun the participle modifies.

EXAMPLE **1. Buzzing mosquitoes swarmed around me.**
1. ***Buzzing—mosquitoes***

GRAMMAR

1. Annoyed, I went inside to watch TV.
2. I woke my sleeping father to ask about mosquitoes.
3. Irritated, he directed me to the encyclopedia.
4. I learned that some flying insects carry diseases.
5. Biting mosquitoes put liquid chemicals into the skin.
6. The swollen skin itches.
7. Sucking blood for food, mosquitoes survive in many different climates.
8. Sometimes you can hear mosquitoes humming.
9. Their vibrating wings make the sound.
10. Mosquitoes, living only a few weeks, may go through as many as twelve generations in a year.

The Participial Phrase

17f. A ***participial phrase*** consists of a participle together with its modifiers and complements. The entire phrase is used as an adjective.

EXAMPLE **Stretching slowly,** the cat jumped down from the windowsill. [The participle *stretching* is modified by the adverb *slowly.*]

The tornado **predicted by the weather forecaster** did not hit our area. [The participle *predicted* is modified by the prepositional phrase *by the weather forecaster.*]

Reading the assignment, she took notes carefully. [The participle *reading* has the direct object *assignment.*]

A participial phrase should be placed close to the word it modifies. Otherwise the phrase may appear to modify another word, and the sentence may not make sense.

REFERENCE NOTE: For information on how to place participial phrases correctly, see pages 642–643.

EXERCISE 11 Identifying Participial Phrases and the Nouns or Pronouns They Modify

Identify the participial phrases in the following sentences. Then, give the word or words each phrase modifies.

EXAMPLE **1. Living over four hundred years ago, Leonardo da Vinci kept journals of his many ideas and inventions.**

1. *Living over four hundred years ago—Leonardo da Vinci*

1. The journals, written in reverse "mirror writing," are more than five thousand pages long.
2. Leonardo drew many pictures showing birds in flight.
3. He hoped that his machines based on his sketches of birds would enable humans to fly.
4. Shown here, his design for a helicopter was the first one in history of motion.

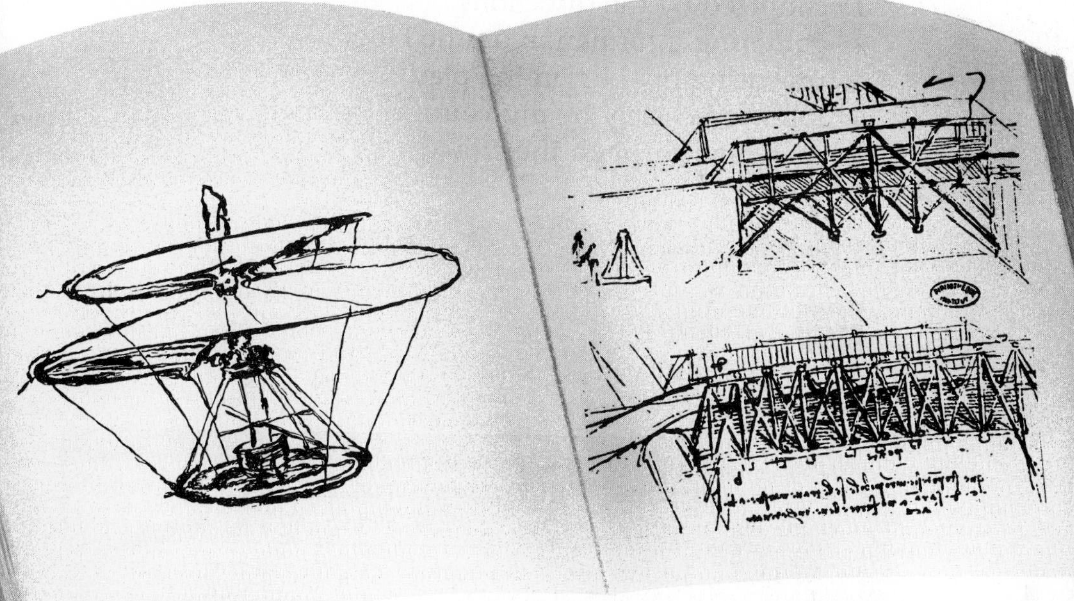

5. Studying the eye, Leonardo understood the sense of sight.
6. He worked hard, filling his journals with sketches like the one above for a movable bridge.

GRAMMAR

7. The solutions reached in his journals often helped Leonardo when he created his artworks.
8. The hands sketched in the journals helped him paint the hands of the *Mona Lisa.*
9. Painting on a large wall, Leonardo created *The Last Supper.*
10. Leonardo, experimenting continually, had little time to paint in his later years.

EXERCISE 12 **Writing Sentences with Participial Phrases**

Write five sentences, using in each sentence a different participial phrase from the following list. [Note: Place a comma after a participial phrase that begins a sentence.]

EXAMPLE 1. cheering for the team
1. *Cheering for the team, we celebrated the victory.*

1. confused by the directions
2. gathering information on the Hopi
3. practicing my part in the play
4. followed closely by my younger brother
5. searching through the crowd

The Infinitive

17g. An ***infinitive*** is a verb form, usually preceded by *to,* that can be used as a noun, an adjective, or an adverb.

INFINITIVES	
USED AS	EXAMPLES
Nouns	**To succeed** is my goal. [*To succeed* is the subject of the sentence.] My ambition is **to teach** Spanish. [*To teach* is a predicate nominative.] She tried **to win.** [*To win* is the direct object of the verb *tried.*]

(continued)

INFINITIVES *(continued)*	
USED AS	EXAMPLES
Adjectives	The place **to meet** tomorrow is the library. [*To meet* modifies the noun *place.*] She is the one **to call.** [*To call* modifies the pronoun *one.*]
Adverbs	Tamara claims she was born **to surf.** [*To surf* modifies the verb *was born.*] This math problem will be hard **to solve** without a calculator. [*To solve* modifies the adjective *hard.*]

NOTE: *To* plus a noun or a pronoun (*to Washington, to her*) is a prepositional phrase, not an infinitive.

PREPOSITIONAL PHRASE I am going **to the mall** today.
INFINITIVE I am going **to shop** for new shoes.

EXERCISE 13 Identifying Infinitives

Identify the infinitives in the following sentences. If a sentence does not contain an infinitive, write *none.*

EXAMPLE **1. I would like to go to New York City someday.**
1. *to go*

1. My first stop would be to visit the Statue of Liberty.
2. Thousands of people go to see the statue every day.
3. They take a boat to Liberty Island.
4. The statue holds a torch to symbolize freedom.
5. The idea of a statue to represent freedom came from a French historian.
6. France gave the statue to the United States in 1884.
7. It was a gift to express the friendship between the two nations.
8. The statue was shipped to this country in 214 cases.
9. In the 1980s, many people helped to raise money for repairs to the statue.
10. The repairs were completed in time to celebrate the statue's 100th anniversary on October 28, 1986.

The Infinitive Phrase

17h. An *infinitive phrase* consists of an infinitive together with its modifiers and complements. It may be used as a noun, an adjective, or an adverb.

EXAMPLES **To be a good gymnast** takes hard work. [The infinitive phrase is used as a noun. The infinitive *to be* has a complement, *a good gymnast.*]

The first person **to fly over both the North Pole and the South Pole** was Richard Byrd. [The infinitive phrase is used as an adjective modifying the noun *person.* The infinitive *to fly* is modified by the prepositional phrase *over both the North Pole and the South Pole.*]

Are you ready **to go to the gym now?** [The infinitive phrase is used as an adverb modifying the adjective *ready.* The infinitive *to go* is modified by the prepositional phrase *to the gym* and by the adverb *now.*]

EXERCISE 14 Identifying Infinitive Phrases

Identify the infinitive phrase in each of the following sentences.

EXAMPLE **1. We went to the park to watch birds.**
1. *to watch birds*

1. A bird is able to control each of its feathers.
2. Birds use their feathers to push their bodies through the air.
3. Human beings learned to build aircraft by studying birds.
4. A bird sings to claim its territory.
5. To recognize the songs of different birds takes practice.
6. By molting (or gradual shedding), birds are able to replace their feathers.

7. Eagles use their feet to catch small animals.
8. Since they have no teeth, many birds have to swallow their food whole.
9. In many cases both parents help to build a nest.
10. Most birds feed their young until the young are ready to fly from the nest.

PICTURE THIS

Wow! Whoever drew this sketch is a good artist. You found this sketch on the bus this morning, and you wish you knew who lost it. What is the artist like? Who is the person in the sketch? You find yourself thinking about these things and making up stories. You decide to write a short story about the artist or about the person in the sketch. Use at least three participial phrases and two infinitive phrases in your story. Underline the phrases you use.

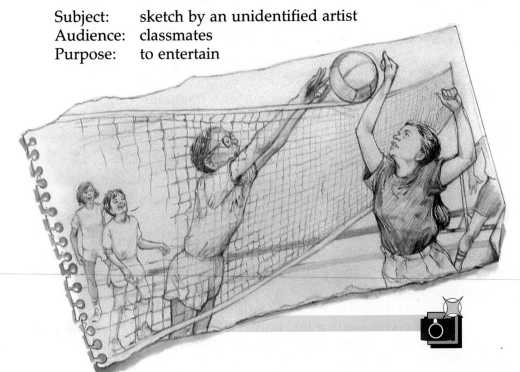

Subject: sketch by an unidentified artist
Audience: classmates
Purpose: to entertain

EXERCISE 15 Writing Sentences with Infinitive Phrases

Write five sentences, using in each sentence a different infinitive phrase from the following list. Try to vary your sentences as much as possible.

EXAMPLE **1.** to see the carved masks of the Haida people
1. *Terry wants to see the carved masks of the Haida people.*

1. to sing with the Boys Choir of Harlem
2. to ask a question about the test
3. to write a poem to his girlfriend
4. to understand the assignment
5. to give a report on the Spanish exploration of California

REVIEW C Identifying and Classifying Participial Phrases and Infinitive Phrases

Identify the participial phrase or the infinitive phrase in each sentence of the following paragraph. Label each phrase as a *participial phrase* or an *infinitive phrase.*

EXAMPLES [1] My family is proud to celebrate our Jewish holidays.
1. *to celebrate our Jewish holidays—infinitive phrase*

[2] Observing Jewish traditions, we celebrate each holiday in a special way.
2. *Observing Jewish traditions—participial phrase*

[1] During Rosh Hashanah we hear the Torah read in our synagogue. [2] Celebrated in September or October, Rosh Hashanah is the Jewish New Year. [3] On this holiday, the rabbi at our synagogue chooses to wear white robes instead of the usual black robes. [4] Representing newness and purity, the white robes symbolize the new year. [5] My favorite food of Rosh Hashanah is the honey cake baked by my grandmother. [6] During this holiday everyone eats a lot, knowing that Yom Kippur, a day of

fasting, is only ten days away. [7] Yom Kippur, considered the holiest day of the Jewish year, is a serious holiday. [8] To attend services like the one you see below is part of my family's Yom Kippur tradition. [9] I am always pleased to see many of my friends and neighbors there. [10] Sunset, marking the end of the day, brings Yom Kippur to a peaceful close.

Review: Posttest 1

A. Identifying and Classifying Prepositional Phrases

Identify each prepositional phrase in the following sentences and classify it as an *adjective phrase* or an *adverb phrase.* Then, give the word that the phrase modifies.

EXAMPLE **1.** The chairs in the kitchen need new cushions.
1. *in the kitchen—adjective phrase; chairs*

1. Cathy Guisewite is the creator of the cartoon strip "Cathy."
2. The Rio Grande is the boundary between Texas and Mexico.

3. Those totem poles come from Washington State.
4. The most popular name for the United States flag is the Stars and Stripes.
5. Heu Feng was a finalist at the international violin competition.
6. Through the window crashed the baseball.
7. I wish I were better at tennis.
8. During the Persian Gulf Conflict, we watched the news often.
9. The first United States space shuttle was launched in 1981.
10. Outside the door the hungry cat waited patiently.

B. Identifying and Classifying Verbal Phrases

Identify the verbal phrase in each of the following sentences. Then, tell whether it is a *participial phrase* or an *infinitive phrase*.

EXAMPLE **1. The snow, falling steadily, formed huge drifts.**
1. *falling steadily—participial phrase*

11. We expect to do well on the test.
12. The bus, slowed by heavy traffic, arrived later than it usually does.
13. Breaking the eggs into the wok, he made egg foo yong.
14. To remain calm is not always easy.
15. She wants to study Spanish in high school.
16. The magazine featuring that article is in the school library.
17. Chilled to the bone, the children finally went inside.
18. Who are the candidates that they plan to support in the election?
19. Bethune-Cookman College, founded by Mary McLeod Bethune, is in Daytona Beach, Florida.
20. Teresa called to ask about tonight's homework assignment.

Review: Posttest 2

Writing Phrases for Sentences

For each of the following sentences, write the kind of phrase that is called for in parentheses.

EXAMPLE **1. ____ , the audience cheered Yo-Yo Ma's performance. (*participial phrase*)**
1. *Clapping loudly, the audience cheered Yo-Yo Ma's performance.*

1. We walked slowly ____. (*adverb phrase*)
2. The people ____ applauded Barbara Jordan's speech. (*adjective phrase*)
3. My little brother is afraid ____. (*adverb phrase*)
4. The water ____ dripped steadily. (*adjective phrase*)
5. ____ we saw many beautiful Navajo rugs. (*adverb phrase*)
6. ____, the principal entered the classroom. (*participial phrase*)
7. Suddenly, ____, the lion pounced. (*participial phrase*)
8. My friends and I like ____. (*infinitive phrase*)
9. ____ is my one ambition. (*infinitive phrase*)
10. She wrote a poem ____. (*participial phrase*)

GRAMMAR

18 THE CLAUSE

Independent and Subordinate Clauses

Diagnostic Test

A. Identifying Clauses

Label each of the following groups of words as a *clause* or *not a clause.*

EXAMPLES **1.** last winter we ice-skated
1. *clause*
2. on the frozen pond
2. *not a clause*

1. until tomorrow
2. for lunch they had tacos
3. their pictures in the newspaper
4. waiting at the corner for the bus

5. because they are twins
6. neither answer is right
7. after the concert last Saturday
8. that honors Rosa Parks
9. which happened before I was born
10. playing first base

B. Classifying Subordinate Clauses

Label each italicized clause in the following sentences as an *adjective clause* or an *adverb clause.* Then give the word or words each clause modifies.

EXAMPLES
1. Manuel's paper route has doubled *since he took it over.*
1. *adverb clause—has doubled*
2. The present *that I bought for Mother's Day* is in my closet.
2. *adjective clause—present*

11. Everyone *who signed up for the marathon* should meet at 8:00 A.M. tomorrow in the parking lot.
12. Tuesday we went to the Mardi Gras Parade, *which is held every year in New Orleans.*
13. Can you go to the park *when school is over today*?
14. The CD *that I wanted to buy* was out of stock.
15. Loretta stayed home today *because she has a bad case of the flu.*
16. I play soccer *so that I will get more exercise.*
17. We met the García family *as we were leaving the grocery store.*
18. My older sister, *who is on the varsity basketball team,* practices after school every day.
19. *Since it was such a beautiful evening,* we decided to take a long walk.
20. The students *whose families observe the Jewish Sabbath* will be excused early on Friday.

GRAMMAR

18a. A ***clause*** is a group of words that contains a verb and its subject and is used as a part of a sentence.

Every clause contains a subject and a verb. However, not all clauses express complete thoughts. Clauses that do express a complete thought are called *independent clauses.* Clauses that do not make complete sense by themselves are called *subordinate clauses.*

The Independent Clause

18b. An ***independent*** (or ***main***) ***clause*** expresses a complete thought and can stand by itself as a sentence.

EXAMPLES I woke up late this morning.
The alarm clock never rang.

When an independent clause stands alone, it is called a sentence. Usually, the term *independent clause* is used only when such a clause is joined with another clause.

SENTENCE **My mother drove me to school.**
INDEPENDENT CLAUSE Since I missed the bus, **my mother drove me to school.**

The Subordinate Clause

18c. A ***subordinate*** (or ***dependent***) ***clause*** does not express a complete thought and cannot stand alone.

A subordinate clause must be joined with at least one independent clause to make a sentence and express a complete thought.

SUBORDINATE CLAUSES since the day we met
that the veterinarian recommended
if the dress is too long

SENTENCES I have liked you **since the day we met.**
We give our hamster the food **that the veterinarian recommended.**
If the dress is too long, we will hem it.

Notice that words such as *since, that,* and *if* signal the beginning of a subordinate clause.

EXERCISE 1 **Identifying Independent and Subordinate Clauses**

For each of the following sentences, label the italicized clause as *independent* or *subordinate.*

EXAMPLE 1. *If you know any modern music history,* you are probably familiar with the Motown sound.
1. *subordinate*

1. Do you recognize any of the entertainers *who are shown in the photographs on the next page?*
2. These performers all had hit records in the 1950s and 1960s *when the music business in Detroit (the Motor City, or "Motown") was booming.*
3. Berry Gordy, *who founded the Motown record label,* began his business in a small office in Detroit.
4. He was a songwriter and producer, and *he was able to spot talent.*
5. Gordy went to clubs to hear local groups *whose sound he liked.*
6. The Miracles, *which was the first group he discovered,* had a lead singer named Smokey Robinson.
7. *Robinson was also a songwriter,* and Gordy included him in the Motown team of writers and musicians.
8. Gordy carefully managed all aspects of the Motown sound, *which is a special combination of rhythm and blues and soul.*

9. Diana Ross and the Supremes, Stevie Wonder, Marvin Gaye, the Four Tops, the Temptations, Gladys Knight and the Pips, and Michael Jackson are just some of the performers *that Gordy discovered.*
10. *As you look at the photographs again,* can you recognize more of these modern music legends?

EXERCISE 2 **Identifying Subordinate Clauses**

Identify the subordinate clause in each of the following sentences.

EXAMPLE 1. When you get up in the morning, do you look at your sleepy face in a mirror?
1. *When you get up in the morning*

1. A mirror is a piece of polished metal or glass that is coated with a substance such as silver.

2. The most common type of mirror is the plane mirror, which is flat.
3. The image that is reflected in a plane mirror is reversed.
4. As you look into a mirror, your left hand seems to be the image's right hand.
5. When an image is reversed, it is called a mirror image.
6. A sailor who looks through the periscope of a submarine is using a system of lenses and mirrors to see above the water's surface.
7. Right-hand rear-view mirrors on cars, which show a wide area of the road behind, are usually convex, or curved outward.
8. Drivers must be careful because convex mirrors make reflected objects appear far away.
9. Because the mirror in a flashlight is concave, or curved inward, it strengthens the light from a small light bulb.
10. When you look in a concave mirror, you see a magnified reflection.

EXERCISE 3 **Writing Sentences with Subordinate Clauses**

Write five sentences by adding an independent clause to each of the following subordinate clauses. Underline the independent clause in each of your sentences. Make your sentences interesting by adding a variety of independent clauses.

EXAMPLE **1.** who lives next door to us
1. *The woman who lives next door to us is a computer programmer.*

1. when I bought the CD
2. who won the contest
3. if my parents agree
4. as Jessye Norman began to sing
5. because we are going to a fiesta

The Adjective Clause

18d. An ***adjective clause*** is a subordinate clause that modifies a noun or a pronoun.

Like an adjective or an adjective phrase, an adjective clause may modify a noun or a pronoun. Unlike an adjective phrase, an adjective clause contains a verb and its subject.

ADJECTIVE	a **blue** flower
ADJECTIVE PHRASE	a flower **with blue petals** [does not have a verb and its subject]
ADJECTIVE CLAUSE	a flower **that has blue petals** [does have a verb and its subject]

An adjective clause usually follows the noun or pronoun it modifies and tells *which one* or *what kind.*

EXAMPLES Emma Willard was the one **who founded the first women's college in the United States.** [The adjective clause modifies the pronoun *one,* telling *which one.*]

I want a bicycle **that I can ride over rough ground.** [The adjective clause modifies the noun *bicycle,* telling *what kind.*]

The Relative Pronoun

An adjective clause is almost always introduced by a *relative pronoun.*

Relative Pronouns

that which who whom whose

These words are called ***relative pronouns*** because they *relate* an adjective clause to the noun or pronoun that the clause modifies.

EXAMPLES A snorkel is a hollow tube **that lets a diver breathe underwater.** [The relative pronoun *that* begins the adjective clause and relates it to the noun *tube.*]

The team's mascot, **which is a horse,** is called Renegade. [The relative pronoun *which* begins the adjective clause and relates it to the noun *mascot.*]

Gwendolyn Brooks is the writer **who is the poet laureate of Illinois.** [The relative pronoun *who* begins the adjective clause and relates it to the noun *writer.*]

Those **whose library books are overdue** must pay fines. [The relative pronoun *whose* begins the adjective clause and relates it to the pronoun *Those.*]

EXERCISE 4 **Identifying Adjective Clauses**

Identify the adjective clause in each of the following sentences. Underline the relative pronoun that begins the clause.

EXAMPLE **1.** The person who wrote the Declaration of Independence was Thomas Jefferson.
1. *who wrote the Declaration of Independence*

1. In his later years, Jefferson lived at Monticello, which he had designed.
2. Jefferson planned a daily schedule that kept him busy all day.
3. He began each day by making a note that recorded the morning temperature.
4. Then he did his writing, which included letters to friends and businesspeople.
5. Afterward, he ate breakfast, which was served around 9:00 A.M.
6. Jefferson, whose property included stables as well as farm fields, went horseback riding at noon.

7. Dinner was a big meal, which began about 4:00 P.M.
8. From dinner until dark, he talked to friends and neighbors who came to visit.
9. He also spent time with his family, which included twelve grandchildren.
10. Jefferson, whose interests ranged from art and architecture to biology and mathematics, read each night.

EXERCISE 5 Writing Appropriate Adjective Clauses

Complete each of the following sentences by adding an adjective clause that will make sense in the blank. Then, underline the relative pronoun. Remember that a clause must contain a verb and its subject.

EXAMPLE **1. We read the Greek legend ____.**
1. ***We read the Greek legend that tells the story of the Trojan horse.***

1. You should proofread every composition ____.
2. My friend ____ is a good student.
3. Mrs. Echohawk ____ was my fifth-grade teacher.
4. We heard a sound ____.
5. Our neighbors ____ are from Fez, Morocco.

PICTURE THIS

You are visiting a small company that creates greeting cards. The artist shown on the next page is a family friend, and she designs cards that will be marketed to young people. She has asked you to help her write messages for the cards that she illustrates. For example, she might design a card with a rabbit on the cover, and you might write *This is a bunny who has something to say: Have a Hoppy Birthday!* Write messages for at least five greeting cards. Use an adjective clause in each message, and circle each relative pronoun. Following each message, write a brief description of a photo or illustration to go with your message.

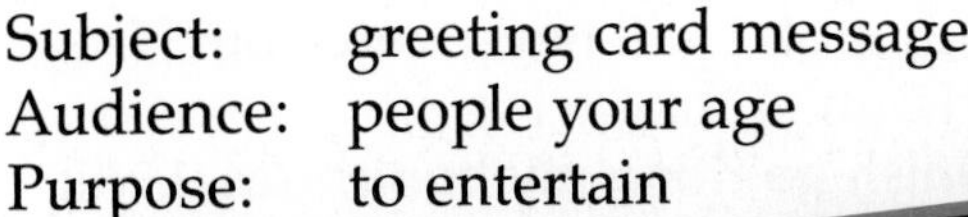

Subject: greeting card messages
Audience: people your age
Purpose: to entertain

The Adverb Clause

18e. An ***adverb clause*** is a subordinate clause that is used as an adverb.

Like an adverb or an adverb phrase, an adverb clause may modify a verb, an adjective, or an adverb. Unlike an adverb phrase, an adverb clause contains a verb and its subject.

ADVERB	**Bravely,** Jason battled a fierce dragon.
ADVERB PHRASE	**With great bravery,** Jason battled a fierce dragon. [does not have a verb and its subject]
ADVERB CLAUSE	**Because Jason was brave,** he battled a fierce dragon. [does have a verb and its subject]

An adverb clause answers the following questions: *How? When? Where? Why? To what extent? How much? How long?* or *Under what conditions?*

EXAMPLES I feel **as though I will never catch up.** [The adverb clause tells *how* I feel.]

After I finish painting my bookcases, I will call you. [The adverb clause tells *when* I will call you.]

I paint **where there is plenty of fresh air.** [The adverb clause tells *where* I paint.]

I have more work to do today **because I didn't paint yesterday.** [The adverb clause tells *why* I have more work to do.]

I will paint **until Mom comes home;** then I will clean my brushes and set the table for supper. [The adverb clause tells *how long* I will paint.]

If I paint for two more hours, I should be able to finish. [The adverb clause tells *under what conditions* I should be able to finish.]

Notice in these examples that adverb clauses may be placed in various positions in sentences. When an adverb clause comes at the beginning, it is usually followed by a comma.

REFERENCE NOTE: For more about punctuating introductory adverb clauses, see page 720.

Subordinating Conjunctions

Adverb clauses begin with *subordinating conjunctions.*

Common Subordinating Conjunctions

after	as soon as	in order that	until
although	as though	since	when
as	because	so that	whenever
as if	before	than	where
as long as	how	though	wherever
as much as	if	unless	while

Some subordinating conjunctions, such as *after, as, before, since,* and *until,* may also be used as prepositions.

PREPOSITION	**Before** sunrise, we left for the cabin.
SUBORDINATING CONJUNCTION	**Before** the sun had risen, we left for the cabin.
PREPOSITION	In the nineteenth century, buffalo skins were used **as** blankets and clothing.
SUBORDINATING CONJUNCTION	Around 1900, **as** the buffalo became nearly extinct, conservationists fought for its protection.

GRAMMAR

EXERCISE 6 **Identifying Adverb Clauses**

Identify the adverb clause in each sentence in the following paragraph. Then write whether the clause tells *when, where, how, why, how much,* or *under what condition.*

EXAMPLE [1] Long before they had a written history, the Chinese were making kites.

1. *Long before they had a written history—when*

[1] Although this story is only a legend, many people believe that a kite like the one pictured on the next page may have saved the people of China's Han Dynasty. [2] The Chinese were about to be attacked by an enemy army when an adviser to the emperor came up with a plan. [3] As the adviser stood beside an open window, his hat was lifted off by a strong wind. [4] He immediately called for a number of kites to be made so that they might be used to frighten the enemy. [5] The kite makers had no trouble finding lightweight bamboo for their kite frames because bamboo is native to China. [6] As soon as each frame was completed, silk was stretched over it. [7] The emperor's adviser attached noisemakers to the kites so that they would produce an eerie sound. [8] He ordered his men to fly the kites in the darkest hour of night because then the enemy would hear the kites but not see them. [9] Unless the adviser had misjudged the enemy,

they would be fooled into thinking that the kites were gods warning them to retreat. [10] According to the legend, the enemy retreated as if they were being chased by a fire-breathing dragon.

Chinese Kites, How to Make and Fly Them, David F. Jue, Charles E. Tuttle Co., Inc. of Tokyo, Japan

REVIEW

Identifying and Classifying Subordinate Clauses

Identify the subordinate clause in each of the following sentences. Then, label each clause as an *adjective clause* or an *adverb clause*.

EXAMPLES
1. American history is filled with stories of people who performed heroic deeds.
1. *who performed heroic deeds—adjective clause*
2. As the American colonists struggled for independence, women played important roles.
2. *As the American colonists struggled for independence—adverb clause*

1. When you study the American Revolution, you may learn about the adventures of a woman known as Molly Pitcher.

2. Molly, whose real name was believed to be Mary Ludwig, was the daughter of farmers.
3. Although she was born in New Jersey, she moved to Pennsylvania.
4. There she married John Hays, who was a barber.
5. Hays joined the colonial army when the Revolution began.
6. Mary Ludwig Hays went to be with her husband in Monmouth, New Jersey, which was the site of a battle on a hot June day in 1778.
7. At first, she carried water to the soldiers so that they would not be overcome by the intense heat.
8. The soldiers nicknamed her "Molly Pitcher" because she carried the water in pitchers.
9. Later, when her husband collapsed from the heat, she took over his cannon.
10. George Washington, who was the commander of the Continental Army, made Molly an honorary sergeant.

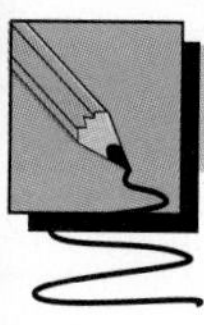

WRITING APPLICATION

Using Subordinating Conjunctions to Explain a Process

Subordinating conjunctions don't just connect ideas. They show the relationships between ideas. Notice how the subordinating conjunctions in the following examples show the different time relationships between the two clauses.

1. Squeeze the trigger of the fire extinguisher **before** you aim the nozzle.
2. Squeeze the trigger of the fire extinguisher **as** you aim the nozzle.
3. Squeeze the trigger of the fire extinguisher **after** you aim the nozzle.

Which of the instructions on the previous page would help you put out a fire efficiently?

Clearly showing relationships between clauses in your writing is always important. However, it is particularly necessary when you are giving instructions or explaining a process.

WRITING ACTIVITY

Your class project for National Safety Week is to write a safety manual. Each class member will write one page of instructions telling what to do in a particular emergency. You may write about a major emergency, such as a fire, an earthquake, or a tornado. Or you may write about a minor emergency, such as a brief power outage, a sprained ankle, or a case of poison ivy. Use subordinating conjunctions to show the relationships between your ideas.

Prewriting Think of a specific emergency that you know how to handle. List the steps that someone should follow in this emergency. Number the steps in order. If you aren't sure of the order or don't know a particular step, stop writing and get the information you need. A health teacher, the school nurse, or an organization such as the Red Cross should be able to provide information. [Remember: Readers will rely on your manual in an emergency. *The information you present must be accurate.*]

Writing Use your prewriting list to begin your first draft. As you write, make your instructions as clear as possible. Define or explain terms that might be unfamiliar to your readers. Be sure that your instructions are in the right order.

Evaluating and Revising Read over your instructions to be sure that you've included all necessary information. Add, cut, or rearrange steps to make the instructions easy to follow. Be sure to use appropriate subordinating conjunctions to make the order of the steps clear. You may want to present your instructions in a numbered list rather than in a paragraph.

Proofreading and Publishing Check your work carefully for any errors in grammar, punctuation, or spelling. For information on punctuating introductory adverb clauses, see page 720. To publish your class safety manual, gather all the pages and input them on a computer or make photocopies. Organize your topics alphabetically, or group them by kinds of emergencies.

Review: Posttest 1

A. Identifying and Classifying Independent and Subordinate Clauses

Label each of the following clauses as either *independent* or *subordinate.*

EXAMPLES
1. when I was eleven years old
1. *subordinate*
2. he was eleven years old
2. *independent*

1. because I have lived in Chile and Ecuador
2. his writing has improved
3. although Gullah is still spoken on South Carolina's Sea Islands
4. when the Philadelphia Phillies won the National League pennant
5. she served as Secretary of Labor
6. that we brought to the Juneteenth picnic
7. everyone laughed
8. who heard the Navajo story about Coyote
9. during the storm the power failed
10. which seemed to be the reason for the delay

GRAMMAR

B. Identifying and Classifying Subordinate Clauses

Identify the subordinate clause in each of the following sentences. Then, label each clause as either an *adjective clause* or an *adverb clause*.

EXAMPLES
1. Today is the day that you are having dinner at my house.
1. *that you are having dinner at my house—adjective clause*
2. I will give you a map so that you can find my house easily.
2. *so that you can find my house easily—adverb clause*

11. If you have never eaten Caribbean food, you are in for a big treat.
12. My mother, who was born and raised in Jamaica, really knows how to cook.
13. Whenever I have a chance, I help her in the kitchen to learn her secrets.
14. My grandmother, whose cooking is even better than my mother's, is making her special sweet potato pone for dessert.
15. Some of the fruits and vegetables that grow in Jamaica are hard to find in the markets around here.
16. Today we are shopping for coconuts, avocados, and callaloo greens, which were introduced to the Caribbean by Africans.
17. We must also remember to buy fresh hot peppers, onions, and spices that are needed for seasoning the meat.
18. Although my mother never uses measuring spoons, she seems to know just how much of each spice to add.
19. As soon as we pay for these items, let's take them to my house.
20. Part of your treat will be to sniff the delicious smells from the kitchen before you even begin eating.

Review: Posttest 2

Writing Sentences with Subordinate Clauses

Write ten different sentences of your own. In each sentence, include a subordinate clause that begins with one of the following words. Underline the subordinate clause. After the sentence, label the subordinate clause as an *adjective clause* or an *adverb clause*.

EXAMPLES
1. so that
1. *We hurried so that we wouldn't miss the bus.—adverb clause*
2. whom
2. *Jim Nakamura, whom I met at summer camp, is now my pen pal.—adjective clause*

1. which
2. before
3. since
4. who
5. than
6. whose
7. as though
8. although
9. that
10. if

19 Kinds of Sentence Structure

Simple, Compound, and Complex Sentences

Diagnostic Test

A. Identifying Independent and Subordinate Clauses

Identify each clause in the following sentences as either an *independent clause* or a *subordinate clause.*

EXAMPLES
1. I waved to them, but they didn't see me.
1. *I waved to them—independent clause; they didn't see me—independent clause*
2. All tennis players who are renting rackets should pay their rental fees today.
2. *All tennis players should pay their rental fees today—independent clause; who are renting rackets—subordinate clause*

1. She raked the leaves, and I mowed the lawn.
2. Lupe and Ben rode their bicycles to the park so that they could watch the fireworks.

3. We chose tacos instead of sandwiches from the cafeteria's menu.
4. The new camp that offers instruction in computer programming will be in session from August 17 through August 28.
5. The rain changed to snow mixed with sleet.
6. At the beach, Mei-Ling and her parents practiced their tai chi exercises.
7. My grandparents, who enjoy exciting vacations, are planning to visit Nepal this year.
8. Since last year I have grown three inches, but I still can't reach the top shelf in the kitchen.
9. Uncle Martin gave me this book by Jamaica Kincaid because he enjoyed it.
10. She wants to be a veterinarian, for she likes to be around animals.

B. Classifying Sentences by Structure

Classify each of the following sentences as a *simple sentence*, a *compound sentence*, or a *complex sentence*.

EXAMPLE **1. The religion of the Muslims is called Islam, and it is based on a belief in one God.**
1. *compound sentence*

11. Muslims live in various parts of the world, though mostly in Africa, the Middle East, and Malaysia.
12. In recent years many Muslims have come to the United States, and they have brought their religion with them.
13. In May 1991, a mosque opened in New York.
14. When the mosque was opened, religious leaders and other Muslims went there to pray.
15. Some worshipers wore the traditional clothing of their homelands, and others were dressed in typical American clothes.
16. Muslims were particularly pleased that the new mosque opened in the spring.

17. The month of fasting called Ramadan had just ended, so the holiday after Ramadan could be celebrated in the new house of worship.
18. Although Muslims share a common religion, their languages differ.
19. Many Muslims speak Arabic, but those in Iran, Turkey, and neighboring countries, for example, speak other languages, too.
20. Of course, Muslims in the United States speak English, or they are learning it as a new language.

The Simple Sentence

19a. A ***simple sentence*** has one independent clause and no subordinate clauses.

EXAMPLES A good **rain** [S] **helps** [V] the farmers.

Up for the rebound **leaped** [V] **Kareem** [S].

A simple sentence may have a compound subject, a compound verb, or both.

EXAMPLES **Burritos** [S] and **fajitas** [S] **are** [V] two popular Mexican dishes. [compound subject]

Susan [S] **read** [V] *The Planet of Junior Brown* and **reported** [V] on it last week. [compound verb]

The huge **dog** [S] and the tiny **kitten** [S] **lay** [V] down in the sunshine and **napped** [V]. [compound subject and compound verb]

EXERCISE 1 Identifying Subjects and Verbs in Simple Sentences

Identify the subject(s) and the verb(s) in each sentence of the following paragraph. [Note: Some sentences have a compound subject, a compound verb, or both.]

EXAMPLE [1] I enjoy urban life but need to escape from the city once in a while.

1. *I—subject; enjoy, need—verbs*

[1] My favorite escape from city life is the green world of Central Park in New York City. [2] Its beautiful woods and relaxing outdoor activities are just a few minutes from our apartment. [3] The enormous size of the park, however, can sometimes be a problem. [4] Often, I take this map along with me for guidance. [5] Using the map, I can easily find the zoo, the bandshell, and the Lost Waterfall. [6] In the summertime my brothers and I row boats on the lake, climb huge rock slabs, and have picnics in the Sheep Meadow. [7] I also watch birds and often wander around the park in search of my favorite species. [8] Last month a pair of purple finches followed me along the pond. [9] Near Heckscher Playground, the birds got tired of the game and flew off. [10] In Central Park my family and I can enjoy a little bit of nature in the middle of a bustling city.

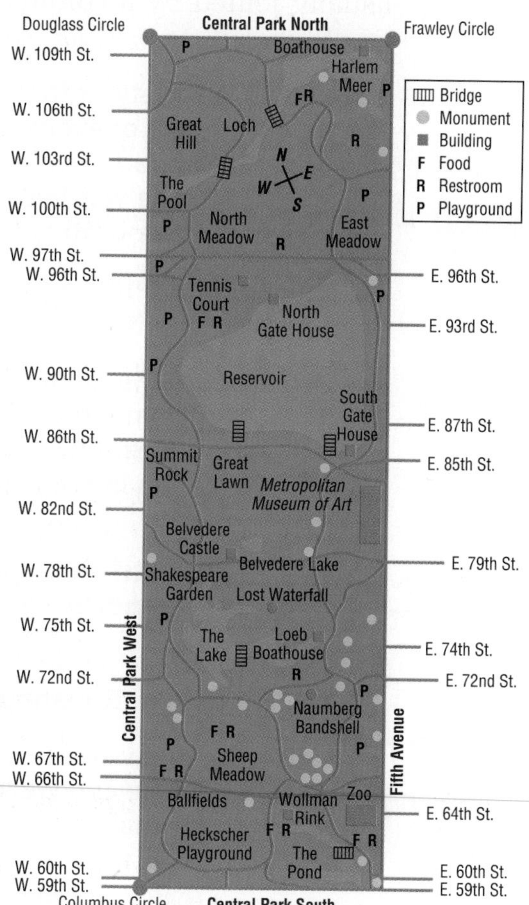

The Compound Sentence

GRAMMAR

19b. A ***compound sentence*** has two or more independent clauses and no subordinate clauses.

INDEPENDENT CLAUSE Melvina wrote about her mother's aunt

INDEPENDENT CLAUSE Leroy wrote about his cousin from Jamaica

COMPOUND SENTENCE Melvina wrote about her mother's aunt, and Leroy wrote about his cousin from Jamaica.

The independent clauses of a compound sentence are usually joined by a comma and a coordinating conjunction (*and, but, or, nor, for, so,* or *yet*).

EXAMPLES A variety of fruits and vegetables should be a part of everyone's diet**, for** they supply many important vitamins.
No one was injured in the fire**, but** several homes were destroyed**, and** many trees burned down.

The independent clauses of a compound sentence may be joined by a semicolon.

EXAMPLE Pedro Menéndez de Avilés founded Saint Augustine, the first permanent settlement in the United States**;** he also established six other colonies in the Southeast.

EXERCISE 2 **Identifying Subjects and Verbs in Compound Sentences**

Identify the subject and verb in each independent clause. Then, give the coordinating conjunction.

EXAMPLE **1.** A newspaper reporter spoke to our class last week, and we learned about careers in journalism.
1. *reporter—subject; spoke—verb; we—subject; learned—verb; and*

1. Ruth Benedict was a respected anthropologist, and Margaret Mead was one of her students.
2. An area's weather may change rapidly, but its climate changes very slowly.
3. Linh Phan lived in Vietnam for many years, so he was able to tell us about Vietnamese foods such as *nuoc mam*.
4. Students may type their reports, or they may write them neatly.
5. Our landlord is kind, yet she will not allow pets in the building.
6. Daniel Boone had no formal education, but he could read and write.
7. Sofia's favorite dance is the samba, and Elena enjoys the merengue.
8. Benjamin Franklin was one of the members of the Constitutional Convention, yet none of his proposals were adopted.
9. Sheena did not play soccer this week, for she had sprained her ankle.
10. They did not watch the shuttle take off, nor did they watch it land.

Distinguishing Compound Sentences from Compound Subjects and Compound Verbs

A simple sentence has only one independent clause. It may have a compound subject or a compound verb or both. A compound sentence has two or more independent clauses. Each independent clause has its own subject and verb. Any of the independent clauses in a compound sentence may have a compound subject, a compound verb, or both.

SIMPLE SENTENCE **Kim** (S) and **Maureen** (S) **read** (V) each other's stories and **made** (V) suggestions for improvements. [compound subject and compound verb]

COMPOUND SENTENCE
S S V
Kim and **Maureen read** each other's
S V
stories, and **they gave** each other suggestions for improvements. [The first independent clause has a compound subject and a single verb. The second independent clause has a single subject and a single verb.]

NOTE: When a subject is repeated after a coordinating conjunction, the sentence is compound.

SIMPLE SENTENCE
S V
We studied about the artist
V
Romare Bearden and **went** to an exhibit of his paintings.

COMPOUND SENTENCE
S V
We studied about the artist
S V
Romare Bearden, and **we went** to an exhibit of his paintings.

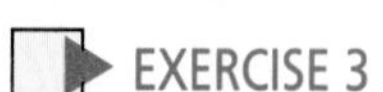

EXERCISE 3 Distinguishing Compound Sentences from Compound Subjects or Compound Verbs

Identify each of the following sentences as either *simple* or *compound.* Then identify the subject(s) and verb(s) in each sentence.

EXAMPLES
1. A rain forest is a tropical evergreen forest and has heavy rains throughout the year.
1. *simple; rain forest—subject; is, has—verbs*
2. The trees and other plants in a rain forest grow close together, and they rise to different heights.
2. *compound; trees, plants—subjects; grow—verb; they—subject; rise—verb*

1. The Amazon River is located in South America and is one of the longest rivers in the world.

2. The Amazon begins in Peru, and it flows across Brazil to the Atlantic Ocean.
3. Of all the rivers in the world, this river carries the most water and drains about one fifth of the earth's fresh water.
4. The Amazon is actually a network of several rivers, but most people think of these combined rivers as only one river.
5. These rivers drain the largest rainy area in the world, and during the flood season, the main river often overflows its banks.
6. Unlike many other rivers, the Amazon does not twist and curve.
7. Instead, it follows a fairly straight course and flows at an average rate of about one and one-half miles an hour.
8. The Amazonian rain forest is only two hundred miles wide along the Atlantic, but it stretches to twelve hundred miles wide at the foot of the Andes Mountains in Peru.
9. The variety of plant life in the Amazonian rain forest is remarkable; in fact, of all rain forests in the world, this area may contain the greatest number of species of plants.
10. Raw materials are shipped directly from ports deep in the rain forest, for oceangoing ships can sail more than two thousand miles up the Amazon.

GRAMMAR

PICTURE THIS

Your community has been given the abandoned theater shown on the next page. Now the local citizens' council must decide what to do with the building. They could sell the theater, they could restore it, or they might find some other use for it. Write a letter to the council, giving your opinion on what should happen to the theater. To make

GRAMMAR

your letter more interesting, vary your sentence structure. Use at least three simple sentences and two compound sentences.

Subject: an abandoned theater
Audience: community leaders
Purpose: to persuade

The Complex Sentence

19c. A ***complex sentence*** has one independent clause and at least one subordinate clause.

Two kinds of subordinate clauses are adjective clauses and adverb clauses. Adjective clauses usually begin with relative pronouns such as *who, whose, which,* and *that.* Adverb clauses begin with subordinating conjunctions such as *after, as, because, if, since,* and *when.*

REFERENCE NOTE: For more information on adjective clauses, see pages 520–521. For more information on adverb clauses, see pages 523–525.

GRAMMAR

EXAMPLES Patricia Roberts Harris, **who served as President Carter's Secretary of Housing and Urban Development,** was the first African American woman Cabinet member. [complex sentence with adjective clause]

When I hear ukulele music, I think of my cousin Alani. [complex sentence with adverb clause]

One interesting annual event **that is held in the Southwest** is the Inter-Tribal Ceremonial, **which involves many different Native American peoples.** [complex sentence with two adjective clauses]

REFERENCE NOTE: For help in deciding when to use commas with subordinate clauses, see pages 713 and 720.

EXERCISE 4 Identifying Subordinate Clauses

Identify the subordinate clause in each of the following sentences. Then, circle the subordinating conjunction or the relative pronoun that begins the subordinate clause.

EXAMPLES **1.** Helen Keller, who overcame severe handicaps, showed courage and determination.

1. *(who) overcame severe handicaps*

2. Keller was fortunate because she had such a skillful and loving teacher.

2. *(because) she had such a skillful and loving teacher*

1. Helen Keller, who is shown in the photographs on the next page, became very ill as a small child.
2. After she recovered from the illness, she could no longer see or hear.
3. Because she could not hear, she also lost her ability to speak.
4. Helen's parents asked Alexander Graham Bell, who trained teachers of people with hearing impairments, for his advice about the child's education.
5. Upon Bell's suggestion, a special teacher, whose name was Annie Sullivan, stayed at the Kellers' home to teach Helen.

6. Sullivan spelled words into Helen's hand as the child touched the object represented by the word.
7. From this basic understanding of language, Helen went on to learn Braille, which is the alphabet used by people with visual impairments.
8. Sullivan, who had been partly cured of blindness herself, remained with Helen for many years.
9. Because she had triumphed over her handicaps, Helen Keller was awarded the Presidential Medal of Freedom.
10. Her autobiography, which is titled *The Story of My Life,* tells about her remarkable achievements.

WRITING APPLICATION

Using a Variety of Sentence Structures in Your Writing

"I'm bored!" That's how a reader responds to writing that uses the same kind of sentence structure over and over again. Using a variety of sentence structures can make your writing more interesting to read.

SIMPLE SENTENCES Josh and I went to the supermarket. Josh watched the lobsters in the fish tank. I picked out some flowers to surprise Mom. We got everything on our shopping list. We paid for our groceries. We walked home.

SENTENCE VARIETY Josh and I went to the supermarket. [simple] While Josh watched the lobsters in the fish tank, I picked out some flowers to surprise Mom. [complex] We got everything on our shopping list. [simple] Then we paid for our groceries, and we walked home. [compound]

GRAMMAR

WRITING ACTIVITY

Anyone can enter the "Win Your Dream Home" Contest. All you have to do is describe your ideal house. Write a letter to the contest judges, describing where your dream house would be and what it would look like. Use a variety of sentence structures to make your letter interesting for the judges to read.

Prewriting Make a list of the special features of the house you want to describe. To help you think of ideas, you may want to look through magazines or books to find pictures of interesting homes. You may also find it helpful to draw a rough diagram of the rooms, yard, and other features you would want. Take notes for details you want to include.

Writing As you write your first draft, use your notes to include vivid details that will give the contest judges a clear picture of your dream house.

Evaluating and Revising Read over your letter to make sure it is interesting and clear. Also, check to see whether you can combine similar ideas by using either compound or complex sentences. Ask an adult to read your letter. Does he or she think your description would impress the contest judges?

Proofreading Check over the grammar and spelling in your letter. Also, make sure that you have used commas correctly in compound sentences and complex sentences. (For information on using commas, see pages 706–722.)

REVIEW A Classifying Simple, Compound, and Complex Sentences

Classify each of the following sentences as *simple*, *compound*, or *complex*.

EXAMPLE **1. The Mississippi River, which is the longest river in the United States, begins in the town of Lake Itasca, Minnesota.**
1. *complex*

1. I drew an illustration for a poem that was written by Robert Hayden.
2. The Olympic skaters felt anxious, but they still performed their routine perfectly.
3. Kamehameha Day is an American holiday that honors the king who united the islands of Hawaii.
4. For the first time in his life, José saw the ocean.
5. If you had a choice, would you rather visit China or Japan?
6. The bull was donated to the children's zoo by the people who bought it at the auction.
7. Lookout Mountain, which is in Tennessee, was the site of a battle during the Civil War.
8. The guide led us through Mammoth Cave, and she explained the difference between stalactites and stalagmites.
9. Wilhelm Steinitz of Austria became famous after he was officially recognized as the first world champion of chess.
10. Amy Tan is the author of the book *The Joy Luck Club*.

REVIEW B Classifying Simple, Compound, and Complex Sentences

GRAMMAR

Classify each sentence in the following paragraphs as *simple, compound,* or *complex.*

EXAMPLE **[1] The Iroquois people traditionally held a Green Corn Festival in August when their crops were ready for harvesting.**

1. *complex*

[1] For the early Iroquois, the Green Corn Festival was a celebration that lasted several days. [2] During the celebration, all children who had been born since midwinter received their names. [3] Tribal leaders made speeches, and adults and children listened to them carefully. [4] In one traditional speech, the leader would give thanks for the harvest. [5] After they had heard the speeches, the people sang and danced.

[6] On the second day of the festival, the people performed the special dance pictured here, and during the dance they gave thanks for the sun, the moon, and the stars. [7] On the third day, the Iroquois gave thanks for the helpfulness of their neighbors and for good luck. [8] The festival ended on the fourth day when teams of young people would play a bowling game. [9] During the festival the people renewed their friendships and rejoiced in their harmony with nature. [10] This Iroquois festival resembles the U.S. Thanksgiving holiday, which has its roots in similar Native American celebrations.

THE CORN DANCE.

GRAMMAR

Review: Posttest 1

A. Identifying and Classifying Clauses

Label each clause in the following sentences as an *independent clause* or a *subordinate clause.*

EXAMPLE 1. We did warm-up exercises before we practiced the difficult routine.
1. *We did warm-up exercises—independent clause; before we practiced the difficult routine—subordinate clause*

1. Students who are interested in attending the science fair at the community college should sign up now.
2. The musical *West Side Story* is a modern version of the story of Romeo and Juliet.
3. The first poem in the book is about spring, and the second one is about autumn.
4. Molasses, which is made from sugar cane, is a thick brown liquid used in human food and animal feed.
5. Before the test we studied the chapter and did the review exercises.
6. We took notes while our teacher discussed the formation of the African nation of Liberia.
7. It rained Saturday morning, but the sun came out in time for the opening of the Special Olympics.
8. The player whose performance is judged as the best receives the Most Valuable Player Award.
9. The tourists went to the Japanese exhibit after they had reached the museum.
10. Not all stringed instruments sound alike, for their shapes and the number of their strings vary.

B. Identifying Simple, Compound, and Complex Sentences

Identify each of the following sentences as *simple, compound,* or *complex.*

EXAMPLE **1. The Museum of Science and Industry, which is in Chicago, features a German submarine captured during World War II.**
1. *complex*

11. Either Ana or Lee will sing the opening song for the international fair.
12. We always visit the Liberty Bell whenever we go to Philadelphia.
13. Have you chosen a topic for your report yet, or are you still making your decision?
14. George Washington Carver's work on soil improvement and plant diseases helped the South in its recovery from the effects of the Civil War.
15. *A Tree Grows in Brooklyn,* which was written by Betty Smith, is one of my favorite books.
16. The call of a peacock sounds very much like that of a person in distress, so its cries can often be quite startling to people.
17. My younger sister and brother enjoy Beatrix Potter's Peter Rabbit stories and usually ask for them at bedtime.
18. The student whose photographs of Native American cliff dwellings won the contest was interviewed on the local news.
19. The house looked completely deserted when I first saw it.
20. The game was tied at the top of the ninth inning, but then Earlene hit a home run.

Review: Posttest 2

Writing Simple, Compound, and Complex Sentences

Write five sentences of your own, following the guidelines given on the next page.

EXAMPLE **1. a simple sentence with a compound subject**
1. ***Jorge and Pilar gave me their recipe for guacamole.***

1. a simple sentence with a compound verb
2. a compound sentence with two independent clauses joined by the coordinating conjunction *and*
3. a compound sentence with two independent clauses joined by the coordinating conjunction *but*
4. a complex sentence with an adjective clause
5. a complex sentence with an adverb clause

20 AGREEMENT

USAGE

Subject and Verb, Pronoun and Antecedent

Diagnostic Test

A. Identifying and Correcting Errors in Subject-Verb Agreement

If the underlined verb in each sentence does not agree with its subject, write the correct form of the verb. If the verb does agree with its subject, write *C*.

EXAMPLE **1. A car with five forward gears cost extra.**
1. ***costs***

1. Don't anybody know how to make egg rolls?
2. "Those Winter Sundays" was written by Robert Hayden.
3. Mathematics are taught every day at 9:00 A.M.

4. Seventy dollars seem like a high price for a pair of skates.
5. Here is your tickets for tomorrow's basketball game, Jennifer.
6. Dolores and Frank wear glasses only for reading.
7. One of the batteries do not work.
8. Everyone except us know some Spanish.
9. My family are originally from Thailand.
10. Neither of these cassette recorders have automatic reverse.

B. Identifying and Correcting Errors in Pronoun-Antecedent Agreement

If the underlined pronoun in each of the following sentences does not agree with its antecedent, write the correct form of the pronoun. If the pronoun does agree with its antecedent, write *C*.

EXAMPLE **1. Someone left their skis here.**
1. ***his or her***

11. Neither of these plants should have their roots disturbed.
12. Did anyone forget their CDs?
13. Either Maria or Louise will receive their award today.
14. Everybody should know their ZIP code.
15. Each student has given their report on an African American folk tale.
16. Every one of the dogs obeyed its owner.
17. Each of the components has its own on-off switch.
18. Will either Hector or Tony read his paper aloud?
19. Not one of the students had finished their science project on time.
20. She borrowed my Navajo silver jewelry and forgot to return them.

Number

Number is the form of a word that indicates whether the word is singular or plural.

20a. When a word refers to one person, place, thing, or idea, it is ***singular*** in number. When a word refers to more than one, it is ***plural*** in number.

SINGULAR	igloo	she	one	child	joy
PLURAL	igloos	they	some	children	joys

REFERENCE NOTE: For more information about forming plurals, see pages 754 and 773–776.

EXERCISE 1 **Classifying Nouns and Pronouns by Number**

Classify each of the following words as *singular* or *plural.*

EXAMPLES
1. girl
1. *singular*
2. rivers
2. *plural*

1. evening
2. wolves
3. women
4. leaf
5. they
6. teeth
7. tacos
8. we
9. thief
10. armies

Agreement of Subject and Verb

20b. A verb agrees with its subject in number.

Two words *agree* when they have the same number. The number of a verb must always agree with the number of its subject.

(1) Singular subjects take singular verbs.

EXAMPLES The **lightning fills** the sky. [The singular verb *fills* agrees with the singular subject *lightning.*]
Jan begins her vacation today. [The singular verb *begins* agrees with the singular subject *Jan.*]

(2) Plural subjects take plural verbs.

EXAMPLES **Cheetahs run** fast. [The plural verb *run* agrees with the plural subject *cheetahs.*]
New **families move** into our neighborhood frequently. [The plural verb *move* agrees with the plural subject *families.*]

When a sentence contains a verb phrase, the first helping verb in the verb phrase agrees with the subject.

EXAMPLES The **motor is** running.
The **motors are** running.

The **girl has** been delayed.
The **girls have** been delayed.

Is anyone filling the piñata?
Are any **students** filling the piñata?

REFERENCE NOTE: Most nouns ending in *–s* are plural (*cheetahs, families*). Most verbs that end in *–s* are singular (*fills, begins*). For more about spelling the plural forms of nouns, see pages 773–776.

EXERCISE 2 Identifying Verbs That Agree in Number with Their Subjects

Choose the form of the verb in parentheses that agrees with the given subject.

EXAMPLE 1. wind (*howls, howl*)
1. *howls*

1. people (*talks, talk*)
2. rain (*splashes, splash*)
3. birds (*flies, fly*)
4. we (*helps, help*)
5. it (*appears, appear*)
6. geese (*hisses, hiss*)
7. night (*falls, fall*)
8. roofs (*leaks, leak*)
9. baby (*smiles, smile*)
10. tooth (*aches, ache*)

EXERCISE 3

Identifying Verbs That Agree in Number with Their Subjects

For each of the following sentences, choose the form of the verb in parentheses that agrees with the subject.

EXAMPLE **1. Special tours (*is, are*) offered at the National Air and Space Museum, Washington, D.C.**
1. *are*

1. This museum (*has, have*) been called the best of all the Smithsonian museums.
2. The huge building (*covers, cover*) three blocks.
3. Twenty-seven showrooms (*offers, offer*) visitors information and entertainment.
4. The different showrooms (*deals, deal*) with various aspects of air and space travel.
5. As you can see, the exhibits (*features, feature*) antique aircraft as well as modern spacecraft.
6. In another area, a theater (*shows, show*) films on a five-story-high screen.
7. A planetarium (*is, are*) located on the second floor.
8. Projectors (*casts, cast*) realistic images of stars on the ceiling.
9. Some tours (*is, are*) conducted by pilots.
10. In addition, the museum (*houses, house*) a large research library.

USAGE

EXERCISE 4 Proofreading for Errors in Subject-Verb Agreement

Most of the following sentences contain errors in subject-verb agreement. If a verb does not agree with the subject, write the correct form of the verb. If a sentence is correct, write *C*.

EXAMPLE **1. More than nineteen million people lives in and around Mexico's capital.**
1. *live*

1. Located in an ancient lake bed, Mexico City have been built on Aztec ruins.
2. Visitors admire the paintings of Diego Rivera at the National Palace.
3. In one of the city's subway stations, an Aztec pyramid still stand.
4. Sculptures grace the Alameda, which is Mexico City's main park.
5. Atop the Latin American Tower, an observatory offer a great view on a clear day.
6. At the National Autonomous University of Mexico, the library's outer walls is famous as works of art.
7. Juan O'Gorman's huge mosaics shows the cultural history of Mexico.
8. Usually, tourists is fascinated by the Great Temple of the Aztecs.
9. Many fiestas fills Mexico City's social calendar.
10. In addition, the city has one of the largest soccer stadiums in the world.

Problems in Agreement

Prepositional Phrases Between Subject and Verb

20c. The number of a subject is not changed by a phrase following the subject.

EXAMPLES The **hero** of those folk tales **is** Coyote. [The verb *is* agrees with the subject *hero.*]
The successful **candidate,** along with two of her aides, **has** entered the auditorium. [The helping verb *has* agrees with the subject *candidate.*]
Scientists from all over the world **have** gathered in Geneva. [The helping verb *have* agrees with the subject *Scientists.*]

REFERENCE NOTE: If the subject is an indefinite pronoun, its number may be determined by a prepositional phrase that follows it. See page 430 for a discussion of indefinite pronouns.

USAGE

EXERCISE 5 Identifying Verbs That Agree in Number with Their Subjects

In the following sentences, choose the form of the verb in parentheses that agrees with the subject.

EXAMPLE 1. The water in the earth's oceans (*cover, covers*) much of the planet's surface.
1. *covers*

1. A tidal wave, despite its name, (*is, are*) not caused by the tides.
2. An eruption beneath the sea (*causes, cause*) a tidal wave.
3. A network of warning signals (*alert, alerts*) people in coastal areas of an approaching tidal wave.
4. The tremendous force of tidal waves (*causes, cause*) great destruction.
5. Walls of earth and stone along the shore (*is, are*) often too weak to protect coastal villages.

EXERCISE 6 Using Correct Subject-Verb Agreement

What do you notice first about the painting shown on the next page? Is it the floating people? the upside down train? the multicolored cat? Look at the painting closely, and identify at least five features you notice. Then, write five sentences about the unusual features you find. Be sure that each of your sentences has correct subject-verb agreement. You may want to compare your findings with those of other students.

EXAMPLE **1.** ***The man in the painting has two faces.***

Marc Chagall, *Paris through the Window*, 1913, Oil on canvas, 53$\frac{1}{2}$ x 55$\frac{3}{4}$ inches, Solomon R. Guggenheim Museum, New York. Gift, Solomon R. Guggenheim, 1937. PHOTO: David Heald copyright Solomon R. Guggenheim Foundation, New York. FN 37.438

Indefinite Pronouns

You may recall that personal pronouns refer to specific people, places, things, or ideas. A pronoun that does not refer to a definite person, place, thing, or idea is called an ***indefinite pronoun.***

PERSONAL PRONOUNS	we	you	she	them
INDEFINITE PRONOUNS	anybody	both	either	everyone

20d. The following indefinite pronouns are singular: *each, either, neither, one, everyone, everybody, no one, nobody, anyone, anybody, someone, somebody.*

EXAMPLES **Each** of the newcomers **was** welcomed to the city.
Neither of these papayas **is** ripe.
Does anybody on the bus speak Arabic?

EXERCISE 7 Choosing Verbs That Agree in Number with Their Subjects

In the following sentences, choose the form of the verb in parentheses that agrees with the subject. Remember that the subject is never part of a prepositional phrase.

EXAMPLE 1. One of these books (*is, are*) yours.
1. *is*

1. Neither of the movies (*was, were*) especially funny.
2. Everybody in those classes (*gets, get*) to see the Balinese dancers.
3. Someone among the store owners (*donates, donate*) the trophy each year.
4. Each of the Washington brothers (*studies, study*) with a Zulu dance instructor.
5. No one on either team (*was, were*) ever in a playoff before.
6. Everyone with an interest in sports (*is, are*) at the tryouts.
7. Anybody with binoculars (*is, are*) popular at a large stadium.
8. Each of our neighbors (*has, have*) helped us plant the community garden.
9. One of the Spanish teachers (*supervises, supervise*) the language lab.
10. Nobody in our family (*is, are*) able to speak Greek well, but we all can speak a little bit.

20e. The following indefinite pronouns are plural: *both, few, many, several.*

EXAMPLES **Few** of our neighbors **have** parakeets.
Many of them **keep** dogs as pets.

USAGE

20f. The indefinite pronouns *all, any, most, none,* and *some* may be either singular or plural.

The number of the pronouns *all, any, most, none,* and *some* is determined by the number of the object in the prepositional phrase following the subject. If the pronoun refers to a singular object, it is singular. If the pronoun refers to a plural object, it is plural.

EXAMPLES **All** of the fruit **looks** fresh. [*All* is singular because it refers to one thing—*fruit.* The verb *looks* is singular to agree with the subject *All*.]

All of the pears **are** ripe. [*All* is plural because it refers to more than one thing—*pears.* The verb *are* is plural to agree with the subject *All*.]

Some of the crowd **has** left. [*Some* is singular because it means "a part" of the crowd. The helping verb *has* is singular to agree with the subject *Some*.]

Some of the fans **are** getting autographs. [*Some* is plural because it refers to more than one fan. The helping verb *are* is plural to agree with the subject *Some*.]

EXERCISE 8 Choosing Verbs That Agree in Number with Their Subjects

For each of the following sentences, choose the form of the verb in parentheses that agrees with the subject.

EXAMPLE 1. All of the new research on dreams (*is, are*) fascinating.
1. *is*

1. Most of our dreams (*occur, occurs*) toward morning.
2. Few of us really (*understand, understands*) the four cycles of sleep.
3. During the cycle known as rapid eye movement (REM), some dreams (*is, are*) very clear.
4. None of my dreams ever (*make, makes*) sense to me.
5. Many of them (*is, are*) about what happened that day.

REVIEW A Identifying Verbs That Agree in Number with Their Subjects

For each sentence in the following paragraph, choose the verb form in parentheses that agrees with the subject.

EXAMPLE **[1] These flying objects probably (*look, looks*) familiar to you.**
1. *look*

[1] Many people throughout the world (*claims, claim*) to have seen objects like these. [2] However, no one (*know, knows*) for sure what they are. [3] They (*resembles, resemble*) huge plates or saucers. [4] Not surprisingly, everyone (*call, calls*) them "flying saucers." [5] Since 1947, they (*has, have*) been officially called unidentified flying objects, or UFOs. [6] The U.S. government (*has, have*) investigated many UFO sightings. [7] The Air Force (*was, were*) responsible for conducting these investigations. [8] Government records (*shows, show*) that more than twelve thousand sightings were reported between 1948 and 1969. [9] Most reported sightings (*has, have*) turned out to be fakes, but others remain unexplained. [10] None of the official reports positively (*proves, prove*) that UFOs are real.

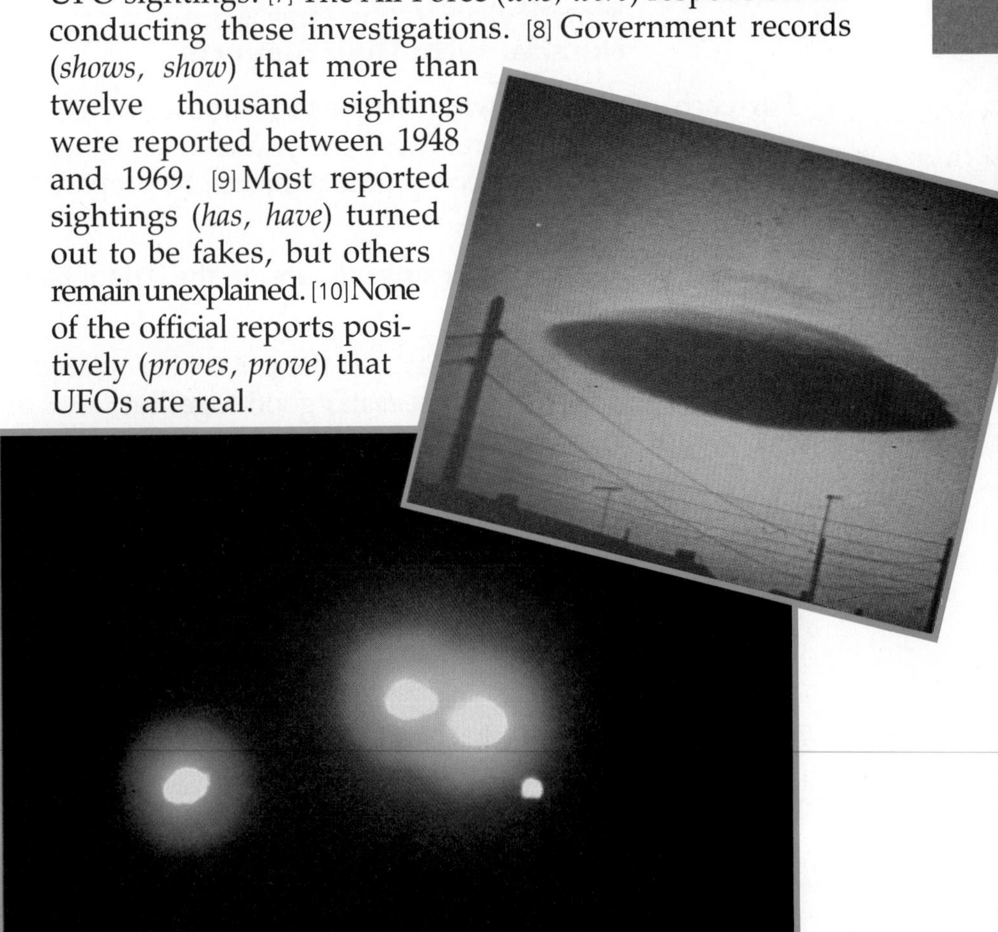

Compound Subjects

20g. Subjects joined by *and* usually take a plural verb.

EXAMPLES Our **dog and cat get** baths in the summer.
Mr. Duffy and his **daughter have** gone fishing.

A compound subject that names only one person or thing takes a singular verb.

EXAMPLES **A famous singer and dancer is** going to speak at our drama club meeting. [One person is meant.]
Macaroni and cheese is my favorite supper. [One combination is meant.]

USAGE

EXERCISE 9 Identifying Verbs That Agree in Number with Their Subjects

For each of the following sentences, choose the correct form of the verb in parentheses. If you choose a singular verb with any of these compound subjects, be prepared to explain why.

EXAMPLE **1.** Chris and her sister (*is, are*) in the school band.
1. *are*

1. (*Is, Are*) the brown bear and the polar bear related?
2. Fruit and cheese (*tastes, taste*) good together.
3. My guide and companion in Bolivia (*was, were*) Pilar, a high school student.
4. New words and new meanings for old words (*is, are*) included in a good dictionary.
5. Mrs. Chang and her daughter (*rents, rent*) an apartment in San Francisco's Chinatown.
6. Both iron and calcium (*needs, need*) to be included in a balanced diet.
7. Mr. Marley and his class (*has, have*) painted a wall-size map of the Caribbean islands.
8. A horse and buggy (*was, were*) once a fashionable way to travel.

9. Tornadoes and hurricanes (*is, are*) dangerous storms.
10. Wind and water (*erodes, erode*) valuable farmland throughout the United States.

20h. Singular subjects joined by *or* or *nor* take a singular verb.

EXAMPLES The chief **geologist or** her **assistant is** due to arrive tonight. [Either one is due, not both.]
Neither a **rabbit nor** a **mole does** that kind of damage in a garden. [Neither one does the damage.]

Plural subjects joined by *or* or *nor* take a plural verb.

EXAMPLES **Either mice or squirrels are** living in our attic.
Neither the **senators nor** the **representatives want** the bill to be vetoed by the president.

20i. When a singular subject and a plural subject are joined by *or* or *nor,* the verb agrees with the subject nearer the verb.

EXAMPLE A **book or flowers** usually **make** an appropriate gift. [The verb agrees with the nearer subject, *flowers.*]
Flowers or a **book** usually **makes** an appropriate gift. [The verb agrees with the nearer subject, *book.*]

Compound subjects that have both singular and plural parts can sound awkward even though they are correct. Whenever possible, revise a sentence to avoid such constructions.

AWKWARD Two small boards or one large one is what we need to patch that hole.
REVISED We need two small boards or one large one to patch that hole.

AWKWARD Neither the lights nor the microwave is working.
REVISED The lights aren't working, and neither is the microwave.

EXERCISE 10 Identifying Verbs That Agree in Number with Their Subjects

Choose the correct form of the verb in parentheses in each of the following sentences. Be able to explain the reason for your choice.

EXAMPLE 1. The club president or the officers (*meets, meet*) regularly with the sponsors.
1. *meet*

1. Neither pens nor pencils (*is, are*) needed to mark the ballots.
2. Either my aunt or my uncle (*is, are*) going to drive us to the lake.
3. That table or this chair (*was, were*) made by hand in Portugal.
4. (*Has, Have*) the sandwiches or other refreshments been served?
5. Index cards or a small tablet (*is, are*) handy for taking notes.
6. Neither that clock nor my watch (*shows, show*) the correct time.
7. One boy or girl (*takes, take*) the part of the narrator.
8. During our visit to Jamaica, a map or a guidebook (*was, were*) my constant companion.
9. The dentist or her assistant (*checks, check*) my braces.
10. Either Japanese poetry or Eskimo myths (*is, are*) going to be the focus of my report.

REVIEW B Proofreading Sentences for Subject-Verb Agreement

Identify each verb that does not agree with its subject in the following sentences. Then supply the correct form of each incorrect verb.

EXAMPLE 1. The players in the photograph on the next page is competing in the most popular sport in the world—soccer.
1. *is—are*

1. One expert in the field of sports have described soccer as the world's favorite type of football.
2. Some sports writers has estimated that there are over thirty million registered soccer players around the globe.
3. Youth leagues and coaching clinics has helped make amateur soccer the fastest-growing team sport in the United States.
4. In Dallas, Texas, neither baseball nor American football attract as many young players as soccer does.
5. Also, more colleges now has varsity soccer teams than football teams.
6. This increase in soccer fans are a trend that started in 1967, when professional teams began playing in the United States.
7. Additional interest were generated when the U.S. Youth Soccer Association was formed.
8. Both males and females enjoys playing this sport.
9. In fact, by the 1980s, many of the soccer teams in the country was women's teams.
10. In the past, professional soccer were mostly a foreign game, but the United States was selected to host the World Cup in 1994.

Other Problems in Subject-Verb Agreement

20j. Collective nouns may be either singular or plural.

A ***collective noun*** is singular in form but names a group of persons, animals, or things.

Common Collective Nouns

audience	committee	group	swarm
class	family	herd	team
club	flock	jury	troop

A collective noun takes a singular verb when the noun refers to the group as a unit. A collective noun takes a plural verb when the noun refers to the individual parts or members of the group.

EXAMPLES The **class were** divided in their opinions of the play. [The members of the class were divided in their opinions.]
The **class has** decided to have a science fair in November. [The class as a unit has decided.]

My **family are** coming from all over the state for the reunion. [The members of the family are coming.]
My **family plans** to attend Beth's graduation. [The family as a unit plans to attend.]

20k. When the subject follows the verb, find the subject and make sure that the verb agrees with it. The subject usually follows the verb in sentences beginning with *here* or *there* and in questions.

EXAMPLES Here **is** my **umbrella.**
Here **are** our **umbrellas.**

USAGE

There **is** a scary **movie** on TV.
There **are** scary **movies** on TV.

Where **was** the **cat**?
Where **were** the **cats**?

Does Jim know the Chens?
Do the **Chens** know Jim?

NOTE: When the subject of a sentence follows the verb, the word order is said to be ***inverted.*** To find the subject of a sentence with inverted order, restate the sentence in normal word order.

INVERTED Here **are** your **gloves.**
NORMAL Your **gloves are** here.

INVERTED **Were you** late, too?
NORMAL **You were** late, too?

INVERTED In the pond **swim** large **goldfish.**
NORMAL Large **goldfish swim** in the pond.

The contractions *here's, there's,* and *where's* contain the verb *is* and should be used only with singular subjects.

EXAMPLES **There's** our new **neighbor.**
Where's my lunch **money**?

REFERENCE NOTE: For more information about contractions, see pages 749–750.

EXERCISE 11 Identifying Verbs That Agree in Number with Their Subjects

Identify the subject in each of the following sentences. Then, choose the correct form of the verb in parentheses.

EXAMPLE **1.** That flock of geese (*migrates, migrate*) each year.
1. *flock—migrates*

1. There (*is, are*) at least two solutions to this Chinese puzzle.
2. The Austrian Olympic team (*was, were*) all getting on different buses.

3. (*Is, Are*) both of your parents from Korea?
4. Here (*comes, come*) the six members of the dance committee.
5. Here (*is, are*) some apples and bananas for the picnic basket.
6. There (*is, are*) neither time nor money for that project.
7. (*Here's, Here are*) the social studies notes I wrote about Mohandas Gandhi.
8. At the press conference, there (*was, were*) several candidates for mayor and two for governor.
9. The family (*has, have*) announced its plans to celebrate Grandma's promotion.
10. Here (*is, are*) some masks carved by the Haida people in Alaska.

USAGE

20l. Words stating amounts are usually singular.

A word or phrase stating a weight, measurement, or an amount of money or time is usually considered one item. Such a word or phrase takes a singular verb.

EXAMPLES Sixteen **ounces equals** one pound.
Ten **feet is** the height of a regulation basketball hoop.
Seventy-five **cents is** enough money for my lunch today.
Two **weeks** never **seems** long enough for vacation.

20m. The title of a book, or the name of an organization or a country, even when plural in form, usually takes a singular verb.

EXAMPLES ***World Tales*** **is** a collection of folk tales retold by Idries Shah. [one book]
The **United Nations has** its headquarters in New York City. [one organization]
The **Philippines is** an island country that is located in the southwest Pacific Ocean. [one country]

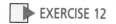

EXERCISE 12 **Identifying Verbs That Agree in Number with Their Subjects**

Choose the correct form of the verb in parentheses in each of the following sentences.

EXAMPLE **1. Three inches (*is, are*) a great deal to grow in one year.**
1. *is*

1. *The Friends* (*is, are*) a book about a girl from the West Indies and a girl from Harlem.
2. Two cups of broth (*seems, seem*) as if it is too little for that recipe.
3. Fifteen feet (*was, were*) the length of the winning long jump.
4. Navarro and Company (*is, are*) selling those jackets.
5. The National Council of Teachers of English (*is, are*) holding its convention in our city this year.
6. The United States (*is, are*) home to many different peoples.
7. Three hours of practice (*is, are*) not unusual for the band.
8. *Arctic Dreams* (*was, were*) written by Barry Lopez.
9. Two weeks of preparation (*has, have*) been enough.
10. Seventy-five cents (*is, are*) the cost of a subway ride.

20n. *Don't* and *doesn't* must agree with their subjects.

The words *don't* and *doesn't* are contractions of *do not* and *does not*. Use *don't* with all plural subjects and with the pronouns *I* and *you*.

EXAMPLES The children **don't** seem nervous.
I **don't** understand.
You **don't** remember.

Use *doesn't* with all singular subjects except *I* and *you*.

EXAMPLES Kim **doesn't** ride the bus.
He **doesn't** play tennis.
It **doesn't** snow here.

USAGE

ORAL PRACTICE

Using *Don't* and *Doesn't*

Read the following sentences aloud, stressing the italicized words.

1. My friend *doesn't* understand the problem.
2. *Doesn't* she want to play soccer?
3. The tomatoes *don't* look ripe.
4. Our school *doesn't* have a gymnasium.
5. Italy *doesn't* border Germany.
6. The geese *don't* hiss at Mr. Waverly.
7. Our Muslim neighbors, the Nassers, *don't* eat pork.
8. He *doesn't* play chess.

EXERCISE 13

Writing Original Sentences with *Don't* and *Doesn't*

You're cleaning out your closet and deciding what to do with the things you don't want any more. You plan to give reusable items to a thrift store, but some things just can't be saved. Here are some of the items you've found:

a flat football
a picture made with glue and beans
a T-shirt with a cartoon on the front
a stuffed toy dinosaur
one red and one green tennis shoe
a bug collection
several *Cricket* magazines
pieces of jigsaw puzzles
a brown sock
dried-up paint brushes

Write five sentences telling why you're getting rid of some of these items. Use *don't* or *doesn't* to agree with a different subject in each sentence.

EXAMPLE **1.** *This stuffed toy dinosaur doesn't have all its stuffing any more.*

20o. A few nouns, though plural in form, take a singular verb.

EXAMPLES **Mathematics seems** easier this year.
Civics is being taught by Ms. Gutierrez.
Mumps is the most uncomfortable disease I've ever had.
The **news was** not encouraging.

REVIEW C Identifying Verbs That Agree in Number with Their Subjects

For each of the following sentences, choose the verb form in parentheses that agrees with the subject.

EXAMPLE 1. New wheelchairs with lifts (*help, helps*) many people reach objects up high.
1. *help*

1. Twenty-five cents (*is, are*) not enough money to buy that newspaper.
2. Everyone in her company (*prefers, prefer*) to take winter vacations.
3. Allen and his parents (*enjoy, enjoys*) the Puerto Rican Day Parade in New York City.
4. Jan (*don't, doesn't*) know the rules for volleyball.
5. Neither the cassette player nor the speakers (*work, works*) on my stereo.
6. There (*is, are*) 132 islands in the state of Hawaii.
7. Many of the place names in California (*comes, come*) from Spanish words.
8. The principal or her assistant (*is, are*) the one who can help you.
9. Home economics (*is, are*) a required course in many schools.
10. A flock of sheep (*was, were*) grazing on the hill.

REVIEW D Proofreading Sentences for Subject-Verb Agreement

Most of the sentences in the following paragraph contain errors in subject-verb agreement. If a verb does not agree with its subject, give the correct form of the verb. If a sentence is correct, write *C*.

EXAMPLE **[1] Here is two pictures of Wang Yani and her artwork.**

1. *are*

[1] There surely is few teenage artists as successful as Yani. [2] In fact, the People's Republic of China regard her as a national treasure. [3] She has shown her paintings throughout the world. [4] A painter since the age of two, Yani don't paint in just one style. [5] Her ideas and her art naturally changes over the years. [6] The painting at the bottom of this page shows one of Yani's favorite childhood subjects. [7] Many of her early paintings features monkeys. [8] In fact, one of her large works picture 112 monkeys. [9] However, most of her later paintings is of landscapes, other animals, and people. [10] As her smile suggests, Yani fill her paintings with energy and life.

Wang Yani, *Little Monkeys and Mummy*

WRITING APPLICATION

Using Subject-Verb Agreement in Formal Writing

You would probably write a thank-you note more neatly than you would write a grocery list. Like penmanship, English usage depends upon the situation. A formal piece of writing calls for special care with language. In formal writing, standard usage, like good penmanship, helps you make a good impression on your audience. Subject-verb agreement is one of the basic rules of standard usage.

NONSTANDARD The last two governors of the state has been highly respected.

STANDARD The last two **governors** of the state **have** been highly respected.

WRITING ACTIVITY

If you could be any person in history, who would you be? Why? Your social studies teacher has asked you to answer these questions in a short composition. Be sure to use correct subject-verb agreement in explaining your choice.

Prewriting First, decide what historical person you would like to be. You can be someone out of ancient history or someone who is alive today. List some types of people such as heads of government, inventors, military leaders, explorers, writers, and artists. Then write the names of people you admire under each type. Select the person you would most like to be and freewrite about that person. As you write, think about why the person is noteworthy and why you would want to be him or her.

Writing Use your freewriting ideas to write your first draft. Begin with a sentence that states the purpose of your composition and identifies your historical figure. Then, give your main reasons for wanting to be that person. If you have several main reasons, you may want to write about each reason in a separate paragraph. Summarize your main points in a conclusion.

Evaluating and Revising Read through your composition and then answer these questions:

- Is it clear what person from history I want to be? If not, revise your main idea statement. For more about writing main ideas, see pages 64–67 and 98.
- Is it clear why I want to be that person? If not, explain your reasons in more detail. See page 69 for more about using supporting details.

Make sure that all subjects and verbs agree in number. Pay special attention to the subject-verb agreement in subordinate clauses. For more about subordinate clauses, see pages 516–525.

Proofreading and Publishing Check your composition for errors in spelling, capitalization, and punctuation. Your class may want to create a display using the compositions and pictures of the people written about. One type of display is a time line. Arrange the compositions and pictures to show where each subject fits in time—from ancient to recent. Another type of display requires a large world map. Use straight pins and yarn to connect each composition to the place on the map where that person lived.

Agreement of Pronoun and Antecedent

A pronoun usually refers to a noun or another pronoun called its ***antecedent.*** Whenever you use a pronoun, make sure that it agrees with its antecedent.

REFERENCE NOTE: For more information about antecedents, see page 428.

20p. A pronoun agrees with its antecedent in number and gender.

Some singular personal pronouns have forms that indicate gender. Feminine pronouns refer to females. Masculine pronouns refer to males. Neuter pronouns refer to things (neither male nor female) and sometimes to animals.

Feminine	she	her	hers
Masculine	he	him	his
Neuter	it	it	its

EXAMPLES **Carlotta** said that **she** found **her** book.
Aaron brought **his** skates with **him.**
The **plant** with mold on **it** is losing **its** leaves.

The antecedent of a personal pronoun can be another kind of pronoun. In such cases, you may need to look in a phrase that follows the antecedent to determine which personal pronoun to use.

EXAMPLES **Each** of the **girls** has offered **her** ideas.
One of the **men** lost **his** key.

Some antecedents may be either masculine or feminine. In such cases, use both the masculine and the feminine forms.

EXAMPLES Every **one** of the parents praised **his or her** child's efforts.
No one in the play forgot **his or her** lines.

NOTE: In conversation, people often use a plural personal pronoun to refer to a singular antecedent that may be either masculine or feminine. This form is becoming more common in writing, too, and it may someday be considered standard written English.

EXAMPLES **Everybody** brought **their** swimsuit.
Each **member** of the club sold **their** tickets.

REFERENCE NOTE: For lists of the different kinds of pronouns, see pages 428–431.

USAGE

(1) Use a singular pronoun to refer to *each, either, neither, one, everyone, everybody, no one, nobody, anyone, anybody, someone,* or *somebody.*

EXAMPLES **Someone** in the class left behind **his or her** pencil.
Each of the snakes escaped from **its** cage.

(2) Use a singular pronoun to refer to two or more singular antecedents joined by *or.*

EXAMPLES Either **Ralph or Carlos** will display **his** baseball card collection.
Nina or Mary will bring **her** CD player.

Sentences with singular antecedents joined by *or* can sound awkward if the antecedents are of different genders. If a sentence sounds awkward, revise it to avoid the problem.

AWKWARD Odessa or Raymond will bring her or his road map.
REVISED Either **Odessa** will bring **her** road map, or **Raymond** will bring **his.**

NOTE: Rules (1) and (2) are often ignored in conversation; however, they should be followed in writing.

(3) Use a plural pronoun to refer to two or more antecedents joined by *and.*

EXAMPLES **Isaac and Jerome** went to the playground so that **they** could practice shooting baskets.
Elena and Roberto sent letters to **their** cousin in Costa Rica.

NOTE: Be sure that any pronoun referring to a collective noun has the same number as the noun.

EXAMPLES The **cast** is giving **its** final performance tonight.
The **cast** are trying on **their** costumes.

EXERCISE 14 Identifying Antecedents and Writing Pronouns That Agree with Them

For each blank in the following sentences, give a pronoun that will complete the meaning of the sentence. Then identify the antecedent or antecedents for that pronoun.

EXAMPLE **1. Dominic or Martin will show ___ slides.**
1. *his—Dominic, Martin*

1. A writer should proofread ___ work carefully.
2. The store sent Paula and Eric the posters that ___ had ordered.
3. Mark or Hector will arrive early so that ___ can help us prepare the dim sum.
4. One of the students raised ___ hand.
5. Each of the dogs ate the scraps that we gave ___.
6. The principal and the Spanish teacher announced ___ plans for the Cinco de Mayo fiesta.
7. Everyone in my class has ___ own writer's journal.
8. Neither recalled the name of ___ first-grade teacher.
9. Anyone may join if ___ collects stamps.
10. Either Vanessa or Marilyn was awarded the blue ribbon for ___ design.

USAGE

REVIEW E Proofreading a Paragraph for Correct Pronoun-Antecedent Agreement

Most of the following sentences contain errors in pronoun-antecedent agreement. Identify each error and give the correct pronoun. If a sentence is correct, write *C*.

EXAMPLE **[1] At the meeting, each member of the Small Business Council spoke about their concerns.**
1. *their—his or her*

[1] Everybody had a chance to express their opinion about the new shopping mall. [2] Mrs. Gomez and Mr. Franklin are happy about his or her new business locations at the mall. [3] Both said that his profits have increased significantly. [4] Neither Mr. Chen nor Mr. Cooper, however, feels that their customers find parking

convenient enough. [5] Anyone shopping at the mall has to park their car too far from the main shopping area. [6] Several members of the council said that the mall has taken away many of their customers. [7] One of the new women on the council then presented their own idea about creating a farmers' market on weekends. [8] Many members said he or she favored the plan, and a proposal was discussed. [9] Each farmer could have their own spot near the town hall. [10] The Small Business Council then agreed to take their proposal to the mayor.

USAGE

PICTURE THIS

You are a sportswriter for the school newspaper and are covering this bicycle race. As the cyclists zoom by, you quickly take notes. Write several sentences that describe this exciting moment in the race. In your sentences, use five of the following pronouns: *her, nobody, his, each, its, one, their, anyone, they*. Remember that a pronoun should agree with its antecedent in number and gender.

Subject: bicycle race
Audience: school newspaper readers
Purpose: to inform

Review: Posttest

A. Identifying Correct Subject-Verb and Pronoun-Antecedent Agreement

Choose the correct word in parentheses in each of the following sentences.

EXAMPLE **1. Some of the paintings (*is, are*) dry now.**
1. *are*

1. Three hours of work (*is, are*) needed for a charcoal drawing.
2. Everybody has offered (*his or her, their*) advice.
3. *Harlem Shadows* (*is, are*) a collection of poems by Claude McKay.
4. Either Stu or Ryan can volunteer (*his, their*) skill in the kitchen.
5. Black beans, rice, and onions (*tastes, taste*) good together.
6. Not one of them has offered (*his or her, their*) help.
7. Sometimes my family (*disagrees, disagree*) with one another, but usually we all get along fairly well.
8. There (*is, are*) a beaded belt and a pair of moccasins in that box.
9. (*Doesn't, Don't*) too many cooks spoil the broth?
10. One of my aunts gave me (*her, their*) silk kimono.

B. Proofreading Sentences for Subject-Verb and Pronoun-Antecedent Agreement

Most of the following sentences contain an agreement error. For each error, identify the incorrect verb or pronoun, and supply the correct form. If the sentence is correct, write *C*.

EXAMPLE **1. Most stargazers has seen points of light shooting across the night sky.**
1. *has—have*

11. These points of light is commonly called shooting stars.
12. Scientists who study outer space calls these points of light meteors.
13. A meteor is a piece of an asteroid that exploded long ago.
14. Each of these pieces are still flying through space on the path of the original asteroid.
15. Most nights, a person is lucky if they can see a single meteor now and then.
16. Throughout the year, however, there is meteor "showers."
17. None of these showers are as big as the ones in August and November.
18. These large showers come at the same time each year.
19. In November 1833, one of the largest meteor showers in history were recorded.
20. Two hundred forty thousand meteors observed in just a few hours are a record that has never been matched!

21 Using Verbs Correctly

USAGE

Principal Parts, Regular and Irregular Verbs, Tense

Diagnostic Test

Using the Past and Past Participle Forms of Verbs

For each of the following sentences, give the correct form (past or past participle) of the verb in parentheses.

EXAMPLE **1. The mayor has (*speak*) at our school's assemblies several times.**
1. *spoken*

1. The sun (*rise*) over the pyramids of Giza in Egypt.
2. We have (*swim*) only three laps.
3. Vera was (*choose*) captain of the volleyball team.
4. I have (*go*) to visit the Grand Canyon twice with my family.
5. The tiny tree frog (*sit*) motionless.
6. Joan has (*write*) a story about aliens from Venus.
7. During lunch hour, Jorge (*do*) his impersonation of Rubén Blades.
8. Someone (*lay*) a mysterious package on my desk.

9. This summer's heat wave has (*break*) all records.
10. Have you (*drink*) all of the tomato juice?
11. The log slowly (*sink*) into the quicksand.
12. The old postcards have (*lie*) in the box for years.
13. Have you ever (*drive*) across the state of Texas?
14. Our local PBS station (*begin*) its fund-raising drive yesterday.
15. Have you (*set*) the paper plates and napkins on the picnic table?
16. Who (*throw*) the ball to first base?
17. I have (*know*) some of my classmates for six years.
18. Kadeem Niles (*take*) the part of Frederick Douglass in the play.
19. The supermarket has (*raise*) the price of eggs.
20. We (*come*) close to winning the tournament.

USAGE

Principal Parts

The four basic forms of a verb are called the ***principal parts*** of the verb.

21a. The principal parts of a verb are the ***infinitive,*** the ***present participle,*** the ***past,*** and the ***past participle.***

Here are the principal parts of two familiar verbs.

INFINITIVE	PRESENT PARTICIPLE	PAST	PAST PARTICIPLE
talk	(is) talking	talked	(have) talked
draw	(is) drawing	drew	(have) drawn

Notice that the present participle and the past participle require helping verbs (forms of *be* and *have*).

The principal parts of a verb are used to express time.

PRESENT TIME He **draws** excellent pictures.
Susan **is drawing** one now.
PAST TIME Last week they **drew** two maps.
She **has** often **drawn** cartoons.
FUTURE TIME Perhaps she **will draw** one for you.
By next Thursday, we **will have drawn** two landscapes.

Because *talk* forms its past and past participle by adding *–ed,* it is called a *regular verb. Draw* forms its past and past participle differently, so it is called an *irregular verb.*

Regular Verbs

21b. A ***regular verb*** forms its past and past participle by adding *–ed* or *–d* to the infinitive form.

INFINITIVE	PRESENT PARTICIPLE	PAST	PAST PARTICIPLE
clean	(is) cleaning	cleaned	(have) cleaned
hope	(is) hoping	hoped	(have) hoped
inspect	(is) inspecting	inspected	(have) inspected
slip	(is) slipping	slipped	(have) slipped

REFERENCE NOTE: Most regular verbs that end in –e drop the –e before adding *–ing.* Some regular verbs double the final consonant before adding *–ing* or *–ed.* For a discussion of these spelling rules, see pages 770–771.

One common error in forming the past or the past participle of a regular verb is to leave off the *–d* or *–ed* ending.

NONSTANDARD Our street use to be more quiet.
STANDARD Our street **used** to be more quiet.

REFERENCE NOTE: For a discussion of standard and nonstandard English, see page 387.

USAGE

ORAL PRACTICE 1

Using Regular Verbs

Read each of the following sentences aloud, stressing the italicized verbs.

1. We are *supposed* to meet at the track after school.
2. The twins *happened* to buy the same shirt.
3. They have already *called* me about the party.
4. Do you know who *used* to live in this house?
5. I *hoped* they could go to the concert with us.
6. The chairs have been *moved* for the dance.
7. That salesclerk has *helped* my mother before.
8. Eli may not have *looked* under the table for the cat.

EXERCISE 1

Writing the Forms of Regular Verbs

For each of the following sentences, fill in the blank with the correct present participle, past, or past participle form of the verb given.

EXAMPLE 1. *learn* Many people today are ___ folk dances from a variety of countries.

1. *learning*

1. *practice* These Spanish folk dancers must have ___ for a long time.
2. *perform* Notice that they are ___ in colorful, native costumes.
3. *wish* Have you ever ___ that you knew how to do any folk dances?

4. *use* Virginia reels ____ to be popular dances in the United States.
5. *promise* Mrs. Stamos, who is from Greece, ____ to teach her daughter the Greek chain dance.
6. *lean* The Jamaican dancer ____ backward before he went under the pole during the limbo competition.
7. *start* The group from Estonia is ____ a dance about a spinning wheel.
8. *request* Someone in the audience has ____ an Irish square dance called "Sweets of May."
9. *dance* During the Mexican hat dance, the girl ____ on the rim of the sombrero.
10. *fill* The Jewish wedding dance ____ the room with music and movement.

Irregular Verbs

21c. An ***irregular verb*** forms its past and past participle in some other way than by adding *–d* or *–ed* to the infinitive form.

Irregular verbs form their past and past participle in three ways:

- by changing vowels *or* consonants

INFINITIVE	PAST	PAST PARTICIPLE
ring	rang	(have) rung
make	made	(have) made

- by changing vowels *and* consonants

INFINITIVE	PAST	PAST PARTICIPLE
do	did	(have) done
go	went	(have) gone

- by making no changes

INFINITIVE	PAST	PAST PARTICIPLE
hurt	hurt	(have) hurt
put	put	(have) put

NOTE: If you are not sure about the principal parts of a verb, look in a dictionary. Entries for irregular verbs list the principal parts of the verb. If the principal parts are not given, the verb is a regular verb.

USAGE

COMMON IRREGULAR VERBS			
INFINITIVE	PRESENT PARTICIPLE	PAST	PAST PARTICIPLE
begin	(is) beginning	began	(have) begun
bite	(is) biting	bit	(have) bitten
blow	(is) blowing	blew	(have) blown
break	(is) breaking	broke	(have) broken
bring	(is) bringing	brought	(have) brought
build	(is) building	built	(have) built
burst	(is) bursting	burst	(have) burst
catch	(is) catching	caught	(have) caught
choose	(is) choosing	chose	(have) chosen
come	(is) coming	came	(have) come
cost	(is) costing	cost	(have) cost
do	(is) doing	did	(have) done
draw	(is) drawing	drew	(have) drawn
drink	(is) drinking	drank	(have) drunk
drive	(is) driving	drove	(have) driven
eat	(is) eating	ate	(have) eaten
fall	(is) falling	fell	(have) fallen
feel	(is) feeling	felt	(have) felt
freeze	(is) freezing	froze	(have) frozen
get	(is) getting	got	(have) got *or* gotten

(continued)

COMMON IRREGULAR VERBS *(continued)*			
INFINITIVE	PRESENT PARTICIPLE	PAST	PAST PARTICIPLE
give	(is) giving	gave	(have) given
go	(is) going	went	(have) gone
grow	(is) growing	grew	(have) grown
know	(is) knowing	knew	(have) known
lead	(is) leading	led	(have) led

USAGE

ORAL PRACTICE 2 **Using Irregular Verbs**

Read each of the following sentences aloud, stressing the italicized verbs.

1. Ellen's sister *drove* her to the mall this afternoon.
2. My parents *came* to the spelling bee last year.
3. I should have *known* the test would be difficult.
4. He's *going* to Cape Canaveral this summer.
5. Maya has been *chosen* to play Emily in *Our Town.*
6. The water pipe *burst* during the ice storm.
7. *Did* you see the northern lights last night?
8. Wyatt *brought* his new computer game to the party.

EXERCISE 2 **Writing the Past and Past Participle Forms of Irregular Verbs**

For each of the following sentences, give the past or past participle form of the verb that will fit correctly in the blank.

EXAMPLE 1. *choose* Sara has ____ her song for the recital.
1. *chosen*

1. *drive* Last summer we ____ to Denver, where we visited the U.S. Mint.
2. *begin* The concert ____ an hour ago.
3. *break* Mike Powell ____ the world long jump record by jumping 29 feet, $4\frac{1}{2}$ inches.
4. *blow* The wind has ____ the tent down.

5. *get* We've ____ tickets to ride *The Silverton.*
6. *fall* People have ____ over that log several times.
7. *do* Mother ____ her best, and she got a promotion.
8. *drink* According to legend, the Aztec emperor Montezuma ____ chocolate.
9. *build* People in Africa ____ large cities hundreds, even thousands, of years ago.
10. *go* You've never ____ to Puerto Rico, have you?

USAGE

MORE COMMON IRREGULAR VERBS			
INFINITIVE	PRESENT PARTICIPLE	PAST	PAST PARTICIPLE
lend	(is) lending	lent	(have) lent
lose	(is) losing	lost	(have) lost
make	(is) making	made	(have) made
meet	(is) meeting	met	(have) met
ride	(is) riding	rode	(have) ridden
ring	(is) ringing	rang	(have) rung
run	(is) running	ran	(have) run
say	(is) saying	said	(have) said
see	(is) seeing	saw	(have) seen
sell	(is) selling	sold	(have) sold
send	(is) sending	sent	(have) sent
shrink	(is) shrinking	shrank	(have) shrunk
sing	(is) singing	sang	(have) sung
sink	(is) sinking	sank	(have) sunk
speak	(is) speaking	spoke	(have) spoken
stand	(is) standing	stood	(have) stood
steal	(is) stealing	stole	(have) stolen
swim	(is) swimming	swam	(have) swum
swing	(is) swinging	swung	(have) swung
take	(is) taking	took	(have) taken
tell	(is) telling	told	(have) told
throw	(is) throwing	threw	(have) thrown
wear	(is) wearing	wore	(have) worn
win	(is) winning	won	(have) won
write	(is) writing	wrote	(have) written

ORAL PRACTICE 3 **Using Irregular Verbs**

Read each of the following sentences aloud, stressing the italicized verbs.

1. When the bell *rang,* we hurried out of the building.
2. The audience was quiet as the acrobats *swung* from the trapeze.
3. That dress *shrank* because it was washed in hot water.
4. Otherwise, Lily would have *worn* it to the dance.
5. Have you *met* the foreign exchange student this year?
6. We were late to the picnic because I *lost* the map.
7. My father *lent* me the money to buy a new watch.
8. Would you believe that Raymond *took* singing lessons?

EXERCISE 3 **Writing the Past and Past Participle Forms of Irregular Verbs**

For each of the following sentences, give the past or past participle form of the verb that will fit correctly in the blank.

EXAMPLE **1.** *see* I have ___ that movie twice already.
1. *seen*

1. *run* Carl Lewis ___ the 100-meter dash in record-breaking time.
2. *sell* My aunt has ___ more houses than any other real estate agent in the city.
3. *speak* The director of the state health department ___ to our class today.
4. *win* Mexican poet Octavio Paz ___ the Nobel Prize for literature.
5. *write* I have ___ some poems, but I am shy about showing them to anyone.
6. *ride* Tamisha's whole family ___ on mules to the bottom of the Grand Canyon.
7. *sing* At the concert, the group ___ my favorite song.

8. *throw* This trash must have been ___ from a car.
9. *swim* Two swans ___ across the lake.
10. *sink* King Arthur's sword Excalibur ___ slowly to the bottom of the lake.

REVIEW A

Writing the Past and Past Participle Forms of Irregular Verbs

For each of the following sentences, give the past or past participle form of the verb that will fit correctly in the blank.

EXAMPLE 1. *tell* Has Alameda ___ you about the book *The Indian Tipi: Its History, Construction, and Use*?

1. *told*

1. *write* Reginald and Gladys Laubin ___ that book and several others about Native American culture.
2. *come* The word *tepee*, or *tipi*, has ___ into English from the Sioux language.
3. *stand* Tepees of various sizes once ___ all across the plains.
4. *see* I have ___ pictures of camps full of decorated tepees.
5. *make* For many years, Native Americans have ___ tepees out of cloth rather than buffalo hides.
6. *build* The Laubins ___ their own tepee and lived in it.
7. *draw* On the outside of their tepees, the Sioux and Cheyenne peoples ___ designs like the ones shown on the next page.
8. *take* Because the Plains peoples followed the animal herds, they needed housing that could be ___ from place to place.
9. *know* Even before reading the book, I ___ that tepee covers were rarely painted inside.
10. *do* Women ___ all the work of making tepees and putting them up.

USAGE

REVIEW B

Writing the Past and Past Participle Forms of Irregular Verbs

For each of the following sentences, give the past or past participle form of the verb that will fit correctly in the blank.

EXAMPLE **1.** ***write*** **I ____ a report on Jim Thorpe.**
1. ***wrote***

1. *blow* Yesterday the wind ____ the leaves into our yard.

2. *break* My pen pal from Australia has never ____ his promise to write once a week.

3. *bring* I ____ the wrong book to class.

4. *burst* The children almost ____ with excitement.

5. *choose* The director ____ James Earl Jones to star in the new series.

6. *come* My aunt and her friend ____ to dinner last night.

7. *do* I have always ___ my homework right after supper.
8. *drink* The guests ___ four quarts of fruit punch.
9. *fall* One of my Russian nesting dolls has ___ off the shelf.
10. *freeze* Has the pond ___ yet?
11. *go* We have never ___ to see the Parthenon in Nashville, Tennessee.
12. *know* Had I ___, I would have called you sooner.
13. *ring* Suddenly the fire alarm ___.
14. *run* Joan Samuelson certainly ___ a good race.
15. *see* I ___ you in line at the movies.
16. *shrink* We dried apples in the sun, and they ___.
17. *speak* After we had ___ to George Takai, who plays Mr. Sulu, we went to the *Star Trek* convention banquet.
18. *throw* You shouldn't have ___ the ball to second base.
19. *write* She has ___ me several long letters.
20. *swim* We ___ out to the float and back.

REVIEW C

Using Past and Past Participle Forms of Irregular Verbs

You've won a radio contest called "Ask a Star." Now you get to interview the celebrity of your choice. You name the star, and the radio station will arrange the interview. Pick a celebrity to interview, and write ten questions to ask him or her. In your questions, use the past or past participle forms of ten of the following verbs. Underline each verb you use.

begin	cost	know	sing
break	do	meet	tell
build	drive	ride	throw
catch	feel	say	wear
choose	get	sell	write

EXAMPLE 1. *Have you really ridden a camel down Hollywood Boulevard?*

PICTURE THIS

The year is 2030. Just ten years ago scientists made great advances in time travel. Now, time-travel booths like this one are common in malls and shopping centers. For a small fee, you can travel to any place at any time in history. You sit down in the booth, fasten your seat belt, and set the dials for the time and place of your choice. When the machine stops, you get out and begin to explore your surroundings. You take notes about what you see so that you won't forget anything when you tell your family and friends about your trip. In your notes, describe how life in this time and place is similar to or different from life as you know it. Use at least ten irregular verbs, underlining each one you use.

Subject: a journey to a different place and time
Audience: your family and friends
Purpose: to inform and entertain

Tense

21d. **The *tense* of a verb indicates the time of the action or of the state of being expressed by the verb.**

Every verb has six tenses.

Present	Past	Future
Present Perfect	Past Perfect	Future Perfect

The following time line shows the relationship between the six tenses.

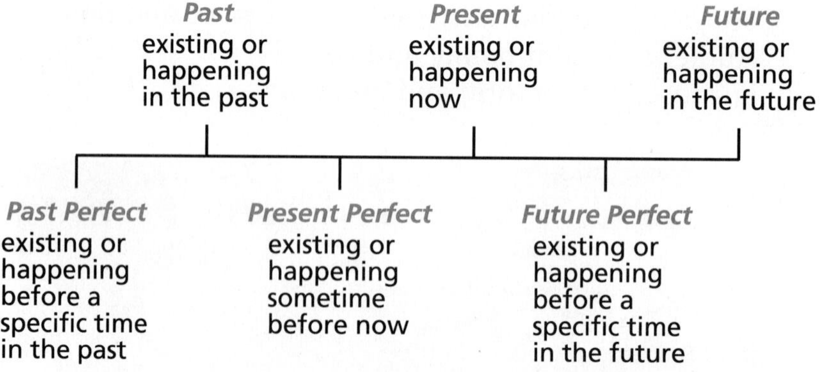
Past
existing or happening in the past
Present
existing or happening now
Future
existing or happening in the future
Past Perfect
existing or happening before a specific time in the past
Present Perfect
existing or happening sometime before now
Future Perfect
existing or happening before a specific time in the future

Listing all the forms of a verb is called *conjugating* the verb.

CONJUGATION OF THE VERB *SEE*	
PRESENT TENSE	
SINGULAR	**PLURAL**
I see	we see
you see	you see
he, she, or it sees	they see

(continued)

CONJUGATION OF THE VERB *SEE* *(continued)*	
PAST TENSE	
SINGULAR	**PLURAL**
I saw	we saw
you saw	you saw
he, she, or it saw	they saw
FUTURE TENSE	
SINGULAR	**PLURAL**
I will (shall) see	we will (shall) see
you will see	you will see
he, she, or it will see	they will see
PRESENT PERFECT TENSE	
SINGULAR	**PLURAL**
I have seen	we have seen
you have seen	you have seen
he, she, or it has seen	they have seen
PAST PERFECT TENSE	
SINGULAR	**PLURAL**
I had seen	we had seen
you had seen	you had seen
he, she, or it had seen	they had seen
FUTURE PERFECT TENSE	
SINGULAR	**PLURAL**
I will (shall) have seen	we will (shall) have seen
you will have seen	you will have seen
he, she, or it will have seen	they will have seen

Consistency of Tense

21e. Do not change needlessly from one tense to another.

When writing about events that take place in the present, use verbs that are in the present tense. When writing about events that occurred in the past, use verbs that are in the past tense.

INCONSISTENT **When we go to the movies, we bought some popcorn.** [*Go* is in the present tense, and *bought* is in the past tense.]

CONSISTENT **When we go to the movies, we buy some popcorn.** [Both *go* and *buy* are in the present tense.]

CONSISTENT **When we went to the movies, we bought some popcorn.** [Both *went* and *bought* are in the past tense.]

USAGE

EXERCISE 4 Revising a Paragraph to Make the Tenses of the Verbs Consistent

Read the following paragraph and decide whether it should be rewritten in the present or past tense. Then rewrite the paragraph, changing the verb forms to make the verb tense consistent.

EXAMPLE [1] I picked up the telephone receiver, but the line is still dead.

1. *I picked up the telephone receiver, but the line was still dead.*

or

I pick up the telephone receiver, but the line is still dead.

[1] Lightning struck our house, and I run straight for cover. [2] "Oh, no!" I exclaim. [3] The electricity had gone out! [4] My parents light candles, and we played a game by candlelight. [5] We know that lightning had hit our telephone answering machine, because it keeps playing the same message over and over. [6] My younger brother asks me what lightning is. [7] "Lightning is a big spark of electricity from a thundercloud," I tell him. [8] He nods. [9] I started to tell him about positive and negative charges creating lightning, but he doesn't understand what I'm talking about and walks away. [10] In the morning, we were all glad when the sun shone and our phone works again.

Six Troublesome Verbs

Sit and *Set*

The verb *sit* means "to be seated" or "to rest." *Sit* seldom takes an object.

The verb *set* means "to place" or "to put (something)." *Set* usually takes an object. Notice that *set* has the same form for the infinitive, past, and past participle.

INFINITIVE	PRESENT PARTICIPLE	PAST	PAST PARTICIPLE
sit	(is) sitting	sat	(have) sat
set	(is) setting	set	(have) set

EXAMPLES Three girls **sat** on the platform. [no object]
Set those geraniums in a sunny place. [Set what? *Geraniums* is the object.]

I **will sit** here for a while. [no object]
I **will set** your dinner on the table. [I will set what? *Dinner* is the object.]

ORAL PRACTICE 4 **Using the Forms of *Sit* and *Set* Correctly**

Read each of the following sentences aloud, stressing the italicized verbs.

1. Darnell and I *sat* down to play a game of chess.
2. After he had been *sitting* for a while, Darnell decided to make banana bread.
3. I *set* the pan on the table.
4. Darnell *set* out the ingredients; then he mixed them.
5. We returned to our game but could not *sit* still for long.
6. We had not *set* the pan in the oven.
7. Then we almost *sat* too long.
8. The pan had been *set* on the wrong rack, and the bread was beginning to burn.

USAGE

EXERCISE 5 Writing the Forms of *Sit* and *Set*

For each blank in the following sentences, supply the correct form of *sit* or *set*.

EXAMPLE **1.** I ____ my suitcase on the rack.
1. *set*

1. On the train to Boston, I ____ next to a middle-aged woman wearing a shawl.
2. She ____ a large basket on the floor by her feet.
3. When the conductor asked her if she would like to ____ it in the baggage rack, she refused.
4. She insisted that the basket must ____ by her feet.
5. As I ____ beside her, I wondered what was in the basket.
6. I ____ my book down and tried to see inside the tightly woven basket.
7. Perhaps I was ____ next to a woman with a picnic lunch to share.
8. Maybe she had ____ next to me because I looked hungry.
9. As the woman ____ her packages down, I watched the basket.
10. A sudden movement of the train caused the basket to open, and inside it ____ a small white rabbit.

Rise and *Raise*

The verb *rise* means "to move upward" or "to go up." *Rise* never takes an object.

The verb *raise* means "to lift (something) up." *Raise* usually takes an object.

INFINITIVE	PRESENT PARTICIPLE	PAST	PAST PARTICIPLE
rise	(is) rising	rose	(have) risen
raise	(is) raising	raised	(have) raised

EXAMPLES **Coretta has already risen from the bench.** [no object]
My brother has raised the curtain. [My brother has raised what? *Curtain* is the object.]

The fans were rising to sing the national anthem. [no object]
Passing cars were raising clouds of dust. [Cars were raising what? *Clouds* is the object.]

ORAL PRACTICE 5

Using Forms of *Rise* and *Raise*

Read each of the following sentences aloud, stressing the italicized verbs.

1. Mount Everest *rises* over 29,000 feet.
2. The flag was *raised* at sunrise.
3. The TV reporter *raised* her voice to be heard.
4. She *rose* from her seat and looked out the window.
5. The constellation Orion had not yet *risen* in the southern sky.
6. They had *raised* the piñata high in the tree.
7. I hope the bread is *rising.*
8. He will be *raising* the bucket from the well.

EXERCISE 6

Identifying the Correct Forms of *Rise* and *Raise*

For each of the following sentences, choose the correct verb of the two in parentheses.

EXAMPLE **1. After the storm, Diana (*rose, raised*) the window.**
1. *raised*

1. The audience (*rose, raised*) for the "Hallelujah Chorus."
2. They used a jack to (*rise, raise*) the car so that they could change the tire.
3. The fire juggler is (*rising, raising*) two flaming batons over his head to signal the start of the show.
4. Some people have trouble remembering that the sun (*rises, raises*) in the east.

USAGE

5. He gently (*rose, raised*) the injured duckling from the lake.
6. Only half of Mauna Kea, a volcano on this island of Hawaii, (*rises, raises*) above the ocean.
7. The proud winner has (*risen, raised*) her trophy so that everyone can see it.
8. The guests have (*risen, raised*) from their seats to see the bride enter.
9. Yeast makes the pizza dough (*rise, raise*).
10. They will (*rise, raise*) the couch while I look under it for the hamster.

USAGE

Lie and *Lay*

The verb *lie* means "to recline," "to be in a place," or "to remain lying down." *Lie* never takes an object.

The verb *lay* means "to put (something) down," "to place (something)." *Lay* usually takes an object.

INFINITIVE	PRESENT PARTICIPLE	PAST	PAST PARTICIPLE
lie	(is) lying	lay	(have) lain
lay	(is) laying	laid	(have) laid

EXAMPLES Rocky Ridge **lies** twenty miles east of here. [no object]

Aunt Martha **lays** her apple dolls in the sun to dry. [Aunt Martha lays what? *Dolls* is the object.]

That bicycle **has lain** in the driveway for a week. [no object]

Dad **has laid** your clean shirts on the bed. [Dad has laid what? *Shirts* is the object.]

ORAL PRACTICE 6

Using Forms of *Lie* and *Lay* Correctly

Read each of the following sentences aloud, stressing the italicized verbs.

1. If you are tired, *lie* down for a while.
2. *Lay* your pencils down, please.
3. Two huge dogs *lay* by the fire.
4. The cat has been *lying* on the new bedspread.
5. Mr. Cortez *laid* the map of Puerto Rico on the table.
6. In our state, snow usually *lies* on the ground until early spring.
7. *Lay* your coats on the bed in my room.
8. After the baby had *lain* down for a nap, she wanted to play.

EXERCISE 7 Identifying the Correct Forms of *Lie* and *Lay*

For each of the following sentences, choose the correct verb of the two in parentheses.

EXAMPLE 1. Marc (*lay, laid*) his new tennis shoes on the floor.
1. *laid*

1. The islands of American Samoa (*lie, lay*) about 4,800 miles southwest of San Francisco.
2. We quickly (*lay, laid*) the crab down when it began to pinch.
3. I don't know where I have (*lain, laid*) my copy of *Chinese Proverbs* by Ruthanne Lum McCunn.
4. Cattle often (*lie, lay*) under trees during sunny days.
5. Many visitors (*lie, lay*) flowers and wreaths at the Vietnam Veterans Memorial in Washington, D.C.
6. My brother, who is sick, has been (*lying, laying*) in bed all day.
7. The postal employee (*lay, laid*) the small package on the scales.
8. (*Lie, Lay*) your backpack down and come see my new comic books.
9. Those clothes will (*lie, lay*) on the floor until you pick them up.
10. You're sore because you've been (*lying, laying*) in one position too long.

REVIEW D **Identifying the Correct Forms of *Sit* and *Set*, *Rise* and *Raise*, *Lie* and *Lay***

For each of the following sentences, choose the correct verb of the two in parentheses.

EXAMPLE **1. The bricklayer (*rose, raised*) from the patio floor and dusted himself off.**
1. *rose*

1. These rocks have (*lain, laid*) here for centuries.
2. (*Sit, Set*) there until your name is called.
3. The nurse (*lay, laid*) her cool hand on the sick child's brow.
4. The cows are (*lying, laying*) in the pasture.
5. The senator and her advisers (*sat, set*) around the huge conference table.
6. After the picnic, everyone (*lay, laid*) on blankets to rest.
7. Smoke (*rose, raised*) from the chimney.
8. The farmhands (*sat, set*) their lunch pails under a tree.
9. Have you been (*sitting, setting*) there all afternoon?
10. The sun has already (*risen, raised*).

REVIEW E **Proofreading a Paragraph for Correct Verb Forms**

Most sentences in the following paragraph contain incorrect verb forms. If a sentence contains the wrong form of a verb, write the correct form. If a sentence is correct, write C.

EXAMPLE **[1] During the 1800s, many German settlers choosed to live in the Hill Country of central Texas.**
1. *chose*

[1] These hardy, determined pioneers builded towns and cleared land for farming. [2] I have went to this town, Fredericksburg, several times. [3] This interesting town lays about eighty miles west of Austin. [4] Fredericksburg

use to be in Comanche territory. [5] Early on, German settlers made peace with the Comanche chiefs. [6] The town then growed rapidly. [7] German-style houses, churches, and public buildings like these raised along the town's central street. [8] On one of our visits, my family set and talked about the town with a woman who was born there. [9] She said that she had spoken German all her life. [10] When we left, she raised a hand and said, *"Auf Wiedersehen"* (until we meet again).

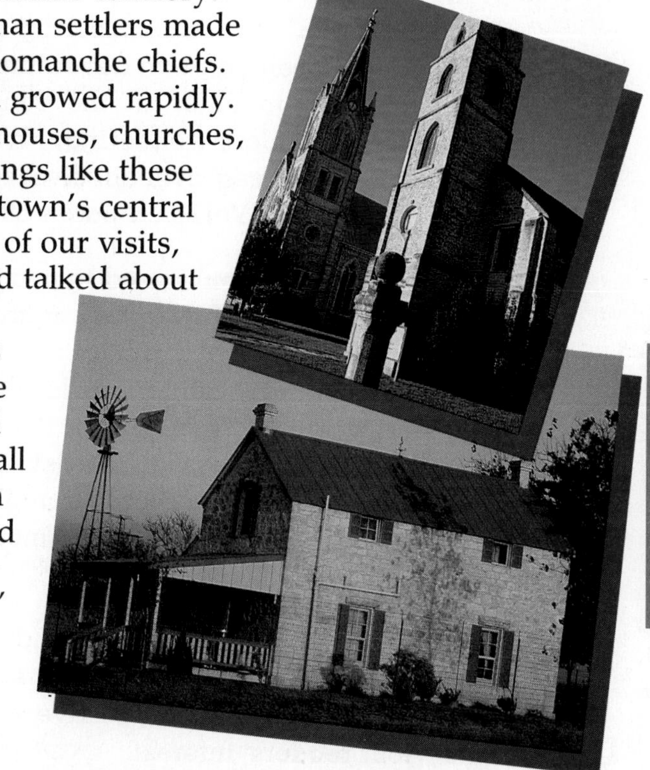

USAGE

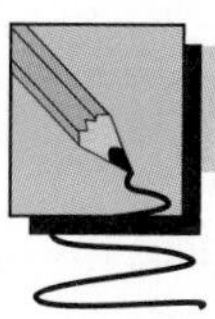

WRITING APPLICATION

Using Different Verb Forms and Tenses in a Story

When you write a story, you use verbs to express the action. The use of correct verb forms and consistent tense helps show your readers the order of events.

INCORRECT FORM AND INCONSISTENT TENSE — The gale wind blowed the tiny boat off course. Huge waves batter the craft. The weary crew will bail out the water.

CORRECT FORM AND CONSISTENT TENSE — The gale wind **blew** the tiny boat off course. Huge waves **battered** the craft. The weary crew **bailed** out the water.

WRITING ACTIVITY

A local writers' club is sponsoring a contest for the best "cliffhanger" opening of an adventure story. Write an exciting paragraph to enter in the contest. Your paragraph should leave readers wondering, "What happens next?" In your paragraph, use at least five verbs from the lists of **Common Irregular Verbs** on pages 584–586.

Prewriting First, you'll need to imagine a suspenseful situation to describe. Maybe your characters will actually be hanging on the edge of a cliff, or maybe they'll be in another type of life-or-death situation. Jot down several ideas for your story opening. Then, choose the one you like best. With that situation in mind, scan the lists of irregular verbs. Note down at least ten verbs that you might be able to use. (You can weed out some of them later.) Include some lively action verbs like *burst, swing, throw.*

Writing As you write your rough draft, think of your readers. Choose words that create a suspenseful, believable scene. Remember that you have only one paragraph to catch your readers' interest.

Evaluating and Revising Ask a friend to read your paragraph. Does your friend find it interesting? Can he or she picture the scene clearly? If not, you may want to add, delete, or revise some details. Check to see if you've used any tired words like *great* or *bad* that you can replace with more specific ones. For more about replacing tired words, see page 391.

Proofreading Check over your spelling, usage, punctuation, and grammar. Be sure that you've used at least five irregular verbs from the lists on pages 584–586. Use your textbook or a dictionary to check the spellings of these verbs. Also, check to make sure the forms are correct and the tenses are consistent.

Review: Posttest

Proofreading Sentences for Correct Verb Forms

If a sentence contains an incorrect past or past participle form of the verb, write the correct form. If a sentence is correct, write *C*.

EXAMPLE **1. Melissa drunk the medicine in one gulp.**
1. *drank*

1. We swum in the lake last weekend.
2. Carlos come from the Dominican Republic.
3. The crow just set there on the barbed wire fence and wouldn't move.
4. I seen that magician on television.
5. The balloon burst with a loud pop.
6. The gypsy raised his tambourine to begin the dance.
7. You should have went with me to the Native American celebration in Gallup, New Mexico.
8. The block of ice shrunk to half its original size.
9. Meanwhile, the water level has rose.
10. I would have wrote to you much sooner, but I lost your address.
11. Sandra throwed the ball to the shortstop.
12. Ms. Lopez has spoke before many civic groups.
13. All of these photographs were taken in Florida's Everglades National Park.
14. The bell has rang for fourth period.
15. While visiting Los Angeles, I run into an old friend in the city's Little Tokyo district.
16. I laid down under a tree to rest.
17. I done everything asked of me.
18. It begun to rain shortly after dusk.
19. Sue lay her pen down and studied the question again.
20. Some of the saucers were broken.

22 USING PRONOUNS CORRECTLY

Nominative and Objective Case Forms

Diagnostic Test

A. Identifying the Correct Forms of Pronouns

For each of the following sentences, choose the correct form of the pronoun in parentheses.

EXAMPLE **1. Mrs. Boyd gave Jeff and (*I, me*) a ride to school.**
1. *me*

1. The closing procession of the powwow will be led by (*he, him*) and the other Dakota dancers.
2. May (*we, us*) choir members leave science class a few minutes early today?
3. (*Who, Whom*) do you think you are, anyway?
4. Please hand out these copies of Consuela's report to (*she, her*) and the committee members.
5. (*He, Him*) and his cat relaxed in the easy chair and listened to the rain.

6. Darnell certainly was enjoying (*himself, hisself*) at the African Heritage Festival last night.
7. The last tennis player to beat Martina Navratilova in straight sets was (*her, she*).
8. (*Who, Whom*) have you asked for help with your math homework?
9. Mom, will you take (*we, us*) tired yard workers out for dinner tonight?
10. Collect about a dozen colorful leaves, and then brush (*they, them*) with a thin coat of shellac.

B. Identifying the Correct Forms of Pronouns

For each of the following sentences, choose the correct form of the pronoun in parentheses.

EXAMPLE **1. The most loyal sports fans at our school are Glenn and (*I, me*).**
1. *I*

11. (*We, Us*) baseball fans are going to the playoff game on Saturday.
12. (*Who, Whom*) will we see at the game?
13. Mario's mother will be driving (*we, us*) and Elena to the stadium.
14. Elena and (*he, him*) volunteered to design a banner.
15. "Tell Jennifer and (*I, me*) your slogan," Glenn said to Mario.
16. "Neither Elena nor (*I, me*) can decide which one we like best," Mario answered.
17. "Well, (*who, whom*) are the two best slogan inventors in the whole school?" I boasted, pointing at Glenn and myself.
18. Last year, the biggest banner was designed by the twins and (*she, her*).
19. They really outdid (*theirselves, themselves*)!
20. You should see the banner designed by (*we, us*) four fans this year, though!

Case

Case is the form of a noun or pronoun that shows its use in a sentence. There are three cases:

- nominative
- objective
- possessive

The form of a noun is the same for both the nominative and the objective cases. For example, a noun used as a subject (nominative case) will have the same form when used as a direct object (objective case).

NOMINATIVE CASE That Ming **vase** is very old. [subject]
OBJECTIVE CASE Who bought the **vase?** [direct object]

A noun changes its form only in the possessive case, usually by adding an apostrophe and an *s*.

POSSESSIVE CASE The Ming **vase's** new owner is pleased.

REFERENCE NOTE: For more information about forming the possessive case of nouns, see pages 746–748.

Unlike nouns, most personal pronouns have different forms for all three cases.

PERSONAL PRONOUNS		
	SINGULAR	
NOMINATIVE CASE	OBJECTIVE CASE	POSSESSIVE CASE
I you he, she, it	me you him, her, it	my, mine your, yours his, her, hers, its
	PLURAL	
NOMINATIVE CASE	OBJECTIVE CASE	POSSESSIVE CASE
we you they	us you them	our, ours your, yours their, theirs

USAGE

NOTE: Some teachers prefer to call possessive forms of pronouns (such as *our, your,* and *their*) adjectives. Follow your teacher's instructions regarding possessive forms.

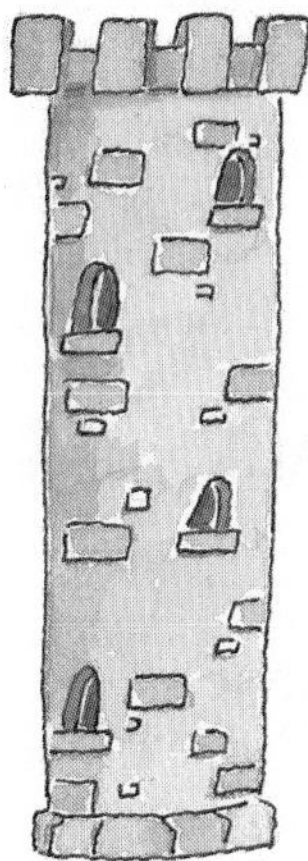

Drawing by Ziegler; © 1988 The New Yorker Magazine, Inc.

The Nominative Case

22a. The subject of a verb is in the nominative case.

EXAMPLES **They** made candles from antique molds. [*They* is the subject of *made.*]
We admired the Navajo rugs. [*We* is the subject of *admired.*]
He and **I** mowed lawns. [*He* and *I* are used together as the compound subject of *mowed.*]

To help you choose the correct pronoun in a compound subject, try each form of the pronoun separately.

EXAMPLE: The guide and (*I, me*) looked for tracks.
I looked for tracks.
Me looked for tracks.
ANSWER: The guide and **I** looked for tracks.

EXAMPLE: (*She, Her*) and (*I, me*) found them.
She found them.
Her found them.
I found them.
Me found them.
ANSWER: **She** and **I** found them.

ORAL PRACTICE 1 **Using Pronouns in Compound Subjects**

Read each of the following sentences aloud, stressing the italicized pronouns.

1. Dr. Chen and *they* discussed the usefulness of herbal medicines.
2. *He* and *I* live next door to each other.
3. *They* and *we* should try to get along better.
4. Yesterday *she* and *they* gave their reports on African American poets.
5. You and *she* left the party early.
6. Since the third grade, you and *I* have been friends.
7. *He* and his family are moving to Puerto Rico.
8. *She* and *I* will miss them.

EXERCISE 1 **Identifying Correct Pronoun Forms**

For each sentence in the following paragraph, choose the correct form of the pronoun in parentheses.

EXAMPLE **1. My friends and (*I*, *me*) like to spend time outdoors.**
1. *I*

[1] Lou and (*I, me*) asked my mother to drive us to a nearby state park. [2] There (*he and I, him and me*) set out on a marked trail through a wooded area. [3] Before long, (*he and I, him and me*) were exploring a snowy area off the beaten track. [4] At dusk Lou and (*I, me*) reluctantly followed our tracks back to the path. [5] (*We, Us*) had had the best time of our lives.

22b. A predicate nominative is in the nominative case.

A ***predicate nominative*** follows a linking verb and identifies or explains the subject of the verb. A pronoun used as a predicate nominative usually follows a form of the verb *be* (such as *am, are, is, was, were, be, been,* or *being*) and identifies the subject.

EXAMPLES The candidates should have been **he** and **she.** [*He* and *she* follow the linking verb *should have been* and identify the subject *candidates.*]
The members of the debating team are **they.** [*They* follows the linking verb *are* and identifies the subject *members.*]

NOTE: Expressions such as *It's me* and *That's her* are acceptable in everyday speaking. However, such expressions should be avoided in writing.

REFERENCE NOTE: For more information about predicate nominatives, see pages 480–481.

ORAL PRACTICE 2 Using Pronouns as Predicate Nominatives

Read each of the following sentences aloud, stressing the italicized pronouns.

1. Were the only Spanish-speaking people you and *they*?
2. The caller could have been *she.*
3. The leaders will be my mother and *he.*
4. The three candidates for class president are you and *we.*
5. That must be the pilot and *he.*
6. The three winners were Frank, May, and *I.*
7. The first ones on the scene were our neighbors and *they.*
8. The speakers at the rally were *she* and Jesse Jackson.

EXERCISE 2 Identifying Correct Pronoun Forms

For each of the following sentences, choose the correct form of the pronoun in parentheses.

EXAMPLE 1. Could it be (*they, them*)?
1. *they*

1. It must be (*them, they*).
2. Two witnesses claimed that the burglar was (*him, he*).

3. Is the last performer (*her, she*)?
4. The next speaker will be (*him, he*).
5. Among the invited guests are Luther and (*us, we*).
6. I knew it was (*her, she*), of course.
7. The hardest workers are Susan, Tranh, and (*me, I*).
8. Can that be (*her, she*) in that Mexican sombrero?
9. The next batter should be (*her, she*).
10. Our newest neighbors are the Blumenthals and (*them, they*).

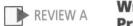

REVIEW A **Writing Sentences That Contain Pronouns in the Nominative Case**

The busy scene you see on the next page was painted by the Mexican American artist Carmen Lomas Garza. It shows one of her childhood birthday parties. The fish-shaped object is a piñata, full of gifts and treats for the children. Carmen is getting ready to take a swing at the piñata. Answer each of the following questions by writing a sentence. Follow the directions after each question.

EXAMPLE **1. What are the kneeling boys in the lower left-hand corner doing? (*Use a plural personal pronoun as the subject.*)**
1. *They are getting ready to play marbles.*

1. What is Carmen using to hit the piñata? (*Use a singular personal pronoun as the subject.*)
2. Whom are the presents on the table for? (*Use a plural personal pronoun as the subject.*)
3. Who will get the gifts and treats inside the piñata? (*Use a person's name and a plural personal pronoun as the compound subject.*)
4. Have you and your classmates ever played a game that requires a blindfold? (*Use a plural and a singular personal pronoun as the compound subject.*)
5. Why does the boy at the far right have presents in his hand? (*Use a singular personal pronoun as the subject.*)

6. What would Carmen say if you asked her, "Who's the birthday girl?" (*Use a singular personal pronoun as a predicate nominative.*)
7. Did Carmen's parents and her grandmother plan the party? (*Use a plural and a singular personal pronoun as a compound predicate nominative.*)
8. Are the baby and his mother standing near the table having a good time? (*Use the baby and a singular personal pronoun as the compound subject.*)
9. Is Carmen's father the man holding the piñata rope? (*Use a singular personal pronoun as a predicate nominative.*)
10. Who are the ones now enjoying Carmen Lomas Garza's long-ago birthday party? (*Use a plural personal pronoun as a predicate nominative.*)

The Objective Case

22c. ***Direct objects*** **and** ***indirect objects*** **of verbs are in the objective case.**

A *direct object* follows an action verb and tells *whom* or *what* receives the action of the verb.

EXAMPLES Mom called **me** to the phone. [*Me* tells *whom* Mom called.]
Julia bought sweet potatoes and used **them** to fill the empanadas. [*Them* tells *what* she used.]

An *indirect object* comes between an action verb and a direct object and tells *to whom* or *to what* or *for whom* or *for what*.

EXAMPLES The hostess handed **her** a name tag. [*Her* tells *to whom* the hostess handed the name tag.]
Mr. Tanaka raises large goldfish; he often feeds **them** rice. [*Them* tells *to what* Mr. Tanaka feeds rice.]

USAGE

To help you choose the correct pronoun in a compound object, try each form of the pronoun separately in the sentence.

EXAMPLE: The teacher chose Luisa and (*I, me*).
The teacher chose *I.*
The teacher chose *me.*
ANSWER: The teacher chose Luisa and **me.**

REFERENCE NOTE: For more information about direct and indirect objects, see pages 474–477.

ORAL PRACTICE 3 Using Pronouns as Direct Objects and Indirect Objects

Read each of the following sentences aloud, stressing the italicized pronouns.

1. I took Joe and *her* to a performance by French mimes.
2. The bus driver let Melba, Joe, and *me* off at the next corner.
3. An usher gave *us* programs.
4. Another usher guided *them* and *me* to our seats.
5. The performers fascinated Melba and *me.*
6. Their costumes delighted the crowd and *her.*
7. No one else impressed Joe and *me* as much as the youngest mime.
8. We watched *her* explore the walls of an invisible room.

EXERCISE 3 **Writing Pronouns Used as Direct Objects and Indirect Objects**

For each blank in the following sentences, give an appropriate pronoun. Use a variety of pronouns, but do not use *you* or *it*.

EXAMPLE 1. Have you seen Kim and ____?
1. *her*

1. The manager hired Susana and ____.
2. Lana sent ____ and ____ invitations.
3. We gave Grandpa López and ____ round-trip tickets to Mexico City.
4. The firefighters rescued ____ and ____.
5. Aunt Coretta showed my cousins and ____ a carved mask from Nigeria.
6. The show entertained the children and ____.
7. The waiter served ____ and ____ a variety of dim sum dumplings.
8. Our team chose ____ and ____ as representatives.
9. The election committee nominated Gerry and ____.
10. The clerk gave Misako and ____ the receipt for the paper lanterns.

REVIEW B **Identifying Correct Pronoun Forms**

For each sentence in the following paragraph, choose the correct form of the pronoun in parentheses.

EXAMPLE 1. Paul told Ms. Ésteban that (*he, him*) and (*I, me*) need a topic for our report.
1. *he, I*

[1] Some of the other students and (*he, him*) thought that there should be more reports on women in American history. [2] (*They, Them*) and their achievements are sometimes overlooked. [3] The picture on the next page, showing Amelia Earhart looking cheerful and confident, interested Paul and (*I, me*). [4] Both (*he, him*) and (*I, me*) were eager to find out more about her contribution to aviation. [5] We learned that it was (*she, her*) who made the

first solo flight by a woman across the Atlantic. [6] The fact that Amelia Earhart was the first pilot to fly from Hawaii to California surprised the rest of the class and (*we, us*), too. [7] In 1937, her navigator and (*she, her*) took off in a twin-engine plane for a trip around the world. [8] After (*they, them*) had completed two thirds of the trip, Earhart and her navigator lost contact with radio operators. [9] Neither the plane nor (*they, them*) were ever sighted again. [10] Ms. Ésteban and (*we, us*) are among the many people still puzzling over this mystery.

USAGE

22d. The ***object of a preposition*** is in the objective case.

A *prepositional phrase* begins with a preposition and ends with a noun or pronoun, called the *object of the preposition.*

EXAMPLES **We waited for them.** [*Them* is the object of the preposition *for.*]

The secret is between him and me. [*Him* and *me* are the compound object of the preposition *between.*]

REFERENCE NOTE: For a list of prepositions, see page 460.

ORAL PRACTICE 4

Using Pronouns as Objects of Prepositions

Read each of the following sentences aloud, stressing the italicized pronouns.

1. Mr. Torres divided the burritos *among them* and *us.*
2. At the game Maria sat *near him* and *her.*
3. Rose walked *toward* Nell and *me.*
4. Sam stood *between him* and *me.*
5. Mom ordered sandwiches *for* Hannah and *her.*
6. "*Without* Squanto and *me,* the Pilgrims won't last through another winter," thought Samoset.
7. I have read biographies *about him* and Martin Luther King, Jr.
8. David's parents gave a bar mitzvah party *for him.*

EXERCISE 4

Choosing Correct Pronouns Used as Objects of Prepositions

For each of the following sentences, choose the correct form of the pronoun in parentheses.

EXAMPLE **1.** Of all the people who traveled with Lewis and Clark, Sacagawea was particularly helpful to (*them, they*).
1. *them*

1. Sacagawea's husband, a guide named Toussaint Charbonneau, joined the expedition with (*her, she*) and their newborn baby.
2. The Shoshone were Sacagawea's people, and she longed to return to (*them, they*).
3. Captain Clark soon realized how important she would be to Lewis and (*he, him*).
4. The land they were traveling through was familiar to (*she, her*).
5. Luckily for (*she, her*) and the expedition, they met a group of friendly Shoshone.
6. From (*they, them*), Sacagawea obtained the ponies that Lewis and Clark needed.

7. Sacagawea's baby boy delighted the expedition's leaders, and they took good care of (*he, him*).
8. In fact, Captain Clark made a promise to (*she, her*) and Charbonneau that he would give the boy a good education.
9. At the age of eighteen, the boy befriended a prince and traveled with (*him, he*) in Europe.
10. Although sources disagree about when Sacagawea died, a gravestone for (*she, her*) in Wyoming bears the date April 9, 1884.

EXERCISE 5 **Writing Sentences That Include Pronouns as Objects of Prepositions**

A day in the life of a guide dog is full of responsibilities. A guide dog leads its owner safely *around* obstacles, *through* traffic, *among* crowds, *up* and *down* stairs, *onto* buses, *into* stores, *under* low-hanging awnings, and *along* busy sidewalks. Write five sentences describing the actions of Duchess as she guides Michael through this busy downtown area. In each sentence, use at least one pronoun as the object of a preposition. In two of your sentences, use a pronoun as part of a compound object.

EXAMPLE 1. *Duchess noticed a group of teenagers in front of a store and guided Michael around them and their bicycles.*

REVIEW C Identifying Correct Pronoun Forms

For each of the following sentences, choose the correct form of the pronoun in parentheses. Then tell what part of the sentence each pronoun is: *subject, predicate nominative, direct object, indirect object,* or *object of a preposition.*

EXAMPLE 1. My brother Pete and (*I, me*) wanted to know more about Elizabeth Blackwell.
1. *I—subject*

1. Mom told Pete and (*I, me*) that Elizabeth Blackwell was the first woman ever to graduate from medical school in the United States.
2. Geneva College granted (*she, her*) a degree in 1849.
3. At first, no male doctor would let her work for (*he, him*) because she was a woman.
4. Pete and (*I, me*) admire Elizabeth Blackwell for not giving up.
5. She wanted to help the poor and opened her own clinic for (*they, them*).
6. Wealthy citizens were soon supporting (*she, her*) and the clinic with donations.
7. Before long, one of the most talked-about topics in medical circles was (*she, her*) and the excellent work she was doing for the poor.
8. Mom and (*we, us*) read more about Dr. Blackwell, and we learned that she opened a medical school just for women.
9. Dr. Blackwell set high standards for students and gave (*they, them*) hard courses of study to complete.
10. Her teaching helped (*they, them*) to become excellent physicians, and she was proud of their success.

USAGE

"It's a new concept in teaching machines. You get 50 points for every grammatical error you blast away!"

PICTURE THIS

You and your family are spending the weekend in a large, unfamiliar city. Too excited to sleep, you watch the traffic and the city lights from the hotel window. As you're watching, you notice this person climbing into a taxi on the street below. You wonder why he is out in the rain on such a dark, chilly night. Is he rushing to meet someone? Is he a doctor called to an emergency? Perhaps he is a spy who must get to the airport in a hurry. You decide to write a brief story based on this scene. Imagine who the man is, where he is coming from, and where he is going. In your story, use pronouns in each of the following ways: as a subject, as a predicate nominative, as a direct object, as an indirect object, or as an object of a preposition.

Subject: a man climbing into a taxi
Audience: yourself
Purpose: to write a story about the man

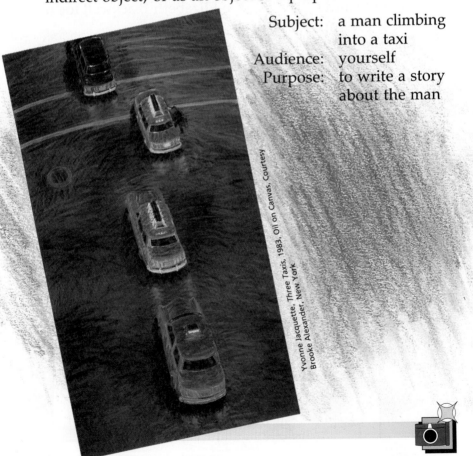

Yvonne Jacquette, *Three Taxis*, 1983, Oil on Canvas, Courtesy Brooke Alexander, New York

Special Pronoun Problems

Who and *Whom*

The pronoun *who* has different forms in the nominative and objective cases. *Who* is the nominative form; *whom* is the objective form.

NOTE: In spoken English, the use of *whom* is becoming less common. In fact, when you are speaking, you may correctly begin any question with *who* regardless of the grammar of the sentence. In written English, however, you should distinguish between *who* and *whom.*

When you need to decide whether to use *who* or *whom* in a question, follow these steps:

STEP 1: Rephrase the question as a statement.
STEP 2: Decide how the pronoun is used in the statement—as subject, predicate nominative, object of the verb, or object of a preposition.
STEP 3: Determine the case of the pronoun according to the rules of standard English.
STEP 4: Select the correct form of the pronoun.

EXAMPLE: (*Who, Whom*) is she?
STEP 1: The statement is *She is* (*who, whom*).
STEP 2: The subject is *she,* the verb is *is,* and the pronoun is the predicate nominative: *She is* (*who, whom*).
STEP 3: A pronoun used as a predicate nominative should be in the nominative case.
STEP 4: The nominative form is *who.*
ANSWER: **Who** is she?

EXAMPLE: (*Who, Whom*) will you invite to the dance?
STEP 1: The statement is *You will invite* (*who, whom*) *to the dance.*
STEP 2: The subject is *you,* and the verb is *will invite.* The pronoun is the direct object of the verb: *You will invite* (*who, whom*).
STEP 3: A pronoun used as a direct object should be in the objective case.
STEP 4: The objective form is *whom.*
ANSWER: **Whom** will you invite to the dance?

ORAL PRACTICE 5

Choosing *Who* or *Whom*

Read each of the following sentences aloud, stressing the italicized pronouns.

1. *Who* is captain of the football team this year?
2. To *whom* did you give your old skateboard?
3. *Whom* will you call to come and pick us up after band practice?
4. *Who* were the first Americans?
5. In the last play of the game, *who* passed the ball to *whom?*
6. *Who*'s that woman in the green kimono?
7. For *whom* did you buy those flowers?
8. *Who* painted that beautiful still life?

USAGE

Pronouns with Appositives

Sometimes a pronoun is followed directly by a noun that identifies the pronoun. Such a noun is called an ***appositive.*** To help you choose which pronoun to use before an appositive, omit the appositive and try each form of the pronoun separately.

EXAMPLE: On Saturdays, (*we, us*) cyclists ride to Mount McCabe and back. [*Cyclists* is the appositive identifying the pronoun.]
We ride to Mount McCabe.
Us ride to Mount McCabe.

ANSWER: On Saturdays, **we** cyclists ride to Mount McCabe and back.

EXAMPLE: The speaker praised (*we, us*) volunteers. [*Volunteers* is the appositive identifying the pronoun.]
The speaker praised *we.*
The speaker praised *us.*

ANSWER: The speaker praised **us** volunteers.

REFERENCE NOTE: For more information about appositives, see page 715.

EXERCISE 6 **Choosing Correct Pronouns**

For each of the following sentences, choose the correct form of the pronoun in parentheses.

EXAMPLE **1. Hanukkah is always an exciting holiday for (*we, us*) Feldmans.**
1. *us*

1. The famous golfer Lee Trevino is a symbol of pride to (*we, us*) Mexican Americans.
2. (*Who, Whom*) will your brother invite to his birthday party?
3. (*Who, Whom*) will be our substitute teacher while Mr. Chen is away?
4. Miss Jefferson, (*we, us*) students want to thank you for all your help.
5. (*Who, Whom*) has Ms. Spears chosen to serve on the Kite Festival committee?
6. Of the three candidates, (*who, whom*) do you have the most confidence in?
7. (*We, Us*) contestants shook hands warmly.
8. To (*who, whom*) do you wish these flowers sent?
9. (*Who, Whom*) do you admire?
10. (*Who, Whom*) is the leftover macaroni and cheese for?

USAGE

Reflexive Pronouns

The reflexive pronouns *himself* and *themselves* can be used as objects. Do not use the nonstandard forms *hisself* and *theirselfs* or *theirselves* in place of *himself* and *themselves.*

NONSTANDARD The secretary voted for hisself in the last election.
STANDARD The secretary voted for **himself** in the last election.

NONSTANDARD The cooks served theirselves some of the won-ton soup.
STANDARD The cooks served **themselves** some of the won-ton soup.

EXERCISE 7 Identifying Correct Pronoun Forms

For each of the following sentences, choose the correct form of the pronoun in parentheses.

1. Before he started to read, Zack asked (*hisself, himself*) three questions to set his purpose.
2. My little brother often falls down, but he never seems to hurt (*hisself, himself*).
3. The guests helped (*theirselves, themselves*) to the nuts and raisins.
4. John Yellowtail enjoys (*himself, hisself*) making fine silver jewelry.
5. If the early settlers wanted cloth, they had to spin it (*theirselves, themselves*).

REVIEW D Identifying Correct Pronoun Forms

For each of the following sentences, choose the correct form of the pronoun in parentheses.

EXAMPLE 1. To me, the two most interesting explorers are (*he, him*) and Vasco da Gama.
1. *he*

1. The team captains will be Jack and (*he, him*).
2. Was the joke played on you and (*he, him*)?
3. We were warned by our parents and (*they, them*).
4. The Washington twins and (*I, me*) belong to the same club.
5. Who are (*they, them*)?
6. Pelé and (*he, him*) both played soccer for the New York Cosmos.
7. "What do you think of (*he and I, him and me*)?" I asked.
8. "You and (*he, him*) are improving," they replied.
9. When Miriam Makeba and the troupe of African musicians arrived, we gave (*she and they, her and them*) a party.
10. Do you remember my sister and (*I, me*)?
11. The coach spoke to (*we, us*) players before the game.

12. The finalists in the talent contest are Alfredo, Sylvia, and (*I, me*).
13. Are you and (*she, her*) going to celebrate Kwanzaa this year?
14. Père Toussaint taught my brother and (*I, me*) to play a Cajun fiddle tune.
15. Mom, Andy gave (*himself, hisself*) the biggest piece of banana bread.
16. Both (*he and she, her and him*) have promised to write us this summer.
17. They congratulated (*themselves, theirselves*) on a job well done.
18. Don't leave without (*he and I, him and me*).
19. (*We, Us*) skiers had a beautiful view from the lift.
20. (*Who, Whom*) were you expecting?

WRITING APPLICATION

Using Nouns to Make the Meaning of Pronouns Clear

Using pronouns to take the place of nouns helps you avoid repeating the same nouns over and over. However, it's important not to use so many pronouns that your reader gets confused.

CONFUSING Steve brought two dog biscuits for Duke. As he walked up the steps, he threw them to him. He lay down happily on some towels and ate them. (*Who walked up the steps? What was thrown? To whom was it thrown? Who lay down? What did he eat?*)

CLEAR Steve brought two dog biscuits for Duke. As Steve walked up the steps, he threw both biscuits to the dog. Duke lay down happily on some towels and ate the biscuits.

Be sure that the pronouns you *do* use refer clearly to their antecedents.

WRITING ACTIVITY

Your favorite radio station is having a "Create a Radio Show" contest. The show will be produced by and for young people. The station has set aside a half-hour of prime time each week for the winning program. Write a letter to the manager of the station explaining what you would like to include in a radio show. The show can have any format you like. It can be like an existing radio show, or it can be something completely new. In your letter, use a variety of pronouns in the nominative case and the objective case. Be sure to include enough nouns so that the meaning of all your pronouns is clear.

Prewriting Discuss your ideas for a radio program with a group of your classmates. List the kinds of entertainment and information you could present. Above all, think about what *you* would like to hear on the radio. Consider how long each part of your show will be. Remember that you have only thirty minutes each week and that part of that time must be devoted to commercials.

Writing As you write your first draft, follow the format for a business letter. (You will find information about business letters on pages 838–842.) Give specific examples of what you want to do on the show, and give reasons for your choices. Remember that even though your ideas may be very creative, your writing must be formal.

Evaluating and Revising Ask the other group members to read your letter to see if your ideas sound interesting and are clearly stated. Ask them if the relationship between each pronoun and its antecedent is clear. If your meaning is not clear, revise your letter. You may need to include more nouns.

Proofreading and Publishing Reread your letter, and correct any remaining errors in usage, spelling, punctuation, or capitalization. Be sure that you have followed the correct format for a business letter. Also, make sure that you have used all pronouns according to the rules for standard written

English. Your class might want to create a bulletin-board display of the letters, titled "WISH—Imagination Radio." With your teacher's permission, the class might vote on the best idea for a show and then produce and tape the pilot episode.

USAGE

Review: Posttest

Correcting Errors in Pronoun Forms

Most of the following sentences contain errors in the use of pronoun forms. For each sentence, identify the error and give the correct pronoun form. If a sentence is correct, write *C*.

EXAMPLE **1. The Garcia children and them grew up together in Texas.**
1. *them—they*

1. Omar and him offered us some *pita,* a Middle Eastern bread.
2. Us basketball players know the value of good sneakers.
3. The computer experts in our class are Rosalinda and her.
4. There's more than a three-year age difference between Edward and I.
5. Pablo and me are planning to visit the Andes Mountains someday.
6. At Passover, my grandparents make gefilte fish and other traditional foods for my cousins and I.
7. Give Suki and him this invitation to the Japanese tea ceremony.
8. Josh made hisself a bookcase in industrial arts class.

9. Two angry hornets chased Earline and she all the way home.
10. The first actors on stage were Jesse and him.
11. Mr. Mendez and us organized a debate about the rights of students.
12. Will you attend the rally with Dominick and me?
13. I helped Kimberly and they with their play about Hiawatha.
14. Jeannette and her know a great deal about Greek myths.
15. The hickory smoke smelled good to we campers.
16. The only seventh-graders in the marching band are Bianca and me.
17. Liang was telling them and me about his birthplace in Hong Kong.
18. Julia and them learned how to use hot wax to make batik patterns on cloth.
19. During most of the marathon, Lionel ran just behind Jim and she.
20. Thomas asked Marvella and he if they wanted to join a gospel chorus.

23 USING MODIFIERS CORRECTLY

Comparison and Placement

Diagnostic Test

A. Correcting Errors in the Use of Modifiers

The following sentences contain errors in the use of modifiers. Rewrite each sentence, correcting the misuse of the modifier in that sentence.

EXAMPLE **1. Linen feels more rougher than silk.**
1. *Linen feels rougher than silk.*

1. These Hawaiian shirts don't have no pockets.
2. This ring is the most expensive of the two.
3. That striped tie would go good with a white shirt.
4. Is a ticket to Mexico more cheaper than a ticket to Canada?
5. Orange juice tastes more sweetly than grapefruit juice.

6. What is the most funniest thing that ever happened to you?
7. I can't hardly take another step.
8. My uncle thinks that Stevie Wonder sings more well than Michael Jackson does.
9. No one is courteouser than Rosa.
10. Ted felt calmly during the test on Greek mythology.

B. Correcting Misplaced Modifiers

Each of the following sentences contains a misplaced modifier. Revise each sentence so that it is clear and correct.

EXAMPLE **1. Hidden in his back pocket, Delbert found the missing ticket.**
1. *Delbert found the missing ticket hidden in his back pocket.*

11. The famous explorer described being attacked by a baboon in today's assembly.
12. Pam examined a plant cell looking through the microscope.
13. Juan read the poem to the class that he had found.
14. My sister promised on Sunday she would take me fishing.
15. Black Hawk was a chief of the Sauk people born in Illinois.
16. The plums are drying in the sun that we picked yesterday morning.
17. My favorite character in this African folk tale that outwits all its enemies is a rabbit.
18. A bird landed on the window sill with a bright red beak.
19. Skateboarding down the street, a large dog chased my brother.
20. The books are now used by many young readers that we donated to the library.

Comparison of Adjectives and Adverbs

A ***modifier*** is a word, a phrase, or a clause that describes another word or limits the meaning of the word. The two kinds of modifiers–adjectives and adverbs—may be used to compare things. In making comparisons, adjectives and adverbs take different forms. The specific form that is used depends upon how many things are being compared. The different forms of comparison are called *degrees of comparison.*

23a. The three degrees of comparison of modifiers are the *positive,* the *comparative,* and the *superlative.*

(1) The ***positive degree*** is used when only one thing is being described.

EXAMPLES This suitcase is **heavy.**
Luís **cheerfully** began the job.

(2) The ***comparative degree*** is used when two things are being compared.

EXAMPLES My suitcase is **heavier** than yours.
He began to talk **more cheerfully** about his plans.

(3) The ***superlative degree*** is used when three or more things are being compared.

EXAMPLES Sylvia's suitcase is the **heaviest** of all.
Of all the boys, Luís worked at the task **most cheerfully.**

NOTE: In conversation, you may hear and use expressions such as *Put your best foot forward* and *May the best team win.* This use of the superlative is acceptable in spoken English. However, in your writing for school and other formal occasions you should generally follow rule (3) above.

Regular Comparison

Most one-syllable modifiers form their comparative and superlative degrees by adding *–er* and *–est*.

POSITIVE	COMPARATIVE	SUPERLATIVE
close	closer	closest
slow	slower	slowest
straight	straighter	straightest
sly	slier	sliest

Notice that both adjectives and adverbs form their degrees of comparison in the same way.

Some two-syllable modifiers form their comparative and superlative degrees by adding *–er* and *–est*. Other two-syllable modifiers form their comparative and superlative degrees by using *more* and *most*.

POSITIVE	COMPARATIVE	SUPERLATIVE
simple	simpler	simplest
easy	easier	easiest
jealous	more jealous	most jealous
swiftly	more swiftly	most swiftly

When you are unsure about which way a two-syllable modifier forms its degrees of comparison, look up the word in a dictionary.

REFERENCE NOTE: For guidelines on how to spell words when adding *–er* or *–est*, see page 771. For a discussion of the information included in dictionary entries, see pages 824–826.

Modifiers that have three or more syllables form the comparative degree by using *more* and the superlative degree by using *most*.

POSITIVE	COMPARATIVE	SUPERLATIVE
powerful	more powerful	most powerful
illegible	more illegible	most illegible
joyfully	more joyfully	most joyfully
attractively	more attractively	most attractively

EXERCISE 1 **Forming the Degrees of Comparison of Modifiers**

Give the forms for the comparative and superlative degrees of the following modifiers. Use a dictionary if necessary.

EXAMPLE **1.** light
1. *lighter; lightest*

1. near
2. proud
3. carefully
4. honestly
5. small
6. tiny
7. timidly
8. enthusiastically
9. safe
10. shady

To show decreasing comparisons, all modifiers form the comparative degree by using *less* and the superlative degree by using *least*.

POSITIVE	COMPARATIVE	SUPERLATIVE
sharp	less sharp	least sharp
costly	less costly	least costly
often	less often	least often
frequently	less frequently	least frequently

Irregular Comparison

The comparative and superlative degrees of some modifiers are not formed by using the regular methods.

POSITIVE	COMPARATIVE	SUPERLATIVE
bad	worse	worst
far	farther	farthest
good	better	best
well	better	best
many	more	most
much	more	most

USAGE

REVIEW A **Writing Comparative and Superlative Forms of Modifiers**

Write the form of the italicized adjective or adverb that will correctly fill the blank in each of the following sentences. You may use a dictionary.

EXAMPLE 1. *unusual* The Corn Palace in Mitchell, South Dakota, is one of the ____ buildings in the United States.
1. *most unusual*

1. *big* The Corn Palace is ____ than I thought it would be.
2. *pretty* People in Mitchell try to make each year's Corn Palace ____ than the one before.
3. *fresh* The building looks the ____ in September after new corn and grasses are put on it.
4. *easy* Some workers find it ____ to saw and nail the corn to panels while others prefer to hang the panels on the building.
5. *good* Which of the huge corn murals on the Corn Palace do you like ____?
6. *mysterious* The enlarged mural of the dancing figure was the ____ to me.
7. *famous* These murals feature Native American scenes designed by Mitchell's ____ artist, Oscar Howe.
8. *interesting* The life of this Sioux artist is the ____ story I've ever heard.

9. *slowly* My parents walked ____ around the Corn Palace than I did and studied every design.
10. *far* The family from Mexico traveled ____ than we did to see the Corn Palace.

Special Problems in Using Modifiers

23b. Use *good* to modify a noun or a pronoun. Use *well* to modify a verb.

EXAMPLES The weather was **good** on the day of the match. [*Good* modifies the noun *weather.*]
If you like pears, here is a **good** one. [*Good* modifies the pronoun *one.*]
The trees are producing **well** this fall. [*Well* modifies the verb phrase *are producing.*]

Good should not be used to modify a verb.

NONSTANDARD Both teams played good.
STANDARD Both teams played **well.**

REFERENCE NOTE: For a discussion of standard and nonstandard English, see page 387.

Well may be used as an adjective meaning "in good health" or "pleasing in appearance."

EXAMPLES **Mom feels quite well today.** [Meaning "in good health," *well* modifies *Mom.*]
Damon looks well in bright colors. [Meaning "pleasing in appearance," *well* modifies *Damon.*]

23c. Use adjectives, not adverbs, after linking verbs.

Linking verbs are often followed by predicate adjectives modifying the subject.

EXAMPLES Ingrid looked **sleepy** [not *sleepily*] this morning. [The predicate adjective *sleepy* modifies the subject *Ingrid.*]
Kadeem felt **uncertain** [not *uncertainly*] about the race. [The predicate adjective *uncertain* modifies the subject *Kadeem.*]

NOTE: Some linking verbs can also be used as action verbs. As action verbs they may be modified by adverbs.

EXAMPLES Ingrid looked **sleepily** at the clock. [*Sleepily* modifies the action verb *looked.*]
Kadeem felt his way **uncertainly** along the hall. [*Uncertainly* modifies the action verb *felt.*]

REFERENCE NOTE: For a list of linking verbs, see page 448.

EXERCISE 2 **Using Adjectives and Adverbs Correctly**

Choose the adjective or adverb in parentheses that will make the sentence correct.

EXAMPLE 1. John seems (*nervous, nervously*) about his speech.
1. *nervous*

1. When we came into the house after ice-skating, the fire felt (*good, well*).
2. The wind blew (*fierce, fiercely*) all night.

3. Tino looked (*good, well*) after his trip to Mexico.
4. We moved (*slow, slowly*) along the trail.
5. Venus looks (*beautiful, beautifully*) tonight.
6. Liang cooked a (*good, well*) meal of vegetables, shrimp, and noodles.
7. We (*sure, surely*) enjoyed seeing you again.
8. We checked the boat (*close, closely*) for leaks.
9. A cup of soup tastes (*good, well*) on a cold day.
10. The ball was caught (*easy, easily*) by the shortstop.

23d. Avoid double comparisons.

A ***double comparison*** is the use of both *–er* and *more* (less) or *–est* and *most* (least) to form a comparison. When you make a comparison, use only one form, not both.

NONSTANDARD This is Kathleen Battle's most finest performance.
STANDARD This is Kathleen Battle's **finest** performance.

NONSTANDARD His hair is more curlier than his sister's.
STANDARD His hair is **curlier** than his sister's.

EXERCISE 3 Revising Sentences to Eliminate Double Comparisons

For each of the following sentences, identify the incorrect modifier. Then give the correct form of the modifier.

EXAMPLES
1. I have been studying more harder lately.
1. *more harder—harder*
2. Frederick Douglass was one of the most brilliantest speakers against slavery.
2. *most brilliantest—most brilliant*

1. Sunday was more rainier than Saturday.
2. That is the most saddest story I have ever heard.
3. Are you exercising more longer than you used to?
4. Native arctic peoples have learned to survive in the most coldest weather.
5. He has a more stronger backhand than his brother.

Double Negatives

23e. Avoid the use of double negatives.

A ***double negative*** is the use of two negative words to express one negative idea.

Common Negative Words

barely	never	none	nothing
hardly	no	no one	nowhere
neither	nobody	not (–n't)	scarcely

NONSTANDARD We couldn't hardly move in the subway car.
STANDARD We **could** hardly move in the subway car.

NONSTANDARD Yolanda didn't eat no breakfast this morning.
STANDARD Yolanda didn't eat **any** breakfast this morning.
STANDARD Yolanda ate **no** breakfast this morning.

EXERCISE 4 **Revising Sentences by Eliminating Double Negatives**

Revise each of the following sentences to eliminate the double negative.

EXAMPLE **1.** I couldn't find no one to go camping with.
1. *I couldn't find anyone to go camping with.*
or
I could find no one to go camping with.

1. I didn't see no one I knew at the game.
2. Early Spanish explorers searched that area of Florida for gold, but they didn't find none.
3. We couldn't hardly hear the guest speaker.
4. The cafeteria didn't serve nothing I like today.
5. Double negatives don't have no place in standard English.

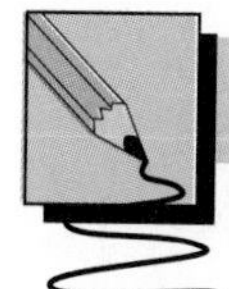

WRITING APPLICATION

Using Clear Comparisons in a Letter

You use comparisons every day to describe changes in the world and in yourself. For instance, your hairstyle may be *shorter* (or *longer*) this year than it was last year. An intersection near your school may be *more dangerous* in the morning than in the afternoon. Complete comparisons help you express your thoughts and observations clearly.

INCOMPLETE The library seems noisier today. [noisier than what?]

COMPLETE The library seems noisier today than it was yesterday.

WRITING ACTIVITY

An anonymous donor has given a large sum of money for improvements to your school. The school's administrators have invited students to suggest practical uses for the money. Write a letter to the administrators describing the improvements you'd like to see. Use at least three comparative and two superlative forms of adjectives and adverbs in your writing.

Prewriting What facilities, equipment, or supplies would make your school a better place? Does your school need a computer lab? more athletic equipment? a bigger library? List all the improvements you can think of. You may want to discuss your ideas with a classmate or a teacher before you select the ones to include in your letter. Also note *why* the improvements are needed. List some ways that these improvements would change life at your school.

Writing As you write your first draft, use your list to help you make clear and accurate comparisons. Keep your audience in mind. The administrators need practical suggestions for how to spend the money. Let them know exactly what improvements your school needs and why. For more about writing persuasion, see Chapter 8.

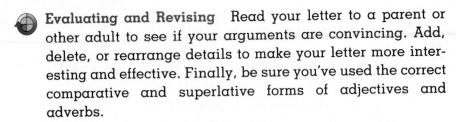

Evaluating and Revising Read your letter to a parent or other adult to see if your arguments are convincing. Add, delete, or rearrange details to make your letter more interesting and effective. Finally, be sure you've used the correct comparative and superlative forms of adjectives and adverbs.

Proofreading Check the form of your letter to make sure it follows the guidelines for business letters (see pages 838–842). Be sure you've used at least three comparative and two superlative forms of adjectives and adverbs. Read through your letter a final time to catch any errors in spelling, grammar, usage, or punctuation.

USAGE

REVIEW B **Using Modifiers Correctly**

Most of the following sentences contain errors in the use of modifiers. Revise each incorrect sentence to eliminate the error. If a sentence is correct, write C.

EXAMPLE 1. My cold is worst today than it was yesterday.
1. *My cold is worse today than it was yesterday.*

1. She is the funnier of the two comedians.
2. Kendo, a Japanese martial art, is more gracefuller than many other sports.
3. No one in our class can play chess as good as Sylvia Yee.
4. Time passes too slow during the summer.
5. After a long swim, she felt good.
6. I wasn't hardly able to hear you.
7. Which of the twins is strongest?
8. Some people don't seem to have no control over their tempers.
9. He hardly ever visits us.
10. Of all the folk dances my grandfather taught me, the polka is the most funnest.

REVIEW C Writing Sentences with Correct Forms of Modifiers

When you watch television, you probably don't think about how a show is created. This diagram of a TV studio shows some of the jobs and equipment involved in producing a show. Which of these jobs might you be interested in doing? Would you rather be in front of the camera or behind the scenes? Imagine that you are working in this studio. Write five sentences describing what you do or telling about the show or your coworkers. Use five of the following items correctly in your sentences. Underline each one you use.

- the superlative of *new*
- the comparative of *good*
- a linking verb and a predicate adjective
- *barely* to express a negative idea
- the positive of *well*
- the superlative of *loud*
- the comparative of *popular*
- a decreasing comparison of *costly*

EXAMPLE **1.** *The new spotlight is better than the old one.*

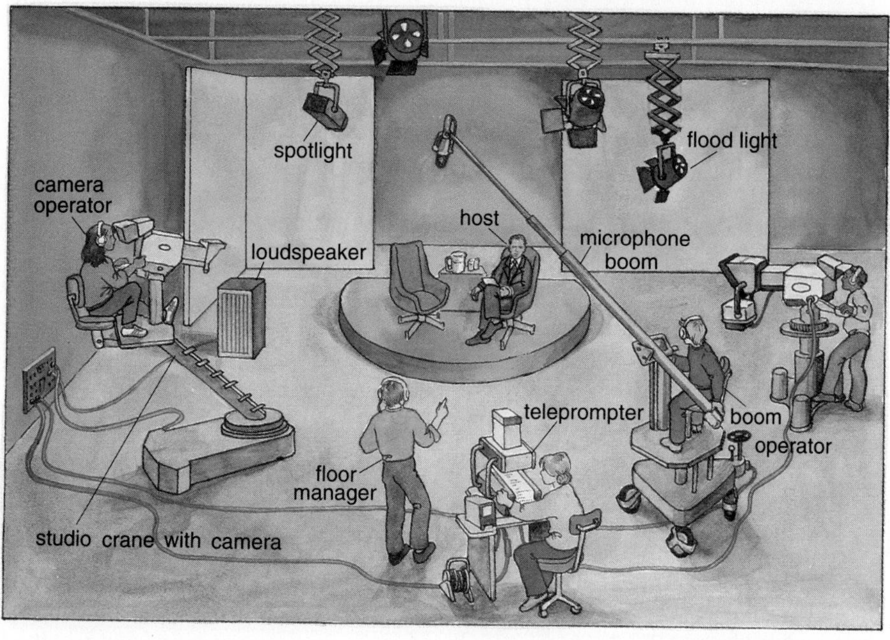

Placement of Modifiers

Notice how the meaning of these sentence changes when the position of the phrase *from Cincinnati* changes.

EXAMPLES The basketball player **from Cincinnati** gave a TV interview for his fans. [The phrase modifies *player.*]

The basketball player gave a TV interview for his fans **from Cincinnati.** [The phrase modifies *fans.*]

From Cincinnati, the basketball player gave a TV interview for his fans. [The phrase modifies *gave.*]

23f. Place modifying phrases and clauses as close as possible to the words they modify.

Prepositional Phrases

A ***prepositional phrase*** begins with a preposition and ends with a noun or a pronoun.

REFERENCE NOTE: For more information about prepositions, see pages 460–464. For more about prepositional phrases, see pages 491–497.

A prepositional phrase used as an adjective should be placed directly after the word it modifies.

MISPLACED The hat belongs to that girl with the green feather.

CLEAR The hat **with the green feather** belongs to that girl.

A prepositional phrase used as an adverb should be placed near the word it modifies.

MISPLACED She read that a new restaurant had opened in today's newspaper.

CLEAR **In today's newspaper** she read that a new restaurant had opened.

Avoid placing a prepositional phrase so that it seems to modify either of two words. Place the phrase so that it clearly modifies the word you intend it to modify.

MISPLACED **Manuel said in the afternoon he would call Janet.** [Does the phrase modify *said* or *would call*?]

CLEAR Manuel said he would call Janet **in the afternoon.** [The phrase modifies *would call.*]

CLEAR **In the afternoon** Manuel said he would call Janet. [The phrase modifies *said.*]

EXERCISE 5 Revising Sentences with Misplaced Prepositional Phrases

The meaning of each of the following sentences is not clear and sensible because the modifying phrase is misplaced. Decide where the phrase belongs; then revise the sentence.

EXAMPLE **1.** In the United States, Zora Neale Hurston grew up in the first self-governed black township.
1. *Zora Neale Hurston grew up in the first self-governed black township in the United States.*

1. That woman was out walking her dog in high heels and a tweed suit this morning.
2. The poster caught my eye on the wall.
3. Hoy taught us with chopsticks how to scoop up rice.
4. Our teacher said on Monday the class would put on a play.
5. Don't forget to take the box to the store with the empty bottles.

EXERCISE 6 Placing Prepositional Phrases Correctly

Rewrite each of the following sentences, adding the prepositional phrase given in parentheses. Be careful to place each prepositional phrase near the word or words it modifies.

EXAMPLE **1. Many paintings show strange, fantastical scenes. (by Marc Chagall)**

1. ***Many paintings by Marc Chagall show strange, fantastical scenes.***

1. Chagall's *The Green Violinist* contains many delightful mysteries and surprises. (for the eye and mind)

2. As you can see in the painting, a gigantic violinist sits among the buildings of a small village. (with a green face and hand)

3. Dark windows look just like the windows of the houses. (on the musician's pants)

4. A man waves to the violinist, and a dog taller than a house seems to smile at the music it hears. (above the clouds)

5. As you look at the painting's bright colors, perhaps you can almost hear the enchanting music. (of the green violinist)

Marc Chagall, *The Green Violinist*, 1923–24, Oil on canvas, 78 × $42\frac{3}{4}$ inches, Solomon R. Guggenheim Museum, New York. Gift, Solomon R. Guggenheim, 1937. Photo: David Heald copyright Solomon R. Guggenheim Foundation, New York. FN 37.446

Participial Phrases

A ***participial phrase*** consists of a verb form—either a present participle or a past participle—and its related words. A participial phrase modifies a noun or a pronoun.

☞ **REFERENCE NOTE:** For more information about participial phrases, see page 504.

Like a prepositional phrase, a participial phrase should be placed as close as possible to the word it modifies.

EXAMPLES **Walking to school,** Celia and James found a wallet. [The participial phrase modifies *Celia* and *James.*]

I. M. Pei, born in China, is a gifted architect. [The participial phrase modifies *I. M. Pei.*]

REFERENCE NOTE: For more about using commas with participial phrases, see pages 713 and 720.

A participial phrase that is not placed next to the noun or pronoun that it modifies is a ***misplaced modifier.***

MISPLACED **Stolen from the media center,** the deputies found the video recorder. [Were the deputies stolen from the media center?]

CLEAR The deputies found the video recorder **stolen from the media center.**

MISPLACED **Sleeping on the roof,** I saw the neighbor's cat. [Was I sleeping on the roof?]

CLEAR I saw the neighbor's cat **sleeping on the roof.**

MISPLACED We're used to the noise **living by the airport.** [Was the noise living by the airport?]

CLEAR **Living by the airport,** we're used to the noise.

A participial phrase that does not clearly and sensibly modify a word in the sentence is a ***dangling modifier.***

DANGLING **Cleaning the attic,** an old trunk was found.

CLEAR **Cleaning the attic, we** found an old trunk.

EXERCISE 7 Revising Sentences with Misplaced or Dangling Participial Phrases

Revise all sentences that contain misplaced or dangling participial phrases. [Hint: You will need to add, delete, or rearrange some words.] Participial phrases that begin or interrupt sentences should be set off by commas. If a sentence is correct, write *C.*

EXAMPLE 1. Made from matzo meal, Rachel shapes tasty dumplings.

1. *Rachel shapes tasty dumplings made from matzo meal.*

1. Pacing in its cage, I watched the lion.
2. Talking on the telephone, Lori did not hear the doorbell.
3. Exploring the cave, a new tunnel was discovered.
4. Wearing a bright orange suit and floppy yellow shoes, the circus featured a clown.
5. Filled with daisies, the girls walked through the field.
6. Reading his part, the actor felt nervous.
7. The turkey was large enough for three families stuffed with sage and bread crumbs.
8. Tired from the long walk through the snow, food and rest were welcomed.
9. Checking the shelves, Judy found the books she needed.
10. Perched in their nest, we saw the young birds.

USAGE

EXERCISE 8 **Writing Sentences with Participial Phrases**

What's going on at the neighbors' house? You were on your way inside your house when loud voices caught your attention. You look next door and see this scene.

Write five sentences about what you see and what happens next. In your sentences, use five of the following participial phrases correctly. Use two of the phrases at the beginning of sentences and three within sentences. [Note: Make sure you use each phrase as a modifier, not as part of a verb phrase.]

- alarmed by the noise
- shaking like a wet dog
- hidden from view
- creeping closer to the door
- lying on the sidewalk
- laughing at the shadow
- perched in the tree
- blinded by the sudden light

EXAMPLE **1.** *The shadow creeping closer to the door frightened me, too.*

Adjective Clauses

An ***adjective clause*** modifies a noun or a pronoun. Most adjective clauses begin with a relative pronoun—*that, which, who, whom,* or *whose.*

REFERENCE NOTE: For more information about adjective clauses, see pages 520–521.

Like adjective phrases, adjective clauses should be placed directly after the words they modify.

MISPLACED The picnic in the park **that we had** was fun. [Did we have the park?]

CLEAR The picnic **that we had** in the park was fun.

MISPLACED The girls thanked their coach **who won the relay race.** [Did the coach win the relay race?]

CLEAR The girls **who won the relay race** thanked their coach.

EXERCISE 9 Revising Sentences with Misplaced Clause Modifiers

Revise each of the following sentences by placing the adjective clause near the word it should modify.

EXAMPLE **1. I showed the fabric to my sister that was made in Kenya.**

1. ***I showed the fabric that was made in Kenya to my sister.***

1. The students received an A who made the first presentation.
2. The kitten belongs to my neighbor that is on the branch.
3. My friend Beverly visited me who lives in Sarasota, Florida.
4. The doctor said that the triplets were healthy who examined them.
5. The cleanup program was supported by all of the students that the president of the seventh-grade class suggested.

PICTURE THIS

You have just witnessed this accident. No one has been hurt, but both drivers are very upset. Each driver insists that the other is to blame. Because you are a witness, the police would like you to describe what happened. Write a brief description of what you saw up to the time of the accident and when the accident occurred. In your description, use at least five adjective clauses.

Subject: traffic accident
Audience: police officers
Purpose: to give an accurate description

REVIEW D **Identifying and Correcting Errors in the Use of Modifiers**

USAGE

Each of the following sentences contains an error in the form or placement of a modifier. Revise each sentence by changing the form of a modifier or by adding, deleting, or rearranging words.

EXAMPLE **1. The record was the sound track of the movie that we heard.**
1. ***The record that we heard was the sound track of the movie.***

1. My stepsister plays both soccer and softball, but she likes soccer best.
2. The waiter brought plates to Terrell and me piled high with spaghetti and meat sauce.
3. Janet's cartoon is more funnier than yours.
4. Barking and growling, the stranger was frightened by the dogs.
5. The German cuckoo clock still runs good after all these years.
6. I didn't do too bad on the geography quiz this morning.
7. Our puppy is much more playfuller than our older dog is.
8. We drove slow past the duck pond to see if any new ducklings had hatched.
9. They never did find no sponsor for their team.
10. I have never been more happier in my life.

REVIEW E Proofreading Sentences for Correct Use of Modifiers

Each of the following sentences contains an error in the form or placement of a modifier. Revise each sentence by changing the form of a modifier or by adding, deleting, or rearranging words.

EXAMPLE **1.** Of all the actors on the TV series *Life Goes On,* Chris Burke is the one I admire more.

1. *Of all the actors on the TV series* Life Goes On, *Chris Burke is the one I admire the most.*

USAGE

1. Born with Down's syndrome, Chris is the younger of four children.
2. Chris decided that he would be a TV star at the age of five.
3. He plays a character on the show whose name is Corky.
4. Chris's acting impressed the director in the pilot show for the series.
5. I read that *Life Goes On* is one of the most popular TV shows in the newspaper.
6. In the picture below, Chris (the most farthest person on the left) takes a break during filming.
7. As you can see, Chris doesn't hardly seem nervous about being a TV star.

8. Saying he has "Up Syndrome," Chris's attitude is usually positive.
9. Chris feels really well when he reads his fan mail, especially letters from other people with Down's syndrome.
10. Fans of the show agree that an actor is a great role model who has overcome many obstacles.

Review: Posttest

A. Revising Sentences by Correcting Errors in the Use of Modifiers

Most of the following sentences contain errors in the form or placement of modifiers. If a sentence has an error, rewrite the sentence correctly. If a sentence is correct, write *C*.

EXAMPLE **1. There wasn't nothing missing.**
1. *There wasn't anything missing.*
or
There was nothing missing.

1. Weigh both packages to see which is heaviest.
2. With care, this car will run good for years.
3. Did you read that Eduardo Mata received an award in the newspaper?
4. We always pass a Czech bakery walking to school.
5. The bean soup tasted good.
6. I think the play *Fiddler on the Roof* is better than the movie.
7. Who is the most smartest person you've ever met?
8. Jason tried to push the huge desk but couldn't hardly move it.
9. The balloons startled the younger children when they burst.
10. A jet taking off can sound more noisier than a jackhammer.

USAGE

B. Revising Sentences by Correcting Errors in the Use of Modifiers

Most of the following sentences contain errors in the form or placement of modifiers. If a sentence has an error, rewrite the sentence correctly. If a sentence is correct, write *C.*

EXAMPLE **1.** This gold and silver French franc is the most prettiest coin I've seen.

1. *This gold and silver French franc is the prettiest coin I've seen.*

11. A coin dealer looked at my collection that has a shop near my house.
12. He examined two old Greek coins but couldn't see no date.
13. The shinier coin looked newer.
14. It turned out to be the oldest of the two, however.
15. I showed one coin to the dealer valued at nearly twenty dollars.
16. He said he couldn't hardly pay more than fifteen dollars for it.
17. If I could bargain good, I might get more for it.
18. Those two coins come from Ireland that have harp designs on them.
19. Collecting coins, my knowledge about other countries and peoples increases.
20. I polished my Saudi Arabian fifty-halala piece good so that I could see the Arabic writing on it.

24 A Glossary of Usage

Common Usage Problems

USAGE

Diagnostic Test

Revising Sentences by Correcting Errors in Usage

In each of the following sets of sentences, one sentence contains an error in usage. Choose the letter of the sentence that contains an error. Revise the sentence, using standard English.

EXAMPLE **1. a.** Bring the books here.
b. I was somewhat embarrassed.
c. Please return these here books.
1. *c. Please return these books.*

1. a. Who's book is it?
b. There is your hat.
c. He is the man who owns the shop.

2. a. I would of gone with you.
b. You're my friend.
c. They're here.

3. a. These kinds of games are challenging.
   b. They bought themselves new shoes.
   c. Can you fix this here shelf?
4. a. I use to know the title of this song.
   b. That headdress looks as if it is genuine.
   c. Set the bucket down on the porch.
5. a. We sat on straw mats called *tatami*.
   b. That fruit salad is real tasty.
   c. You ought to try it.
6. a. If we had liked it, we would have bought it.
   b. The cat jumped off of the chair.
   c. Please wait outside the office.
7. a. She looks like her sister.
   b. They went somewhere together.
   c. He acts like he is tired.
8. a. I made less mistakes this time.
   b. My brother is learning how to dive.
   c. Jack is somewhat nervous.
9. a. I like this type of pen.
   b. I know how come he won.
   c. Marco served himself some meatloaf.
10. a. The monkey scratched its head.
    b. It's not here.
    c. We had ought to check the weather report.
11. a. Our chorus sang good.
    b. Clog dancing gives you a good workout.
    c. Sofía plays the castanets well.
12. a. I looked everywhere.
    b. The balloon burst.
    c. Bring the box over there.
13. a. You should have been there.
    b. Tom and Sabrena they are in my English class.
    c. It's been a cold winter.
14. a. We shared the popcorn among the three of us.
    b. From here she looks like Karen.
    c. Where is the lake at?
15. a. Bill looks as if he is upset.
    b. The milk smells badly.
    c. We had scarcely enough books for everyone.

16. a. They sang a lot of ballads.
    b. The meal was alright.
    c. Alan had already left.
17. a. Everyone can go accept Ramón.
    b. She worked for half an hour.
    c. I rode an elephant.
18. a. Marco grew up in Honduras.
    b. The musicians were already to begin playing.
    c. They divided the task among the six workers.
19. a. Use less water in the mixture.
    b. Music makes me feel good.
    c. We looked everywheres for red suede shoes.
20. a. That kimono looks good on you.
    b. Where did you get them shoes?
    c. They raised the price of stamps.

This chapter contains an alphabetical list, or glossary, of many common problems in English usage. You will notice throughout the chapter that some examples are labeled *standard* or *nonstandard*. ***Standard English*** is the most widely accepted form of English. It is used in *formal* situations, such as speeches and compositions for school, and in *informal* situations, such as conversations and everyday writing. ***Nonstandard English*** is language that does not follow the rules and guidelines of standard English.

REFERENCE NOTE: For more discussion of standard and nonstandard English, see page 387.

a, an Use *a* before words beginning with a consonant sound. Use *an* before words beginning with a vowel sound. Keep in mind that the *sound*, not the actual letter, that a word begins with determines whether *a* or *an* should be used.

EXAMPLES They are building **a** hospital near our house.
I bought **a** one-way ticket.
I would like **an** orange.
We worked for **an** hour.

accept, except *Accept* is a verb; it means "to receive." *Except* may be either a verb or a preposition. As a verb, it means "to leave out." As a preposition, *except* means "excluding."

EXAMPLES Ann **accepted** the gift.
No one will be **excepted** from writing a research paper.
All my friends will be there **except** Jorge.

ain't Avoid this word in speaking and writing; it is nonstandard English.

all right Used as an adjective, *all right* means "satisfactory" or "unhurt." Used as an adverb, *all right* means "well enough." *All right* should always be written as two words.

EXAMPLES Your science project looks **all right** to me. [adjective]
Judy cut her toe, but she is **all right** now. [adjective]
I did **all right** in the drama club tryouts. [adverb]

a lot *A lot* should always be written as two words.

EXAMPLE I have read **a lot** of Native American folk tales.

already, all ready *Already* means "previously." *All ready* means "completely prepared."

EXAMPLES By the time my mother came home, I had **already** cooked dinner.
The students were **all ready** for the trip.

among See **between, among.**

anywheres, everywheres, nowheres, somewheres Use these words without the final *–s*.

EXAMPLE Did you go **anywhere** [not *anywheres*] today?

as See **like, as.**

as if See **like, as if.**

at Do not use *at* after *where.*

NONSTANDARD Where are the Persian miniatures at?
STANDARD Where are the Persian miniatures?

bad, badly *Bad* is an adjective. It modifies nouns and pronouns. *Badly* is an adverb. It modifies verbs, adjectives, and adverbs.

EXAMPLES The fruit tastes **bad.** [The predicate adjective *bad* modifies *fruit.*]
Don't treat him **badly.** [The adverb *badly* modifies the verb *do treat.*]

NOTE: The expression *feel badly* has become acceptable, though ungrammatical, informal English.

INFORMAL Carl felt badly about losing the race.
FORMAL Carl felt **bad** about losing the race.

EXERCISE 1 **Identifying Correct Usage**

Choose the correct word or words in parentheses in each of the following sentences.

EXAMPLE 1. Navajo people came to the Southwest from (*somewhere, somewheres*) in the North.
1. *somewhere*

1. One group of Navajos settled in the region where the Pueblo people (*lived, lived at*).
2. Pueblo artists (*already, all ready*) used powdered paint to make sacred, or religious, pictures on the earth floors of their lodges.
3. The Navajos (*excepted, accepted*) the idea of sacred painting, but they changed the ceremony into sand painting.
4. When the Navajo artists were (*all ready, already*) to begin the ceremony, they gathered in a circle, as shown in the picture on the next page.
5. (*A, An*) artist skilled in sand painting knew which designs to use for different purposes.

6. For example, he might make a certain design when things were not (*all right, alright*) in the community.
7. If someone were injured or feeling (*badly, bad*), the Navajo sand painter would use his art to help heal that person.
8. The ceremony sometimes lasted for several days—(*anywheres, anywhere*) up to nine days, in fact.
9. The traditional art of sand painting (*ain't, hasn't*) disappeared, and artists still take part in the ceremonies.
10. At sunset, the sand paintings are carefully swept away, and the designs are recorded nowhere (*accept, except*) on Navajo blankets, in photographs, and in the artist's imagination.

between, among Use *between* when referring to two things at a time, even though they may be part of a group consisting of more than two.

EXAMPLES Who sits **between** you and Sue?

Between the last three track meets, I trained very hard. [Although there were more than two meets, the training occurred between any two of them.]

There isn't much difference **between** these three brands of juice. [Although there are more than two brands, each one is being compared with the others separately.]

Use *among* when referring to a group rather than to separate individuals.

EXAMPLES We divided the tacos and burritos **among** the five of us.
There was much disagreement **among** the governors about the new tax plan. [The governors are thought of as a group.]

bring, take *Bring* means "to come carrying something." *Take* means "to go carrying something." Think of *bring* as related to *come, take* as related to *go.*

EXAMPLES **Bring** that chair here.
Now **take** this one over there.

bust, busted Avoid using these words as verbs. Use a form of either *burst* or *break.*

EXAMPLES The pipe **burst** [not *busted*] after the storm.
The Japanese raku ware vase **broke** [not *busted*] when it fell.

can't hardly, can't scarcely The words *hardly* and *scarcely* are negative words. They should never be used with another negative word.

EXAMPLES I **can** [not *can't*] **hardly** wait to hear your new CD.
We **had** [not *hadn't*] **scarcely** enough food for everyone at the Juneteenth picnic.

REFERENCE NOTE: For more on double negatives, see page 636.

could of Do not write *of* with the helping verb *could.* Write *could have.* Also avoid *ought to of, should of, would of, might of,* and *must of.*

EXAMPLES Abdul could **have** [not *of*] helped us.
You should **have** [not *of*] hung the piñata higher.

don't, doesn't See page 567.

except See **accept, except.**

USAGE

USAGE

everywheres See **anywheres,** etc.

fewer, less *Fewer* is used with plural words. *Less* is used with singular words. *Fewer* tells "how many," *less* tells "how much."

EXAMPLES We had expected **fewer** guests.
Please use **less** salt.

good, well *Good* is always an adjective. Never use *good* to modify a verb; use *well,* which is an adverb.

NONSTANDARD The steel-drum band played good.
STANDARD The steel-drum band played **well.**

Although it is usually an adverb, *well* may be used as an adjective to mean "healthy."

EXAMPLE I did not feel **well** yesterday.

NOTE: *Feel good* and *feel well* mean different things. *Feel good* means "to feel happy or pleased." *Feel well* simply means "to feel healthy."

EXAMPLES Helping others makes me feel **good.**
I went home because I didn't feel **well.**

had of See **of.**

had ought, hadn't ought The verb *ought* should never be used with *had.*

NONSTANDARD You had ought to learn to dance the polka.
You hadn't ought to be late for class.
STANDARD You **ought** to learn to dance the polka.
You **oughtn't** to be late for class.
or
You **should** learn to dance the polka.
You **shouldn't** be late for class.

EXERCISE 2 **Identifying Correct Usage**

Choose the correct word or words in parentheses in each of the following sentences.

EXAMPLE 1. Bike riders (*had ought, ought*) to know some simple rules of safety.
1. *ought*

1. Just about (*everywheres, everywhere*) you go these days you see people riding bikes.
2. Riders who wear helmets have (*fewer, less*) major injuries than riders who don't.
3. When my aunt came for a visit, she (*brought, took*) her bicycle with her.
4. In choosing clothes, cyclists (*can hardly, can't hardly*) go wrong by wearing bright, easy-to-see colors.
5. On busy streets, groups of cyclists should ride in single file and leave space (*among, between*) their bikes in case of sudden stops.
6. Members of cycling clubs may decide (*between, among*) themselves on special communication signals.
7. A cyclist who is involved in an accident should not try to ride home, even if he or she seems to feel (*well, good*).
8. If possible, call a family member or friend who can (*bring, take*) both the rider and the bike home.
9. A tire that is punctured can usually be patched, but you may not be able to fix one that has (*burst, busted*).
10. Many of the cycling accidents that happened last year (*could of, could have*) been avoided if cyclists and motorists had been more careful.

USAGE

REVIEW A **Proofreading a Paragraph for Correct Usage**

Each sentence in the following paragraph contains an error in English usage. Identify each error. Then write the correct usage.

EXAMPLE [1] I should of known that the painting on the next page was done by Grandma Moses.
1. *should of—should have*

[1] My art teacher gave me a assignment to write a report about any artist I chose. [2] Of all the artists that I could of chosen, Grandma Moses appealed to me the most. [3] I went to the library and looked for a quiet place where I could do my research at. [4] I learned that Anna Mary Robertson Moses didn't start painting until she was all ready in her seventies. [5] By then, her children were grown, and she had less responsibilities. [6] Grandma Moses had no art teacher accept herself. [7] As you can see in the self-portrait *Rockabye,* Grandma Moses felt well about her role as a grandmother. [8] She holds one baby in her lap while the other one rocks in a cradle among the artist and the dog. [9] You can't hardly help feeling that she really loves these children. [10] My report is already for class now, and I can't wait to tell my classmates about this remarkable artist.

he, she, they Do not use an unnecessary pronoun after a noun. This error is called the ***double subject.***

NONSTANDARD	Isiah Thomas he was named Most Valuable Player.
STANDARD	Isiah Thomas was named Most Valuable Player.

hisself, theirself, theirselves These words are nonstandard English. Use *himself* and *themselves.*

EXAMPLES Bob hurt **himself** [not *hisself*] during the game.
They served **themselves** [not *theirselves*] last.

how come In informal English, *how come* is often used instead of *why.* In formal English, *why* is always preferred.

INFORMAL I know how come he's upset.
FORMAL I know **why** he is upset.

its, it's *Its* is a personal pronoun in the possessive case. *It's* is a contraction of *it is* or *it has.*

EXAMPLES The kitten likes **its** new home. [possessive pronoun]
We have Monday off because **it's** the Rosh Hashanah holiday. [contraction of *it is*]
It's been a long day. [contraction of *it has*]

kind, sort, type The words *this, that, these,* and *those* should agree in number with the words *kind, sort,* and *type. This* and *that* are singular. *These* and *those* are plural.

EXAMPLES **That kind** of watch is expensive. [singular]
Those kinds of jokes are silly. [plural]

kind of, sort of In informal English, *kind of* and *sort of* are often used to mean "somewhat" or "rather." In formal English, *somewhat* or *rather* is preferred.

INFORMAL I feel kind of tired.
FORMAL I feel **somewhat** tired.

learn, teach *Learn* means "to acquire knowledge." *Teach* means "to instruct" or "to show how."

EXAMPLES My brother is **learning** how to drive.
The driving instructor is **teaching** him.

less See **fewer, less.**

lie, lay See page 598.

like, as *Like* is a preposition and therefore introduces a prepositional phrase. In informal English, *like* is often used as a conjunction meaning "as." In formal English, *as* is always preferred.

EXAMPLES Your uncle's hat looked **like** a sombrero. [*Like* introduces the phrase *like a sombrero.*]
Marcia trained every day **as** the coach had suggested. [*As the coach had suggested* is a clause and needs the conjunction *as* (not the preposition *like*) to introduce it.]

REFERENCE NOTE: For more information about prepositional phrases, see pages 491–497. For more information about clauses, see Chapter 18.

like, as if, as though In formal written English, *like* should not be used for the subordinating conjunction *as if* or *as though.*

EXAMPLES The Swedish limpa bread looks **as if** [not *like*] it is ready.
The car looks **as though** [not *like*] it needs to be washed.

might of, must of See **could of.**

nowheres See **anywheres,** etc.

EXERCISE 3 Identifying Correct Usage

Choose the correct word or words in parentheses in each of the following sentences.

EXAMPLE 1. Young rattlesnakes (*learn, teach*) themselves to use their rattles by imitating their parents.
1. *teach*

1. (*Its, It's*) a sound that most people have learned to dread.
2. As you can see on the next page, the snake's rattle consists of "buttons" of flesh at the end of (*its, it's*) tail, which are shaken against rings of loose skin.

3. The rings of skin (*themselves, theirselves*) are fragile and can break.
4. (*As, Like*) zookeepers have discovered, snakes that rattle at visitors all day may damage their rattles.
5. (*These kind, These kinds*) of snakes are highly poisonous, but they do not attack unless threatened.
6. Not all scientists agree about (*how come, why*) certain snakes have rattles.
7. According to many scientists, rattlesnakes (*they use, use*) the rattling sound to frighten enemies.
8. Other scientists believe that the rattles may act (*like, as*) signals allowing snakes to communicate with each other.
9. As the photograph shows, snakes don't have ears; however, they are (*sort of, rather*) sensitive to sound vibrations.
10. When people hear a rattlesnake, they react (*like, as if*) the situation is an emergency—and it is.

USAGE

of Do not use *of* with prepositions such as *inside, off,* and *outside.*

EXAMPLES We waited **outside** [not *outside of*] the theater for the ticket window to open.
The glass fell **off** [not *off of*] the table.
Only Muslims are allowed **inside** [not *inside of*] the city of Mecca in Saudi Arabia.

Of is also unnecessary with *had*.

EXAMPLE **If we had** [not *had of*] **tried harder, we would have won.**

ought to of See **could of.**

real In informal English, the adjective *real* is often used as an adverb meaning "very" or "extremely." In formal English, *very* or *extremely* is preferred.

INFORMAL Basenji puppies are real quiet because they don't bark.
FORMAL Basenji puppies are **very** quiet because they don't bark.

rise, raise See pages 596–597.

she, he, they See **he,** etc.

should of See **could of.**

sit, set See page 595.

some, somewhat Do not use *some* for *somewhat* as an adverb.

NONSTANDARD I like classical music some.
STANDARD I like classical music **somewhat.**

USAGE

PICTURE THIS

The year is 2045. You are a new crew member on a space station. The amazing view shown on the next page is your first glimpse of Earth from your new quarters. Write a letter to a friend back home describing what you see and explaining how the view makes you feel. In your letter, correctly use five of the following words or expressions.

already	hardly	ought	real
as if	good	its	except
like	less	it's	well

Subject:	the view of Earth from space
Audience:	a friend
Purpose:	to describe the view and your reaction to it

somewheres See **anywheres,** etc.

sort See **kind,** etc.

sort of See **kind of,** etc.

take See **bring, take.**

teach See **learn, teach.**

than, then *Than* is a conjunction. *Then* is an adverb.

EXAMPLES I sing better **than** I act.
We'll eat first, and **then** we'll ride our bikes.

that See **who,** etc.

that there See **this here, that there.**

their, there, they're *Their* is the possessive form of *they.* *There* is used to mean "at that place" or to begin a sentence. *They're* is a contraction of *they are.*

EXAMPLES Do you have **their** CDs?
The lake is over **there.**
There are five movie theaters in town.
They're writing a report on the poet Américo Paredes.

theirself, theirselves See **hisself,** etc.

them *Them* should not be used as an adjective. Use *these* or *those.*

EXAMPLE Where did you put **those** [not *them*] papers?

they See **he,** etc.

this here, that there The words *here* and *there* are not needed after *this* and *that.*

EXAMPLE I like **this** [not *this here*] Chinese dragon kite, but I like **that** [not *that there*] one better.

this kind, sort, type See **kind,** etc.

try and In informal English, *try and* is often used for *try to.* In formal English, *try to* is preferred.

INFORMAL I will try and be there early.
FORMAL I will **try to** be there early.

type See **kind,** etc.

EXERCISE 4 **Identifying Correct Usage**

Choose the correct word or words in parentheses in each of the following sentences.

EXAMPLE 1. The Amish people (*try and, try to*) maintain a simple, traditional way of life.
1. *try to*

1. In the early 1700s, the Amish were not allowed to practice (*their, they're, there*) religion in Germany and Switzerland.
2. Hearing that there was more freedom in North America (*than, then*) in Europe, the Amish came to the New World.
3. Since that time, they have remained (*outside of, outside*) the mainstream of American life.
4. The Amish work (*real, very*) hard at producing organically grown crops.

5. In Amish communities such as (*this, this here*) one, modern conveniences such as telephones, cars, and televisions are not used.
6. The closeness of Amish family life is evident in the way (*these, them*) people build their homes.
7. (*They're, There, Their*) are often three generations—grandparents, parents, and children—living in a large compound made up of several houses.
8. Pictures and photographs are not allowed (*inside of, inside*) Amish homes, but the Amish brighten their plain houses with colorful pillows, quilts, and rugs.
9. If an Amish person gets sick, he or she is almost always cared for by family members rather (*than, then*) by a doctor.
10. The Amish way of life might surprise you (*somewhat, some*), yet Amish communities have thrived in North America for nearly three hundred years.

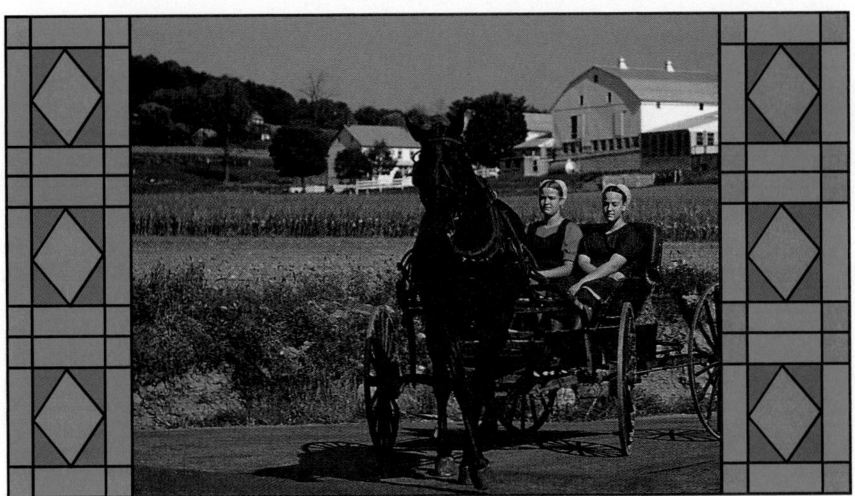

use to, used to Be sure to add the *–d* to *use. Used to* is in the past form.

EXAMPLE Gail **used to** [not *use to*] be on the softball team.

way, ways Use *way,* not *ways,* in referring to a distance.

EXAMPLE Do we have a long **way** [not *ways*] to go?

well See **good, well.**

when, where Do not use *when* or *where* incorrectly in writing a definition.

NONSTANDARD A *homophone* is when a word sounds like another word but has a different meaning and spelling.

STANDARD A *homophone* is a word that sounds like another word but has a different meaning and spelling.

where Do not use *where* for *that.*

EXAMPLE Did you read in the newsletter **that** [not *where*] the teen center is closing?

who, which, that The relative pronoun *who* refers to people only. *Which* refers to things only. *That* refers to either people or things.

EXAMPLES Jolene is the one **who** called. [person]
Here is the salad, **which** is my favorite part of the meal. [thing]
The book **that** you want is here. [thing]
He is the salesperson **that** helped me choose the gift. [person]

who, whom See page 619.

whose, who's *Whose* is the possessive form of *who.* *Who's* is a contraction of *who is* or *who has.*

EXAMPLES **Whose** book is this? [possessive pronoun]
Who's the new student? [contraction of *who is*]
Who's read "A Walk to the Jetty"? [contraction of *who has*]

without, unless Do not use the preposition *without* in place of the conjunction *unless.*

EXAMPLE I can't go **unless** [not *without*] I ask Dad.

would of See **could of.**

your, you're *Your* is the possessive form of *you*. *You're* is the contraction of *you are.*

EXAMPLES **Your** Saint Patrick's Day party was great!
You're a good friend.

EXERCISE 5 Identifying Correct Usage

Choose the correct word or words in parentheses in the following sentences.

EXAMPLE 1. Last week I received a letter from Sandra, (*who's, whose*) a good friend of mine.
1. *who's*

1. When I opened the envelope, I saw (*where, that*) she had sent me these chopsticks and these instructions.

2. "I thought you'd like (*you're, your*) own pair of chopsticks, with instructions for how to use them," Sandra wrote.
3. Instructions like the ones Sandra sent me are helpful because chopsticks can be hard to use (*unless, without*) you are shown how.

4. In the letter, Sandra told me (*that, where*) she and her family had taken a trip to visit her grandparents in New York City.
5. Because Sandra lives in a small town, she wasn't (*use, used*) to the crowds.
6. She especially enjoyed visiting Chinatown, (*which, who*) is located on Manhattan Island.
7. While her family was eating in a Chinese restaurant, one of the servers, (*which, who*) was very helpful, showed her how to use chopsticks.
8. "(*Your, You're*) not going to believe this," she wrote, "but by the end of the meal, I was using chopsticks quite well."
9. *Etiquette* is (*when you use good manners, the use of good manners*), and Sandra claimed, "It was only proper etiquette to use chopsticks to eat Chinese food."
10. I'll write Sandra that I have a long (*ways, way*) to go before I'm an expert in using chopsticks.

REVIEW B Writing Original Sayings with Correct Usage

People throughout the world pass knowledge along from one generation to another. In many cases, such knowledge is stated in a sentence or two called a *folk saying.* While these sayings express bits of wisdom, they are also often humorous. You've probably heard some of the following folk sayings:

If you carry a light, you'll not fear the dark.
It is easier to hear a secret than to keep it.
Learn to behave from those who cannot.
Don't count your chickens before they're hatched.
Slow and steady wins the race.
A penny saved is a penny earned.
Lost time is never found again.

Write five sayings of your own. Base each saying on your own experiences or on things you've been told. In your sayings, include the correct use of one of the words in five of the following items. Underline each of these words that you use.

good, well	like, as	who, which, that
its, it's	rise, raise	whose, who's
kind, sort, type	than, then	without, unless
learn, teach	way, ways	your, you're

EXAMPLE **1.** *A horse that keeps walking can go a long way, as long as it doesn't walk in circles.*

WRITING APPLICATION

Using Formal English in a Speech

At formal occasions, you probably wear your best clothes and use your best manners. That's expected. In formal writing and speaking situations, people expect you to "dress up" your language. Of course, you can't put a report or a speech in a tuxedo, but you can express your ideas in formal standard English.

INFORMAL / NONSTANDARD I'm real upset that the mayor's Clean Air Commission ain't come up with a plan for shutting down that there incinerator.

FORMAL / STANDARD I am extremely upset that the mayor's Clean Air Commission has not thought of a plan for shutting down that incinerator.

WRITING ACTIVITY

A local television station has started a new program called *Sound-Off*. Each speaker on the program gets five minutes on the air to express an opinion about a community issue. Some of the issues that have been addressed are crime prevention, pet leash laws, and the addition of more leagues for youth sports. Choose a topic that you think is important, and write a speech to submit to the TV station. Use only formal standard English in your speech.

Prewriting First, choose a specific topic that interests you. You might ask friends, classmates, or relatives to help you brainstorm some ideas. After you've selected your topic, jot down some notes about it. List important facts and information about the issue. Do you have all the information you need? If not, do some research at your school or local library. Also be sure to include your own feelings and opinions about your topic. Finally, make a rough outline of what you want to say.

Writing Use your notes and outline to help you write a draft of your speech. Try to write a lively introduction that will grab your listeners' attention. In your introduction, give a clear statement of opinion. (For more about statements of opinion, see page 248.) Then discuss each supporting point in a paragraph or two. Conclude your speech by restating your main point.

Evaluating and Revising Ask a friend to time you as you read your speech aloud. Then, ask your friend the following questions:

- Is the main idea clear?
- Does the speech give useful information?
- Is the speech convincing?
- Did you hear any informal expressions?

Use the **Glossary of Usage** in this chapter to help you revise any informal or nonstandard usages. If your speech runs longer than five minutes, you'll need to cut or revise some information.

Proofreading Read your speech slowly to check for any errors in grammar, spelling, or punctuation. Be sure that you have correctly spelled the names of people and organizations. (For more about capitalizing proper names, see pages 676–678.)

Review: Posttest

Revising Sentences by Correcting Errors in Usage

Each of the following sentences contains an error in usage. Write each sentence correctly, using standard formal English.

EXAMPLE **1. They did they're best to help.**
1. *They did their best to help.*

1. We are already for our trip to Washington, D.C.
2. Can you tell the difference among these three baseball mitts?
3. Please take those packages to me.
4. Elena had a cold, but she is feeling good now.
5. Mr. Chang he is my t'ai chi ch'uan instructor.
6. Will you learn me how to throw a baseball?
7. May I borrow that there collection of Cheyenne folk tales?
8. Tara might of come with us, but she had to baby-sit.
9. We use to live in Karachi, Pakistan.
10. She is the woman which owns the Great Dane.
11. I dropped the pictures, but I think they're alright.
12. I read in the newspaper where Mayor Alvarez will visit our school.
13. Their the best players on the team.
14. The pipes busted last winter.
15. We cannot go sailing without we wear life jackets.
16. Her new apartment is bigger then her last one.
17. The group went everywheres together.
18. Lydia acted like she was bored.
19. *Antonyms* are when words are opposite in meaning.
20. I hope that you will except my apology.
21. Have you played you're new Natalie Cole CD?
22. Do you know how come the library is closed today?
23. They can't hardly wait for their vacation.
24. I feel well when I am with my friends.
25. Those kind of movies make me laugh.

25 Capital Letters

Rules for Capitalization

MECHANICS

Diagnostic Test

Proofreading Sentences for Correct Capitalization

For each of the following sentences, find the words that should be capitalized but are not. Write the words correctly.

EXAMPLE **1. The Mississippi river lies west of illinois.**
1. *River, Illinois*

1. At the crossbay supermarket, i bought a can of jensen's soup, a loaf of garfield bread, and a box of zoom soapflakes.
2. Aunt janice, who lives in holbrook, arizona, took me to visit petrified forest national park.
3. The rosenbach museum and library in philadelphia is open to the public tuesday through Sunday.
4. The bijou theater is next to my junior high school.
5. In world history class, we learned about queen elizabeth I, the defeat of the spanish armada, and the age of exploration.

6. Ares, hera, and zeus are greek gods whose roman names are mars, juno, and jupiter.
7. *The wind in the willows* is a famous children's book.
8. Dave's housewares store has moved from sixteenth avenue to front street.
9. The lozi people in africa live near the Zambezi river.
10. "Stopping by woods on a snowy evening" is by robert frost, an american poet from new england.
11. Do you know when david souter was appointed to the supreme court?
12. Next monday is memorial day.
13. When we traveled through the south, we visited the antietam national battlefield at sharpsburg, maryland.
14. Shirley ling came from hong kong last year, and she is teaching us about chinese culture.
15. Cayuga lake stretches north from ithaca, new york.
16. The main religion in indonesia is islam, but there are many indonesian buddhists and hindus.
17. My older sister, who goes to lincoln high school, is taking spanish, history, mathematics II, and art.
18. Carlos and i had sandwiches made of polish ham with german mustard on french bread.
19. We turned west onto route 95 and stayed on it for five miles.
20. George copway, who was born in canada, wrote about his people, the ojibwa.

25a. Capitalize the first word in every sentence.

EXAMPLES **That dog knows several tricks. It will shake hands or roll over when I tell it to.**

The first word of a direct quotation should begin with a capital letter, whether or not the quotation starts the sentence.

EXAMPLE **Mrs. Hernandez said, "Don't forget to bring your contributions for the bake sale."**

Traditionally, the first word of every line of poetry begins with a capital letter.

EXAMPLE **I**n the night
The rain comes down.
Yonder at the edge of the earth
There is a sound like cracking,
There is a sound like falling.
Down yonder it goes on slowly rumbling.
It goes on shaking.

A Papago poem, "In the Night"

NOTE: Some modern poets do not follow this style. If you are quoting from a poem, be sure to follow the capitalization that the poet uses.

REFERENCE NOTE: For information about using capital letters in quotations, see pages 737–738.

25b. Capitalize the pronoun *I*.

EXAMPLE This week **I** have to write two papers.

25c. Capitalize proper nouns.

A ***proper noun*** names a particular person, place, thing, or idea. Such a word is always capitalized. A ***common noun*** names a kind or type of person, place, thing, or idea. A common noun is not capitalized unless it begins a sentence or is part of a title.

PROPER NOUNS	COMMON NOUNS
Central **H**igh **S**chool	high school
Saturday	day
Barbara **J**ordan	woman
Cambodia	country
Lassie	dog
USS ***N**autilus*	submarine

REFERENCE NOTE: For information about using capital letters in abbreviations, see pages 703–704.

Some proper nouns consist of more than one word. In these names, short prepositions (those of fewer than five letters) and articles (*a, an, the*) are not capitalized.

EXAMPLES **H**ouse of **R**epresentatives
Ivan the **T**errible

REFERENCE NOTE: For more discussion of proper nouns, see page 424.

(1) Capitalize the names of persons.

EXAMPLES **M**onica **S**one, **A**aron **N**eville, **M**rs. **A**brams, **C**harlayne **H**unter-**G**ault

(2) Capitalize geographical names.

TYPE OF NAME	EXAMPLES	
Continents	Europe Antarctica	South America Asia
Countries	Australia El Salvador	Egypt Finland
Cities, Towns	Miami Los Angeles	Indianapolis Manila
States	Tennessee Rhode Island	Delaware Wyoming
Islands	Aleutian Islands Crete	Long Island Isle of Pines
Bodies of Water	Amazon River Chesapeake Bay Suez Canal	Lake Ontario Jackson's Pond Indian Ocean
Streets, Highways	Main Street Eighth Avenue	Canary Lane Ventura Highway

NOTE: In a hyphenated street number, the second part of the number is not capitalized.

EXAMPLE West Thirty-fourth Street

MECHANICS

TYPE OF NAME	EXAMPLES	
Parks and Forests	**Y**osemite **P**ark **S**herwood **F**orest	**E**verglades **N**ational **P**ark
Mountains	**C**atskills **M**ount **F**uji	**M**ount **E**verest **A**lps
Sections of the Country	**N**ew **E**ngland the **W**est	**C**orn **B**elt the **S**outheast

NOTE: Words such as *east, west, north,* or *south* are not capitalized when the words merely indicate *direction.*

EXAMPLES A car was going **w**est on Oak Street. [direction]
The **S**outh has produced some of America's great writers. [section of the country]

EXERCISE 1 Correcting Errors in Capitalization

Each of the following sentences contains errors in capitalization. Correct these errors either by changing capital letters to small letters or by changing small letters to capital letters.

EXAMPLE **1.** The original Settlers of hawaii came from the marquesas islands and tahiti.
1. *settlers, Hawaii, Marquesas Islands, Tahiti*

1. our Class is studying about hawaii.
2. The Hawaiian islands are located in the pacific ocean, nearly twenty-four hundred miles West of san francisco, california.
3. Hawaii became the fiftieth State in the united states in 1959.
4. Our teacher, ms. Jackson, explained that the Capital City is honolulu, and it is located on the southeast Coast of oahu island.
5. The largest of the Islands is hawaii.
6. On the southeast shore of hawaii island is hawaii volcanoes national park.
7. Ms. Jackson asked, "can anyone name one of the Volcanoes there?"

8. Since i have been reading about National Parks, i raised my hand.
9. "The Park has two active volcanoes, mauna Loa and kilauea," I answered.
10. "This picture shows how lava from kilauea's eruption threatened everything in its path in 1989," I added.

(3) Capitalize names of organizations, teams, businesses, institutions, and government bodies.

TYPE OF NAME	EXAMPLES	
Organizations	Drama Club Girl Scouts	Modern Language Association
Teams	Boston Celtics Dallas Cowboys	Los Angeles Dodgers
Businesses	Sears, Roebuck and Co.	Fields Department Store
Institutions	Westside Regional Hospital	Roosevelt Junior High School
Government Bodies	United Nations Peace Corps York City Council	Office of Management and Budget

MECHANICS

NOTE: Do not capitalize such words as *hotel, theater,* or *high school* unless they are part of the name of a particular building or institution.

EXAMPLES

Capital Theater	a theater
Lane Hotel	the hotel
Taft High School	this high school

EXERCISE 2 **Using Capitalization Correctly**

Mark Twain and his famous character Huckleberry Finn had many adventures on the Mississippi River. It's a big, long river with room for many adventures! Write your own short story about traveling on the Mississippi. Use the map below to tell about the journey. In your story, use at least five words from the map. Remember to capitalize all names of persons and geographical names.

EXAMPLE *Early on the fourth day, Jason and she knew they were in Kentucky.*

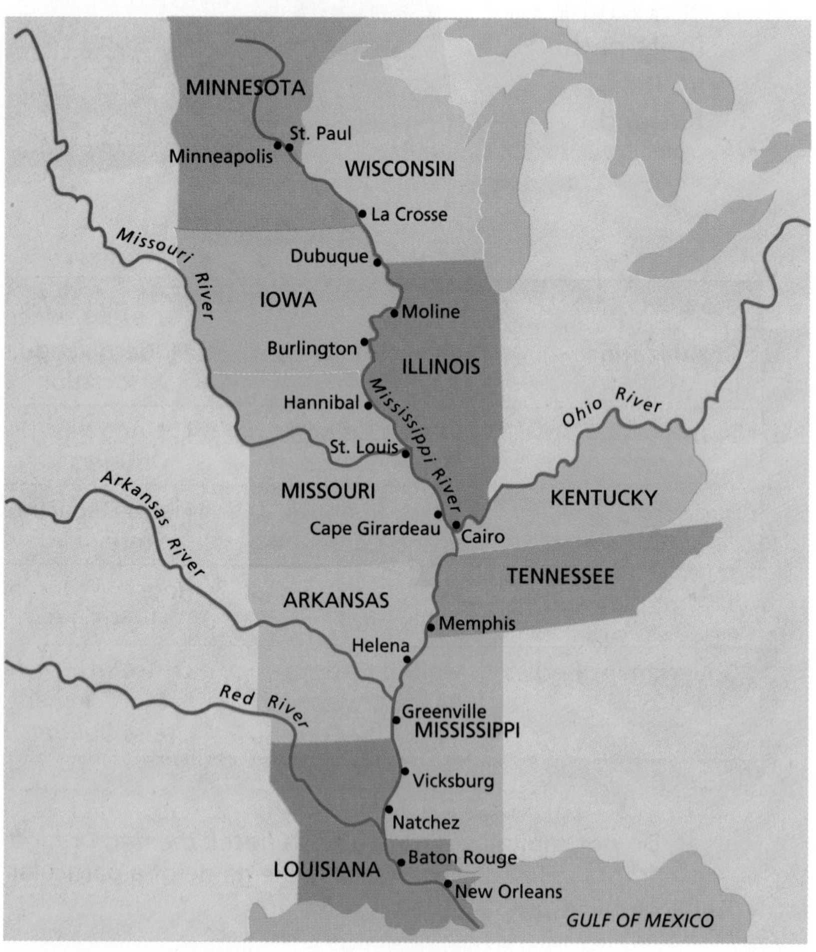

(4) Capitalize the names of historical events and periods, special events, and calendar items.

MECHANICS

TYPE OF NAME	EXAMPLES	
Historical Events and Periods	**R**evolutionary **W**ar **M**iddle **A**ges **R**enaissance	**U**nited **S**tates **B**icentennial **A**ge of **R**eason
Special Events	**T**exas **S**tate **F**air **S**pecial **O**lympics	**S**uper **B**owl **F**estival of **S**tates
Calendar Items	**M**onday **F**ebruary	**M**emorial **D**ay **T**hanksgiving **D**ay

NOTE: Do *not* capitalize the name of a season unless it is part of a proper name.

EXAMPLES the **f**all semester
the Quebec **W**inter Carnival

(5) Capitalize the names of nationalities, races, and peoples.

EXAMPLES **M**exican, **N**igerian, **C**aucasian, **I**roquois

NOTE: The words *black* and *white* may or may not be capitalized when they refer to races.

EXAMPLE In the 1960s, both **B**lacks and **W**hites [*or* **b**lacks and **w**hites] worked to end segregation.

(6) Capitalize the brand names of business products.

EXAMPLES **L**ux soap, **G**eneral **E**lectric stove, **P**epsi **C**ola bottle [Notice that the names of the types of products are not capitalized.]

(7) Capitalize the names of ships, trains, airplanes, and spacecraft.

TYPE OF NAME	EXAMPLES	
Ships	***Q**ueen **E**lizabeth 2*	***K**on **T**iki*
Trains	***C**ity of **N**ew **O**rleans*	***O**rient **E**xpress*
Airplanes	***A**ir **F**orce **O**ne*	***S**pruce **G**oose*
Spacecraft	***V**oyager II*	***S**putnik*

MECHANICS

(8) Capitalize the names of buildings and other structures.

EXAMPLES **S**ydney **O**pera **H**ouse, **W**orld **T**rade **C**enter, **A**swan **D**am, **E**iffel **T**ower, **B**rooklyn **B**ridge

(9) Capitalize the names of monuments and awards.

TYPE OF NAME	EXAMPLES	
Monuments	**S**tatue of **L**iberty **L**incoln **M**emorial	**T**omb of the **U**nknown **S**oldier
Awards	**E**mmy **A**ward **N**obel **P**rize	**D**istinguished **S**ervice **M**edal

(10) Capitalize the names of religions and their followers, holy days, sacred writings, and specific deities.

TYPE OF NAME	EXAMPLES	
Religions and Followers	**J**udaism **H**induism	**C**hristian **M**uslim
Holy Days	**E**aster **R**amadan	**Y**om **K**ippur **C**hristmas **E**ve
Sacred Writings	**K**oran **B**ible	**T**almud **U**panishads
Specific Deities	**G**od **A**llah	**J**ehovah **K**rishna

NOTE: The word *god* is not capitalized when it refers to a god of ancient mythology. The names of specific gods *are* capitalized.

EXAMPLE The king of the Norse **g**ods was **O**din.

(11) Capitalize the names of planets, stars, and other heavenly bodies.

EXAMPLES **M**ercury, **V**enus, **S**irius, **A**ndromeda, **U**rsa **M**ajor

MECHANICS

NOTE: The words *earth, moon,* and *sun* are not capitalized unless they are used along with the names of other heavenly bodies that are capitalized.

EXAMPLES Oceans cover three fourths of the **e**arth's surface.
Which is largest—Saturn or **E**arth?

EXERCISE 3 **Proofreading Sentences for Correct Capitalization**

For each of the following sentences, supply capital letters where they belong.

EXAMPLE **1.** Each arbor day the students at franklin junior high school plant a tree.
1. *Arbor Day, Franklin Junior High School*

1. The golden gate bridge spans the entrance of san francisco bay.
2. Yosemite national park in california has the nation's highest waterfall.
3. The peace corps became an agency of the federal government by an act of congress.
4. On august 4, 1984, upper volta, a nation in africa, changed its name to burkina faso.
5. Thousands of cherokee people live in the smoky mountains in and around cherokee, north carolina.
6. To stop flooding in the south, the tennessee valley authority, a government agency, built thirty-nine dams on the tennessee river and the streams that flow into it.
7. The first two states to be admitted to the united states were delaware and pennsylvania.
8. On new year's day, many fans crowd into football stadiums for the annual bowl games.
9. The rose bowl is the oldest of these annual football bowl games.
10. A noted scholar, thomas jefferson, founded the university of virginia.

EXERCISE 4 Proofreading Paragraphs for Correct Capitalization

In the following paragraphs all capital letters have been omitted. Rewrite the paragraphs, using capitals wherever they are needed.

the branford mall is the largest in melville county. it is on jefferson parkway, two miles north of duck lake state park and the big bridge that crosses duck lake. across the parkway from the mall is the new branford high school with its parking lots, playing fields, and stadium, home of the branford panthers. near the mall are the american legion hall, bowlerama, and king skating rink.

the mall has two jewelry stores, nicholson's department store, the palace cinema, and thirty-five other businesses. they range from small stationery stores to the finest restaurant in the midwest. the restaurant larue is run by marie and jean larue, who are from france. also in the mall is the american paper box company, which sells boxes for every packaging need. an outlet store for northwestern leather goods of chicago sells uffizi purses and wallets.

MECHANICS

REVIEW A Correcting Errors in Capitalization

Each of the following sentences contains errors in capitalization. Correct these errors by either changing capital letters to small letters or changing small letters to capital letters.

EXAMPLE **1. African americans in massachusetts have played an important part in american history.**
1. Americans, Massachusetts, American

1. In Boston, the Crispus attucks monument is a memorial to attucks and the other men who died in the boston Massacre.
2. According to many Historians, attucks was a former slave who fought against the british in the american Revolution.

3. The department of the Interior has made the Home of maria baldwin a historic building in cambridge.
4. Baldwin was a Leader in the league for Community Service, an Organization to help the Needy.
5. One of the founders of the National association for the Advancement of colored people, w.e.b. Du Bois, was born in great Barrington, Massachusetts.
6. A marker stands on the Spot where Du Bois lived.
7. Jan ernst matzeliger, who lived in lynn, invented a machine that made Shoes easier and cheaper to manufacture.
8. The nantucket whaling Museum has information about Peter green, a Sailor and Second Mate on the ship *john Adams.*
9. During a storm at sea, Green saved the Ship and crew after the Captain and First Mate had drowned.
10. Use the Map of Massachusetts shown above to locate the Towns and Cities in which these notable african Americans lived.

25d. Capitalize proper adjectives.

A ***proper adjective*** is formed from a proper noun and is always capitalized.

PROPER NOUN	PROPER ADJECTIVE
Greece	Greek theater
Mars	Martian moons
Darwin	Darwinian theory
Japan	Japanese tea ceremony

25e. Do *not* capitalize the names of school subjects, except course names followed by a number and languages.

EXAMPLES **history, typing, mathematics, English, Spanish, Latin, History 101, Music III, Art Appreciation I**

MECHANICS

EXERCISE 5 Proofreading Sentences for Correct Capitalization

In each of the following sentences, find the word or words that should be capitalized but are not. Write the words correctly.

EXAMPLE **1. Rosa said we were eating real mexican *fajitas.***
1. *Mexican*

1. The program featured russian ballet dancers.
2. The european Common Market helps improve international trade.
3. The scandinavian countries include both Norway and Sweden.
4. In geography, we learned about the platypus and the koala, two australian animals.
5. Many great english plays were written during the elizabethan age.

6. I am planning to take computer I next year.
7. On the floor was a large persian rug.
8. England, France, Scotland, Russia, and the United States played important roles in canadian history.
9. The back yard was decorated with chinese lanterns.
10. Have you ever tasted indian rice pudding?

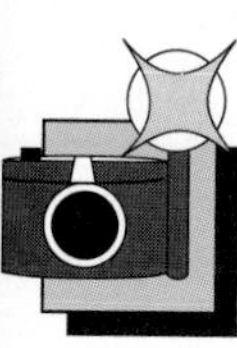

PICTURE THIS

The year is 1845. You and your family are pioneers traveling west in one of these covered wagons. You are using this map to find your way from Independence to Los Angeles. Write a letter describing your journey to a friend back in Independence. You may want to tell about your fellow pioneers, the towns you've passed through, or the rivers and stretches of land you've crossed. You may also want to mention some of the people, places, and things you miss back home. In your letter, use at least three proper nouns and two proper adjectives.

Subject: heading west in a covered wagon
Audience: a friend
Purpose: to describe your journey

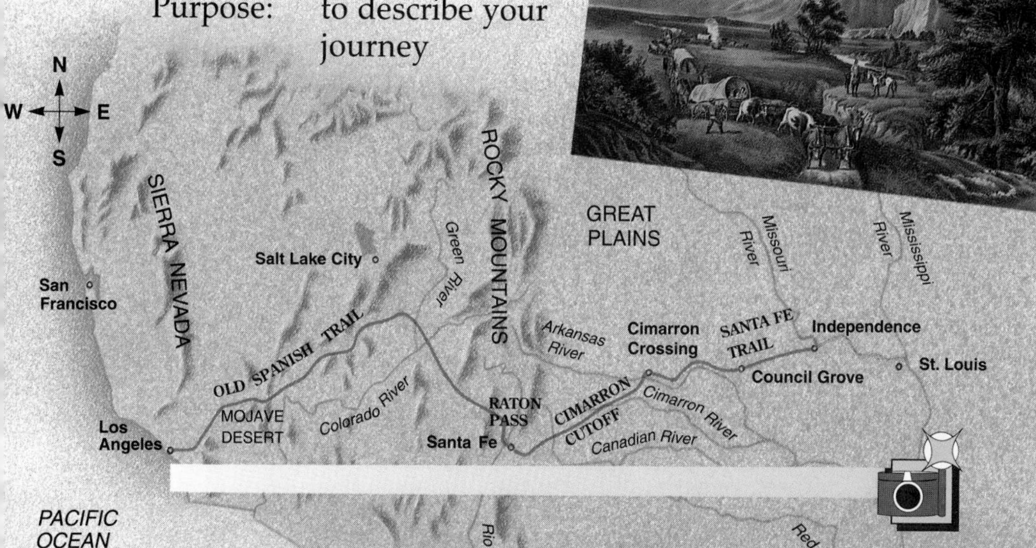

25f. Capitalize titles.

(1) Capitalize the title of a person when the title comes before a name.

EXAMPLES **P**resident Lincoln **M**rs. Wendell
Mayor Bradley **C**ommissioner Rodriguez

REFERENCE NOTE: For more information about abbreviations, see pages 703–704.

(2) Capitalize a title used alone or following a person's name only when you want to emphasize the title of someone holding a high office.

EXAMPLE The **S**ecretary of Defense held a news conference.
Lien Fong, class **s**ecretary, read the minutes.

A title used by itself in direct address is usually capitalized.

EXAMPLES Is it very serious, **D**octor?
How do you do, **S**ir [*or* sir]?

(3) Capitalize a word showing a family relationship when the word is used before or in place of a person's name.

EXAMPLES We expect **U**ncle **F**red and **A**unt **H**elen soon.
We always go to **G**randma **L**owery's house for Thanksgiving dinner.
Both **M**om and **D**ad work at the hospital.

Do not capitalize a word showing a family relationship when a possessive comes before the word.

EXAMPLE We asked Pedro's **m**other and his **a**unt Celia to be chaperons.

(4) Capitalize the first and last words and all important words in titles of books, magazines, newspapers, poems, short stories, movies, television programs, works of art, and musical compositions.

MECHANICS

Unimportant words in titles include

- articles (*a, an, the*)
- coordinating conjunctions (*and, but, for, nor, or, so, yet*)
- prepositions of fewer than five letters (such as *by, for, on, with*)

TYPE OF NAME	EXAMPLES	
Books	*The Mask of Apollo* *Mules and Men* *The Foxfire Book*	*Chicano Authors: Inquiry by Interview*
Magazines	*Popular Mechanics* *Ebony*	*Seventeen* *Sports Illustrated*
Newspapers	*The Miami Herald* the *Houston Post*	*The Wall Street Journal*
Poems	"Season at the Shore"	"In Time of Silver Rain"
Short Stories	"The Night the Bed Fell"	"Zlateh the Goat"
Movies	*Dances with Wolves*	*It's a Wonderful Life*
Television Programs	*Life Goes On* *In Living Color*	*Star Trek: The Next Generation*
Works of Art	*Mona Lisa* *David*	*The Old Guitarist* *Mankind's Struggle*
Musical Compositions	"America the Beautiful"	*The Marriage of Figaro*

NOTE: The article *the* before a title is not capitalized unless it is the first word of the title.

EXAMPLES My father reads the ***Wall Street Journal.***
Does she work for ***The Georgia Review***?

REFERENCE NOTE: For guidelines on what titles are italicized, see pages 735–736. For guidelines on what titles are enclosed in quotation marks, see pages 743–744.

MECHANICS

EXERCISE 6 Proofreading Sentences for Correct Capitalization

Write the following sentences, using capitals wherever they are needed.

EXAMPLE 1. The series *all creatures great and small* is being rerun on public television.

1. *The series* All Creatures Great and Small *is being rerun on public television.*

1. While waiting to interview mayor ward, I read an article in *newsweek.*
2. Have you read leslie marmon silko's poem "story from bear country"?
3. You have probably seen a picture of *the thinker*, one of rodin's best-known sculptures.
4. On television last night we saw a movie called *the three faces of eve.*
5. This year voters will elect a president and several united states senators.
6. Uncle nick read aloud from francisco jiménez's short story "the circuit."
7. The reporter asked, "Can you tell us, senator inouye, when you plan to announce the committee's final decision?"
8. The main speaker was dr. andrew holt, a former president of the university of tennessee.
9. Besides uncle don, our visitors included aunt pat, aunt jean, both of my grandmothers, and my great-grandfather.
10. The president met with his advisers before he spoke to the nation.

REVIEW B Proofreading Sentences for Correct Capitalization

Each of the following sentences contains at least one error in capitalization. Write correctly the words that require capital letters.

MECHANICS

EXAMPLE 1. The waters of the caribbean are pleasantly warm.
1. *Caribbean*

1. The greeks believed that zeus, the king of the gods, lived on mount olympus.
2. The *titanic* sank after hitting an iceberg off the coast of newfoundland.
3. My cousin collects scandinavian pottery.
4. Stephanie is taking english, math II, biology, and world history.
5. On friday we were cheered by the thought that monday, memorial day, would be a holiday.
6. that chair is made of teakwood.
7. I wanted to name my persian cat after the chief justice of the supreme court.
8. In *roots,* alex haley, a famous journalist, traces the history of his family.
9. She usually travels to boston on american airlines.
10. The quaker oats company has introduced a new corn cereal.

REVIEW C **Proofreading a Paragraph for Correct Capitalization**

Each sentence in the following paragraph contains at least one error in capitalization. Write correctly the words that require capital letters.

EXAMPLE [1] Before the thanksgiving holidays, i learned some interesting facts about africa in my history II class.
1. *Thanksgiving, I, Africa, History II*

[1] My teacher, mr. davidson, told us about the mighty kingdoms and empires that existed for hundreds of years in africa. [2] some of these kingdoms dated back to the time of the roman empire. [3] Others rose to power during the period known as the middle ages in europe. [4] For many years, the people in the kingdom of cush did iron-work and traded along the nile river. [5] Later, the cush

were defeated by the people of axum, led by king ezana. [6] As you can see in the map below, kingdoms in west africa developed between lake chad and the atlantic ocean. [7] Three of these kingdoms were ghana, mali, and songhai. [8] These kingdoms established important trade routes across the sahara desert. [9] Tombouctou's famous university attracted egyptian and other arab students. [10] I read more about these african kingdoms and empires in our textbook, *world history: people and nations.*

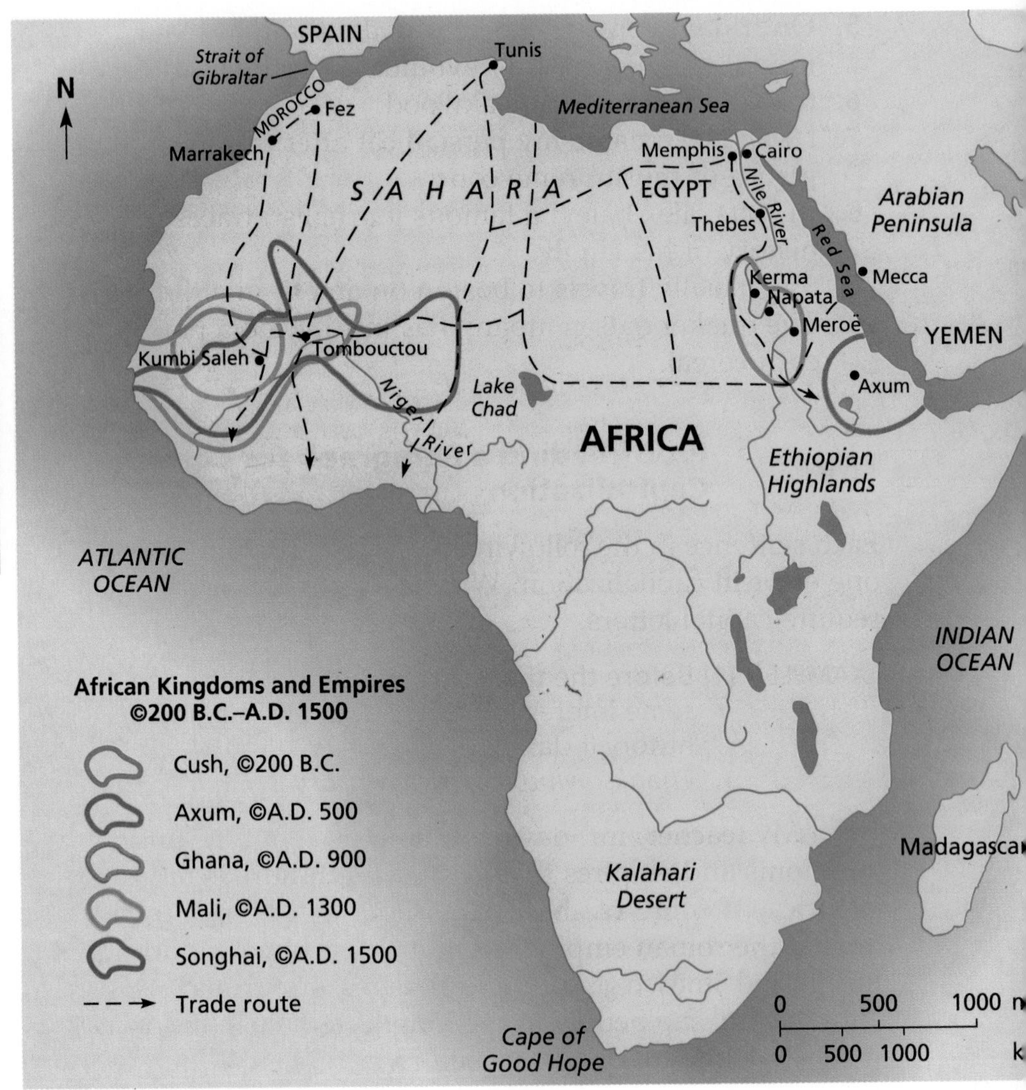

WRITING APPLICATION

Using Capital Letters to Make Your Writing Clear

Used correctly, capital letters help your readers understand your writing. Capital letters signal that you mean a particular person, place, thing, or idea. Compare the following sentences:

I'd like to see the **w**hite **h**ouse.
I'd like to see the **W**hite **H**ouse.

The capital letters in the second sentence completely change the meaning of the sentence. The second sentence refers to the home of the President of the United States, not to just any "white house."

MECHANICS

WRITING ACTIVITY

Students in your class have become pen pals with students in another country. You have been given the name of someone to write to. Write a letter to your pen pal introducing yourself and telling about your school and your community. In your letter, be sure to use capitalization correctly.

Prewriting Note down the information you want to give in your letter. You may wish to include some of the following information:

- your age
- a description of yourself
- your favorite books, movies, actors, or musicians
- the name of your school
- the courses you are taking in school this year
- some clubs, organizations, or special activities you participate in
- a description of your community
- some special places, events, or attractions in your community or state

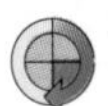

Writing As you write your draft, keep in mind that your pen pal may not recognize names of some people, places, and things in the United States. For example, he or she may not recognize the names of your favorite movies or musical groups. Be sure to use correct capitalization and even brief explanations to make your meaning clear.

Evaluating and Revising Read through your letter carefully. Have you left out any important information? Are any parts of your letter confusing? If so, you may want to add, cut, or revise some details. Is the tone of your letter friendly? Have you followed the correct form for a personal letter? (For more about personal letters, see page 836.)

Proofreading Read over your letter carefully to check for any errors in grammar, spelling, or punctuation. Use the rules in this chapter to help you double-check your capitalization.

MECHANICS

REVIEW D **Correcting Errors in Capitalization**

Each of the following sentences contains errors in capitalization. Correct these errors by either changing capital letters to small letters or changing small letters to capital letters.

EXAMPLE 1. On june 25, 1876, the Sioux and cheyenne warriors defeated general george a. Custer and his Troops.
1. *June, Cheyenne, General George A., troops*

1. The Defeat of gen. custer occurred at the battle of the little bighorn.
2. In december of 1890, many Sioux were killed by the Soldiers in a battle at wounded Knee creek in south Dakota.

3. Both Battles have become part of american History, remembered by artists, writers, and filmmakers.
4. In the late nineteenth century, the sioux Artist Kicking bear painted the *Battle Of The little Bighorn.*
5. The painting, done on muslin Cloth, is shown below.

Kicking Bear (Sioux), *Battle of the Little Big Horn,* 1898, Courtesy of the Southwest Museum, Los Angeles. Photo #184.

6. Kicking bear, who himself fought in the Battle, painted at the pine Ridge agency in south Dakota, where he lived.
7. soldiers who fought against kicking Bear described him as courageous.
8. The well-known American Poet Stephen vincent benét wrote about the battle of wounded knee in a Poem called "american names."
9. More recently, the author Dee brown wrote about the native americans of the west in his book *bury my Heart at Wounded knee.*
10. In 1970, the movie *Little big Man* told the story of a 121-year-old man who survived the Battle against general Custer.

Review: Posttest

Proofreading Sentences for Correct Capitalization

For each of the following sentences, write the words in the sentence that require capitalization. If a sentence is correct, write *C*.

EXAMPLE **1. Next saturday rachel and i will get to watch the filming of our favorite TV show.**
1. *Saturday, Rachel, I*

1. The curtiss soap corporation sponsors the television show called *three is two too many*.
2. The show's theme song is "you and i might get by."
3. My favorite actor on the show is joe fontana, jr., who plays the lovable dr. mullins.
4. The female lead, janelle bledsoe, used to go to our junior high school right here in houston, texas.
5. The action takes place out west, just after the civil war ended.
6. The program is on monday nights, except during the summer.
7. One episode took place at a fourth of july picnic, where dr. mullins challenged the local sheriff to a pie-eating contest.
8. Ms. Bledsoe plays a teacher who is married to Mr. reginald wilson foster II, president of the flintsville National bank.
9. Mrs. foster teaches latin, home economics, and arithmetic I at flintsville's one-room school.
10. One local character, uncle ramón, once played a practical joke on judge grimsby right outside the mayor's office.
11. Some people, including my mother, think that the program is silly, but my father enjoys watching it occasionally.
12. Even i don't think it will receive an emmy from the academy of television arts and sciences.

13. When grandma murray and aunt edna from mobile, alabama, visited us, they watched the program.
14. In that monday night's show, an alien named romax from the planet zarko came to town and stayed at the sidewinder hotel.
15. The alien, who looked like United States president zachary taylor, spoke english perfectly and could read people's minds.
16. He settled a dispute between the union pacific railroad and the flintsville ranchers' association.
17. In another show a united states senator and romax discussed their views of justice.
18. In the silliest show, the people in the next town, longview, thought that a sea monster was living a few miles north in lake cranberry and reported it to the national bureau of endangered species.
19. A week later, mayor murdstone lost his only copy of his secret recipe for irish stew and saw the recipe in the next issue of the *flintsville weekly gazette.*
20. One time a mysterious stranger appeared, claiming he had sailed to the east around cape horn on the ship *the gem of the ocean.*
21. Another time, wealthy landowner mabel platt hired the law firm of crum, lockwood, and tarr to sue mayor murdstone and threatened to take the case all the way to the united states supreme court.
22. In the next episode, a buddhist priest, who just happened to be traveling through the west on his way back to china, stopped off in flintsville and gave some of the townsfolk a few lessons in manners.
23. Once, when someone mistakenly thought he had found gold down at cutter's creek, thousands of prospectors flocked to flintsville, including three bank-robbing members of the feared gumley gang.
24. The programs are taped before an audience in the universal theater in los angeles, california.
25. You can get tickets to be in the audience by writing to curtiss soap corporation, 151 holly avenue, deerfield, michigan 49238.

SUMMARY STYLE SHEET	
Names of Persons	
Emilio Estevez	an actor
Marie Curie	a scientist
Crazy Horse	a leader
Geographical Names	
Fifty-first Street	a dead-end street
Little Rock	the capital of Arkansas
Hidalgo	a county in New Mexico
in the South	traveling south
Kenya	a country in Africa
Galápagos Islands	a group of islands
Indian Ocean	the ocean between Africa and Australia
Everglades National Park	a park in Florida
Appalachian Mountains	hiking in the mountains
Names of Heavenly Bodies	
Jupiter, Venus, Earth	the surface of the earth
Ursa Minor	a constellation
Milky Way	a spiral galaxy
Names of Teams, Organizations, Businesses, Institutions, Government Bodies	
Overton Owls	a softball team
Westboro Writers' Club	the members of the club
American Printing Company	the company she works for
East Side High School	the local high school
Department of Energy	a department of the government
Names of Historical Events and Periods, Special Events, Calendar Items	
Battle of the Little Bighorn	a fierce battle
Ice Age	at an early age
Travis County Fair	a large fair
Veterans Day	a national holiday
June	summer

(continued)

MECHANICS

SUMMARY STYLE SHEET *(continued)*

Names of Nationalities, Races, Religions	
Turkish	a **n**ationality
Caucasian	a **r**ace
Judaism	a **r**eligion
God	a **g**od of **G**reek mythology
Names of Buildings, Monuments, Awards	
Copley **H**otel	a fancy **h**otel
the **G**eneral **A**ssembly **B**uilding	a United Nations **b**uilding
Washington **M**onument	a national **m**onument
Names of Trains, Ships, Airplanes, Spacecraft	
***S**uper **C**hief*	a **t**rain
***T**itanic*	a **s**hip
***A**ir **F**orce **O**ne*	an **a**irplane
***C**hallenger*	a **s**pace **s**huttle
Brand Names	
Nike shoes	**r**ed **s**hoes
Fab detergent	**l**aundry **d**etergent
Names of Languages, School Subjects	
English, **D**utch, **C**ree, **S**panish	a **f**oreign **l**anguage
Algebra I, **B**iology II, **M**usic 104	**a**lgebra, **b**iology, **m**usic
Titles	
Senator **S**uarez	a **s**enator from my state
President of the United States	the **p**resident of the club
Aunt **M**artha	my **a**unt
How are you, **A**unt?	
***U**p from **S**lavery*	a **b**ook
***T**een*	a **m**agazine
***T**he **N**ew **Y**ork **T**imes*	a **n**ewspaper
"**H**ector the **C**ollector"	a **p**oem
"**T**he **H**ouse on **M**ango **S**treet"	a **s**hort **s**tory
***T**eenage **M**utant **N**inja **T**urtles*	a **m**ovie, a **p**lay
***A** **D**ifferent **W**orld*	a **t**elevision **p**rogram
***T**he **P**umpkin **P**atch*	a **p**ainting
"**T**he **S**tar-**S**pangled **B**anner"	a **n**ational **a**nthem

MECHANICS

26 PUNCTUATION

End Marks, Commas, Semicolons, Colons

MECHANICS

Diagnostic Test

Using End Marks, Commas, Semicolons, and Colons to Punctuate Sentences Correctly

The following sentences lack necessary punctuation. Write each sentence, inserting the correct punctuation.

EXAMPLE **1. After I read my history assignment I did my other homework but I did not finish it**
1. *After I read my history assignment, I did my other homework, but I did not finish it.*

1. The following students gave their reports yesterday Carlos Sue and Alan
2. Tanay's grandfather carved this beautiful soapstone cooking pot
3. Have you met Ellen who has recently transferred to our school
4. Calling Simon's name I ran to the door

5. Her new address is 151 Mesa Drive El Paso TX 79912
6. Have you listened to that Bill Cosby tape Felix
7. You will let me know of course if you can't attend
8. Mia will conduct the meeting Gary recently elected secretary will take the minutes
9. Looking out at the harsh bright glare Angela closed the curtains
10. Carlos Montoya picked up the guitar positioned his fingers on the fingerboard just before the frets and strummed a few chords of a flamenco song.
11. If you hurry you can get home before 9 00 PM
12. Help This is an emergency
13. By the way Rosalinda have you seen any of the re-releases of Alfred Hitchcock's old movies
14. Dave hit a long fly ball toward the fence but Phil was there to make the catch
15. *El Norte* which is one of my favorite movies is about a brother and sister fleeing Central America
16. Performed in Spanish the movie that we saw had English subtitles
17. Nicaragua Panama and Honduras are in Central America Peru and Chile are in South America
18. One of our cats Gypsy scooted through the door across the room and out the window
19. The Lock Museum of America a fascinating place in Terryville Conn has over twenty thousand locks on display.
20. Could the surprise gift be in-line skates or a new football or tickets to a concert

End Marks

An ***end mark*** is a mark of punctuation placed at the end of a sentence. *Periods, question marks,* and *exclamation points* are end marks.

26a. Use a period at the end of a statement.

EXAMPLES The chess player considered his next move.
Tea is grown in Sri Lanka.

26b. Use a question mark at the end of a question.

EXAMPLES Did you see the exhibit of Benin bronzes?
What time is it?

26c. Use an exclamation point at the end of an exclamation.

EXAMPLES What a high bridge!
Look at how bright the moon is!

26d. Use either a period or an exclamation point at the end of a request or a command.

EXAMPLES Please call the dog. [a request]
Call the dog! [a command]

EXERCISE 1 **Adding End Marks to Sentences**

Rewrite each of the following sentences, adding the necessary end marks.

EXAMPLE **1.** Did you know that a choreographer is a person who creates dance steps
1. *Did you know that a choreographer is a person who creates dance steps?*

1. Why is Katherine Dunham called the mother of African American dance
2. She studied anthropology in college and won a scholarship to visit the Caribbean
3. In Haiti, she was inspired by the dances she saw
4. When Dunham returned to the United States, she toured the country with her own professional dance company

5. How I admire such a talented person
6. Look at the beautiful costume and jewelry worn by Dunham in the photograph below
7. How many honors has Dunham's creativity won her
8. She was named to the Hall of Fame of the National Museum of Dance in Saratoga, New York
9. She was also given the National Medal of Arts Award for exploring Caribbean and African dance
10. The editors of *Essence* magazine praised Dunham for helping to break down racial barriers

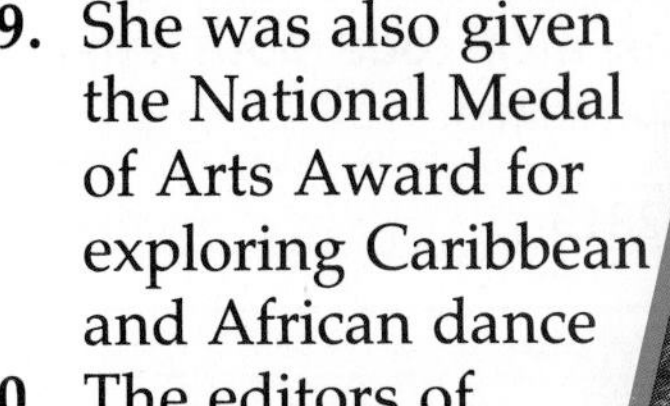

26e. Use a period after most abbreviations.

TYPES OF ABBREVIATIONS	EXAMPLES
Personal Names	F. Scott Fitzgerald Livie I. Durán W.E.B. Du Bois
Titles Used with Names	Mr. Mrs. Ms. Jr. Sr. Dr.
Organizations and Companies	Co. Inc. Corp. Assn.

NOTE: Abbreviations for government agencies and some widely used abbreviations are written without periods. Each letter of the abbreviation is capitalized.

EXAMPLES UN, FBI, PTA, NAACP, PBS, CNN, YMCA, VHF

TYPES OF ABBREVIATIONS	EXAMPLES
Addresses	Ave. St. Rd. Blvd. P.O. Box
States	Tex. Penn. Ariz. Wash.

NOTE: A two-letter state abbreviation without periods is used only when it is followed by a ZIP code. Both letters of the abbreviation are then capitalized.

EXAMPLE Orlando, **FL** 32819

TYPES OF ABBREVIATIONS	EXAMPLES
Times	A.M. P.M. B.C. A.D.
Units of Measure	oz. lb. in. ft. yd. mi.

NOTE: Abbreviations for metric units of measure are usually written without periods and are not capitalized.

EXAMPLES mm, kg, dl

If you're not sure whether to use periods with abbreviations, look in a dictionary.

NOTE: When an abbreviation with a period ends a sentence, another period is not needed. However, a question mark or an exclamation point is used as needed.

EXAMPLES We will arrive by 3:00 P.M.
Can you meet us at 3:30 P.M.?

MECHANICS

EXERCISE 2 Creating and Writing Abbreviations

Abbreviations provide a quick way to express information. Think of how inconvenient it would be to have to write 10 ante meridiem instead of 10 A.M. Create five abbreviations that you think would be handy timesavers. Use each one in a sentence that tells what it stands for. Be sure to use periods after each letter in your abbreviations.

EXAMPLE *I.A.F. means "I'm almost finished," an abbreviation students use when they've nearly completed their homework.*

PICTURE THIS

Suddenly last night, monster tomatoes began attacking your town! They're so huge that they have crushed cars, knocked down buildings, and caused general panic. When the attack started, you grabbed your camera and got this amazing shot of one of the giant tomatoes chasing two friends of yours. But now your camera won't work because it is drenched with tomato juice. You remember that you have a small notebook in your pocket. Jot down a description of the attack so that the rest of the world will know what happened. Use all three types of end marks in your description.

Subject: monster tomatoes attacking your town
Audience: people who haven't seen the attack
Purpose: to inform by giving a clear description

Commas

End marks are used to separate complete thoughts. *Commas,* however, are used to separate words or groups of words within a complete thought.

Items in a Series

26f. Use commas to separate items in a series.

A series is a group of three or more items written one after another. The items in a series may be words, phrases, or clauses.

WORDS IN A SERIES
January, February, and March are all summer months in the Southern Hemisphere. [nouns]
The engine rattled, coughed, and stalled. [verbs]
The baby was happy, alert, and active after her nap. [adjectives]
PHRASES IN A SERIES
There were fingerprints at the top, on the sides, and on the bottom. [prepositional phrases]
Cut into pieces, aged for a year, and well dried, the wood was ready to burn. [participial phrases]
To pitch in a World Series game, to practice medicine, and to run for mayor are all things I hope to do some day. [infinitive phrases]
CLAUSES IN A SERIES
We sang, we danced, and we played trivia games. [short independent clauses]

NOTE: Only *short* independent clauses in a series may be separated by commas. Independent clauses in a series are usually separated by semicolons.

Always be sure that there are at least three items in the series; two items do not need a comma between them.

INCORRECT You will need a pencil, and plenty of paper.
CORRECT You will need a pencil and plenty of paper.

NOTE: In your reading, you will find that some writers omit the comma before the *and* joining the last two items of a series. Nevertheless, you should form the habit of always including this comma. Sometimes a comma is necessary to make your meaning clear. Notice how the comma affects the meaning in the following examples.

EXAMPLES Mom**,** Jody and I want to go to the movies. [Mom is being asked for her permission.]
Mom**,** Jody**,** and I want to go to the movies. [Three people want to go to the movies.]

Including a comma before the last item in a series is never incorrect; therefore, it is usually best to do so.

When all the items in the series are joined by *and* or *or,* do not use commas to separate them.

EXAMPLES Take water **and** food **and** matches with you.
I will take a class in karate **or** judo **or** aikido next year.

EXERCISE 3 Proofreading Sentences for the Correct Use of Commas

Some of the following sentences need commas; others do not. If a sentence needs commas, write the word before each missing comma and add the comma. If a sentence is correct, write *C*.

EXAMPLE **1.** Seal the envelope stamp it and mail the letter.
1. *envelope, it,*

1. The mountains and valleys of southern Appalachia were once home to the Cherokee people.
2. Cleveland Toledo and Dayton are three large cities in Ohio.

3. The captain entered the cockpit checked the instruments and prepared for takeoff.
4. Luisa bought mangos and papayas and oranges.
5. The speaker took a deep breath and read the report.
6. My dog Rover can roll over walk on his hind feet and catch a tennis ball.
7. The neighbors searched behind the garages in the bushes and along the highway.
8. Ruben Blades is an attorney an actor and a singer.
9. Eleanor Roosevelt's courage her humanity and her service to the nation will always be remembered.
10. Rivers overflowed in Virginia and North Carolina.

26g. Use a comma to separate two or more adjectives that come before a noun.

EXAMPLES Jupiter is a large, strange planet.
Zina Garrison played a powerful, brilliant game.

Do not place a comma between an adjective and the noun immediately following it.

INCORRECT My spaniel is a fat, sassy, puppy.
CORRECT My spaniel is a fat, sassy puppy.

Sometimes the final adjective in a series is closely connected to the noun. When the adjective and the noun are linked in such a way, do not use a comma before the final adjective.

EXAMPLES A huge **horned owl** lives in those woods. [not *huge, horned owl*]
An unshaded **electric light** hung from the ceiling. [not *unshaded, electric light*]

To see whether a comma is needed, insert *and* between the adjectives (*unshaded and electric,* for example). If *and* sounds awkward there, don't use a comma.

REFERENCE NOTE: When an adjective and a noun are closely linked, they may be considered one word. Such a word is called a *compound noun.* For more about compound nouns, see page 423.

MECHANICS

EXERCISE 4 Proofreading Sentences for the Correct Use of Commas

Most of the following sentences need commas. If a sentence needs any commas, write the word before each missing comma and add the comma. If a sentence is correct, write *C*.

EXAMPLE **1. Juanita Chen and I are making enchiladas.**
1. *Juanita, Chen, and I are making enchiladas.*
or
Juanita, Chen and I are making enchiladas.

1. In judo class I learned that skill balance and timing are more important than strength.
2. Among Robert Fulton's interests were a steam warship and the submarine.
3. Smoking is a costly dangerous habit.
4. In the human ear, the hammer anvil and stirrup carry sound waves to the brain.
5. Buffalo Bill was a Pony Express rider a scout and a touring stunt performer.
6. "The Masque of the Red Death" is a famous horror story by Edgar Allan Poe.
7. According to Greek mythology, the three Fates spin the thread of life measure it and cut it.
8. LeVar Burton plays the intelligent likable character Geordi on *Star Trek: The Next Generation.*
9. Burton also starred in the popular award-winning miniseries *Roots.*
10. Falstaff begged for mercy in a fight ran away and later bragged about his bravery in battle.

EXERCISE 5 **Creating Menu Descriptions**

Your parents have opened a restaurant, and they are eager to attract customers. Your job is to list today's specials on a sign outside the restaurant. List at least five food items and give a short description of each one. Try to make the foods sound appealing. Be sure to use commas between a series of adjectives. [Remember: Do not use a comma between an adjective and the noun it modifies.]

EXAMPLE *Delicious homemade chicken soup served with a fresh garden salad and refreshing iced tea—$2.75*

Compound Sentences

26h. Use a comma before *and, but, for, or, nor, so,* and *yet* when they join independent clauses in a compound sentence.

EXAMPLES Tamisha offered to get tickets**,** and I accepted.
They had been working very hard**,** but they didn't seem especially tired.
The twins were excited**,** for they were going to day care for the first time.

MECHANICS

NOTE: *So* is often overused. If possible, try to reword a sentence to avoid using *so*.

EXAMPLE It was late, so we went home.
REVISED Because it was late, we went home.

When the independent clauses are very short, the comma before *and, but,* or *or* may be omitted.

EXAMPLES It rained and it rained.
She's going but I'm not.
Come with us or meet us there.

NOTE: Always use a comma before *nor, for, so,* or *yet* joining independent clauses.

EXAMPLE I don't know much about modern art**,** yet I enjoy the work of Mark Rothko.

Don't be confused by a simple sentence with a compound verb. A simple sentence has only one independent clause.

SIMPLE SENTENCE WITH COMPOUND VERB	Usually we **study** in the morning and **play** tennis in the afternoon.
COMPOUND SENTENCE	Usually we study in the morning**,** and we play tennis in the afternoon. [two independent clauses]

REFERENCE NOTE: For more about compound sentences, see pages 536–538. For more about simple sentences with compound verbs, see page 534.

EXERCISE 6 Correcting Compound Sentences by Adding Commas

Some of the following sentences are compound and need additional commas. If a sentence needs a comma, write the word before the missing comma and add the comma. If the sentence is correct, write *C*.

EXAMPLE 1. Native American artists have a heritage dating back thousands of years and many of them use this heritage to create modern works.
1. *years,*

1. Today's artists may work with many nontraditional materials but they use traditional techniques.
2. In the photograph on the next page, you can see the work of the Tohono O'odham artist Mary Thomas and begin to appreciate this basket-weaver's skill.
3. The baskets in the photograph are woven in the "friendship design" and show a circle of human figures in a prayer ceremony.
4. Yucca, banana yucca root, and devil's claw are used to make these baskets and each plant's leaves are a different color.
5. The Navajo artist Danny Randeau Tsosie learned about his heritage from his grandmother.
6. She taught him songs and explained the meaning of the different ceremonies.

7. Christine Nofchissey McHorse learned the skill of pottery making from her grandmother and she can make beautiful bowls.
8. McHorse has an unusual style for her designs combine traditional Navajo and Pueblo images.
9. Native American jewelry makers often use pieces of turquoise and coral found in North America but they also use other stones from around the world.
10. Native American art may look very modern yet some of its symbols and patterns are quite old.

MECHANICS

Interrupters

26i. Use commas to set off an expression that interrupts a sentence.

Two commas are needed if the expression to be set off comes in the middle of the sentence. One comma is needed if the expression comes first or last.

EXAMPLES Our neighbor, Ann Myers, is a fine golfer.
Naturally, we expect to win.
My answer is correct, I think.

(1) Use commas to set off nonessential participial phrases or nonessential subordinate clauses.

A ***nonessential*** (or ***nonrestrictive***) phrase or clause adds information that isn't needed to understand the meaning of the sentence. Such a phrase or clause can be omitted without changing the main idea of the sentence.

NONESSENTIAL PHRASES	My sister, **listening to her radio,** did not hear me.
	Paul, **thrilled by the applause,** took a bow.
NONESSENTIAL CLAUSES	*Out of Africa*, **which I saw again last week,** is my favorite movie.
	I reported on *Secret of the Andes*, **which was written by Ann Nolan Clark.**

Do not set off an ***essential*** (or ***restrictive***) phrase or clause. Since such a phrase or clause tells *which one(s),* it cannot be omitted without changing the meaning of the sentence.

ESSENTIAL PHRASES	The people **waiting to see Arsenio Hall** whistled and cheered. [Which people?]
	A bowl **made by Maria Martínez** is a collector's item. [Which bowl?]
ESSENTIAL CLAUSES	The dress **that I liked** has been sold. [Which dress?]
	The man **who tells Navajo folk tales** is Mr. Platero. [Which man?]

NOTE: A clause beginning with *that* is usually essential.

REFERENCE NOTE: For more about phrases, see Chapter 17. For more about subordinate clauses, see pages 516–525.

EXERCISE 7 Adding Commas with Nonessential Phrases and Clauses

Some of the following sentences need commas to set off nonessential phrases and clauses. Other sentences are correct without commas. If a sentence needs commas, write the word that comes before each missing comma and add the comma. If the sentence is correct, write *C*.

EXAMPLE **1.** This photograph which was taken near Ellis Island shows a family of immigrants from Eastern Europe.
1. *photograph, Island,*

1. Millions of immigrants who came to the United States between about 1892 and 1954 stopped at Ellis Island which is in Upper New York Bay.
2. Families arriving from Europe were examined and interviewed there.

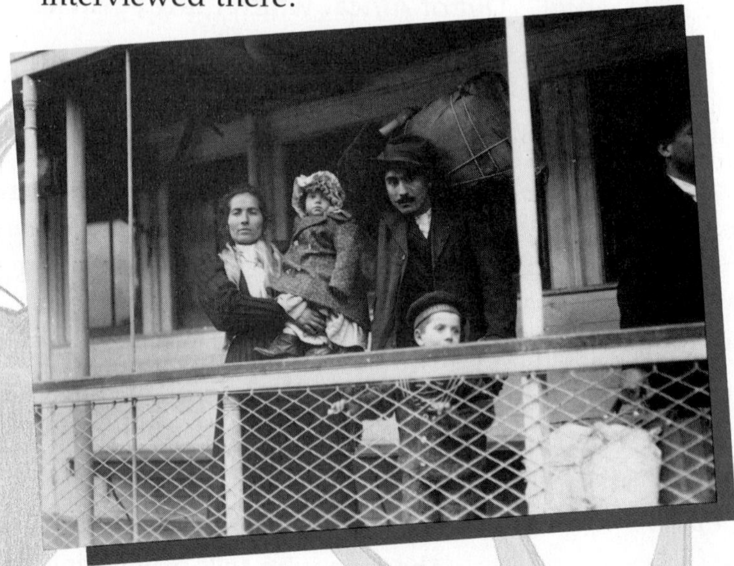

3. The island and its buildings which were closed to the public for many years are now part of the Statue of Liberty National Monument.
4. In 1990, Ellis Island rebuilt as a museum was officially opened to the public.
5. Visitors who wish to see the museum can take a ferry ride from Manhattan Island.
6. The museum's lobby crowded with steamer trunks and other old baggage is the visitors' first sight.
7. One special attraction in the museum consists of audiotapes and videotapes that describe the immigrants' experiences.

8. The Registry Room which is on the second floor sometimes held as many as five thousand people.
9. The immigrants who came from many countries hoped to find freedom and a happier life in America.
10. Immigrants who came to the United States brought with them the value of hard work and a variety of skills that helped to make our country great.

(2) Use commas to set off appositives and appositive phrases that are nonessential.

An ***appositive*** is a noun or a pronoun used to explain or identify another noun or pronoun.

EXAMPLES Vernon**, my cousin,** was born in Jamaica.
Jamaica**, a popular island for tourists,** is in the Caribbean Sea.

Do not use commas to set off an appositive that is essential to the meaning of a sentence.

EXAMPLES My sister **Alicia** is at basketball practice. [The speaker has more than one sister and must give a name to identify which sister.]
My sister**, Alicia,** is at basketball practice. [The speaker has only one sister and is giving her name as added information.]

MECHANICS

EXERCISE 8 Proofreading Sentences for the Correct Use of Commas with Appositives

For each of the following sentences, identify the appositive or appositive phrase. Supply commas where needed. [Hint: Not all of the appositives require commas.]

EXAMPLE 1. Mars one of the closest planets can be seen without a telescope.
1. *Mars, one of the closest planets,*

1. The whole class has read the novel *Old Yeller*.
2. Shana Alexander a former editor of *McCall's* was the main speaker.

3. Do you own a thesaurus a dictionary of synonyms and antonyms?
4. The Galápagos Islands a group of volcanic islands in the Pacific Ocean were named for the Spanish word meaning "tortoise."
5. Rubber an elastic substance quickly restores itself to its original size and shape.
6. This bowl is made of clay found on Kilimanjaro the highest mountain in Africa.
7. The North Sea an arm of the Atlantic Ocean is rich in fish, natural gas, and oil.
8. Jamake Highwater a Blackfoot/Eastern Band Cherokee writes about the history of his people.
9. At Gettysburg a town in Pennsylvania an important battle of the Civil War was fought.
10. My friend Juanita is teaching me to make tortillas.

EXERCISE 9 Writing Sentences with Appositives

In this painting by Frederic Remington, cowboys break for a midday meal at the chuck wagon. If you'd worked hard on the ranch all morning, you'd gladly join them! Write

Frederick Remington, *The Midday Meal*, Remington Art Memorial Museum, Ogdensburg, New York.

five sentences about these cowboys and their meal. In your sentences, use five of the following groups of words as appositives or appositive phrases. Be sure that you insert commas wherever they are needed.

EXAMPLE **1.** *The new cook, Jake Thompson, makes great chili.*

the last day on the trail
a terrible cook
our two visitors
the newest ranch hand
the wildest horse in the territory
Jake Thompson
an unusual feast
a good place to eat chow
beans and cornbread again
my partner

(3) Use commas to set off words that are used in direct address.

EXAMPLES **Ben,** please answer the doorbell.
Mom needs you**, Francine.**
Would you show me**, Kadeem,** where the craft store is?

MECHANICS

EXERCISE 10 Correcting Sentences by Adding Commas with Words Used in Direct Address

Identify the words in direct address from the following sentences. Insert commas before, after, or both before and after the words, as needed.

EXAMPLE **1.** Listen folks to this amazing announcement!
1. *, folks,*

1. Andrea when are you leaving for Detroit?
2. Pay attention now class.
3. Let us my sisters and brothers give thanks.
4. Please Dad may I use your computer?
5. Senator please summarize your tax proposal.

(4) Use commas to set off parenthetical expressions.

A ***parenthetical expression*** is a side remark that adds information or relates ideas.

EXAMPLES Carl**, on the contrary,** prefers soccer to baseball.
To tell the truth, Jan is one of my best friends.

Common Parenthetical Expressions

by the way	in fact	of course
for example	in my opinion	on the contrary
however	I suppose	on the other hand
I believe	nevertheless	to tell the truth

Some of these expressions are not always used as parenthetical expressions.

EXAMPLES **Of course** it is true. [not parenthetical]
That is**, of course,** an Indian teakwood screen. [parenthetical]

I suppose we ought to go home now. [not parenthetical]
He'll want a ride**, I suppose.** [parenthetical]

MECHANICS

EXERCISE 11 Correcting Sentences by Adding Commas with Expressions That Interrupt

The following sentences contain parenthetical expressions that require commas. Write the parenthetical expressions, inserting commas as needed.

EXAMPLE **1.** As a matter of fact even a small refracting telescope gives a good view of Saturn's rings.
1. *As a matter of fact,*

1. You don't need a telescope however to see all the beautiful sights in the night sky.
2. For instance on a summer night you can view the Scorpion, the Serpent, and the Serpent Bearer.

3. By the way you should not overlook the Milky Way.
4. The Milky Way in fact is more impressive in the summer than at any other time of year.
5. Hercules of course is an interesting constellation.
6. Studying the constellations is in my opinion a most interesting hobby.
7. It takes an active imagination however to spot some constellations.
8. The Archer for example is hard to see unless you're familiar with a constellation map like this one.
9. The Scorpion on the other hand is quite clearly outlined.
10. Astronomy is a fascinating science I think.

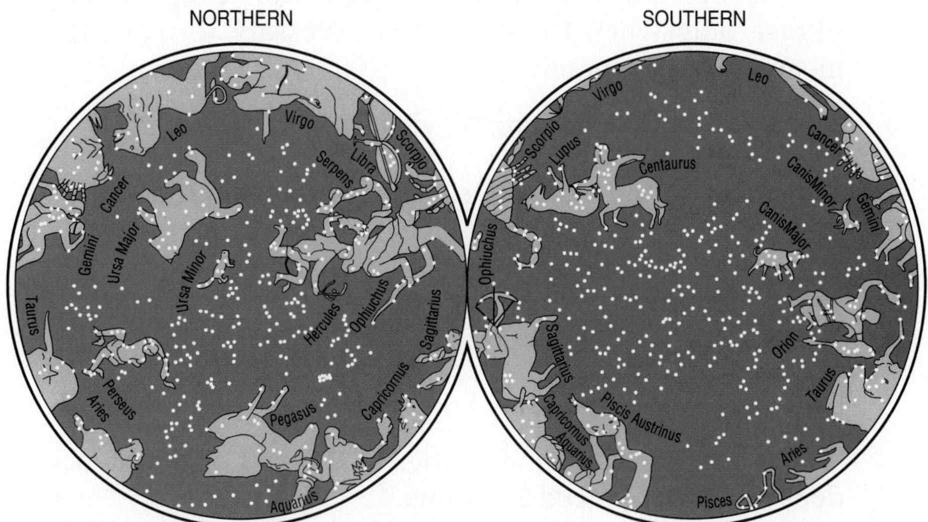

Introductory Words, Phrases, and Clauses

26j. Use a comma after certain introductory elements.

(1) Use a comma after *yes, no,* or any mild exclamation such as *well* or *why* at the beginning of a sentence.

EXAMPLES **Yes,** you may borrow my bicycle.
Why, it's Lena!
Well, I think you are wrong.

(2) Use a comma after an introductory participial phrase.

EXAMPLES **Beginning a new school year,** Zelda felt somewhat nervous.

Greeted with applause from the fans, Rashid ran out onto the field.

(3) Use a comma after two or more introductory prepositional phrases.

EXAMPLE **At the bottom of the hill,** you will see the baseball field.

Use a comma after a single introductory prepositional phrase only when the comma is necessary to make the meaning of the sentence clear.

EXAMPLES In the morning they left. [clear without a comma]

In the morning**,** sunlight streamed through the window. [The comma is needed so that the reader does not read "morning sunlight."]

(4) Use a comma after an introductory adverb clause.

EXAMPLE **After I finish my homework,** I will go to the park.

An adverb clause that comes at the end of a sentence does not usually need a comma.

EXAMPLE I will go to the park **after I finish my homework.**

MECHANICS

EXERCISE 12 Adding Commas with Introductory Elements

If a comma is needed in a sentence, write the word before the missing comma and add the comma. If a sentence is punctuated correctly, write *C.*

EXAMPLE **1.** Walking among the lions the trainer seemed unafraid.

1. *lions,*

1. At our school students eat lunch in the cafeteria.
2. Although Jesse Jackson did not win the 1984 or 1988 Democratic presidential nomination he raised many important issues.
3. On the desk in the den you will find your book.
4. Yes I enjoyed the fajitas that Ruben made.
5. Walking home from school Rosa saw her brother.
6. When I go to bed late I have trouble waking up in the morning.
7. Well we can watch *True Colors* or play checkers.
8. Seeing the calculators in the store window George decided to go in and buy one.
9. At the stoplight on the corner of the next block they made a right turn.
10. Because pemmican remained good to eat for several years it was a practical food for many Native American peoples.

Conventional Situations

26k. Use commas in certain conventional situations.

(1) Use commas to separate items in dates and addresses.

EXAMPLES **She was born on January 26, 1981, in Cheshire, Connecticut.**
A letter dated November 26, 1888, was found in the old house at 980 West Street, Davenport, Iowa.

Notice that a comma separates the last item in a date or in an address from the words that follow it. However, a comma does *not* separate a month and a day (*January 26*) or a house number and a street name (*980 West Street*).

NOTE: Use the correct ZIP Code on every envelope you address. The ZIP Code follows the two-letter state abbreviation without any punctuation between it and the state.

EXAMPLE **Fargo, ND 58102**

EXERCISE 13 Using Commas Correctly

Rewrite each of the following sentences, inserting commas wherever they are needed.

EXAMPLE **1. I received a package from my friend who lives in Irving Texas.**
1. *I received a package from my friend who lives in Irving, Texas.*

1. On May 25 1935 Jesse Owens tied or broke six world track records.
2. The American Saddle Horse Museum is located at 4093 Iron Works Pike Lexington KY 40511.
3. Marian Anderson was born on February 27 1902 in Philadelphia Pennsylvania.
4. Our ZIP code address is Ames IA 50010.
5. Ocean City New Jersey is a popular seaside resort.

(2) Use a comma after the salutation of a friendly letter and after the closing of any letter.

EXAMPLES **Dear Dad,** **Dear Sharon,**
With love, **Yours truly,**

MECHANICS

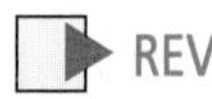

REVIEW A Proofreading Sentences for the Correct Use of Commas

Write each word in the following sentences that should be followed by a comma and add the comma after the word.

EXAMPLE **1. The substitute's name is Mr. Fowler I think.**
1. *Fowler,*

1. What time is your appointment Kevin?
2. My aunt said to forward her mail to 302 Lancelot Drive Simpsonville SC 29681.
3. George Washington Carver a famous scientist had to work hard to afford to go to school.
4. Quick violent flashes of lightning caused an average of 14,300 forest fires a year in the United States.

5. My cousin Lono sent me a note on a postcard from Pahala Hawaii.
6. A single branch stuck out of the water and the beaver grasped it in its paws.
7. The beaver by the way is a rodent.
8. This hard-working mammal builds dams lodges and canals.
9. The lodges of American beavers built with their entrances underwater are marvels of engineering.
10. The beaver uses its large tail which is flattened as a rudder.

REVIEW B **Proofreading Sentences for the Correct Use of Commas**

For the following sentences, write each word that should be followed by a comma and add the comma.

EXAMPLE **1. Kyoto's palaces shrines and temples remind visitors of this city's importance in Japanese history.**

1. *palaces, shrines,*

1. The Procession of the Eras celebrated every autumn takes place in Kyoto.
2. Kyoto a beautiful city was Japan's capital for more than one thousand years.
3. The Procession of the Eras festival which celebrates Kyoto's history begins on October 22.
4. The beautiful solemn procession is a remarkable sight.
5. At the beginning of the festival priests offer special prayers.
6. Portable shrines are carried through the streets and thousands of marchers follow.
7. The photograph on the next page for example shows marchers dressed as ancient warriors.
8. Because the marchers near the front represent recent history they wear costumes from the nineteenth-century Royal Army Era.

9. Marching at the end of the procession archers wear costumes from the eighth-century Warrior Era.

10. The procession is in fact a rich memorial to Kyoto's long and varied history.

Semicolons

A ***semicolon*** looks like a combination of a period and a comma, and that is just what it is. A semicolon separates complete thoughts as a period does. A semicolon also separates items within a sentence as a comma does.

26l. Use a semicolon between independent clauses if they are not joined by *and, but, or, nor, for, so,* or *yet.*

EXAMPLES Jimmy took my suitcase upstairs**;** he left his own in the car.

After school, I went to band practice**;** then I studied in the library for an hour.

26m. Use a semicolon rather than a comma before a coordinating conjunction to join independent clauses that contain commas.

CONFUSING I wrote to Ann, Ramona, and Mai, and Jean notified Latoya and Sue.

CLEAR I wrote to Ann, Ramona, and Mai**;** and Jean notified Latoya and Sue.

NOTE: Semicolons are most effective when they are not overused. Sometimes it is better to separate a compound sentence or a heavily punctuated sentence into two sentences rather than to use a semicolon.

ACCEPTABLE In the tropical jungles of South America, it rains every day, sometimes all day**;** the vegetation there, some of which is found nowhere else in the world, is lush, dense, and fast-growing.

BETTER In the tropical jungles of South America, it rains every day, sometimes all day**.** The vegetation there, some of which is found nowhere else in the world, is lush, dense, and fast-growing.

EXERCISE 14 **Using Semicolons Correctly**

Most of the following sentences have a comma where there should be a semicolon. If the sentence needs a semicolon, write the words before and after the missing semicolon and insert the punctuation mark. If the sentence does not need a semicolon, write *C*.

EXAMPLE **1.** Human beings have walked on the moon, they have not yet walked on any of the planets.

1. *moon; they*

1. Miyoko finished her homework, then she decided to go outside.
2. Each January some people predict the major events of the upcoming year, but they are seldom accurate.
3. Tie these newspapers together with string, put the aluminum cans in a bag.

4. I called Tom, Paul, and Francine, and Fred called Amy, Carlos, and Brad.
5. Reading is my favorite pastime, I love to begin a new book.
6. In 1991, Wellington Webb was elected mayor of Denver, he became the first African American to hold that office.
7. The two companies merged, and they became the largest consumer goods firm in the nation.
8. Your grades have improved, you definitely will pass the course.
9. I want to work with animals someday, I might even become a veterinarian.
10. We haven't seen the movie, for it hasn't come to our town yet.

Colons

26n. Use a colon before a list of items, especially after expressions such as *the following* or *as follows.*

EXAMPLES You will need these items for map work**:** a ruler, colored pencils, and tracing paper.
Jack's pocket contained the following items**:** a key, half an apple, a piece of gum, and two rusty nails.
The primary colors are as follows**:** red, blue, and yellow.

Never use a colon directly after a verb or a preposition. Omit the colon or reword the sentence.

INCORRECT This marinara sauce is made of: tomatoes, bay leaves, onions, oregano, and garlic.
CORRECT This marinara sauce is made of the following ingredients**:** tomatoes, bay leaves, onions, oregano, and garlic.

INCORRECT My stepsister's favorite sports are: basketball, tennis, swimming, and bowling.

CORRECT My stepsister's favorite sports are basketball, tennis, swimming, and bowling.

CORRECT My stepsister's favorite sports are the following ones**:** basketball, tennis, swimming, and bowling.

26o. Use a colon between the hour and the minute.

EXAMPLES **8:30** A.M., **10:00** P.M.

26p. Use a colon after the salutation of a business letter.

EXAMPLES Dear Sir or Madam**:** Dear Mrs. Foster**:** To Whom It May Concern**:** Dear Dr. Christiano**:**

26q. Use a colon between chapter and verse in referring to passages from the Bible.

EXAMPLE John 1**:**1
Ruth 1**:**15–17

EXERCISE 15 **Using Colons and Commas Correctly**

Make each of the following word groups into a complete sentence by supplying an appropriate list or time. Insert colons and commas where they are needed.

EXAMPLE **1.** The test will begin at *[time]*
1. *The test will begin at 9:30* A.M.

1. My classes this year are as follows *[list]*
2. You will need these supplies for your project *[list]*
3. So far we have studied the following punctuation marks *[list]*
4. Meet me at the mall at *[time]*
5. My favorite foods are *[list]*

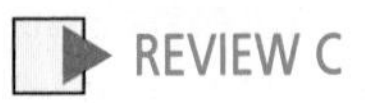

REVIEW C

Using End Marks, Commas, Semicolons, and Colons Correctly

The sentences in the following paragraph lack necessary end marks, commas, semicolons, and colons. Write each sentence, inserting the correct punctuation.

EXAMPLE [1] **What an unusual clever caring way to help animals**

1. ***What an unusual, clever, caring way to help animals!***

[1] Animal lovers have you heard about the Sanctuary for Animals [2] Founded by Leonard and Bunny Brook the sanctuary is a safe home for all kinds of animals [3] Through the years hundreds of stray unwanted and abused animals have found a home at the sanctuary [4] It is located on the Brooks' land in Westtown New York [5] On their two hundred acres the Brooks take care of the following animals camels lions elephants even this Australian kangaroo as well as dogs and cats [6] Of course Mr. and Mrs. Brook also raise chickens keep horses and look after their other farm animals [7] The Brooks their family and their friends care for animals like this baby cougar they also let

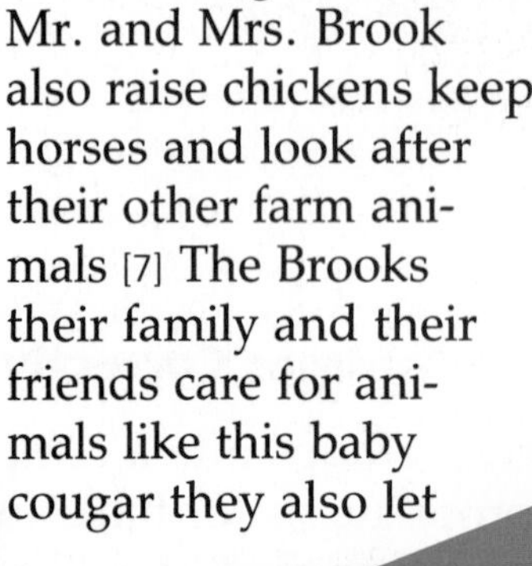

the animals work for themselves [8] How do the animals work [9] The Brooks formed the Dawn Animal Agency and their animals became actors and models [10] You may have seen this camel or some of the other animals in magazines movies television shows and commercials

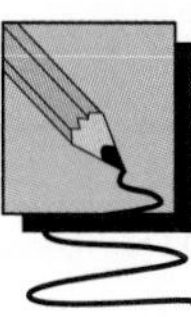

WRITING APPLICATION

Using Punctuation to Make Your Meaning Clear

When you talk, you have many different ways to make your meaning clear. You pause between ideas, raise and lower your voice, and gesture with your hands. When you write, your words and punctuation have to do all the work. Punctuation helps separate your ideas and show the relationships between them. Notice how changing punctuation changes the meaning in the following sentences.

EXAMPLES We'll hold the carwash on Saturday**,** and on Monday we'll be able to buy the new baseball uniforms.

We'll hold the carwash on Saturday and on Monday**.** We'll be able to buy the new baseball uniforms.

I'll help wash cars with Jeff and Carla**,** and Susan will put up flyers around town.

I'll help wash cars with Jeff**,** and Carla and Susan will put up flyers around town.

MECHANICS

WRITING ACTIVITY

Your class is sponsoring a carwash to raise money for a special project or trip. You've been chosen to write an announcement about the carwash for publication in a community newsletter. Write a brief announcement telling when and where the carwash will be, how much it will cost, what the money will be used for, and any other important details. In your announcement be sure to use end marks, commas, semicolons, and colons correctly.

Prewriting List the information that you'll include in your announcement. Clearly state the purpose of the carwash—what your class will spend the money on. You may also want to tell how much money the class needs to raise. Make sure you've included all the facts people will need to know about the time, location, and cost of the carwash.

Writing As you write your draft, remember that the purpose of your announcement is to attract customers. Write an attention-grabbing first sentence that explains the purpose of the carwash. Be sure to present all your information in clear, complete sentences. Add any important details that you didn't list earlier.

Evaluating and Revising Ask a friend to read your announcement. Is it clear and straightforward? Does it convince your friend that the carwash is for a good cause? If not, revise, rearrange, or add details.

Proofreading As you proofread your announcement, pay special attention to your use of punctuation. Remember to check the placement of colons in expressions of time.

Review: Posttest

Using End Marks, Commas, Semicolons, and Colons Correctly

The following sentences lack necessary end marks, commas, semicolons, and colons. Write each sentence, inserting the correct punctuation.

EXAMPLE **1. Snakes lizards and crocodiles are reptiles**
1. ***Snakes, lizards, and crocodiles are reptiles.***

1. Toads and frogs on the other hand are amphibians
2. Some turtles live on land others live in lakes streams or oceans
3. Although turtles have no teeth they can bite with their strong hard beaks
4. The terms *turtle* and *tortoise* are interchangeable but *tortoise* usually refers to a land dweller.
5. The African pancake tortoise which has a flat flexible shell has a unique means of defense.
6. Faced with a threat it takes the following precautions it crawls into a narrow crack in a rock takes a deep breath and wedges itself in tightly
7. Because some species of tortoises are endangered they cannot be sold as pets
8. Three species of tortoises that live in the United States are the desert tortoise the gopher tortoise and the Texan tortoise.
9. The gopher tortoise lives in the Southeast but the desert tortoise comes from the Southwest
10. The Indian star tortoise now an endangered species is very rare
11. As this kind of tortoise grows older its shell grows larger the number of stars increases and their pattern becomes more complex
12. The Indian star tortoise requires warmth sunlight and a diet of green vegetables
13. Living in fresh water soft-shelled turtles have long flexible noses and fleshy lips
14. Their shells are not really soft however but are covered by smooth skin
15. Wanda may I introduce you to my pet turtle Pokey
16. Pokey who has been part of our family for years is a red-eared turtle.
17. When my parents got Pokey he was only two inches in diameter

18. Pokey has been in my family for fifteen years and he could easily live to be fifty
19. If you look at the design on Pokey's shell you can get a good idea of his age
20. Don't you agree with me Wanda that a turtle makes a good pet

SUMMARY OF USES OF THE COMMA

26f Use commas to separate items in a series—words, phrases, and clauses.

26g Use a comma to separate two or more adjectives that come before a noun.

26h Use a comma before *and*, *but*, *for*, *or*, *nor*, *so*, and *yet* when they join independent clauses.

26i Use commas to set off an expression that interrupts a sentence.

(1) Use commas to set off nonessential participial phrases and nonessential subordinate clauses.

(2) Use commas to set off appositives and appositive phrases that are nonessential.

(3) Use commas to set off words used in direct address.

(4) Use commas to set off parenthetical expressions.

26j Use a comma after certain introductory elements.

(1) Use a comma after *yes, no,* or any mild exclamation such as *well* or *why* at the beginning of a sentence.

(2) Use a comma after an introductory participial phrase.

(3) Use a comma after two or more introductory prepositional phrases.

(4) Use a comma after an introductory adverb clause.

26k Use a comma in certain conventional situations.

(1) Use commas to separate items in dates and addresses.

(2) Use a comma after the salutation of a friendly letter and after the closing of any letter.

27 PUNCTUATION

Underlining (Italics), Quotation Marks, Apostrophes, Hyphens, Parentheses, Dashes

MECHANICS

Diagnostic Test

Using Underlining (Italics), Quotation Marks, Apostrophes, Hyphens, Parentheses, and Dashes

The following sentences contain errors in the use of underlining (italics), quotation marks, apostrophes, hyphens, parentheses, or dashes. Write each sentence correctly.

EXAMPLE **1. My mother's note said, "Please buy celery, rye bread, and milk.**
1. ***My mother's note said, "Please buy celery, rye bread, and milk."***

1. Sharon she's my youngest cousin asked me to tell her a bedtime story.
2. "Did you know," asked Kathy, "that the novel *Don Quixote* has seventy four chapters"?

3. "Have you ever read Robert Hayden's poem 'Those Winter Sundays?" asked Jorge.
4. "Whos your favorite professional baseball player?" asked Don.
5. Randall Jarrell wrote both fiction and nonfiction, but hes best known for his poetry.
6. Many people misspell the word *accommodate* by leaving out one c.
7. "Meet me at 2:30 sharp; don't be late, my mother's note read.
8. The reading list included the novel Island of the Blue Dolphins.
9. My complaint was that the sandwiches we ate at the beach were three fourths sand.
10. In English class today, we read the poem Sisters, which was written by Lucille Clifton.
11. "Can you volunteer just two hours worth of your time a week?" asked Mrs. Jackson.
12. The bearded man you probably guessed is really the jewel thief in disguise.
13. "A group of twenty one students is not a two thirds majority of our class," Stan stated.
14. This coupon is for a free enchilada at Pedros Lunch Palace on Oak Street.
15. The librarian told me that the only copy of the book *Childrens Songs* had been checked out for more than two weeks.
16. Ms. Liu said, Turn to Chapter 7, 'Multiplying Fractions.'"
17. "What is the origin of the word inoculate?" Derrick asked Dr. Jackson.
18. "The state of Massachusetts was named after a Native American people that lived in that area" Jessica said.
19. She added, "The word *Massachusett* also refers to that peoples language."
20. Aunt Rosie and Uncle Fred went to the Bahamas on the cruise ship Princess.

MECHANICS

Underlining (Italics)

Italics are printed letters that lean to the right—*like this.* When you write or type, you show that a word should be *italicized* by underlining it. If your composition were to be printed, the typesetter would set the underlined words in italics. For example, if you type

Madeleine L'Engle wrote A Wrinkle in Time.

the sentence would be printed like this:

Madeleine L'Engle wrote *A Wrinkle in Time.*

NOTE: If you use a personal computer, you can probably set words in italics yourself. Most word-processing software and many printers can produce italic type.

27a. Use underlining (italics) for titles of books, plays, periodicals, films, television programs, works of art, long musical compositions, ships, aircraft, and spacecraft.

TYPE OF NAME	EXAMPLES	
Books	*A Wind in the Door*	*Watership Down* *Mules and Men*
Plays	*Our Town* *Hamlet*	*I Never Sang for My Father*
Periodicals	the *Houston Post* *Essence*	*National Geographic*
Films	*The Maltese Falcon*	*Cry Freedom*
Television Programs	*The Golden Girls*	*In Living Color*
Works of Art	*Starry Night* *The Dream*	*Watson and the Shark*
Long Musical Compositions	*Carmen* *An American in Paris*	*Music for the Royal Fireworks*
Ships	the *Titanic* the *Pequod*	the *USS Eisenhower*
Aircraft	the *Silver Dart* the *Hindenburg*	the *Deperdussin Racer*
Spacecraft	*Soyuz XI*	*Atlantis*

NOTE: The article *the* before the title of a newspaper is often neither italicized nor capitalized when it is written within a sentence.

EXAMPLE Would you like to subscribe to **the** *Chicago Tribune*?

REFERENCE NOTE: For examples of titles that are not italicized but are enclosed in quotation marks, see page 744.

27b. Use underlining (italics) for words, letters, and figures referred to as such.

EXAMPLES I often confuse the words *accept* and *except.*
Don't forget to double the final *n* before you add *–ing* in words like *running.*
Can you tell whether he wrote a *4* or a *9*?

EXERCISE 1 Using Underlining (Italics) Correctly

For each of the following sentences, write each word or item that should be italicized and underline it.

EXAMPLE 1. Mike Royko writes a column for the Chicago Tribune.
1. *Chicago Tribune*

1. The British spell the word humor with a u after the o.
2. In Denmark, you might see the spelling *triatlon* for the word triathlon.
3. The current Newsweek has an informative article on the famine in Africa.
4. Our school paper, the Norwalk Valley News, is published weekly.
5. Luis Valdez wrote and directed La Bamba, a movie about the life of Richie Valens.
6. The Oceanic is one of the ocean liners that sail to the Caribbean.
7. The movie Dances with Wolves has some of the most beautiful photography that I have ever seen.
8. Our local theater group is presenting The Time of Your Life, a comedy by William Saroyan.

9. Lindbergh's Spirit of St. Louis is on display at the museum, along with the Wright brothers' Flyer and Gemini IV.
10. The best novel that I read during vacation was The Summer of the Swans.

Quotation Marks

27c. Use quotation marks to enclose a ***direct quotation***—a person's exact words.

Be sure to place quotation marks both before and after a person's exact words.

EXAMPLES Emma Lazarus wrote the famous quotation on the Statue of Liberty, which begins with the words **"**Give me your tired, your poor. . . .**"**
"When the bell rings,**"** said the teacher, **"**leave the room quietly.**"**

Do not use quotation marks for an ***indirect quotation***—a rewording of a direct quotation.

DIRECT QUOTATION Tom predicted, **"**It will be a close game.**"** [Tom's exact words]
INDIRECT QUOTATION Tom predicted that it would be a close game. [not Tom's exact words]

27d. A direct quotation begins with a capital letter.

EXAMPLES Maria said, "The *carne asada* isn't ready yet, but please help yourself to the guacamole."
While he was in prison, Richard Lovelace wrote a poem containing the well-known quotation "Stone walls do not a prison make."

27e. When the expression identifying the speaker interrupts a quoted sentence, the second part of the quotation begins with a small letter.

EXAMPLES "Lightning has always awed people," explained Mrs. Worthington, "and many of us are still frightened by it."

"The time has come," insisted the speaker, "to improve our educational program."

A quoted sentence that is divided in this way is called a *broken quotation.* Notice that each part of a broken quotation is enclosed in a set of quotation marks.

When the second part of a divided quotation is a sentence, it begins with a capital letter.

EXAMPLE "I can't go today," I said. "**A**sk me tomorrow."

27f. A direct quotation is set off from the rest of the sentence by a comma, a question mark, or an exclamation point, but not by a period.

Set off means "to separate." If a quotation comes at the beginning of a sentence, a comma follows it. If a quotation comes at the end of a sentence, a comma comes before it. If a quoted sentence is interrupted, a comma follows the first part and comes before the second part.

EXAMPLES Bernie said**,** "Science is more interesting than history."

"I especially like to do experiments**,**" Velma commented.

"Yes**,**" Juan added**,** "Bernie loves to do experiments, too."

When a quotation ends with a question mark or an exclamation point, no comma is needed.

EXAMPLES "Is that a good video game**?**" Jane wanted to know.

"I'll say it is**!**" Debbie exclaimed.

MECHANICS

EXERCISE 2 **Punctuating Quotations**

For each of the following sentences, insert commas, quotation marks, and capital letters where they are needed. If a sentence is correct, write *C.*

EXAMPLE **1.** Let's go to a horror movie this afternoon, said Bob.

1. *"Let's go to a horror movie this afternoon," said Bob.*

1. When I shrieked in fear, the usher warned me to be quiet.
2. At the same time, Bob whispered it's only a movie—calm down!
3. He pointed out that the people around us were getting annoyed.
4. I quietly replied I'm sorry.
5. You shouldn't have screamed, he complained.
6. From now on I said to him I promise I'll try to be quiet.
7. When the lights came on, Bob said it's time to go.
8. Outside the theater he muttered something about people who shouldn't go to horror movies.
9. But I can't help it I explained.
10. You were even afraid Bob protested during the credits!

27g. A period or a comma should always be placed *inside* the closing quotation marks.

EXAMPLES "The Ramses exhibit begins over there**,**" said the museum guide.

Darnell replied, "I'm ready to see some ancient Egyptian jewelry and artwork**.**"

27h. A question mark or an exclamation point should be placed inside the closing quotation marks when the quotation itself is a question or an exclamation. Otherwise, it should be placed outside.

EXAMPLES "How far have we come**?**" asked the exhausted man. [The quotation is a question.]

Who said, "Give me liberty or give me death"**?** [The sentence, not the quotation, is a question.]

"Jump!" ordered the firefighter. [The quotation is an exclamation.]

I couldn't believe it when he said, "No, thank you"! [The sentence, not the quotation, is an exclamation.]

When both the sentence and the quotation at the end of the sentence are questions (or exclamations), only one question mark (or exclamation point) is used. It is placed inside the closing quotation marks.

EXAMPLE Did Josh really say, "What's Cinco de Mayo?"

EXERCISE 3 Punctuating and Capitalizing Quotations

For each of the following sentences, insert capital letters, quotation marks, and other marks of punctuation where needed.

EXAMPLE 1. Ashley Bryan wore traditional African clothes when he came to our school Elton said

1. *"Ashley Bryan wore traditional African clothes when he came to our school," Elton said.*

1. Oh, like the clothes Mr. Johnson showed us in class Janell exclaimed
2. Elton asked have you read any of Ashley Bryan's books about African culture
3. I've read Janell quickly replied the one titled *Beat the Story-Drum, Pum-Pum*
4. I'd like to read that again Elton said those African folk tales are wonderful
5. Mrs. Ray thinks *Walk Together Children* is excellent Janell said
6. Isn't that Elton asked about Negro spirituals
7. You're right Janell answered and Bryan wrote that spirituals are America's greatest contribution to world music
8. She added he grew up in New York City and began writing stories and drawing when he was still in kindergarten

9. Did you know Elton asked that he illustrated his own books

10. This is one of the woodcuts Bryan made to illustrate *Walk Together Children* he added.

EXERCISE 4 Revising Indirect Quotations to Create Direct Quotations

Revise each of the following sentences by changing the indirect quotation to a direct quotation. Be sure to use capital letters and punctuation wherever necessary.

EXAMPLE **1.** I asked my grandmother if she would like to help us paint our float.

1. *"Grandma," I asked, "would you like to help us paint our float?"*

1. Mayor Alaniz announced that he would lead the parade this year.

2. Ms. Feldman asked me what my plans for the big parade were.

3. I answered that my brother and I were building a float.

4. She exclaimed that she thought that was terrific.

5. Ron remarked that our float probably had something to do with sports.

27i. When you write dialogue (conversation), begin a new paragraph every time the speaker changes.

EXAMPLE The young man smiled, and said, "My old master, now let me tell you the truth. My home is not so far away. It is quite near your temple. We have been old neighbors for many years."

The old monk was very surprised. "I don't believe it. You, young man, will have your joke. Where is there another house round here?"

"My master, would I lie to you? I live right beside your temple. The Green Pond is my home."

"You live in the pond?" The old monk was even more astonished.

"That's right. In fact," said Li Aiqi, in a perfectly serious tone, "I'm not a man at all. I am a dragon."

from "Green Dragon Pond," a Bai folk tale

REFERENCE NOTE: For more information on writing dialogue, see pages 140 and 194.

27j. When a quotation consists of several sentences, put quotation marks only at the beginning and the end of the whole quotation.

EXAMPLE "Mary Elizabeth and I will wait for you at Robertson's Drug Store. Please try to get there as soon as you can. We don't want to be late for the concert," Jerome said before he rushed off down the hall.

27k. Use single quotation marks to enclose a quotation within a quotation.

EXAMPLES Brandon added, "My mom always says, 'Look before you leap.'"

"Did Ms. Neuman really say, 'It's all right to use your books and your notes during the test'?" asked Sakura.

PICTURE THIS

Watch out! You and a friend are making sure that no one gets hurt at your little sister's birthday party. If this child hits the piñata hard enough, it will break open. Then all the small toys and treats inside will fall out, and the children will rush for them. Breaking open piñatas, which are papier-mâché figures like this one, is a Latin American party custom. It's also popular in the United States. As you watch the children, you and your friend talk about the scene. Write a short conversation about what you see and hear. Be sure to use quotation marks and punctuation correctly.

Subject: a piñata contest
Audience: a friend
Purpose: to talk about what's happening

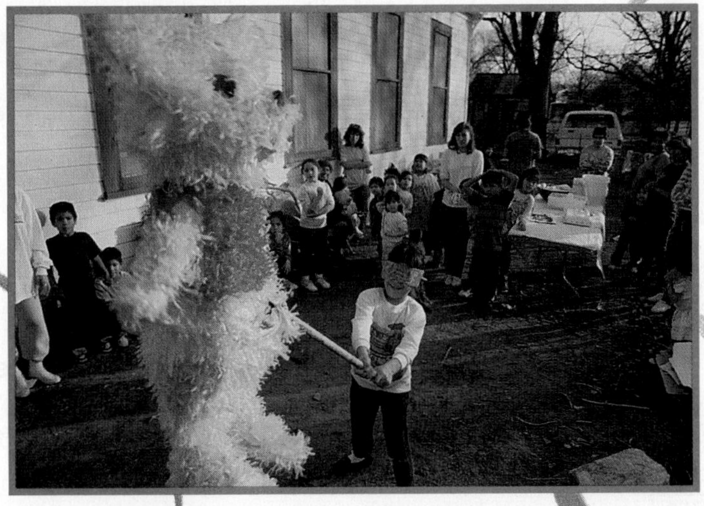

27l. Use quotation marks to enclose the titles of short works such as short stories, poems, articles, songs, episodes of television programs, and chapters and other parts of books.

TYPE OF NAME	EXAMPLES
Short Stories	"A Day's Wait" "The Medicine Bag" "The Circuit"
Poems	"In Time of Silver Rain" "Birdfoot's Grampa" "Annabel Lee"
Articles	"Rooting for the Home Team" "Annie Leibovitz: Behind the Images" "The Storytelling Renaissance"
Songs	"La Cucaracha" "The Star-Spangled Banner" "Swing Low, Sweet Chariot"
Episodes of Television Programs	"Cheap Is Cheap" "This Side of Paradise" "Growing Up Hispanic"
Chapters and Other Parts of Books	"The Natural World" "The Myths of Greece and Rome" "The Double Task of Language"

REFERENCE NOTE: For examples of titles that are italicized, see page 735.

EXERCISE 5 **Punctuating Quotations**

Insert quotation marks where they are needed in each of the following items. If a sentence is correct, write *C.*

EXAMPLE **1. Let's sing 'The Ballad of Gregorio Cortez,' suggested Jim.**
1. *"Let's sing 'The Ballad of Gregorio Cortez,'" suggested Jim.*

1. Lani, have you seen my clarinet? asked Rob. It was on this table. I need it for my lesson this afternoon.
2. The most interesting chapter in *The Sea Around Us* is The Birth of an Island.
3. Didn't Benjamin Franklin once say, Time is money? asked Myra.
4. My favorite Langston Hughes poem is As I Grew Older, said Mom.

5. Lea Evans said, One of the greatest changes in architecture has been in the design of churches. They no longer follow traditional forms. Churches have been built that are shaped like stars, fish, and ships.
6. The latest issue of *Discover* has a fascinating picture of a shark that swallowed an anchor.
7. Do you know which character asked What's in a name? in *Romeo and Juliet*? I asked.
8. Yes, answered Li. My mother used to say that to me when I was a little girl. That's how I first heard of Shakespeare.
9. A human hand has more than twenty-seven bones and thirty-five muscles! exclaimed Marcus. No wonder it can do so much.
10. There is an article called The Customers Always Write in today's newspaper.

REVIEW A **Punctuating Paragraphs**

Revise the following paragraphs, using quotation marks and other marks of punctuation wherever necessary. Remember to begin a new paragraph each time the speaker changes. If a sentence is correct, write *C.* [Note: The punctuation marks that are already included in the exercise are correct.]

EXAMPLE [1] **Mr. Brown asked Can you baby-sit tonight?**
1. *Mr. Brown asked, "Can you baby-sit tonight?"*

[1] Last night I baby-sat for the Browns, a new family on our block. [2] Come in Mrs. Brown greeted me. [3] You must be Lisa. [4] Hello, Mrs. Brown I replied. [5] I'm looking forward to meeting the children. [6] First Mrs. Brown explained I want you to meet Ludwig. [7] Is he a member of the family I asked. [8] In a way replied Mrs. Brown as she led me to the kitchen and pointed to an aging dachshund. [9] That is Ludwig. [10] He rules this house and everyone in it.

[11] Mr. Brown entered the kitchen and introduced himself. [12] I see that you've met Ludwig he said. [13] Yes

Mrs. Brown answered for me. [14] Why don't you give Lisa her instructions while I go find the children?

[15] If Ludwig whines said Mr. Brown give him a dog biscuit. [16] Should I take him for a walk I asked. [17] No replied Mr. Brown. [18] Just let him out into the yard.

[19] Mrs. Brown came back into the kitchen with the children. [20] Did my husband remind you to cover Ludwig when he falls asleep she asked. [21] I'll remember I promised [22] But what should I do for the children? [23] Don't worry said Mr. Brown. [24] They'll behave themselves and go to bed when they're supposed to. [25] As I told you laughed Mrs. Brown Ludwig rules this house and everyone in it, even the sitter!

Apostrophes

Possessive Case

The ***possessive case*** of a noun or a pronoun shows ownership or relationship.

OWNERSHIP	RELATIONSHIP
Kathleen's desk	**anybody's** guess
his bat	an **hour's** time
their car	**horse's** mane

27m. To form the possessive case of a singular noun, add an apostrophe and an *s.*

EXAMPLES a boy**'s** cap　　Cleon**'s** pen
the baby**'s** toy　　Charles**'s** opinion

NOTE: A proper noun ending in *s* may take only an apostrophe to form the possessive case if the addition of *'s* would make the name awkward to say.

EXAMPLES Philippines**'** government
Ms. Rodgers**'** cat

EXERCISE 6 **Using Apostrophes for Singular Possessives**

For each sentence in the following paragraph, identify the word that needs an apostrophe. Then, write the word correctly punctuated.

EXAMPLE [1] The Prado in Madrid, Spain, is one of the worlds greatest museums.
1. *worlds—world's*

[1] Shown here is one of the Prados paintings by Diego Velázquez, *Las Meninas.* [2] Velázquezs painting is known in English as *The Maids of Honor.* [3] In the center of the canvas is Princess Margarita, the royal couples daughter. [4] To the princesss right, a kneeling maid of honor offers her something to drink. [5] To the royal childs left, another maid of honor curtsies. [6] On the far left of the canvas, you can see the artists own image, for he has painted himself! [7] The palaces other important people, such as the chamberlain and a court jester, also appear. [8] The faces of Margaritas parents are reflected in the mirror on the back wall. [9] In the foreground, the royal dog ignores a young guests invitation to play. [10] This paintings fame has grown since it was painted in 1656, and each year millions of people see it while visiting the Prado.

Diego Velázquez, *Las Meninas*, Prado, Madrid, Scala/Art Resource.

27n. To form the possessive case of a plural noun that does not end in *s*, add an apostrophe and an *s*.

EXAMPLES **mice's tracks** **men's hats**
children's games **teeth's enamel**

27o. To form the possessive case of a plural noun ending in *s*, add only the apostrophe.

EXAMPLES **cats' basket** **four days' delay**
brushes' bristles **the Carsons' bungalow**

NOTE: Do not use an apostrophe to form the *plural* of a noun. Remember that the apostrophe shows ownership or relationship.

INCORRECT Three girls' lost their tickets.
CORRECT Three **girls** lost their tickets. [plural]
CORRECT Three **girls'** tickets were lost. [plural possessive]

MECHANICS

EXERCISE 7 Writing Possessives

Rewrite each of the following expressions by using the possessive case. Be sure to insert an apostrophe in the right place.

EXAMPLE 1. food for the dog
1. *the dog's food*

1. the nominee of the party
2. the clothes of the babies
3. the grades of my sister
4. the name tags of the guests
5. the dish for the cat

EXERCISE 8 Writing Sentences with Plural Possessives

Write the plural form of each of the following words. After each plural form, write a sentence using the possessive form of that plural.

1. dog
2. plumber
3. goose
4. friend
5. woman

27p. Do not use an apostrophe with possessive personal pronouns.

EXAMPLES **Is that sticker yours or mine?**
Our cat is friendlier than theirs.
His report on Cherokee folk tales was as good as hers.

REFERENCE NOTE: For more about possessive personal pronouns, see pages 606–607.

27q. To form the possessive case of some indefinite pronouns, add an apostrophe and an *s.*

EXAMPLES neither's homework
everyone's choice
somebody's jacket

REFERENCE NOTE: For more about indefinite pronouns, see page 430.

EXERCISE 9 **Writing Possessives of Indefinite Pronouns**

Rewrite each of the following expressions by using the possessive case of each indefinite pronoun. Be sure to insert an apostrophe in the right place.

EXAMPLE **1. the park for everyone**
1. *everyone's park*

1. the stereo that belongs to somebody
2. the footprints of anyone
3. the fault of nobody
4. the turn of either
5. the opinion of another

Contractions

27r. Use an apostrophe to show where letters have been omitted (left out) in a contraction.

A ***contraction*** is a shortened form of a word, a number, or a group of words. The apostrophe in a contraction shows where letters or numerals have been left out.

Common Contractions

I am	I'm	they had	they'd
1993	'93	where is	where's
let us	let's	we are	we're
of the clock	o'clock	he is	he's
she would	she'd	you will	you'll

The word *not* can be shortened to *n't* and added to a verb, usually without any change in the spelling of the verb.

EXAMPLE	is not	is**n't**	has not	has**n't**
	are not	are**n't**	have not	have**n't**
	does not	does**n't**	had not	had**n't**
	do not	do**n't**	should not	should**n't**
	was not	was**n't**	would not	would**n't**
	were not	were**n't**	could not	could**n't**
EXCEPTIONS	will not	**won't**	cannot	**can't**

Be careful not to confuse contractions with possessive pronouns.

CONTRACTIONS	POSSESSIVE PRONOUNS
It's Friday. [*It is*] **It's** been a pleasure. [*It has*]	**Its** nest is over there.
Who's your server? [*Who is*] **Who's** been practicing the piano? [*Who has*]	**Whose** backpack is this?
You're late. [*You are*]	**Your** mom called
They're arriving soon. [*They are*] **There's** the path. [*There is*]	**Their** parakeet is friendly. That rose bush is **theirs.**

MECHANICS

EXERCISE 10 Using Apostrophes in Contractions Correctly

For each of the following sentences, write the word or words requiring an apostrophe and insert the apostrophe. Be sure to spell the word correctly. If a sentence is correct, write *C*.

EXAMPLE **1. Arent you going with us at one oclock?**
1. *Aren't; o'clock*

1. Wed better chain our bicycles to the rack.
2. That old cars seen better days, hasnt it?
3. She wasnt too happy to see us.
4. Whose ringing the doorbell?
5. We wont forget how helpful youve been.
6. Im certain youll be invited.
7. Whose turn is it to take attendance?
8. Anns an excellent swimmer, but she cant dive.
9. Its almost time to leave, isnt it?
10. Im sure theyll show up before its over.

EXERCISE 11 Punctuating Contractions

For each sentence in the following paragraph, identify the word that needs an apostrophe to indicate a contraction. Then, write the word correctly.

EXAMPLE [1] **Whats the best route from Lawrenceville, New Jersey, to Newtown, Pennsylvania?**
1. *What's*

[1] Theres one especially pretty route you can take to get there. [2] I think youll enjoy the drive. [3] You shouldnt go due west directly. [4] Youve got to go north or south first. [5] Its easier to go south on Route 206 to Route U.S. 1, cross the Delaware River, and then go north on Route 32 to Yardley. [6] From Yardley, turn left on Route 322, and in a little while Im sure you will find yourself in Newtown. [7] If youd prefer a different route, go south on Route 206 to Route 546 and make a right turn to go west. [8] After you cross the Delaware River and the road becomes 532, dont

turn until Linton Hill Road. [9] When you turn left onto Linton Hill Road, it wont be long before you arrive in Newtown. [10] Heres a map you can use to help you find your way.

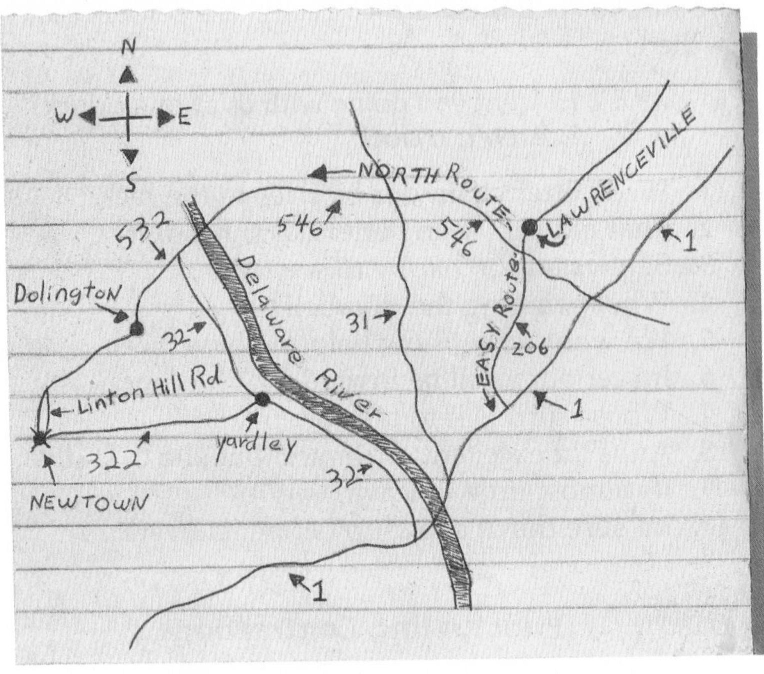

EXERCISE 12 **Writing Contractions**

For each sentence in the following paragraph, write the contraction of the underlined word or words.

EXAMPLE [1] **If you think it should have been easy to visit the building shown on the next page, guess again!**

1. ***should've***

[1] It is the Potala Palace in Lhasa, Tibet, which my parents and I visited last year. [2] The city of Lhasa is two miles high in the Himalaya Mountains, and we could not move around much because the lack of oxygen made us tired. [3] The Potala Palace is the former residence of the Tibetan spiritual leader, who has been living in exile in

India. [4] Because this palace is a holy shrine, pilgrims do not mind traveling on foot from all over the country to worship there. [5] After they have bought yak butter in the city square, they take it to the palace as an offering. [6] From the photograph, you cannot imagine how steep those stairs on the right are! [7] Because it would have taken a long time to climb them, our bus driver took us directly to the rear entrance on the left. [8] Once inside, we spent hours exploring the palace, but we were not able to visit most of its more than one thousand rooms! [9] I am sure we would never have found our way out without our guide, who led us to an exit on the right. [10] Walking down the stairs was not too hard, and soon we were in the beautiful central square in the Himalayan sunshine!

EXERCISE 13 **Writing Contractions**

Write a suitable contraction for the blank in each of the following sentences.

1. ____ my sweater?
2. ____ lying on the beach.
3. We ____ help you right now.
4. ____ dinner ready?
5. They ____ played that game before.

Plurals

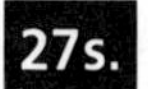

27s. Use an apostrophe and an *s* to form the plurals of letters, numerals, and signs, and of words referred to as words.

EXAMPLES **Your *o*'s look like *a*'s, and your *u*'s look like *n*'s.**
There are three *5*'s in his telephone number.
One sign of immature writing is too many *and*'s.
There are two *o*'s, two *k*'s, and three *e*'s in the word *bookkeeper.*

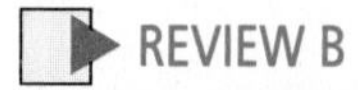

REVIEW B **Using Underlining (Italics) and Apostrophes Correctly**

For each of the following sentences, add underlining or apostrophes as necessary. The punctuation already supplied is correct.

EXAMPLE 1. One of my brothers college textbooks is History of Art by H. W. Janson.
1. *brother's; History of Art*

1. Whos the painter who inspired the musical play Sunday in the Park with George?
2. Hes Georges Seurat, one of Frances greatest painters.
3. "The young childrens reactions to Jacob Lawrences paintings were surprising," Angie said.
4. Didnt you read the review in Rolling Stone of the movie Vincent & Theo?

5. Its about Vincent van Gogh and his brother, who often supported him.
6. "I like Jasper Johns," Rick said, "but I cant tell if that is one of Johnss paintings."
7. Have you ever tried counting all the 2s or 4s in his Numbers in Color painting?
8. On a class trip to Chicago, we saw the bronze statue The Great Horse by Duchamp-Villon.
9. In our group, everybodys favorite painting is Cow's Skull: Red, White and Blue by Georgia O'Keeffe.
10. "On PBS, Ive seen an American Playhouse program about O'Keeffes life," Joyce said.

Hyphens

27t. Use a hyphen to divide a word at the end of a line.

EXAMPLES In my opinion, what this salad needs is some cu-
cumber slices.
Will you and Marguerite help me put the silver-
ware on the table?

When dividing a word at the end of a line, remember the following rules:

(1) Divide a word only between syllables.

INCORRECT Mr. Morrison looked around with a bewildered expression.
CORRECT Mr. Morrison looked around with a bewildered expression.

(2) Do not divide a one-syllable word.

INCORRECT Exercises like push-ups help to develop strength of the arm muscles.
CORRECT Exercises like push-ups help to develop
strength of the arm muscles.

(3) Do not divide a word so that one letter stands alone.

INCORRECT The seating capacity of the new stadium is e-
normous.

CORRECT The seating capacity of the new stadium is enormous.

27u. Use a hyphen with compound numbers from *twenty-one* to *ninety-nine* and with fractions used as modifiers.

EXAMPLES During a leap year, there are twenty-nine days in February.

Congress may override a president's veto by a two-thirds majority. [*Two-thirds* is an adjective that modifies *majority.*]

The pumpkin pie was so good that only one sixth of it is left. [*One sixth* is not used as a modifier. Instead, *sixth* is a noun modified by the adjective *one.*]

MECHANICS

EXERCISE 14 **Using Hyphens Correctly**

Write a number—using words, not numerals—to fit the blank in each sentence. Use hyphens where they are needed.

EXAMPLE **1.** The sum of ten and fifteen is ____.
1. *twenty-five*

1. January, March, May, July, August, October, and December are the months that have ____ days.
2. ____ of the moon is visible from the earth, but the other half can be seen only from outer space.
3. In twenty years I will be ____ years old.
4. I used ____ cup, which is 25 percent of the original one cup.
5. Our seventh-grade class has ____ students, fifteen boys and twelve girls.

REVIEW C **Punctuating Sentences Correctly**

Rewrite the following sentences, inserting underlining, quotation marks, commas, apostrophes, and hyphens as necessary.

EXAMPLE **1. For the talent show, Leila recited Poes poem The Raven.**
1. *For the talent show, Leila recited Poe's poem "The Raven."*

1. Queen Hatshepsut seized the throne of Egypt in 1503 B.C. and ruled for twenty one years.
2. Whos borrowed my scissors? demanded Jean.
3. Its hard to decide which authors story I should read first.
4. A weeks vacation never seems long enough.
5. After wed eaten supper, we decided to watch an old episode of Star Trek.
6. The driver shouted Move to the rear of the bus!
7. We didnt eat any salmon during our visit to Oregon.
8. I wasnt sorry admitted the clerk to see those picky customers leave.
9. Very Short on Law and Order is my favorite chapter in Andrew Garcia's autobiographical book Tough Trip Through Paradise.
10. Our new phone number starts with two 6s and ends with two 4s.

Parentheses

27v. Use parentheses to enclose material that is added to a sentence but is not considered of major importance.

EXAMPLES Emilio Aguinaldo **(**1869–1964**)** was a Filipino patriot and statesman.

Mom and Dad bought a kilim **(**ki lēm'**)** rug from our Turkish friend Ali.

Material enclosed in parentheses may be as short as a single word or as long as a short sentence. A short sentence in parentheses may stand alone or be contained within another sentence. Notice that a sentence within a sentence is not capitalized and has no end mark.

EXAMPLES Please be quiet during the performance. **(Take crying babies to the lobby.)**

Jack Echohawk **(he's Ben's cousin)** told us about growing up on a reservation.

EXERCISE 15 **Correcting Sentences by Adding Parentheses**

Insert parentheses where they are needed in the following sentences.

EXAMPLE **1.** My bicycle I've had it for three years is a ten-speed.

1. *My bicycle (I've had it for three years) is a ten-speed.*

1. At the age of thirteen, Jennifer Capriati began playing tennis my favorite sport professionally.
2. Elijah McCoy 1843–1929 invented a way to oil moving machinery.
3. I had to buy a new pocket calculator. My old one stopped working.
4. Charlemagne shär′lə mān′ was one of Europe's most famous rulers.
5. Lian Young she's a friend of mine told our class about her school in China.

Dashes

A *parenthetical expression* is a word or phrase that breaks into the main thought of a sentence. Parenthetical expressions are usually set off by commas or parentheses.

MECHANICS

EXAMPLES Grandma Moses, **for example,** started painting in her seventies.

The butler **(Theo Karras)** was the detective's first suspect.

REFERENCE NOTE: For more about using commas with parenthetical expressions, see page 718. For more about using parentheses, see pages 757–758.

Some parenthetical elements need stronger emphasis. In such cases, a dash is used.

27w. Use a dash to indicate an abrupt break in thought or speech.

EXAMPLES The right thing to do—I know it'll be hard—is to apologize.

"Do you think Ann will mind—I really hope she won't—if I borrow her sunglasses?" asked Melody.

EXERCISE 16 **Correcting Sentences by Adding Dashes**

Insert dashes where they are needed in the following sentences.

EXAMPLE **1.** The school lunchroom it was a dull green has been painted a cheery yellow.

1. *The school lunchroom—it was a dull green—has been painted a cheery yellow.*

1. Fireflies I can't remember where I read this make what is called cold light.
2. Roberto has always wanted to be can't you guess? an astronaut.
3. Randy Travis I really want to see his concert has a new song out.
4. Do you mind I don't if Jill and Mandy go to the mall with us?
5. The best way to learn how to swim that is, after you've learned the basic strokes is to practice.

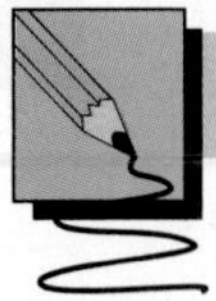

WRITING APPLICATION

Using Quotations in Reports

In persuasive and informative essays, a direct quotation can sometimes be more effective than a secondhand paraphrase. However, a quotation can be confusing and misleading if it isn't correctly capitalized and punctuated.

CONFUSING Inés Torro, manager of the Waste Disposal Department, said by the end of December, weekly recycling pickup will be available in all areas of the city.

CLEAR Inés Torro, manager of the Waste Disposal Department, said**,** **"B**y the end of December, weekly recycling pickup will be available in all areas of the city.**"**

MECHANICS

WRITING ACTIVITY

Your social studies class is taking a survey of people's attitudes toward recycling. Interview at least three people from different households in your community. Ask them specific questions to find out

- whether they think recycling is important
- what items, if any, they recycle
- whether they find it easy or difficult to recycle
- how they think recycling could be made easier for people in the community

Based on the information you gather, write a brief report about recycling in your community. In your report, quote several people's exact words.

Prewriting First, think of several questions to ask. Word your questions so that they can't be answered with a simple *yes* or *no*. Next, decide whom you want to interview. You might interview friends, family members, or neighbors. Begin each interview by recording the person's name, age, and occupation. During the interview, write down or tape-record what the person says. (If you want to tape the interview, make sure you have the person's permission first.) If you write down the interview, be sure to write the person's answers word for word. (You may need to ask the person to speak slowly.) When all your interviews are completed, compare your interviewees' responses. How are they similar? How are they different? What conclusions can you draw about attitudes toward recycling in your community? Jot down some notes to help you organize your information.

Writing In the first paragraph of your draft, give a statement that sums up the main idea of your report. Then, use your interviewees' answers to support your main idea. Since you can't quote every word, you'll need to choose your quotations carefully. Quote words and sentences that accurately represent each person's answers and attitudes. Clearly identify each person that you quote. Conclude your report by restating your main idea.

Evaluating and Revising After you've completed your first draft, reread your main idea. Does the body of your report support that idea? If not, rethink and revise your main idea. Make sure the body of your report follows a logical order. As you organize your report, you may need to add, cut, or rearrange details. Be sure that all direct quotations are correctly quoted. Also, be sure that you have not used a person's words or ideas without giving him or her credit.

Proofreading and Publishing As you proofread your report, check your quotations against your notes. Be sure you've spelled people's names correctly. Finally, make sure that you've put quotation marks around direct quotations and that you've capitalized and punctuated all quotations correctly. You and your classmates can share your findings and suggestions with the person or agency in charge of recycling in your community. As a class, write a letter that summarizes your findings.

Review: Posttest

A. Proofreading Sentences for the Correct Use of Apostrophes, Quotation Marks, Underlining (Italics), Hyphens, Parentheses, and Dashes

Revise each of the following sentences so that apostrophes, quotation marks, underlining, hyphens, parentheses, or dashes are used correctly. [Note: A sentence may contain more than one error.]

EXAMPLE **1. "May I borrow your copy of 'Life' magazine? Phil asked Alan.**
1. *"May I borrow your copy of <u>Life</u> magazine?" Phil asked Alan.*

1. Boris Karloff (his real name was William Henry Pratt played the monster in the original movie version of Frankenstein.
2. "Ive never known—do you? what the word 'kith' means," Phil said.
3. Its just a simple word," Anna said, "that refers to family and friends."
4. I've heard that the programs announcer and inter viewer will be Connie Chung, a favorite of mine.
5. Alan said that "Norma couldn't understand why twenty two people had voted against having the dance on a Friday night.
6. "A two thirds majority of the mens team hadnt played before", Shawn said.
7. Fred said, This magazine article titled *Luxury Liners of the Past* is interesting".
8. "Does the public library have copies of the 'Lakota Times' or any other Native American newspapers"? Tanya asked.
9. My sisters' like to read folk tales in books such as the one in Two Ways to Count to Ten by Ruby Dee.
10. The Lopezes's cat I dont think they know is living in our garage." Mary said.

MECHANICS

B. Punctuating Quotations Correctly

For each of the following sentences, add quotation marks where they are needed.

EXAMPLE **1. I wonder why so many people enjoy collecting things, said J. D.**
1. *"I wonder why so many people enjoy collecting things," said J. D.*

11. I know I do! Julia exclaimed.
12. Tomás said, My grandmother once said, It's the thrill of the hunt.
13. Do you collect anything as a hobby? Josh asked Marsha, who had just entered the room.
14. No, Marsha answered, but I know a person who collects old cameras and antique costume jewelry.
15. My aunt collects John McCormack's records, Kevin said. Do you know who he is?
16. I'm not sure, Julia said, but I think that he was an Irish singer.
17. Yes, he sang in the opera; he also sang popular Irish songs such as The Rose of Tralee, Kevin said.
18. My stepbrother has a collection of arrowheads. He hasn't been collecting them very long, Sydney said.
19. You should see Mrs. Webb's collection of Chinese jade carvings, J. D. said. It's great!
20. Some people—I'm sure you know—have unusual collections, Josh said. For instance, my aunt collects old shoelaces.

28 SPELLING

Improving Your Spelling

MECHANICS

Good Spelling Habits

Practicing the following techniques can help you spell words correctly.

1. **To learn the spelling of a word, pronounce it, study it, and write it.** Pronounce words carefully. Mispronunciation can cause misspelling. For instance, if you say *ath • a • lete* instead of *ath • lete,* you will probably spell the word wrong.

   - First, make sure that you know how to pronounce the word correctly, and then practice saying it.
   - Second, study the word. Notice any parts that might be hard to remember.
   - Third, write the word from memory. Check your spelling.
   - If you misspelled the word, repeat the three steps of this process.

2. **Use a dictionary.** When you find that you have misspelled a word, look it up in a dictionary. Don't guess about the correct spelling.

3. **Spell by syllables.** A ***syllable*** is a word part that can be pronounced by itself.

EXAMPLE **thor • ough** [two syllables]
sep • a • rate [three syllables]

Instead of trying to learn how to pronounce and spell a whole word, break it up into its syllables whenever possible. It's easier to learn a few letters at a time than to learn all of them at once.

REFERENCE NOTE: For information on using the dictionary to determine the syllables in a word, see page 825.

EXERCISE 1 Spelling by Syllables

Look up the following words in a dictionary, and divide each one into syllables. Pronounce each syllable correctly, and learn to spell the word by syllables.

1. legislature
2. perspire
3. modern
4. temperature
5. probably
6. similar
7. library
8. definition
9. recognize
10. awkward

4. **Proofread for careless spelling errors.** Reread your writing carefully, and correct any mistakes and unclear letters. For example, make sure that your *i*'s are dotted, and your *t*'s crossed, and your *g*'s don't look like *q*'s.

5. **Keep a spelling notebook.** Divide each page into four columns:

COLUMN 1 Correctly spell the word you missed. (Never enter a misspelled word.)
COLUMN 2 Write the word again, dividing it into syllables and marking its accents.
COLUMN 3 Write the word once more, circling the spot that gives you trouble.
COLUMN 4 Jot down any comments that might help you remember the correct spelling.

Here is an example of how you might make entries for two words that are often misspelled.

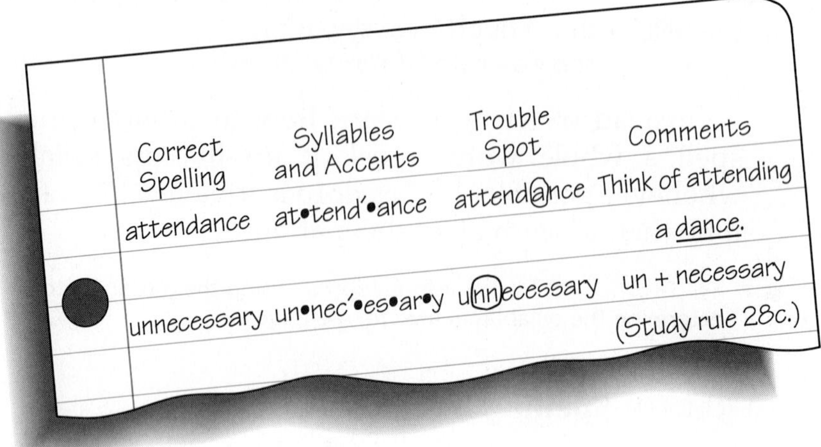

Correct Spelling
Syllables and Accents
Trouble Spot
Comments
attendance
at•tend′•ance
attendance
Think of attending a dance.
unnecessary
un•nec′•es•ar•y
unnecessary
un + necessary (Study rule 28c.)

Spelling Rules

ie and *ei*

28a. Write *ie* when the sound is long *e*, except after *c*.

EXAMPLES **chief, brief, believe, yield, receive, deceive**
EXCEPTIONS **seize, leisure, either, neither, weird**

Write *ei* when the sound is not long *e*, especially when the sound is long *a*.

EXAMPLES **sleigh, veil, freight, weight, height, foreign**
EXCEPTIONS **friend, mischief, ancient, pie**

You may find this time-tested verse a help.

I before e
Except after *c*,
Or when sounded like *a*,
As in *neighbor* and *weigh*.

If you use this rhyme, remember that "*i* before *e*" refers only to words in which these two letters stand for the sound of long *e*, as in the examples under rule 28a.

EXERCISE 2 Writing Words with *ie* and *ei*

Add the letters *ie* or *ei* to correctly spell each of the following words.

EXAMPLE **1. conc . . . t**
1. *conceit*

1. dec . . . ve
2. n . . . ther
3. rec . . . ve
4. h . . . ght
5. fr . . . nd
6. l . . . sure
7. misch . . . f
8. w . . . ght
9. . . . ght
10. sl . . . gh
11. fr . . . ght
12. n . . . ghbor
13. c . . . ling
14. shr . . . k
15. rec . . . pt
16. p . . . ce
17. r . . . gn
18. th . . . r
19. s . . . ze
20. br . . . f

EXERCISE 3 Proofreading a Paragraph to Correct Spelling Errors

The following paragraph contains ten spelling errors involving the use of *ie* and *ei*. For each sentence, write the misspelled word or words correctly. If a sentence has no spelling error, write *C*.

EXAMPLE **[1] Last summer I recieved an airline ticket as a birthday gift.**
1. *received*

[1] I used the ticket to fly to Puerto Rico with my freind Alicia to see my grandmother and other relatives. [2] We flew to San Juan, where my grandmother's nieghbor, Mr. Sanchez, met us and drove us to my grandmother's house. [3] When we got there, all of my relatives—aunts, uncles, cousins, neices, nephews—came to welcome us. [4] They couldn't beleive that niether of us had ever been to Puerto Rico before, so the next day, they took us sightseeing. [5] First we went to Humacao, which, as you can see on the map on the next page, is located on the Caribbean. [6] Then we drove along the coast to Ponce, the island's cheif city after San Juan. [7] Continuing north from Ponce, we thought that we'd take a liesurely drive on this mountain road, *Ruta Panoramica,* which means "Panoramic

Road." [8] However, the road turned and twisted so much that I was releived to get back on the main road. [9] After we had a breif rest, we explored the western part of the island. [10] Within two days, Puerto Rico no longer seemed foriegn to us.

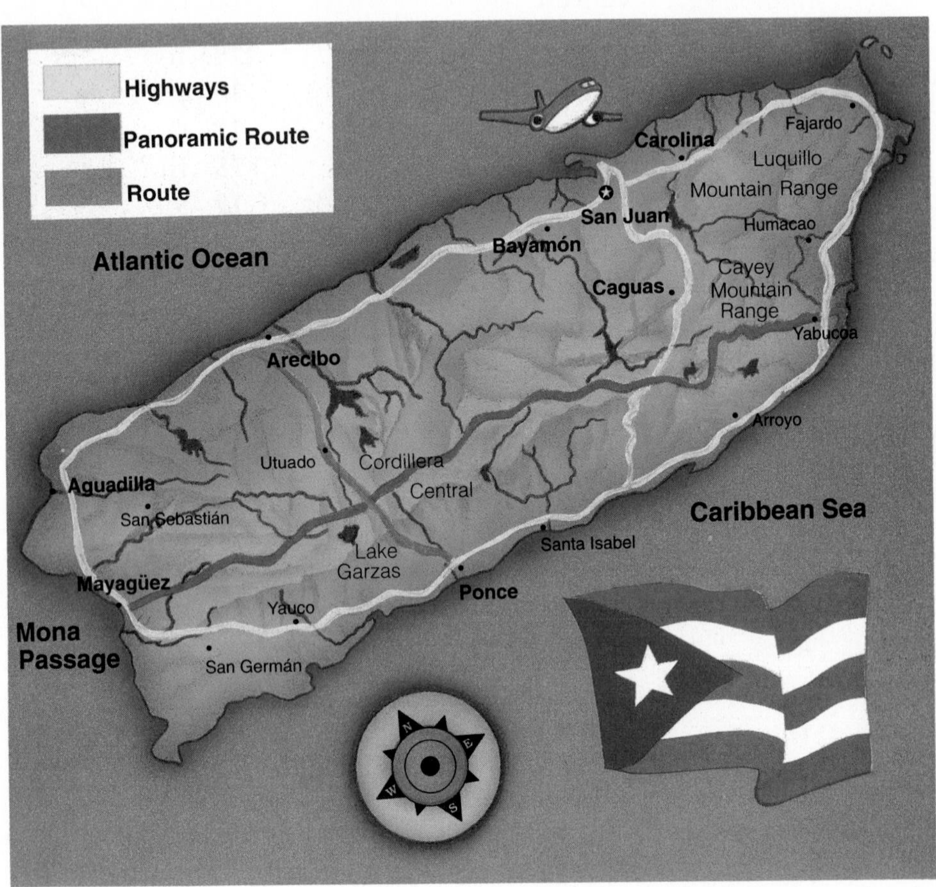

MECHANICS

–cede, –ceed, and –sede

28b. The only word ending in *–sede* is *supersede.* The only words ending in *–ceed* are *exceed, proceed,* and *succeed.* All other words with this sound end in *–cede.*

EXAMPLES con**cede,** re**cede,** pre**cede**

Prefixes and Suffixes

A ***prefix*** is a letter or a group of letters added to the beginning of a word to change its meaning. A ***suffix*** is a letter or a group of letters added to the end of a word to change its meaning.

28c. When adding a prefix to a word, do not change the spelling of the word itself.

EXAMPLES il + legal = **illegal**
un + natural = **unnatural**
dis + appear = **disappear**
mis + spent = **misspent**

EXERCISE 4 Spelling Words with Prefixes

Spell each of the following words, adding the prefix given.

EXAMPLE **1.** semi + circle
1. *semicircle*

1. il + legible
2. un + necessary
3. im + partial
4. in + offensive
5. im + mortal
6. mis + spell
7. dis + satisfy
8. dis + approve
9. mis + understand
10. over + rule

28d. When adding the suffix –*ness* or –*ly* to a word, do not change the spelling of the word itself.

EXAMPLES sudden + ness = sudden**ness**
truthful + ly = truthful**ly**
still + ness = still**ness**
final + ly = final**ly**

EXCEPTION For most words that end in *y*, change the *y* to *i* before –*ly* or –*ness.*

EXAMPLES kindly + ness = kindl**iness**
day + ly = da**ily**

MECHANICS

28e. Drop the final silent e before a suffix beginning with a vowel.

Vowels are the letters *a, e, i, o, u,* and sometimes *y.* All other letters of the alphabet are ***consonants.***

EXAMPLES nice + est = nic**est**
love + able = lov**able**

EXCEPTION Keep the silent e in words ending in *ce* and *ge* before a suffix beginning with *a* or *o.*

EXAMPLES notice + able = notic**eable**
courage + ous = courag**eous**

28f. Keep the final e before a suffix beginning with a consonant.

EXAMPLES care + less = car**eless**
plate + ful = plat**eful**
false + hood = fals**ehood**

EXCEPTIONS argue + ment = argu**ment**
true + ly = tru**ly**

F W WNT T TLK RLLY GD, W'LL HV T NVNT VWLS.
THAVES 10-16

FRANK & ERNEST reprinted by permission of NEA, Inc.

 EXERCISE 5 **Spelling Words with Suffixes**

Spell each of the following words, adding the suffix given.

EXAMPLE **1.** joy + ful
1. *joyful*

1. hopeful + ly
2. happy + ness
3. sincere + ly
4. write + ing
5. desire + able
6. change + able
7. cross + ing
8. advance + ment
9. true + ly
10. easy + ly

28g. For words ending in *y* preceded by a consonant, change the *y* to *i* before any suffix that does not begin with *i*.

EXAMPLES friendly + er = friendl**ier**
beauty + ful = beaut**iful**
carry + ing = carry**ing**

Words ending in *y* preceded by a vowel do not change their spelling before a suffix.

EXAMPLES key + ed = key**ed**
pay + ment = pay**ment**

EXCEPTIONS lay—laid say—said

28h. Double the final consonant before adding *–ing, –ed, –er,* or *–est* to a one-syllable word that ends in a single consonant preceded by a single vowel.

EXAMPLES sit + ing = si**tting**
hop + ed = ho**pped**
dim + er = di**mmer**

With a one-syllable word ending in a single consonant that is *not* preceded by a single vowel, do not double the consonant before adding *–ing, –ed, –er,* or *–est*.

EXAMPLES reap + ed = reap**ed** neat + est = neat**est**
cold + er = cold**er** hold + ing = hold**ing**

EXERCISE 6 **Spelling Words with Suffixes**

Spell each of the following words, adding the suffix given.

EXAMPLE **1.** beauty + ful
1. *beautiful*

1. bay + ing
2. silly + ness
3. drop + ed
4. deny + ing
5. pity + less
6. swim + er
7. sly + est
8. hurry + ed
9. tap + ing
10. clean + er

REVIEW A Proofreading a Paragraph for Correct Spelling

Most of the following sentences contain words that have been misspelled. Write each misspelled word correctly. If a sentence is correct, write *C*.

EXAMPLE [1] Remember the beautyful bonsai trees in the *Karate Kid* movies?

1. *beautiful*

[1] Bonsai trees can live to be hundreds of years old, yet you can quickly create one of your own in an afternoon. [2] Simpley use these pictures as you proceed through the following steps.

[3] First, you'll need an inxpensive plant (such as a juniper), some soil, some moss, and a shallow bowl. [4] When you are chooseing a plant, try to get one with a trunk that has some of its roots showing so that your tree will look old. [5] Make a carful study of your plant, and decide how you want the bonsai to look in the bowl. [6] Then, cut or pinch away undesireable branches and leaves until the plant looks like a tree. [7] After triming your plant, remove most of the large roots so that the plant can stand in the bowl. [8] Cover the remaining roots with soil, and if the weather is mild, put your bonsai in a shaded place outside. [9] You don't have to water your plant dayly, but you should keep the soil moist. [10] After your plant has healled, you will have many years of enjoyment from your bonsai.

Forming the Plural of Nouns

28i. Observe the following rules for spelling the plural of nouns:

(1) To form the plural of most nouns, add –s.

SINGULAR	girl	cheese	task	monkey	banana
PLURAL	girls	cheeses	tasks	monkeys	bananas

REFERENCE NOTE: Make sure that you do not confuse the plural form of a noun with its possessive form. For a discussion of possessive forms of nouns, see pages 746–748.

(2) Form the plural of nouns ending in *s, x, z, ch,* or *sh* by adding *–es.*

SINGULAR	moss	wax	waltz	birch	dish
PLURAL	mosses	waxes	waltzes	birches	dishes

NOTE: Proper nouns usually follow this rule, too.

EXAMPLES the Nuñezes
the Williamses

EXERCISE 7 Spelling the Plural of Nouns

Spell the plural form of each of the following nouns.

EXAMPLE 1. match
1. *matches*

1. box
2. crash
3. wrench
4. address
5. church
6. index
7. Gómez
8. ditch
9. miss
10. tax

(3) Form the plural of nouns ending in *y* preceded by a consonant by changing the *y* to *i* and adding *–es.*

SINGULAR	lady	hobby	county	strawberry
PLURAL	**ladies**	**hobbies**	**counties**	**strawberries**

EXCEPTION With proper nouns, simply add *–s.*
EXAMPLES the **Applebys,** the **Trilbys.**

(4) Form the plural of nouns ending in *y* preceded by a vowel by adding *–s.*

SINGULAR	toy	journey	highway	Wednesday
PLURAL	**toys**	**journeys**	**highways**	**Wednesdays**

(5) Form the plural of most nouns ending in *f* by adding *–s.* The plural of some nouns ending in *f* or *fe* is formed by changing the *f* to *v* and adding either *–s* or *–es.*

SINGULAR	gulf	belief	knife	loaf	wolf
PLURAL	**gulfs**	**beliefs**	**knives**	**loaves**	**wolves**

NOTE: When you are not sure about how to spell the plural of a noun ending in *f* or *fe,* look in a dictionary.

(6) Form the plural of nouns ending in *o* preceded by a vowel by adding *–s.* The plural of many nouns ending in *o* preceded by a consonant is formed by adding *–es.*

SINGULAR	patio	ratio	veto	hero
PLURAL	**patios**	**ratios**	**vetoes**	**heroes**

EXCEPTIONS **Eskimo—Eskimos** **silo—silos**

MECHANICS

Form the plural of most musical terms ending in *o* by adding *–s.*

SINGULAR	piano	alto	solo	trio
PLURAL	**pianos**	**altos**	**solos**	**trios**

NOTE: To form the plural of some nouns ending in *o* preceded by a consonant, you may add either *–s* or *–es.*

SINGULAR	banjo	mosquito	flamingo
PLURAL	**banjos**	**mosquitos**	**flamingos**
	or	*or*	*or*
	banjoes	**mosquitoes**	**flamingoes**

(7) The plural of a few nouns is formed in irregular ways.

SINGULAR	man	mouse	foot	ox	child
PLURAL	**men**	**mice**	**feet**	**oxen**	**children**

EXERCISE 8 **Spelling the Plural of Nouns**

Spell the plural form of each of the following nouns.

EXAMPLE **1.** industry
1. *industries*

1. turkey
2. studio
3. chief
4. soprano
5. puppy
6. self
7. chimney
8. baby
9. tomato
10. echo

(8) Form the plural of compound nouns consisting of a noun plus a modifier by making the modified noun plural.

SINGULAR	sister-in-law	coat-of-arms
PLURAL	**sisters-in-law**	**coats-of-arms**
SINGULAR	Chief of State	editor in chief
PLURAL	**Chiefs of State**	**editors in chief**

REFERENCE NOTE: For more on compound nouns, see page 423.

(9) The plural of a few compound nouns is formed in irregular ways.

SINGULAR	**eight-year-old**	**tie-up**	**drive-in**
PLURAL	**eight-year-olds**	**tie-ups**	**drive-ins**

(10) Some nouns are the same in the singular and the plural.

SINGULAR AND PLURAL **deer** **sheep** **salmon** **Sioux**

(11) Form the plural of numerals, letters, signs, and words referred to as words by adding an apostrophe and *–s*.

SINGULAR	**1800**	***B***	**&**
PLURAL	**1800's**	***B*'s**	**&'s**

NOTE: In your reading you may notice that some writers do not use apostrophes to form the plurals of numerals, letters, signs, and words referred to as words. However, using an apostrophe is never wrong. Therefore, it is best always to use the apostrophe.

MECHANICS

EXERCISE 9 Spelling the Plural of Nouns

Spell the plural form of each of the following nouns.

EXAMPLE **1. push-up**
1. *push-ups*

1. side-wheeler
2. moose
3. mother-in-law
4. 1930
5. *m*
6. thirteen-year-old
7. trout
8. governor-elect
9. Chinese
10. commander in chief

Shoe, by Jeff MacNelly, reprinted by permission: Tribune Media Services.

Words Often Confused

People often confuse the words in each of the following groups. Some of these words are ***homonyms,*** which means that their pronunciations are the same. However, these words have different meanings and spellings. Other words in the following groups have the same or similar spellings yet have different meanings.

accept	[verb] *to receive; to agree to* The Lanfords would not *accept* our gift.
except	[preposition] *with the exclusion of; but* Everyone *except* Lauren agreed.
advice	[noun] *a recommendation for action* What is your mother's *advice?*
advise	[verb] *to recommend a course of action* She *advises* me to take the camp job.
affect	[verb] *to act upon; to change* Does bad weather *affect* your health?
effect	[noun] *result; consequence* What *effect* does the weather have on your health?
already	*previously* We have *already* studied the customs of the Navajo people.
all ready	*all prepared* or *in readiness* The crew is *all ready* to set sail.

MECHANICS

EXERCISE 10 **Choosing Between Words Often Confused**

From each pair in parentheses, choose the word or words that will make the sentence correct.

EXAMPLE 1. All of us (*accept, except*) Josh forgot our tickets.
1. *except*

1. By the time Melba arrived, Roscoe had (*already, all ready*) baked the sweet potatoes.
2. One of the purposes of the Cabinet is to (*advice, advise*) the president.
3. The soft music had a soothing (*affect, effect*) on the tired child.
4. The girls were (*already, all ready*) for the sleigh ride.
5. The arrival of Buddhism in Japan had an enormous (*affect, effect*) on Japanese culture.
6. The snow has melted everywhere (*accept, except*) in the mountains.
7. The doctor's (*advice, advise*) was to drink plenty of fluids and to rest.
8. Sarita was happy to (*accept, except*) the invitation to the party.
9. Reading the newspaper usually (*affects, effects*) my ideas about current events.
10. What do you (*advice, advise*) me to do?

altar	[noun] *a table or stand at which religious rites are performed* There was a bowl of flowers on the *altar*.
alter	[verb] *to change* Another hurricane may *alter* the shoreline near our town.
altogether	*entirely* It is *altogether* too cold for swimming.
all together	*everyone in the same place* Will our class be *all together* at the Ramses exhibit?

brake	[noun] *a device to stop a machine* I used the emergency *brake* to prevent the car from rolling downhill.
break	[verb] *to fracture; to shatter* Don't *break* that mirror!
capital	*a city, the location of a government* What is the *capital* of this state?
capitol	*building; statehouse* The *capitol* is on Congress Avenue.
cloths	*pieces of cloth* I need some more cleaning *cloths.*
clothes	*wearing apparel* I decided to put on warm *clothes.*

MECHANICS

EXERCISE 11 Choosing Between Words Often Confused

From each pair in parentheses, choose the word or words that will make the sentence correct.

EXAMPLE **1.** If it rains, we will (*altar, alter*) our plans.
1. *alter*

1. My summer (*cloths, clothes*) are loose and light.
2. In England, you can still see remains of (*altars, alters*) built by early tribes.
3. Going down a steep mountain, a bicyclist can wear out a set of (*brakes, breaks*).
4. You should use soft (*cloths, clothes*) to clean silver.
5. The cold weather did not (*altar, alter*) Ling's plans for the Chinese New Year celebration.
6. Accra is the (*capital, capitol*) of Ghana.
7. Put the pieces of the vase (*altogether, all together*), and I will try to repair it.

8. Did he (*brake, break*) his promise?
9. On the dome of the (*capital, capitol*) stands a large bronze statue.
10. The audience was (*altogether, all together*) charmed by the mime's performance.

coarse	[adjective] *rough, crude, not fine* The *coarse* sand acts as a filter.
course	[noun] *path of action; series of studies* [also used in the expression *of course*] What is the best *course* for me to take? You may change your mind, *of course.*
complement	[noun] *something that completes* Red shoes are a good *complement* to that outfit.
compliment	[verb] *to praise someone;* [noun] *praise from someone* Mrs. Katz *complimented* Jean on her speech. Thank you for the *compliment*.
council	*a group of people who meet together* The mayor's *council* has seven members.
councilor	*a member of a council* The mayor appointed seven *councilors*.
counsel	[noun] *advice;* [verb] *to give advice* He needs legal *counsel* on this matter. His attorney will *counsel* him before the hearing.
counselor	*one who advises* Mr. Jackson is the guidance *counselor* for the seventh grade.

des´ert [noun] *a dry, barren, sandy region; a wilderness*
This cactus grows only in the *desert.*

desert´ [verb] *to abandon; to leave*
Good sports do not *desert* their teammates.

dessert´ [noun] *the final course of a meal*
Let's have fresh peaches for *dessert.*

EXERCISE 12

Choosing Between Words Often Confused

From each pair in parentheses, choose the word that will make the sentence correct.

EXAMPLE **1. At the end of dinner, we ate (*desert, dessert*).**
1. *dessert*

1. The city (*council, counsel*) will not meet unless seven of the ten (*councilors, counselors*) are present.
2. The patient received (*council, counsel*) from the doctor on the best (*coarse, course*) to a speedy recovery.
3. Chutney and yogurt are often the (*complements, compliments*) of Indian food.
4. When we visited Cairo, we saw the Nile River, of (*coarse, course*).
5. Juan is preparing the enchiladas, and I'm making *piedras* for (*desert, dessert*) tonight.
6. Marilyn made a hand puppet out of (*coarse, course*) burlap.
7. The major would not (*desert, dessert*) her regiment.
8. I want your (*council, counsel*), not your (*complements, compliments*).
9. My mother and father both took part in Operation (*Dessert, Desert*) Storm.
10. Our camp (*councilor, counselor*) suggested that we eat fruit for (*desert, dessert*).

formally *with dignity; following strict rules or procedures*
We must behave *formally* at the reception.

formerly *previously; at an earlier date*
Formerly, people thought travel to the moon was impossible.

---

hear [verb] *to receive sounds through the ears*
You can *hear* a whisper through these walls.

here [adverb] *in this place*
How long have you lived *here?*

---

its [possessive form of *it*]
That book has lost *its* cover.

it's [contraction of *it is* or *it has*]
It's the coldest winter anyone can remember.
It's not rained for two months.

---

lead [verb, present tense, rhymes with *feed*] *to go first, to be a leader*
Can she *lead* us out of this tunnel?

led [verb, past tense of *lead*] *went first*
Elizabeth Blackwell *led* the movement for hospital reform.

lead [noun, rhymes with *red*] *a heavy metal; graphite used in a pencil*
There is no *lead* in a *lead* pencil.

---

loose [adjective, rhymes with *moose*] *not tight*
This belt is too *loose.*

lose [verb] *to suffer loss*
Fran will *lose* the argument if she doesn't check her facts.

passed [verb, past tense of *pass*] *went by*
He *passed* us five minutes ago.

past [noun] *that which has gone by;* [preposition] *beyond*; [adjective] *ended*
Good historians make the *past* come alive.
We rode *past* your house.
That era is *past*.

EXERCISE 13

Choosing Between Words Often Confused

From each pair in parentheses, choose the word that will make the sentence correct.

EXAMPLE **1. Kaya (*lead, led*) us to the ceremonial lodge.**
1. *led*

1. The woman who (*formally, formerly*) (*lead, led*) the band moved to Alaska.
2. We do not expect to (*loose, lose*) any of our backfield players this year.
3. We (*passed, past*) three stalled cars this morning on our way to school.
4. "Why did you (*lead, led*) us (*hear, here*)?" the angry group demanded.
5. Can you (*hear, here*) the difference between the CD and the album?
6. The workers removed the (*lead, led*) pipes from the old house.
7. How did the ship break (*loose, lose*) from both of its anchors?
8. The guests are to dress (*formally, formerly*) for the inauguration ball.
9. "I think (*it's, its*) time for a pop quiz," announced Mrs. Ferrari.
10. Has the school bus already gone (*passed, past*) our street, Tiffany?

peace	*quiet order and security* World *peace* is the goal of the United Nations.
piece	*a part of something* Lian bought that *piece* of silk in Hong Kong.
plain	[adjective] *unadorned, simple, common;* [noun] *a flat area of land* Jeans were part of his *plain* appearance. A broad, treeless *plain* stretched before them.
plane	[noun] *a flat surface; a tool; an airplane* Use an inclined *plane* to move that couch. I have just learned how to use a carpenter's *plane.* Have you ever flown in a *plane*?
principal	[noun] *the head of a school;* [adjective] *chief, main* The *principal* spoke of the *principal* duties of students.
principle	[noun] *a rule of conduct; a fundamental truth* Action should be guided by *principles.*
quiet	[adjective] *still and peaceful; without noise* The forest was very *quiet.*
quite	[adverb] *wholly or entirely; to a great extent* Some students are already *quite* sure of their career plans.
shone	[verb, past tense of *shine*] *gleamed; glowed* The moon *shone* softly over the grass.
shown	[verb, past participle of *show*] *revealed* Tamisha has *shown* me how to crochet.

EXERCISE 14 Choosing Between Words Often Confused

From each pair in parentheses, choose the word that will make the sentence correct.

EXAMPLE **1. Mr. Ramírez used a (*plain, plane*) to smooth the board.**
1. *plane*

1. Each drop of water (*shone, shown*) like crystal.
2. Motor vehicles are one of the (*principal, principle*) sources of air pollution in our cities.
3. If you don't hurry, you'll miss your (*plain, plane*).
4. The (*principal, principle*) of trust can lead to world (*peace, piece*).
5. Jan has (*shone, shown*) me how to change a tire.
6. It is clear that Luisa is acting on (*principal, principle*), not from a personal motive.
7. On Christmas Eve we always sing carols and have a (*peace, piece*) of fruitcake.
8. "What a (*quiet, quite*) Fourth of July," said Gloria.
9. "For once," the (*principal, principle*) announced with a smile, "you don't have to be (*quiet, quite*)."
10. (*Plain, Plane*) fruits and vegetables can provide a delicious and nutritious meal.

EXERCISE 15 Proofreading for Words Often Confused

In the following paragraph, identify the ten misspelled words. Then give the correct spelling of each word.

EXAMPLE **[1] Some portraits are quiet striking.**
1. *quiet—quite*

[1] The painting on the next page is by Rembrandt, one of the principle painters of the seventeenth century. [2] The portrait, probably of a rabbi in Amsterdam, is quiet lovely even though it is relatively plane. [3] The painting illustrates one of Rembrandt's main artistic principals, the strong contrast between light and dark. [4] Light is shown

only on the rabbi's face, hands, and a peace of clothing. [5] The rest of the painting is quiet dark, creating a somber plain that highlights these lighted features. [6] The rabbi is shone in a state of piece, and the lack of detail in the painting gives an impression of quite elegance.

Van Rijn Rembrandt, *Portrait of an Old Man*, Florence, Uffizi, Scala/Art Resource

stationary	[adjective] *in a fixed position* Is that chalkboard *stationary?*
stationery	[noun] *writing paper* Do you have any white *stationery?*

than	[a conjunction used in comparisons] Alaska is bigger *than* Texas.
then	[adverb] *at that time* If she will see me after class, we can talk about it *then.*

their	[possessive form of *they*] Can you understand *their* message?
there	[adverb] *a place*; [also used to begin a sentence] Let's meet *there*. *There* are toys hidden inside the piñata.
they're	[contraction of *they are*] *They're* all from Guam.
threw	[verb, past tense of *throw*] *hurled* Ted *threw* me the mitt.
through	[preposition] I can't see *through* the lens.

Choosing Between Words Often Confused

From each pair or group in parentheses, choose the word that will make the sentence correct.

EXAMPLE **1. When will we arrive (*their, they're, there*)?**
1. *there*

1. That noise is from a jet plane going (*threw, through*) the sound barrier.
2. The stars appear to be (*stationary, stationery*), but we know that (*their, there, they're*) moving at very high speeds.
3. Thailand is much larger (*than, then*) South Korea.
4. The pitcher (*threw, through*) a curve ball.
5. A (*stationary, stationery*) store usually sells paper, pencils, and other supplies.
6. We started our trip in Barcelona and (*than, then*) traveled north to Madrid.
7. The girls brought (*their, there, they're*) displays for the science fair.
8. A moving target is much harder to hit (*than, then*) a (*stationary, stationery*) one.

9. Each time Chris got a free throw, he lobbed the ball neatly (*threw, through*) the net to score one point.
10. (*Their, They're, There*) first rehearsal will be after school today.

to	[preposition] We are going *to* Mexico.
too	[adverb] *also; more than enough* Audrey is going, *too.* Kazuo used *too* much miso; consequently, the soup was very salty.
two	*one plus one* We bought *two* sets of chopsticks.
weak	[adjective] *feeble; not strong* Melinda's illness has left her very *weak.*
week	[noun] *seven days* Let's practice again next *week.*
weather	[noun] *the condition of the atmosphere* The *weather* seems to be changing.
whether	[conjunction] *if* We don't know *whether* to expect rain or snow.
who's	[contraction of *who is* or *who has*] *Who's* going to the museum? "*Who's* been eating my porridge?" asked Papa Bear.
whose	[possessive form of *who*] *Whose* report was the most original?
your	[possessive form of *you*] What is *your* middle name?
you're	[contraction of *you are*] *You're* my best friend.

EXERCISE 17 Choosing Between Words Often Confused

From each pair or group in parentheses, choose the word that will make the sentence correct.

EXAMPLE **1. What are (*your, you're*) plans for celebrating Juneteenth?**
1. ***your***

1. (*Who's, Whose*) the present Secretary of State of the United States?
2. My stepsister and I built (*to, too, two*) snow forts on our front lawn.
3. "(*Your, You're*) late," my friend complained.
4. Would you be able to stand the (*weather, whether*) in Alaska?
5. That sounds like a (*weak, week*) excuse to me.
6. (*Your, You're*) dog is (*to, too, two*) sleepy to learn any new tricks.
7. "(*Who's, Whose*) boots and mittens are these?" Mrs. Allen asked.
8. The pilot must quickly decide (*weather, whether*) to parachute to safety or try to land the crippled plane.
9. Spring break starts next (*weak, week*).
10. My family is going (*too, to, two*) New Orleans for the holidays.

EXERCISE 18 Writing Sentences with Words Often Confused

You are the new meteorologist for a local television station. Tonight is your first broadcast, and you still haven't written your script. Using the weather map on the next page, write five sentences for your script. In each sentence, use one of the words from the following list. Underline each one you use.

to	weak	whose
two	weather	your
too	whether	you're
week	who's	

EXAMPLE **1.** ***I'll let you know whether you'll need an umbrella this weekend, right after these messages.***

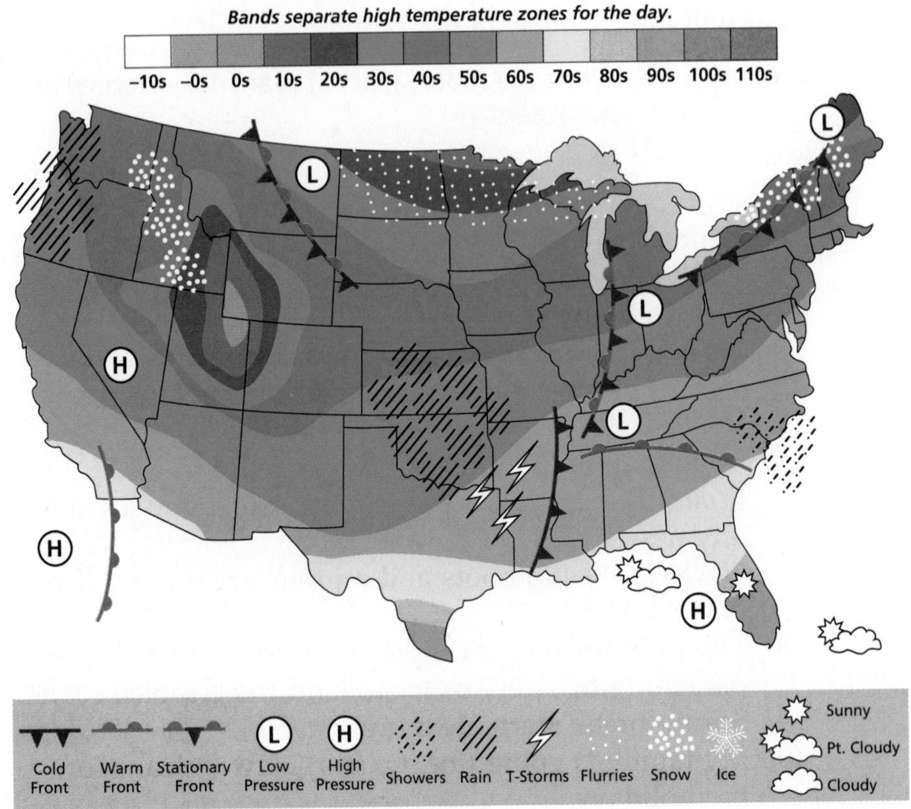

MECHANICS

REVIEW B Choosing Between Words Often Confused

From each pair or group in parentheses, choose the word or words that will make the sentence correct.

EXAMPLE **My parents asked my [1] (*advice, advise*) about where we should spend our vacation.**
1. *advice*

Last March, my family could not decide [1] (*weather, whether*) to visit Boston or Philadelphia. Finally, we decided on Boston, the [2] (*capital, capitol*) of Massachusetts. We drove [3] (*to, too, two*) the city in three days. Even my parents could not conceal [4] (*their, there, they're*) excitement. We did not [5] (*loose, lose*) a moment. Boston [6] (*formally, formerly*) was "the hub of the universe," and we discovered that [7] (*it's, its*) still a fascinating city.

Everyone in my family [8] (*accept, except*) me had eaten lobster, and I ate my first one in Boston. I was not [9] (*altogether, all together*) certain how to eat the lobster, but my doubt did not [10] (*affect, effect*) my appetite. My parents insisted that pear yogurt was a strange [11] (*desert, dessert*) to follow lobster, but I would not [12] (*altar, alter*) my order. After the pear yogurt, I asked for a small [13] (*peace, piece*) of pie, but my father told me to be [14] (*quiet, quite*).

While in Boston, we walked up and down the streets just to [15] (*hear, here*) the strange accent of the Bostonians. [16] (*Their, There, They're*) especially noted for [17] (*their, there, they're*) pronunciation of *a*'s and *r*'s.

We had not been in Boston long before the [18] (*weather, whether*) bureau predicted a big snowstorm for the area. Since we had not taken the proper [19] (*cloths, clothes*) for snow, we decided to return home. On the way back, we were [20] (*already, all ready*) making plans for another visit to Boston.

50 Commonly Misspelled Words

As you study the following words, pay particular attention to the letters in italics. These letters generally cause the greatest difficulty in correctly spelling the words.

a*ch*e	col*o*r	fr*ie*nd	re*a*dy	ti*re*d
ag*ai*n	cou*gh*	g*u*ess	s*ai*d	toni*gh*t
a*l*ways	cou*l*d	ha*l*f	s*a*ys	tri*es*
ans*w*er	c*o*untry	ho*u*r	sen*s*e	tr*o*uble
bel*ie*ve	d*ai*ly	inst*ea*d	sh*oe*s	*u*pon
b*u*ilt	doct*o*r	l*ai*d	sin*c*e	us*in*g
b*u*sy	do*esn't*	min*ute*	spec*ia*l	w*ea*r
b*u*y	do*n't*	of*t*en	stra*igh*t	w*o*men
ca*n*not	e*a*rly	*on*ce	tho*ugh*	wo*n't*
ca*n't*	ea*s*y	pa*i*d	thr*ough*	*w*rite

MECHANICS

200 Spelling Words

absence
absolutely
acceptance
accommodate
accumulate
achieve
acquire
across
advertisement
against

aisles
among
announce
anxiety
apologize
apparent
appreciation
arctic
arguing
argument

arithmetic
assistance
associate
attacked
attendance
attitude
attorney
audience
basis
beginning

benefit
bicycle
bough
bouquet
brief
brilliant
bureau
business
candidate
career

careless
carrying
ceased
ceiling
choice
college
committee
completely
conceive
conscience

conscious
control
correspondence
courteous
criticize
curiosity
decision
definite
describe
description

desirable
discipline
divine
efficiency
eighth
eliminate
embarrass
equipment
especially
exactly

excellent
execute
existence
experience
experiment
explanation
extremely
familiar
favorite
February

field
fierce
finally
foliage
foreign
fortunately
forty
fourth
genius
genuine

government
governor
grammar
guarantee
height
heir
humorous
hungrily
icicles
imaginary

immediately
independent
intelligence
interest
interpret

jealous
judgment
knowledge
laboratory
leisure

license
liquor
loneliness
losing
luxury
magazine
marriage
mathematics
meant
medicine

mischief
muscle
museum
necessary
nervous
nineteen
ninety
occasion
occur
occurrence

opinion
opportunity
opposite
originally
particularly
patience
perceive
performance
permanent
personal

physical
picnic
possess
preferred
privilege
probably
professor
pursue
realize
receive

recommend
referred
religion
repetition
rhythm
safety
satisfy
scene
schedule
seize

separate
shining
similar
society
speech
strength
studying
succeed
success
surprise

suspicion
sympathy
teammates
technique
temperament

temporary
theory
thorough
tomorrow
tongue

tournament
tragedy
transferred
treasury
uncomfortable
university
unnecessary
unusually
vacuum
vague

various
veil
vicinity
villain
violence
warrior
wholly
whose
writing
yield

PART THREE

RESOURCES

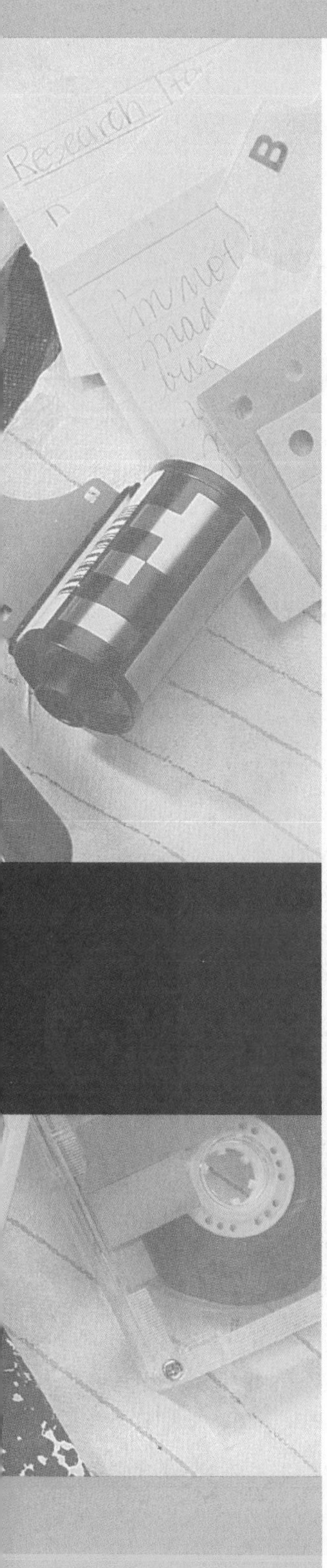

RESOURCES

29 Speaking

Skills and Strategies

Effective speaking takes a little practice. Fortunately, you can learn some simple techniques that will allow you to speak confidently in almost any speaking situation. Whenever you speak, you can improve your effectiveness if you think about

- your purpose (What are you trying to say?)
- your topic (What are you speaking about?)
- your audience (Who are your listeners?)

The Communication Cycle

Communicating is a two-way process. First, a speaker communicates feelings or ideas to the listeners. Then the listeners respond to the speaker's message. This response is called *feedback.*

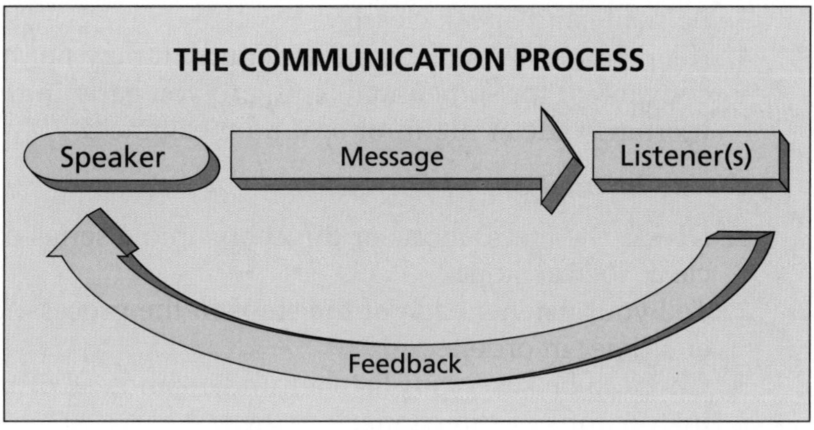

Speaking Informally

Impromptu Speaking

At times you will need to speak to a group of people without having time to plan what you will say. This is called an ***impromptu speech.*** Here are some suggestions.

1. *Think about your purpose.* (Do you want to give information to your audience? to persuade them?)
2. *Think about your topic.* (What's the main thing you need to say? If you have time, add details to explain your main ideas.)
3. *Think about your audience.* (Does what you're saying suit the time, the place, and the people that you are speaking to?)

Speaking Socially

In most social situations, you need to remember to speak clearly and politely.

Speaking on the Telephone

1. Call people at times that are convenient for them.
2. Identify yourself; then state your reason for calling.

3. Be polite and speak clearly.
4. Keep your call to a reasonable length. It may not be convenient for someone to speak to you early in the morning, late at night, or around mealtimes.

Giving Instructions or Directions

1. Divide the instructions or directions into a series of clear, logical steps.
2. Tell your listener each of the steps in the process, one at a time, in order.
3. Check to be sure your listener understands all of the instructions or directions.
4. Repeat any instructions that are not clear.

Making Social Introductions

1. Have confidence. If no one else introduces you, introduce yourself to other people.
2. When you introduce others, identify them by name.
3. When you are introducing others, it is customary to speak first to
   - a person of higher job position
   - an older person before a younger person
   - the person you know best

Speaking Formally

Preparing a Speech

A formal speech is one that you give at a specific time and place. When you give this kind of speech, you usually have the chance to prepare carefully beforehand.

Planning Your Speech

When you prepare your speech, you will need to consider your purpose for speaking. The following chart shows some common types of speeches, arranged according to their purpose.

SPEECH CONSIDERATIONS		
PURPOSE	DESCRIPTION OF SPEECH	EXAMPLES OF SPEECH TITLES
To inform	gives facts or general information or explains how to do something	Dinosaurs Once Lived in West Texas How to Take Good Snapshots
To persuade	attempts to change an opinion or attempts to get listeners to act	Why Everyone Should Recycle How Volunteering Can Make a Difference
To entertain	relates an amusing story or incident	My Most Embarrassing Moment

Considering Your Audience

When you plan your speech, you also need to consider your audience's interests.

THINKING ABOUT YOUR AUDIENCE		
QUESTIONS ABOUT AUDIENCE	ANSWER	YOUR SPEECH WILL NEED
What does the audience already know about this subject?	very little	to give background details to listeners
	a little	to give at least some background details
	a lot	to focus only on interesting points
How interested will the audience be in this subject?	very interested	to keep your listeners' interest
	only a little interested	to focus on aspects most interesting to your listeners
	uninterested	to convince your listeners that this topic is important

Organizing Your Speech Notes

The most common type of speech is a speech you give using note cards. First, you prepare an outline of your main points. Next, you make note cards for each of the main points. Then, when you give your speech, you talk directly to the audience. You can refer to your note cards whenever you need to remember your main points.

Here are some suggestions for making note cards.

1. Write each main idea on a separate note card.
2. Make a special note card for anything that you might need to read word for word (such as a quotation, a series of dates, or statistics that are too difficult to memorize).
3. Include a special note card to tell you when to show a chart, diagram, graphic, drawing, model, or other visual materials.
4. Number your completed note cards to help you keep them in the correct order.

Giving Your Speech

Speaking Effectively

To give an effective speech, you'll need to use your voice and your gestures to help express your meaning to your listeners. Here are some pointers to use when you are speaking.

1. *Stand confidently.* Stand up straight and look alert. Use comfortable and appropriate movements to emphasize your words.
2. *Speak clearly.* Speak loudly enough so that everyone can hear you. Pronounce your words carefully.
3. *Look at your audience.* When you speak, look directly at your audience. Speak directly to them.
4. *Use a normal way of speaking.* Your voice gives your audience clues that help them understand what points you want to emphasize.

Speaking in Front of an Audience

It's normal to feel nervous about speaking in front of an audience. But you can use the following suggestions to help you stay in command.

1. *Be prepared.* Organize your material carefully. Practice using your note cards and any special information or visuals you plan to use during your speech.
2. *Practice your speech.* Each time you rehearse, pretend you're actually giving your speech.
3. *Remember your purpose.* Focus on what you want to tell your audience and how you want them to react instead of worrying about yourself.

Special Speaking Situations

Making Announcements

When you make an announcement, your main goal is to provide information. Follow these guidelines.

1. Write out your announcement. Be sure to include all the important facts. Add important details that will interest your listeners.
2. When it's time to give your announcement, first get your audience's attention. Then announce your message slowly and clearly.

Making an Introduction

Sometimes a short introduction is given before a speech or before a dramatic performance. An introduction gets the audience's attention. It also gives an audience any necessary background information. For example, an introduction may explain details about the performance or presentation. (Include information about the speaker or the subject of a speech.) Or, it might include background information about a dramatic work, the actors, or the author of a theatre work being presented.

Group Discussions

Setting a Purpose

You probably work in groups in many of your classes. The goal of group discussions is to accomplish a specific purpose. This purpose may be

- to discuss and share ideas
- to cooperate in group learning
- to solve a problem
- to arrive at a group decision or to make a group recommendation

To help your group decide about your purpose, find out how much time will be allowed. Then you'll need to identify what your group will be expected to accomplish within the time allowed.

Assigning Roles

Everyone involved in a group discussion should have a specific role. Each role has special responsibilities. For example, your group may choose a chairperson to help keep the discussion moving smoothly. Someone else may be chosen as the secretary, or reporter (recorder), who has the responsibility of taking notes during the discussion.

Usually, a group establishes a plan, or outline, for the order of topics to follow in a discussion. This plan may be established by the chairperson, or sometimes the entire group may discuss and organize the plan for the discussion.

A Chairperson's Responsibilities

1. Announce the topic and establish a plan.
2. Follow the plan.
3. Encourage each member to take part.
4. Help group members stay on track. Avoid disagreements and distractions.

A Secretary's or Reporter's Responsibilities

1. Take notes about important information.
2. Prepare a final report.

A Participant's Responsibilities

1. Take an active part in the discussion.
2. Ask questions and listen attentively to others.
3. Cooperate and share information.

Oral Interpretation

Oral interpretation is more like acting in a play than giving a speech. When you give an oral interpretation, you read a piece of literature expressively to your listeners. To indicate the meaning of the selection, you use facial expressions, your voice, gestures, and movements to interpret the literary work for your listeners.

Choosing a Selection

The purpose of an oral interpretation is to entertain. An oral interpretation is usually planned, so you should have enough time to select your literary piece and practice your presentation.

The material you choose for your presentation depends on several different factors, such as

- who your audience is (what their interests are and how willing they are to be an attentive audience)
- how long a presentation you plan to make (can vary greatly, from very short to very long)
- what the occasion or situation is (material suited to one occasion may not work well in another)
- how expressive an interpretation you want to give (can vary, from readings that require a lot of acting to mildly expressive pieces)

Think about the kind of story you would choose to read to a group of six-year-olds during story hour. You would probably want a story with lots of action, and you would want characters whose voices and movements you could act out to amuse and entertain your young listeners.

Now think about what might be an appropriate reading for a presentation at a parent-teacher banquet near Thanksgiving. Perhaps you would select a literary work that suits the holiday coming up, or that has characters or a situation that would interest your audience. An older audience of enthusiastic parents and teachers will probably be more willing to pay attention to a longer, more serious selection than an audience of six-year-olds would.

Here are suggestions for finding a literary work for an oral interpretation.

SELECTING AN ORAL INTERPRETATION

TYPE OF LITERATURE	DESCRIPTION OF POSSIBLE SELECTION
poem	a poem that tells a story, such as an epic poem
	a poem that has a speaker (using the word *I*) or a conversation between characters
	a poem that is expressive of a particular emotion
short story	a brief story, or portion of a story, that has ■ a beginning, middle, and end ■ either a narrator who tells the story (using *I*) or characters who talk to one another (using dialogue in quotation marks)
play	a short play, or one scene from a play, that has ■ a beginning, middle, and end ■ one or more characters with dialogue

You may need an introduction for your interpretation. This introduction may set the scene, tell something about the author of the piece of literature you're presenting, or give details that tell your audience about important events that have already taken place in the story.

Adapting Material

You may be able to find just the right piece of literature. It may already be the perfect length. It may have just the right number of characters, with dialogue that tells the part of the story you want to tell. But sometimes you need to shorten a short story, a long poem, or a play. This shortened version is called a *cutting*. To make a cutting, follow these suggestions.

1. Decide where the part of the story you want to use should begin and where it should end.
2. Cut out parts that don't contribute to the portion of the story you are telling.
3. From a short story, cut dialogue tags such as *she whispered sadly*. Instead, use these clues to tell you how to act out the characters' words.

Presenting an Oral Interpretation

After you've chosen a piece of literature to present, you can prepare a ***reading script.*** A reading script is usually typed (double-spaced or written neatly with space between each line). You can then mark this script to help you when you are reading your selection. For example, you can underline words to remind you to use special emphasis when you say them. Or you can mark a slash (/) to show where you plan to take a breath or pause briefly to create suspense. You might write a word or two or a brief note as a reminder of the emotion that you want to express when you say a character's words.

Rehearse your presentation several different ways until you feel that you have found the most effective. Practice in front of your mirror. Then try out your reading on friends, classmates, or relatives.

Use your voice to suit your meaning. Vary your body movements and your voice to show that you are portraying different characters and to show important emotions (such as fear or joy).

Review

EXERCISE 1 Speaking Socially

For each of the situations, explain how you might handle the conversation. What would you say to be polite and to be clear?

1. You're calling to congratulate a classmate who has won a science award.
2. You've invited a new classmate to study at your house. Give directions on how to get to your house from the school.
3. You're standing in front of the school, talking to your new teacher. Your mother arrives. Introduce your mother to your teacher.
4. Explain to your classmates how to make or repair something (such as how to bake bread or repair a bicycle tire). Make sure you provide all the necessary information and give the steps in order. Repeat or summarize all necessary instructions.
5. At a baseball game, you realize that the person sitting next to you is a classmate you like but do not know well. Introduce yourself.

EXERCISE 2 Making an Announcement

Write an announcement for an upcoming event. The event can be real, or you can make up the details. Give all the necessary information.

EXERCISE 3 Preparing and Giving a Speech

Choose a topic for a short, two- to three-minute speech to give to your English class. Think about your audience and your purpose when choosing your speech topic. Prepare note cards for your speech. Then give your speech to the class, following the guidelines for speaking effectively on page 800.

EXERCISE 4 Conducting a Group Discussion

Select a group chairperson to lead a discussion on a topic your teacher assigns or one of your own choosing. Establish a plan for the discussion and assign roles. The purpose for the discussion is to make a list of the group's findings about the topic. Here are some suggestions for a topic your group might discuss.

1. activities that every community should provide for young people
2. ways to improve teacher-student relationships
3. the most important thing we can do to improve the future
4. leadership qualities and how to develop them
5. how to reduce gang violence

EXERCISE 5 Presenting an Oral Interpretation

Select a literary work or a suitable portion of a piece of literature. Prepare a script for a three-minute oral interpretation to present to your class. Write a brief introduction telling the title and author of the selection. Present your interpretation to your class.

30 LISTENING

Strategies for Active Listening

Listening is not as simple as it sounds. You constantly hear noises and sounds of one kind or another. But you probably don't really *listen* to very many of them. In other words, hearing and listening are not the same thing. Hearing just happens. But listening is an active process. Listening requires that you think as well as hear.

Listening with a Purpose

Keep your purpose in mind as you listen. This will help you be a more effective listener. Common purposes for listening are

- for enjoyment or entertainment
- to gain information
- to understand information or an explanation
- to evaluate or form an opinion

Listening for Information

Listening for Details

When you listen for information, you need to listen for details that answer the basic *5W-How?* questions: *Who? What? When? Where? Why?* and *How?* As you listen to whoever is speaking, try to find answers for each of these questions.

Listening to Instructions

Careful listening is important when you are given assignments, instructions, or directions. Follow these guidelines.

1. Identify each separate step. Listen for words that tell you when each step ends and the next one begins. These words may include *first, second, third, next, then,* and *last* or *finally.*
2. Listen to the order of the steps. Take notes whenever it is necessary.
3. Imagine yourself completing each step in order.
4. Make sure you have all the instructions and understand them. Ask questions if you are unclear about any step.

Listening Politely

Follow these guidelines to be a polite and effective listener.

1. Look at the speaker. When you pay attention, the speaker can tell that you are interested in what he or she has to say.
2. Respect the speaker. Be tolerant of individual differences, such as a speaker's accent, customs, race, or religion.
3. Don't interrupt the speaker.

4. Pay attention. Don't whisper, fidget, or make other types of noises or actions that could distract other listeners.
5. Try to understand the speaker's point of view. Also, be aware of how your own point of view affects the way you judge what others have to say.
6. Don't judge too soon. Listen to the speaker's entire message before you evaluate the speech.

Using the LQ2R Method

The LQ2R study method is especially helpful when you are listening to a speaker who is giving information or instructions.

L *Listen* carefully to information as it is being presented. Focus your attention only on the speaker, and don't allow yourself to be distracted.

Q *Question* yourself as you listen. Make a list of questions as they occur to you.

R *Recite* in your own words the information as it is being presented. Summarize information in your mind or jot down notes as you listen.

R *Re-listen* as the speaker concludes the presentation. The speaker may sum up, or repeat, major points of the presentation.

REFERENCE NOTE: For more information about study methods, see pages 845–862.

Taking Notes

You can't write down every word a speaker says. Instead, write only the key words or important phrases the speaker uses. Translate difficult terms into your own words.

REFERENCE NOTE: For more about note taking, see pages 854–855.

Interviewing

An interview is a special listening situation. When you interview someone, you usually ask someone who is an expert or has special knowledge about a subject to speak to you and give you information about what he or she knows. Interviews are good sources for obtaining interesting and up-to-date information. Follow these suggestions to conduct an effective interview.

Preparing for the Interview

- Decide what information that you really want to ask about most.
- Make a list of questions to ask.
- Make an appointment for the interview. Be on time.

Conducting the Interview

- Be courteous and patient. Give the person you are interviewing time to answer each question that you ask. Respect what the person you are interviewing has to say, even if you disagree.
- Listen carefully to each answer that the person you are interviewing gives to the questions you ask. If the person gives you an answer that confuses you, or if you're not sure you understand what the person means, you may want to ask some follow-up questions to be clear about the information the person is giving you.
- It is polite to tell the person you are interviewing how you plan to use the information you are asking for. For example, if you plan to use the person's exact words in a report, it is usually best to tell the person as you begin the interview and ask permission to quote him or her directly.
- Thank the person for granting you the interview.

Following up on the Interview

- Review your notes to be sure they are clear.
- Write a summary of the interview as soon as possible.

Critical Listening

When you listen critically, you think carefully about what you hear. You analyze and then evaluate the ideas being presented.

GUIDELINES FOR LISTENING CRITICALLY	
Find main ideas.	What are the most important points? Listen for clue words, such as *major, main, most important,* or similar words.
Identify significant details.	What dates, names, or facts does the speaker use to support main ideas? What kinds of examples or explanations are used to support the main ideas?
Distinguish between facts and opinions.	A ***fact*** is a statement that can be proved to be true. (May is the fifth month.) An ***opinion*** is a belief or a judgment about something. It cannot be proved to be true. (Cherry pie is better than apple pie.)
Note comparisons and contrasts.	Are some details compared or contrasted with others?
Understand cause and effect.	Does the speaker say or hint that some events cause others to occur? Or does the speaker suggest that some events are the result of others?
Predict outcomes and draw conclusions.	What reasonable conclusions or predictions can you make from the facts and evidence you have gathered from the speech?

REFERENCE NOTE: For more information about interpreting and analyzing information, see pages 849–852.

Understanding Persuasive Techniques

To get you to believe in something or to take some action, speakers may use one of the common persuasive techniques listed below. Learning to recognize these techniques can help you understand a speaker's message. It can also help you avoid being "taken in" by arguments that are not based on logic or reason.

COMMON PERSUASIVE TECHNIQUES USED BY SPEAKERS	
Bandwagon	Users of this technique urge you to "jump on the bandwagon" by suggesting that you should do or believe something because "everyone" is doing it. The idea is to make you think you're missing out if you don't join in.
Testimonial	Experts or famous people sometimes give a personal "testimony" about a product or idea. However, the person giving the testimonial may not really know much about that particular product or idea.
Emotional appeals	This technique uses words that appeal to your emotions rather than to your logic or reason.
"Plain folks"	Ordinary people (or people who pretend to be ordinary) are often used to persuade others. People tend to believe others who seem to be similar to themselves.
False cause and effect	This technique is used to suggest that because one event happened first, it caused a second event to occur. However, the two events may not actually have a cause-and-effect relationship.

Review

EXERCISE 1 Listening for Information

Make up five questions similar to those that follow. Read them aloud, pausing briefly to allow your classmates time to jot down their answers. Have listeners check their answers to see how accurately they listened.

1. In the series of numbers *6—1—8—3—4*, the fourth number is ____.
2. In this list, *in—off—but—for—how*, the word beginning with *o* is ____.
3. Here is the order for pairs: first, Josh and Erika; then, Graciella and Cindy; last, Roberto and Quan. Which group is Cindy in?
4. The Colorado River is in Arizona, the Sabine River is in Texas, and the Columbia River is in Oregon. Where is the Sabine River?
5. Here are six colors: red, green, yellow, blue, purple, orange. Which color is second?

EXERCISE 2 Preparing Interview Questions

Think of an elected official, a celebrity, or an individual from history that you would like to interview. Then prepare ten questions you would like to be able to ask that person in an interview. Follow the steps for preparing for an interview on page 811.

EXERCISE 3 Listening to a Speech

Listen to a short speech presented by your teacher in class. Take brief notes. Then respond to the following questions about the speech.

1. What are the main ideas of the speech?
2. Does the speech contain details that support the main points in the speech? If so, identify several of them.

3. Can you distinguish between facts and opinions mentioned in the speech?
4. Does the speech contain comparisons and contrasts?
5. Do some events in the speech cause other events to happen?

EXERCISE 4 **Identifying Persuasive Techniques**

Identify the persuasive technique used in each of the following items.

1. "You should buy Yummies," says Jo Jo Jackson, champion skeet-shooter. "They'll help start your day off with a bang!"
2. "Everyone's joining our crusade for reforming the school system. Sign up to do your part now!"
3. "Those big spenders in Washington are ruining our country!"
4. "Our candidate for City Council is shown with her husband and two lovely children in front of their attractive, yet modest, home."
5. Because Jim forgot to wear his lucky bowling shirt, he lost the first three games of the tournament.

31 The Library/ Media Center

Finding and Using Information

In the library or media center you can find information on many subjects. But you need to know how to find it.

The Arrangement of a Library

Every book in a library has a number and letter code, the book's ***call number.*** The call number tells you how the book has been classified and where to find it.

DEWEY CLASSIFICATION OF NONFICTION		
NUMBERS	SUBJECT AREAS	EXAMPLES OF SUBDIVISIONS
000–099	General Works	encyclopedias, handbooks
100–199	Philosophy	psychology, ethics, personality
200–299	Religion	bibles, mythology, theology
300–399	Social Sciences	government, law, economics
400–499	Languages	dictionaries, grammars
500–599	Science	general science, mathematics
600–699	Technology	engineering, inventions
700–799	The Arts	music, theater, recreation
800–899	Literature	poetry, drama, essays
900–999	History	biography, geography, travel

In most school libraries nonfiction books are classified and arranged using the Dewey decimal system. The Dewey decimal system assigns a number to each nonfiction book according to its subject.

Biographies are often shelved in a separate section of the library, apart from other nonfiction books with a special call number of their own. Libraries arrange biographies in alphabetical order according to the last name of the person the book is about. Two or more biographies of the same person are put in alphabetical order according to the last name of the author.

Arrangement of Fiction

In most libraries, fiction books are placed in a section separate from the nonfiction books. The books in the fiction section of a library are arranged alphabetically by their author's last name. Two or more books written by the same author are arranged alphabetically by the first word of their titles (not counting *A, An,* or *The*). Sometimes collections of short stories are kept separate from other works of fiction.

The Card Catalog

To find the book you want, find the call number in the library's ***card catalog.*** The card catalog is a cabinet of small drawers containing cards. These cards are arranged in alphabetical order by title, author, or subject. Books of fiction have at least two cards in the catalog—a *title card* and an *author card.* Or, if a book is nonfiction, it will have a third card—a *subject card.* Occasionally, you may find *"see"* or *"see also"* cards. These cards tell you where to go in the card catalog to find additional information on a subject.

An ***on-line catalog*** is a version of the card catalog stored on a computer. It contains the same information as a regular catalog. An on-line catalog can display author, title, or subject information just like a regular card catalog.

INFORMATION IN THE CARD CATALOG

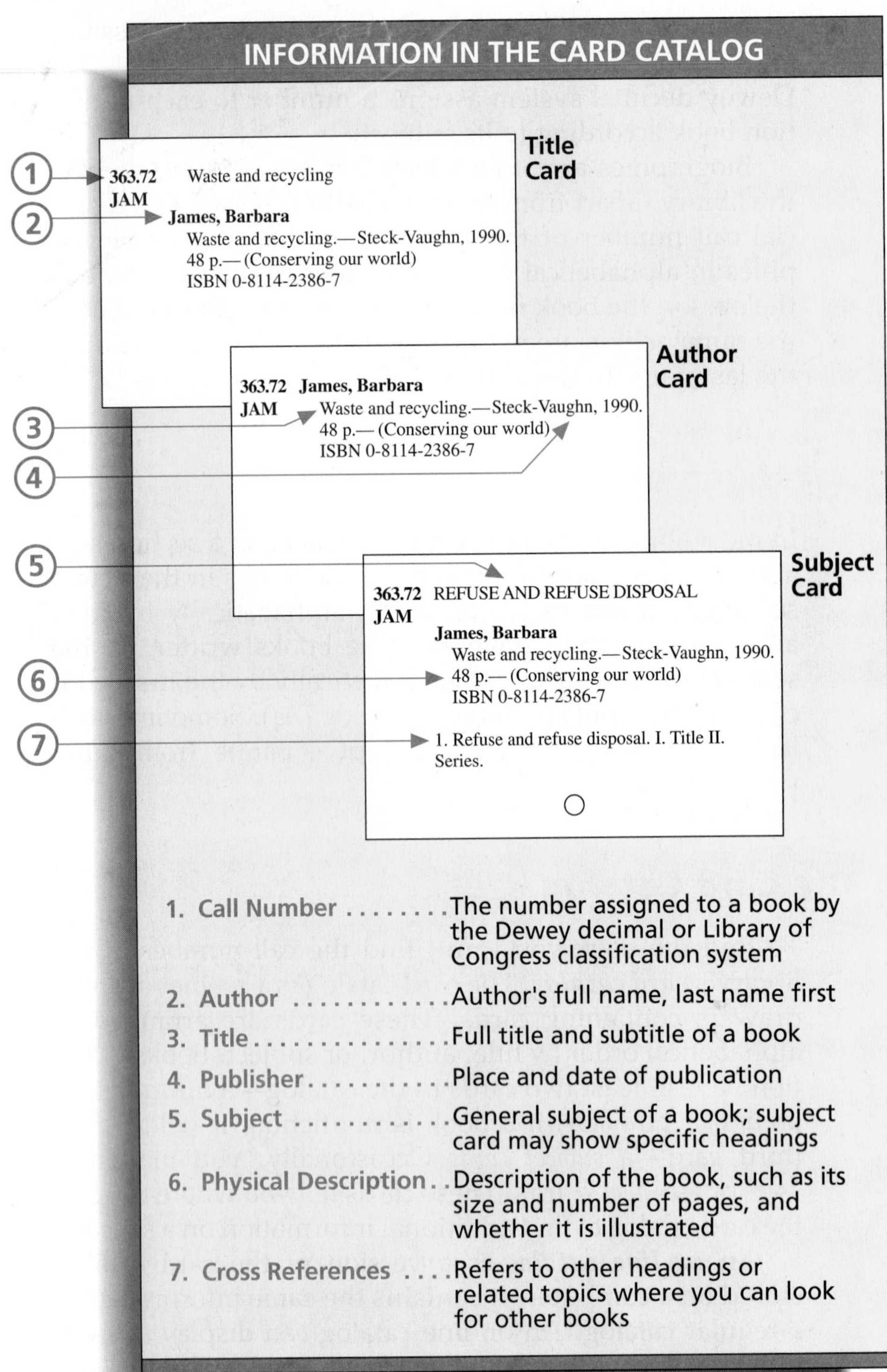

Title Card
1
363.72 Waste and recycling
JAM
2
James, Barbara
Waste and recycling.—Steck-Vaughn, 1990.
48 p.—(Conserving our world)
ISBN 0-8114-2386-7
Author Card
363.72 James, Barbara
JAM
3
Waste and recycling.—Steck-Vaughn, 1990.
48 p.—(Conserving our world)
4
ISBN 0-8114-2386-7
5
Subject Card
363.72 REFUSE AND REFUSE DISPOSAL
JAM
James, Barbara
Waste and recycling.—Steck-Vaughn, 1990.
6
48 p.—(Conserving our world)
ISBN 0-8114-2386-7
7
1. Refuse and refuse disposal. I. Title II. Series.

1. **Call Number** . . . . The number assigned to a book by the Dewey decimal or Library of Congress classification system
2. **Author** . . . . Author's full name, last name first
3. **Title** . . . . Full title and subtitle of a book
4. **Publisher** . . . . Place and date of publication
5. **Subject** . . . . General subject of a book; subject card may show specific headings
6. **Physical Description** . . Description of the book, such as its size and number of pages, and whether it is illustrated
7. **Cross References** . . . . Refers to other headings or related topics where you can look for other books

Parts of a Book

Information is often easier to find if you know how to use the parts of a book effectively. The title, the table of contents, and the index are examples of the types of information that can be found in the different parts of a book.

INFORMATION FOUND IN PARTS OF A BOOK	
PART	INFORMATION
Title page	gives full title, author, publisher, and place of publication
Copyright page	gives date of first publication and of any revisions
Table of contents	lists titles of chapters or sections of the book and their starting page numbers
Appendix	provides additional information about subjects found in the book; maps and charts are sometimes found here
Glossary	in alphabetical order defines difficult or technical words found in the book
Bibliography	lists sources used to write the book; gives titles of works on related topics
Index	lists topics mentioned in the book and page numbers on which they can be found

Reference Materials

The *Readers' Guide*

The most current information on many topics is found in magazines rather than in books. To find a magazine article, use the *Readers' Guide to Periodical Literature.* The *Readers' Guide* indexes articles, poems, and stories from more than 150 magazines. In the *Readers' Guide,* magazine articles are listed alphabetically by author and by subject. These headings are printed in boldfaced capital letters.

Information in *Readers' Guide* entries is abbreviated. In the front of the *Readers' Guide* these abbreviations are explained.

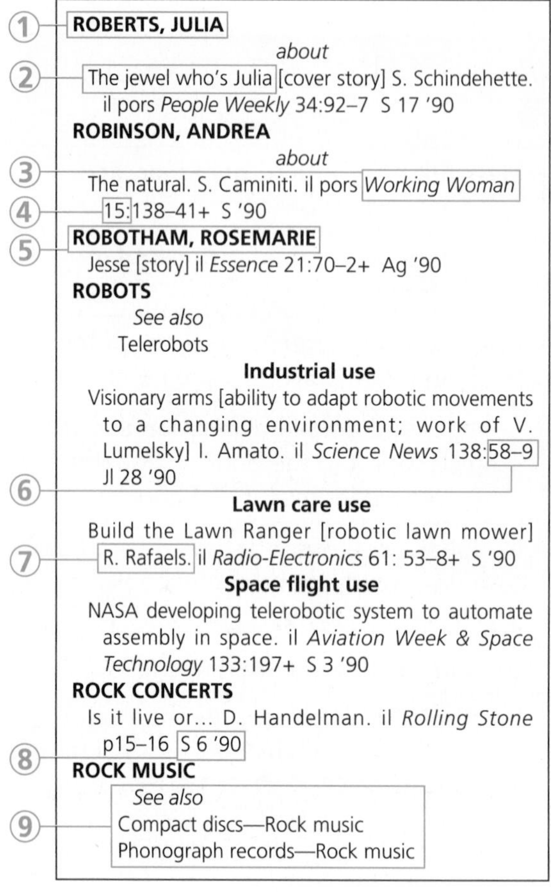

ROBERTS, JULIA

about

The jewel who's Julia [cover story] S. Schindehette. il pors *People Weekly* 34:92–7 S 17 '90

ROBINSON, ANDREA

about

The natural. S. Caminiti. il pors *Working Woman* 15:138–41+ S '90

ROBOTHAM, ROSEMARIE

Jesse [story] il *Essence* 21:70–2+ Ag '90

ROBOTS

See also

Telerobots

Industrial use

Visionary arms [ability to adapt robotic movements to a changing environment; work of V. Lumelsky] I. Amato. il *Science News* 138:58–9 Jl 28 '90

Lawn care use

Build the Lawn Ranger [robotic lawn mower] R. Rafaels. il *Radio-Electronics* 61: 53–8+ S '90

Space flight use

NASA developing telerobotic system to automate assembly in space. il *Aviation Week & Space Technology* 133:197+ S 3 '90

ROCK CONCERTS

Is it live or... D. Handelman. il *Rolling Stone* p15–16 S 6 '90

ROCK MUSIC

See also

Compact discs—Rock music

Phonograph records—Rock music

1. **Subject entry**
2. **Title of article**
3. **Name of magazine**
4. **Volume number of magazine**
5. **Author entry**
6. **Page reference**
7. **Author of article**
8. **Date of magazine**
9. **Subject cross-reference**

Special Reference Sources

The ***vertical file*** is a special filing cabinet containing up-to-date materials. These materials may include newspaper clippings or government and information pamphlets.

Microforms are pages from various newspapers and magazines that are reduced to miniature size. The two most common type are *microfilm* (a roll or reel of film) and *microfiche* (a sheet of film). You view them by using a special projector to enlarge the images to a readable size.

Some libraries store reference sources on computers. Ask your librarian what database systems your library has. A ***database*** is information that is stored on computer for easy retrieval.

Reference Works

Most libraries devote a section entirely to reference books that contain information on many subjects.

REFERENCE WORKS		
TYPE	DESCRIPTION	EXAMPLES
Encyclopedias	▪ multiple volumes ▪ articles arranged alphabetically by subject ▪ source for general information	*Collier's Encyclopedia* *Compton's Encyclopedia* *The World Book Encyclopedia*
General Biographical References	▪ information about the lives and accomplishments of outstanding people	*Current Biography* *The International Who's Who* *Webster's New Biographical Dictionary*
Atlases	▪ maps and geographical information	*Atlas of World Cultures* *National Geographic Atlas of the World*
Almanacs	▪ up-to-date information about current events, facts, statistics, and dates	*The Information Please Almanac, Atlas & Yearbook* *The World Almanac and Book of Facts*
Books of Synonyms	▪ lists more interesting or more exact words to express ideas	*Roget's International Thesaurus* *Webster's New Dictionary of Synonyms*

Newspapers

Most daily newspapers are divided into sections that contain a wide variety of features and types of writing. Newspaper writers write for different purposes. And readers, like you, read the newspaper for purposes of your own. The following chart shows some of the different contents that you will find in a typical daily newspaper.

WHAT'S IN A NEWSPAPER?

WRITER'S PURPOSE/ TYPE OF WRITING	READER'S PURPOSE	READING TECHNIQUE
to inform news stories sports	to gain knowledge or information	Ask yourself the *5W-How?* questions (page 33).
to persuade editorials comics reviews ads	to gain knowledge, to make decisions, or to be entertained	Identify points you agree or disagree with. Find facts or reasons the writer uses.
to be creative or expressive comics columns	to be entertained	Identify ways the writer interests you or gives you a new viewpoint or ideas.

Review

EXERCISE 1 Using the Parts of a Book

Tell which part or parts of a book you would check to find the following information.

1. a list of page numbers that deal with a specific topic
2. the meaning of a technical term used often in the book
3. a list of the sources used to write the book
4. the place where the book was published
5. how many times the book has been revised

EXERCISE 2 **Using the Library**

Answer the following questions to show your understanding of the information resources in the library.

1. In order, which of the following books would be shelved first: *Winter Thunder* by Mari Sandoz, or *Nisei Daughter* by Monica Sone?
2. Use the sample *Readers' Guide* entry on page 820 to find the title of an article written by S. Caminiti about Andrea Robinson. What magazine printed this article?
3. Use the card catalog or the on-line catalog in your library to find a biography of a famous person. Write the book title, the author's name, and the call number.
4. Tell which reference book you might use to find the names of the countries that border Yugoslavia.
5. Tell which reference book might contain recent statistics on the total population of the United States.

EXERCISE 3 **Exploring the Newspaper**

Using a copy of the daily newspaper from home or your library, answer the following questions.

1. Is there a special identification or title for each section of this newspaper? Explain.
2. Find an article that gives you information about a specific event in world news, sports, or entertainment. Find answers to the *5W-How?* questions (*Who? What? Where? When? Why? How?*) in the details of this article.
3. Find an editorial or a letter to the editor. Identify what the writer wants you to think or do. What facts or opinions does the writer use to try to persuade you?
4. Find a comic that you think is intended to persuade you. Find another comic that you think is intended just for fun. Explain your selection.
5. Find an advertisement or classified ad that makes you want to buy the item offered. What do you find most effective about the ad?

32 THE DICTIONARY

Types and Contents

Types of Dictionaries

There are many types of dictionaries. Each type contains different kinds of information. However, all dictionaries contain certain general features.

TYPES OF DICTIONARIES		
TYPE AND EXAMPLE	NUMBER OF WORDS	NUMBER OF PAGES
Unabridged *Webster's Third International Unabridged Dictionary*	460,000	2,662
College or Abridged *Webster's Ninth New Collegiate Dictionary*	160,000	1,563
School *The Lincoln Writing Dictionary*	35,000	932
Paperback *The Random House Dictionary*	74,000	1,056

RESOURCES

A SAMPLE ENTRY

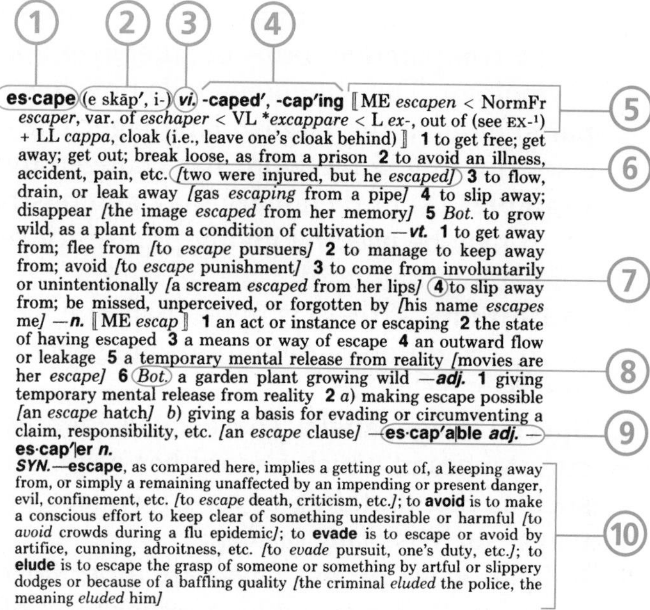

es·cape (e skāp′, i-) *vi.* **-caped′, -cap′ing** ⟦ME *escapen* < NormFr *escaper*, var. of *eschaper* < VL **excappare* < L *ex-*, out of (see EX-[1]) + LL *cappa*, cloak (i.e., leave one's cloak behind)⟧ **1** to get free; get away; get out; break loose, as from a prison **2** to avoid an illness, accident, pain, etc. [two were injured, but he *escaped*] **3** to flow, drain, or leak away [gas *escaping* from a pipe] **4** to slip away; disappear [the image *escaped* from her memory] **5** *Bot.* to grow wild, as a plant from a condition of cultivation —***vt.*** **1** to get away from; flee from [to *escape* pursuers] **2** to manage to keep away from; avoid [to *escape* punishment] **3** to come from involuntarily or unintentionally [a scream *escaped* from her lips] **4** to slip away from; be missed, unperceived, or forgotten by [his name *escapes* me] —***n.*** ⟦ME *escap*⟧ **1** an act or instance or escaping **2** the state of having escaped **3** a means or way of escape **4** an outward flow or leakage **5** a temporary mental release from reality [movies are her *escape*] **6** *Bot.* a garden plant growing wild —***adj.*** **1** giving temporary mental release from reality **2** *a*) making escape possible [an *escape* hatch] *b*) giving a basis for evading or circumventing a claim, responsibility, etc. [an *escape* clause] —**es·cap′a|ble** ***adj.*** —**es·cap′|er** ***n.***

SYN.—**escape**, as compared here, implies a getting out of, a keeping away from, or simply a remaining unaffected by an impending or present danger, evil, confinement, etc. [to *escape* death, criticism, etc.]; to **avoid** is to make a conscious effort to keep clear of something undesirable or harmful [to *avoid* crowds during a flu epidemic]; to **evade** is to escape or avoid by artifice, cunning, adroitness, etc. [to *evade* pursuit, one's duty, etc.]; to **elude** is to escape the grasp of someone or something by artful or slippery dodges or because of a baffling quality [the criminal *eluded* the police, the meaning *eluded* him]

From *Webster's New World Dictionary.* © 1986 by Merriam-Webster Inc., publisher of Merriam-Webster ® Dictionaries. Reprinted by permission of Merriam-Webster Inc.

1. **Entry word.** The entry word shows the correct spelling of a word. An alternate spelling may also be shown. The entry word shows how the word should be divided into syllables, and may also show if the word should be capitalized.
2. **Pronunciation.** The pronunciation of a word is shown using accent marks, phonetic symbols or diacritical marks. Each ***phonetic symbol*** represents a specific sound. ***Diacritical marks*** are special symbols placed above letters to show how they sound. Dictionaries provide guides to the meanings and use of diacritical marks or phonetic symbols.
3. **Part-of-speech labels.** These labels are usually abbreviated and show how the entry word should be used in a sentence. Some words may be used as more than one part of speech. In this case, a part-of-speech label is provided before the set of definitions that matches each label.

4. **Other forms.** Sometimes your dictionary shows spellings of plural forms of nouns, tenses of verbs, or the comparative forms of adjectives and adverbs.
5. **Etymology.** The ***etymology*** tells how a word (or its parts) entered the English language. The etymology also shows how the word has changed over time.
6. **Examples.** Your dictionary may demonstrate how a word may be used by giving phrases or sentences containing that word.
7. **Definitions.** If there is more than one meaning for a word, the different definitions are separated by numbers or letters.
8. **Special usage labels.** These labels identify the circumstances in which a word has a special meaning, such as *Bot.* (botany), or how it is used in special ways, such as *Slang* or *Rare.*
9. **Related word forms.** These are other forms of the entry word. For example, another form of the word might be shown that is created by adding suffixes or prefixes. Or a common phrase might be shown in which the entry word appears.
10. **Synonyms and antonyms.** Words that are similar in meaning are ***synonyms.*** Words that are opposite in meaning are ***antonyms.*** Dictionaries may list synonyms and antonyms at the end of some word entries.

EXERCISE 1 Using the Dictionary to Check for Capitalization

Look up the following words in a dictionary and explain when they are and are not capitalized. Your dictionary may not give capitalized uses for all the words.

1. president
2. roman
3. arctic
4. ping-pong
5. mason

EXERCISE 2 **Dividing Words into Syllables**

Divide the following words into syllables. Use the same method to show syllable division that your dictionary uses.

1. habitat
2. turmoil
3. diamond
4. incomplete
5. mediterranean

EXERCISE 3 **Finding Part-of-Speech Labels**

Look up each of the following words in a dictionary. Give all the parts of speech listed for each word and an example of how the word is used as each part of speech.

EXAMPLE **1.** elastic
1. *adj.—an elastic waistband*
n.—lined with elastic

1. fall
2. interview
3. record
4. mask
5. base

EXERCISE 4 **Identifying the Usage Labels of Words**

Look up the following words in a college dictionary and write the usage label or labels given for the word, if any.

1. foul
2. relief
3. grub
4. master
5. degree

EXERCISE 5 **Finding Synonyms for Words**

Write all the synonyms you can think of for each of the following words. Then use a dictionary to check your list and to add to it.

1. fear
2. mix
3. enormous
4. part
5. rich

33 Vocabulary

Learning and Using New Words

You constantly learn new words from your parents and friends, from subjects you study, and from books, television, and games. You can also learn the meanings of word parts and how they are combined to form new words.

Building a Vocabulary

One good way to build your vocabulary is to start a word bank. When you see or hear a new word, write the word and its definition in a section of your notebook. Always check the definition and pronunciation of any unfamiliar words in your dictionary.

Using Word Parts

Many English words can be divided into parts. If you know the meanings of various word parts, you can often determine the meanings of many unfamiliar words.

A word part added to the beginning of a word is called a ***prefix.*** A word part added to the end of a word is called a ***suffix.*** Prefixes and suffixes can't stand alone. They must be added to other words or word parts.

A ***base word*** can stand alone. It is a complete word all by itself, although other word parts may be added to it to make new words.

PREFIX	BASE WORD	SUFFIX	NEW WORD
bi–	week	–ly	biweekly
un–	comfort	–able	uncomfortable

Roots, like prefixes and suffixes, can't stand all alone. Roots can combine with one or more word parts to form words.

WORD ROOT	MEANING	EXAMPLES
–dict–	to speak	dictate, dictionary
–ject–	to throw	project, reject
–voc–	to call	vocation, vocal
–vis–	to see	visual, invisible

COMMONLY USED PREFIXES		
PREFIXES	MEANINGS	EXAMPLES OF PREFIXES + BASE WORDS
anti–	against, opposing	antisocial, antiviral
bi–	two	biannual, bicultural
co–	with, together	codefendant, coordinate
dis–	away, from, opposing	disarm, disconnect
in–	not	inappropriate, ineffective
inter–	between, among	interaction, interstate
mis–	badly, not, wrongly	misconduct, misshape

COMMONLY USED PREFIXES *(continued)*		
PREFIXES	MEANINGS	EXAMPLES
non–	not	nonactive, nonfatal
post–	after, following	postdated, postwar
pre–	before	predawn, preview
re–	back, again	replay, restock
semi–	half, partly	semidarkness, semisweet
sub–	under, beneath	subgroup, subplot
trans–	across, beyond	transfer, transform
un–	not, reverse of	uneven, untrue

REFERENCE NOTE: For guidelines on spelling when adding prefixes, see page 769.

COMMONLY USED SUFFIXES		
SUFFIXES	MEANINGS	EXAMPLES OF BASE WORDS + SUFFIXES
–able	able, likely	adaptable, changeable
–ate	become, cause	activate, invalidate
–dom	state, condition	freedom, kingdom
–en	make, become	darken, weaken
–ful	full of, characteristic of	joyful, truthful
–hood	condition, quality	childhood, sisterhood
–ion	action, condition	liberation, protection
–ize	make, cause to be	dramatize, Americanize
–ly	in a characteristic way	blandly, swiftly
–ment	result, action	enchantment, payment
–ness	quality, state	peacefulness, sadness
–or	one who	actor, editor
–ous	characterized by	joyous, murderous
–ship	condition, state	friendship, hardship
–y	condition, quality	dirty, jealousy

REFERENCE NOTE: For guidelines on spelling when adding suffixes, see pages 769–771.

Learning New Words from Context

The *context* of a word includes all the other words and sentences that surround it. These surrounding words often provide valuable clues to meaning.

USING CONTEXT CLUES	
TYPE OF CLUE	EXPLANATION
Definitions and Restatements	Look for words that define the term or restate it in other words. ■ The university owns a *seismograph,* a machine for measuring the force of earthquakes.
Examples	Look for examples used in context that reveal the meaning of an unfamiliar word. ■ There are many types of literary *genres,* such as novels, short stories, poems, and plays.
Synonyms	Look for clues that indicate an unfamiliar word is similar to a familiar word. ■ For a beginner, the *novice* played well.
Antonyms	Look for clues that indicate an unfamiliar word is opposite in meaning to a familiar word. ■ The speaker was *strident,* not soft-spoken.
Comparison and Contrast	Look for clues that indicate that an unfamiliar word is compared to or contrasted with an unfamiliar word or phrase. ■ A *salvo* of cheers burst, like a sudden thunderstorm, from the onlookers. ■ Unlike Sofía, who is wise and sensible, Pierce is often *fatuous.*
Cause and Effect	Look for clues that indicate an unfamiliar word is related to the cause or the result of an action, feeling, or idea. ■ Since our trip was *curtailed,* we came home early.

Choosing the Right Word

Since many English words have several meanings, you must look at *all* the definitions given in the dictionary for any particular word. Always think about the context of an unfamiliar word. Then determine the definition that best fits the given context.

Dictionaries sometimes provide sample contexts to show the various meanings of a word. Compare each of the sample contexts given in the dictionary with the context of a new word to make sure you've found the meaning that fits.

Synonyms and Antonyms

Synonyms are words that have nearly the same meaning. For example, here are some pairs of synonyms: happy—glad, big—large, and beautiful—lovely. However, ***antonyms*** are words that have nearly the opposite meaning. For example, here are some pairs of antonyms: happy—sad, big—small, and beautiful—ugly.

When you look up a word in a dictionary, you will often find several synonyms listed. To help you distinguish between synonyms, some dictionaries give *synonym articles*—brief explanations of a word's synonyms and how they differ in meaning. Dictionaries sometimes also list antonyms at the end of an entry for a word.

EXERCISE 1 Using Prefixes to Define Words

For each of the following words, give the prefix used and its meaning. Give the meaning of the whole word. Use a dictionary if necessary.

1. bilingual
2. misfire
3. antilabor
4. preheat
5. nondairy
6. transatlantic
7. interdenominational
8. postgraduate
9. semiprecious
10. subnormal

EXERCISE 2 **Adding Suffixes to Words**

To each of the following words add the suffix in parentheses that follows the word. Then give the meaning of each new word and its part of speech. Use a dictionary if necessary to find the meaning or the spelling of each new word. [Note: Be careful. Remember that some words change their spelling when a suffix is added.]

1. appease (–ment)
2. official (–dom)
3. like (–able)
4. civil (–ize)
5. spite (–ful)
6. state (–hood)
7. envy (–ous)
8. haste (–en)
9. grit (–y)
10. author (–ship)

EXERCISE 3 **Using Context Clues**

Use context clues to choose the word or phrase that best fits the meaning of each italicized word.

a. beautiful
b. entertaining
c. considering
d. dropped sharply
e. round
f. reacting
g. myths
h. nicknames

1. Sharria spends as much time *pondering* what to wear to school as she does thinking about her homework.
2. The earth is *spherical,* like a ball.
3. Ludlow was known by various *sobriquets,* including Lumpy and Pokey.
4. Emiliano thought the tiny blue insect was *exquisite,* not hideous as his aunt believed.
5. Because the temperature *plummeted,* we decided to build a fire.

EXERCISE 4 **Selecting the Correct Context**

For each sentence below, write the word from the following list that best fits the sentence. Use a dictionary to find the definition that best fits the context for each word.

flawless	intrude
caliber	eliminate
pummel	moderate
incite	envelop

1. The concert was so long that the director decided to ___ two songs.
2. The dark fog seemed to ___ the cottage.
3. On the field trip, the class stopped for lunch at a restaurant that had ___ prices.
4. The fiery speaker was able to ___ the crowd.
5. The final report of the year should be a work of high ___.

34 LETTERS AND FORMS

Style and Contents

Letters are an important form of communication. Everyone likes to get letters. To receive letters, however, you usually have to write your share. It is important to learn how to write effective social and business letters. You will also find there are a few general rules you should follow when you complete printed forms.

Types of Letters

Like all other forms of communication, letters have a purpose and an intended audience.

LETTERS		
TYPE	PURPOSE	AUDIENCE
Personal	to express emotions and ideas	close friends or relatives
Social	to express appreciation or to communicate information about a specific event	close friends or social acquaintances
Business	to inform a business that you need its services, or to tell how well or badly a service was performed	a business or organization

RESOURCES

Writing Letters

Personal Letters

A ***personal letter*** is often the best way to communicate, even with someone you know well. In conversations—face-to-face or on the telephone—other people or time schedules may intrude. Personal letters, however, often get their receiver's complete attention. Unlike conversations, letters last. People often save personal letters and read them many times. A friendly letter is a gesture of friendship, containing a personal message from the sender to the receiver, such as best wishes for an upcoming holiday. When you're writing a personal letter, remember to write about things that interest you and the person you're writing to.

Social Letters

Social letters are usually for a specific purpose or in response to a specific event. The most common types of social letters are thank-you letters, invitations, and letters of regret.

Thank-you Letters

You write thank-you letters when you want to thank someone for taking the time, trouble, or expense to do something for you. Thank the person, then try to add a personal note. For example, if you're thanking someone for a gift, tell why the gift is special to you.

Invitations

An invitation should include specific information about the occasion, such as the time and place and any other special details your guests might need to know (such as that everyone may bring a friend, should dress casually, or is expected to bring food).

Letters of Regret

You write a ***letter of regret*** when you receive an invitation to an event that you will not be able to attend. You should especially respond in writing to invitations that include the letters *R.S.V.P.* (in French, an abbreviation for "please reply").

You should always respond quickly enough so that the person who is inviting you can accurately count the number of guests to prepare for. If the planned event is very soon, you may want to telephone the person to say that you can't come. But another consideration is politeness. Even if you have telephoned to say you won't attend, it's still polite to send a follow-up letter of regret.

5455 Blackstone Street
Chicago, IL 60615
March 20, 1992

Dear Felicia,

I was so happy to receive your invitation to your birthday slumber party next Friday evening. I really would like to be there. Unfortunately, my parents had already made plans for the whole family for that night.

Thank you very much for inviting me. I hope you have a happy birthday and a lot of fun at your party.

Your friend,

Bianca

Business Letters

The Parts of a Business Letter

Business letters follow a particular form. There are six parts of a business letter; they are

(1) the heading
(2) the inside address
(3) the salutation
(4) the body
(5) the closing
(6) the signature

Block Style

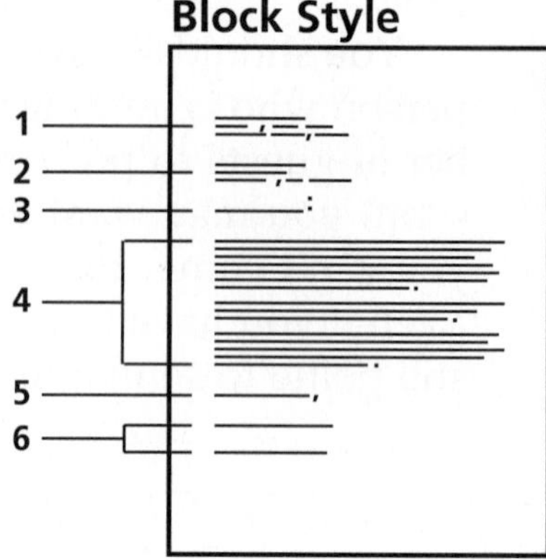

Modified Block Style

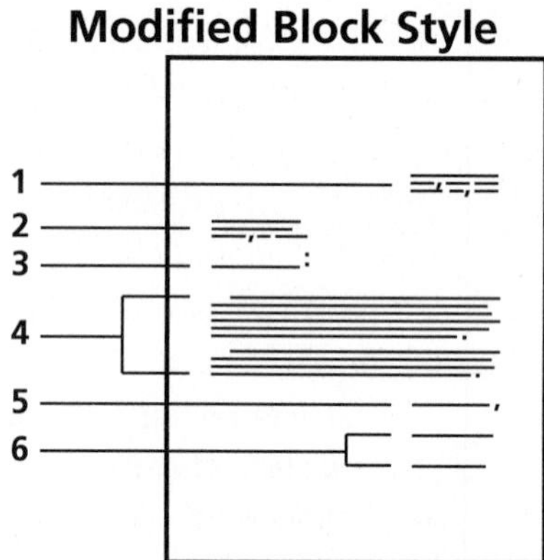

These six parts are usually arranged in one of the two most common styles used for business letters.

The ***block form*** places each part of the letter at the left margin of the page. A blank space is left between each paragraph in the body of the letter. Each paragraph is not indented.

The ***modified block form*** arranges the heading, the closing, and your signature just to the right of an imaginary line that extends down the center of the page. The middle parts of the letter all begin at the left margin. Each paragraph is indented.

The Heading. The heading usually has three lines:

- your street address
- your city, state, and ZIP code
- the date the letter was written

The Inside Address. The inside address gives the name and address of the person you are writing.

- If you're directing your letter to someone by name, use a courtesy title (such as *Mr., Ms., Mrs.,* or *Miss*) or a professional title (such as *Dr.* or *Professor*) in front of the person's name. After the person's name, include the person's business title (such as *Editor, Business Manager,* or *Department Chairperson*).
- If you don't have a person's name, use a business title or position title (such as *Store Manager* or *Complaints Department*).

The Salutation. The salutation is your greeting to the person you're writing.

- In a business letter, the salutation ends with a colon (such as in *Dear Mayor Williams:*). If you are writing to a specific person, use the person's name (such as *Dear Ms. Stokes*).
- If you don't have the name of a specific person, use a general salutation, such as *Dear Sir or Madam,* or *Ladies and Gentlemen.* Or, you can use a department or a position title (such as *Activity Director* or *Head of Division*), with or without the word *Dear.*

The Body. The body contains the message of your letter. Leave a blank line between paragraphs in the body of the letter.

The Closing. You should end your letter politely. There are several standard phrases that are often used to close business letters such as *Sincerely, Respectfully yours,* or *Yours truly*.

The Signature. Your signature should be handwritten in ink directly below the closing. Your name should be typed or printed neatly just below your signature.

Types of Business Letters

The Request or Order Letter. In a ***request letter,*** you write to request a product or service. For example, you might write to an art museum to request a schedule of hours it is open and any fees that are charged. In an ***order letter,*** you ask for something specific, such as a free brochure advertised in a magazine. You may also need to write an order letter to ask for a product by mail that appears in a magazine or advertisement without a printed order form.

When you are writing a request or order letter, remember the following points.

1. State your request clearly.
2. If you need to receive information, enclose a stamped envelope addressed to yourself. You are asking a favor of the persons you're writing to, so it's polite not to expect them to pay for the reply.
3. Make your request long before you need whatever you are requesting. Allow the persons to whom you have sent your request enough time to fit their reply into their normal schedule.
4. If you want to order something, include all important information. For example, give the size, color, brand name, or any other specific information. If there are costs involved, add the amount carefully.

The Complaint or Adjustment Letter. When you do not receive services or products that you have reason to expect, you may wish to write a ***complaint*** or ***adjustment letter.*** Remember these points.

1. Send your letter as soon as possible.
2. Be specific in your letter. Include the following details:
   - why you are unhappy (with the product or service)
   - how you were affected (lost time or money)
   - what solution you believe will correct the problem
3. Read your letter over to make sure it's calm and courteous.

The Appreciation or Commendation Letter. In an ***appreciation*** or ***commendation letter,*** you tell someone—a specific person, a group of people, a business, or an organization—that he, she, or they did a good job with a product or service. Be specific about exactly what action or idea of this person's you are commending. For example, if your city's mayor has just proposed some new summer recreation programs that you feel teenagers need, you might want to write an appreciation letter to thank him or her for being concerned with good recreation facilities and healthful programs for the city's young people.

210 Valley View Place
Minneapolis, MN 55419
March 10, 1993

Sgt. Latrice Jeffreys
Second Precinct Police Station
850 Second Avenue South
Minneapolis, MN 55402

Dear Sgt. Jeffreys:

Thank you very much for coming to speak to our school about safety. We are aware of this issue and how much it can affect our lives. It's good to know that there are so many things we can do ourselves to keep from becoming victims of crime.

I hope you will continue to speak to students about this very important subject. We should all know what our part is in fighting crime.

Sincerely yours,

Ingrid Johansen

Ingrid Johansen

Appearance of a Business Letter

Follow these suggestions to give your letter the best possible appearance.

- Use plain, white, unlined $8\frac{1}{2}'' \times 11''$ paper.
- Type your letter if possible (single-spaced, with an extra line between paragraphs). Or, write your letter by hand, using black or blue ink. Be as neat as possible. Try to avoid cross-outs, smudges, erasures, and inkblots. Check your letter for typing errors and misspellings, and correct them neatly.
- Leave equal margins on the sides, top, and bottom of the page.
- Use only the front of each page. If your letter is more than one page, leave a one-inch margin at the bottom of the first page and finish the letter on the next page.

Addressing an Envelope

The return address goes in the top left-hand corner of the envelope. The name and address of the person to whom the letter is written is in the center of the envelope. On the envelope for a business letter, the name and address to which the letter is being sent should exactly match the inside address of the letter.

Tama Wuliton
2703 Bryant Road
Dana Point, CA 92629

Clasprite Paperclip Company
1605 S. Noland Rd., Building 6
Borita, CA 92002

Completing Printed Forms

When you fill out a form, your purpose is to give clear, complete information. The following guidelines will help you complete all types of forms.

HOW TO FILL OUT FORMS

1. Look over the entire form before you begin.
2. Look for, and follow, special instructions (such as "Type or print" or "Use a pencil").
3. Read each item carefully.
4. Supply all the information requested. If a question does not apply to you, write "does not apply," or use either a dash or the symbol *N/A* (meaning "not applicable").
5. When you're finished, make sure nothing is left blank. Also, check for errors and correct them neatly.
6. Mail the form to the correct address or give it to the correct person.

Review

EXERCISE 1 **Writing a Social Letter**

Write a social letter for one of the following situations, or make up one of your own.

1. A friend's mother baked you cookies for your birthday and sent you a thoughtful card.
2. You have been invited to a friend's house party but cannot attend because your grandparents will be in town for an overnight visit on the date of the party.
3. You are planning a movie-watching party at your house. Write a letter of invitation including all the information your guests would need to know.

EXERCISE 2 Writing a Business Letter

Write a business letter for one of the situations below. Use your own return address, but make up any other information you need to write the letter. Address an envelope for your letter. Fold the letter neatly and place it into the envelope. (Do not mail the letter.)

1. Your parents said you could spend two weeks this summer at the youth camp of your choice. Write to the Circle Q Summer Camp, located at 3333 Route 1, Festus, Missouri 63028.
2. Write a letter of appreciation or commendation to an individual or organization you would like to thank or congratulate for outstanding efforts or performance.

EXERCISE 3 Completing a Form

For each numbered blank, write what you would put in that blank if you filled out this form.

INFORMATION FORM

NAME 1	BIRTHDAY 2
NICKNAME 3	PHONE # 4
ADDRESS 5	
PARENT OR GUARDIAN 6	WORK # 7

	TEACHER	ROOM #	HOBBIES AND INTERESTS
PERIOD 0	8	9	10
PERIOD 1			
PERIOD 2			
PERIOD 3			
PERIOD 4			
PERIOD 5			
PERIOD 6			
PERIOD 7			

35 Studying and Test Taking

Using Skills and Strategies

Good grades are almost always a sign of good study skills. If you develop good study habits, you can earn better grades with less last-minute panic before tests. You might not have to study harder to improve your grades. You might be able to study smarter, instead.

Planning a Study Routine

RESOURCES

Plan a study schedule that will help you study successfully. When you map out a schedule, stick to it. Here are some suggestions:

1. *Know your assignments.* Write down all the assignments you have and their due dates. Be sure you understand the instructions for each assignment.
2. *Make a plan.* Break large assignments into small steps. Keep track of when you should be finished with each step.
3. *Concentrate when you study.* Set aside a time and a place to focus your attention on your assignments.

Strengthening Study Skills

Reading and Understanding

The way you read depends on what you're reading and why you are reading it. Your reading rate should match your purpose for reading. Here are some common purposes for reading.

READING RATES AND THEIR PURPOSE		
READING RATE	PURPOSE	EXAMPLE
Scanning	Reading for specific details	Looking in your math book for the page that has the explanation for solving a problem
Skimming	Reading for main points or important ideas	Looking through the chapter headings, charts, and time lines of your history book to review for a test
Reading for mastery	Reading closely to understand and remember	Reading a new chapter in your science book to plan for an in-class writing assignment

Writing to Learn

Writing can help you learn. When you write, you are forced to put your thoughts in order. You may use writing to analyze a problem, record your observations, or work out all the details of a plan. See the following chart for examples of types of writing that can help you explore and make decisions about your ideas.

TYPE OF WRITING	PURPOSE	EXAMPLE
Freewriting	To help you focus your thoughts	Writing for ten minutes to explore plot ideas for a creative writing assignment
Autobiographies	To help you examine the meaning of important events in your life	Writing about your hopes for the future on the day of your sister's wedding
Diaries	To help you recall your impressions and express your feelings	Writing about your reactions to a speech made by a guest speaker in your history class
Journals and Learning Logs	To help you record your observations, descriptions, solutions, and questions	Jotting down notes for a biology class discussion while watching a bird building its nest
	To help you define or analyze information, or propose a solution	Listing reasons for and against a plan of action to help you decide to do it or not

Using a Word Processor as a Writing Tool

The word processor is a wonderful tool for writing. You can use it to help you plan, draft, and edit your writing. Almost every step of the writing process is easier if you use a word processor.

Prewriting. With a little practice, you can type quickly on a word processor. You can then rewrite your notes or ideas without having to recopy or retype them.

Writing First Drafts. You can write, revise, and rearrange your ideas as often as you want. Then you can use the printer to produce a hard copy, or printout.

Evaluating. The word processor is great for trying out different versions. Just save your original document. Then, on a copy of the document, type in your changes. If you don't like the revisions, you still have the original.

Revising. You can easily type in changes on a word processor. Then you can print a clean copy without having to rewrite or retype the unchanged portions.

Proofreading. Some word processors can check spelling or find errors in punctuation or sentence structure.

Writing the Final Version. It's simple to print a final copy with a word processor. You can even print multiple copies with your printer.

Using the SQ3R Method

SQ3R is the name of a study method that was developed by Francis Robinson, an educational psychologist. The SQ3R study method includes five simple steps.

S *Survey* the entire assignment. If you're studying a chapter in a textbook, look quickly at the headings, subheadings, terms in boldface and italics, charts, outlines, illustrations, and summaries.

Q *Question* yourself. List questions that you want to be able to answer after reading the selection.

R *Read* the material carefully to find answers to your questions. Take notes as you read.

R *Recite* in your own words answers to each of the questions you wanted to be able to answer.

R *Review* the material by rereading quickly, looking over your questions, and recalling the answers.

The SQ3R method will help you read material more carefully. When you read actively, you are more likely to remember what you read.

Interpreting and Analyzing Information

Writers of essays, articles, and textbook chapters organize ideas and relate them to one another. If you can interpret and analyze the relationship of ideas, you will understand more of whatever you read.

Stated Main Idea. The main idea of a passage is the most important point the writer is making. Sometimes the main idea is stated. This means the author may clearly state the main idea in one or two sentences.

Implied Main Idea. Sometimes the main idea is not stated. There may not be one or two sentences that tell the major point the writer is making. Instead, the main idea may be implied. You may have to figure out for yourself the central idea that ties all the other ideas together.

HOW TO FIND THE MAIN IDEA

- Skim the passage. (What topic do the sentences have in common?)
- Identify the general topic. (What is the passage about?)
- Identify what the passage says about the topic. (What's the message of the passage as a whole?)
- State the meaning of the passage in your own words.
- Review the passage. (If you have correctly identified the main idea, all the other ideas will support it.)

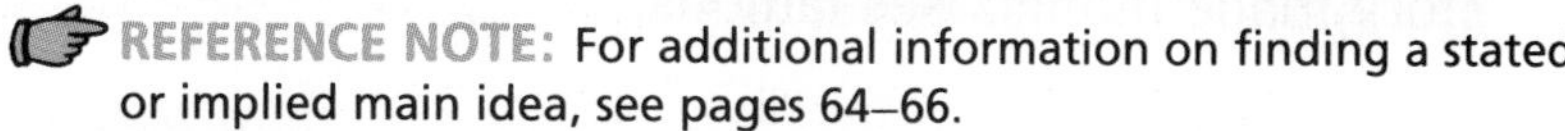

REFERENCE NOTE: For additional information on finding a stated or implied main idea, see pages 64–66.

Recognizing Relationships Among Details

Sometimes you have to work to understand the meaning of a reading passage. First, you need to understand the main idea. Then you need to look at how the details are related to the main idea and to each other.

FINDING RELATIONSHIPS AMONG DETAILS	
Identify specific details.	What details answer questions such as *Who? What? When? Where? Why?* and *How?* (*5W-How?* questions)?
Distinguish between fact and opinion.	What information can be proved true or false? What statements express a personal belief or attitude?
Identify similarities and differences.	How are the details similar to or different from one another?
Understand cause and effect.	Do earlier events affect later ones?
Identify an order of organization.	In what kind of order are the details arranged? Are they in chronological order, spatial order, order of importance, or some other pattern or order?

Reading Passage

In the story "Rikki-tikki-tavi," by Rudyard Kipling, a young English boy living in India rescues a young mongoose from drowning. Later in the story, the grateful, brave mongoose saves the lives of the boy and his parents by killing two cobras that plan to kill the humans. Kipling's story made mongooses famous.

Sample Analysis

OPINION: How did the mongoose in Kipling's story feel about humans?
ANSWER: *Rikki-tikki-tavi felt grateful to the humans for saving him. He felt brave when he was killing the cobras.*

Scientists who became interested in the mongoose proved that, just as Kipling said, mongooses could kill poisonous snakes. The mongoose is a small animal, similar to a ferret, that makes its home in Africa and some parts of Asia. Cobras and other poisonous snakes are only part of the mongoose's strange daily menu. Mongooses also feed on rodents, including rats, and insects, including wasps. A mongoose will even eat a scorpion.

Many people think that mongooses are immune to the poisonous venom of a snake. Others believe that mongooses know where to find a plant to eat that will keep a snake's venom from being harmful. But a mongoose only succeeds in killing a poisonous snake because it is faster than the snake. When a mongoose attacks a snake, it bites through the snake's spine right behind its head. The mongoose then holds on to the snake's head until the snake has completely stopped struggling.

In the past, people brought mongooses to Hawaii and the West Indies, hoping that they would kill some of the rats and snakes on those islands. Instead, the mongooses hunted rare birds that were easier to catch and kill than rodents and reptiles. Because of the mongooses' unpredictable eating habits, they are allowed in the United States only for zoos and scientific research.

FACT: What is the mongoose's defense against the venom of a snake?
ANSWER: *The only defense of the mongoose is its quickness.*

DETAILS: Mongooses can be found inhabiting which three continents?
ANSWER: *Mongooses can be found in Africa and some parts of Asia.*

SIMILARITY: How is the mongoose like a ferret?
ANSWER: *The mongoose is small in size like a ferret and similar in appearance.*

CAUSE AND EFFECT: Why did the United States decide that people would not be allowed to import mongooses?
ANSWER: *Mongooses that were imported into Hawaii and the West Indies did not control pests as expected. They did not eat rats and snakes. Instead, they ate rare birds.*

Applying Reasoning Skills

To understand what you read, you have to think about the ideas. These ideas are like clues, and you have to act like a detective to analyze evidence that you find in your reading. When you think critically, you may draw *conclusions*. ***Conclusions*** are decisions based on facts and evidence that are drawn from your reading.

Sometimes, thinking critically means that you must make *inferences*. ***Inferences*** are decisions based on evidence that is only hinted at, or implied, in what you have read. For example, when you analyze the reading passage on pages 850–851, you might draw these conclusions or inferences.

> Mongooses can survive in many different habitats. (Evidence: Mongooses are found on two continents. Also, mongooses eat all sorts of animals that live in many types of environments—deserts, mountains, or forests.)
>
> The cobra is a dangerous creature. (Evidence: Only one animal, the mongoose, will hunt and kill the cobra.)

A ***valid conclusion*** is firmly established by facts, evidence, or logic. An ***invalid conclusion***, however, is one that is not supported by facts or logic. For example, it is invalid to conclude that mongooses are considered pests in their natural habitat. This conclusion is not consistent with facts in the reading passage. In the passage you find that the mongoose's diet in its natural environment consists mainly of animals that are considered pests by humans.

HOW TO DRAW CONCLUSIONS	
Gather all the evidence.	What facts or details have you learned about the subject?
Evaluate the evidence.	What do the facts and details tell you about the subject?
Make appropriate connections.	What can you reasonably conclude from the evidence?

Analyzing Graphics and Illustrations

Many times, a book or article will include visuals such as diagrams, maps, graphs, and illustrations. These visuals often make information clearer and easier to understand than if it is written out.

A paragraph filled with details is often difficult to understand. Graphics and illustrations help you understand relationships between sets of facts. For example, the pie charts below show the distribution of farm work in the United States.

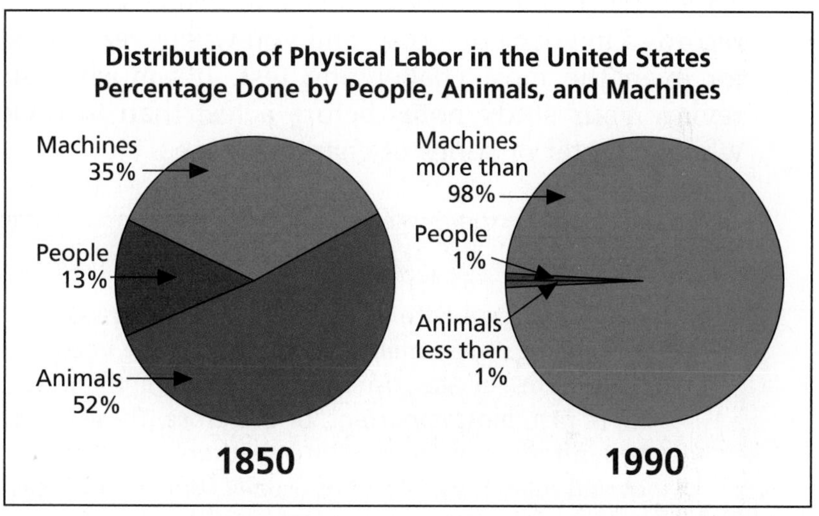

Looking at these graphs, you can quickly compare the overall amount of farm work performed by machines today with the amount performed by machines in 1850. Graphs like these can help you understand information more easily.

Applying Study Methods

Various study methods are simply different ways of organizing and handling information. The following are some of the most common methods:

- taking notes
- classifying
- organizing information visually
- outlining
- paraphrasing
- summarizing
- memorizing

Taking Notes

Taking accurate notes during a reading assignment or in class is worth the extra effort. Detailed information will be recorded in your notebook, and you will be ready to study for even the most challenging test. It's much easier to review your study notes before a test than to review a whole chapter or series of chapters.

HOW TO TAKE STUDY NOTES

1. Identify and take note of the main ideas in class or your reading. These main ideas should be the headings in your notes. In class, listen for key words and phrases, such as *first, most important,* or *therefore.* These words often introduce main ideas. In a textbook, chapter headings and related subheadings usually contain key ideas.
2. Keep your notes brief. Use abbreviations and summarize material in your own words.
3. Include brief examples or details, if you can. Important examples or details can help you recall the main ideas.
4. Review your notes soon after you have written them to be sure you have included all important information.

Here's an example of careful study notes about the reading passage on pages 850–851. The notes show the main ideas as headings. Underneath these main headings are grouped important details that relate to each heading. You can see that not every detail from the passage appears in these notes. Only the most important details are listed.

Mongooses

"Rikki-tikki-tavi"

- Story written by Rudyard Kipling
- Boy in India saves mongoose from drowning
- Mongoose kills two cobras—saves boy and family
- Story made people interested in mongooses

Characteristics of mongooses

- Small and ferret-like
- Live in Africa and Asia
- Eat poisonous snakes, rodents, and insects (including wasps and scorpions)

Mongooses and snakes

- Mongooses not immune to snake venom
- Don't seek out special plant to counter venom
- Mongoose's advantage is quickness
- Mongoose bites through snake's spine behind its head; holds on until snake dies
- Mongooses brought to Hawaii and West Indies to eat poisonous snakes—ate rare birds instead (thus not allowed in U.S. except for research and zoos)

Classifying

Classifying is arranging information into categories or groups. All the items that are in a category or group are related to each other. The name or description of the category shows the relationship between the various items in the group. For example, the name *sports* is the label of a category that could include various items, such as *baseball*, *basketball*, *hockey*, or *soccer*.

EXAMPLE What do the following birds have in common? penguins, chickens, emus, ostriches

ANSWER They are all birds that can't fly.

You also use classification when you identify patterns. For example, look at the relationship between the following sequence of numbers.

What's the next number in the series?

3 6 12 24 48 ____?____

ANSWER The first number in this series, *3,* is doubled to produce the second number, *6.* The second number is then doubled to produce the third number, *12.* This doubling goes on (*12* doubled is *24, 24* doubled is *48*). Then, to produce the next number in the series, you would double *48.* The answer is *96.*

Organizing Information Visually

Sometimes, new information is easier to understand if you organize it visually. A map, diagram, or chart is easier to understand than the same information provided in paragraph form.

For example, the passage that follows compares different poisonous snakes.

There are many kinds of venomous snakes. Rattlesnakes, for example, are found throughout the Western Hemisphere. They range from two to eight feet in length. The likelihood of a human dying as a result of a rattler's bite is low. The same is true for the bite of a cottonmouth. Cottonmouths are found from West Virginia to Texas. They can reach up to five feet in length. The coral snake is smaller, ranging from two to four feet in length. The coral snake, which may be found south of Canada in both North and South

America, is very deadly. King cobras, found throughout southern Asia, may reach a length of sixteen feet. The king cobra's bite is not usually deadly. The Cape cobra, however, is very deadly. This snake reaches up to seven feet in length and is found in southern Africa. One of the largest and most deadly snakes is the black mamba. This snake reaches up to fourteen feet in length and is found in southern and central Africa. Almost all of the people who are attacked by a black mamba die if they do not receive medical treatment immediately after being bitten.

It would be very difficult to identify all the snakes and all of their differences and similarities if you just read this passage and tried to remember all the details. However, if you made a chart like the one below, you would find the information in the paragraph much easier to remember.

VENOMOUS SNAKES			
TYPE OF SNAKE	LENGTH	LIKELIHOOD OF DEATH IF BITTEN (UNTREATED)	LOCATION
rattlesnake	2–8 ft.	low	W. Hemisphere
cottonmouth	up to 5 ft.	low	W. Virginia to Texas
coral snake	2–4 ft.	high	south of Canada; North and South America
king cobra	up to 16 ft.	low	southern Asia
Cape cobra	up to 7 ft.	high	southern Africa
black mamba	up to 14 ft.	very high	southern and central Africa

Outlining

An ***outline*** helps you organize important information. In an outline, the ideas are arranged in an order and in a pattern that makes their relationship to one another clear.

Sometimes you might want to make a formal outline by using Roman numerals for headings and capital letters for subheadings. For taking notes in your classes, however, you might want to use a faster method. An informal outline helps organize information quickly.

FORMAL OUTLINE FORM

I. Main Point
    A. Supporting Point
        1. Detail
            a. Information or detail

INFORMAL OUTLINE FORM

Main idea
    Supporting detail
    Supporting detail
    Supporting detail

Paraphrasing

When you ***paraphrase,*** you restate someone else's ideas in your own words. A paraphrase often helps explain ideas that are expressed in complicated or unfamiliar terms.

For example, the first part of President Lincoln's Gettysburg Address is: "Fourscore and seven years ago, our fathers brought forth on this continent, a new nation conceived in Liberty, and dedicated to the proposition that all men are created equal." You might paraphrase this as: "Eighty-seven years ago, our ancestors established here in America a new country that was committed to freedom and to the idea that every person is born equal."

When you write a paraphrase, it will usually be about the same length as the original. This means that you will probably not use paraphrasing for long passages of writing. However, you may sometimes be asked (usually in language arts classes) to paraphrase a short passage, such as a poem.

Here is an example of a poem and its paraphrase.

Those Winter Sundays
by Robert Hayden

Sundays too my father got up early
and put his clothes on in the blueblack cold,
then with cracked hands that ached
from labor in the weekday weather made
banked fires blaze. No one ever thanked him.

I'd wake and hear the cold splintering, breaking.
When the rooms were warm, he'd call,
And slowly I would rise and dress,
fearing the chronic angers of that house,

Speaking indifferently to him,
who had driven out the cold
and polished my good shoes as well.
What did I know, what did I know
of love's austere and lonely offices?

Here is a possible paraphrase of the poem.

The speaker in the poem is talking about his father. Each day the father would rise in the early morning, while the house was still cold, to build a fire. The father's hands were cracked and aching from his week's work. He was never thanked for his hard work.

On these cold mornings, the speaker would awake to the sounds of his father splitting wood. When the house had warmed, his father would call him downstairs. The speaker would slowly get dressed.

Unlike the house, which could be warmed, relations between the father and son remained cold and distant. The son expressed no thanks for the fires his father built or the shoes his father polished for him. The son later realizes that he was unaware of the love and commitment that motivated his father's daily routine.

Follow these guidelines when you write a paraphrase.

HOW TO PARAPHRASE

1. Read the selection carefully before you begin.
2. Be sure you understand the main idea of the selection. Look up unfamiliar words in a dictionary.
3. Determine the tone of the selection. (What is the attitude of the writer toward the subject of the selection?)
4. Identify the speaker in fictional material. (Is the poet speaking, or is it a character in the poem?)
5. Write your paraphrase in your own words. Shorten long sentences or stanzas. Use your own, familiar vocabulary, but follow the same order of events or ideas that is used in the selection.
6. Check to be sure that the ideas in your paraphrase of a selection match the ideas that are expressed in the original selection.

You also use paraphrasing when you write a research report. Make sure to cite the source of whatever you paraphrase. It's important to give credit for someone else's words or ideas.

REFERENCE NOTE: For more about giving appropriate credit to sources when writing reports, see page 329.

Summarizing

A *summary* is a brief restatement of the main ideas expressed in a piece of writing. Like a paraphrase, a summary expresses another person's ideas in your own words. However, a summary is shorter than a paraphrase. A summary shortens the original material, presenting only the most important points.

When you summarize, you think critically about the material that you are condensing. You make decisions and draw conclusions about what to include in the summary and what to leave out.

HOW TO SUMMARIZE

1. Skim the selection you wish to summarize.
2. Read the passage again closely. This time, look for the main ideas and notice all of the details that support each main idea.
3. Write your summary in your own words. Include only the main ideas and the most important supporting points.
4. Evaluate and revise your summary, checking to see that you have covered the most important points. Make sure that the information in your summary is clearly expressed and that the person reading your summary can follow your ideas.

Here's a sample summary of the reading passage found on pages 316–317.

> The cheetah is the fastest land animal. It lives in Arabia, Africa, and parts of Asia. The cheetah's body is built more like a dog's than a cat's. Its claws are dull except for the claw on the inside of the foreleg. Cheetahs have a bad sense of smell, but they have good eyesight. A cheetah may be seven feet long from the head to the tip of the tail. Unlike most big cats, it can be easily tamed; a cheetah will even purr when it is happy. Cheetahs have been clocked at amazing speeds of up to 80 miles per hour.

Memorizing

When you take tests and quizzes, you need to memorize the information that you are to be tested on. One long effort to memorize study material the night before a test will not be very effective. Instead, you'll find that frequent, short, focused sessions are more likely to help you remember information. On the following page are some hints for memorizing effectively.

HOW TO MEMORIZE	
Memorize key concepts.	Whenever possible, condense the material you need to remember.
Rehearse the material in different ways.	Copy the material by hand or recite the material out loud.
Invent memory games.	Form a word from the first letters of important terms, or make up rhymes to help you remember facts and details.

Improving Test-Taking Skills

Preparing for Different Kinds of Tests

Nervousness before a test is normal. However, you can channel the energy that comes from being nervous to help you do well on the test. Your attitude is the key.

HOW TO PREPARE FOR A TEST
Plan for success. Do everything you can to help you perform your best on the test. Identify the material to be covered on the test. Then make a plan that allows enough time to take notes, study, and review the material.
Be confident. If you have studied thoroughly, you know you are prepared. During the test, pay attention only to reading and answering the test questions.
Keep trying. Be determined to keep improving. Your efforts will help you improve your study effectiveness.

Objective questions and *essay questions* are two basic ways that your knowledge can be tested. There are specific ways to prepare for each type of test.

Objective Tests

There are many kinds of objective test questions. Some examples are multiple-choice, true/false, matching, reasoning or logic, or short-answer questions. Objective questions test you on specific information, such as names, terms, dates, or definitions. Most objective test questions have only one correct answer.

To prepare for objective tests, you will need to review specific information from your textbook and your notes. The study skills listed earlier in this chapter will help you prepare for objective tests.

HOW TO STUDY FOR OBJECTIVE TESTS

1. Identify important terms, facts, or ideas in your textbook and class notes.
2. Review the information in more than one form. For example, you may be responsible for defining literary terms. Make flashcards. Practice identifying the definition from the term, then identify the term from its definition.
3. Practice and rehearse factual information. Go over the items you have had difficulty with until you know them well.
4. If possible, briefly review all the information shortly before the actual test.

Your study strategies may be slightly different for each type of objective test. If you have to define key terms, then study using flashcards. If problem-solving questions are on the test, work out practice problems and check your answers with your textbook.

Taking Different Kinds of Objective Tests

Before you begin an objective test, quickly scan the questions. Knowing the number of items on the test helps you decide how to budget your time for each item. Here are some strategies for handling specific kinds of objective test questions.

Multiple-Choice Questions. With a multiple-choice question, you select a correct answer from a number of choices.

EXAMPLE **1.** Mongooses are effective as hunters of poisonous snakes because
A mongooses know where to find an herb that acts as an antidote for snake venom.
(B) mongooses are quicker than most snakes.
C mongooses are immune to snake venom.
D mongooses know when to find snakes sleeping.

HOW TO ANSWER MULTIPLE-CHOICE QUESTIONS	
Read the question or statement carefully.	■ Make sure you understand the key question or statement you are given before you look at the answer choices. ■ Look for words such as *not* or *always.* These words limit your choice of answers.
Read all the choices before selecting an answer.	■ Eliminate choices that you know are incorrect. This improves your chances of choosing correctly among the remainder. ■ Think carefully about the remaining choices. Select the one that makes the most sense.

True/False Questions. In a true/false question, you are asked to decide whether a certain statement is true or false.

EXAMPLE **1.** T (F) In both 1850 and 1990 in the United States, people did less farm work than machines.

HOW TO ANSWER TRUE/FALSE QUESTIONS	
Read the statement carefully.	■ The whole statement is false if any part of it is false.
Look for word clues.	■ Words such as *always* or *never* limit a statement. ■ A statement is true only if it is entirely and always true.

Matching Questions. Matching questions ask you to match the items in one list with the items in another list.

Directions: Match the name of the snake in the left-hand column with its natural home in the right-hand column.

C **1.** king cobra **A** southern Africa
D **2.** black mamba **B** from West Virginia to Texas
A **3.** Cape cobra **C** southern Asia
B **4.** cottonmouth **D** central and southern Africa

HOW TO ANSWER MATCHING QUESTIONS	
Read the directions carefully.	Sometimes you won't use all the items listed in one column. Other items may be used more than once.
Scan the columns.	If you match items you know first, you'll have more time to evaluate items you are less sure about.
Complete the rest of the matching.	Make your best guess on remaining items.

Reasoning or Logic Questions. This type of question tests your reasoning abilities more than your knowledge of a particular subject. You often find reasoning or logic questions on standardized tests. You may be asked to

RESOURCES

identify the relationship between several items (usually words, pictures, or numbers).

Reasoning questions might ask you to identify a pattern in a number sequence (as in the example on page 856) or ask you to predict the next item in a sequence.

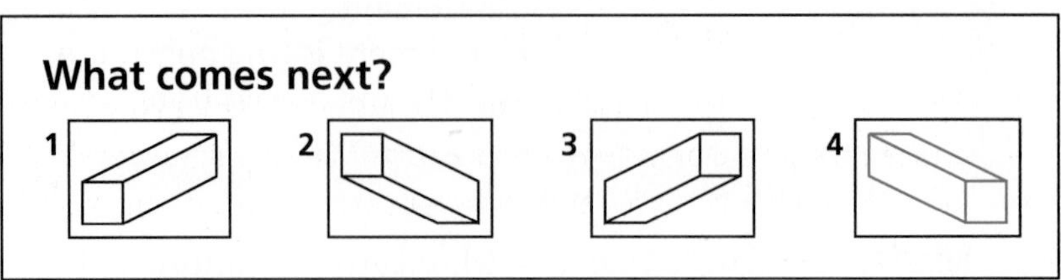

In this sequence of three drawings, the front of the block is in a different corner of the box each time. Therefore, in its final position the front of the block must be in the lower right corner of the box.

HOW TO ANSWER REASONING OR LOGIC QUESTIONS	
Be sure you understand the instructions.	Reasoning or logic questions are often multiple-choice. On some tests, however, you may need to write a word or phrase, complete a number sequence, or even draw a picture for your answer.
Analyze the relationship implied in the question.	Look at the question carefully to gather information about the relationship of the items.
Draw reasonable conclusions.	Evaluate the relationship of the items to decide your answer.

One special type of reasoning and logic question is an analogy question. In an analogy you recognize the relationship between two words and identify two other words that have a similar relationship.

EXAMPLE **1.** Directions: Select the appropriate pair of words to complete the analogy.

GLASS : MILK :: ______________

A glass : cup
B ice : iced tea
C bowl : soup
D cow : grass

In this analogy, you would express the relationship of items in the form of a sentence or question: "A *glass* is used to hold *milk.*" What other pair of words has the same relationship?

You would then test all the choices to see which one fits best. For example, to test the first choice, *A,* you would say, "Does a *glass* hold a *cup*? (No.)" For the second, you'd say, "Does *ice* hold *iced tea*? (No.)" For the third choice, you'd say, "Does a *bowl* hold *soup*? (Yes.)" Now look at the last choice, *D.* "Does a *cow* hold *grass*? (Yes, but only when the cow eats grass.)"

You now have two possibilities for answers, *C* and *D.* To choose between them, you would decide which pair of words is more like the relationship of a *glass* to the *milk* it holds. You might reason that both *milk* and *soup* are foods for humans and a *glass* and a *bowl* are both dishes. Maybe *grass* is food, but not for humans, nor is a *cow* like a *dish.* Therefore, the best choice is *C.*

Short-Answer Questions. Short-answer questions ask for short, precise responses. Instead of choosing from among a set of choices, you write the answer yourself.

Some short-answer questions (such as labeling a map or diagram, or fill-in-the-blank questions) can be answered with one or a few words. Other types of short-answer questions require you to give a full, written response, usually one or two sentences in length.

EXAMPLE Describe how a mongoose kills a snake.
ANSWER *The mongoose bites through the snake's spine right behind its head. The mongoose then holds onto the snake until it stops struggling.*

HOW TO RESPOND TO SHORT-ANSWER QUESTIONS	
Read the question carefully.	Some questions have more than one part. You will have to include an answer to each part to receive full credit.
Plan your answer.	Briefly decide what you need to include in the answer.
Be as specific as possible in your answers.	Give a full, exact answer.
Budget your time.	Begin by answering those questions you are certain about.

Essay Tests

Essay tests measure how well you understand a subject. Essay answers are usually a paragraph or more in length.

HOW TO STUDY FOR ESSAY TESTS
1. Read assigned material carefully. 2. Make an outline of main points and important details. 3. Create your own essay questions and practice writing answers. 4. Evaluate and revise your practice answers. Check your answers by your notes and textbook. Also check the composition section of this textbook for help in writing.

Taking Essay Tests

There are certain steps you should take before you begin an essay test. Quickly scan the questions. How many questions will you need to answer? Do you need to choose from several items? Which of them do you think you can answer best? After you have determined the answers to these questions, plan how much time to spend on each essay answer. Then stay with the schedule.

Read the question carefully. You may be asked for an answer that contains several parts.

Pay attention to important terms in the question. Essay questions on tests usually require specific tasks to be accomplished in the answer. Each task is expressed with a verb. If you become familiar with the key verbs and what kind of response each one calls for, this knowledge can help you to write a more successful essay.

ESSAY TEST QUESTIONS		
KEY VERB	TASK	SAMPLE QUESTION
argue	Take a viewpoint on an issue and give reasons to support this opinion.	Argue whether or not your school should start a recycling or a landscaping project.
analyze	Take something apart to see how each part works.	Analyze the life cycle of the chicken.
compare	Point out likenesses.	Compare word processors and typewriters.
contrast	Point out differences.	Contrast Cinderella and Snow White.
define	Give specific details that make something unique.	Define the term *divisor* as it is used in math.
demonstrate	Provide examples to support a point.	Demonstrate the importance of a balanced diet to good health.

ESSAY TEST QUESTIONS *(continued)*		
KEY VERB	TASK	SAMPLE QUESTION
describe	Give a picture in words.	Describe how Tom Sawyer convinces all his friends to whitewash his fence.
discuss	Examine in detail.	Discuss the term *cause and effect.*
explain	Give reasons.	Explain the need for protecting an endangered species.
identify	Point out specific characteristics.	Identify the types of clouds.
list	Give all steps in order or all details about a subject.	List the steps for opening a lock with a combination.
summarize	Give a brief overview of the main points.	Summarize the tale of Beauty and the Beast.

Take a moment to use prewriting strategies. Consider the key verbs in the question. Then jot down a few notes or an outline to help you decide what you want to say. Write notes or a rough outline on scratch paper.

Evaluate and revise as you write. You probably can't redo your whole essay, but you can edit and improve it.

QUALITIES OF A GOOD ESSAY ANSWER

- The essay is well organized.
- The main ideas and supporting points are clearly presented.
- The sentences are complete and well written.
- There are no distracting errors in spelling, punctuation, or grammar.

Review

EXERCISE 1 Choosing an Appropriate Reading Rate

Identify the reading rate that best fits each of the following situations.

1. You are looking at a test just handed to you to decide how much time you need to allot to each section.
2. You are looking in your grammar book for the section on the proper use of a semicolon.
3. You are reading a chapter in your history book and will be tested on it in two days.
4. You are reviewing the main points of the same chapter in your history book the night before your test.
5. You are looking in a textbook chapter for the answer to a question on your review sheet.

EXERCISE 2 Applying the SQ3R Method

Use the SQ3R method while reading a textbook chapter that you need to read for a class. List at least five questions and write a brief answer to each one.

EXERCISE 3 Analyzing Details in a Passage

Answer the following questions about the reading passage on pages 850–851.

1. Give two facts or details about mongooses (other than those noted in the sample analysis).
2. Why was the mongoose brought to Hawaii and the West Indies?
3. How did the mongoose in Kipling's story save the lives of the boy and his family?
4. What two myths about the mongoose's ability to kill poisonous snakes are discussed in the reading passage?
5. Under what conditions may a mongoose be brought into the United States?

EXERCISE 4 Drawing Conclusions and Making Inferences

Using the reading passage on pages 850–851, identify the evidence or explain the reasoning that you might use to make the following inferences or draw the following conclusions.

1. The mongoose is important for controlling the cobra population.
2. Mongooses are clever animals.
3. People in Asia, Africa, and southern Europe probably consider the mongoose a very valuable member of the animal kingdom.
4. Mongooses are not timid.
5. The mongoose is able to kill almost any kind of snake in the world.

EXERCISE 5 Interpreting Graphic Information

Using the chart on page 857, answer each of the following questions.

1. What is the longest venomous snake shown on the chart?
2. Which snake's bite would be most likely to kill you if you were left untreated after its attack?
3. Which snakes can be found somewhere in North America?
4. Which of the snakes shown on the chart is the smallest?
5. Where are king cobras found? Cape cobras?

EXERCISE 6 Analyzing Your Note-Taking Method

Select a homework assignment in your science, social studies, or English textbook. Take study notes, following the guidelines on page 854 regarding ways to take effective study notes. Be prepared to share your notes in class and to explain how you took notes.

EXERCISE 7 **Identifying Classifications**

For each of the following groups, identify the category.

1. tile, carpet, Oriental rug, linoleum
2. bed, cot, bunk, couch
3. basket, purse, suitcase, shopping bag
4. beagle, dachshund, retriever, Doberman pinscher
5. sandals, tennis shoes, hightops, boots

EXERCISE 8 **Applying Visual Organization**

After reading the paragraph below, make a chart of its contents. Use your graphic to answer the numbered questions on page 874. [Hint: Your completed chart should have two columns: one labeled "Reptiles" and one labeled "Amphibians."]

Reptiles and amphibians are two of the three classes of cold-blooded vertebrates. Reptiles and amphibians can appear to be very similar, but they are actually very different. First, reptiles are a larger class of animals than amphibians. For example, the largest reptiles, pythons and anacondas, can grow to be over thirty feet long. By contrast, the largest of the amphibians, the Japanese giant salamander, is only five feet long. Second, their appearance is different. The skin of a reptile is scaly, while an amphibian's skin is smooth and sometimes even slimy. Reptiles breathe only with their lungs. Amphibians breathe with gills when they are young and with lungs as adults. Some amphibians retain their gills and have both lungs and gills as adults. In addition, all amphibians take in oxygen through their skins. Third, their mating habits differ. Amphibians mate during rainy periods, while reptiles mate in the spring. Reptiles are born on land, while amphibians are born in water or on moist ground. Reptiles are either hatched from eggs or are born live. Amphibians always hatch from eggs.

1. How is the skin of a reptile different from the skin of an amphibian?
2. Which is a larger class of animals: reptiles or amphibians?
3. What is the difference, in feet, between the largest reptile and the largest amphibian?
4. Do reptiles breathe differently than amphibians? Explain.
5. How do reptiles and amphibians differ in their place of birth?

EXERCISE 9 **Paraphrasing a Poem**

Paraphrase the following excerpt from "A Psalm of Life" by Henry Wadsworth Longfellow.

Not enjoyment, and not sorrow,
  Is our destined end or way;
But to act, that each to-morrow
  Find us farther than today.

from "A Psalm of Life"
by Henry Wadsworth Longfellow

EXERCISE 10 **Analyzing Essay Questions**

Identify the key verb that states the specific task in each of the following essay questions. Do not write an essay response. Instead, state briefly what you would need to do to answer each question.

1. Contrast the temperaments of Rip and Dame Van Winkle in Washington Irving's "Rip Van Winkle."
2. Explain the importance of the U.S. Constitution at the time it was written.
3. Discuss the importance of setting in the poem "The Highwayman" by Alfred Noyes.
4. List the steps of the rain cycle.
5. Demonstrate the importance of imagery in the poem "A Dream Deferred" by Langston Hughes.

APPENDIX

DIAGRAMING SENTENCES

A ***sentence diagram*** is a picture of how the parts of a sentence fit together. It shows how the words in the sentence are related.

Subjects and Verbs (pages 400–411)

To diagram a sentence, first find the simple subject and the simple predicate, or verb, and write them on a horizontal line. Then separate the subject and verb with a vertical line. Keep the capital letters but leave out the punctuation marks, except in cases such as *Mr.* and *July 1, 1992.*

EXAMPLE **Horses gallop.**

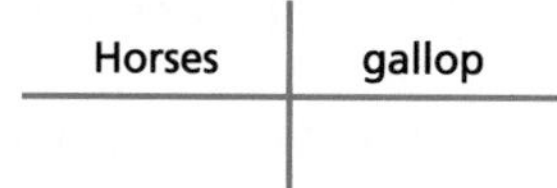

Questions (page 407)

To diagram a question, first make the question into a statement. Then diagram the sentence. Remember that in a diagram, the subject always comes first, even if it does not come first in the sentence.

EXAMPLE **Are you going?**

you | Are going

The examples on the previous page are easy because each sentence contains only a simple subject and a verb. Now look at a longer sentence.

EXAMPLE **A quiet, always popular pet is the goldfish.**

To diagram the simple subject and verb of this sentence, follow these steps.

Step 1: Separate the complete subject from the complete predicate.

complete subject	complete predicate
A quiet, always popular pet	is the goldfish.

Step 2: Find the simple subject and the verb.

simple subject	verb
pet	is

Step 3: Draw the diagram.

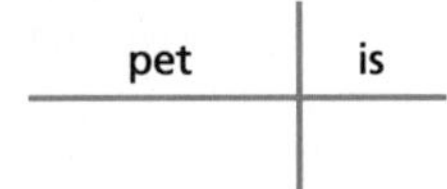

Understood Subjects (pages 415–416)

To diagram an imperative sentence, place the understood subject *you* in parentheses on the horizontal line.

EXAMPLE **Clean your room.**

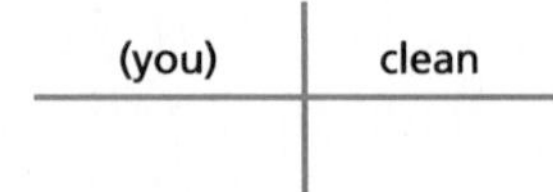

EXERCISE 1 Diagraming Simple Subjects and Verbs

Diagram only the simple subject and verb in each of the following sentences. Remember that simple subjects and verbs may consist of more than one word.

EXAMPLE **1. Gwendolyn Brooks has been the poet laureate of Illinois.**

Gwendolyn Brooks	has been

1. My friend Angela just returned from Puerto Rico.
2. She was studying Spanish in San Juan.
3. Listen to her stories about her host family.
4. She really enjoyed her trip.
5. Have you ever been to Puerto Rico?

Compound Subjects (page 409)

To diagram a compound subject, put the subjects on parallel lines. Then put the connecting word (the conjunction) on a dotted line that joins the subject lines.

EXAMPLE **Sharks** and **eels** can be dangerous.

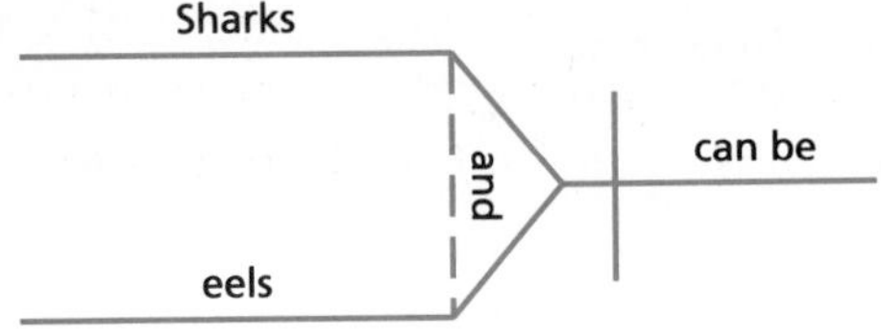

Compound Verbs (page 411)

To diagram a compound verb, put the two verbs on parallel lines. Then join them by a dotted line on which you write the connecting word.

EXAMPLE The cowboy **swung** into the saddle and **rode** away.

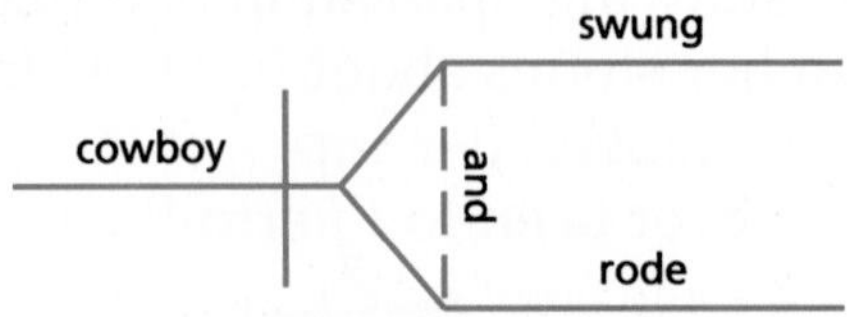

This is how a compound verb is diagramed when it has a helping verb.

EXAMPLE Alice Walker **has written** many books and **received** several prizes for them.

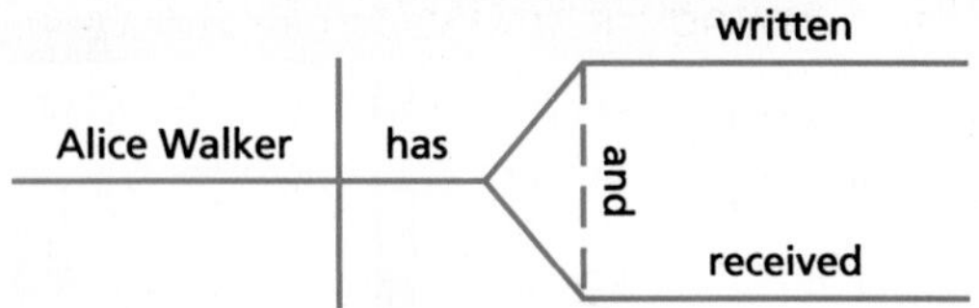

Compound Subjects and Compound Verbs (pages 409–411)

A sentence with both a compound subject and a compound verb combines the patterns for each.

EXAMPLE **Rosa Parks** and **Martin Luther King, Jr., saw** a problem and **did** something about it.

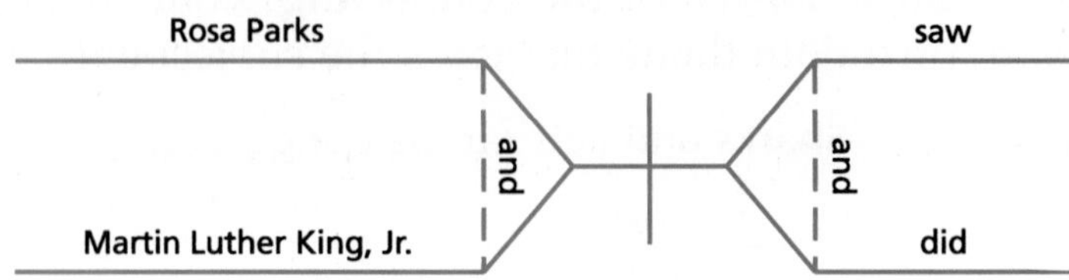

Sometimes parts of a compound subject or a compound verb are joined by correlative conjunctions, such as *both . . . and.* Correlatives are diagramed like this:

EXAMPLE **Both** Luisa **and** Miguel can sing.

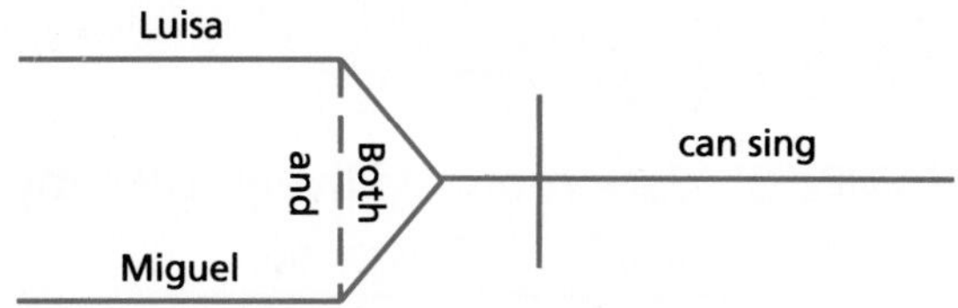

EXERCISE 2 Diagraming Compound Subjects and Compound Verbs

Diagram the simple subjects and the verbs in the following sentences. Include the conjunctions that join the compound subjects or the compound verbs.

EXAMPLE **1. Both Whitney Houston and Ray Charles are going on tour and cutting new albums.**

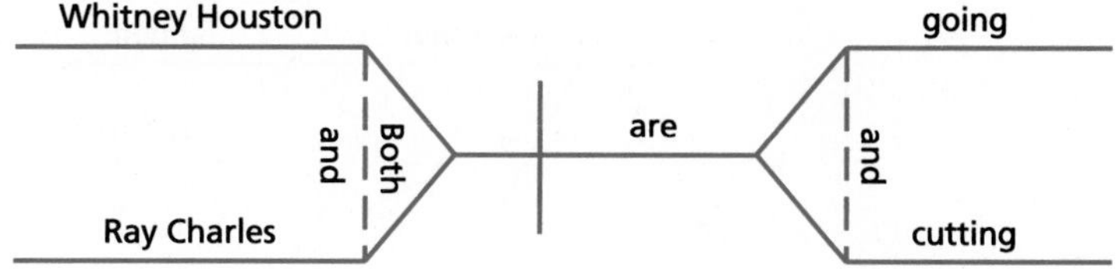

1. Everyone knows and likes Mr. Karras.
2. Hurricanes and tornadoes are frequent during the summer.
3. Julio and Rosa were frying tortillas and grating cheese for the tacos.
4. Both Jade Snow Wong and Amy Tan have written books about their childhoods in San Francisco's Chinatown.
5. Elena and I grabbed our jackets and took the bus to the mall.

Adjectives and Adverbs

Adjectives and adverbs are written on slanted lines connected to the words they modify. Notice that possessive pronouns are diagramed in the same way adjectives are.

Adjectives (pages 434–437)

EXAMPLES **dark** room **a lively** fish **my best** friend

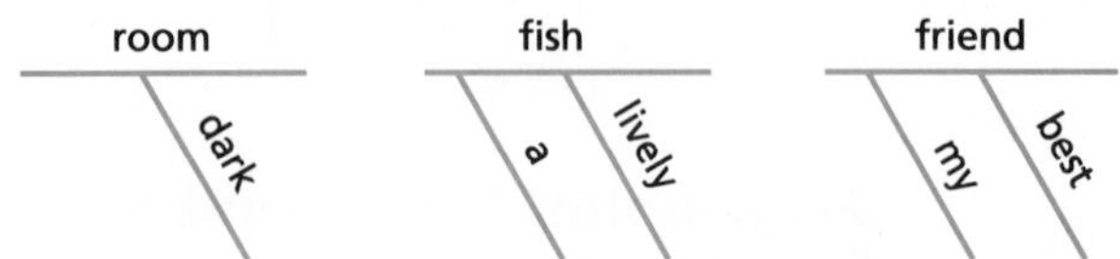

EXERCISE 3 Diagraming Sentences with Adjectives

Diagram the subjects, verbs, and adjectives in the following sentences.

EXAMPLE **1. A huge silver spaceship landed in the field.**

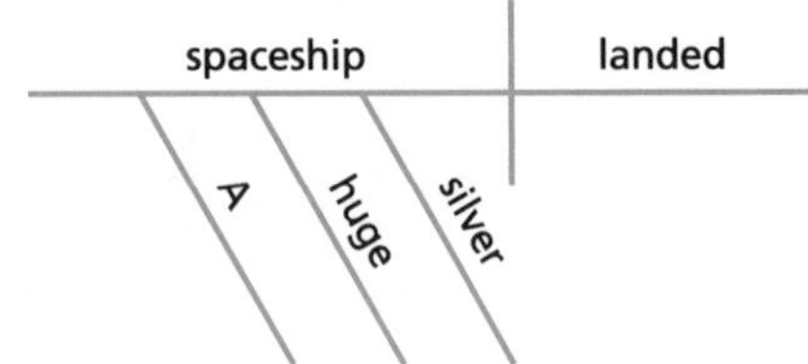

1. The horror movie will soon be finished.
2. The soft, silky kitten played with a shoelace.
3. A tall red-headed woman walked into the room.
4. The funniest television show stars Bill Cosby.
5. A weird green light shone under the door.

Adverbs (pages 454–457)

EXAMPLES walks **briskly** arrived **here late**

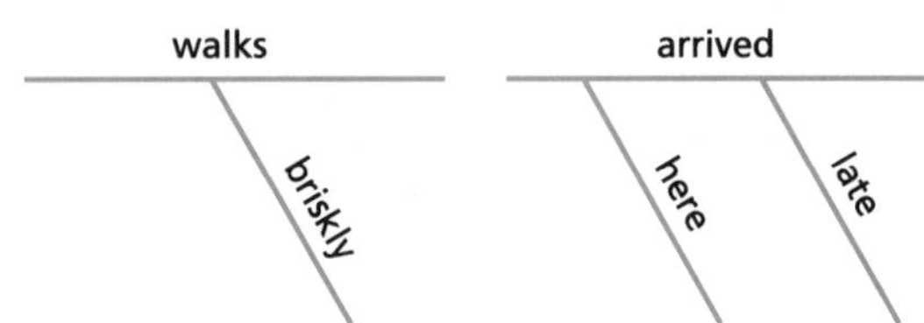

When an adverb modifies an adjective or another adverb, it is placed on a line connected to the word it modifies.

EXAMPLES a **very happy** child drove **rather slowly**

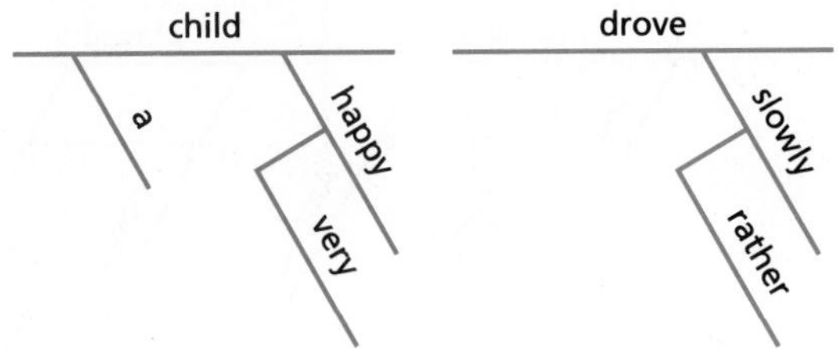

This **extremely rare** record will **almost certainly** cost a great deal.

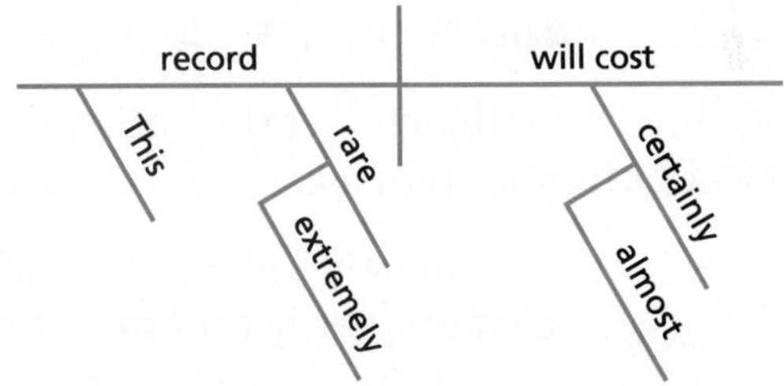

Conjunctions and Modifiers (pages 465–466)

When a modifier applies to only one part of the compound subject, it is diagramed like this:

EXAMPLE Benjamin Davis, Sr., and **his** son worked **hard** and rose **quickly** through the military.

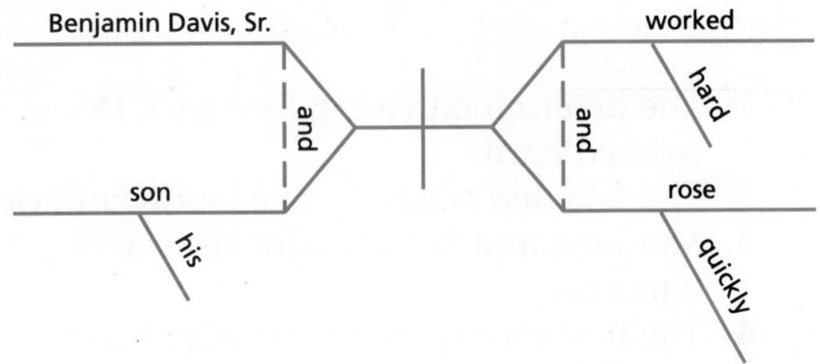

When a conjunction joins two modifiers, it is diagramed like this:

EXAMPLE **The English and American musicians played slowly and quite beautifully.**

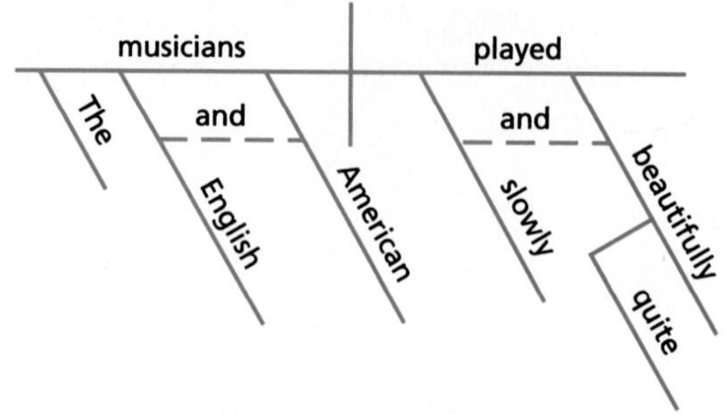

EXERCISE 4 Diagraming Sentences with Adjectives and Adverbs

Diagram the subjects, verbs, adjectives, and adverbs in the following sentences.

EXAMPLE **1. A relatively unknown candidate won the election easily and rather cheaply.**

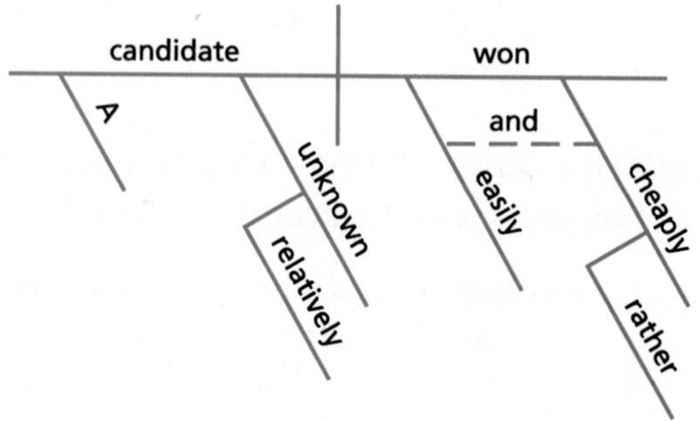

1. The determined young Frederick Douglass certainly worked hard.
2. The talented actress spoke loudly and clearly.
3. Mei-Ling and her younger sister will arrive early tomorrow.
4. The best musicians always play here.
5. Generally that glue does not work very well.

Objects (pages 474–477)

Direct Objects (pages 474–475)

A direct object is diagramed on the horizontal line with the subject and verb. A vertical line separates the direct object from the verb. Notice that this vertical line does not cross the horizontal line.

EXAMPLE **We like pizza.**

Compound Direct Objects (page 475)

EXAMPLE **Lizards eat flies and earthworms.**

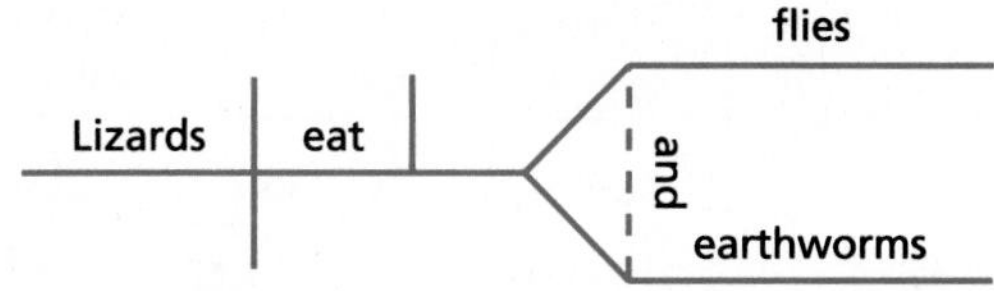

Indirect Objects (page 477)

An indirect object is diagramed on a horizontal line beneath the verb. The verb and the indirect object are joined by a slanting line.

EXAMPLE **Marisol brought me a piñata.**

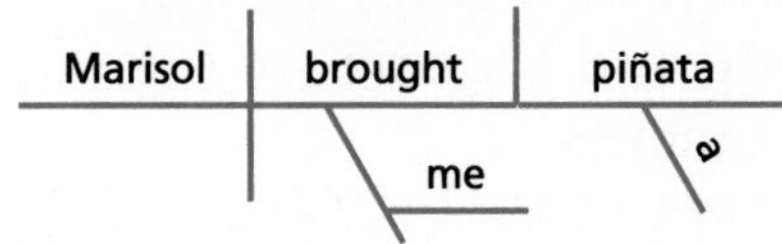

Compound Indirect Objects (page 477)

EXAMPLE **Tanya gave the singer and the dancer cues.**

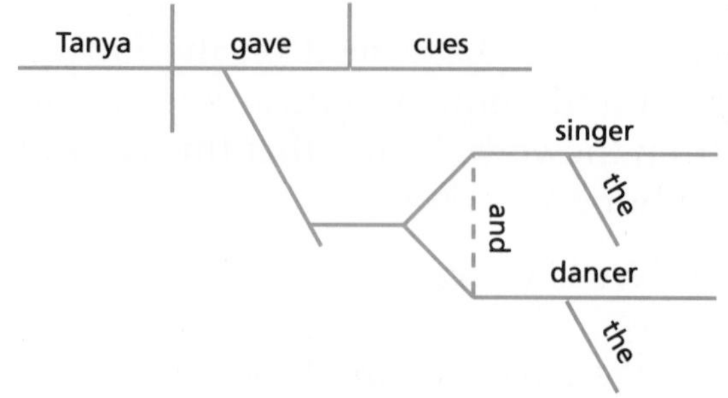

EXERCISE 5 **Diagraming Direct and Indirect Objects**

Diagram the following sentences.

EXAMPLE **1. I gave the clerk a dollar.**

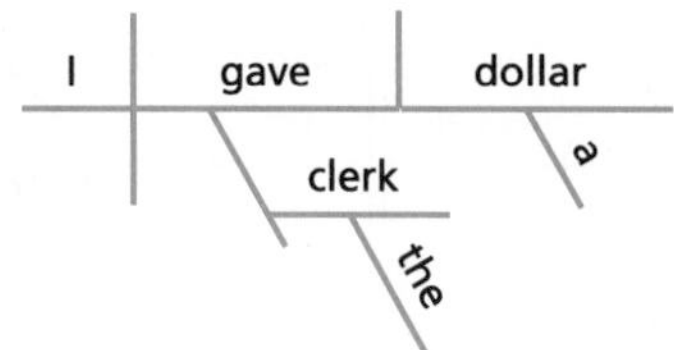

1. Several businesses bought our school computer equipment.
2. He sent the American Red Cross and Goodwill Industries his extra clothes.
3. My aunt knitted Violet and me sweaters.
4. Kim drew us a quick sketch.
5. Gerardo and Wendie are organizing the play and the refreshments.

Subject Complements (pages 480–482)

A subject complement is diagramed on the horizontal line with the subject and the verb. It comes after the verb. A line slanting toward the subject separates the subject complement from the verb.

Predicate Nominatives (pages 480–481)

EXAMPLE Barbra Streisand is a famous **singer.**

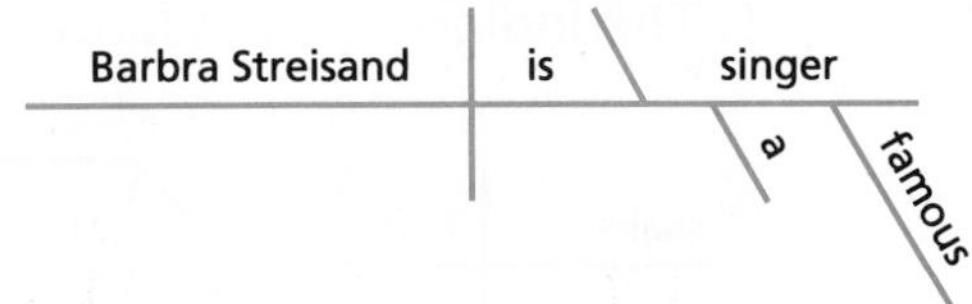

Compound Predicate Nominatives (page 481)

EXAMPLE Clara is a **student** and a volunteer **nurse.**

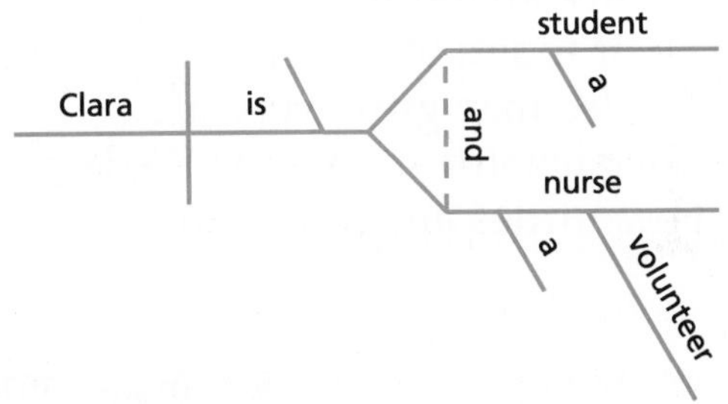

Predicate Adjectives (page 482)

EXAMPLE She was extremely **nice.**

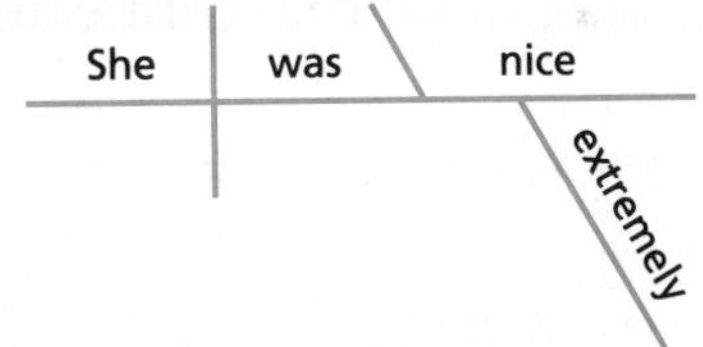

Compound Predicate Adjectives (page 482)

EXAMPLE We were **tired** but very **happy.**

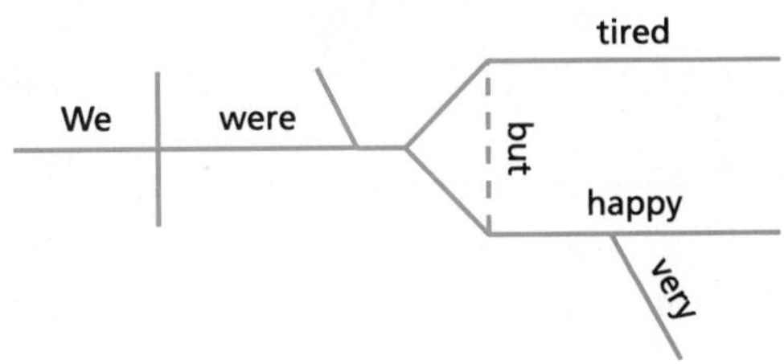

EXERCISE 6 Diagraming Sentences

Diagram the following sentences.

EXAMPLE **1. The indigo snake is large and shiny.**

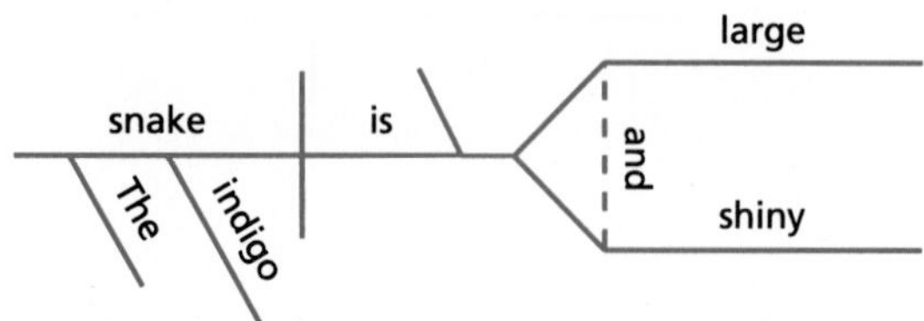

1. Turtles are reptiles.
2. Their tough bills look sharp and strong.
3. Turtles may grow very old.
4. The alligator snapper is the largest freshwater turtle.
5. Few turtles are dangerous.

Prepositional Phrases (pages 491–497)

A prepositional phrase is diagramed below the word it modifies. Write the preposition on a slanting line below the modified word. Then write the object of the preposition on a horizontal line connected to the slanting line.

Adjective Phrases (pages 493–494)

EXAMPLES traditions **of the Sioux** gifts **from Nadine and Chip**

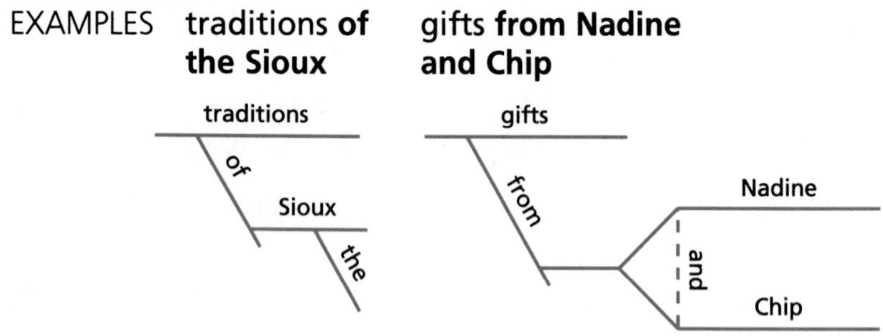

Adverb Phrases (pages 496–497)

EXAMPLES awoke early **in the morning**

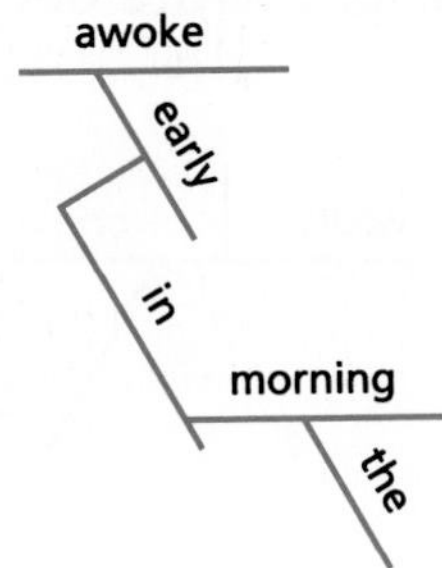

search **for the gerbil and the hamster**

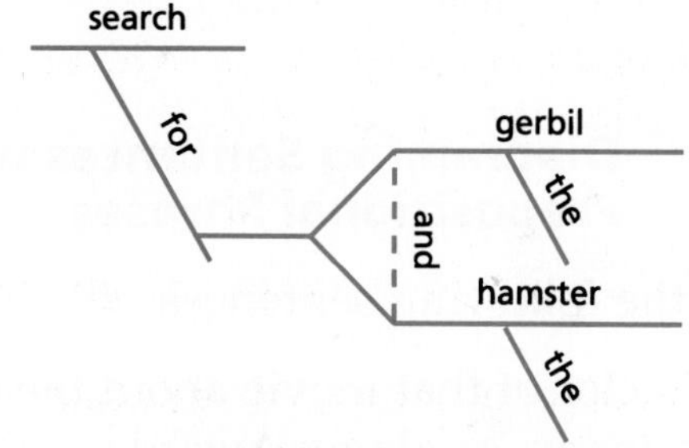

Two prepositional phrases may modify the same word.

EXAMPLE The tour extends **across the country** and **around the world.**

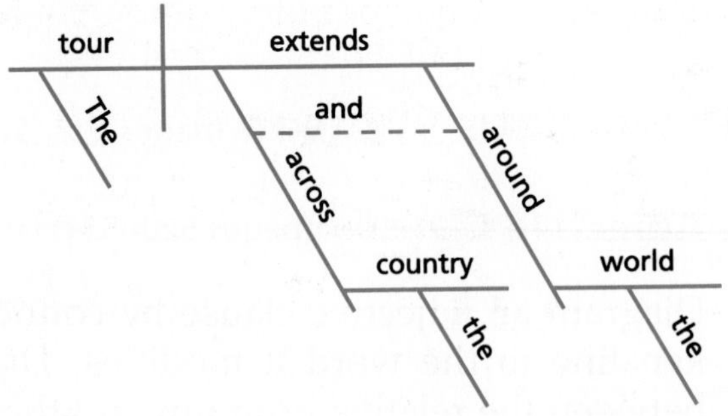

When a prepositional phrase modifies the object of another preposition, the diagram looks like this:

EXAMPLE **Richard Wright wrote one of the books on that subject.**

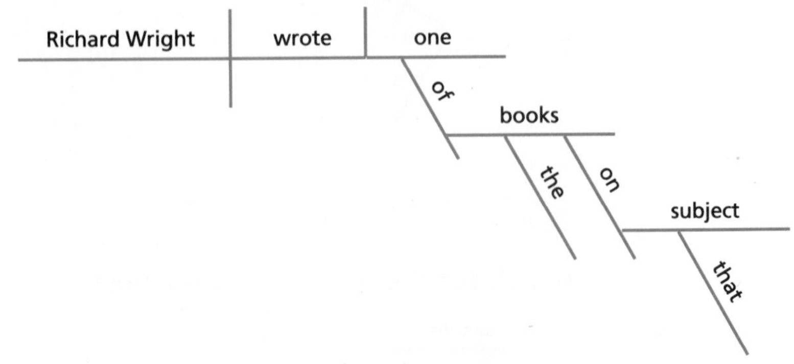

EXERCISE 7 **Diagraming Sentences with Prepositional Phrases**

Diagram the following sentences.

1. The director of that movie about the Civil War was chosen for an Academy Award.
2. A play about Cleopatra will be performed tonight.
3. Leroy practices with his band and by himself.
4. Stevie Wonder has written songs about love and freedom.
5. The scientist worked late into the night.

Subordinate Clauses (pages 516–525)

Adjective Clauses (pages 520–521)

Diagram an adjective clause by connecting it with a broken line to the word it modifies. Draw the broken line between the relative pronoun and the word that it relates to. [Note: The words *who, whom, whose, which,* and *that* are relative pronouns.] The adjective clause is diagramed below the independent clause.

EXAMPLES **The students whose projects are selected will attend the regional contest.**

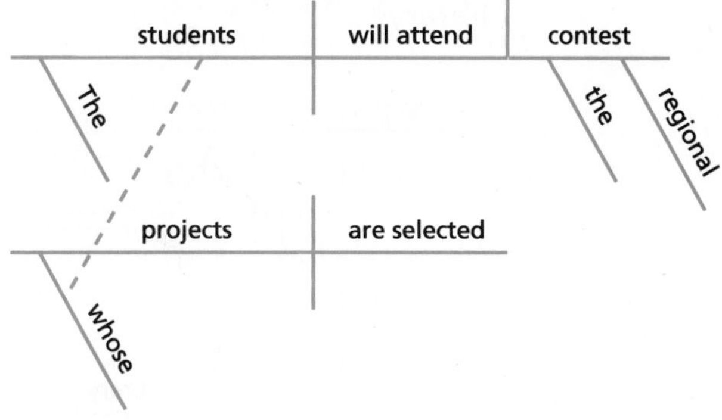

Adverb Clauses (pages 523–525)

Diagram an adverb clause by using a broken line to connect the adverb clause to the word it modifies. Place the subordinating conjunction that introduces the adverb clause on the broken line. [Note: The words *after, because, if, since, unless, when,* and *while* are common subordinating conjunctions.] The adverb clause is diagramed below the independent clause.

EXAMPLE **If I study for two more hours,** I will finish my homework.

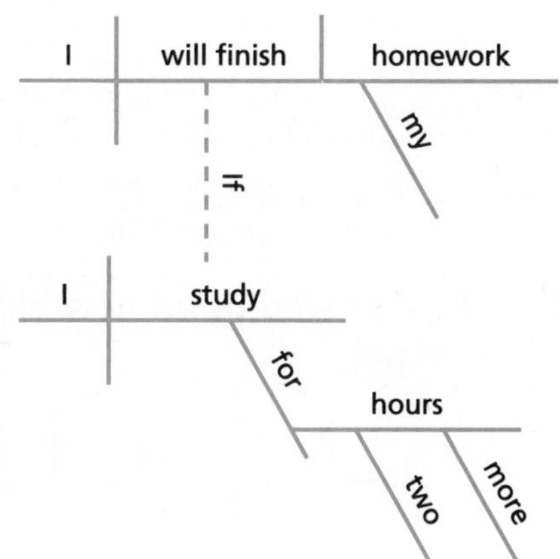

EXERCISE 8 **Diagraming Sentences with Adjective Clauses and Adverb Clauses**

Diagram the following sentences.

EXAMPLE **1. Will you stop by my house after you go to the library?**

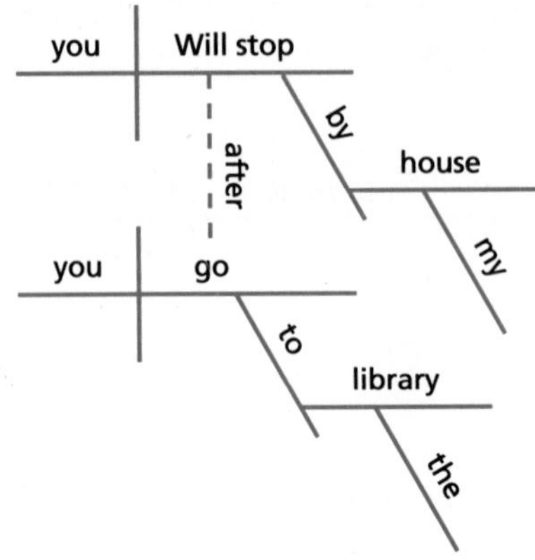

1. Proverbs are sayings that usually give advice.
2. Because the day was very hot, the cool water felt good.
3. The problem that worries us now is the pollution of underground sources of water.
4. If it does not rain tomorrow, we will visit Crater Lake.
5. Janice and Linda found some empty seats as the movie started.

The Kinds of Sentence Structure (pages 534–541)

Simple Sentences (page 534)

EXAMPLE **Ray showed us his new bike.** [one independent clause]

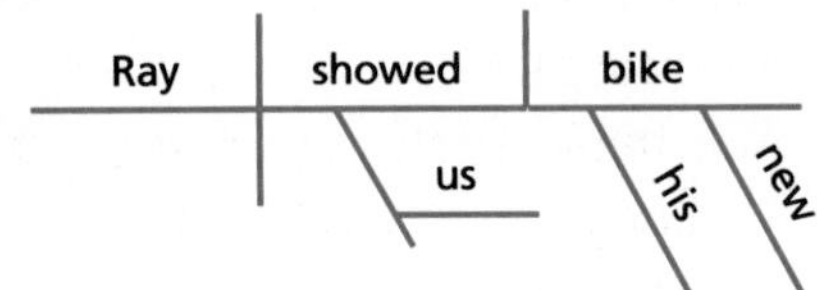

Compound Sentences (pages 536–538)

The second independent clause in a compound sentence is diagramed below the first and is joined to it by a coordinating conjunction. [The coordinating conjunctions are *and, but, for, or, nor, so,* and *yet.*]

EXAMPLE **Ossie Davis wrote the play, and Ruby Dee starred in it.** [two independent clauses]

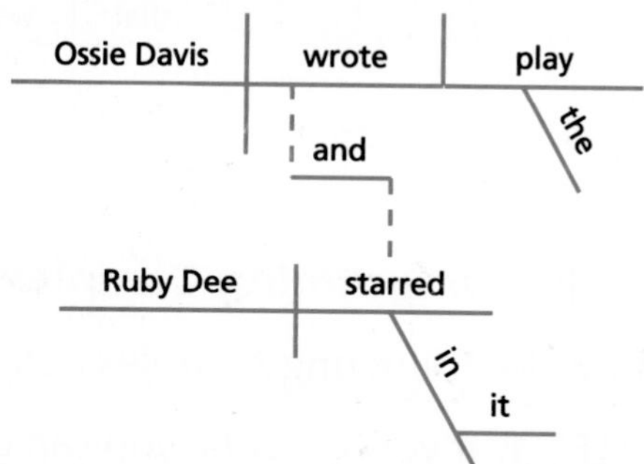

EXERCISE 9 Diagraming Compound Sentences

Diagram the following compound sentences.

EXAMPLE **1. Lucas likes that new CD, but I have not heard it.**

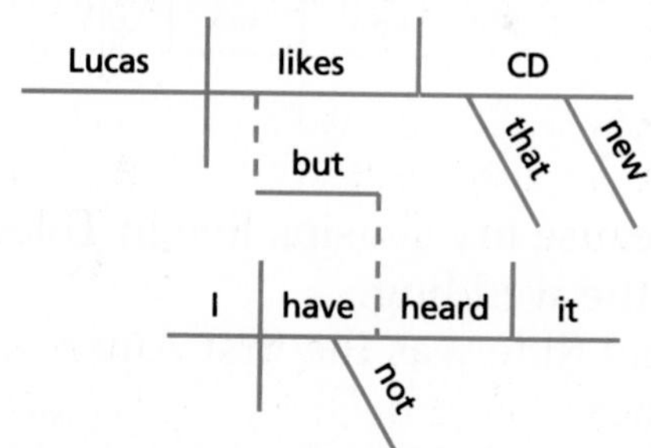

1. We went to the mall, and everyone had a good time.
2. Miriam celebrates Hanukkah, and she told our class about the holiday.
3. Luis Alvarez was an atomic scientist, but his son became a geologist.
4. Do you like basketball, or do you prefer hockey?
5. Sandy Koufax is my baseball hero, but my sister prefers Hank Aaron.

Complex Sentences (pages 540–541)

EXAMPLE Altovise has a carving **that was made in Nigeria.** [one independent clause and one subordinate clause]

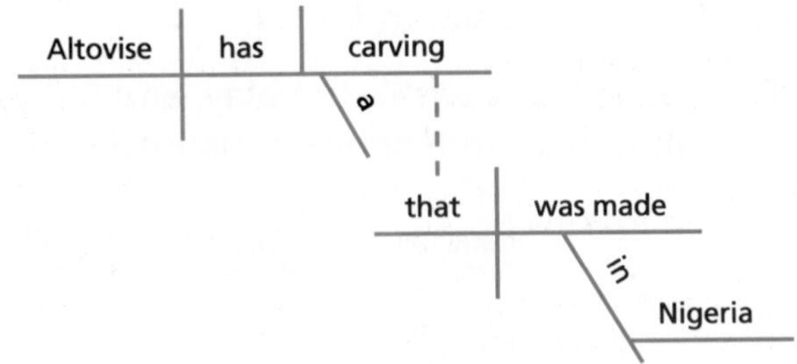

EXERCISE 10 Diagraming Complex Sentences

Diagram the following complex sentences.

EXAMPLE **1.** If you see Lola, you can give her this book.

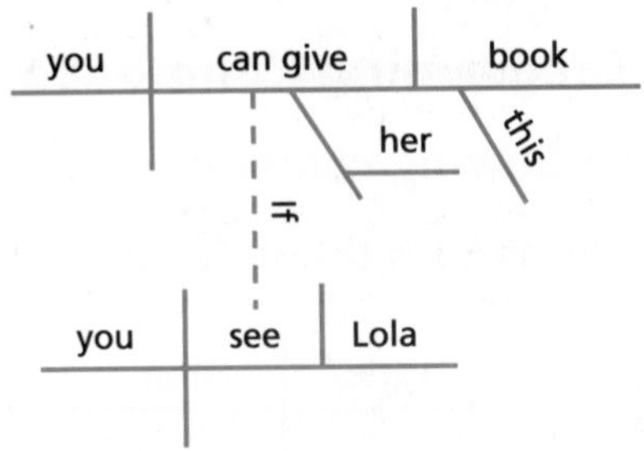

1. Because my cousins live in Toledo, they took a plane to the wedding.
2. Sally Ride was the first American woman who flew in space.
3. Although Wilma Rudolph had been a very sick child, she became a top Olympic athlete.
4. All three of the children screamed as the roller coaster began its descent.
5. The amusement park that we like best offers two free rides to frequent customers.

Glossary of Terms

A

Action verb An action verb is a verb that expresses physical or mental action. (See page 444.)

Adjective An adjective is a word that modifies a noun or a pronoun. (See page 434.)

Adjective clause An adjective clause is a subordinate clause that modifies a noun or a pronoun. (See page 520.)

Adjective phrase An adjective phrase is a prepositional phrase that modifies a noun or a pronoun. (See page 493.)

Adverb An adverb is a word that modifies a verb, an adjective, or another adverb. (See page 454.)

Adverb clause An adverb clause is a subordinate clause that is used as an adverb. (See page 523.)

Adverb phrase An adverb phrase is a prepositional phrase that modifies a verb, an adjective, or another adverb. (See page 496.)

Agreement Agreement refers to the correspondence, or match, between grammatical forms. (See Chapter 20.)

Aim An aim is one of the four basic purposes, or reasons, for writing. (See pages 7 and 24.)

Antecedent An antecedent is a noun or pronoun to which a pronoun refers. (See page 428.)

Antonym An antonym is a word with the opposite meaning of another word. (See page 832.)

Appositive An appositive is a noun or a pronoun that explains or identifies another noun or pronoun. (See page 715.)

B

Body The body of a composition is one or more paragraphs that state and develop the composition's main points. (See page 107.)

Brainstorming Brainstorming is a way a writer finds ideas for writing by making a list of all thoughts about a subject without stopping to judge the ideas. (See page 29.)

C

Case Case is the form of a noun or pronoun that shows its use in a sentence. (See page 606.)

Chronological order Chronological order is a way a writer arranges details in a paragraph or composition according to when events or actions take place. (See page 79.)

Clause A clause is a group of words that contains a verb and its subject and is used as a part of a sentence. (See page 516.)

Cliché A cliché is a vague and overused expression. (See page 391.)

Clustering Clustering is a way a writer finds writing ideas and gathers information by breaking a large subject into its smaller parts, using circles and lines to create a diagram of his or her thoughts. (See page 31.)

Coherence Coherence, in a paragraph or composition, means that a writer has clearly arranged and connected all ideas. (See pages 74 and 108.)

Colloquialism A colloquialism is a casual, colorful expression used in everyday conversation. (See page 389.)

Comparative degree Comparative degree is the form a modifier takes when two things are being compared. (See page 629.)

Comparing Comparing means telling how things are alike. (See page 82.)

Complement A complement is a word or group of words that completes the meaning of a verb. (See page 473.)

Complex sentence A complex sentence has one independent clause and at least one subordinate clause. (See page 540.)

Compound sentence A compound sentence has two or more independent clauses and no subordinate clauses. (See pages 368 and 536.)

Compound subject A compound subject consists of two or more subjects that are joined by a connecting word and have the same verb. (See pages 366, 409, and 560.)

Compound verb A compound verb consists of two or more verbs that are joined by a connecting word and have the same subject. (See page 411.)

Conclusion (1) A conclusion restates the main idea in different words, sums up the ideas in the composition, and brings it to a definite close. (See pages 109 and 336.) **(2)** A conclusion is a decision reached by reasoning from clearly expressed facts and evidence found in a reading passage or other materials. (See page 852.)

Conflict A conflict is a situation that holds a problem or challenge for a character in a story. (See page 186.)

Conjunction A conjunction is a word that joins words or groups of words. (See page 465.)

Connotation The connotation of a word is the word's emotional meanings suggested by or associated with that word. (See page 390.)

Context The context of a word includes the surrounding words and the way the word is used. (See page 831.)

Contrasting Contrasting means telling how things are different from one another. (See page 82.)

Creative writing Creative writing is writing that aims at creating literature: stories, poems, songs, and plays. (See page 7.)

D

Declarative sentence A declarative sentence makes a statement and is followed by a period. (See page 415.)

Denotation The denotation of a word is its direct, plainly expressed meaning—the meaning a dictionary lists. (See page 390.)

Description Description is a way a writer develops a paragraph or composition by using sensory details to describe something. (See page 77.)

Dialect A dialect is a variety of a language used by a particular group of people. (See page 385.)

Dialogue Dialogue consists of the words that characters say in a story. (See page 194.)

Direct object A direct object is a noun or pronoun that receives the action of a transitive verb. (See page 474.)

Double negative A double negative is the use of two negative words to express one negative idea. (See page 636.)

E

Essential clause/Essential phrase An essential (or **restrictive**) clause or phrase is one that is necessary to the meaning of the sentence. (See page 713.)

Evaluating Evaluating is the stage in the writing process in which a writer goes over a draft, making judgments about its strengths and weaknesses in content, organization, and style. (See pages 6 and 46.)

Evaluation Evaluation is a way a writer develops a paragraph or composition by making judgments, telling what is good or bad about a subject. (See page 84.)

Exclamatory sentence An exclamatory sentence shows excitement or expresses strong feeling and is followed by an exclamation point. (See page 416.)

Expressive writing Expressive writing is writing that aims at expressing a writer's feelings and thoughts. (See page 7.)

F

Figure of speech A figure of speech is a word or a group of words that have a meaning other than what they actually say. (See page 164.)

***5W-How?* questions** The *5W-How?* questions—*Who? What? Where? When? Why? How?*—are questions a writer uses to collect information about a subject. (See page 33.)

Freewriting Freewriting is a way of finding ideas for writing which a writer writes whatever pops into his or her head. (See page 28.)

H

Helping verb A helping verb helps the main verb to express action or a state of being. (See page 451.)

Homonyms Homonyms are words that are spelled differently and that mean different things, but are pronounced alike. (See page 777.)

"How-to" process writing "How-to" process writing is a form of writing in which a writer tells a step-by-step story of how to do something. (See page 216.)

I

Imperative sentence An imperative sentence gives a command or makes a request and is followed by either a period or an exclamation point. (See page 415.)

Independent clause An independent, or **main,** clause expresses a complete thought and can stand by itself as a sentence. (See page 516.)

Indirect object An indirect object is a noun or pronoun that comes between the verb and the direct object and tells *to whom* or *for whom* the action of the verb is done. (See page 477.)

Inference An inference is a decision that is made based on evidence that is hinted at or implied. (See page 852.)

Infinitive (1) An infinitive is one of the four principal, or basic, parts of a verb. (See page 580.) **(2)** An infinitive is a verbal, usually preceded by *to,* that can be used as a noun, an adjective, or an adverb. (See page 506.)

Infinitive phrase An infinitive phrase consists of an infinitive together with its modifiers and complements. (See page 508.)

Informative writing Informative writing is writing that aims at giving facts or information, or explaining something. (See page 7.)

Interjection An interjection is a word that expresses strong emotion. (See page 467.)

Interrogative sentence An interrogative sentence asks a question and is followed by a question mark. (See page 416.)

Intransitive verb An intransitive verb expresses action (or tells something about the subject) without passing the action to a receiver. (See page 446.)

Introduction An introduction begins a composition and should catch the readers' interest and present the main idea. (See page 104.)

Irregular verb An irregular verb is a verb that forms its past and past participle in some other way than by adding *–d* or *–ed* to the infinitive form. (See page 583.)

Jargon Jargon is special language that is used by a particular group of people. (See page 392.)

Linking verb A linking verb is a verb that expresses a state of being and links, or connects, the subject of a sentence with a word in the predicate that explains or describes the subject. (See page 447.)

List of sources A list of sources, or **Works Cited** list, tells what sources of information were used in a report. (See page 336.)

Logical order Logical order is a way of grouping ideas by what makes sense. (See page 82.)

M

Main idea A main idea is what a writer wants to say about a topic. It is the idea that a paragraph or composition is organized around. (See pages 64 and 98.)

Metaphor A metaphor is a figure of speech that compares two things directly, without using the words *like* or *as.* A metaphor says that something *is* something else. (See page 165.)

Modifier A modifier is a word, a phrase, or a clause that describes another word or limits the meaning of the word. (See page 629.)

Narration Narration is a way a writer develops a paragraph or composition by telling about events or actions as they change over a period of time. (See page 78.)

Nonessential clause/Nonessential phrase A nonessential (or **nonrestrictive**) clause or phrase adds information that is not needed to understand the meaning of the sentence. It is set off by commas. (See page 713.)

Noun A noun is a word that names a person, place, thing, or idea. (See page 423.)

Number Number is the form of a word that indicates whether the word is singular or plural. (See page 551.)

O

Object of the preposition The noun or pronoun that ends a prepositional phrase is the object of the preposition that begins the phrase. (See page 491.)

Order of importance Order of importance is a way of arranging details in a paragraph or composition according to how important the details are—most to least important, or the opposite. (See pages 84 and 160.)

P

Paraphrase A paraphrase is a restatement of someone's ideas in different words. (See page 858.)

Parenthetical expression A parenthetical expression is a side remark that adds information or relates ideas. (See page 718.)

Participial phrase A participial phrase consists of a participle together with its modifiers and complements. (See page 504.)

Participle A participle is a verb form that can be used as an adjective. (See page 502.)

Personal narrative A personal narrative is a form of writing in which an author explores and shares the meaning of an experience that was especially important to him or her. (See Chapter 4.)

Persuasive essay A persuasive essay is a form of writing in which a writer supports an opinion and tries to persuade an audience. (See Chapter 8.)

Persuasive writing Persuasive writing is writing that aims at persuading people to think or act in a certain way. (See page 7.)

Phrase A phrase is a group of related words that is used as a single part of speech and does not contain a verb and its subject. (See page 490.)

Plot The plot is the series of events that follow each other in a story. (See page 191.)

Positive degree Positive degree is the form a modifier takes when only one thing is being described. (See page 629.)

Predicate The predicate is the part of a sentence that says something about the subject. (See page 404.)

Predicate adjective A predicate adjective is an adjective that follows a linking verb and describes the subject of a sentence. (See page 482.)

Predicate nominative A predicate nominative is a noun or pronoun that follows a linking verb and explains or identifies the subject of a sentence. (See page 480.)

Prefix A prefix is a letter or group of letters added to the beginning of a word to create a new word with a different meaning. (See page 769.)

Preposition A preposition is a word that shows the relationship between a noun or pronoun and another word in the sentence. (See page 460.)

Prepositional phrase A prepositional phrase is a group of words beginning with a preposition and ending with a noun or a pronoun. (See pages 461 and 491.)

Prewriting Prewriting is the first stage in the writing process. In this stage, a writer thinks and plans, decides what to write about, collects ideas and details, and makes a plan for presenting ideas. (See pages 6 and 26.)

Principal parts of a verb The principal parts of a verb are a verb's four basic forms: the *infinitive,* the *present participle,* the *past,* and the *past participle.* (See page 580.)

Pronoun A pronoun is a word used in place of a noun or more than one noun. (See page 428.)

Proofreading Proofreading is the stage of the writing process in which a writer carefully reads a revised draft to correct mistakes in grammar, usage, and mechanics. (See pages 6 and 53.)

Publishing Publishing is the last stage of the writing process. In this stage, a writer makes a final, clean copy of a paper and shares it with an audience. (See pages 6 and 54.)

Purpose Purpose, or **aim,** is the reason for writing or speaking.(See pages 7, 24, and 37.)

Regular verb A regular verb is a verb that forms its past and past participle by adding *–d* or *–ed* to the infinitive form. (See page 581.)

Report A report is a form of writing in which a writer presents factual information that he or she has discovered through reading and asking questions about a topic. (See Chapter 10.)

Revising Revising is the stage of the writing process in which a writer goes over a draft, making changes in its content, organization, and style in order to improve it. (See pages 6 and 49.)

Run-on sentence A run-on sentence is two or more complete sentences run together as one. (See page 358.)

Sensory details Sensory details are words used to describe one of the five senses—sight, sound, touch, taste, and smell. (See page 69.)

Sentence A sentence is a group of words that has a subject and a verb and expresses a complete thought. (See page 398.)

Sentence fragment A sentence fragment is a group of words that looks like a sentence but does not express a complete thought. (See pages 355 and 398.)

Setting The setting is where and when a story takes place. (See page 190.)

Simile A simile is a figure of speech that compares two basically unlike things, using the words *like* or *as.* (See page 164.)

Simple sentence A simple sentence has one independent clause and no subordinate clauses. (See page 534.)

Slang Slang consists of made-up words and old words used in new ways. (See page 389.)

Spatial order Spatial order is a way of arranging details in a paragraph or composition by ordering them according to their location—from near to far, left to right, and so on. (See pages 77 and 160.)

Statement of opinion A statement of opinion is a sentence in which a writer clearly states a topic and his or her opinion about it. (See page 248.)

Subject The subject is the part of a sentence that tells whom or what the sentence is about. (See page 400.)

Subject complement A subject complement completes the meaning of a linking verb and identifies or describes the subject. (See page 480.)

Subordinate clause A subordinate, or **dependent,** clause does not express a complete thought and cannot stand alone as a sentence. (See page 516.)

Subordinating conjunction A subordinating conjunction begins an adverb clause and shows the relationship between the adverb clause and the word or words that the clause modifies. (See page 524.)

Suffix A suffix is a letter or group of letters added to the end of a word to create a new word with a different meaning. (See page 769.)

Summary A summary is a brief restatement of the main ideas expressed in a piece of writing. (See page 860.)

Superlative degree Superlative degree is the form a modifier takes when three or more things are being compared. (See page 629.)

Supporting sentences Supporting sentences are sentences in a paragraph or composition that give details or information to explain or prove the main idea. (See page 69.)

Syllable A syllable is a word part that can be pronounced by itself. (See page 765.)

Synonym A synonym is a word that has a meaning similar to, but not exactly the same as, another word. (See page 832.)

T

Topic sentence A topic sentence is the sentence that states the main idea of a paragraph. (See page 65.)

Transitional words and phrases Transitional words and phrases connect ideas in a paragraph or composition by showing why and how ideas and details are related. (See pages 74 and 108.)

Transitive verb A transitive verb is an action verb that expresses an action directed toward a person or thing. (See page 446.)

U

Unity Unity, in a paragraph or composition, means that all the sentences or paragraphs work together as a unit to express or support one main idea. (See pages 71 and 107.)

V

Verb A verb is a word that expresses an action or a state of being. (See page 444.)

Verbal A verbal is a form of a verb used as a noun, an adjective, or an adverb. (See page 502.)

Verb phrase A verb phrase contains one main verb and one or more helping verbs. (See pages 405 and 451.)

W

"What if?" questions Asking "What if?" questions is a way of thinking creatively that can help a writer spark his or her imagination to explore ideas for writing. (See page 34.)

Writer's journal A writer's journal is a written record of what happens in a person's life, and how he or she feels and thinks. The journal can be a sourcebook for writing ideas. (See page 27.)

Writing Writing is the stage in the writing process in which a writer puts his or her ideas into sentences and paragraphs, following a plan for presenting the ideas. (See pages 6 and 44.)

Writing process The writing process is the series of stages or steps that a writer goes through to develop ideas and to communicate them clearly in a piece of writing. (See pages 6 and 24.)

Glossary

This glossary is a short dictionary of words found in the professional writing models in this textbook. The words are defined according to their meanings in the context of the writing models.

Pronunciation Key

Symbol	Key Words	Symbol	Key Words
a	asp, fat, parrot	b	bed, fable, dub, ebb
ā	ape, date, play, break, fail	d	dip, beadle, had, dodder
ä	ah, car, father, cot	f	fall, after, off, phone
e	elf, ten, berry	g	get, haggle, dog
ē	even, meet, money, flea, grieve	h	he, ahead, hotel
i	is, hit, mirror	j	joy, agile, badge
ī	ice, bite, high, sky	k	kill, tackle, bake, coat, quick
ō	open, tone, go, boat	l	let, yellow, ball
ô	all, horn, law, oar	m	met, camel, trim, summer
oo	look, pull, moor, wolf	n	not, flannel, ton
o͞o	ooze, tool, crew, rule	p	put, apple, tap
yo͞o	use, cute, few	r	red, port, dear, purr
yoo	cure, globule	s	sell, castle, pass, nice
oi	oil, point, toy	t	top, cattle, hat
ou	out, crowd, plow	v	vat, hovel, have
u	up, cut, color, flood	w	will, always, swear, quick
ʉr	urn, fur, deter, irk	y	yet, onion, yard
ə	a in ago	z	zebra, dazzle, haze, rise
	e in agent	ch	chin, catcher, arch, nature
	i in sanity	sh	she, cushion, dash, machine
	o in comply	th	thin, nothing, truth
	u in focus	*th*	then, father, lathe
ər	perhaps, murder	zh	azure, leisure, beige
		ŋ	ring, anger, drink

Abbreviation Key

adj.	adjective	*prep.*	preposition
adv.	adverb	*vi.*	intransitive verb
n.	noun	*vt.*	transitive verb
pl.	plural		

A

ag • ate [ag'it] ***n.*** A marble made of a hard stone, usually striped or clouded in color.

ap • pren • tice [ə pren'tis] ***adj.*** Beginning.

ar • rest • ing [ə rest'iŋ] ***adj.*** Attracting immediate and full attention.

at • ta • ché [at' ə shā') ***n.*** A person who works for his or her own country in another country.

awed [ôd] ***adj.*** Feeling respect and wonder.

B

bay • o • net [bā'ə net'] ***n.*** A kind of blade attached to the barrel of a rifle.

blus • ter • y [blus'tər ē] ***adj.*** Windy, with clouds; stormy.

bo • lo tie [bō'lō tī] ***n.*** A cord worn around the neck with a decorated fastener to tighten the neck loop.

braille [brāl] ***n.*** A system of writing used by the blind in which patterns of raised dots are felt by the fingers.

buck • skin [buk'skin'] ***n.*** A yellow-gray horse.

bur • dock [bur'däk'] ***n.*** A plant with large leaves and purple flowers.

butte [byo͞ot] ***n.*** A lone steep hill in an area of flat land.

C

car • mine (kär'min] ***adj.*** Red or purplish-red.

check [chek] ***vt.*** To hold back.

chlo • rine [klôr'ēn] ***n.*** A chemical used to clean water.

com • mo • tion [kə mō'shən] ***n.*** Noisy confusion.

com • pe • tent [käm'pə tənt] ***adj.*** Very capable; skilled.

con • fines [kän'fīns'] ***n.*** A fenced in or limited area.

con • sume [kən so͞om'] ***vt.*** To eat up.

Co • pen • hag • en [kō' pən hā'gən] ***n.*** The capital city of Denmark.

Crazy Horse [krā'zē hôrs] ***n.*** *c.* 1842–1877. A famous chief of the Dakotas.

D

dep • re • cat • ing • ly [dep'rə kāt'in lē] ***adv.*** In a disapproving manner.

de • scend [dē send'] ***vi.*** To come down.

de • scend • ant [dē sen'dənt] ***n.*** One who is the son, daughter, grandchild, great-grandchild, etc., of a certain person.

de • te • ri • o • rate [dē tir'ē ə rāt] ***vi.*** To become poorer in quality.

dor • sal [dôr'səl] ***adj.*** On the back.

E

en • trance [en trans'] ***vt.*** To fill with delight.

e • phem • er • al [ē fem'ər əl] ***adj.*** Short-lived.

e • rode [ē rōd'] ***vi.*** To wear away until gone.

ex • ten • sive • ly [ek sten'siv lē] ***adv.*** To a great extent; covering a wide variety.

F

fast [fast] ***vi.*** To go without food.

fa • tigue [fə tēg'] ***n.*** Exhaustion; weariness.

for • feit [fôr'fit] ***vt.*** To lose or give up something in payment for a mistake in a game.

for • mat [fôr'mat'] ***n.*** Form.

fume [fyo͞om] ***vi.*** To show annoyance.

G

great·coat [grāt′kōt′] ***n.*** A heavy overcoat.

green·house [grēn′hous′] ***adj.*** Helping to trap the sun's rays in the earth's atmosphere, which may be causing climates all over the earth to gradually become hotter.

guf·faw [gu fô′] ***vi.*** To laugh loudly and roughly.

H

har·assed [hə rasd′] ***adj.*** Troubled and busy.

ha·ven [hā′vən] ***n.*** A safe place.

hid·e·ous [hid′ē əs] ***adj.*** Horrible to see or hear about.

hu·man·oid [hyōō′mə noid] ***adj.*** A creature with human characteristics.

hyp·not·ic [hip nät′ik] ***adj.*** Causing a sleep-like condition.

I

i·de·al·ism [ī dē′əl iz′əm] ***n.*** Thought based on the way one wishes things to be.

in·di·ca·tion [in′ di kā′shən] ***n.*** A sign; something that suggests.

in·fer·tile [in furt″l] ***adj.*** Not able to grow plants.

in·step [in′step′] ***n.*** The upper part of the arch of the foot.

in·ter·spe·cies [in′tər spē′shēz] ***adj.*** Between two different kinds of creatures or species.

ir·i·des·cent [ir′ i des′ənt] ***adj.*** Showing shiny colors that change when an object is moved.

J

Ju·bi·lee [jōō′bə lē′] ***n.*** A cry of joy.

ju·ve·nile [jōō′və nīl′] ***adj.*** Immature; lacking adult skill or experience.

K

knead [nēd] ***vt.*** To mix and work dough or clay by folding and pressing with the hands.

L

las·so [las′ō] ***n.*** A long rope with a movable loop on the end for catching cattle.

M

ma·neu·ver [mə nōō′vər] ***n.*** A planned movement.

meth·ane [meth′ān′] ***n.*** A colorless, odorless gas given off by rotting or digested plants.

mi·nus·cule [mi nus′kyōōl′] ***adj.*** Very small.

Mo·ses [mō′zəz] ***n.*** A person in the Bible who led his people out of slavery, usually pictured as a tall, old man with a long, white beard.

N

nat·u·ral·ist [nach′ər əl ist] ***n.*** A person who studies nature.

Na·zi [nät′sē] ***adj.*** Done by the political party that controlled Germany under Hitler from 1933 to 1945.

neu·ro·bi·ol·o·gist [nōō′rō bī äl′ə jist] ***n.*** A scientist who is an expert on the nervous system.

O

ob·jec·tive·ly [əb jek′tiv lē] ***adv.*** Without opinion for or against.

oc·cu·pied [äk′yōō pīd] ***adj.*** Captured and being run by a foreign government.

o·cean·ar·i·um [ō′shə ner′ē əm] ***n.*** A large aquarium for fish and animals from the ocean.

P

pad • dy [pad'ē] ***n.*** A rice field, partly under water.

pal • sied [pôl'zēd] ***adj.*** Paralyzed; often small from lack of use.

perch [purch] ***n.*** A freshwater fish.

per • se • cu • tion [pur'si kyoo'shən] ***n.*** The cruel or harsh treatment of someone for believing differently.

pre • ma • ture • ly [prē'mə toor' lē] ***adv.*** Too early.

pro • ces • sion [prō sesh'ən] ***n.*** A group moving forward together.

Q

quest [kwest] ***n.*** A journey in search of something of value.

R

raf • ter [raf'tər] ***n.*** A board that helps hold up a roof.

rain • forest [rān fôr'ist] ***n.*** A thick, evergreen forest in a tropical area that receives rain year-round.

re • it • er • ate [rē it'ə rāt'] ***vt.*** To repeat.

rem • i • nisce [rem'ə nis'] ***vi.*** To think and talk about memories of past events.

rep • er • toire [rep'ər twär'] ***n.*** The range of special skills that a performer is familiar with and prepared to demonstrate.

Re • sist • ance [ri zis'təns] ***n.*** The organized secret work of the people in a captured country fighting against the foreign country that has captured it.

rimed cou • plet [rīmd kup'lit] ***n.*** Two rhyming lines that are the same length, one written just after the other.

rouse [rouz] ***vi.*** To cause someone to act.

ru • pee [rōō'pē] ***n.*** The basic money unit of India.

S

sa • cred [sā'krid] ***adj.*** Holy; spiritually perfect or pure.

sage [sāj] ***n.*** A plant that is dried and used for seasoning; it was once believed to have healing powers.

sau • ci • ly [sô'si lē] ***adv.*** In a bright, lively way.

sheep • ish • ly [shēp'ish lē] ***adv.*** In an embarrassed manner.

sil • ver [sil'vər] ***vt.*** To cover with a silvery color.

Sioux [sōō] ***n.*** A North American Indian people of the Northern Plains.

so • ber [sō'bər] ***vt.*** To make someone be serious.

sound • ing [soun'diŋ] ***n.*** The act of measuring the depth of water using sound.

soy • a [soi'ə] ***n.*** A plant of the pea family.

spat [spat] ***n.*** A heavy cloth or leather covering worn over the upper part of a shoe.

T

te • pee [tē' pē] ***n.*** A cone-shaped tent made of animal skins stretched over poles.

ter • mi • nate [tur'mə nāt'] ***vt.*** To put an end to.

tract [trakt] ***n.*** A large area of land.

trem • o • lo [trem'ə lō'] ***n.*** A trembling sound made by rapidly repeating the same tone.

V

ve • ran • da [və ran'də] ***n.*** A long, open porch.

vi • cious [vish'əs] ***adj.*** Intense; mean.

vi • sion [vizh'ən] ***adj.*** Having to do with seeing unreal, dreamlike images in the mind.

Index

A

INDEX

INDEX

C

INDEX

INDEX

D

E

INDEX

F

I

J

K

L

INDEX

S

T

INDEX

U

V

W

Y

Z

Acknowledgments

For permission to reprint copyrighted material, grateful acknowledgment is made to the following sources:

American Way: From "Dream of the Blue Dolphins" by Michael DiLeo from *American Way,* the magazine of American Airlines. Copyright © 1991 by American Airlines.

Andrews and McMeel, A Universal Press Syndicate Company: From *The Pre-History of the Far Side, A 10th Anniversary Exhibit* by Gary Larson. Copyright © 1980, 1981, 1982, 1983, 1984 by the Chronicle Publishing Company; copyright © 1984, 1985, 1986, 1987, 1988, 1989 by Universal Press Syndicate.

Arte Público Press: From "The Jacket" from *Small Faces* by Gary Soto. Copyright © 1986 by Gary Soto.

Bradbury Press, an Affiliate of Macmillan, Inc.: From *Hatchet* by Gary Paulsen. Copyright © 1987 by Gary Paulsen.

Broadside Press: From "Questions and Answers" by Dudley Randall from *A Capsule Course in Black Poetry Writing* by Gwendolyn Brooks, Keorapetse Kgositsile, Haki R. Madhubuti, and Dudley Randall. Copyright © 1975 by Gwendolyn Brooks Blakely, Keorapetse Kgositsile, Haki R. Madhubuti, and Dudley Randall.

Jean Caldwell. Quotation by Madeleine L'Engle from an interview with Jean Caldwell from *On Being a Writer,* edited by Bill Strickland. Copyright © 1982 by Jean Caldwell.

Carlinsky & Carlinsky, Inc.: From "Kites" by Dan Carlinsky from *Boy's Life,* May 1974. Copyright © 1974 by Dan Carlinsky.

The Christian Science Monitor: Quotation by Fairfax Cone from *The Christian Science Monitor,* March 20, 1963. Copyright © 1963 by The Christian Science Monitor.

Dial Books for Young Readers, a division of Penguin Books USA Inc.: From *Roll of Thunder, Hear My Cry* by Mildred D. Taylor. Copyright © 1976 by Mildred D. Taylor.

Doubleday, a division of Bantam, Doubleday Dell Publishing Group, Inc.: From *Mighty Hard Road: The Story of Cesar Chavez* by James P. Terzian and Kathryn Cramer. Copyright © 1970 by Doubleday & Company, Inc. From "I'm from Out of the Beech" from *I Wish I Could Give My Son a Wild Raccoon* by Eliot Wigginton. Copyright © 1976 by Reading is Fundamental.

Dutton, an imprint of New American Library, a division of Penguin Books USA, Inc.: From *Insects, The Creeping Conqueror and Human History* by Carson I. A. Ritchie. Copyright © 1979 by Carson I. A. Ritchie.

Harcourt Brace Jovanovich, Inc.: "The Marble Champ" from *Baseball in April and Other Stories* by Gary Soto. Copyright © 1990 by Gary Soto.

HarperCollins Publishers: From "Hard Times" from *Black Elk: The Secret Ways of a Lakota* by Wallace H. Black Elk and William S. Lyon. Copyright © 1990 by Wallace H. Black Elk and William S. Lyon. From "One day a month, go without meat" from *Two Minutes a Day for a Greener Planet* by Marjorie Lamb. Copyright © 1990 by Marjorie Lamb.

Henry Holt and Company, Inc.: From "A Runaway Slave" from *Chariot In the Sky: A Story of the Jubilee Singers* by Arna Bontemps. Copyright 1951 by Arna Bontemps. Copyright © 1979 by Mrs. Arna (Alberta) Bontemps. "Stopping by Woods on a Snowy Evening" from *The Poetry of Robert Frost,* edited by Edward Connery Lathem. Copyright 1923, © 1969 by Holt, Rinehart and Winston. Copyright 1951 by Robert Frost.

Houghton Mifflin Company: From *Carlota* by Scott O'Dell. Copyright © 1977 by Scott O'Dell. All rights reserved.

Gary L. Johnson: From "A Son's Challenge" by Gary L. Johnson from *Reader's Digest,* September 1991. Copyright © 1991 by Gary L. Johnson.

Kalmbach Publishing Company: From "The Spaceport Mermaids" by Greg Walz-Chojnacki from *Odyssey,* vol. 12, no. 10, October 1990. Copyright © 1990 by Kalmbach Publishing Co.

Lion Books, Publisher, Scarsdale, NY: "Ubuhlali and Umnaka-Beaded Necklaces and Bangles" from *African Crafts.* Published by and copyright © Lion Books, Publisher, Scarsdale, NY.

Little, Brown and Company: From *Nisei Daughter* by Monica Sone. Copyright © 1953 and copyright renewed © 1981 by Monica Sone.

Liveright Publishing Corporation: "Those Winter Sundays" from *Collected Poems* by Robert Hayden, edited by Frederick Glaysher. Copyright © 1985 by Erma Hayden.

Lothrop, Lee and Shepard Books a division of William Morrow & Co., Inc.: From "Green Dragon Pond" from *The Spring of Butterflies,* translated by He Liyi. Copyright © 1985 by William Collins Sons & Co. Ltd.

Macmillan Publishing Company: From "My Aunt" from *Meet My Folks* by Ted Hughes. Copyright © 1961, 1973 by Ted Hughes.

Margaret K. McElderry Books, an imprint of Macmillan Publishing Company: From *A Jar of Dreams* by Yoshiko Uchida. Copyright © 1981 by Yoshiko Uchida.

William Morrow and Company, Inc./ Publishers, New York: From *Willie Bea and the Time the Martians Landed* by Virginia Hamilton. Copyright © 1983 by Virginia Hamilton Adoff. From *To Space and Back* by Sally Ride with Susan Okie. Copyright © 1986 by Sally Ride and Susan Okie. "A Drink for Crow" from *Stories to Solve: Folktales from Around the World,* told by George Shannon. Copyright © 1985 by George W. B. Shannon.

National Dairy Board, America's Dairy Farmers: Ad, "When your potassium comes with dairy calcium, you don't need a bunch." Copyright © 1990 by the National Dairy Board.

National Wildlife Federation: "Cures from the Jungle" by Whitney Hair from "Dear Ranger Rick" from *Ranger Rick* magazine, vol. 24, no. 8, August 1990. Copyright © 1990 by National Wildlife Federation. From "Meet-a-Cheetah" by Fred Johnson from *Ranger Rick* magazine, January 1969. Copyright © 1969 by National Wildlife Federation.

New American Library, a division of Penguin Books USA Inc.: From *The Sayings of Confucius* by James R. Ware. Copyright © 1955, 1983 by James R. Ware.

New York Magazine: Quotation by Barbara Costikyan from "Holiday Entertaining" from *New York,* October 22, 1984. Copyright © 1984 by New York Magazine. All rights reserved.

Newsweek, Inc.: From "A Doll Made to Order" from *Newsweek,* December 9, 1985. Copyright © 1985 by Newsweek, Inc. All rights reserved.

Omni International, Ltd.: From "The Dinner Party" by Mona Gardner from *Saturday Review,* January 31, 1942. Copyright © 1942 by Saturday Review.

Philomel Books, a division of The Putnam Publishing Group: From *A White Romance* by Virginia Hamilton. Copyright © 1987 by Virginia Hamilton.

The Pushcart Press: From a quotation by Maxwell Perkins from *The Writer's Quotation Book, a literary companion,* edited by James Charlton. Copyright © 1980 by The Pushcart Press.

Marian Reiner: Haiku by Basho from *Cricket Songs: Japanese haiku,* translated by Harry Behn. Copyright © 1964 by Harry Behn.

The Saturday Evening Post, a division of The Benjamin Franklin Literary and Medical Society, Inc.: From "Kachinas: Sacred Drama of the Hopis" by Lonnie Dyer from *Young World* magazine. Copy-right © 1976 by The Saturday Evening Post.

School Library Journal: From a book review by Louise L. Sherman on *Number the Stars* by Louis Lowry from *School Library Journal,* vol. 35, no. 7, March 1989. Copyright © 1989 by Reed Publishing, USA.

Charles Scribner's Sons, an imprint of Macmillan Publishing Company: From "Jody's Discovery" from *The Yearling* by Marjorie Kinnan Rawlings. Copyright © 1938 by Marjorie Kinnan Rawlings, copyright renewed © 1966 by Norton Baskin.

Virginia Driving Hawk Sneve: "The Medicine Bag" by Virginia Driving Hawk Sneve from *Boy's Life,* 1975. Copyright © 1975 by Virginia Driving Hawk Sneve.

Texas A & M University Press: From *Journal of an Indian Trader: Anthony Glass and the Texas Trading Frontier, 1790–1810,* edited by Dan L. Flores. Copyright © 1985 by Dan L. Flores.

Universal Press Syndicate: From "Coyote Places the Stars" from *Giving Birth to Thunder, Sleeping With His Daughter: Coyote Builds North America* by Barry Lopez. Copyright © 1977 by Barry Holstun Lopez.

University of California Press: From "In the Night" from *Singing for Power: The Song Magic of the Papago Indians of Southern Arizona* by Ruth Murray Underhill. Copyright © 1938, 1966 by Ruth Murray Underhill.

University of Nebraska Press: From "Across the Big Water" from *Black Elk Speaks: Being the Life Story of a Holy Man of the Oglala Sioux* as told through John G. Neihardt (Flaming Rainbow). Copyright © 1932, 1959, 1972 by John G. Neihardt. Copyright © 1961 by John G. Neihardt Trust.

Viking Penguin, a division of Penguin Books USA Inc.: "How to Eat Like a Child" from *How to Eat Like a Child* by Delia Ephron. Copyright © 1977, 1978 by Delia Ephron.

Webster's New World Dictionaries, A Division of Simon & Schuster, New York, NY: From the entry "escape" from *Webster's New World Dictionary of American English,* Third College Edition. Copyright © 1988 by Simon & Schuster, Inc.

Westminister/John Knox Press: From *Winter Thunder* by Mari Sandoz. Copyright © 1951 by The Curtis Publishing Company. Copyright © 1954 by Mari Sandoz. From *My Diary - My World* by Elizabeth Yates. Copyright © 1981 by Elizabeth Yates.

H. W. Wilson Company: Entries for "Roberts, Julia" through "Rock Music" from *Readers' Guide to Periodical Literature,* October 25, 1990, Vol. 90, No. 12. Copyright © 1991 by The H.W. Wilson Company.

PHOTO CREDITS

Abbreviations used: (t)top, (c)center, (b)bottom, (l)left, (r)right.

TABLE OF CONTENTS: Page vi, Nawrocki Stock Photo; vii, David Young-Wolff/PhotoEdit; viii, Archive Photos; x, Kobel Collection/SuperStock; xii, NASA; xiii, Culver Pictures; xv(t), Ted Horowitz/The Stock Market; xv(c), HRW Photo by Russell Dian; xv(b), Bev Rehkop/Unicorn Stock Photo; xvi(t), James Balog/Black Star; xvi(b), Christopher Arenc/AlaskaPhoto Collection/AllStock; xvii, The Granger Collection, New York; xix(t), Mary Messenger; xix(b), UPI/Bettmann Newsphotos; xxi, Norma Morrison; xxii(l), xxii(r), Michael Ochs Archives/Venice, CA; xxv, Camerique; xxxii, Bob Daemmrich/The Image Works; xxxiv, HBJ Photo by Stephanie Maize; xxxv(l), Courtesy Dudley Randall; xxxv(r), Ed Crabtree.

INTRODUCTION: Page 2, Bob Daemmrich Photography; 4, Blair Seitz/Seitz & Seitz; 5, Elena Rooraid/PhotoEdit; 6, Marc Deville/Gamma-Liaison; 7, Bonnie Kamin/Comstock.

CHAPTER 1: Page 21, Courtesy Dudley Randall; 27(l), 27(r), Myrleen Ferguson/PhotoEdit; 29(l), 29(r), Prettyman/PhotoEdit; 30, David R. Frazier Photolibrary; 33, HRW Photo by Ken Lax; 34(l), Lorraine Rorke/The Image Works; 34(r), Rosebush Vision/Phototake NY; 37, 38(l), David R. Frazier Photolibrary; 38(r), Ric Noyle/Visual Impact Hawaii; 40, Paolo Koch/Photo Researchers Inc.; 42(l), 42(r), 45, 50, Nawrocki Stock Photo; 52(l), Focus on Sports; 52(c), Usman Khan; 52(r), Arnold Michlin/PhotoEdit; 57, Michael & Barbara Reed/Animals, Animals.

CHAPTER 2: Page 60, Smithsonian Institution; 62, Topham/The Image Works; 64(l), Tom Bean/DRK Photo; 64(r), David Young-Wolff/PhotoEdit; 66, HRW Photo by Eric Beggs/Shoes courtesy RunTex, Austin, Texas; 68, Charles Palek/Animals, Animals; 70, Tony Freeman/PhotoEdit; 72, R. Hamilton Smith/FPG; 73, David R. Frazier Photolibrary; 75(l), Shostal Associates/SuperStock; 75(r), Jim Cartier/Photo Researchers, Inc.; 76, Lawrence Migdale; 78, Myrleen Ferguson/PhotoEdit; 83, Aaron Haupt/David R. Frazier Photolibrary; 85(l), Stan Osolinski/FPG; 85(r), Lee Kuhn/FPG; 87(l), Grant Heilman/Grant Heilman Photography; 87(r), Phil Schermeister/Photographers Aspen; 89(l), Reuters/Bettmann Newsphotos; 89(r), M. Richards/PhotoEdit.

CHAPTER 3: Page 95(t), Pat and Rae Hagan/Bruce Coleman Inc.; 95(b), Jeff Foott/Bruce Coleman Inc.; 96, Pat and Rae Hagan/Bruce Coleman Inc.; 97(tl), FourByFive/SuperStock; 98, Archive Photos; 99(l), David R. Frazier Photolibrary; 99(r), Tony Freeman/PhotoEdit; 101, 103(l), 103(r), M. Richards/PhotoEdit; 105, Hans Reinhard/Bruce Coleman Inc.; 109(l), 109(r), Runk/Schoenberger/Grant Heilman; 111, Shostal Associates/SuperStock; 112(l), FourByFive/SuperStock; 112(r), Shostal Associates/SuperStock; 113, The Photo Source/SuperStock.

CHAPTER 4: Page 123, Tom McCarthy/Unicorn Stock Photo; 124(l), Richard Hutchins/PhotoEdit; 124(r), David Young-Wolff/PhotoEdit; 125, Tony Freeman/PhotoEdit; 126, Walter Chandoha; 128, George D. Lepp/Comstock; 131, David E. Kennedy/TexaStock; 132, DiMaggio/Kalish/Peter Arnold Inc.; 134, Tom Murphy/SuperStock; 139, Frank Siteman/The Picture Cube; 142, Ed Crabtree; 144(l), Tony Freeman/PhotoEdit; 144(r), Mary Messenger; 146, SuperStock.

CHAPTER 5: Page 154, David DeLossy/The Image Bank; 157, Kobal Collection/SuperStock; 159, Tony Freeman/PhotoEdit; 161, Alfred B. Thomas; 162, Chuck O'Rear/Westlight; 163, HRW Photo Library; 164, Gary W. Griffen/Animals, Animals; 171, Richard Hutchings/PhotoEdit; 175(t), 175(l), 175(r), HRW Photo by Eric Beggs; 176, SuperStock.

CHAPTER 6: Page 185(l), 185(r), Walt Disney Pictures/Shooting Star; 187(l), Shostal Associates/SuperStock; 187(r), FourByFive/SuperStock; 188, Richard Hutchings/InfoEdit; 190(l), Spectrum/Bavaria/Viesti Associates, Inc.; 190(r), S. Chester/Comstock; 194, Comstock; 199, FourByFive/SuperStock; 200, Neal and Molly Jansen/Shostal Associates/SuperStock; 205, David Young-Wolff/PhotoEdit; 207(t), Shostal Associates/SuperStock; 207(b), Geffen 1986/Kobal Collection/SuperStock.

CHAPTER 7: Page 217(l), David R. Frazier Photolibrary; 217(r), Lawrence Migdale; 220, Bob Daemmrich/The Image Works; 221, HRW Photo by Eric Beggs; 223, Camerique; 224(t) Murray Alcosser/The Image Bank; 224(b), Robert Frerck/Odyssey, Chicago; 226, SuperStock; 229, FourBy Five/SuperStock; 237, NASA; 238, Larry Kolvoord/Viesti Associates, Inc.; 241, Treasure Island, R.L. Stevenson, J.B. Lippincott Company.

CHAPTER 8: Page 247, Grant Heilman/Grant Heilman Photography; 248, Culver Pictures; 249(l), UPI/Bettmann Newsphotos; 249(r), Witt/Sipa-Press; 250, Frank Siteman/The Picture Cube; 251, Dan Helms/Duomo; 253, Jack S. Grove/Tom Stack & Associates; 255, Eric Sander/Gamma-Liaison; 257, Grant Heilman Photography; 258, R. Azoury/Sipa-Press; 260, Al Tielemans/Duomo; 264, UPI/Bettmann; 266, Norma Morrison; 271, Culver Pictures, Inc.; 273, Richard Shiell/Earth Scenes.

CHAPTER 9: Page 293, Elena Rooraid/PhotoEdit; 302, HBJ Photo by Stephanie Maize; 304(l), D. Cavagnaro/DRK Photo; 304(r), John Shaw/Tom Stack & Associates; 309, HRW Photo by John Langford; 312, Jerry Howard/Positive Images; 313, UPI/Bettmann.

CHAPTER 10: Page 317, Gunter Ziesler/Peter Arnold, Inc.; 321(t), Bettmann Newsphotos;

321(r), Gunter Ziesler/Peter Arnold, Inc.; 321(b), NASA/Sipa-Press; 323(l), C. Canet/M.C.R. Communication/Gamma-Liaison; 323(c), Brian Lovell/ Nawrocki Stock Photo; 323(r), Luca Gavagna/ Photo Researchers, Inc.; 325(l), 325(r), John Cancalosi/DRK Photo; 327(t), SuperStock; 327(c), Melinda Berge/DRK Photo; 327(r), Paul Conklin/ PhotoEdit; 327(b), Edward C. Cohen/SuperStock; 328, Haley/Sipa-Press; 338, Scott Camazine/ Photo Researchers; 339, Stephen J. Kraseman/ DRK Photo; 341, Annie Griffiths/DRK Photo; 345, Charles Krebs/Allstock; 346, David R. Frazier Photolibrary; 351(l), Bev Rehkop/Unicorn Stock Photo; 351(c), HRW Photo by Russell Dian; 351(r), Ted Horowitz/The Stock Market; 353, Lawrence Migdale.

CHAPTER 11: Page 355, UPI/Bettmann; 357, Richard Alan Wood/Animals, Animals; 361, NASA/JPL Photo; 365, James Balog/Black Star; 366(l), Christopher Arend/AlaskaPhoto Collection/Allstock; 366(r), Nancy Simmerman/AlaskaPhoto Collection/AllStock; 369(l), 369(c), 369(r), Lawrence Migdale; 371, Breck P. Kent/Animals, Animals; 374, U.S. Army Photograph/HRW Photo Library; 377, Al Grotell.

CHAPTER 12: Page 381, The Granger Collection, NY; 388, Art Wolfe/AllStock; 393, The Bettmann Archive.

CHAPTER 13: Page 399, C.C. Lockwood/DRK Photo; 403, UPI/Bettmann Newsphotos; 406(t), Harriet Gans/The Image Works; 406(l), NPS Photo by Kepa Maly/Hawaii Volcanoes National Park; 406(r) George Hunter/H.Armstrong Roberts, Inc.; 410(l), Nicholas deVore III; 410(r), Runk/Schoenberger/Grant Heilman; 410(b), David Hiser/Photographers/Aspen; 417, Fred Ward/Black Star.

CHAPTER 14: Page 432, Mary Messenger; 438(l), B. Thomas/H. Armstrong Roberts; 438(r), Tom McHugh/Photo Researchers, Inc.

CHAPTER 15: Page 445, Bob Daemmrich/The Image Works; 451(t), Blair Seitz/Seitz & Seitz; 451(l), Jeff Reed/The Stock Shop; 451(r), SuperStock; 453, Norma Morrison; 459, Herb Segars/ Earth Scenes; 468, Arthur Tilley/Tony Stone Worldwide/Chicago Ltd.

CHAPTER 16: Page 476, 483, SuperStock; 487(l), HRW Photo by Russell Dian; 487(r), Norma Morrison.

CHAPTER 17: Page 492, Camerique; 495, Ken Yimm/UPI/Bettmann; 505, The Granger Collection, NY; 511, Bill Aron/PhotoEdit.

CHAPTER 18: Page 518, Michael Ochs Archives/ Venice CA.

CHAPTER 19: Page 523, 540, Tony Freeman/ PhotoEdit; 542(l), 542(r), 545, Culver Pictures, Inc.

CHAPTER 20: Page 553(l), Paul Conklin; 553(c), Jake McGuire/Washington Stock Photo, Inc.; 553(r), Paul Conklin; 559(t), Novosti/Sipa-Press; 559(b), Francois/Figaro/Gamma; 563, David Madison/Duomo; 570(t), Zheng Zhensun; 576, Lisa Pomerantz/The Image Bank.

CHAPTER 21: Page 582, Camerique; 601(t), Reagan Bradshaw; 601(b), Bob Daemmrich/ The Image Works.

CHAPTER 22: Page 614, FPG International.

CHAPTER 23: Page 633(l), 633(r), Cameramann International, Ltd.; 648, Len Hekel/© 1991 Capital Cities/ABC, Inc.

CHAPTER 24: Page 656(l), 656(r), Nawrocki Stock Photo; 663, Marty Cordano/DRK Photo; 667, Renato Rotolo/Gamma Liaison.

CHAPTER 25: Page 679, Bruce Asato, Honolulu Advertiser/Sipa Press; 687, SuperStock.

CHAPTER 26: Page 703, Brian Lanker; 705, Four Square Productions, Inc.; 712, Jerry Jacka; 714, International Museum of Photography at George Eastman House; 724, The Japan National Tourist Organization, New York; 728, Sanctuary for Animals, Westtown, New York.

CHAPTER 27: Page 743, Kennedy/TexaStock; 753, SuperStock.

CHAPTER 28: Page 772, S.E. Byrne/Lightwave.

Illustration Credits

Brian Battles—110, 200, 205, 225, 227, 271, 312, 353, 359, 363, 511, 687, 743, 824

Linda Blackwell—152, 183, 204, 245, 263

Keith Bowden—70, 248, 355, 361, 387, 413, 505, 540, 663, 665, 714, 752, 768

Rondi Collette—xxii, xxvi, 518, 523, 639, 669

Chris Ellison—146, 166, 168, 307, 348, 349, 483

Richard Erickson—260, 716

Janice Fried—61, 173

John Hanley—90

Mary Jones—xxviii, xxix, 607, 644, 770

Linda Kelen—xvii, xxvii, xxix, 71, 193, 201, 213, 214, 215, 268, 382, 389, 391, 616, 646

Susan B. Kemnitz—10, 11, 13, 15, 16, 195, 197

Rich Lo—xii, 27, 42, 123, 132, 207, 237, 276, 278, 357, 450, 451, 589

Judy Love—ix, xiv, xxxi, 65, 119, 120, 239, 269, 281, 283, 284, 287, 289, 291, 509, 618

Yoshi Miyake—377

Richard Murdock—48, 209

Precision Graphics—500, 535, 680, 685, 692, 719, 790

Jack Scott—106, 266, 318, 378

Chuck Solway—591

Troy Thomas—xi, 180–181, 182–183, 545

Nancy Tucker—67, 79, 81, 418, 498, 772

DEAN
CORNWELL

LLOYD C. DOUGLAS

The Robe

Illustrated by Dean Cornwell

PEOPLES BOOK CLUB

CHICAGO

Dedicated with appreciation
to
Hazel McCann
who wondered what became of
The Robe

This is a special edition published exclusively for the members of the PEOPLES BOOK CLUB, P. O. BOX 6570A, Chicago, Illinois. It was originally published by Houghton Mifflin Co.

MANUFACTURED IN THE UNITED STATES OF AMERICA

LIST OF ILLUSTRATIONS

THE DICE GAME — *Front Endpaper*

Demetrius did not look at the lonely man again. Marcellus, Paulus, and four or five others were lounging in a small circle on the ground.

THE SLAVE MARKET — *Following page 28*

Father had bought Demetrius six years ago and presented him to Marcellus on his seventeenth birthday. He selected his slaves with the same discriminating care that he exercised when purchasing beautiful statuary and other art objects.

PONTIUS PILATE'S BANQUET — *Following page 92*

Demetrius slowly bowed his head and handed Marcellus the Robe; then stood with slumped shoulders while his master tugged it on over the sleeves of his toga. A gale of appreciative laughter went up, and there was tumultuous applause.

MARCELLUS AND MIRIAM IN THE GARDEN — *Following page 220*

There was a peculiar tone-quality in her low voice that Marcellus could not define, except that its warmth was entirely unselfconscious and sincere.

LIST OF ILLUSTRATIONS

Chapter I

Because she was only fifteen and busy with her growing up, Lucia's periods of reflection were brief and infrequent; but this morning she felt weighted with responsibility.

Last night her mother, who rarely talked to her about anything more perplexing than the advantages of clean hands and a pure heart, had privately discussed the possible outcome of Father's reckless remarks yesterday in the Senate; and Lucia, flattered by this confidence, had declared maturely that Prince Gaius wasn't in a position to do anything about it.

But after she had gone to bed, Lucia began to fret. Gaius might indeed overlook her father's heated comments about the extravagances and mismanagement of his government, if he had had no previous occasion for grievance against the Gallio family. There was, however, another grievance that no one knew about except herself—and Diana. They would all have to be careful now or they might get into serious trouble.

The birds had awakened her early. She was not yet used to their flutterings and twitterings, for they had returned much sooner than usual, Spring having arrived and unpacked before February's lease was up. Lucia roused to a consciousness of the fret that she had taken to bed with her. It was still there, like a toothache.

Dressing quietly so as not to disturb Tertia, who was soundly sleeping in the alcove—and would be alarmed when she roused to find her mistress's couch vacant—Lucia slipped her sandals softly over the exquisitely wrought mosaics that led from her bedchamber and through her parlor into the long corridor and down the wide stairway to the spacious hall and out into the vast peristyle where she paused, shielding her eyes against the sun.

For the past year or more, Lucia had been acutely conscious of her increasing height and rapid development into womanhood; but here on this expanse of tessellated tiling she always felt very insignificant. Everything in this immense peristyle dwarfed her; the tall marble columns that supported the vaulted roofs, the stately statues standing in their silent dignity on the close-clipped lawn, the high silver spray of the fountain. No matter how old she became, she would be ever a child here.

Nor did it make her feel any more mature when, proceeding along the patterned pavement, she passed Servius whose face had been as bronzed and deep-lined when Lucia was a mere toddler. Acknowledging with twinkling fingers and a smile the old slave's grave salute, as he brought the shaft of his spear to his wrinkled forehead, she moved on to the vine-covered pergola at the far end of the rectangle.

There, with her folded arms resting on the marble balustrade that overlooked the terraced gardens, the arbors, the tiled pool, and commanded a breath-taking view of the city and the river, Lucia tried to decide whether to tell Marcellus. He would be terrifically angry, of course, and if he did anything about it at all he might make matters worse; but—somebody in the family must be informed where we stood in the opinion of Gaius before any more risks were taken. It was unlikely, thought Lucia, that she would have an opportunity to talk alone with her brother until later in the day; for Marcellus had been out—probably all night—at the Military Tribunes' Banquet, and wouldn't be up before noon; but she must resolve at once upon a course of action. She wished now that she had told Marcellus last summer, when it had happened.

The soft whisper of sandal-straps made her turn about. Decimus the butler was approaching, followed by the Macedonian twins bearing silver trays aloft on their outspread palms. Would his mistress, inquired Decimus with a deep bow, desire her breakfast served here?

'Why not?' said Lucia, absently.

Decimus barked at the twins and they made haste to prepare the table while Lucia watched their graceful movements with amused curiosity, as if observing the antics of a pair of playful terriers. Pretty things, they were; a little older than she, though not so tall; agile and shapely, and as nearly alike as two peas. It was the first time that Lucia had seen them in action, for they had been purchased only a week ago. Apparently Decimus, who had been training them, thought they were ready now for active duty. It would be interesting to see how they performed, for Father said they had been brought up in a home of refinement and were probably having their first experience of serving a table. Without risking an inquiring glance at the young woman who stood watching them, they proceeded swiftly but quietly with their task. They were both very white, observed Lucia, doubtless from confinement in some prisonship.

One of Father's hobbies, and his chief extravagance, was the possession of valuable slaves. The Gallio family did not own very many, for Father considered it a vulgar, dangerous, and ruinously expensive vanity to have swarms of them about with little to do but eat, sulk, and conspire. He selected his slaves with the same discriminating care that he exercised when purchasing beautiful statuary and other art objects. He had no interest in public sales. Upon the return of a military expedition from some civilized country, the commanding officers would notify a few of their well-to-do acquaintances that a limited number of high-grade captives were available; and Father would go down, the day before the sale, and look them over, learn their history, sound them out, and if he found anything he wanted to add to his household staff he would bid. He never told anyone in the family how much he had paid for their slaves, but it was generally felt that he had never practiced economy in acquiring such merchandise.

Most of the people they knew were in a constant dither about their slaves; buying and selling and exchanging. It wasn't often that Father disposed of one; and when, rarely, he had done so, it was because the slave had mistreated another over whom he had some small authority. They had lost an excellent cook that way, about a year ago. Minna had grown crusty and cruel toward the kitchen crew, scolding them loudly and knocking them about. She had been warned a few times. Then, one day, Minna had slapped Tertia. Lucia wondered, briefly, where Minna was now. She certainly did know how to bake honey cakes.

You had to say this for Father: he was a good judge of people. Of course, slaves weren't people, exactly; but some of them were almost people. There was Demetrius, for example, who was at this moment marching through the colonnade with long, measured strides. Father had bought Demetrius six years ago and presented him to Marcellus on his seventeenth birthday. What a wonderful day that was, with all their good friends assembled in the Forum to see Marcellus—clean-shaven for the first time in his life—step forward to receive his white toga. Cornelius Capito and Father had made speeches, and then they had put the white toga on Marcellus. Lucia had been so proud and happy that her heart had pounded and her throat had hurt, though she was only nine then, and couldn't know much about the ceremony except that Marcellus was expected to act like a man now—though sometimes he forgot to, when Demetrius wasn't about.

Lucia pursed her full lips and grinned as she thought of their relationship; Demetrius, two years older than Marcellus, always so seriously respectful, never relaxing for an instant from his position as a slave; Marcellus, stern and dignified, but occasionally forgetting to be the master and slipping absurdly into the rôle of intimate friend. Very funny, it was sometimes. Lucia loved to watch them together at such moments. Of course she had about the same relation to Tertia; but that seemed different.

Demetrius had come from Corinth, where his father—a wealthy shipowner—had taken a too conspicuous part in defensive politics. Everything had happened at once in Demetrius' family. His father had been executed, his two elder brothers had been given to the new Legate of Achaea, his patrician mother had committed suicide; and Demetrius—tall, handsome, athletic—had been brought to Rome under heavy guard, for he was not only valuable but violent.

Lucia remembered when, a week before Marcellus' coming of age, she had heard Father telling Mother about his purchase of the Corinthian slave, only an hour earlier. She had been much impressed—and a little frightened, too.

'He will require careful handling for a while,' Father was saying. 'He has seen some rough treatment. His keeper told me I had better sleep with a dagger under my pillow until the Corinthian cooled down. It seems he had badly beaten up one of his guards. Ordinarily, of course, they would have dealt with him briefly and decisively; but they were under orders to deliver him uninjured. They were quite relieved to get him off their hands.'

'But is this not dangerous?' Mother had inquired anxiously. 'What might he not do to our son?'

'That,' Father had replied, 'will be up to Marcellus. He will have to win the fellow's loyalty. And he can do it, I think. All that Demetrius needs is an assurance of fair play. He will not expect to be petted. He is a slave, and he knows it—and hates it; but he will respond to decent discipline.' And then Father had gone on to say that after he had paid the money and signed the documents, he had himself led Demetrius out of the narrow cell; and, when they were in the open plaza, had unlocked his chains; very carefully, too, for his wrists were raw and bleeding. 'Then I walked on ahead of him,' Father had continued, 'without turning to see whether he was following me. Aulus had driven me down and was waiting in the chariot at the Appian Gate, a few yards away. I had planned to bring the Corinthian back with me. But, as we neared the chariot, I decided to give him instructions about how to reach our villa on foot.'

'Alone?' Mother had exclaimed. 'Was that not very risky?'

'Yes,' Father had agreed, 'but not quite so risky as to have brought him here as a shackled prisoner. He was free to run away. I wanted him to be in a position to decide whether he would rather take a chance with us than gamble on some other fate. I could see that my gestures of confidence had surprised and mellowed him a little. He said—in beautiful Greek, for he had been well educated, "What shall I do, sir, when I arrive at your villa?" I told him to inquire for Marcipor, who would advise him. He nodded, and stood fumbling with the rusty chains that I had loosed from his hands. "Throw them away," I said. Then I mounted the chariot, and drove home.'

'I wonder if you will ever see him again,' Mother had said; and, in answer to her question, Marcipor appeared in the doorway.

'A young Corinthian has arrived, Master,' said Marcipor, a Corinthian himself. 'He says he belongs to us.'

'That is true,' Father said, pleased with the news. 'I bought him this morning. He will attend my son, though Marcellus is to know nothing of this for the present. Feed him well. And provide him with a bath and clean clothing. He has been imprisoned for a long time.'

'The Greek has already bathed, Master,' replied Macipor.

'Quite right,' approved Father. 'That was thoughtful of you.'

'I had not yet thought of it,' admitted Marcipor. 'I was in the sunken garden, supervising the building of the new rose arbor, when this Greek appeared. Having told me his name, and that he belonged here, he caught sight of the pool—'

'You mean'—expostulated Mother—'that he dared to use our pool?'

'I am sorry,' Marcipor replied. 'It happened so quickly I was unable to thwart it. The Greek ran swiftly, tossing aside his garments, and dived in. I regret the incident. The pool will be drained immediately, and thoroughly cleansed.'

'Very good, Marcipor,' said Father. 'And do not rebuke him; though he should be advised not to do that again.' And Father had laughed, after Marcipor had left the room. Mother said, 'The fellow should have known better than that.' 'Doubtless he did,' Father had replied. 'But I cannot blame him. He must have been immensely dirty. The sight of that much water probably drove him temporarily insane.'

One could be sure, reflected Lucia, that Marcipor hadn't been too hard on poor Demetrius; for, from that day, he had treated him as if he were his own son. Indeed, the attachment was so close that slaves more recently acquired often asked if Marcipor and Demetrius were not somehow related.

* * * * * *

Demetrius had reappeared from the house now, and was advancing over the tiled pavement on his way to the pergola. Lucia wondered what errand was bringing him. Presently he was standing before her, waiting for a signal to speak.

'Yes, Demetrius?" she drawled.

'The Tribune,' he announced, with dignity, 'presents his good wishes for his sister's health and happiness, and requests that he be permitted to join her at breakfast.'

Lucia brightened momentarily; then sobered, and replied, 'Inform your master that his sister will be much pleased—and tell him,' she added, in a tone somewhat less formal, 'that breakfast will be served here in the pergola.'

After Demetrius had bowed deeply and was turning to go, Lucia sauntered past him and proceeded along the pavement for several yards. He followed her at a discreet distance. When they were out of earshot, she paused and confronted him.

'How does he happen to be up so early?' she asked, in a tone that was neither perpendicular nor oblique, but frankly horizontal. 'Didn't he go to the banquet?'

'The Tribune attended the banquet,' replied Demetrius, respectfully. 'It is of that, perhaps, that he is impatient to speak.'

'Now don't tell me that he got into some sort of mess, Demetrius.' She tried to invade his eyes, but the bridge was up.

'If so,' he replied, prudently, 'the Tribune may wish to report it without the assistance of his slave. Shall I go now?'

'You were there, of course, attending my brother,' pursued Lucia. And when Demetrius bowed an affirmative, she asked, 'Was Prince Gaius there?' Demetrius bowed again, and she went on, uncertainly, 'Did you—was he—had you an opportunity to notice whether the Prince was in good humor?'

'Very,' replied Demetrius—'until he went to sleep.'

'Drunk?' Lucia wrinkled her nose.

'It is possible,' deliberated Demetrius, 'but it is not for me to say.'

'Did the Prince seem friendly—toward my brother?' persisted Lucia.

'No more than usual.' Demetrius shifted his weight and glanced toward the house.

Lucia sighed significantly, shook her black curls, and pouted.

'You can be very trying sometimes, Demetrius.'

'I know,' he admitted ruefully. 'May I go now? My master—'

'By all means!' snapped Lucia. 'And swiftly!' She turned and marched back with clipped steps to the pergola. Something had gone wrong last night, or Demetrius wouldn't have taken that frozen attitude.

Decimus, whose instinct advised him that his young mistress was displeased, retreated to a safe distance. The twins, who had now finished laying the table, were standing side by side awaiting orders. Lucia advanced on them.

'What are you called?' she demanded, her tone still laced with annoyance.

'I am Helen,' squeaked one of them, nervously. 'My sister is Nesta.'

'Can't she talk?'

'Please—she is frightened.'

Their long-lashed eyes widened with apprehension as Lucia drew closer, but they did not flinch. Cupping her hands softly under their round chins, she drew up their faces, smiled a little, and said, 'Don't be afraid. I won't bite you.' Then—as if caressing a doll—she toyed with the tight little curls that had escaped from Helen's cap. Turning to Nesta, she untied and painstakingly retied her broad sash. Both girls' eyes were swimming. Nesta stopped a big tear with the back of her hand.

'Now, now,' soothed Lucia, 'don't cry. No one is going to hurt you here.' She impulsively abandoned the lullaby, drew herself erect, and declared proudly: 'You belong to Senator Marcus Lucan Gallio! He paid a great price for you—because you are valuable; and—because you are valuable—you will not be mistreated. . . . Decimus'—she called, over her shoulder—'see that these pretty children have new tunics; white ones—with coral trimmings.' She picked up their hands, one by one, and examined them critically. 'Clean,' she remarked, half aloud—'and beautiful, too. That is good.' Facing Decimus, she said: 'You may go now. Take the twins. Have them bring the food. My brother will have breakfast with me here. You need not come back.'

Lucia had never liked Decimus very well; not that there was any particular ground for complaint, for he was a perfect servant; almost too deferential, a chilling deference that lacked only a little of being sulkiness. It had been Lucia's observation that imported slaves were more comfortable to live with than the natives. Decimus had been born in Rome and had been in their family for almost as long as Lucia could remember. He had a responsible position; attended to all the purchasing of supplies for their tables, personally interviewed the merchants, visited the markets, met the foreign caravans that brought spices and other exotics from afar; a very competent person indeed, who minded his own business, kept his own counsel, and carried himself with dignity. But he was a stranger.

One never could feel toward Decimus as one did toward good old Marcipor who was always so gentle—and trustworthy too. Marcipor had managed the business affairs of the family for so long that he probably knew more about their estate than Father did.

Decimus bowed gravely now, as Lucia dismissed him, and started toward the house, his stiff back registering disapproval of this episode that had flouted the discipline he believed in and firmly exercised. The Macedonians, their small even teeth flashing an ecstatic smile, scampered away, hand in hand, without waiting for formal permission. Lucia stopped them in their tracks with a stern command.

'Come back here!' she called severely. They obeyed with spiritless feet and stood dejectedly before her. 'Take it easy,' drawled Lucia. 'You shouldn't romp when you're on duty. Decimus does not like it.'

They looked up shyly from under their long lashes, and Lucia's lips curled into a sympathetic grin that relighted their eyes.

'You may go now,' she said, abruptly resuming a tone of command. Lounging onto the long marble seat beside the table, she watched the twins as they marched a few paces behind Decimus, their spines straight and stiff as arrows, accenting each determined step with jerks of their heads from side to side, in quite too faithful imitation of the crusty butler. Lucia chuckled. 'The little rascals,' she muttered. 'They deserve to be spanked for that.' Then she suddenly sobered and sat studiously frowning at the rhythmic flexion of her sandaled toes. Marcellus would be here in a moment. How much—if anything—should she tell her adored brother about her unpleasant experience with Gaius? But first, of course, she must discover what dreadful thing had happened last night at the Tribunes' Banquet.

* * * * * *

'Good morning, sweet child!' Marcellus tipped back his sister's head, noisily kissed her between the eyes, and tousled her hair, while Bambo, his big black sheep-dog, snuggled his grinning muzzle under her arm and wagged amiably.

'Down! Both of you!' commanded Lucia. 'You're uncommonly bright this morning, Tribune Marcellus Lucan Gallio. I thought you were going to a party at the Club.'

'Ah—my infant sister—but what a party!' Marcellus gingerly touched his finely moulded, close-cropped, curly head in several ailing areas, and winced. 'You may well be glad that you are not—and can never be—a Tribune. It was indeed a long, stormy night.'

'A wet one, at any rate, to judge from your puffy eyes. Tell me about it—or as much as you can remember.' Lucia scooped Bambo off the marble lectus with her foot, and her brother eased himself onto the seat beside her. He laughed, reminiscently, painfully.

'I fear I disgraced the family. Only the dear gods know what may come of it. His Highness was too far gone to understand, but someone will be sure to tell him before the day is over.'

Lucia leaned forward anxiously, laid a hand on his knee, and searched his cloudy eyes.

'Gaius?' she asked, in a frightened whisper. 'What happened, Marcellus?'

'A poem,' he muttered, 'an ode; a long, tiresome, incredibly stupid ode, wrought for the occasion by old Senator Tuscus, who, having reached that ripeness of senescence where Time and Eternity are mistaken for each other—'

'Sounds as if you'd arrived there, too,' broke in Lucia. 'Can't you speed it up a little?'

'Don't hurry me, impatient youth,' sighed Marcellus. 'I am very frail. As I was saying, this interminable ode, conceived by the ancient Tuscus to improve his rating, was read by his son Antonius, also in need of royal favor; a grandiloquent eulogy to our glorious Prince.'

'He must have loved the flattery,' observed Lucia, 'and of course you all applauded it. You and Tullus, especially.'

'I was just coming to that,' said Marcellus, thickly. 'For hours there had been a succession of rich foods and many beverages; also a plentitude of metal music interspersed with Greek choruses—pretty good—and an exhibition of magic—pretty bad; and some perfunctory speeches, of great length and thickness. A wrestling-match, too, I believe. The night was far advanced. Long before Antonius rose, my sister, if any man among us had been free to consult his own desire, we would all have stretched out on our comfortable couches and slept. The gallant Tullus, of whose good health you are ever unaccountably solicitous, sat across from me, frankly asleep like a little child.'

'And then you had the ode,' encouraged Lucia, crisply.

'Yes—we then had the ode. And as Antonius droned on—and on—he seemed to recede farther and farther; his features became dimmer and dimmer; and the measured noise he was making sounded fainter and fainter, as my tortured eyes grew hotter and heavier—'

'Marcellus!' shouted Lucia. 'In the name of every immortal god! Get on with it!'

'Be calm, impetuous child. I do not think rapidly today. Never again shall I be anything but tiresome. That ode did something to me, I fear. Well—after it had been inching along for leagues and decades, I suddenly roused, pulled myself together, and gazed about upon the distinguished company. Almost everyone had peacefully passed away, except a few at the high table whose frozen smiles were held with clenched teeth; and Antonius' insufferable young brother, Quintus, who was purple with anger. I can't stomach that arrogant pup and he knows I despise him.'

'Gaius!' barked Lucia, in her brother's face, so savagely that Bambo growled. 'I want to know what you did to offend Gaius!'

Marcellus laughed whimperingly, for it hurt; then burst into hysterical guffaws.

'If the Glorious One had been merely asleep, quietly, decently, with his fat chins on his bosom—as were his devoted subjects—your unfortunate brother might have borne it. But our Prince had allowed his head to tip far back. His mouth—by no means a thing of beauty, at best—was open. The tongue protruded unprettily and the bulbous nose twitched at each resounding inhalation. Our banquet-hall was deathly quiet, but for Antonius and Gaius, who shared the floor.'

'Revolting!' muttered Lucia.

'A feeble word, my sister. You should give more heed to your diction. Well—at that fateful moment Antonius had reached the climax of his father's ode with an apostrophe to our Prince that must have caused a storm on Mount Parnassus. Gaius was a Fountain of Knowledge! The eyes of Gaius glowed with Divine Light! When the lips of Gaius moved, Wisdom flowed and Justice smiled! . . . Precious child,' went on Marcellus, taking her hand, 'I felt my tragic mishap coming on, not unlike an unbeatable sneeze. I suddenly burst out laughing! No—I do not mean that I chuckled furtively into my hands: I threw back my head and roared! Howled! Long, lusty yells of insane laughter!' Reliving the experience, Marcellus went off again into an abandon of undisciplined mirth. 'Believe me—I woke everybody up—but Gaius.'

'Marcellus!'

Suddenly sobered by the tone of alarm in his sister's voice, he looked into her pale, unsmiling face.

'What is it, Lucia?' he demanded. 'Are you ill?'

'I'm—afraid!' she whispered, weakly.

He put his arm about her and she pressed her forehead against his shoulder.

'There, there!' he murmured. 'We've nothing to fear, Lucia. I was foolish to have upset you. I thought you would be amused. Gaius will be angry, of course, when he learns of it; but he will not venture to punish the son of Marcus Lucan Gallio.'

'But—you see—' stammered Lucia, 'it was only yesterday that Father openly criticized him in the Senate. Had you not heard?'

'Of course; but the Pater's strong enough to take care of himself,' declared Marcellus, almost too confidently to be convincing. There was a considerable pause before his sister spoke. He felt her body trembling.

'If it were just that one thing,' she said, slowly, "perhaps it might be overlooked. But—now you have offended him. And he was already angry at me.'

'You!' Marcellus took her by the shoulders and stared into her worried eyes. 'And why should Gaius be angry at you?'

'Do you remember, last summer, when Diana and her mother and I were guests at the Palace on Capri—and Gaius came to visit the Emperor?'

'Well? Go on!' demanded Marcellus. 'What of it? What did he say? What did he do?'

'He tried to make love to me.'

'That loathsome beast!' roared Marcellus, leaping to his feet. 'I'll tear his dirty tongue out! I'll gouge his eyes out with my thumbs! Why haven't you told me this before?'

'You have given the reason,' said Lucia, dejectedly. 'I was afraid of the tongue-tearing—and eye-gouging. Had my brother been a puny, timid man, I might have told him at once. But my brother is strong and brave—and reckless. Now that I have told him, he will kill Gaius; and my brother, whom I so dearly love, will be put to death, and my father, too, I suppose. And my mother will be banished or imprisoned, and—'

'What did Mother think about this?' broke in Marcellus.

'I did not tell her.'

'Why not? You should have done so—instantly!'

'Then she would have told Father. That would have been as dangerous as telling my brother.'

'You should have told the Emperor!' spluttered Marcellus. 'Tiberius is no monument to virtue, but he would have done something about that! He's not so very fond of Gaius.'

'Don't be foolish! That half-crazy old man? He would probably have gone into one of his towering tantrums, and scolded Gaius in the presence of everybody; and then he would have cooled off and forgotten all about it. But Gaius wouldn't have forgotten! No—I decided to ignore it. Nobody knows—but Diana.'

'Diana! If you thought you had such a dangerous secret, why should you tell that romping infant Diana?'

'Because she was afraid of him, too, and understood my reasons for not wanting to be left alone with him. But Diana is not a baby, Marcellus. She is nearly sixteen. And—if you pardon my saying so—I think you should stop mussing her hair, and tickling her under the chin, when she comes here to visit me—as if she were five, and you a hundred.'

'Sorry! It hadn't occurred to me that she would resent my playful caresses. I never thought of her except as a child—like yourself.'

'Well—it's time you realized that Diana is a young woman. If she resents your playful caresses, it is not because they are caresses but because they are playful.' Lucia hesitated; then continued softly, her eyes intent on her brother's gloomy face. 'She might even like your caresses—if they meant anything. I think it hurts her, Marcellus, when you call her "Sweetheart." '

'I had not realized that Diana was so sensitive,' mumbled Marcellus. 'She is certainly stormy enough when anything displeases her. She was audacious enough to demand that her name be changed.'

'She hated to be called Asinia, Marcellus,' said Lucia, loyally. 'Diana is prettier, don't you think?'

'Perhaps,' shrugged Marcellus. 'Name of a silly goddess. The name of the Asinius stock is noble; means something!'

'Don't be tiresome, Marcellus!' snapped Lucia. 'What I am saying is: Diana would probably enjoy having you call her "Sweetheart"—if—'

Marcellus, who had been restlessly panthering about, drew up to inspect his sister with sudden interest.

'Are you trying to imply that this youngster thinks she is fond of me?'

'Of course! And I think you're pretty dumb, not to have noticed it! Come and sit down—and compose yourself. Our breakfast is on the way.'

Marcellus glanced casually in the direction of the house; then stared frowningly; then rubbed his eyes with his fists, and stared again. Lucia's lips puckered into a reluctant grin.

'In truth, my sister,' he groaned, 'I am in much worse condition than I had supposed.'

'You're all right, Tribune,' she drawled. 'There really are two of them.'

'Thanks! I am relieved. Are they as bright as they are beautiful?' he asked, as the twins neared.

'It is too early to tell. This is their first day on duty. Don't frighten them, Marcellus. They're already scared half out of their wits. They have never worked before . . . No, no, Bambo! Come here!'

Rosy with embarrassment, the Macedonians began unburdening their silver trays, fussily pretending they were not under observation.

'Cute little things; aren't they?' chirped Marcellus. 'Where did Father pick them up?'

'Don't!' whispered Lucia. She rose and walked to the balustrade, her brother sauntering after her. They turned their faces toward the city. 'What did Tullus think of what you did?' she asked, irrelevantly.

'Tell me'—Marcellus ignored her query—'is there anything peculiar about these slaves that makes you so extraordinarily considerate?'

Lucia shook her head, without looking up—and sighed.

'I was just thinking,' she said, at length, 'how I might feel if I were in their place.' Her troubled eyes lifted to meet his look of inquiry. 'It is not impossible, Marcellus, that I may soon find myself in some such predicament. . . . You wouldn't like that. Would you?'

'Nonsense!' he growled, out of the corner of his mouth. 'You're making too great a disaster of this! Nothing's going to happen. I'll see to that.'

'How?' demanded Lucia. 'How are you going to see to it?'

'Well'—temporized Marcellus—'what do you think I should do—short of going to that ugly reptile with an apology?'

Lucia brightened a little and laid her hand on his arm.

'Do that!' she pleaded. 'Today! Make peace with him, Marcellus! Tell him you were drunk. You were; weren't you?'

'I'd rather be flogged—in the market-place!'

'Yes—I know. And perhaps you will be. Gaius is dangerous!'

'Ah—what could he do? Tiberius would not permit his half-witted stepson to punish a member of the Gallio family. It's common knowledge that the old man despises him.'

'Yes—but Tiberius consented to his regency because Julia demanded it. And Julia still has to be reckoned with. If it came to a decision whether that worn-out old man should stand up for the Gallio family—against Gaius—with his shrewish wife screaming in his ears, I doubt that he would trouble himself. Julia would stop at nothing!'

'The vindictive old—' Marcellus paused on the edge of a kennel word.

'Think it over.' Lucia's tone was brighter, as if she felt herself gaining ground. 'Come—let us eat our breakfast. Then you will go to Gaius, and take your medicine. Praise him! Flatter him! He can stand any amount of it. Tell him he is beautiful! Tell him there's nobody in the whole Empire as wise as he is. Tell him he is divine! But—be sure you keep your face straight. Gaius already knows you have a keen sense of humor.'

* * * * * *

Having decided to accept his sister's counsel, Marcellus was anxious to perform his unpleasant duty and be done with it. Prudence suggested that he seek an interview through the formal channels and await the convenience of the Prince; but, increasingly impressed by the gravity of his position, he resolved to ignore the customary court procedure and take a chance of seeing Gaius without an appointment. By appearing at the Palace shortly before noon, he might even be lucky enough to have a few minutes alone with the Prince before anyone had informed him about last night's mishap.

At ten, rejuvenated by a hot bath, a vigorous massage by Demetrius, and a plunge in the pool, the Tribune returned to his rooms, dressed with care, and sauntered downstairs. Observing that the library door was ajar, he paused to greet his father, whom he had not seen since yesterday. The handsome, white-haired Senator was seated at his desk, writing. He glanced up, nodded, smiled briefly, and invited Marcellus to come in.

'If you are at liberty today, my son, I should be pleased to have you go with me to inspect a span of matched Hispanian mares.'

'I should like to, sir; but might tomorrow serve as well? I have an important errand to do; something that cannot be put off.' There was a note of anxiety in the Tribune's voice that narrowed the wise old eyes.

'Nothing serious, I trust.' Gallio pointed to a vacant seat.

'I hope not, sir.' Marcellus sat tentatively on the broad arm of the chair as a fair compromise between candid reticence and complete explanation.

'Your manner,' observed his father, pointedly, 'suggests that you are worried. I have no wish to intrude upon your private perplexities, but is there anything I might do for you?'

'I'm afraid not, sir; thank you.' After a moment of indecision, Marcellus slowly slid into the chair and regarded his distinguished parent with a sober face. 'If you have the time, I will tell you.'

Gallio nodded, put down his stylus, and leaned forward on his folded arms encouragingly. It was quite a long narrative. Marcellus did not spare himself. He told it all. At one juncture, he was half-disposed to introduce Lucia's dilemma as relevant to his own; but decided against it, feeling that their pater was getting about all he could take for one session. He concluded, at length, with the declaration that he was going at once to apologize. Gallio, who had listened attentively but without comment, now shook his leonine head and shouted 'No!' He straightened and shook his head again. 'No!—No, no!'

Amazed by his father's outburst, for he had anticipated his full approval, Marcellus asked, 'Why not, sir?'

'The most dangerous implement a man can use for the repair of a damaged relationship is an abject apology.' Gallio pushed back his huge chair and rose to his full height as if preparing to deliver an address. 'Even in the most favorable circumstances, as when placating an injured friend, a self-abasing apology may do much harm. If the friend is contented with nothing less, he should not be served with it at all; for his friendship is not worth its upkeep. In the case of Gaius, an apology would be a fatality; for you are not dealing here with a gentleman, but with a congenital scoundrel. Your apology will imply that you expect Gaius to be generous. Generosity, in his opinion, is a sign of weakness. By imputing it to him, you will have given him further offense. Gaius has reasons to be sensitive about his power. Never put yourself on the defensive with a man who is fretting about his own insecurity. Here, he says, is at least one opportunity to demonstrate my strength.'

'Perhaps you are right, sir,' conceded Marcellus.

'Perhaps? Of course, I am right!' The Senator walked to the door, closed it softly, and resumed his seat. 'And that is not all,' he went on. 'Let me refresh your mind about the peculiar relations in the imperial family which explain why Gaius is a man to be watched and feared. There is old Tiberius, alternately raging and rotting in his fifty-room villa on Capri; a pathetic and disgusting figure, mooning over his necromancies and chattering to his gods—My son,' Gallio interrupted himself, 'there is always something fundamentally wrong with a rich man or a king who pretends to be religious. Let the poor and helpless invoke the gods. That is what the gods are for—to distract the attention of the weak from their otherwise intolerable miseries. When an emperor makes much ado about religion, he is either cracked or crooked. Tiberius is not crooked. If he is cracked, the cause is not far to seek. For a score of years he has nursed a bitter grudge against his mother for demanding that he divorce Vipsania—the only creature he ever loved—'

'I think he is fond of Diana,' interjected Marcellus.

'Right! And why? He is fond of the child because she is Vipsania's granddaughter. Let us remember that he was not a bad ruler in his earlier days. Rome had never known such prosperity; not even under Julius. As you know, when Vipsania passed out of his life, Tiberius went to pieces; lost all interest in the Empire; surrounded himself with soothsayers, mountebanks, priests, and astrologers. Presently his mind was so deranged by all this nonsense that he consented to marry Julia, whom he had despised from childhood.' The Senator chuckled, not very pleasantly, and remarked: 'Perhaps that was why he wished to be relieved of all his administrative duties. He found that to hate Julia as adequately as she deserved to be hated, he had to make it a full-time occupation. So—there was the vixenish Julia, together with the obnoxious offspring she had whelped before he married her. And he has not only hated Julia: he has been deathly afraid of her—and with good reason—for she has the morbid mind of an assassin—and the courage, too.'

'Lucia says the old gentleman never touches his wine, at table, until the Empress has tasted it,' put in Marcellus, 'but she thought that was just a little family joke.'

'We will not disturb your young sister with any other interpretation,' advised the Senator, 'but it is no joke; nor is Tiberius merely trying to be playful when he stations a dozen Numidian gladiators at the doors and windows of his bedchamber. . . . Now, these facts are, I suspect, never absent very long from Gaius' mind. He knows that the Emperor is half-insane; that his mother lives precariously; and that if anything should happen to her his regency would last no longer than it takes a galley to clear for Crete with a deposed prince on board.'

'Were that to happen,' broke in Marcellus, 'who would succeed Gaius?'

'Well—' Gallio slighted the query with a shrug. 'It will not happen. If anyone dies, down there, it won't be Julia. You can depend on that.'

'But—just supposing—' persisted Marcellus. 'If, for any reason—accident, illness, or forthright murder—Julia should be eliminated—and Gaius, too, in consequence—do you think Tiberius might put Asinius Gallus on the throne?'

'It is possible,' said Gallio. 'The Emperor might feel that he was making tardy amends to Vipsania by honoring her son. And Gallus would be no mean choice. No Roman has ever commanded more respect than Pollio, his learned sire. Gallus would have the full support of our legions—both at home and abroad. However'—he added, half to himself—'a brave soldier does not inevitably make a wise monarch. Your military commander has only a foreign foe to fight. All that he requires is tactics and bravery. An emperor is forever at war with a jealous court, an obstreperous Senate, and a swarm of avaricious landholders. What he needs is a keen scent for conspiracy, a mind crafty enough to outmaneuver treachery, a natural talent for duplicity—and the hide of an alligator.'

'Thick enough to turn the point of a stiletto,' assisted Marcellus.

'It is a hazardous occupation,' nodded Gallio, 'but I do not think our excellent friend Gallus will ever be exposed to its dangers.'

'I wonder how Diana would like being a princess,' remarked Marcellus, absently. He glanced up to find his father's eyes alight with curiosity.

'We are quite far afield, aren't we; discussing Diana?' observed Gallio, slyly. 'Are you interested in her?'

'Not any more than Lucia is,' replied Marcellus, elaborately casual. 'They are, as you know, inseparable. Naturally, I see Diana almost every day.'

'A beautiful and amazingly vivacious child,' commented the Senator.

'Beautiful and vivacious,' agreed Marcellus—'but not a child. Diana is nearly sixteen, you know.'

'Old enough to be married: is that what you are trying to say? You could hardly do better—if she can be tamed. Diana has fine blood. Sixteen, eh? It is a wonder Gaius has not noticed. He might do himself much good in the esteem of the Emperor—and he certainly is in need of it—if he should win Diana's favor.'

'She loathes him!'

'Indeed? Then she has talked with you about it?'

'No, sir. Lucia told me.'

There was a considerable interval of silence before Gallio spoke again, slowly measuring his words.

'In your present strained relation to Gaius, my son, you would show discretion, I think, if you made your attentions to Diana as inconspicuous as possible.'

'I never see her anywhere else than here, sir.'

'Even so: treat her casually. Gaius has spies everywhere.'

'Here—in our house?' Marcellus frowned incredulously.

'Why not? Do you think that Gaius, the son of Agrippa, who never had an honest thought in his life, and of Julia, who was born with both ears shaped like keyholes, would be too honorable for that?' Gallio deftly rolled up the scroll that lay at his elbow, indicating that he was ready to put aside his work for the day. 'We have discussed this fully enough, I think. As for what occurred last night, the Prince's friends may advise him to let the matter drop. Your best course is to do nothing, say nothing—and wait developments.' He rose and straightened the lines of his toga. 'Come! Let us ride to Ismael's camp and look at the Hispanians. You will like them; milk-white, high-spirited, intelligent—and undoubtedly expensive. Ismael, the old rascal, knows I am interested in them, unfortunately for my purse.'

Marcellus responded eagerly to his father's elevated mood. It was almost as if the shrewd Marcus Lucan Gallio had firmly settled the unhappy affair with Gaius. He opened the door for the Senator to precede him. In the atrium, leaning against a column, lounged Demetrius. Coming smartly to attention he saluted with his spear and followed a few paces behind the two men as they strolled through the vasty rooms and out to the spacious western portico.

'Rather unusual for Demetrius to be loitering in the atrium,' remarked Marcellus in a guarded undertone.

'Perhaps he was standing there,' surmised Gallio, 'to discourage anyone else from loitering by the door.'

'Do you think he may have had a special reason for taking that precaution?'

'Possibly. He was with you at the banquet; knows that you gave offense to Gaius; concludes that you are in disfavor; and, by adding it all up, thinks it is time to be vigilant.'

'Shall I ask him if he suspects that there are spies in the house?' suggested Marcellus.

Gallio shook his head.

'If he observes anything irregular, he will tell you, my son.'

'I wonder who this is coming.' Marcellus nodded toward a uniformed Equestrian Knight who had just turned in from the Via Aurelia. 'We're to be honored,' he growled. 'It is Quintus, the younger Tuscus. The Prince has been seeing much of him lately, I hear.'

The youthful Tribune, followed by a well-mounted aide, rode briskly toward them; and, neglecting to salute, drew a gilded scroll from the belt of his tunic.

'I am ordered by His Highness, Prince Gaius, to deliver this message into the hands of Tribune Marcellus Lucan Gallio,' he barked, haughtily. The aide, who had dismounted, carried the scroll up the steps and handed it over.

'His Highness might do well to employ messengers with better manners,' drawled Marcellus. 'Are you to await an answer?'

'Imperial commands require obedience; not replies!' shouted Quintus. He pulled his horse about savagely, dug in his spurs, and made off, pursued by his obsequious aide.

'Gaius is prompt,' commented the Senator. There was satisfaction on his face as he watched his son's steady hands, and the cool deliberateness with which he drew his dagger and thrust the point of it through the wax. Unrolling the ostentatious document, Marcellus held it at an angle where his father might share its contents. Gallio read it aloud, in a rasping undertone.

Prince Gaius Drusus Agrippa to Trib. Marcellus Lucan Gallio:

Greeting:

> The courage of a Military Tribune should not be squandered in banquet-halls. It should be serving the Empire in positions where reckless audacity is honorable and valorous. Tribune Marcellus Lucan Gallio is commanded to report, before sunset, at the Praetorium of Chief Legate M. Cornelius Capito, and receive his commission.

Marcellus rolled up the scroll, tossed it negligently to Demetrius, who thrust it into the breast of his tunic; and, turning to his father, remarked, 'We have plenty of time to go out and see Ismael's horses.'

The Senator proudly drew himself erect, gave his son a respectful bow, strutted down the marble steps; and, taking the bridle reins, mounted his mettlesome black gelding. Marcellus beckoned to Demetrius.

'You heard that message?' he queried, abruptly.

'Not if it was private, sir," countered Demetrius.

'Sounds a bit malicious,' observed Marcellus. 'The Prince evidently wishes to dispose of me.'

'Yes, sir,' agreed Demetrius.

'Well—I brought this upon myself,' said Marcellus. 'I shall not order you to risk your life. You are at liberty to decide whether—'

'I shall go with you, sir.'

'Very good. Inspect my equipment—and look over your own tackle, too.' Marcellus started down the steps, and turned to say, soberly, 'You're going to your death, you know.'

'Yes, sir,' said Demetrius. 'You will need some heavier sandals, sir. Shall I get them?'

'Yes—and several pairs for yourself. Ask Marcipor for the money.'

After a lively tussle with the bay, who was impatient to overtake her stable-mate, Marcellus drew up beside the Senator, and they slowed their horses to a trot.

'I tarried for a word with Demetrius. I shall take him with me.'

'Of course.'

'I told him he might decide.'

'That was quite proper.'

'I told him he might never come back alive.'

'Probably not,' said the Senator, grimly, 'but you can be assured that he will never come back alone.'

'Demetrius is a very sound fellow—for a slave,' observed Marcellus.

The Senator made no immediate rejoinder, but his stern face and flexed jaw indicated that his reflections were weighty.

'My son,' he said at length, staring moodily down the road, 'we could use a few men in the Roman Senate with the brains and bravery of your slave, Demetrius.' He pulled his horse down to a walk. ' "Demetrius is a sound fellow—for a slave"; eh? Well— his being a slave does not mean that what he thinks, what he says, and what he does are unimportant. One of these days the slaves are going to take over this rotted Government! They could do it tomorrow if they were organized. You might say that their common desire for liberty should unite them, but that is not enough. All men want more liberty than they have. What the Roman slaves lack is leadership. In time, that will come. You shall see!' The Senator paused so long, after this amazing declaration, that Marcellus felt some response was in order.

'I never heard you express that opnion before, sir. Do you think there will be an uprising—among the slaves?'

'It lacks form,' replied Gallio. 'It lacks cohesion. But some day it will take shape; it will be integrated; it will develop a leader, a cause, a slogan, a banner. Three-fourths of this city's inhabitants either have been or are slaves. Daily our expeditionary forces arrive with new shiploads of them. It would require a very shrewd and powerful Government to keep in subjugation a force three times its size and strength. But—look at our Government! A mere hollow shell! It has no moral fiber! Content with its luxury, indolence, and profligacy, its extravagant pageants in honor of its silly gods; ruled by an insane dotard and a drunken nonentity! So, my son, Rome is doomed! I do not venture to predict when or how Nemesis will arrive—but it is on its way. The Roman Empire is too weak and wicked to survive!'

Chapter II

Cornelius Capito was not in when Marcellus called at three to learn what Gaius had planned for him. This was surprising and a bit ominous too. The conspicuous absence of the Chief Legate, and his deputizing of a young understrapper to handle the case, clearly meant that Capito had no relish for an unpleasant interview with the son of his lifelong friend.

The Gallios had walked their horses for the last two miles of the journey in from Ismael's camp where the Senator had declined to purchase the Hispanian mares at the exorbitant price demanded by the avaricious old Syrian, though it was plain to see that the day's events had dulled his interest in the negotiation.

The Senator's mind was fully occupied now with speculations about Cornelius. If anybody in Rome could temper the punitive assignment which Gaius intended for his son, it would be the Commander of the Praetorian Guard and Chief of the Legates who wielded an enormous power in the making of appointments.

Slipping into a reminiscent—and candidly pessimistic—mood, the elder Gallio had recited the deplorable story they both knew by heart, the dismal epic of the Praetorian Guard. Marcellus had been brought up on it. As if his son had never heard the tale before, the Senator began away back in the time when Julius Caesar had created this organization for his own security. Picked men they were, with notable records for daring deeds. As the years rolled on, the traditions of the Praetorian Guard became richer. A magnificent armory was built to house its battle trophies, and in its spacious atrium were erected bronze and marble tablets certifying to the memorable careers of its heroes. To be a member of the Praetorian Guard in those great—long since outmoded—days when courage and integrity were valuable property, was the highest honor the Empire could bestow.

Then, Gallio had continued gloomily, Augustus—whose vanity had swollen into a monstrous, stinking, cancerous growth—had begun to confer honorary memberships upon his favorites; upon Senators who slavishly approved his mistakes and weren't above softening the royal sandal-straps with their saliva; upon certain rich men who had fattened on manipulations in foreign loot; upon wealthy slave-brokers, dealers in stolen sculpture; upon provincial revenue-collectors; upon almost anybody indeed who could minister to the diseased Augustan ego, or pour ointment on his itching avarice. And thus had passed away the glory and distinction of the Praetorian Guard. Its memberships were for sale.

For a little while, Tiberius had tried to arrest its accelerating descent into hell. Cornelius Capito, who had so often led his legion into suicidal forays that a legend had taken shape about him—for were not the gods directing a man whose life was so cheaply held and so miraculously preserved?—was summoned home to be Commander of the Praetorian Guard. Capito had not wanted the office, but had obeyed the command. With the same kind of recklessness that had won him honors on many a battle-field, he had begun to clean up the discredited institution. But it hadn't been long until hard pressure on Tiberius made it necessary for the Emperor to caution the uncompromising warrior about his honest zeal. He mustn't go too far in this business of cleansing the Praetorian Guard.

'It was then,' declaimed Gallio, 'that brave old Capito discovered, to his dismay, why Tiberius had called him to be the Commander; simply to use his name as a deodorant!'

Marcellus had realized, at this juncture of his father's painful reflections, that the remainder of the story would be somewhat embarrassing; for it concerned the Military Tribunes.

'If Augustus had only been content'—the Senator was proceeding according to schedule—'with his destruction of the Praetorian Guard! Perhaps, had he foreseen the result of his policy there, not even his rapacious greed could have induced him to work the same havoc with the Order of Tribunes. But you know what happened, my son.'

Yes—Marcellus knew. The Order of Tribunes had been honorable too. You had to be a Tribune, in deed and in truth, if you wanted to wear its insignia. Like the Praetorian Guard, it too was handsomely quartered. Tribunes, home on furlough or recovering from injuries or awaiting orders, took advantage of the library, the baths, the commissary that the Empire had provided for them. Then Augustus had decided to expand the Order of Tribunes to include all sons of Senators and influential taxpayers. You needn't ever have shouted an order or spent a night in a tent. If your father had enough money and political weight, you could wear the uniform and receive the salute.

Marcellus liked to think that his own case was not quite so indefensible as most of them. He had not been a mere playboy. At the Academy he had given his full devotion to the history of military campaigns, strategy, and tactics. He was an accomplished athlete, expert with the javelin, a winner of many prizes for marksmanship with the bow. He handled a dueling sword with the skill of a professional gladiator.

Nor had his recreations been profitless. Aristocratic youths, eligible to the hierarchy of public offices, disdained any actual practice of the fine arts. They affected to be critics and connoisseurs of painting and sculpture, but would have experienced much embarrassment had they been caught with a brush or chisel in hand. Independent of this taboo, Marcellus had taken a serious interest in sculpture, much to the delight of his father, who—upon observing that he had a natural genius for it—had provided him with competent tutors.

But—sometimes he had been appropriately sensitive about his status as a Military Tribune when, as happened infrequently, some *real* Tribune showed up at the ornate clubhouse, bronzed and battered and bandaged, after grueling months on active duty.

However—Marcellus said to himself—it wasn't as if he had no qualifications for military service. He was abundantly prepared to accept a commission if required to do so. Occasionally he had wished that an opportunity for such service might arise. He had never been asked to take a command. And a man would be a fool, indeed, to seek a commission. War was a swinish business, intended for bullies who liked to strut their medals and yell obscenities at their inferiors and go for weeks without a bath. He could do all this if he had to. He didn't have to; but he had never been honestly proud of his title. Sometimes when Decimus addressed him as 'Tribune'—which was the surly fellow's custom on such occasions as serving him his late breakfast in bed—Marcellus was tempted to slap him, and he would have done so had he a better case.

They had ridden in silence for a little time, after the Senator had aired his favorite grievances.

'Once in a while,' continued Gallio, meditatively, 'crusty Capito—like blind Samson of the Hebrew myth—rouses to have his way. I am hopeful that he may intervene in your behalf, my son. If it is an honorable post, we will not lament even though it involves peril. I am prepared to hand you over to danger—but not to disgrace. I cannot believe that my trusted friend will fail to do his utmost for you, today. I bid you to approach him with that expectation!'

His father had seemed so confident of this outcome that the remainder of their ride had been almost enjoyable. Assured that the gruff but loyal old warrior, who had helped him into his first white toga, would see to it that no indignities were practiced on him by a petulant and vengeful Prince, Marcellus set off light-heartedly to the impressive headquarters of the Chief Legate.

Accompanied by Demetrius, who was himself a striking figure in the saddle, he rode through the increasingly crowded streets on the way to the huge circular plaza, around half of which were grouped the impressive marble buildings serving the Praetorian Guard and ranking officials of the army. To the left stretched a vast parade-ground, now literally filled with loaded camel caravans and hundreds of pack-asses.

An expedition was mobilizing, ready for departure on the long trip to Gaul. The plaza was a stirring scene! Banners fluttered. The young officers were smart in their field uniforms. The legionaries were alert, spirited, apparently eager to be on their way. Maybe an experience of this sort would be stimulating, thought Marcellus.

Unable to ride into the plaza, because of the congestion, they dismounted in the street, Marcellus handing his reins to Demetrius, and proceeding through the narrow lane toward the Praetorium. The broad corridors were filled with Centurions awaiting orders. Many of them he knew. They smiled recognition and saluted. Perhaps they surmised that he was here on some such business as their own, and it gave him a little thrill of pride. You could think what you liked about the brutishness and griminess of war, it was no small honor to be a Roman soldier—whatever your rank! He shouldered his way to the open door leading into Capito's offices.

'The Commander is not in,' rasped the busy deputy. 'He ordered me to deliver this commission to you.'

Marcellus took the heavily sealed scroll from the fellow's hand, hesitated a moment, half-inclined to inquire whether Capito expected to return presently, decided against it; turned, and went out, down the broad steps and across the densely packed plaza. Demetrius, seeing him coming, led the horses forward and handed his master the bay mare's bridle-reins. Their eyes met. After all, thought Marcellus, Demetrius had a right to know where we stood in this business.

'I have not opened it yet,' he said, tapping the scroll. 'Let us go home.'

* * * * * *

The Senator was waiting for him in the library.

'Well—what did our friend Capito have for you?' he asked, making no attempt to disguise his uneasiness.

'He was not there. A deputy served me.' Marcellus laid the scroll on the desk and sat down to wait while his father impatiently thrust his knife through the heavy seals. For what seemed a very long time the narrowed eyes raced the length of the pompous manifesto. Then Gallio cleared his throat, and faced his son with troubled eyes.

'You are ordered to take command of the garrison at Minoa,' he muttered.

'Where's Minoa?'

'Minoa is a villainously dirty little port city in southern Palestine.'

'I never heard of it,' said Marcellus. 'I know about our forts at Caesarea and Joppa; but—what have we at this Minoa?'

'It is the point of departure for the old trail that leads to the Dead Sea. Most of our salt comes from there, as you probably know. The duty of our garrison at Minoa is to make that road safe for our caravans.'

'Doesn't sound like a very interesting job,' commented Marcellus. 'I was anticipating something dangerous.'

'Well—you will not be disappointed. It is dangerous enough. The Bedouins who menace that salt trail are notoriously brutal savages. But because they are independent gangs of bandits, with hideouts in that rocky desert region, we have never undertaken a campaign to crush them. It would have required five legions.' The Senator was speaking as if he were very well informed about Minoa, and Marcellus was listening with full attention.

'You mean these desert brigands steal the salt from our caravans?'

'No—not the salt. They plunder the caravans on the way in, for they have to carry supplies and money to hire laborers at the salt deposits. Many of the caravans that set out over that trail are never heard from again. But that isn't quite all,' the Senator continued. 'We have not been wasting very good men in the fort at Minoa. The garrison is composed of a tough lot of rascals. More than half of them were once commissioned officers who, for rank insubordination or other irregularities, are in disfavor with the Government. The lesser half is made up of an assortment of brawlers whose politics bred discontent.'

'I thought the Empire had a more prompt and less expensive method of dealing with objectionable people.'

'There are some cases,' explained the Senator, 'in which a public trial or a private assassination might stir up a protest. In these instances, it is as effective—and more practical—to send the offender to Minoa.'

'Why, sir—this is equivalent to exile!' Marcellus rose, bent forward over his father's desk, and leaned his weight on his white-knuckled fists. 'Do you know anything more about this dreadful place?'

Gallio slowly nodded his head.

'I know all about it, my son. For many years, one of my special duties in the Senate—together with four of my colleagues—has been the supervision of that fort.' He paused, and began slowly rising to his feet, his deep-lined face livid with anger. 'I believe that was why Gaius Drusus Agrippa—' The Senator savagely ground the hated name to bits with his teeth. 'He planned this for my son—because he knew—that I would know—what you were going into.' Raising his arms high, and shaking his fists in rage, Gallio shouted, 'Now I would that I were religious! I would beseech some god to damn his soul!'

* * * * *

Cornelia Vipsania Gallio, who always slightly accented her middle name—though she was only a stepdaughter to the divorced spouse of Emperor Tiberius—might have been socially important had she made the necessary effort.

If mere wishing on Cornelia's part could have induced her husband to ingratiate himself with the Crown, Marcus Lucan Gallio could have belonged to the inner circle, and any favor he desired for himself or his family might have been granted; or if Cornelia herself had gone to the bother of fawning upon the insufferable old Julia, the Gallio household might have reached that happy elevation by this shorter route. But Cornelia lacked the necessary energy.

She was an exquisite creature, even in her middle forties; a person of considerable culture, a gracious hostess, an affectionate wife, an indulgent mother, and probably the laziest woman in the whole Roman Empire. It was said that sometimes slaves would serve the Gallio establishment for months before discovering that their mistress was not an invalid.

Cornelia had her breakfast in bed at noon, lounged in her rooms or in the sunny garden all afternoon, drowsed over the classics, apathetically swept her slim fingers across the strings of her pandura; and was waited on, hand and foot, by everybody in the house. And everybody loved her, too, for she was kind and easy to please. Moreover, she never gave orders—except for her personal comfort. The slaves—under the competent and loyal supervision of Marcipor; and the diligent, if somewhat surly, dictatorship of Decimus in the culinary department—managed the institution unaided by her counsel and untroubled by her criticism. She was by nature an optimist, possibly because fretting was laborious. On rare occasions, she was briefly baffled by unhappy events, and at such times she wept quietly—and recovered.

Yesterday, however, something had seriously disturbed her habitual tranquillity. The Senator had made a speech. Paula Gallus, calling in the late afternoon, had told her. Paula had been considerably upset.

Cornelia was not surprised by the report that her famous husband was pessimistic in regard to the current administration of Roman government, for he was accustomed to walking the floor of her bedchamber while delivering opinions of this nature; but she was shocked to learn that Marcus had given the Senate the full benefit of his accumulated dissatisfactions. Cornelia had no need to ask Paula why she was so concerned. Paula didn't want Senator Gallio to get himself into trouble with the Crown. In the first place, it would be awkward for Diana to continue her close friendship with Lucia if the latter's eminent parent persisted in baiting Prince Gaius. And, too, was there not a long-standing conspiracy between Paula and Cornelia to encourage an alliance of their houses whenever Diana and Marcellus should become romantically aware of each other?

Paula had not hinted at these considerations when informing Cornelia that the Senator was cutting an impressive figure on some pretty thin ice, but she had gone so far as to remind her long-time friend that Prince Gaius —while notably unskillful at everything else—was amazingly resourceful and ingenious when it came to devising reprisals for his critics.

'But what can I do about it?' Cornelia had moaned languidly. 'Surely you're not hoping that I will rebuke him. My husband would not like to have people telling him what he may say in the Senate.'

'Not even his wife?' Paula arched her patrician brows.

'Especially his wife,' rejoined Cornelia. 'We have a tacit understanding that Marcus is to attend to his profession without my assistance. My responsibility is to manage his home.'

Paula had grinned dryly; and, shortly after, had taken her departure, leaving behind her a distressing dilemma. Cornelia wished that the Senator could be a little less candid. He was such an amiable man when he wanted to be. Of course, Gaius was a waster and a fool; but—after all—he was the Prince Regent, and you didn't have to call him names in public assemblies. First thing you knew, they'd all be blacklisted. Paula Gallus was far too prudent to let Diana become involved in their scrapes. If the situation became serious, they wouldn't be seeing much more of Diana. That would be a great grief to Lucia. And it might affect the future of Marcellus, too. It was precious little attention he had paid to the high-spirited young Diana, but Cornelia was still hopeful.

Sometimes she worried, for a moment or two, about Marcellus. One of her most enjoyable dreams posed her son on a beautiful white horse, leading a victorius army through the streets, dignifiedly acknowledging the plaudits of a multitude no man could number. To be sure, you didn't head that sort of parade unless you had risked some perils; but Marcellus had never been a coward. All he needed was a chance to show what kind of stuff he was made of. He would probably never get that chance now. Cornelia cried bitterly; and because there was no one else to talk to about it, she bared her heart to Lucia. And Lucia, shocked by her mother's unprecedented display of emotion, had tried to console her.

But today, Cornelia had quite disposed of her anxiety; not because the reason for it had been in any way relieved, but because she was temperamentally incapable of concentrating diligently upon anything—not even upon a threatened catastrophe.

* * * * * *

About four o'clock (Cornelia was in her luxurious sitting-room, gently combing her shaggy terrier) the Senator entered and without speaking dropped wearily into a chair, frowning darkly.

'Tired?' asked Cornelia, tenderly. 'Of course you are. That long ride. And you were disappointed with the Hispanian horses, I think. What was the matter with them?'

'Marcellus has been ordered into service,' growled Gallio, abruptly.

Cornelia pushed the dog off her lap and leaned forward interestedly.

'But that is as it should be, don't you think? We had expected that it might happen some day. Perhaps we should be glad. Will it take him far away?'

'Yes.' The Senator nodded impressively. 'Far away. He has been ordered to command the fort at Minoa.'

'Command! How very nice for him! Minoa! Our son is to be the commander—of the Roman fort—at Minoa! We shall be proud!'

'No!' Gallio shook his white head. 'No!' We shall not be proud! Minoa, my dear, is where we send men to be well rid of them. They have little to do there but quarrel. They are a mob of mutinous cut-throats. We frequently have to appoint a new commander.' He paused for a long, moody moment. 'This time the Senate Committee on affairs at Minoa was not consulted about the appointment. Our son had his orders directly from Gaius.'

This was too much even for the well-balanced Cornelia. She broke into a storm of weeping; noisily hysterical weeping; her fingers digging frantically into the glossy black hair that had tumbled about her shapely shoulders; moaning painful and incoherent reproaches that gradually became intelligible. Racked with sobs, Cornelia amazed them both by crying out, 'Why did you do it, Marcus? Oh—why did you have to bring this tragedy upon our son? Was it so important that you should denounce Gaius—at such a

The Slave Market

Father had bought Demetrius six years ago and presented him to Marcellus on his seventeenth birthday. . . . He selected his slaves with the same discriminating care that he exercised when purchasing beautiful statuary and other art objects.

From page 3 of text

DEAN

cost to Marcellus—and all of us? Oh—I wish I could have died before this day!'

Gallio bowed his head in his hands and made no effort to share the blame with Marcellus. His son was in plenty of trouble without the added burden of a rebuke from his overwrought mother.

'Where is he?' she asked, thickly, trying to compose herself. 'I must see him.'

'Packing his kit, I think,' muttered Gallio. 'He is ordered to leave at once. A galley will take him to Ostia where a ship sails tomorrow.'

'A ship? What ship? If he must go, why cannot he travel in a manner consistent with his rank? Surely he can charter or buy a vessel, and sail in comfort as becomes a Tribune.'

'There is no time for that, my dear. They are leaving tonight.'

'They? Marcellus—and who else?'

"Demetrius.'

'Well—the gods be thanked for that much!' Cornelia broke out again into tempestuous weeping. 'Why doesn't Marcellus come to see me?' she sobbed.

'He will, in a little while,' said Gallio. 'He wanted me to tell you about it first. And I hope you will meet him in the spirit of a courageous Roman matron.' The Senator's tone was almost severe now. 'Our son has received some very unhappy tidings. He is bearing them manfully, calmly, according to our best traditions. But I do not think he could bear to see his mother destroy herself in his presence.'

'Destroy myself!' Cornelia, stunned by the words, faced him with anguished eyes. 'You know I could never do a thing like that—no matter what happened to us!'

'One does not have to swallow poison or hug a dagger, my dear, to commit suicide. One can kill oneself and remain alive physically.' Gallio rose, took her hand, and drew Cornelia to her feet. 'Dry your tears now, my love,' he said gently. 'When Marcellus comes, let him continue to be proud of you. There may be some trying days ahead for our son. Perhaps the memory of an intrepid mother will rearm him when he is low in spirit.'

'I shall try, Marcus.' Cornelia clung to him hungrily. It had been a long time since they had needed each other so urgently.

* * * * * *

After Marcellus had spent a half-hour alone with his mother—an ordeal he had dreaded—his next engagement was with his sister. Father had informed Lucia, and she had sent word by Tertia that she would be waiting for him in the pergola whenever it was convenient for him to come.

But first he must return to his rooms with the silk pillow his mother had insisted on giving him. It would be one more thing for Demetrius to add to their already cumbersome impedimenta, but it seemed heartless to refuse the present, particularly in view of the fine fortitude with which she had accepted their mutual misfortune. She had been tearful, but there had been no painful break-up of her emotional discipline.

Marcellus found the luggage packed and strapped for the journey, but Demetrius was nowhere to be found. Marcipor, who had appeared in the doorway to see if he might be of service, was queried; and replied, with some reluctance and obvious perplexity, that he had seen Demetrius on his horse, galloping furiously down the driveway, fully an hour ago. Marcellus accepted this information without betraying his amazement. It was quite possible that the Greek had belatedly discovered the lack of some equipment necessary to their trip, and had set off for it minus the permission to do so. It was inconceivable that Demetrius would take advantage of this opportunity to make a dash for freedom. No, decided Marcellus, it wouldn't be that. But the incident needed explanation, for if Demetrius had gone for additional supplies he would not have strapped the luggage until his return.

Lucia was leaning against the balustrade, gazing toward the Tiber where little sails reflected final flashes of almost horizontal sunshine, and galleys moved so sluggishly they would have seemed not to be in motion at all but for the rhythmic dip of the long oars. One galley, a little larger than the others, was headed toward a wharf. Lucia cupped her hands about her eyes and was so intent upon the sinister black hulk that she did not hear Marcellus coming.

He joined her without words, and circled her girlish waist tenderly. She slipped her arm about him, but did not turn her head.

'Might that be your galley?' she asked, pointing. 'It has three banks, I think, and a very high prow. Isn't that the kind that meets ships at Ostia?'

'That's the kind,' agreed Marcellus, pleased that the conversation promised to be dispassionate. 'Perhaps that is the boat.'

Lucia slowly turned about in his arms and affectionately patted his cheeks with her soft palms. She looked up, smiling resolutely, her lips quivering a little; but she was doing very well, her brother thought. He hoped his eyes were assuring her of his approval.

'I am so glad you are taking Demetrius,' she said, steadily. 'He wanted to go?'

'Yes,' replied Marcellus, adding after a pause, 'Yes—he quite wanted to go.' They stood in silence for a little while, her fingers gently toying with the knotted silk cord at the throat of his tunic.

'All packed up?' Lucia was certainly doing a good job, they both felt. Her voice was well under control.

'Yes.' Marcellus nodded with a smile that meant everything was proceeding normally, just as if they were leaving on a hunting excursion. 'Yes, dear—all ready to go.' There was another longer interval of silence.

'Of course, you don't know—yet'—said Lucia—'when you will be coming home.'

'No,' said Marcellus. After a momentary hesitation he added, 'Not yet."

Suddenly Lucia drew a long, agonized 'Oh!'—wrapped her arms tightly around her brother's neck, buried her face against his breast, and shook with stifled sobs. Marcellus held her trembling body close.

'No, no,' he whispered. 'Let's see it through, precious child. It's not easy; but—well—we must behave like Romans, you know.'

Lucia stiffened, flung back her head, and faced him with streaming eyes aflame with anger.

'Like Romans!' she mocked. 'Behave like Romans! And what does a Roman ever get for being brave—and pretending it is fine—and noble—to give up everything—and make-believe it is glorious—glorious to suffer—and die—for Rome! For Rome! I hate Rome! Look what Rome has done to you—and all of us! Why can't we live in peace? The Roman Empire—Bah! What is the Roman Empire? A great swarm of slaves! I don't mean slaves like Tertia and Demetrius; I mean slaves like you and me—all our lives bowing and scraping and flattering; our legions looting and murdering—and for what? To make Rome the capital of the world, they say! But why should the whole world be ruled by a lunatic like old Tiberius and a drunken bully like Gaius? I hate Rome! I hate it all!'

Marcellus made no effort to arrest the torrent, thinking it more practical to let his sister wear her passion out—and have done with it. She hung limp in his arms now, her heart pounding hard.

'Feel better?' he asked, sympathetically. She slowly nodded against his breast. Instinctively glancing about, Marcellus saw Demetrius standing a few yards away with his face averted from them. 'I must see what he wants,' he murmured, relaxing his embrace. Lucia slipped from his arms and stared again at the river, unwilling to let the imperturbable Greek see her so nearly broken.

'The daughter of Legate Gallus is here, sir,' announced Demetrius.

'I can't see Diana now, Marcellus,' put in Lucia, thickly. 'I'll go down through the gardens, and you talk to her.' She raised her voice a little.

'Bring Diana to the pergola, Demetrius.' Without waiting for her brother's approval, she walked rapidly toward the circular marble stairway that led to the arbors and the pool. Assuming that his master's silence confirmed the order, Demetrius was setting off on his errand. Marcellus recalled him with a quiet word and he retraced his steps.

'Do you suppose she knows?' asked Marcellus, frowning.

'Yes, sir.'

'What makes you think so?'

'The daughter of Legate Gallus appears to have been weeping, sir.'

Marcellus winced and shook his head.

'I hardly know what to say to her,' he confided, mostly to himself, a dilemma that Demetrius made no attempt to solve. 'But'—Marcellus sighed—'I suppose I must see her.'

'Yes, sir,' said Demetrius, departing on his errand.

Turning toward the balustrade, Marcellus watched his sister's dejected figure moving slowly through the arbors, and his heart was suffused with pity. He had never seen Lucia so forlorn and undone. It was not much wonder if she had a reluctance to meet Diana in her present state of collapse. Something told him that this impending interview with Diana was likely to be difficult. He had not often been alone with her, even for a moment. This time they would not only be alone, but in circumstances extremely trying. He was uncertain what attitude he should take toward her.

She was coming now, out through the peristyle, walking with her usual effortless grace, but lacking animation. It was unlike Demetrius to send a guest to the pergola unattended, even though well aware that Diana knew the way. Damn Demetrius!—he was behaving very strangely this afternoon. Greeting Diana might be much more natural and unconstrained if he were present. Marcellus sauntered along the pavement to meet her. It was true, as Lucia had said; Diana was growing up—and she was lovelier in this pensiveness than he had ever seen her. Perhaps the bad news had taken all the adolescent bounce out of her. But, whatever might account for it, Diana had magically matured. His heart speeded a little. The elder-brotherly smile with which he was preparing to welcome her seemed inappropriate if not insincere, and as Diana neared him, his eyes were no less sober than hers.

She gave him both hands, at his unspoken invitation, and looked up from under her long lashes, winking back the tears and trying to smile. Marcellus had never faced her like this before, and the intimate contact stirred him. As he looked deeply into her dark eyes, it was almost as if he were discovering her; aware, for the first time, of her womanly contours, her finely sculptured brows, the firm but piquant chin, and the full lips—now parted with painful anxiety—disclosing even white teeth, tensely locked.

'I am glad you came, Diana.' Marcellus had wanted this to sound fraternal, but it didn't. He was intending to add, 'Lucia will want to see you presently'—but he didn't; nor did he release her hands. It mystified him that she could stand still that long.

'Are you really going—tonight?' she asked, in a husky whisper.

Marcellus stared into her uplifted eyes, marveling that the tempestuous, teasing, unpredictable Diana had suddenly become so winsome.

'How did you know?' he queried. 'Who could have told you so soon? I learned about it myself not more than three hours ago.'

'Does it matter—how I found out?' She hesitated, as if debating what next to say. 'I had to come, Marcellus,' she went on, bravely. 'I knew you would have no time—to come to me—and say good-bye.'

'It was very—' He stopped on the verge of 'kind,' which, he felt, would be too coolly casual, and saw Diana's eyes swimming with tears. 'It was very dear of you,' he said, tenderly. Marcellus clasped her hands more firmly and drew her closer. She responded, after a momentary reluctance.

'I wouldn't have done it, of course,' she said, rather breathlessly—'if the time hadn't been so short. We're all going to miss you.' Then, a little unsteadily, she asked, 'Will I hear from you, Marcellus?' And when he did not immediately find words to express his happy surprise, she shook her head and murmured, 'I shouldn't have said that, I think. You will have more than enough to do. We can learn about each other through Lucia.'

'But I shall want to write to you, dear,' declared Marcellus, 'and you will write to me—often—I hope. Promise!'

Diana smiled mistily, and Marcellus watched her dimples deepen—and disappear. His heart skipped a beat when she whispered, 'You will write to me tonight? And send it back from Ostia—on the galley?'

'Yes—Diana!'

'Where is Lucia?' she asked, impetuously reclaiming her hands.

'Down in the arbors,' said Marcellus.

Before he realized her intention, Diana had run away. At the top of the stairs she paused to wave to him. He was on the point of calling to her—to wait a moment—that he had something more to say; but the utter hopelessness of his predicament kept him silent. What more, he asked himself, did he want to say to Diana? What promise could he make to her—or exact of her? No—it was better to let this be their leave-taking. He waved her a kiss—and she vanished down the stairway. It was quite possible—quite probable indeed—that he would never see Diana again.

Moodily, he started toward the house; then abruptly turned back to the pergola. The girls had met and were strolling, arm in arm, through the rose arbor. Perhaps he was having a final glimpse of his lovable young sister, too. There was no good reason why he should put Lucia to the additional pain of another farewell.

It surprised him to see Demetrius ascending the stairway. What errand could have taken him down to the gardens, wondered Marcellus. Perhaps he would explain without being queried. His loyal Corinthian was not acting normally today. Presently he appeared at the top of the stairs and approached with the long, military stride that Marcellus had often found difficult to match when they were out on hunting trips. Demetrius seemed very well pleased about something; better than merely pleased. He was exultant! Marcellus had never seen such an expression on his slave's face.

'Shall I have the dunnage taken down to the galley now, sir?' asked Demetrius, in a voice that betrayed recent excitement.

'Yes—if it is ready.' Marcellus was organizing a question, but found it difficult, and decided not to pry. 'You may wait for me at the wharf,' he added.

'You will have had dinner, sir?'

Marcellus nodded; then suddenly changed his mind. He had taken leave of his family, one by one. They had all borne up magnificently. It was too much to ask of them—and him—that they should undergo a repetition of this distress in one another's presence.

'No,' he said, shortly. 'I shall have my dinner on the galley. You may arrange for it.'

'Yes, sir.' Demetrius' tone indicated that he quite approved of this decision.

Marcellus followed slowly toward the house. There were plenty of things he would have liked to do, if he had been given one more day. There was Tullus, for one. He must leave a note for Tullus.

* * * * * *

Upon meeting in the arbor, Lucia and Diana had both wept, wordlessly. Then they had talked in broken sentences about the possibilities of Marcellus' return, his sister fearing the worst, Diana wondering whether some pressure might be brought to bear on Gaius.

'You mean'—Lucia queried—'that perhaps my father might—'

'No.' Diana shook her head decisively. 'Not your father. It would have to be done some other way.' Her eyes narrowed thoughtfully.

'Maybe your father could do something about it,' suggested Lucia.

'I don't know. Perhaps he might, if he were here. But his business in Marseilles may keep him stationed there until next winter.'

'You said good-bye to Marcellus?' asked Lucia, after they had walked on a little way in silence. She questioned Diana's eyes and smiled pensively as she watched the color creeping up her cheeks. Diana nodded and pressed Lucia's arm affectionately, but made no other response.

'How did Demetrius get down here so fast?' she asked, impulsively. 'He came for me, you know, telling me Marcellus was leaving and wanted to see me. Just now I passed him. Don't tell me that slave was saying good-bye—like an equal?'

'It was rather strange,' admitted Lucia. 'Demetrius had never spoken to me in his life, except to acknowledge an order. I hardly knew what to make of it, Diana. He came out here, saluted with his usual formality, and delivered a little speech that sounded as if he had carefully rehearsed it. He said, "I am going away with the Tribune. I may never return. I wish to bid farewell to the sister of my master and thank her for being kind to her brother's slave. I shall remember her goodness." Then he took this ring out of his wallet—'

'Ring?' echoed Diana, incredulously. 'Hold still. Let me look at it,' she breathed. Lucia held up her hand, with fingers outspread, for a closer inspection in the waning light. 'Pretty; isn't it?' commented Diana. 'What is that device—a ship?'

'Demetrius said,' continued Lucia, ' "I should like to leave this with my master's sister. If I come back, she may return it to me. If I do not come back, it shall be hers. My father gave it to my mother. It is the only possession I was able to save." '

'But—how queer!' murmured Diana. 'What did you say to him?'

'Well—what could I say?' Lucia's tone was self-defensive. 'After all—he is going away with my brother—at the risk of his own life. He's human; isn't he?'

'Yes—he's human,' agreed Diana, impatiently. 'Go on! What did you say?'

'I thanked him,' said Lucia, exasperatingly deliberate, 'and told him I thought it was wonderful of him—and I do think it was, Diana—to let me keep his precious ring; and—and—I said I hoped they would both come home safely—and I promised to take good care of his keepsake.'

'That was all right, I suppose,' nodded Diana, judicially. 'And—then what?' They had stopped on the tiled path, and Lucia seemed a little confused.

'Well,' she stammered, 'he was still standing there—and I gave him my hand.'

'You didn't!' exclaimed Diana. 'To a slave?'

'To shake, you know,' defended Lucia. 'Why shouldn't I have been willing to shake hands with Demetrius? He's as clean as we are; certainly a lot cleaner than Bambo, who is always pawing me.'

'That's not the point, Lucia, whether Demetrius' hands are cleaner than Bambo's feet—and you know it. He is a slave, and we can't be too careful.' Diana's tone was distinctly stern, until her curiosity overwhelmed her indignation. 'So—then'—she went on, a little more gently—'he shook hands with you.'

'No—it was ever so much worse than that.' Lucia grinned at the sight of Diana's shocked eyes. 'Demetrius took my hand, and put the ring on my finger—and then he kissed my hand—and—well—after all, Diana—he's going away with Marcellus—maybe to die for him! What should I have done? Slap him?'

Diana laid her hands on Lucia's shoulders and looked her squarely in the eyes.

'So—then—after that—what happened?'

'Wasn't that enough?' parried Lucia, flinching a little from Diana's insistent search.

'Quite!' After a pause, she said, 'You're not expecting to wear that ring; are you, Lucia?'

'No. There's no reason why I should. It might get lost. And I don't want to hurt Tertia.'

'Is Tertia in love with Demetrius?'

'Mad about him! She has been crying her eyes out, this afternoon, the poor dear.'

'Does Demetrius know?'

'I don't see how he could help it.'

'And he doesn't care for her?'

'Not that way. I made him promise he would say good-bye to her.'

'Lucia—had it ever occurred to you that Demetrius has been secretly in love with you—maybe for a long time?'

'He has never given me any reason to think so,' replied Lucia, rather vaguely.

'Until today, you mean,' persisted Diana.

Lucia meditated an answer for a long moment.

'Diana,' she said soberly, 'Demetrius is a slave. That is true. That is his misfortune. He was gently bred, in a home of refinement, and brought here in chains by ruffians who weren't fit to tie his sandals!' Her voice trembled with suppressed anger. 'Of course'—she went on, bitterly ironical—'their being Romans made all the difference! Just so you're a Roman, you don't have to know anything—but pillage and bloodshed! Don't you realize, Diana, that everything in the Roman Empire today that's worth a second thought on the part of any decent person was stolen from Greece? Tell me!—how does it happen that we speak Greek, in preference to Latin? It's because the Greeks are leagues ahead of us, mentally. There's only one thing we do better: we're better butchers!'

Diana frowned darkly.

With her lips close to Lucia's ear, she said guardedly, 'You are a fool to say such things—even to me! It's too dangerous! Isn't your family in enough trouble? Do you want to see all of us banished—or in prison?'

* * * * *

Marcellus stood alone at the rail of the afterdeck. He had not arrived at the wharf until a few minutes before the galley's departure; and, going up to the cramped and stuffy cabin to make sure his heavy luggage had been safely stowed, was hardly aware that they were out in the river until he came down and looked about. Already the long warehouse and the docks had retreated into the gloom, and the voices sounded far away.

High up on an exclusive residential hillside, two small points of light flickered. He identified them as the brasiers at the eastern corners of the pergola. Perhaps his father was standing there at the balustrade.

Now they had passed the bend and the lights had disappeared. It was as if the first scroll of his life had now been written, read, and sealed. The pink glow that was Rome had faded and the stars were brightening. Marcellus viewed them with a strange interest. They seemed like so many unresponsive spectators; not so dull-eyed and apathetic as the Sphinx, but calmly observant, winking occasionally to relieve the strain and clear their vision. He wondered whether they were ever moved to sympathy or admiration; or if they cared, at all.

After a while he became conscious of the inexorable rasp of sixty oars methodically swinging with one obedience to the metallic blows of the boatswain's hammers as he measured their slavery on his huge anvil. . . . Click! Clack! Click! Clack!

Home—and Life—and Love made a final, urgent tug at his spirit. He wished he might have had an hour with Tullus, his closest friend. Tullus hadn't even heard what had happened to him. He wished he had gone back once more to see his mother. He wished he had kissed Diana. He wished he had not witnessed the devastating grief of his sister. . . . Click! Clack! Click! Clack!

He turned about and noticed Demetrius standing in the shadows near the ladder leading to the cabins. It was a comfort to sense the presence of his loyal slave. Marcellus decided to engage him in conversation; for the steady hammer-blows, down deep in the galley's hull, were beginning to pound hard in his temples. He beckoned. Demetrius approached and stood at attention. Marcellus made the impatient little gesture with both hands and a shake of the head which, by long custom, had come to mean, 'Be at ease! Be a friend!' Demetrius relaxed his stiff posture and drifted over to the rail beside Marcellus where he silently and without obvious curiosity waited his master's pleasure.

'Demetrius'—Marcellus swept the sky with an all-inclusive arm—'do you ever believe in the gods?'

'If it is my master's wish, I do,' replied Demetrius, perfunctorily.

'No, no,' said Marcellus, testily, 'be honest. Never mind what I believe. Tell me what you think about the gods. Do you ever pray to them?'

'When I was a small boy, sir,' complied Demetrius, 'my mother taught us to invoke the gods. She was quite religious. There was a pretty statue of Priapus in our flower garden. I can still remember my mother kneeling there, on a fine spring day, with a little trowel in one hand and a basket of plants in the other. She believed that Priapus made things grow. . . . And my mother prayed to Athene every morning when my brothers and I followed the teacher into our schoolroom.' He was silent for a while; and then, prodded by an encouraging nod from Marcellus, he continued: 'My father offered libations to the gods on their feast-days, but I think that was to please my mother.'

'This is most interesting—and touching, too,' observed Marcellus. 'But you haven't quite answered my question, Demetrius. Do you believe in the gods—now?'

'No, sir.'

'Do you mean that you don't believe they render any service to men? Or do you doubt that the gods exist, at all?'

'I think it better for the mind, sir, to disbelieve in their existence. The last time I prayed—it was on the day that our home was broken up. As my father was led away in chains, I knelt by my mother and we prayed to Zeus—the Father of gods and men—to protect his life. But Zeus either did not hear us; or, hearing us, had no power to aid us; or, having power to aid us, refused to do so. It is better, I think, to believe that he did not hear us than to believe that he was unable or unwilling to give aid. . . . That afternoon my mother went away—upon her own invitation—because she could bear no more sorrow. . . . I have not prayed to the gods since that day, sir. I have cursed and reviled them, on occasions; but with very little hope that they might resent my blasphemies. Cursing the gods is foolish and futile, I think.'

Marcellus chuckled grimly. This fine quality of contempt for the gods surpassed any profanity he had ever heard. Demetrius had spoken without heat. He had so little interest in the gods that he even felt it was silly to curse them.

'You don't believe there is any sort of supernatural intelligence in charge of the universe?' queried Marcellus, gazing up into the sky.

'I have no clear thought about that, sir,' replied Demetrius, deliberately. 'It is difficult to account for the world without believing in a Creator, but I do not want to think that the acts of men are inspired by superhuman beings. It is better, I feel, to believe that men have devised their brutish deeds without divine assistance.'

'I am inclined to agree with you, Demetrius. It would be a great comfort, though, if—especially in an hour of bewilderment—one could nourish a reasonable hope that a benevolent Power existed—somewhere—and might be invoked.'

'Yes, sir,' conceded Demetrius, looking upward. 'The stars pursue an orderly plan. I believe they are honest and sensible. I believe in the Tiber, and in the mountains, and in the sheep and cattle and horses. If there are gods in charge of them, such gods are honest and sound of mind. But if there are gods on Mount Olympus, directing human affairs, they are vicious and insane.' Apparently feeling that he had been talking too much, Demetrius stiffened, drew himself erect, and gave the usual evidences that he was preparing to get back on his leash. But Marcellus wasn't quite ready to let him do so.

'Perhaps you think,' he persisted, 'that all humanity is crazy.'

'I would not know, sir,' replied Demetrius, very formally, pretending not to have observed his master's sardonic grin.

'Well'—hectored Marcellus—'let's narrow it down to the Roman Empire. Do you think the Roman Empire is an insane thing?'

'Your slave, sir,' answered Demetrius, stiffly, 'believes whatever his master thinks about that.'

It was clear to Marcellus that the philosophical discussion was ended. By experience he had learned that once Demetrius resolved to crawl back into his slave status, no amount of coaxing would hale him forth. They both stood silently now, looking at the dark water swirling about the stern.

The Greek is right, thought Marcellus. That's what ails the Roman Empire: it is mad! That's what ails the whole world of men. *Mad!* If there is any Supreme Power in charge, He is *mad!* The stars are honest and sensible. But humanity is *insane!* . . . Click! Clack! Click! Clack!

Chapter III

After the tipsy little ship had staggered down past the Lapari Islands in the foulest weather of the year, and had tacked gingerly through the perilous Strait of Messina, a smooth sea and a favorable breeze so eased Captain Manius' vigilance that he was available for a leisurely chat.

'Tell me something about Minoa,' urged Marcellus, after Manius had talked at considerable length about his many voyages: Ostia to Palermo and back, Ostia to Crete, to Alexandria, to Joppa.

Manius laughed, down deep in his whiskers.

'You'll find, sir, that there is no such place as Minoa.' And when Marcellus' stare invited an explanation, the swarthy navigator gave his passenger a lesson in history, some little of which he already knew.

Fifty years ago, the legions of Augustus had laid siege to the ancient city of Gaza, and had subdued it after a long and bitter campaign that had cost more than the conquest was worth.

'It would have been cheaper,' observed Manius, 'to have paid the high toll they demanded for travel on the salt trail.'

'But how about the Bedouins?' Marcellus wondered.

'Yes—and the Emperor could have bought off the Bedouins, too, for less than that war cost. We lost twenty-three thousand men, taking Gaza.'

Manius went on with the story. Old Augustus had been beside himself with rage over the stubborn resistance of the defense—composed of a conglomeration of Egyptians, Syrians, and Jews, none of whom were a bit squeamish at the sight of blood, and never took prisoners and were notoriously ingenious in the arts of torture. Their attitude, he felt, in willfully defying the might of the Empire demanded that the old pest-hole Gaza should be cleaned up. Henceforth, declared Augustus, it was to be known as the Roman city of Minoa; and it was to be hoped that the inhabitants thereof, rejoicing in the benefits conferred upon them by a civilized state, would forget that there had ever been a municipality so dirty, unhealthy, quarrelsome, and altogether nasty as Gaza.

'But Gaza,' continued Manius, 'had been Gaza for seventeen centuries, and it would have taken more than an edict by Augustus to change its name.'

'Or its manners, either, I daresay,' commented Marcellus.

'Or its smell,' added Manius, dryly. 'You know, sir,' he went on, 'the crusty white shore of that old Dead Sea is like a salt lick beside a water-hole in the jungle where animals of all breeds and sizes gather and fight. This has been going on longer than any nation's history can remember. Occasionally some animal bigger than the others has shown up, driving all the rest of them away. Sometimes they have ganged on the big fellow and chased him off, after which the little ones have gone to fighting again among themselves. Well—that's Gaza for you!'

'But the salt lick,' put in Marcellus, 'is not at Gaza; but at the Dead Sea.'

'Quite true,' agreed Manius, 'but you don't get to the Dead Sea for a lick at the salt unless Gaza lets you. For a long time the lion of Judah kept all the other animals away, after he had scared off the Philistine hyenas. Then the big elephant Egypt frightened away the lion. Then Alexander the tiger jumped onto the elephant. Always after a battle the little fellows would come sneaking back, and claw the hides off one another while the big ones were licking their wounds.'

'And what animal came after the tiger?' prodded Marcellus, though he knew the answer.

'The Roman eagle,' replied Manius. 'Flocks and swarms of Roman eagles, thinking to pick the bones; but there were plenty of survivors not ready to have their bones picked. That,' he interrupted himself to remark, 'was how we lost three-and-twenty thousand Romans—to get possession of the old salt lick.'

'A most interesting story,' mused Marcellus, who had never heard it told just that way.

'Yes,' nodded Manius, 'an interesting story; but the most curious part of it is the effect that these long battles had upon the old city of Gaza. After every invasion, a remnant of these foreign armies would remain; deserters and men too badly crippled to travel home. They stayed in Gaza—a score of different breeds—to continue their feuds.' The Captain shook his head and made a wry face. 'Many will tell you of the constant quarreling and fighting in port cities such as Rhodes and Alexandria where there is a mixed population composed of every known tint and tongue. Some say the worst inferno on any coast of our sea is Joppa. But I'll vote for Gaza as the last place in the world where a sane man would want to live.'

'Perhaps Rome should clean up Gaza again,' remarked Marcellus.

'Quite impossible! And what is true of old Gaza is equally true of all that country, up as far as Damascus. The Emperor could send in all the legions that Rome has under arms, and put on such a campaign of slaughter as the world has never seen; but it wouldn't be a permanent victory. You can't defeat a Syrian. And as for the Jews!—you can kill a Jew, and bury him, but he'll climb out alive!' Noting Marcellus' amusement, Manius grinningly elaborated, 'Yes, sir—he will climb right up the spade-handle and sell you the rug he'd died in!'

'But'—queried Marcellus, anxious to know more about his own job—'doesn't our fort at Minoa—or Gaza, rather—keep order in the city?'

'Not at all! Hasn't anything to do with the city. Isn't located in the city, but away to the east in a most desolate strip of desert sand, rocks, and scratchy vegetation. You will find only about five hundred officers and men—though the garrison is called a legion. They are there to make the marauding Bedouins a bit cautious. Armed detachments from the fort go along with the caravans, so that the brigands will not molest them. Oh, occasionally'—Manius yawned widely—'not very often—a caravan starts across and never comes back.'

'How often?' asked Marcellus, hoping the question would sound as if he were just making conversation.

'Well—let's see,' mumbled Manius, squinting one eye shut and counting on his battered fingers. 'I've heard of only four, this past year.'

'Only four,' repeated Marcellus, thoughtfully. 'I suppose that on these occasions the detachment from the fort is captured too.'

'Of course,' drawled Manius.

'And put into slavery, maybe?'

'No—not likely. The Bedouins don't need slaves; wouldn't be bothered with them. Your Bedouin, sir, is a wild man; wild as a fox and sneaking as a jackal. When he strikes, he slips up on you from the rear and lets you have it between your shoulder blades.'

'But—doesn't the garrison avenge these murders?' exclaimed Marcellus.

Manius shook his head and drew a crooked grin.

'That garrison, sir, does not amount to much, if you'll excuse my saying so. None of them care. They're poorly disciplined, poorly commanded, and haven't the slightest interest in the fort. Ever so often they have a mutiny and somebody gets killed. You can't expect much of a fort that sheds most of its blood on the drillground.'

* * * * * *

That night Marcellus felt he should confide his recent information to Demetrius. In a quiet voice, as they lay in their adjacent bunks, he gave his Corinthian a sketch of the conditions in which they were presently to find themselves, speaking his thoughts as freely as if his slave were jointly responsible for whatever policy might be pursued.

Demetrius had listened in silence throughout the dismaying recital, and when Marcellus had concluded he ventured to remark laconically, 'My master must command the fort.'

'Obviously!' responded Marcellus. 'That's what I am commissioned to do! What else—indeed?' And as there was no immediate reply from the other bunk, he added, testily, 'What do you mean?'

'I mean, sir—if the garrison is unruly and disorderly, my master will exact obedience. It is not for his slave to suggest how this may be accomplished; but it will be safer for my master if he takes full command of the fort instantly—and firmly!'

Marcellus raised up on one elbow and searched the Greek's eyes in the gloom of the stuffy cabin.

'I see what you have in mind, Demetrius. Now that we know the temper of this place, you think the new Legate should not bother about making himself agreeable, but should swagger in and crack a few heads without waiting for formal introductions.'

'Something like that,' approved Demetrius.

'Give them some strong medicine; eh? Is that your idea?'

'When one picks up a nettle, sir, one should not grasp it gently. Perhaps these idle men would be pleased to obey a commander as well-favored and fearless as my master.'

'Your words are gracious, Demetrius.'

'Almost any man, sir, values justice and courage. My master is just—and my master is also bold.'

'That's how your master got into this predicament, Demetrius,' chuckled Marcellus ironically—'by being bold.'

Apparently unwilling to discuss that unhappy circumstance, but wanting to support his end of the conversation, Demetrius said, 'Yes, sir,' so soberly that Marcellus laughed. Afterward there was such a long hiatus that it was probable the Corinthian had dropped off to sleep, for the lazy roll of the little ship was an urgent sedative. Marcellus lay awake for an hour, consolidating the plan suggested by his shrewd and loyal Greek. Demetrius, he reflected, is right. If I am to command this fort at all, I must command it from the moment of my arrival. If they strike me down, my exit will be at least honorable.

* * * * * *

It was well past mid-afternoon on the eighth day of March when Captain Manius maneuvered his unwieldy little tub through the busy roadstead of Gaza, and warped her flank against a vacant wharf. His duties at the moment were pressing, but he found time to say good-bye to the young Tribune with something of the somber solicitude of the next of kin bidding farewell to the dying.

Demetrius had been among the early ones over the rail. After a while he returned with five husky Syrians to whom he pointed out the burdens to be carried. There were no uniforms on the dirty wharf, but Marcellus was not disappointed. He had not expected to be met. The garrison had not been advised of his arrival. He would be obliged to appear at the fort unheralded.

Gaza was in no hurry, probably because of her great age and many infirmities. It was a full hour before enough pack-asses were found to carry the baggage. Some more time was consumed in loading them. Another hour was spent moving at tortoise speed through the narrow, rough-cobbled, filthy streets, occasionally blocked by shrieking contestants for the right of way.

The Syrians had divined the Tribune's destination when they saw his uniform, and gave him a surly obedience. At length they were out on a busy, dusty highway, Marcellus heading the procession on a venerable, half-shed camel, led by the reeking Syrian with whom Demetrius—by pantomime—had haggled over the price of the expedition. This bargaining had amused Marcellus; for Demetrius, habitually quiet and reserved, had shouted and gesticulated with the best of them. Knowing nothing about the money of Gaza, or the rates for the service he sought, the Corinthian had fiercely objected to the Syrian's first three proposals, and had finally come to terms with savage mutters and scowls. It was difficult to recognize Demetrius in this new rôle.

Far ahead, viewed through the billowing clouds of yellow dust, appeared an immensely ugly twelve-acre square bounded by a high wall built of sunbaked brick, its corners dignified by tall towers. As they drew nearer, a limp Roman banner was identified, pendent from an oblique pole at the corner.

An indolent, untidy sentry detached himself from a villainous group of unkept legionaries squatting on the ground, slouched to the big gate, and swung it open without challenging the party. Perhaps, thought Marcellus, the lazy lout had mistaken their little parade for a caravan that wanted to be convoyed. After they had filed through into the barren, sunblistered courtyard, another sentry ambled down the steps of the praetorium and stood waiting until the Tribune's grunting camel had folded up her creaking joints. Demetrius, who had brought up the rear of the procession, dismounted from his donkey and marched forward to stand at his master's elbow. The sentry, whose curiosity had been stirred by the sight of the Tribune's insignia, saluted clumsily with a tarnished sword in a dirty hand.

'I am Tribune Marcellus Gallio!' The words were clipped and harsh. 'I am commissioned to take command of this fort. Conduct me to the officer in charge.'

'Centurion Paulus is not here, sir.'

'Where is he?'

'In the city, sir.'

'And when Centurion Paulus goes to the city, is there no one in command?'

'Centurion Sextus, sir; but he is resting, and has given orders not to be disturbed.'

Marcellus advanced a step and stared into the sulky eyes.

'I am not accustomed to waiting for men to finish their naps,' he growled. 'Obey me—instantly! And wash your dirty face before you let me see it again! What is this—a Roman fort—or a pigsty?'

Blinking a little, the sentry backed away for a few steps; and, turning, disappeared through the heavy doors. Marcellus strode heavily to and fro before the entrance, his impatience mounting. After waiting for a few minutes, he marched up the steps, closely followed by Demetrius, and stalked through the gloomy hall. Another sentry appeared.

'Conduct me to Centurion Sextus!' shouted Marcellus.

'By whose orders?' demanded the sentry, gruffly.

'By the orders of Tribune Marcellus Gallio, who has taken command of this fort. Lead on—and be quick about it!'

At that moment a near-by door opened and a burly, bearded figure emerged wearing an ill-conditioned uniform with a black eagle woven into the right sleeve of his red tunic. Marcellus brushed the sentry aside and confronted him.

'You are Centurion Sextus?' asked Marcellus; and when Sextus had nodded dully, he went on, 'I am ordered by Prince Gaius to command this fort. Have your men bring in my equipment.'

'Well—not so fast, not so fast,' drawled Sextus. 'Let's have a look at that commission.'

'Certainly,' Marcellus handed him the scroll; and Sextus, lazily unrolling it, held it close to his face in the waning light.

'I suggest, Centurion Sextus,' rasped Marcellus, 'that we repair to the Legate's quarters for this examination. In the country of which I am a citizen, there are certain courtesies—'

Sextus grinned unpleasantly and shrugged.

'You're in Gaza now,' he remarked, half-contemptuously. 'In Gaza, you will find, we do things the easy way, and are more patient than our better-dressed equals in Rome. Incidentally,' added Sextus, dryly, as he led the way down the hall, 'I too am a Roman citizen.'

'How long has Centurion Paulus been in command here?' asked Marcellus, glancing about the large room into which Sextus had shown him.

'Since December. He took over, temporarily, after the death of Legate Vitelius.'

'What did Vitelius die of?'

'I don't know, sir.'

'Not of wounds, then," guessed Marcellus.

'No, sir. He had been ailing. It was a fever.'

'It's a wonder you're not all sick,' observed Marcellus, dusting his hands, distastefully. Turning to Demetrius he advised him to go out and stand guard over their equipment until it was called for.

Sextus mumbled some instructions to the sentry, who drifted away.

'I'll show you the quarters you may occupy until Commander Paulus returns,' he said, moving toward the door. Marcellus followed. The room into which he was shown contained a bunk, a table, and two chairs. Otherwise it was bare and grim as a prison cell. A door led into a smaller unfurnished cubicle.

'Order another bunk for this kennel,' growled Marcellus. 'My slave will sleep here.'

'Slaves do not sleep in the officers' row, sir,' replied Sextus, firmly.

'My slave does!'

'But it's against orders, sir!'

'There are no orders at this fort—but mine!' barked Marcellus.

Sextus nodded his head, and a knowing grin twisted his shaggy lips as he left the room.

* * * * * *

It was a memorable evening at the fort. For years afterward the story was retold until it had the flavor of a legend.

Marcellus, accompanied by his orderly, had entered the big mess-hall to find the junior officers seated. They did not rise, but there were no evidences of hostility in the inquisitive glances they turned in his direction as he made his way to the round table in the center of the room. A superficial survey of the surrounding tables informed Marcellus that he was the youngest man present. Demetrius went directly to the kitchen to oversee his master's service.

After a while, Centurion Paulus arrived, followed by Sextus who had apparently waited to advise his chief of recent events. There was something of a stir when they came striding across the room to the center table. Sextus mumbled an ungracious introduction. Marcellus rose and was ready to offer his hand, but Paulus did not see it; merely bowed, drew out his chair, and sat. He was not drunk, but it was evident that he had been drinking. His lean face, stubbly with a three-days' beard, was unhealthily ruddy; and his hands, when he began to gobble his food, were shaky. They were also dirty. And yet, in spite of his general appearance, Paulus bore marks of a discarded refinement. This man, thought Marcellus, may have been somebody, once upon a time.

'The new Legate; eh?' drawled Paulus, with his mouth full. 'We have had no word of his appointment. However'—he waved a negligent hand, and helped himself to another large portion from the messy bowl of stewed meat—'we can go into that later; tomorrow, perhaps.' For some minutes he wolfed his rations, washing down the greasy meat with noisy gulps of a sharp native wine.

Having finished, Paulus folded his hairy arms on the table and stared insolently into the face of the young interloper. Marcellus met his cloudy eyes steadily. Each knew that the other was taking his measure, not only as to height and weight—in which dimensions they were approximately matched, with Paulus a few pounds heavier, perhaps, and a few years older—but, more particularly, appraising each other's timber and temper. Paulus drew an unpleasant grin.

'Important name—Gallio,' he remarked, with mock deference. 'Any relation to the rich Senator?'

'My father,' replied Marcellus, coolly.

'Oh-ho!' chuckled Paulus. 'Then you must be one of these clubhouse Tribunes.' He glanced about, as conversations at the adjoining tables were throttled down. 'One would think Prince Gaius could have found a more attractive post for the son of Senator Gallio,' he went on, raising his voice for the benefit of the staff. 'By jove—I have it!' he shouted, hilariously, slapping Sextus on the shoulder. 'The son of Marcus Lucan Gallio has been a bad boy!' He turned again to Marcellus. 'I'll wager this is your first command, Tribune.'

'It is,' replied Marcellus. The room was deathly still now.

'Never gave an order in your life; eh?' sneered Paulus.

Marcellus pushed back his chair and rose, conscious that three score of interested eyes were studying his serious face.

'I am about to give an order now!' he said, steadily. 'Centurion Paulus, you will stand and apologize for conduct unbecoming an officer!'

Paulus hooked an arm over the back of his chair, and grinned.

'You gave the wrong order, my boy,' he snarled. Then, as he watched Marcellus deliberately unsheathing his broadsword, Paulus overturned his chair as he sprang to his feet. Drawing his sword, he muttered, 'You'd better put that down, youngster!'

'Clear the room!' commanded Marcellus.

There was no doubt in anyone's mind now as to the young Tribune's intention. He and Paulus had gone into this business too far to retreat. The tables were quickly pushed back against the wall. Chairs were dragged out of the way. And the battle was on.

At the beginning of the engagement, it appeared to the audience that Paulus had decided to make it a brief and decisive affair. His command of the fort was insecurely held, for he was of erratic temper and dissolute habits. Obviously he had resolved upon a quick conquest as an object lesson to his staff. As for the consequences, Paulus had little to lose. Communication with Rome was slow. The tenure of a commander's office was unstable and brief. Nobody in Rome cared much what happened in the fort at Minoa. True—it was risky to kill the son of a Senator, but the staff would bear witness that the Tribune had drawn first.

Paulus immediately forced the fight with flailing blows, any one of which would have split his young adversary in twain had it landed elsewhere than on Marcellus' parrying sword. Entirely willing to be on the defensive for a while, Marcellus allowed himself to be rushed backward until they had almost reached the end of the long mess-hall. The faces of the junior officers, ranged around the wall, were tense. Demetrius stood with clenched fists and anxious eyes as he saw his master being crowded back toward a corner.

Step by step, Paulus marched into his retreating antagonist, raining blow after blow upon the defensive sword until, encouraged by his success, he saw his quarry backing into a quite hopeless position. He laughed—as he decreased the tempo of his strokes, assured now of his victory. But Marcellus believed there was a note of anxiety in the tone of that guttural laugh; believed also that the decreased fury of the blows was not due to the heavier man's assurance—but because of a much more serious matter. Paulus was getting tired. There was a strained look on his face as he raised his sword-arm. It was probably beginning to ache. Paulus was out of training. Life at Minoa had slowed him up. We take things easy in Gaza.

As they neared the critical corner, Paulus raised his arm woodenly to strike a mighty blow; and, this time, Marcellus did not wait for it to descend, but slashed his sword laterally so close to Paulus' throat that he instinctively threw back his head, and the blow went wild. In that instant,

Marcellus wheeled about quickly. It was Paulus now who was defending the corner.

Marcellus did not violently press his advantage. Wearied by his unaccustomed exercise, Paulus was breathing heavily and his contorted mouth showed a mounting alarm. He had left off flailing now; and, changing his tactics for a better strategy, seemed to be remembering his training. And he was no mean swordsman, Marcellus discovered: at least, there had been a time, no doubt, when Paulus might have given a good account of himself in the arena.

Marcellus caught sight of Demetrius again, and noted that his slave's face was eased of its strain. We were on familiar ground now, doing battle with skill rather than brute strength. This was ever so much better. Up till this moment, Marcellus had never been engaged in a dueling-match where his adversary had tried to hew him down with a weapon handled as an axe is swung. Paulus was fighting like a Roman Centurion now; not like a common butcher cleaving a beef.

For a brief period, while their swords rang with short, sharp, angry clashes, Marcellus gradually advanced. Once, Paulus cast his eyes about to see how much room was left to him; and Marcellus obligingly retreated a few steps. It was quite clear to every watcher that he had voluntarily donated Paulus a better chance to take care of himself. There was a half-audible ejaculation. This maneuver of the new Legate might not be in keeping with the dulled spirit of Minoa, but it stirred a memory of the manner in which brave men dealt with one another in Rome. The eyes of Demetrius shone with pride! His master was indeed a thoroughbred. 'Eugenos!' he exclaimed.

But Paulus was in no mood to accept favors. He came along swiftly, with as much audacity as if he had earned this more stable footing, and endeavored to spar Marcellus into a further retreat. But on that spot the battle was permanently located. Paulus tried everything he could recall, weaving, crouching, feinting—and all the time growing more and more fatigued. Now his guard was becoming sluggish and increasingly vulnerable. On two occasions, the spectators noted, it would have been simple enough for the Tribune to have ended the affair.

And now—with a deft maneuver—Marcellus brought the engagement to a dramatic close. Studying his opportunity, he thrust the tip of his broadsword into the hilt-housing of Paulus' wearied weapon, and tore it out of his hand. It fell with a clatter to the stone floor. Then there was a moment of absolute silence. Paulus stood waiting. His posture did him credit, they all thought; for, though his face showed the shock of this stunning surprise, it was not the face of a coward. Paulus was decisively defeated, but he had better stuff in him than any of them had thought.

Marcellus stooped and picked up the fallen broadsword by its tip, drew back his arm with the slow precision of a careful aim, and sent it swiftly—end over end over end through the mess-hall—to the massive wooden door where it drove its weight deep into the timber with a resounding thud. Nobody broke the stillness that followed. Marcellus then reversed his own sword in his hand, again took a deliberate aim, and sent the heavy weapon hurtling through the air toward the same target. It thudded deep into the door close beside the sword of Paulus.

The two men faced each other silently. Then Marcellus spoke; firmly but not arrogantly.

'Centurion Paulus,' he said, 'you will now apologize for conduct unbecoming an officer.'

Paulus shifted his weight and drew a long breath; half-turned to face the tightening ring of spectators; then straightened defiantly, folded his arms, and sneered.

Marcellus deliberately drew his dagger from his belt, and stepped forward. Paulus did not move.

'You had better defend yourself, Centurion,' warned Marcellus. 'You have a dagger; have you not? I advise you to draw it!' He advanced another step. 'Because—if you do not obey my order—I intend to kill you!'

It wasn't easy for Paulus, but he managed to do it adequately. Demetrius remarked afterward that it was plain to be seen Centurion Paulus was not an accomplished orator, which Marcellus thought was a very droll comment.

After Paulus had stammered through his glum, impromptu speech, Marcellus responded, 'Your apology is accepted, Centurion. Now perhaps there is something else that you might think it timely to say to your fellow officers. I have not yet been officially presented to them. As the retiring Commander, it is, I feel, your right to extend this courtesy.'

Paulus fully found his voice this time, and his announcement was made in a firm tone.

'I am introducing Tribune Marcellus Gallio, the Legate of this legion, and Commander of this fort.'

There was a concerted clatter of swords drawn in salute—all but the sword of paunchy old Sextus, who pretended to be adjusting his harness.

'Centurion Sextus!' called Marcellus, sharply. 'Bring me my sword!'

All eyes watched Sextus plod awkwardly over to the big door and tug the sword out of the thick planking.

'Bring the sword of Centurion Paulus, also!' commanded Marcellus.

Sextus worked the second broadsword out of the timber, and came with heavy feet and a dogged air. Marcellus took the heavy weapons, handed Paulus his, and waited to receive Sextus' salute. The hint was taken without further delay. Paulus also saluted before sheathing his sword.

'We will now finish our dinner,' said Marcellus, coolly. 'You will restore the tables to their places. Breakfast will be served to the staff tomorrow morning at five. All officers will be smooth-shaven. There will be an inspection on the parade-ground at six, conducted by Lieutenant-Commander Paulus. That will do.'

Paulus had asked, respectfully enough, to be excused as they returned to their table, and Marcellus had given him permission to go. Sextus was trailing along after him, without asking leave; and upon being sharply asked if he had not forgotten something, mumbled that he had finished his dinner.

'Then you will have time,' said Marcellus, 'to clear the Commander's quarters, so that I may occupy those rooms tonight.'

Sextus acknowledged the order and tramped heavily to the door. Appetites were not keen, but the staff made a show of finishing dinner. Marcellus lingered at his table. At length, when he rose, they all stood in their places. He bowed and left the room, followed by Demetrius. As they passed the open door of the Commander's rooms, on their way to the quarters which had been assigned them earlier, it was observed that a dozen slaves were busily engaged in making the place ready for occupancy.

After a few minutes, the men came and transferred their various gear to the Commander's quarters. When they were alone, Marcellus sat down behind the big desk. Demetrius stood at attention before him.

'Well, Demetrius?' Marcellus raised his brows inquiringly. 'What is on your mind?'

Demetrius brought the shaft of his spear to his forehead in salute.

'I wish to say, sir, that I am much honored to be the slave of the Commander of Minoa.'

'Thanks, Demetrius,' smiled Marcellus, wearily. 'We will have to wait—and see—who commands Minoa. This is a tough outfit. The preliminary skirmish was satisfactory; but—making peace is always more difficult than making war.'

For the next few days the nerves of the legion were tense. The new Legate had demonstrated his determination to be in full authority, but it was by no means clear whether that authority would be maintained on any other terms than a relentless coercion.

Paulus had suffered a severe loss of prestige, but his influence was still to be reckoned with. He was obeying orders respectfully, but with such grim taciturnity that no one was able to guess what was going on in his mind. Whether he was not yet fully convalescent from the wounds dealt to his pride, or was sullenly deliberating some overt act of revenge, remained to be seen. Marcellus had formed no clear opinion about this. Demetrius planted his bunk directly inside the door, every night, and slept with his dagger in his hand.

After a week, the tension began to relax a little as the garrison became accustomed to the new discipline. Marcellus issued crisp orders and insisted upon absolute obedience; not the sluggish compliance that had been good enough for Gaza, but a prompt and vigorous response that marched with clipped steps and made no tarrying to ask foolish questions or offer lame excuses.

It had seemed wise to the new Commander to let his more personal relations with the staff develop naturally without too much cultivation. He showed no favoritism, preserved his official dignity, and in his dealings with his fellow officers wasted no words. He was just, considerate, and approachable; but very firm. Presently the whole organization was feeling the effect of the tighter regulations, but without apparent resentment. The men marched with a fresh vigor and seemed to take pride in keeping their equipment in order. The appearance and morale of the officers had vastly improved.

Every morning, Paulus, now second in command, came to the office of Marcellus for instructions. Not a word had passed between them, relative to their dramatic introduction. Their conversations were conducted with icy formality and the stiffest kind of official courtesy. Paulus, faultlessly dressed, would appear at the door and ask to see the Commander. The sentry would convey the request. The Commander would instruct the sentry to admit the Centurion. Paulus would enter and stand straight as an arrow before the official desk. Salutes would be exchanged.

'It is necessary to replace six camels, sir.'

'Why?' The query would snap like a bowstring.

'One is lame. Two are sick. Three are too old for service.'

'Replace them!'

'Yes, sir.'

Then Paulus would salute and stalk out. Sometimes Marcellus wondered whether this frosty relationship was to continue forever. He hoped not. He was getting lonesome in the remote altitude to which he had climbed for sake of maintaining discipline. Paulus was, he felt, an excellent fellow; embittered by this exile, and morally disintegrated by the boredom and futility of his desert life. Marcellus had resolved that if Paulus showed the slightest inclination to be friendly, he would meet the overture halfway; but not a step further. Nor would he take the initiative.

As for Sextus, Marcellus had very little direct contact with him, for Sextus received his orders through Paulus. The big, gruff fellow had been punctilious in his obedience, but very glum. At the mess-table he had nothing to say; ate his rations with a scowl, and asked to be excused.

One evening, after ten days had passed, Marcellus noticed that Sextus' chair was vacant.

'Where is he?' demanded the Commander, nodding toward the unoccupied place.

'Broke his leg, sir,' answered Paulus.

'When?'

'This afternoon, sir.'

'How?'

'Stockade gate fell on him, sir.'

Marcellus immediately rose and left the table. After a moment, Paulus followed and overtook him on the way to Sextus' quarters. They fell into step, and marched side by side with long strides.

'Bad break?'

'Clean break. Upper leg. Not much mangled.'

Sextus was stretched out on his back, beads of sweat on his forehead. He glanced up and made an awkward gesture of greeting.

'Much pain?' inquired Marcellus.

'No, sir.' Sextus gritted his teeth.

'Gallant liar!' snapped Marcellus. 'Typical Roman lie! You wouldn't admit you were in pain if you'd been chopped to mincemeat! That bunk is bad; sags like a hammock. We will find a better one. Have you had your dinner?'

Sextus shook his head; said he didn't want anything to eat.

'Well—we'll see about that!' said Marcellus, gruffly.

By inspection hour, next morning, the story had spread through the acres of brown tents that the new Commander—who had had them all on the jump and had strutted about through the camp with long legs and a dark frown—had gone to the kitchen of the officers' mess and had concocted a nourishing broth for old Sextus; had moved him to airier quarters; had supervised the making of a special bed for him.

That day Marcellus became the Commander of the fort at Minoa. That night Demetrius did not take his dagger to bed with him; he didn't even bother to lock the door.

* * * * * *

The next morning, Paulus pushed the sentry aside at the Commander's quarters and entered without more ceremony than a casual salute. Marcellus pointed to a vacant chair and Paulus accepted it.

'Hot day, Centurion Paulus,' remarked Marcellus.

'Gaza does not believe in pleasant weather, sir. The climate suits the temper of the people. It's either hot or cold.' Paulus tipped back his chair and thrust his thumbs under his belt. 'The Jews have an important festival, sir. They observe it for a week when the moon is full in the month they call Nisan. Perhaps you know about it.'

'No—never heard of it,' admitted Marcellus. 'Is it any of our business?'

'It's their annual Passover Week,' explained Paulus, 'celebrating their flight from Egypt.'

'What have they been doing down in Egypt?' asked Marcellus indifferently.

'Nothing—lately,' grinned Paulus. 'This happened fifteen centuries ago.'

'Oh—that! Do they still remember?'

'The Jews never forget anything, sir. Every year at this season, all the Jews who can possibly get there go to Jerusalem to "eat the Passover," as their saying is; but most of them are quite as much interested in family reunions, games, sports, auctions, and all manner of shows. Caravans of merchandise come from afar to market their wares. Thousands crowd the city and camp in the surrounding hills. It is a lively spectacle, sir.'

'You have been there, it seems.'

'On each of the eleven years since I was sent to this fort, sir,' nodded Paulus. 'The Procurator in Jerusalem—I think you know that his office outranks all of the other Palestinian establishments—expects detachments from the forts at Capernaum, Caesarea, Joppa, and Minoa to come and help keep order.'

'An unruly crowd, then?' surmised Marcellus.

'Not very, sir. But always, when that many Jews assemble, there is the usual talk of revolution. They wail sad chants and prattle about their lost heritage. So far as I know, this unrest has never amounted to anything more alarming than a few street brawls. But the Procurator thinks it is a good thing, on these occasions, to have a conspicuous display of Roman uniforms—and a bit of drill-work in the vicinity of the Temple.' Paulus chuckled, reminiscently.

'Do we get a formal notice?'

'No, sir. The Procurator does not trouble himself to send a courier. He takes it for granted that a detachment from Minoa will show up.'

'Very well, Paulus. How many men do we send, and when do they go?'

'A company, sir; a full hundred. It is a three-day journey. We should start the day after tomorrow.'

'You may arrange for it then, Paulus. Would you like to command the detachment, or have you had enough of it?'

'Enough of it! By no means, sir! This expedition is the only bright event of the year! And if I may venture to suggest, Tribune, you yourself might find this a most refreshing diversion.'

'On your recommendation, I shall go. What is the nature of the equipment?'

'It is not very burdensome, sir. Because it is a gala occasion, we carry our best uniforms. You will be proud of your command, I think; for it is a reward of merit here to be chosen for this duty, and the men are diligent in polishing their weapons. Otherwise we pack nothing but provisions for tenting and meals on the way. We are put up in commodious barracks in Jerusalem, and the food is of an uncommonly fine quality, furnished by certain rich men of the city.'

'What?' Marcellus screwed up his face in surprise. 'Do they not resent Roman rule in Jerusalem?'

Paulus laughed ironically.

'It is the common people who feel the weight of the Roman yoke, sir. As for the rich, many of whom collect the tribute for Tiberius—and keep a quarter of it for themselves—they are quite content. Oh—publicly, of course, the nabobs have to make a show of lamenting the loss of their kingdom; but these fat old merchants and money-lenders would be quite upset if a real revolution got started. You will find that the city fathers and the Procurator are thick as thieves, though they pretend to be at odds.'

'But this is amazing, Paulus! I had always supposed that the Jews were passionately patriotic, and uncompromising in their bitter hatred of the Empire.'

'That is quite true, sir, of the common people. Very zealous, indeed! They keep hoping for their old independence. Doubtless you have heard of their ancient myth about a Messiah.'

'No. What's a Messiah?'

'The Messiah is their deliverer, sir. According to their prophets, he will appear, one day, and organize the people to accomplish their freedom.'

'I never heard of it,' admitted Marcellus, indifferently. 'But small wonder. I haven't had much interest in religious superstitions.'

'Nor I!' protested Paulus. 'But one hears quite a little about this Messiah business during Passover Week.' He laughed at the recollection. 'Why, sir—you should see them! Sleek, paunchy old fellows, swathed from their whiskers to their sandals in voluminous black robes, stalking through the streets, with their heads thrown back and their eyes closed, beating their breasts and bleating about their lost kingdom and bellowing for their

Messiah! Pouf! They don't want any other kingdom than the one that stuffs their wallets and their bellies. They don't want a Messiah—and if they thought there was the slightest likelihood of a revolution against Roman domination they would be the first to stamp it out.'

'They must be a precious lot of hypocrites!' growled Marcellus.

'Yes, sir,' agreed Paulus, 'but they set a fine table!'

For a little while, the Tribune sat silently shaking his head in glum disgust.

'I know the world is full of rascality, Paulus, but this beats anything I ever heard of!'

'It is rather sickening, sir,' conceded Paulus. 'The sight that always makes me want to slip a knife under one of those pious arms upraised in prayer, is the long procession of the poor and sick and blind and crippled trailing along after one of these villainous old frauds, under the impression that their holy cause is in good hands.' He interrupted himself to lean over the arm of his chair for a better view of the doorway, and caught sight of Demetrius standing in the hall within sound of their voices. Marcellus' eyes followed.

'My Greek slave keeps his own counsel, Centurion,' he said, in a confidential tone. 'You need not fear that he will betray any private conversation.'

'What I was going to say, sir,' continued Paulus, lowering his voice—'this political situation in Jerusalem, revolting as it sounds, is not unusual.' He leaned halfway across the desk, and went on in a guarded whisper, 'Commander—that's what holds the Empire together! If it were not for the rich men in all of our subjugated provinces—men whose avarice is greater than their local patriotism—the Roman Empire would collapse!'

'Steady, Paulus!' warned Marcellus. 'That's a dangerous theory to expound! You might get into trouble—saying such things.'

Paulus stiffened with sudden wrath.

'Trouble!' he snarled, bitterly. 'I did get into trouble, sir, that way! I was fool enough to be honest in the presence of Germanicus! That'—he added, only half audibly—'was how I—a Legate—earned my passage to Minoa to become a Centurion! But—by the gods—what I said was true! The Roman Empire was consolidated, and is now supported, by the treachery of rich provincials, willing to sell out their own people! This strategy is not original with us, of course! Rome learned the trick from Alexander. He learned it from the Persians, who had learned it in Egypt. Buy up the big men of a little country—and—pouf!—you can have the rest of them for nothing!' Paulus' face was flushed with anger, and after his seditious speech he sat with clenched hands, flexing the muscles of his jaw. Then he faced

Marcellus squarely, and muttered: 'Valor of Rome! Bah! I spit on the valor of Rome! Valor of treachery! Valor of gold! Valor of hurling the poor at one another on the battle-field, while the big ones are off in a corner selling them out! The great and proud Roman Empire!' Paulus brought his fist down with a bang on the desk. 'I spit on the Roman Empire!'

'You are very indiscreet, Paulus,' said Marcellus, seriously. 'For remarks of that sort, you could have your pelt pulled off. I hope you do not often let yourself go like that.'

Paulus rose and hitched up his broad belt.

'I had no fear of speaking my mind to you, sir,' he said.

'What makes you think I wouldn't give you away?' asked Marcellus.

'Because'—replied Paulus, confidently—'you believe in real valor—the kind that demands courage!'

Marcellus drew an appreciative smile.

'It is a wonder, Paulus,' he said, thoughtfully, 'that the ordinary rank and file do not take things into their own hands.'

'Pouf! What can they do?' scoffed Paulus, with a shrug. 'They're nothing but sheep, with no shepherd! Take these Jews, for example: now and then, some fiery fellow goes howling mad over the raw injustice, and gets up on a cart, and lets out a few shrieks—but they dispose of him in a hurry!'

'Who shuts him up? The rich men?'

'Well—not directly. We're always called in to do the dirty work. It's obvious that Rome can't permit such uprisings; but it is the rich and greedy provincials who nip revolutions in the bud.'

'Damned scoundrels!' exclaimed Marcellus.

'Yes, sir,' assented Paulus, his gusty storm having blown out—'but you will find that these damned scoundrels in Jerusalem know good wine when they see it, and aren't mean about sharing it with the Roman legions. That'—he added, with cool mockery—'is to encourage us to be on the lookout for any foolhardy patriot who squeaks about the lost kingdom!'

Chapter IV

The first day's journey, from Gaza to Ascalon, was intolerably tedious, for the deep-rutted highway was crowded with creeping caravans and filthy with dust.

'It will be better tomorrow,' promised Melas, amused by the grotesque appearance of Demetrius who had rewound his turban about his face until only his eyes were visible.

'Let us hope so!' grumbled the Corinthian, tugging at the lead-donkey that was setting off toward a clump of thistles. 'But how will it be better? These snails are all crawling to Jerusalem; are they not?'

'Yes—but we leave the highway at Ascalon,' explained Melas, 'and take a shorter road through the hills. The caravans do not travel it. They're afraid of the Bedouins.'

'And we aren't?'

'We're too many for them. They wouldn't risk it.'

Centurion Paulus' stocky, bow-legged, red-headed Thracian was enjoying himself. Not often was Melas in a position to inform his betters; and, observing that the status of Demetrius was enviable compared to his own, it had made him quite expansive to be on such friendly terms with the new Legate's well-spoken slave.

'It isn't the camels that stir up the dust,' advised Melas, out of his long experience. 'Your camel lifts his big, padded paws and lays them down on top of the soft dirt. It's the asses that drag their feet. But I hate camels!'

'I am not very well acquainted with camels,' admitted Demetrius, willing to show some interest in his education.

'Nobody is,' declared Melas. 'You can live with a camel for years and treat him as your brother, but you can never trust him. See that?' He tapped a badly disfigured nose. 'I got that up in Gaul, a dozen years ago. The fleas and flies were driving my master's old Menepthah crazy. I spent the better part of two days rubbing olive oil into his mangy hide. And he stood like a rock, and purred like a cat; because he liked it. When I was all through, he turned around and kicked me in the face.'

Demetrius laughed, as was expected, and inquired what sort of revenge Melas had considered appropriate, a query that delighted him, for there was more of the story.

'I was so blind mad,' continued Melas, 'that I did the same thing to him—only Menepthah saw it coming and grabbed my foot. Ever have a camel bite you? Now—an ass,' he expounded, 'or a dog, will snap and nip and nibble at you; but if he is going to bite, he tells you. Your camel never lets you into the secret. When he bites, nobody knows what is in his mind— but himself. I was laid up for two weeks, the time Menepthah bit my foot. I don't like camels,' he added, reasonably enough, his new friend thought.

'They can't be blamed much for wanting to get even,' observed Demetrius. 'It's a pretty rough life, I suppose.'

Melas seemed to be weighing this bland comment on his not very sensitive scales as they trudged along, and presently gave Demetrius a long, appraising look out of the tail of his eye. His lip curled in a sour grin. At length he ventured to give his thoughts an airing; having a care, however, to keep them in leash.

'It doesn't do much good—trying to get even. Take your slave, now: he can't get anywhere that way. Camels and asses and slaves are better off minding their masters.' And when Demetrius did not comment, Melas added, encouragingly, 'Or—don't you think so?'

Demetrius nodded, without interest. He had no desire to discuss this matter.

'If you're going to serve another man, at all,' he remarked casually, 'it's only good sense to serve him well.'

'That's what I always say,' approved Melas, with such exaggerated innocence that Demetrius wondered whether the fellow was making a smug pretense of lily-white loyalty—or recklessly toying with a piece of crude irony. He thought it might be interesting to find out.

'Of course, slavery is a bit different from the employment of freedmen,' experimented Demetrius. 'If a freedman finds his work distasteful, he can leave it, which is ever so much better than keeping on at it—and shirking it. The slave does not have this choice.'

Melas chuckled a little.

'Some slaves,' he remarked, 'are like asses. They snap at their masters, and get slapped for it. They sit down and balk, and get themselves whipped and kicked. There's no sense in that. And then there are some slaves that behave like camels; just keep going on, and taking it, no matter how they're used'—Melas' tone was getting noticeably metallic, to match his heavy scowl—'and, one day—when the master is drunk, maybe—the poor beast pays him off.'

'And then what?' demanded Demetrius.

Melas shrugged, sullenly.

'Then he'd better run away,' he concluded. Presently he muttered an afterthought: 'Not much chance for a camel. Once in a while a slave gets away. Three years ago'—Melas lowered his voice, though there was no need of this precaution as they were far at the rear of the procession, and the furtive quality of the Thracian's tone hinted at a conspiratorial confidence. 'It was on this same trip—three years ago. Commander Vitelius' slave, as cheerful and obedient as anybody you ever met—Sevenus, by name—managed to lose himself the next to the last day in Jerusalem. Nobody knows what became of him.' Melas stepped nearer and muttered out of the corner of his mouth: 'Nobody but me. Sevenus left for Damascus. Wanted me to go along. Sometimes I've wished I had taken him up. It's easy enough. We're more or less on our own in Jerusalem. The officers have themselves a good time. Don't want the slaves hanging about. Bad for discipline.' Melas winked significantly. 'The Centurions like to play a little.'

Demetrius listened without comment to this lengthy speech; and Melas, a bit anxious, searched his eyes for advice as to the safety of proceeding farther.

'Of course, it's no secret,' he proclaimed, doffing his air of mystery. 'Everybody at Minoa knows about it—all but what I just told you.'

Demetrius knew he was making a mistake when he asked the question that implied a personal interest in this matter, but the story had stirred his curiosity.

'What made this fellow Sevenus think he had a chance of freedom in Damascus?'

Melas' eyes relighted.

'Why—Damascus is Syrian. Those people up there hate Rome like poison! The old city's full of Roman slaves, they say; living right out in the open, too; making no attempt to hide. Once you get there, you're safe as a bug in a donkey's ear.'

* * * * * *

Early next morning, their caravan broke camp and moved off through the bare hills over a winding road which narrowed frequently, in long ravines and deep wadies, to a mere bridlepath that raveled out yesterday's compact pilgrimage into a single thread.

It was a desolate country, practically uninhabited. Small herds of wild goats, almost indistinguishable from the jagged brown rocks on the treeless hillsides, grouped to stare an absurd defiance of any attempted trespass upon their domain. In the valleys, the spring rains had fraudulently invited an occasional tuft of vegetation to believe it had a chance of survival. Beside a blistered water-hole a brave little clump of violets drooped with thirst.

Demetrius was finding pleasure in this stage of the journey. The landscape was uninspiring, but it refreshed his spirit to be out in the open and at a comfortable distance from the uncouth Melas whose favorite topic had become disquieting. There was little doubt but the Thracian was building up toward a proposal of escape; either that, or was harboring an even more sinister design to engage him in a conspiracy and then expose him. Of course, this suspicion might be quite unfair to the fellow; but it would be dangerous to take any risks. No matter what he, himself, might say to Melas, on this touchy matter, it could easily become a weapon in the garrulous Thracian's hand, in the event he were to be miffed about something or made envious of the unusual privileges accorded to the Commander's more fortunate slave. Demetrius had resolved to be painstakingly prudent in any conversation with Melas, and—as much as possible—avoid being alone with him. Besides, there was much to think about, left over from a discussion between Marcellus and Paulus, last night; a most provocative—and highly amusing—survey of the gods, conducted by two men who had no piety at all. A good deal of it had been shockingly irreverent, but undeniably entertaining.

Late yesterday afternoon, when the company had halted near a spring—on city property, a mile northeast of Ascalon—Demetrius had been happy to receive a summons to attend his master, for he had begun to feel lonesome and degraded. He was amazed at the smart appearance of the camp. Almost by magic the brown tents had risen in four precise rows, the commissary had unpacked and set up its field equipment, chairs and tables and bunks had been unfolded and put in order. Banners were flying. Sentries were posted. The local Roman representative—a seedy, unprepossessing old fellow, with the bright pink nose of a seasoned winebibber, accompanied by three obsequious Jewish merchants—came out to read and present an illuminated scroll which eloquently (and untruthfully) certified to Ascalon's delight that the famed Legion of Minoa had deigned to accept the city's poor but cheerful hospitality. They had brought with them four huge wineskins bulging with the best of the native product, and were invited to remain for supper, after the Commander had formally replied—

with his staff ranged stiffly to the rear of him—that Minoa was fully as glad to be in Ascalon as Ascalon was to entertain Minoa, which his slave considered deliciously droll.

After the evening meal had been disposed of, and his immediate duties performed, Demetrius had stretched out on the ground in the shadow of the Commander's tent—a quite imposing tent, it was, larger than the others, trimmed with red flouncing, red silk curtains at the entrance, and a canopy over the doorway supported by slanting spear-shafts. With his fingers interlaced behind his head, Demetrius lay gazing up at the stars, marveling at their uncommon brightness, and effortlessly listening to the subdued voices of his master and Paulus, lounging in camp-chairs under the gaudy canopy. Apparently the visitation of the local dignitaries, who had now left for home, accounted for the conversation. Paulus was holding forth with the leisurely drawl of an amateur philosopher—benign, tolerant, and a little bit tight. Demetrius cocked an ear. Occasionally, in such circumstances, a man imprudently spoke his honest convictions about something; and, if Paulus had any convictions, it might be interesting to learn what they were.

'The Jews,' Paulus was saying, 'are a queer people. They admit it themselves; brag about it, in fact; no other people like them in the whole world. For one thing, they're under a special divine protection. Their god, Jehovah—they have only one, you know—isn't interested in anybody else but the Jews. Of course, there would be nothing positively immoral about that belief, if it weren't for the fact that their Jehovah created the world and all its inhabitants; but has no use for any of the other people; says the Jews are his children. Presumably the rest of the world can look out for itself. If they'd just admit that Jehovah was a sort of local deity—'

'Oh—but we do the same thing, Paulus; don't we?' rejoined Marcellus. 'Isn't Jupiter a sort of general superintendent of the universe, with unlimited jurisdiction?'

'Not at all; not at all, sir,' protested Paulus, lazily. 'Jupiter hasn't any interests in the Egyptians, but he doesn't claim he made them what they are, and then despised them for being no better. And he never said that the Syrians are a lousy lot, for not lighting bonfires on his feast-day. And Jupiter never said he was going to see that the Romans had the best of it—all the time.'

'Did Jehovah say that to the Jews?'

Demetrius laughed silently. He had suspected that Marcellus wasn't very well informed about the various religions, but his master's almost complete ignorance on the subject was ludicrous.

'Why—certainly!' Paulus was orating. 'Started them off in a garden where he had grown a fruit they were forbidden to eat. Of course they ate it, not to satisfy their hunger but their curiosity.'

'One would think Jehovah might have been delighted over their curiosity,' put in Marcellus, 'seeing that every good thing we have was discovered through someone's inquisitiveness.'

'Yes—but this made Jehovah angry,' explained Paulus, 'so he pitched them out into the desert, and let them get tricked into slavery. Then he told them how to escape, and turned them loose in a wilderness. Then he promised them a land of their own—'

'And this is it!' laughed Marcellus. 'What a promised land!'

'There isn't a more worthless strip of country in the world!' declared Paulus. 'And now the Jews have lost control of it. You'd think that after about fifteen hundred years of hard knocks, poverty, and slavery, these specially favored children of Jehovah would begin to wonder whether they might not be better off without so much divine attention.'

'Perhaps that accounts for this Messiah business that you spoke about, the other day. Maybe they've given up hope that Jehovah will take care of them, and think the Messiah might improve their fortunes when he comes. Do you suppose that's what they have in mind? It's not unreasonable. I daresay that's the way we and the Greeks accumulated so many gods, Paulus. When one god gets weary and impotent, another fresher god takes over. Didn't old Zeus retire once in favor of his son Apollo?'

'Not for long,' remembered Paulus. 'Apparently the weather hadn't been very good, so young Apollo decided he would manage the sun; and ran amuck with it. Old Zeus had to straighten out the tangle for the boy. Now—there's sense in a religion like that, Tribune. Our gods behave the way we do, naturally, because we made them the way we are. Everybody gets tired of the dictatorial old man, and eventually he gets tired too; decides to let his son run the business—whether it's growing gourds or managing the planets; but he never thinks the young fellow is competent, so he keeps on interfering until presently there is a row. That's why our religion is such a comfort to us,' Paulus continued, elaborately ironical.

'I'm afraid you're not very pious,' commented Marcellus. 'If the gods hear what you are saying, they may not like it. They might think you doubted their reality.'

'Not at all, sir! It's men like me who really believe in their reality. They're authentic—the gods! Some of them want war, some want peace, some of them don't know what they want—except an annual feast-day and a big parade. Some give you rest and sleep, some drive you insane. Some you are expected to admire, and some you are expected to hate, and all of them are never quite happy unless they are frightening you and assured that you are afraid. This is sensible. This is the way life is! . . . But these Jews! There they are, with only one god; and he is perpetually right, perpetually good, wise, loving. Of course he is stubborn, because they are stubborn; doesn't approve of pleasure, because they never learned how to play; never makes any mistakes, because the Jew never makes any mistakes. Tribune, Jehovah can't help being a pessimist. The Jews are a pessimistic people.'

'Maybe Jehovah thinks it is a good thing for his children to endure hardship,' speculated Marcellus; 'toughens their fiber, knocks off their surplus fat, keeps them in fighting trim. I believe he has a good idea there, Paulus. Sometimes I've thought that Rome would be better off if we patricians had to scratch for a living, and stole less from the neighbors.'

There was a considerable pause at this point in the sacrilegious discussion, and Demetrius had wondered whether they hadn't about exhausted themselves and their subject. But not quite.

'Rome will have that problem solved for her, one of these days,' Paulus was muttering, ominously. 'The scepter is passed around, Commander. Egypt has her day in the sunshine. Darius tramps about, scaring everybody for an hour or two. Alexander sobs because there's no one left to be subdued. The Caesars drive their chariots over Alexander's world; so drunk with power that they can't even bear to let these poor Hebrews own a few acres of weeds and snakes. . . . Ho-hum!'

Demetrius had yawned, too, and wished they would go to bed.

'But it will be somebody else's turn—soon,' said Paulus.

'When?' asked Marcellus, exactly as Demetrius thought he might.

'Well—if justice were served to crazy old Tiberius and his addled stepchild,' deliberated Paulus, 'I should think it might be someone else's turn tomorrow—or by the end of next week, at the latest. . . . How about a little more wine, Tribune?'

Demetrius had sat up, ready for the summons. It came instantly, and he presented himself.

'Fill Centurion Paulus' cup,' ordered Marcellus. 'No—none for me.'

And then Demetrius had gone back into the shadow of the tent to resume his waiting. The conversation had taken a queer turn now.

'Paulus,' his master was saying, 'you believe that the gods are manufactured by men. If it isn't an impertinent question—did you ever try to make one?'

Demetrius, sauntering today along through a narrow ravine, almost oblivious of the long procession single-filing on ahead, laughed as he recalled that extraordinary question and its absurd answer.

'No,' Paulus had replied, 'but it isn't too late. Shall I make one for you now?'

'By all means!' chuckled Marcellus. 'I assume that when you have him completed he will closely resemble yourself.'

'Well—not too closely; for this god I'm going to invent is good. He doesn't just pretend to be good. He really is good! He takes a few bright men into his confidence—not necessarily Romans or Greeks or Gauls; just so they're honest and intelligent—and entrusts them with some important tasks. He tells one man how to cure leprosy, and others how to restore sight to the blind and hearing to the deaf. He confides the secrets of light and fire; how to store up summer heat for use in winter; how to capture the light of day and save it to illumine the night; how to pour idle lakes onto arid land.' Paulus had paused, probably to take another drink.

'Very good, Centurion,' Marcellus had commented, thoughtfully. 'If you'll set up your god somewhere, and get him to producing these effects, he can have all my trade.'

'Perhaps you might like to assist in his creation, sir,' suggested Paulus, companionably.

Demetrius had not expected the quite serious speech that followed. As it proceeded, he raised up one elbow and listened intently.

'It occurs to me, Paulus,' Marcellus was saying, soberly, 'that this god of yours, who seems a very fine fellow indeed, might well consider a revision of the present plan for removing men from this world. What happens to us is something like this: a man spends his active life striving to accomplish a few useful deeds, and eventually arrives at the top of his powers; honored—we will say—and a good example to his community. Then he begins to go into a decline; loses his teeth and his hair; his step slows, his eyes grow dim, his hearing is dulled. This disintegration frets him, and he becomes gusty and irascible, like an old dog. Now he retires to a sunny corner of the garden with a woolen cap and a rug around his legs, and sits there in everybody's way until it is time for him to take to his bed with grievous aches and pains which twist him into revolting postures. When no dignity is left to him, nor any longer deserved, he opens his sunken mouth and snores for a few days, unaware of his inglorious end. Now—I think your new god should do something about this, Paulus.'

'We will take it up with him, sir,' promised Paulus, agreeably. 'How would you like to have the matter handled?'

Apparently this required a bit of concentration, for the reply was delayed a little while. When it came, Marcellus' tone had abandoned all trace of persiflage and was deeply sincere.

'When a Roman of our sort comes of age, Paulus, there is an impressive ceremony by which we are inducted into manhood. Doubtless you felt, as I did, that this was one of the high moments of life. Well do I remember—

the thrill of it abides with me still—how all of our relatives and friends assembled, that day, in the stately Forum Julium. My father made an address, welcoming me into Roman citizenship. It was as if I had never lived until that hour. I was so deeply stirred, Paulus, that my eyes swam with tears. And then good old Cornelius Capito made a speech, a very serious one, about Rome's right to my loyalty, my courage, and my strength. I knew that tough old Capito had a right to talk of such matters, and I was proud that he was there! They beckoned to me, and I stepped forward. Capito and my father put the white toga on me—and life had begun!'

There was an interval of silence here. Demetrius, much moved by this recital, had strained to hear above his own accented heartbeats, for the reminiscence had been spoken in a tone so low that it was almost as if Marcellus were talking to himself.

'Now—I think your god should ordain that at the crowning moment of a mature man's career; at the apex; when his strength has reached its zenith; when his best contribution has been made; let your god ordain that another assembly be held, with all present who know and revere this worthy man. And who among us would not strive to be worthy, with such a consummation in prospect? Let there be a great assembly of the people. Let there be an accounting of this man's deeds; and, if he has earned a lofty eulogy, let it be spoken with eloquence.'

'And then?' demanded Paulus. 'A valedictory, perhaps?'

'No,' Marcellus had decided, after a pause. 'Let the man keep silent. He will have no need to explain his deeds, if they were worth emulation. He will arise, and his peers will remove his toga; and it will be treasured; perhaps conferred upon another, some day, for courageous action. It would be a great responsibility to wear such a garment, Paulus.' There was another long pause.

'I think the god should prescribe that this event occur in the waning of a golden afternoon in springtime. There should be a great chorus, singing an elegiac ode. And while the triumphant music fills the air—with the vast assembly standing reverently—let the honored man march erectly and with firm step from the rostrum—and out—to face the sunset! Then—let him vanish! And be seen no more!'

After he had gone to bed, last night, and the camp was quiet, except for the footfalls and jangling side-arms of the sentries, Demetrius had pondered long and deeply over this strange conceit—the making of a better god!

This morning, as he marched through the barren hills, towing a file of stupid donkeys who had as much control over their destiny as had he over his own, Demetrius wondered what he might have said if they had invited him to add a desirable attribute to their imaginary deity. Doubtless the world would be a more comfortable place to live in if, as Paulus had suggested, some plan were arrived at for a better distribution of light and heat. And perhaps it would bring a man's days to a more dramatic conclusion if, as his master had so beautifully visioned, the human career might close with music and pageantry instead of a tedious glissade into helpless senility; though, as things stood, a man's lack of honor at the end of his life seemed quite compatible with his absurd plight at life's beginning. If Marcellus proposed to add dignity to a man's departure from the world, he should also pray for a more dignified arrival.

No—such idle speculations were a mere waste of opportunity if one had a chance to mend the world. There were other needs of far greater import. Surely, this amazingly honest deity whom Marcellus and Paulus had invoked would want to do something about the cruel injustice of men in their dealings, one with another. With hot indignation, Demetrius reconstructed the painful scene of that day when Roman ruffians forced the doors, and threw his beautiful mother aside as they stalked into his honored father's library to bind him and carry him away to his death.

This nobler god—if he had any interest in justice, at all—would appear, at such a tragic moment, and sternly declare, 'You can't *do* that!'

Demetrius repeated the words aloud—over and over—louder and louder—until the high-walled ravine believed in them, and said so.

'*You can't do that!*' he shouted, so loudly that Melas—far on ahead—turned to look back inquiringly.

* * * * * *

They had all but reached the end of their journey now. For the past hour their caravan had been plodding up a long hill. At its crest, a very impressive spectacle had confronted them. They were gazing down upon Jerusalem, whose turrets and domes were aglow with the smouldering fire of sunset.

'Gorgeous!' Marcellus had murmured.

All day, Demetrius had marched beside his master's tall camel, happy to be relieved of his unpleasant duties at the rear. Early in the forenoon, they had come to the junction of the lonesome valley road and a highway running up from Hebron. All along the thoroughfare were encampments of caravans, making no sign of preparation for travel.

'Is this not strange, Paulus?' Marcellus had inquired. 'Why aren't they on the road?'

'It's the Sabbath day, sir,' answered Paulus. 'Jews can't travel on the last day of the week. It's against their law.'

'Can't move at all, eh?'

'Oh—practically not. They may proceed a little way—what they call a Sabbath day's journey—two thousand cubits. Look, sir.' Paulus pointed down the road. 'Two thousand of their cubits would take them to that group of olive trees. That's as far as a Jew can go from his residence on the Sabbath.'

'Quite inconvenient,' observed Marcellus, idly.

'For the poor people—yes.' Paulus laughed. 'The rich, as usual, have their own way of circumventing the law.'

'How's that?'

'Well, sir; in their interpretation of this statute, any place where a man has a possession is considered his residence. If a rich man wants to visit somebody ten miles away, on the Sabbath, he sends his servants on ahead, a day earlier, and they deposit along the road—at two-thousand-cubit intervals—such trifling articles as an old sandal, a cracked pot, a worn-out rug, a scroll-spool; and thus prepare the way for their law-abiding lord.'

'Do you mean that—seriously?' inquired Marcellus.

'Yes—and so do they. I tell you, sir, these rich Jews will go to more bother about the external appearance of their religion than any people on earth. And they do it with straight faces, too. It is a great mistake to be playful with them about it. They've deceived themselves so long that they really think they're honest. Of course,' he added, wryly, 'the opulent Jew has no monopoly on self-deception. All our rich and influential men, whatever their race or country, are subject to this unhappy malady. It must be a tragic condition to possess great wealth and a sensitive conscience. I never thought much about this before,' he rambled on, 'but I doubt not the sophists could prove self-deception to rate high among the cardinal virtues. None but the noble would heap upon himself so much sham and shame in the cause of righteousness.'

'Paulus, you're a cynic—and an uncommonly bitter one,' drawled Marcellus. 'By the way—what must these people, along the roadside, think of our disregard of their holy Sabbath?'

'Pouf! They expect nothing better of us. And I'm not sure they'd like it if we laid up for the day in honor of their beliefs. In their opinion, we could defile their religion worse by recognizing it than by ignoring it. They don't want anything from us—not even our respect. They can't be blamed, of course,' Paulus added. 'No man should be asked to think highly of a master who has robbed him of his liberty.'

Demetrius had turned his face away, at that speech, pretending an interest in a tented caravan resting on a neighboring slope. He wondered whether his master thought this remark of the Centurion's was injudicious; wondered whether he wished his slave had not overheard it.

* * * * *

Early the next morning, the militia from Minoa broke camp and prepared to complete the journey into the city. Demetrius had been glad to see the sunrise. It was the first night, since he had been the slave of Marcellus, that he had slept beyond the sound of his master's call. After the encampment had been made, late yesterday afternoon, the Legate and four of the senior staff officers had decided to ride on into Jerusalem. None of the slaves, except the Syrian camel-boys, had been taken along. Demetrius, left to guard Marcellus' effects, had slept in the ornate tent alone.

Rousing at dawn, he had drawn the curtains aside, and was amazed at the tide of traffic already on the highway; processions of heavily laden camels, rhythmically lifting their haughty noses at every step; long trains of pack-asses, weighted with clumsy burdens; men, women, children, slaves—all carrying bundles and baskets and boxes of every shape and size. The pestilential dust rolled high.

With the speed and skill of long experience, the contingent from Minoa leveled their camp, rolled up the tents, packed the stores, and took to the road. Proudly the uniformed company marched down the highway, the pilgrims scurrying to the stone fences at the trumpet's strident command. But the pack-train did not fare so well. The laden asses from Minoa, not carrying banners or blowing trumpets or wearing the Roman uniform, were considered by the travelers as of no more importance than a similar number of pack-asses from anywhere else.

Melas, ever anxious to display large knowledge to the newcomer, seemed highly amused by Demetrius' efforts to keep his string of donkeys in hand. It was quite apparent that the unkempt Thracian was enjoying the Corinthian's dilemma. At a disadvantage in Demetrius' company, the odds were all in his favor now. He wasn't as cultured as the Legate's slave, but when it came to managing pack-asses in a dense crowd of uncivil travelers, Melas was in a position to offer counsel. He looked back and grinned patronizingly.

It was a peculiar crowd! In Rome, on a feast-day, there was plenty of rough jostling and all manner of rudeness. Arrogant charioteers thought nothing of driving their broad iron wheels over the bare feet of little children. People on foot treated one another with almost incredible discourtesy. One favorite method of making one's way through a crowd was to dive in with both hands full of mud and filth scooped up from the street. Few cared to debate the right of way with persons thus armed. No—Rome had won no prizes for the politeness of her gala-day multitudes. But in spite of her forthright brutality, Rome—on such occasions—was hilarious. Her crowds sang, cheered, laughed! They were mischievous, merciless, vulgar—but they were merry!

There was no laughter in this pilgrim throng that crowded the widening avenue today. This was a tense, impassioned, fanatical multitude; its voice a guttural murmur as if each man canted his own distresses, indifferent to the mumbled yearnings of his neighbors. On these strained faces was an expression of an almost terrifying earnestness and a quality of pietistic zeal that seemed ready to burst forth into wild hysteria; faces that fascinated Demetrius by the very ugliness of their unabashed contortions. Not for all the wealth of the world would he have so bared his private griefs and longings to the cool stare of the public. But apparently the Jews didn't care who read their minds. All this, thought the Corinthian, was what the sight of their holy city had done to their emotions.

Suddenly, for no reason at all that Demetrius could observe, there was a wave of excitement. It swept down over the sluggish swollen stream of zealots like a sharp breeze. Men all about him were breaking loose from their families, tossing their packs into the arms of their overburdened children, and racing forward toward some urgent attraction. Far up ahead the shouts were increasing in volume, spontaneously organizing into a concerted reiterated cry; a single, magic word that drove the multitude into a frenzy.

Unable to keep his footing in this onrushing tide, Demetrius dragged and pushed his stubborn charges to the roadside where Melas stood savagely battering his tangled donkeys over their heads with his heavy cudgel.

'Crack them on the nose!' yelled Melas.

'I have no club,' shouted Demetrius. 'You take them!'

Melas, pleased to have his competency appealed to, grasped the lead-strap to the other string of donkeys and began laying on the discipline with a practiced hand. While he was thus engaged, Demetrius set off after the hurrying crowd, forcing his way with the others until the congestion was too dense for further progress. Wedged tight against his arm, and grinning up into his face, was another Greek, older but smaller than himself; a slave, easily recognizable as such by the slit in his ear-lobe. Impudently the ill-scented little fellow bent about for a glimpse of Demetrius' ear; and, having assured himself of their social equality, laughed fraternally.

'Athens,' he announced, by way of introduction.

'Corinth,' returned Demetrius, crisply. 'Do you know what is going on?'

'They're yelling something about a king. That's all I can make of it.'

'Understand their language?'

'A little. Just what I've picked up on these trips. We come up every year with a load of spices.'

'You think they've got somebody up front who wants to be their king? Is that it?'

'Looks like it. They keep howling another word that I don't know—Messiah. The man's name, maybe.'

Demetrius impulsively turned about, thrust a shoulder into the steaming mass, and began pushing through to the side of the road, followed closely—to his distaste—by his diminutive countryman. All along the way, men were recklessly tearing branches from the palms that bordered the residential thoroughfare, indifferent to the violent protests of property-owners. Running swiftly among the half-crazed vandals, the Greeks arrived at the front of the procession and jammed their way into it.

Standing on tiptoe for an instant in the swaying crowd, Demetrius caught a fleeting glimpse of the obvious center of interest, a brown-haired, bareheaded, well-favored Jew. A tight little circle had been left open for the slow advance of the shaggy white donkey on which he rode. It instantly occurred to Demetrius that this coronation project was an impromptu affair for which no preparation had been made. Certainly there had been no effort to bedeck the pretender with any royal regalia. He was clad in a simple brown mantle with no decorations of any kind, and the handful of men—his intimate friends, no doubt—who tried to shield him from the pressure of the throng, wore the commonest sort of country garb.

The huzzas of the crowd were deafening. It was evident that these passionate zealots had all gone stark, raving mad! Paulus had drawn a very clear picture of the Jew's mood on these occasions of the holy festival commemorative of an ancient flight from bondage.

Again Demetrius, regaining his lost balance, stretched to full height for another look at the man who had somehow evoked all this wild adulation. It was difficult to believe that this was the sort of person who could be expected to inflame a mob into some audacious action. Instead of receiving the applause with an air of triumph—or even of satisfaction—the unresponsive man on the white donkey seemed sad about the whole affair. He looked as if he would gladly have had none of it.

'Can you see him?' called the little Athenian, who had stuck fast in the sticky-hot pack an arm's length away.

Demetrius nodded without turning his head.

'Old man?'

'No—not very,' answered Demetrius, candidly remote.

'What does he look like?' shouted the Athenian, impatiently.

Demetrius shook his head—and his hand, too—signaling that he couldn't be bothered now, especially with questions as hard to answer as this one.

'Look like a king?' yelled the little Greek, guffawing boisterously.

Demetrius did not reply. Tugging at his impounded garments, he crushed his way forward. The surging mass, pushing hard from the rear, now carried him on until he was borne almost into the very hub of the procession that edged along, step by step, keeping pace with the plodding donkey.

Conspicuous in the inner circle, as if they constituted the mysterious man's retinue, were the dozen or more who seemed stunned by the event that obviously had taken them by surprise. They too were shouting, erratically, but they wore puzzled faces, and appeared anxious that their honored friend would measure up a little more heroically to the demands of this great occasion.

It was quite clear now to Demetrius that the incident was accidental. It was quite understandable, in the light of Paulus' irreverent comments on the Passover celebration. All these proud, poverty-cursed, subjugated pilgrims, pressing toward their ancient shrine, would be on the alert for any movement that savored of revolt against their rapacious foe. It needed only the shout—'Messiah!'—and they would spring into action without pausing to ask questions. That explained it, believed Demetrius. In any case, whoever had started this wild pandemonium, it was apparent that it lacked the hero's approbation.

The face of the enigmatic Jew seemed weighted with an almost insupportable burden of anxiety. The eyes, narrowed as if in resigned acceptance of some inevitable catastrophe, stared straight ahead toward Jerusalem. Perhaps the man, intent upon larger responsibilities far removed from this pitiable little coronation farce, wasn't really hearing the racket at all.

So deeply absorbed had Demetrius become, in his wide-eyed study of the young Jew's face, that he too was beginning to be unmindful of the general clamor and confusion. He moved along with inching steps, slanting his body against the weight of the pressing crowd, so close now to the preoccupied rider that with one stride he could have touched him.

Now there was a temporary blocking of the way, and the noisy procession came to a complete stop. The man on the white donkey straightened, as if roused from a reverie, drew a deep sigh, and slowly turned his head. Demetrius watched, with parted lips and a pounding heart.

The meditative eyes, drifting about over the excited multitude, seemed to carry a sort of wistful compassion for these helpless victims of an aggression for which they thought he had a remedy. Everyone was shouting,

shouting—all but the Corinthian slave, whose throat was so dry he couldn't have shouted, who had no inclination to shout, who wished they would all be quiet, quiet! It wasn't the time or place for shouting. Quiet! This man wasn't the sort of person one shouted at, or shouted for. Quiet! That was what this moment called for—Quiet!

Gradually the brooding eyes moved over the crowd until they came to rest on the strained, bewildered face of Demetrius. Perhaps, he wondered, the man's gaze halted there because he alone—in all this welter of hysteria—refrained from shouting. His silence singled him out. The eyes calmly appraised Demetrius. They neither widened nor smiled; but, in some indefinable manner, they held Demetrius in a grip so firm it was almost a physical compulsion. The message they communicated was something other than sympathy, something more vital than friendly concern; a sort of stabilizing power that swept away all such negations as slavery, poverty, or any other afflicting circumstance. Demetrius was suffused with the glow of this curious kinship. Blind with sudden tears, he elbowed through the throng and reached the roadside. The uncouth Athenian, bursting with curiosity, inopportunely accosted him.

'See him—close up?' he asked.

Demetrius nodded; and, turning away, began to retrace his steps toward his abandoned duty.

'Crazy?' persisted the Athenian, trudging alongside.

'No.'

'King?'

'No,' muttered Demetrius, soberly—'not a king.'

'What is he, then?' demanded the Athenian, piqued by the Corinthian's aloofness.

'I don't know,' mumbled Demetrius, in a puzzled voice, 'but—he is something more important than a king.'

Chapter V

After the camp had been set up near the suburban village of Bethany, Marcellus and his staff continued down the long hill into the city. There was very little traffic on the streets, for the people were keeping the Sabbath.

Though Paulus had not exaggerated Jerusalem's provision for the representatives of her Roman Emperor, the young Legate of Minoa was not prepared for his first sight of the majestic Insula of the Procurator.

As they halted their weary camels at twilight before the imposing façade of Rome's provincial seat, Marcellus sat in speechless admiration. No one needed to inform a stranger that this massive structure was of foreign origin, for it fairly shouted that it had no relation whatever to its mean environment.

Apparently the architects, sculptors, and landscape artists had been advised that expense was the least of their problems. Seeing the Jews had it to pay for, explained Paulus, the Emperor had not been parsimonius, and when Herod—the first Procurator—had professed a grandiose ambition 'to rebuild this brick city in marble,' Augustus had told him to go as far as he liked.

'And you can see that he did,' added Paulus, with an inclusive gesture made as proudly as if he had done it himself.

True, Jerusalem wasn't all marble. The greater part of it was decidedly shabby, dirty, and in need of repair. But Herod the Great had rebuilt the Temple on a magnificent scale and then had erected this Insula on a commanding elevation far enough away from the holy precincts to avoid an unhappy competition.

It was a huge quadrangle stronghold, dominating the very heart of Jerusalem. Three spacious levels of finely wrought mosaic pavement, united by marble steps and balustrades with pedestals bearing the exquisitely sculptured busts of eminent Romans, terraced up from the avenue to the colonnaded portal of the Praetorium. On either side of the paved area sloped an exotic garden of flowers and ornamental shrubbery watered from marble basins in which lavish fountains played.

'These fountains,' said Paulus, in a discreet undertone, 'were an afterthought. They were installed only seven years ago, when Pilate came. And they caused an uprising that brought all the available troops to the new Procurator's rescue.'

'Were you in it, too, Paulus?' asked Marcellus.

'Indeed—yes! We were all here, and a merry time it was. The Jew has his little imperfections, but he is no coward. He whines when he trades, but he is no whimperer in battle. He hates war and will go to any length to preserve the peace; but—and this was something Pontius Pilate didn't know—there is a point where you'd better stop imposing on a Jew.'

'Well, go on then about the fountains,' urged Marcellus, for the sight of the water had made him impatient for a bath.

'Pilate's wife was responsible for it. They had been down in Crete for many years where Pontius had been the Prefect. You can grow anything in Crete, and the lady was dismayed to find herself in such an arid country as Judea. She begged for gardens. Gardens must have water. To have that much water there must be an aqueduct. Aqueducts are expensive. There was no appropriation to cover this item. So—the new Procurator helped himself to some funds from the Temple treasury, and—'

'And the battle was on,' surmised Marcellus.

'You have said it, sir,' declared Paulus, fervently. 'And it stayed on for seven exciting months. Pilate nearly lost his post. Two thousand Jews were killed, and nearly half that many Romans. It would have been better, I suppose, if Tiberius had transferred Pilate to another position. The Jews will never respect him; not if he stays here a thousand years. He makes every effort to humor them, remembering what they can do to him if they wish. He is here to keep the peace. And he knows that the next time there is a riot, his term of office will expire.'

'It's a wonder the Jews do not raise a general clamor for his removal,' speculated Marcellus.

'Ah—but they don't want him removed,' laughed Paulus. 'These rich and wily old merchants and money-lenders, who pay the bulk of the taxes and exercise a great deal of influence, know that Pilate is not in a position to dictate harsh terms to them. They hate him, of course, but they wouldn't like to see him go. I'll wager that if the Emperor appointed another man to the office of Procurator, the Sanhedrin would protest.'

'What's the Sanhedrin?' inquired Marcellus.

'The Jewish legislative body. It isn't supposed to deal with any matters except religious observances; but—well—when the Sanhedrin growls, Pontius Pilate listens!' Paulus shouted to the squatting camel-boys, and the apathetic beasts plodded on. 'But I do not wish to convey the idea, sir,' continued the Centurion, 'that Pilate is a nobody. He is in a very unfortunate predicament here. You will like him, I think. He is a genial fellow, and deserves a more comfortable Prefecture.'

They had moved on then, around the corner, to the section of the vast barracks assigned to the garrison from Minoa. Three sides of the great quadrangle had been equipped for the accommodation of troops, the local constabulary occupying less than a third of it. Now the entire structure was filled almost to capacity. The whole institution was alive. The immense parade-ground, bounded by the two-story stone buildings, was gay with the uniforms of the legions arriving from the subordinate Palestinian forts. The banners of Caesarea, Joppa, and Capernaum, topped by the imperial ensign, added bright color to the teeming courtyard.

Marcellus was delighted with the appointments of the suite into which he was shown. They compared favorably with the comforts to be had at the Tribunes' Club in Rome. It was the first time he had been entirely at ease since the night he had left home.

After a while Paulus came in to see if his young Commander had everything he wanted.

'I am writing some letters,' he said. '*The Vestris* should arrive at Joppa by tomorrow or next day, and will probably sail for home before the end of the week. You remember, sir, she was just coming into the harbor at Gaza as we passed through.'

'Thanks, Paulus, for reminding me,' said Marcellus. 'It is a good suggestion.'

* * * * * *

He had not written to Diana since the night of his departure on the galley to Ostia. That had been a difficult letter to compose. He was very deeply depressed. After several unsatisfactory attempts to tell her how sorry he was to leave her and with what impatience he would await their next meeting—in the face of his serious doubt that he should ever see her again—his letter had turned out to be a fond little note of farewell, containing neither fatuous promises nor grim forebodings. The lovely Diana would be cherished in his thoughts, he wrote, and she was not to worry about him.

Many times, on the long voyage to Gaza, he had begun letters that were never finished. There was so little to say. He would wait until there was something of interest to report. On the last day before making port, he had written a letter to his family, dry as the little ship's log, promising to do better next time.

The early days at Minoa had been eventful enough to furnish material for a letter, but his new duties had kept him occupied. Tonight he would write to Diana. He could tell her honestly that things were ever so much better than he had expected. He would explain how he happened to be in Jerusalem. He would tell her that he was handsomely quartered, and describe the appointments of the Insula. It would need no gilding. Marcellus' dignity, sadly battered by the punitive assignment to discredited Minoa, had been immeasurably restored. He was almost proud of his Roman citizenship. He could write Diana now with some self-confidence.

For two hours, under the light of the three large stone lamps bracketed on the wall beside his desk, he reviewed the important events of his life at Minoa. He didn't say how arid, how desolate, how altogether unlovely was the old fort and its environs; nor did he exhaust the details of his first day's experience there.

'The acting Commander,' he wrote, 'was a bit inclined to be surly, and did not overdo his hospitality when I arrived; but a little later he decided to co-operate, and we are now the best of friends. I quite like this Centurion Paulus. Indeed I hardly know what I should do without him, for he knows all the traditions of the fort; what things must be done, and the right time and way to do them.'

Marcellus was enjoying his work on the letter. It gave him a glow of pleasure to inform Diana of these things which now made up his life. It was almost as if they belonged to each other; almost as an absent husband might write to his wife.

The scroll, when he should paste the sheets of papyrus end to end, would be a bulky one. Before it quite outgrew its spindle-rims, he must bring it to a close with something from his heart. This was not quite so easy to do.

For a long time he sat deliberating what should be his proper attitude. Should he obey his feelings and tell Diana, without reserve, how much she had been in his thoughts, how dear she was to him, and how ardently he wished their separation was over? Would that be fair? Diana was young, so full of life. Was it right to encourage her in the hope that he might be coming home some day to claim her? Was it right to let Diana believe that he entertained that hope himself? Might it not be more honest to tell her frankly that there was no likelihood of his return for a long time; years, perhaps? Of course Diana already knew the circumstances. And he had casually mentioned of Paulus that he had been sent to Minoa eleven years ago; and had not been home since his appointment. She could draw her own dismaying conclusions. At length, Marcellus finished his letter almost to his satisfaction.

'You know, Diana, what things I would be saying to you if we were together. At the far distance which separates us—in miles, and who can tell how much of time?—it is enough to say that your happiness will always be mine. Whatever things make you sad, dear girl, sadden me also. A ship—*The Vestris*—is reported to be arriving at Joppa. She called at Gaza. I am impatient to return to the fort, for I may find a letter from you there. I fondly hope so. Demetrius will come in tomorrow morning and deliver this scroll to the Insula's courier who meets *The Vestris*. She sails soon. Would I were a passenger!'

* * * * * *

Demetrius had never been so restless. Of course, whenever he had paused to contemplate his hopeless position in the scheme of things, his life held out no promise. But gradually he had become inured to his fate. He was a slave, and nothing could be done about it. Comparing himself to a free man, his lot was wretched indeed; but when he contrasted the terms of his slavery with the cruel conditions imposed upon most of the people in bondage, he was fortunate.

In the house of Gallio, he had been treated with every consideration due a servant. And his life had become so inextricably related to the life of Marcellus that his freedom—even if it were offered him—might cost him more in companionship than it was worth in liberty of action. As for his deep affection for Lucia, it was, he knew, wholly unrequited. He couldn't have had Lucia, if he had been as free as a sea-gull. Such common-sense reflections as these had saved his mind and reconciled him to his destiny.

Now his bland little philosophy had ceased to comfort him. Not only was his small world in disarray, but the whole institution of human existence had become utterly futile, meaningless, empty, a mere mockery of something that had had sublime possibilities, perhaps, but had been thrown away; lost beyond recovery!

He had tried to analyze his topsy-turvy mind and find reasons for his heavy depression. For one thing, he was lonely. Marcellus had not willfully ignored him, since their arrival in Jerusalem, but it was apparent that slaves were not welcome in the officers' quarters except when actually on duty. When their service was performed, they were to clear out. Demetrius had not been accustomed to such treatment. He had been his master's shadow for so long that this new attitude of indifference was as painful as a physical wound.

Again and again, he said to himself that Marcellus probably felt unhappy too, and maybe deplored the necessity to exclude him from his friendship. Demetrius had been made to feel his slavery as he had never felt it before, not since the day that he had been sold to Senator Gallio.

But there was another cause of Demetrius' mental distress. It was the haunting memory of the beseeching eyes into which he had gazed momentarily on the road into the city. Afterward, he had sat for hours, in a brown study, trying to define those eyes, and had arrived at the conclusion that they were chiefly distinguished by their loneliness. It was so apparent that the little group of men, who had tried to keep the crowd from pressing too hard, were disappointed. Whatever it was that the noisy fanatics wanted him to do, it was the wrong thing. You could see that, at a glance. It was a wonder they couldn't see it themselves. Everybody there had urged him to lead a cause in which—it was so obvious!—he had no interest. He was a lonely man. The eyes hungered for an understanding friend. And the loneliness of this mysterious man had somehow communicated with the loneliness of Demetrius. It was a loneliness that plainly said, 'You could all do something about this unhappy world, if you would; but you won't.'

Three days had passed now, singularly alike in program. Melas had been almost too attentive in his capacity of uninvited guide to the sights of the city. It was inevitable that they should be thrown into each other's company. Their duties were light and briefly accomplished. As Melas had foreseen, you looked after your master at mealtime, polished his equipment, helped him into his complicated military harness in the morning and out of it at night. The rest of the time was yours.

Breakfast was served at dawn, after which the troops turned out on the parade-ground for routine inspection. Then a small detachment of each contingent returned to their respective barracks to be on call while the main bodies—commanded by junior officers and led by the larger, but no more splendidly accoutered, Legion of the Procurator—marched smartly into the street.

It was a stirring sight and Demetrius—his tasks completed for the morning—liked to watch the impressive parade as, four abreast, the gaily uniformed soldiers strutted around the corner, stood like statues while the colors were dipped before the proud portals of the Praetorium, and proceeded down the avenue to the Temple, passing in their march the quite pretentious marble residence of Caiaphas, the High Priest. Caiaphas did not rate a salute; neither did the Temple.

On two occasions, Demetrius, attended by Melas as voluntary commentator, trailed along at the rear of the procession. On an equivalent occasion in Rome, hundreds would have followed such a parade; but not here. Perhaps the people were too sullen, perhaps they hated Rome too much. Perhaps, again, they lacked the vitality to pick up their heels and keep pace with the long steps of the soldiers. Demetrius had seen plenty of rags and tatters and blind beggars and hopeless cripples, but never in such numbers or in such dire distress. His own native Corinth had its share of misery, but its wretchedness was on display mostly in the port area. Athens—he had been there once with his father and brothers when he was twelve—had plenty of poverty, but it also had beautiful parks and exquisite works of art. This Jerusalem—that called itself a holy city—was horrible; its streets crowded with disease and deformities and verminous mendicants. Other cities had their faults; hateful ones, too. But Jerusalem? Not much wonder the strange man on the white donkey had been lonely!

The return of the troops to the Insula was made by a circuitous route which bisected the center of the market district where hucksters and customers scrambled to give the legionaries plenty of room as they went striding arrogantly down the narrow street, their manner saying that Emperor Tiberius mustn't be detained even at the cost of a few trampled toes. If a recumbent camel, indifferent to the dignity of the Empire, remained seated in the middle of the road, Rome did not debate the right of way, but opened the formation and pretended that the sullen beast was an island. Occasionally a balky pack-ass was similarly deferred to by the armed forces of Tiberius. Everybody else sought the protection of doorways and alleys.

This rambling route included the Roman Consulates, a not very imposing group of official residences, where brief pauses were made to salute the imperial arms rather than the imperial representatives of Samaria, Decapolis, and Galilee.

'You watch them,' advised Melas, 'when they stop to salute Herod's house. It's funny.'

And it was funny. Herod, who handled Rome's diplomatic dealings with Galilee, which were reputed to be trivial and infrequent, had made himself very well-to-do, but the homage paid to his establishment was perfunctory enough to constitute a forthright insult.

'I've heard them say,' Melas had explained, 'that this Herod fellow would like to be the Procurator. That's why Pilate's Legion begins the salute with the thumb to the nose. Maybe that's orders: I don't know.'

Back at the parade-ground, the companies were dismissed for the day. By twos and threes the men swaggered down into the congested business zone, capitalizing the privileges of their resplendent garb and glittering weapons, rejoicing alike in the shy admiration of the olive-tinted girls and the candid hatred of the merchants whose wares they impudently pawed and pilfered.

In the afternoon, the majority of the troops strolled out to the small arena, south of the city, and watched the games—footraces, discus-hurling, javelin-throwing, wrestling—tame sports, but better than none. No gladiatorial combats were permitted, nor any other amusing bloodshed. Immediately outside of the arena but within its compound, every conceivable type of imposture flourished. Many of the mountebanks were from far distances. There were magicians from India, pygmies from Africa, Syrian fortune-tellers. Patently crooked gambling wheels and other games of chance beguiled many a hard-earned shekel. Innumerable booths dispensed lukewarm, sickeningly sweet beverages of doubtful origin, flyblown figs, and dirty confections.

To the Romans, accustomed at home to more exciting events on their festal days, the arena and its accessories had but little charm. To the country people, it was a stupendous show, especially for the younger ones. Most of their elders, mightily concerned with the sale of pottery, rugs, shawls, assorted homespun, sandals, saddles, bracelets, bangles, and ornamental trifles in leather, wood, and silver, remained downtown in the thick of serious trade.

As for Marcellus and his staff, and the ranking officers of the other garrisons, their chief diversion—aside from lounging in the baths—was gambling. After the first day, spent in making ceremonious calls upon the Procurator and the Consuls, and a bit of sight-seeing, the staff members idled in their sumptuous quarters.

There seemed to be an unlimited supply of wine, and it was apparent that the officers were making abundant use of it. On two occasions, Centurion Paulus had not appeared at the evening dinner, and many another place was vacant at the well-provided tables in the ornate mess-hall. Demetrius had been pleased to note that his master was exercising a little more discretion than some of the others, but it was evident that he too was relieving his boredom by the only available method. It was to be hoped that the week could be brought to an end without a row. The materials for quarrels were all at hand; the wine, the dice, the idleness. It had never taken very much liquor to make Marcellus reckless. Paulus, when drunk, was surly and sensitive. Demetrius had begun to count the hours until it would be time to take to the road. Minoa had its disadvantages, but it was a safer and more attractive place than Jerusalem.

He wished he could find out what had become of the man who didn't want to be king of this country. One day he had broached the subject to the Thracian; but Melas, who knew everything, knew nothing about this; had quite forgotten the little furor on the hill.

'The patrol probably scared him back to the country,' surmised Melas.

'Perhaps they put him in prison,' wondered Demetrius.

'He'd be lucky,' laughed Melas. 'Men who gather up big crowds around them are better off in jail, this week, than on the street.'

'Do you know where the prison is?' Demetrius had inquired, suddenly inspired with an idea.

Melas gave him a quizzical glance. No, he didn't know where the prison was and didn't want to know. Prisons were fine places to stay away from. Any man was a fool to visit a friend in prison. First thing you knew, they'd gobble you up, too. No, sir! Melas had had enough of prisons to last him the rest of his life.

One afternoon—it was their fourth day in Jerusalem—Demetrius went out alone over the road on which they had come into the city, and on up the long hill until he reached the place where he had seen the lonely man with the beseeching eyes. He easily recognized the spot: there were dusty and broken palm branches scattered along the roadside, poor shreds of a brief and doubtful glory.

Retracing his steps slowly to the brow of the hill, he turned aside into a public park where well-worn paths wound through a grove of ancient olive trees, gnarled and twisted as if they had shared with the hapless Jews a long, stubborn withstanding of persecution. He sat there in the shade for an hour looking down over Jersusalem. You'd think a city thirty-five centuries old would have a little more to show for its experience. For that matter, the whole world seemed incapable of learning anything useful. Jerusalem wanted her freedom. What would she do with freedom if she had it? Everybody in the world wanted more freedom; freedom to do and be what?

Suppose—it was inconceivable—but suppose the Jews contrived to drive the Romans out? Then what? Would they then leave off quarreling among themselves, and forget their old party differences, and work together for the good of their country? Would the rich landlords and money-lenders ease up on the poor? If they disposed of the Romans, would they feed the hungry and care for the sick and clean the streets? Why—they could do all that now, if they wished. The Romans wouldn't stop them. The Romans would be glad enough to see such improvements, for some of them had to live there too.

What was the nature of this bondage that Jerusalem so bitterly resented? That noisy pack of fanatics on the road, the other day, thought their trouble was with the Roman Government. If they could find a leader strong enough to free them from Rome, they would set up a kingdom of their own. That, they seemed to think, would make everything right. But would it? How would a revolution help the mass of the people? Once a new Government was in the saddle, a small group of greedy men would promptly impose upon the public. Maybe this lonely man from the country knew that. This tatterdemalion throng wanted him to be their king; wanted him to live at the Insula, instead of Pilate. Then the few, who had helped him into power, would begin to make themselves great. But Jerusalem would continue to be what she was now. A change of masters wouldn't help the people.

Demetrius rose and sauntered back to the main thoroughfare, surprised to see that so few travelers were on the road. It still lacked two hours of sunset. Something important must be going on to have drawn the traffic off the highway; yet the city seemed unusually quiet.

He walked slowly down the hill, his thoughtful mood persisting. What kind of government would solve the world's problems? As matters stood, all governments were rapacious. People everywhere endured their rulers until they had gained strength enough to throw them off and take on another load of tyranny. The real trouble wasn't located at the capital, but in the immediate neighborhood, in the tribe, in the family, in themselves. Demetrius wished he might talk with the lonely man from the country, and learn what he thought of government; how, in his opinion, a better freedom might be found.

It suddenly occurred to him that the impudent little Athenian might know what had become of the man who didn't want to be a king. He quickened his steps, resolved to make inquiries for a caravan with spices to sell.

Down in the city, nearly all of the usual activity had ceased. What had become of everybody? Even in the market area, there were very few traders about. Accosting a bearded old Greek, who was laboriously folding a bundle of rugs, Demetrius inquired what was up; where were the people? The tired old man shrugged and grinned, without making a reply. It was evident that he thought the young fellow was trying to be playful.

'Has anything happened?' persisted Demetrius, soberly.

The old man tied his bundle and sat on it, puffing from his exertion. Presently he regarded his fellow countryman with fresh interest.

'You trying to say,' he exclaimed, 'that you honestly don't know what's happening? My boy, this is the night of the Jewish Passover. All the Jews are in their houses. And those who haven't houses have crawled in somewhere under shelter.'

'For how long?'

'Until morning. Tomorrow they will be out early, for it is the last day of Passover Week, and there will be much business. But—where have you been, that you didn't know?'

Demetrius was amused at the old man's comments on his ignorance.

'I've never been here before,' he said. 'I know nothing about the Jews' customs. For the past two hours I've been out on the hill. There's an olive grove.'

'I know.' The old man nodded. 'They call it the Garden of Gethsemane. Not much there to see. Ever on Mars' Hill—in Athens?'

'Yes; beautiful!'

'These people can't make any statues. It's against their religion. Can't carve anything.'

'There's a lot of carving on the Temple,' said Demetrius.

'Yes—but they didn't do it.' The old man rose and shouldered his burden.

'I wonder if you know where I might find a caravan from Athens that deals in spices,' asked Demetrius.

'Oh, yes. You mean Popygos. He's down by the old tower. You passed his place when you came in from the hill. Popygos. Better keep your hand on your wallet.'

'Would he rob a fellow Greek?'

'Popygos would rob his grandmother.'

Demetrius grinned and bade the grizzled old merchant good-bye. He started toward the Insula. It was too late to go back looking for the spice caravan. He would find it tomorrow. People were very much alike, wherever you found them. The Jews hated their government. So did the Greeks. But a change of government wouldn't help. That wasn't the trouble. The trouble was that the people couldn't change each other or themselves. The rug merchant discredited the spice merchant. Popygos would rob his grandmother. But that wasn't Tiberius Caesar's fault. Tiberius was a bad Emperor, no doubt; but under any other government the grandmother of Popygos would be no more safe than she was now. The lonely man from the country probably knew that. He didn't want to be a king. No matter who was king, you'd better keep your hand on your wallet. The world was in serious need of something—but it wasn't something that a new king could furnish.

* * * * * *

Demetrius did not wait to watch the early morning inspection. As soon as he had finished serving his master's breakfast, he made off alone. Already the streets were crowded. You had to pick your way carefully through the market district or you might tramp on some reckless huckster sitting cross-legged on the narrow sidewalk surrounded by his pitiful little stock of merchandise; a few crude earthenware jugs, perhaps. Here sat a shapeless bundle of rags that turned out to be an old woman with three eggs and a melon for sale. The roadway was choked with pack-animals unloading into the little bazaars. Everywhere emaciated arms stretched out for a penny. Loathsome sores were unwrapped and put on display accompanied progressively by a wheedle, a whine, a hiss, and a curse. A hollow-chested old man with empty, fly-infested eye-sockets apathetically blew a plaintive squawk from a decrepit flageolet. Now the street narrowed into a dark, pestilential cavern that declined over a series of broad stone steps, slippery with refuse, swarming with beggars and mangy, half-starved dogs. According to Centurion Paulus, the Jews believed that they were created in the image of their god. Demetrius held his nose and hurried through this assortment of divine reproductions, having a care not to brush against them.

The caravan was not hard to find. Near the old tower, overlooking the little Kedron River, there was an open plaza where the road to the west began. A pungent aroma—distinctly refreshing after a trip through the market—guided Demetrius to his destination. A welcoming voice halted him.

'Ho, adelphos!' shouted the garrulous little Athenian. Demetrius was honestly glad to see him, though at any other time or place he wouldn't have liked to be hailed as brother by this intrusive fellow. They shook hands. 'I was hoping to see you again. My name is Zenos. I don't think I told you.'

'I am Demetrius. You have a pleasant location here.'

'Right! Plenty of room, and we see everything. You should have been here last night. Much excitement! They arrested this Nazarene, you know. Found him up there in the old park.'

'Nazarene? I hadn't heard. What had he done?' asked Demetrius, without interest.

'Why—you know! The man we saw on the white donkey, the other day.'

Demetrius came alive and pressed a flock of inquiries. Zenos was delighted to have so much information to dispense. Troops from the Insula had been on the lookout for this Jesus ever since Sunday noon. Last night they had captured him; brought him, and his little band of friends, back into the city.

'But what had he done?' demanded Demetrius, impatiently.

'Well—they arrested him for stirring up the people, and for wanting to be a king. Popygos says if they convict him of treason, it will go hard with him.'

'Treason! But that's nonsense!' exclaimed Demetrius, hotly. 'That man doesn't want to upset the Government; doesn't want to have anything to do with the Government; neither this Government nor any other. Treason? They're all crazy!'

'No—they're not crazy,' objected Zenos. 'The people who run the Temple have got to dispose of him somehow, or he'll ruin their business. Haven't you heard what he did over there—same day we saw him?'

'Not a word. What happened?'

'What happened! Plenty! You see—the Temple is where the people make sacrifices; buy animals and burn them; nasty mess, bad smell; but their god likes the idea. So—the loggia—or whatever they may call it—is crowded full of animals for sale. The people bring their money, and the money-changers—just inside the door—convert it into Temple money'—Zenos laughed heartily. 'And everybody says that these bankers make a fat thing of it, too.'

'Do you mean to say that they sell animals inside of that beautiful Temple?' asked Demetrius, incredulously.

'In an arcaded court done in marble!' declared Zenos, solemnly nodding his head. 'In a court with gorgeous tiled paving; walls and ceiling in the finest mosaic you ever saw; nothing nicer in Athens. And they have it full of calves and sheep and pigeons. You can imagine how it looks—but you can't imagine how it stinks! You've got to go there and smell it! Well—this Jesus came in from the country—away up in Galilee some place—and went into the Temple—and didn't like it; said it was not the place to sell animals. And he must have caught on to the thievery, too, for he made short work of the money-changers.'

'What?' doubted Demetrius.

Zenos laughed delightedly over his friend's bewilderment.

'Yes, sir! If you'll believe it—he didn't look like a man who would risk it— this Jesus picked up a whip and began slashing about'—Zenos elaborately cracked an imaginary whip a dozen times in swift succession. 'Just as if he owned the whole establishment! Crack! Zip! Lash! Crash! Slash!—and out they came. It was wonderful! Out galloped the calves and the priests and the sheep and the bankers and the air was full of pigeons and feathers. And Jesus upset the money-tables. It poured out over the floor—shekels and drachmas and denarii—big money, little money, good money, bad money; swarms of pilgrims down on their hands and knees fighting for it. Thrilling sight! I wouldn't have missed it!' Zenos glanced over his shoulder and muttered, 'Here comes the old man. He's sore today. His best customers are all busy attending to this Jesus.'

The door of the largest tent had been drawn aside and a paunchy old fellow with graying hair and beard had stepped out and was waddling toward them. It had been a long time since Demetrius had seen anyone so barbarously festooned with jewelry; heavy silver chains around his neck and depending to his middle, rings on his fingers, rings in his ears, bracelets, anklets. He paused to regard Demetrius with an appraising scowl.

'He's from Corinth.' Zenos pointed with his thumb. 'We got acquainted on the road.'

'I see you wear a Roman tunic,' observed Popygos, crossly.

'My master,' explained Demetrius, respectfully, 'commands the fort at Minoa.'

'It would have been well,' said Popygos, 'if the Roman guard had let the Jews settle their own quarrels today. Everybody in Jerusalem who has so much as two shekels to rub together is mixed up with the case of this man from Nazareth. Now that the Government is in it, the affair will go on all day. And tomorrow is the Jews' Sabbath.'

'And they can't do business on the Sabbath,' remarked Demetrius, for something to say.

Old Popygos stroked his whiskers reflectively.

'I have been making this trip for three-and-twenty years,' he said, 'and we have sold fewer goods this time than ever before. It gets worse and worse. Always some big squabble, Passover Week, to keep my best customers from coming for their cloves and cinnamon.' Popygos upended a reed basket and sat down, jingling. 'I can remember a time,' he went on, deliberately, 'when they didn't have so many rackets. Now you take this thing that happened down here at the Temple, last Sunday. A few years ago, they were quite peaceful. The country people came in to do the Passover business and a little trading. Always brought a dove in a cage, if they were very poor, or a lamb or a calf, if they could afford it. That was for the Temple. The priests burned the offering—or said they did. They must have, from the way it reeked down around there. Then these Temple people got a little smarter. A man from the country would bring a lamb and the priests would examine it and find a wart on its belly—or some small blemish. So that lamb wouldn't do. But they could take his damaged lamb and give him a good one for it, if he would pay a cash difference. Then the blemished lamb was ready to sell to the next customer.'

'Rather dirty trading,' commented Demetrius. 'Not much wonder this Nazarene objected.'

'Well—it won't do any good,' drawled Popygos. 'At least, it hasn't done him any good.'

'What will they do to him?' wondered Demetrius. 'Put him in prison?'

'Hardly! I understand they took him last night to the High Priest's house and tried him for making a disturbance in the Temple. Defiling the Temple—that was what they charged him with.' Popygos broke into bitter laughter. 'As if anybody could defile a Temple that had been turned into a stable. Of course they had enough people on their side to convict him, so they all rushed over to the Insula and got Pilate out of bed to hear the case. He told them that they had better settle it among themselves, if it was just another Temple brawl. But the rich old fellows wouldn't let the Procurator off so easily as that. They said this Jesus was trying to make himself a king. Pilate didn't take any stock in that, of course. So he suggested that they whip him and let him go.'

'And did they whip him?' asked Demetrius, anxiously.

'That they did! And quite heavily, too. Then somebody in the crowd yelled, "Kill the Galilean!" Pilate pricked up his ears, at that. "If this man is a Galilean," he said, "try him before Herod. He handles all Galilean matters." '

'Did they take him there?' asked Demetrius.

'Took him there,' nodded Popygos, 'and Herod had a good time tormenting him, thinking that would please the Temple crowd and the fat money-lenders. He had the soldiers whip Jesus again; then dressed him in some old scarlet regalia, and pretended to do homage to him. Some drunken lout rolled up a thornbush and put it on his head for a crown. But the money-bags were not satisfied with the show. They wanted this Jesus put to death—'

'To death!' shouted Demetrius.

'Yes. And they knew that nobody could give that order but Pilate. So—they all went back to the Insula.'

'And then what happened?' demanded Demetrius.

Popygos shook his head and twitched a shoulder.

"That's all I know,' he said. 'Diophanos the goldsmith, who was there and told me this, had to come back to his bazaar.'

'Perhaps the trial is still going on at the Insula,' said Demetrius, restlessly.

'You'd better keep away from there,' warned Popygos. 'No good comes from mixing into business like that.'

'But my master may need me,' said Demetrius. 'I must go. I hope you have a safe journey home, sir. Good-bye, Zenos.'

* * * * * *

While still some distance away, Demetrius, who had quickened his pace until he was almost running, saw a compact crowd gathered about the main entrance to the Praetorium. He hurried up the steps and stood at the edge of the tensely occupied audience, receiving dark glances from his well-dressed Jewish neighbors as he appeared beside them. There were no poor people present.

The Procurator was standing within the colonnade, surrounded by a detachment of palace guards. On the highest level of the terraced flagging, a company of troops, four ranks deep, stood stiffly at attention. In front of them, standing alone, was the captive. Questions were being asked and answered in a language Demetrius could not understand. He concluded it was Aramaic, for that was the tongue spoken by the tempestuous crowd on the road. He left his place and edged around until he was at the extreme right. Now he could see the profile of the lonely man. Yes—he was wearing the crown of thorns that Popygos had reported. The blood had run down from his forehead until his face was streaked with it. His hands were tied. His coat had been pulled back off his bare shoulders, showing livid whip-welts. Some of them were bleeding. But he seemed not to be conscious of his injuries. The Procurator's interrogations—whatever they were—proceeded quietly, the prisoner, with uplifted face, as quietly answering them in a respectful but self-confident tone. Occasionally a low dissenting mutter ran through the sullen crowd that stood with eyes squinted and mouths open to hear the testimony.

So intently had Demetrius been watching the victim's face that he had barely glanced about. It now occurred to him to look for Marcellus. The front rank was composed of officers representing the various forts. Paulus was among them, resolutely erect, but swaying rhythmically. Immediately behind him stood a single line of troops from Minoa. Marcellus was not to be seen.

Now the Procurator was speaking in a louder voice. It brought an instant, concerted, angry roar from the civilian audience. Demetrius maneuvered to a position where he could get a better view of the judge. Now he saw Marcellus, standing with the other Legates at the immediate left of the Procurator. He wondered whether his master really knew what was going on. Unless someone was at hand to act as interpreter, Marcellus probably had no notion what all this was about. Demetrius knew the exact meaning of the slightest expression on his master's face. At the moment, it conveyed a good deal of bewilderment, and about the same amount of boredom. It was evident that Marcellus wished he were somewhere else.

Procurator Pilate seemed quite confused. The hostile attitude of his influential audience had rattled him. He turned aside and gave an order to one of the guards, who retired within the wide doorway. Presently he was back with a huge silver basin. Pilate dipped his hands in it, and flicked water from his fingers. The crowd roared again, but this time it was a cry of vengeful triumph. It was clear that a decision had been made; equally apparent that the decision had satisfied the prosecution. Now Demetrius understood what was meant by the pantomime with the basin. Pilate was washing his hands of the case. The people were to have their way, but they were to consider themselves responsible for the judgment. As for the Procurator, he didn't care to have the prisoner's blood on his hands. Demetrius felt that his master would undoubtedly understand. Even if he knew nothing about the case, he would know that Pilate had made a decision against his own inclinations.

Now Pilate had turned to Marcellus, who had stepped forward saluting. There was a brief, inaudible colloquy. Marcellus bowed in acknowledgment of an order, saluted again; and, descending the steps, approached Paulus and gave him some instructions. Paulus barked a command, and the Minoa contingent advanced, formed a line by twos, and executed a smart right-about. Led by Marcellus, with Paulus to the immediate rear of him, the troops marched through the crowd that opened a passage for them. One soldier of the final pair paused to grasp the dangling rope that bound the condemned man's hands. It was a rough and apparently unanticipated jerk, for it nearly drew the prisoner off his feet. The legionaries were marching with long strides.

Not many of the crowd fell in behind the procession. Most of them coagulated into muttering little groups, wagging their beards in sour satisfaction. Demetrius wondered what was to be the fate of this Jesus. He had received the death penalty; no question about that. Nothing less would have appeased the people. He would probably be taken to the courtyard of some prison to face a detachment of archers. On the other side of the street, a small company of pale-faced, poorly dressed, badly frightened men from the country seemed trying to decide whether to follow. After a moment, a few of them did; but they were in no hurry to catch up. These people were undoubtedly Jesus' friends. It was a pity, Demetrius thought, that they had shown up so meanly. The man surely deserved a more loyal support.

Undecided whether to trail along after the procession or wait at the barracks for his master's return, Demetrius stood for some time irresolute. Presently Melas joined him, grinning feebly.

'What are they going to do with him?' inquired Demetrius, unsteadily.

'Crucify him,' said Melas.

'Crucify him!' Demetrius' voice was husky. 'Why—he hasn't done anything to deserve a death like that!'

'Maybe not,' agreed Melas, 'but that's the order. My guess is that the Procurator didn't want to have it done, and thinks it may stir up some trouble for him. That's why he gave Minoa the job; didn't want his own legion mixed up in it. Minoa's pretty far away, and a tough outfit.' Melas chuckled. He was glad to belong to a tough outfit. Minoa didn't mind a little brutality.

'Are you going along?' asked Demetrius.

Melas scowled and shook his head.

'No—nothing for me to do there. Had you thought of going? It's not a very pretty business: I can tell you that! I saw it done—once—over in Gaul. Soldier stabbed his Centurion. They nailed him up for that. It took all day. You could hear him cry for half a league. The big black birds came before he died and—'

Demetrius shook his head, made an overhand protest, and swallowed convulsively. Melas grinned and spat awkwardly. Then he turned and started ambling slowly back toward the barracks, leaving Demetrius standing there debating with himself what to do.

After a while he moved along woodenly after Melas. Reaching his master's silent and empty quarters, he sat down and tried to compose himself. His heart was beating so hard it made his head ache.

Then he rose and found a drink of water. It occurred to him that Marcellus too might want a drink before this dreadful business was over. He filled a small jug, and started; walking slowly, for he didn't want to go.

Ever since he had looked into this Jesus' eyes, Demetrius had thought of him as the lonely man whom nobody understood; not even his close friends. Today he would be a lonely man indeed.

Pontius Pilate's Banquet

Demetrius slowly bowed his head and handed Marcellus the Robe; then stood with slumped shoulders while his master tugged it on over the sleeves of his toga. A gale of appreciative laughter went up, and there was tumultuous applause.

From page 107 of text

Chapter VI

One of the Insula's ten companies was absent from inspection. Marcellus noticed the diminished strength of the Procurator's Legion, but thought little of it. Whatever might be the nature of the business that had called out these troops so early in the day, it was of no concern to Minoa.

But when Julian, the Capernaum Commander who was taking his turn as officer of the day, glumly announced that the customary parade was canceled and that all the legionaries would return to their barracks to await further orders, Marcellus' curiosity was stirred. Returning to his quarters, he sent for Paulus, confident that this ever-active fountain of gossip could explain the mystery.

After a considerable delay, the Centurion drifted in unsteadily with flushed cheeks and bloodshot eyes. His Commander regarded him with unconcealed distaste and pointed to a chair into which the dazed and untidy Paulus eased himself gently.

'Do you know what's up?' inquired Marcellus.

'The Procurator,' mumbled Paulus, 'has had a bad night.'

'So have you, from all appearances,' observed Marcellus, frostily. 'What has been going on—if it isn't a secret?'

'Pilate is in trouble.' Paulus' tongue was clumsy, and he chewed out his words slowly. 'He is in trouble with everybody. He is even in trouble with good old Julian, who says that if the man is a Galilean, Capernaum should have been detailed to police the trial at Herod's court.'

'Would you be good enough to tell me what you are talking about?' rasped Marcellus. 'What man? What trial? Begin at the beginning, and pretend I don't know anything about it.'

Paulus yawned prodigiously, scrubbed his watery eyes with shaky fingers, and began to spin a long, involved yarn about last night's experiences. An imprudent carpenter from somewhere up in Galilee had been tried for disturbing the peace and exciting the people to revolt. A few days ago, he had become violent in the Temple, chasing the sacrificial animals out into the street, upsetting the money-tills, and loudly condemning the holy place as a den of robbers. 'A true statement, no doubt,' commented Paulus, 'but not very polite.'

'The fellow must be crazy,' remarked Marcellus.

Paulus pursed his swollen lips judicially and shook his head.

'Something peculiar about this man,' he muttered. 'They arrested him last night. They've had him up before old Annas, who used to be the High Priest; and Caiaphas, the present High Priest; and Pilate—and Herod—and—'

'You seem to know a lot about it,' broke in Marcellus.

Paulus grinned sheepishly.

'A few of us were seeing the holy city by moonlight,' he confessed. 'Shortly after midnight we ran into this mob and tagged along. It was the only entertainment to be had. We were a bit tight, sir, if you'll believe it.'

'I believe it,' said Marcellus. 'Go on, please, with whatever you can remember.'

'Well—we went to the trials. As I have said, we were not in prime condition to understand what was going on, and most of the testimony was shrieked in Aramaic. But it was clear enough that the Temple crowd and the merchants were trying to have the man put to death.'

'For what happened at the Temple?'

'Yes—for that, and for going about through the country gathering up big crowds to hear him talk.'

'About what?'

'A new religion. I was talking with one of Pilate's legionaries who understands the language. He said this Jesus was urging the country people to adopt a religion that doesn't have much to do with the Temple. Some of the testimony was rubbish. One fellow swore the Galilean had said that if the Temple were torn down he could put it up again in three days. Stuff like that! Of course, all they want is a conviction. Any sort of testimony is good enough.'

'Where does the matter stand now?' asked Marcellus.

'I got a plenty of it at Herod's court, and came back before daybreak; dead on my feet. They had just decided to have another trial before Pilate, directly after breakfast. They are probably at the Insula now. Pilate will have to give them what they want—and'—Paulus hesitated, and then continued grimly—'what they want is a crucifixion. I heard them talking about it.'

'Shall we go over?' queried Marcellus.

'I've had enough, sir, if you'll excuse me.' Paulus rose with an effort and ambled uncertainly across the room. In the doorway he confronted a sentinel, garbed in the Insula uniform, who saluted stiffly.

'The Procurator's compliments,' he barked, in a metallic tone. 'The ranking officers and a detachment of twenty men from the Minoa Legion will attend immediately in the Procurator's court.' With another ceremonious salute, he backed out and strutted down the corridor without waiting for a reply.

'I wonder what Pilate wants of us,' reflected Marcellus, uneasily, searching the Centurion's apprehensive eyes.

'I think I can guess,' growled Paulus. 'Pilate doesn't confer honors on Minoa. He's going to detail us to do something too dirty and dangerous for the local troops; doesn't want his precious legion mixed up in it. The Minoa contingent will be leaving tomorrow. If any trouble results, we will be out of reach.' He hitched up his belt and left the room. Marcellus stood irresolute for a moment and followed, intending to ask Paulus to order out the detachment. Through the half-open door to the Centurion's quarters, he saw him greedily gulping from an enormous cup. He strode angrily into the room.

'If I were you, Paulus,' he said, sternly, 'I shouldn't drink any more at present. You've already had much too much!'

'If I were you,' retorted Paulus, recklessly, 'I would take as much of this as I could hold!' He took a couple of uncertain steps toward Marcellus, and faced him with brazen audacity. 'You're going to crucify a man today!' he muttered. 'Ever see that done?'

'No.' Marcellus shook his head. 'I don't even know how it is done. You'll have to tell me.'

Paulus carefully picked his way back to the table where the grotesquely shaped wineskin sat. Refilling the big cup, he handed it, dripping, to his Commander.

'I'll show you—when we get there,' he said, huskily. 'Drink that! All of it! If you don't, you'll wish you had. What we're going to do is not a job for a sober man.'

Marcellus, unprotesting, took the cup and drank.

'It isn't just that the thing is sickeningly cruel,' continued Paulus. 'There's something strange about this man. I'd rather not have anything to do with it!'

'Afraid he'll haunt you?' Marcellus paused at the middle of the cup, and drew an unconvincing grin.

'Well—you wait—and see what you think!' murmured Paulus, wagging his head mysteriously. 'The witnesses said he acted, at the Temple, as if it were his own personal property. And that didn't sound as silly as you might think, sir. At old man Annas' house, I'm bound if he didn't act as if he owned the place. At Caiaphas' palace, everybody was on trial—but this Jesus! He was the only cool man in the crowd at the Insula. He owns that, too. Pilate felt it, I think. One of the witnesses testified that Jesus had professed to be a king. Pilate leaned forward, looked him squarely in the face, and said, "Are you?" Mind, sir, Pilate didn't ask him, "Did you say you were a king?" He said, "Are you?" And he wasn't trying to be sarcastic, either.'

'But that's nonsense, Paulus! Your wine-soaked imagination was playing tricks on you!' Marcellus walked across the table and poured himself another cupful. 'You get out the troops,' he ordered, resolutely. 'I hope you'll be able to stand straight, over at the Insula. You're definitely drunk, you know.' He took another long drink, and wiped his mouth on the back of his hand. 'So—what did the Galilean say to that—when Pilate asked him if he was king?'

'Said he had a kingdom—but not in the world,' muttered Paulus, with a vague, upward-spiraling gesture.

'You're worse than drunk,' accused Marcellus, disgustedly. 'You're losing your mind. I think you'd better go to bed. I'll report you sick.'

'No—I'm not going to leave you in the lurch, Marcellus.' It was the first time Paulus had ever addressed the Commander by his given name.

'You're goo-fellow, Paulus,' declared Marcellus, giving him his hand. He retraced his way to the wineskin. Paulus followed and took the cup from his hand.

'You have had just the right amount, sir,' he advised. 'I suggest that you go now. Pilate will not like it if we are tardy. He has endured about all the annoyance he can take, for one morning's dose. I shall order out the detachment, and meet you over there.'

* * * * * *

With a purposely belated start, and after experiencing much difficulty in learning the way to the place of execution—an outlying field where the city's refuse was burned—Demetrius did not expect to arrive in time to witness the initial phase of the crucifixion.

Tardy as he was, he proceeded with reluctant steps; very low in spirit, weighted with a dejection he had not known since the day of his enslavement. The years had healed the chain-scars on his wrists: fair treatment at the hands of the Gallio family had done much to mend his heart: but today it seemed that the world was totally unfit for a civilized man to live in. Every human institution was loaded with lies. The courts were corrupt.

Justice was not to be had. All rulers, big and little, were purchasable. Even the temples were full of deceit. You could call the roll of all the supposed reliances that laid claim to the people's respect and reverence, and there wasn't one of them that hadn't earned the bitter contempt of decent men!

Though accustomed to walk with long strides and clipped steps, Demetrius slogged along through the dirty streets with the shambling gait of a hopeless, faithless, worthless vagabond. At times his scornful thoughts almost became articulate as he passionately reviled every tribunal and judiciary, every crown and consistory in the whole, wide, wicked world. Patriotism! How the poets and minstrels loved to babble about the high honor of shedding one's blood. Maybe they, too, had been bought up. Old Horace: maybe Augustus had just sent him a new coat and a cask of wine when he was inspired to write, 'How sweet and glorious to die for one's country!' Nonsense! Why should any sane man think it pleasant or noble to give up his life to save the world? It wasn't fit to live in; much less die for! And it was never going to be any better. Here was this foolhardy Galilean, so thoroughly enraged over the pollution of a holy place that he had impulsively made an ineffective little gesture of protest. Doubtless nineteen out of every twenty men in this barren, beaten, beggared land would inwardly applaud this poor man's reckless courage; but, when it came to the test, these downtrodden, poverty-cursed nobodies would let this Jesus stand alone—without one friend—before the official representatives of a crooked Temple and a crooked Empire.

Loyalty? Why should any man bother himself to be loyal? Let him go out on his own, and protect himself the best he can. Why should you spend your life following at the heels of a Roman master, who alternately confided in you and humiliated you? What had you to lose, in self-respect, by abandoning this aristocrat? It wasn't hard to make one's way to Damascus.

It was a dark day for Demetrius. Even the sky was overcast with leaden, sullen clouds. The sun had shone brightly at dawn. For the past half-hour, an almost sinister gloom had been thickening.

As he neared the disreputable field, identifiable for some distance by the noisome smoke that drifted from its smouldering corruptions, he met many men walking rapidly back to the city. Most of them were well-fed, well-dressed, pompous, preoccupied; men of middle age or older, strutting along in single file, as if each had come alone. These people, surmised Demetrius, were responsible for the day's crime. It relieved him to feel that the worst of it was over. They had seen the public assassination to a successful conclusion, and were now free to return to their banks and bazaars. Some, doubtless, would go to the Temple and say their prayers.

After the last straggling group of mud hovels had been passed, the loathsome, garbage-littered field lay before him. He was amazed to see how much pollution had been conveyed to this place, for the city's streets had not shown so huge a loss of filth. A fairly clean, narrow path led toward a little knoll that seemed to have been protected. Demetrius stopped—and looked. On the green knoll, three tall crosses stood in a row. Perhaps it had been decided, as an after-thought, to execute a couple of the Galilean's friends. Could it be possible that two among them, crazed by their leader's impending torture, had attempted to defend him? Hardly: they didn't have it in them: not the ones he had seen that day on the road: not the ones he had seen, this morning.

Forcing his unwilling feet, he advanced slowly to within less than a stadium of the gruesome scene. There he came to a stop. The two unidentified men were writhing on their crosses. The lonely man on the central cross was still as a statue. His head hung forward. Perhaps he was dead, or at least unconscious. Demetrius hoped so.

For a long time he stood there, contemplating this tragic sight. The hot anger that had almost suffocated him was measurably cooled now. The lonely man had thrown his life away. There was nothing to show for his audacious courage. The Temple would continue to cheat the country people who came in to offer a lamb. Herod would continue to bully and whip the poor if they inconvenienced the rich. Caiaphas would continue to condemn the blasphemies of men who didn't want the gods fetched to market. Pilate would deal out injustice—and wash his dirty hands in a silver bowl. This lonely man had paid a high price for his brief and fruitless war on wickedness. But—he had spoken: he had acted. By tomorrow, nobody would remember that he had risked everything—and lost his life—in the cause of honesty. But—perhaps a man was better off dead than in a world where such an event as this could happen. Demetrius felt very lonely too.

There was not as large a crowd as he had expected to see. There was no disorder, probably because the legionaires were scattered about among the people. It was apparent, from the negligence of the soldiers' posture, as they stood leaning on their lances, that no rioting had occurred or was anticipated.

Demetrius moved closer in and joined the outer rim of spectators. Not many of the well-to-do, who had been conspicuous at the Insula, were present. Most of the civilians were poorly dressed. Many of them were weeping. There were several women, heavily veiled and huddled in little groups, in attitudes of silent, hopeless grief. A large circle had been left unoccupied below the crosses.

Edging his way slowly forward, occasionally rising on tiptoe to search for his master, Demetrius paused beside one of the legionaries who, recognizing him with a brief nod, replied to his low-voiced inquiry. The Commander and several other officers were on the other side of the knoll, at the rear of the crosses, he said.

'I brought him some water,' explained Demetrius, holding up the jug. The soldier showed how many of his teeth were missing.

'That's good,' he said. 'He can wash his hands. They're not drinking water today. The Procurator sent out a wineskin.'

'Is the man dead?' asked Demetrius.

'No—he said something awhile ago.'

'What did he say? Could you hear?'

'Said he was thirsty.'

'Did they give him water?'

'No—they filled a sponge with vinegar that had some sort of balm in it, and raised it to his mouth; but he wouldn't have it. I don't rightly understand what he is up there for—but he's no coward.' The legionary shifted his position, pointed to the darkening sky, remarked that there was going to be a storm, and moved on through the crowd.

Demetrius did not look at the lonely man again. He edged out into the open and made a wide détour around to the other side of the knoll. Marcellus, Paulus, and four or five others were lounging in a small circle on the ground. A leather dice-cup was being shaken negligently, and passed from hand to hand. At first sight of it, Demetrius was hotly indignant. It wasn't like Marcellus to be so brutally unfeeling. A decent man would have to be very drunk indeed to exhibit such callous unconcern in this circumstance.

Now that he was here, Demetrius thought he should inquire whether there was anything he could do for his master. He slowly approached the group of preoccupied officers. After a while, Marcellus glanced up dully and beckoned to him. The others gave him a brief glance and resumed their play.

'Anything you want to tell me?' asked Marcellus, thickly.

'I brought you some water, sir.'

'Very good. Put it down there. I'll have a drink presently.' It was his turn to play. He shook the cup languidly and tossed out the dice.

'Your lucky day!' growled Paulus. 'That finishes me.' He stretched his long arms and laced his fingers behind his head. 'Demetrius,' he said, nodding toward a rumpled brown mantle that lay near the foot of the central cross, 'hand me that coat. I want to look at it.'

Demetrius picked up the garment and gave it to him. Paulus examined it with idle interest.

'Not a bad robe,' he remarked, holding it up at arm's length. 'Woven in the country; dyed with walnut juice. He'll not be needing it any more. I think I'll say it's mine. How about it, Tribune?'

'Why should it be yours?' asked Marcellus, indifferently. 'If it's worth anything, let us toss for it.' He handed Paulus the dice-cup. 'High number wins. It's your turn.'

There was a low mutter of thunder in the north and a savage tongue of flame leaped through the black cloud. Paulus tossed a pair of threes, and stared apprehensively at the sky.

'Not hard to beat,' said Vinitius, who sat next him. He took the cup and poured out a five and a four. The cup made the circle without bettering this cast until it arrived at Marcellus.

'Double six!' he called. 'Demetrius, you take care of the robe.' Paulus handed up the garment.

'Shall I wait here for you, sir?' asked Demetrius.

'No—nothing you can do. Go back to the Insula. Begin packing up. We want to be off to an early start in the morning.' Marcellus looked up at the sky. 'Paulus, go around and see how they are doing. There's going to be a hard storm.' He rose heavily to his feet, and stood swaying. Demetrius wanted to take his arm and steady him, but felt that any solicitude would be resented. His indignation had cooled now. It was evident that Marcellus had been drinking because he couldn't bear to do this shameful work in his right mind. There was a deafening, stunning thunderclap that fairly shook the ground on which they stood. Marcellus put out a hand and steadied himself against the central cross. There was blood on his hand when he regained his balance. He wiped it off on his toga.

A fat man, expensively dressed in a black robe, waddled out of the crowd and confronted Marcellus with surly arrogance.

'Rebuke these people!' he shouted, angrily. 'They are saying that the storm is a judgment on us!'

There was another gigantic crash of thunder.

'Maybe it is!' yelled Marcellus, recklessly.

The fat man waved a menacing fist.

'It is your duty to keep order here!' he shrieked.

'Do you want me to stop the storm?' demanded Marcellus.

'Stop the blasphemy! These people are crying out that this Galilean is the Son of God!'

'Maybe he *is!*' shouted Marcellus. '*You* wouldn't know!' He was fumbling with the hilt of his sword. The fat man backed away, howling that the Procurator should hear of this.

Circling the knoll, Demetrius paused for a final look at the lonely man on the central cross. He had raised his face and was gazing up into the black sky. Suddenly he burst forth with a resonant call, as if crying to a distant friend for aid.

A poorly dressed, bearded man of middle age, apparently one of the Galilean's friends from the country, rushed out of the crowd and ran down the slope weeping aloud in an abandon of grief. Demetrius grasped him by the sleeve as he stumbled past.

'What did he say?'

The man made no reply, tore himself loose, and ran on shouting his unintelligible lamentations.

Now the dying Galilean was looking down upon the crowd below him. His lips moved. His eyes surveyed the people with the same sorrow they had expressed on the road when the multitude had hailed him as their king. There was another savage burst of thunder. The darkness deepened.

Demetrius rolled up the Robe and thrust it inside his tunic, pressing it tightly under his arm. The intimate touch of the garment relieved his feeling of desolation. He wondered if Marcellus might not let him keep the Robe. It would be a comfort to own something that this courageous man had worn. He would cherish it as a priceless inheritance. It would have been a great experience, he felt, to have known this man; to have learned the nature of his mind. Now that there would be no opportunity to share his friendship, it would be an enduring consolation to possess his Robe.

Turning about, with swimming eyes, he started down the hill. It was growing so dark now that the narrow path was indistinct. He flung a backward look over his shoulder, but the descending gloom had swallowed up the knoll.

By the time he reached the city streets, night had fallen on Jerusalem, though it was only mid-afternoon. Lights flickered in the windows. Pedestrians moved slowly, carrying torches. Frightened voices called to one another. Demetrius could not understand what they were saying, but their tone was apprehensive, as if they were wondering about the cause of this strange darkness. He wondered, too, but felt no sense of depression or alarm. The sensation of being alone and unwanted in an unfriendly world had left him. He was not lonely now. He hugged the Robe close to his side as if it contained some inexplicable remedy for heartache.

Melas was standing in the corridor, in front of Paulus' door, when he arrived at the barracks. Demetrius was in no mood to talk, and proceeded to his master's quarters, Melas following with his torch.

'So—you went out there; eh?' said the Thracian, grimly. 'How did you like it?' They entered the room and Melas applied his torch to the big stone lamps. Receiving no answer to his rough query, he asked, 'What do you think this is; an eclipse?'

'I don't know,' replied Demetrius. 'Never heard of an eclipse lasting so long.'

'Maybe it's the end of the world,' said Melas, forcing an uncouth laugh.

'That will be all right with me,' said Demetrius.

'Think this Jesus has had anything to do with it?' asked Melas, half in earnest.

'No,' said Demetrius, 'I shouldn't think so.'

Melas moved closer and took Demetrius by the arm.

'Thought any more about Damascus?' he whispered.

Demetrius shook his head indifferently.

'Have you?' he asked.

'I'm going—tonight,' said Melas. 'The Procurator always gives a dinner to the officers on the last night. When it is over, and I have put the Centurion to bed—he'll be tight as a tambourine—I'm leaving. Better come with me. You'll wait a long time for another chance as good as this one.'

'No—I'm not going,' said Demetrius firmly.

'You'll not tell on me, will you?'

'Certainly not.'

'If you change your mind, give me a wink at the banquet.' Melas sauntered toward the door. Demetrius, thinking he had gone, drew out the Robe and unfolded it under the light.

'What have you there?' queried Melas, from the doorway.

'His Robe,' said Demetrius, without turning.

Melas came back and regarded the blood-stained garment with silent interest.

'How do you happen to have it?' he asked, in an awed tone.

'It belongs to the Legate. The officers tossed for it. He won it.'

'I shouldn't think he'd want it,' remarked Melas. 'I'm sure I wouldn't. It will probably bring him bad luck.'

'Why *bad* luck?' demanded Demetrius. 'It belonged to a brave man.'

* * * * *

Marcellus came in, dazed, drunk, and thoroughly exhausted. Unbuckling his sword-belt, he handed it to Demetrius, and sank wearily into a chair.

'Get me some wine,' he ordered, huskily.

Demetrius obeyed; and, on one knee, unlaced his master's dusty sandals while he drank.

'You will feel better after a cold bath, sir,' he said, encouragingly.

Marcellus widened his heavy eyes with an effort and surveyed his slave with curiosity.

'Were you out there?' he asked, thickly. 'Oh, yes; I remember now. You were there. You brought j-jug water.'

'And brought back his Robe,' prompted Demetrius.

Marcellus passed his hand awkwardly across his brow and tried to dismiss the recollection with a shuddering shrug.

'You will be going to the dinner, sir?' asked Demetrius.

'Have to!' grumbled Marcellus. 'Can't have off-cers laughing at us. We're tough—at Minoa. Can't have ossifers—orfficers—chortling that sight of blood makes Minoa Legate sick.'

'Quite true, sir,' approved Demetrius. 'A shower and a rub-down will put you in order. I have laid out fresh clothing for you.'

'Very good,' labored Marcellus. 'Commanner Minoa never this dirty before. Wha's that?' He raked his fingers across a dark wet smudge on the skirt of his toga. 'Blood!' he muttered. 'Great Roman Empire does big brave deed! Wins bloody battle!' The drunken monologue trailed off into foggy incoherences. Marcellus' head sank lower and lower on his chest. Demetrius unfastened the toga, soaked a towel in cold water, and vigorously applied it to his master's puffed face and beating throat.

'Up you come, sir!' he ordered, tugging Marcellus to his feet. 'One more hard battle to fight, sir. Then you can sleep it off.'

Marcellus slowly pulled himself together and rested both hands heavily on his slave's shoulders while being stripped of his soiled clothing.

'I'm dirty,' he mumbled to himself. 'I'm dirty—outside and inside. I'm dirty—and ashamed. Unnerstand—Demetrius? I'm dirty and ashamed.'

'You were only obeying orders, sir,' consoled Demetrius.

'Were you out there?' Marcellus tried to focus his eyes.

'Yes, sir. A very sorry affair.'

'What did you think of him?'

'Very courageous. It was too bad you had it to do, sir.'

'I wouldn't do it again,' declared Marcellus, truculently—'no matter who ordered it! Were you there when he called on his god to forgive us?'

'No—but I couldn't have understood his language.'

'Nor I—but they told me. He looked directly at me after he had said it. I'm afraid I'm going to have a hard time forgetting that look.'

Demetrius put his arm around Marcellus to steady him. It was the first time he had ever seen tears in his master's eyes.

* * * * * *

The Insula's beautiful banquet-hall had been gaily decorated for the occasion with many ensigns, banners, and huge vases of flowers. An orchestra, sequestered in an alcove, played stirring military marches. Great stone lamps on marble pillars brightly lighted the spacious room. At the head table, a little higher than the others, sat the Procurator with Marcellus and Julian on either side and the Commanders from Caesarea and Joppa flanking them. Everyone knew why Marcellus and Julian were given seats of honor. Minoa had been assigned a difficult task and Capernaum had a grievance. Pilate was glum, moody, and distraught.

The household slaves served the elaborate dinner. The officers' orderlies stood ranged against the walls, in readiness to be of aid to their masters, for the Procurator's guests—according to a long-established custom—had come here to get drunk, and not many of them had very far to go.

The representatives of Minoa were more noisy and reckless than any of the others, but it was generally conceded that much latitude should be extended in their case, for they had had a hard day. Paulus had arrived late. Melas had done what he could to straighten him up, but the Centurion was dull and dizzy—and surly. The gaiety of his table companions annoyed him. For some time he sat glumly regarding them with distaste, occasionally jerked out of his lethargy by a painful hiccough. After a while his fellow officers took him in hand, plying him with a particularly heady wine which had the effect of whipping his jaded spirits into fresh activity. He tried to be merry; sang and shouted; but no one could understand anything he said. Presently he upset his tall wine-cup, and laughed uproariously. Paulus was drunk.

It pleased Demetrius to observe that Marcellus was holding his own with dignity. He was having little to say, but Pilate's taciturnity easily accounted for that. Old Julian, quite sober, was eating his dinner with relish, making no effort to engage the Procurator in conversation. The other tables were growing louder and more disorderly as the evening advanced. There was much boisterous laughter; many rude practical jokes; an occasional unexplained quarrel.

The huge silver salvers, piled high with roasted meats and exotic fruits, came and went; exquisitely carved silver flagons poured rare wines into enormous silver goblets. Now and then a flushed Centurion rose from the couch on which he lounged beside his table, his servant skipping swiftly across the marble floor to assist him. After a while they would return. The officer, apparently much improved in health, would strut back to his couch and resume where he had left off. Many of the guests slept, to the chagrin of their slaves. So long as your master was able to stagger out of the room and unburden his stomach, you had no cause for humiliation; but if he went to sleep, your fellow slaves winked at you and grinned.

Demetrius stood at attention, against the wall, immediately behind his master's couch. He noted with satisfaction that Marcellus was merely toying with his food, which showed that he still had some sense left. He wished, however, that the Commander would exhibit a little more interest in the party. It would be unfortunate if anyone surmised that he was brooding over the day's events.

Presently the Procurator sat up and leaned toward Marcellus, who turned his face inquiringly. Demetrius moved a step forward and listened.

'You are not eating your dinner, Legate,' observed Pilate. 'Perhaps there is something else you would prefer.'

'Thank you; no sir,' replied Marcellus. 'I am not hungry.'

'Perhaps your task, this afternoon, dulled your appetite,' suggested Pilate, idly.

Marcellus scowled.

'That would be a good enough reason, sir, for one's not being hungry,' he retorted.

'A painful business, I'm sure,' commented Pilate. 'I did not enjoy my necessity to order it.'

'Necessity?' Marcellus sat up and faced his host with cool impudence. 'This man was not guilty of a crime, as the Procurator himself admitted.'

Pilate frowned darkly at this impertinence.

'Am I to understand that the Legate of Minoa disputes the justice of the court's decision?'

'Of course!' snapped Marcellus. 'Justice? No one knows better than the Procurator that this Galilean was unjustly treated!'

'You are forgetting yourself, Legate!' said Pilate, sternly.

'I did not initiate this conversation, sir,' rejoined Marcellus, 'but if my candor annoys you, we can talk about something else.'

Pilate's face cleared a little.

'You have a right to your opinions, Legate Marcellus Gallio,' he conceded, 'though you certainly know it is unusual for a man to criticize his superior quite so freely as you have done.'

'I know that, sir,' nodded Marcellus, respectfully. 'It is unusual to criticize one's superior. But this is an unusual case.' He paused, and looked Pilate squarely in the eyes. 'It was an unusual trial, an unusual decision, an unusual punishment—and the convict was an unusual man!'

'A strange person, indeed,' agreed Pilate. 'What did you make of him?' he asked, lowering his voice confidentially.

Marcellus shook his head.

'I don't know, sir,' he replied, after an interval.

'He was a fanatic!' said Pilate.

'Doubtless. So was Socrates. So was Plato.'

Pilate shrugged.

'You're not implying that this Galilean was of the same timber as Socrates and Plato!'

The conversation was interrupted before Marcellus had an opportunity to reply. Paulus had risen and was shouting at him drunkenly, incoherently. Pilate scowled, as if this were a bit too much, even for a party that had lost all respect for the dignity of the Insula. Marcellus shook his head and signed to Paulus with his hand that he was quite out of order. Undeterred, Paulus staggered to the head table, leaned far across it on one unstable elbow, and muttered something that Demetrius could not hear. Marcellus tried to dissuade him, but he was obdurate and growing quarrelsome. Obviously much perplexed, the Commander turned and beckoned to Demetrius.

'Centurion Paulus wants to see that Robe,' he muttered. 'Bring it here.'

Demetrius hesitated so long that Pilate regarded him with sour amazement.

'Go—instantly—and get it!' barked Marcellus, angrily.

Regretting that he had put his master to shame, in the presence of the Procurator, Demetrius tried to atone for his reluctant obedience by moving swiftly. His heart pounded hard as he ran down the corridor to the Legate's suite. There was no accounting for the caprice of a man as drunk as Paulus. Almost anything could happen, but Paulus would have to be humored.

Folding the blood-stained, thorn-rent Robe over his arm, Demetrius returned to the banquet-hall. He felt like a traitor, assisting in the mockery of a cherished friend. Surely this Jesus deserved a better fate than to be abandoned—even in death—to the whims of a drunken soldier. Once, on the way, Demetrius came to a full stop and debated seriously whether to obey—or take the advice of Melas—and run.

Marcellus glanced at the Robe, but did not touch it.

'Take it to Centurion Paulus,' he said.

Paulus, who had returned to his seat, rose unsteadily; and, holding up the Robe by its shoulders, picked his way carefully to the head table. The room grew suddenly quiet, as he stood directly before Pilate.

'Trophy!' shouted Paulus.

Pilate drew a reproachful smile and glanced toward Marcellus as if to hint that the Legate of Minoa might well advise his Centurion to mend his manners.

'Trophy!' repeated Paulus. 'Minoa presents trophy to the Insula.' He waved an expansive arm toward the banners that hung above the Procurator's table.

Pilate shook his head crossly and disclaimed all interest in the drunken farce with a gesture of annoyance. Undaunted by his rebuff, Paulus edged over a few steps and addressed Marcellus.

'Insula doesn't want trophy!' he prattled idiotically. 'Very well! Minoa keep trophy! Legate Marcellus wear trophy back to Minoa! Put it on, Legate!'

'Please, Paulus!' begged Marcellus. 'That's enough.'

'Put it on!' shouted Paulus. 'Here, Demetrius; hold the Robe for the Legate!' He thrust it into Demetrius' hands.

Someone yelled, 'Put it on!' And the rest of them took up the shout, pounding the tables with their goblets. 'Put it on!'

Feeling that the short way out of the dilemma was to humor the drunken crowd, Marcellus rose and reached for the Robe. Demetrius stood clutching it in his arms, seemingly unable to release it. Marcellus was pale with anger.

'Give it to me!' he commanded, severely. All eyes were attentive, and the place grew quiet. Demetrius drew himself erect, with the Robe held tightly in his folded arms. Marcellus waited a long moment, breathing heavily. Then suddenly drawing back his arm he slapped Demetrius in the face with his open hand. It was the first time he had ever ventured to punish him.

Demetrius slowly bowed his head and handed Marcellus the Robe; then stood with slumped shoulders while his master tugged it on over the sleeves of his toga. A gale of appreciative laughter went up, and there was tumultuous applause. Marcellus did not smile. His face was drawn and haggard. The room grew still again. As a man in a dream, he fumbled woodenly with the neck of the garment, trying to pull it off his shoulder. His hands were shaking.

'Shall I help you, sir?' asked Demetrius, anxiously.

Marcellus nodded; and when Demetrius had relieved him of the Robe, he sank into his seat as if his knees had suddenly buckled under him.

"Take that out into the courtyard,' he muttered, hoarsely, 'and burn it!'

Demetrius saluted and walked rapidly across the hall. Melas was standing near the doorway. He moved in closer as Demetrius passed.

'Meet me—at midnight—at the Sheep Gate,' he whispered.

'I'll be there,' flung back Demetrius, as he hurried on.

* * * * * *

'You seem much shaken.' Pilate's tone was coolly derisive. 'Perhaps you are superstitious.'

Marcellus made no reply. It was as if he had not heard the sardonic comment. He took up his wine-cup in a trembling hand and drank. The other tables, now that the unexpected little drama had been played out, resumed their banter and laughter.

'I suspect that you have had about enough for one day,' added the Procurator, more considerately. 'If you wish to go, you may be excused.'

'Thank you, sir,' replied Marcellus, remotely. He half-rose from his couch, but finding that his knees were still weak, sank down again. Too much attention had already been focused on him: he would not take the risk of an unfortunate exit. Doubtless his sudden enfeeblement would soon pass. He tried to analyze this curious enervation. He had been drinking far too much today. He had been under a terrific emotional strain. But even in his present state of mental confusion, he could still think straight enough to know that it wasn't the wine or the day's tragic task. This seizure of unaccountable inertia had come upon him when he thrust his arms into the sleeves of that Robe! Pilate had taunted him about his superstition. Nothing could be farther from the truth: he was not superstitious. Nobody had less interest in or respect for a belief in supernatural persons or powers. That being true, he had not himself invested this Robe with some imagined magic.

He realized that Pilate was looking him over with contemptuous curiosity. His situation was becoming quite embarrassing. Sooner or later he would be obliged to stand up. He wondered if he could.

A palace guard was crossing the room, on his way to the head table. He came to a halt as he faced the Procurator, saluted stiffly, and announced that the Captain of *The Vestris* had arrived and wished to deliver a letter to Legate Marcellus Lucan Gallio.

'Bring it here,' said Pilate.

'Captain Fulvius wishes to deliver it with his own hands, sir,' said the guard.

'Nonsense!' retorted Pilate. 'Tell him to give you the letter. See that the Captain has his dinner and plenty of wine. I shall have a word with him in the morning.'

'The letter, sir,' said the guard, impressively, 'is from the Emperor!'

Marcellus, who had listened with scant interest, now leaned forward and looked at the Procurator inquisitively.

'Very well,' nodded Pilate. 'Tell him to come in.'

The few minutes of waiting seemed long. A letter from the Emperor! What manner of message would be coming from crazy old Tiberius? Presently the bronzed, bearded, bow-legged sailor ambled through the room, in tow of the guard. Pilate greeted him coolly and signed for him to hand the scroll to Marcellus. The Captain waited, and the Procurator watched out of the tail of his eye, while the seals were broken. Marcellus thrust a shaky dagger through the heavy wax, slowly unrolled the papyrus, and ran his eye over the brief message. Then he rolled up the scroll and impassively addressed the Captain.

'When are you sailing?' There was nothing in Marcellus' tone to indicate whether the letter from Emperor Tiberius bore good tidings or bad. Whatever the message was, it had not stirred him out of his strange apathy.

'Tomorrow night, sir. Soon as we get back to Joppa.'

'Very good,' said Marcellus, casually. 'I shall be ready.'

'We should leave here an hour before dawn, sir,' said the Captain. 'I have made all arrangements for your journey to the port. The ship will call at Gaza to pick up whatever you may wish to take with you to Rome.'

'How did you happen to deliver this letter to Legate Marcellus Gallio in Jerusalem?' inquired Pilate, idly.

'I went to the Minoa fort, sir, and they told me he was here.' The Captain bobbed an awkward leave-taking and followed the guard from the hall. Pilate, unable to restrain his curiosity any longer, turned to Marcellus with inquiring eyes.

'If congratulations are in order,' he said, almost deferentially, 'may I be the first to offer them?'

'Thank you,' said Marcellus, evasively. 'If it is agreeable with you, sir, I shall go now.'

'By all means,' approved Pilate, stiffening. 'Perhaps you need some assistance,' he added, as he observed Marcellus' struggle to rise. 'Shall I send for your servant?'

Clutching the table for support, Marcellus contrived to get to his feet. For a moment, as he steadied himself, he was unsure whether his legs would bear his weight until he had crossed the banquet-hall. Clenching his hands, he massed his will into a determined effort to walk. With short, infirm steps, he began the long journey to the door, so intent upon it that he had failed to give his distinguished host so much as a farewell glance. He was immeasurably relieved when, having passed through the door and into the broad corridor, he could brace a hand against the wall. After he had proceeded for some distance down the hall, he came to an arched doorway that opened upon the spacious courtyard. Feeling himself quite unable to go farther, he picked his way—with the caution of an old man—down the steps. On the lower step, he sat down heavily, in the darkness that enveloped the deserted parade-ground, wondering whether he would ever regain his strength.

Occasionally, during the next hour, he made tentative efforts to rise; but they were ineffectual. It struck him oddly that he was not more alarmed over his condition. Indeed, this lethargy that had attacked him physically had similarly disqualified his mind.

The fact that his exile, which had threatened to ruin his life, was now ended, did not exult his spirit. He said, over and over to himself, 'Marcellus, wake up! You are free! You are going home! You are going back to your family! You are going back to Diana! The ship is waiting! You are to sail tomorrow! What ails you, Marcellus?'

Once he roused to brief attention as the figure of a man with a pack on his shoulder neared his darkened doorway. The fellow was keeping close to the wall, proceeding with stealthy steps. It was Paulus' slave. He had the furtive air of a fugitive. As he passed Marcellus, he gave a sudden start at the sight of him sitting there; and, taking to his heels, vanished like a frightened antelope. Marcellus thought this faintly amusing, but did not smile. So—Melas was running away. Well—what of it? The question arrived and departed with no more significance than the fitful flicker in the masses of exotic shrubbery where the fireflies played.

After what seemed like a very long time, there came the sound of sandals scraping along the marble corridor, and thick, tired voices. The banquet was over. Marcellus wondered dully whether he should make his presence known to them as they passed, but felt powerless to come to a decision. Presently the footsteps and voices grew fainter and fainter, down the corridor. After that, the night seemed more dark. But Marcellus did not have a sense of desolation. His mind was inert. He laboriously edged his way over to the marble pillar at the right of the arch; and, leaning against it, dreamlessly slept.

* * * * * *

Demetrius had spent a busy hour in the Legate's suite, packing his master's clothing and other equipment for the journey he would be making, in the morning, back to Minoa. He had very few misgivings about escaping from his slavery, but the habit of waiting on Marcellus was not easy to throw off. He would perform this final service, and be on his way to liberty. He might be captured, or he might experience much hardship; but he would be free! Marcellus, when he sobered, would probably regret the incident in the banquet-hall; might even feel that his slave had a just cause for running away.

He hadn't accomplished his freedom yet, but he was beginning to experience the sense of it. After he had strapped the bulky baggage, Demetrius quietly left the room and returned to his own small cubicle at the far end of the barracks occupied by the contingent from Minoa, where he gathered up his few belongings and stowed them into his bag. Carefully folding the Galilean's Robe, he tucked it in last after packing everything else.

It was, he admitted, a very irrational idea, but the softness of the finely woven, homespun Robe had a curiously quality. The touch of it had for him a strangely calming effect, as if it were a new reliance. He remembered a legend from his childhood, about a ring that bore the insignia of a prince. And the prince had given the ring to some poor legionary who had pushed him out of an arrow's path. And, years afterward, when in great need, the soldier had turned the ring to good account in seeking an audience with the prince. Demetrius could not remember all the details of the story, but this Robe seemed to have much the same properties as the prince's ring. It was in the nature of a surety, a defense.

It was a long way to the Sheep Gate, but he had visited it before on one of his solitary excursions, lured there by Melas' information that it was now rarely used except by persons coming into the city from the villages to the north. If a man were heading for the Damascus road, and wished to avoid a challenge, the Sheep Gate offered the best promise. Demetrius had been full of curiosity to see it. He had no intention of running away; but thought it might be interesting to have a glimpse of a road to freedom. Melas had said it was easy.

The gate was unguarded; deserted, indeed. Melas had not yet arrived, but his tardiness gave Demetrius no concern. Perhaps he himself was early. He lounged on the parched grass by the roadside, in the shadow of the crumbling limestone bastion, and waited.

At length he heard the rhythmic lisps of sandal-straps, and stepped out into the road.

'Anyone see you go?' asked Melas, puffing a little as he put down his pack for a momentary rest.

'No. Everything was quiet. How about you?'

'The Legate saw me leave.' Melas chuckled. 'He gave me a fright. I was sneaking along the barracks wall, in the courtyard, and came upon him.'

'What was he doing there?' demanded Demetrius, sharply.

'Just sitting there—by himself—in a doorway.'

'He recognized you?'

'Yes—I feel sure he did; but he didn't speak. Come! Let's not stand here any longer. We must see how far we can travel before sunrise.' Melas led the way through the dilapidated gate.

'Did the Legate appear to be drunk?' asked Demetrius.

'N-no—not very drunk,' said Melas, uncertainly. 'He left the hall before any of the others; seemed dizzy and half out of his head. I was going to wait and put my mean old drunkard to bed, but they kept on at it so long that I decided to leave. He probably won't miss me. I never saw the Centurion that drunk before.'

They plodded on through the dark, keeping to the road with difficulty. Melas stumbled over a rock and cursed eloquently.

'You say he seemed out of his head?' said Demetrius, anxiously.

'Yes—dazed—as if something had hit him. And out there in that archway, he had a sort of empty look in his face. Maybe he didn't even know where he was.'

Demetrius' steps slowed to a stop.

'Melas,' he said, hoarsely, 'I'm sorry—but I've got to go back to him.'

'Why—you—' The Thracian was at a loss for a strong enough epithet. 'I always thought you were soft! Afraid to run away from a fellow who strikes you in the face before a crowd of officers; just to show them how brave he is! Very well! You go back to him and be his slave forever! It will be tough! He has lost his mind!'

Demetrius had turned and was walking away.

'Good luck to you, Melas,' he called, soberly.

'Better get rid of that Robe!' shouted Melas, his voice shrill with anger. 'That's what drove your smart young Marcellus out of his mind! He began to go crazy the minute he put it on! Let him be. He is accursed! The Galilean has had his revenge!'

Demetrius stumbled on through the darkness, Melas' raging imprecations following him as far as the old gate.

'Accursed!' he yelled. 'Accursed!'

Chapter VII

ALTHOUGH winter was usually brief on the Island of Capri there was plenty of it while it lasted—according to Tiberius Caesar who detested it. The murky sky depressed his spirit. The raw dampness made his creaking joints ache. The most forlorn spot, he declared, in the Roman Empire.

The old man's favorite recreation, since committing most of his administrative responsibilities to Prince Gaius, was residential architecture. He was forever building huge, ornate villas on the lofty skyline of Capri; for what purpose not even the gods knew.

All day long through spring, summer, and autumn, he would sit in the sun—or under an awning if it grew too hot—and watch his stonemasons at work on yet another villa. And his builders had respect for these constructions too, for the Emperor was an architect of no mean ability. Nor did he allow his aesthetic taste to run away with his common sense. The great cisterns required for water conservation on a mountaintop were planned with the practical skill of an experienced plumber and concealed with the artistry of an idealistic sculptor.

There were nine of these exquisite villas now, ranged in an impressive row on the highest terrain, isolated from one another by spacious gardens, their architectural genre admitting that they had been derived from the mind and purse of the jaded, restless, irascible old Caesar who lived in the Villa Jovis which dominated them all—a fact further illuminated by the towering pharos rising majestically from the center of its vast, echoing atrium.

Tiberius hated winter because he could not sit in the sun and watch his elaborate fancies take on form and substance. He hadn't very long to live, and it enraged him to see the few remaining days slipping through his bony fingers like fine sand through an hourglass.

When the first wind and rain scurried across the bay to rattle the doors and pelt the windows of his fifty-room palace, the Emperor went into complete and embittered seclusion. No guests were welcome. Relatives were barred from his sumptuous suite. No deputations were received from Rome; no state business was transacted.

Prince Gaius, whom he despised, quite enjoyed this bad weather, for while the Emperor was in hibernation he felt free to exercise all the powers entrusted to him—and sometimes a little more. Tiberius, aware of this, fumed and snuffled, but he had arrived at that stage of senescence where he hadn't the energy to sustain his varied indignations. They burned white-hot for an hour—and expired.

Through the short winter, no one was allowed to see the decaying monarch but his personal attendants and a corps of bored physicians who packed his old bones in hot fomentations of spiced vinegar and listened obsequiously to his profane abuse.

But the first ray of earnest sunshine always made another man of him. When its brightness spread across his bed and dazzled his rheumy eyes, Tiberius kicked off his compresses and his doctors, yelled for his tunic, his toga, his sandals, his cap, his stick, his piper, his chief gardener, and staggered out into the peristyle. He shouted orders, thick and fast; and things began to hum. The Emperor had never been gifted with much patience, and nobody expected that he would miraculously develop this talent at eighty-two. Now that spring had been officially opened with terrifying shrieks and reckless cane-waving, the Villa Jovis came to life with a suddenness that must have shocked the conservative old god for whom the place had been named. The Macedonian musicians and Indian magicians and Ionian minstrels and Rhodesian astrologers and Egyptian dancing girls were violently shelled out of their comfortable winter sloth to line up before his fuming majesty and explain why—at the expense of a tax-harried, poverty-cursed Empire—they had been living in such disgusting indolence.

For the sake of appearances, a servant would then be dispatched to the Villa Dionysus—the name of his aged wife's palace had been chosen with an ironical chuckle—to inquire about the health of the Empress, which was the least of the old man's anxieties. It would not have upset him very much to learn that Julia wasn't so well. Indeed, he had once arranged for the old lady's assassination, an event which had failed to come off only because the Empress, privily advised of the engagement planned for her, had disapproved of it.

This season, spring had arrived much earlier than usual, blasting everything into bloom in a day. The sky was full of birds, the gardens were full of flowers, the flowers were full of bees, and Tiberius was full of joy. He wanted somebody to share it with him; somebody young enough to respond with exultation to all this beauty: who but Diana!

So—that afternoon a courier, ferrying across to Neapolis, set forth on a fast horse, followed an hour later by the most commodious of the royal carriages—stuffed with eider-down pillows as a hint that the return journey from Rome to Capri, albeit hard to take, should be made with dispatch; for the distinguished host was not good at waiting. His letter, addressed to Paula Gallus, was brief and urgent. Tiberius did not ask whether it would be convenient for her to bring Diana to Capri; and, if so, he would send for them. He simply advised her that the carriage was on the way at full gallop, and that they were to be prepared to take it immediately upon its arrival.

* * * * * *

At dusk on the third day of their hard travel, Paula and Diana had stepped out of the imperial barge onto the Capri wharf; and, climbing wearily into the luxurious litters awaiting them, had been borne swiftly up the precipitous path to the Villa Jovis. There the old Emperor had met them with a pathetic eagerness, and had mercifully suggested that they retire at once to their baths and beds, adding that they were to rest undisturbed until tomorrow noon. This inspired announcement Paula Gallus received with an almost tearful gratitude and made haste to avail herself of its benefits.

Diana, whose physical resources had not been so thoroughly depleted, lingered, much to the old man's delight; slipped her hand through his arm and allowed herself to be led to his private parlor, where, when he had sunk into a comfortable chair, she drew up a stool; sat, with her shapely arms folded on his emaciated knee, and looked up into his deep-lined face with a tender affection that made the Emperor clear his throat and wipe his hawk-like nose.

It was so good of him, and so like him, she said, to want her to come. And how well he was looking! How glad he must be to see spring come again. Now he would be out in the sunshine, every day, probably supervising some new building. What was it going to be, this season: another villa, maybe? Diana smiled into his eyes.

'Yes,' he replied, gently, 'another villa. A truly beautiful villa.' He paused, narrowing his averted eyes thoughtfully. 'The most beautiful of them all, I hope. This one'—Tiberius gave her an enigmatic smile—'this one is for the sweet and lovely Diana.' He did not add that this idea had just now occurred to him. He made it sound as if he were confiding a plan that had been long nurtured in secret.

Diana's eyes swam and sparkled. She patted the brown old hand tenderly. With a husky voice she murmured that he was the very dearest grandfather anyone ever had.

'And you are to help me plan the villa, child,' said Tiberius, warmly.

'Was that why you sent for me?' asked Diana.

The old man pursed his wrinkled lips into a sly smile and lied benevolently with slow nods of his shaggy white head.

'We will talk about it tomorrow,' he promised.

'Then I should get to bed at once,' she decided, springing to her feet. 'May I have breakfast with you, Grandfather?'

Tiberius chuckled amiably.

'That's too much to ask of you, my sweet,' he protested. 'You must be very tired. And I have my breakfast at dawn.'

'I'll be with you!' announced Diana. She softly patted him on the head. 'Good night, Your Majesty.' Dropping to one knee, she bowed ceremoniously and rising retreated—still facing him—until she reached the door where she paused, puckered her smiling lips, and pantomimed a kiss.

The aged Emperor of Rome was much pleased.

* * * * * *

It was high noon and the day was bright. Not for a long time had Tiberius enjoyed himself so fully. This high-spirited girl was renewing his interest in life. She had matured beyond belief since he had last seen her. He responded to her radiant vitality with an almost adolescent yearning. Had Diana hinted that she would like to have the Island of Capri, Tiberius would have handed it to her without pausing to deliberate.

After breakfast they had walked to the far east end of the enchantingly lovely mall, Diana ecstatic, the Emperor bumbling along with short steps and shorter breaths, scraping the mosaic pavement with his sandal-heels. Yes, he panted, there was plenty of room at the far end of the row for a magnificent villa. Nothing, he declared, could ever obstruct this splendid view. He stopped, clutched at Diana's arm for steadiness, and pointed toward the northeast with a shaky cane. There would always be old Vesuvius to greet you in the morning. 'And do you not see the sunlight glinting from the white roofs of Pompeii and Herculaneum? And across there, close at hand, is sleepy little Surrentum. You can sit at your window and see everything that is going on in Surrentum.'

Observing that the old man's legs were getting wobbly, Diana had suggested that they turn aside here and rest in the arbor that marked the eastern boundary of the new—and still unoccupied—Villa Quirinus. The Emperor slumped heavily into a rustic chair and mopped his perspiring brow, his thin, mottled hand trembling as if palsied. For some time they sat in silence, waiting for the old man to recuperate. His lean face was contorted and his jaw chopped convulsively.

'You have grown to be a beautiful woman, Diana!' he remarked, in a thin treble, after blandly invoicing her charms with the privileged eyes of eighty-two. 'You will probably be married one of these days.'

Diana's bright smile slowly faded and her heavy lashes fell. She shook her curly, blue-black head and drew what seemed a painful little sob through locked teeth. Tiberius snorted impatiently and pounded the pavement with his cane.

'Now what's the trouble?' he demanded. 'In love with the wrong man?'

'Yes.' Diana's face was sober and her reply was a mere whisper. 'I don't mind telling you, Grandfather,' she went on, with overflowing eyes, 'I'm in love with Marcellus.'

'Well—why not? What's the matter with Marcellus?' The old man leaned forward to peer into her unhappy eyes. 'It would be a most excellent alliance,' he went on. 'There isn't a more honorable man in the Empire than Gallio. And you are fond of Lucia. By all means—marry Marcellus! What's to hinder?'

'Marcellus,' murmured Diana, hopelessly, 'has been sent far away—to be gone for years, perhaps. He has been put in command of the fort at Minoa.'

'Minoa!' yelled Tiberius, straightening his sagging spine with an indignant jerk. 'Minoa!' he shrilled—'that dirty, dried-up, pestilential, old rat-hole? Who ordered him to do that, I'd like to know?'

'Prince Gaius,' exploded Diana, swept with sudden anger.

'Gaius!' The Emperor pried himself up by his elbows, struggled to his feet, and slashed the air with his cane. His leaky old eyes were boiling. 'Gaius!' he shrieked. 'The misbegotten, drunken, dangerous fool! And what made him think he could do that to the son of Marcus Lucan Gallio? To Minoa—indeed! Well!—we'll see about that!' He clawed at Diana's arm. 'Come! Let us return to the villa! Gaius will hear from his Emperor!'

Leaning heavily on her, and wasting his waning strength on savage screams of anger, Tiberius shuffled along toward the Villa Jovis, pausing occasionally to shout long vituperations composed of such ingenious sacrileges and obscenities that Diana was more astounded than embarrassed. On several occasions she had witnessed the old man's grumpiness when annoyed. This was the first time she had seen him in one of his celebrated rages. It was commonly believed that the Emperor, thoroughly roused, went temporarily insane. There was a rumor—probably slanderous—that he had been known to bark like a dog; and bite, too.

Deaf to Diana's urgent entreaty that he should rest a little while before dictating the message to Gaius, the old man began howling for his chief scrivener while they were still trudging through the peristyle. A dozen dignified servants approached from all directions, making as if they would be of service, but keeping a discreet distance. Diana finally got the fuming Emperor as far as the atrium, where she dumped him onto a couch and into the solicitous hands of the Chamberlain; then scurried away to her room, where she flung herself down on her bed, with her face buried in the pillow, and laughed hysterically until she cried.

After a while, she repaired her face at the mirror; and, slipping across the corridor, tapped gently at her mother's door. She pushed it open and peeped in. Paula Gallus stirred and sleepily opened one eye.

'Mother!' Diana crossed the room and sat down on the edge of the bed. 'What do you think?' she whispered, dramatically. 'He's going to bring Marcellus home!'

'Well,' said Paula, from a considerable distance, 'that's what you had planned to make him do; wasn't it?'

'Yes—but isn't it wonderful?' insisted Diana.

'It will be, when he has done it,' drawled Paula. 'You'd better stand over him—and see that he doesn't forget all about it.'

'Oh—he wouldn't forget! Not this time! Never was anyone so angry! Mother—you should have seen him! He was terrific!'

'I know,' yawned Paula. 'I've seen him.'

'Well—in spite of everything,' declared Diana, 'I think he's an old darling!'

'He's an old lunatic!' mumbled Paula.

Diana pressed her cheek against her mother's heart.

'Marcellus is coming back,' she murmured ecstatically. 'Gaius will be very angry to have his orders flouted—but he won't be able to do a thing about it; will he?' And when Paula did not immediately reply, Diana added, anxiously, 'Will he, Mother?'

'Not at present—no.' Paula's tone carried a hint of warning. 'But we must keep it in mind that Tiberius is a very old man, my dear. He shouts and stamps and slobbers on himself—and forgets, in an hour or two, what it was that had upset him. Besides, he is going to die, one of these days.'

'And then Gaius will be the Emperor?' Diana's voice was full of trouble.

'Nobody knows, dear.'

'But he hates Gaius! You should have heard him!'

'Yes—but that's not imperial power: that's just an angry old man's noise. Julia and her little clique will appoint the next Emperor. It may not be Gaius. They quarrel frequently.'

'I've often wondered whether Tiberius might not appoint Father. I know he likes him.'

'Not a chance in a thousand.' Paula waved aside the suggestion with a languid hand.

'But Father is a great man!' declared Diana, loyally.

Paula nodded and her lips curled into a grim smile.

'Great men do not become Emperors, Diana,' she remarked, bitterly. 'It's against the rules. Your father is not eligible. He has no talent for treachery. He is brave and just. And—besides—he is not epileptic. . . . Now—you had better run along and see that the letter gets safely started on its way.'

Diana took a few steps; and, returning slowly, sat down on the bed again. She smiled mysteriously.

'Let's have it,' encouraged Paula. 'It seems to be a secret—yes?'

'Mother—he is going to build a great villa for me!'

Paula grinned.

'Nonsense!' she muttered. 'By noon he won't remember that he ever said such a thing. At least I sincerely hope he doesn't. Imagine your living here!'

'Marcellus, too,' said Diana. 'He wants Marcellus to live here, I think.'

'And do what?'

'We didn't talk about that.'

Paula ran her fingers gently over Diana's hand.

'Well—be sure you don't introduce the subject. Let him talk. Promise him anything. He'll forget. You don't want a villa on Capri. You don't want Marcellus living here in this hateful atmosphere. Hot-headed as he is, you would be a widow in a week! Go, now, child! Make him write that letter!'

* * * * *

Lucia's intuition told her that Marcellus was on board this galley. For an hour—ever since its black prow had nosed around the bend, and the three banks of long oars had pushed the heavy hull into full view—she had been standing here alone in the pergola, leaning against the balustrade, intently watching.

If *The Vestris* had experienced no delays, she could have arrived in Ostia as early as the day before yesterday. Father had cautioned them to be patient. Watched pots were slow to boil. It was a long voyage from Joppa, and *The Vestris* had several ports to make on the way home. But even Father, in spite of his sensible advice, was restless as a caged fox; you could tell from the way he invented time-killing errands for himself.

The whole villa was on edge with impatience to have Marcellus safely home. Tertia was in a flutter of excitement for two good reasons: she was eager for the return of Marcellus, of course; and she was beside herself with anxiety to see Demetrius. It was a pity, thought Lucia, that Demetrius had been so casual in his attitude toward Tertia. Marcipor drifted about from room to room, making sure that everything was in first-class order. Mother had ordered gay new draperies for Marcellus' suite. The only self-possessed person in the household was Mother. She had wept happily when Diana came to tell them what had happened; but was content to wait calmly.

As for Lucia, she had abandoned all pretence of patience. All yesterday afternoon, and again today, she had waited in the pergola, watching the river. Sometimes she would leave her post and try to stroll in the rose arbors—now in their full June glory—but in a few minutes her feet would turn back, of their own accord, to the observation point at the east end of the pergola.

As the galley crept up the river, veering toward the docks, Lucia's excitement increased. She knew now that her brother was one of the passengers, probably fidgeting to be off. If her guess were correct, it would not be long now until they would see him. He would hire a carriage at the wharf and come fast. Wouldn't Father be surprised? He wasn't expecting Marcellus today; had gone over beyond the Aventine to look at a new riding horse: it was to be a homecoming present. Maybe Marcellus would be here when Father returned.

It was going to be a great pity that Diana would not be at home to welcome him. Tiresome old Tiberius had sent for her again, and there was nothing she could do but obey him.

'Will he keep on pestering her like that?' Lucia had wondered.

'She must not offend him,' Father had said, seriously. 'The old man is malicious enough to hand Marcellus over to the Prince, if Diana fails to humor him.' After a moment of bitter reflection, he had muttered, 'I am afraid the child is in an awkward—if not dangerous—position. And while we are not directly responsible for it, her predicament worries me.'

'But—the Emperor wouldn't harm Diana!' she had exclaimed. 'That old man?'

Father had growled deep in his throat.

'A Caesar,' he had snarled, contemptuously, 'is capable of great wickedness—up to and including his last gasp—though he should live a thousand years!'

'I don't believe you like the Emperor,' she had said, impishly, to cool him off, as she made for the door. He had grunted crossly—and grinned.

You could just see the hinder part of the galley now, as it slipped into its berth. Lucia had been on this tension for so long that she was ready to fly into bits. She couldn't wait here another instant! The servants might think it strange if she went alone to the entrance gate. But this was a special occasion. Returning to the house, she ran on through to the imposing portico, down the marble steps, and set off briskly on the long, shaded driveway that wound through the acacias and acanthuses and masses of flowering shrubbery. A few slaves, ending their day's work in the formal gardens, raised their eyes inquisitively. At a little distance from the ornate bronze gates, Lucia, flushed and nervous, sat down on a stone bench, resolved to hold herself together until the great moment.

After what seemed a very long time, a battered old public chariot, drawn by two well-lathered horses, turned in from the busy avenue. Beside the driver stood Demetrius, tall, tanned, and lean. He sighted her instantly, clutched the driver's arm, handed him a coin and dismissed him. Stepping down, he walked quickly toward her, and Lucia ran to meet him. His face, she observed, was grave, though his eyes had lighted as she impulsively gave him her hands.

'Demetrius!' she cried. 'Is anything wrong? Where is Marcellus?'

'There was no carriage at the wharf,' he explained. 'I came for a better conveyance.'

'Is my brother not well?' Still holding his hands, Lucia searched his eyes anxiously. He flinched a little from this inquisition, and his reply was evasive.

'No—my master is not—my master did not have a pleasant voyage.'

'Oh—that!' She smiled her relief. 'I thought my brother was a better sailor. Was he sick all the way?'

Demetrius nodded non-committally. It was plain to see he was holding something back. Lucia's eyes were troubled.

'Tell me, Demetrius!' she pleaded, huskily. 'What ails my brother?' There was a disturbingly long silence.

'The Tribune had a very unhappy experience, the day before we sailed.' Demetrius was speaking slowly, measuring his words. 'It is too long a story to tell you now, for my master is at the wharf awaiting me. He has been deeply depressed and is not yet fully recovered. He did not sleep well on the ship.'

'Stormy weather?' suggested Lucia.

'A smooth sea,' went on Demetrius, evenly. 'But my master did not sleep well; and he ate but little.'

'Was the food palatable?'

'No worse than food is on ships, but my master did not eat; and therefore he suffers of weakness. . . . May I go quickly now—and get the large carriage for him?'

'Demetrius—you are trying to spare me, I think.' Lucia challenged his eyes with a demand for the whole truth.

'Your brother,' said Demetrius, deliberately, 'is moody. He prefers not to talk much, but does not like to be left alone.'

'But he did want to come home; didn't he?' asked Lucia, wistfully.

'Your brother,' replied Demetrius, gloomily, 'does not want *anything*.' He glanced up the driveway, restlessly. 'Shall I go now?'

Lucia nodded, and Demetrius, saluting with his spear, turned to go. She moved forward and fell into step with him. He lagged to walk behind her. She slowed her pace. He stopped.

'Please precede me,' he suggested, gently. 'It is not well that a slave should walk beside his master's sister.'

'It is a stupid rule!' flashed Lucia.

'But—a *rule!*' Demetrius' impatience had sharpened his tone. Instantly he saw that he had offended her. Her cheeks were aflame and her eyes were swimming. 'I am sorry,' he murmured, contritely. 'I did not mean to hurt you.'

'It was my fault,' she admitted. Turning abruptly, she led the way with long, determined steps. After they had proceeded for a little way in silence, Lucia—her eyes straight ahead—declared bitterly, 'I hate this whole business of slavery!'

'I don't care much for it myself,' rejoined Demetrius, dryly.

It was the first time he had been amused for nearly two months. Half-turning suddenly, Lucia caught him wearing a broad grin. Her lips curved into a fleeting, reluctant smile. Squaring her shapely shoulders, she quickened her swinging stride and marched on, Demetrius lengthening his steps as he followed, stirred by the rhythm of her graceful carriage.

She paused where the driveway divided to serve the great house and the stables. Demetrius stood at attention.

'Tell me truly,' she begged, in a tone that disposed of his slavery, 'is Marcellus' mind affected?'

Demetrius accepted his temporary freedom and spoke without constraint. 'Marcellus has had a severe shock. Perhaps he will improve, now that he is back home. He will make an effort to show his interest, I think. He has promised me that much. But you must not be startled if he stops talking—in the middle of a remark—and seems to forget what you were talking about. And then—after a long wait—he will suddenly ask you a question—always the same question—' Demetrius averted his eyes, and seemed unwilling to proceed further.

'What is the question?' insisted Lucia.

'He will say, "Were you out there?" '

'Out where?' she asked, frowning mystifiedly.

Demetrius shook his head and winced.

'I shall not try to explain that,' he said. 'But when he asks you if you were out there, you are to say, "No!" Don't ask him, "Where?" Just say, "No!" And then he will recover quickly, and seem relieved. At least, that was the way the conversation went when we were on *The Vestris*. Sometimes he would talk quite freely with the Captain—almost as if nothing was the matter. Then he would suddenly lose interest and retreat inside himself. Then he would inquire, "Were you out there?" And Captain Fulvius would say, "No." Then Marcellus would be pleased, and say, "Of course—you weren't there. That is good. You should be glad." '

'Did the Captain know what he was talking about?' inquired Lucia.

Demetrius nodded, rather grudgingly, she thought.

'Why can't you tell me?' Her tone was almost intimate.

'It's—it's a long story,' he stammered. 'Perhaps I may tell you—sometime.'

She took a step nearer, and lowering her voice almost to a whisper, asked, 'Were *you* "out there"?' He nodded reluctantly, avoiding her eyes. Then, impetuously abandoning the last shred of reserve, he spoke on terms of equality.

'Don't question him, Lucia. Treat him exactly as you have always done. Talk to him about anything—but Jerusalem. Be careful not to touch this sore spot. Maybe it will heal. I don't know. It's very deep—and painful—this mental wound.'

Her cheeks had flushed a little. Demetrius had made full use of the liberty she had given him: he had spoken her name. Well—why not? Who had a better right? They all owed much to this devoted slave.

'Thanks, Demetrius,' she said, gently. 'It was good of you to tell me what to do.'

At that, he abruptly terminated his brief parole, snapped to a stiff, military posture; looked through her without seeing her as he made a ceremonious salute; turned—and marched away. Lucia stood for a moment, indecisively, watching his dignified retreat with softened eyes.

* * * * * *

For the first hour after his arrival, it was difficult to reconcile Marcellus' behavior and his slave's warning. Parting from Demetrius, Lucia had hurried upstairs with the appalling news, and before she had finished devastating her mother with these sad tidings of her brother's predicament, her father had returned. There was little to be said. They were awed, stunned. It was as if they had learned of Marcellus' death, and were waiting for his body to be brought home.

It was a happy surprise, therefore, when he breezed in with unusually affectionate greetings. True, he was alarmingly thin and his face was haggard; but good food and plenty of rest (boomed Father, confidently) would quickly restore him to full weight and vitality. As for his mental condition, Demetrius' report had been wholly incorrect. What, indeed, had ailed the fellow—to frighten them with the announcement that his master was moody and depressed? Quite to the contrary, Marcellus had never been so animated!

Without pausing to change after his journey, he had seemed delightfully eager to talk. In Mother's private parlor, they had drawn their chairs close together, at his suggestion; though Marcellus had not sat down himself. He had paced about, like a caged animal, talking rapidly with an almost boisterous exuberance, pausing to toy with trifles on his mother's table, halting to peer out at the window, but continuing to chatter about the ship, the ports of call, the aridity of Gaza, the crude life at Minoa. Under normal conditions, the family might have surmised that he had had too much wine. It wasn't like Marcellus to talk so incessantly, or so fast. But they were glad enough that it wasn't the other thing! He was excited over his homecoming; that was all. They listened attentively, their eyes shining. They laughed gaily at his occasional drolleries and cheered him on!

'Do sit down, boy!' Mother had urged, tenderly, at his first full stop. 'You're tired. Don't wear yourself out.'

So—Marcellus had sat down, in the very middle of a stirring story about the bandits who infested the old salt trail, and his voice had become less strident. He continued talking, but more slowly, pausing to grope for the right word. Presently his forced gaiety acknowledged his fatigue, and he stopped—quite suddenly, too, as if he had been interrupted. For an instant his widened eyes and concentrated expression made him appear to have seen or heard something that had commanded his full attention. They watched him with silent curiosity, their hearts beating hard.

'What is it, Marcellus?' asked Mother, trying to steady her voice. 'Would you like a drink of water?'

He tried unsuccessfully to smile, and almost imperceptibly shook his head, as the brightness faded from his eyes. The room was very quiet.

'Perhaps you had better lie down, my son,' suggested Father, trying hard to sound casual.

Marcellus seemed not to have heard that. For a little while his breathing was laborious. His hands twitched, and he slowly clenched them until the thin knuckles whitened. Then the seizure passed, leaving him sagged and spiritless. He nervously rubbed his forehead with the back of his hand. Then he slowly turned his pathetically sad face toward his father, stared at him curiously, and drew a long, shuddering sigh.

'Were you—were you—out there—sir?' he asked, weakly.

'No—my son.' It was the thin voice of an old, old man.

Marcellus made a self-deprecating little chuckle, and shook his head, as if decrying his own foolishness. He glanced about with an attempted smile, vaguely questing their eyes for an opinion of this strange behavior. He swallowed noisily.

'Of course, you weren't,' he said, disgusted with himself. 'You have been here—all the time; haven't you?' Then he added, in a tired voice, 'I think I should go to bed now, Mother.'

'I think so too,' said Mother, softly. She had made an earnest effort not to let him see how seriously she had been affected, but at the sight of his drooping head, she put both hands over her eyes and sobbed. Marcellus looked toward her pleadingly, and sighed.

'Will you call Demetrius, Lucia?' he asked, wearily.

She stepped to the door, thinking to send Tertia, but it was unnecessary. Demetrius, who obviously had been waiting in the corridor, just outside the door, entered noiselessly and assisted his master to his feet.

'I'll see you—all—in the morning,' mumbled Marcellus. He leaned heavily on his slave as they left the room. Lucia made a little moan and slipped away quietly. The Senator bowed his head in his hands, and was silent.

* * * * * *

Marcus Lucan Gallio had not made a quick and easy decision when he resolved to have a confidential, man-to-man conference with Demetrius. The Senator punctiliously practiced the same sort of justice in dealing with his slaves that he had ever proudly observed in his relations with freedmen; but he also believed in firm discipline for them. Sometimes it annoyed him when he observed a little gesture of affection—almost a caress, indeed!—in Lucia's attitude toward Tertia; and on a couple of occasions (though this was a long time ago) he had had to remind his son that the way to have a good slave was to help him keep his place.

Gallio had an immense respect for Marcellus' handsome and loyal Corinthian. He would have trusted him anywhere and with anything, but he had never broken over the inexorable line which he felt should be drawn, straight and candid, between master and slave. It had now come to pass that he must invite Demetrius to step across that social boundary; for how else could he hope to get the full truth about the circumstances which had made such sad havoc of his son's mind?

Two days had passed, Marcellus remaining in his room. Gallio had gone up several times to see him, and had been warmly but shyly welcomed. A disturbing constraint on Marcellus' part, a forced amiability, an involuntary shrinking away from a compassionate contact lest it inadvertently touch some painfully sensitive lesion—these strange retreats, in pathetic combination with an obvious wish to show a filial affection, constituted a baffling situation. Gallio didn't know how to talk with Marcellus about it; feared he might say the wrong thing. No—Demetrius had the key to it. He must make Demetrius talk. In the middle of the afternoon, he sent for him to come to the library.

Demetrius entered and stood at attention before Gallio's desk.

'I wish to have a serious talk with you, Demetrius, about my son. I am greatly disturbed. I shall be grateful to you for a full account of whatever it is that distresses him.' The Senator pointed to the chair opposite his desk. 'You may sit down, if you like. Perhaps you will be more comfortable.'

'Thank you, sir,' said Demetrius, respectfully. 'I shall be more comfortable standing, if you please, sir.'

'As you choose,' said Gallio, a bit curtly. 'It occurred to me that you might be able to speak more freely—more naturally—if you sat.'

'No, sir, thank you,' said Demetrius. 'I am not accustomed to sitting in the presence of my betters. I can speak more naturally on my feet.'

'Sit down!' snapped Gallio. 'I don't want you towering over me, answering questions in stiff monosyllables. This is a life-and-death matter! I want you to tell me everything I ought to know—without reserve!'

Demetrius laid his heavy, metal-studded, leather shield on the floor, stood his spear against a pillar, and sat down.

'Now, then!' said Gallio. 'Let's have it! What ails my son?'

'My master was ordered to bring a detachment of legionaries to Jerusalem. It was a custom, during the annual festival of the Jews, for representations from the various Palestinian forts to assemble at the Procurator's Insula, presumably to keep order, for the city was crowded with all sorts.'

'Pontius Pilate is the Prefect of Jerusalem: is that not true?'

'Yes, sir. He is called the Procurator. There is another provincial governor residing in Jerusalem.'

'Ah—I remember. A vain fellow—Herod. A rascal!'

'Doubtless,' murmured Demetrius.

'Jealous of Pilate, I am told.'

'No one should be jealous of Pilate, sir. He permits the Temple to dictate to him. At least he did, in the case I must speak of.'

'The one that concerns my son?' Gallio leaned forward on his folded arms and prepared to listen attentively.

'May I inquire, sir, whether you ever heard of the Messiah?'

'No—what is that?'

'For hundreds of years the Jews have been expecting a great hero to arise and liberate them. He is their promised Messiah. On these yearly feast-weeks, the more fanatical among them are on the alert, thinking he may appear. Occasionally they have thought they had found the right man—but nothing much ever came of it. This time—' Demetrius paused, thoughtfully, stared out at the open window, and neglected to finish the sentence.

'There was a Jew from the Province of Galilee'—he continued—'about my own age, I should think, though he was such an unusual person that he appeared almost independent of age—or time—'

'You saw him, then?'

'A great crowd of country people tried to persuade him that he was the Messiah; that he was their King. I saw that, sir. It happened the day we arrived.'

' "Tried to persuade him" you say.'

'He had no interest in it, at all, sir. It appears that he had been preaching, mostly in his own province, to vast throngs of people; a simple, harmless appeal for common honesty and kindness. He was not interested in the Government.'

'Probably advised them that the Government was bad,' surmised Gallio.

'I do not know, sir; but I think he could have done so without violating the truth.'

The crow's-feet about Gallio's eyes deepened a little.

'I gather that you thought the Government was bad, Demetrius.'

'Yes, sir.'

'Perhaps you think all governments are bad.'

'I am not acquainted with all of them, sir,' parried Demetrius.

'Well,' observed Gallio, 'they're all alike.'

'That is regrettable,' said Demetrius, soberly.

'So—then—the young Galilean repudiated kingship—and got into trouble, I suppose, with his admirers—'

'And the Government, too. The rich Jews, fearing his influence in the country, insisted on having him tried for treason. Pilate, knowing he had done no wrong, made an effort to acquit him. But they would have him condemned. Against his will, Pilate sentenced him to death.' Demetrius hesitated. 'Sentenced him to be crucified,' he went on, in a low tone. 'The Commander of the fort at Minoa was ordered to conduct the execution.'

'Marcellus? Horrible!'

'Yes, sir. He fortunately was blind drunk when he did it. A seasoned Centurion, of the Minoa staff, had seen to that. But he was clear enough to realize that he was crucifying an innocent man—and—well, as you see, sir, he didn't get over it. He dismisses it from his mind for a while—and then it all sweeps over him again, like a bad dream. He sees the whole thing—so vividly that it amounts to acute pain! It is so real to him, sir, that he thinks everybody else must have known something about it; and he asks them if they do—and then he is ashamed that he asked.'

Gallio's eyes widened with sudden understanding.

'Ah!' he exclaimed. ' "Were you out there?" So—that's it!'

'That is it, sir; but not quite all.' Demetrius' eyes traveled to the window and for a moment he sat tapping his finger-tips together as if uncertain how to proceed. Then he faced the Senator squarely and went on. 'Before I tell you the rest of it, sir, I should like to say that I am not a superstitious person. I have not believed in miracles. I am aware that you have no faith in such things, and you may find it very hard to accept what I must now tell you.'

'Say on, Demetrius!' said Gallio, thumping his desk impatiently.

'This Jesus of Galilee wore a simple, brown, homespun Robe to the cross. They stripped it off and flung it on the ground. While he hung there, dying, my master and a few other officers sat near-by playing with dice. One took up this Robe and they cast for it. My master won it. Later in the evening, there was a banquet at the Insula. Everyone had been drinking to excess. A Centurion urged my master to put on the Robe.'

'Shocking idea!' grumbled Gallio. 'Did he do it?'

'He did it—quite unwillingly. He had been very far gone in wine, in the afternoon, but was now steadied. I think he might have recovered from the crucifixion horror if it had not been for the Robe. He put it on—*and he has never been the same since!*'

'You think the Robe is haunted, I suppose.' Gallio's tone was almost contemptuous.

'I think something happened to my master when he put it on. He tore it off quickly, and ordered me to destroy it.'

'Very sensible! A poor keepsake!'

'I still have it, sir.'

'You disobeyed him?'

Demetrius nodded.

'My master was not at himself when he gave that order. I have occasionally disobeyed him when I felt that the command was not to his best interest. And now I am glad I kept the Robe. If it was the cause of his derangement, it might become the instrument of his recovery.'

'Absurd!' expostulated Gallio. 'I forbid you to let him see it again!'

Demetrius sat silent while Gallio, rising angrily, paced the floor. Presently he stopped short, rubbed his jaw reflectively, and inquired:

'Just *how* do you think this Robe might be used to restore my son's mind?'

'I do not know, sir,' Demetrius confessed. 'I have thought about it a great deal. No plan has suggested itself.' He rose to his feet and met the Senator's eyes directly. 'It has occurred to me that we might go away for a while. If we were alone, an occasion might arise. He is quite on the defensive here. He is confused and ashamed of his mental condition. Besides—there is something else weighing heavily on his mind. The daughter of Legate Gallus will return soon. She will expect my master to call on her, and he is worrying about this meeting. He does not want her to see him in his present state.'

'I can understand that,' said Gallio. 'Perhaps you are right. Where do you think he should go?'

'Is it not customary for a cultured young man to spend some time in Athens? Should he decide to go there—either to attend lectures or practice some of their arts—no questions would be asked. Your son has always been interested in sculpture. My belief is that it will be difficult to do very much for him while he remains here. He should not be confined to the house; yet he knows he is in no condition to see his friends. The word may get about that something is wrong. This would be an embarrassment for him—and the family. If it is your wish, sir, I shall try to persuade him to go to Athens. I do not think it will require much urging. He is very unhappy.'

'Yes—I know,' muttered Gallio, half to himself.

'He is so unhappy'—Demetrius lowered his voice to a tone of intimate confidence—'that I fear for his safety. If he remains here, Diana may not find him alive when she returns.'

'You mean—Marcellus might destroy himself rather than face her?'

'Why not? It's a serious matter with him.'

'Have you any reason to believe that he has been contemplating suicide?'

Demetrius was slow about replying. Drawing a silver-handled dagger from the breast of his tunic, he tapped its keen blade against the palm of his hand. Gallio recognized the weapon as the property of Marcellus.

'I think he has been toying with the idea, sir,' said Demetrius.

'You took this from him?'

Demetrius nodded.

'He thinks he lost it on the boat.'

Gallio sighed deeply; and, returning to his desk, he sat down, drew out a sheet of papyrus and a stylus, and began writing rapidly in large letters. Finishing, he affixed his seal.

'Take my son to Athens, Demetrius, and help him recover his mind. But no man should ask a slave to accept such a responsibility.' He handed the document to Demetrius. 'This is your certificate of manumission. You are a free man.'

Demetrius stared at the writing in silence. It was hard for him to realize its full significance. Free! Free as Gallio! He was his own man! Now he could speak—even to Lucia—as a freedman! He was conscious of Gallio's eyes studying him with interest as if attempting to read his thoughts. After a long moment, he slowly shook his head and returned the document to the Senator.

'I appreciate your generosity, sir,' he said, in an unsteady voice. 'In any other circumstance, I should be overjoyed to accept it. Liberty means a great deal to any man. But I think we would be making a mistake to alter the relationship between my master and his slave.'

'Would you throw away your chance to be free'—demanded Gallio, huskily—'in order to help my son?'

'My freedom, sir, would be worthless to me—if I accepted it at the peril of Marcellus' recovery.'

'You are a brave fellow!' Gallio rose and walked across the room to his huge bronze strong-box. Opening a drawer, he deposited the certificate of Demetrius' release from bondage. 'Whenever you ask for it,' he declared, 'it will be here, waiting for you.' He was extending his hand; but Demetrius, pretending not to have seen the gesture, quickly raised his spear-shaft to his forehead in a stiff salute.

'May I go now, sir?' he asked, in the customary tone of servitude.

Gallio bowed respectfully—as to a social equal.

* * * * * *

No one in the household had been more distressed than Marcipor, who did not feel at liberty to ask questions of anybody but Demetrius, and Demetrius' time had been fully occupied. All day he had paced about restlessly, wondering what manner of tragedy had befallen Marcellus whom he idolized.

When the door of the library opened, after the lengthy interview, Marcipor, waiting impatiently in the atrium, came forward to meet Demetrius. They clasped hands silently and moved away together into an alcove.

'What is it all about, Demetrius?' asked Marcipor, in a guarded tone. 'Is it something you can't tell me?'

Demetrius laid a hand on the older Corinthian's shoulder and drew him closer.

'It is something I *must* tell you,' he murmured. 'Come to my room at midnight. I cannot tarry now. I must go back to him.'

After the villa was quiet and Demetrius was assured that Marcellus was asleep, he retired to his adjacent bedchamber. Presently there was a light tap on the door, and Marcipor entered. They drew their chairs close and talked in hushed voices until the birds began to stir in the pale blue light of the oncoming dawn. It was a long, strange story that Demetrius had to tell. Marcipor wanted to see the Robe. Demetrius handed it to him, and he examined it curiously.

'But *you* don't believe there is some peculiar power in this garment; do you?' asked Marcipor.

'I don't know,' admitted Demetrius. 'If I said, "Yes—I do believe that," you would think I was going crazy; and if I feared I was crazy, I wouldn't be a fit person to look after Marcellus, who unquestionably *is* crazy—and needs my care. So—I think I had better say that there's nothing in this Robe that you don't put into it yourself—out of your own imagination. As for me—I saw this man, and—well—that makes all the difference. He was not an ordinary person, Marcipor. I could be easily persuaded that he was divine.'

'That seems an odd thing for you to say, Demetrius,' disapproved Marcipor, studying his face anxiously. 'You're the last man I would have picked for it.' He stood up, and held the Robe out at arm's length. 'Do you care if I put it on?'

'No—he wouldn't care—if you put it on,' said Demetrius.

'Who do you mean—wouldn't care?' Marcipor's face was puzzled. 'Marcellus?'

'No—the man who owned it. He didn't object to my having it, and you are as honest as I am.'

'By the gods, Demetrius,' muttered Marcipor. 'I believe you *are* a bit touched by all this grim business. How do you know he didn't object to your having his Robe? That's foolish talk!'

'Well—be it foolish or not—when I touch this Robe it—it does something to me,' stammered Demetrius. 'If I am tired, it rests me. If I am dejected, it revives my spirits. If I am rebellious over my slavery, it reconciles me. I suppose that is because—when I handle his Robe—I remember his strength—and courage. Put it on—if you want to, Marcipor. Here—let me hold it for you.'

Marcipor slipped his long arms into the sleeves, and sat down.

'It *is* strangely warm,' he said. 'My imagination, I suppose. You have told me of his deep concern for the welfare of all other people; and—quite naturally—his—Robe—' Marcipor's groping words slowed to a stop, and he gave Demetrius a perplexed wisp of a smile.

'I'm not as crazy as I look; eh?' grinned Demetrius.

'What *is* it?' asked Marcipor, in a husky whisper.

'Well—whatever it *is*,' said Demetrius, 'it's *there!*'

'Peace?' queried Marcipor, half to himself.

'And confidence,' added Demetrius.

'And—one need not worry—for everything—will come out—all right.'

Chapter VIII

AT SUNSET on the last day of the month which Julius Caesar—revising the calendar—had named for himself, Marcellus and his slave sighted the Parthenon from a decrepit vehicle that rated a place in the Athenian Museum of Antiquities. It was with mingled feelings that Demetrius renewed acquaintance with his native land.

Had his business in the Grecian capital been more urgent, and had he been of normal mind, the erstwhile Legate of the Legion at Minoa might have fretted over the inexcusable tedium of their voyage.

He and Demetrius had embarked on the Greek ship *Clytia* for the sole reason that they wanted to leave Rome without delay and *The Clytia's* sailing was immediate. In no other respect was this boat to be recommended. Primarily a cargo vessel built expressly for wheat shipments to the Imperial City, the battered old hulk usually returned to Greece in ballast, except for certain trivial consignments of furniture and other household gear for Roman envoys in the provinces.

There were no private accommodations for passengers. All nine of them shared the same cabin. There was only one deck. At the stern a primitive kitchen, open to the sky, was at the disposal of fare-paying voyagers who were expected to cook their own meals. *The Clytia* had the raw materials for sale at a nice profit.

Almost too handy to the kitchen and adjacent dining-table a half-dozen not very tidy pens confined a number of unhappy calves and sheep, and a large crate of dilapidated fowls. Upon embarkation there had also been a few pigs, but a Jewish merchant from Cytherea had bought them, on the second day out, and had unceremoniously offered them to Neptune—with his unflattering compliments, for he was not a good sailor.

Amidship in the vicinity of *The Clytia's* solitary mast a constricted area of deck space, bounded by a square of inhospitable wooden benches, served as promenade and recreation center. Beside the mast a narrow hatchway descended steeply into the common cabin which was lighted and ventilated by six diminutive ports. Upon the slightest hint of a fresh breeze these prudent little ports were closed. *The Clytia* made no attempt to pamper her passengers. Indeed, it was doubtful whether any other craft plying between Ostia and Piraeus was equipped to offer so comprehensive an assortment of discomforts.

The grimy old ship's only grace was her love of leisure. She called everywhere and tarried long; three days and nights, for example, in unimportant Corfu where she had only to unload a bin of silica and take on a bale of camel's-hair shawls; four whole days in Argostoli where she replenished her water-casks, discharged a grateful passenger, and bought a crate of lemons. She even ambled all the way down to Crete, for no better cause than to leave three blocks of Carrara marble and acquire a case of reeking bull-hides for conversion into shields. While in port, one of her frowsy old hawsers parted, permitting *The Clytia* to stave a galley that lay alongside; and another week had passed before everybody was satisfied about that and clearance was ordered for the next lap of the interminable cruise.

Had Marcellus been mentally well, he would surely have found these delays and discomforts insupportable. In his present mood of apathetic detachment, he endured his experiences with such effortless fortitude that Demetrius' anxiety about him mounted to alarm. Marcellus had no natural talent for bearing calmly with annoyances, however trivial; and it worried the Corinthian to see his high-spirited master growing daily more and more insensitive to his wretched environment. As for himself, Demetrius was so exasperated by all this boredom and drudgery that he was ready to jump out of his skin.

Vainly he tried to kindle a spark of interest in the wool-gathering mind of Marcellus. The Senator had provided his son with a small but carefully selected library; classics, mostly, and Demetrius had tactfully endeavored to make him read; but without success.

For the better part of every fair day, Marcellus would sit silently staring at the water. Immediately after breakfast he would pick his way forward through the clutter that littered the deck; and, seating himself on a coil of anchor-cable near the prow, would remain immobile with his elbows on his knees and his chin in his hands, gazing dully out to sea. Demetrius would give him time to get himself located, and then he too would saunter forward with a few scrolls under his arm and sprawl at full length on a battened hatch close by. Sometimes he would read a paragraph or two aloud and ask a question. On these occasions, Marcellus would sluggishly return from a remote distance to make a laconic reply, but it was obvious that he preferred not to be molested.

Although Demetrius' chief concern was to beguile his master's roving mind, he himself was finding food for reflection. Never before had he found opportunity for so much uninterrupted reading. He was particularly absorbed by the writings of Lucretius. Here, he thought, was a wise man.

'Ever read Lucretius, sir?' he asked, one afternoon, after an hour's silence between them.

Marcellus slowly turned his head and deliberated the question.

'Indifferently,' he replied, at length.

'Lucretius thinks it is the fear of death that makes men miserable,' went on Demetrius. 'He's for abolishing that fear.'

'A good idea,' agreed Marcellus, languidly. After a long wait, he queried, 'How does he propose to do it?'

'By assuming that there is no future life,' explained Demetrius.

'That would do it,' drawled Marcellus—'provided the assumption would stay where you had put it.'

'You mean, sir, that the assumption might drag its anchor in a gale?'

Marcellus smiled wanly at the seagoing metaphor, and nodded. After a meditative interval, he said:

'For some men, Demetrius, the fear of death might be palliated by the belief that nothing more dreadful could possibly happen to them than had already happened—in their present existence. Perhaps Lucretius has no warrant for saying that all men fear death. Some have even sought death. As for me—I am not conscious of that fear; let death bring what it will. . . . But does Lucretius have aught to say to the man who fears life?'

Demetrius was sorry he had introduced the conversation, but he felt he should not abandon it abruptly; assuredly not at this dismaying juncture.

'Lucretius concedes that all life is difficult, but becoming less so as men evolve from savagery to civilization.' Demetrius tried to make this observation sound optimistic. Marcellus chuckled bitterly.

' "As men evolve from savagery," eh! What makes him think men are evolving from savagery?' He had an impatient gesture, throwing the idea away with a toss of his hand. 'Lucretius knew very little about what was going on in the world. Lived like a mole in a burrow. Lived on his own fat like a bear in winter. Went wrong in his head at forty, and died. "Evolving from savagery"? Nonsense! Nothing that ever went on in the jungle can compare with the bestiality of our life today!' Marcellus' voice had mounted from a monologic mutter to a high-tensioned harangue. ' "Evolving from savagery"!' he shouted. 'You know better than that. *You were out there!*'

Demetrius nodded soberly.

'It was very sad,' he said, 'but I think you have reproached yourself too much, sir. You had no alternative.'

Marcellus had retreated into his accustomed lethargy, but he suddenly roused, clenching his fists.

'That's a lie, Demetrius, and you know it! There *was* an alternative! I could have set the Galilean free! I had enough of those tough fellows from Minoa with me to have dispersed that mob!'

'Pilate would have court-martialed you, sir. It might have cost you your life!'

'My life!' shouted Marcellus. 'It *did* cost me my life! Far better to have lost it honorably!'

'Well,' soothed Demetrius, gently, 'we should try to forget about it now. In Athens you can divert your mind, sir. Are you not looking forward with some pleasure to your studies there?'

There was no reply. Marcellus had turned his back and was again staring at the sea.

On another day, Demetrius—imprudently, he felt afterward—ventured to engage his moody master again in serious talk.

'Lucretius says here that our belief that the gods are concerned with our human affairs has been the source of nothing but unhappiness to mankind.'

'Of course,' muttered Marcellus—'and he was a fool for believing that the gods exist, at all.' After *The Clytia* had swayed to and fro sleepily for a couple of stadia, he mumbled, 'Lucretius was crazy. He knew too much about the unknowable. He sat alone—and thought—and thought—until he lost his mind. . . . That's what I'm doing, Demetrius.'

* * * * * *

In a less perturbed state of mind, Marcellus—thoroughly fatigued by the long journey—would have been gaily excited over the welcome he received at the hands of his Athenian host, though this warm reception was not altogether unexpected.

When Marcus Lucan Gallio was in his early twenties, he had spent a summer in Athens, studying at the famous old Academy of Hipparchus, and lodging in the exclusive House of Eupolis which had been conducted by one family for five generations. Old Georgias Eupolis, his host, treated the patrons of his establishment as personal guests. You had to be properly vouched for if you sought accommodations there; but having been reliably introduced, nothing was too good for you.

The cool hauteur of the House of Eupolis in its attitude toward applicants was not mere snobbery. Athens was always filled with strangers. The city had more than a hundred inns, and all but a half-dozen of them were notorious. The typical tavern-keeper was a panderer, a thief, and an all-around rascal; and, for the most part, his clients were of the same feather. The Athenian inn that hoped to maintain a reputation for decency had to be critical of its registrants.

Apparently young Gallio had made a favorable impression, for when he left the House of Eupolis old Georgias had broken a silver drachma in two; and, handing one half to Marcus, had attached a little tablet of memoranda to the other which he had put away for safe-keeping.

'Whoever presents your piece of that drachma, my son,' Georgias had said, 'will be welcome here. You will not lose it, please.'

Arriving now at dusk in the shaded courtyard of the fine old hostelry, Marcellus had silently handed the broken coin to the churlish porter who had stepped out of the shadow to question them. Immediately the slave's behavior had changed from surly challenge to alert deference. Bowing and scraping he had made haste to carry the little talisman to his master. In a few moments the genial proprietor—a well-groomed man of forty—had come down the stone steps of the vine-clad portico, offering a smile and outstretched hands. Marcellus had stepped out of the antiquated chariot, announcing that he was the son of Gallio.

'And how are you addressed, sir?' asked the inkeeper.

'I am a Tribune. My name is Marcellus.'

'Your father is well remembered here, Tribune Marcellus. I hope he is alive and well.'

'He is, thank you. Senator Gallio sends his greetings to your house. Though it was a very long time ago, my father hopes his message of affection for Georgias may still be delivered.'

'Alas! My venerable father has been gone these ten years. But in his name, I give you welcome. My name is Dion. The House of Eupolis is yours. Come in! I can see you are weary.'

He turned to Demetrius.

'The porter will help you with your burdens, and show you where you are to sleep.'

'I wish my slave to share my own quarters,' put in Marcellus.

'It is not customary with us,' said Dion, a bit coolly.

'It is with me,' said Marcellus. 'I have been subjected lately to considerable hardship,' he explained, 'and I am not well. I do not wish to be alone. Demetrius will lodge with me.'

Dion, after a momentary debate with himself, gave a shrug of reluctant consent, and signed to Marcellus to precede him into the house.

'You will be responsible for his conduct,' he said, crisply, as they mounted the steps.

'Dion,' said Marcellus, pausing at the doorway, 'had this Corinthian his freedom, he would appear at an advantage in any well-bred company. He has been gently brought up; is a person of culture, and brave withal. The House of Eupolis will come to no dishonor on his account.'

The well-worn appointments of the spacious andronitis, into which entrance was had directly from the front door, offered a substantial, home-like comfort.

'If you will be seated, Marcellus,' advised Dion, recovering his geniality, 'I shall find the other members of my family. Then—because you are tired—I shall show you to your rooms. Will you be with us long?'

Marcellus lifted an indecisive hand.

'For some time, I think,' he said. 'Three months; four; six: I do not know. I want quiet. Two bedchambers, a small parlor, and a studio. I might want to amuse myself with some modeling.' Dion said he understood, and would be able to provide a suitable suite.

'And you will face the garden,' he said, as he moved toward the stairs. 'We have some exceptionally fine roses, this year.'

Demetrius entered as Dion disappeared and came to the chair where Marcellus sat.

'Have you learned, sir, where we are to go?' he asked.

'He will tell us. Remain here until he comes,' said Marcellus, wearily.

Presently they appeared, and he rose to meet them; Dion's comely wife, Phoebe, who, having learned the identity of their guest, was genuinely cordial; and Ino, Dion's widowed elder sister, who thought she saw in Marcellus a strong resemblance to the young man she had admired so much.

'Once we thought,' said Dion, with a teasing smile for his sister, 'that something might come of it.'

'But we Greeks are never comfortable anywhere else,' explained Ino, which made Marcellus wonder if their friendship hadn't been serious.

No one had paid any attention to Demetrius, which was entirely natural, for Dion had probably advised the family that Marcellus was accompanied by his slave.

At the first pause in the conversation, Ino turned to him inquiring if he wasn't a Greek. Demetrius bowed a respectful affirmative.

'Where?' inquired Ino.

'Corinth.'

'You have been in Athens before?'

'Once.'

'Do you read?'

'Sometimes.'

Ino laughed a little. Glancing toward her brother, she was aware that he disapproved of this talk. So did Marcellus, she noticed. Demetrius retreated a step and straightened to a sentry's posture. There was a momentary constraint before general conversation was resumed.

While they talked, a tall, strikingly beautiful girl sauntered in through the front door, apparently having just arrived from without the grounds, for she wore an elaborately fringed and tasseled pink himation, drawn about her so tightly that it accented her graceful figure. Her mother reached out an affectionate hand as she came into the circle.

'Our daughter, Theodosia,' she said. 'My child, our guest is Marcellus, the son of Marcus Gallio, of whom you have often heard your father speak.'

Theodosia gave him a bright smile. Then her dark, appraising eyes drifted over his shoulder and surveyed Demetrius with interest. He met her look of inquiry with what was meant to be a frown. This only added to Theodosia's curiosity. Obviously she was wondering why no one was inclined to introduce him.

It was an awkward moment. Marcellus did not want to hurt Demetrius. He felt it would be cruel to remark, casually, 'That man is my slave.' He heartily wished afterward that he had done so, instead of merely trying to be humane.

'This is Demetrius,' he said.

Theodosia took a step forward, looked up into Demetrius' face, and gave him a slow smile that approved of him first with her candid eyes and then with pouting lips. Demetrius gravely bowed with stiff dignity. Theodosia's eyes were puzzled. Then, after a little hesitation—for unmarried women were not accustomed to shaking hands with men, unless they were close relatives—she offered him her hand. Demetrius stared straight ahead and pretended not to see it.

'He's a slave,' muttered her father.

'Oh,' said Theodosia. 'I didn't know.' Then she looked up into Demetrius' eyes again. He met her look, this time, curiously. 'I'm sorry,' she murmured. Aften an instant she stammered in a tone that was almost intimate, 'It is too bad—that we have to—to be this way—I think. I hope we have not—I didn't mean—' She floundered to a stop as Demetrius, with an understanding smile, nodded that it was all right, and she wasn't to fret about it.

'We will show you to your suite now,' said Dion, abruptly.

Marcellus bowed to the women and followed his host, Demetrius marching stiffly behind him. Theodosia stared after them until they disappeared. Then she gave a quick little sigh and turned a self-defensive smile on her aunt.

'Forget it, child,' murmured Ino, sensibly. 'How could you know he was a slave; certainly wasn't dressed like one; certainly didn't look like one. And we don't have slaves standing about in here.'

'Well—it shouldn't have happened,' said Phoebe, crossly. 'You'll have to be careful now. If he takes any advantage of this, you must snub him—properly!'

'Wasn't he snubbed—properly?' wondered Theodosia.

'With words, perhaps,' remarked Aunt Ino, with a knowing grin.

* * * * * *

After a week, Demetrius, who had counted heavily upon this sojourn in Athens to relieve his master's deep dejection, began to lose heart.

Upon their arrival at the House of Eupolis, Marcellus had been welcomed so warmly—and had responded to these amenities so gratefully—that Demetrius felt they had already gone a long way toward solving the distressing problem.

The new environment was perfect. Their sunny rooms on the ground floor looked out upon a gay flower-garden. In their stone-flagged little peristyle, comfortable chairs extended an invitation to quiet reading. Surely no one at all interested in sculpture could have asked for a better opportunity than the studio afforded.

But it was of no use. Marcellus' melancholy was too heavy to be lifted. He was not interested in Demetrius' suggestion that they visit the Acropolis or Mars' Hill or some of the celebrated galleries.

'How about strolling down to the agora?' Demetrius had pleaded, on the second morning. 'It's always interesting to see the country people marketing their produce.'

'Why don't you go?' countered Marcellus.

'I do not like to leave you alone, sir.'

'That's true,' nodded Marcellus. 'I dislike being alone.'

He wouldn't even go to see the Temple of Heracles, directly across the street, within a boy's arrow of where he sat slowly examining his fingers. Demetrius expected that he would surely want to show some civility to the Eupolis family. Dion had called twice, frankly perplexed to find his guest so preoccupied and taciturn. Theodosia had appeared, one morning, at the far end of the garden; and Marcellus, observing her, had come in from the peristyle, apparently to avoid speaking to her.

Demetrius thought he knew what was keeping Marcellus away from the Eupolis family. He never could tell when one of these mysterious seizures would arrive to grip him until the sweat streamed down his face, in the midst of which he would stun somebody with the incomprehensible query,

'Were you out there?' Not much wonder he didn't care to have a friendly chat with Theodosia.

True, it was not absolutely necessary for Marcellus to make further connections with his host's family. Meals were sent over to their suite. Household slaves kept their rooms in order. Demetrius had practically nothing to do but wait—and keep a watchful but not too solicitous eye on his master. It was very trying, and he was bored almost to death.

On the morning of the eighth day, he resolved to do something about it.

'If you are not quite ready to do any modeling, sir,' he began, 'would you object if I amused myself with some experiments in clay?'

'Not at all,' mumbled Marcellus. 'I know this must be very tiresome for you. By all means, get the clay.'

So—that afternoon, Demetrius dragged the tall, stout modeling-table into the center of the studio and began some awkward attempts to mould a little statuette. After a while, Marcellus came in from his perpetual stupor in the peristyle and sat down in the corner to watch. Presently he chuckled. It was not a pleasantly mirthful chuckle, but ever so much better than none. Realizing that his early adventure in modeling was at least affording some wholesome entertainment, Demetrius persisted soberly in the production of a bust that would have made a dog laugh.

'Let me show you.' Marcellus came over to the table and took up the clay. 'To begin with, it's too dry,' he said, with something like critical interest. 'Get some water. If you're going to do this at all, you may as well give yourself a chance.'

Now, thought Demetrius, we have solved our problem! He was so happy he could hardly keep his joy out of his face, but he knew that Marcellus would resent any felicitations. All afternoon they worked together; rather, Marcellus worked, and Demetrius watched. That evening Marcellus ate his supper with relish and went early to bed.

After breakfast the next morning, it delighted Demetrius to see his master stroll into the studio. He thought he would leave him alone. Perhaps it would be better for him to work without any distraction.

In a half-hour, Marcellus trudged out to the peristyle and sat down. He was pale. His forehead was beaded with perspiration. His hands were trembling. Demetrius turned away with a deep sigh. That night he decided to do the thing he had resolved to do if all other expedients failed. It would be drastic treatment. In Marcellus' mental condition, it might indeed be the one tragic move that would put him definitely over the border line. But he couldn't go on this way! It was worth a trial.

After Marcellus had retired, Demetrius went over to the kitchen and asked Glycon, the steward, whether he could tell him the name of a first-class weaver: he wanted to have a garment mended for his master. Glycon was prompt with the information. Of course! A skillful weaver? Who but old Benjamin? That would be down near the Theater of Dionysus. Anybody could tell you, once you got to the theater.

'Benjamin sounds like a Jew,' remarked Demetrius.

'So he is,' nodded Glycon, 'and a fine old man; a scholar, they say.' Glycon laughed. 'There's one Jew not interested in getting rich. I've heard it said that if Benjamin doesn't like your looks he won't do business with you.'

'Perhaps he wouldn't care to talk with a slave,' wondered Demetrius.

'Oh—that wouldn't matter to Benjamin,' Glycon declared. 'Why should it? Haven't his own people rattled plenty of chains?'

* * * * * *

All the next day until mid-afternoon, Marcellus sat slumped in his big chair outside the doorway, staring dully at the garden. In the adjacent studio, Demetrius disinterestedly toyed with the soft clay, listening for any movement in the little peristyle. Twice he had gone out, with an assumption of cheerfulness, to ask questions which he thought might stir his moody master's curiosity about his absurd attempts at modeling; but there was no response.

The situation had now become so desperate that Demetrius felt it was high time to make the dangerous experiment which—if everything else failed—he had resolved to try. His heart beat rapidly as he turned away from the table and went to his own room, and his hands were trembling as he reached into the depths of the large sailcloth bag in which the cherished Galilean garment had been stowed.

It had been many weeks since he had seen it himself. He had had no privacy on *The Clytia*, and the enchanted Robe that had so profoundly affected Marcellus' mind had not been unpacked since they had left Rome.

Sitting down on the edge of his couch, Demetrius reverently unfolded it across his knees. Again he had this strange sensation of tranquility that had come to him when he had handled the Robe in Jerusalem. It was a peculiar sort of calmness; not the calmness of inertia or indifference, but the calmness of self-containment. He was stilled—but strengthened.

There had never been any room in his mind for superstition. He had always disdained the thought that any sort of power could be resident in an inanimate object. People who believed in the magical qualities of insensate things were either out-and-out fools, or had got themselves into an emotional state where they were the easy victims of their own inflamed imagination. He had no patience with otherwise sensible men who carried lucky stones in their pockets. It had comforted him to feel that although he was a slave his mind was not in bondage.

Well—be all that as it might—the solid fact remained that when he laid his hands upon the Galilean's Robe, his agitation ceased. His nervous anxiety vanished. After the previous occasion when he had sensed this, he had told himself that the extraordinary experience could be accounted for on the most practical, common-sense terms. This Robe had been worn by a man of immense courage; effortless, inherent, built-in, automatic courage! Demetrius had seen this Jesus on trial, serene and self-assured with the whole world arrayed against him, with death staring him in the face, and not one protesting friend in sight. Was it not natural that his Robe should become a symbol of fortitude?

With far too much time on his hands during these recent weeks, Demetrius had deliberated upon this phenomenon until he had arrived at the reasonable explanation of his own attitude toward the thorn-torn garment: it was a symbol of moral strength, just as his mother's ring was a symbol of her tender affection.

But now!—with the Robe in his suddenly steadied hands—he wasn't so sure about the soundness of his theory. There was a power clinging to this homespun Galilean Robe which no cool rational argument was fit to cope with. Indeed, it seemed rather impudent to attempt an analysis of its claims upon his emotions.

Folding the Robe across his arm, Demetrius walked confidently to the open door. Marcellus slowly turned his head with a listless expression of inquiry. Then his eyes gradually widened with terror, his face a contorted mask of amazement and alarm. He swallowed convulsively and slowly bent backward over the broad arm of his chair, recoiling from the thing that had destroyed his peace.

'I have learned of a good weaver, sir,' said Demetrius, calmly. 'If you have no objections, I shall have him mend this Robe.'

'I told you'—Marcellus' dry throat drained the life out of his husky tone—'I ordered you—to destroy—that thing!' His voice rose, thin and shrill. 'Take it away! Burn it! Bury the ashes!' Pulling himself to his feet, he staggered to the corner of the peristyle, with the feeble steps of an invalid; and, hooking an arm around the pillar, he cried: 'I had not thought this of you, Demetrius! You have known the nature of my distress! And now—you come coolly confronting me with this torturing reminder; this haunted thing! I tell you—you have gone too far with your callous disobedience! I had always treated you as a friend—you who were my slave. I am finished with you! I shall sell you—in the market-place!' Thoroughly spent with rage, Marcellus slumped down upon the stone bench. 'Leave me,' he muttered, hoarsely. 'I can bear no more! Please go away!'

Demetrius slowly and silently withdrew into the house, shaking his head. His experiment had failed. It had been exactly the wrong thing to do. The patient, wearisome game of restoring Marcellus was now lost. Indeed, he was ever so much worse off; quite out of reach.

Returning to his own small bedchamber, Demetrius sat down, with the Robe still clutched tightly in his arms, and wondered what should be the next step to take. Curiously enough, Marcellus' complete breakdown had not upset him: he was unspeakably sorry, but self-controlled. The hysterical threat of being sold in the agora did not disturb him. Marcellus would not do that. Nor was he going to permit himself to be offended by the savagery of his master's rebuke. If ever Marcellus needed him, it was now.

Clearly the next thing to be done was to do nothing. Marcellus must be given time to compose himself. There would be no sense in trying to reason with him in his present state. It would be equally futile to plead for pardon. Marcellus had far better be left alone for a while.

Laying the folded Robe across the top of the capacious gunny-bag, Demetrius slipped quietly out through the front door and strolled through the cypress grove toward the street. Deeply preoccupied, he did not see Theodosia—in the swing—until he was too close to retreat unobserved. She straightened from her lounging posture, put down the trifle of needlework beside her, and beckoned to him. He was quite lonesome enough to have welcomed her friendly gesture, but he disliked the idea of compromising her. Theodosia was evidently a very willful girl, accustomed to treating the conventions with saucy indifference.

With undisguised reluctance, he walked toward the swing; and, at a little distance, drew up erectly to listen to whatever she might want to say. He was far from pleased by the prospect of getting them both into trouble, but there was no denying that Theodosia made a very pretty picture in the graceful white peplos girdled with a wide belt of paneled silver, a scarlet ribbon about her head that accented the whiteness of her brow, and gaily beaded sandals much too fragile for actual service.

'Why is it,' she demanded, with a comradely smile, 'that we see nothing of your master? Have we offended him? Does he disapprove of us? Tell me, please. I am dying of curiosity.'

'My master has not been well,' replied Demetrius, soberly.

'Ah—but there's more to it than that.' Theodosia's dark eyes were narrowed knowingly as she slowly nodded her blue-black head. 'You're troubled too, my friend. Needn't tell me you're not. You are worried about him. Is that not so?'

It was evident that this girl was used to having her own way with people.

She was so radiant with vitality that even her impudence was forgivable. Demetrius suddenly surprised them both with a candid confession.

'It is true,' he admitted. 'I am worried—beyond the telling!'

'Is there anything that we can do?' Theodosia's eager eyes were sincerely sympathetic.

'No,' said Demetrius, hopelessly.

'He has puzzled me,' persisted Theodosia. 'When you arrived, the other night, Marcellus struck me as a person who was trying to get away from something. He didn't really want to talk to us. You know that. He was polite enough—but very anxious to be off. I can't think it was because he did not like us. He had the air of one wanting to escape. It's clear enough that he is not hiding from the law; for surely this is no place for a fugitive.'

Demetrius did not immediately reply, though Theodosia had paused several times to give him a chance to say something. He had been busy thinking. As he stood listening to this bright girl's intuitive speculations, it occurred to him that she might be able to offer some sensible advice, if she knew what the problem was. Indeed, it would be better for her to know the facts than to harbor a suspicion that Marcellus was a rascal. He knew that Theodosia was reading in his perplexed eyes a half-formed inclination to be frank. She gave him an encouraging smile.

'Let's have it, Demetrius,' she murmured, intimately. 'I won't tell.'

'It is a long story,' he said, moodily. 'And it would be most imprudent for the daughter of Eupolis to be seen in an extended conversation with a slave.' He lowered his voice confidentially. 'Your father is already annoyed, you know, because you made the mistake of treating me cordially.'

Theodosia's pretty lips puckered thoughtfully.

'I do not think anyone is watching us,' she said, glancing cautiously toward the house. 'If you will walk briskly down the street, as if setting out on an errand, and turn to the right at the first corner—and again to the right, at the next one—you will come to a high-walled garden to the rear of that old temple over there.'

Demetrius shook his head doubtfully.

'Priests are notorious spies,' he said. 'At least they are in Rome, and it was true of them in Corinth. Doubtless it is the same here in Athens. I should think a temple would be about the last place that people would go for a private talk. We might find ourselves under suspicion of discussing a plot.'

Theodosia flushed a little—and gave him a mischievous smile.

'We will not be suspected of sedition,' she promised. 'I shall see to that. Two very good friends will have come to the garden—not to arrange for poisoning the Prefect's porridge—but to exchange pleasant compliments.'

Demetrius' heart quickened, but he frowned.

'Don't you think,' he asked, prudently, 'that you are taking a good deal for granted by trusting quite so much in the honesty of a slave?'

'Yes,' admitted Theodosia. 'Go quickly now. I'll join you presently.'

Deeply stirred by the anticipation of this private interview, but obliged to view it with some anxiety, Demetrius obeyed. Theodosia's almost masculine directness assured him that she was quite beyond a cheap flirtation, but there was no denying her winsome regard for him. Well—we would know, pretty soon, whether she was really concerned about Marcellus, or enlivening a dull afternoon with a bit of adventure. It was conceivable, of course, that both of these things might be true.

As he neared the old wall, Demetrius firmly pressed his gray bandeau down over the ear that denied him a right to talk on terms of equality with a free woman. It gave him a rather rakish appearance which, he felt, might not be altogether inappropriate if this meeting was to be staged as a rendezvous. Sauntering in through the open gate, he strolled to the far end of the arbor and sat down on the commodious marble lectus. A well-nourished priest, in a dirty brown cassock, gave him an indifferent nod, and resumed his hoeing.

He did not have long to wait. She was coming out of the temple, into the cloister, swinging along with her independent head held high. Demetrius stood to wait for her. It was hard to break an old habit, and his posture was stiffly conventional.

'Sit down!' she whispered. 'And don't look so serious.'

He did not have to dissemble a smile as he obeyed her, for her command had been amusing enough. She dropped down close beside him on the stone seat and gave him both hands. The priest leaned on his hoe and sanctioned their meeting with an informed leer. Then he looked a bit puzzled. Presently he dropped the hoe, deliberately cut a large red rose, and waddled toward them, his shifty little eyes alive with inquiry. Drawing an almost sinister smile, he presented the rose to Theodosia. She thanked him prettily and raising it to her face inhaled luxuriously. The priest, with his curiosity about them still unsatisfied, was backing away.

'Put your arm around me,' she muttered, deep in the rose, 'and hold me tight—as if you meant it.'

Demetrius complied, so gently, yet so competently, that the priest wagged his shaggy head and ambled back to his weeds. Then, apparently deciding that he had done enough work for one day, he negligently trailed the hoe behind him as he plodded away to disappear within the cloister, leaving them in sole possession of the quiet garden.

Reluctantly withdrawing his arm as Theodosia straightened, Demetrius remarked, with a twinkle, 'Do you suppose that holy beast might still be watching us—through some private peek-hole?'

'Quite unlikely,' doubted Theodosia, with a gently reproving smile.

'Perhaps we should take no risks,' he cautioned, drawing her closer.

She leaned back in his arm without protest.

'Now'—she said, expectantly—'begin at the beginning and tell me all about it. The Tribune is afraid of something—or somebody. Who is it? What is it?'

Demetrius was finding it difficult to launch upon his narrative. Theodosia's persuasive warmth was distracting his mind.

'You are very kind to me,' he said, softly.

'I should have had a brother,' she murmured. 'Let's pretend you are. You know—I feel that way about you—as if we'd known each other a long time.'

Resolutely pulling himself together, Demetrius began his story, not at the beginning but at the end.

'Marcellus,' he declared soberly, 'is afraid of a certain Robe—a brown, homespun, blood-stained Robe—that was worn by a man he was commanded to crucify. The man was innocent—and Marcellus knows it.'

'And the Robe?' queried Theodosia.

It was—as he had threatened—a long story; but Demetrius told it all, beginning with Minoa—and the journey to Jerusalem. Frequently Theodosia detained him with a question.

'But—Demetrius,' she interrupted, turning to look up into his face, 'what was there about this Jesus then that made him seem to you such a great man? You say he was so lonely and disappointed, that morning, when the crowd wanted him as their king: but what had he done to make so many people admire him so much?'

Demetrius had to admit he didn't know.

'It is hard to explain,' he stammered. 'You had a feeling that he was sorry for all of these people. This may sound very foolish, Theodosia; but it was as if they were homeless little children crying for something, and—'

'Something he couldn't give them?' she wondered, thoughtfully.

'There you have it!' declared Demetrius. 'It was something he couldn't give them, because they were too little and inexperienced to understand what they needed. Maybe this will seem a crazy thing to say: it was almost as if this Galilean had come from some far-away country where people were habitually honest and friendly and did not quarrel; some place where the streets were clean and no one was greedy, and there were no beggars, no thieves, no fights, no courts, no prisons, no soldiers; no rich, no poor.'

'You know there's no place like that,' sighed Theodosia.

'They asked him, at his trial—I'll tell you about that presently—whether he was a king; and he said he had a kingdom—but—it was not in the world.'

Theodosia glanced up, a bit startled, and studied his eyes.

'Now don't tell me you believe anything like that,' she murmured, disappointedly. 'You don't look like a person who would—'

'I'm not!' he protested. 'I don't know what I believe about this Jesus. I never saw anyone like him: that's as far as I can go.'

'That's far enough,' she sighed. 'I was afraid you were going to tell me he was one of the gods.'

'I take it you don't believe in the gods,' grinned Demetrius.

'Of course not! But do go on with your story. I shouldn't have interrupted.'

Demetrius continued. Sometimes it was almost as if he were talking to himself, as he reviewed the tragic events of that sorry day. He relived his strange emotions as the darkness settled over Jerusalem at mid-afternoon. Theodosia was very quiet, but her heart was beating hard and her eyes were misty.

'And he didn't try to defend himself—at all?' she asked, huskily; and Demetrius, shaking his head, went on to tell her of the gambling for the Robe, and what had happened that night at the Insula when Marcellus had been forced to put it on.

When he had finished his strange story, the sun was low. Theodosia rose slowly, and they walked arm in arm toward the cloister.

'Poor Marcellus,' she murmured. 'It would have to be something very exciting indeed—to divert his mind.'

'Well—I've tried everything I can think of,' sighed Demetrius. 'And now I'm afraid he has completely lost confidence in me.'

'He thinks the Robe is—haunted?'

Demetrius made no answer to that; and Theodosia, tugging at his arm, impulsively brought him to a stop. She invaded his eyes, one at a time, bewildered.

'But—*you* don't believe that! Do you?' she demanded.

'For my unhappy master, Theodosia, the Robe is haunted. He is convinced of it—and that makes it so—for him.'

'And what do *you* think? Is it haunted for *you?*'

He avoided her eyes for a moment.

'What I am going to say may sound silly. When I was a very little boy, and had fallen down and hurt myself, I would run into the house and find my mother. She would not bother to ask me what in the world I had been doing to bruise myself that way; or scold me for not being more careful. She would take me in her arms and hold me until I was through with my weeping, and everything was all right again. Perhaps my skinned knee still hurt, but I could bear it now.' He looked down tenderly into Theodosia's soft eyes. 'You see—my mother was always definitely on my side—no matter how I came by my mishaps.'

'Go on,' she said. 'I'm following you.'

'Often I have thought—' He interrupted himself to interpolate, 'Slaves get very lonesome, my friend!—Often I have thought there should be—for grown-up people—some place where they could go—when badly hurt—and find the same kind of assurance that a little child experiences in his mother's arms. Now—this Robe—it isn't haunted—for me—but—'

'I think I understand, Demetrius.'

After a moment's silence, they separated, leaving as they had arrived. Demetrius went out through the gate in the old wall. His complete review of the mysterious story had had a peculiar effect on him. Everything seemed unreal, as if he had spent an hour in a dream-world.

The clatter of the busy street, when he had turned the corner, jangled him out of his reverie. It occurred to him—and he couldn't help smiling—that he had spent a long time with his arm around the highly desirable Theodosia, almost oblivious of her physical charms. And he knew she had not been piqued by his fraternal attitude toward her. The story of Jesus—inadequately as Demetrius had related it out of his limited information—was of an emotional quality that had completely eclipsed their natural interest in each other's affections. Apparently the Galilean epic, even when imperfectly understood, had the capacity for lifting a friendship up to very high ground.

* * * * * *

It was quite clear now to Marcellus that the time for decisive action had arrived. Life, under these humiliating conditions, was no longer to be endured.

He had not fully shared his father's earnest hope that a sojourn in Athens—with plenty of leisure and no embarrassing social responsibilities—would relieve his mental strain. He knew that he would be carrying his burden along with him.

It was possible, of course, that time might dim the tragic picture that filled his mind. He would pursue a few distracting studies, give his restless hands some entertaining employments, and try to resume command of his thoughts.

But it was hopeless. He had no interest in anything! Since his arrival in Athens—far from experiencing any easing of the painful nervous tension—he had been losing ground. The dread of meeting people and having to talk with them had deepened into a relentless obsession. He was afraid to stir from the house. He even shunned the gardeners.

And now—he had gone to pieces. In an utter abandonment of all emotional control, he had made a sorry spectacle of himself in the sight of his loyal slave. Demetrius could hardly be expected to maintain his patience or respect much longer.

This afternoon, Marcellus had been noisy with his threats and recriminations. At the rate he was breaking up, by tomorrow afternoon he might commit some deed of violence. It was better to have done with this dreadful business before he brought harm to anyone else.

His people at home would be grieved when they learned the sad tidings, but bereavement was ever so much easier to bear than disgrace. As he sat there in the peristyle, with his head in his hands, Marcellus made a mental leave-taking of those he had loved best. He saw Lucia, in the shaded pergola, her slim legs folded under her as she sat quietly reading. He briefly visited his distinguished father in his library. He didn't worry so much about his father's reception of the bad news. Senator Gallio would not be surprised: he would be relieved to know that the matter was settled. Marcellus went up to his mother's room, and was glad to find her quietly sleeping. He was thankful that his imagination had at least spared him the anguish of a tearful parting.

He bade good-bye to Diana. They were together in the pergola, as on that night when he had left for Minoa. He had taken her in his arms, but rather diffidently, for he felt he would not be coming back; and it wasn't quite honest to make promises. This time he held Diana tightly—and kissed her.

Demetrius had unquestionably deceived him about the dagger he had bought in Corfu. It had been believed that the silver-handled dagger he had carried for years had been lost somehow on *The Vestris*. Marcellus had doubted that. Demetrius, alarmed over his melancholy state, had taken the weapon from him. However—the theft had been well enough meant. Marcellus had not pressed the matter; had even consented unprotestingly to the theory that the dagger was lost. At Corfu, he had found another. It was less ornamental than serviceable. Next day after leaving Corfu, it was missing. Marcellus had thought it unlikely that any of his fellow passengers would steal a dagger of such insignificant value. Demetrius had it: there was no question about that. Very likely, if he searched his slave's gunny-sack, he would find both of them.

Of course, it was possible that Demetrius might have thrown the weapons overboard, but he was so scrupulously honest that this seemed improbable. Demetrius would hold them against the arrival of a day when he thought it safe to restore them.

Unbuckling the belt of his tunic and casting it aside, Marcellus entered the Corinthian's small bedchamber, and saw the gunny-sack on his couch. His hands were trembling as he moved forward toward it; for it was no light matter to be that close to death.

Now he stopped! There it was—the *Thing!* He slowly retreated and leaned against the wall. Ah!—so the ingenious Demetrius had anticipated his decision! He was going to defend his stolen daggers with the Robe! Marcellus clenched his hands and growled. He would have it out with this Thing!

Resolutely forcing his feet to obey, he moved slowly to the couch and stretched out a shaking hand. The sweat was pouring down his face and his legs were so weak he could hardly stand. Suddenly he brought his hand down with a violent movement as if he were capturing a living thing.

For a long moment Marcellus stood transfixed, his fingers buried in the long-feared and hated garment. Then he sat down on the edge of the couch and slowly drew the Robe toward him. He stared at it uncomprehendingly; held it up to the light; rubbed it softly against his bare arm. He couldn't analyze his peculiar sensations, but something very strange had happened to him. His agitation was stilled. Rising, as if from a dream, he laid the Robe over his arm and went out into the peristyle. He sat down and draped it across the broad arms of his chair. He smoothed it gently with his hand. He felt a curious elation; an indefinable sense of relief—relief from everything! A great load had been lifted! He wasn't afraid any more! Hot tears gathered in his eyes and overflowed.

After a while he rose and carried the Robe back to Demetrius' room, placing it where he had found it. Unaccustomed to his new sense of well-being, he was puzzled about what to do next. He went into the studio and laughed at Demetrius' poor little statuette. The house wasn't quite large enough to hold him; so, donning his toga, he went out into the garden.

It was there that his slave found him.

Demetrius had approached the house with a feeling of dread. He knew Marcellus well enough to surmise that he wasn't going to be able to endure much more humiliation.

Entering the house quietly, he looked into his master's bedchamber and into the studio. Then he went out to the peristyle. His heart sank.

Then he saw Marcellus sauntering in the garden. He walked toward him eagerly, realizing instantly that a great change had come over him.

'You are feeling better, sir! Are you not?' said Demetrius, staring into his face incredulously.

Marcellus' lips twitched as he smiled.

'I have been away from you a long time, Demetrius,' he said, unsteadily.

'Yes, sir. I need not tell you how glad I am that you have returned. Is there anything I can do for you?'

'Did you tell me that you had learned of a good weaver; one who might mend that Robe?'

Enlightenment shone in Demetrius' eyes.

'Yes, sir!'

'After we have had our supper,' said Marcellus, 'we will try to find him.' He sauntered slowly toward the house, Demetrius following him, his heart almost bursting with exultation. When they reached the peristyle, Demetrius could no longer keep silent.

'May I ask you, sir, what happened?' he queried. 'Did you touch it?'

Marcellus nodded and drew a bewildered smile.

'I was hoping you would, sir,' said Demetrius.

'Why? Have you had any strange experiences with it?'

'Yes, sir.'

'What did it do to you?'

'I can't quite define it, sir,' stammered Demetrius. 'There's a queer energy—belonging to it—clinging to it—somehow.'

'Don't you know that's a very crazy thing to say?' demanded Marcellus.

'Yes, sir. I have tried to account for it. I saw him die, you know. He was very brave. Perhaps I invested this Robe with my own admiration for his courage. When I look at it, I am ashamed of my own troubles, and I want to behave with fortitude, and——'

He paused, uncertain how to proceed.

'And that explains it, you think?' persisted Marcellus.

'Y-yes, sir,' stammered Demetrius. 'I suppose so.'

'There's more to it than that, Demetrius, and you know it!'

'Yes, sir.'

Chapter IX

Waking at dawn, Marcellus was ecstatic to find himself unencumbered by the weight that so long had oppressed him. It was the first time he had ever realized the full meaning of freedom.

Pausing at Demetrius' open door he noted with satisfaction that his loyal slave, whose anxiety had been as painful as his own, was still soundly sleeping. That was good. Demetrius deserved a rest—and a forthright apology, too.

Not since that summer when, at fifteen, Marcellus was slowly convalescing from a serious illness, had he experienced so keen an awareness of life's elemental properties. The wasting fever had left him weak and emaciated; but through those days of his recovery his senses had been abnormally alert. Especially in the early morning: all colors were luminous, all sounds were intensified, all scents were heady concentrates of familiar fragrances.

Until then, the birds chirped and whistled, each species shrieking its own identifying cry; but it was silly to say that they sang. Now the birds sang, their songs melodious and choral. The dawn breeze was saturated with a subtle blend of newmown clover and sweetish honeysuckle, of jasmine and narcissus, welcoming him back to life's brightness and goodness. An occasional cool wisp of dank leaf-mould and fresh-spaded earth momentarily sobered him; and then he would rejoice that he had escaped their more intimate acquaintance.

For those few days, as a youth, Marcellus had been impressed by his kinship with all created things. It stilled and steadied his spirit to find himself so closely integrated with Nature. Then, as he regained his bodily vigor, this peculiar sensitivity gradually ceased to function. He still enjoyed the colors and perfumes of the flowers, the liquid calls of the birds, and the insistent hum of little winged creatures; but his brief understanding of their language was lost in the confusion of ordinary work and play. Nor did he expect ever to reclaim that transient rapture. Perhaps it could be experienced only when one's physical resources had ebbed to low tide, and one's fragility had made common cause with such other fragile things as hummingbirds and heliotrope.

This morning, to his happy amazement, that higher awareness had returned, filling him with a mystifying exaltation. He had somehow recaptured that indefinable ecstasy.

It had rained softly in the night, bathing the tall sycamores until their gaily fluttering leaves reflected glints of gold. The air was heavy with the scent of refreshed roses. Perhaps it was on such a morning, mused Marcellus, that Aristophanes had composed his famous apostrophe to the Birds of Athens.

Doubtless it was inevitable that yesterday afternoon's strange experience should have produced a sequence of varied reactions. The immediate effect of his dealings with the Robe had been a feeling of awe and bewilderment, quickly followed by an exhilaration bordering on hysteria. But the protracted neural strain had been so relentless, and had taken such a heavy toll, that this sudden release of tension had produced an almost paralyzing fatigue. Marcellus had gone supperless to bed and had slept like a little child.

Rousing, wide-awake, with an exultant sense of complete cleansing and renewal, he had wished he could lift his eyes and hands in gratitude to some kindly spirit who might be credited with this ineffable gift. As he sat there in the rose-arbor, he mentally called the roll of the classic gods and goddesses, questing a name worthy of homage; but he could think of none who deserved his intellectual respect; much less his reverence. He had been singularly blest; but the gift was anonymous. For the first time in his life, Marcellus envied all naïve souls who believed in the gods. As for himself, he was incapable of belief in them.

But this amazing experience with the Robe was something that could not be dismissed with a mere 'I do not understand; so—let it be considered a closed incident.'

No—it was a problem that had to be dealt with, somehow. Marcellus gave himself to serious reflection. First of all, the Robe had symbolized that whole shameful affair at Jerusalem. The man who wore it had been innocent of any crime. He had been unfairly tried, unjustly sentenced, and dishonorably put to death. He had borne his pain with admirable fortitude. Was 'fortitude' the word? No—murmured Marcellus—the Galilean had something else besides that. The best that 'fortitude' could accomplish was courageous endurance. This Jesus had not merely endured. It was rather as if he had confronted his tragedy!—*had gone to meet it!*

And then—that night at the Insula—dully sobering from a whole day's drunkenness, Marcellus had gradually roused to a realization that he—in the face of this incredible bravery—had carried out his brutal work as if the victim were an ordinary criminal. The utter perfidy of his behavior had suddenly swept over him like a storm, that night at Pilate's banquet. It was not enough that he had joined hands with cowards and scoundrels to crucify this Jesus. He had consented to ridicule the dead hero by putting on his blood-stained Robe for the entertainment of a drunken crowd. Not much wonder that the torturing memory of his own part in the crime had festered—and burned—and poisoned his spirit! Yes—that part of it was understandable. And because the Robe had been the instrument of his torture, it was natural, he thought, that he should have developed an almost insane abhorrence of it!

Yesterday afternoon, its touch had healed his wounded mind. How was he to evaluate this astonishing fact? Perhaps it was more simple than it seemed: perhaps he was making it all too difficult. He had shrunk from this Robe because it symbolized his great mistake and misfortune. Now—compelled by a desperate circumstance to lay his hands upon the Robe—his obsession had vanished! Was this effect purely subjective—or was the Robe actually possessed of magical power?

This latter suggestion was absurd! It was preposterous! It offended every principle he had lived by! To admit of such a theory, he would have to toss overboard all his reasonable beliefs in an impersonal, law-abiding universe—and become a confessed victim of superstition.

No—he could not and would not do that! There was no magic in this Robe! It was a mere tool of his imagination. For many weeks it had symbolized his crime and punishment. Now it symbolized his release. His remorse had run its full measure through the hourglass and the time had come for him to put his crime behind him. The touch of the Robe in his hands had simply marked the moment for the expiration of his mental punishment. He was not going to admit that the Robe was invested with power.

Today he would find that weaver and have the Robe repaired. He would at least show it that much honor and respect. It was nothing more than a garment—but it deserved to be handled with gratitude—and reverence! Yes—he would go that far! He could honestly say that he reverenced this Robe!

Demetrius had joined him now, apologetic for tardiness.

'I am glad you could sleep,' smiled Marcellus. 'You have had much worry—on my account. In my unhappiness, I have been rough with you. You have been quite understanding, Demetrius, and immensely patient. I am sorry for the way I have treated you; especially yesterday. That was too bad!'

'Please, sir!' pleaded Demetrius. 'I am so glad you are well again!'

'I think we will try to find your weaver, today, and see if he can mend the Robe.'

'Yes, sir. Shall I order your breakfast now?'

'In a moment. Demetrius—in your honest opinion—is that Robe haunted?'

'It is very mysterious, sir.' Demetrious was spacing his words deliberately. 'I had hoped that you might be able to throw a little light on it. May I ask what conclusion you have come to?'

Marcellus sighed and shook his head.

'The more I think about it,' he said, slowly, 'the more bewildering it is!' He rose, and moved toward the house.

'Well, sir,' volunteered Demetrius, at his elbow, 'it isn't as if we were *required* to comprehend it. There are plenty of things that we are not expected to understand. This may be one of them.'

* * * * * *

Across the street from the main entrance to the sprawling, open-air Theater of Dionysus, there was a huddle of small bazaars dealing in such trifles as the playgoers might pick up on their way in; sweetmeats, fans, and cushions. At the end of the row stood Benjamin's little shop, somewhat aloof from its frivolous neighbors. There was nothing on the door to indicate the nature of Benjamin's business; nothing but his name, burned into a cypress plank, and that not plainly legible; dryly implying that if you didn't know Benjamin was a weaver—and the oldest and most skillful weaver in Athens—you weren't likely to be a desirable client.

Within, the shop was suffocatingly stuffy. Not a spacious room to begin with, it contained—besides the two looms, one of them the largest Marcellus had ever seen—an ungainly spinning-wheel, a huge carding device, and bulky stores of raw materials; reed baskets heaped high with silk cocoons, big bales of cotton, bulging bags of wool.

Most of the remaining floor space was occupied by the commodious worktable on which Benjamin sat, cross-legged, deeply absorbed in the fine hem he was stitching around the flowing sleeve of an exquisitely wrought chiton. He was shockingly lean and stooped, and his bald head seemed much too large for his frail body. A long white beard covered his breast. His shabby robe was obviously not worn as a specimen of his handicraft. Behind him, against the wall and below the window-ledge, there was a long shelf well filled with scrolls whose glossy spools showed much handling.

Benjamin did not look up until he had reached the end of his thread; then, straightening with a painful grimace, he peered at his new clients with a challenge that wrinkled his long nose and uptipped his lip, after the manner of an overloaded, protesting camel. Except for the beady brightness of his deeply caverned eyes, Benjamin was as old as Jehovah—and as cross, too, if his scowl told the truth about his disposition.

Marcellus advanced confidently with Demetrius at his elbow.

'This garment,' he began, holding it up, 'needs mending.'

Benjamin puckered his leathery old mouth unpleasantly, sniffed, licked his thumb, and twisted a fresh thread to a sharp point.

'I have better things to do,' he declaimed, gutturally, 'than darn holes in old coats.' He raised his needle to the light, and squintingly probed for its eye. 'Go to a sailmaker,' he added, somewhat less gruffly.

'Perhaps I should not have bothered you with so small a matter,' admitted Marcellus, unruffled. 'I am aware that this garment is of little practical value, but it is a keepsake, and I had hoped to have it put in order by someone who knows how.'

'Keepsake, eh!' Old Benjamin reached for the Robe with a pathetically thin hand and pawed over it with well-informed fingers. 'A keepsake,' he mumbled. 'And how did this get to be a keepsake?' He frowned darkly at Marcellus. 'You are a Roman; are you not? This Robe is as Jewish as the Ten Commandments.'

'True!' conceded Marcellus, patiently. 'I am a Roman, and the Robe belonged to a Jew.'

'Friend of yours, I suppose.' Benjamin's tone was bitterly ironical.

'Not exactly a friend—no. But he was a brave Jew and well esteemed by all who knew him. His Robe came into my hands, and I wish to have it treated with respect.' Marcellus leaned closer to watch as the old man scratched lightly at a dark stain with his yellow finger-nail.

'Died fighting—maybe,' muttered Benjamin.

'It was a violent death,' said Marcellus, 'but he was not fighting. He was a man of peace—set upon by enemies.'

'You seem to know all about it,' growled Benjamin. 'However—it is naught to me how you came by this garment. It is clear enough that you had no hand in harming the Jew, or you would not think so highly of his old Robe.' Thawing slightly, he added, 'I shall mend it for you. It will cost you nothing.'

'Thanks,' said Marcellus, coolly. 'I prefer to pay for it. When shall I call?'

Benjamin wasn't listening. With his deep-lined old face upturned toward the window he was inspecting the Robe against the light. Over his thin shoulder he beckoned Marcellus to draw closer.

'Observe, please. It is woven without a seam; all in one portion. There is only one locality where they do that. It is up in the neighborhood of the Lake Gennesaret, in Galilee.' Benjamin waggled his beard thoughtfully. 'I have not seen a piece of Galilean homespun for years. This is from up around Capernaum somewhere, I'd say.'

'You are acquainted with that country?' inquired Marcellus.

'Yes, yes; my people are Samaritans, a little way to the south; almost on the border.' Benjamin chuckled grimly. 'The Samaritans and the Galileans never had much use for one another. The Galileans were great Temple people, spending much time in their synagogues, and forever leaving their flocks and crops to look after themselves while they journeyed to Jerusalem for the ceremonies. They kept themselves poor with their pilgrimages and sacrifices. We Samaritans didn't hold with the Temple.'

'Why was that?' wondered Marcellus.

Benjamin swung his thin legs over the edge of the table and sat up prepared to launch upon an extended lecture.

'Of course,' he began, 'you have heard the story of Elijah.'

Marcellus shook his head, and Benjamin regarded him with withering pity; then, apparently deciding not to waste any more time, he drew up his legs again, folded them comfortably, and resumed his rethreading of the needle.

'Was this Elijah one of the gods of Samaria?' Marcellus had the misfortune to inquire.

The old man slowly put down his work and seared his young customer with a contemptuous stare.

'I find it difficult to believe,' he declared, 'that even a Roman could have accumulated so much ignorance. To the Jew—be he Samaritan, Galilean, Judean, or of the dispersed—there is but one God! Elijah was a great prophet. Elisha, who inherited his mantle, was also a great prophet. They lived in the mountains of Samaria, long before the big temples and all the holy fuss of the lazy priests. We Samaritans have always worshiped on the hilltops, in the groves.'

'That sounds quite sensible to me,' approved Marcellus, brightly.

'Well,' grunted the old man, 'that's no compliment to our belief; though I suppose you intended your remark to be polite.'

Marcellus spontaneously laughed outright, and Benjamin, rubbing his long nose, grinned dryly.

'You are of a mild temper, young man,' he observed.

'That depends, sir, upon the nature of the provocation,' said Marcellus, not wishing to be thought weak. 'You are my senior—by many, many years.'

'Ah—so—and you think an old man has a right to be rude?'

'Apparently we share the same opinion on that matter,' drawled Marcellus, complacently.

Benjamin bent low over his work, chuckling deep in his whiskers.

'What is your name, young man?' he asked, after a while, without looking up; and when Marcellus had told him, he inquired, 'How long are you to be in Athens?'

The query was of immense interest to Demetrius. Now that conditions had changed, Marcellus might be contemplating an early return to Rome. He had not yet indicated what his intentions were, or whether he had given the matter any thought at all.

'I do not know,' replied Marcellus. 'Several weeks, perhaps. There are many things I wish to see.'

'How long have you been here?' asked Benjamin.

Marcellus turned an inquiring glance toward Demetrius, who supplied the information.

'Been on Mars' Hill?' queried the old man.

'No,' replied Marcellus, reluctantly.

'Acropolis?'

'Not yet.'

'You have not been in the Parthenon?'

'No—not yet.'

'Humph! What have you been doing with yourself?'

'Resting,' said Marcellus. 'I've recently been on two long voyages.'

'A healthy young fellow like you doesn't need any rest,' scoffed Benjamin. 'Two voyages, eh? You're quite a traveler. Where were you?'

Marcellus frowned. There seemed no limit to the old man's inquisitiveness.

'We came here from Rome,' he said, hoping that might be sufficient.

'That's one voyage,' encouraged Benjamin.

'And—before that—we sailed to Rome from Joppa.'

'Ah—from Joppa!' Benjamin continued his precise stitching, his eyes intent upon it, but his voice was vibrant with sudden interest. 'Then you were in Jerusalem. And how long ago was that?'

Marcellus made a mental calculation, and told him.

'Indeed!' commented Benjamin. 'Then you were there during the week of the Passover. I am told there were some strange happenings.'

Demetrius started; restlessly shifted his weight, and regarded his master with anxiety. Benjamin's darting glance, from under shaggy eyebrows, noted it.

'Doubtless,' replied Marcellus, evasively. 'The city was packed with all sorts. Anything could have happened.' He hitched at his belt, and retreated a step. 'I shall not interfere with your work any longer.'

'Come tomorrow—a little before sunset,' said Benjamin. 'The Robe will be ready for you. We will have a glass of wine together—if you will accept the hospitality of my humble house.'

Marcellus hesitated for a moment before replying, and exchanged glances with Demetrius who almost imperceptibly shook his head as if saying we had better not risk a review of the tragedy.

'You are most kind,' said Marcellus. 'I am not sure—what I may be doing—tomorrow. But—if I do not come, I shall send for the Robe. May I pay you now?' He reached into the breast of his tunic.

Benjamin continued stitching, as if he had not heard. After a long minute he searched Marcellus' eyes.

'I think,' he said slowly, patting the Robe with gentle fingers, 'I think you do not want to talk—about this Jew.'

Marcellus was plainly uncomfortable, and anxious to be off.

'It is a painful story,' he said, shortly.

'All stories about Jews are painful,' said Benjamin 'May I expect you tomorrow?'

'Y-yes,' agreed Marcellus, indecisively.

'That is good,' mumbled Benjamin. He held up his bony hand. 'Peace be upon you!'

'Er—thank you,' stammered Marcellus, uncertain whether he, in turn, was expected to confer peace upon the old Jew. Maybe that would be a social error. 'Farewell,' he said, finally, feeling he would be safe to leave it at that.

Outside the shop, Marcellus and Demetrius traded looks of mutual inquiry and sauntered across the road to the empty theater.

'Odd old creature,' remarked Marcellus. 'I'm not sure that I want to see any more of him. Do you think he is crazy?'

'No,' said Demetrius—'far from it. He is a very wise old man.'

'I think you feel that I should be making a mistake to come back here tomorrow.'

'Yes, sir. Better forget all about that now.'

'But—I wouldn't have to talk about that wretched affair in Jerusalem,' protested Marcellus. 'I can simply say that I do not want to discuss it.' His tone sounded as if he were rehearsing the speech he intended to make on that occasion. 'And that,' he finished, 'ought to settle it, I think.'

'Yes, sir; that ought to settle it,' agreed Demetrius—'but it won't. Benjamin will not be easily put off.'

They strolled down the long grass-grown aisle toward the deserted stage.

'Do you know anything about the customs and manners of the Jews, Demetrius?' queried Marcellus, idly.

'Very little, sir, about their customs.'

'When old Benjamin said, "Peace be upon you," what should I have replied? Is there a formulated answer to that?'

' "Farewell" is correct usage, sir, I think,' said Demetrius.

'But I did say that!' retorted Marcellus, returning with a bound from some faraway mental excursion.

'Yes, sir,' agreed Demetrius. He hoped they were not already slipping back into that pool of painful reflection.

They retraced their steps to the theater entrance.

'I wonder how much the old man knows about Galilee,' mused Marcellus.

'He will tell you tomorrow.'

'But—I'm not going back tomorrow! I don't want to have this matter reopened. I intend to put the whole thing out of my mind!'

'That is a wise decision, sir,' approved Demetrius, soberly.

* * * * * *

It was immediately apparent that this firm resolution was to be enforced. Leaving the Theater of Dionysus, they strolled through the agora where Marcellus paused before the market booths to exchange a bit of banter with rosy-cheeked country girls and slip copper denarii into the grimy incredulous hands of their little brothers and sisters. Then they went up on Mars' Hill and spent an hour in the sacred grove where the great of the Greeks had turned to stone.

Turning aside from the main path, Marcellus sat down on a marble bench, Demetrius standing a little way distant. Both were silently reflective. After an interval, Marcellus waved an arm toward the stately row of mutilated busts.

'Demetrius, it has just occurred to me that there isn't a warrior in the lot! You Greeks are hard fighters, when you're put to it; but the heroes who live forever in your public gardens are men of peace. Remember the Forum? Sulla, Antony, Scipio, Camillus, Julius, Augustus—all tricked out in swords and helmets! But look at this procession of Greeks, marching up the hill! Socrates, Epicurus, Herodotus, Solon, Aristotle, Polybius! Not a fighter among them!'

'But—they all look as if they'd been to war, sir,' jested Demetrius.

'Ah, yes—*we* did that!' said Marcellus, scornfully. 'Our gallant Roman legions; our brave illiterates!' He sat scowling for a moment; then went on, with unaccustomed heat: 'Demetrius—I say damn all men who make war on monuments! The present may belong to the Roman Empire by force of conquest; but, by all the gods, the past does not! A nation is surely of contemptible and cowardly mind that goes to battle against another nation's history! It didn't take much courage to come up here and hack the ears off old Pericles! I daresay the unwashed, drunken vandal who nicked his broadsword on the nose of Hippocrates could neither read nor write! There's not much dignity left in a nation that has no respect for the words and works of geniuses who gave the world whatever wisdom and beauty it owns!'

Deeply stirred to indignation, he rose and strode across the path, and faced the bust of Plato.

'That man!—for example—*he* has no nationality! *He* has no fatherland! *He* has no race! No kingdom—in this world—can claim him—or destroy him!' Abruptly, Marcellus stopped in the midst of what promised to be an oration. He stood silent, for a moment; then walked slowly toward Demetrius, and stared into his eyes.

'Do you know, Demetrius—that is what the Galilean said of himself!'

'I remember,' nodded Demetrius. 'He said his kingdom was not of the world—and nobody knew what he meant.'

'I wonder'—Marcellus' voice was dreamy. 'Perhaps—some day—he'll have a monument—like Plato's. . . . Come—let us go! We had decided to be merry, today; and here we've been owling it like old philosophers.'

It was late in the afternoon before they reached the inn. When they were drawing within sight of it, Marcellus remarked casually that he must call on the Eupolis family.

'I should have done so earlier,' he added, casually. 'Upon my word, I don't believe I've seen any of them since the night we arrived!'

'They will be glad to see you, sir,' said Demetrius. 'They have inquired about you frequently.'

'I shall stop and see them now,' decided Marcellus, impulsively. 'You may return to our suite. I'll be back presently.'

After they had separated, Demetrius reflected with some amusement that this renewal of acquaintance, after so strange a lapse, would be of much interest to the Eupolis household. Perhaps Theodosia would want to tell him about it.

Then he fell to wondering what she would think about himself in this connection. Had he not been so alarmed over his master's condition that he had confided his distress to her? And here was Marcellus—supposedly mired in an incurable despair—drifting in to call, as jauntily as if he had never fretted about anything in his life! Would Theodosia think he had fabricated the whole story? But she couldn't think that! Nobody could invent such a tale!

After a while one of the kitchen slaves came to announce that the Tribune would be dining with the family. Demetrius grinned broadly as he sauntered out alone to the peristyle. He wondered what they would talk about at dinner. The occasion would call for a bit of tact, he felt.

* * * * *

Early the next morning Marcellus donned a coarse tunic and set to work at his modeling-table with the air of a professional sculptor. Demetrius hovered about, waiting to be of service, until it became evident that nothing was desired of him today but his silence, perhaps his absence. He asked if he might take a walk.

Theodosia had set up a gaily colored target near the front wall that bounded the grounds and was shooting at it from a stadium's distance. She made a pretty picture in the short-sleeved white chiton, a fringe of black curls escaping her scarlet bandeau. As Demetrius neared, he was surprised to see that she was using a man's bow, and although she was not drawing it quite to top torsion her arrows struck with a clipped, metallic ping that represented an unusual strength, for a girl. And the shots were well placed, too. Demetrius reflected that if Theodosia wanted to, she could do a lot of damage with one of those long, bone-tipped arrows.

She smiled and inquired whether he had any suggestions for her. He interpreted this as an invitation to join her; but, reluctant, as before, to compromise them both by appearing in conversation together, he did not turn aside from the graveled driveway.

'I think your marksmanship is very good,' he halted to say. 'You surely need no instruction.'

She flushed a little, and drew another arrow from the quiver that leaned against the stone lectus. Demetrius could see that she felt rebuffed as she turned away. Regardless of consequences, he sauntered toward her.

'Are you too busy for a quiet talk?' she asked, without looking at him.

'I was hoping you might suggest it,' said Demetrius. 'But we can't talk here, you know.'

'Ssss—*ping!*' went the arrow.

'Very well,' said Theodosia. 'I'll meet you—over there.'

Walking quickly away, Demetrius made the circuitous trip to the Temple garden. Apparently the priests were occupied with their holy employments, whatever they were, for no one was in sight. His heart speeded a little when he saw Theodosia coming. It was a new experience to be treated on terms of equality, and he was not quite sure how this amenity should be viewed. He needed and wanted Theodosia's friendship—but how was he to interpret the freedom with which she offered it? Should she not have some compunctions about private interviews with a slave? It was a debatable question whether this friendship was honoring him, or merely demoting her.

Theodosia sat down by him, without a greeting, and regarded him soberly, at such short range that he noted the little flecks of gold in her dark eyes.

'Tell me about the dinner-party,' said Demetrius, wanting to get it over with.

'Very strange; is it not?' There was nothing ironical in her tone. 'He is entirely recovered.'

Demetrius nodded.

'I was afraid you might think I had misrepresented the facts,' he said. 'I could not have blamed you.'

'No—I believed what you told me, Demetrius, and I believe it still. Something happened. Something very important happened.'

'That is true. He found the Robe, while I was absent, and came by an entirely different attitude toward it. Once he had touched it, his horror of it suddenly left him. Last night he slept. Today he has been his usual self. I think his obsession has been cured. I don't pretend to understand it!'

'Naturally—I have thought of nothing else all day,' confessed Theodosia. 'If it was the Robe that had tormented Marcellus, it must have been a new view of the Robe that restored him. Maybe it's something like this: I keep a diary, Demetrius. Every night, I write a few things I wish to remember. If someone who does not know me should read a page where I am happy and life is good, he might have quite a different impression of me than if he read the other side of the papyrus where I am a cynic, a stoic; cold and bitter. Now—you and Marcellus recorded many different thoughts on that Galilean Robe. Yours were sad, mostly, but they did not chide you. Marcellus recorded memories on it—and they afflicted him.'

She paused, her eyes asking whether this analogy had any merit at all. Demetrius signed to her to go on.

'You told me that this Jesus forgave them all, and that Marcellus had been much moved by it. Maybe, when he touched the Robe again, this impression came back to him so strongly that it relieved his remorse. Does that sound reasonable?'

'Yes—but wouldn't you think, Theodosia, that after having had an experience like that—a sort of illumination, setting him free of his phobias—

Marcellus would be in a great state of exaltation? True—he was ecstatic, for a while; but his high moment was brief. And for the most of the day, yesterday, he acted almost as if nothing had happened to him.'

'My guess is that he is concealing his emotions,' ventured Theodosia. 'Maybe he feels this more deeply than you think.'

'There is no reason for his being reticent with me. He was so stirred by his experience, the night before last, that he was half-indignant because I tried to regard it rationally.'

'Perhaps that is why he doesn't want to discuss it further. He thinks the problem is too big for either of you, so he's resolved not to talk about it. You say he had a high moment—and then proceeded as if the experience had been of no consequence. Well—that's natural; isn't it? We can't live on mountain-tops.' Theodosia's eyes had a faraway look, and her voice was wistful.

'My Aunt Ino,' she continued, 'once said to me, when I was desperately lonely and blue, that our life is like a land journey, too even and easy and dull over long distances across the plains, too hard and painful up the steep grades; but, on the summits of the mountain, you have a magnificent view—and feel exalted—and your eyes are full of happy tears—and you want to sing—and wish you had wings! And then—you can't stay there, but must continue your journey—you begin climbing down the other side, so busy with your footholds that your summit experience is forgotten.'

'You have a pretty mind, Theodosia,' said Demetrius, gently.

'That was my Aunt Ino's mind I was talking about.'

'I am sorry you were lonely and depressed, Theodosia.' Absently he rubbed his finger-tips over the small white scar on his ear. 'I shouldn't have thought you were ever sad. Want to talk about it?'

Her eyes had followed his hand with frank interest.

'Not all slaves have had their ears marked,' she said, pensively. 'Your position is tragic. I know that. There is something very wrong with a world in which a man like you must go through life as a slave. But—really—is there much to choose between your social condition and mine? I am the daughter of an innkeeper. In your case, Demetrius, it makes no difference that you were brought up in a home of refinement and well endowed with a good mind: wicked men put you into slavery—and there you are! And where am I? It makes no difference that my father, Dion, is a man of integrity, well versed in the classics, acquainted with the arts, and bearing himself honorably before the men of Athens, as did his father Georgias. He is an innkeeper. Perhaps it would have been better for me if I had not been taught to love things beyond my social station.'

'But—Theodosia, your advantages have made your life rich,' said Demetrius, consolingly. 'You have so much to make you happy; your books, your music, your boundless vitality, your beautiful clothes——'

'I have no place to wear my nice clothes,' she countered, bitterly, 'and I have no use for my vitality. If the daughter of an innkeeper wants to be happy, she should conform to the traditions. She should be noisy, pert, and not above petty larcenies. Then she could have friends—of her own class.' Her eyes suddenly flooded. 'Demetrius,' she said, huskily, 'sometimes I think I can't bear it!'

He slipped his arm about her, and they sat for a long moment in silence. Then she straightened, and regarded him soberly.

'Why don't you run away?' she demanded, in a whisper. 'I would—if I were a man.'

'Where would you go?' he asked, with an indulgent grin.

Theodosia indicated with a negligent gesture that the question was of secondary importance.

'Anywhere,' she murmured vaguely. 'Sicily—maybe. They say it is lovely—in Sicily.'

'It's a land of thieves and cutthroats,' declared Demetrius. 'It is in the lovely lands that life is most difficult, Theodosia. The only places where one may live in peace—so far as I know—are arid desolations where nothing grows and nothing is covetable.'

'Why not Damascus? You thought of that once, you know.'

'I should die of loneliness up there.'

'You could take me along.' She laughed lightly, as she spoke, to assure him the remark was intended playfully, but they quickly fell silent. Rousing from her reverie, Theodosia sat up, patted her bandeau, and said she must go.

Demetrius rose and watched her as she drifted gracefully away; then resumed his seat and unleashed his thoughts. He was becoming much too fond of Theodosia, and she was being too recklessly generous with her friendship. Perhaps it would be better to avoid any more private talks with her, if he could do so without hurting her feelings. She was very desirable and her tenderness was endearing. The freedom with which she confided in him and the artless candor of her attitude—sometimes but little short of a caress—had stirred him deeply. Until now, whatever devotion he had to offer a woman was silently, hopelessly given to Lucia. As he reflected upon his feeling for her now, Lucia was in the nature of a shrine. Theodosia was real! But he was not going to take advantage of her loneliness. There was nothing he could ever do for her. They were both unhappy enough without exchanging unsecured promises. He was a slave—but not a thief.

The day was still young and at his disposal; for Marcellus did not want him about. Perhaps that was because he wished to be undistracted while he made experiments with his modeling-clay; perhaps, again, he needed solitude for a reshaping of his preconceived theories about supernatural phenomena.

Strolling out of the Temple garden, Demetrius proceeded down the street which grew noisier and more crowded as he neared the agora. He aimlessly sauntered through the vasty market-place, savoring the blended aromas of ground spices, ripe melons, roasted nuts, and fried leeks; enjoying the polyglot confusion. Emerging, he lounged into a circle gathered about a blind lute-player and his loyal dog; drifted across the cobbled street to listen to a white-bearded soothsayer haranguing a small, apathetic company from the portico of an abandoned theater; was jostled off the pavement by a shabby legionary who needed much room for his cruise with a cargo of wine. Time was beginning to hang heavy on his hands.

It now occurred to him that he might trump up some excuse to have a talk with Benjamin. Purchasing a small basket of ripe figs, he proceeded to the weaver's house; and, entering, presented himself before the old man's worktable.

'So—he decided not to come; eh?' observed Benjamin, glancing up sourly and returning immediately to his stitches. 'Well—you're much too early. I have not finished. As you see, I am at work on it now.'

'I did not come for the Robe, sir.' Demetrius held out his gift. 'It was a long day, and I had no employment. I have been strolling about. Would you like some figs?'

Benjamin motioned to have the basket put down on the table beside him; and, taking one of the figs, slowly munched it, without looking up from his work. After a while, he had cleared his mouth enough to be articulate.

'Did you say to yourself, "I must take that cross old Jew some of these nice figs"?—or did you say, "I want to ask Benjamin some questions, and I'll take the figs along, so he'll think I just dropped in to be friendly"?'

'They're quite good figs, sir,' said Demetrius.

'So they are.' Benjamin reached for another. 'Have one yourself,' he mumbled, with difficulty. 'Why did you not want him to come back and see me today? You were afraid I might press him to talk about that poor, dead Jew? Well—and why not? Surely a proud young Roman need not shrink from the questions of an old weaver—an old Jewish weaver—in subjugated Athens!'

'Perhaps I should let my master speak for himself. He has not instructed me to discuss this matter.'

'I daresay you are telling the truth; albeit frugally,' grinned Benjamin. 'You would never be mistaken for a sieve. But why may we not do a little honest trading? You came to ask questions. Very well; ask them. Then—I shall ask questions of you. We will put all of the questions on the table, and bargain for answers. Is that not fair enough?'

'I'm afraid I don't quite understand,' parried Demetrius.

'Well—for one thing—I noticed yesterday that you were surprised and troubled when I showed knowledge of strange doings in Jerusalem, last Passover Week; and I think you would like to ask me how much I know about that. Now—I shall be glad to tell you, if you will first answer some questions of mine.' Benjamin glanced up with a sly, conspiratorial smile. 'I shall give you an easy one first. Doubtless you were in Jerusalem with your master: did you happen to see the Galilean whom they crucified?'

'Yes, sir,' replied Demetrius, promptly.

'Very good. What manner of man was he?' Benjamin put down his work, and leaned forward with eager interest. 'You are a bright fellow, for a slave—and a heathen. Was there anything—anything peculiar—about this Galilean? How close did you get to him? Did you hear him speak?'

'My first sight of the Galilean was on the morning of our entrance into Jerusalem. There was a great crowd accompanying him into the city. Not knowing the language, I did not fully understand the event; but learned that this large multitude of country people wanted to crown him king. They were shouting "Messiah!" I was told that these people were always looking for a great leader to deliver them from political bondage; he would be the "Messiah." So—the crowd shouted "Messiah!"—and waved palms before him, as if he were a king.'

Benjamin's eyes were alert and his shrunken mouth was open, the puckered lips trembling.

'Go on!' he demanded, gutturally, when Demetrius paused.

'I forced my way into the pack until I was almost close enough to have touched him. He was indeed an impressive man, sir, albeit simply clad——'

'In this?' Benjamin caught up the Robe in his shaking hands and pushed it toward Demetrius, who nodded—and went on.

'It was quite evident that the man was not enjoying the honor. His eyes were brooding; full of sadness; full of loneliness.'

'Ah!—wait a moment, my friend!' Benjamin turned to his shelf of scrolls; drew out one that had seen much handling; turned it rapidly to the passage he sought; and read, in a deep sonorous tone: ' "—a man of sorrows—acquainted with grief——" This is the prophecy of Yeshayah. Proceed, please! Did he speak?'

'I did not hear him speak—not that day.'

'Ah!—so you saw him again!'

'When he was tried—at the Insula, a few days later—for treason.'

'You saw that?'

Demetrius nodded.

'What was his behavior there?' asked Benjamin. 'Did he plead for mercy?'

'No—he was quite composed. I could not understand what he said; but he accepted his sentence without protest.'

Benjamin excitedly spread open his ancient scroll.

'Listen, my friend! This, too, is from the prophecy of Yeshayah. "He was oppressed and afflicted, yet he opened not his mouth." '

'He did talk,' remembered Demetrius, 'but very calmly—and confidently. That was thought strange, too; for he had been cruelly whipped.'

Benjamin read again from the scroll in an agitated voice: ' "He was wounded for our transgressions—and with his stripes we are healed." '

'Whose transgressions'—wondered Demetrius—'the Jews'?'

'Yeshayah was a Jewish prophet, my friend,' replied Benjamin. 'And he was foretelling the coming of a Jewish Messiah.'

'That means then that the Messiah's injuries would not be borne in the interest of any other people?' persisted Demetrius. 'If that is true, I do not think this Jesus was the Messiah! Before he died, he forgave the Roman legionaries who had nailed him to the cross!'

Benjamin glanced up with a start.

'How do you know that?' he demanded.

'So it was said by those who stood by,' declared Demetrius. 'It was heard by all.'

'This is a strange thing!' murmured Benjamin. Presently he roused from a long moment of deep meditation. 'Now—you may ask me questions, if you wish,' he said.

'I think you have answered my queries, sir. I thought you might tell me something more about the Messiah—and you have done so. According to the writings, he was to come as the champion of the Jewish people. The man I saw had no wish to be their champion. It made him unhappy when they urged kingship upon him. At his trial he said he had a kingdom—but it was not in the world.'

'Where then—if not in the world?' rasped Benjamin.

'You are much wiser than I, sir. If you do not know, it would be presumptuous for a pagan slave to attempt an explanation.'

'You are sarcastic, my young friend,' grumbled Benjamin.

'No, sir—I am entirely sincere—and bewildered. I think this Jesus was interested in *everybody!* I think he was *sorry for everybody!*' Demetrius paused, and murmured apologetically, 'Perhaps I have been talking too freely, sir.'

'You have a right to talk,' conceded Benjamin. 'I am a Jew—but I believe that our God is the father of mankind. Peradventure the Messiah—when he comes to reign over the Jews—will establish justice for all.'

'I wish I could study these ancient prophecies,' said Demetrius.

'Well'—Benjamin shrugged—'and why not? Here they are. You have a good mind. If you have much time, and little to do, learn to read them.'

'How?'

'I might help you,' said Benjamin, amiably. He swung his thin legs over the edge of the table. 'You will excuse me now,' he added, abruptly. 'I must prepare my noonday meat.' Without further words of leave-taking, he moved slowly toward a door at the rear, and disappeared.

* * * * * *

Evidently Benjamin had finished his day's labor, for the sleek-topped worktable was unoccupied. A door in the far corner behind the largest room, unnoticed by Marcellus on his previous visit, stood hospitably ajar. He walked toward it.

In pleasant contrast to the stifling confusion of the overcrowded shop, Benjamin's private quarters were simply but tastefully furnished. The orange-and-blue rug that covered the entire floor was of fine workmanship. There were three comfortable chairs and footstools, a couch with a pair of camel's-hair saddle-bags for a pillow, and a massive metal-bound chest. An open case of deep shelves, fitted around either side and below a large window, was filled to capacity with ancient scrolls.

A farther door opposite gave upon a shaded, stone-flagged court. Assuming that the old man expected him to proceed, Marcellus crossed the room. Benjamin, surprisingly tall in his long black robe and tasseled skull-cap, was laying a table in the center of his high-walled vine-thatched peristyle.

'I hope I am not intruding,' said Marcellus.

'It is never an intrusion,' said Benjamin, 'to pass through an open door in Athens. You are welcome.' He pointed to one of the rug-covered chairs by the table and put down the two silver goblets from his tray.

'I had not know that you lived here, at your shop,' remarked Marcellus, for something to say.

'For two reasons,' explained Benjamin, laying an antique knife beside the brown barley-loaf. 'It is more convenient, and it is prudent. One does not leave a shop unguarded in this city.'

'Or any other city of my acquaintance,' commented Marcellus.

'Such as—' Benjamin drew out his chair and sat.

'Well—such as Rome, for example. We are overrun with slaves. They are notorious thieves, with no regard for property rights.'

Benjamin laughed gutturally.

'The slave is indeed a predatory creature,' he remarked dryly. 'He makes off with your best sandals when the only thing you have stolen from him is his freedom.' He raised his cup and bowed to Marcellus. 'Shall we drink to the day when no man is another man's property?'

'Gladly!' Marcellus sipped his wine. It was of good vintage. 'My father,' he asserted, 'says the time will come when Rome must pay dearly for enslaving men.'

'He does not approve of it? Then I presume he owns no slaves.' Benjaman was intent upon evenly slicing the bread. Marcellus flushed a little at the insinuation.

'If slavery were abolished,' he said, defensively, 'my father would be among the first to applaud. Of course—as the matter stands—'

'Of course,' echoed Benjamin. 'Your father knows it is wrong, but other men of his social station practice it. In his opinion, it is better to be wrong than eccentric.'

'If I may venture to speak for my father,' said Marcellus, calmly, 'I do not think he has elaborated a theory of that nature. He is a man of integrity and generosity. His slaves are well treated. They probably have better food and shelter in our home—'

'I can readily believe that,' interrupted Benjamin. 'They have more to eat than they might have if they were free. Doubtless that is also true of your horses and dogs. The question is: Are men and beasts of the same category? Is there no essential difference between them in respect to the quality of their value? If a healthy, hard-working ass can be had for ten drachmas, and an able-bodied man can be had for two silver talents, the difference in their worth is purely quantitative. It is at that point that I find human slavery abhorrent. It is an offense to the majesty of the human spirit; for if any man deserves to be regarded as of the same quality as a beast of burden, then no man has any dignity left. I, Benjamin, believe that all men are created in the image of God.'

'Is that a Jewish conception?' asked Marcellus.

'Yes.'

'But wealthy Jews own slaves; do they not?' Marcellus raised the question casually as if it didn't matter much how or whether the old man answered it, but the charge stirred Benjamin to instant attention.

'Ah—there you have tapped one of the roots of our trouble!' he exclaimed. 'The Jew professes to believe that humanity was created in the image of God. Thus he affirms that God is his spiritual father. But that can be true only if he declares that all men are the children of God. Either they all are—or none! I, Benjamin, think they all are! Therefore, when I enslave another man, placing him at one with the cattle in the fields, I throw my whole case away.'

Marcellus broke his bread and amiably conceded that it didn't seem quite right for one man to own another. It was no way to regard a fellow human, he said, even if you treated him kindly. A man shouldn't be made to feel that he was just another animal.

'Oh—as for that'—Benjamin dismissed this idea with an indifferent wave of his thin arm—'you don't rob a slave of his divine character when you buy him and hitch him to a plow, between an ox and an ass. He has had no choice in the matter. It isn't he who has demoted mankind: it is *you!* He is still free to believe that God is his spiritual father. But *you* aren't! Now, you take the case of that handsome Greek who trails about after you. Slavery hasn't stopped *him* from being one of the sons of God, if he wants to consider himself so; but his slavery has made *you* a relative of the beasts, because that is your conception of man's value.'

'I am not much of a philosopher,' admitted Marcellus, carelessly. 'Perhaps, after I've been in Athens awhile, lounging on Mars' Hill, observing the spinning of sophistical cobwebs—'

'You'll be able to tie up sand with a rope,' assisted Benjamin, in the same temper. 'But what we're talking about is more than a pedantry. It is a practical matter. Here is your great Roman Empire, sending out its ruthless armies in all directions to pillage and persecute weak nations; bringing home the best of their children in stinking slave-ships, and setting the old ones at hard labor to pay an iniquitous tribute. Eventually the Roman Empire will collapse—'

'My father thinks that,' interposed Marcellus. 'He says that the Romans, with their slave labor, are getting softer and fatter and lazier, every day; and that the time will come—'

'Yes, yes—the time will come—but that won't be the reason!' declaimed Benjamin. 'The Romans will be crushed, but not because they are too fat. It will be because they have believed that all men are beasts. Enslaving other men, they have denied their own spiritual dignity. Not much wonder that your Roman gods are a jest and a mockery in the sight of all your intelligent people. What do *you* want with gods—you who think that men are like cattle, to be led by a halter? Why should *you* look to the gods, when your dog doesn't?'

Benjamin paused in his monologue to refill their goblets. He had been much stirred, and his old hand was trembling.

'I am a Jew,' he went on, 'but I am not unconversant with the religion of other races. Time was when your Roman deities were regarded with some respect. Jove meant something to your ancestors. Then the time came when Julius Caesar became a god, more important than Jove. Only the down-trodden any longer believed in the classic deities who controlled the sunrise and the rain, who dealt out rewards and punishments, who tempered the wind for the mariner, and filled the grape with goodness. And why—let me ask you—did Caesar make a mockery of the Roman religion? Ah—that was when the Romans had achieved enough military power to enslave other nations, buying and selling men, and driving them in herds. By that act they declared that all men—including themselves, of course—were of no relation to the gods! Vain and pompous Caesar was god enough when it became established that all men were animals!'

'I don't believe any sensible person ever thought that Julius was a god,' protested Marcellus.

'Down in his heart—no,' agreed Benjamin. 'Nor Caesar, himself, I dare say!'

'Is it your belief, then, that if the Romans abolished slavery they would think more highly of the old gods, and by their reverence make themselves more noble?'

Benjamin chuckled derisively.

'An "if" of such magnitude,' he growled, 'makes the rest of your question ridiculous.'

'Well—as for me'—Marcellus had tired of the subject, as his tone candidly announced—'I have no interest in the gods, be they classic or contemporary.'

'How do you account for the universe?' demanded Benjamin.

'I don't,' replied Marcellus. 'I didn't know that I was expected to.' And then, feeling that this rejoinder was more impolite than amusing, he added quickly: 'I should be glad to believe in a supernatural being, if one were proposed who seemed qualified for that office. It would clarify many a riddle. Yesterday you were saying that your people—the Samaritans—worshiped on the mountain-tops. I can cheerfully do that too if I'm not required to personify the sunrise and the trees.'

'We do not personify the objects of nature,' explained Benjamin. 'We believe in one God—a Spirit—creator of all things.'

'Somewhere I have heard it said'—Marcellus' eyes were averted thoughtfully—'that the Jews anticipate the rise of a great leader, a champion, a king. He is to set them free and establish an enduring government. Do you Samaritans believe that?'

'We do!' declared Benjamin. 'All of our great prophets have foretold the coming of the Messiah.'

'How long have you been looking for him?'

'For many centuries.'

'And you are still hopeful?'

Benjamin stroked his long beard thoughtfully.

'The expectation ebbs and flows,' he said. 'In periods of national calamity there has been much talk of it. In times of great hardship and persecution, the Jews have been alert to discover among themselves some wise and brave man who might give evidence of messianic powers.'

'And never found one to qualify?' asked Marcellus.

'Not the real one—no.' Benjamin paused to meditate. 'It is a queer thing,' he went on. 'In a time of great need, when powerful leadership is demanded, the people—confused and excited—hear only the strident voices of the audacious, and refuse to listen to the voice of wisdom which, being wise, is temperate. Yes—we have had many zealous pretenders to messiahship. They have come and gone—like meteors.'

'But—in the face of all these disappointments, you sustain your faith that the Messiah will come?'

'He will come,' murmured Benjamin. 'Of course, every generation thinks its own problems are severe enough to warrant his coming. Ever since the Roman occupation, there has been a revival of interest in the ancient predictions. Even the Temple has pretended to yearn for the Messiah.'

'Pretended?' Marcellus raised his brows.

'The Temple is fairly well satisfied with things as they are,' grumbled Benjamin. 'The Roman Prefects grind the poor with vicious taxation, but they are careful about imposing too hard on the priests and the influential rich. The Temple would be embarrassed, I fear, if the Messiah put in an appearance. He might want to make some changes.' The old man seemed to be talking mostly to himself now, for he did not bother to explain what he meant.

'He might discharge the merchants, perhaps, who sell sacrificial beasts to the poor at exorbitant prices?' asked Marcellus, artlessly.

Benjamin rallied from his reminiscent torpor and slowly turned an inquiring gaze upon his pagan guest.

'How do you happen to know about that iniquity?' he asked slyly.

'Oh—I heard it discussed in Jerusalem.' Marcellus made it sound unimportant. 'It seems there had been a little protest.'

'A little protest?' Benjamin lifted an ironical eyebrow. 'It must have been quite an insistent protest to have come to the ears of a visiting Roman. What were you doing there—if I may venture to ask?'

'It was Empire business,' replied Marcellus, stiffly. He rose, readjusting the folds of his toga. 'I must not outstay my welcome,' he said, graciously. 'You have been most kind. I am indebted. May I have the Robe now?'

Benjamin withdrew, returning almost immediately. Marcellus examined the Robe in the waning light.

'It is well done,' he said. 'No one would know it had ever been torn.'

'But you,' said Benjamin, gravely. Marcellus shifted his position, uneasily, avoiding the old man's eyes. 'These stains'—added Benjamin—'I tried to remove them. They will not come out. You have not told me about this poor Jew. He was brave, you said; and died at the hands of his enemies. Was he a Galilean, perhaps?'

'I believe so,' replied Marcellus, restlessly. He folded the Robe over his arm, and extended his hand in farewell.

'Was his name Jesus?' Benjamin's insistent voice had dropped to a mere guttural whisper.

'Yes—that was his name,' admitted Marcellus, grudgingly. 'How did you know?'

'I learned of the incident from a long-time friend, one Popygos, a dealer in spices. He was in Jerusalem during this last Passover Week. Tell me'—Benjamin's tone was entreating—'how did you come by this Robe?'

'Does it matter?' countered Marcellus, suddenly haughty.

Benjamin bowed obsequiously, rubbing his thin hands.

'You must forgive me for being inquisitive,' he murmured. 'I am an old man, without family, and far from my native land. My scrolls—the history of my race, the words of our great prophets—they are my meat and drink, my young friend! They are a lamp unto my feet and a light upon my path. They are my heritage. My daily work—it is nothing! It busies my fingers and brings me my food; but my soul, my life—it is hidden and nourished in words so fitly spoken they are as apples of gold in pictures of silver!' Benjamin's voice had risen resonantly and his deep-lined face was enraptured.

'You are fortunate, sir,' said Marcellus. 'I, too, am fond of the classics bequeathed to us by men of great wisdom—Plato, Pythagoras, Parmenides—'

Benjamin smiled indulgently and wagged his head.

'Yes, yes—it was through their works that you were taught how to read—but not how to live! They who spoke the Hebrew tongue understood the words of life! Now—you see—my young friend—throughout these prophecies there runs a promise. One day, a Messiah shall arise and reign! His name shall be called Wonderful! And of his kingdom there shall be no end! No certain time is set for his coming—but he will come! Think you then that it is a mere idle curiosity in me to inquire diligently about this Jesus, whom so many have believed to be the Messiah?'

'I would hear more about these predictions,' said Marcellus, after a meditative pause.

'Why not?' Benjamin's deep set eyes lighted. 'I love to think of them. I shall gladly tell you; thought it would be better if you could read them for yourself.'

'Is Hebrew difficult?' asked Marcellus.

Benjamin smiled and shrugged.

'Well—it is no more difficult than Greek, which you speak fluently. Naturally—it is more difficult than Latin.'

'Why—"naturally"?' snapped Marcellus, frowning.

'Forgive me,' retreated Benjamin. 'Perhaps the Greek asks more of the mind because the Greek writers—' The old man politely floundered to a stop.

'The Greek writers thought more deeply,' assisted Marcellus. 'Is that what you're trying to say? If so—I agree with you.'

'I meant no offense,' reiterated Benjamin. 'Rome has her poets, satirists, eulogists. There are many interesting little essays by your Cicero; rather childish. They pick flowers, but they do not sweep the sky!' Benjamin caught up a worn scroll from the table and deftly unrolled it with familiar hands. 'Listen, friend!—"When I consider thy heavens, the work of thy fingers, the moon and the stars which thou hast ordained, what is man that thou art mindful of him?" '

'Rather pessimistic, I'd say,' broke in Marcellus, 'albeit it sounds sensible enough.'

'But wait!' cried Benjamin. 'Let me go on, please!—"Thou hast made him a little lower than the angels, and hast crowned him with glory and honor." Ah—there is richness in the Hebrew wisdom! You should acquaint yourself with it!'

'For the present, I shall have to content myself with such choice bits of it as you may be good enough to offer me, from time to time,' said Marcellus. 'I am doing some sculpturing now, and it will claim my full attention.' He laid a small silk bag of silver on the table. 'Please accept this—for mending the Robe.'

'But I do not wish to be paid,' said Benjamin, firmly.

'Then give it to the poor,' said Marcellus, impatiently.

'Thank you.' Benjamin bowed. 'It has just occurred to me that if you would know something of this ancient Jewish lore—and are quite too busy to study it for yourself—you might permit your Greek slave to learn the language. I should be glad to instruct him. He is intelligent.'

'It is true that Demetrius is bright. May I ask how you discovered it?'

'He spent an hour here today.'

'Indeed! What was his errand?'

Benjamin shrugged the query away as of no consequence.

'He was sauntering about, and paid me a friendly call; brought me some figs; asked me some questions.'

'What manner of questions?'

'He may tell you if you ask him,' said Benjamin, dryly. 'He is your property; is he not?'

'I do not own his thoughts,' retorted Marcellus. 'Perhaps you have imputed to me a more brilliant talent for brutality than I possess.'

Old Benjamin smiled, almost benevolently, shook his head slowly, and laid a thin hand on Marcellus' broad shoulder.

'No—I do not think you are cruel, my son,' he declared, gently. 'But you are an unfortunate representative of a cruel system. Perhaps you cannot help yourself.'

'Perchance—when your Messiah comes,' rejoined Marcellus, crisply, still smarting under the old man's condescension, 'he may make some valuable suggestions.' He turned to go.

'By the way,' said Benjamin, following to the door, 'how long, after the crucifixion of Jesus, did you remain in Jerusalem?'

'I left the city before sunrise, the next morning,' replied Marcellus.

'Ah!' reflected Benjamin, stroking his white beard. 'Then you heard nothing further—about him?'

'What more was there to hear? He was dead.'

'Do you'—the old man hesitated—'do you know that—for a certainty?'

'Yes,' declared Marcellus. 'I am sure of it.'

'Were you there?' Benjamin's cavernous eyes insisted upon a direct answer. It was slow in coming.

'I saw him die,' admitted Marcellus. 'They pierced his heart, to make sure, before they took him down.'

To his amazement, Benjamin's seamed face lighted with a rapturous smile.

'Thank you, my friend!' he said, brightly. 'Thank you—for telling me!'

'I had not supposed my painful words would make you glad,' said Marcellus, in a tone of bewilderment. 'This Jesus was a brave man! He deserved to live! Yet you seem pleased to be assured that he was put to death!'

'There have been many rumors,' said Benjamin, 'many idle tales, reporting that the drunken legionaries left the scene before he died, and that the friends of the Galilean rescued and revived him.'

'Well—I happen to know that such tales are untrue!' said Marcellus, firmly. 'The executioners were drunk enough, but they killed the Galilean, and when they left—he was dead! This is not hearsay with me. *I know!*'

'You are speaking important words, my son!' Benjamin's voice was husky with emotion. 'I am glad you came today! I shall hope to see more of you, sir.' He raised his bony hand over Marcellus' head. His arm was trembling. 'The Lord bless you and keep you,' he intoned, reverently. 'The Lord make his face to shine upon you, and be gracious unto you. The Lord lift up his countenance upon you, and give you peace.'

There was a long moment of silence before Marcellus stirred. Much perplexed, and uncertain what was expected of him, he bowed respectfully to Benjamin; and, without further words, walked slowly through the shop and out into the twilight.

Chapter X

Now that Diana was expected back from Capri almost any day, the Gallio family felt that some explanation must be contrived to account for the sudden departure of Marcellus.

Unquestionably word had already reached Tiberius that *The Vestris* had arrived with Marcellus as her most important passenger. Diana would be eager to see him, and she had every reason to believe that he would be waiting impatiently for her return.

Lucia was for telling her that Marcellus had come home in such frail health that an immediate change of climate seemed imperative, though Diana would inquire about the nature of his malady, and wonder in what respect the climate of Athens was so highly esteemed.

Cornelia had weakly suggested that perhaps there were better physicians in Athens. Diana might be satisfied with that, she thought, or said she did; but this was nonsense, for everybody knew that most of the really good Athenian physicians had been imported to Rome.

'No,' Senator Gallio had observed judiciously, 'you are both in error. When there is some serious explaining to be done, no contraption is as serviceable as the truth. Let her have it. If Diana and my son are in love, as you two seem to think, she has a right to know the story and it is our duty to tell her. It should not be difficult.' With everything thus sensibly settled, the Senator rose and was leaving his wife's boudoir when their daughter halted him.

'Assuming that I have it to do,' said Lucia, maturely, 'how much of the story is to be told?'

Her father made the query of no great importance with a negligent flick of his fingers.

'You can say that your brother was required to conduct the crucifixion of a Jewish revolutionist; that the experience was a shock; that it plunged him into a deep melancholy from which he has not yet fully recovered; that we thought it best for him to seek diversion.'

'Nothing, then,' mused Lucia, 'about those dreadful seizures of remorse—and the haunted look—and that odd question he insisted on asking, against his will?'

'Mmm—no,' decided the Senator. 'That will not be necessary. It should be sufficient to say that Marcellus is moody and depressed.'

'Diana will not be contented with that explanation,' declared Lucia. 'She is going to be disappointed, embarrassed, and indignant. Quite aside from their fondness for each other, it was no small thing she did for Marcellus in having him recalled from exile. And she will think it very strange indeed that a Roman Tribune should be so seriously disturbed by the execution of a convict.'

'We are all agreed on that,' glumly conceded the Senator. 'I do not pretend to understand it. My son has never been lacking in courage. It is not like him to fall ill at the sight of blood.'

'Perhaps it would be better,' put in Cornelia, suddenly inspired, 'if we omit all reference to that dreadful crucifixion, and simply say that Marcellus wanted to do some sculpturing, and attend some lectures, and—'

'So urgently,' scoffed Lucia, 'that he couldn't wait a few days to see the girl who was responsible for bringing him home.'

Her mother sighed, took another stitch in her embroidery, and murmured that her suggestion did sound rather silly, an afterthought that her relatives accepted without controversy.

'He promised me he would write to her,' remembered Lucia.

'Well—we cannot wait for that,' said her father. 'It might be weeks. Diana will want to know—now! Better tell her everything, Lucia. She will get it out of you, in any case. A young woman bright enough to extort valuable favors from our crusty old Emperor will make her own deductions about this—no matter what you tell her.'

'If she really loves him,' cooed Cornelia, 'she will forgive him—anything!'

'Doubtless,' agreed her husband, dryly, moving toward the door.

'I'm afraid you do not know Diana very well,' cautioned Lucia. 'She has had no training that would fit her to understand. She idolizes her father, who would as lief kill a man as a mouse. I do not think she is experienced in forgiving people for being weak.'

'That doesn't sound like you, Lucia,' reproved her mother, gently, when the Senator was out of hearing. 'One would almost think you were not sympathetic with your brother. Surely—you do not think Marcellus weak; do you?'

'Oh—I don't know what to think,' muttered Lucia, dismally. 'What is there to think?' She put both her hands over her eyes and shook her head.

'We've lost Marcellus, Mother,' she cried. 'He was so manly! I loved him so much! It is breaking my heart.'

* * * * * *

But if the problem of dealing out the bad news to Diana was perplexing, it was simple as compared with the dilemma that arose on the following afternoon when an impressively uniformed Centurion was shown in, bearing an ornate, official scroll addressed to Marcellus. It was from the Emperor. The Centurion said he was expected to wait for instructions, adding that the royal carriage would call early in the morning.

'But my son is not here,' said Gallio. 'He has sailed for Athens.'

'Indeed! That is most unfortunate!'

'I gather that you are acquainted with the nature of this message.'

'Yes, sir; it is no secret. The Emperor has appointed Tribune Marcellus to be the Commander of the Palace Guard. We are all much pleased, sir.'

'I sincerely regret my son's absence, Centurion. Perhaps I should send a message with you to the Emperor.' Gallio reflected for a moment. 'No—I shall go and explain to him in person.'

'Very good, sir. Will it be agreeable to start at dawn?'

So—they started at dawn, though it was not particularly agreeable, a swift drive from Rome to Neapolis being rated by the Senator as a doubtful pleasure. Moreover, he had no great relish for his errand. He was not unacquainted with the techniques of persuasive debate, but the impending interview with the Emperor would be unpleasant; for Tiberius had no patience and Gallio had no case. The horses galloped over the deep-rutted cobbles, the big carriage bounced, the painful hours dragged, the Senator's head ached. All things considered, it was not an enjoyable excursion, and by the time he reached the top of Capri, at midnight, there was nothing left in him but a strong desire to go to bed.

The Chamberlain showed him to a sumptuous apartment and Gallio sank into a chair utterly exhausted. Two well-trained Macedonians began unpacking his effects, laying out fresh linen. Another slave drew water for his bath while a big Nubian, on his knees, unlaced the Senator's sandals. A deferential Thracian came with a welcome flagon of chilled wine. Then the Chamberlain reappeared.

'The Emperor wishes to see you, sir,' he reported, in an apologetic tone.

'Now?' Gallio wrinkled his nose distastefully.

'If you please, sir. His Majesty had left orders to have Tribune Marcellus shown into his presence immediately upon his arrival. When told that

Senator Gallio had come instead, the Emperor said he would give him an audience at once.'

'Very well,' sighed Gallio. Signing to the Nubian to relace his sandals, the weary man rose stiffly and followed along to the Emperor's lavishly appointed suite.

The old man was sitting up in bed, bolstered about with pillows, his nightcap rakishly askew. A half-dozen attendants were fluttering about, inventing small errands.

'Out!' he yelled, as the Senator neared the imperial couch; and they backed nimbly away—all but the Chamberlain. 'You, too!' shrilled Tiberius—and the Chamberlain tiptoed to the door. Peering up into Gallio's face, the Emperor regarded him with a surly look of challenge.

'What is the meaning of this?' he squeaked. 'We confer a great honor upon your son, who has done nothing to deserve it, only to learn that—without so much as a by-your-leave—he has left the country. You, his father, have come to explain. Well!—be about it, then! High time somebody explained!'

'Your Majesty,' began Gallio, with a deep bow, 'my son will be very unhappy when he learns that he has unwittingly offended his Emperor, to whom he owes so much.'

'Never mind about that!' barked Tiberius. 'Get on with it! And make it short! I need my rest! They were a pack of fools to wake me up for no better cause—and you were a fool to let them! You, too, should be in bed. You have had a hard trip. You are tired. Sit down! Don't stand there like a sentry! I command you to sit down! You are an old, old man. Sit down—before you fall down!'

Gallio gratefuly sank into the luxurious chair by the Emperor's massive golden bed, pleased to observe that the royal storm was subsiding somewhat.

'As Your Majesty has said, it is too late in the night for a lengthy explanation. My son Marcellus was appointed Legate of the Legion at Minoa—'

'Yes, yes—I know all about that!' spluttered Tiberius. 'We rescinded the order of that addlepated scamp in Rome and brought your son back. And then what?'

'From Minoa, sire, he was ordered to Jerusalem to help preserve the peace during the Jews' annual festival. A small but turbulent revolutionary party became active. Its leader was tried for treason and condemned to death by crucifixion.'

'Crucifixion, eh? Must have been a dangerous character.'

'I did not understand it so, Your Majesty. He was a young Jew of no great repute, a harmless, mild-mannered, peace-loving fellow from one of the outlying provinces—Galilee, I believe. It seems he had grossly offended the Temple authorities.'

'Indeed!' Tiberius leaned forward with sudden interest. 'What did he do?'

'It is their custom, sire, to sell sacrificial animals in the court of the Temple. The priests profit by it, demanding high prices from the poor. This Galilean was enraged over the fraud and the sacrilege; took up a drover's whip, and lashed the priests and the beasts out of the Temple and into the street, and—'

'Hi! Hi!' yelled Tiberius, so loudly that the Chamberlain put his head in at the door. 'Here—you! Worthless eavesdropper! Bring wine for Senator Gallio. We, ourself, shall have wine! Hi! Hi! Mild-mannered, peace-loving Galilean whipped the prating priests out into the street, eh? Not much wonder they crucified him. He was a reckless fellow, indeed! But when does your son appear in this story?'

'He was ordered to crucify the Jew—and it made him ill.' Gallio paused to sip his wine slowly, while the old man snuffled and bubbled into the huge goblet which the Chamberlain held to his lips.

'Ill?' Tiberius grinned sourly and belched. 'Sick at his stomach?'

'Sick in his head. If it is your pleasure, sire, I shall tell you about it,' said Gallio; and when Tiberius had nodded assent, he proceeded to an account of Marcellus' depression and strange behavior, and their decision to send him to Athens, where, they hoped, he might find mental diversion.

'Well!' grunted Tiberius. 'If your sensitive son cannot endure the scent of warm blood, we would not urge him to undertake the protection of our person. We had understood from the young daughter of Gallus that he was a brave man. In her sight he is highly esteemed, and it was to please her that we brought him home—and appointed him to command the Villa Guard. It is well for her that his weakness is made manifest before he has had an opportunity to bring disgrace upon her.'

This was too bitter a dose for Gallio to take without protest.

'Your Majesty places me in a difficult position,' he declared, riskily. 'It would be most unseemly in me to express a contrary opinion; yet the Emperor would surely consider me mean and cowardly did I not venture some defense of my own flesh and blood!'

Tiberius slobbered in the depths of his goblet for a moment that seemed very long to Gallio. At length he came up wheezing.

'Very—hic—well! Say on!' The old man scrubbed his wet chin with the back of a mottled hand. 'Defend your son!'

'Marcellus is not a weakling, sire. He is proud and brave; worthy of his Roman citizenship and his rank as a Tribune. I do not fully understand why he should have been so affected by the crucifixion of this Jew, except that—'

'Go on! Except what?'

'He thinks the Galilean was innocent of any crime deserving so severe a punishment. The Procurator himself declared the man innocent and tried to argue in his behalf.'

'And then condemned him to death? What manner of justice does the Empire administer in Jerusalem? Who is the Prefect now—this sleek and slimy fellow—what's his name—Herod?'

'They tried him before Herod, yes—but it was Pontius Pilate who sentenced him. Pilate is the Procurator.'

Tiberius laughed bitterly, coughed, and spat on the silk sleeve of his robe.

'Pontius Pilate,' he snarled reminiscently. 'He's the dizzy one who built that damned aqueduct. Wife wanted gardens. Had to have water. Robbed the Temple to build aqueduct. Fool! Had all the Jews in turmoil. Cost us thousands of legionaries to put down the riots. Had we to do it again, we would let Pilate settle his own account with the Jews! I never thought much of the fellow, letting his silly, spoiled wife lead him about by the nose.' The Emperor paused for breath. 'An impotent nobody,' he added, 'afraid of his wife.' Having grimly pondered this final observation, Tiberius startled his guest by breaking forth in a shrill drunken guffaw. 'You are at liberty to laugh, too, Gallio,' he shouted. 'Afraid of his wife! Impotent nobody—'fraid of wife! Hi! Hi!'

Gallio grinned obligingly, but did not join in the Emperor's noisy hilarity over his self-debasing joke. Tiberius was drunk, but he would be sober again—and he might remember.

'And this serpent—Herod!' The Emperor rubbed his leaky old eyes with his fists, and rambled on, thickly. 'Well do we know of his perfidies. A loathsome leech, fattening on the blood of his countrymen. Gallio—I have waged war in many lands. I have enslaved many peoples. I have put their brave defenders to death. But—though I commanded their warriors to be slain, I had much respect for their valor. But—this Herod! This verminous vulture! This slinking jackal!—pretending to represent the interests of his conquered fellow Jews—while licking our sandal-straps for personal favors!—what a low creature he is! Yes, yes—I know—it is to the Empire's advantage to have such poltroons in high office throughout all our provinces—selling out their people—betraying them—' Exhausted by his long speech, Tiberius broke off suddenly, gulped another throatful of wine, dribbled a stream of it down his scrawny neck, explored his lips with a clumsy tongue, retched, and muttered, 'I hate a traitor!'

'I have sometimes wondered, sire,' remarked Gallio, thinking some rejoinder was expected, 'whether it really is to the advantage of the Empire when we allow treacherous scoundrels like Herod to administer the affairs of our subjugated provinces. Is it safe? Does it pay? Our subjects are defrauded, but they are not deceived. Their hatred smoulders, but it is not quenched.'

'Well—let them hate us, then,' growled Tiberius, tiring of the subject—'and much good may it do them! The Roman Empire does not ask to be loved. All she demands is obedience—prompt obedience—and plenty of it!' His voice shrilled, truculently. 'Let them hate us! Let the whole world hate us!' He clenched his gnarled old fists. The Chamberlain gently stroked his pillow to soothe his passion, and ducked as one of the bony elbows shot up unexpectedly in his direction.

Presently the heavy old head drooped. The Chamberlain ventured a beseeching glance at the Senator who half-rose from his chair, uncertain whether to take the initiative in a withdrawal. Tiberius roused and swallowed hard, making a wry face.

'We have gone far afield, Gallio,' he mumbled. 'We were discussing your frail son. He crucified a harmless Jew, and the injustice of it put him to bed, eh? And weeks afterward, he is still brooding. Very peculiar! How do you account for it?'

'The case is full of mystery, sire,' sighed Gallio. 'There is one small matter of which I have not spoken. It concerns this Jew's Robe.'

'Eh?' Tiberius leaned forward, spurred to curiosity. 'Robe? What about a robe?'

Gallio debated with himself, for a moment, how best to proceed, half-sorry he had alluded to the incident.

'My son was accompanied by his Greek slave, a quite intelligent fellow. It is from him that I have this feature of the story. It seems that when the Galilean was crucified, his discarded Robe lay on the ground, and my son and other officers—whiling the time—cast dice for it. Marcellus won it.'

Tiberius was sagging into his pillows, disappointed with so dull a tale.

'That night,' continued Gallio, 'there was a banquet at Pilate's Insula. According to the slave, my son was far from happy, but there was nothing peculiar in his behavior during or after the crucifixion. He had been drinking heavily, but otherwise was of normal mind. At the banquet, one of his staff officers from Minoa, far gone with wine, urged him to put on this Jew's Robe.' Gallio paused, and the old man's face showed a renewed interest.

'Well?' he queried, impatiently. 'Did he put it on?'

Gallio nodded.

'Yes—and he has never been the same since.'

'Ha!' exclaimed the Emperor, brightening. 'Now we are getting some place with this story! Does your son think the Jew laid a curse on his Robe?'

'It is hard to say what my son thinks, sire. He is very reticent.'

Suddenly a light shone in the old man's eyes.

'Ah—I see! That is why you sent him to Athens! He will consult the learned astrologers, soothsayers, and those who commune with the dead! But why Athens? There are better men at Rhodes. Or, you might have sent him here! There are no wiser men than my Rhodesian, Telemarchus!'

'No—Your Majestry; we did not send Marcellus to Athens to consult the diviners. We urged him to go away, for a time, so that he might not be embarrassed by meeting friends in his unhappy state of mind.'

'So—the dead Jew's Robe is haunted?' Tiberius smacked his lips. This tale was much to his liking. 'The Jews are a queer people; very religious; believe in one god. Evidently this Galilean was a religious fanatic, if he got himself into trouble with the Temple; had some new kind of religion, maybe.'

'Did your Majesty ever hear of the Messiah?' inquired Gallio.

The Emperor's jaw slowly dropped and his rheumy eyes widened.

'Yes,' he answered, in a hoarse whisper. 'He that is to come. They're always looking for him, Telemarchus says. They've been expecting him for a thousand years, Telemarchus says. He that is to come—and set up a kingdom.' The old man chuckled, mirthlessly. 'A kingdom, Telemarchus says; a kingdom that shall have no end; and the government shall be upon his shoulder. Telemarchus says it is written. I let him prattle. He is old. He says the Messiah will reign, one day, in Rome! Hi! Hi! I let Telemarchus prattle. Were he younger, by a century or two, I would have him whipped for his impudence. A Messiah—huh! A kingdom—pouf! Well'—Tiberius returned from his rumbling monologue—'what were you starting to say about the Messiah?'

'Nothing, sire—except that there was a strong feeling among the common people—my son's slave says—that this Galilean Jew was the promised Messiah.'

'What?' shouted Tiberius. 'You don't believe that, Gallio!'

'I am not religious, sire.'

'What do you mean—you're not religious? You believe in the gods; do you not?'

'I have no convictions on the subject, Your Majesty. The gods are remote from my field of study, sire.'

Tiberius scowled his stern disapproval.

'Perhaps Senator Gallio will presently be telling us that he does not believe his Emperor is divine!'

Gallio bowed his head and meditated a reply.

'How about it?' demanded the old man, hotly. 'Is the Emperor divine?'

'If the Emperor thought he was divine,' replied Gallio, recklessly, 'he would not need to ask one of his subjects to confirm it.'

This piece of impudence was so stunning that Tiberius was at a loss for appropriate words. After a long, staring silence he licked his dry lips.

'You are a man of imprudent speech, Gallio,' he muttered, 'but honest withal. It has been refreshing to talk with you. Leave us now. We will have further conversation in the morning. We are sorry your son cannot accept our appointment.'

'Good night, sire,' said Gallio. He retreated toward the door. Something in his weighted attitude stirred the old man's mellowed mind to sympathy.

'Stay!' he called. 'We shall find a place for the son of our excellent Gallio. Marcellus shall do his sculpture and attend the learned lectures. Let him dabble in the arts and drowse over the philosophies. Let him perfect himself in logic and metaphysics. By the gods!—there are other things needful at this court besides watching at keyholes and strutting with swords! Your son shall be our preceptor. He shall lecture to us. We are weary of old men's counsel. Marcellus shall give us a youthful view of the mysteries. Gallio—inform your son of our command!'

'Your Majesty is most kind,' murmured the Senator, gratefully. 'I shall advise my son of your generous words, sire. Perhaps this appointment may help to restore his ailing mind.'

'Well—if it doesn't'—the old man yawned mightily—'it won't matter. All philosophers are sick in the head.' He grinned, slowly sank back into his pillows, and the leathery lips puffed an exhausted breath. The Emperor of Rome was asleep.

* * * * * *

Informed by the Chamberlain that His Imperial Majesty was not yet awake, the Senator breakfasted in his room and set out for a walk. It had been many years since he had visited Capri; not since the formal opening of the Villa Jovis when the entire Senate had attended the festivities, memorable for their expensiveness rather than their impressiveness. Although fully informed about the enormously extravagant building operations on the island, he had not clearly pictured the magnitude of these undertakings. They had to be seen to be believed! Tiberius might be crazy, but he was an accomplished architect.

Walking briskly on the broad mosaic pavement to the east end of the mall, Gallio turned aside to a shaded arbor, sank into a comfortable chair, and dreamily watched the plume of blue smoke floating lazily above Vesuvius. Somehow the sinister old mountain seemed to symbolize the Empire; tremendous power under compression; occasionally spewing forth sulphurous fumes and molten metals. Its heat was not the kind that warmed and cheered, nor did its lava grow harvests. Vesuvius was competent only as a destroyer. They who dwelt in its shadow were afraid.

The same thing was true of the Empire, reflected Gallio. 'Let them hate us!' old Tiberius had growled. 'Let the whole world hate us!' Long before the Caesars, that surly boast had brought disaster to the Persians, the Egyptians, and the Greeks. Nemesis had laughed at their arrogance, and swept them—cursing impotently—into servitude.

Gallio wondered if he would be alive to witness the inevitable break-up of the Empire. What plans had Nemesis in mind for the disposal of Rome? What would be the shape of the new dynasty? Who would arise—and whence—to demolish the thing that the Caesars had built? Last night the disgusting old drunkard Tiberius had seemed almost frightened when he rehearsed the cryptic patter of the Jewish prophets. 'He that is to come.' Ah, yes—Tiberius saw the crisis nearing! Maybe the superstitious old fellow had never defined his exact reasons for being so deeply interested in the oracles and enchantments and ponderous nonsense of his avaricious soothsayers and stargazers; but that was *it!* Tiberius saw the Empire drifting toward the cataract! 'He that is to come!' Well—somebody would come—and the government would be upon his shoulder—but he wouldn't be a Jew! That was impossible! That was ridiculous!

Completely absorbed by his grim speculations, Gallio did not observe Diana's arrival until she stood directly before him, tall, slim, vital. She smiled and graciously held out her hand.

It was the first time he had had an opportunity for conversation with her, beyond the brief greetings they had exchanged when she came to visit Lucia. Until lately, Diana was only a little girl, shy and silent in his presence, but reputed to be high-spirited almost to the extent of rowdiness. In recent weeks, apprised of a growing attachment between his son and the daughter of Gallus, he had become somewhat more aware of her; but, this morning, it was almost as if he had never seen her before. Diana had grown up. She had taken on the supple grace and charming contours of a woman. She was beautiful! Gallio did not wonder that Marcellus had fallen in love with her.

He came to his feet, bowed deeply, and was warmed by her firm handclasp. Her steady eyes were set wide apart, framed in long, curling lashes, and arched by exquisitely modeled brows. The red silk bandeau accented the blue-blackness of her hair, the whiteness of her patrician forehead, the pink flush on her cheeks. Gallio looked into the level eyes with frank admiration. They were quite disturbingly feminine, but fearless and forthright as the eyes of a man; an inheritance from her father, perhaps. Gallus had a delightful personality, and an enviable poise, but—just underneath his amiability—there was the striking strength of a coiled spring in a baited trap. Diana's self-possessed smile and confident handclasp instantly won the Senator's respect, though the thought darted through his mind that the arrestingly lovely daughter of Gallus was equipped with all the implements for having her own way, and—if any attempt were made to thwart her—would prove to be a handful indeed.

'May I join you, Senator Gallio?' Diana's full lips were girlish, but her well-disciplined voice was surprisingly mature.

'Please sit down, my dear.' The Senator noted the easy grace of her posture as she took the chair opposite, artless but alert. 'I was hoping to have a talk with you,' he went on, resuming his seat.

Diana smiled encouragingly, but made no rejoinder; and Gallio, measuring his phrases, proceeded in a manner almost didactic:

'Marcellus came home from his long voyage, a few days ago, ill and depressed. He was grateful—we are all grateful, Diana—for your generous part in bringing him back to us. Marcellus will be eager to express his deep appreciation. But—he is not ready to resume his usual activities. We have sent him away—to Athens—hopeful that a change of environment may divert his gloomy mind.'

Gallio paused. He had anticipated an involuntary exclamation of surprise and regret; but Diana made no sound; just sat there, keenly attentive, alternately studying his eyes and his lips.

'You see'—he added—'Marcellus has had a severe shock!'

'Yes—I know,' she nodded, briefly.

'Indeed? How much do you know?'

'Everything you told the Emperor.'

'But—the Emperor is not yet awake.'

'I have not seen him,' said Diana. 'I had it from Nevius.'

'Nevius?'

'The Chamberlain.'

Gallio stroked his cheek thoughtfully. This Nevius must be quite a talkative fellow. Diana interpreted his dry smile.

'But you had intended to tell me, had you not?' she reminded him. 'Nevius is not a common chatterer, sir: I must say that for him. He is very close-mouthed. Sometimes,' she went on, ingenuously, 'it is difficult to make Nevius tell you everything that is going on at the Villa.'

The Senator's lips slowly puckered and his shoulders twitched with a silent chuckle. He was on the point of asking her if she had ever thought of taking up diplomacy as a profession; but the matter at issue was too serious for badinage. He grew suddenly grave.

'Now that you know—about Marcellus—I need not repeat the painful story.'

'It is all very strange.' Diana's averted eyes were troubled. 'According to Nevius, it was an execution that upset Marcellus.' Her expressive eyes slowly returned to search the Senator's sober face. 'There must be more to it than that, sir. Marcellus has seen cruel things done. Who has not? Is not the arena bloody enough? Why should Marcellus sink into grief and despair because he had to put a man to death?—no matter who—no matter how! He has seen men die!'

'This was a crucifixion, Diana,' said the Senator, quietly.

'And perfectly ghastly, no doubt,' she agreed, 'and Nevius says there was much talk of the man's innocence. Well—that wasn't Marcellus' fault. He didn't conduct the trial, nor choose the manner of execution. I can understand his not wanting to do it, but—surely no amount of brooding is going to bring this poor Jew back to life! There is a mystery behind it, I think. Nevius had a tale about a haunted Robe—and darkness in the middle of the afternoon—and a confused jumble about a predicted Messiah, or something like that. Does Marcellus think he has killed a person of great importance? Is that what's fretting him?'

'I shall tell you the very little that I know about it, Diana, and you may draw your own conclusions. As for me, it has been difficult to arrive at any sensible solution to the problem.' Gallio frowned studiously. 'For ages, the Jewish prophets have predicted the coming of a champion of their people's liberty. This fearless chieftain would restore the Jews' kingdom. Indeed, the traditional forecast—according to Emperor Tiberius, who is learned in all occult matters—is of wider scope, prefiguring a king with a more extensive dominion than the mere government of poor little Palestine.'

'Somebody the size of the Caesars?' wondered Diana.

'At least,' nodded Gallio, with a brief, contemptuous grin. 'Now—it happens that a very considerable number of Jews thought they had reason to believe that this Galilean, whom the Temple executives and the Roman provincial government tried for treason and heresy, was their promised Messiah—'

'But—surely'—broke in Diana—'Marcellus doesn't believe anything like that! He's the last person in the world!'

'That is true,' agreed Gallio. 'He is not superstitious. But—according to Demetrius, who was present throughout the whole affair, it was a strange occasion. The Jew's demeanor at the trial was, to say the least, unusual.

Demetrius says everybody was on trial but the prisoner; says the man's behavior on the cross was heroic. And Demetrius is a cold-blooded fellow, not accustomed to inventing lies.'

'What do you think about the Robe?' queried Diana.

'I have no ideas,' confessed the Senator. 'Marcellus had had a hard day. He was nervous, ashamed, overwrought. He may have been a victim of his own imagination. But—when he put on that Robe—it did something to him! We may not like the implications of this problem—but—well—there it is! You doubtless think it is silly to believe that the Jew's Robe is haunted—and so do I. All such idiotic prattle is detestable to me! I do not believe there is any energy resident in an inanimate thing. As for the Messiah legend, I have no interest in it. Whether the Galilean was justly accused, or not, is a closed incident, of no concern to me. But—after all of these considerations are dismissed, either as foolish or finished—Marcellus is worrying himself into madness. That much, at least, we know—for a fact.' Gallio rubbed his wrinkled brow and drew a hopeless sigh.

'Nevius says the Emperor wants Marcellus to come to Capri as a teacher,' said Diana, after the brief silence between them. 'We don't want him to do that; do we, sir?'

'I find it difficult to see Marcellus in that rôle,' agreed Gallio. 'He has but scant respect for the kind of learning that engages the mind of the Emperor.'

'Do you think he will consent?'

'Well'—Gallio made a helpless little gesture—'Marcellus may not have much choice in the matter. He is, at present, able to remain in Athens. But when he comes home, he will have to obey the Emperor's order, whether he enjoys it or not.'

Suddenly Diana leaned forward, her face clouded with anxiety.

'Tell him not to come home,' she whispered. 'He mustn't come here!' She rose, and Gallio, mystified, came to his feet, regarding her with serious interest. 'I must tell you something,' she went on, nervously. She took him by the arm and pointed to a long row of stakes, with little flags fluttering on them. 'This is where the Emperor is going to build the beautiful new villa. He is drawing the plans for it now. When it is finished, it is to be mine.'

Gallio stared.

'Yours?' he said, woodenly. 'Do you mean you want to live here—under the thumb of this cruel, crazy old man?'

Diana's eyes were full of tears. She shook her head, and turned her face away, still holding tightly to the Senator's arm.

'He suggested it, sir, when I was pleading with him to bring Marcellus home,' she confided, brokenly. 'It wasn't exactly a condition to his promise to send for Marcellus; but—he seems now to think it was. I thought he would forget about it. He forgets almost everything. But—I'm afraid he means to go through with it. That is why he wants Marcellus here. It is to be our villa.'

'Well,' soothed Gallio. 'Why not, then? Is it not true that Marcellus and you are in love?'

Diana nodded and bent her head.

'There will be much trouble if he comes to Capri,' she said, huskily. Then, dashing the tears from her eyes and facing Gallio squarely, she said: 'I must tell you all about it. Please don't try to do anything. Gaius has been here twice recently. He wants me to marry him. The Emperor will not let me go home. I have written to my mother and I know the letter was not delivered.'

'I shall tell her to come to you—at once!' declared Gallio, hotly.

'No, no—not yet—please!' Diana clutched his arm with both hands. 'Maybe there will be some other way out! I must not put my mother in danger!'

'But—Diana—you can't stay here—under these conditions!'

'Please! Don't say—or do—anything.' She was trembling.

'What are you afraid of, my dear?' demanded Gallio.

'I am afraid of Gaius!' she whispered.

Chapter XI

At sunrise on the seventh day of September a market gardener with fresh fruits and vegetables for the House of Eupolis reported that *The Vestris* had been sighted off Piraeus.

Feeling sure there must be letters for him on the ship, and unwilling to await their sluggish delivery through the Tetrarch's Insula in the city, Marcellus engaged a port-wagon and set off at once, accompanied by Demetrius.

Ordinarily the slave would have sat by the driver; but, of late, Demetrius and his master had been conducting all of their conversations in Aramaic. It was not an easy tongue, and when they spoke they enunciated carefully, watching each other's lips. This morning they sat side by side in the rear seat of the jolting wagon, and anyone casually observing them would not have guessed that one of these young men owned the other. Indeed—Demetrius was taking the lead in the conversation, occasionally criticizing his master's accent.

Every morning after breakfast, for several weeks, Demetrius had gone to Benjamin's shop for instruction, spending the day until late afternoon. The old weaver had not asked to be recompensed for his services as a pedagogue. It would be a pleasure to him, he had said. But as the days went by, Demetrius began to be useful in the shop, quickly picking up deftness in carding and spinning. In the evenings, he relayed his accumulated knowledge of Aramaic to Marcellus who, unwilling to be in Benjamin's debt, had presented him—over his protest—with two great bales of long-fibered Egyptian cotton and several bags of selected wools from the Cyprian Mountains where fleeces were appropriate to a severe climate.

Benjamin, who had no talent for flattery, had been moved to volunteer the statement—after a month had passed—that Demetrius was making surprising progress. If that were true, Demetrius had remarked, it was because he had received such clear instruction, to which Benjamin had replied that the best way to learn anything is to explain it to somebody else. Marcellus was receiving his Aramaic on the first bounce, but getting it thoroughly; for Demetrius was holding him to it with a tactful but relentless tyranny.

On the way to Piraeus, they were engaged in an animated discussion of the Ten Commandments, Marcellus approving of them, Demetrius complaining that they were unjust. On occasions, he became so enthusiastic in advocating his cause that he abandoned the Aramaic and took to the Greek, much to his master's amusement.

'Here, you!' shouted Marcellus. 'No talking about the Jewish Commandments in a heathen language!'

'But, sir, they are so unfair! "Thou shalt not steal." Very good; but there is no Commandment enjoining the man of property to deal generously with the poor, so they would have no wish to steal! "Thou shalt not covet!" Good advice; no doubt. But is it fair to tell the poor man he musn't be envious of the rich man's goods—and then forget to admonish the rich man that he has no right to be so selfish?'

'Oh—you're just looking at it from the slave angle,' drawled Marcellus. 'You're prejudiced. The only fault I can find with the Commandments is their injunction against sculpture. This Jehovah was certainly no patron of the arts.'

'That was to keep them from making idols,' explained Demetrius.

'I know—but what's the matter with idols? They're usually quite artistic. The ordinary run of people are bound to worship something: it had better be something lovely! Old Zeus didn't raise a row when the Greek sculptors carved a flock of gods—all shapes and sizes—take your pick. There must be forty of them on Mars' Hill! They even have one up there in honor of "The Unknown God." '

'I wonder what Zeus thought of that one?' speculated Demetrius.

'He probably laughed,' said Marcellus. 'He does laugh, sometimes, you know. I think that's the main trouble with Jehovah. He doesn't laugh.'

'Maybe he doesn't think the world is very funny,' observed Demetrius.

'Well, that's his fault, then,' said Marcellus, negligently. 'If he created it, he should have made it a little funnier.'

Demetrius made no reply to that.

'I believe that's the silliest thing I ever said in my life!' reflected Marcellus, soberly.

'Oh—I wouldn't go so far as to say that, sir,' rejoined Demetrius, formally. They both laughed. This study of Aramaic was making their master-slave relationship very difficult to sustain.

* * * * * *

Captain Fulvius, roaring orders to the sweating slaves, stared strangely at Marcellus as he came on deck; then beamed with sudden recognition and grasped him warmly by the hand.

'You are well again, sir!' he boomed. 'That is good! I hardly knew you. Many's the time I have thought about you. You were a very sick man!'

'I must have tried your patience, Captain,' said Marcellus. 'All is well now, thank you.'

'Ho! Demetrius!' Fulvius offered his hand, somewhat to Marcellus' surprise. 'I haven't forgotten that good turn you did me, son, on the voyage down from Joppa.'

'I hadn't heard about that,' said Marcellus, turning a questioning glance toward Demetrius.

'It was nothing, sir,' murmured Demetrius.

'Nothing!' shouted Fulvius. 'The fellow saves my life, and now declares it was nothing! Demetrius, you should be put in chains for that!' He turned to Marcellus. 'You were too ill to be interested in the story, sir; so we did not bother you with it. A mad slave—it gets quite hot down in the bottom tier, sir—managed to slip his bracelet, one night, when we were standing off Alexandria; sneaked up on deck, and had a belaying-pin raised to dash my brains out. And your Demetrius got there just in time!'

'I am glad I happened to be standing by, sir,' said Demetrius.

'So am I!' declared the Captain, fervently. 'Well—it's good to see you both. There are letters for you, I notice, Legate. I asked the Tribune to take them to you when he went to deliver the message from the Emperor, but he is a haughty young fellow; said he was not a common errand-boy.'

'Message from the Emperor?' queried Marcellus, uneasily.

'You have not yet received it, then? Perhaps you passed the magnificent Tribune on the way. Will you stay and break bread with us?'

'It would be a pleasure, Captain Fulvius; but I should return without delay. This Tribune may be waiting.'

'Aye! He will be waiting and fuming; a restless fellow, who takes his duties hard; a very important fellow, too, who likes to give orders.' Fulvius sighed unhappily. 'And I shall have him on my hands for another threescore and five days, at least; for he is bearing a message also to Pontius Pilate in Jerusalem—and returns on *The Vestris.*'

'Can't you pitch him overboard?' suggested Marcellus.

'I can,' grinned Fulvius, 'but my wife is expecting me back in Ostia by early December. Legate, if you can spare Demetrius for the day, shall he not tarry with me?'

Marcellus was about to give his consent, but hesitated.

'He may come tomorrow, Fulvius, if you wish it. Perhaps he had best return with me now. This message from the Emperor might make some alterations in our plans.'

'Thank you, Captain Fulvius,' said Demeterius. 'I shall come if I can.'

Marcellus was more eager than the shambling horses to return to the city, but even at their plodding gait it was an uncomfortable ride, certainly not conducive to the pleasant perusal of letters, for the dusty, deep-rutted highway was crammed with lumbering wagons and overburdened camel-trains, requiring frequent excursions to the ill-conditioned roadside.

He slit the seal of his father's bulky scrawl, happy to note that it contained also messages from his mother and Lucia. Diana's letter—he was surprised to find it addressed from Capri—might have been read first had the circumstances been more favorable. Marcellus revolved the scroll in his hands and decided he would enjoy it later in private.

'Evidently the daughter of Gallus had occasion to reopen her letter after sealing it,' he remarked, more to himself than Demetrius, who sat idly observant as his master inspected the scroll.

'The overlaid wax seems of a slightly different color, sir,' commented Demetrius.

More painstakingly, Marcellus examined the scroll again, picking at the second application of wax with the point of his dagger.

'You're right,' he muttered. 'The letter has been tampered with.'

'By a woman,' added Demetrius. 'There is her finger-mark.'

Frowning with annoyance, Marcellus tucked Diana's scroll into the breast of his tunic, and began silently reading his father's letter. He had just returned from Capri—he wrote—where he had explained his son's sudden departure.

'It was imperative that I should be entirely frank with the Emperor'—the letter went on—'because you had no more than reached open sea before a message arrived appointing you——'

'Demetrius—I bid you listen to this!' exclaimed Marcellus. 'The Emperor has appointed me Commander of the Guard—at Capri! Doubtless that is the import of the message I am receiving today. Commander of the Guard at Capri! What do you suppose the Commander of the Capri Guard has to do?'

The intimate tone meant that Demetrius was not only temporarily emancipated, but would probably be reproached if he failed to make prompt use of his privilege to speak on terms of equality.

'Taste soup, I should think,' he ventured. 'And sleep in his uniform—with one eye open.'

'While his slave sleeps with both eyes open,' remarked Marcellus in the same manner. 'I dare say you're right. The island is a hotbed of jealousy and conspiracy. One's life wouldn't be worth a punched denarius.' Resuming the letter, he read on for a time with a deepening scowl.

'I am not receiving that appointment,' he glanced up to say. 'My father advises me that the Emperor has something else in mind. Let me read you:—"He was much interested in what I felt obliged to tell him of your unpleasant experience in Jerusalem. And when I informed him that this crucified Jew was thought by some to have been the Messiah——" ' Marcellus suddenly broke off and stared into Demetrius' face. 'How do you suppose my father found that out?' he demanded.

'I told him,' said Demetrius, with prompt candor. 'Senator Gallio insisted on a full account of what happened up there. I thought it due you, sir, that an explanation be made—seeing you were in no condition to make it yourself.'

'That's true enough,' admitted Marcellus, grimly. 'I hope you did not feel required to tell the Senator about the Galilean's Robe.'

'Yes, sir. The Robe was responsible for your—your illness. The story—without the Robe—would have been very confusing.'

'You mean—it was quite clear—with the Robe included?'

'No, sir. Perhaps that part of it will always be a mystery.'

'Well—let us get on with this.' Marcellus took up the scroll and resumed his reading aloud:—' "The Emperor was stirred to an immense curiosity, for he is deeply learned in all of the religions. He has heard much about the messianic prophecies of the Jews. He wishes you to pursue your studies in Athens, especially concerning the religions, and return to Capri as a teacher." A *teacher!*' Marcellus laughed, self-derisively; but Demetrius did not smile. 'Do you not think this funny, Demetrius?' he insisted. 'Can you picture *me*—lecturing to that menagerie?'

'No, sir,' replied Demetrius, soberly, 'I do not think this is funny. I think it is a disaster!'

'You mean—I'll be bored?'

'Worse than bored!' exclaimed Demetrius, recklessly. 'It is a contemptible position, if you ask me, sir! The Emperor is said to have a large contingent of astrologers, diviners of oracles, ghost-tenders, dream-mechanics and all that sort of thing—clustered about him. It would be a sorry business for my master to be engaged in!'

Marcellus had begun to share the Corinthian's seriousness.

'You think he wants me to teach a mess of superstitious nonsense?'

'Yes,' nodded Demetrius. 'He wants to hear some more about that Robe.'

'But that isn't superstitious nonsense!' objected Marcellus.

'No—not to us—but it will be little else than that by the time Emperor Tiberius and his soothsayers are through discussing it.'

'You feel deeply about this, Demetrius,' said Marcellus, gently.

'Well, sir—I don't want to see the Robe reviled by that loathsome old man—and his crew of lunatics.'

Marcellus pretended to be indignant.

'Are you aware, Demetrius, that your references to the Emperor of Rome might be considered bordering on disrespect?' They both grinned, and Marcellus took up his father's letter again, reading aloud, slowly:

> I doubt whether you would have any relish for this employment, my son. The Emperor is of strange, erratic mind. However—this is his command, and you have no choice but to obey. Fortunately, you are permitted to remain in Athens for a reasonable length of time, pursuing your studies. We are all eager to have you back in Rome, but I cannot counsel you to speed your return.

There was no reference to Diana. Marcellus thought this odd, for surely Diana must have been at the Villa Jovis while his father was there. He was anxious to read her letter. It disquieted him to know that she was a guest on that sinister island. Someone had opened her scroll. Someone was spying on her. It was not a safe place for Diana.

* * * * * *

The House of Eupolis was apparently in a great state of excitement. It was not every day that a flashily uniformed Tribune arrived with a message from the Emperor of Rome; and the whole establishment—habitually reserved—was undeniably impressed by the occasion.

Dion, grave-faced and perspiring freely, was pacing up and down the driveway as the battered old port-wagon entered the gate.

'You must make haste, Marcellus!' he pleaded, in a frightened voice, as they pulled up beside him. 'There is a message from the Emperor! The Tribune has been waiting in a rage, shouting that if you did not soon arrive he would report our house to the Tetrarch!'

'Be at ease, Dion,' said Marcellus, calmly. 'You are not at fault.' Dismissing the carriage, he proceeded up the driveway, passing a huddle of scared garden-slaves who stared at him with awe and sympathy. Theodosia and her Aunt Ino hovered about her mother who sat stiffly apprehensive in the swing. The pompous figure of the Tribune strutted imperiously before the entrance to the house.

Instantly Marcellus recognized Quintus Lucian! So—that was why the fellow was showing off. Gaius' pet—Quintus! Doubtless the creature had had no stomach for his errand. That explained his obnoxious conduct on the ship. Gaius was probably in a red-hot fury because the old man at Capri had gone over his head with orders for Marcellus' return from Minoa; and now the Emperor had sent this detestable Quintus with a message—and there hadn't been anything that Quintus, or Gaius, either, could do about it.

'And how long shall the Emperor's envoy be kept waiting?' he snarled, as Marcellus drew nearer with Demetrius following at a few paces.

'I had not been advised to be on the alert for a message from His Majesty,' rejoined Marcellus, trying to keep his temper. 'But now that I am here, Tribune Quintus, I suggest that you perform your errand with the courtesy that a Roman expects from an officer of his own rank.'

Quintus grunted crossly and handed over the gaudily gilded imperial scroll.

'Are you to wait for a reply?' inquired Marcellus.

'Yes—but I advise you not to keep me waiting long! His Majesty's envoys are not accustomed to wasting their time at Greek inns.' The tone was so contemptuous that it could have only one meaning. Demetrius moved forward a step and stood at attention. Marcellus, white with anger, made no retort.

'I shall read this in private, Quintus,' he said, crisply, 'and prepare a reply. You may wait—or you may return for it—as you prefer.' As he strode away, he muttered to Demetrius, 'You remain here.'

After Marcellus had disappeared, on his way to his suite, Quintus swaggered toward Demetrius and faced him with a surly grin.

'You his slave?' He nodded in the general direction Marcellus had taken.

'Yes, sir.'

'Who is the pretty one—by the swing?' demanded Quintus, out of the corner of his mouth.

'She is the daughter of Eupolis, sir,' replied Demetrius, stiffly.

'Indeed! We must make her acquaintance while we wait.' Shouldering past Demetrius, he stalked haughtily across the lawn, accenting each arrogant step with a sidewise jerk of his helmet. Dion, pale and flustered, scurried along toward the swing. Demetrius slowly followed.

With elegantly sandaled feet wide apart and arms akimbo, Quintus halted directly before Theodosia, ignoring the others, and looked her over with an appraising leer. He grinned, disrespectfully.

'What's your name?' he demanded, roughly.

'That is my daughter, sir!' expostulated Dion, rubbing his hands in helpless entreaty.

'You are fortunate, fellow, to have so fair a daughter. We must know her better.' Quintus reached for her hand, and Theodosia recoiled a step, her eyes full of fear. 'Timid; eh?' He laughed contemptuously. 'Since when was the daughter of a Greek innkeeper so frugal with her smiles?'

'But I implore you, Tribune!' Dion's voice was trembling. 'The House of Eupolis has ever been respectable. You must not offend my daughter!'

'Must not—indeed!' crowed Quintus. 'And who are you—to be advising the envoy of the Emperor what he must not do? Be gone, fellow!' He thrust out an arm toward Phoebe and Ino. 'You, too!' he barked. 'Leave us!'

Deathly white, Phoebe rose unsteadily and took a few steps, Ino supporting her. Dion held his ground for a moment, panting with impotent anger, but began edging out of range as their enemy fumbled for his dagger.

'What are you doing here, slave?' shouted Quintus, turning savagely to Demetrius.

'My master ordered me to remain, sir,' replied Demetrius; then, to Theodosia, 'You had better go with your father to the house.'

Purple with rage, Quintus whipped out his dagger and lunged forward. Demetrius sprang to meet the descending arm which he caught at the wrist with a tiger-claw grip of his right hand while his left crashed into the Tribune's face. It was a staggering blow that took Quintus by complete surprise. Before he could regain his balance, Demetrius had sent another full-weight drive of his left fist into the Tribune's mouth. The relentless finger-nails cut deep into his wrist and the dagger fell from his hand. The battle was proceeding too rapidly for Quintus. Dazed and disarmed, he struck wildly, blindly, while Demetrius, pressing forward step by step, continued to shoot stunning blows into the mutilated face.

Quintus was quite at his mercy now, and Demetrius knew it would be simple enough to administer the one decisive upper-cut to the jaw that would excuse the Emperor's envoy from any further participation in the fight; but a strong desire had laid hold on him to see how much damage could be inflicted on the Tribune's face before he finally put him away. It was becoming a quite sanguinary engagement. Both of Demetrius' fists were red with blood as they shot into the battered eyes and crashed against the broken nose. Quintus was making no defense now. Bewildered and blinded with blood, he yielded ground with staggering steps until he had been driven backward to a huge pine where he put out a hand for support. He breathed with agonized, whistling sobs.

'You'll die for this!' he squeaked, through swollen lips.

'Very well!' panted Demetrius. 'If I'm to die for punishing you—!'

Grabbing Quintus by the throat-strap of his helmet, he completed the ruin of his shockingly mangled face. Then, satisfied with his work, he deliberately drew back his arm and put his full strength behind an ultimate drive at the point of the Tribune's jaw. The knees buckled and Quintus sank limply to the ground.

The Eupolis family had withdrawn some distance while the punishment was being administered. Now Dion came running up, ghastly pale.

'Have you killed him?' he asked, hoarsely.

Demetrius, breathing heavily, was examining his bruised and bleeding hands. He shook his head.

'We will all be thrown into prison,' moaned Dion.

'Don't think of trying to escape,' advised Demetrius. 'Stay where you are —all of you. You had nothing to do with it. That can be proved.' He started to walk away toward his master's suite.

'Shall I do anything for this fellow?' called Dion.

'Yes—bring a basin of water and towels. He will be coming around presently. And if he shows fight, send for me—and tell him that if I have to do this again, I shall kill him!'

Very much spent, Demetrius walked slowly to their quarters and proceeded through to the peristyle where Marcellus sat at the table writing, his face brightly animated. He did not look up from his letter.

'Demetrius! The Emperor commands me to go to Palestine and learn what is to be known—at first hand—about the Galilean!' Marcellus' voice was vibrant. 'Could anything have been more to my liking? Tiberius wants to know how much truth there is in the rumor that Jesus was believed to be the Messiah. As for me—I care naught about that! I want to know what manner of man he was! What a chance for us, Demetrius! We will pursue our Aramaic diligently with old Benjamin. Come early spring, we will journey into Galilee!' He signed his name to the letter, put down his stylus, pushed back his chair, looked up into Demetrius' pale face. 'Why—what on earth have you been doing?' he demanded.

'The Tribune,' said Demetrius wearily.

Marcellus sprang to his feet.

'What? You haven't been fighting—with Quintus!'

'Not exactly fighting,' said Demetrius. 'He insulted the family—Theodosia in particular—and I rebuked him.'

'Well—from the look of your hands, I should say you had done a good job. But—Demetrius!—this is very serious! Greek slaves can't do that—not to Roman Tribunes—no matter how much it is needed!'

'Yes—I know, sir. I must run away. If I remain here, you will try to defend me—and get into trouble. Please—shall I not go—at once?'

'By all means!' insisted Marcellus. 'But—where will you go? Where can you go?'

'I don't know, sir. I shall try to get out into the country, into the mountains, before the news spreads.'

'How badly is Quintus hurt?' asked Marcellus, anxiously.

'He will recover,' said Demetrius. 'I used no weapons. His eyes are swollen shut—and his mouth is swollen open—and the last few times I hit him on the nose, it felt spongy.'

'Has he gone?'

'No—he was still there.'

Marcellus winced and ran his fingers through his hair.

'Go—wash your hands—and pack a few things for your journey.' Walking past Demetrius, he went to his bedroom and unlocking his strong-box filled a silk bag with gold and silver talents and other coins of smaller value. Returning, he sat down at the table, took up his stylus, wrote a page, stamped it with his heavy seal ring, rolled it, and thrust it into a scroll. 'Here you are,' he said, when Demetrius reappeared. 'This money will befriend you for the present—and this scroll contains your manumission. I shall remain here until spring; the ides of March, approximately. Then I shall go to Jerusalem. I cannot tell how long I may be touring about in the Palestinian provinces; all summer, certainly; perhaps longer. Then I am to return to Capri and report to the Emperor. For that I have no relish; but we will not borrow trouble.'

'Would I were going with you, sir!' exclaimed Demetrius.

'I shall miss you, Demetrius; but your first duty now is to put yourself quickly out of danger. Try to let me know, as soon as safety permits, where you are in hiding. Remember that I shall be burning with desire to learn that you have not been apprehended! Notify me of your needs. If you are captured, I shall leave no stone unturned to effect your deliverance.'

'I know that, sir.' Demetrius' voice was unsteady. 'You are very kind. I shall take the money. As for my freedom—not now.' He laid the scroll on the table. 'If I were caught with this on me, they might think you had rewarded me for punishing Quintus.' Drawing himself stiffly to attention, he saluted with his spear. 'Farewell, sir. I am sorry to go. We may never meet again.'

Marcellus reached out his hand.

'Good-bye, Demetrius,' he said, huskily. 'I shall miss you sorely. You have been a faithful friend. You will be much in my thoughts.'

'Please tell Theodosia why I did not tarry to bid her farewell,' said Demetrius.

'Anything between you two?' inquired Marcellus, with sudden interest.

'That much—at least,' admitted Demetrius.

They silently gripped each other's hands—and Demetrius sped away through the rose garden.

Marcellus moved slowly back into the house, relocked his strong-box, and went out by the front door. Dion was approaching, pale and agitated.

'You have heard, sir?' he asked, anxiously.

'How is he?' inquired Marcellus.

'Sitting up—but he is an unpleasant sight. He says he is going to have us all punished.' Dion was shaken with fear.

'Tell me—what really happened?'

'The Tribune showed much disrespect for Theodosia. Your slave remonstrated, and the Tribune lunged at him with his dagger. After that—well—your Demetrius disarmed him and began striking him in the face with his fists. It was a very brutal beating, sir. I had not thought your gentle-spoken slave could be so violent. The Tribune is unrecognizable! Has your slave hidden himself?'

'He is gone,' said Marcellus, much to Dion's relief.

Proceeding through the grove, they came upon the wretched Quintus, sitting slumped under the tall pine, dabbing at his mutilated face with a bloody towel. He looked up truculently and squinted through the slim red slit in a purpling eye.

'When I inform the Tetrarch,' he claimed, thickly, 'there will be prison for you—and beheadings for the others.'

'What had you thought of telling the Tetrarch, Quintus?' inquired Marcellus, with a derisive grin. 'And what do you think they will say, at the Insula, when you report that after you had insulted a respectable young woman, and had tried to stab a slave who intervened, you let the fellow disarm you and beat you with his bare hands until you couldn't stand up? Go, Quintus, to the Insula!' went on Marcellus, mockingly. 'Let them all see how you look after having had a duel with a Greek slave! The Tetrarch will probably tell you it was disgraceful enough for a Roman Tribune to be engaged in a fight with a slave, even if he had come out of it victorious! Come, then; let us go to the Insula, Quintus. I shall accompany you. I wouldn't miss it for the world!'

Quintus patted his face gingerly.

'I shall not require your assistance,' he muttered.

'Let me put you up, sir,' wheedled Dion, 'until you feel better.'

'That is a good suggestion,' advised Marcellus. 'Dion certainly owes you nothing for playing the scoundrel on his premises, but if he is willing to give you shelter until you are fit to be seen, you would be wise to accept his offer. I understand you are sailing on *The Vestris*, the day after tomorrow. Better stay under cover here, and go directly to the ship when she is ready to put off. Then none of your acquaintances at the Insula will have an amusing story to tell about you, next time he visits Rome.'

'I shall have that slave of yours whipped to ribbons!' growled Quintus.

'Perhaps you might like to do it yourself!' retorted Marcellus. 'Shall I summon him?'

* * * * * *

The gray days were short, cold, and tiresome. Marcellus had discovered how heavily he had leaned on his Corinthian slave, not only for personal service but friendship and entertainment. Demetrius had become his alter ego. Marcellus was lost and restless without him.

Nothing interesting happened. The days were all alike. In the morning he went early to old Benjamin's shop for his regular ration of Aramaic, offered mostly in the form of conversation. At noon he would return to the inn and spend the rest of the daylight in his studio, hacking away without much enthusiasm or inspiration on a marble head that resembled Diana Gallus less and less, every day. It was still apparent that she was a girl, a Roman girl, a quite pretty girl; but no one would have guessed that she was Diana.

And perhaps this was to be accounted for, surmised Marcellus, by the increasing vagueness of Diana on the retina of his imagination. She was very far away—and retreating. He had had two letters from her. The first, from Capri, had been written in haste. She knew all about the Emperor's orders that he was to continue his studies in Athens and then proceed to Jerusalem and the northern provinces of Palestine for authentic information about that mysterious young Jew.

As for herself, Diana said, the Emperor had insisted on her remaining at Capri for a few weeks; and, in view of his valued favors, she had decided to do so. He had been very kind; he was lonesome; she must stay.

Her second letter had been written from home. It, too, sounded as if the carriage were waiting and someone were reading the words over her shoulder. The letter was friendly enough, solicitous of his welfare, but wanting in the little overtones of tenderness and yearning. It was as if their love had been adjourned to await further development in some undated future. Marcellus re-read this letter many times, weighing and balancing its phrases, trying to decide whether Diana had been taking extra precautions in case the scroll were read by a third party, or whether she was losing interest in their affection. It might be one or the other: it might indeed be both. Her words were not softly whispered. They were gentle—but clearly audible. And they made him very lonesome.

It was an important occasion, therefore, when the long letter arrived from Demetrius. A light snow had fallen in the night and the sky was heavily overcast. Marcellus had stood for a long time at the studio window debating whether to go to Benjamin's shop today. But the light was too poor for sculpturing. And the old man would be expecting him. With a mood to fit the sullen sky, he made his way to the shop where Benjamin greeted him with bright-eyed excitement.

'Here is a letter for you!'

'Indeed! Why was it sent here?'

'In my care. Addressed to me—but intended for you. It was brought by a slave attached to a caravan, and delivered here last night by Zenos, the noisy boy who runs errands for my friend Popygos. Demetrius, as you will see, is in Jerusalem. I read that much of it. Your slave is prudent. Fearing a letter addressed to you might be examined and reveal his whereabouts, he has sent it to me.' Benjamin laughed as he handed over the scroll. 'Now you will have an opportunity to put your Aramaic to practical use. It's very good Aramaic, too!' he added proudly.

Marcellus drew up a stool beside the worktable, unrolled the end of the long sheet of papyrus, and began reading aloud, with occasional hesitations and appeals to Benjamin who delightedly came to his rescue.

> Esteemed Master (read Marcellus), I am writing this on the Jewish Sabbath in the upper chamber of an old house overlooking the Kidron, no great distance from the Temple area. I share this room with one Stephanos, a Greek of my own age, whom the Jews call Stephen. He is intelligent, well-informed, and friendly. At present he is absent, on some mysterious errand; possibly the same business that kept him out, last night, until shortly before dawn.
>
> I arrived in Jerusalem but three days ago. You will be curious to learn the manner of my departure from Athens. Confident of Fulvius' friendship, I ran to Piraeus, boarded *The Vestris*, and confided my dilemma. Fulvius hid me in the hold. When the ship stood well out to sea, on the second day, I was brought on deck where I enjoyed full liberty. We had an important passenger who was recovering from an accident that had disfigured his face. He kept to his cabin until we had cleared from Alexandria. Recognizing me, he ordered Fulvius to put me in irons, which Fulvius refused to do, saying that I had paid my passage. This was untrue, though I had offered to pay. Fulvius told the distinguished passenger that if he wished he could have me apprehended at the next port.
>
> We anchored at nightfall in the Bay of Gaza, and Fulvius secretly put me ashore in the small boat. Providing myself with a few necessities, I journeyed on foot over the same route taken by the Legion from Minoa to Jerusalem. In a desolate wady, some twelve parasangs northeast of Ascalon, I was captured and robbed by Bedouins, who did not otherwise harm me, and permitted my escape. The weather was

extremely cold and I was lightly clad. That country is sparsely settled, as you may recall. The few inhabitants are poor, and hostile to strangers. I learned to relish warm goat-milk and frosted corn; and I was stoned while pillaging withered leeks from an ill-kept garden. I discovered that eggs, sucked from the shell, are delicious, and that a sleepy cow does not resent sharing her warmth with a wayfarer seeking shelter in her stall. The cattle of Judea are hospitable. On the last night of my journey, I was pleasantly surprised by being permitted to sleep in the stable of a tavern in the village of Bethlehem. In the morning the innkeeper sent his servant with a dish of hot broth and a small loaf of wheaten bread. The servant said it was a custom of the inn to befriend impoverished travelers. I observed that on the corner of the napkin, in which the bread was brought, there was embroidered the figure of a fish. It stirred my curiosity a little because a similar design had been burned with an iron into the timber of the stable-door. After leaving Bethlehem I noticed, at two road-crossings, the crude outline of a fish, drawn in the sand, and surmised that the device might indicate the direction taken by someone who wished to leave this cryptic advice for another person following. Not knowing what it meant—or caring very much—I dismissed the matter from my mind.

Arriving in Jerusalem, hungry and footsore, I decided to seek the house of a weaver, hoping I might be given some small tasks to provide me with food and shelter. In this I was most fortunate. At the shop of Benyosef I was kindly received by Stephanos, who works there. Learning that I am a Greek, and having been informed that I had done some carding and spinning for Benjamin in Athens, whose name Stephanos recognized, he commended me to Benyosef, and I was given employment. The wage is small, but consistent with the service I render, and is ample to sustain me for the present. Stephanos bade me lodge with him.

Of course, his interest in me is due, primarily, to the fact that I am a Greek. His people were long ago of Philippi, his great-grandparents having fled for refuge in Jerusalem when Macedonia was subjugated. It seems that there are hundreds of Greeks here, whose ancestors migrated to Jerusalem for the same reason. Not many of them are literate; and Stephanos, who is a student of the classics, longs for congenial company. He seemed pleased when, in response to his queries, I told him I was at least somewhat conversant with Greek literature.

On our first evening together, after we had eaten supper and were talking of many things relating to the unhappy Greeks, Stephanos idly drew the outline of a fish on the back of a papyrus tablet; and, pushing it across the table, raised his brows inquiringly.

I told him it signified nothing to me, though I had seen the symbol before. He then asked me if I had not heard of Jesus, the Galilean. I admitted that I had—but not very much—and would be interested in hearing more. He said that the people who believed in the teachings of Jesus were being so savagely persecuted that they met only in secret. This fish-emblem had been adopted as their method of identifying themselves to others of similar belief. He did not tell me how they came to use this device. Jesus was not a fisherman, but a carpenter.

Stephanos went on to say that Jesus advocated freedom for all men. 'Surely a slave should ally himself with such a cause,' he said. I told him I was deeply concerned, and he promised to tell me more about Jesus when there was an opportunity.

The house of Benyosef, I am discovering, is not only a weaver's shop, but a secret meeting-place for the men who were intimate friends of Jesus. My position here is so lowly and menial that my presence is unnoticed by the sober men who come neither to buy nor sell, but to slip in quietly and sit beside the old man, whispering while he whacks his ancient loom. (Benjamin would laugh at that loom.)

Yesterday a heavily bearded man of great strength and stature spent an hour in low-voiced conversation with Benyosef and two young fellows, in a far corner of the shop. Stephanos said they were Galileans. The huge man, he said, was called 'The Big Fisherman,' and the younger men, who were brothers, he referred to as 'The Sons of Thunder.' 'The Big Fisherman' seems a very forceful man. Perhaps he is the leader of the party, though why there should be a party at all, or so much secrecy, now that their Jesus is dead and his cause is lost, I do not pretend to understand. They all act as if they were suppressing some excitement. It does not resemble the excitement of fear; rather that of expectancy. They behave as if they had found something valuable and had hidden it.

This afternoon, a tall, well-favored man from the country came into the shop and was greeted with much warmth. I gathered that they had not seen him for some time. When the day's work was done, and Stephanos and I were on the way to our lodging, I remarked of this man that he seemed an amiable person whom everyone liked, and he unexpectedly confided that the man was Barsabas Justus, of Sepphoris in Galilee. He then went on to say that Jesus had appointed twelve friends to serve as his accredited disciples. One of them, Judas of Kerioth, had betrayed Jesus' whereabouts to the priests. After his master's arrest, he was filled with remorse and hanged himself. The eleven disciples met later to elect a successor to this Judas, though why they felt the necessity to do that, after Jesus was dead, Stephanos did not explain.

They voted on two men who had followed Jesus about through the provinces, hearing him speak to the people and witnessing many strange deeds of which Stephanos may tell me when he is in a mood to speak more freely. I think he wants first to make sure that I will respect his confidence. One of these two men, Matthias by name, was elected to succeed the traitor Judas. The other man is this Barsabas Justus.

I venture to suggest, sir, that when you come to Jerusalem to make inquiries about Jesus' career, you could not do better than to contrive the acquaintance of a man like Barsabas Justus. This will not be easy to do. These friends of Jesus are watched closely for any indication that they are attempting to extend or preserve his influence. The Temple authorities evidently feel that the teachings of the Galilean contain the seeds of revolution against the established religion, and the Insula has probably been persuaded that the sooner everybody forgets about Jesus, the more likely it may be that this next Passover season can be celebrated without a political uprising.

During these past three days I have given much thought to a plan which might assist you in getting up into Galilee without exciting suspicion. You could appear in Jerusalem as a connoisseur of homespun fabrics, particularly interested in the products of Galilean household looms. Let it be known that such textiles are now highly esteemed in Rome. Inquire in the bazaars for such fabrics and pay generously for a few articles. They are not considered as of much value here, but might quickly become so if you permit yourself to be well cheated in two or three shops. Rumor spreads rapidly in this city.

In the course of your search for Galilean homespun you would naturally call at the house of Benyosef where you might let it be known that you contemplate a trip into the region around Capernaum to look for textiles. You could inquire whether it would be possible to employ, as a guide, some man well acquainted with that country.

Of the several Galileans who visit the shop, Barsabas Justus would be the most likely, I think, to accept such employment. The man they call 'The Big Fisherman' is too passionately absorbed in whatever he is doing in the city and 'The Sons of Thunder' appear to be weighted with duties, but Barsabas Justus seems to have fewer responsibilities. Unquestionably he is your man—if you can get him.

My belief is that they will scatter when Passover Week approaches, for the Insula will be on the alert, and these Galileans will want to avoid useless trouble. I suggest that you plan to arrive here about a month before the Passover. Spring will be approaching, and the country will be beautiful. It will be more prudent if you do not recognize me, even if we meet face to face; for, unless I am mistaken, Stephanos will—by that time—have taken me into his full confidence, and it would be most unfortunate if he suspected collusion between us. Stephanos does not know that I have ever been in Jerusalem before. If I can contrive a secret meeting when you come, I shall be overjoyed to talk with you, but I think you should ignore me completely. If a private conference is practical, I shall arrange for it and let you know—somehow.

Marcellus glanced up at Benjamin—and grinned.

'That boy should have been a Jew!' declared the old man. 'He has a keen mind—and is cunning.'

'Yes,' agreed Marcellus, dryly. 'I can see that a study of Aramaic has done wonders for him. He is crafty. However—this advice sounds sensible enough; don't you think?'

'I doubt it, my friend. This is a game that will have to be played with the utmost care,' warned Benjamin. 'The Jews have no reasons for trusting the Romans. Their confidence will not be easily won.'

'Do you think I might be able to pass myself off for a merchant?' inquired Marcellus, doubtfully.

'A good way to find out,' suggested Benjamin, with a twinkle, 'is to go over here to David Sholem's bazaar and buy something; and then go across the street and try to sell it to old Aaron Barjona.' They both laughed.

'But—seriously,' said Marcellus. 'Do you think I might be able to get into Galilee by any such scheme as the one Demetrius suggests?'

'Not a chance!' scoffed Benjamin.

'Not if I offer the fellow a handsome wage?'

Benjamin shook his head decisively.

'No—not for a handsome wage. This Barsabas Justus may have much to give that you would like to know; but he will have nothing to sell.'

'You advise me not to attempt it?'

The old man laboriously threaded a needle, with many grotesque squints and grimaces. Having accomplished it, he grinned, triumphantly, and deftly rolled a tight knot into the end of the thread.

'It might be worth trying,' he grunted. 'These Galileans may be bigger fools than we think.'

Chapter XII

WITH almost no conversation they had eaten their lunch under an old fig tree, a little distance from the highway, and were now lounging in the shade.

Justus had stretched out his long frame on the grass, and with his fingers laced behind his shaggy head was staring up through the broad leaves into a bland April sky, his studious frown denoting perplexity.

Marcellus, reclining against the tree-trunk, moodily wished himself elsewhere. He was restless and bored. Old Benjamin's pessimistic forecast that this proposed expedition into Samaria and Galilee would be a disappointment had turned out to be correct.

Arriving in Jerusalem two weeks ago, Marcellus had acted fully upon Demetrius' written advice. Having engaged lodgings at the best inn, a commodious old house with a garden, halfway up the hill toward the suburb of Bethany, registering in the name of 'M. Lucan,' he had proceeded deliberately to bewilder the downtown bazaars with inquiries for homespun fabrics and garments—particularly articles of Galilean origin. He went from one shop to another, naïvely admiring the few things they showed him; recklessly purchasing robes and shawls at the first price quoted, professing to be immensely pleased to have them at any cost. And when the merchants confessed, with unfeigned lamentations, that their stock of Galilean textiles had run low, he upbraided them for their lack of enterprise.

Then he had laid up, for a few days, lounging in the garden of the inn, re-reading The Book of Yeshayah—old Benjamin's farewell gift—and waiting for the rumor of his business transactions to be whispered about among the clothing dealers. It was very trying to be so close to Demetrius and unable to communicate with him. One day he almost persuaded himself that this elaborate scheme for getting into Galilee was unnecessarily fantastic, and he half-resolved to go down to Benyosef's shop and explain, in the most forthright manner, that he had a desire to talk with men who had known Jesus in his own community. But, upon reflection, he saw that such a course might embarrass Demetrius; so he abandoned this impulsive procedure and impatiently bided his time.

At mid-afternoon on the fifth day of that second week, he went to the house of Benyosef, sauntering in casually to give the impression that he really wanted to do business; for he had observed that, in Jerusalem, the serious customer with his mind set on something he intended to buy invariably tried to disguise his interest. The most ridiculous subterfuges were practiced. The customer would stroll in pretending he had come to meet a friend, or that he had lost his bearings and wanted to know how to find Straight Street. On the way out he would pause to finger some article of merchandise. Apparently these childish tricks deceived nobody. The more indifferent the customer was, the more attentively the merchant hovered about him. It was evident that all business in the Holy City was so full of mendacity that a man who gave evidence of an honest purpose was immediately suspected of rank imposture.

Pausing indecisively in the open doorway of Benyosef's shop, Marcellus glanced about in search of Demetrius. It was not going to be easy, after this long separation, to confront his loyal friend with the cool stare of a stranger. A survey of the cluttered shop failed to reveal the presence of Demetrius, but Marcellus was not sure whether he was disappointed or relieved; for he had dreaded this moment.

The clatter of the two antiquated looms slowed and ceased as he made his way toward the venerable weaver who, he felt, must be old Benyosef himself. If the aged Jew was alarmed at the presence of an urbane young Roman in his house, he gave no sign of it. He maintained his seat on the bench of his loom, methodically polite but not obsequious. Marcellus briefly stated his errand. Benyosef shook his long white beard. His weaving, he said, was all custom work. He had nothing made up to sell. If his client wished to order a coat, they would gladly make it for him, and it would be a good one. But as for homespun, it might be found in the bazaars; or, better, in the country. And with that laconic announcement, he deftly scooted a wooden shuttle through the open warp and gave the thread a whack with the beam that made the old loom shudder. It was apparent that so far as Benyosef was concerned the interview had terminated.

Four other men had been mildly interested—and a dark, handsome boy of twelve, who had stopped romping with a dog to listen. One of the men was a young Greek with a refined face, seated at a ramshackle loom adjacent to Benyosef's. Marcellus surmised that this might be Demetrius' friend Stephanos.

Near the wall, behind the looms, sat two men who bore a marked resemblance, one in his early thirties, the other considerably younger. They were deeply tanned, and simply dressed in country garb, their rustic, well-worn sandals indicating that they were accustomed to long journeys on foot. This pair, obviously brothers, might easily qualify as 'The Sons of Thunder,' though the appellation did seem rather incongruous, for they appeared benign enough, especially the younger whose expressive eyes had a marked spiritual quality. He would have passed more reasonably as a mystic than an agitator.

The fourth man, who sat in the corner on an inverted tub, was probably sixty. He, too, was an outlander, to judge by his homely dress and the shagginess of his gray-streaked hair and beard. Bronzed and bushy, he seemed out of place under a roof. During the brief colloquy, he had sat gently stroking his beard with the back of his hand, his brown eyes drifting lazily from old Benyosef to the eccentric Roman who, for some obscure reason, wanted to purchase articles of homespun.

At first sight of him, Marcellus thought this might be the man Demetrius had referred to as 'The Big Fisherman.' He was big enough. But another glance at the reposeful posture and the amiable smile assured Marcellus that if 'The Big Fisherman' was a man of energy and something of a party leader, the hairy one who lounged on the tub must be someone else, conceivably Barsabas Justus.

Now that the looms had gone into action again, Marcellus had begun to doubt whether this was the time or place to introduce his question about the possibility of finding a guide, but Benyosef had remarked that one might hope to buy homespun in the country; so the query would be natural enough. As if this were a fresh inspiration, Marcellus inquired, in his best Aramaic, and addressing them all impartially, whether they knew of a man —well acquainted in the northern provinces—who might be employed to accompany him on a leisurely tour.

Benyosef, ceasing his racket, scowled thoughtfully, but made no comment. The older brother shook his head. The younger calmly stared through and beyond the inquirer as if he had not heard. The Greek, who might be Stephanos, slowly turned about and faced the big man in the corner.

'You could go, Justus,' he said. 'You were intending to go home, anyhow; weren't you?'

'How long do you want to stay?' rumbled Justus, after some deliberation.

'Two weeks, perhaps, or three—or a month.' Marcellus tried not to sound too urgent. 'Once I am up there, and have found my way about,' he added, 'you could leave me—if you had other things to do.'

'When do you want to start?' inquired Justus, with a little more interest.

'Soon as possible. How about the day after tomorrow?'

'The day after tomorrow,' put in Benyosef, reproachfully, 'is the Sabbath of the Lord our God!'

'Sorry,' mumbled Marcellus. 'I had forgotten.'

'Don't you Romans ever observe a day of rest, young man?' demanded Benyosef, enjoying his right to be querulous.

'The Romans rest oftener than we do,' drawled Justus, encouraged to this audacity by the broad grin with which Marcellus had met the old man's impertinence.

'But not oftener than *you do!*' growled Benyosef, darting his bright little eyes at Justus.

This was good for a chuckle. Even the younger brother turned about and smiled a little. As if to prove himself a man of action, Justus rose and led the way to a wooden bench in front of the house. Marcellus, with a nod to the others, followed. So did the boy, who sat beside them, hugging his knees.

With more resourcefulness than Marcellus had expected, Justus led the conversation about necessary arrangements for the journey. They would need a small string of pack-asses, he said, to carry camp equipment; for some of the smaller villages offered very poor accommodations. Four asses would be sufficient, he thought, to pack everything including whatever might be purchased.

'Will you buy the asses for me, and the camping tackle?' asked Marcellus. 'Doubtless you could make better terms. How much money will it take?' He unstrapped his wallet.

'You are trusting me to buy these things?' inquired Justus.

'Why not? You look honest.' Noting that this comment had brought a little frown, he added, 'You would not be an acceptable visitor at old Benyosef's shop if you were unscrupulous.'

Justus gave him a long sidewise look without turning his head.

'What do you know about old Benyosef—and his shop?' he queried gruffly.

Marcellus shrugged.

'The place is of good repute,' he answered, negligently. 'Benyosef has been in business for a long time.'

'That means nothing,' retorted Justus. 'Plenty of rascals stay in business for a long time.' And when Marcellus had agreed to that with a nod, and an indifferent 'Doubtless,' Justus said: 'There will be no need to buy pack-asses. You can hire them—and a boy to drive them. Hire the tent, too, and everything else.'

'Will you see to it, then? Let us be on our way early on the first day of the week.' Marcellus rose. 'How much will you expect for your services?'

'I am willing to leave that to you, sir,' said Justus. 'As you heard Stephen say, I had intended going home in a few days to Sepphoris in Galilee. This journey will not inconvenience me. I have nothing to do at present. My time is of little value. You may provide me with food and shelter. And I could use a new pair of sandals.'

'Well—I mean to do better than that by you,' declared Marcellus.

'A new robe, then," suggested Justus, holding up a frayed sleeve.

'With pleasure.' Marcellus lowered his tone and said, 'Pardon the question, but—but'—he hesitated—'you are a Jew; are you not?'

Justus chuckled and nodded, stroking his whiskers.

When they parted, a moment later, with a definite understanding to meet at the Damascus Gate soon after sunrise on the next morning after the Sabbath, Marcellus felt confident that the journey would be rewarding. Justus was a friendly old fellow who would tell him everything he wanted to know. He was just the type to enjoy reminiscence.

With his errand satisfactorily performed and nothing in particular to do, Marcellus strolled back toward the busy, ill-flavored market-place where he idled past the booths and stalls, pausing to listen, with amusement and disgust, to the violent rages of hucksters and shoppers over deals relating to one small pickled fish or a calf's foot. Vituperations rent the air. Unpleasant comments were made by customers reflecting on the merchants' ancestry. Insults were screamed, and ignored, and forgotten, which—had they been exchanged in a Roman barracks—would have demanded an immediate blood atonement. At one booth, where he stopped to witness an almost incredible scene involving the disputed price of a lamb kidney, Marcellus was a bit surprised to find, close beside him, the boy he had seen at Benyosef's shop.

Having had more than enough of the market-place, he decided to return to his inn. It was a long tramp. Turning about, at the top of the steps leading to the entrance, Marcellus looked down toward the city. The boy from Benyosef's was sauntering down the street. It was more amusing than annoying to have been followed. On second thought—these people were quite within their rights to investigate him as far as they could. Perhaps they wanted to know at what manner of place he was stopping. Had he been a guest at the Insula, they would have had nothing further to do with him.

That evening, as he sat in the walled garden of the inn, after supper, studying the ancient scroll that Benjamin had given him, Marcellus glanced up to find Stephanos standing before him.

'May I speak with you privately?' asked Stephanos, in Greek.

They walked to the far end of the garden, and Marcellus signed to him to sit down.

'You were surprised not to find Demetrius,' began Stephanos. 'About a fortnight after he wrote to you, he had the misfortune to be recognized on the street by the Tribune with whom he had had trouble in Athens. No effort was made to apprehend him, but he believed that the Tribune might seek revenge. In that case his friends at Benyosef's shop might be involved—and we are in no position to defend ourselves.'

'Where did he go, Stephanos?' asked Marcellus, deeply concerned.

'I do not know, sir. He returned to our lodgings and awaited me. We sat up and talked nearly all through the night. Several of our men were in a secret meeting at Benyosef's shop. We joined them an hour before dawn. Demetrius, having bade us farewell, slipped away before the sun rose. He will return when it is safe; when the Tribune has left. You may leave a letter for him with me, if you like, or send it later in my care—should you find a messenger who can be trusted. He confided to me that you were coming and asked me to explain his absence. None of the others were told.' Stephanos lowered his voice, and continued, 'Demetrius also confided your reasons for wanting to visit Galilee.'

'Just how much did he tell you?' Marcellus studied the Greek's face.

'Everything,' replied Stephanos, soberly. 'You see, sir, he wanted to make sure that Justus would go along with you. He felt that I might be of some service in arranging this. And when he began to explain the nature of your interest in Jesus—with much hesitation, and many mysterious gaps in the story—I urged him to make a clean breast of the whole business; and he did You can trust me to keep your secret.'

Marcellus had no rejoinder ready to meet this startling announcement, For a time he sat quietly deliberating.

'Are they suspicious of me, at Benyosef's shop?' he asked, at length. 'I was followed, this afternoon.'

'Young Philip is my nephew, sir,' explained Stephanos. 'I needed to know where you were lodging. You need have no anxiety about Philip. He will not talk. No one at the shop will learn of our meeting. I feared, for a moment, this morning, that John might recognize you, but apparently he did not. He is a dreamy fellow.'

'How could he have recognized me?' asked Marcellus.

'John was at the crucifixion, sir. Perhaps you may recall the young man who tried to comfort Jesus' mother.'

'His mother! She was there? How dreadful!' Marcellus bowed his head and dug his finger-tips into his temples.

'It was indeed, sir,' muttered Stephanos. 'I was there. I recognized you instantly when you came into the shop, though of course I was expecting you. I think you may feel sure that John did not remember.'

'You have been very kind, Stephanos. Is there any way in which I can serve you?'

'Yes, sir.' The Greek lowered his voice to a whisper. 'Have you the Robe?'

Marcellus nodded.

"May I see it?' asked Stephanos.

'Yes,' said Marcellus. 'Come with me.'

* * * * * *

They had been on the road for three days now, and the name of Jesus had not been mentioned. For all his apparent ingenuousness, Justus was surprisingly profound. His ready smile promised a childish capitulation to your wishes. His deference to your rating as a well-to-do young Roman was graciously tendered. But your negligent prediction that Justus would be eager to talk about Jesus had turned out to be incorrect. You were learning that there were a few things which not even a wealthy, well-dressed Roman could acquire either by cajolery, command, or purchase; and one of these things was the story of Jesus.

It had never occurred to Marcellus that an occasion could arise when his Roman citizenship might be an inconvenience. If you were a Roman and had plenty of money, you could have what you wanted, anywhere in the world. Doors and gates were swung open, bars and bridges were let down, tables were set up, aliens climbed out of public vehicles to give you their seats, merchants made everybody else stand aside while they attended to your caprices. If you arrived late at the wharf, the boat waited. If there was only one commodious cabin, the rich Jew surrendered it without debate. When you said Come, people came; when you said Go, they went.

But if you had journeyed on foot into the impoverished little provinces north of Jerusalem, ostensibly to purchase homespun, but actually to make inquiries concerning a certain penniless carpenter who had moved about in that region, your Roman citizenship was a nuisance and your money was of no aid.

The project—as Marcellus had originally conceived it—had presented no problems. Barsabas Justus, full of zeal for his new cause, would be bubbling with information about his hero. Perhaps he might even have designs on you as a possible convert. He would be eager to introduce you to the country people who had often met this strange Galilean face to face. You would be shown into their homes to see the outgivings of their household looms and, before you had a chance to sit down, they would be reciting stories of enchanted words and baffling deeds.

Well—it hadn't come out that way. True, the country people had welcomed you at their little wayside inns, had greeted you respectfully on the highway, had shown you their fabrics, had politely answered your random questions about their handicrafts; but they had had nothing to say about this Jesus. They were courteous, hospitable, friendly; but you, who had often been a stranger in strange places, had never felt quite so lonesome before. They all shared a secret; but not with you. Justus would present you to a household and tell them why you had come and they would make haste to bring out the best specimens of their weaving. And presently, the father of the family and Justus would exchange a covert glance of mutual understanding and quietly drift out of the room. After a while, your hostess would excuse herself, leaving you with auntie and the children; and you knew that she had slipped away to join her husband and Justus.

The very air of this country was full of mystery. For instance, there was this fish-emblem; figure of a fish, freshly cut into the bark of a sycamore, scrawled with a stick into the sand by the roadside, chalked on a stone fence, scratched into a bare table at a village inn. Demetrius had said it was the accepted token of the new movement to practice the teachings of Jesus.

On the second day out, Marcellus, hoping to make Justus talk, had asked casually:

'What's all this—about fish?'

And Justus had replied:

'That's what we live on—up here—fish.'

Marcellus had been miffed a little by this evasion. He resolved to ask no more questions.

* * * * * *

Marcellus, lounging against the fig tree, studied the tanned face of old Justus, and wondered what he was thinking about; wondered, too, how long he was likely to lie there gazing wide-eyed at the sky. Justus gave no sign that he was aware of his client's restlessness.

After a while, Marcellus came slowly to his feet and sauntered over toward the pack-asses which the cloddish young driver—sound asleep under a tree—had staked out to graze.

Noticing with indignation that the lead donkey's bridle was buckled so short that the unhappy creature's mouth had been torn by the bit and was bleeding, he tugged the torturing harness off over the long ears; and, sitting down on the grass, proceeded to lengthen the straps by punching new holes with the point of his dagger. It was not an easy task, for the leather was old and stiff; and before he had put the bridle together again, the donkey-boy had roused and was watching him with dull curiosity.

'Come here, stupid one!' barked Marcellus. 'I shall not tolerate any cruelty to these beasts.' He reached into his wallet and drew out a copper coin. 'Go you to that house—or the next—or the next—and get some ointment—and don't come back here without it!'

After the dolt had set off, shambling down the road, Marcellus rose, carelessly patted the old donkey on the nose, and returned to find Justus sitting up, smilingly interested.

'You like animals,' he observed, cordially.

'Yes,' said Marcellus—'some animals. I can't say that I am particularly fond of donkeys; but it irritates me when I see them mistreated. We will have to keep an eye on that dunce!'

Justus nodded approvingly. Marcellus sat down beside him, aware that his guide was studying him with the air of having made a new acquaintance.

'Do you like flowers?' asked Justus, irrelevantly, after a length, candid, and somewhat embarrassing inspection.

'Of course,' drawled Marcellus. 'Why not?'

'This country is full of wild flowers. It's the season for them. Later, it is very dry, and they wither. They are especially abundant this year.' Justus made a slow, sweeping gesture that covered the sloping hillside. 'Look, sir, what a wide variety.'

Marcellus followed the tanned finger as the gentle voice identified the blossoms with what seemed like confident knowledge; pink mustard, yellow mustard, blue borage, white sage, rayed umbel, plantain, bugle-weed, marigold, and three species of poppies.

'You must be an ardent lover of nature, Justus,' commented Marcellus.

'Only in the last couple of years, sir. I used to pass the flowers by without seeing them, as almost every man does. Of course I recognized the useful plants; flax and wheat, oats and barley and clover; but I never thought much about flowers until I made the close acquaintance of a man who knew all about them.'

Justus had again stretched out on the grass, and his tone had become so dreamily reminiscent that Marcellus, listening with suspended breath, wondered if—at last—the soft-voiced Galilean might be about to speak of his lost friend.

'He knew all about flowers,' reiterated Justus, with a little shake of his head, as if the recollection were inexpressibly precious. Marcellus thought of asking whether his friend had died or left the country, seeing that Justus' reference to him sounded as if it belonged to the past; but decided not to be too intrusive with his questions.

'You would have thought,' Justus was saying, half to himself, 'that the flowers were friends of his, the way he talked about them. One day he bade some of us, who were walking with him, to stop and observe a field of wild lilies. "See how richly they are clad!" he said. "They do no work. They do not spin. Yet even King Solomon did not have such raiment." '

'A lover of beauty,' commented Marcellus. 'But probably not a very practical fellow. Did he not believe in labor?'

'Oh, yes—he believed that people should be industrious,' Justus had been quick to declare, 'but he held that most of them spent too much time and thought on their bodies; clothing—and food—and hoarding—and bigger barns—and the accumulation of things.'

'Sounds as if he wasn't very thrifty.' Marcellus grinned as he said it, so it wouldn't seem a contemptuous criticism; but Justus, staring at the sky, did not see the smile, and the comment brought a frown.

'He was not indolent,' said Justus, firmly. 'He could have had things, if he'd wanted them. He was a carpenter by occupation—and a skillful one too. It was a pleasure to see him handle keen-edged tools. When he mortised timbers they looked as if they had grown that way. There was always a fair-sized crowd about the shop, watching him work; children all over the place. He had a way with children—and animals—and birds.' Justus laughed softly, and exhaled a nostalgic sigh. 'Yes—he had a way with him. When he would leave the shop to go home, there was always a lot of children along—and dogs. Everything belonged to him; but he never owned anything. He often said that he pitied people who toiled and schemed and worried and cheated to possess a lot of things; and then had to stand guard over them to see that they weren't stolen or destroyed by moths and rust.'

'Must have been an eccentric person,' mused Marcellus, 'not to want anything for his own.'

'But he never thought he was poor!' Justus raised up on one elbow, suddenly animated. 'He had the spirit of truth. Not many people can afford that, you know.'

'What an odd thing to say!' Marcellus had stared into Justus' eyes, until the older man grinned a little.

'Not so odd, when you stop to think about it. A talent for truth is real property. If a man loves truth better than things, people like to be around where he is. Almost everybody wishes he could be honest, but you can't have the spirit of truth when your heart is set on dickering for *things*. That's why people hung about this carpenter and listened to everything he said:

Marcellus and Miriam in the Garden

There was a peculiar tone-quality in her low voice that Marcellus could not define, except that its warmth was entirely unselfconscious and sincere.

From page 231 of text

he had the spirit of truth. Nobody had to be on guard with him; didn't have to pretend; didn't have to lie. It made them happy and free as little children.'

'Did everybody respond to him—that way?' asked Marcellus, seriously.

'Almost everybody,' nodded Justus. 'Oh—sometimes people who didn't know him tried to deceive him about themselves, but'—he grinned broadly as if remembering an occasion—'but, you see, sir, he was so perfected in the truth that you couldn't lie to him, or pretend to be what you weren't. It simply couldn't be done, sir; either by word, tone, or manner! And as soon as people found that out, they dropped their weapons and defenses, and began to speak the truth, themselves! It was a new experience for some of them, and it gave them a sensation of freedom. That's why they liked him, sir. They couldn't lie to him, and so they told the truth—and—the truth set them free!'

'That's a new thought!' declared Marcellus. 'Your friend must have been a philosopher, Justus. Was he a student of the classics?'

Justus was briefly puzzled, and presently shook his head.

'I do not think so,' he replied. 'He just—*knew!*'

'I don't suppose he had very many admirers among the well-to-do,' ventured Marcellus—'if he discouraged the accumulation of property.'

'You would have been surprised, sir!' declared Justus. 'Plenty of rich men listened. I recall, one time a wealthy young nobleman followed him about for a whole afternoon; and before he left he came up closer and said, "How can I get that—what you have?" '

Justus paused so long and the look in his eyes grew so remote that Marcellus wondered whether he had drifted off to thinking about something else.

'And then—what did your carpenter say?'

'Told him he was too heavily weighed with *things*,' replied Justus. ' "Give your things away," he said, "and come along with me." '

'Did he?'

'No—but he said he wished he could. He went away quite depressed, and we were all sorry, for he was indeed a fine young fellow.' Justus shook his head, and smiled pensively. 'I suppose that was the first time he had ever really wanted something that he couldn't afford.'

'This carpenter must have been a very unusual man,' remarked Marcellus. 'He appears to have had the mind of a dreamer, a poet, an artist. Did he draw, perhaps—or carve?'

'Jews do not draw—or carve.'

'Indeed? How then do they express themselves?'

'They sing,' replied Justus—'and tell stories.'

'What manner of stories?'

'Oh—the legends of our people, mostly; the deeds of our great ones. Even the little children can recite the traditions and the prophecies.' Justus smiled benevolently, and seemed about to confide an incident. 'I have a grandson, sir. His name is Jonathan. We called him Jonathan because he was born with a crooked foot, like Jonathan of old—the son of King Saul. Our Jonathan is seven. You should hear him tell the story of the Creation, and the Great Flood, and the Exodus.'

'The Exodus?' Marcellus searched his memory.

'You do not know, sir?' Justus was tolerant but surprised.

'I know what the word means,' said Marcellus, defensively. 'Exodus is a going-away, or a road out; but I do not recall a story about it.'

'I thought everyone knew the history of our people's escape from bondage in Egypt,' said Justus.

'Oh—that!' recalled Marcellus. 'I didn't know that was an escape. Our history teachers insist that the Jews were expelled from Egypt.'

'That,' declared Justus, indignantly, 'is a vicious untruth! The Pharaoh tried to keep our fathers there—in slavery—to till their soil and build their monuments.'

'Well—no matter,' drawled Marcellus. 'There's nothing we can do about it now. I'll accept your version of the story, if you want to tell me.'

'Little Jonathan will recite it for you when we visit Sepphoris. He is a bright boy.' Justus' sudden anger had cooled.

'It is easy to see you are fond of him, Justus.'

'Yes—little Jonathan is all we have. My wife entered into her rest many years ago. My daughter Rebecca is a widow. Jonathan is a great comfort to us. Perhaps you know how it is, sir, in a home where a child is sick or crippled. He gets a little more care; a little more love, maybe, to make up for it. Jonathan still gets it, though he is all well now.'

'Well?' queried Marcellus. 'His foot—you mean?'

Justus nodded slowly, turning his face away.

'Is that not unusual?' persisted Marcellus.

The crow's-feet on Justus' temple deepened and his face was sober as he nodded again without looking up. It was plain now that he did not wish to be questioned further. Presently he tugged himself loose from his meditative mood, returned with a smile, stretched his long, bronzed arms, and rose to his feet.

'It is time we moved on, sir,' he declared, 'if we expect to reach Sychar by sunset. The town does not have a good inn. We will make camp this side, near Jacob's well. Ever hear of Jacob, sir?' He grinned, good-humoredly.

'I believe not, Justus,' confessed Marcellus. 'Is it such a good well?'

'No better than plenty of other wells, but a landmark; fifteen centuries old.'

They were on the highway again. The lout with the browsing donkeys had dragged his stubborn caravan out of the weeds. Justus turned about; and, shielding his eyes with his cupped hands, gazed intently down the road over which they had come. Marcellus' curiosity was rekindled. It was not the first time that Justus had stopped to look backward. And whenever they had come to a crossing, he had paused to look carefully in all directions. He did not seem to be apprehensive of danger. It was rather as if he had made an appointment to meet someone up here. Marcellus was on the point of asking if that were true, but discreetly decided it was none of his business.

For more than three hours they plodded along the dusty highway, not meeting many travelers, not making much conversation. It was late afternoon. A half-mile ahead, a cluster of sycamores was sighted and a few scattered dwellings.

'There are the outskirts of Sychar,' said Justus, lengthening his stride.

In a little while they reached the little suburb, a sleepy, shabby community of whitewashed, flat-roofed houses. In its center, by the roadside, was the historic well. Two women were walking away with water-jars on their shoulders. A third was arriving. Justus' steps lagged to give her time to draw up the huge bucket and fill her jar. She glanced apathetically in their direction, put down her jar, stared; and then proceeded vigorously with her task. Hurriedly filling the jar, and spilling much water about her feet, she shouldered her burden and made off toward one of the small houses.

'Have we alarmed her?' asked Marcellus, grinning. 'I had not thought we looked so fierce.'

'She is not frightened,' said Justus soberly.

It was a large well. The ancient stonework around it was of the height of a sheep, and broad enough to be sat upon comfortably. Justus, who had suddenly become preoccupied, sank wearily onto the ledge with his back toward the small group of dwellings. After standing about for some moments, wondering how long they were to linger here, Marcellus sat down on the opposite side to wait until Justus was ready to move on. His eyes idly followed the rapidly retreating figure of the woman until she entered one of the houses.

Almost immediately she reappeared without her water-jar and ran across the highway to a neighbor; entered, and came out in a moment accompanied by another younger and more attractive woman. They stood for a while looking toward the well; then advanced slowly, stopping frequently to parley, their faces full of perplexity.

'That woman is coming back, Justus, and bringing another along, and they are not coming for water,' drawled Marcellus.

Justus roused with a little jerk and turned his head. Then he rose and walked toward the woman who came quickly to meet him. They held a brief, low-voiced conversation, Justus solemnly shaking his head. The younger woman, her eyes—very pretty eyes, too—wide with curiosity, continued to press her queries, and Justus shook his head, as if saying, No—no—no. Finally he tipped his head slightly in Marcellus' direction, and the woman's eyes instantaneously followed the gesture. Justus was cautioning them not to pursue the matter, whatever it was.

Then the older woman left them and began slowly retracing her steps toward her house; and Justus, frowning heavily and nodding what seemed to be a reluctant consent, turned back toward the well. Yes—he would try to talk with her again, his manner plainly said. He would talk with her again, as soon as he could do so without arousing the curiosity of this Roman.

After Justus had unpacked their camping equipment and put up the sleeping-tent under a pair of rangy sycamores, he had mumbled something about having to go back to the village for bread, though Marcellus knew they had enough for their supper and suspected that his more urgent errand was to talk with that woman again; for his manner had made it plain that he wished to go alone.

Wearied by the long day's tramp and annoyed by his guide's secretiveness, he flung himself down on the rug that Justus had spread in front of the tent and moodily watched the sun going down over the tree-tops and house-roofs of the village.

Why did Justus want to have a private interview with this woman? What did they have to talk about? Something quite serious, apparently. Perhaps they would discuss this mystery. But why should there be a mystery? The Galilean was dead. Who was going to persecute these people for what the carpenter had said or done; or for their tender remembrance of him?

Marcellus was offended. Surely Justus had no reason to think that he had come up into this poverty-stricken land to harass the simple-hearted country-folk. There was no occasion for this fellow to treat him as if he were an ordinary eavesdropper!

Well—if Justus did not trust him, it was conceivable that he might secretly go through his belongings, looking for some evidence. If he did so—he would get a stunning surprise! There was one article of Galilean homespun, at the bottom of his gunny-bag, that Justus must not see!

Chapter XIII

It was well on toward sunset when they sighted Cana, after a fatiguing tramp from the village of Nain where Justus' insistence on observing the Sabbath had kept them off the road for a day—one of the most tedious and profitless days that Marcellus had ever experienced.

Justus had gone to the little synagogue in the morning. Had he been invited, Marcellus would have accompanied him, so hard up was he for diversion in an unkempt town where there was nothing of interest to see or do. But Justus had set off alone, after assuring Marcellus that there were ample provisions for his noonday meal.

About the middle of what threatened to be an interminable afternoon, Marcellus, lounging on the ground in front of the tent, observed Justus returning in the company of an elderly woman and a tall, sober-faced young man. They walked slowly, preoccupied with serious conversation. When within a stadium of the camp, they came to a stop and continued their earnest talk for a long time. Then the woman and the young man who, Marcellus surmised, might have been her son, reluctantly turned back toward the village, arm in arm, while Justus came on wearing a studious frown.

Marcellus knew it was childish to feel any resentment over the quite obvious disinclination of Justus to acquaint him with his local friends. When there was trading in prospect, Justus was promptly polite with his introductions, but he was making it plain that their relationship was strictly on a business basis.

It wasn't that Marcellus had any considerable interest in meeting this gray-haired woman, or the thoughtful young man on whose arm she leaned affectionately; but he couldn't help feeling a bit chagrined over the snubbing. Of course, in all fairness to Justus, he reflected, the fellow had contracted only to take him into households where homespun might be purchased. He had not promised to introduce the young Roman merchant as his friend. Nor could Justus be expected to know—nor might he be permitted to suspect—that his patron had no interest whatsoever in this merchandising, but wanted only to meet and talk with persons who had known Jesus.

Returning to the tent, with an absent nod toward his idle client, Justus had sat silently staring at the distant hills. Occasionally Marcellus stole a glance in his direction, but he was completely oblivious. It could not be divined whether this retreat into silence was of a piece with Sabbath observance or whether some new reason accounted for his taciturnity.

Early the next morning, Justus had been suddenly animated with a desire to be on the highway. Breakfast was dispatched at top speed. The pack-asses and their socially inferior custodian were advised that there would be no nonsense on this day's journey. The sun was hot, but the determined guide led the little caravan with long, swinging strides. Marcellus was mightily relieved when, at high noon, Justus turned off the road and pointed to a near-by clump of olives.

'Shall we rest now, and eat?' he inquired.

'By all means!' panted Marcellus, mopping his brow. 'Is this Cana such an interesting city, then, that we must walk our legs off to get there today?'

'I am sorry to have pressed you,' said Justus. 'I did not explain because I wanted to give you a pleasant surprise at the end of the day. There is a young woman in Cana who sings every evening in the park.'

'Indeed!' muttered Marcellus, wearily. 'Well—she'd better be good!'

'She is good.' Justus began unpacking their lunch. 'The people of Cana have their supper early; and afterward a great many of them—both young and old—assemble about the fountain where this crippled girl sings the songs that our people love. Her family and the neighbors carry her there on her cot, and the people sit down and listen until dark.'

'Extraordinary!' commented Marcellus, rubbing his lame muscles. 'You say she's a cripple? I shall want to meet her. At the rate we're traveling, by the end of the day she and I may have a common cause.'

Justus acknowledged the raillery with a grin, broke a wheaten loaf, gave half of it to Marcellus, and seated himself on the grass.

'Miriam is a beautiful young woman,' he went on, munching his bread hungrily. 'She is about twenty-two now. Some seven years ago she was suddenly stricken with paralysis. That would have been a great misfortune in any case, but for Miriam it was a calamity. She had been very active in games, and a leader in the children's sports. Now she was unable to walk. Moreover, she added to her unhappiness by resenting her affliction, spending her days in such pitiful lamentations that her parents were beside themselves with grief, and their house was in mourning.'

'I take it that you knew them well,' contributed Marcellus, mildly interested.

'Not at that time,' admitted Justus, 'but the day came when that part of Miriam's story was quite widely discussed. For all of three years she lay on her bed, inconsolable, peevish, so embittered by her trouble that she rejected all the kindly efforts made to divert her mind. As time passed, she refused to admit her friends into her room; and sat alone, sullen and smouldering with rebellion.'

'And now she sings? What happened?'

'Now she sings,' nodded Justus; adding, after a meditative moment: 'I do not know the particulars, sir. I am not sure that anyone does. Miriam refuses to discuss it. Her parents profess not to know. When people have inquired of them, they have replied, "Ask Miriam." '

'Perhaps they are telling the truth when they say they do not know.' Marcellus was becoming concerned. 'Surely they could have no motive for refusing to explain the improvement in their daughter's disposition.'

Justus had nodded a few times, without comment.

'Maybe Miriam herself doesn't know,' speculated Marcellus, hopeful that the story had not come to an end. 'Maybe Miriam found that she had finally exhausted her resentment—and might as well make the best of it.' He paused to give Justus a chance to contradict this inexpert opinion; and, meeting no rejoinder, ventured another guess. 'Maybe she woke up one morning and said to herself, "I've been making everybody miserable. I'm going to pretend that I'm happy. I'll be cheerful—and sing!" Maybe she just reached that decision, after proving that the other course was futile.'

'Maybe,' murmured Justus, remotely.

'But you don't think so,' declared Marcellus, after a long interval of silence.

'I don't know.' Justus shook his head decisively. 'One of her girl friends, whom she hadn't seen for a couple of years, was to be married. They had urgently pleaded with Miriam to attend the wedding, but she would not go; and all that day she wept bitterly. But—that evening—when her parents returned from the wedding-feast—she met them with gladness; and sang!'

'Amazing!' exclaimed Marcellus. 'And has she a voice—really?'

'You may decide that for yourself, sir, when you hear her,' said Justus. 'And you may meet her in her home tomorrow. Naomi, her mother, does beautiful weaving. I shall take you there. She may have some things that might interest you. If you are rested now, sir, shall we be on our way?'

* * * * * *

They pitched their tent at the edge of little Cana, ate their supper quickly, and walked to the center of the village, overtaking many people headed in the same direction. Already fifty or more were seated on the ground in semicircular rows facing a natural fountain that gently welled up into the huge brick basin.

'I suppose this is Cana's drinking water,' said Marcellus, as they moved toward an unoccupied spot on the lawn.

'It is warm water,' said Justus. 'Hot springs abound in this region.' They seated themselves cross-legged on the ground.

'Is it thought to be a healing water?' asked Marcellus.

'Yes—but not by the people of Galilee. Travelers come from afar to bathe in the water from these springs.'

'Oh? Then Cana sees many strangers.'

'Not so many in Cana. They go mostly to Tiberias, on the Lake Gennesaret. It is a more important city, and possesses much wealth. It is only the rich who come to bathe in medicinal waters.'

'And why is that?' inquired Marcellus. 'Do not the poor believe in the virtue of these hot springs?'

Justus laughed. It was a deep, spontaneous laugh that he seemed to enjoy; an infectious laugh that evoked companionable chuckles in their vicinity, where many men and women had recognized the big, gentle-voiced neighbor from Sepphoris. Marcellus was discovering something new and interesting about Justus. He was naturally full of fun. You wouldn't have suspected it. He had been so serious; so weighted.

'The poor do not have the diseases, sir, that these springs are supposed to cure,' explained Justus. 'Only men accustomed to rich foods and an abundance of fine wines seek these healing waters. The Galileans do not suffer of ills arising from such causes.'

It was delicious irony, because so free of any bitterness. Marcellus admired the tone of the appreciative laughter that came from their candidly eavesdropping neighbors. His heart warmed toward them. He was going to feel at home with them.

'That's a new thought, Justus,' he replied, 'and a sound one. I never considered it before, but it is a fact that hot springs are intended for gluttons and winebibbers. Now that you speak of it, I recall having heard something about this city of Tiberias on Lake Gennesaret.'

'Often called the Sea of Galilee,' nodded Justus, 'but not by the Galileans.' The crowd seated about them had grown attentive, tilting its head at a favorable angle, frankly interested.

'Big lake?' wondered Marcellus.

'Big enough to be stormy. They have some rough gales.'

'Any fishing?'

Justus nodded indifferently, and a middle-aged man sitting in front of them turned his head, plainly wanting to say something. Marcellus caught his dancing eye, and raised his brows encouragingly.

'That's one of the diseases that poor people can afford, sir,' remarked the man, 'fishing!' Everybody laughed merrily at that.

'Do they catch them?' inquired Marcellus.

'Yes,' drawled Justus, 'they have caught them—all of them—a long time ago.' This sally was good, too; and the friendly hilarity increased the circle of listeners. Marcellus felt that they were showing quite an amiable attitude toward him; perhaps because he was sponsored by Justus who, it seemed, everyone knew; and, besides, Marcellus was doing fairly well with his Aramaic.

'But they still fish?' he inquired, artlessly.

A shrill childish voice unexpectedly broke in, from up the row a little way.

'Once they caught a great lot of them!' shouted the lad.

'Sh-sh!'—came a soft, concerted caution from his kin.

All eyes were now turning toward the fountain where a cot was being borne in from the street. The girl was sitting up, propped about with pillows. In her bare, shapely arms she hugged a small harp.

The sculptor in Marcellus instantly responded. It was a finely modeled, oval face, white with a pallor denoting much pain endured; but the wide-set, long-lashed eyes had not been hurt. Her abundant hair, parted in the middle, framed an intelligent brow. Her full lips were almost gay, as they surveyed the crowd.

Two men followed, carrying wooden trestles, and the cot was lifted up until everyone could see. A deep hush fell upon the people. Marcellus was much impressed by the unusual scene, and found himself wishing that the girl wouldn't try to sing. The picture was perfect. It was imprudent to risk spoiling it.

Miriam gently swept the strings of her harp with slim, white fingers. Then her face seemed to be transfigured. Its momentary gaiety had faded, and there had come an expression of deep yearning. It was clear that she had left them now, and was putting out on an enchanted excursion. The luminous eyes looked upward, wide with far vision. Again she lightly touched the harp-strings.

The voice was a surprisingly deep, resonant contralto. That first tone, barely audible at its beginning, swelled steadily until it began to take on the pulsing vibration of a bell. Marcellus felt a quick tightening of his throat, a sudden suffusion of emotion that burned and dimmed his eyes. Now the song took wings!

'*I waited patiently for the Lord—and He inclined unto me—and heard my cry.*'

All around Marcellus heads were bent to meet upraised hands; and stifled sobs, with childish little catches of breath in them, were straining to be quiet. As for himself, he sat staring at the entranced girl through uncontrollable tears. He shook them out of his eyes—and stared!

'*And He hath put a new song in my mouth!*' exulted Miriam.

Justus slowly turned his head toward Marcellus. His seamed face was contorted and his eyes were swimming. Marcellus touched his sleeve and nodded soberly. Their gaze returned to the enraptured girl.

'*Then I said, "Lo—I come." In the volume of the Book it is written of me, "I delight to do Thy will, O God—and Thy law is in my heart!"*'

The song was ended and the close-packed crowd drew a deep sigh. Neighbors slowly turned their faces toward their best beloved, smiled wistfully with half-closed eyes, and shook their heads, lacking words to tell how deeply they had been moved. After an interval Miriam found her wings again. Marcellus reached for occasional phrases of her triumphant song, while rushing about in his heart to reacquaint himself with instinctive longings of his own. It was coming to an end now, even as the last rays of sunset filled the sky.

'*To give light to them that sit in darkness and in the shadow of death,*' sang Miriam, '*and to guide our feet in the way of peace.*'

Twilight was falling. The men bore Miriam away. The crowd silently scattered and took to the highway. It pleased Marcellus that Justus, trudging by his side in the darkness, did not ask him if he had liked Miriam's voice, or whether he had not been impressed by the unusual occasion.

* * * * * *

The home of Reuben and Naomi, at the northern extremity of the village, was more commodious and occupied a larger parcel of ground than most of the residences in Cana. The white-walled house, well back from the road, was shaded by tall sycamores. In the spacious front yard were many fruit trees, now gay and fragrant with blossoms; and on either side of this area there was an apparently prosperous vineyard.

It was with some difficulty that Marcellus had curbed his impatience to visit this home where he hoped to meet the crippled girl with the radiant face and the golden voice. Justus had seemed willfully tedious at the two places where they had called on their way; and had it not been imprudent, Marcellus would have dispatched these small transactions by purchasing whatever was offered.

'Let us first speak to Miriam,' said Justus, unlatching the gate. 'I see her sitting in the arbor.'

They crossed the neatly clipped grass-plot and sauntered toward the shaded arbor where Miriam sat alone. She wore a white himation trimmed with coral at the throat and flowing sleeves, but no jewelry except a slim silver chain about her neck with a tiny pendant—a fish—carved from a seashell. On the table beside her cot was the harp and a small case of scrolls. Her curly head was bent attentively over the lace medallion she was knitting. As they approached, she glanced up, recognizing Justus, and smiled a welcome.

'Oh—you needn't explain, Barsabas Justus,' she said when, after presenting Marcellus, he had added that the young man was interested in Galilean fabrics. 'Everybody in Cana knows about it.' She smiled into Marcellus' eyes. 'We are all excited, sir, over your visit; for it isn't often that anyone comes here to trade.'

There was a peculiar tone-quality in her low voice that Marcellus could not define, except that its warmth was entirely unself-conscious and sincere. Frequently he had observed, upon being introduced to young women, that they had a tendency to soar off into an impetuous animation, pitching their blithe remarks in a shrill key as if from a considerable distance. Miriam's voice was as unaffected and undefended as her smile.

'Naomi is at home?' asked Justus.

'In the house. Will you find her? I think she and Father are expecting you.'

Justus turned away, and Marcellus was uncertain whether to follow. Miriam helped him to a gratifying decision by pointing to a chair.

'I heard you sing,' he said. 'It was the most—' He paused to grope for an appropriate word.

'How do you happen to speak Aramaic?' she interposed gently.

'I don't—very well,' said Marcellus. 'However'—he went on more confidently—'even your own countrymen might find it difficult to describe your singing. I was deeply moved by it.'

'I am glad you wanted to tell me that.' Miriam pushed aside the pillow on which the lace medallion had been pinned, and faced him with candid eyes. 'I wondered a little what you might think. I saw you there with

Justus. I had never sung for a Roman. It would not have surprised me if you had been amused; but would have hurt me.'

'I'm afraid we have a bad reputation in these provinces,' sighed Marcellus.

'Of course,' said Miriam. 'The only Romans we see in Cana are legionaries, marching down the street, so haughtily, so defiantly'—She straightened and swaggered her pretty shoulders, accenting her militant pantomime with little jerks of her head—'as if they were saying—' She paused and added, apologetically, 'But perhaps I should not tell you.'

'Oh—I know what we always seem to say when we strut,' assisted Marcellus. He protruded his lips with an exaggerated show of arrogance, and carried on with Miriam's march—' *"Here—we come—your—lords—and—mas—ters!"* '

They both laughed a little, and Miriam resumed her needlework. Bending over it attentively, she inquired:

'Are there many Romans like you, Marcellus Gallio?'

'Multitudes! I make no claim to any sort of uniqueness.'

'I never talked with a Roman before,' said Miriam. 'But I supposed they were all alike. They look alike.'

'In their uniforms, yes; but under their spiked helmets and shields, they are ordinary creatures with no relish for tramping the streets of foreign cities. They would much prefer to be at home with their families, hoeing in their gardens and tending their goats.'

'I am glad to know that,' said Miriam. 'It is so unpleasant to dislike people—and so hard not to think badly of the Romans. Now I shall say that great numbers of them wish they were at home with their gardens and goats; and I shall hope,' she went on, with a slow smile, 'that their desire may be fulfilled. Do you have a garden, sir?'

'Yes—we have a garden.'

'But no goats, I think.'

'There is no room for them. We live in the city.'

'Do you have horses?'

'Yes.'

'In Galilee,' drawled Miriam, 'horses require more room than goats. Would you like to tell me about your home?'

'Gladly. Our family consists of our parents and my sister Lucia and myself.'

'Does your father take care of the garden while you are abroad?'

'Well—not personally—no,' replied Marcellus, after a little hesitation; and when she glanced up from under her long lashes with an elder-sisterly grin, he asked, 'Are you having a good time?'

She nodded companionably.

'I might have known that you kept a gardener,' she said, 'and a maid-servant too, no doubt.'

'Yes,' assented Marcellus, casually.

'Are they—slaves?' asked Miriam, in a tone that hoped not to give offense.

'Yes,' admitted Marcellus, uncomfortably, 'but I can assure you they are not mistreated.'

'I believe that,' she said, softly. 'You couldn't be cruel to anyone. How many slaves have you?'

'I never counted them. A dozen, perhaps. No—there must be more than that. Twenty—maybe.'

'It must seem odd to own other human beings,' reflected Miriam. 'Do you keep them locked up, when they're not working?'

'By no means!' Marcellus dismissed the query with a toss of his hand. 'They are free to go anywhere they please.'

'Indeed!' exclaimed Miriam. 'Don't they ever run away?'

'Not often. There's no place for them to go.'

'That's too bad.' Miriam sighed. 'They'd be better off in chains; wouldn't they? Then maybe they could break loose. As it is, the whole world is their prison.'

'I never thought about it before,' pondered Marcellus. 'But I suppose the whole world is a prison for everyone. Is anybody entirely free? What constitutes freedom?'

'The truth!' answered Miriam, quickly. 'The truth sets anyone free! If it weren't so, I might feel quite fettered myself, Marcellus Gallio. My country is owned by a foreign master. And, because of my lameness, I may seem to have very little liberty; but my spirit is free!'

'You are fortunate,' said Marcellus. 'I should give a great deal to experience a liberty independent of all physical conditions. Did you work out that philosophy for yourself? Was it a product of your illness, perhaps?'

'No, no!' She shook her head decisively. 'My illness made a wretched slave of me. I did not earn my freedom. It was a gift.'

Marcellus kept silent, when she paused. Perhaps she would explain. Suddenly her face lighted, and she turned toward him with an altered mood.

'Please forgive me for being inquisitive about you,' she said. 'I sit here all day with nothing new happening. It is refreshing to talk with someone from the outside world. Tell me about your sister Lucia. Is she younger than you?'

'Much.'

'Younger than I?'

'Six years younger,' ventured Marcellus, smiling into her suddenly widened eyes.

'Who told you my age?'

'Justus.'

'How did he happen to do that?'

'He was telling me, before we arrived in Cana, about your singing. He said that you never knew you could sing until—one day—you found that you had a voice—and sang. Justus said it came all unexpectedly. How do you account for it—if it isn't a secret?'

'It is a secret,' she said, softly.

They were coming around the corner of the house now—Naomi, first, with her arms full of robes and shawls, followed by Justus and Reuben. Marcellus came to his feet and was introduced. Reuben rather diffidently took the hand that Marcellus offered him. Naomi, apparently pleased by their guest's attitude, smiled cordially. It was easy to see the close resemblance of mother and daughter. Naomi had the same dimples in her cheeks.

'We have always gone to Jerusalem to attend the Passover at this season,' she said, spreading out her wares across the back of a chair. 'This year we shall not go. That is why I happen to have so many things on hand.'

Marcellus assumed his best business manner. Taking up a brown robe, he examined it with professional interest.

'This,' he said, expertly, 'is typically Galilean. A seamless robe. And excellent workmanship. Evidently you have had much practice in weaving this garment.'

Naomi's gratified expression encouraged him to speak freely. He felt he was making a good case for himself as a connoisseur of homespun, and could risk an elaboration of his knowledge, particularly for Justus' information.

'A weaver of my acquaintance in Athens,' he went on, 'told me something about this robe. He was formerly of Samaria, I believe, and was quite familiar with Galilean products.' He glanced toward Justus, and met an inquisitive stare, as if he were searching his memory for some related fact. Now his eyes lighted a little.

'There was a young Greek working for Benyosef, a short time ago,' remarked Justus. 'I heard him say he had been with a weaver in Athens named Benjamin, from whom he had learned to speak Aramaic. Might this have been the same weaver?'

'Why—yes!' Marcellus tried to enjoy the coincidence. 'Benjamin is well respected in Athens. He is a good scholar, too.' He chuckled a little.

'Benjamin quite insists on speaking Aramaic with anyone whom he suspects of knowing the language.'

'He must have found you pleasant company, sir,' remarked Justus. 'I have noticed that you use many terms which are colloquial with the Samaritans.'

'Indeed!' said Marcellus, taking up a shawl, and returning his attention to Naomi. 'This is excellent wool,' he assured her. 'Is it grown here in Galilee?'

'In our own madbra,' replied Reuben, proudly.

'Madbra?' repeated Marcellus. 'In the desert?'

Justus laughed.

'See, Reuben?' he exclaimed. 'When the Samaritans say "madbra," they mean barren land.' He turned to Marcellus. 'When we say "madbra," we mean pasture. "Bara" is our word for desert.'

'Thanks, Justus,' said Marcellus. 'I'm learning something.' He dismissed this small episode by concentrating on the shawl. 'It is beautifully dyed,' he said.

'With our own mulberries,' boasted Naomi.

'Had I known you were acquainted with Benjamin,' persisted Justus, 'I should have told you about this young Greek, Demetrius; a most thoughtful fellow. He left suddenly, one day. He had been in some trouble—and was a fugitive.'

Marcellus politely raised his brows, but made it clear enough, by his manner, that they had other things to talk about.

'I shall want the shawl,' he said, 'and this robe. Now—let us see what else.' He began fumbling with the garments, hoping he had not seemed abrupt in disregarding the comments about Demetrius.

Presently Justus sauntered away toward the vineyard, and Reuben followed him.

'Why don't you show Marcellus Gallio those pretty bandeaus, Mother?' suggested Miriam.

'Oh—they're nothing,' said Naomi. 'He wouldn't bother with them.'

'May I see them?' asked Marcellus.

Naomi obligingly moved away, and Marcellus continued to inspect the textiles with exaggerated concern.

'Marcellus.' Miriam's tone was confidential.

He glanced up and met her level eyes inquiringly.

'Why did you lie to Justus?' she insisted, just above a whisper.

'Lie to him?' parried Marcellus, flushing.

'About that Greek. You did not want to talk about him. Perhaps you know him. Tell me, Marcellus. What are you? You're not a merchant. I know that. You have no real interest in my mother's weaving.' Miriam waited for a reply, but Marcellus had not recovered his self-possession. 'Tell me,' she coaxed, softly. 'What are you doing up here—in Galilee—if it isn't a secret?'

He met her challenging smile with an attempted casualness.

'It is a secret,' he said.

Chapter XIV

JUSTUS was coolly polite today, but remote. He was beginning to be skeptical about Marcellus. Yesterday at Reuben's house a few facts, unimportant when considered singly, had taken on size once they were strung together.

Marcellus, whose Aramaic was distinctly of the Samaritan variety, had recklessly volunteered that he knew old Benjamin, the weaver in Athens, who had derived from Samaria.

Demetrius, the handsome young Greek who had recently been in Benyosef's employ, also knew old Benjamin; had worked for him; and the Aramaic he spoke was loaded with Samaritan provincialisms. Clearly there was some sort of tieup between Marcellus and this fugitive slave, though the Roman had pretended not to have known him, and had shown no interest in the story of his hasty flight from Benyosef's shop. Doubtless Marcellus knew about it, and had reasons for wanting to evade any discussion of it. It all went to prove that you couldn't trust a Roman.

At sunset yesterday, Justus had strolled down the street by himself, making it clear that his Roman patron's company was not desired. For a little while Marcellus had debated the propriety of going alone to the fountain. His anxiety to hear Miriam sing again decided the matter.

The whole town was there and seated when he quietly joined the crowd at its shaded outskirts. No notice was taken of him, for Miriam had at that moment arrived and all eyes were occupied. Marcellus sat on the ground, a little way apart, and experienced the same surge of emotion that had swept through him on the previous evening. Now that he had talked with her, Miriam's songs meant even more. He had been strangely drawn to this girl. And he knew that she had been sincerely interested in him. It was not, in either case, a mere transient infatuation. There had been nothing coyly provocative in Miriam's attitude. She wanted only to be his friend, and had paid him the high compliment of assuming that he was bright enough to understand the nature of her unreserved cordiality.

As he sat there in the darkness, alternately stilled and stirred by her deep, vibrant, confident tones, he found himself consenting to the reality of her honest faith. His inherent, built-in skepticism yielded to a curious wistfulness as she sang, *'In the shadow of thy wings will I make my refuge. . . . My heart is fixed. . . . Awake, my glory! Awake, my harp!'* Miriam couldn't walk—but she could fly.

Justus had briefly announced that they would be leaving early in the morning for his home town, Sepphoris, where he must attend to some errands.

'Will we be coming back through Cana?' Marcellus had asked.

'If it is your wish, yes,' Justus had replied, 'but we have seen everyone here who has weaving for sale.'

There wasn't much to be said after that. Marcellus could think of no reasonable excuse for a return to Cana. He couldn't say, 'I must have another private talk with Miriam.' No—he would have to go, leaving her to wonder what manner of rôle he had been playing. Given one more day, one more confidential chat with Miriam, he might have told her why he was here in Galilee.

When the last song was ended, he waited in the shadows for the crowd to disperse. Justus, he observed, had moved forward to join Reuben's party as it made its way to the street. It would be quite possible to overtake this slow-moving group and say farewell to Miriam. Perhaps she might be glad if he did. But on second thought that seemed inadvisable. It might prove embarrassing to both of them. Perhaps Reuben and Naomi shared the obvious suspicions of Justus that there was something irregular about this Roman's tour of Galilee. After lingering indecisively until the little park was cleared, Marcellus, deeply depressed and lonely, slowly retraced his way to the little camp reproaching himself for having unnecessarily given them cause to distrust him. He saw now that it would have been much more sensible if he had told Justus, at the outset, why he wanted to visit Galilee. Of course, Justus, in that event, might have refused to conduct him; but the present situation was becoming intolerable. Marcellus was very unhappy. He would have given much for a talk with Demetrius tonight. Demetrius was resourceful. Had he been along, by this time he would have found means for penetrating the reticence of these Galileans.

* * * * * *

It was nearing midday now. They had not exchanged a word for more than an hour. Justus, who had been tramping on ahead, paused to wait for Marcellus to come abreast of him. He pointed to a house on a near-by shady knoll.

'We will stop there,' he said, 'though it is likely that Amasiah and Deborah have gone to Jerusalem. They weave excellent saddle-bags and sell them to the bazaars when they attend the Passover.'

A stout, middle-aged woman came sauntering through the yard to meet them as they turned in at the gate, her face suddenly beaming as she recognized Justus. No—Amasiah was not at home. Yes—he had gone to Jerusalem.

'And why not you, Deborah?' asked Justus.

'Surely you know,' she sighed. 'I have no wish ever to see the Holy City again. Nor would Amasiah have gone but to sell the saddle-bags.' She turned inquiring eyes toward Marcellus, and Justus introduced him with cool formality, explaining his mission. Deborah smiled briefly and murmured her regret that they had nothing to sell. No—everything had gone with Amasiah.

'All but a little saddle-blanket I made for Jasper,' she added. 'I can show it to you.' They moved toward the house, and Deborah brought out the saddle-blanket, a thick, well-woven trifle of gay colors. 'Jasper can get along without it, if you want it.' She nodded toward a diminutive, silver-gray donkey, browsing in the shade.

'I suppose Jasper is a little pet,' surmised Marcellus, lightly.

'Jasper is a little pest,' grumbled Deborah. 'I am too heavy to ride him any more, and Amasiah says he isn't worth his keep in a pack-train.'

'Would you like to sell him?' inquired Marcellus.

'You wouldn't have any use for him,' said Deborah, honestly.

'How much would you want?' persisted Marcellus.

'What's he worth, Justus?' asked Deborah, languidly.

Justus sauntered over to the donkey, pulled his shaggy head up out of the grass, and looked into his mouth.

'Well—if he's worth anything at all, which is doubtful, except maybe for a child to play with—he should bring twelve to fifteen shekels.'

'Has he any bad habits?' inquired Marcellus.

'Eating,' said Deborah, dryly.

'But he won't run away.'

'Oh, no; he won't run away. That would be too much of an effort.' They all laughed but Jasper, who sighed deeply.

'I'll give you fifteen shekels for the donkey and the blanket,' bargained Marcellus.

Deborah said that was fair enough, and added that there was quite a good saddle too, and a bridle that had been made especially for Jasper. She brought them. It was a well-made saddle, and the bridle was gaily ornamented with a red leather top-piece into which a little bell was set.

'How about twenty-five shekels for everything?' suggested Marcellus.

Deborah tossed the saddle across the donkey's back and began fastening the girths. Marcellus opened his wallet. Justus, watching the pantomime, chuckled. It relieved Marcellus to see him amused about something.

Jasper was reluctant to leave the grass-plot, but showed no distress when it came time to part with Deborah, who had led him as far as the gate. Marcellus took the reins and proceeded to the highway, Justus lingering for a private word with Deborah.

Late in the afternoon they reached the frowsy fringe of little Sepphoris, a typical Galilean village. Everybody waved a hand or called a greeting to Justus as the big fellow trudged on with lengthening strides. Soon they were nearing the inevitable public plaza. A small boy broke loose from a group of children playing about the brick-walled well and came running toward Justus with exultant shouts. He was a handsome lad with a sensitive face, a tousle of curly black hair, and an agile body. Justus quickened his steps and caught the little fellow up in his arms, hugging him hungrily. He stopped and turned about, his eyes brightly proud.

'This is my Jonathan!' he announced, unnecessarily.

The boy gave his grandfather another strangling embrace and wiggled out of his arms. He had sighted Jasper.

'Is this your donkey?' he cried.

'Perhaps you would like to ride him,' said Marcellus.

Jonathan climbed on, and Marcellus adjusted the stirrup-straps, a score of children gathering about with high-keyed exclamations. Justus stood by, stroking his beard, alternately smiling and frowning.

'What's his name?' asked Jonathan, as Marcellus put the reins in his hands. His small voice was shrill with excitement.

'His name is Jasper,' said Marcellus. 'You may have him, Jonathan. He is your donkey now.'

'Mine!' squeaked Jonathan. He gazed incredulously at his grandfather.

'This gentleman,' said Justus, 'is my friend, Marcellus Gallio. If he says the donkey is yours, it must be so.' He turned to Marcellus, and said, above the children's shouts of amazement at Jonathan's good fortune, 'That is most generous of you, sir!'

'Is he one of us, Grandfather?' Jonathan pointed a finger at his benefactor.

The two men exchanged quick glances; one frankly mystified, the other somewhat embarrassed.

'You *are* one of us,' declared Jonathan, 'or you wouldn't give your things away!'

Again Marcellus invaded Justus' eyes, but received no answer.

'Are you rich?' demanded Jonathan, immensely forthright.

'No one has ever said "yes" to that question, Jonathan,' laughed Marcellus, as Justus mumbled an unintelligible apology for his grandson's impertinence.

'But—you must be rich,' insisted Jonathan, 'to be giving your things away. Did Jesus tell you to do that?' He thrust his small face forward and studied Marcellus' eyes with childish candor. 'You knew Jesus; didn't you? Did my grandfather tell you that Jesus straightened my foot—so I can walk and run?'

The children were quiet now. Marcellus found himself confronted with the necessity of making a public address, and was appropriately tongue-tied. After a difficult interval, he stammered:

'Y-yes—your grandfather told me—about your foot, Jonathan. I am very glad it got well. That is fine!'

'Let us go now,' muttered Justus, uneasily. 'My house is close by. Come! I want you to meet my daughter.'

Marcellus needed no urging. They proceeded up the street, their numbers increasing as they went. The news had traveled fast. People came out of their houses, wide-eyed with curiosity; children of all sizes ran to join the procession. One small boy on crutches, dangling a useless leg, waited for the parade, his pinched face alight with wonder. Justus stepped to the side of the road and gave him a friendly pat on the head as he passed.

Now they had arrived at the modest little home. The dooryard was scrupulously tidy. The narrow walk was bordered with tulips. Rebecca, a gentle-voiced, plain-featured matron of thirty-five, met them, considerably puzzled by all the excitement. Justus, on the doorstep, briefly explained; and, with a new cordiality, presented Marcellus.

'Oh—you shouldn't have done that, sir,' murmured Rebecca, though her shining eyes were full of appreciation. 'That is quite an expensive gift to make to a little boy.'

'I'm fully repaid,' smiled Marcellus. 'It is evident that the donkey is a success.'

'Look, Mother!' shouted Jonathan, waving his arm. 'It's *mine!*'

Rebecca nodded and smiled, and the noisy pack moved on in the wake of the town's young hero.

'This is a great day for Jonathan,' said Rebecca, as she led the way into their small, frugally furnished parlor.

'Yes, yes,' sighed Justus, sinking into a chair. He was frowning thoughtfully. 'It's a great day for the lad—but Jonathan's pretty young for a responsibility like that.'

'Oh—he's old enough,' remarked Marcellus. 'That lazy little donkey really should belong to a child. Jonathan will get along with him splendidly.'

'As for that—yes,' agreed Justus, soberly. He stroked his beard moodily, nodded his head several times and muttered to himself, 'Yes, yes; that's a good deal to expect of a little boy.' Then suddenly brightening he said to his daughter, 'Rebecca, we will pitch Marcellus Gallio's tent there beside the house. And he will have his meals with us.'

'Of course, Father,' responded Rebecca, promptly, giving their guest a hospitable smile. 'Is there anything you are enjoined not to eat, sir?' And when Marcellus looked puzzled, she hesitatingly explained, 'I am not acquainted with the Roman customs. I thought perhaps your religion—like ours—forbids your eating certain things.'

'Oh, no,' declared Marcellus, amiably. 'My religion has never inconvenienced anyone—not even me.' He quickly repented of this flippancy when he observed that his remark had drawn down the corners of his host's mouth.

'Do you mean that your people have no religion at all?' queried Justus, soberly.

'No religion!' protested Marcellus. 'Why—we have gods on every corner!'

'Idols—you mean,' corrected Justus, dourly.

'Statues,' amended Marcellus. 'Some of them quite well done, too. Imported from Greece, most of them. The Greeks have a talent for it.'

'And your people worship these—statues?' wondered Justus.

'They seem to, sir. I suppose some of them are really sincere about it.' Marcellus was tiring of this inquisition.

'But you, personally, do not worship these things,' persisted Justus.

'Oh—by no means!' Marcellus laughed.

'Then you do not believe in any Supreme Power?' Justus was shocked and troubled.

'I admit, Justus, that all the theories I have heard on this subject are unconvincing. I am open to conviction. I should be glad indeed to learn of a reliable religion.'

Rebecca, scenting a difficult discussion, moved restlessly to the edge of her chair, smiling nervously.

'I shall go and prepare your supper,' she said, rising. 'You men must be starving.'

'I didn't mean to be offensive, Justus,' regretted Marcellus, when Rebecca had left the room. 'You are a sincerely religious person, and it was thoughtless of me to speak negligently of these matters.'

'No harm done,' said Justus, gently. 'You wish you could believe. That is something. Is it not true, in our life, that they find who seek? You are a man of good intent. You are kind. You deserve to have a religion.'

Marcellus couldn't think of an appropriate rejoinder to that, so he sat silent, waiting for further directions. After a moment, Justus impulsively slapped his big brown hands down on his knees in a gesture of adjournment; and, rising, moved toward the door.

'Let us put up your tent, Marcellus,' he suggested kindly. It was the first time he had spoken Marcellus' name without the formal addition of 'Gallio.'

* * * * * *

Shortly after the family supper, which he had been too busy to attend, Jonathan appeared at the open front of the brown tent. He stood with his feet wide apart, his arms akimbo, and an expression of gravity on his sensitive lips. It was apparent that the day's experiences had aged him considerably.

Marcellus, writing at the small collapsible table, put down his stylus, regarded his caller with interest, and grinned. He mistakingly thought he knew what had been going on in Jonathan's mind. At the outset, his amazing windfall had dizzied him into a state of emotional instability that had made his voice squeaky and his postures jerky; but now that the crowd had gone home, and Jasper had been shown into the unoccupied stall beside the cow, and had been hand-fed with laboriously harvested clover, Jonathan's excitement had cooled. He was becoming aware of his new status as a man of affairs, a man of property, sole owner and proprietor of a donkey, the only man of his age in all Sepphoris who owned a donkey. Even his grandfather didn't own a donkey. Marcellus felt that Jonathan's behavior was approximately normal for a seven-year-old boy, in these circumstances.

'Well—did you put him up for the night?' he inquired, as one man to another.

Jonathan pursed his lips and nodded gravely.

'Will you come in and sit down?'

Jonathan came in and sat down, crossing his legs with mature deliberation.

'Did Jasper behave pretty well?'

Jonathan nodded several times, facing the ground.

Marcellus felt in need of some cooperation, but pursued his inquiries hopefully.

'Didn't bite anybody? Or kick anybody? Or lie down in his harness and go to sleep on the road?'

Jonathan shook his head slowly, without looking up, his tongue bulging his cheek.

Not having conversed with a small boy for many years, Marcellus began to realize that it wasn't as simple a matter as he had supposed.

'Well!' he exclaimed brightly. 'That's fine! Is there anything else you'd like to tell me about it?'

Jonathan glumly raised his head and faced Marcellus with troubled eyes. He swallowed noisily.

'Thomas asked me to let him ride,' he muttered, thickly.

'Something tells me that you refused,' ventured Marcellus.

Jonathan nodded remorsefully.

'I shouldn't fret about that,' went on Marcellus, comfortingly. 'You can let Thomas ride tomorrow. Perhaps he shouldn't have expected you to lend him your donkey on the very first day you had him. Is this Thomas a good friend of yours?'

'Did you see the boy with the crutches; the one with the limber leg?'

'The little boy your grandfather stopped to speak to?'

Jonathan nodded.

'Well—you can make it all up to Thomas,' cooed Marcellus, maternally. 'He'll have plenty of chances to ride. See here—if you feel so upset about this, why don't you run over to Thomas' house now and tell him he may ride Jasper, first thing in the morning.'

'They're going away tomorrow,' croaked Jonathan, dismally. 'Thomas and his mother. They don't live here. They live in Capernaum. They came here because his grandmother was sick. And she died. And now they're going back to Capernaum.'

'That's too bad,' said Marcellus. 'But it isn't your fault. If you're troubled about it, perhaps you'd better talk it over with your grandfather. Did you ever sleep in a tent, Jonathan?'

Jonathan shook his head, the gloom lifting a little.

'There's another cot we can set up,' said Marcellus. 'You go and talk to your grandfather about Thomas, and ask your mother if you may sleep in the tent.'

Jonathan grinned appreciatively and disappeared.

It was impossible not to overhear the conversation, for Justus was seated near the open window within an arm's reach of the tent. After a while,

Marcellus became conscious of the deep, gentle voice of Justus and the rather plaintive treble of his troubled grandson. Immensely curious to learn how all this was coming out, he put down his stylus and listened.

'When Jesus told people to give their things away, he said that just to rich people; didn't he, Grandfather?'

'Yes—just to people who had things they could divide with others.'

'Is Marcellus rich?'

'Yes—and he is very kind.'

'Did Jesus tell him to give his things away?'

There was a long pause here that made Marcellus hold his breath.

'I do not know, Jonathan. It is possible.'

There was another long silence, broken at length by the little boy.

'Grandfather—why didn't Jesus heal Thomas' leg?'

'I don't know, son. Perhaps Jesus wasn't told about it.'

'That was too bad,' lamented Jonathan. 'I wish he had.'

'Yes,' sighed Justus. 'That would make things much easier for you; wouldn't it?'

'I'm glad he straightened my foot,' murmured Jonathan.

'Yes—that was wonderful!' rumbled Justus. 'Jesus was very good to you! I know that if you could do anything for Jesus, you would be glad to; wouldn't you?'

'I couldn't do anything for Jesus, Grandfather,' protested Jonathan. 'How could I?'

'Well—if you should find that there was something Jesus hadn't done, because they hadn't told him about it; something he would have wanted to do, if he had known; something he would want to do now, if he were still here—'

'You mean—something for Thomas?' Jonathan's voice was thin.

'Had you thought there was something you might do for Thomas?'

Little Jonathan was crying now; and from the sound of shifting positions within the room, Marcellus surmised that Justus had taken his unhappy grandson in his arms. There was no more talk. After a half-hour or more, Jonathan appeared, red-eyed and fagged, at the door of the tent.

'I'm going to sleep with Grandfather,' he gulped. 'He wants me to.'

'That's right, Jonathan,' approved Marcellus. 'Your grandfather hasn't seen you for a long time. You may play in the tent tomorrow, if you like.'

Jonathan lingered, scowling thoughtfully and batting his eyes.

'Would it be all right with you if I gave Jasper away?' he asked, with an effort.

'To Thomas, maybe?' wondered Marcellus.

Jonathan nodded, without looking up.

'Are you sure you want to?'

'No—I don't want to.'

'Well—you're a pretty brave little boy, Jonathan! I'll say that for you!" declared Marcellus. This fervent praise, being altogether too much for Jonathan, led to his sudden disappearance. Marcellus untied his sandal-straps and lounged on his cot as the twilight deepened. This Jesus must have been a man of gigantic moral power. He had been dead and in his grave for a year now, but he had stamped himself so indelibly onto the house of Justus that even this child had been marked! The simile intrigued him for a moment. It was as if this Jesus had taken a die and a hammer—and had pounded the image of his spirit into this Galilean gold, converting it into the coins of his kingdom! The man should have lived! He should have been given a chance to impress more people! A spirit like that—if it contrived to get itself going—could make the world over into a fit habitation for men of good will! But Jesus was dead! A little handful of untutored country people in Galilee would remember for a few years—and the great light would be extinguished. It would be a pity! Little Jonathan would give up his donkey to a crippled boy, but only Sepphoris would ever know about it. Miriam would sing her inspired songs—but only for sequestered little Cana. Jesus' kingdom belonged to the world! But its coinage was good only in the shabby villages of Galilee. He would write that, tomorrow, to Demetrius.

* * * * *

Marcellus ate his breakfast alone, Rebecca attentive but uncommunicative. He had ventured upon several commonplace remarks to which she had replied, amiably enough, in listless monosyllables. Yes—Jonathan and his grandfather had had their breakfast early. No—she didn't think they would be gone long.

After he had eaten, Marcellus returned to the tent and continued writing the letter he had begun to Demetrius; writing it in Greek; with no plans for its delivery. Everybody who was likely to be journeying to Jerusalem at this season had already gone.

Presently Justus appeared at the tent-door. Marcellus signed to him to come in, and he eased himself onto a camp-chair.

'Well,' began Marcellus, breaking a lengthy silence, 'I suppose little Jonathan has done a generous deed—and broken his heart. I am sorry to have caused him so much distress.'

'Do not reproach yourself, Marcellus. It may turn out well. True—the child is a bit young to be put to such a severe test. We can only wait and see how he behaves. This is a great day for Jonathan—if he can see it through.' Justus was proud—but troubled.

'See it through!' echoed Marcellus. 'But he has seen it through! Hasn't he given his donkey to the crippled lad? You don't think he may repent of his gallantry, and ask Thomas to give the donkey back; do you?'

'No, no—not that! But they're all down there on the corner telling Jonathan what a fine little fellow he is. You should have heard them—when Thomas and his mother set off—Thomas riding the donkey and his mother walking alongside, so happy she was crying. And all the women caressing Jonathan, and saying, "How sweet! How kind! How brave!" ' Justus sighed deeply. 'It was too bad! But—of course—I couldn't rebuke them. I came away.'

'But—Justus!' exclaimed Marcellus. 'Surely it is only natural that the neighbors should praise Jonathan for what he did! It was no small sacrifice for a little boy! Isn't it right that the child should be commended?'

'Commended—yes,' agreed Justus, 'but not praised overmuch. As you have said, this thing has cost Jonathan a high price. He has a right to be rewarded for it—in his heart. It would be a great pity if all he gets out of it is smugness! There is no vanity so damaging to a man's character as pride over his good deeds! Let him be proud of his muscles, his fleetness, his strength, his face, his marksmanship, his craftsmanship, his endurance—these are the common frailties that beset us all. But when a man becomes vain of his goodness, it is a great tragedy! My boy is very young and inexperienced. He could be so easily ruined by self-righteousness, almost without realizing what ailed him.'

'I see what you mean!' declared Marcellus. 'I agree with you! This thing will either make Jonathan strong—beyond his years—or it will make a little prig of him! Justus—let's get out of here before the neighbors have had a chance to ruin him. We'll take him along with us! What do you say?'

Justus' eyes lighted. He nodded an enthusiastic approval.

'I shall speak with his mother,' he said. 'We will pack up and leave—at once!'

'That's sensible,' said Marcellus. 'I was afraid you might insist on Jonathan's remaining here—just to see how much of this punishment he could take.'

'No!' said Justus. 'It wouldn't be fair to overload the little fellow. He has done very well indeed. It is time now that we gave him a helping hand. We too have some obligations in this case, my friend!'

'You're right!' Marcellus began rolling up the letter he had just finished. 'I got Jonathan into this mess, and I'll do my best to help him through it without being damaged.'

Justus had no more than had time to enter the house until Jonathan put in an appearance at the door of the tent, wearing the wan, tremulous smile of a patient burden-bearer.

'Hi!—Jonathan,' greeted Marcellus, noisily. 'I hear you got young Thomas started on his way. That's good. What do you want with a donkey, anyhow? You have two of the best legs in town.' Busily preoccupied with the blankets he was folding up and stuffing into a pack-saddle, he absently chattered on, half to himself, 'A boy who was once a cripple—and then was cured—should be so glad he could walk that he would never want to ride!'

'But Jasper was such a nice donkey,' replied Jonathan, biting his lip. 'Everybody said they didn't know how I could give him up.'

'Well—never mind what everybody said!' barked Marcellus. 'Don't let them spoil it for you now! You're a stout little fellow—and that's the end of it! Here!—blow your nose—and give me a hand on this strap!'

Justus showed up in time to hear the last of it. He winced—and grinned.

'Jonathan,' he said, 'we are taking you with us on a few days' journey. Your mother is packing some things for you.'

'*Me?* I'm going along?' squealed Jonathan. 'Oh!' he raced around the corner of the tent, shouting gleefully.

Justus and Marcellus exchanged sober glances.

'That was a brutal thing I did just now!' muttered Marcellus.

' "Faithful are the wounds of a friend," ' said Justus. 'Jonathan will recover. He already has something new to think about—now that he is going with us.'

'By the way, Justus, where *are* we going?'

'I had thought of Capernaum next.'

'That can wait. We might overtake Thomas and Jasper. We don't want to see any more of them today. Let's go back to Cana. It will do little Jonathan good to have a look at Miriam.'

Justus tried to conceal a broad grin by tugging at his beard.

'Perhaps it would do you good too, Marcellus,' he ventured. 'But will you not be wasting your time? We have seen everything there is for sale—in Cana.'

Suddenly Marcellus, who had been tossing camp equipment into a wicker box, straightened and looked Justus squarely in the eyes.

'I think I have bought all the homespun I want,' he announced, bluntly. 'What I have been learning about this Jesus has made me curious to hear more. I wonder if you will help me meet a few people who knew him—people who might be willing to talk about him.'

'That would be difficult,' said Justus, frankly. 'Our people have no reasons for feeling that they can talk freely with Romans. They would find it hard to understand why a man of your nation should be making inquiries about Jesus. Perhaps you are not aware that the Romans put him to death. Maybe you do not know that the legionaries—especially in Jerusalem—are on the alert for any signs that the friends of Jesus are organized.'

'Do you suspect me of being a spy, Justus?' asked Marcellus, bluntly.

'No—I do not think you are a spy. I do not know what you are, Marcellus; but I am confident that you have no evil intent. I shall be willing to tell you some things about Jesus.'

'Thank you, Justus.' Marcellus drew from his tunic the letter he had written. 'Tell me: how may I send this to Jerusalem?'

Justus frowned, eyeing the scroll suspiciously.

'There is a Roman fort at Capernaum,' he muttered. 'Doubtless they have messengers going back and forth, every few days.'

Marcellus handed him the scroll and pointed to the address.

'I do not want this letter handled through the Capernaum fort,' he said, 'or the Insula at Jerusalem. It must be delivered by a trusted messenger into the care of the Greek, Stephanos, at Benyosef's shop.'

'So you do know that slave Demetrius,' commented Justus. 'I thought as much.'

'Yes—he is *my* slave.'

'I had wondered about that, too.'

'Indeed! Well—what else had you wondered about? Let's clean it all up, while we're at it.'

'I have wondered what your purpose was in making this trip into Galilee,' said Justus, brightening a little.

'Well—now you know; don't you?'

'I am not sure that I do.' Justus laid a hand on Marcellus' arm. 'Tell me this: did you ever see Jesus; ever hear him talk?'

'Yes,' admitted Marcellus, 'but I could not understand what he said. At that time I did not know the language.'

'Did you study Aramaic so you could learn something about him?'

'Yes—I had no other interest in it.'

'Let me ask one more question.' Justus lowered his voice. 'Are you one of us?'

'That's what I came up here to find out,' said Marcellus. 'Will you help me?'

'As much as I can,' agreed Justus, 'as much as you are able to comprehend.'

Marcellus looked puzzled.

'Do you mean that there are some mysteries here that I am not bright enough to understand?' he demanded, soberly.

'Bright enough—yes,' rejoined Justus. 'But an understanding of Jesus is not a mere matter of intelligence. Some of this story has to be accepted by faith.'

'Faith comes hard with me,' frowned Marcellus. 'I am not superstitious.'

'So much the better,' declared Justus. 'The higher the price you have to pay, the more you will cherish what you get.' Impulsively throwing aside his coat, he began pulling up tentstakes. 'We will talk more about this later,' he said. 'It is time we were on our way if we hope to reach Cana by sunset.' Suddenly he straightened with a new idea. 'I have it!' he exclaimed. 'We will go to Nazareth! It is much nearer than Cana. Nazareth was Jesus' home town. His mother lives there still. She will not hesitate to talk freely with you. When she learns that you—a Roman—saw her son, and were so impressed that you wanted to know more about him, she will tell you everything!'

'No—no!' exclaimed Marcellus, wincing. 'I have no wish to see her.' Noting the sudden perplexity on Justus' face, he added, 'I feel sure she would not want to talk about her son—to a Roman.'

* * * * * *

For the first three miles, Jonathan frolicked about the little caravan with all the aimless extravagance of a frisky pup, dashing on ahead, inexpertly throwing stones at the crows, and making many brief excursions into the fields. But as the sun rose higher, his wild enthusiasm came under better control. Now he was content to walk sedately beside his grandfather, taking long strides and feeling very manly. After a while he took his grandfather's hand and shortened his steps at the request of his aching legs.

Preoccupied with their conversation, which was weighty, Justus had been only vaguely aware of the little boy's weariness; but when he stumbled and nearly fell, they all drew up in the shade, unloaded the pack-train, and reapportioned their burdens so that the smallest donkey might be free for a rider. Jonathan made no protest when they lifted him up.

'I wish I had kept that nice saddle,' he repined.

'No, you don't,' drawled Marcellus. 'When you give anything away, make a good job of it. Don't skimp!'

'Our friend speaks truly, my boy,' said Justus. 'The donkey will carry you safely without a saddle. Let us move on, and when the sun is directly overhead, we will have something to eat.'

'I'm hungry now!' murmured Jonathan.

'The bread will taste better at noon,' advised Justus.

'I'm hungry, too,' intervened Marcellus, mercifully. As he unstrapped the hamper, he added, out of the corner of his mouth, 'He's only a baby, Justus. Don't be too hard on him.'

Justus grumbled a little over the delay and the breakdown of discipline, but it was easy to see that he had been mellowed by Marcellus' gentle defense of the child. A token lunch was passed about, and presently they were on the highway again.

'You would have been delighted with the mind of Jesus,' said Justus, companionably. 'You have a generous heart, Marcellus. How often he talked about generosity! In his opinion there was nothing meaner than a mean gift. About the worst thing a man could do to himself or a fellow creature was to bestow a grudged gift. It was very hard on a man's character to *give* away something that should have been *thrown* away! That much of Jesus' teachings you could accept, my friend, without any difficulty.'

'That is a friendly comment, Justus, but you do me too much credit,' protested Marcellus. 'The fact is—I have never in my life given anything away that impoverished me in the least. I have never given anything away that I needed or wanted to keep. I suppose Jesus parted with everything he had.'

'Everything!' said Justus. 'He had nothing but the garments he wore. He held that if a man had two coats, he should give one away. During his last year with us he wore a good robe. Perhaps he would have given that away, too, if it hadn't been given to him in peculiar circumstances.'

'Would you like to tell me about it?' asked Marcellus.

'There was an ill-favored woman in Nazareth who was suspected of practicing witchcraft. She was a dwarfish person with an ugly countenance, and walked alone, friendless and bitter. The children cried after her on the road. And so a legend spread that Tamar had an evil eye. One Sabbath day the neighbors heard her loom banging, and warned her against this breaking of the law; for many of our people have more respect for the Sabbath than they have for one another. Tamar did not heed the warning and she was reported to the authorities who came in upon her, on a Sabbath morning, and destroyed her loom which was her living. Perhaps you can guess the rest of the story,' said Justus.

'It was fortunate for Tamar that Jesus was a good carpenter,' remarked Marcellus. 'But what did the authorities think of his coming to Tamar's aid? Did they accuse him of being sympathetic with Sabbath-breakers?'

'That they did!' declared Justus. 'It was at a time when the priests were on the alert to find him at fault. The people often urged him to speak in the village synagogues, and this displeased the rabbis. They were always haranguing the people about their tithes and sacrificial offerings. Jesus talked about friendship and hospitality to strangers and relief for the poor.'

'But—didn't the rabbis believe in friendship and charity?' wondered Marcellus.

'Oh, yes—of course. They took it for granted that everybody was agreed on that.'

'In theory, at least,' surmised Marcellus.

'Exactly! In theory. But securing funds to support the synagogue—that was practical! They had to talk constantly about money. It left them no time to talk about the things of the spirit.'

'Well—go on about Tamar,' interposed Marcellus. 'I suppose Jesus reconstructed her loom——and she wove him the Robe.'

'Right! And he wore it until he died.'

'Were you there—when he died?' asked Marcellus, uneasily.

'No—I was in prison.' Justus seemed disinclined to enlarge upon this matter; but, when questioned, told the story briefly. A few days before his trial for treason and disturbing the peace, Jesus had impulsively driven hucksters and bankers out of the Temple. Several of his friends had been arrested and thrown into prison on the charge of having gathered up some of the scattered coins from the pavement. The accusation was untrue, Justus insisted, but they were kept in prison for a fortnight. 'It was all over,' he said, sadly, 'when we were released. As for the Robe—the Roman soldiers gambled for it—and carried it away with them. We often wondered what became of it. It could have no value—for them.'

It was noon now, and a halt was made in a little grove where there was a spring and a green grass-plot for grazing. The donkeys were unburdened and tethered. The food was unpacked; a wineskin, a basket of bread, a parcel of smoked fish, an earthenware jar of cooked barley, a box of sun-cured figs. They spread a blanket on the ground for little Jonathan, who, stuffed to repletion and wearied by the journey, promptly tumbled down to sleep. Justus and Marcellus, lounging on the grass, pursued a low-voiced conversation.

'Sometimes thoughtless people misunderstood his attitude toward business,' Justus was saying. 'His critics noised it about that he had contempt for barter and trade; that he had no respect for thrift and honest husbandry.'

'I had wondered about that,' said Marcellus. 'There has been much talk about his urging people to give things away. It had occurred to me that this could be overdone. If men recklessly distributed their goods to all comers, how could they provide for their own dependents?'

'Let me give you an illustration,' said Justus. 'This subject came up, one day, and Jesus dealt with it in a story. He was forever contriving simple little fables. He said, a man with a vineyard wanted his grapes picked, for they were now ripe. Going down to the public market, he asked a group of idlers if they wanted a job. They said they would work all day for one denarius.'

'Rather high,' observed Marcellus.

'Rather! But the grapes had to be picked immediately, and the man wasn't in a position to argue; so he took them on. By noon, it was apparent that he would need more help. Again in the market-place he asked the unemployed what they would take to work that afternoon. And they said, "We will leave that up to you, sir." Well—when evening came, the men who had dickered with him for one denarius were paid off according to agreement. Then came the men who had worked shorter hours, leaving the wages to the owner's generosity.'

'So—what did he do?' wondered Marcellus, sincerely interested.

'Gave every man a denarius! All the way up and down the line—one denarius! He even gave a denarius to a few who hadn't worked more than an hour!'

'That might have started a row,' surmised Marcellus.

'And indeed it *did!* The men who had worked all day complained bitterly. But the owner said, 'I paid the price you had demanded. That was according to contract. These other men made no demands, but relied on my good will." '

'Excellent!' exclaimed Marcellus. 'If a man drives a hard bargain with you and you are forced to concede to it, you have no obligation to be generous. But if he lets *you* say how much he should have, that's likely to cost you something!'

'There you are!' nodded Justus. 'You have a right to weigh it out by the pennyworth, if the other fellow haggles. But if he leaves it up to you, the measure you give must be pressed down, shaken together, and running over!'

'Justus,' declared Marcellus, 'if it became a custom for people to deal with one another that way, the market-place wouldn't be quite so noisy; would it?'

'And all men would be better off,' said Justus. 'People wouldn't have to be taxed to employ patrols to keep the peace. And—as the idea spread,' he added, dreamily, 'all of the armies could be demobilized. That would lift a great weight off the shoulders of the people. And once they had experienced this more abundant life that Jesus proposed, it is not likely they would want to return to the old way.'

For some time they sat in silence, each busy with his own thoughts.

'Of course—it's utterly impractical,' declared Marcellus. 'Only a little handful would make the experiment, and at ruinous cost. The great majority would sneer and take advantage of them, considering them cowardly and feebleminded for not defending their rights. They would soon be stripped of everything!'

'That's true,' admitted Justus. 'Stripped of everything but *the great idea!* But, Marcellus, that idea is like a seed. It doesn't amount to much if you expect immediate returns. But if you're willing to plant it, and nourish it—'

'I suppose,' remarked Marcellus, 'it is as if some benefactor appeared in the world with a handful of new grain which, if men should feed on it, would give them peace and prosperity.'

'Very good,' approved Justus, 'but that handful of grain would not go very far unless it were sowed and reaped and sowed again and again. Jesus talked about that. Much of this seed, he said, would never come up. Some of it would lodge in the weeds and brambles. Some of it would fall upon stony ground. But a little of it would grow.'

'Justus—do you honestly believe there's any future for a theory like that—in this greedy world?' Marcellus was deeply in earnest.

'Yes—I do!' declared Justus. 'I believe it because he believed it! He said it would work like yeast in meal; slowly, silently; but—once it began—nothing could ever stop it. Nobody would ever be able to shut it off—or dig it up—or tear it out!'

'But—why did it begin—up here—in poor little Galilee—so remote from the main centers of world development?' wondered Marcellus.

'Well'—reflected Justus—'it had to begin *somewhere!*' After a moment of meditation, he faced Marcellus with a sly grin. 'Do you think this seed might have had a better chance to take root and grow, if it had fallen on the streets in Rome?'

'I think the question answers itself,' conceded Marcellus.

Justus reached over and patted the little boy's tanned cheek.

'On—now—to Cana,' he said, scrambling to his feet.

In a few minutes they were on the highway, Justus leading with long, swinging strides, indulging in a reminiscent monologue.

'How often we came over this road together!' he was recalling. 'Jesus loved Cana better than any other town in Galilee.'

'Better than Nazareth?' queried Marcellus.

'They never quite appreciated his spirit in Nazareth,' explained Justus. 'You know how it is. A prophet has no standing in his own community. The Nazarenes used to say, "How can this man have any wisdom? Don't *we* know him?" '

'Apparently they didn't rate very high in their own esteem,' laughed Marcellus.

'It was natural,' said Justus, sobering. 'He had grown up with them. He never held it against them that they did not respond to his teachings as they did in Cana and Capernaum. It was in Cana that he first exercised the peculiar powers you will be hearing about. I don't suppose anyone has told you what happened there, one day, at a wedding.'

'No,' replied Marcellus, attentively. 'What happened?'

It was a story of some length, and Justus was so particular about the small details that Marcellus immediately surmised its importance. Anna, the daughter of Hariph and Rachel, was to be married. Hariph was a potter, an industrious fellow, but by no means prosperous, and the expense of the wedding dinner for Anna was not easy for them. However, Hariph was going to see his child properly honored. Anna was very popular, and Hariph and Rachel had a host of relatives. Everybody was invited and everybody came.

'Were you there, Justus?'

'No—that was before I knew Jesus. The story of what occurred, that day, quickly spread far and wide. I don't mind telling you that when I heard it, I doubted it.'

'Get on with it, please!' insisted Marcellus.

'Jesus arrived late. The wedding rites had been performed, and the guests had been at table for some time when he appeared. Poor Hariph was unhappy. He had not provided enough wine for so large a crowd. His predicament was whispered into Jesus' ear.'

Justus tramped on for half a stadium in moody silence.

'Maybe it is not the time yet to tell you this,' he muttered. 'You will not believe it. I did not believe it when they told me! Jesus slipped away from the table, and went to the small serving-room. He saw some of Hariph's earthenware jars in the little court outside, and told the servants to fill them with water. Then, having instructed them to serve it to the guests, he went back and resumed his place at the table. When the water was served, *it was wine!*'

'No—Justus—no!' exclaimed Marcellus. 'This spoils the story of Jesus!'

'I was afraid you weren't ready for it, my friend,' regretted Justus.

'Oh—but there must have been some better explanation of that wine,' insisted Marcellus. 'Jesus comes in with that radiant personality; everyone loving him. And even the water they drank in his presence tasted like wine! And so—this other utterly preposterous tale got bruited about.'

'Have it your own way, Marcellus,' consented Justus, kindly. 'It does not offend me that you doubt the story. You can believe in the wisdom and goodness of Jesus without that.'

They proceeded, without further conversation, up the long hill where, at the crest, Justus stopped, cupped his eyes with his big, brown hands, and gazed intently down the narrow road as far as he could see; a familiar, though unexplained, occurrence. The best Marcellus could make of these frequent long-range observations was his belief that Justus was expecting to meet someone by appointment. Today he thought of asking about it, but decided to wait until Justus wanted to tell him.

While they tarried, at the top of the hill, for the pack-train to overtake them, Marcellus broke the silence with a query.

'Did you not tell me, Justus, that Miriam discovered her matchless voice while her family was absent from home, attending a wedding-feast to which she had been invited—and had refused to go?'

'Yes,' assented Justus. 'It was Anna's wedding.'

'Jesus arrived late at the wedding,' remembered Marcellus.

'Yes.' Justus nodded and they exchanged a look of mutual understanding.

'I wonder what made him late,' reflected Marcellus.

'I, too, have often wondered about that,' said Justus, quietly.

'Do you suppose he might have asked Miriam not to tell?'

'It is possible.'

'So far as you know, Justus,' persisted Marcellus, 'did he ever confer a great gift upon someone—and request the beneficiary to keep it a secret?'

'Yes,' said Justus. 'There were many evidences of such events.'

'How do you explain that?' Marcellus wanted to know.

'Jesus found any public display of charity very offensive,' said Justus. 'Had it been possible, I think he would have preferred to do all of his generous deeds in secret. On one occasion he said to a great throng that had gathered on a hillside to hear him talk, "When you make gifts, do not let them be seen. Do not sound a trumpet that you may receive praise. When you do your alms-giving, let not your left hand know what your right hand is doing. No one but your Father will see. Only your Father will reward you." '

'What did he mean, Justus—about your Father rewarding you—if no one else knows? Take little Jonathan's case, for example: if nobody had learned about his giving his donkey to the crippled lad, would he have been secretly rewarded?'

'Of course!' declared Justus. 'If no one had known about the gift, Jonathan's heart would have overflowed with happiness. You wouldn't have heard him wishing that he had kept the saddle!'

'But the child had no way of keeping the matter quiet!' expostulated Marcellus.

'True,' nodded Justus. 'That was not Jonathan's fault, but his misfortune.'

'Do you think that peculiar radiance of Miriam's can be accounted for by her having kept her secret? In her case, she was not the donor. She was the recipient!'

'I know,' agreed Justus. 'If the recipient doesn't tell, then the donor is rewarded in his heart. It is thus that the recipient helps him to obtain his reward.'

'But now that Jesus is dead,' argued Marcellus, with a puzzled look, 'Miriam is free to tell her secret; is she not?'

Justus stroked his beard, thoughtfully.

'Probably not,' he murmured. 'If she were—she would tell.'

Chapter XV

THEY had reached Cana too late to hear Miriam sing, but Marcellus thought it was just as well, for Jonathan was so tired and sleepy that he could hardly hold his head up.

By the time they had pitched camp, washed off their dust, eaten a light supper, and put the little boy to bed, many voices could be heard; villagers strolling home in the moonlight from their customary rendezvous at the fountain.

Justus sauntered out to the street. Marcellus, wearily stretched at full length on his cot, heard him talking to a friend. After a while he returned to say he had been informed by Hariph the potter that Jesse, the son of Beoni, was leaving early in the morning for Jerusalem. Doubtless he would carry the letter to Demetrius.

'Very good!' Marcellus handed him the scroll and unstrapped his coin purse. 'How much will he expect?'

'Ten shekels should be enough.' There was an expression of satisfaction in Justus' face and tone, perhaps because the letter had been given up so casually. His look said that there could be nothing conspiratorial in this communication. 'Jesse will probably be over here presently,' he added. 'Hariph will tell him. He lives hard by the home of Beoni.'

'You can talk with him,' said Marcellus. 'I am going to sleep.'

And he did; but after a while the murmur of low-pitched voices roused him. He raised up on his elbow, and through the open tent-door the white moonlight showed Justus and a stocky, shaggy-haired man of thirty, seated cross-legged on the ground. Jesse, the son of Beoni, was rumbling gutturally about the business that was taking him to Jerusalem. He was going to attend the annual camel auction. They always had it at the end of Passover. Many caravans from afar, having disposed of their merchandise, offered their pack-animals for sale rather than trek them home without a pay-load. You could get a sound, three-year-old she-camel for as little as eighty shekels, Jesse said. He hoped to buy six, this time. He could easily sell them in Tiberias for a hundred or better. Yes—he made this trip every year. Yes—he would gladly carry Justus' letter to the Greek who worked for Benyosef. And when Justus asked him how much, Jesse said, 'Nothing at all. It's no bother.'

'But it isn't my letter,' explained Justus. 'It is sent by this Roman, Marcellus Gallio, who is up here buying homespun. He's there in the tent, asleep.'

'Oh—that one! My mother told me about him. It is strange that he should want our simple weaving. No one ever thought it was valuable. Well—if it is his letter, and not yours, he should pay me eight shekels.'

'He will give you ten.' The coins were poured clinking into Jesse's hand.

'Eight is enough,' said Jesse. 'You keep the other two.'

'But I have done nothing to earn them,' protested Justus. 'They are yours. I think the Roman would prefer to give you ten.'

Jesse chuckled—not very pleasantly.

'Since when have the Romans turned soft-hearted?' he growled. 'I hope there is nothing queer about this scroll. They tell me the jail in Jerusalem is alive with vermin. How about it, Justus? You ought to know.' Jesse laughed at his own grim jest. 'You lodged there for a couple of weeks last spring.'

Marcellus could not hear Justus' rejoinder. Perhaps he had merely grinned or scowled at Jesse's bucolic raillery.

'You can trust Marcellus,' said Justus, confidently. 'He is a man of good will. Not all Romans are crooked, Jesse. You know that.'

'Yes, yes,' consented Jesse. 'As the saying goes, "Every Jew has his Roman." Mine happens to be Hortensius.'

'You mean the Centurion, over in Capernaum, whose orderly Jesus cured of a palsy? Did you have dealings with him, Jesse?'

'I sold him four camels—shortly before that affair of his servant. Three for a hundred each. I told him he could have the other one for sixty because she was spavined. And he said, "She doesn't limp. What did you pay for her?" And I said, "Eighty—but I didn't know the spavin was bad until we were on the road two days." And he said, "She seems to be all right now." And I said, "She's rested. But she'll go lame on a long journey with anything of a load." And he said, "You needn't have told me." Then he said, "Do you know Jesus?" And I said, "Yes." And he said, "I thought so." And then he said, "Let's split the cost of the spavin. I'll give you seventy." And I said, "That's fair enough." And then I said, "Do you know Jesus, sir?" And he said, "No—but I heard him talk, one day." And then I asked him, just as if we were equals, "Are you one of us?" And he was busy counting out the money, and didn't answer that; but when he handed it to me he said—that was four years ago, and I looked younger than now—he said, "You keep on listening to Jesus, boy! You'll never be rich—but you'll never be poor!" '

'I'm glad you told me that, Jesse,' said Justus. 'You see what happened there? Hortensius heard Jesus talk about how people ought to treat one another. And maybe he wondered whether anybody was trying to practice it. And then you told him the truth about the spavined camel. And he began to believe that Jesus had great power.'

Jesse laughed.

'So you think the camel deal had something to do with his believing that Jesus could cure his sick orderly.'

'Why not?' It was Justus' turn to chuckle. 'I suppose the Centurion decided that any man who could influence a Jewish camel-drover to tell the truth about a spavin should be able to heal the sick. But'—Justus' tone was serious now—'however Hortensius came by his faith, he had plenty of it. I was there that day, Jesse. The Centurion came forward—a fine figure, too, in full uniform—and said, very deferentially, that his servant was sick unto death. Would Jesus heal him? "You need not trouble to come to my house, sir," he said. "If you will say that my servant is healed, that will be sufficient." Jesus was much pleased. Nothing like that had happened before. None of us had ever been that sure. He said to Hortensius, "You have great faith. Your wish is granted." '

'And then'—recollected Jesse—'they say that almost everyone in the crowd set off at top speed for Hortensius' house.'

'Yes,' said Justus, 'and they never did agree on a story. One report had it that the restored orderly met Hortensius at the gate. Some said the fellow was recovered and sitting up in bed. Others told that when the Centurion returned, the orderly was saddling a horse to ride to Capernaum. You know how these rumors get about. I suppose the fact is that none of these curious people was admitted to the Centurion's grounds.'

'But the man did recover, that day, from his sickness; didn't he?' Jesse insisted.

'He did, indeed!' declared Justus. 'I heard him say so. By the way—think you that Hortensius will be made Commander of the fort at Capernaum, now that old Julian has been promoted to succeed Pilate?'

'No such luck for Galilee!' grumbled Jesse. 'Everyone likes Hortensius. He is a just man, and he would be friendly to our cause. That old fox Herod will see to it that someone tougher than Hortensius gets the job. The thing that surprises me is the appointment of lazy old Julian to the Insula at Jerusalem.'

'Perhaps it's because Julian is lazy that the Temple crowd wanted him as their Procurator,' suggested Justus. 'The more indolent and indifferent he is, the more power will be exercised by the High Priest. He will let Caiaphas do anything he pleases. There are times, Jesse,' went on Justus, thoughtfully, 'when a weak, lazy, vacillating man—of good intent—is more to be feared than a crafty and cruel man. He shuts his eyes—and lets the injustices and persecutions proceed. In truth, our cause would have been better served if Pilate had remained.'

'Does anyone know what has become of Pilate?' asked Jesse.

'Sent back to Crete, I understand. Better climate. The rumor is that Pontius Pilate is a sick man. He hasn't made a public appearance for all of a year.'

'Why—that goes back to the crucifixion!' said Jesse. 'Do you mean that Pilate hasn't been seen in public since that day?'

'That's what they say. Benyosef thinks Pilate's sickness is mental.'

'Well—if that's the case, a change of climate will do him no good,' remarked Jesse. 'Hariph says he heard that there's talk of transferring the Commander of the fort at Minoa to Capernaum.'

'Impossible!' muttered Justus. 'They wouldn't dare! It was the legion from Minoa that put Jesus to death!'

'Yes—I know that,' said Jesse. 'I think, too, that it's just idle talk. Hariph didn't say where he'd picked it up. Someone told him that this Paulus from Minoa would probably be our next Commander. If so—we will have to be more careful than ever.'

Justus sighed deeply and rose to his feet.

'I must not keep you longer, Jesse. You have a long day ahead of you. Salute Benyosef for me, and any of the others who may have returned, now that the Passover is at an end. And'—he laid a hand on Jesse's shoulder—'keep watchful eyes on the roads, for no one knows the day—or the hour—' His deep voice throttled down to a whisper. They shook hands and Jesse drifted away.

With his face turned toward the tent-wall, Marcellus feigned sleep when Justus entered quietly. For a long time he lay wide awake, pondering the things he had overheard. So—it hadn't been so easy for Pilate. Pilate had washed his hands in the silver basin, but apparently the Galilean's blood was still there. So—Julian was in command at Jerusalem: Caiaphas could have his own way now. Julian wouldn't know; wouldn't care if he did know what persecutions were practiced on the little handful that wanted to keep the memory of Jesus alive. It wouldn't be long until old Benyosef and his secretive callers would have to give it all up. And perhaps Paulus was to be sent up here to keep Galilee in order. Well—maybe Paulus wouldn't be as hard on them as they feared. Paulus wasn't a bad fellow. Paulus had been forced to take part in the crucifixion of Jesus. That didn't mean he had approved of it. It was conceivable that Paulus might even take an interest in the Galilean friends of Jesus. But they would never accept his friendship. The very sight of him would be abhorrent. Justus' comments had made that clear. A man who had had anything to do with nailing their adored Jesus to the cross could never hope to win their good will, no matter how generously he treated them.

Marcellus realized now that he had been quite too sanguine in believing that his sincere interest in the story of Jesus might make it safe for him to confide in Miriam. He had been telling himself that Miriam—uncannily gifted with sympathetic understanding—would balance his present concern about Jesus against the stark facts of his part in the tragedy. Miriam, he felt, would be forgiving. That was her nature; and, besides, she liked him, and would give him the benefit of whatever doubts intruded. Perhaps he would not need to go the whole way with his confession. It might be enough to say that he had attended the trial of Jesus, and had seen him die. Whether he could bring himself to be more specific about his own participation in this shameful business would depend upon her reaction as he proceeded.

But he knew now that such a conversation with Miriam was unthinkable! Justus, too, was a fair-minded person to whom one might safely confide almost anything; but Justus had revolted against the shocking suggestion that an officer from *Minoa* might be sent to preserve the peace of Galilee. 'They wouldn't dare!' Justus had muttered through locked teeth.

No—he couldn't tell Miriam. Perhaps it would be more prudent if he made no effort to see her alone.

* * * * * *

Hariph the potter, upon whom Cana relied for most of its information on current events, had risen at daybreak with the remembrance that Reuben had mentioned his need of a few wine-jars. Although it lacked some three months of the wine-pressing season, this was as good a time as any to learn Reuben's wishes. Too, he thought Reuben might be glad to learn that Barsabas Justus had arrived in Cana, last evening, with his small grandson—the one who, crippled from birth, had been made sound as any boy ever was—and the handsome young Roman who, for some obscure reason, was buying up homespun at better than market prices. To this might be added the knowledge that Jesse, the son of Beoni, had been engaged by this Marcellus to carry an important letter to Jerusalem. After these items had been dealt out to Reuben, piecemeal, he could be told that Justus would be taking his grandson to see Miriam.

And so it happened that when the three callers sauntered across Reuben's well-kept lawn, at mid-forenoon, instead of taking the family by surprise they discovered that their visit was awaited.

Feeling that little Jonathan might enjoy a playmate, Miriam had sent for her nine-year-old cousin Andrew, who lived a mile farther out in the country. And Andrew's widowed mother, Aunt Martha, had been invited too, which had made her happy, for she had not seen Justus in recent months. There were many questions she wanted to ask him.

They were all in the arbor, grouped about Miriam who was busy with the inevitable embroidery. She was very lovely, this morning, with a translucent happiness that made her even prettier than Marcellus had remembered. After greetings and introductions had been attended to—the artless sincerity of Miriam's welcome speeding Marcellus' pulse—they all found seats. Miriam held out a slim hand to Jonathan and gave him a brooding smile that brought him shyly to her side.

'You must be a very strong boy, Jonathan,' she told him, 'keeping up with these big men on a journey, all the way from Sepphoris.'

'I rode a donkey—most of the time,' he mumbled, self-consciously; then, with more confidence, 'I had a nicer donkey—of my own. His name was Jasper.' He pointed a finger vaguely in Marcellus' direction without looking at him. 'He gave Jasper to me. And I gave him to Thomas, because Thomas is lame.'

'Why—what a lovely thing to do!' exclaimed Miriam. Her shining eyes drifted past Jonathan and gave Marcellus a heart-warming glance, and then darted to Justus, whose lips were drawn down to a warning frown. 'I suppose Thomas really needs a donkey,' she went on, accepting Justus' hint. 'It must have made you very happy to do that for him.'

Jonathan smiled wanly, put one brown bare foot on top of the other, and seemed to be meditating a dolorous reply. Divining his mood, Miriam intercepted with a promising diversion.

'Andrew,' she called, 'why don't you take Jonathan to see the conies. There are some little ones, Jonathan, that haven't opened their eyes yet.'

This suggestion was acted upon with alacrity. When the children had scampered away, Naomi turned to Marcellus.

'What's all this about the donkey?' she inquired, smiling.

Marcellus recrossed his long legs and wished that he had been included in the expedition to inspect the conies.

'I think Jonathan has told it all,' he replied, negligently. 'I found a lazy little donkey that nobody wanted and gave him to Jonathan. There was a lame lad in the neighborhood and Jonathan generously presented him with the donkey. We thought that was pretty good—for a seven-year-old.'

'But we don't want his good-heartedness to go to his head,' put in Justus, firmly. 'He's already much impressed.'

'But Jonathan is only a child, Barsabas Justus,' protested Miriam.

'Of course!' murmured Martha.

'I know,' mumbled Justus, stroking his beard. 'But we can't have him spoiled, Miriam. If you have an opportunity, speak to him about it. . . . Well, Reuben, what's the prospect for the vineyard?'

'Better than usual, Justus.' Reuben slowly rose from his chair. 'Want to walk out and have a look at the vines?'

They ambled away. Presently Naomi remembered something she had to do in the kitchen. Aunt Martha, with a little nod and a smile, thought she might help. Miriam bent over her work attentively as they disappeared around the corner of the house.

'You have been much in my thoughts, Marcellus,' she said softly, after a silence which they both had been reluctant to invade with some casual banality.

'You can see that I wanted to come back.' Marcellus drew his chair closer.

'And now that you're here'—Miriam smiled into his eyes companionably—'what shall we talk about first?'

'I am much interested in the story of that carpenter who did so many things for your people.'

Miriam's eyes widened happily.

'I knew it!' she cried.

'How could you have known it?' wondered Marcellus.

'Oh'—archly—'by lots of little things—strung together. You knew nothing about textiles, nor does good old Justus, for that matter. You have had no experience in bargaining. It was clear that you were in Galilee on some other errand.'

'True—but what made you think I was interested in Jesus?'

'Your choosing Justus to conduct you. He saw as much of Jesus as anyone except Simon and the Zebedee boys who were with him constantly. But you had me quite mystified.' She shook her head and laughed softly. 'Romans are under suspicion. I couldn't understand why Justus had consented to come up here with you. Then it came out that you knew the Greek who works for Benyosef. He must have planned your meeting with Justus, for surely that was no accident! The men who frequent Benyosef's shop are friends of Jesus. So—I added it all up—and—'

'And concluded that I had employed Justus to inform me about Jesus,' interposed Marcellus. 'Well—your deduction is correct, though I must say that Justus seems to know a great deal that he isn't confiding in me.'

'Have you told him why you are interested in Jesus?' Miriam studied his eyes as she waited for his reply.

'Not fully,' admitted Marcellus, after some hesitation. 'But he is not suspicious of my motive.'

'Perhaps if you would tell Justus exactly how you happened to become interested in Jesus, he might be more free to talk,' suggested Miriam; and when Marcellus failed to respond promptly, she added, 'I am full of curiosity about that, myself.'

'That's a long story, Miriam,' muttered Marcellus, soberly.

'I have plenty of time,' she said. 'Tell me, Marcellus.'

'A year ago, I was in Jerusalem—on business—' he began, rather uncertainly.

'But not buying homespun,' she interjected, when he paused.

'It was government business,' Marcellus went on. 'I was there only a few days. During that time, there was a considerable stir over the arrest of this Galilean on a charge of treason. I was present at the trial where he was sentenced to death. It seemed clear that the man was innocent. The Procurator himself said so. I had much difficulty putting the matter out of my mind. Everything indicated that Jesus was a remarkable character. So—when I had occasion to come to Jerusalem again, this spring, I decided to spend a few days in Galilee, and learn something more about him.'

'What was it—about Jesus—that so deeply impressed you?' Miriam's tone entreated full confidence.

'His apparently effortless courage, I think,' said Marcellus. 'They were all arrayed against him—the Government, the Temple, the merchants, the bankers, the influential voices, the money. Not a man spoke in his behalf. His friends deserted him. And yet—in the face of cruel abuse—with a lost cause—and certain death confronting him—he was utterly fearless.' There was a thoughtful pause. 'It was impossible not to have a deep respect for a person of that fiber. I have had an immense curiosity to know what manner of man he was.' Marcellus made a little gesture to signify that he had ended his explanation.

'That wasn't such a very long story, after all, Marcellus,' remarked Miriam, intent upon her work. 'I wonder that you were so reluctant to tell it. Did you, perhaps, omit to tell Justus some of the things you have just told me?'

'No,' said Marcellus. 'I told him substantially the same thing.'

'But I thought you said you had not told him fully!'

'Well—what I have told you and Justus is sufficient, I think, to assure you that my interest is sincere,' declared Marcellus. 'At least, Justus appears to be satisfied. There are some stories about Jesus which he hints at—but refuses to tell—because, he says, I am not ready to be told. Yesterday he was lamenting that he had talked about that wedding-feast where the guests thought the water tasted like wine.'

'You didn't believe it.' Miriam smiled briefly. 'I do not wonder. Perhaps Justus is right. You weren't prepared for such a story.' A slow flush crept up her cheeks, as she added, 'And how did he happen to be talking of Anna's wedding?'

'We had been hoping to reach Cana in time to hear you sing,' said Marcellus, brightly, glad to have the conversation diverted. 'Naturally that led to comments about your sudden discovery of your inspiring voice. Justus had told me previously that it had occurred on the day of a wedding-feast. I pressed the subject, and he admitted that your strange experience had happened on the same day.'

'The changing of water into wine—that was too much for you,' laughed Miriam, sympathetically. 'I'm not surprised. However'—she went on, seriously—'you seem to have had no trouble believing in my discovery that I could sing. It has completely transformed my life—my singing. It instantly made me over into another kind of person, Marcellus. I was morbid, helpless, heart-sick, self-piteous, fretful, unreasonable. And now—as you see—I am happy and contented.' She stirred him with a radiant smile, and asked, softly, 'Is that so much easier to understand than the transformation of water into wine?'

'Shall I infer, then, that there was a miracle performed in your case, Miriam?' asked Marcellus.

'As you like,' she murmured, after some hesitation.

'I know you prefer not to discuss it,' he said, 'and I shall not pursue you with queries. But—assuming that Jesus spoke a word that made you sing—why did he not add a word that would give you power to walk? He straightened little Jonathan's foot, they say.'

Miriam pushed her embroidery aside, folded her arms, and faced Marcellus with a thoughtful frown.

'I cannot tell you how I came by my gift,' she said, 'but I do not regret my lameness. Perhaps the people of Cana are more helped by the songs I sing—from my cot—than they might be if I were physically well. They all have their worries, agonies, defeats. If I had been made whole, perhaps they would say, "Oh—it's easy enough for Miriam to sing and rejoice. Miriam has no trouble. Why indeed shouldn't she sing?"'

'You're a brave girl!' declared Marcellus.

She shook her head.

'I do not feel that I merit much praise, Marcellus. There was a time when my lameness was a great affliction—because I made it an affliction. It afflicted not only me but my parents and all my friends. Now that it is not an affliction, it has become a means of blessing. People are very tender in their attitude toward me. They come to visit me. They bring me little gifts. And, as Jesus said so frequently, it is more blessed to give than to receive. I am fortunate, my friend. I live in an atmosphere of love. The people of Cana frequently quarrel—but not with me. They are all at their best—with me.' She flashed him a sudden smile. 'Am I not rich?'

Marcellus made no response, but impulsively laid an open hand on the edge of the cot, and she gave him hers with the undeliberated trust of a little child.

'Shall I tell you another strange story, Marcellus?' she asked, quietly. 'Of course Justus must have told you that after Jesus had done some amazing things in our Galilean villages, the news spread throughout the country, and great crowds followed him wherever he went; hundreds, thousands; followed along for miles and miles and days and days! Men in the fields would drop their hoes and run to the road as the long procession passed; and then they too would join the throng, maybe to be gone from home for a week or more, sleeping in the open, cold and hungry, completely carried away! Nothing mattered—but to be close to Jesus! Well—one day—he was entering Jericho. You haven't been to Jericho, have you? No—you came up through Samaria. Jericho is one of the larger towns of Judea. As usual, a big crowd followed him and the whole city rushed to the main thoroughfare as the word spread that he had come. At that time, the Chief Revenue Officer of Jericho was a man named Zacchaeus—'

'A Greek?' broke in Marcellus.

'No—he was an Israelite. His name was Zaccai, really; but being in the employ of the Roman Government—' Miriam hesitated, colored a little, and Marcellus eased her embarrassment with an understanding grin.

'You needn't explain. These provincial officers usually alter their names as soon as they begin to curry favor with their foreign masters. It's fashionable now to have a Greek name; much smarter and safer than to have a Roman name. I think I know something about this Zaccai—alias Zacchaeus—without meeting him. He is a common type of rascally tax-collector; disloyal to everybody—to the Government—and his own countrymen. We have them in all of our provinces throughout the Empire. You can't have an empire, Miriam, without scoundrels in the provincial seats of government. Think you that Tiberius could govern faraway Hispania and Aquitania unless certain of their men betrayed their own people? By no means! When the provincial officers go straight, the Empire goes to pieces!

. . . But—pardon the interruption, Miriam, and the long speech. Tell me about Zacchaeus.'

'He was very wealthy. The people of Jericho feared and hated him. He had spies at every keyhole listening for some rebellious whisper. Anyone suspected of grumbling about the Government was assessed higher taxes, and if he protested, he was charged with treason. Zacchaeus had built a beautiful home on a knoll at the southern boundary of Jericho and lived like a prince. There were landscaped gardens and lagoons—and scores of servants.'

'But no friends,' surmised Marcellus.

'Neither among the rich nor poor; but Zacchaeus did not care. He had contempt for their hatred. Well—on this day—having heard that Jesus was proceeding toward Jericho, Zacchaeus came down into the city for a glimpse of him. The waiting crowd was so dense that he abandoned his carriage and struggled through the multitude to reach a spot where he might see. A legionary, recognizing him, assisted him to climb up into the fork of a tree, though this was forbidden to anyone else. Presently Jesus came down the street with his large company, and stopped by the tree. He called to Zacchaeus, addressing him by name, though they had never met, saying, "May I dine with you today?" '

'And what did the people of Jericho think of that?' wondered Marcellus.

'They were indignant, of course,' said Miriam. 'And Jesus' closest friends were very unhappy. Zacchaeus had been so mean—and now Jesus had singled him out for special attention. Many said, "This Galilean is no better than the priests, who are ever truckling to the rich." '

'I suppose Zacchaeus made the most of their discomfiture,' commented Marcellus.

'He was much flattered; hurried down from the tree and swaggered proudly at Jesus' side as the procession moved on. And when they arrived at his beautiful estate, he gave orders that the multitude might enter the grounds and wait—'

'While he and his guest had dinner,' assisted Marcellus. 'They must not have liked that.'

'No—they were deeply offended; but they waited. And saw Jesus enter the great marble house of Zacchaeus. After they had sat waiting for almost an hour, Zacchaeus came out and beckoned to the people. They scrambled to their feet and ran to hear what he might say. He was much disturbed. They could see that something had happened to him. The haughtiness and arrogance was gone from his face. Jesus stood a little way apart from him, sober and silent. The great multitude stood waiting, every man holding his breath and staring at this unfamiliar face of Zacchaeus. And then he spoke, humbly, brokenly. He had decided, he said, to give half of all he owned to feed the poor. To those whom he had defrauded, he would make abundant restitution.'

'But—what had happened?' demanded Marcellus. 'What had Jesus said to him?'

Miriam shook her head.

'Nobody knows,' she murmured; then, with averted, reminiscent eyes, she added, half to herself: 'Maybe he didn't say anything at all. Perhaps he looked Zacchaeus squarely in the eyes until the man saw—reflected there—the image of the person he was meant to be.'

'That is a strange thing to say,' remarked Marcellus. 'I'm afraid I don't understand.'

'Many people had that experience,' said Miriam, softly. 'When Jesus looked directly into your eyes—' She broke off suddenly, and leaned far forward to face him at close range. 'Marcellus,' she went on, in an impressive tone lowered almost to a whisper, 'if you had ever met Jesus—face to face—and he had looked into your eyes until—until you couldn't get away—you would have no trouble believing that he could do *anything—anything he pleased!* If he said, "Put down your crutches!" you would put them down. If he said, "Pay back the money you have stolen!" you would pay it back.'

She closed her eyes and relaxed against the cushions. Her hand, still in his, was trembling a little.

'And if he said, "Now you may sing for joy!" ' ventured Marcellus, 'you would sing?'

Miriam did not open her eyes, but a wisp of a smile curved her lips. After a moment, she sat up with suddenly altered mood, reclaimed her hand, patted her curls, and indicated that she was ready to talk of something far afield.

'Tell me more about this Greek who worked for Benyosef,' she suggested. 'Evidently he too is interested in Jesus, or he wouldn't have had the confidence of the men who meet one another there.'

'It will be easy to talk about Demetrius,' replied Marcellus, 'for he is my closest friend. In appearance he is tall, athletic, handsome. In mind, he is widely informed, with a sound knowledge of the classics. At heart, he is loyal and courageous. As to his conduct, I have never known him to do an unworthy thing.' Marcellus paused for a moment, and went on resolutely. 'When I was seventeen, my father presented Demetrius to me—a birthday gift.'

'But—you said he is your closest friend!' exclaimed Miriam. 'How can that be? Does he not resent being enslaved?'

'No man can be expected to like slavery, Miriam; but, once you have been a slave, there is not very much you could do with your freedom if you achieved it. I have offered Demetrius his liberty. He is free to come and go as he likes.'

'You must have been a good master, Marcellus,' said Miriam, gently.

'Not always. At times—especially during the past year—I have made Demetrius very unhappy. I was moody, restless, wretched, sick.'

'And why was that?' she asked. 'Would you like to tell me?'

'Not on this fair day,' rejoined Marcellus, soberly. 'Besides—I am well now. I need not burden you with it.'

'As you please,' she consented. 'But—how did Demetrius happen to be working in Benyosef's shop?'

'That is a long story, Miriam.'

'You—and your long stories,' she put in, dryly.

Marcellus feigned a wince—and smiled.

'Briefly, then—we were in Athens. Through no fault of his, and in defense of some helpless people, Demetrius engaged in combat with a man who held a position of authority, but had not been advised that a blow delivered by this Greek slave would stun on ox. It was a well-justified battle, albeit one-sided and of short duration. But we thought it prudent for Demetrius to lose no time increasing the distance between himself and the Athenian jail. So—he drifted to Jerusalem, and because he had some knowledge of carding and spinning—'

'And how had he picked that up?' asked Miriam, busy again with her precise stitches.

'At a weaver's shop in Athens. He was studying Aramaic under the weaver's instruction—and made himself useful.'

'Was that where you got your Aramaic, Marcellus?'

'Yes.'

'Did you learn carding and spinning, too?'

'No,' laughed Marcellus. 'Just Aramaic—such as it is.'

'That was in preparation for this tour of Galilee, I think,' ventured Miriam. 'And when you have learned all you wish to know about Jesus—what then?'

'My plans are uncertain.' Marcellus frowned his perplexity. 'I must go back to Rome, though my return is not urgent. Naturally I want to rejoin my family and friends, but—'

Miriam took several little stiches before she looked up to ask, almost inaudibly—'But what?'

'Something tells me I am going to feel quite out of place in Rome,' he confessed. 'I have been much impressed by what I have heard of your brave

Galilean's teachings about human relations. They seem so reasonable, so sensible. If they became popular, we could have a new world. And, Miriam, we must have a new world! Things can't go on this way! Not very much longer!'

Miriam put down her work and gave him her full attention. She had not seen him in such a serious mood before.

'During these past few days,' he went on, 'I have had a chance to look at the world from a different angle. It wasn't that I had never stopped to think about its injustice, its waste, its tragic unhappiness. But—out here in this quiet country—I lie at night, looking up at the stars, and suddenly I recall Rome!—its greed and gluttony at the top; its poverty and degredation growing more and more desperate all the way down to the bottom of damp dungeons and galleys and quarries. And Rome rules the world! The Emperor is a lunatic. The Prince Regent is a scoundrel. They rule the world! Their armies control the wretched lives of millions of people!' He paused, patted a damp brow, and muttered, 'Forgive me, my friend, for haranguing you.'

'Would it not be wonderful,' exclaimed Miriam, 'if Jesus were on the throne?'

'Impossible!' expostulated Marcellus.

'Maybe not,' said Miriam, quietly.

He studied her eyes, wondering if she were really serious, and was amazed at her sober sincerity.

'You can't be in earnest!' he said. 'Besides—Jesus is dead.'

'Are you sure of that?' she asked, without looking up.

'I agree that his teachings are not dead, and something should be done to carry them to as many people as can be reached!'

'Do you intend to tell your friends about him—when you go home?'

Marcellus sighed.

'They would think me crazy.'

'Would your father think you were crazy?'

'He would, indeed! My father is a just man of generous heart, but he has contempt for people who interest themselves in religion. He would be embarrassed—and annoyed, too—if I were to discuss these things with our friends.'

'Might he not think it brave of you?'

'Brave? Not at all! He would think it was in very bad taste!'

Justus and Reuben were sauntering in from the vineyard, much occupied with their low-voiced conversation.

'How long will you be here, Marcellus?' asked Miriam, with undisguised concern. 'Will I see you again; tomorrow, maybe?'

'Not tomorrow. We go to Capernaum tomorrow, Justus says. He wants me to meet an old man named Nathanael. Ever hear of him?'

'Of course! You will like him. But you are coming back to Cana, aren't you, before you return to Jerusalem?'

'I'd like to.'

'Please. Now you let me have a word with Justus, alone; will you?'

'Justus,' said Marcellus, as the men approached, 'I shall go back to the village, and meet you there at your convenience.'

He offered his hand to Reuben, who clasped it cordially. Evidently Justus had given Reuben a friendly account of him.

'Good-bye, Miriam,' he said, taking her hand. 'I shall see you next week.'

'Good-bye, Marcellus,' she said. 'I shall be looking for you.' The bearded Galilean stood by and watched them exchange a lingering look. Reuben frowned a little, as if the situation perplexed him. The frown said that Reuben didn't want his girl hurt. This Roman would go away and forget all about her, but Miriam would remember.

'You're coming back this way, then,' said Reuben to Justus, as Marcellus moved away.

'It seems so.' Justus grinned.

'Let me tell Naomi that you will tarry and break bread with us,' said Reuben.

When they were alone, Miriam motioned to Justus to sit down beside her.

'Why don't you tell Marcellus everything?' she asked. 'He is deeply concerned. It seems he knows so little. He was in Jerusalem and attended the trial at the Insula, heard Jesus sentenced to death, and knows that he was crucified. And that is all. So far as he is aware, the story of Jesus ended that day. Why haven't you told him?'

'I intend to, Miriam, when he is prepared to hear it. He would not believe it if I were to tell him now.' Justus moved closer and lowered his voice. 'I thought perhaps you would tell him.'

'I almost did. Then I wondered if you might not have some reason—unknown to me—for keeping it a secret. I think Marcellus has a right to know everything now. He thinks it such a pity that no plans have been made to interest people in Jesus' teachings. Can't you tell him about the work they are doing in Jerusalem—and Joppa—and Caesarea? He hasn't the faintest idea of what is going on!'

'Very well,' nodded Justus. 'I shall tell him—everything.'

'Today!' urged Miriam.

'Tell me truly, daughter,' said Justus, soberly. 'Are you losing your heart to this foreigner?'

Miriam took several small, even stitches before she looked up into his brooding eyes.

'Marcellus doesn't seem a bit foreign to me,' she said, softly.

* * * * * *

Aimlessly sauntering back to the tent Marcellus began sorting over the homespun he had accumulated, wondering what he should do with it. Now that there was no longer any reason for pretending an interest in such merchandise, the articles already purchased were of no value to him. The thought occurred—and gave him pleasure—that he might take them to Miriam. She would be glad to see that they were distributed among the poor.

He took up a black robe and held it against the light. It was of good wool and well woven. He had paid twenty shekels for it. Fifteen would have been enough, but the woman was poor. Besides, he had been trying to make a favorable impression on Justus by dealing generously with his fellow countrymen.

With nothing better to entertain him, Marcellus sat down on the edge of his cot, with the robe in his hands, and indulged in some leisurely theorizing on the indeterminate value of this garment. If you computed the amount of skilled labor invested by the woman who wove it, on a basis of an adequate wage per hour for such experienced workmanship, the robe was easily worth thirty shekels. But not in Sepphoris, where she lived; for the local market was not active. In Sepphoris it was worth twelve shekels. A stranger would have been asked fifteen. Marcellus had made it worth twenty. Now it wasn't worth anything!

He would give it to Miriam, who had no use for it, and it still wouldn't be worth anything until she had donated it to someone who needed it. At that juncture, the robe would begin to take on some value again, though just how much would be difficult to estimate. If the man who received this excellent robe should be inspired by it to wash his hands and face and mend his torn sandals—thereby increasing public confidence in his character, and enabling him to find employment at a better wage—the robe might eventually turn out to be worth more than its original cost. If the man who received it was a lazy scalawag, he might sell it for whatever it would fetch, which wouldn't be much; for no person of any substance would want—at any price—a garment that had been in the possession of this probably verminous tramp. You could amuse yourself all day with speculations concerning the shifting values of material things.

Marcellus had been doing an unusual amount of new thinking, these past few days, on the subject of property. According to Justus, Jesus had had much to say about a man's responsibility as a possessor of material things. Hoarded things might easily become a menace; a mere fire-and-theft risk; a breeding-ground for destructive insects; a source of worry. Men would have plenty of anxieties, but there was no sense in accumulating worries over *things!* That kind of worry destroyed your character. Even an unused coat, hanging in your closet; it wasn't merely a useless thing that did nobody any good; it was an active agent of destruction to your life. And your *life* must be saved, at all costs. What would it advantage a man—Jesus had demanded—if he were to gain the whole world—and lose his own life?

A bit bewildered by this statement, Marcellus had inquired:

'What did he mean, Justus, about the importance of saving your own life? He didn't seem to be much worried about losing his! He could have saved it if he had promised Pilate and the priests that he would go home and say nothing more to the people about his beliefs.'

'Well, sir'—Justus had tried to explain—'Jesus didn't mean quite the same thing that you have in mind when he talked about a man's life. You see—Jesus wasn't losing his life when they crucified him, but he would have lost it if he had recanted and gone home. Do you understand what I mean, Marcellus?'

'No—I can't say that I do. To speak that way about life is simply trifling with the accepted definition of the word. I believe that when a man is dead, he has lost his life; perhaps lost it in a good cause; perhaps still living—for a little while—in the memory of those who believed in him and cherished his friendship. But if our human speech is of any use at all, a man who is dead has lost his life.'

'Not necessarily,' protested Justus. 'Not if his soul is still alive. Jesus said we need have no fear of the things that kill the body. We should fear only the things that kill the soul.' And when Marcellus had shrugged impatiently, Justus had continued, 'The body isn't very important; just a vehicle; just a kit of tools—to serve the soul.' He had chuckled over Marcellus' expression of disgust. 'You think that sounds crazy; don't you?' he added, gently.

'Of course!' Marcellus had shrugged. 'And so do you!'

'I admit it's not easy to believe,' conceded Justus.

And then Marcellus had stopped in the road—they were on their way from Sepphoris to Cana—and had delivered what for him was a long speech.

'Justus,' he began, 'I must tell you candidly that while I am much interested in the sensible philosophy of your dead friend Jesus, I hope you will not want to report any more statements of that nature. I have a sincere respect for this man's mind, and I don't wish to lose it.'

He had half-expected Justus to be glum over this rebuke, but the big fellow had only grinned and nodded indulgently.

'I didn't mean to be offensive,' said Marcellus.

'I am not troubled,' said Justus, cordially. 'It was my fault. I was going too fast for you; offering you meat when you should have milk.'

* * * * * *

He tossed the black robe aside and examined a white shawl with a fringe. He couldn't imagine his mother wearing it, but the woman who had made it had been proud of her handiwork. He remembered how reluctant she was to see it go out of her little house, down on the Samaritan border somewhere. She should have been permitted to keep the shawl. It meant more to her than it could possibly mean to anyone else. Such things should never be sold; or bought, either. Marcellus recalled the feeling of self-reproach he had often experienced at lavish banquets in Rome where the wines were cooled with ice that had been brought from the northern mountains by relays of runners who sometimes died of exhaustion. No honest man could afford such wine. It had cost too much.

Well—he would give all of these garments to Miriam. She would put them to good use. But—wouldn't it be rather ungracious to let Miriam know that these things, fabricated with great care by her own fellow countrymen, weren't worth carrying away?

'But they are gifts,' he would say to Miriam. 'The people who receive them will be advantaged.'

And then Miriam would have a right to say, though she probably wouldn't, 'How can they be gifts, Marcellus, when they are only useless things that you don't want to be bothered with?'

And then, assuming that Miriam had said that, he could reply:

'But so far as the people are concerned who get these things, they would be gifts; wouldn't you say?'

'No,' he thought she might reply, 'they would never be gifts. You see, Marcellus—' And then she would go on to explain again how Jesus had felt about gifts.

He pitched the heavy white shawl back onto the pile of homespun and glanced up to see a tall, lean, rugged-faced fellow standing at the door of the tent. The visitor grinned amiably and Marcellus invited him to come in. He eased himself down on a camp-stool, crossed his long legs, and said his name was Hariph.

'Doubtless you came to see Justus,' said Marcellus, cordially. 'He is at Reuben's house. If you call this afternoon, I think he will be here.'

Hariph nodded, but made no move to go; sat slowly swinging his pendent foot and nursing his elbows on his knee while he candidly surveyed the furniture of the tent, the heap of homespun, and the urbane stranger from Rome.

'I think I have heard Justus speak of you,' said Marcellus, feeling that if Hariph meant to stay awhile some conversation might be appropriate. 'You are a potter, I believe. You make water-jars—and wine-jars—and things like that.'

Hariph nodded and the grin widened a little.

'Tell me,' went on Marcellus, hopefully, 'is it customary to use the same sort of jar either for wine or water?'

'Oh, yes, sir,' replied Hariph, with deliberate professional dignity. 'Many do that. Water or wine—it's all the same. Oil, too. Same pot.'

'But I suppose that after you've had oil in a pot, you wouldn't want to put wine in it,' observed Marcellus, sensibly enough, he thought.

'No—that wouldn't be so good,' agreed Hariph. 'The wine would taste of oil.'

'The same thing might be true, I daresay, of water in a jar that had held wine,' pursued Marcellus. 'The water might taste like wine.'

Hariph stopped swinging his foot and gazed squintingly toward the street, the fine lines on his temple deepening. Marcellus surmised that the town gossip was trying to decide whether it would be prudent to discuss the matter. After some delay, he turned to his young host and gratified him by saying:

'Did Justus tell you?'

'Yes.'

'Did you believe it?' asked Hariph.

'No,' replied Marcellus, firmly. 'I should be much interested in hearing what you think about it.'

'Well, sir,' rejoined Hariph, 'we ran out of wine at the wedding of my daughter Anna, and when Jesus came he made wine—out of water. I don't know how. I just know that he did it.'

'Did you taste it?'

'Yes, sir. I never tasted wine like that—before or since.'

'What was it—a heavy, potent wine?'

'N-no, sir.' Hariph screwed up his face indecisively. 'It was of a delicate flavor.'

'Red?' queried Marcellus.

'White,' remembered Hariph.

'White as water?'

'Yes, sir.' Hariph's eyes collided briefly with Marcellus' dry smile, and drifted away. Nothing further was said for a long moment.

'I am told that everyone was very fond of Jesus,' remarked Marcellus.

'Indeed they were, sir!' responded Hariph. 'He came late, that day. You should have seen them when he appeared; the shouts of greeting; many leaving their places to crowd about him. It was so, wherever he went, sir. Nobody had eyes for anyone else.'

'Had you ever kept wine in those jars, Hariph?' asked Marcellus.

'Yes, sir,' admitted Hariph.

Marcellus nodded his head slowly and grinned.

'Well—thank you for telling me,' he said. 'I was almost sure there must be an explanation.' He rose, significantly. 'I am glad you called, Hariph. Shall I tell Justus you will be back later?'

Hariph had not risen. His face was perplexed.

'If it was only that one thing, sir,' he said, quite unaffected by his dismissal—'if it had been only that one time—'

Marcellus sat down again and gave respectful attention.

'But—from that day on, sir,' continued Hariph, deliberately, 'there were many strange happenings.'

'So I have heard,' admitted Marcellus. 'Let me ask you: did you see any of these mysterious things done, or did you just learn about them from others? Strange stories always grow in the telling, you know.'

'Has anyone told you,' asked Hariph, 'how Jesus fed a crowd of five thousand people when he had nothing but a little basketful of bread and a couple of smoked fish?'

'No,' said Marcellus, eagerly. 'Tell me, please.'

'Perhaps Justus will tell you, if you ask him. He was there. He was closer to it—when it happened.'

'Were you there, Hariph?'

'Yes—but I was rather far back in the crowd.'

'Well, tell me what you saw. I shall be much interested in your view of it. Where did all this happen?"

'It wasn't so very long after our wedding. Jesus had begun going about through the villages, talking with the people, and large crowds were following him.'

'Because of what he said?' interposed Marcellus.

'Partly—but mostly because of the reports that he was healing all manner of diseases, and giving blind men their sight, and—'

'Do you believe that—about the blind men?'

'Yes, sir!' declared Hariph. 'I saw one man who could see as well as you can, sir.'

'Had you known him before?'

'No, sir,' confessed Hariph. 'But his neighbors said he had been blind for years.'

'Did you know them—his neighbors?'

'No, sir. They were from down around Sychar.'

'That kind of testimony,' observed Marcellus, judicially, 'wouldn't get very far in a court of law; but you must have some good reason for believing it. . . . Well—go on, please, about the strange feast.'

'Always there were big crowds following him,' continued Hariph, undismayed by the Roman's incredulity. 'And sometimes they weren't easy to handle. Everybody wanted to be close enough to see these wonderful things happen; and you never could tell when it would be. It's no small matter, sir'—Hariph interrupted himself to comment—'when one of your own neighbors, as you might say, who had grown up with the other youngsters of his village, and had worked at a carpenter's bench, takes to talking as nobody else had ever talked; and stopping in the middle of a speech to point his finger at some old man who might be standing in the front row, with his mouth open and both hands cupped behind his ears, trying to hear—and suddenly the old man yells "Ahhh!"—and begins dancing up and down, shouting, "I can hear! I can hear! I can hear!" And Jesus wouldn't have stopped talking: he would just point at the man—and he could hear!'

'Did you ever see Jesus do that, Hariph?' demanded Marcellus.

'No, sir—but there were plenty who did; people whose word you could trust, too!'

'Very well,' consented Marcellus, indulgently. 'Now tell me about the feeding of the five thousand people. You say you saw that?'

'It was this way, sir. It all began over in Capernaum. A lot of strange things had happened, and the news had spread abroad until a great crowd had collected, a disorderly crowd it was; for nobody was trying to keep them from pushing and jostling and tramping on one another.'

'It's a wonder they didn't call out the legionaries,' said Marcellus. 'There's a fort at Capernaum.'

'Yes—and many of the soldiers were there; but I don't think the priests and elders of the city wanted the crowd to be kept in order. They probably hoped something would happen, a bad accident, maybe, so that Jesus could be arrested for disturbing the peace.'

'But didn't he have a few close friends who might have demanded the people to cease this confusion?'

'Yes, sir—Jesus had many close friends. He named twelve of them to be known as his disciples. But they had no authority to give orders to that big crowd. They were really beside themselves to know what to do. Reuben and I had gone over to Capernaum—like everybody else—to see what was going on. When we arrived, the people were milling about in the central plaza. I never was in such a press, sir! Men and women with sick children in their arms, being pushed roughly in the swaying pack. Blind men. Half-dead people on cots, carried by their friends. There were even lepers in the crowd.' Hariph chuckled grimly. 'Nobody jostled *them!*'

'It's a wonder they weren't arrested,' put in Marcellus.

'Well, sir,' drawled Hariph, 'when a leper is out on his own, not even a legionary is anxious to lay hands on him. And you couldn't blame the poor lepers, sir. They hoped to be healed, too.'

'Is Jesus supposed to have healed lepers, Hariph?' Marcellus' tone was loaded with doubt.

'Yes, sir. . . . Well, when the crowd became unmanageable, Jesus began retreating down toward the shore. Several of his disciples had run on ahead and engaged a boat. And before the people realized what was happening, Jesus and his twelve closest friends were pulling away from the beach.'

'Wasn't that a rather heartless thing to do?' queried Marcellus.

'He had tried to talk to them, sir, but there was too much confusion. You see—the people who crowded in about him hadn't come to hear him talk, but to witness some strange thing. They wouldn't even give way to the cripples or the blind or the very sick ones borne on cots. And then, too, Jesus had just received bad news. One of his best friends, whom old Herod Antipas had thrown into prison, had just been beheaded. Word of it came to Jesus while he was trying to deal with that unruly mob. You can't blame him, sir, for wanting to get away.'

'Quite to the contrary, Hariph!' declared Marcellus. 'It's gratifying to hear that he could be puzzled about something. It was lucky that there was a boat available. Was the crowd enraged?'

'Oh—they behaved each according to his own temper,' remembered Hariph. 'Some shook their fists and shouted imprecations. Some shook their heads and turned away. Some wept. Some stood still and said nothing, as they watched the boat growing smaller.'

'And what did you and Reuben do?'

'Well, sir—we decided to go home. And then somebody noticed that the boat was veering toward the north. A great shout went up, and the people began racing toward the beach. It seemed likely that the party in the boat was making for some place up in the neighborhood of Bethsaida.'

'How far was that?' inquired Marcellus.

'For the boat—about six miles. For the crowd—nearly nine. It was a hot day and rough going. That country up there is mostly desert. But everybody went, or so it seemed. It was a singular sight, sir, that long procession stumbling over the stones and through the dried weeds. It was far past midday when we found them.'

'Did Jesus seem annoyed when the crowd arrived?'

'No—just sorry,' murmured Hariph. 'His face was sad. The people were so very tired. They weren't pushing one another—not after that trip!' He laughed a little at the recollection.

'Did he chide them for the way they behaved in Capernaum?'

'No, sir. He didn't say anything for a long time. The people flung themselves down to rest. Justus told me afterward that Simon urged Jesus to talk to them, but he wanted to wait until all of them had arrived; for some were carrying their sick, and were far behind. He didn't speak a word until they were all there. And then he stood up and began to talk. He did not reprove us for trailing him to this place, nor did he have aught to say of the people's rudeness. He talked about all of us being neighbors. We were all one family. Everyone was very quiet. There wasn't a sound—but the voice of Jesus. And remember, sir; there were five thousand people in that crowd!' Hariph's chin twitched involuntarily. He cleared his throat. Marcellus studied his face soberly.

'I am not one to weep easily, sir,' he went on, huskily. 'But there was something about those words that brought the tears. There we were—nothing but a great crowd of little children—tired and worn out—and here was a man—the only man there—and all the rest of us nothing but quarrelsome, stingy, greedy, little children. His voice was very calm, but—if you can believe me, sir—his words were as ointment on our wounds. While he talked, I was saying to myself, "I have never lived! I have never known how to live! This man has the words of life!" It was as if God Himself were speaking, sir! Everybody was much moved. Men's faces were strained and their tears were flowing.' Hariph wiped his eyes with the backs of his hands.

'After a while,' he continued, brokenly, 'Jesus stopped talking and motioned to some who had carried a sick man all that long way, and they brought their burden and put it down at Jesus' feet. He said something to the sick man. I could not hear what it was. And the sick man got up! And so did everybody else—as if Jesus had suddenly pulled us all to our feet. And everyone drew a gasp of wonder!' Hariph grinned pensively and faced Marcellus directly with childishly entreating eyes. 'Do you believe what I am telling you, sir?'

'It is difficult, Hariph,' said Marcellus, gently. 'But I think you believe what you are saying. Perhaps there is some explanation.'

'That may be, sir,' said Hariph, politely. 'And then there were many, many others who went to Jesus to be healed of their diseases; not jostling to be first, but waiting their turn.' He hesitated for a moment, embarrassed. 'But I shall not weary you with that,' he went on, 'seeing you do not believe.'

'You were going to tell me how he fed them,' prompted Marcellus.

'Yes, sir. It was growing late in the afternoon. I had been so moved by the things I had heard and seen that I had not thought of being hungry. Reuben and I, knowing there would be nothing out there to eat, had stopped at a market-booth in Capernaum and had bought some bread and cured fish. In any other kind of crowd, we would have eaten our luncheon. But now that we had begun to feel hungry, I was ashamed to eat what I had before the faces of the men about me; for, as I have said, Jesus had been talking about us all being of one family, and how we ought to share what we had with one another. I should have been willing to divide with the man next to me; but I didn't have much more than enough for myself. So—I didn't eat; nor did Reuben.'

'I daresay there were plenty of men in the crowd who faced the same dilemma,' surmised Marcellus.

'Well—the disciples were around Jesus telling him he had better dismiss the people, so they could go to the little villages and buy food. Justus told me afterward that Jesus only shook his head and told them that the people would be fed. They were much bewildered and worried. There was a small boy, sitting very close and overhearing this talk. He had a little basket, his own lunch, not very much; just enough to feed a boy. He went to Jesus with his basket and said he was willing to share what he had.'

Marcellus' eyes lighted, and he leaned forward attentively.

'Go on!' he demanded. 'This is wonderful.'

'Yes—it really was wonderful, sir. Jesus took the basket and held it up for the people to see. And then he told how the boy wanted to share his food with all of the people. And he looked up and thanked God for the little boy's gift. It was very, very quiet, sir. Then he began breaking the small loaves into bits, and the fish he tore into little shreds; and he gave these fragments to his disciples and told them to feed the people.'

'Did the crowd laugh?' asked Marcellus.

'Well—no, sir. We didn't laugh, though almost everyone smiled over such a big crowd being fed on almost nothing, as you might say. As I told you, I had been ashamed to bring out the food I had, and now I was ashamed not to; so I unwrapped my bread and fish, and broke off a piece, and offered it to the man next to me.'

'Wonderful!' shouted Marcellus. 'Was he glad to get it?'

'He had some of his own,' said Hariph, adding, quickly, 'But there were plenty of people who did not have any food along with them, sir. And everyone was fed, that day! After it was over, they gathered up a dozen basketfuls of fragments, left over.'

'It sounds as if some other people, besides you and Reuben, had had the forethought to bring some provisions along,' speculated Marcellus. 'They probably wouldn't have gone out into the desert with empty baskets. This is really a marvelous story, Hariph!'

'You believe it, sir?' Hariph was happily surprised.

'Indeed I do! And I believe it was a miracle! Jesus had inspired those stingy, selfish people to be decent to one another! It takes a truly great man to make one harmonious family out of a crowd like that! I can't understand the healing, Hariph; but I believe in the feeding! And I'm glad you wanted to tell me!'

Chapter XVI

They were on the way from Cana to Capernaum. All day their narrow road had been gaining altitude, not without occasional dips into shallow valleys, but tending upward toward a lofty plateau where the olive-green terrain met an azure sky set with masses of motionless white clouds.

It had been a fatiguing journey, with many pauses for rest, and as the shadows slanted farther to the east, the two men trudged the steepening grade in silence, leaving the little pack-train far behind. They were nearing the top now. Justus had promised that they would make camp in the lee of the great rock they had sighted two hours ago. There was a cool spring, he said, and plenty of forage. He hoped they would find the spot untenanted. Yes—he knew the place well. He had camped there many times. There was a splendid view. Jesus had loved it.

Throughout this tour of Galilee, Marcellus had paid very little attention to the physical characteristics of the province. Until now, the landscape had been unremarkable, and he had been fully preoccupied by the strange business that had brought him here. Marcellus had but one interest in this otherwise undistinguished land of rock-strewn fields, tiny vineyards, and apathetic villages drowsing in the dust around an ancient well. He was concerned only about a mysterious man who had walked these winding roads, a little while ago, with crowds of thousands surging about him.

It was not easy today, on this sleepy old highway, to picture either the number or the temper of that multitude. The people must have come from long distances, most of them, for this country was not thickly populated. Nor was it easy to imagine the confusion, the jostling, the shouting. Such Galileans as Marcellus had seen were not emotional, not responsive; a bit stolid, indeed.

That weary, weather-beaten woman, leaning on her hoe, in the frowsy little garden they had just passed—had she, too, bounded out of her kitchen, leaving their noonday pottage on the fire, to join in that curious throng?

This bearded man in the meadow—her husband, obviously; now sluggishly mowing wisps of grass with his great-grandfather's scythe—had he run panting to the edge of the crowd, trying to scramble through the sweating pack for a glimpse of the face of Jesus?

It was almost incredible that this silent, solemn, stodgy province could ever have been haled out of its age-long lethargy and stirred to such a pitch of excitement. Even Justus, looking back upon it all, could only shake his shaggy head and mutter that the whole affair was quite beyond comprehension. You could think what you liked about the miracles, reflected Justus, soberly: many of the people were hysterical and had reported all manner of strange occurrences, some of which had never been satisfactorily confirmed. The air had been full of wild rumors, Justus said. A few Nazarenes had been quoted as remembering that when Jesus was a lad, at play with them, he had fashioned birds of clay, and the birds had come to life and had flown away. You could hear such tales by the score, and they had confused the public's estimate of Jesus, making him seem a mountebank in the opinion of many intelligent people.

But these passionate throngs of thousands who followed, day after day, indifferent to their hunger and discomfort—all Galilee knew that this was true because all Galilee had participated. You might have good reasons for doubting the validity of some of these miracle stories, but you couldn't doubt this one! Obscure little Galilee, so slow and stupid that its bucolic habits and uncouth dialect were stock jokes in Judea, had suddenly come alive! Its dull work was abandoned. Everybody talking at once! Everybody shouting questions which nobody tried to answer! Camels were left standing in their harness, hitched to water-wheels. Shuttles were left, midway of the open warp. Tools lay scattered on the floor of the carpenter shop. Plows stopped in the furrow. Fires burned out in the brick-kiln. Everybody took to the road, on foot, on donkeys, on carts, on crutches. Helpless invalids who couldn't be left were bundled up on stretchers and carried along. Nothing mattered but to follow the young man who looked into your eyes and made you well—or ashamed—or tightened your throat with longing for his calm strength and floral purity.

Now the bright light had gone out. The great crowds had scattered. The inspired young man was dead. Galilee had gone back to sleep. It was a lonesome land. Perhaps the Galileans themselves were now conscious of its loneliness, after having briefly experienced this unprecedented activity.

Marcellus wished he knew how much of Jesus' influence still remained alive. Of course, you could depend upon a few of them—those who had known him best and owed him much—to remember and remember until they died; people like Miriam. Or were there any more like Miriam? Justus had said that some of these Galileans had been completely transformed, almost as if they had been born again. Certain men of low estate had learned new occupations. Certain beggars had become productive. A few publicans had become respected citizens. Women who had been known as common scolds were going about doing deeds of kindness. But perhaps the majority had been unable to hold on to their resolutions. He must press Justus for some more information about that.

Now they had arrived at the top of the terrain, every step adding depth to the view. Far to the north lay a range of snow-capped mountains. A few steps farther on, and the distant turrets and domes of a modern city glistened in the declining sun. There was no need to inquire its name: it had to be Tiberias. Marcellus lengthened his stride to keep pace with Justus who was moving swiftly toward the northern rim, turning his head from side to side, and peering intently in all directions, as if he had expected to meet a friend up here.

Suddenly the whole breath-taking panorama was spread before them and Marcellus had his first sight of the deep-blue lake that had figured so much in his guide's conversation. It had been around this little sea that Jesus had spent most of his days. Justus dropped wearily to the ground, folded his arms, and sat in silent contemplation of the scene. Marcellus, a little way apart, reclined on his elbows. Far in the distance was a slanting sail. All along the shoreline, flat-roofed villages straggled down to the water's edge.

After a long interval, Marcellus stirred.

'So—this is the Sea of Galilee!' he said, half to himself.

Justus nodded slowly. Presently he pointed to the farthest settlement that could be seen.

'Capernaum,' he said. 'Eight miles.'

'I daresay this lake has some tender memories for you, Justus,' remarked Marcellus. 'Tell me,' he went on, with a slow gesture that swept the landscape, 'has the general behavior of those people been greatly altered by the career of Jesus?'

'It is hard to say,' replied Justus. 'They do not talk much about it. They are afraid. The Roman fort is close by. One could easily get into trouble by asking questions. One only knows what has happened in the lives of one's friends. I expect to visit some of them while we are here.'

'Will I see them?' inquired Marcellus, doubtfully.

'Not many,' said Justus, frankly. 'You will see old Bartholomew, as I told you. He has a story I want you to hear. Bartholomew will not be afraid to talk to you, after I assure him it will be safe.' He turned about and faced Marcellus with a reminiscent smile. 'You might be interested in knowing how Jesus and Bartholomew first met. The old man was sitting out in his little fig orchard, one morning, when Jesus and Philip passed the house. And Jesus cheerily waved a hand and said, "Peace be upon you, Nathanael!"'

'I thought his name was Bartholomew,' put in Marcellus.

'That's the amusing part of it,' chuckled Justus. 'It is not customary with us to call venerable men by their given names. I don't suppose old Bartholomew had heard himself called Nathanael for at least twoscore years. And here was this young stranger taking an immense liberty with him.'

'Was he offended?' asked Marcellus, with a grin.

'Well—perhaps not seriously offended, but certainly astonished. He called Jesus to come to him, perhaps intending to take him to task for what looked like a bit of impudence. Philip told me the story. He said that old Bartholomew was looking stern as he waited for Jesus to approach. Then his eyes widened and softened; and he smiled and said, "You knew my name." "Yes," replied Jesus, "and because it means 'Godgiven' it is fitting, for you are an Israelite of high integrity."'

'That should have pleased the old man,' observed Marcellus.

'It did,' said Justus, soberly. 'It made him a disciple.'

'You mean—he came along—and followed after Jesus?'

'Yes. There was something strange about that. The old man had long since taken to his chair in the garden, thinking his active days were ended. But he got up and went along with Jesus—and he rarely left his side for nearly three years.'

'His vigor was restored?' Marcellus' face showed disbelief.

'No—he was still an old man. It was hard work for him to keep up with the others. He got very weary indeed, and he wheezed and panted like any other hard-pressed old man—'

'But he came along,' assisted Marcellus.

'Yes—Bartholomew came along. No one else would have ventured to call him Nathanael—but Jesus did, invariably. And Bartholomew liked it.'

'Perhaps Jesus did that to keep the old man going,' suggested Marcellus. 'Maybe it made him feel younger.'

'Well—it wasn't only Bartholomew who felt young and immature in the company of Jesus.' Justus frowned and stroked his beard, his habit when groping for an elusive memory. 'With the exception of John, all of the close friends and disciples of Jesus were older than he—but he was our senior—by years and years. Sometimes, after we had slipped away for an hour's rest, he would say, "Come, children: we must be on our way." But no one smiled—or thought it peculiar.'

'He seemed remote?' asked Marcellus.

Justus deliberately pondered a reply, then shook his head.

'No—not remote. He was companionable. You wanted to get closer to him—as if for protection. I think that's why the people were always crowding about him—until he hardly had room to move.'

'That must have put him under a great strain,' said Marcellus. 'Didn't he ever seem weary?'

'Very, very weary!' remarked Justus. 'But he never protested. Sometimes men would brace a shoulder against the crowd and push their way in, knocking others off their footing, but I can't recall that he ever rebuked anyone for it. . . . Marcellus, did you ever see a flock of little chickens climbing over one another to get under the hen's wings? Well—the hen doesn't seem to notice; just holds out her feathers, and lets them scramble in. That was his attitude. And that was our relation to him.'

'Very strange!' murmured Marcellus, abstractedly. 'But I think—I understand—what you mean,' he added, as from a distance.

'You couldn't!' declared Justus. 'You think you understand—but—you would have had to know Jesus to comprehend what I am saying. Some of us were old enough to have been his father—but we were just—just little chickens! Take Simon, for example. Simon was always the leader among the disciples. I hope you meet him when you go back to Jerusalem. Simon is a very forceful, capable man. Whenever Jesus happened to be absent from us, for an hour, Simon was far and away the big man of the company, everyone deferring to him. But—when Jesus would rejoin us'—Justus grinned, pursed his lips, and slowly shook his head—'Simon was just a little boy; just a humble, helpless little boy! A little chicken!'

'And Bartholomew—he was a little chicken, too?'

'Well,' deliberated Justus, 'not quite in the same way, perhaps. Bartholomew never expressed his opinions so freely as Simon when Jesus was away from us. He didn't have quite so far to drop—as Simon. It was amazing how much fatigue the old fellow could endure. He attended the last supper they had together on the night Jesus was betrayed. But when the news came in that the Master had been arrested, it was too much for Bartholomew. He was very sick. They put him to bed. By the time he recovered—it was all over.' Justus closed his eyes, sighed deeply, and an expression of pain swept his face. 'It was all over,' his lips repeated, soundlessly.

'He must be quite infirm, by this time,' said Marcellus, anxious to lift the gloom.

'About the same,' said Justus. 'Not much older. Not much weaker.' He grinned a little. 'Bartholomew has a queer idea now. He thinks he may never die. He sits all day in the fig orchard, when the weather is fair.'

'Looking up the road, perhaps,' speculated Marcellus—'and wishing he might see Jesus again, coming to visit him.'

Justus had been gazing down at the lake. Now he turned his eyes quickly toward Marcellus and stared into his face. After a rather tense moment, which left Marcellus somewhat bewildered, Justus returned his gaze to the lake.

'That is exactly what old Bartholomew does,' he murmured. 'All day long. He sits—watching the road.'

'Old men get strange fancies,' commented Marcellus.

'You don't have to be old,' said Justus, 'to get strange fancies.'

The little caravan, which had lagged on the last steep climb, now shuffled over the shoulder of the hill. Jonathan came running across, and snuggled down beside Justus.

'When do we have supper, Grandfather?' he wheedled.

'Quite soon, son,' answered Justus, gently. 'Go and help the boy unload. We will join you presently.' Little Jonathan scampered away.

'The lad seems in quite good spirits today,' observed Marcellus.

'That's Miriam's work,' declared Justus. 'She had a long talk with Jonathan yesterday. I think we need not worry about him now.'

'That conversation must have been worth hearing,' said Marcellus.

'Jonathan didn't seem inclined to talk about it,' said Justus, 'but he was deeply impressed. You noticed how quiet he was, last night.'

'I doubt whether there is another young woman—of Miriam's sort—in the whole world!' announced Marcellus, soberly.

'There is a widow in Capernaum,' said Justus. 'Perhaps you may have an opportunity to meet her. She spends all of her time with the very poor who have sickness in their houses. Her name is Lydia. You might be interested in her story.'

'Tell me, please.' Marcellus sat up and gave attention.

'Lydia lost her husband, Ahira, while still quite a young woman. I do not know how it is in your country, but with us the predicament of a young widow is serious. She goes into retirement. Lydia was one of the most beautiful girls in Capernaum so everyone said. Ahira had been a man of considerable wealth, and their home was in keeping with his fortune. Shortly after his death, Lydia became grievously afflicted with an ailment peculiar to women, and gradually declined until her beauty faded. Her family was most sympathetic. At great expense, they summoned the best physicians. They carried her to many healing springs. But nothing availed to check her wasting disease. The time came when it was with great difficulty that she could move about in her room. And now the whole country began to be stirred by reports of strange things that Jesus had done for many sick people.' Justus hesitated, seemingly in doubt as to his procedure with the story. Marcellus waited with mounting curiosity.

'I think I had better tell you,' continued Justus, 'that it wasn't always easy for substantial people to have an interview with Jesus. As for the poor, they had no caste to lose. Most of them were in the habit of begging favors, and were not reticent about crowding in wherever they thought it it might be to their advantage. But men and women in better circumstances—no matter how much they wanted to see Jesus—found it very hard to put down their natural pride and push into that clamorous multitude. Jesus regretted this matter. Often and often, he consented to talk alone with important men, late in the night, when he sorely needed his rest.'

'Men who wanted to be privately cured of something?' asked Marcellus.

'Doubtless—but I know of some cases in which very influential men, who had no malady at all, invited Jesus into their homes for a long conference. Once we waited at the gate of Nicodemus ben Gorion, the most widely known lawyer of this region, until the cocks crew in the early morning. And there was nothing the matter with Nicodemus; at least, nothing physical.'

'Do you suppose he was warning Jesus to cease his work?' wondered Marcellus.

'No. Nicodemus came out with him, that night, as far as the gate. Jesus was talking earnestly to him. When they parted, each man laid a hand on the other's shoulder. We only do that with social equals. Well—as I had meant to say—it would have taken a lot of courage for a gently bred woman of means to have invaded the crowd that thronged about Jesus.'

'That's quite understandable,' agreed Marcellus.

'One day, when Jesus was speaking in the public plaza in Capernaum, a well-to-do man named Jairus pushed his way through the crowd. The people made way for him when someone spoke his name. It was plain to see that he was greatly excited. He went directly to Jesus and said that his little daughter was sick unto death. Would Jesus come at once? Without asking any questions, Jesus consented, and they started down the principal street, the crowd growing larger as they went. When they passed Lydia's house, she watched them from the window, and saw Jairus, whom she knew, walking at Jesus' side.'

'Where were you, Justus?' asked Marcellus. 'You seem quite familiar with these details.'

'As it happened, it was in the neighborhood of Lydia's house that I joined the crowd. I had come with a message for Simon, who had serious illness at home. His wife's mother was sick, and had become suddenly worse. I was as close to Jesus as I am to you when this thing happened. I don't suppose Lydia would have attempted it if she hadn't seen Jairus in the throng. That must have given her confidence. Summoning all her poor strength, she ran down the steps and into that crowd, desperately forced her way through, and struggled on until she was almost at Jesus' side. Then, her courage must have failed her; for, instead of trying to speak to him, she reached out and touched his Robe. I think she was frightened at her own audacity. She turned quickly and began forcing her way out.'

'Why didn't some of you call Jesus' attention to her?' asked Marcellus.

'Well'—defended Justus—'there was a great deal of confusion—and it all happened so quickly—and then she was gone. But, instantly, Jesus stopped and turned about. "Who touched me?" he demanded.'

'You mean—he felt that contact—through his Robe?' exclaimed Marcellus.

Justus nodded—and went on.

'Simon and Philip reminded him that there were so many crowding about. Almost any of them might have brushed against him. But he wasn't satisfied with that. And while he stood there, questioning them, we heard this woman's shrill cry. They opened the way for her to come to him. It must have been a very trying moment for Lydia. She had lived such a sheltered life. The crowd grew suddenly quiet.'

Justus' voice was husky as he recovered the scene.

'I saw many pathetic sights, through those days,' he continued, 'but none more moving. Lydia came slowly, with her head bowed and her hands over her eyes. She knelt on the ground before Jesus and confessed that she was the one who had touched him. Then she lifted her eyes, with the tears running down her cheeks, and cried, "Master! I have been healed of my affliction!" '

Overcome by his emotions, Justus stopped to wipe his eyes on his sleeve. Steadying his voice with an effort, he went on:

'Everyone was deeply touched. The people were all in tears. Jairus was weeping like a child. Even Jesus, who was always well controlled, was so moved that his eyes were swimming as he looked down into Lydia's face. Marcellus—that woman gazed up at him as if she were staring into a blinding sunshine. Her body was shaking with sobs, but her face was enraptured! It was beautiful!'

'Please go on,' insisted Marcellus, when Justus fell silent.

'It was a very tender moment,' he said, thickly. 'Jesus gave her both of his hands and drew her gently to her feet; and then, as if he were speaking to a tearful little child,' he said, "Be comforted, my daughter, and go in peace. Your faith has made you whole." '

'That is the most beautiful story I ever heard, Justus,' said Marcellus, soberly.

'I hardly know why I told you,' muttered Justus. 'I've no reason to think you could believe that Lydia was cured of her malady merely by touching Jesus' Robe.'

He sat waiting, with an almost wistful interest, for a further comment from Marcellus. It was one thing to say of a narrative that it was a beautiful story; it was quite another thing to concede its veracity. Marcellus had been adept in contriving common-sense explanations of these Galilean mysteries. The story of Lydia's healing had obviously moved him, but doubtless he would come forward presently with an attempt to solve the problem on natural grounds. His anticipated argument was so long in coming that Justus searched his face intently, astonished at its gravity. He was still more astounded when Marcellus replied, in a tone of deep sincerity:

'Justus—I believe every word of it!'

* * * * * *

Notwithstanding his weariness, Marcellus had much difficulty in going to sleep that night. Justus' story about Lydia had revived the memory of his own strange experiences with the Robe. It had been a long time since he had examined his mind in respect to these occurrences.

He had invented reasons for the amazing effects the Robe had wrought in his own case. His explanation was by no means conclusive or satisfying, but he had adopted it as less troublesome than a forthright admission that the Robe was haunted.

The case, viewed rationally, began with the fact that he had had a very serious emotional shock. The sight of a crucifixion was enough to leave scars on any decent man's soul. To have actually conducted a crucifixion was immeasurably worse. And to have crucified an innocent man made the whole affair a shameful crime. The memory of it would be an interminable torture, painful as a physical wound. Not much wonder that he had been so depressed that all his mental processes had been thrown into disarray.

There was that night at the Insula when he had drunkenly consented to put on the blood-stained Robe. Apparently his weighted remorse over the day's tragedy had reached a stage where it could not endure this one more perfidy. A wave of sickening revulsion had swept through him, as if some punitive power—resident in the Robe—had avenged the outrage.

For a long time Marcellus had suffered of that obsession. The Robe was possessed! He shuddered when he thought of it. The Robe had become the symbol of his crime and shame.

Then had come his remarkable recovery, that afternoon in Athens. His mental affliction had reached a moment of crisis. He could bear it no longer. The only way out was by suicide. And at that critical juncture, the Robe had stayed his hand.

For a few hours thereafter, Marcellus had been completely mystified. When he tried to analyze the uncanny thing that had happened to him, his mind refused to work on it. Indeed, he had been so ecstatic over his release from the bondage of his melancholia that he was in no mood to examine the nature of his redemption. Such brief and shallow reasoning as he put upon it was as futile as an attempt to evaluate some fantastic, half-forgotten dream.

The time came when he could explain his recovery even as he had explained his collapse. The Robe had been a focal point of interest on both occasions. But—did the Robe actually have anything to do with it? Wasn't it all subjective?

The explanation seemed sound and practical. His mind had been deeply wounded, but now it had healed. Evidently the hour had arrived, that afternoon in the cottage at the inn, when his harassed mind determined to overthrow the torturing obsession. It was a reasonable deduction, he felt. Nature was always in revolt against things that thwarted her blind but orderly processes. For many years a tree might wage a slow and silent warfare against an encumbering wall, without making any visible progress. One day the wall would topple; not because the tree had suddenly laid hold upon some supernormal energy, but because its patient work of self-defense and self-release had reached fulfillment. The long-imprisoned tree had freed itself. Nature had had her way.

Marcellus had contented himself with this explanation. He had liked the analogy of the tree and the wall; had liked it so well that he had set it to work on other phases of his problem. You had had a peculiar experience that had forced you to a belief in the supernatural. But your mind—given a chance to resume its orderly functions—would begin to resist that untenable thought. It wasn't natural for a healthy mind to be stultified by alleged supernatural forces. No matter how convincing the evidences of supernatural power, one's mind would proceed—automatically, involuntarily—to push this intrusive concept away, as a tree-root pushes against an offending wall.

Until long after midnight, Marcellus lay on his cot, wide awake, re-examining his own rationalizings about the Robe in the light of Lydia's experience, and getting nowhere with it. He had impulsively told Justus that he believed the story. There was no reason to doubt the good man's integrity; but, surely, somewhere along the line there must be an explanation. Maybe Lydia's malady had run its course, that day, needing only this moment of high emotional stress to effect her release. He silently repeated this over and over, trying to make it sound reasonable; trying to make it stick. Then he agreed with himself that his theory was nonsense, and drifted off to sleep.

Rousing with a start, Marcellus cautiously raised up on one elbow and peered out through the open tent-door. In the gray-blue, predawn twilight he dimly saw the figure of a tall, powerfully built, bearded man. It was quite too dark to discern the intruder's features.

His attitude did not denote furtiveness. He stood erect, apparently attempting to identify the occupants of the tent, and probably finding it impossible. Presently he moved away.

As soon as he had disappeared, Marcellus arose, quietly strapped his sandals, buckled his belt, and slipped out. There had been nothing sinister in this unexpected visitation. Obviously the man was neither a thief nor an ordinary prowler. He had not acted as if he had plans to molest the camp. It was quite conceivable that he had arranged to meet Justus up here and had been delayed. Finding the campers still asleep, he had probably decided to wait awhile before making himself known.

This seemed a reasonable surmise, for upon their arrival at the hilltop yesterday afternoon Justus had scrutinized the terrain as if expecting to be joined here by some acquaintance; though that was a habit of his; always scanning the landscape whenever an elevation presented a farther view; always peering down cross-roads; always turning about with a start whenever a door opened behind him.

It was still too dark to explore the terrain in quest of the mysterious visitor. Marcellus walked slowly toward the northern rim of the narrow plateau where he and Justus had sat. Low in the east, beyond the impenetrable darkness that mapped the lake, the blue was beginning to fade out of the gray. Now the gray was dissolving on the horizon and a long, slim ribbon of gleaming white appeared. Outspread lambent fingers reached up high, higher, higher into the dome from beyond a dazzling, snow-crowned mountain. Now the snow was touched with streaks of gold. Marcellus sat down to watch the dawn arrive.

At not more than a stadium's distance, also facing the sunrise, sat the unidentified wayfarer, not yet aware that he was observed. Apparently absorbed by the pageant in the east, he sat motionless with his long arms hugging his knees. As the light increased, Marcellus noted that the man was shabbily dressed and had no pack; undoubtedly a local resident; a fisherman, perhaps, for the uncouth knitted cap, drawn far down over his ears, was an identifying headgear affected by sailors.

With no wish to spy on the fellow, Marcellus noisily cleared his throat.

The stranger slowly turned his head; then arose nimbly and approached. Halting, he waited for the Roman to speak first.

'Who are you?' asked Marcellus? 'And what do you want?'

The newcomer ran his fingers through his beard, and smiled broadly. Then he tugged off the wretched cap from a swirl of tousled hair.

'This disguise,' he chuckled, 'is better than I had thought.'

'Demetrius!' Marcellus leaped to his feet and they grasped each other's hands. 'Demetrius!—how did you find me? Have you been in trouble? Are you being pursued? Where did you come by such shabby clothes? Are you hungry?'

'I learned yesterday afternoon in Cana that you were on the way to Capernaum. I have not been in much trouble, and am not now pursued. The clothes'—Demetrius held up his patched sleeves, and grinned—'are they not befitting to a vagrant? I had plenty to eat, last night. Your donkey-boy helped me to my supper and lent me a rug.'

'Why didn't you make yourself known?' asked Marcellus, reproachfully.

'I wanted to see you alone, sir, before encountering Justus.'

'Proceed, then,' urged Marcellus, 'and tell me as much as you can. He will be waking presently.'

'Stephanos told you of my flight from Jerusalem—'

'Have you been back there?' interrupted Marcellus.

'No, sir; but I contrived to send Stephanos a message, and he wrote me fully about your meeting.' Demetrius surveyed his master from head to foot. 'You are looking fit, sir, though you've lost a pound or two.'

'Walking,' explained Marcellus. 'Good for the torso; bad for the feet. Keep on with your story now. We haven't much time.'

Demetrius tried to make it brief. He had fled to Joppa, hoping to see his master when his ship came in. He had been hungry and shelterless for a few days, vainly seeking work on the docks.

'One morning I saw an old man dragging a huge parcel of green hides along the wharf,' he went on. 'I was so desperate for employment that I shouldered the reeking pelts and carried them to the street. The old Jew trotted alongside protesting. When I put the loathsome burden down, he offered me two farthings. I refused, saying he had not engaged me. He then asked what I would take to carry the hides to his tannery, a half-mile up the street that fronted the beach. I said I would do it for my dinner.'

'No details, Demetrius!' insisted Marcellus, impatiently. 'Get on with it!'

'These details are important, sir. The old man wanted to know what part of Samaria I had come from. Perhaps you have discovered that our Aramaic is loaded with Samaritan dialect. His people had lived in Samaria. His name was Simon. He talked freely and cordially, asking many questions. I told him I had worked for old Benjamin in Athens, which pleased him, for he knew about Benjamin. Then I confided that I had worked for Benyosef in Jerusalem. He was delighted. At his house, hard by the tannery, he bade me bathe and provided me with clean clothing.' Demetrius grinned at his patches. 'This is it,' he said.

'You shall have something better,' said Marcellus. 'I am a clothing merchant. I have everything. Too, too much of everything. So—what about this old Simon?'

'He became interested in me because I had worked for Benyosef, and asked me if I were one of them, and I said I was.' Demetrius studied Marcellus' face. 'Do you understand what I mean, sir?' he asked, wistfully.

Marcellus nodded, rather uncertainly.

'Are you, really—one of them?' he inquired.

'I am trying to be, sir,' responded Demetrius. 'It isn't easy. One is not allowed to fight, you know. You just have to take it—the way he did.'

'You're permitted to defend yourself; aren't you?' protested Marcellus.

'*He* didn't,' replied Demetrius, quietly.

Marcellus winced and shook his head. They fell silent for a moment.

'That part of it,' went on Demetrius, 'is always going to be difficult; too difficult, I fear. I promised Stephanos, that morning when I left Jerusalem, that I would do my best to obey the injunctions—and in less than an hour I had broken my word. Simon Peter—he is the chief of the disciples—the one they call "The Big Fisherman"—he baptized me, just before dawn, in the presence of all the others in Benyosef's shop, and, sir—'

'Baptized you?' Marcellus' perplexity was so amusing that Demetrius was forced to smile, in spite of his seriousness.

'Water,' he explained. 'They pour it on you, or put you in it, whichever is more convenient—and announce that you are now clean, in Jesus' name. That means you're one of them, and you're expected to follow Jesus' teachings.' Demetrius' eyes clouded and he shook his head self-reproachfully as he added, 'I was in a fight before my hair was dry.'

Marcellus tried to match his slave's remorseful mood, but his grin was already out of control.

'What happened?' he asked, suppressing a chuckle.

Demetrius glumly confessed his misdemeanor. The legionaries had a habit of stopping unarmed citizens along the road, compelling them to shoulder their packs. A great hulk of a soldier had demanded this service of Demetrius and he had refused to obey. Then there was the savage thrust of a lance. Demetrius had stepped out of the way, and the legionary had drawn up for another onslaught.

'In taking the lance from him,' continued Demetrius, 'I broke it.'

'Over his head, I suspect,' accused Marcellus.

'It wasn't a very good lance, sir,' commented Demetrius. 'I am surprised that the army doesn't furnish these men with better equipment.'

Marcellus laughed aloud. 'And then what?' he urged.

'That was all. I did not tarry. Now that I have broken my promise'—Demetrius' tone was repentant—'do you think I can still consider myself a Christian? Do you suppose I'll have to be baptized again?'

'I wouldn't know,' mumbled Marcellus, busy with his own thoughts. 'What do you mean—"a Christian"?'

'That's the new name for people who believe in Jesus. They're calling Jesus "The Christos"—meaning "The Anointed." '

'But that's Greek! All of these people are Jews; aren't they?'

'By no means, sir! This movement is traveling fast—and far. Simon the tanner says there are at least three hundred banded together down in Antioch.'

'Amazing!' exclaimed Marcellus. 'Do you suppose Justus knows?'

'Of course.'

'This is astounding news, Demetrius! I had considered the whole thing a lost cause! How could it stay alive—after Jesus was dead?'

Demetrius stared into his master's bewildered eyes.

'Don't you—haven't you heard about that, sir?' he inquired, soberly. 'Hasn't Justus told you?'

Both men turned at the sound of a shrill shout.

'Who is the child?' asked Demetrius, as Jonathan came running toward them. Marcellus explained briefly. The little boy's pace slowed as he neared them, inquisitively eyeing the stranger.

'Grandfather says you are to come and eat now,' he said moving close to Marcellus, but giving full attention to the unexplained man in the shabby tunic.

'Do you catch fish?' he asked. 'Have you a boat? Can I ride in it?'

'This man's name is Demetrius,' said Marcellus. 'He is not a fisherman, and he does not own a boat. He borrowed the cap.'

Demetrius smiled and fell in behind them as Marcellus, with the little boy's hand in his, walked toward the tent. Jonathan turned around, occasionally, to study the newcomer who followed with measured steps.

Justus, busily occupied at the fire, a few yards from the tent, glanced up with a warm smile of recognition and a word of greeting, apparently not much surprised at the arrival of their guest.

'May I take over, sir?' asked Demetrius.

'It is all ready; thank you,' said Justus. 'You sit down with Marcellus, and I shall serve you.'

Demetrius bowed and stepped aside. Presently Justus came to the low table he had improvised by drawing a couple of packing-cases together, and served Marcellus and Jonathan with the broiled fish and honey cakes. Jonathan motioned with his head toward Demetrius and looked up anxiously into Marcellus' face.

'Why doesn't he come and eat with us?' he inquired.

Marcellus was at a loss for a prompt and satisfactory reply.

'You needn't worry about Demetrius, son,' he remarked, casually. 'He likes to stand up when he eats.'

Instantly he divined that he had taken the wrong turn. Justus, who was sitting down opposite them, with his own dish, frowned darkly. He had some deep convictions on the subject of slavery. It was bad enough, his glum expression said, that Demetrius should be Marcellus' slave. It was intolerable that this relationship should be viewed so casually.

Jonathan pointed over his shoulder with his half-eaten cake in the direction of Demetrius who was standing before the fire, dish in hand, apparently enjoying his breakfast.

'That man stands up when he eats, Grandfather!' he remarked in a high treble. 'Isn't that funny?'

'No,' muttered Justus, 'it is not funny.' With that, he left the table, and went over to stand beside the slave.

Marcellus decided not to make an issue of it and proceeded to some lively banter with Jonathan, hoping to distract the child's attention.

Demetrius surveyed Justus' grim face and smiled.

'You mustn't let this slave business distress you, sir,' he said, quietly. 'My master is most kind and considerate. He would gladly give his life for me, as I would for him. But—slaves do not sit at table with their masters. It is a rule.'

'A bad rule!' grumbled Justus, deep in his throat. 'A rule that deserves to be broken! I had thought better of Marcellus Gallio.'

'It is a small matter,' said Demetrius, calmly. 'If you wish to make my slavery easier, please think no more of it, sir.'

At that, Justus' face cleared a little. There was no use making a scene over a situation that was none of his business. If Demetrius was contented, there wasn't much more to be said.

After they had eaten, Justus carried a dish of food out to the donkey-boy, Jonathan trotting along, still perplexed about the little episode.

'Grandfather,' he shrilled, 'Marcellus Gallio treats Demetrius no better than we treat our donkey-boy.'

Justus frowned, but made no attempt to explain. His grandson had given him something new to think about. In the meantime, Demetrius had joined Marcellus, his bearded lips puckered as he tried to discipline a grin.

'Perhaps it will clear the air for everybody, sir,' he said, 'if I go on by myself to Capernaum. Let me meet you, late this afternoon.'

'Very well,' consented Marcellus. 'Ask Justus where he proposes to stop. But—are you sure it is prudent for you to go down to Capernaum? We have a fort there, you know.'

'I shall be watchful, sir,' promised Demetrius.

'Take this!' Marcellus poured a handful of coins into his palm. 'And keep your distance from that fort!'

* * * * * *

Demetrius, unencumbered, made good progress down the serpentine road to the valley floor. The air was hot. He carried his shabby coat and the disreputable cap under his arm. The lake-shore on this side was barren and unpopulated. Tossing off his clothing, he waded out and swam joyously, tumbled about like a dolphin, floated on his back, churned the water with long overhand strokes, luxuriating in his aquatics, and the thorough cleansing. He came out shaking his mop of hair through his fingers, the blazing sun drying him before he reached the little pile of patched and faded garments.

Tiberias gleamed white in the mid-forenoon sun. The marble palace of Herod Antipas, halfway up the hill, appropriately set apart from the less noble but surprisingly lavish residences, glistened dazzlingly. Demetrius imagined he could see a sinuous shimmer of heat enveloping the proud structure, and was glad he did not have to live there. He was not envious of Herod's privilege to spend the summer here. However, he reflected, the family had probably sought a more congenial altitude for the hot season, leaving a small army of servants to sweat and steal and quarrel until the weather eased with the coming of autumn.

He had reached the little city now, and proceeded on through it, keeping close to the beach, where many fishing-boats had been drawn up on the sand, and the adjacent market-booths reeked of their merchandise. Occasionally he was viewed with a momentary curiosity by small groups of apathetic loungers, sitting cross-legged in the shade of dirty foodshops. The air was heavy with decaying fruit and the stench of rancid oil sizzling in tarnished pans. It had been a long time since breakfast, and Demetrius had had an unusual amount of exercise.

He tarried before one of the unpleasant foodstalls. The swarthy cook scowled, and waved his wooden spoon at the shabby traveler with the uncouth cap—and no pack.

'Be on your way, fellow!' he commanded. 'We have nothing to give you.'

Demetrius jingled his money, and made a wry face.

'Nor have you anything to sell that a dog would eat,' he retorted.

The greasy fellow instantly beamed with a wheedling smile, lifting his shoulders and elbows into a posture of servitude. It was this type of Jew that Demetrius had always despised, the Jew who was arrogant, noisy, and abusive until he heard a couple of coins clink. Immediately you were his friend, his brother, his master. You could pour out a torrent of invective on him now, if you liked. He would be weather-proofed and his smile undiminished. He had heard the pennies.

'Oh—not so bad as that, sir!' exclaimed the cook. 'The evil smell'—he wagged a confidential thumb toward the neighboring booth—'it is that one who defiles the air with his stale perch and wretched oil.' Tipping a grimy kettle forward, he stirred its steaming contents, appreciatively sucking his lips. 'Delicious!' he murmured.

A tousled, red-eyed legionary sauntered up from the waterfront, rested an elbow on the end of the high table, and sourly sniffed the heavy scent of burning fat. His uniform was dirty. Apparently he had slept where he fell. Doubtless he was ready for food now. He gave Demetrius a surly stare.

'Have a bowl of this fine pottage, Centurion,' coaxed the cook. 'Choice lamb—with many costly spices. A great helping for only two farthings.'

Demetrius repressed a grin. 'Centurion'—eh? Why hadn't the Jew gone the whole way and addressed the debauched legionary as 'Legate'? But perhaps he knew where to stop when dishing up flattery. The unkempt Roman snarled a curse, and rubbed his clammy forehead with his dirty brown bandeau. The cook took up an empty bowl and smiled encouragingly at Demetrius, who scowled and shook his head.

'None for me,' he muttered, turning away.

'I'll have some!' declared the legionary, truculently, slapping an empty wallet.

The cook's eager face collapsed, but he was not in a position to refuse the penniless soldier. With a self-piteous shrug, he half-filled the bowl and put it down on the filthy table.

'Business is so bad,' he whined.

'So is your pottage,' mumbled the legionary, nursing a hot mouthful. 'Even that slave would have none of it.'

'Slave, sir?' The cook leaned over the high table to have another look at the tall Greek, who was moving leisurely up the street. 'He has a wallet full of money. Good money, too—from the sound of it! A thief, no doubt!'

The legionary put down his spoon. His lip curled in a crafty grin. If an overdue soldier could reappear at the fort with a prisoner in tow, he might make a better case for his absence all night.

'Hi—you!' he shouted. 'Come back here!'

Demetrius hesitated, turned, held a brief parley with himself, and retraced his steps. It would do no good to attempt an escape in the neighborhood of a fort.

'Did you call me, sir?' he asked quietly.

'How do you happen to be in Tiberias alone, fellow?' The legionary wiped his stubbled chin. 'Where is your master? Don't pretend you're not a slave—with that ear.'

'My master is on the way to Capernaum, sir. He sent me on to seek out a desirable camping-place.'

This sounded reasonable. The legionary untidily helped himself to another large spoonful of the pottage.

'Who is your master, fellow? And what is he doing in Capernaum?'

'A Roman citizen, sir; a merchant.'

'A likely tale!' snorted the legionary. 'What manner of merchandise does a Roman find in Capernaum?'

'Homespun, sir,' said Demetrius. 'Galilean rugs and robes.'

The legionary chuckled scornfully and scraped the bottom of his bowl with a shaky spoon.

'Greek slaves are usually better liars than that,' he growled. 'You must think me a fool. A slave in rags and patches, seeking a camp-site for a Roman who comes all the way to little Capernaum to buy clothing!'

'And with much money on him!' shrilled the cook. 'A robber he is!'

'Shut up, pig!' bellowed the legionary. 'I should take you along, were you not so filthy.' Setting his soiled bandeau at a jaunty angle, he rose, tightened his belt, belched noisily, and motioned to Demetrius to fall in behind him.

'But why am I apprehended, sir?' demanded Demetrius.

'Never mind about that!' snarled the legionary. 'You can tell your story at the fort.' With an exaggerated swagger, he marched stiffly up the street without turning to see whether his captive was following.

Demetrius hesitated for a moment, but decided that it would be foolhardy to attempt an escape in a vicinity so well patrolled. He would go along to the fort and try to send a message to Marcellus.

Beyond the limits of Tiberias the grim old sand-colored barracks loomed up on the arid hillside. Above the center of the quadrangle reared the parapets of the inevitable praetorium. The legionary strutted on toward the massive wooden gate. A sentry sluggishly unbarred the heavy barricade. They passed into the treeless, sun-blistered drill-ground and on between orderly rows of brown tents, unoccupied now, for it was noon and the legion would be in the mess-hall. Presently they brought up before the relatively impressive entrance to the praetorium. A gray-haired guard made way for them.

'Take this slave below and lock him up,' barked the legionary.

'What's your name, fellow?' demanded the guard.

Demetrius told him.

'And your master's name?'

'Lucan—a Roman citizen.'

'Where does he live?'

'In Rome.'

The guard gave the disheveled legionary an appraising glance. Demetrius thought he saw some hesitancy on the part of the older man.

'What's the charge?' asked the guard.

'Suspicion of theft,' said the legionary. 'Lock him up, and let him explain later how he happens to be wandering about, away from his master, dressed like a fisherman—and with a wallet full of money.'

'Write his name on the slate, then,' said the guard. 'The Centurion is at mess.'

The legionary fumbled with the chalk, and handed it to Demetrius.

'Can you write your name, slave?' he inquired gruffly.

In spite of his predicament, Demetrius was amused. It was obvious that neither of these Romans could write. If they couldn't write, they couldn't read. He took the chalk and wrote:

'Demetrius, Greek slave of Lucan, a Roman encamped in Capernaum.'

'Long name—for a slave,' remarked the legionary. 'If you have written anything else—'

'My master's name, sir.'

'Put him away, then,' said the legionary, turning to go. The old guard tapped on the floor with his lance and a younger guard appeared. He signed with a jerk of his head that Demetrius should follow, and strode off down the corridor to a narrow stairway. They descended to the prison. Bearded faces appeared at the small square apertures in the cell-doors; Jewish faces, mostly, and a few tough-looking Bedouins.

Demetrius was pushed into an open cell at the far end of the narrow corridor. A perpendicular slit, high in the outer wall, admitted a frugal light. The only furniture was a wide wooden bench. Anchored to the masonry lay a heavy chain with a rusty manacle. The guard ignored the chain, retreated into the corridor, banged the heavy door shut and pushed the bolt.

Slumping down on the bench, Demetrius surveyed his cramped quarters, and wondered how long he would have to wait for some official action in his case. It suddenly occurred to him that if the dissipated legionary suspected the entry on the slate he might have thought it safer to rub it out. In that event, the new prisoner stood a good chance of being forgotten. Perhaps he should have made a dash for it when he had an opportunity. Assuming a speedy trial, how much should he tell? It would be difficult to explain Marcellus' business in Galilee. Without doubt, old Julian the Legate was under orders to make short work of this Christian movement. There was no telling what attitude he might take if he learned that Marcellus had been consorting with these disciples of Jesus.

As his eyes became accustomed to the gloom, Demetrius noticed a shelf in the corner bearing an earthenware food-basin and a small water-fowl. He had been hungry an hour ago. Now he was thirsty. Moving to the door he crouched—for the barred port was not placed for a tenant of his height—and looked across the narrow corridor into a pair of inquisitive Roman eyes framed in the opposite cell-door. The eyes were about the same age as his own, and seemed amused.

'When do we get food and water?' asked Demetrius, in circus Latin.

'Twice,' replied the Roman, amiably. 'At mid-morning—you should have arrived earlier—and again at sunset. Praise the gods—I shan't be here for the next feeding. I'm getting out this afternoon. My week is up.'

'I can't wait until sunset for water,' muttered Demetrius.

'I'll wager you ten sesterces you'll wait until they bring it to you,' drawled the Roman. He straightened to relieve his cramped position, revealing a metal identification tablet on the chain around his neck.

'What is your legion?' inquired Demetrius, seeing his neighbor was disposed to be talkative.

'Seventeenth: this one.'

'Why aren't you in the legion's guardhouse,' ventured Demetrius, 'instead of down in this hole with the civilians?'

'The guardhouse is full,' chuckled the legionary.

'Was there a mutiny?' inquired Demetrius.

Not a mutiny, the legionary explained. They had had a celebration. Julian the Legate had been transferred to Jerusalem. The new Legate had brought a detachment of fifty along with him from his old command, to guard him on the journey. During the festivities, much good wine had flowed; much good blood, too, for the detachment from Minoa was made up of quarrelsome legionaries—

'From Minoa!' exclaimed Demetrius. 'Is Tribune Paulus your new Legate?'

'Indeed he is!' retorted the legionary. 'And plenty hard! Old Julian was easy-going. This fellow has no mercy. As for the fighting, it was nothing; a few dagger cuts, a couple of bloody noses. One man from Minoa lost a slice off his ear.' He grinned reminiscently. 'I sliced it off,' he added, modestly. 'It didn't hurt him much. And he knew it was accidental.' After a little pause, 'I see somebody nicked you on the ear.'

'That wasn't accidental,' grinned Demetrius, willing to humor the legionary, who laughed appreciatively, as if it were a good joke on the Greek that he had been enslaved.

'Did you run away?' asked the Roman.

'No—I was to have joined my master in Capernaum.'

'He'll get you out. You needn't worry. He's a Roman, of course.'

'Yes,' said Demetrius, 'but he doesn't know I'm here.' He lowered his voice. 'I wonder if you could get a message to him. I'd gladly give you something for your trouble.'

The legionary laughed derisively.

'Big talk—for a slave,' he scoffed. 'How much? Two denarii, maybe?'

'I'll give you ten shekels.'

'That you won't!' muttered the legionary. 'I don't want any of that kind of money, fellow!'

'I didn't steal it,' declared Demetrius. 'My master gave it to me.'

'Well—you can keep it!' The legionary scowled and moved back from the door.

Demetrius sat down dejectedly on the bench. He was very thirsty.

Chapter XVII

Of course it was sheer nonsense to say that you had full confidence in Nathanael Bartholomew's integrity but disbelieved his eye-witness account of the storm.

Nor could you clarify this confusion by assuming that the old man had been a victim of hallucination. Bartholomew wasn't that type of person. He was neither a liar nor a fool.

According to his story, told at great length as they sat together in his little fig orchard, Jesus had rebuked a tempest on the Sea of Galilee; had commanded the gale to cease, and it had obeyed his voice—instantly! Jesus had spoken and the storm had stopped! Bartholomew had snapped his dry old fingers. Like *that!*

And the story wasn't hearsay. Bartholomew hadn't heard it from a neighbor who had got it from his cousin. No, sir! The old man had been in the boat that night. He had heard and seen it all! If you couldn't believe it, Bartholomew would not be offended; but it was *truth!*

The tale was finished now. The aged disciple sat calmly fanning his wrinkled neck, drawing his long, white beard aside and loosening the collar of his robe. Marcellus, with no further comments to offer and no more questions to ask, frowned studiously at his own interlaced fingers, conscious of Justus' inquisitive eyes. He knew they expected him to express an opinion; and, after a silence that was becoming somewhat constrained, he obliged them by muttering to himself, 'Very strange! Very strange indeed!'

The dramatic story had been told with fervor, told with an old man's verbosity, but without excitement. Bartholomew wasn't trying to persuade you; nor was he trying to convert you. He had nothing to sell. Justus had asked him to tell about that storm, and he had done so. Perhaps it was his first opportunity for so complete a recital of all its incidents. Certainly it was the first time he had ever told the story to someone who hadn't heard it.

Shortly after Demetrius had set off alone, that morning, the little caravan had proceeded slowly down the winding road to the valley; had skirted the sparsely populated lake-shore to Tiberias where the ostentatious Roman palaces on the hills accented the squalor of the waterfront; had followed the beach street through the city; had passed the frowning old fort, and entered the sprawling suburbs of Capernaum.

Jonathan had been promised a brief visit with Thomas—and the donkey; so they had turned off into a side street where, after many inquiries, they had found the little house and an enthusiastic welcome. Upon the urgent persuasion of Thomas and his mother, Jonathan was left with them, to be picked up on the morrow. Everybody agreed that the donkey recognized Jonathan, though the elders privately suspected that the sugar which had been melting in the little boy's warm hand for the past two hours might have accounted for Jasper's flattering feat of memory.

Regaining the principal thoroughfare, they had moved on toward the business center of the town which had figured so prominently in Justus' recollections of Jesus. They had halted for a moment in front of Lydia's home, and Justus was for making a brief call, but Marcellus dissuaded him as it was nearing midday and a visit might be inopportune.

The central plaza had seemed familiar. The synagogue—ironically more Roman than Jewish in its architecture, which was understandable because Centurion Hortensius had furnished the money—spread its marble steps fanwise into the northern boundary of the spacious square, exactly as Marcellus had pictured it; for it was from these steps that Jesus had addressed massed multitudes of thousands. It was almost deserted now, except for the beggars, tapping on the pavement with their empty bowls; for everybody who had a home to go to was at his noonday meal.

Marcellus felt he had been here many times before. Indeed he was so preoccupied with identifying the cherished landmarks that he almost forgot they were to have met Demetrius here. Justus had reminded him, and Marcellus had looked about apprehensively. It would be a very awkward situation if Demetrius had been arrested. He had no relish for an interview with old Julian; not while on his present mission. Justus relieved his anxiety somewhat by saying he had told Demetrius where they would make camp, on the grounds of the old Shalum Inn; but what could be detaining Demetrius in the meantime?

'Perhaps he misunderstood me,' suggested Justus.

'It's possible,' agreed Marcellus, 'but unlikely. Demetrius has a good ear for instructions.'

They had sauntered down to the beach, strewn with fishing-boats drawn up on the shingle, leaving the donkey-boy to keep an eye out for Demetrius.

Justus had suggested that they eat their lunch on the shore. After waiting a half-hour for the Greek to show up, they had packed their lunch kit and proceeded northward, Marcellus anxious but still hopeful of meeting his loyal slave at the inn. It was a quiet spot—the Inn of Ben-Shalum—with spacious grounds for travelers carrying their own camping equipment. No one had seen anything of a tall Greek slave. Hastily unpacking, they put up the tent in the shade of two tall sycamores, and made off toward the home of Bartholomew, a little way up the suburban street.

And now the old man had ended the story they had come to hear. In its preliminary phases, episodes had been introduced which bore no closer relation to the eventful storm than that they had occurred on the same day. Jesus had been very weary that night; so weary that he had slept at the height of the gale and had had to be awakened when it became clear that the little ship was foundering. Such deep fatigue had to be accounted for; so Bartholomew had elaborated the day's activities.

Sometimes, for a considerable period, the husky old voice would settle deep in the sparse white beard and rumble on in an almost inaudible monotone, and you knew that Bartholomew had deserted you and Justus for the great crowd that sat transfixed on a barren coast—a weary, wistful, hungry multitude of self-contained people who, in the melting warmth of Jesus' presence, had congealed into one sympathetic family, for the sharing of their food.

'A clean, bright lad,' Bartholomew was mumbling to himself; 'a nephew of Lydia's, who had none of her own; he spent most of his time at her house. She had packed his little basket.'

And then, suddenly remembering his guests, Bartholomew had roused from his reverie to tell Marcellus all about Lydia's strange healing; and Justus had not intervened with a hint that their young Roman friend had already heard of her experience. Having finished with Lydia—and Jarius, too, whose little daughter had been marvelously restored that day—the old man had drifted back to his memories of the remarkable feast in the desert.

'The boy must have been sitting at the Master's feet,' he soliloquized, with averted eyes. 'He must have been sitting there all the time; for when Jesus said we would now eat our supper, there he was—as if he had popped up from nowhere—holding out his little basket.'

It had taken Bartholomew a long time to tell of that strange supper; the sharing of bread, the new acquaintances, the breaking down of reserve among strangers, the tenderness toward the old ones and the little ones. . . . And then the tempo of the tale speeded. Wisps of chill wind lashed the parched reeds. Dark clouds rolled up from the northeast. The old man swept them on with a beckoning arm; black clouds that had suddenly darkened the sky. There was a low muttering of thunder. The crowd grew apprehensive. The people were scrambling to their feet, gathering up their families, breaking into a run. The long procession was on its way home.

Darkness came on fast, the lowering black clouds lanced by slim, jagged, red-hot spears that spilled torrents splashing onto the sun-parched sand. Philip was for rushing to shelter in the little village of Bethsaida, two miles east. Peter was for beaching the big boat and using the mainsail for cover. And when they were all through making suggestions, Jesus said they would embark at once and return to Capernaum.

'He said we had nothing to fear,' went on Bartholomew, 'but we were afraid, nevertheless. Some of them tried to reason with him. I said nothing, myself. Old men are timid,' he paused to interpolate, directly to Marcellus. 'When there are dangers to be faced, old men should keep still, for there's little they can do, in any case.'

'I should have thought,' commented Marcellus, graciously, 'that an elderly man's experience would make him a wise counselor—on any occasion.'

'Not in a storm, young man!' declared Bartholomew. 'An old man may give you good advice, under the shade of a fig tree, on a sunny afternoon; but—not in a storm!'

The boat had been anchored in the lee of a bit of a cove, but it was with great difficulty that they had struggled through the waves and over the side. Unutterably weary, Jesus had dropped down on the bare bench near the tiller and they had covered him up with a length of drenched sail-cloth.

Manning the oars, they had maneuvered into open water, had put out a little jib and promptly hauled it in, the tempest suddenly mounting in fury. No one of them, Bartholomew said, had ever been out in such a storm. Now the boat was tossed high on the crest, now it was swallowed up, gigantic waves broke over their heads, the flood pounded them off their seats and twisted the oars out of their hands. The tortured little ship was filling rapidly. All but four oars had been abandoned now. The rest of the crew were bailing frantically. But the water was gaining on them. And Jesus slept!

Justus broke into the narrative here as Bartholomew—whose vivid memory of that night's hard work with a bailing-bucket brought big beads of perspiration out on his deep-lined forehead—had paused to wield his palm-leaf fan.

'You thought Jesus should get up and help; didn't you?' Justus was grinning broadly.

The old man's lips twitched with a self-reproachful smile.

'Well,' he admitted, 'perhaps we did think that after getting us into this trouble he might take a hand at one of the buckets. Of course'—he hastened to explain—'we weren't quite ourselves. We were badly shaken. It was getting to be a matter of life or death. And we were completely exhausted—the kind of exhaustion that makes every breath whistle and burn.'

'And so—you shouted to him,' prodded Justus.

'Yes! We shouted to him!' Bartholomew turned to address Marcellus. '*I* shouted to him! "Master!" I called. "We are going to drown! The boat is sinking! Don't you care?" ' The old man dropped his head and winced at the memory. 'Yes'—he muttered, contritely. '*I* said that—to my Master.'

After a moment's silence, Bartholomew drew a deep sigh, and continued. Jesus had stirred, had sat up, had stretched out his long, strong arms, had rubbed his fingers through his drenched hair.

'Not alarmed?' inquired Marcellus.

'Jesus was never alarmed!' retorted Bartholomew, indignantly. 'He rose to his feet and started forward, wading through the water, hands reaching up to steady him as he made for the housing of the mainmast. Climbing up on the heavy planking, he stood for a moment with one arm around the mast, looking out upon the towering waves. Then he raised both arms high. We gasped, expecting him to be pitched overboard. He held both hands outstretched—and spoke! It was not a shrill shout. It was rather as one might soothe a frightened animal. "Peace!" he said. "Peace! Be still!" '

The climax of the story had been built up to such intensity that Marcellus found his heart speeding. He leaned forward and stared wide-eyed into the old man's face.

'Then what?' he demanded.

'The storm was over,' declared Bartholomew.

'Not *immediately!*' protested Marcellus.

Bartholomew deliberately raised his arm and snapped his brittle old fingers.

'Like *that!*' he exclaimed.

'And the stars came out,' added Justus.

'I don't remember,' murmured Bartholomew.

'Philip said the stars came out,' persisted Justus, quietly.

'That may be,' nodded Bartholomew. 'I don't remember.'

'Some have said that the boat was immediately dry,' murmured Justus, with a little twinkle in his eyes as if anticipating the old man's contradiction.

'That was a mistake,' sniffed Bartholomew. 'Some of us bailed out water all the way back to Capernaum. Whoever reported that should have helped.'

'How did you all feel about this strange thing?' asked Marcellus.

'We hadn't much to say,' remembered Bartholomew. 'I think we were stunned. There had been so much confusion—and now everything was quiet. The water, still coated with foam, was calm as a pond. As for me, I experienced a peculiar sensation of peace. Perhaps the words that Jesus spoke to the storm had stilled us too—in our hearts.'

'And what did *he* do?' asked Marcellus.

'He went back to the bench by the tiller and sat down,' replied Bartholomew. 'He gathered his Robe about him, for he was wet and chilled. After a while he turned to us, smiled reproachfully, and said, as if speaking to little children, "Why were you so frightened?" Nobody ventured to answer that. Perhaps he didn't expect us to say anything. Presently he reclined, with his arm for a pillow, and went to sleep again.'

'Are you sure he was asleep?' asked Justus.

'No—but he was very quiet and his eyes were closed. Perhaps he was thinking. Everyone thought he was asleep. There was very little talk. We moved to the center of the boat and looked into each other's faces. I remember Philip's whispering, "What manner of man is this—that even the winds and waves obey him?" '

The story was finished. Marcellus, for whose benefit the tale had been told, knew they were waiting for him to say whether he believed it. He sat bowed far forward in his chair, staring into the little basket he had made of his interlaced fingers. Bartholomew wasn't willfully lying. Bartholomew was perfectly sane. But—by all the gods!—you couldn't believe a story like *that!* A man—speaking to a storm! Speaking to a storm as he might to a stampeded horse! And the storm obeying his command! No!—you couldn't have any of *that!* He felt Justus' friendly eyes inquiring. Presently he straightened a little, and shook his head.

'Very strange!' he muttered, without looking up. 'Very strange indeed!'

* * * * * *

The afternoon was well advanced when the gray-haired captain of the guard came down to free the legionary who had sliced off the ear of a visiting fellow-in-arms from Minoa.

Demetrius listened attentively at the little port in his door as his neighbor's bolt was drawn, hoping to overhear some formal conversation relative to the prisoner's release; but was disappointed. Neither man had spoken. The heavy door was swung back and the legionary had emerged. The captain of the guard had preceded him down the dusky corridor. The sound of their sandals, scraping on the stone floor, died away.

Shortly afterward there was a general stir throughout the prison; guttural voices; unbolting of doors and rattling of heavy earthenware bowls and basins; the welcome sound of splashing water. Feeding time had arrived and was being greeted with the equivalent of pawing hoofs, clanking chains, and nostril-fluttering whimpers in a stable. Demetrius' mouth and throat were dry; his tongue a clumsy wooden stick. His head throbbed. He couldn't remember ever having been that thirsty; not even in the loathsome prison-ship on the way from Corinth to Rome, long years ago.

It seemed they would never reach his end of the corridor. He hoped the water would hold out until they came to his cell. That was all he wanted—water! As for food, it didn't matter; but he had to have water—*now!*

At length they shuffled up to his door, unbolted it, and swung it wide open. Two burly, brutish, ear-slit Syrian slaves appeared in the doorway. The short, stocky one, with the spade beard, deep pockmarks, and greasy hands, plunged his gourd-dipper into an almost empty bucket of malodorous pottage and pointed angrily to the food-basin on the shelf. Demetrius, with nothing on his mind but his consuming thirst, had been waiting with his water-bowl in hand. He reached up for the food-basin, and the surly Syrian dumped the gourdful of reeking hot garbage into it. Then he rummaged in the bottom of a filthy bag and came up with a small loaf of black bread which he tossed onto the bare bench. It bounced and clattered like a stone.

Retreating to make room for his companion, the stocky one edged out into the corridor and the tall one entered with a large water-jar on his shoulder. Half-crazed with thirst, Demetrius held his water-bowl high. The Syrian, with a crooked grin, as if it amused him to see a Greek in such a predicament, tipped the jar, and from its considerable height poured a stream that overflowed the bowl, drenching the prisoner's clothing. There was hardly more than a spoonful left. The Syrian was backing toward the door.

'Give me water!' demanded Demetrius, huskily.

The fellow sneered, tipped the jar again, and poured the remainder of the water over Demetrius' feet. Chuckling, but vigilant, he moved back into the doorway.

Though the bowl was not large, it was heavy and sturdy pottery, and in the hand of a man as recklessly thirsty and angry as Demetrius it was capable of doing no small amount of damage. But for the thick mop of kinky hair that covered his forehead, the bowl might have cracked the Syrian's skull, for it was delivered with all the earnestness that Demetrius could put into it.

Dropping the water-jar, which broke into jagged fragments, the dizzied Syrian, spluttering with rage, whipped out a long dagger from his dirty sash, and lunged forward. Hot pottage would not have been Demetrius' choice of weapons, but it was all he had to fight with; so he threw it into his assailant's face. Momentarily detained by this unexpected onslaught, the Syrian received another more serious blow. Raising the heavy food-basin in both hands, Demetrius brought it down savagely on the fellow's forearm, knocking the dagger from his hand.

Unarmed, the Syrian reeled back into the corridor where the stocky one, unable to force his way into the cell, was waiting the outcome of the battle. Demetrius took advantage of this moment to pick up the dagger. With the way cleared, the stocky one—dagger in hand—was about to plunge in; but when he saw that the prisoner had armed himself, he backed out and began swinging the door shut.

Unwilling to be trapped and probably killed with a lance thrust through the port, Demetrius threw his weight against the closing door and forced his way out into the corridor. Excited by the confusion, the prisoners set up a clamor of encouraging shouts that brought the elderly Captain of the guard and three others scurrying down the stone stairway. They paused, a few feet from the engagement. One of the younger guards was for rushing in to separate them, but the Captain put out an arm and barred the way. It wasn't every day that you could see a determined fight waged with daggers. When angry men met at close range with daggers, it was rough sport.

Cautious in their cramped quarters, the contestants were weaving about, taking each other's measure. The Syrian, four inches shorter but considerably outweighing the Greek, crouched for a spring. One of the younger guards emptied his flat wallet into his hand.

'Two shekels and nine denarii on the Syrian pig,' he wagered. The others shook their heads. The Greek was at a disadvantage. The dagger was the favorite weapon with the Syrians—a dagger with a long, curving blade. The Syrian considered it good strategy to slip up behind an enemy in the dark and let him have it between the ribs a little below and to the right of the left shoulder. On such occasions one needed a long knife. Demetrius was not unfamiliar with daggers, but had never practiced with one that had been especially contrived for stabbing a man in the back.

He was finding his borrowed weapon unwieldy in this narrow corridor. It was close-in fighting and decidedly dangerous business. The tall Syrian lurked far back in the darkness behind his companion. The stocky one, facing an appreciative audience of guards, seemed eager to bring the event to an early conclusion. They were sparring actively now, their clashing blades striking sparks in the gloom. Demetrius was gradually retreating, quite definitely on the defensive. The guards backed away to give them a chance. The pace of the fighting increased, the Syrian forcing the action.

'Ha!' he shouted; and a dark, red streak showed up on the Greek's right sleeve, above the elbow. An instant later, a long gash appeared across the back of the Syrian's hand. He gave a quick fling of his arm to shake off the blood, but not quick enough. A cut had opened over his collar-bone, dangerously close to his throat. He retreated a step. Demetrius pursued his advantage, and added another gash to his antagonist's hand.

'*On guard*—Greek!' shouted the Captain. The tall Syrian in the rear had drawn back his arm to hurl a chunk of the broken waterjar. Demetrius dodged, at the warning, and the murderous missile grazed the side of his head.

'Enough!' yelled the Captain. Grasping Demetrius' shoulder, he pushed him aside, the younger guards followed with lances poised to strike.

'Come out of there, vermin!' the Captain ordered. The Syrians sullenly obeyed, the stocky one yielding his bloody dagger as he squeezed by the guards. The procession started down the corridor and up the stairs. Arriving on the main floor, the Captain led the way along the spacious hall, and out into the courtyard. Water was brought, wounds were laved and crudely bandaged. Demetrius grabbed a water-jar, and drank greedily. The cut on his arm was deep and painful, and the wide abrasion on his temple burned, but now that he had had a drink, nothing else mattered much.

The Captain gave a command to proceed and they re-entered the praetorium, turned to the left at a broad marble staircase, and ascended to the second floor. A sentry informed the guard at an imposing door that Captain Namius wished to see the Legate. The guard disappeared, returning presently with a curt nod. They advanced through the open door and filed into the sumptuous courtroom, brightly lighted with great lamps suspended from beautifully wrought chains.

Demetrius' wounds were throbbing, but he was not too badly hurt to be amused. Paulus, rattling a leather dice-cup, was facing Sextus across the ornately carved table that dominated the dais at the far end of the room. So—Paulus, transferred to the command of the fort at Capernaum, had brought his old gambling companion along. The guards and their quarry, preceded by two sentries in gay uniforms, marched forward. Legate Paulus glanced disinterestedly in their direction and returned his attention to the more important business in hand. Shaking the cup, he poured out the dice on the polished table, and shrugged. Sextus grinned, took the cup, shook it languidly, poured it out—and scowled. Paulus laughed, and sat down in the huge chair behind the table. Centurion Sextus came to attention.

'What is it, Namius?' yawned Paulus.

'The Syrians were fighting this Greek prisoner, sir.'

'What about?' asked Paulus, impatiently.

Captain Namius didn't know. The Syrian slaves were feeding the prisoners, and 'somehow got mixed up with this Greek.'

'Step nearer, Greek.' Paulus' eyes had narrowed. He was searching his memory. Demetrius stepped forward, scowling to keep from smiling. Sextus leaned over and mumbled something. Paulus' eyes lighted. He nodded and grinned dryly.

'Take the Syrians away for the present, Captain,' he said. 'I would talk with this Greek.' He waited until the guards and the Syrians had left the room.

'Are you badly hurt, Demetrius?' asked Paulus, kindly.

'No, sir.' Demetrius was becoming aware that the room was slowly revolving and growing dark. The Legate's ruddy face was blurred. He heard Paulus bark an order and felt the edge of a chair pushed up behind him. He slumped down in it weakly. A sentry handed him a glass of wine. He gulped it. Presently the vertigo cleared. 'I am sorry, sir,' he said.

'How do you happen to be here, Demetrius?' inquired Paulus. 'But no—that can wait. Where is your master?'

Demetrius told him.

'Here?—in Capernaum!' exclaimed Paulus. 'And whatever brings the excellent Tribune Marcellus to this sadly pious city?'

'My master has taken a fancy to Galilean homespun, sir. He has been touring about, looking for—such things.'

Paulus frowned darkly and stared into Demetrius' face.

'Is he well—in his head, I mean?'

'Oh, yes, sir,' said Demetrius, 'quite so, sir.'

'There was a rumor—' Paulus did not finish the sentence, but it was evident that he expected a rejoinder. Demetrius, unaccustomed to sitting in the presence of his betters, came unsteadily to his feet.

'The Tribune was ill, sir, for several months. He was deeply depressed. He went to Athens—and recovered.'

'What was he so depressed about, Demetrius?' asked Paulus; and when the reply was not immediately forthcoming, he added, 'Do I know?'

'Yes, sir,' said Demetrius.

'Something cracked—when he put on that Robe—at the Procurator's banquet.'

'Yes, sir. It did something to him.'

'I remember. It affected him strangely.' Paulus shook himself loose from an unpleasant recollection. 'Now—for your case. Why are you here?'

Demetrius explained in a few words, and when Paulus inquired about the fight, he replied that he had wanted water and the Syrian wouldn't give it to him.

'Bring Captain Namius in!' commanded Paulus. A sentry went out and returned almost immediately with the guards and the Syrians. The examination proceeded swiftly. Namius gave an account of the duel in the corridor.

'We stopped it,' he concluded, 'when this Syrian picked up a shard of the broken water-jar and threw it at the Greek.'

'Take him out and give him thirty-nine lashes with a bull-whip!' shouted Paulus. 'Lock the other pig up—and don't try to fatten him. That will be all, Captain.'

'And the Greek, sir?' asked Namius.

'Put him to bed, and have the physician attend to his cuts.'

Namius gave an order. The guards made off with the Syrians.

'Shall I go now, sir?' asked Demetrius.

'Yes—with the Captain. No—wait. You may go, Namius. I shall summon you.' Paulus watched the retreating figure of the old guard until he reached the door; then, glancing about the room, he said quietly, 'You may all go.' He looked up over his shoulder. 'You, too, Sextus. I want a word alone with Demetrius.'

* * * * * *

They had almost nothing to say to each other on the way back to the inn. Justus, preoccupied and somehow elevated, as if the afternoon with Bartholomew had reinvigorated his spirit, strode along with confident steps.

As for Marcellus, the old disciple's story had impressed and disturbed him. Had he never known of Jesus until today, and Bartholomew had said, 'I heard this man speak to a storm—and the storm ceased,' he could have dismissed that statement as utterly preposterous. But the testimony about Jesus' peculiar powers had been cumulative. It had been coming at him from all directions.

Marcellus' footsteps lagged as his thoughts became more involved. Justus, appreciating his dilemma, gave him an understanding smile, lengthened his stride, and moved on alone, leaving his bewildered patron to follow at his leisure.

The trouble was: once you began to concede that there might be an element of truth in some of these stories, it was unreasonable to draw an arbitrary line beyond which your credulity would not go. It was childish to say, 'Yes—I believe Jesus could have done *this* extraordinary thing, but I don't believe he could have done *that!*'

Some of the stories permitted a common-sense explanation. Take Hariph's naïve account of the wedding-feast, for example. That wasn't hard to see through. The porous water-jars had previously held wine. Of course you had to concede the astounding effect of Jesus' personality on the wedding-guests who loved, admired, and trusted him. Not everybody could have made that water taste like wine. You were willing to grant that. Mean and frugal fare could be made pleasantly palatable when shared with a well-loved friend. If the water-into-wine episode had been the only example of Jesus' inexplicable power, it would present no problem at all. But there was Miriam's sudden realization that she possessed an inspired voice; had made this amazing discovery on the same day that the other thing had happened in the home of Hariph. If you consented to Miriam's story—and its truth was self-evident—you might as well accept Hariph's. And there was the strange feeding of the five thousand. You could explain that without difficulty. Under Jesus' persuasive words about human brotherhood, they had shared their food. You had to concede nothing here but the tremendous strength of Jesus' personality, which you were glad enough to do because you believed in it yourself. Demosthenes had wrought wonders with his impassioned appeals to the Greeks. Such infusions of courage and honesty required no miracle.

But there was little Jonathan. The whole town of Sepphoris knew that Jonathan had been born a cripple. Of course you could maintain that Jesus could have manipulated that crooked little foot and reduced its dislocation; and if that were the only story of Jesus' surprising deeds, your explanation might suffice. To be sure, that leaves the entire population of Sepphoris believing something that wasn't true; but even that was possible. There was no limit to the credulity of unsophisticated people. Indeed, they rather liked to believe in the uncanny.

There was Lydia, healed of a long-time disease by touching Jesus' Robe. Well—you couldn't say that was impossible in the face of your own experience. You had impulsively told Justus that you believed it, and Justus felt that you were ready to hear about the storm. If you believed that Jesus' supernormal power could heal the physical and mental sickness of those who merely touched his Robe, by what reasoning do you disbelieve that he could still a storm? Once you impute to him supernormal power, what kind of impertinence consents to your drawing up an itemized list of the peculiar things he can and cannot do? Yet this storm story was too, too much! Here you have no human multitude yielding to the entreating voice. This is an inanimate, insensible tempest! No human being—however persuasive—could still a storm! Concede Jesus *that* power, and you admit that he was *divine!*

'I have taken the liberty of asking Shalum to bake us a fish,' announced Justus, as Marcellus slowly sauntered toward the tent. 'We will have supper at the inn. It will be a relief from my poor cooking.'

'Very well,' agreed Marcellus, absently. 'Haven't seen anything of Demetrius?'

'No—and I inquired at the inn.'

'I had almost forgotten about the poor fellow,' confessed Marcellus. 'There has been much to think about, this afternoon.'

'If Demetrius has been arrested, he will give an account of himself,' said Justus, reassuringly. 'You will learn his whereabouts promptly, I think. They will surrender him—for a price—no matter what the indictment is. Valuable slaves don't stay long in jail. Shall we go to supper now, sir?'

The dining-hall had accommodations for only a score of guests, but it was tastefully appointed. Because the lighting facilities in small town hostelries were not good, travelers dined early. The three dignified Pharisees, whose commodious tent had been pitched in the sycamore grove during the afternoon, occupied a table in the center of the room. Two centurions from the fort were enjoying their wine at a table by a western window while they waited to be served. Shalum—grizzled, bow-legged, obsequious—led the way to a corner table, bowing deeply when Justus introduced his friend.

'Is he a Christian?' asked Marcellus, as Shalum waddled away.

Justus blinked with surprise, and Marcellus grinned.

'Yes,' said Justus, in a barely audible tone that strongly counseled caution.

'You didn't think I knew that word; did you?' murmured Marcellus.

Justus did not reply; sat with arms folded, staring out into the garden.

'Demetrius picked it up in Joppa,' explained Marcellus, quietly.

'We must be careful,' admonished Justus. 'Pharisees have small hearts, but big ears.'

'Is that a saying?' Marcellus chuckled.

'Yes—but not a loud saying,' warned Justus, breaking one of the small brown loaves. He raised his voice a little and said, casually, 'Shalum bakes good bread. Have some.'

'You come here frequently?'

'This is the first time for a year and a half,' confided Justus. 'Last time I was in this room, it was full. Shalum gave a dinner for Jesus. All of the disciples and a few others were here; and there must have been a hundred outside. Shalum fed them too.'

'Nothing secret about it then.'

'No—not then. The priests were already plotting how they might destroy his influence with the people, but they were not yet openly hostile.'

'That's strange,' said Marcellus. 'When Jesus was alive and an active menace to the priests' business, no effort was made to keep his doings a secret. Now that he is dead and gone—you must talk about him in whispers.'

Justus looked Marcellus squarely in the eyes—and smiled. He seemed about to make some rejoinder, but refrained. An old servitor came with their supper; the baked fish on a large platter, lentils in cream, stewed figs, and a pitcher of wine. It was an attractive meal and they were hungry.

'Did you sit close to Jesus at that dinner?' asked Marcellus, after some moments devoted to their food.

'No—I sat with Matthias, over yonder by the door.'

'Where did Jesus sit?' inquired Marcellus.

'There,' nodded Justus, 'where you're sitting.'

Marcellus started.

'No one should ever sit here!' he declared.

Justus' eyes mellowed, and he approved Marcellus' sentiment with a comradely smile.

'You talk like a Christian yourself, my friend,' he murmured; adding, after a moment, 'Did you enjoy Bartholomew's story?'

'It wasn't meant to be enjoyed!' retorted Marcellus. 'I confess I'm thoroughly bewildered by it. Bartholomew is a fine old man. I'm convinced that he believes his story true.'

'But you don't believe it,' said Justus.

'Bartholomew made one statement, Justus, that may throw a little light on the matter. Do you remember his saying that he felt at peace, that he felt calmed, when Jesus spoke to the storm? Maybe that's where the storm was stilled, the storm in these men's minds! Jesus spoke to their fears, and they were reassured.'

'Does that explanation content you?' asked Justus, soberly.

'Of course not!' admitted Marcellus. 'But—see here, Justus! You can't have Jesus stopping a storm!'

'Why not?' asked Justus, gently.

'Why not! Don't you realize that he has to be superhuman to do that? Can't you see that such an act makes him a *god?*'

'Well—and if it does—'

'Then you're left with a lot more explaining to do. Suppose you say that Jesus is divine; a god! Would he permit himself to be placed under arrest, and dragged about in the night from one court to another, whipped and reviled? Would he—this god!—consent to be put to death on a cross? A god, indeed! Crucified—dead—and buried!'

Justus sat for a moment, saying nothing, staring steadily into Marcellus' troubled eyes. Then he leaned far forward, grasped his sleeve, and drew him close. He whispered something into Marcellus' ear.

'No, Justus!' declared Marcellus, gruffly. 'I'm not a fool! I don't believe that—and neither do you!'

'But—*I saw him!*' persisted Justus, unruffled.

Marcellus swallowed convulsively, and shook his head.

'Why do you want to say a thing like that to me?' he demanded, testily. 'I happen to know it isn't true! You might make some people believe it—but not me! I hadn't intended to tell you this painful thing, Justus, but—*I saw him die!* I saw a lance thrust deep into his heart! I saw them take his limp body down—dead as ever a dead man was!'

'Everybody knows that,' agreed Justus, calmly. 'He was put to death and laid away in a tomb. And on the morning of the third day, he came alive, and was seen walking about in a garden.'

'You're mad, Justus! Such things don't happen!'

'Careful!' warned Justus. 'We mustn't be overheard.'

Pushing his plate away, Marcellus folded his arms on the table. His hands were trembling.

'If you think Jesus is alive,' he muttered, 'where is he?'

Justus shook his head, made a hopeless little gesture with both hands, and drew a long sigh.

'I don't know,' he said, dreamily, 'but I do know he is alive.' After a quiet moment, Justus brightened a little. 'I am always looking for him,' he went on. 'Everytime a door opens. At every turn of the road. At every street-corner. At every hillcrest.'

Marcellus' eyes had widened, and he nodded understandingly.

'I knew you were always expecting to meet someone,' he said. 'If you persist in that habit, you'll lose your mind.' Neither man spoke for some moments. Marcellus looked toward the door. 'Do you mean to say,' he asked cautiously, 'that you wouldn't be surprised if Jesus came in here now—and asked Shalum to serve him his supper?'

Justus repressed a smile at the sight of Marcellus' almost boyish expression of complete bafflement.

'No,' he replied, confidently. 'I shouldn't be surprised, at all. I confess I was badly shaken the first time I saw him. As you say, such things don't happen. They're quite impossible. Had I been alone, I should have doubted my senses—and my sanity, too.'

'Where was this?' demanded Marcellus, as seriously as if he expected to believe the story.

'At Benyosef's house; quite a little company of us; ten days after Jesus had been put to death. We had had a simple supper together. The sun had set, but the lamps had not yet been lighted. There had been much talk about Jesus' reappearance. Several of the disciples claimed to have seen him. I, for one, didn't believe it; though I kept still. There had been a lot of confusing reports. On the morning of the third day, some women had gone to the sepulcher and found it empty. One of them said she had seen Jesus, walking in the garden; said he had spoken to her.'

'Hysterical, I dare say,' put in Marcellus.

'That's what I made of it,' admitted Justus. 'And then there was a story that two men had seen him on the highway and asked him to have supper with them at an inn.'

'Reliable people?'

'I didn't know them. One was a man named Cleopas, a cousin of Alphaeus. I never heard the other man's name.'

'Sounds like poor testimony.'

'It occurred that way to me,' said Justus. 'Several of the disciples declared he had come into the room where they were sitting, that same night. But—they were terribly wrought up, and I thought they might have imagined seeing him, what with so many strange reports flying about—'

'Naturally!' agreed Marcellus. 'Once the stories started, the hallucinations multiplied. Well—go on. You were at Benyosef's house—'

'John had been telling how he looked and what he said—'

'He's that dreamy young fellow, eh?'

'Yes—that's the one,' Justus went on, undisturbed by the implications of Marcellus' query. 'And when John had finished his story, Thomas stood up and spoke his mind—and my mind, too. "I don't believe a word of it!" he shouted. "And I don't intend to believe it until I have seen him with my own eyes—and touched his wounds with my hands!"'

'He was a bold fellow,' remarked Marcellus. 'Was John offended?'

'I don't know,' said Justus, absently. 'He didn't have much time to be offended. Jesus was standing there—at Thomas' elbow.'

'No—Justus!'

'Yes—with the same compassionate smile we all knew so well.'

'A specter?'

'Not at all! He was a little thinner. You could see the effects of the bad treatment he had suffered. There were long scratches on his forehead. He held his hands out to Thomas—'

'Did you all gather about him?' asked Marcellus, with a dry throat.

'No—I think we were stunned. I'm sure I was. I couldn't have moved if I had tried. There was complete silence. Jesus stood there, holding out his hands and smiling into Thomas' eyes. You could see the deep wounds in his palms. "Touch them," he said, gently. This was too much for Thomas. He covered his face with his hands and cried like a child.'

The dining-room had cleared. Twilight was settling. Shalum came over to inquire if there was anything else he could do for them. Marcellus glanced up bewilderedly at this summons back to reality.

'I have been telling my friend some things about Jesus,' said Justus.

'Yes, yes,' nodded Shalum. 'Once, when he honored my poor house, he was seated there, sir, where you are sitting.'

'Did he rise and speak—at the dinner?' asked Marcellus.

'He did not rise to speak,' remembered Justus.

'He told a story,' said Shalum. 'It seems someone had asked him to explain what was meant by "my neighbor" as it is written in our law. And Jesus told a fable about a man who was traveling from Jerusalem to Jericho—a dangerous road—and beset by Bedouins who stripped, robbed, and wounded him, leaving him half-dead. A priest came along and saw him, but passed on. A Levite, too, paused—but went his way. Then a Samaritan came—we do not care much for Samaritans up here, sir—and tied up the man's wounds—and took him to an inn. "Which of these men," he asked, "was a neighbor to him who fell among thieves?" '

'That was easily answered, I think,' observed Marcellus. 'Had I been here, I should have asked another question. I am told that Jesus did not believe in fighting—regardless of the circumstances. Now, if the brave Samaritan had arrived while the Bedouins were beating the life out of this unfortunate fellow, what was he supposed to do; join in the defense, or wait until the robbers had completed their work—and fled?'

Shalum and Justus exchanged looks of inquiry, each inviting the other to reply.

'Jesus was interested in binding up wounds,' said Justus, solemnly; 'not in inflicting them.'

'Does that answer your question, sir?' inquired Shalum.

'No,' said Marcellus. 'Perhaps we should go, Justus. It is growing dark.' They rose. 'The fish was good, Shalum. Let us have another for breakfast.'

Taking up the little lantern that Shalum had provided, Justus led the way across the well-kept grounds to the tent where he lighted their larger one and hung it to the center pole. Marcellus unlaced his sandal-thongs, took off his belt, and lounged on his cot, his eyes following Justus as he made his bed.

'And then what happened,' asked Marcellus, 'after Thomas looked at the wounds?'

'Benyosef filled a supper-plate, and offered it to Jesus,' said Justus, sitting down on the edge of his cot. 'There was a piece of broiled fish, a small loaf, and some honey in the comb. And Jesus took it—and ate.'

'Not just a spirit then,' commented Marcellus.

'I don't know,' mumbled Justus, uncertainly. 'He ate it—or some of it. The day was fading fast. Philip suggested that the lamps be lighted. Andrew, who was near the door to an adjoining room, went out and returned with a taper. Old Benyosef held up a lamp and Andrew lighted it. Jesus was not there.'

'Vanished?' Marcellus sat up.

'I don't know. It was getting dark in there. He might have gone out through the door. But nobody heard it open or close.'

'Had he come in through the door?'

'I don't know. I didn't hear it. The first I knew, he was standing there beside Thomas. And then—when the lamp was lighted—he wasn't there.'

'What do you suppose became of him?'

'I don't know.' Justus shook his head.

There was a long silence.

'Ever see him again?' asked Marcellus.

Justus nodded.

'Once more,' he said, 'about a month afterward. But in the meantime, he was seen up here in Galilee. A very unfortunate thing happened on the night Jesus was tried. When they had him before old Annas, Simon was waiting in the courtyard where the legionaries had built a fire. A servant-girl said to Simon, "Aren't you a friend of this Galilean?" And Simon said, "No—I don't know him." '

'But I thought Simon was a leader among the disciples,' remarked Marcellus.

'That's what made it so bad,' sighed Justus. 'Ordinarily, Simon is a bold fellow, with plenty of courage. But he certainly did himself no credit that night. He followed along, at a distance, when they took Jesus to the Insula, and waited, across the street, while the trial was held. I don't know where he went after the procession started out toward the place of execution, or where he spent the night and the next day. I heard him confess it all. He was sick with remorse, and hurried back home.'

'So—Simon wasn't present on that first occasion when the disciples thought they saw Jesus.'

'No—but Jesus told them to be sure and tell Simon.'

'Did Jesus know that Simon had denied his friendship?'

'Oh, yes—he knew. You see that's why he was so anxious to have Simon know that everything was all right again. Well—the next morning, the Zebedee brothers and Thomas decided to take old Bartholomew home. He had been sick. They put him on a donkey and set out for Galilee where they found Peter, restless and heart-sore, and told him what had happened.

He was for rushing back to Jerusalem, but they counseled him to wait; for the news of Jesus' return was being noised about, and the priests were asking questions. And Benyosef's shop was being watched. So—that night, they all went fishing. In the early morning, at sunrise, they left off and sailed toward the east shore. Bartholomew said that when they were within about two hundred cubits of the beach—chilled and drowsy from their long night on the water—they were suddenly roused by a loud shout and a splash. Simon had jumped overboard and was swimming. They all leaped up to see what had come over Simon. And they saw Jesus standing at the water's edge, waiting. It was a very tender meeting, he said, for Simon had been quite broken-hearted.'

'And then'—Marcellus' voice was impatient—'did he vanish—as before?'

'Not at once. They broiled fish for breakfast on the beach. He sat and talked with them for above an hour, showing special attention to Simon.'

'What did he talk about?'

'Their future duties,' replied Justus, 'to remember and tell the things he had taught. He would come back, he said, though he could not tell them the day or the hour. They were to be on the alert for his coming. After they had eaten, someone suggested that they return to Capernaum. They had beached the boat, and all hands—except Jesus—fell to work, pushing off into the water. Bartholomew was up in the bow, rigging a sail. The others scrambled over the side and shipped the oars. When they looked about for Jesus, he was nowhere to be seen.'

'But he appeared again—another time?'

'The last time he was seen,' said Justus, 'I was present. It was on a hill top in Judea, a few miles north of Jerusalem. Perhaps I should tell you that the disciples and other friends of Jesus were closely watched, through those days. Such meetings as we had were late in the night and held in obscure places. In Jerusalem, the Temple people had the legionaries of the Insula patrolling the streets in search of us. Up here in Galilee, Herod Antipas and Julian the Legate had threatened death to anyone who so much as spoke Jesus' name.'

'They too believed that he had returned to life?' inquired Marcellus.

'Perhaps not. I don't know. But they knew they had failed to dispose of him. They thought the people would soon forget and settle down to their old ways; but it soon appeared that Jesus had set some forces in motion—'

'I don't understand,' broke in Marcellus. 'What forces?'

'Well—for one thing—the Temple revenues were falling off. Hundreds of people, accustomed to paying tithes, stayed away from the synagogues whose priests had persecuted Jesus. There was no violence; but in the market-places throughout all Judea, Samaria, and Galilee, merchants who had thought to win favor with the authorities by denouncing Jesus found that their business was failing. The Christians were patronizing one another. It was apparent that they were in collusion and had a secret understanding. An edict was published prohibiting any assembly of Jesus' adherents. We agreed among ourselves to hold no more meetings until such time as it might be more prudent.'

'How many Christians were there in Jerusalem, at that time?' asked Marcellus. 'A score, perhaps?'

'About five hundred that had declared themselves. One afternoon, about five weeks after the crucifixion, Alphaeus came to my house saying that Simon had called a meeting. A week hence, we were to assemble shortly after sunrise on a hill, quite off the highway, where we had often spent a day of rest when Jesus was with us. Knowing it was dangerous to be seen on the roads in company with others of our belief, we journeyed singly. It was a beautiful morning. As I came to the well-remembered footpath that led across the fields toward the hills, I saw—in the early dawn-light—several men preceding me; though I could identify none but Simon, who is a tall man. As the grade grew steeper, I overtook old Bartholomew leaning on his staff, already tired and laboring for breath.'

'He had walked all that way from Capernaum?' asked Marcellus.

'And had spent the whole week at it,' said Justus. 'But it seemed that the hill would be too much for him. I counseled him not to try; that his heart might fail him; but he wouldn't listen. So I gave him an arm and we trudged along slowly up the winding path that became more difficult with every turn. Occasionally we had glimpses of the others, widely separated, as they climbed the rugged grade. We were about halfway up when Bartholomew stopped, pointed with his staff, and hoarsely shouted, "Look you! On the rock!" I looked up—and there he was! He was wearing a white robe. The sunshine made it appear dazzling. He was standing on the big white rock—at the summit—waiting.'

'Were you amazed?'

'No—not amazed; but eager to press on. Bartholomew urged me to leave him. He would make it alone, he said. But the good old man was half-dead with weariness, so I supported him the rest of the way. When we came out at length on the little plateau in a shady grove, we saw him. Jesus was standing, with both arms outstretched in a gesture of blessing. The disciples were kneeling about his feet. Simon, with his great hands covering his face, had bowed over until his head nearly touched the ground. Poor old Bartholomew, much moved and thoroughly spent, couldn't take another step. He fell to his knees. So did I, though we were at least a hundred cubits from the others. We bowed our heads.' Justus' voice broke, and for a moment he was overcome with emotion. Marcellus waited silently for him to regain his self-control.

'After a while,' continued Justus, thickly, 'we heard the murmuring of voices. We raised our eyes. He was gone.'

'Where, Justus? Where do you think he went?' asked Marcellus, huskily.

'I don't know, my friend. I only know that he is alive—and I am always expecting to see him. Sometimes I feel aware of him, as if he were close by.' Justus smiled faintly, his eyes wet with tears. 'It keeps you honest,' he went on. 'You have no temptation to cheat anyone, or lie to anyone, or hurt anyone—when, for all you know, Jesus is standing beside you.'

'I'm afraid I should feel very uncomfortable,' remarked Marcellus, 'being perpetually watched by some invisible presence.'

'Not if that presence helped you defend yourself against yourself, Marcellus. It is a great satisfaction to have someone standing by—to keep you at your best.' Justus suddenly came to his feet, and went to the door of the tent. A lantern was bobbing through the trees.

'Someone coming?' inquired Marcellus, sitting up.

'A legionary,' muttered Justus.

'News of Demetrius, perhaps.' Marcellus joined Justus at the tent-door. A tall legionary stood before them.

'I bear a message,' he announced, 'from Legate Paulus to Tribune Marcellus Lucan Gallio.'

'*Tribune!*' murmured Justus—in an agitated voice.

'The Legate presents his compliments,' continued the legionary, in formal tones, 'and desires his excellent friend, Tribune Marcellus, to be his guest tonight at the fort. If it is your wish, you may accompany me, sir, and I shall light your way.'

'Very good,' said Marcellus. 'I shall be ready in a moment. Tarry for me at the gate.'

The legionary brought up his spear in a salute and marched away.

'Apparently Demetrius is safe!' exclaimed Marcellus, brightly.

'And I have betrayed my people!' moaned Justus, sinking down on his cot. 'I have delivered my friends into the hands of their enemies!'

'No—Justus—no!' Marcellus laid a hand on his shoulder. 'All this may seem disquieting to you, but I assure you I am not a spy! It is possible I may befriend you and your people. Wait for me here. I shall return by midday tomorrow.'

Justus made no response; sat dejectedly, with his face in his hands, until Marcellus' footsteps faded away. It was a long night of agony and remorse. When the first pale blue light appeared, the heavy-hearted Galilean gathered up his few belongings; made his way to the silent street, and trudged along, past the old fort, to the plaza. For a long time, he sat on the marble steps of the synagogue, and when the sun had risen he proceeded to the little house where he had left Jonathan.

Thomas' mother was in the kitchen, preparing breakfast.

'You are early,' she said. 'I was not expecting you so soon. I hope all is well with you,' she added, searching his troubled face.

'I wish to be on the road as soon as may be,' he replied.

'But where is your young Roman—and your little pack-train?'

'They are remaining here,' said Justus. 'Jonathan and I are going home.'

Chapter XVIII

PAULUS had been in command of the fort at Capernaum only a week, but he already knew he wasn't going to like it here.

For a dozen years he had been hoping to get out of Minoa. It was a disgrace to be stationed there, and the Empire meant you to realize that an appointment to this fort was a degradation.

The buildings were ugly and shabby, the equipment bad, the climate abominable. No provision had ever been made for an adequate water-supply. On the sun-blistered grounds there wasn't a tree, a flower, or a blade of grass; not even a weed. The air was always foul with yellow, abrasive dust. You couldn't keep clean if you wanted to, and after a few months at Minoa you didn't care.

The garrison was lazy, surly, dirty, and tough. With little to do, except occasional brief and savage raids on the Bedouins, discipline was loose and erratic. There were no decent diversions; no entertainment. When you couldn't bear the boredom and discomfort another minute, you went down to Gaza and got drunk, and were lucky if you didn't get into a bloody brawl.

As for that vicious old city, was not Gaza known throughout the world for the squalor of its stinking kennels where the elderly riff-raff of a half-dozen quarrelsome races screamed imprecations, and the younger scum swapped unpleasant maladies, and the hapless stranger was stripped and robbed in broad daylight? Gaza had her little imperfections; there was no doubt about that. But she had docks and wharves and a spacious harbor. Little coastal ships tied up to her piers; bigger ships lay at anchor in her bay. You strolled down to watch them come and go, and felt you were still in contact with the outside world. Sometimes ships' officers would come out to the fort for a roistering evening; sometimes military men you had known in Rome would visit you while their vessel took on cargo.

Paulus' unexpected appointment to Capernaum had been received with hilarious joy. He had never been there, but he had heard something about its quiet charm. Old Julian had been envied his post.

For one thing—the fort was within a half-hour's ride of Tiberias, that ostentatious seat of the enormously wealthy sycophant, Herod Antipas. Paulus had no notion he was going to like this toad: he had nothing but contempt for these provincial lickspittles who would sell their own sisters for a smile from some influential Roman; but Herod frequently entertained interesting guests who, though they might despise him, must make a show of honoring his position as Tetrarch of Galilee and Peraea.

And Capernaum, everyone said, was beautiful; ringed by green hills, with snow-capped mountains in the distance. There was a lovely inland sea. The people were docile. They were reputed to be melancholy over the execution of their Jesus, but they were not violently resentful. Doubtless that problem would solve itself if you gave it time. Old Julian's tactics—listening at the keyholes of cottages for revolutionary talk, the posting of harsh edicts, floggings and imprisonments—what did they accomplish but to band these simple, harmless people together for mutual sympathy? Of course, if the foolhardy fishermen persisted in making a nuisance of their cult, you would have to punish them, or get yourself into trouble with Herod. That's what you would be there for—to keep the peace.

Now that you were here, you had much more peace than you had bargained for. Had the gods ever ordained such quiet nights? Paulus had not fully appreciated this oppressive silence for the first day or two. There was the novelty of settling into his immeasurably better quarters. He proudly inspected the trim pleasure-craft that Herod had placed at the disposal of the Legate. He luxuriated in the well-equipped baths, thinking kindly of old Julian whom he had never had any use for.

The fort buzzed with activity. A fairly large contingent from Minoa had accompanied Paulus. There had been the usual festivities at the Insula in Jerusalem during Passover Week—though Paulus had been moody and taciturn, anxious to have it over with, and move on. His retinue had come along to Capernaum, for defense on the journey as well as to dignify his inauguration. A generous dinner had been served after the ceremonies to which Herod—represented by a deputy—had contributed lavish supplies of potent wine. It was a noisy night. Heads had been cracked, noses flattened, more urgent arguments had been settled with knives. Paulus had filled the courtroom with battered celebrants; had crowded the guardhouse; had stormed and shouted oaths new to the local legionaries; and, well pleased with his first day's duties, had gone to bed tight as a drum.

Next day, the Minoa contingent had left for home—all but Sextus. At the last minute, Paulus—with a premonition of loneliness—had told Sextus to remain, at least for a time. And when the last of them had disappeared, a strange quietness settled over the fort. That night, after Sextus had ambled off early to bed, Paulus sat by his window watching the moonlight on the lake. Except for Sextus' snoring, the silence was profound. Perhaps it had been a mistake to retain Sextus. He wasn't very good company, after all.

What did one do for diversion in Capernaum? The little town was sound asleep. The Herod family was away. Tiberias was dead as a doornail. If this was a sample of life at Capernaum, you had been better off at Minoa.

The days trudged along, scraping their sandal-heels; sitting down, now and then, for a couple of hours, while Time remained standing. Paulus, strolling in the courtyard, paused before the sundial, read its laconic warning, 'Tempus fugit,' and sourly remarked to Sextus, 'It's apparent that old Virgil never visited Capernaum.'

After a week, Paulus was so restless that he even thought of contriving some errand to Jerusalem, though his recent visit there had been lacking in interest. Perhaps that was because the insufferable young Quintus, who had been sent by the Crown to reshuffle the Palestinian commands, was too, too much in evidence. Paulus, who was a good hater, had never despised anybody so quickly, so earnestly. Quintus was a vain, overbearing, patronizing, strutting peacock; he was an insolent, ill-mannered puppy; he was a pompous ass! In short, Paulus didn't like him at all. But Quintus would have sailed for home by now. Maybe Quintus was what had ailed Jerusalem, this time.

* * * * * *

It was late afternoon. The sun was setting. Paulus and Sextus had been apathetically shaking the old leather dice-cup on the long table in the courtroom. Sextus yawned cavernously and wiped his eyes.

'If it's bedtime,' drawled Paulus, 'perhaps we'd better light the lamps.' He clapped his hands. A guard scurried up. Paulus pointed to the lamps. The guard saluted and made haste to obey. 'Nine,' mumbled the Legate, handing the dice-cup to his drowsy friend.

At this juncture, old Namius had come in with three disheveled slaves. Somewhere, Paulus felt, he had seen that tall Greek. Sextus jogged his memory. Ah—Demetrius! He had always liked Demetrius, in spite of his cool superiority. Demetrius was a haughty fellow, but you had respect for him. Paulus suddenly recalled having seen an announcement, posted at the Insula in Jerusalem, offering a reward for the capture of a Greek slave belonging to Tribune Marcellus Gallio. The bulletin said that the Greek had assaulted a Roman citizen in Athens, and was thought to be in hiding in Jerusalem. So—here he was. Somebody had gathered him in. But no—a brief examination revealed that Demetrius had been arrested on suspicion. He had been loitering; he was shabby; he had money. In prison he had fought the rascally Syrians who denied him water. So much for that. Then Paulus had wanted to know about Marcellus, who had been reported crazy—or the next thing to it—and was delighted to learn that his friend was in the neighborhood.

But before he could release Demetrius, he must learn something about this charge against him. If it were true that he had struck a Roman, and run away, you couldn't dismiss him so easily. Paulus put them all out, including Sextus, who didn't like it.

'Demetrius'—Paulus frowned judiciously—'what have you to say about this report that you are a fugitive; that you struck a Roman citizen in Athens? That is very serious, you know!'

'It is true, sir,' replied Demetrius, without hesitation. 'I found it necessary to punish Tribune Quintus severely.'

'Quintus!' shouted the Legate. 'You mean to say you struck Quintus?' He leaned forward over the desk, eyes beaming. 'Tell me all about it!'

'Well, sir—the Tribune came to the Inn of Eupolis with a message for my master. While waiting for the reply, he made himself grossly offensive to the daughter of the innkeeper. They are a highly respected family, sir, and the young woman was not accustomed to being treated like a common trollop. Her father was present, but feared to intervene lest they all be thrown into prison.'

'So—you came to the damsel's rescue, eh?'

'Yes, sir.'

'Don't you know you can be put to death for so much as touching a Roman Tribune?' demanded Paulus, sternly; and when Demetrius had slowly and remorsefully nodded his head, the Legate's frown relaxed, and he asked, in a confidential tone, 'What did you do to him?'

'I struck him in the face with my fist, sir,' confessed Demetrius. 'And—once I had struck him—I knew I had committed a crime punishable by death, and couldn't make my position any worse, so—'

'So—you hit him again, I think,' surmised Paulus, with mounting interest. 'Did he fight back?'

'No, sir. The Tribune was not expecting that first blow, and was unprepared for the next one.'

'In the face?' Paulus' eyes were wide and bright.

'Many times, sir,' admitted Demetrius.

'Knock him down?'

'Oh, yes, sir; and held him up by his helmet-strap, and beat his eyes shut. I was very angry, sir.'

'Yes—I can see that you were.' Paulus put both hands over his suddenly puffed cheeks and stifled something like a hiccough. 'And then you ran off?'

'Without a moment's delay, sir. There was a ship sailing. The Captain befriended me. Tribune Quintus was on board, and would have had me apprehended, but the Captain let me escape in the small boat at Gaza. From there I walked to Jerusalem.'

'Didn't the Captain know he could be punished for that?' growled Paulus. 'What was his name?'

'I cannot remember, sir,' regretted Demetrius, after some hesitation.

'That is undoubtedly a lie,' said Paulus, 'but you are to be commended for your loyalty. So, then, you went to Jerusalem. Why?'

'My master expected to come shortly.'

'What did you do there?'

Demetrius told him of the weaver's shop. Paulus grew interested again. 'I understand there is a weaver's shop where the leaders of the Jesus-people meet. What was the name of your weaver?'

'Benyosef, sir.'

'That was the name! And how did you happen to be in that company, Demetrius? Are you, perhaps, one of these—these—what do they call them—Christians?'

'Yes, sir,' confessed Demetrius, tardily. 'Not a very good one; but I believe as they do.'

'You can't!' shouted Paulus. 'You have a good mind! You don't mean to tell me that you believe all this nonsense—about Jesus returning to life, and being seen on various occasions!'

'Yes, sir,' said Demetrius. 'I am sure that is true.'

'But—see here!' Paulus stood up. 'You were out there, that day, and saw him die!'

'Yes, sir. I am sure he died; and I am sure he is alive.'

'Have you seen him?' Paulus' voice was unsteady.

Demetrius shook his head and the Legate grinned.

'I hadn't thought,' he said, dryly, 'that you could be taken in by such a story. Men who die do not return. Only fools think so!' Paulus sat down again, relaxing in his chair. 'But you are not a fool. What makes you believe that?'

'I heard the story from a man who did see him; a man of sound mind; a man who does not lie.' Demetrius broke off, though it was evident he would have said more.

'Very well; go on!' commanded the Legate.

'It did not surprise me very much,' continued Demetrius. 'There never was a person like that before. Surely—you, sir, must have noticed that. He had something nobody else ever had! I don't believe he was an ordinary man, sir.'

'How do you mean—not ordinary? Are you trying to say that you think he was something else than a man? You don't think he was a god?'

'Yes, sir,' said Demetrius, firmly. 'I think he was—and is—a god!'

'Nonsense! Don't you know we are locking up people for saying things like that about this dead Galilean?' Paulus rose impetuously and paced back and forth behind the long table. 'I mean to let you go—for your master's sake; but'—he stopped suddenly and shook a warning finger—'you are to clear out of Galilee—and there's to be no more talk about this Jesus. And if you ever tell anyone that you told me about your assault on Quintus—and I learn of it—I'll have you flogged! Do you understand? I'll have you stripped and lashed with a bull-whip!'

'Thank you, sir,' said Demetrius, gratefully. 'I am very sorry that I struck him.'

'Then you don't deserve your freedom,' growled Paulus. 'That's why I am turning you loose—and now you're sorry you did it. And you believe that dead men come to life. You're crazy!' He clapped his hands, and a guard stalked in. 'Make this Greek comfortable,' he barked. 'Have the physician attend to his cuts. Give him a good supper and a bed. He is to be released from prison.'

Demetrius wincingly brought his arm up in a salute, and turned to follow.

'One more thing!' rasped Paulus, to the guard. 'When you have finished with the Greek, return here. I want you to carry a message to Shalum's Inn. Make haste!'

* * * * * *

Marcellus was pleased to observe that Paulus' promotion had not altered his manner. The easy informality of their friendship was effortlessly resumed.

A small table had been laid in the Legate's handsomely furnished suite; a silver cake-tray, a bowl of fresh fruit, a tall flagon of wine. Paulus, clean-shaven, wearing an expensive white toga and a red silk bandeau that accented the whiteness of his close-cropped hair, was a distinguished figure. He met his guest in the doorway and embraced him warmly.

'Welcome, good Marcellus!' he exclaimed. 'And welcome to Galilee; though, if you have been touring about up here, you may be better acquainted with this province than I.'

'It is a delight to see you again, Paulus!' rejoined Marcellus. 'All my good wishes for the success and happiness of your new command! It was most generous of you to send for me.'

With his arm around Marcellus' shoulders, Paulus guided his friend to a chair by the table, and sauntered to its mate on the other side.

'Come; sit down.' He filled their goblets. 'Let us drink to this happy meeting. Now you must tell me what brings you into my quiet little Galilee.'

Marcellus smiled, raised the goblet to the level of his eyes, and bowed to his host.

'It would take an hour to explain my errand, Paulus,' he replied, sipping his wine. 'A long story—and a somewhat fantastic one, too. In short, the Emperor ordered me to learn something more about the Galilean whom we put to death.'

'A painful business for you, I think,' frowned Paulus. 'I still reproach myself for placing you in such an unhappy position that night at the Procurator's banquet. I did not see you again, or I should have tried to make amends. If it is not too late to say so I am sorry it happened. I was drunk.'

'We all were,' remembered Marcellus. 'I bore you no ill-will.'

'But it wasn't drunkenness that ailed you, sir, when you groped your way out of that banquet-hall. When you put on the dead man's Robe, something happened to you. Even I, drunk as I was, could see that. By the gods!—I thought you must have sighted a ghost!' Raising his goblet, Paulus drank deeply; then, shrugging his dour mood aside, he brightened. 'But why revive unpleasant memories? You were a long time ill. I heard of it and was sad. But now you are quite recovered. That is well. You are the picture of health, Marcellus. Drink—my friend! You have hardly tasted your wine; and it is good.'

'Native?' Marcellus took another sip.

Paulus grinned; then suddenly stiffened to pantomime an attitude of cool hauteur.

'My eminent patron,' he declaimed, with elaborate mockery, 'my exalted lord, the ineffable Herod Antipas—Tetrarch of Galilee and Peraea, robber of the poor, foot-washer of any titled Roman that comes within reach—he sent the wine. And though Herod himself may be a low form of life, his wine is noble.' Slipping easily out of his august rôle, Paulus added, casually, 'I have had no native wine yet. By the way—the country people have a story that our Jesus once supplied a wedding-party with a rare vintage that he made by doing some incantations over a water-pot. There are innumerable yarns of this order. Perhaps you have heard them.'

Marcellus nodded, but did not share the Legate's cynical amusement.

'Yes,' he said, soberly. 'I have heard them. They are very hard to understand.'

'Understand!' echoed Paulus. 'Don't tell me you have tried to understand them! Have we not plenty of such legends in Rome—tales that no one in his right senses gives a second thought to?'

'Yes—I know, Paulus,' agreed Marcellus, quietly, 'and I should want to be among the last to believe them; but—'

At the significant pause, Paulus stood up, busying himself with refilling their goblets. He offered the silver cake-tray, which Marcellus declined, and sat down again with a little gesture of impatience.

'I hope you aren't going to say that these Galilean stories are credible, Marcellus,' he remarked, coolly.

'This Jesus was a strange man, Paulus.'

'Granted! By no means an ordinary man! He had a peculiar kind of courage, and a sort of majesty—all his own. But I hope you don't believe that he changed water into wine!'

'I do not know, Paulus,' replied Marcellus, slowly. 'I saw a child who had been born with a crippled foot; now as active as any other little boy.'

'How do you know he was born with a crippled foot?' demanded Paulus.

'The whole village knew. There was no reason why they should have invented the story for my benefit. They were suspicious of me. In fact, the boy's grandfather, my guide, was reluctant to talk about it.'

'Well—you can be sure there is some reasonable explanation,' rasped Paulus. 'These people are as superstitious as our Thracian slaves. Why—they even believe that this man came to life—and has been seen!'

Marcellus nodded thoughtfully.

'I heard that story for the first time about an hour ago, Paulus. It is amazing!'

'It is preposterous!' shouted Paulus. 'These fools should have contented themselves with tales of water changed to wine—and the magical healing of the sick.' Paulus drank again, noisily. His ruddy face showed annoyance as he watched Marcellus absently toying with the stem of his goblet, his eyes averted. 'You know well enough that the Galilean was dead!' he stormed, angrily. 'No one can tell you or me that he came to life!' Drawing up the sleeve of his toga, Paulus tapped his muscular forearm with measuring fingers, and shrilled, 'I thrust my spear into his chest that deep!'

Marcellus glanced up, nodded, and dropped his eyes again, without comment. Paulus suddenly leaned forward over the table, and brought his fist down with a thump.

'By the gods! Marcellus'—he shouted—'*you believe it!*'

There was a tense silence for a long moment. Marcellus stirred and slowly raised his eyes, quite unruffled by the Legate's outburst.

'I don't know what to believe, Paulus,' he said, quietly. 'Of course my natural reaction is the same as yours; but—there is a great mystery here, my friend. If this story is a trumped-up lie, the men who have been telling it at the risk of their lives are quite mad; yet they do not talk like madmen. They have nothing to gain—and everything to lose—by reporting that they saw him.'

'Oh—I'll concede that,' declared Paulus, loftily. 'It's no uncommon thing for a fanatic to be reckless with his life; but—look you, Marcellus!—however difficult that is to understand—you can't have a dead man coming back from his grave! Why—a man who could overcome death, could—'

'Exactly!' broke in Marcellus. 'He could do anything! He could defy any power on earth! If he cared to, he might have the whole world for his kingdom!'

Paulus drank greedily, spilling some of it on the table.

'Odd thing to say,' he muttered, thickly. 'There was some talk at his trial—about his kingdom: remember? Pilate asked him—absurdly enough, I thought—if he were a king.' Paulus chuckled mirthlessly. 'He said he was—and it shook Pilate a little, too. Indeed—it stunned everybody, for a minute; just the cool audacity of it. I was talking with Vinitius, that night at the banquet, and he said the Galilean explained that his kingdom was not in the world; but—that doesn't mean anything. Or does it?'

'Well—it certainly wouldn't mean anything if *I* said it,' replied Marcellus. 'But if a man who had been out of this life were able to return from—from wherever he had been—he might conceivably have a kingdom elsewhere.'

'You're talking rubbish, Marcellus,' scoffed Paulus. 'I'll assist you,' he went on, drunkenly. 'You are my guest, and I must be polite. If it's so—that a dead man—with some kind of elsewhere-kingdom—has come back to life:—mind you, now, I know it isn't so—but if it's so—I'd rather it were this Jesus than Quintus or Julian or Pilate—or the half-witted Gaius that old Julia whelped.' He laughed boisterously at his own absurdity. 'Or old Tiberius! By the gods!—when crazy old Tiberius dies, I'll wager he stays dead! By the way—do you mean to go back and tell the old fool this story? He'll believe it, you know, and it will scare the very liver out of him!'

Marcellus grinned tolerantly, reflecting that the Legate—albeit pretty drunk—had said something worth thinking about.

'Good idea, Paulus,' he remarked. 'If we're going to have a king who knows how to outlive all the other kings, it might be a great thing for the world if he were a person of good deeds and not evil ones.'

The Legate's face sobered, and Marcellus, noting his serious interest, enlarged upon his impromptu idea.

'Consider these tales about Jesus, Paulus. He is reputed to have made blind men see: there is no story that he made any man blind. He is said to have changed water into wine; not wine into water. He made a crippled child walk; he never made any child a cripple.'

'Excellent!' applauded Paulus. 'The kings have been destroyers, despoilers. They have made men blind, crippled, broken.' He paused, and went on, muttering half to himself, 'Wouldn't the world be surprised if once it should have a government that came to the rescue of the blind and sick and lame? By the gods!—I wish this absurd tale about the Galilean were true!'

'Do you mean that, Paulus, or are you jesting?' demanded Marcellus, earnestly.

'Well'—compromised the Legate—'I'm as serious as the matter warrants, seeing it hasn't a leg to stand on.' His forehead wrinkled in a judicial frown. 'But—see here, Marcellus, aren't you going in for this Jesus business a little too far for your own good?'

Marcellus made no reply, other than an enigmatic pursing of the lips. Paulus grinned, shrugged, and replenished his goblet. His manner said they would drop that phase of the subject.

'What else do they say about him, up here in the country?' he asked negligently. 'You seem to have been making inquiries.'

'They have a story in Cana,' replied Marcellus, casually, 'about a young woman who discovered she could sing. The people think Jesus was responsible for it.'

'Taught her to sing?'

'No. One day she found that she could sing. They believe he had something to do with it. I heard her, Paulus. There hasn't been anything quite like it—so far as I know.'

'Indeed!' enthused Paulus. 'I must tell the Tetrarch. It's part of my business, you know, to please the old rascal. He may invite her to entertain one of his banquets.'

'No, Paulus, please!' protested Marcellus. 'This girl has been gently bred. Moreover, she is a cripple; can't stand up; never leaves the neighborhood.'

'He gave her a voice, and left her a cripple; eh?' Paulus grinned. 'How do you explain that?'

'I don't explain it; I just report it. But—I sincerely hope you will say nothing about her to Herod. She would feel very much out of place in his palace, if what I have heard about him is correct.'

'If what you've heard is revolting,' commented Paulus, bitterly, 'it's correct. But if you are so concerned about these Christians, it might be to their advantage if one of their daughters sang acceptably for the lecherous old fox.'

'No!' snapped Marcellus, hotly. 'She and her family are friends of mine. I beg of you not to degrade her with an invitation to meet Herod Antipas or any member of his household!'

Paulus agreed that they were a precious lot of scoundrels, including Herod's incorrigible daughter Salome. A dangerous little vixen, he declared, responsible for a couple of assassinations, and notoriously unchaste. He chuckled unpleasantly, and added that she had come by her talents honestly enough, seeing that her father—if he was her father—hadn't even the respect of the Sanhedrin, and her mother was as promiscuous as a cat. He snorted contemptuously, and drank to take the taste of them out of his mouth. Marcellus scowled, but made no comment. Presently he became aware that Paulus was regarding him with a friendly but reproachful inspection.

'I wonder if you realize, Marcellus,' Paulus was saying, 'that your keen concern for these Christians might sometime embarrass you. May I talk to you about that, without giving offense?'

'Why not, Paulus?' replied Marcellus, graciously.

'Why not? Because it may sound impertinent. We are of the same rank. It does not behoove me to give you advice—much less injunctions.'

'Injunctions?' Marcellus' brows lifted a little. 'I'm afraid I don't understand.'

'Let me explain, then. I assume you know what has been happening in Palestine during the past year. For a few weeks, after the execution of the Galilean, his movement appeared to be a closed incident. The leaders of his party scattered, most of them returning to this neighborhood. The influential men of Jerusalem were satisfied. There were sporadic rumors that Jesus had been seen in various places after his death, but nobody with any sense took these tales seriously. It was expected that the whole affair would presently be forgotten.'

'And then it revived,' remarked Marcellus, as Paulus paused to take another drink.

'Revived is not the word. It hadn't died. Undercover groups had been meeting in many cities. For a few months there were very few outward signs of it. The authorities had contempt for it, feeling that it was a thing of no importance, either as to size or quality. Then—one day—it began to dawn on the priests that their synagogues were not being patronized; the tithes were not paid. Then the merchants observed that their business was increasingly bad. In Jericho, more than half of the population now make no secret of their affiliations. In Antioch, the Christians are quite outspoken; adding daily to their numbers. Nor is interest in this party limited to the poor and helpless, as was at first supposed. Nobody knows how many there are in Jerusalem, but the Temple is beside itself with anxiety and anger, prodding the Insula to do something drastic. Old Julian is being harassed by the priests and merchants, who are making it plain that he must act—or resign.'

'What does he think of doing about it?' inquired Marcellus.

'Well'—Paulus flicked his hands in a baffled gesture—'it's obvious that the movement cannot be tolerated. It may look innocuous to a casual visitor like yourself; but, to the solid respectables of Jerusalem, it is treason, mutiny, blasphemy, and a general disintegration of their established ways. Julian doesn't want a bloody riot on his hands, and has been playing for time; but the city fathers are at the end of their patience.'

'But—surely they can't find much fault with the things Jesus taught,' interposed Marcellus. 'He urged kindness, fair dealing, good will. Don't the influential men of Palestine believe in letting the people treat one another decently?'

'That isn't the point, Marcellus, and you know it,' argued Paulus, impatiently. 'These Christians are refusing to do business on the old basis. More and more they are patronizing one another. Why—right here in little Capernaum—if you don't have the outline of a fish scrawled on the door of your shop, it doesn't pay to open up.' He studied his friend's interested face—and grinned. 'I suppose you know what that fish stands for.'

Marcellus nodded—and smiled broadly.

'No—it isn't a bit funny!' warned Paulus, grimly. 'And I must strongly counsel you that the less you see of these Christians, the better it will be for'—he checked himself, and finished lamely in a tone almost inaudible—'for all of us.'

'But—for me—in particular, I think you mean,' said Marcellus.

'Have it your own way.' Paulus waved his arm. 'I'm not having a good time—saying these things to you. But—I don't want to see you get into trouble. And you easily could, you know! When the pressure is put on, it's going to get rough! The fact that you're a Roman Tribune will not count for much—once the stampede begins! We are going to make war on the Christians, Marcellus, no matter who they are! Why don't you clear out before you are apprehended? Take your slave—and go!'

'I do not know where he is,' admitted Marcellus.

'Well—I do,' grinned Paulus. 'He is in bed, somewhere here in the fort.'

'A prisoner?'

'No—but he ought to be.' The Legate laughingly recounted the afternoon's revelations. 'By the way,' he ended, 'did you see him destroy Quintus?'

Marcellus, who had been much amused by the recital, shook his head.

'I saw the Tribune shortly afterward,' he said. 'The work had been well done, I assure you.'

'It gratified me to hear about it,' said Paulus, 'as I have no respect for Quintus and his misfortunes do not annoy me; but'—he grew suddenly serious—'this was no light offense, and may yet have to be settled for. Your Demetrius is free to go, but I hope he will not linger in this country; at least, not in my jurisdiction. Nor you, Marcellus! Consider your predicament: your slave is wanted for assaulting a Tribune; moreover, he is known to have been in close association with the Christian party in Jerusalem. He can be apprehended on either count. Now—it may be assumed that you know all this. In short, you have been harboring a criminal and a Christian; and your own position as a friend of the Christians is of no advantage to you. What do you intend to do about it?'

'I had thought of remaining in Palestine for a few weeks, before proceeding to Rome,' said Marcellus. 'I have no definite plans.'

'Better have some plans!' advised Paulus, sternly. 'Your situation is more hazardous than you think. It will do your pious Galilean friends no good to have you championing their cause. I tell you candidly that they are all in imminent danger of arrest. I advise you to pack your travel equipment early in the morning, go quietly across country to Joppa, and take the first ship that heads for home.'

'Thanks for the counsel, Paulus,' replied Marcellus, non-committally. 'May I have a word with Demetrius now?'

Paulus frowned darkly and dismissed the request with a gesture of exasperation.

'The fact that your Greek slave is a superior fellow and your friend,' he said, crisply, 'does not alter his status in the opinion of my own retinue. I suggest that you wait until morning to see him.'

'As you like,' said Marcellus, unruffled.

Paulus rose unsteadily.

'Let us retire now,' he said, more cordially, 'and meet for breakfast at sunrise. Then'—he smiled meaningly—'if you will insist upon leaving at once, I shall speed you on your way. I shall do better than that: I shall order a small detachment of legionaries, acquainted with the less traveled roads, to see you safely to Joppa.'

'But I am not going to Joppa, Paulus,' declared Marcellus, firmly. 'I am not leaving Palestine until I have fully satisfied myself about this story of the Galilean's return to life.'

'And how are you to do that?' demanded Paulus. 'By interviewing a few deluded fishermen, perhaps?'

'That's one way of putting it,' rejoined Marcellus, unwilling to take offense. 'I want to talk with some of the leaders.'

'They are not here now,' said Paulus. 'The foremost of them are in Jerusalem.'

'Then I am going to Jerusalem!'

For a moment, Paulus, with tight lips, deliberated a reply. A sardonic grin slowly twisted his mouth.

'If you start tomorrow for Jerusalem,' he predicted ominously, 'you should arrive about the right time to find them all in prison. Then—unless you are more prudent than you appear to be at present—you will get into a lot of trouble.' He clapped his hands for the guard. 'Show the Tribune to his room,' he ordered. Offering his hand, with his accustomed geniality, he smiled and said, 'I hope you rest well. We will see each other in the morning.'

Chapter XIX

THEY entered the city unchallenged two hours before sunset. The sentries at the Damascus Gate did not so much as bother to ask Marcellus his name or what manner of cargo was strapped to the tired little donkeys. It was evident that Jerusalem was not on the alert.

The journey from Capernaum had been made with dispatch, considering the travelers were on foot. By rising before dawn and keeping steadily at it—even through the sultry valleys, where all prudent rested in the shade while the sun was high—the trip had been accomplished in three days.

Warned by Paulus' grim forecast of drastic action about to be taken against the Christians, Marcellus had expected to encounter arrogant troops and frightened people, but the roads were quiet and the natives were going about their small affairs with no apparent feeling of insecurity. If it were true that a concerted attack on them had been planned, it was still a well-guarded secret.

Their leave-taking of Capernaum had been almost without incident. Arriving early at the tent, they found that Justus had disappeared. Shalum had no explanation to offer. The mother of little Thomas, when they stopped at her home to make inquiries, had no more to say than that Justus and Jonathan had left for Sepphoris an hour ago. Marcellus had a momentary impulse to follow them and reassure Justus; but, remembering Paulus' injunction that the Galileans would now be better served if he gave them no further attention, he proceeded on his way with many misgivings. It was no small matter to have lost Justus' friendship. He wanted to stop in Cana and have a farewell word with Miriam, but decided against it.

After supper that first night out—they had camped in a meadow five miles southeast of Cana—Marcellus had insisted on hearing all about Demetrius' experiences with the Christians in Jerusalem, especially with reference to their belief in the reappearance of Jesus. The Greek was more than willing to tell everything he knew. There was no uncertainty in his mind about the truth of the resurrection story.

'But—Demetrius—that is impossible, you know!' Marcellus had declared firmly when his slave had finished.

'Yes, I know, sir,' Demetrius had admitted.

'But you believe it!'

'Yes, sir.'

'Well—there's no sense to be made out of that!' grumbled Marcellus, impatiently. 'To admit a thing's impossible, and in the next breath confess your belief in it, leaves your argument in very bad shape.'

'If you will pardon me, sir,' ventured Demetrius, 'I was not arguing. You asked me: I told you. I am not trying to persuade you to believe in it. And I agree that what I have been saying doesn't make sense.'

'Then the story is nonsense!' reasoned Marcellus; and after he had given his slave ample time to reply, he added crisply, 'Isn't it?'

'No, sir,' reiterated Demetrius, 'the story is true. The thing couldn't happen; but it did.'

Feeling that this sort of conversation didn't have much to recommend it, Marcellus had mumbled good night and pretended to sleep.

On the next day and the day thereafter, the subject had been discussed on the road, as profitlessly. Jesus had been seen after his death. Such things didn't happen; couldn't happen. Nevertheless, he had been seen; not once, but many times; not by one man only, but by a score. Demetrius was advised that he was losing his mind. He conceded the point without debate and offered to change the subject. He was told that he had been duped and deluded, to which accusation he responded with an indulgent nod and a smile. Marcellus was thoroughly exasperated. He wanted to talk about it; wanted Demetrius to plead his case, if he had one, with an air of deep conviction. You couldn't get anywhere with a man who, when you called him a fool, calmly admitted it.

'I never would have thought, Demetrius,' Marcellus had said, taking pains to make it sound derisive, 'that a man with as sound a mind as yours would turn out to be so childishly superstitious!'

'To tell you the truth, sir,' Demetrius had replied, 'I am surprised at it myself.'

They had been trudging along, with Marcellus a little in advance, stormily vaunting his indignation over his slave's stubborn imbecility, when it suddenly occurred to him that he wasn't having it out with Demetrius—but with himself. He swung about, in the middle of an angry sentence, and read—in his companion's comradely grin—a confirmation of his discovery. Falling into step, he walked along in silence for a while.

'Forgive me, Demetrius,' he said, self-reproachfully. 'I have been very inconsiderate.'

Demetrius smiled broadly.

'I understand fully, sir,' he said. 'I went through all that, hour after hour, day after day. It is not easy to accept as the truth something that one's instinct rejects.'

'Well, then'—deliberated Marcellus—'let us, just for sake of argument, batter our instincts into silence and accept this, for the moment, as the truth. Consider the possibilities of a man with a divine personality who, if he wants to, can walk up to Emperor Tiberius, without fear, and demand his throne!'

'He will not want to,' rejoined Demetrius. 'If he were that sort of person, he would have demanded Pilate's seat. No—he expects to come into power another way; not by demoting the Emperor, but by inspiring the people. His rule will not begin at the top. It will begin at the bottom—with the common people.'

'Bah!' scoffed Marcellus. 'The common people, indeed! What makes you think they have it in them to set up a just government? Take this weak-spined little handful of pious fishermen, for example: how much courage is to be expected of them? Why—even when their Jesus was on trial for his life, they were afraid to speak out in his defense. Except for two or three of them, they let him go to his death alone!'

'True, sir,' said Demetrius, 'but that was before they knew he could overcome death.'

'Yes, but Jesus' ability to overcome death wouldn't make their lives any more secure than they were before.'

'Oh—yes, sir!' exclaimed Demetrius. 'He promised them that they too would live forever. He said that he had overcome death—not only for himself—but for all who had faith in him.'

Marcellus slowed to a stop, thrust his thumbs under his belt, and surveyed his slave with a frown of utter mystification.

'Do you mean to say that these crazy fishermen think they are going to live forever?' he demanded.

'Yes, sir—forever—with him,' said Demetrius, quietly.

'Ridiculous!' snorted Marcellus.

'It seems so, sir,' agreed Demetrius. 'But if they sincerely believe that—whether it is true or not will have no bearing on their behavior. If a man considers himself stronger than death, he has nothing to fear.'

'Then why are these people in hiding?' asked Marcellus, reasonably enough, he thought.

'They have their work to do, sir. They cannot be too reckless with their lives. It is their duty to tell the story of Jesus to as many as can be reached. Every man of them expects to be killed, sooner or later, but—it won't matter. They will live on—somewhere else.'

'Demetrius—do you believe all this nonsense yourself?' asked Marcellus, pityingly.

'Sometimes,' mumbled Demetrius. 'When I'm with them, I believe it.' He tramped on moodily through the dust, his eyes on the road. 'It isn't easy,' he added, half to himself.

'I should say not!' commented Marcellus.

'But, sir,' declared Demetrius, 'the fact that an idea is not easy to understand need not disparage it. Are we not surrounded with facts quite beyond our comprehension?' He stretched a long arm toward the hillside, gay with flowers. 'We can't account for all that diversity of color and form—and we don't have to. But they are facts.'

'Well—that's beside the point,' protested Marcellus. 'Stick to your business, now, and don't let your mind wander. We'll agree that all life's a mystery. Proceed with your argument.'

'Thank you, sir,' grinned Demetrius. 'Now—these disciples of Jesus honestly believe that the world will eventually be ruled by faith in his teachings. There is to be a universal government founded on good will among men. Whoever believes and practices this has the assurance that he will live forever. It isn't easy to believe that one may live forever. I grant you that, sir.'

'And not much easier to believe that the world could be governed by good will,' put in Marcellus.

'Now—the Emperor,' went on Demetrius, 'rules the world by force. That is not easy. Thousands of men have to lose their lives to support this form of government. Germanicus leads an expedition into Acquitania, promising his Legates riches in captured goods and slaves if they follow and obey him at the risk of their lives. They take that chance. Many of them are killed and have nothing to show for their courage. Jesus promises everlasting life as a reward for those who follow and obey him in his effort to bring peace to the world. His disciples believe him, and—'

'And take that chance,' interposed Marcellus.

'Well, sir; it isn't a more hazardous chance than the legions take who follow Germanicus,' insisted Demetrius. 'This faith in Jesus is not easy, but that doesn't make it nonsense—if you will pardon my speaking so freely.'

'Say on, Demetrius!' approved Marcellus. 'You are doing well, considering what kind of material you have to work with. Tell me—do you, personally, expect to live on here forever—in some spectral form?'

'No.' Demetrius shook his head. 'Somewhere else. He has a kingdom—somewhere else.'

'And you truly believe that!' Marcellus studied his slave's sober face as if he had never seen it before.

'Sometimes,' replied Demetrius.

Neither had anything to say for a while. Then, coming to an abrupt halt, the Greek faced his master with an expression of self-confidence.

'This faith,' he declared deliberately, 'is not like a deed to a house in which one may live with full rights of possession. It is more like a kit of tools with which a man may build him a house. The tools will be worth just what he does with them. When he lays them down, they will have no value until he takes them up again.'

* * * * * *

It was nearly sundown when Demetrius arrived at the shop of Benyosef, for much time had been consumed in the congested streets on the way to the inn where Marcellus had stopped on his previous visit to Jerusalem. The travel equipment and Galilean purchases had to be unloaded and stored. The man who owned the donkeys had to be paid off. Marcellus was eager for a bath and fresh clothing. Having made his master comfortable and having attended to his own reconditioning, Demetrius had set off to find Stephanos.

Since his course led directly past Benyosef's, he decided to look in; for it was possible that his friend was still at work. The front door was closed and bolted. Going around to the side door which admitted to the family quarters, he knocked; but there was no response. This seemed odd, for the aged Sarah never went anywhere, and would surely be here at suppertime.

Perplexed, Demetrius hastened on to the shabby old house where he had lodged with Stephanos. Here, too, the doors were locked and apparently everyone was gone. A short distance up the street, a personable young Jew, John Mark, lived with his widowed mother and an attractive young cousin, Rhoda. He decided to call there and inquire, for Stephanos and Mark were close friends, though he had often wondered whether it wasn't the girl that Stephanos went to see.

He found Rhoda locking the high wicket-gate and preparing to leave with a well-filled basket on her arm. She greeted him warmly, and Demetrius noted that she was prettier than ever. She seemed to have matured considerably in his absence.

'Where is everybody?' he inquired, after a brief account of the closed houses he had visited.

'Oh—don't you know?' Rhoda handed him the basket and they moved toward the gate. 'We all have supper together now. You must come with me.'

'Who have supper together?' wondered Demetrius.

'The Christians. Simon began it many weeks ago. They leased the old building where Nathan had his bazaar. We all bring food every evening, and share it. That is,' she added, with an impatient little shrug, 'some of us bring food—and all of us share.'

'It doesn't sound as if it was much fun,' observed Demetrius.

'Well'—Rhoda tossed her curly head—'it hasn't turned out as Simon had expected.'

They were walking rapidly, Demetrius taking long strides to keep pace with the clipped steps that seemed to be beating time for some very vigorous reflections. He decided not to be too inquisitive.

'How is Stephanos?' he asked, with a sly smile that Rhoda tried unsuccessfully to dodge.

'You will see him presently,' she replied, archly. 'Then you may judge for yourself.'

'Rhoda'—Demetrius sounded at least sixty—'those pink cheeks tell me that something has been going on here since I left. If this means what I think, I am happy for both of you.'

'You know too much, Uncle Demetrius,' she retorted, with a prim smile. 'Can't Stephen and I be friends—without—'

'No—I don't think so,' interjected Demetrius. 'When is it going to be, Rhoda? Will I have time to weave a tablecloth for you?'

'A little one.' She flashed him a bright smile.

Promising that he would borrow a loom and begin work early in the morning, if his master could spare him the time, Demetrius found his curiosity mounting in regard to these daily suppers.

'How many people come?' he asked.

'You will be surprised! Three hundred or more. Many have disposed of their property in the country and are living here now; quite a colony of them. At least a hundred take all of their meals at the Ecclesia.'

'The Ecclesia,' repeated Demetrius. 'Is that what you call it? That's Greek, you know. Most of you are Jews; are you not? How did you happen to call your headquarters the Ecclesia?'

'Stephen,' said Rhoda, proudly. 'He said it was a suitable name for such an assembly. Besides—fully a third of the Christians are Greeks.'

'Well—it's a comfort to see the Jews and Greeks getting together on something,' remarked Demetrius. 'Just one big, happy family; eh?' he added, with some private misgivings.

'It's big enough: no question about that!' murmured Rhoda; and then, making hasty amends for this comment, she continued, 'Most of them are deeply in earnest, Demetrius. But there are enough of the other kind to spoil it.'

Peter and Marcellus at Golgotha

'I was not here that day,' rumbled the deep, throaty voice. 'I did not stand by him in the hour of his anguish.' Peter drew a deep sigh.

From page 372 of text

DEAN

'Quarreling; are they? I'm afraid they won't get very far with this new idea that what the world needs is good will.'

'That's what Stephen says,' approved Rhoda. 'He is quite disappointed. He thinks this whole business—of having all the Christians live together—is a mistake. He believes they should have stayed at home and kept on with their daily work.'

'What's the rumpus about?' Demetrius couldn't help asking.

'Oh—the same old story,' sighed Rhoda. 'You Greeks are stingy and suspicious and oversensitive about your rights, and—'

'And you Jews are greedy and tricky,' broke in Demetrius, with a grin.

'We're *not* greedy!' exclaimed Rhoda.

'And we Greeks are not stingy!' retorted Demetrius. They both laughed.

'That's a good little picture of the rumpus,' said Rhoda. 'Poor Simon. He had such high hopes for the Ecclesia. I was so sorry for him, last night, I could have cried. After supper he made us a serious talk, repeating some of the words of Jesus about loving one another, even those who mistreat us; and how we were all the children of God, equal in his sight, regardless of our race. And—if you'll believe it—right while Simon was speaking, an old man from the country, named Ananias, got up and stamped out!'

Demetrius could think of no appropriate comment. It gave him a sickish feeling to learn that so lofty an ideal had fallen into such disrepute in the hands of weak people. Rhoda sensed his disappointment.

'But please don't think that Simon is held lightly,' she went on. 'He has great influence! The people believe in him! When he walks down the street, old men and women sitting at their windows beg him to stop and talk with them. Stephen says they even bring out their sick ones on cots so that he may touch their foreheads as he passes. And—Demetrius—it's wonderful how they all feel toward Stephen, too. Sometimes I think that if anything ever happened to Simon—' Rhoda hesitated.

'Stephen might be the leader?' asked Demetrius.

'He is big enough for it!' she declared. 'But don't tell him I said that,' she added. 'He would think it a great misfortune if anything happened to Simon.'

They were nearing the rangy old bazaar now. Several women were entering with baskets. A few men loitered about the open door. No legionaries were to be seen. Apparently the Christians were free to go and come as they pleased.

Rhoda led the way into the large, bare, poorly lighted room, crowded with men, women, and children, waiting beside the long tables on which food was being spread. Stephanos advanced with a welcoming smile.

'Adelphos Demetrius!' he exclaimed, extending both hands. 'Where did you find him, Rhoda?'

'He was looking for you.' Her tone was tenderly possessive.

'Come, then,' he said. 'Simon will want to see you. You're thin, my friend. What have they been doing to you?'

Demetrius flinched involuntarily as Stephanos squeezed his arm.

'A little accident,' he explained. 'It's not quite healed.'

'How did you do it?' asked Rhoda. 'You've a cut on your wrist too; a bad one!'

Demetrius was spared the necessity of replying, Stephanos coming to his rescue with a little pantomime of pursed lips and a slight shake of his head for Rhoda's benefit.

'You were fighting, I think,' she whispered, with a reproving grin. 'Christians don't fight, you know.' Impishly puckering a meaningful little smile at Stephanos, she added, 'They don't even fret about things.' Preoccupied, Stephanos missed this sally, and beckoned to Demetrius to follow him.

* * * * * *

Conversation on the way back was forced and fragmentary. John Mark and his mother walked on ahead. The tall Greeks followed on either side of Rhoda, who felt dwarfed and unimportant, for it was evident, by their taciturnity, that they wanted to be alone with each other. She did not resent this. She was so deeply in love with Stephanos that anything he did was exactly right, even when he so plainly excluded her from his comradeship with Demetrius.

After a hasty good night at Mark's gate, the Greeks sauntered down the street toward their lodgings, silently at first, each waiting for the other to speak. Stephanos' steps slowed.

'Well—what did you think of it?' he demanded, bluntly. 'Tell me truly.'

'I'm not quite sure,' temporized Demetrius.

'But you are!' snapped Stephanos. 'You have seen our Christian Ecclesia in action. If you are not quite sure, that means you think we have taken the wrong road!'

'Very well,' consented Demetrius, with an indulgent chuckle. 'If that's what you think, why not go on and tell me what you think? You've had a better chance to form an opinion. I haven't seen your Ecclesia do anything yet—but eat. What else is it good for? I'm bound to say, Stephanos, that if I were selecting a company of people to engage in some dangerous tasks requiring endless faith and courage, I might have skipped a few who were present tonight.'

'There you are!' lamented Stephanos. 'That's what ails it. Jesus commands us to carry on his work, no matter at what cost in privation, pain, and hazard of life; and all we've accomplished is a free boarding-house and loafing-place for anybody who will say, "I believe." '

'Doubtless Simon's intentions were good,' observed Demetrius, feeling that he was expected to make some comment.

'Excellent!' agreed Stephanos. 'If everybody connected with the Ecclesia had the bravery and goodness of Simon Peter, the institution might develop great power. You see—at the beginning, what he wanted was a close-knit body of men who would devote their full time to this work. He thought they could inspire one another if they lived together. You remember how it was at the shop, Demetrius, the disciples spending hours in conference. Simon wanted to increase this circle, draw in other devoted men, and weld them together in spirit and purpose.'

'And made the circle a little too large?' suggested Demetrius.

Stephanos came to a halt, and moodily shook his head.

'The whole plan was unsound,' he said, disconsolately. 'Simon announced that any Christian might sell his property and bring the proceeds to the Ecclesia with the promise that his living would be provided for.'

'No matter how much or little he had?' queried Demetrius.

'Right! If you owned a farm or a vineyard, you sold it—probably at a sacrifice—and brought Simon the money. If you had nothing but a few chickens, a milk-goat, and a donkey, you came with the money you'd got from that. And all would live together in brotherly love.'

Gloomily Stephanos recited the misadventures of this unhappy experiment. The word had quickly spread that any Christian family could insure its living by joining the Ecclesia. There was no lack of applicants. Simon had rejoiced to see the large number of people who professed to be Christians. At an all-night conference in Benyosef's shop, Simon had been almost beside himself with happiness. The kingdom was growing!

'That night,' continued Stephanos, 'it was decided that Simon should remain to oversee our Ecclesia. The others were to see how nearly ready the Christians were to attempt similar projects in Joppa, Caesarea, Antioch, and other good-sized cities. So—they scattered; John, James, Philip, Alphaeus, Matthew—' Stephanos made an encircling gesture that included all the rest of them. 'Simon is impetuous, you know. When he captures an idea, he saddles and bridles it and rides away at a gallop!'

'And the Ecclesia grew!' assisted Demetrius.

'In numbers—yes! Large families, with next to nothing, moved in to live in idleness, lustily singing hymns and fervent in prayer, but hardly knowing what it was all about, except that they had three meals a day and plenty of good company.'

'And how did the other people like it, the ones who had owned considerable property?'

'Well—that was another problem. These people began to feel their superiority over the indigents. The more money you had contributed to the Ecclesia, the more right you thought you had to dictate the policies of the institution.' Stephanos drew an unhappy smile. 'Only this morning, one arrogant old fellow, who had been impudent and cross over something Simon had said, was discovered to have cheated in his dealings with the Ecclesia, and when Simon confronted him with it, he went into such a mad rage that he had a stroke. Died of it! And Simon will probably get the blame for it.'

'It must be very discouraging,' said Demetrius.

'That isn't all!' sighed Stephanos. 'This daily supper! Many merchants are coming to these meetings now—bringing their food along; I must give them credit for that—but quite clearly patronizing the Ecclesia to make friends for business reasons. In short—the Ecclesia is becoming too, too popular!'

'What's to be done about it?' Demetrius wanted to know.

Stephanos moved on slowly, shaking his head.

'Demetrius—until this Ecclesia began to take in boarders, the Christian community in Jerusalem was a reckonable force. Men continued their gainful occupations, careful to deal honestly and charitably, eager to live according to Jesus' commandments, and talking of his way of life to all who would give heed. And in the evening they would assemble to hearten one another. Simon would stand up and challenge them to greater efforts. He would repeat the words of Jesus, and renew their strength. He was magnificent!' Stephanos stopped again and faced his friend sadly. 'You heard him tonight—squandering his splendid energies in wheedling a lot of selfish, bickering people to forget their little squabbles and stop nagging one another. Did you notice that weak, solicitous smile on his face as he entreated them to be more generous with their gifts to the Ecclesia? Well—that wasn't Simon! That wasn't the Simon who fired the hearts of the men who used to meet in the night to repledge their all to the cause of our Christos! It is a disgrace!' Stephanos clenched both hands in his tousled hair and shook his head hopelessly. 'Is it for this,' he cried, 'that Jesus suffered on the cross—and died—and rose again?'

'Have you talked with Simon about it?' asked Demetrius, after a discreet interval.

'Not lately. A couple of weeks ago, when it became evident there was going to be an open ruction between the Jews and Greeks, several of us inquired whether we could do anything to help him, and he appointed seven of us to oversee the fair apportioning of food and clothing; but—Demetrius—my feeling for Jesus and his worth to the world is a sort of exalted passion that can't bring itself down to the low level of listening patiently to ill-mannered quarrels over whether Bennie Issacher was given a better coat than little Nicolas Timonodes.'

Demetrius snorted his sympathetic disgust and suggested that his friend would do well to keep away from such annoyances.

'I mean to do just that!' declared Stephanos. 'I made a decision tonight. I'm not going back there, any more!'

'It is possible,' said Demetrius, 'that Julian may soon solve the Ecclesia's difficulties. Had you heard anything about an attack? My master thinks the Christians are presently to be set upon by the Insula.'

Stephanos laughed bitterly.

'If the Procurator waits a little while, the Ecclesia will destroy itself, and save him the bother. But—tell me—how does your Roman master feel about Jesus, now that he has been in Galilee?'

'Much impressed, Stephanos. He finds it difficult to believe that Jesus came alive, but he considers him the greatest man who ever lived. He wants to talk with you. He was deeply touched when you asked to see the Robe, and were so moved by the sight of it.'

'He still has it, I suppose,' murmured Stephanos. 'Do you think he would let me see it again, Demetrius? So much has happened, lately, to depress me. Do you know—my friend—that when I touched the Robe, that night, it—it did something for me! I can't explain it—but—'

'Let us go to the inn!' said Demetrius, impetuously. 'Now! He will still be up, and glad to see you. I think you need to have a talk with each other.'

'Are you sure he won't think it an intrusion?' asked Stephanos, anxiously.

'No—he will welcome you. It will be good for you both.'

Once the decision was made, Stephanos set the pace with long, determined strides.

'Are you going to tell the Tribune about the Ecclesia?' he asked.

'By no means!' declared Demetrius. 'I believe that Marcellus is on the way to becoming a Christian. He is infatuated with the story of Jesus, and talks of nothing else. If he decides to be a Christian, he will be a good one and a brave one; you can depend on that! But we mustn't expose him to things that might disgust him. If he knew that some of his companions in this cause were mere quarrelsome idlers, he might not want to debase himself.'

'Those are hard words, my friend,' said Stephanos.

'It gave me no pleasure to say them,' rejoined Demetrius. 'But I know the Tribune very well. It is true he has been brought up as a pagan, but he is particular about the company he keeps.'

* * * * * *

They found Marcellus alone and reading. He greeted them warmly, showing an instant interest in Stephanos, who was ready with an apology for the untimely call.

'There is no one I would rather see, Stephanos,' he said, cordially, offering him a chair. 'You sit down too, Demetrius. You men have had a pleasant reunion, I think.'

'Did you have an interesting journey in Galilee, sir?' asked Stephanos, rather shyly.

'Interesting—and bewildering,' replied Marcellus. 'Justus was a good guide. I heard many strange stories. It is difficult to believe them—and difficult not to believe them.' He paused, his expression inviting a rejoinder; but Stephanos, at a disadvantage in the presence of this urbane Roman, merely nodded, with averted eyes.

'I was greatly attracted by old Nathanael Bartholomew,' went on Marcellus.

'Yes,' said Stephanos, after a tongue-tied interval.

Demetrius, growing restless, thought he would come to his timid compatriot's rescue.

'I think Stephanos would like to see the Robe, sir,' he suggested.

'Gladly!' agreed Marcellus. 'Will you find it for him, Demetrius?'

After some moments in the adjoining room, during which time Marcellus and Stephanos sat silent, Demetrius returned and laid the folded Robe across his friend's knees. Stephanos gently smoothed it with his finger-tips. His lips were trembling.

'Would you like to be alone—for a little while?' asked Marcellus, softly. 'Demetrius and I can take a walk in the garden.'

Stephanos gave no sign that he had heard. Gathering the Robe up into his arms, he glanced at Marcellus and then at Demetrius, with a new light of assurance in his eyes.

'This was my Master's Robe!' he announced, in confident tones, as if delivering a public address. 'He wore it when he healed the sick and comforted the sorrowing. He wore it when he spoke to the multitudes as no man has ever spoken. He wore it when he went to the cross to die—for *me*—a humble weaver!' Stephanos boldly searched Marcellus' astonished face. 'And for *you*—a wealthy Tribune!' He turned toward Demetrius. 'And for *you*—a slave!'

Marcellus leaned forward on the arms of his chair, baffled by the suddenly altered manner of the Greek who had thrown aside his reticence to declare his faith in such resonant tones.

'You killed my Lord, Tribune Marcellus!' went on Stephanos, boldly.

'Stephanos! Please!' entreated Demetrius.

Marcellus held up a cautioning hand toward his slave.

'Proceed, Stephanos!' he commanded.

'It was forgivable,' went on Stephanos, rising to his feet, 'for you did not know what you were doing. And you are sorry. The Temple and the Insula killed him! And they did not know what they were doing. But they are not sorry—and they would do it again—tomorrow!' He took a step toward Marcellus, who rose from his chair, and stood, as one receiving an order. 'You—Tribune Marcellus Gallio—can make amends for what you have done! He forgave you! I was there! I heard him forgive you! Make friends with him! He is alive! I have seen him!'

Demetrius was at his elbow now, murmuring half-articulate entreaties. Gently taking the Robe from him, he tugged him back to his chair. They all sat down, and there was a long moment when no one spoke.

'Forgive me, sir,' said Stephanos, contritely. He clumsily rubbed the back of a nervous hand across his brow. 'I have been talking too freely.'

'You need no reproach yourself, Stephanos,' replied Marcellus, huskily. 'You have not offended me.'

There was a long, constrained silence which no one seemed disposed to break. Stephanos rose.

'It is late,' he said. 'We should go.'

Marcellus held out his hand.

'I am glad you came, Stephanos,' he said, soberly. 'You are welcome to come again. . . . Demetrius—I shall see you here in the morning.'

* * * * * *

Badly shaken and perplexed, Marcellus sat for an hour staring at the wall. At length, he was overcome by the day's fatigue. Stretching out on his bed, he fell asleep. Shortly before dawn he was roused by hoarse cries and shrill screams accompanied by savage commands and thudding blows. It was not unusual, at an inn, to be annoyed at almost any hour of the day by loud lamentations signifying that some hapless kitchen-slave was being flogged; but this pandemonium, which seemed to emanate from the courtyard below, sounded as if the whole establishment was in trouble.

Marcellus pushed his long legs over the edge of his bed, walked to the window, and looked down. Instantly he knew what was happening. Julian's threatened day of wrath had arrived. A dozen legionaries, in full battle equipment, were clubbing the household slaves into a corner of the courtyard. Evidently other troops were inside, chasing their quarry out. The entire lower floor was in confusion. There were blows and protestations, scuffling of feet, splintering of door-panels. Presently there was a scurry of sandals on the stairs. Marcellus' door was thrown open.

'Who are you?' bawled a brutish voice.

'I am a Roman citizen,' replied Marcellus, coolly. 'And you would do well, fellow, to show better manners when you enter the room of a Tribune.'

'We have no manners today, sir,' retorted the legionary, with a brief grin. 'We are searching for Christians.'

'Indeed!' growled Marcellus. 'And does Legate Julian think these poor, harmless people are important enough to warrant all this racket at daybreak?'

'The Legate does not tell me what he thinks, sir,' scored the legionary, 'and it is not customary for ordinary troops to ask him. I am obeying orders, sir. We are rounding up all the Christians in the city. You are not a Christian, and I am sorry I have disturbed you.' He was retreating into the hall.

'Stay!' shouted Marcellus. 'How do you know I am not a Christian? Can't a Roman Tribune be a Christian?'

The legionary chuckled, shrugged, tugged off his heavy metal helmet, and wiped his dripping forehead with a swipe of his rough sleeve.

'I've no time for jesting, sir, if the Tribune will excuse me.' He resumed his helmet, saluted with his spear, and stamped down the hall.

The cries outside were subsiding now. Apparently the evacuation had been completed. A terrified group of slaves had huddled against the area wall, nursing their bruises. Apart from them a little way stood a few shabbily clad, frightened guests. The aging wife of Levi, the innkeeper, hovered close to them. She was pale, and her head kept jerking up involuntarily with some nervous quirk. Marcellus wondered whether she did that all the time or only when she was badly scared.

The tall, handsome Centurion marched forward, faced the victims, shouted for silence, drew out an impressive scroll to its full length, and in a dry crackle read an edict. It was pompously phrased. There was to be no further assembling of the blasphemers who called themselves Christians. There was to be no further mention, in public or private, of the name of Jesus the Galilean, who had been found guilty of treason, blasphemy, and offenses against the peace of Jerusalem. This edict was to be considered the first and last official warning. Disobedience would be punishable by death.

Rolling up the scroll, the Centurion barked an order, the detachment stiffened, he stalked toward the street, they fell in behind him. After a moment, one old retainer, with blood oozing through the sparse white hair on his temple and trickling down over his bare shoulder, quietly crumpled into a shapeless heap. A slave-girl of twenty stooped over him and cried aloud. A bearded Greek bent down and listened with his ear against the old man's chest. He raised up and shook his head. Four of them picked up the limp body and moved off slowly toward the servants' quarters, most of the others trudging dejectedly after them. The innkeeper's wife turned slowly about. Her head was bobbing violently. She pointed to a fallen broom. A limping slave with a crooked back took up the broom and began ineffectively sweeping the tiled pavement. Except for him, the courtyard was empty now. Marcellus turned away from the window, scowling.

'Brave old Julian!' he muttered. 'Brave old Roman Empire!'

He finished his dressing and went below. Levi met him at the foot of the stairs with much bowing and fumbling of hands. He hoped the Tribune had not been disturbed by all the commotion. And would he have his breakfast served at once? Marcellus nodded.

'We will have less trouble with these Christians now,' declared Levi, to assure his Roman guest that his sympathies were with the Insula.

'Had they been causing you trouble?' asked Marcellus, negligently.

Levi hunched his shoulders, spread out his upturned fingers, and smirked. 'It is enough that their sect is in disfavor with the Government,' he parried, discreetly.

'That wasn't what I asked you,' growled Marcellus. 'Have these Christians, who were being knocked about here this morning, given you any cause for complaint? Do they steal, lie, fight? Do they get drunk? Are they brawlers? Tell me—what sort of people are they?'

'In truth, sir,' admitted Levi, 'I cannot complain of them. They are quiet, honest, and faithful. But, sir, as the Insula has decreed, we cannot tolerate blasphemy!'

'Blasphemy? Rubbish!' snarled Marcellus. 'What does the Insula know or care about blasphemy? What is it that these people blaspheme, Levi?'

'They have no respect for the Temple, sir.'

'How could they, when the Temple has no respect for itself?'

Levi shrugged a polite disapproval, though he still smiled weakly.

'The religion of our people must be protected, sir,' he murmured, piously.

Marcellus made a little grimace and sauntered out into the sunny arcade where he found, laying his breakfast table, the slave-girl who had been so deeply grieved over the old man's death in the courtyard. Her eyes were red with weeping, but she was going about her duties competently. She did not look up when Marcellus took his seat.

'Was that old man related to you?' he asked, kindly.

She did not reply. Sudden tears overflowed her eyes and ran down her cheeks. In a moment she moved away, obviously to return to the kitchen for his breakfast. Levi strolled toward his table.

'How was this girl related to the old man they killed?' asked Marcellus.

'He was her father,' said Levi, reluctantly.

'And you are making her serve the table?'

Levi's shoulders, elbows, eyebrows, and palms came up in a defensive gesture.

'Well—it is her regular task, sir. It is not my fault that her father was killed.'

Marcellus rose, and regarded his host with cool contempt.

'And you prate about your religion! What a mean fellow you are, Levi!' He strode toward the door.

'But, please, sir!' begged Levi. 'I myself shall serve you! I am sorry to have given offense!' He toddled off toward the kitchen. Marcellus, angrily returning to his table, wondered if the loathsome creature would slap the girl for unwittingly creating an awkward incident.

* * * * * *

Demetrius had risen at daybreak so that he might have time to do an errand at the Ecclesia before going on to attend his master at the inn. He had tried to dress without waking his friend who, he knew, had spent a restless night; but Stephanos roused and sat up, rubbing his eyes.

'I'll see you this evening,' whispered Demetrius, as if his companion were still asleep and shouldn't be awakened. 'Shall I meet you here?'

'At the Ecclesia,' mumbled Stephanos.

'Thought you weren't going there any more.'

'I can't let good old Simon down, Demetrius. He is alone, now that the other disciples are away on missions.'

Tiptoeing out of the house, Demetrius walked rapidly toward the Ecclesia, where he hoped to have a private word with Simon. It had seemed almost disloyal not to counsel with Stephanos about this, but Marcellus had insisted upon secrecy. He wanted an interview with Simon. Demetrius was to arrange for it, if he could. There had been no opportunity to ask Simon, last night. Perhaps he would have a better chance to see him alone this morning before the day's activities began.

The Ecclesia was already astir. Cots were being folded up and put away to make room for tables. Tousled, half-dressed children of all sizes were racing about, babies were crying, old men were crouching in out-of-the-way corners, scowling meditatively as they stroked their patriarchal beards. The women were bustling back and forth between the kitchen at the rear and the breakfast-tables which their men were setting up. Demetrius approached the nearest group and inquired for Simon. One of them glanced about, and pointed. Simon was standing by a window, quite apart from the others, brooding over a tattered scroll. Even in this relaxed position there was something majestic about this huge Galilean. If only he had a suitable setting and a courageous constituency, thought Demetrius, Simon would have great weight. The man was of immense vitality and arresting personality, a natural leader. Not much wonder the people wanted him to lay his hands upon their sick.

Approaching, Demetrius waited to be recognized. Simon glanced up, nodded soberly, and beckoned to him.

'Sir, my master—Marcellus Gallio—earnestly desires a conversation with you, at your convenience,' said Demetrius.

'He that went into Galilee with Justus?' queried Simon. 'To look for homespun—or so he said.'

'My master did acquire a large quantity of homespun, sir,' said Demetrius.

'And what else?' asked Simon, in his deep voice.

'He became much interested in the life of Jesus, sir.'

'I think he had that before he went,' rumbled Simon, studying Demetrius' eyes. 'I think that was why he went.'

'Yes, sir,' conceded Demetrius. 'That was his real object in going to Galilee. He is deeply concerned—but full of questions. At present he is at Levi's inn. May I tell him you will talk with him—in private?'

'I will talk with him—on the morrow—at mid-afternoon,' said Simon. 'And as he desires privacy, let him come to me in the refuse-field, north of the city, the place they call Golgotha. There is a path through the field which leads to a knoll in the center of it.'

'I know where it is, sir.'

'Then show him the way. Bid him come alone.' Simon rolled up the scroll; and, inattentive to Demetrius' murmured thanks, walked toward the tables. There was a whispered demand for silence, and the confusion ceased, except for the crying of a baby. Those who were seated rose. In a powerful, resonant voice, Simon began to read.

> The people that walked in darkness have seen a great light. They that dwell in the shadow of death, upon them the light shines. For unto us a child is born. Unto us a son is given. The government shall be upon his shoulder.

There was a clamor at the entrance, and all eyes turned apprehensively. Crisp commands were being shouted. The frightened people did not have long to wait in anxiety. The doors burst open, and a whole company of Legionaries marched in, deploying fanwise as they advanced. With their spears held horizontally, breast-high, they moved rapidly forward, pushing the terrified Christians before them. Some of the older ones fell down in their excitement. They were ruthlessly prodded to their feet and shoved on in the wake of the scurrying pack that was massing against the rear wall.

Demetrius, who had remained near the window quite apart from the residents, found himself in the position of a spectator. The troops swept on relentlessly. Simon, a towering figure, stood his ground. He was alone, now, all the others having huddled at the wall. The Centurion shouted an order, and the company halted. He strode arrogantly toward Simon and faced him with a sardonic grin. They were of the same height, both magnificent specimens of manhood.

'Are you, then, the one they call The Fisherman?' demanded the Centurion.

'I am!' answered Simon, boldly. 'And why are you here to break up a peaceful assembly? Has any one of us committed a crime? If so—let him be taken for trial.'

'As you wish,' snapped the Centurion. 'If you want to be tried for blasphemy and treasonable utterances, the Procurator will accommodate you. . . . Take him away!'

Simon turned about and faced his desperate people.

'Be of good cheer!' he shouted. 'Make no resistance! I shall come back to you!'

'That you will not!' broke in the Centurion. In obedience to a sharp command and a sweep of his sword, two burly legionaries leaped forward, caught Simon by the arms, whirled him about, and started for the door. The company pressed forward toward the defenseless crowd. The Centurion called for silence. Palefaced women nervously cupped their hands over the mouths of their screaming children. An edict was read. By order of the Procurator, there was to be no further assembling of the blasphemers who called themselves Christians.

Demetrius began slowly edging his way along the wall in the direction of the front door. He caught fragments of the Centurion's announcement. This building was to be vacated immediately. Anyone found on the premises hereafter would be taken into custody. The name of Jesus, the blasphemer and traitor, was never again to be spoken.

'Away with you now!' yelled the Centurion. 'Back to your homes! And do not inquire for your Fisherman! You will not see him any more!'

As he neared the door, realizing that the speech had ended and the troops would be promptly moving out, Demetrius speeded his going, ran to the street and crossed it, dodged into a narrow alley, pursued it to the next street, slowed to a brisk walk, and proceeded to Levi's inn. Everything was quiet there. He entered and moved toward the stairway leading to Marcellus' quarters. Levi, observant, called him back.

'Your master is out,' he said.

'Do you know where he went, sir?' inquired Demetrius, anxiously.

'How should I?' retorted Levi.

Thinking that Marcellus might have left instructions in his room, Demetrius asked and was granted permission to go upstairs. A Greek slave-girl was putting the room to rights. She recognized him and smiled shyly. Informed of his errand, she joined in the search for a message.

'Did you see my master this morning?' asked Demetrius.

She shook her head.

'We had much trouble here, a little while ago,' she said.

Demetrius pressed her for particulars, and she told him what had occurred. He went to the window and stood for a long moment, looking out, trying to imagine what might be Marcellus' reaction to this cruel business. He would be very angry, no doubt. He would want to do something about it, perhaps. It was not inconceivable that Marcellus might go to Julian and remonstrate. The more Demetrius deliberated on this possibility, the more reasonable it seemed. It would be an audacious thing to do, but Marcellus was impetuous enough to attempt it. After all—the word of a Tribune should have some weight.

He turned about and met the Greek girl's eyes. They were friendly but serious. Glancing cautiously toward the open door, she moved closer to him and whispered, 'Are you one of us?'

Demetrius nodded soberly, and she gave him an approving smile. With a sudden burst of interest in her duties, she began folding and patting the blankets on the bed, as if suspicious that she might be found idling.

'Better stay off the streets today,' she said, softly, out of the corner of a pretty mouth. 'Go down to the kitchen. You'll be safe there.'

'Thanks,' said Demetrius. 'That's not a bad idea. Besides—I'm hungry.' He was crossing the room. The girl laid her hand on his sleeve as he passed her.

'Does your master know you are one of us?' she whispered.

Demetrius was not sure how this question should be answered, so he gave her an enigmatic smile which she was free to interpret as she chose, and left the room. The ever-present Levi met him at the foot of the stairs and unexpectedly informed him that it was a fine morning.

'Beautiful!' agreed Demetrius, aware that the Jew was sparring for news.

'Had your master left instructions for you?' asked Levi, amiably.

'I am to have my breakfast, sir, and await his return.'

'Very good,' said Levi. 'Go to the kitchen. They will serve you.' He tagged along as far as the door. 'I suppose everything was quiet on the streets this morning.'

'It was still quite early, sir, when I left my lodgings,' replied Demetrius, unhelpfully.

After his breakfast of bread, milk, and sun-cured figs, he paced restlessly up and down the small area bounded by the servants' quarters. Nobody seemed inclined to talk. The girl who had served him was crying. He resolved to stroll over to the Insula and wait outside. Something told him that Marcellus was there. Where else could he be?

* * * * * *

Having finished his breakfast, which Levi himself had served with a disgusting show of servility, Marcellus began to be apprehensive about the safety of Demetrius, who, he felt, should have arrived by this time unless he had encountered some trouble.

He did not know where Stephanos lived, but they could tell him at Benyosef's shop. Then it occurred to him that Benyosef's might have been visited by the legionaries. Doubtless they knew it was a meeting-place of the disciples of Jesus, and might be expected to deal severely with anyone found there. Prudence suggested that he keep out of that storm-center. If Demetrius had been arrested, it would be sensible to wait until order had been restored. Then he could learn where his slave was, and make an effort to have him released.

The obsequious Levi helped him to a decision. Marcellus was stalking up and down in the courtyard, feverishly debating what to do, when the Jew appeared in the doorway, obviously much interested in his guest's perturbation. Levi did not say anything; just stood there slowly blinking his brightly inquisitive eyes. Then he retreated into the little foyer and emerged a moment later carrying a chair, as to say that if the Tribune knew what was good for him today, he would stay where he was and avoid getting into trouble. Marcellus scowled, lengthened his stride; and, without a backward glance, marched down the steps to the street.

To reach Benyosef's shop, it was necessary to traverse a few blocks on the rim of the congested market district where the shabby hovels of the very poor huddled close to the reeking alleys. Here there was much excitement, frantic chatter, and gesticulations. Marcellus slowed his steps near one vociferous group of slatternly people and learned that the Christians' meeting-place had been invaded, emptied, and locked up. The leaders had been dragged off to prison. Simon the Fisherman was to be beheaded.

Marcellus quickened his pace. A little way down the street, in the vicinity of Benyosef's shop, a crowd had gathered. At the edge of it, apparently waiting for orders, ranged a company of legionaries, negligently leaning on their spears. Someone in the middle of the crowd was making an impassioned speech. In a moment Marcellus had drawn close enough to recognize the voice.

It was Stephanos. Bareheaded, and in the brown tunic he wore at his loom, he had evidently been dragged out for questioning; and from the sullen silence of the throng, it was to be inferred that these people were willing to wait patiently until the reckless Greek had incriminated himself.

Taller than most, Marcellus surveyed the spectators with curiosity to discover what manner of men they were. Instantly he divined the nature of this audience. They were well dressed, for the most part, representing the more substantial element from the business district. There was a sprinkling of younger priests, too. The face of the crowd was surly, but everybody was listening in a tense silence.

Stephanos was not mincing his words. He stood there boldly, in the open circle they had formed about him, his long arms stretched out in an appeal to reason—but by no means an appeal for mercy. He was not defiant, but he was unafraid.

It was no rabble-rousing speech addressed to the emotions of ignorant men, but a scathing indictment of Jerusalem's leaders who, Stephanos declared, had been unwilling to recognize a cure for the city's distresses.

'You have considered yourselves the Chosen People!' he went on, audaciously. 'Your ancestors struggled out of one bondage into another, century after century, ever looking for a Deliverer, and never heeding your great teachers when they appeared with words of wisdom! Again and again, inspired leaders have risen among your people, only to be thwarted and reviled—not by the poor and needy—but by such as *you!*'

A concerted growl rumbled through the angry crowd.

'Which of the prophets,' demanded Stephanos, 'did your fathers not persecute? And now you have become the betrayers—and murderers—of the Just One!'

'Blasphemer!' shouted an imperious voice.

'You!' exclaimed Stephanos, sweeping the throng with an accusing hand—'you—who claim to have received your law at the hands of angels—how have you kept it?'

There was an infuriated roar, but no one moved to attack him. Marcellus wondered how much longer the suppressed fury of these maddened men would tolerate this rash excoriation.

From far back on the fringe of the crowd, someone hurled a cobblestone. It was accurately thrown and struck Stephanos on the cheekbone, staggering him. Instinctively he reached up a hand to wipe away the blood. Another stone, savagely hurled by a practiced hand, crashed against his elbow. A loud clamor rose. For an instant, Marcellus hoped it might be a protest against this lawless violence, but it was quickly evident that the hoarse shouts were in denunciation of the speech, and not the stoning. A vengeful yell gave sinister applause to the good aim of another stone as it struck the Greek full in the face. Two more, not so well thrown, went over Stephanos' head and drove into the crowd. Trampling upon one another, the dignitaries on the other side of the open circle scurried for cover against the walls and fences. Stephanos, shielding his bleeding head with his arms, backed away slowly from the hostile throng, but the stones kept coming.

The Centurion barked an order now and the legionaries sprang into action, plowing roughly through the pack, tossing men right and left, with utter disregard of their importance. Marcellus, who had been standing beside a tall soldier, followed him through, and was surprised to see him jab his elbow into the face of a stocky priest whose ponderous dignity hadn't permitted him to move swiftly enough. Now the legionaries were lined up inside the semicircle of spectators. They had made a fence of their spears. The stones were coming faster now, and with telling effect. Marcellus began to realize that this was no impulsive, impromptu incident. The better citizens were not throwing stones, but without doubt they had planned that the stones should be thrown. The men who were doing it were expert.

Stephanos was down now, on his elbows and knees, trying to protect his head with one bleeding hand. The other arm hung limp. The crowd roared. Marcellus recognized that bestial cry. He had heard it many a time in the Circus Maximus. He pushed his way on to the side of the tall legionary who, after a glance in his direction, made room for him.

Several of the younger men in the shouting multitude now decided to take a hand in the punishment. The Centurion pretended not to notice when they dodged under the barricade of spears. Their faces were deeply flushed and contorted with rage. There was nothing more they could do to Stephanos, who had crumpled on the ground, but perhaps the stones they threw were to be merely tokens of their willingness to share the responsibility for this crime.

Marcellus' heart ached. There had been nothing he could do. Had Julian been there, he might have protested, but to have denounced the Centurion would have done no good. The fellow was obeying his orders. Poor Stephanos lay dead, or at least unconscious, but the dignitaries continued to stone him.

Immediately in front of Marcellus—on the other side of the barrier—

stood a young, bookish man, wearing a distinctive skull-cap with a tassel, evidently a student. He was of diminutive stature, but sturdily built. His hands were clenched and his rugged face was twisted with anger. Every thudding stone that beat upon the limp body had his approval. Marcellus studied his livid face, amazed that a man of his seeming intelligence could be so viciously pleased by such an exhibition of inhuman brutality.

Presently a fat man, in an expensive black robe, ducked through the line, took off his robe, and tossed it to the short one, bidding him hold it. Another man of lofty dignity followed his friend in; and, handing his robe also to the bow-legged scholar, began clawing up a stone from the pavement.

Marcellus, towering over the short-legged fellow, leaned forward and demanded, sternly, 'What harm had he done to *you?*'

The little man turned about and glanced up impudently into Marcellus' eyes. He was a malicious creature, but no fool. It was a face to be remembered.

'He is a blasphemer!' he shouted.

'How does the crime of blasphemy compare with murder?' growled Marcellus. 'You seem to be a learned man. Perhaps you know.'

'If you will come to the Rabbinical School tomorrow, my friend,' replied the little man, suddenly cooled by the prospect of airing his theology, 'I shall enlighten you. Ask for Saul—of Tarsus,' he added, proudly. 'I am a Roman citizen—like yourself, sir.'

There were no stones flying now. The crowd was growing restless. The young theologian had handed back the robes he had held and was shouldering out through the loosening throng. The legionaries were still maintaining their barricade, but were shifting their weight uneasily as if impatient to be off. The Centurion was soberly talking, out of the corner of his mouth, to a long-bearded Jew in an impressive black robe. The multitude was rapidly disintegrating.

Marcellus, with brooding eyes fixed on the broken body of the gallant Greek, thought he saw a feeble movement there. Stephanos was slowly rising up on one elbow. A hush fell over the people as they watched him rise to his knees. The blood-smeared face looked up, and the bruised lips were parted in a rapturous smile. Suddenly Stephanos raised his arm aloft as if to clutch a friendly hand.

'I see him!' he shouted, triumphantly. 'I see him! My Lord Jesus—take me!' The eyes closed, the head dropped, and Stephanos crumpled down among the stones.

The spectators, momentarily stunned, turned to go. Men did not pause to ask questions. They scurried away as if frightened. Marcellus' heart was pounding and his mouth was dry. But he found himself possessed of a curious exaltation. His eyes were swimming, but his face trembled with an involuntary smile.

He turned about and looked into the bewildered eyes of the tall legionary.

'That was a strange thing, sir!' muttered the soldier.

'More strange than you think!' exclaimed Marcellus.

'I would have sworn the Greek was dead! He thought he saw someone coming to rescue him!'

'He *did* see someone coming to rescue him!' shouted Marcellus, ecstatically.

'That dead Galilean, maybe?' queried the legionary, nervously.

'That Galilean is not dead, my friend!' declared Marcellus. 'He is more alive than any man here!'

Thoroughly shaken, his lips twitching with emotion, Marcellus moved away with the scattering crowd. His mind was in a tumult. At the first corner, he turned abruptly and retraced his steps. Nobody was interested in Stephanos now. The troops from the Insula, four abreast, were disappearing down the street. None of the friends of the intrepid Greek had yet ventured to put in an appearance. It was quite too soon to expect that any of them would take the risk.

Dropping to one knee beside the battered corpse, Marcellus gently drew aside the matted hair and gazed into the impassive face. The lips were still parted in a smile.

After a long time, old Benyosef hobbled out of the shop. His eyes were red and swollen with weeping. He approached diffidently, halting a few steps away. Marcellus looked up and beckoned to him and he came, pale with fright. Stooping over, with his wrinkled hands bracing his feeble knees, he peered into the quiet face. Then he searched Marcellus' eyes inquisitively, but without recognition.

'It was a cruel death, sir,' he whimpered.

'Stephanos is not dead!' declared Marcellus. 'He went away with Jesus!'

'I beg of you—do not mock our faith, sir!' pleaded Benyosef. 'This has been a sad day for us who believe in Jesus!'

'But did he not promise you that if you believe in him, you will never die?'

Benyosef slowly nodded his head, staring into Marcellus' eyes incredulously.

'Yes—but *you* do not believe that, sir!' he mumbled.

Marcellus rose and laid his hand on the old man's thin arm.

'Jesus may never come for me, Benyosef,' he said, quietly, 'and he may never come for you—but he came for Stephanos! Go, now, and find a younger man to help me. We will carry the body into your shop.'

Still pale with fright, the neighbors gathered about the mangled form of Stephanos as it lay on the long table in Benyosef's work-room. They were all crying. Rhoda's grief was inconsolable. Some of the men regarded Marcellus with suspicion that he might be there to spy upon them. It was no time to explain that he felt himself one of them. Presently he was aware of Demetrius at his elbow, and importuned him to stay and be of service.

Taking Benyosef by the arm, he led the tearful old man into the corner back of his loom.

'There is nothing I can do here,' he said, laying some gold coins in the weaver's hand. 'But I have a request of you. When Justus comes again to Jerusalem, tell him I saw Stephanos welcomed into Jesus' kingdom, and am persuaded that everything he told me—in Galilee—is the truth.'

* * * * * *

It had been a long day for Simon, sitting there heavily manacled in the darkness. At noon they had brought him some mouldy bread and a pitcher of water, but he had not eaten; he was too heartsick for that.

For the first hour after his incarceration, derisive voices from adjoining cells had demanded to know his name, his crime, and when he was to die. With noisy bravado, they jested obscenely about their impending executions, and taunted him for being too scared to speak. He had not answered them, and at length they had wearied of reviling him.

The wooden bench on which he sat served also as a bed. It was wider than the seat of a chair, and Simon could not rest his back against the wall. This unsupported posture was fatiguing. Sometimes he stretched his huge frame out on the bench, but with little ease. The wall was damp, as was the floor. Huge rats nibbled at his sandals. The heavy handcuffs cut his wrists.

He thought that he could have borne these discomforts and the threat of a death sentence with a better fortitude had he been able to leave behind him a determined organization to carry on the work that had been entrusted to him. Obviously he had blundered. Perhaps it had been a mistake to establish the Ecclesia. Maybe the time had not come for such a movement. He had been too impatient. He should have let it grow, quietly, unobtrusively, like yeast in meal, as Jesus had said.

What, he wondered, would become of the Christian cause now, with all of them scattered and in hiding? Who would rise up as their leader? Philip? No—Philip was a brave and loyal fellow, but—he lacked boldness. The leader would have to be audacious. John? No. James? No. They had the heart for it, but not the voice. There was Stephen. Stephen might do it—but not in Jerusalem. The Jews would insist on an Israelite, as perhaps they should; for the Christian heritage was of the Hebrew people.

Why had the Master permitted this dreadful catastrophe? Had he changed his plans for the prosecution of his work? Had he lost confidence in the leader he had appointed? Simon's memory reconstructed the eventful day when Jesus had said to him, 'Simon—I shall call you Peter; Peter the Rock! I shall build on this Rock!' Simon closed his eyes and shook his head as he compared the exultation of that moment with the utter hopelessness of his present plight.

When night fell, a guard with a flickering torch noisily unlocked each cell in turn and another replenished the water-pitcher. Noting that his bread had not been eaten, the guard did not give him any more; nor did he offer any comment. Perhaps it was not unusual for men, awaiting death, to take but little interest in food.

At feeding time there had been much rattling of chains and scuffling of feet, but everything was quiet now. Simon grew drowsy, slumped back uncomfortably with his head and shoulders against the old wall, and slept. After a while, he found himself experiencing a peculiar dream; peculiar in that it didn't seem like a dream, though he knew it was, for it couldn't be real. In his dream, he roused, amazed to find that the manacles had slipped from his hands and were lying open on the bench. He lifted his foot. The weight was gone. He drew himself up and listened. Everything was quiet but the rhythmic breathing of his fellow prisoners. He had never had a dream of such keen vividness.

Simon stood up and stretched his long arms. He took three or four short steps toward the cell-door, slipping his sandals along the stone floor as he felt his way in the darkness. There was no sound of the scuffling of his sandals on the flagging. Except for this, the dream was incredibly real. He put out his hand and touched the heavy, nail-studded door. It noiselessly retreated. He advanced his hand to touch the door again. It moved forward. He took another step—and another. There had never been such a dream! Simon was awake and could feel his heart pounding, and the rapid pulse-beat in his neck; but he knew he was still asleep on the bench.

He put his hand against the damp wall and moved on with cautious steps that made no sound. At the end of the long corridor, a feeble light showed through the iron bars of a door. As he neared it the door swung open so slowly and noiselessly that Simon knew the thing was unreal! He walked through with firmer steps. In the dim light he saw two guards sitting on the floor, with their arms around their knees and their heads bent forward in sleep. They did not stir. He proceeded toward the massive entrance gates, recognizing the ponderous lock that united them. He expected his dream to swing them open, but they had not moved. He put his hand on the cold metal, and pushed, but the heavy gates remained firm.

By this he knew that the dream was over, and he would rouse to find himself manacled in his cell. He was chilly. He wrapped his robe more tightly about him, surprised that he still had the unimpeded use of his hands. He glanced about, completely bewildered over his strange mental condition. Suddenly his eye lighted on a narrow gate, set within one of the greater gates. It was open. Simon stepped through, and it closed behind him without a sound. He was on the street. He started to walk briskly. At a crossing, he stumbled against a curbing in the darkness. Surely this rough jar would waken him. Simon stood still, looked up at the stars, and laughed softly for joy. He was awake! He had been delivered from prison!

What to do now? Where to go? With lengthened steps, he made his way to Benyosef's, where all was dark. He moved on to the home of John Mark. A frail light showed from an upstairs window. He tapped at the high wicket gate. After a little delay, the small port in the gate was opened and he saw the frightened face of Rhoda.

She screamed and fled to the open house-door.

'It is Simon!' he heard her shout. 'Simon has returned from the dead!'

Rushing back to the gate, she unbolted it and drew it open. Her eyes were swollen with weeping, but her face was enraptured. She threw her arms around Simon, hugging him fiercely.

'Simon!' she cried. 'Jesus has brought you back from death! Did you see Stephen? Is he coming too?'

'Is Stephen dead, Rhoda?' asked Simon, sadly.

Her grip relaxed, and she slumped down into a dejected little figure of hopeless grief. Simon raised her up tenderly and handed her over to Mark's mother.

'We heard they had killed you,' said Mark.

'No,' said Simon. 'I was delivered from prison.'

They moved slowly into the house, Rhoda weeping inconsolably. The place was crowded with Christians. Their grieving eyes widened and their drawn faces paled as Simon entered, for they had thought him dead. They made way for him in silence. He paused in the midst of them. Some great experience had come to Simon. He had taken on a new dignity, a new power. Slowly he raised his hand and they bowed their heads.

'Let us pray,' said Peter the Rock.

'Blessed be God who has revived our hope. Though in great heaviness for a season, let us rejoice that this trial of our faith—more precious than gold—will make us worthy of honor when our Lord returns.'

* * * * *

After walking up and down on the other side of the street facing the Insula for an hour or more, Demetrius' anxiety overwhelmed his patience. He must have been mistaken in his surmise that Marcellus would visit Julian himself on behalf of the persecuted Christians.

Abandoning his vigil, he made off rapidly for Benyosef's shop. While still a long way off, he began meeting well-dressed, sullen-faced men, apparently returning from some annoying experience. When he saw the sunshine glinting on the shields of an approaching military force, Demetrius dodged into an alley, and continued the journey by a circuitous route.

In spite of the edict prohibiting any further assembly of Christians, fully a score were crowded into the shop, silently gathered about a dead body. To his amazement, Demetrius saw his master in the midst of the people, almost as if he were in charge. He shouldered his way through the sorrowing group. Rhoda was down on her knees before the body, sobbing piteously. It seemed very unreal to find Stephanos, with whom he had talked only a few hours ago, lying here broken and dead.

Marcellus had taken him aside, when he had regained his composure.

'You remain with them, Demetrius,' he had said. 'Assist them with the burial. My presence here is an embarrassment. They cannot account for my interest, and are suspicious. I am going back to the inn.'

'Did you see this happen, sir?' Demetrius had asked.

'Yes.' Marcellus drew closer and said confidentially, 'And much more happened than appears here! I shall tell you—later.'

After they had put poor Stephanos away—and no one had molested them while on their errand—Demetrius had returned home with John Mark, thinking he would be free presently to rejoin Marcellus at the inn. But Mark's mother, Mary, and Rhoda too, had insisted so urgently on his remaining with them that he dared not refuse. When their unwanted supper had been disposed of and darkness had fallen, friends of the family began to arrive singly and by twos and threes until the lower rooms were filled. No one acted as a spokesman for the pensive party. There was much low-voiced conversation about a vision that appeared to Stephen before he died, but none of them had been close enough to know exactly what had happened. Demetrius had not attached much significance to the rumors. The only one who felt confident was Rhoda.

And then, to the utter amazement of everyone, Simon had arrived; a more important, more impressive figure than he had been before. He seemed reluctant to tell the details of his release from prison; but, by whatever process that had come to pass, the experience had built Simon up. He even seemed taller. They all felt it, and were shy about initiating conversation with him; hesitant about asking questions. Oddly enough, he had quietly announced that henceforth they should call him Peter.

Beckoning John Mark apart, Demetrius had suggested that they ask Simon Peter to lodge there. As for himself, he would cheerfully surrender his room and return to the inn. So—it had been arranged that way and Demetrius had slipped out unobtrusively. It was nearing midnight when he tapped at Marcellus' door, finding him awake and reading. They had talked in whispers until daybreak, their master-slave relationship completely ignored in their earnest discussion of the day's bewildering experiences.

'I too am a Christian!' Marcellus had declared, when he had finished his account of the stoning of Stephanos, and it seemed to Demetrius that the assertion had been made with more pride than he had ever put into 'I am a Roman!' It was very strange, indeed, this complete capitulation of Marcellus Gallio to a way of belief and behavior so foreign from his training and temperament.

Early in the afternoon, Demetrius accompanied him to the edge of the disreputable field that was called Golgotha. They were quiet as they approached it. Acrid smoke curled lazily from winnows of charred refuse. In the distance a grass-covered knoll appeared as a green oasis in a desert.

'Do you remember the place, sir?' asked Demetrius, halting.

'Vaguely,' murmured Marcellus. 'I'm sure I couldn't have found it. Is it clear in your memory, Demetrius?'

'Quite so. I came late. I could see the crosses from here, and the crowd.'

'What was I doing when you arrived?' asked Marcellus.

'You and the other officers were casting dice.'

'For the Robe?'

'Yes, sir.'

Neither spoke for a little while.

'I did not see the nailing, Demetrius,' said Marcellus, thickly. 'Paulus pushed me away. I was glad enough to escape the sight. I walked to the other side of the knoll. It has been a bitter memory, I can tell you.'

'Well, sir,' said Demetrius, 'here is the path. I shall wait for you at the inn. I hope you will not be disappointed, but it seems unlikely that Simon Peter would try to keep his appointment.'

'He will come, I think,' predicted Marcellus. 'Simon Peter is safer from arrest today than he was yesterday. Both the Insula and the Temple have tried to convince the public that the Christians have no legal or moral sanction for their beliefs. Having captured their leader, with the expectation of making a tragic example of him, they are now stunned by the discovery that their victim has walked out of prison. Neither Julian nor Herod will want to undertake an explanation of that event. I think they will decide that the less said or done now, in the case of The Big Fisherman, the better it will be for everybody concerned. I fully expect Simon Peter will meet me here—unless, in all the confusion, he has forgotten about it.'

* * * * * *

Peter had not forgotten. Marcellus saw him coming, a long way off, marching militantly with head up and a swinging stride that betokened a confident mind. The man had leadership, reflected the admiring watcher.

As The Big Fisherman neared the grassy knoll, however, his steps slowed and his shoulders slumped. He stopped and passed an unsteady hand over his massive forehead. Marcellus rose and advanced to meet him as he mounted the slight elevation with plodding feet. Peter extended his huge hand, but did not speak. They sat down on the grass near the deep pits where the crosses had stood, and for a long time they remained in silence.

At length, Peter roused from his painful meditation and glanced at Marcellus with heavy eyes, which drifted back to the ground.

'I was not here that day,' rumbled the deep, throaty voice. 'I did not stand by him in the hour of his anguish.' Peter drew a deep sigh.

Marcellus did not know what to say, or whether he was expected to say anything. The big Galilean sat ruefully studying the palms of his hands with a dejection so profound that any attempt to relieve it would have been an impertinence. Now he regarded Marcellus with critical interest, as if noting him for the first time.

'Your Greek slave told me you were interested in the story of Jesus,' he said, soberly. 'And it has come to me that you were of friendly service, yesterday, when our brave Stephen was taken away. Benyosef thought he heard you profess the faith of a Christian. Is that true, Marcellus Gallio?'

'I am convinced, sir,' said Marcellus, 'that Jesus is divine. I believe that he is alive, and of great power. But I have much to learn about him.'

'You have already gone far with your faith, my friend!' said Peter, warmly. 'As a Roman, your manner of living has been quite remote from the way of life that Jesus taught. Doubtless you have done much evil, for which you should repent if you would know the fullness of his grace. But I could not ask you to repent until I had told you of the wrongs which I have done. Whatever sins you may have committed, they cannot compare to the disloyalty for which I have been forgiven. He was my dearest friend—and, on the day that he needed me, I swore that I had never known him.'

Peter put his huge hands over his eyes and bowed his head. After a long moment he looked up.

'Now'—he said—'tell me how much you know about Jesus.'

Marcellus did not immediately reply, and when he did so, his words were barely audible. He heard himself saying, as if someone else were speaking:

'I crucified him.'

* * * * *

The sun was low when they rose to return to the city. In those two hours, Marcellus had heard the stirring details of a story that had come to him previously in fragments and on occasions when his mind was unprepared to appreciate them.

They had found a strange kinship in their remorse, but Peter—fired by his inspiring recollections of the Master-man—had declared it was the future that must concern them now. He had daring plans for his own activities. He was going to Caesarea—to Joppa—perhaps to Rome!

'And what will you do, Marcellus?' he asked, in a tone of challenge.

'I am going home, sir.'

'To make your report to the Emperor?'

'Yes, sir.'

Peter laid his big hand heavily on Marcellus' knee and earnestly studied his eyes.

'How much are you going to tell him—about Jesus?' he demanded.

'I am going to tell the Emperor that Jesus, whom we thought dead, is alive—and that he is here to establish a new kingdom.'

'It will take courage to do that, my young brother! The Emperor will not like to hear that a new kingdom is coming. You may be punished for your boldness.'

'Be that as it may,' said Marcellus, 'I shall have told him the truth.'

'He will ask you how you know that Jesus lives. What will you say?'

'I shall tell him of the death of Stephanos—and the vision that he had. I am convinced that he saw Jesus!'

'Emperor Tiberius will want better proof than that.'

Marcellus was silently thoughtful. It was true, as Peter had said, such testimony would have very little weight with anyone disinclined to believe. Tiberius would scoff at such evidence, as who would not? Senator Gallio would say, 'You saw a dying man looking at Jesus. How do you know that is what he saw? Is this your best ground of belief that your Galilean is alive? You say he worked miracles: but you, personally, didn't see any.'

'Come,' said Peter, getting to his feet. 'Let us go back to the city.'

They strode along with very little to say, each immersed in his thoughts. Presently they were in the thick of city traffic. Peter had said he was going back to John Mark's house. Marcellus would return to the inn. Now they were passing the Temple. The sun was setting and the marble steps—throughout the day swarming with beggars—were almost deserted.

One pitiful cripple, his limbs twisted and shrunken, sat dejectedly on the lowest step, waggling his basin and hoarsely croaking for alms. Peter slowed to a stop. Marcellus had moved on, a little way, but drifted back when he observed that Peter and the beggar were talking.

'How long have you been this way, friend?' Peter was saying.

'Since my birth, sir,' whined the beggar. 'For God's sake—an alms!'

'I have no money,' confessed Peter; then, impulsively, he went on—'but such as I have I give you!' Stretching out both hands to the bewildered cripple, he commanded, 'In the name of Jesus—stand up—and walk!' Grasping his thin arms, he tugged the beggar to his feet—and he stood! Amazed—and with pathetic little whimpers—half-laughing, half-crying, he slipped his sandals along the pavement; short, uncertain, experimental steps—but he was walking. Now he was shouting!

A crowd began to gather. Men of the neighborhood who recognized the beggar were pushing in to ask excited questions. Peter took Marcellus by the arm and they moved on, walking for some distance in silence. At length Marcellus found his voice, but it was shaky.

'Peter! How did you do that?'

'By the power of Jesus' spirit.'

'But—the thing's impossible! The fellow was born crippled! He had never taken a step in his life!'

'Well—he will walk now,' said Peter, solemnly.

'Tell me, Peter!' entreated Marcellus. 'Did you know you had this power? Have you ever done anything like this before?'

'No—not like this,' said Peter. 'I am more and more conscious of his presence. He dwells in me. This power—it is not mine, Marcellus. It is his spirit.'

'Perhaps he will not appear again—except in men's hearts,' said Marcellus.

'Yes!' declared Peter. 'He will dwell in men's hearts—and give them the power of his spirit. But—that is not all! *He will come again!*'

Chapter XX

It was common knowledge that Rome had the noisiest nights of any city in the world, but one needed a quiet year abroad to appreciate this fully.

Except for the two celebrated avenues intersecting at the Forum—the Via Sacra and the Via Nova—which were grandly laid with smooth block of Numidian marble, all of the principal thoroughfares were paved with cobblestones ranging in size from plums to pomegranates.

To relieve the congestion in these cramped, crooked streets and their still narrower tributaries, an ordinance—a century old—prohibited the movement of market-carts, delivery wagons, or any other vehicular traffic from sunrise to sunset, except imperial equipages and officially sanctioned parades on festal occasions.

Throughout the daylight hours, the business streets were gorged with milling crowds on foot, into which the more privileged ruthlessly rode their horses or were borne on litters and portable chairs; but when twilight fell, the harsh rasp and clatter of heavy iron wheels grinding the cobblestones set up a nerve-racking cacophony accompanied by the agonized squawk of dry axles, the cracking of whips, and the shrill quarrels of contenders for the right of way; nor did this maddening racket cease until another day had dawned. This was every night, the whole year round.

But the time to see and hear Rome at her utmost was during the full of a summer moon when much building construction was in progress, and everybody who had anything to haul took advantage of the light. Unable to sleep, thousands turned out in the middle of the hideous night to add their jostling and clamor to the other jams and confusions. Shopkeepers opened up to serve the meandering insomniacs with sweets and beverages. Hawkers barked their catch-penny wares; minstrels twanged their lyres and banged their drums; bulging camel-trains doggedly plodded through the protesting throng, trampling toes and tearing tunics; great wagons loaded with lumber and hewn stone plowed up the multitude, pitching the furrows against the walls and into open doorways. All nights in Rome were dreadful, and the more beautiful nights were dangerous.

Long before their galley from Ostia had rounded the bend that brought the city into full view on that bright June midnight of their homecoming, Marcellus heard the infernal din as he had never heard it before; heard it as no one could hear it without the preparation of a month's sailing on a placid summer sea.

The noise had a new significance. It symbolized the confounded outcry of a competitive world that had always done everything the hard way, the mean way, and had very little to show for its sweat and passion. It knew no peace, had never known peace, and apparently didn't want any peace.

Expertly the galley slipped into its snug berth to be met by a swarm of yelling porters. Demetrius, one of the first passengers over the rail, returned in a moment with a half-dozen swarthy Thracians who made off with their abundant luggage. Engaging another port-wagon for themselves, the travelers were soon swallowed up in a bedlam of tangled traffic through which they inched along until Marcellus, weary of the delay, suggested that they pay off the driver and continue on foot.

He had forgotten how insufferably rude and cruel the public could be. Massed into a solid pack, it had no intelligence. It had no capacity to understand how, if everyone calmly took his turn, some progress might be made. Even the wild animals around a water-hole in the jungle had more sense than this surly, selfish shoving mob.

Marcellus' own words, spoken with such bland assurance to the cynical Paulus, flashed across his mind and mocked him. The kingdom of good will, he had declared, would not come into being at the top of society. It would not be handed down from a throne. It would begin with the common people. Well—here were your common people! Climb up on a cart, Marcellus, and tell the common people about good will. Admonish them to love one another, aid one another, defer to one another; and so fulfill the law of Christ. But—look out!—or they will pelt you with filth from the gutters; for the common people are in no mood to be trifled with.

* * * * * *

The reunion of the Gallio family, an hour later, was one of the happiest experiences of their lives. When Marcellus had left home a year ago, shaky, emaciated, and mentally upset, the three who remained mourned for him almost as if he were dead. True, there had been occasional brief letters assuring them that he was well, but there was a conspicuous absence of details concerning his experiences and only vague intimations of a desire to come home. Between the lines they read, with forebodings, that Marcellus was still in a state of mental upheaval. He had seemed very far away, not only in miles but in mind. The last letter they had received from him, a month ago, had said, in closing, 'I am trailing an elusive mystery for the Emperor. Mysteries are his recreation. This one may turn out to be something more serious than a mere pastime.' The Senator had sighed and shaken his head as he slowly rolled up the scroll.

But now Marcellus had come back as physically fit as a gladiator, mentally alert, free of his despondency, in possession of his natural zest and enthusiasm.

And something else had been added, something not easy to define, a curious radiance of personality. There was a new strength in Marcellus, a contagious energy that vitalized the house. It was in his voice, in his eyes, in his hands. His family did not at first ask him what this new thing was, nor did they let him know that it was noticeable; neither did they discuss it immediately with one another. But Marcellus had acquired something that gave him distinction.

The Senator had been working late in his library. He had finished his task, had put away his writing materials, and had risen from his desk-chair when he heard confident footsteps.

Leaving Demetrius in the driveway to await the arrival of their luggage, Marcellus—joyfully recognized by the two old slaves on guard at the front door—had walked swiftly through to the spacious atrium. His father's door was partly open. Bursting in on him unceremoniously, he threw his arms around him and hugged him breathless. Although the Senator was tall and remarkably virile for his years, the Tribune's overwhelming vitality completely engulfed him.

'My son! My son!' Gallio quavered, fervently. 'You are well again! Strong again! Alive again! The gods be praised!'

Marcellus pressed his cheek against his father's and patted him on the back.

'Yes, sir!' he exclaimed. 'More alive than ever! And you, sir, grow more handsome every day! How proud I am to be your son!'

Lucia, in her room, suddenly stirred in her sleep, sat up wide-awake, listened, tossed aside the silk covers, listened again with an open mouth and a pounding heart.

'Oh!' she called. 'Tertia! My robe! Tertia! Wake up! Hurry! My sandals! Marcellus is here!' Racing down to the library, she threw herself into her brother's arms, and when he had lifted her off her feet and kissed her, she cried, 'Dear Marcellus—you are well!'

'And you—my sweet—are beautiful! You have grown up; haven't you?'

He lightly touched her high coronet of glossy black hair with caressing fingers. 'Lovely!'

The Senator put his arms around both of them, to their happy surprise, for it was not his custom to be demonstrative with his affection.

'Come,' he said gently. 'Let us go to your mother.'

'It is very late,' said Marcellus. 'Should we waken her?'

'Of course!' insisted Lucia.

They crowded through the doorway, arm in arm. In the dimly lit atrium, a little group of the older servants had assembled, tousled and sleepy, their anxious eyes wondering what to expect of the son and heir who, on his last visit home, had been in such a distressing state of mind.

'Ho!—Marcipor!' shouted Marcellus, grasping the outstretched hand. 'Hi!—Decimus!' It wasn't often that the stiff and taciturn butler unbent, but he beamed with smiles as he thrust out his hand. 'How are you, Tertia!' called Marcellus to the tall, graceful girl descending the stairs. They all drew in closer. Old Servius was patted on the shoulder, and the wrinkled, toothless mouth chopped tremulously while the tears ran unchecked.

'Welcome! Welcome!' the old man shrilled. 'The gods bless you, sir!'

'Ah—Lentius!' hailed Marcellus. 'How are my horses?' And when Lentius had made bold to reply that Ishtar had a filly, three months old—which made them all laugh merrily as if this were a good joke on somebody—Marcellus sent them into another gale of laughter by demanding, 'Bring in the filly, Lentius! I must see her at once!'

There were more than a score of slaves gathered in the atrium now, all of them full of happy excitement. There had never been such an utter collapse of discipline in the Gallio household. Long-time servants, accustomed to moving about soberly and on tiptoe, heard themselves laughing hilariously—laughing here in the atrium!—laughing in the presence of the Senator! And the Senator was smiling, too!

Marcellus was brightening their eyes with his ready recognition, calling most of them by name. A pair of pretty Macedonian twins arrived, hand in hand, dressed exactly alike; practically indistinguishable. He remembered having had a glimpse of them, two years ago, but had forgotten their names. He looked their way, and so did everyone else, to their considerable embarrassment.

'Are you girls sisters?' he inquired.

This was by far the merriest thing that anyone had said, and the atrium resounded with full-throated appreciation.

'Decimus!' shouted the Senator, and the laughter ceased. 'You will serve supper! In an hour! In the banquet-room! With the gold service! Marcipor!—let all the lamps be lighted! Throughout the villa! And the gardens!'

Marcellus brushed through the scattering crowd and bounded up the stairs. Cornelia met him in the corridor, outside her door, and he gathered her hungrily into his arms. They had no adequate words for each other; just stood there, clinging together, Cornelia smoothing his close-cropped hair with her soft palm and sobbing like a child, while the Senator, with misty eyes, waited a little way apart, fumbling with the silk tassels on his broad sash.

Her intuition suggesting that Marcellus and their emotional mother might need a quiet moment alone together, Lucia had tarried at the foot of the staircase for a word with Decimus about the supper. All the other servants had scurried away to their duties, their very sandal-straps confiding in excited whispers that this was a happy night and a good place to be.

'Not too much food, Decimus,' Lucia was saying. 'Some fresh fruit and cold meats and wine—and a nut-cake if there is one. But don't cook anything. It is late, and the Senator will be tired and sleepy before you have time to prepare an elaborate dinner. Serve it in the big dining-room, as he said, and use the gold plate. And tell Rhesus to cut an armful of roses—red ones. And let the twins serve my brother. And—'

With suddenly widened eyes, she sighted Demetrius—tall, tanned, serious, and handsome—entering the atrium. Dismissing the butler with a brief nod, Lucia held her arm high and waved a welcome, her flowing sleeve baring a shapely elbow. Decimus, keenly observant, scowled his displeasure and stalked stiffly away.

Advancing with long strides, Demetrius came to a military halt before her, bowed deferentially, and was slowly bringing up his spear-shaft to his forehead in the conventional salute when Lucia stepped forward impulsively, laying both hands on his bronzed arms.

'All thanks, good Demetrius,' she said, softly. 'You have brought Marcellus home—well and strong as ever. Better than ever!'

'No thanks are due me for that,' he rejoined. 'The Tribune needed no one to bring him home. He is fully master of himself now.' Demetrius raised his eyes and regarded her with frank admiration. 'May I tell the Tribune's sister how very—how very well she is looking?'

'Why not—if you think so?' Lucia, toying with her amber beads, gave him a smile that meant to be non-committal. 'There is no need asking you how you are, Demetrius. Have you and the Tribune had some exciting experiences?' Her eyes were wincingly exploring a long, new scar on his upper arm. He glanced down at it with a droll grin. 'How did you get that awful cut?' she asked, squeamishly.

'I met a Syrian,' said Demetrius. 'They are not a very polite people.'

'I hope you taught him some of the gentle manners of the Greeks,' drawled Lucia. 'Tell me—did you kill him?'

'You can't kill a Syrian,' said Demetrius, lightly. 'They die only of old age.'

Lucia's little shrug said they had had enough of this banter and her face slowly sobered to a thoughtful frown.

'What has happened to my brother?' she asked. 'He seems in such extraordinarily high spirits.'

'He may want to tell you—if you give him time.'

'You're different, too, Demetrius.'

'For the better, I hope,' he parried.

'Something has expanded you both,' declared Lucia. 'What is it? Has Marcellus been elevated to a more responsible command?'

Demetrius nodded enthusiastically.

'Will his new assignment take him into danger?' she asked, suddenly apprehensive.

'Oh, yes, indeed!' he answered, proudly.

'He doesn't appear to be worrying much about it. I never saw him so happy. He has already turned the whole villa upside-down with his gaiety.'

'I know. I heard them.' Demetrius grinned.

'I hope it won't spoil them,' she said, with dignity. 'They aren't used to taking such liberties; though perhaps it will not hurt—to have it happen—this once.'

'Perhaps not,' said Demetrius, dryly. 'It may not hurt them—to be really happy—this once.'

Lucia raised her brows.

'I am afraid you don't understand,' she remarked, coolly.

'I'm afraid I do,' he sighed. 'Had you forgotten that I too am a slave?'

'No.' She gave a little toss of her head. 'But I think you have.'

'I did not mean to be impudent,' he said, contritely. 'But what we are talking about is very serious, you know; discipline, slavery, mastery, human relations—and who has a right to tell others when they may be happy.'

Lucia searched his face with a frown.

'Well—I hope my brother's genial attitude towards our servants is not going to make us lose our control of this house!' she snapped, indignantly.

'It need not,' said Demetrius. 'He believes in a little different kind of control; that is all. It is much more effective, I think, than controlling by sharp commands. More pleasant for everybody; and, besides, you get better service.'

Marcellus was calling to her from the head of the stairs.

Marcellus and Diana at Capri

She had developed into a mature woman in his absence. In his recollections of her, Diana was a beautiful girl . . . but now she was far more lovely than he had remembered.

From page 394 of text

DEAN CORNWELL

'I am sorry I spoke impatiently, Demetrius,' she said, as she moved away. 'We are so glad you are home again.'

He met her level eyes and they smiled. He raised his spear-shaft to salute. She pursed her lips, shook her head, and made a negligent gesture. 'Never mind the salute,' she said—'this once.'

Marcipor, who had been lingering impatiently in the alcove, waiting for this conversation to end, came forward as Lucia disappeared up the stairway. He fell into step with Demetrius and they strolled out through the peristyle into the moonlight.

'It is amazing—how he has recovered!' said Marcipor. 'What happened to him?'

'I shall tell you fully when there is an opportunity; later tonight, if possible. Marcellus has become an ardent believer. He toured through Galilee—'

'And you?' asked Marcipor. 'Were you not with him?'

'Only part of the time. I spent many weeks in Jerusalem. I have much to tell you about that. Marcipor—the Galilean is alive!'

'Yes—we have heard that.'

' "We"?—and who are "we"?' Demetrius took hold of Marcipor's arm and drew him to a sudden halt.

'The Christians in Rome,' replied Marcipor, smiling at his friend's astonishment.

'Has it then come to Rome—so soon?'

'Many months ago—brought by merchants from Antioch.'

'And how did you find out?'

'It was being whispered about in the markets. Decimus, who is forever deriding the Greeks, was pleased to inform me that certain superstitious traders from Antioch had brought the report of a Jewish carpenter who had risen from the dead. Remembering what you had told me about this man, I was devoured with curiosity to hear more of it.'

'And you found the men from Antioch?' encouraged Demetrius.

'The next day. They were quite free to talk, and their story sounded convincing. They had had it from an eye-witness of many astounding miracles—one Philip. Seeking to confirm it, several of them went to Jerusalem where they talked with other men who had seen this Jesus after his death—men whose word they trusted. All that—added to what you had reported—gave me cause to believe.'

'So—you are a Christian!' Demetrius' eyes shone. 'You must tell the Tribune. He will be delighted!'

Marcipor's face grew suddenly grave.

'Not yet—Demetrius. My course is not clear. Decimus made it his business to inform the Senator of this new movement, describing it as a revolution against lawful authority.'

'Has the Senator done anything about it?'

'Not that I know of, but is it not natural that his feeling toward the Christians should be far from complacent? He associates all this with his son's misfortunes. Now—if Marcellus is told that we have a large body of believers here in Rome, he might impetuously throw himself into it. That would be dangerous. The Christians are keeping under cover. Already the patrols are beginning to make inquiries about their secret meetings. We must not cause a breach between Marcellus and his father.'

'Very well, Marcipor,' agreed Demetrius. 'We will not tell the Tribune, but he will find it out; you may be sure of that. And as for estrangement, it is inevitable. Marcellus will not give up his belief, and it is quite unlikely that the Senator could be persuaded of its truth. Old men do not readily change their opinions. However—this new cause cannot wait, Marcipor, until all the opinionated old men have approved of it. This story of Jesus is our only hope that freedom and justice may come. And if it is to come—at all—it must begin now!'

'I believe that,' said Marcipor—'but still—I shouldn't like to see Marcellus offend his father. The Senator is not going to live long.'

'There was just such a case reported to Jesus,' said Demetrius. 'I had this from a Galilean who heard the conversation. A young man, very much impressed that it was his duty to come out openly for this new way of life, said to Jesus, "My father is an old man, sir, with old views. This new religion is an offense to him. Let me first bury my father, and then I shall come—and follow." '

'That sounds reasonable,' put in Marcipor, who was sixty-seven.

'Jesus didn't think so,' went on Demetrius. 'It was high time for a drastic change in men's belief and behavior. The new message couldn't wait for the departure of old men with old views. Indeed, these old men were already dead. Let them be buried by other dead ones.'

'Did he say that?' queried Marcipor.

'Well—something like that.'

'Sounds rather rough—to me—coming from so gentle a person.'

Demetrius slipped his hand affectionately through the older Corinthian's arm.

'Marcipor—let us not make the mistake of thinking that, because this message of Jesus concerns peace and good will, it is a soft and timid thing that will wait on every man's convenience, and scurry off the road, to hide in the bushes, until all other things go by! The people who carry this torch are going to get into plenty of trouble. They are already being whipped and imprisoned! Many have been slain!'

'I know, I know,' murmured Marcipor. 'One of the traders from Antioch told me of seeing a young Greek stoned to death by a mob in Jerusalem. Stephanos was his name. Did you—by any chance—know him?'

'Stephanos,' said Demetrius, sadly, 'was my closest friend.'

* * * * * *

Marcellus had not finished his breakfast when Marcipor came in to say that Senator Gallio was in his library and would be pleased to have a talk with the Tribune at his early convenience.

'You may tell the Senator that I shall be down in a few minutes,' said Marcellus.

He would have preferred to postpone, for a few days, this serious interview with his father. It would be very difficult for the Senator to listen to his strange story with patience or respect. For some moments Marcellus sat staring out the open window, while he absently peeled an orange that he didn't intend to eat, and tried to decide how best to present the case of Jesus the Galilean; for, in this instance, he would be more than an advocate. Marcellus would be on trial, too.

Marcus Lucan Gallio was not a contentious man. His renown as a debater in the Senate had been earned by diplomacy; by his knowing when and how much to concede, where and whom to appease, and the fine art of conciliation. He never doggedly pursued an argument for vanity's sake. But he was proud of his mental morality.

If, for example, he became firmly convinced that at all times and everywhere water seeks a level, there would be no use in coming to him with the tale that on a certain day, in a certain country, at the behest of a certain man, water was observed to run uphill. He had no time for reports of events which disregarded natural laws. As for 'miracles,' the very word was offensive. He had no tolerance for such stories and not much more tolerance for persons who believed in them. And because, in his opinion, all religions were built on faith in supernatural beings and supernatural doings, the Senator was not only contemptuous of religion, but admitted a candid distaste for religious people. Anybody who went in for such beliefs was either ignorant or unscrupulous. If a man, who had any sense at all, became a religious propagandist, he needed watching; for, obviously, he meant to take advantage of the feebleminded who would trust him because of his piety. Some people—according to Senator Gallio—seemed to think that a pious man was inevitably honest, whereas the facts would show that piety and integrity were categorically irrelevant. It was quite proper for old Servius to importune his gods. One could even forgive old Tiberius for his consuming interest in religion, seeing that he was out of his head. But there was no excuse for such nonsense in a healthy, educated man.

Marcellus had been treated with deep sympathy when he had come home a year ago. He had suffered a great shock and his mind was temporarily unbalanced. He couldn't have said anything too preposterous for his father's patience. But now he was sound in body and mind. He would tell the Senator this morning an amazing story of a man who had healed all manner of diseases; a man who, having been put to death on a cross, rose from his grave to be seen of many witnesses. And this would undoubtedly make the Senator very angry—and disgusted. 'Bah!' he would shout. 'Nonsense!'

* * * * * *

This forecast of his father's probable attitude had been appallingly accurate. It turned out to be a very unhappy interview. From almost the first moment, Marcellus sensed strong opposition. He had decided to begin his narrative with Jesus' unjust trials and crucifixion, hoping thus to enlist the Senator's sympathy for the persecuted Galilean, but he was not permitted to build up his case from that point.

'I have heard all that, my son,' said Gallio, crisply. 'You need not review it. Tell me of the journey you made into the country where this man lived.'

So—Marcellus had told of his tour with Justus; of little Jonathan, whose crippled foot had been made strong; of Miriam, who had been given a voice; of Lydia, who had found healing by a touch of his Robe; of old Nathanael Bartholomew, and the storm at sea—while his father gazed steadily at him from under shaggy frowning brows, offering no comments and asking no questions.

At length he had arrived at the phase of the story where he must talk of Jesus' return to life. With dramatic earnestness he repeated everything that they had told him of these reappearances, while the lines about the Senator's mouth deepened into a scowl.

'It all sounds incredible, sir,' he conceded, 'but I am convinced that it is true.' For a moment, he debated the advisability of telling his father about the miracle he had seen with his own eyes—Peter's healing of the cripple. But no—that would be too much. His father would tell him he had been imposed upon by these miracle stories reported to him by other men. But there would be nothing left for the Senator to say except 'You lie!' if he told him that he himself had seen one of these wonders wrought.

'On the testimony of a few superstitious fishermen!' growled Gallio, derisively.

'It was not easy for me to accept, sir,' admitted Marcellus, 'and I am not trying to persuade you of it. You asked me to tell you what I had learned about Jesus, and I have told you truly. It is my belief that this Galilean is still alive. I think he is an eternal person, a divine person with powers that no king or emperor has ever possessed, and I further believe that he will eventually rule the world!'

Gallio chuckled bitterly.

'Had you thought of telling Tiberius that this Jesus intends to rule the world?'

'I may not need to say that to Tiberius. I shall tell him that Jesus, who was put to death, is alive again. The Emperor can draw his own conclusions.'

'You had better be careful what you say to that crazy old man,' warned Gallio. 'He is insane enough to believe you, and this will not be pleasant news. Don't you know he is quite capable of having you punished for bringing him a tale like that?'

'He can do no more than kill me,' said Marcellus, quietly.

'Perhaps not,' drawled Gallio; 'but even so light a punishment as death—for an aspiring young man—might be quite an inconvenience.'

Marcellus humored his father's grim jest with a smile.

'In sober truth, sir, I do not fear death. There is a life to come.'

'Well—that is an ancient hope, my son,' conceded Gallio, with a vague gesture. 'Men have been scrawling that on their tombs for three thousand years. The only trouble with that dream is that it lacks proof. Nobody has ever signaled us from out there. Nobody has ever come back to report.'

'Jesus did!' declared Marcellus.

Gallio sighed deeply and shook his head. After a moody silence, he pushed back his chair and walked slowly around the big desk, as Marcellus rose to meet his approach.

'My son,' he said, entreatingly, laying his hands on the broad shoulders, 'go to the Emperor and tell him what you have learned of this Galilean prophet. Quote Jesus' words of wisdom. They are sensible and should do Tiberius much good if he would heed them. Tell him—if you must—about the feats of magic. The old man will believe them, and the more improbable they are the better they—and you—will please him. That, in my opinion, should be sufficient.'

'Nothing about Jesus' return to life?' inquired Marcellus, respectfully.

'Why should you?' demanded Gallio. 'Take a common-sense view of your predicament. Through no fault of yours, you have had an unusual experience, and are now obliged to report on it to the Emperor. He has been mad for a dozen years or more and everybody in Rome knows it. He has surrounded himself with scores of scatter-brained philosophers, astrologers, soothsayers, and diviners of oracles. Some of them are downright impostors and the rest of them are mentally unhinged. If you tell Tiberius what you have told me, you will be just one more monkey added to his menagerie.'

It was strong medicine, but Marcellus grinned; and his father, feeling that his argument was gaining ground, went on, pleadingly.

'You have a bright future before you, my son, if you will it so; but not if you pursue this course. I wonder if you realize what a tragedy may be in the making for you—for all of us! It will be a bitter experience for your mother, and your sister, and your father, to know that our friends are telling one another you have lost your mind; that you are one of the Emperor's wise fools. And what will Diana say?' he continued, earnestly. 'That beautiful creature is in love with you! Don't you care?'

'I do care, sir!' exclaimed Marcellus. 'And I realize that she may be sadly disappointed in me, but I have no alternative. I have put my hand to this plow—and I am not turning back!'

Gallio retreated a step and lounged against his desk, with a sly smile.

'Wait until you see her before you decide to give her up.'

'I am indeed anxious to see her, sir.'

'Will you try to meet her, down there, before you talk to Tiberius?'

'If possible, yes sir.'

'You have made your arrangements for the voyage?'

'Yes, sir. Demetrius has seen to it. We leave this evening. Galley to Ostia. To Capri on *The Cleo*.'

'Very good,' approved Gallio, much encouraged. He slapped Marcellus on the back. 'Let us take a walk in the gardens. And you haven't been to the stables yet.'

'A moment, please, sir—before we go.' Marcellus' face was serious. 'I know you have a feeling that everything is settled now, according to your wish, and I would be happy to follow your counsel if I were free to do so.'

'Free?' Gallio stared into his son's eyes. 'What do you mean?'

'I feel obliged, sir, to tell the Emperor of Jesus' return to life.'

'Well, well, then,' consented Gallio, brusquely, 'if you must talk about that, let it be as a local rumor among the country people. You don't have to tell Tiberius that you believe it! If you want to say that a few fishermen thought they saw him, that should discharge your obligation. You have no personal knowledge of it. *You* didn't see him!'

'But I saw a man who did see him, sir!' declared Marcellus. '*I saw this man looking at him!*'

'And that constitutes proof—in your opinion?' scoffed Gallio.

'In this instance—yes, sir! I saw a Greek stoned for his Christian belief. He was a brave man, ready to risk his life for his faith. I knew him, and trusted him. When everyone thought him dead, he raised up, smiled, and shouted, "*I see him!*" And—*I know that he saw him!*'

'But you don't have to tell that to Tiberius!' said Gallio, testily.

'Yes, sir! Having heard and seen that, I should be a coward if I did not testify to it! For I, too, am a Christian, sir! I cannot do otherwise!'

Gallio made no reply. With bent head, he turned away slowly and left the room, without a backward glance.

Lamenting his father's disappointment, Marcellus sauntered out to the pergola, feeling sure that Lucia would be waiting for him. She saw him coming and ran to meet him. Linking their arms, she tugged him along gaily toward their favorite rendezvous.

'What's the matter?' she insisted, shaking his arm. 'Have a row with the Senator?'

'I hurt his feelings,' muttered Marcellus.

'I hope you weren't talking to him about that awful business up there in Jerusalem that made you sick!'

'No, dear; but I was telling him about that man—and I would be glad to tell you, too.'

'Thanks, my little brother!' chaffed Lucia. 'I don't want to hear a word of it! High time you forgot all about it! . . . Here, Bambo! . . . Make a fuss over him, Marcellus. He hardly knows you.' Her lips pouted. 'Neither do I,' she murmured. 'Aren't you ever going to be happy any more? Last night we all thought you were well again. I was so glad I lay awake for hours, hugging myself for joy! Now you're blue and moody.' Big tears stood in her eyes. 'Please, Marcellus!'

'Sorry, sister.' He put his arm around her. 'Let us go look at the roses. . . . Here, Bambo!'

Bambo strolled up and consented to have his head patted.

* * * * * *

The Emperor had not been well for many weeks. Early in April, while rashly demonstrating how tough he was, the old man had ambled down to the uncompleted villa on the easternmost end of the mall in a drenching rain and had taken a severe cold, the effects of which had depleted his not too abundant vitality.

In normal circumstances Tiberius, customarily careful of his health, would have taken no such risk; or, having taken it, would have gone at once to bed, fuming and snorting, to be packed in hot fomentations and doctored with everything that the court physicians could devise.

But on this occasion the Emperor, having renewed his youth—or at least having attained his second childhood—had sat about with Diana in the dampness of the new villa, wet to the skin, after which he had sauntered back to the Jovis pretending to have enjoyed the rain and refusing to permit anyone to aid him, though it was clear enough that he was having a hard chill: he had sneezed sloppily in the Chamberlain's face while hoarsely protesting that he was sound as a nut.

That the young daughter of Gallus had been innocently but unmistakably responsible for this dangerous imprudence—and many another hazardous folly on the part of the aging Emperor—was now the unanimous opinion of the household staff.

The beauteous Diana was getting to be a problem. For the first few weeks after her arrival, more than a year ago, the entire population of Capri—with the exception of the Empress Julia, whose jealousy of her was deep and desperate—had rejoiced in the girl's invigorating influence on Tiberius. His infatuation for Diana had done wonders for him. Boyishly eager to please her, he was living more temperately, not only in what he ate and drank, but in what he said and did. Not often now was the Emperor noticeably intoxicated. His notorious tantrums were staged less frequently and with less violence. When annoyed, he still threw things at his ministers, but it had been a long time since he had barked at or bitten anyone. And whereas he had frequently humiliated them all by slogging about the grounds looking like the veriest ragamuffin, now he insisted on being shaved almost every morning and was keenly interested in his costumes.

This had met the enthusiastic approval of everybody whose tenure of office was in any way related to his own—and that included almost everyone on Capri, ministers, minstrels, physicians, dancers, gardeners, vintners, tailors, astrologers, historians, poets, cooks, guards, carpenters, stonemasons, sculptors, priests, and at least three hundred servants, bond and free. The longer they could keep the Emperor alive, the better for their own careers; and the more contented he was, the less arduous their task of caring for him.

It was quite natural, therefore, that Diana should be popular. The poets in residence composed extravagant odes appropriately extolling her beauty, and—with somewhat less warrant—her sweet and gentle disposition, for she was of uncertain temper and not at all reticent about expressing her feelings when displeased.

But, as time went on, it began to be whispered about that the infirm

Emperor, in trying to show off for Diana, was wearing himself out. He was at her nimble heels from sunrise to sunset, in all weathers, fiercely gouging the graveled paths with his cane as they toured the island, and wheezing up and down stairs in her lavish new villa which seemed almost as far from completion as it had been six months previously, though a hundred skilled workmen had been hard at it every day. Nothing was ever quite fine enough. Mantels had to be taken down and rebuilt, again and again. Mosaic floors and walls were ripped out and done over. One day the old man had testily remarked that he didn't believe the villa would ever be completed, an impromptu forecast which, albeit spoken lightly, turned out to be a sound prediction.

For some time considerable sympathy was felt for Diana. Though no one knew certainly—for she was far too wise to confide fully in anyone connected with this university of gossip, intrigue, and treachery—it was generally believed that the brilliant and beautiful girl was being detained at Capri against her personal wishes. This seemed to be confirmed by the fact that on the occasions of her mother's visits, every few weeks, Diana would weep piteously when the time came for Paula's departure. There might be certain advantages in being the sole object of the Emperor's devotion; but, considered as a permanent occupation, it left a good deal to be desired.

A legend had gradually taken form and size concerning Diana's prospects. The Chamberlain, in his cups, had confided to the Captain of the Guard that the comely daughter of Legate Gallus was in love with the son of Senator Gallio, a probably hopeless attachment, seeing that the young Tribune was sick in the head and had been spirited out of the country. This information was soon common knowledge.

No one was more interested in Diana's aspirations than old Julia, who contrived to inspect every letter she sent and received. And it was believed that Julia relayed copies of all such correspondence to Gaius; for, on each occasion of having spied upon Diana's letters, she had dispatched a scroll to the Prince by special messenger.

During the winter, Gaius had not visited Capri; but, advised of the Emperor's indisposition, he had come in latter April, attended by a foppish retinue, and had spent a week, pretending to be much concerned over the old man's ill-health, but fully enjoying the nightly banquets which Tiberius had ordered.

On these occasions the Emperor—barely able to hold his weary head up—drowsed and roused and grinned like a skull and drowsed again, a ludicrous caricature of imperial power. On his right, but paying no attention to him, reclined old Julia, wigged, painted, ablaze with jewels and shockingly cadaverous, smirking and fawning over Gaius who lounged beside her.

None of the fifty dissolute sycophants, who sprawled about the overloaded tables, dared risk exchanging a wink or a smile, but it was an amusing pantomime, with the Emperor half-asleep and the Empress disgustingly pawing at the gold-embroidered sleeve of the Prince while he, disdainfully indifferent to her caresses, leaned far forward to make amorous grimaces at Diana, on the other side of Tiberius, stripping her with his experienced, froglike eyes, while she regarded him with the cool detachment of one reading an epitaph on an ancient monument.

This had been privately enjoyed by almost everybody but Celia, the beautiful but feather-headed wife of Quintus and niece of Sejanus, long-time friend and adviser of Tiberius. Celia was beside herself with an anxiety she could not disguise. She would have been ready to kill Diana had the girl shown Gaius the slightest encouragement, but she was also much annoyed over Diana's frosty disinterest in the Prince's attentions. Who indeed did this young Gallus think she was—to be so haughty? She had better mend her manners! The crazy old man she was leading about—like a dog on a leash—would be dying one of these fine days; and then where would she be?

It had been a depressing week for Celia. Ever since Quintus had been sent abroad on some state mission of high importance, she had been the center of interest at the Prince's social functions, serving as hostess and enjoying his candid and clumsy preferment. At first it had been believed that Gaius was showing her special favors to ingratiate himself with old Sejanus, who held a strong hand on the imperial purse-strings. But as time went on, and the Prince's visits at Celia's villa were of daily occurrence, this flattery had gone to her head and she had made the mistake of snubbing many friends who, though they had endured her snobberies for diplomacy's sake, were carefully preparing to avenge themselves when an opportune moment arrived. It had been Celia's hope that the Prince would find further business for her husband in foreign parts, but now it had been announced that Quintus was returning presently. As if that were not dismaying enough, Gaius was giving his full attention to Diana.

On the last day of this visit to the Emperor, Celia had arranged what she thought was a private moment with the Prince—though there were few conversations on Capri which the whole island didn't know by nightfall—and tearfully took him to task for his recent indifference.

'I thought you liked me,' she whimpered.

'Not when your nose is red,' he grumbled. 'You'd better stop making yourself ridiculous.'

'Can't you send Quintus away again?' she wheedled.

'That braying ass?' retorted Gaius. 'We trust him with an ambassadorial errand, and he gets himself slapped all over the campus of a Greek inn by an unarmed slave!'

'I don't believe it!' shrilled Celia. 'It's a story someone invented to discredit him! I thought you were Quintus' friend.'

'Bah! Quintus' only friend is his mirror! Had I cared for your husband, would I have made a cuckold of him?'

Celia had wept hysterically.

'You liked me well enough," she cried, 'until you came here and noticed this Gallus girl's curves! And it's plain to see she despises you! What an impudent creature she is!'

'Mind you don't plan to do her some injury!' growled Gaius, clutching her arm roughly. 'You would better forget all about her now, and be contented with your husband when he comes.' He chuckled infuriatingly. 'You and Quintus are admirably suited to each other.'

'You can't do this to me!' she shouted, reckless with rage. 'Where will you stand with Sejanus when I tell him you have treated me like an ordinary trollop?'

Gaius shrugged.

'Where will *you* stand—when you tell him that?' he sneered.

Whereupon Celia had sought comfort in a call on the Empress, suddenly remembering a social duty which most of the rest forgot in the confusion of departure.

Julia had been surprisingly effusive; and Celia, red-eyed and outraged, was a ready victim to the Empress' sympathetic queries.

'Poor Gaius!' sighed old Julia. 'So impressionable! So lonesome! And so beset with cares! You must make allowances for him, my dear. And he really is in love, I think, with the daughter of Gallus. It would not be a bad alliance. Gallus is a great favorite with the army, at home and abroad. Indeed—Gallus *is* the army! And if my son is to succeed to the throne, he needs the good will of our legions. Furthermore—as you have seen for yourself, the Emperor is so foolishly fond of Diana that her marriage with Gaius would practically insure my son's future.'

'But Diana hates him!' cried Celia. 'Anyone can see that!'

'Well—that is because she thinks she is in love with the half-crazy son of Gallio.' Julia's thin lips puckered in an omniscient smile. 'She will get over that. Perhaps—if you would like to square accounts with the luscious Diana, you might give yourself no bother to deny the reports that Marcellus is insane.' And with that, the Empress had kissed Celia and waved her out.

Wiping her lips vigorously, Celia returned to the Jovis where the party was assembling for conveyance down the mountain to the imperial barge. She was still hopeful that Gaius, on the return trip, would repent of his discourtesies and restore her to his favor.

'Where is the Prince?' she inquired, with forced brightness, of her cousin Lavilla Sejanus, as the slave-borne chairs were being filled.

'He isn't going back to the city with us,' Lavilla had had malicious pleasure in replying. 'I daresay he wants to have a quiet visit with Diana.'

'Well—he can have her!' retorted Celia, hotly.

'Don't be too sure of that!' shrilled Minia, Laville's younger sister, who was thought to have been wholly occupied with the conversation she was having with Olivia Varus, in the chair beside her.

'Diana is waiting for Marcellus Gallio to come back,' put in Olivia.

'Much good that will do her,' sniffed Celia. 'Marcellus has lost his mind. That's why they sent him away.'

'Nonsense!' scoffed Lavilla. 'The Emperor sent him away to make some sort of investigation—in Athens—or somewhere. Think he would have sent a crazy man?'

'Why not?' giggled Minia.

'Who told you that, Celia?' demanded Olivia.

'The Empress!' declared Celia, impressively. 'I don't think it's a secret.'

'Neither do I,' drawled Lavilla. 'It may have been—but it isn't now.'

'Why should you care?' inquired Minia, languidly.

'Well—I rather like Marcellus,' said Lavilla, 'and Diana, too. It's unfortunate to have such a story strewn about. Besides—I don't believe it!'

'But the Empress told me!' snapped Celia, indignantly.

Lavilla arched her brows, pursed her lips, and shrugged.

'I wonder why,' she said.

* * * * * *

It was mid-afternoon when *The Cleo* sighted the island and another hour had passed before she tied up at the wharf. It had been a perfect day. Marcellus had never seen the Bay of Neapolis so blue. Demetrius was left at the docks to oversee the conveyance of their luggage to the Villa Jovis.

Engaging a waiting chair, Marcellus was borne up the long flight of marble steps, and the sinuous path, and more steps, and another path, luxuriating in the ruinously expensive beauty with which the Emperor had surrounded himself. The old man might be crazy, but he was an artist.

Now that they had come up to the plateau, Tiberius' wonder city—dominated by the massive Jovis—gleamed white in the June sunshine. Lean old philosophers and fat old priests lounged in the arbors, and on the graveled paths that bounded the pools other wise men strolled with their heads bent and their hands clasped behind them. Were all of the Emperor's counselors old men? Naturally they would be. It aged Marcellus to face the prospect of joining forces with these doddering ancients.

It surprised and gratified him that he had so little explaining to do in accounting for his presence. He spoke his name to the patrol and they passed him without examination. He told the porter who he was and the porter sent another with a message to the Captain of the Guard, who came without delay and led him through the vasty peristyle into the cool, high-ceilinged atrium where, presently, the Chamberlain entered to greet him with much deference.

The Emperor, who was resting, would be made aware of Tribune Marcellus' arrival. Meantime—would the Tribune be pleased to go to the apartment which had been prepared for him?

'I was expected, then?' asked Marcellus.

'Oh, yes, sir,' replied Nevius. 'His Majesty had learned of Tribune Marcellus' arrival in Rome.'

It was a sumptuous suite that they showed him, with a small, exquisitely appointed peristyle of its own, looking out upon a colorful garden. A half-dozen Nubians were preparing his bath. A tall Macedonian slave came with a flagon of wine, followed by another bearing a silver salver filled with choice fruits.

Marcellus stepped out into the peristyle, frowning thoughtfully. It was an unexpectedly lavish reception he was having at the hands of the Emperor. His rank entitled him to certain courtesies, but the attention he was receiving needed a better explanation. It was flattering enough, but perplexing. Demetrius had arrived now, and the porters had brought the luggage. The Chamberlain came out to announce that the Tribune's bath was ready.

'And at your convenience, sir,' added Nevius, 'the daughter of Gallus will receive you—in the garden—at her villa.'

* * * * * *

They had offered to conduct him, but Marcellus preferred to go alone after receiving general directions. Diana's villa! And what did Diana want with a villa—at Capri? Or did she want a villa? Or was it the old man's idea?

He was approaching it now, involuntarily slowing his steps as he marveled at its grace and symmetry. It was a large house, but conveyed no impression of massiveness. The Doric columns of the portico were not ponderous;

the carving on the lintel was light and lacy. It was an immense doll's house, suggestive of something an ingenious confectioner might have made of white sugar.

A guard met him on the tessellated pavement and led the way in and through the unfurnished atrium, ceiled with blue in which gold stars were set; and on to the peristyle where many workmen glanced down from the scaffoldings with casual interest in the guest. Beyond lay the intentions of a terraced garden. Pointing to the pergola that was on the southern rim of the plateau, the guard retraced his steps and Marcellus proceeded with lengthened stride, full of happy anticipation.

Diana was leaning against the marble balustrade, looking out upon the sea. Sensitive to his coming, perhaps hearing his footsteps, she slowly turned about; and, resting her elbows on the broad stone railing, waited his approach with a sober, wide-eyed stare which Marcellus easily interpreted. She was wondering—and with deep apprehension—whether he had fully recovered from his mental sickness; whether there would be constraint in their meeting. Her eyes were a little frightened, and she involuntarily pressed the back of her hand against her lips.

Marcellus had no time to regard the attractive costume she wore, the gracefully draped white silk stola with the deep crimson border at the throat, the slashed sleeves loosely clasped with gold buttons, the wide, tightly bound girdle about the hips, the pearl-beaded crimson coronet that left a fringe of black curls on her white forehead; but Diana was an enchanting picture. She had developed into a mature woman in his absence. In his recollections of her, Diana was a beautiful girl. Sometimes he had wondered, when abroad, whether he might have idealized her too extravagantly; but now she was far more lovely than he had remembered. His happiness shone in his face.

Slowly she advanced to meet him, tall and regal in the caressing lines of the white stola, her full lips parting in a tentative smile that was gaining confidence with every step. She extended her hands, as he neared her, still studying him with a yearning hope.

'Diana!' he exclaimed hopefully. 'Dearest Diana!' Grasping her hands, he smiled ecstatically into her uplifted eyes.

'Have you really come back to me, Marcellus?" she murmured.

He drew her closer and she came confidently into his arms, reached up her hand and laid her palm gently on his cheek. Her long lashes slowly closed and Marcellus tenderly kissed her eyes. Her hand moved softly around his neck, suddenly tightening, almost fiercely, as his lips touched hers. She drew a quick, involuntary breath, and raced his heart with her unrestrained answer to his kiss. For a long moment they clung to each other, deeply stirred.

'You are adorable!' whispered Marcellus, fervently.

With a contented sigh, Diana childishly snuggled her face against his breast while he held her tightly to him. She was trembling. Then, slowly disengaging herself from his arms, she looked up into his face with misty, smiling eyes.

'Come—let us sit down,' she said softly. 'We have much to talk about.' The timbre of her voice had altered too. It had deepened and matured.

Marcellus followed her graceful figure to the marble lectus that gave an entrancing view of the sea, and they sat, Diana facing him with a brooding concern.

'Have you seen the Emperor?' she asked; and when he shook his head absently—as if seeing the Emperor was a matter of small importance—she said, soberly, 'Somehow I wish you didn't have to talk with him. You know how eccentric he has been; his curiosity about magic and miracles and stars and spirits—and such things. Lately he has been completely obsessed. His health is failing. He doesn't want to talk about anything else but metaphysical things.'

'That's not surprising,' commented Marcellus, reaching for her hand.

'Sometimes—all day long and far into the night,' she went on, in that new, deep register that made every word sound confidential, 'he tortures his poor old head with these matters, while his queer sages sit in a circle about his bed, delivering long harangues to which he tries to listen—as if it were his duty.'

'Perhaps he is preparing his mind for death,' surmised Marcellus.

Diana nodded with cloudy eyes.

'He has been impatient for your return, Marcellus. He seems to think that you may tell him something new. These old men!' She flung them away with a scornful gesture. 'They exhaust him; they exasperate him; and they impose upon him—cruelly! That horrible old Dodinius, who reads oracles, is the worst of the lot. Always, at the Feast of the New Moon, he slaughters a sheep, and performs some silly ceremonies, and pretends he has had a revelation. I don't know how.'

'They count the warts on the sheep's underpinning, I think,' recalled Marcellus, 'and they examine the entrails. If a certain kink in an intestine points east, the answer is "Yes"—and the fee is five hundred sesterces.'

'Well'—Diana dismissed the details with a slim hand—'however it is accomplished, dirty old Dodinius does it; and they say that he has occasionally made a true prediction. If the weather is going to be stormy, he always knows it before anyone else.'

'Perhaps he feels the change in his creaking hinges,' suggested Marcellus.

'You're a confirmed skeptic, Marcellus.' She gave him a sidelong glance that played at rebuking him. 'There should be no frivolous comments about these holy men. Dodinius' best forecast was when he discovered that Annaeus Seneca was still living, next day after the report had come that the old poet was dead. How he divined that, the gods only know; but it was true that Seneca had drifted into a deathlike coma from which he recovered—as you know.'

'You don't suppose he hired Seneca to play dead,' ventured Marcellus, with a chuckle.

'My dear—if Annaeus Seneca wanted to connive with somebody, it wouldn't be an old dolt like Dodinius,' Diana felt sure. Dropping the badinage, she grew serious. 'About ten days ago, it was revealed to him—so he insists—that the Emperor is going to live forever. He hasn't found it easy to convince the Emperor, for there is quite a lot of precedent to overcome; but you will find His Majesty immensely curious about this subject. He wants to believe Dodinius; sends for him, first thing in the morning, to come and tell him again all about the revelation; and Dodinius, the unscrupulous old reptile, reassures him that there can be no doubt of it. Isn't that a dreadful way to torment the Emperor in his last days when he should be allowed to die in peace?'

Marcellus, with eyes averted, nodded non-committally.

'Sometimes, my dear'—Diana impulsively leaned forward, shaking her head in despair—'it makes me hot with shame and loathing that I have to live here surrounded by these tiresome men who fatten on frauds! All one ever hears, on this mad island, is a jumble of atrocious nonsense that no healthy person, in his right mind, would give a second thought to! And now—as if the poor old Emperor hadn't heard enough of such stupid prattle—Dodinius is trying to persuade him to live forever.'

Marcellus made no comment on that; sat frowningly gazing out on the sea. Presently he stirred, returned, and put his arm about her shoulders.

'I don't know what you have come to tell the Emperor, Marcellus,' continued Diana, yielding to his caress, 'but I do know it will be honest. He will want to know what you think of this crazy notion that Dodinius has put into his head. This may call for some tact.'

'Have you a suggestion?' asked Marcellus.

'You will know what to say, I think. Tiberius is a worn-out old man. And he certainly doesn't look very heroic. But there was a time when he was brave and strong. Perhaps—if you remind him—he will be able to remember. He wasn't afraid to die when he was vigorous and had something to live for.' Diana lightly traced a pattern on Marcellus' forearm with her finger-tips. 'Why should that weary old man want to live forever? One would think he should be glad enough to put his burden down—and leave all these scheming courtiers and half-witted prophets—and find his peace in oblivion.'

Marcellus bent over her and kissed her lips, and was thrilled by her warm response.

'I love you, dear!' he declared, passionately.

'Then—take me away from here,' she whispered. 'Take me some place where nobody is insane—and nobody talks metaphysical rubbish—and nobody cares about the future—or the past—or anything but just now!' She hugged him closer to her. 'Will you, Marcellus? The Emperor wants us to live here. That's what this horrible villa is about.' Diana's voice trembled. 'I can't stay here! I can't! I shall go mad!' She put her lips close to his ear. 'Let us try to slip away. Can't we bribe a boat?'

'No, darling,' protested Marcellus. 'I shall take you away, but not as a fugitive. We must bide our time. We don't want to be exiles.'

'Why not?' demanded Diana. 'Let us go some place—far, far away—and have a little house—and a little garden—close by a stream—and live in peace.'

'It is a beautiful picture, dear,' he consented, 'but you would soon be lonely and restless; and besides—I have some important work to do that can't be done—in a peaceful garden. And then, too—there are our families to consider.'

Diana relaxed in his arms, earnestly thinking.

'I'll be patient,' she promised, 'but don't let it be too long. I am not safe here.'

'Not safe!' exclaimed Marcellus. 'What are you afraid of?'

Before she could reply, they both started—and drew apart—at the sound of footsteps. Glancing toward the villa, Marcellus saw the guard approaching who had directed him to the pergola.

'Tiberius is too feeble and preoccupied to be of any protection to me,' said Diana, in a low voice. 'The Empress is having more and more to say about our life here on this dreadful island. Gaius comes frequently to confer with her—'

'Has that swine been annoying you?' broke in Marcellus.

'I have managed to avoid being alone with him,' said Diana, 'but old Julia is doing her utmost to—'

The guard had halted, a little distance away.

'Yes—Atreus?' inquired Diana, turning toward him.

'The Emperor is ready to receive Tribune Marcellus Gallio,' said the guard deferentially.

'Very well,' nodded Marcellus. 'I shall come at once.'

The guard saluted and marched stiffly away.

'When and where do we meet, dear?' asked Marcellus, rising reluctantly. 'At dinner, perhaps?'

'Not likely. The Emperor will want to have you all to himself this evening. Send me a message—to my suite at the Jovis—when you are at liberty. If it is not too late, I may join you in the atrium. Otherwise, let us meet here in the pergola, early in the morning.' Diana held out her hand and Marcellus kissed it tenderly.

'Does this Atreus belong to you?' he asked.

Diana shook her head.

'I brought only two maids from home,' she said. 'All the others who attend me belong here. Atreus is a member of the guard at the Jovis. He follows me about wherever I go.'

'Is he to be trusted?' asked Marcellus, anxiously.

Diana shrugged—and drew a doubtful smile.

'How can one tell who is to be trusted in this hotbed of conspiracy? Atreus is respectful and obliging. Whether he would take any risks in my behalf—I don't know. Whether he is now on his way to tell old Julia that he saw you kiss me—I don't know. I shouldn't care to bet much on it—either way.' Diana rose, and slipped her arm through his. 'Go, now,' she whispered. 'The poor old man will be waiting—and he is not patient. Come to me—when you can.'

Marcellus took her in his arms and kissed her.

'I shall be thinking of nothing else,' he murmured—'but you!'

* * * * * *

The last time Marcellus had seen the Emperor—and that at a considerable distance—was on the opening day of the Ludi Florales, eleven years ago. Indeed, it was the last time that anyone had seen him at a public celebration.

His recollection was of an austere, graying man, of rugged features and massive frame, who paid but scant attention to the notables surrounding him in the imperial box, and even less to the spectacles in the arena.

Marcellus had not been surprised at the glum detachment of this dour-faced man; for it was generally known that Tiberius, who had always detested crowds and the extravagance of festivals, was growing alarmingly morose. Elderly men—like Senator Gallio—who could remember the wanton profligacy of Augustus, and had rejoiced in the Tiberian economies which had brought an unprecedented prosperity to Rome, viewed the Emperor's increasing moodiness with sympathetic regret. The younger generation, not quite so appreciative of the monarch's solid virtues, had begun to think him a sour and stingy old spoil-sport, and earnestly wished he would die.

Tiberius had not fully accommodated them in this respect, but he had done the next thing to it; for, not long afterward, he had taken up his residence on Capri, where his subsequent remoteness from the active affairs of government was almost equivalent to an abdication.

That had been a long time ago; and as Marcellus—in full uniform—sat in the spacious, gloomy atrium, waiting to be summoned into the imperial bedchamber, he prepared his mind for the sight of a very old man. But nobody could prepare himself for an interview with this old man who, on first sight, seemed to have so little of life left in him; but, when stirred, was able to mobilize some surprisingly powerful reserves of mental and physical vigor.

The Emperor was propped up in his pillows, an indistinct figure, for the sun was setting and the huge room was full of shadows. Nothing appeared to be alive in the massive bed but the cavernous eyes that had met Marcellus at the door and accompanied him through the room to the straight-backed chair. The face in the pillows was a scaffolding of bulging bones thinly covered with wrinkled parchment. The neck was scrawny and yellow. Under the sparse white hair at Tiberius' sunken temple a dogged artery beat slow but hard, like the tug of an exhausted oar at the finish of a long race. The bony hand that pointed to the chair—which had been drawn up uncomfortably close to the bedside—resembled the claw of an old eagle.

'Your Majesty!' murmured Marcellus, bowing deeply.

'Sit down!' rumbled Tiberius, testily. 'We hope you have learned something about that haunted Robe!' He paused to wheeze asthmatically. 'You have been gone long enough to have found the river Styx—and the Jews' Garden of Eden! Perhaps you rode home on the Trojan Horse—with the Golden Fleece for a saddle-blanket!'

The old man turned his head to note the effects of his acidulous drollery, and Marcellus—thinking that the Emperor might want his dry humor appreciated—risked a smile.

'Funny; is it?' grumped Tiberius.

'Not if Your Majesty is serious,' replied Marcellus, soberly.

'We are always serious, young man!' Digging a sharp elbow into his pillow, the Emperor drew himself closer to the edge of the bed. 'Your father had a long tale about the crucifixion of a mad Galilean in Jerusalem. That fellow Pilate—who forever gets himself into trouble with the Jews—ordered you to crucify this fanatic, and it went to your head.' The old man licked his dry lips. 'By the way—how is your head now?'

'Quite well, Your Majesty,' responded Marcellus, brightly.

'Humph! That's what every crazy man thinks. The crazier he is, the better he feels.' Tiberius grinned unpleasantly, as one fool to another, and added, 'Perhaps you think your Emperor is crazy.'

'Crazy men do not jest, sire,' parried Marcellus.

Tiberious screwed up a mouth that looked like the neck of an old, empty coin-purse, and frowningly cogitated on this comforting thought.

'How do you know they don't?' he demanded. 'You haven't seen all of them—and there are no two alike. But'—suddenly irritable—'why do you waste the Emperor's time with such prattle? Be on with your story! But wait! It has come to our ears that your Greek slave assaulted the son of old Tuscus with his bare hands. Is this true?'

'Yes—Your Majesty,' admitted Marcellus, 'it is true. There was great provocation; but that does not exonerate my slave, and I deeply regret the incident.'

'You're a liar!' muttered Tiberius. 'Now we shall believe nothing you say! But—tell us that story first.'

The malicious old eyes grew brighter as Marcellus obediently reported the extraordinary episode under the trees at the House of Eupolis, and by the time Quintus had been unrecognizably disfigured by the Greek's infuriated fists the Emperor was up on one elbow, his face beaming.

'And you still have this slave?' barked Tiberius. 'He should have been put to death! What will you take for him?'

'I should not like to sell him, sire; but I shall gladly lend him to Your Majesty—for as long as—'

'Long as we live; eh? rasped the old man. 'A few weeks; eh? Perhaps we may live longer! Perhaps your Emperor may never die!' The lean chin jutted forward challengingly. 'Is that silly?'

'It is possible for a man to live forever,' declared Marcellus.

'Rubbish!' grunted Tiberius. 'What do you know about it?'

'This Galilean, sire,' said Marcellus, quietly. 'He will live forever.'

'The man you killed? He will live forever? How do you make that out?'

'The Galilean came to life, sire.'

'Nonsense! You probably bungled the crucifixion. Your father said you were drunk. Did you stay until it was over—or can you remember?'

Yes—Marcellus had stayed. A Centurion had driven his spear deep into the dead man's heart—to make doubly sure. There was no question about his death. The third day afterward, he had come to life, and had been seen on many occasions by different groups of people.

'Impossible!' yelled Tiberius. 'Where is he now?'

Marcellus didn't know. But he did know that this Jesus was alive; had eaten breakfast with friends on a lake-shore in Galilee; had appeared in people's houses. Tiberious propped himself up on both elbows and stared, his chin working convulsively.

'Leaves footprints when he walks,' resumed Marcellus. 'Turns up unexpectedly. Talks, eats, shows his wounds which—for some curious reason—do not heal. Doesn't bother to open the door when he enters. People have a queer feeling of a presence beside them; they look about, and there he is.'

Tiberius glanced toward the door and clapped his dry old hands. The Chamberlain slipped in noiselessly and instantly, as if—upon being summoned—he hadn't had far to come.

'Lights—stupid one!' shouted the old man, shrilly. He snuggled down, shivered, and drew the covers up over his emaciated shoulder. 'Proceed,' he muttered. 'Doesn't open the door; eh?'

'Two men are walking along the highway, late afternoon, discussing him,' went on Marcellus, relentlessly. 'Presently he falls into step with them. They invite him to supper at an inn, some twelve miles from Jerusalem.'

'Not a ghost, then!' put in Tiberius.

'Not a ghost; but this time he does not eat. Breaks the bread, murmurs thanks to his God, and disappears. Enters a house in Jerusalem, a few minutes later; finds friends at supper—and eats.'

'Might show up almost anywhere; eh?' speculated Tiberius, adding, half to himself, 'Probably not if the place were well guarded.' And when Marcellus had let this observation pass without hazarding an opinion, the old man growled, 'What do you think?'

'I think it wouldn't make any difference,' ventured Marcellus. 'He will go where he pleases. He opens the eyes of the blind and the ears of the deaf; heals lepers, paralytics; lunatics. I did not believe any of these things, Your Majesty, until it was impossible not to believe them. He can do anything!'

'Why, then, did he let them put him to death?' demanded Tiberius.

'Your Majesty, well versed in the various religions, will remember that among the Jews it is customary to make a blood offering for crimes. It is believed that the Galilean offered himself as an atonement gift.'

'What crimes had *he* committed?' asked Tiberius.

'None, sire! He was atoning for the sins of the world.'

'Humph! That's an ingenious idea.' Tiberius pondered it gravely, his eyes on the ceiling. 'All the sins; everybody's sins! And, having attended to that, he comes alive again, and goes about. Well—if he can make atonement for the sins of the whole world, it's presumable that he knows what they are and who has committed them. Cosmic person; eh? Knows all about the whole world; eh? Are you fool enough to believe all that?'

'I believe—Your Majesty'—Marcellus was proceeding carefully, spacing his words—'that this Jesus—can do whatever he wills to do—whenever—wherever—and to whomever he pleases.'

'Including the Emperor of Rome?' Tiberius' tone recommended prudence.

'It is conceivable, sire, that Jesus might visit the Emperor, at any time;

but, if he did, it would surely be in kindness. Your Majesty might be greatly comforted.'

There was a long, thoughtful moment before Tiberius wanted more information about the strange appearances and disappearances. 'Quite absurd—making himself visible or invisible—at will. What became of him, while invisible? Did he—did he blot himself out?'

'The stars do not blot themselves out, sire,' said Marcellus.

'Your reasoning is, then, that this person might be in the room *now*, and we unable to see him.'

'But Your Majesty would have nothing to fear,' said Marcellus. 'Jesus would have no interest in the Emperor's throne.'

'Well—that's a cool way to put it, young man!' growled Tiberius. 'No interest in the throne; eh? Who does this fellow think he is?'

'He thinks he is the Son of God!' said Marcellus, quietly.

'And you!' Tiberius stared into his eyes. 'What do you think?'

'I think, sire, that he is divine; that he will eventually claim the whole world for his kingdom; and that this kingdom will have no end.'

'Fool!—Do you think he will demolish the Roman Empire?' shouted the old man.

'There will be no Roman Empire, Your Majesty, when Jesus takes command. The empires will have destroyed one another—and themselves. He has predicted it. When the world has arrived at complete exhaustion, by wars and slaveries, hatreds and betrayals, he will establish his kingdom of good will.'

'Nonsense!' yelled Tiberius. 'The world can't be ruled by good will!'

'Has it ever been tried, Your Majesty?' asked Marcellus.

'Of course not! You're crazy! And you're too young to be that crazy!' The Emperor forced a laugh. 'Never has so much drivel been spoken in our presence. We are surrounded by wise old fools who spend their days inventing strange tales; but you have outdone them all. We will hear no more of it!'

'Shall I go, then, Your Majesty?' inquired Marcellus, coming to the edge of his chair. The Emperor put out a detaining hand.

'Have you seen the daughter of Gallus?' he asked.

'Yes, Your Majesty.'

'You are aware that she loves you, and has waited these past two years for your return?'

'Yes, Your Majesty.'

'She was deeply grieved when you came back to Rome, a year ago, and were ashamed to see her because of the sickness in your head. But—hopeful of your recovery—she has had eyes for no one else. And now—you return to her polluted with preposterous nonsense! You, who are so infatuated with kindness and good will—what does Diana think of you now? Or have you informed her how cracked you are?'

'We have not talked about the Galilean, sire,' said Marcellus, moodily.

'This young woman's happiness may mean nothing to you—but it means everything to us!' The Emperor's tone was almost tender. 'It is high time, we think, that you take some steps to deal fairly with her. Let there be no more of this folly!'

Marcellus sat with clouded eyes, making no reply when Tiberius paused to search his face.

'We now offer you your choice!' The old voice was shrill with anger. 'You will give up all this Jesus talk, and take your rightful place as a Roman Tribune and the son of an honored Roman Senator—or you will give up the daughter of Gallus! We will not consent to her marriage with a fool! What say you?'

'Will Your Majesty permit me to consider?' asked Marcellus, in an unsteady voice.

'For how long?' demanded Tiberius.

'Until noon tomorrow.'

'So be it, then! Noon tomorrow! Meantime—you are not to see Diana. A woman in love has no mind. You might glibly persuade her to marry you. She would repent of it later. This decision is not for the daughter of Gallus to make. It is all yours, young man! . . . That will do! You may go!'

Stunned by the sudden turn of affairs and the peremptory dismissal, Marcellus rose slowly, bowed, and moved toward the door where the old man testily halted him.

"Stay! You have talked of everything but the haunted Robe. Let us hear about that before you go. We may not see you again.'

Returning to his chair, Marcellus deliberately reported his own strange restoration, traceable to the Robe; told also of Lydia's marvelous recovery. Having secured the Emperor's attention, he recited tales of other mysterious occurrences in and about Capernaum; spoke of the aged Nathanael Bartholomew; and Tiberius—with an old man's interest in another old man's story—showed enough curiosity about the storm on the lake to warrant the telling of it—all of it. When they wakened Jesus at the crest of the tempest, Tiberius sat up. When Jesus, wading through the flooded boat, mounted the little deck and stilled the storm as a man soothes a frightened horse—

'That's a lie!' yelled the Emperor, sinking back into his pillows; and when Marcellus had no more to say, the old man snorted: 'Well—go on!

Go on! It's a lie—but a new lie! We will say that for it! Plenty of gods know how to stir up storms: this one knows how to stop them! . . . By the way—what became of that haunted Robe?'

'I still have it, sire.'

'You have it here with you? We would like to see it.'

'I shall send for it, Your Majesty.'

The Chamberlain was instructed to send for Demetrius. In a few moments, he appeared; tall, handsome, grave. Marcellus was proud of him; a bit apprehensive, too, for it was easy to see that the Emperor was instantly interested in him.

'Is this the Greek who slaughters Roman Tribunes with his bare hands?' growled Tiberius. 'Nay—let him answer for himself!' he warned Marcellus, who had begun to stammer a reply.

'I prefer to fight with weapons, Your Majesty,' said Demetrius, soberly.

'And what is your favorite weapon?' barked Tiberius. 'The broadsword? The dagger?'

'The truth, Your Majesty,' replied Demetrius.

The Emperor frowned, grinned, and turned to Marcellus.

'Why—this fellow's as crazy as you are!' he drawled; then, to Demetrius, 'We had thought of keeping you as one of our bodyguard, but—' He chuckled. 'Not a bad idea! The truth; eh? Nobody else on this island knows how to use that weapon. You shall stay!'

Demetrius' expression did not change. Tiberius nodded to Marcellus, who said, 'Go—and fetch the Galilean Robe.' Demetrius saluted deeply and made off.

'What manner of miracle will be wrought upon the Emperor, do you think?' inquired Tiberius, with an intimation of dry bravado.

'I do not know, sire,' replied Marcellus, gravely.

'Perhaps you think we would better not experiment with it.' Tiberius' tone made a brave show of indifference, but he cleared his throat huskily after he had spoken.

'I should not presume to advise Your Majesty,' said Marcellus.

'If you were in our place—' Tiberius' voice was troubled.

'I should hesitate,' said Marcellus.

'You're a superstitious fool!' growled the Emperor.

Demetrius was re-entering with the brown Robe folded over his arm. Tiberius' sunken eyes narrowed. Marcellus rose; and, taking the Robe from Demetrius, offered it to the old man.

The Emperor reached out his hand, tentatively. Then, slowly recoiling, he thrust his hand under the covers. He swallowed noisily.

'Take it away!' he muttered.

Chapter XXI

Many a Roman of high distinction would have been overwhelmed with joy and pride by a summons to have breakfast at the bedside of the Emperor, but Diana's invitation distressed her.

Since late yesterday afternoon she had been dreamily counting the hours until she could keep her early morning engagement with Marcellus. She was so deeply in love with him that nothing else mattered. Now the happy meeting would have to be postponed; perhaps abandoned altogether if last night's prolonged interview in the imperial bedchamber had turned out badly.

Until after midnight, Diana—disinterestedly jabbing uneven stitches into an embroidery pattern—had listened to every footfall in the corridors, alert for a message. At length she had persuaded herself that Marcellus thought it too late to disturb her. After a restless night, she had welcomed the dawn; had stood at the window, impatient, ecstatic, waiting for the moment when—with any degree of prudence—she might slip out of the Villa Jovis and speed to her enchanted pergola.

And now the message had come from the Emperor. Concealing her disappointment from the servants, Diana made ready to obey the summons. While her maids fluttered about, helping her into gay colors—which usually brightened the old man's dour mood—she tried to imagine what might have happened. Perhaps Tiberius had proposed some project for Marcellus which would amount to his imprisonment on this wretched island. Knowing how anxious she was to leave Capri, Marcellus might have tried to decline such an offer. In that case, Diana—deeply obligated to the Emperor—would be asked to use her influence. Her intuition warned her that this breakfast with Tiberius might be a very unhappy occasion.

Dispatching Acteus to inform Marcellus that she could not keep her engagement, Diana practiced a few bright smiles before her mirror; and, resolutely holding on to one of them, marched into the imperial presence.

'How very good of Your Majesty!' she exclaimed. 'I hope I have not kept you waiting. Are you famished?'

'We have had our breakfast,' sulked Tiberius, 'an hour ago.' He jabbed a sharp, brown thumbnail into the ribs of the Chamberlain who was fussing with the pillows. 'Pour a goblet of orange juice for the daughter of Gallus—and then get out! All of you!'

'Not feeling so well?' purred Diana.

'Don't try to joke with us, young woman!' snorted the old man. 'That will do now!' he yelled, at the Chamberlain. 'Stop pottering—and be gone! And close the door!'

'I wish I could do something,' sympathized Diana, when they were alone.

'Well—perhaps you can! That's why we sent for you!'

'I'll do my best, Your Majesty.' Diana held her big goblet in both hands to keep it from trembling.

'We had a long talk with your handsome fool.' Tiberius boosted his tired bones over to the edge of the big bed, and scowled into Diana's anxious eyes. 'You said that old Dodinius was crazy. Compared to this Marcellus, Dodinius is a ray of light!'

'I'm sorry,' murmured Diana. 'I was with him for an hour, yesterday afternoon, and he talked sensibly enough.'

'Perhaps you did not discuss the one thing that touches him off. Do you know he has become convinced that this Jesus is divine—and has intentions to rule the whole world?'

'Oh, no—please!' entreated Diana, suddenly sickened.

'You ask him! You won't have to ask him! You just say, "Jesus"—and see what happens to you!'

'But—naturally'—stammered Diana, loyally—'Marcellus would want to tell Your Majesty everything about this poor dead Jew, seeing that's why he was sent abroad.'

'Poor dead Jew—indeed!' shrilled Tiberius. 'This Galilean came to life again! Went about the country! Walked, talked, ate with people! Still going about, they think! Likely to turn up anywhere!'

'Perhaps they didn't kill him,' suggested Diana.

'Of course they killed him!' snarled Tiberius.

'And Marcellus thinks he came to life: did he see him?'

'No—but he believes it. And he has it that this Jesus is a god, who will take command of the world and rule it without armies.'

Diana winced and shook her head.

'I thought he was fully recovered,' she said, dismally. 'This sounds as if he were worse off than ever. What are we to do?'

'Well—if there is anything to be done, you will have to do it yourself.

May we remind you that our interest in this mad young Tribune is solely on your account? It was for your sake that we brought him back from that fort at Minoa. For your sake, again, we found an errand for him outside the country to give him time to recover his mind. We see now that we sent him to the wrong place—but it is too late to correct that mistake. He knows that he is under a heavy obligation to you. Besides—he loves you. Perhaps you can prevail upon him to abandon his interest in this Galilean.' The old man paused, shook his head slowly, and added, 'We doubt whether you can do anything. You see, my child, he really believes it!'

'Then—why not let him believe it?' insisted Diana. 'I love him—no matter what he believes about that—or anything! He won't pester me with this crazy idea; not if I tell him I have no interest in it.'

'Ah—but there's more to it than that, young woman!' declared Tiberius, sternly. 'It isn't as if Marcellus, as a casual traveler in Galilee, had happened upon this strange story and had become convinced of its truth. In that case, he might regard it as a seven-day wonder—and let it go at that. As the matter stands, he probably considers himself bound to do something about it. He crucified this Jesus! He has a debt to pay! It's a bigger debt—by far—than the one he owes you!'

'Did he say that, Your Majesty?' asked Diana, deeply hurt.

'No—he did not say that. But your Marcellus, unfortunately, is a young man of strong will and high integrity. This is going to cause him a great deal of trouble—and you, too, we surmise. He will feel obligated to take part in this Jesus movement.'

'Movement?' echoed Diana, mystifiedly.

'Nothing less—and it has in it the seeds of revolution. Already, throughout our Palestinian provinces, thousands are professing that this Jesus is the Christos—the Anointed One—and are calling themselves Christians. The thing is moving rapidly, up through Macedonia, down through Mesopotamia; moving quietly, but gathering strength.'

Diana listened with wide, incredulous eyes.

'You mean—they might try to overthrow the Empire?'

'Not by force. If some foolhardy fellow were to stand up on a cart and yell at these captive people to take up arms against their masters, they would know that was hopeless. But—here comes a man without an army; doesn't want an army; has no political aspirations; doesn't want a throne; has no offices to distribute; never fought a battle; never owned a sword; hasn't a thing to recommend him as a leader—except'—Tiberius lowered his voice to a throaty rumble—'except that he knows how to make blind men see, and cripples walk; and, having been killed for creating so much excitement, returns from the dead, saying, "Follow me—and I will set you free!" Well—why shouldn't they follow him—if they believe all that?' The old man chuckled mirthlessly. 'There's more than one kind of courage, my child,' he soliloquized, 'and the most potent of all is the reckless bravery of people who have nothing to lose.'

'And you think Marcellus is one of these Christians?' queried Diana.

'Of course he is! Makes no bones about it! He had the audacity to tell us—to our face—that the Roman Empire is doomed!'

'Why—what an awful thing to say!' exclaimed Diana.

'Well—at least it's a dangerous thing to say,' mumbled Tiberius; 'and if he is fool enough to blurt that out in the presence of the Emperor, he is not likely to be prudent in his remarks to other people.'

'He might be tried for treason!' feared Diana.

'Yes—but he wouldn't care. That's the trouble with this new Galilean idea. The people who believe it are utterly possessed! This Jesus was tried for treason—and convicted—and crucified. But he rose from the dead—and he will take care of all who give up their lives as his followers. They have no fear. Now—you set a thing like that in motion—and there'd be no end to it!'

'But what has Marcellus to gain by predicting doom for the Empire?' wondered Diana. 'That's quite absurd, I think.'

'Had you thought the Roman Empire might last forever?' rasped Tiberius.

'I never thought much about it,' admitted Diana.

'No—probably not,' mumbled the old man, absently. He lay for some time staring at the high-vaulted ceiling. 'It might be interesting,' he went on, talking to himself—'it might be interesting to watch this strange thing develop. If it could go on—the way it seems to be going now—nothing could stop it. But—it won't go on—that way. It will collapse—after a while. Soon as it gets into a strong position. Soon as it gets strong enough to dictate terms. Then it will squabble over its offices and spoils—and grow heady with power and territory. The Christian afoot is a formidable fellow—but—when he becomes prosperous enough to ride a horse—' Tiberius suddenly broke out in a startling guffaw. 'He! he! he!—when he gets a horse! Ho! ho! ho!—a Christian on horseback will be just like any other man on horseback! This Jesus army will have to travel on foot—if it expects to accomplish anything!'

Diana's eyes widened as she listened, with mingled pity and revulsion, to the mad old Emperor's prattle. He had talked quite rationally for a while. Now he was off again. By experience she knew that his grim amusement would promptly be followed by an unreasonable irascibleness. She moved to the edge of her chair, as to inquire whether she might go now. The old man motioned her back.

'Your Marcellus has another audience with us at noon,' he said, soberly. 'We told him we had no intention of permitting you to throw yourself away by marrying a man who has anything to do with this dangerous Jesus business. If he goes in for it seriously—and we have no doubt he intends to—he will lose his friends—and his life, too. Let him do it if he likes; but he shall not drag you along! We told him he must choose. We told him if he did not abandon this Christian party at once, we would give you in marriage to Gaius.'

'Oh—please—no!' begged Diana.

'We admit,' chuckled Tiberius, 'that Gaius has his little faults; but he can make a Princess of you! You may not think it an ideal alliance, but you will be happier as a Princess than as the wife of a crazy man in love with a ghost!'

'What did he say,' Diana whispered, 'when you told him you would give me to Gaius?'

'He wanted until noon—today—to consider.' The old man raised up on his elbow to note the effect of this shocking announcement. His grin slowly faded when he saw how painfully she had been wounded.

'He had to have time to consider,' she reflected, brokenly—'to consider—whether he would let me be handed over—to Gaius!'

'Yes—and our opinion is that he will let that happen! Regardless of his love for you, my child, he will not give up his Jesus!' Tiberius shook a long bony finger directly in her face. 'That's what we meant when we told you that this Christian movement is no small thing! Men who believe in it will give up everything! With Marcellus, nothing else matters. *Not even you!*'

'Then—perhaps there is no reason why I should talk to him,' said Diana, hopelessly. 'It would only hurt us both.'

'Oh—it's worth a trial. We pledged him not to talk with you until he had come to a decision, but we shall send him word that he is released from his promise. Perhaps you can help him decide.'

Diana rose and moved toward the door.

'Better not confront him with our threat to give you to Gaius,' called the old man. 'You are not supposed to know that.'

* * * * * *

They sat close together on the marble lectus in the sequestered pergola, silently gazing out upon a calm summer sea. It lacked less than a half-hour of noon now and Marcellus would have to be going; for he had an urgent appointment with an old man, and old men—whatever their faults—had a high regard for punctuality.

Everything, it seemed, had been said. Diana, emotionally exhausted, leaned her head against Marcellus' shoulder. Sometimes an involuntary sob tore into her breathing, and his arm would tighten about her protectingly.

When they had met here, three hours ago, Diana thought she had reason to hope that their love would solve the problem. Marcellus, strong but tender, had disclosed a depth of passion that had shaken them both. Nothing could tear them apart now; nothing! Diana was ecstatic. There could be no trouble for them now. So long as they had each other, let the world do what it liked. Let the Empire stand or fall! Let this Jesus go about forever doing good and ruling men by good will, or let him fail of it, and the world go on fighting and starving as it had always been fighting and starving: they had each other, and nothing could separate them! She hungrily raised her face to meet his kisses. He felt her heart pounding. They were one!

'Come, now,' Diana had whispered, breathlessly, 'let us sit down—and make some plans.'

They sat, very close together, and very much aware of each other, until Diana drew a little apart and shook her head. Her eyes were radiant, but her lips were trying to be resolute.

'Please—Marcellus!' she murmured, unsteadily. 'Talk to me! Let us decide what we will say to the Emperor. He wants me to be happy, and he knows I love you. Why not ask him to give you something to do in Rome?'

'But he expects you to live here,' Marcellus reminded her.

'Perhaps we can talk him out of that,' hoped Diana. 'My villa is not finished. Ill as he is, Tiberius knows he cannot supervise it. I think it worries him. He may be glad enough to have done with it. Let us tell him we want to go back to Rome—at least for a while—and visit our people—and be married. Maybe he will consent.'

'He might,' agreed Marcellus, from a considerable distance. 'There's no telling what the Emperor will think—about anything.'

'And then'—went on Diana, with girlish enthusiasm—'you could do all the things you liked to do, and renew your old friendships—and go to the Tribunes' Club—'

Marcellus frowned.

'Well—what's the matter with the Tribunes' Club?' demanded Diana. 'You used to spend half your time there—in the gymnasium and the baths.' Marcellus leaned forward with his elbows on his knees and stared moodily at his interlaced fingers.

'That was before I knew what it had cost to erect that marble club-house,' he said, soberly.

'Oh, my dear—why can't you leave off fretting over things you can't help?' implored Diana. 'It distresses you that the marble was quarried by slaves. Well—and so was this marble we're sitting on—and the marble that went into your villa at home. Let's agree it's too bad that some people are slaves; but—what are you going to do about it—all by yourself?'

Marcellus sighed deeply and shook his head. Then, suddenly straightening, he faced her with a surprisingly altered mood, his eyes alight.

'Diana—I am bursting to tell you a story—about a man—about a remarkable man!'

'If he's the man I think you mean'—Diana's face had lost its animation—'I'd really rather you didn't. He has caused you so much unhappiness, and I think it is time you put him out of your mind. I don't believe he has been good for you.'

'Very well,' consented Marcellus, the smile fading from his eyes. 'As you like.' He fell silent.

Impetuously, Diana moved closer to him, repentant.

'I shouldn't have said that,' she whispered. 'Tell me about him.'

Marcellus was well prepared for this opportunity. He had given much thought to what he would say when the time came for him to tell Diana about Jesus. It would not be easy to make her understand. All of her instincts would be in revolt. She would be deeply prejudiced against the story. He had carefully planned the speech he would make to her, in which he must explain Jesus as a divine liberator of the world's oppressed. But now—with Diana's warm and supple contours snuggled close against him, he decided to abandon this larger appraisal and deal more simply with his story. He began by telling her about Jonathan and the donkey.

'Why—what a perfectly mean thing to do to that little boy!' she exclaimed, when Jonathan sorrowfully gave up his donkey to Thomas.

'It was a severe test,' admitted Marcellus, 'but it made a little man of Jonathan.'

'And why did they want Jonathan to be a little man?' queried Diana, making it clear that if she were obliged to listen to this Galilean story, she reserved the right to make comments and ask questions. 'I should have thought,' she went on, innocently, 'that Jonathan would have been ever so much more attractive as a little boy.'

Conceding that the phrase, 'little man,' had not been skillfully chosen, Marcellus thought he should tell her how children felt toward Jesus; how—according to Justus—they swarmed about him in his carpenter shop; how, when Jesus went home in the evening, a crowd of little ones accompanied him. And dogs.

'Well—I'm glad about the dogs,' drawled Diana. 'From what I had heard of his goodness, I had supposed that dogs might feel rather embarrassed in his company.' Instantly she realized that this flippancy had stung. Marcellus recoiled as if she had slapped him.

'His goodness was not negative, Diana, and it was not smug, and it was not weak,' declared Marcellus. 'May I reconstruct your picture of him?'

'Please do,' murmured Diana, absently. She caressingly retied the heavy silk cord at the throat of his tunic, and smiled into his sober eyes from under her long lashes, her full lips offering a forthright invitation. Marcellus swallowed hard, and gave her a fraternal pat on the cheek. She sighed and shouldered back under his arm.

Then he told her all about Miriam; all about the wedding feast—and Miriam's voice.

'And she never could sing before?'

'No—she had never wanted to sing before.'

'And you talked with her—and heard her sing? You liked her, I think. Was she pretty?'

'Very!'

'Jewess?'

'Yes.'

'They are very pretty, sometimes,' conceded Diana. 'It's too bad she was a cripple.'

'She didn't mind being lame. This other gift was so very important.'

'Why didn't Jesus let her walk?'

'Sounds as if you thought he could,' commented Marcellus, encouraged.

'Well'—replied Diana, defensively—'you think he could; don't you? I'm taking your word for it.'

'Miriam thinks she can do more good to the unfortunate in her town if she, too, has a disability—'

'And can sing—in spite of her affliction,' interposed Diana. 'She must be a fine person.'

'She hadn't been a fine person,' said Marcellus—'not until this strange thing happened to her.'

'Was she in love with Jesus?'

'Yes—everybody was.'

'You know what I mean.'

'No—I don't think she was. Not that way.'

Diana thoughtfully rubbed her cheek against Marcellus' sleeve.

'Wasn't Jesus in love with anyone?' she murmured.

'Everyone,' said Marcellus.

'Perhaps he thought it was wrong—to love just one person—above all others.'

'I think that might have been wrong—for him. You see, Diana, Jesus was not an ordinary person. He had unusual powers, and felt that his life belonged to the public.'

'What other things did he do?' Diana's curiosity seemed to be more serious. 'There was little Jonathan's foot, and Miriam's voice—'

'I must tell you about Lydia.'

But—before he went into the story of Lydia's touching the Robe, Marcellus thought he should review his own peculiar experiences with it. Diana grew indignant as he relived that tragic night at the Insula in Jerusalem when Paulus had forced him to put on the Galilean's Robe.

'This poor Jesus had suffered enough!' she exclaimed. 'They had no right to make a mockery of his clothes! And he had been so brave—and had done no wrong!'

Heartened by her sympathy, Marcellus had gone on to tell her all about that afternoon in Athens when—desperate over his mental condition—he had decided to destroy himself.

'You may find it hard to understand, dear, how a person could come to a decision to take his own life.'

'Oh, no!' Diana shook her head. 'I can understand that, Marcellus. I could easily come to that decision—in certain circumstances.'

'It is a lonely business—suicide,' muttered Marcellus.

'Perhaps that is why I can understand it,' said Diana. 'I am well acquainted with loneliness.'

Then Marcellus proceeded to tell her about his finding of the Robe, and the peculiar effect it had on him. Diana looked up into his face, her eyes swimming with tears.

'There's no use trying to explain,' he went on. 'I gathered up the Robe in my hands—and it healed my mind.'

'Maybe that was because you knew it had belonged to another lonely man,' suggested Diana.

'Curiously enough,' said Marcellus, 'that was the sensation I had when I held the Robe in my arms. Some strange friendship—a new, invigorating friendship—had come to my rescue. The painful tension was relaxed. Life was again worth living.' He gravely studied her brooding eyes. 'I wonder if you believe what I am saying.'

'Yes, dear—I believe it; and, considering your earlier experience with his Robe, I am not very much surprised.' She was silent for a moment, and then said, 'Tell me now about this Lydia.'

It was quite a lengthy story, with many unforeseen excursions. Diana had remarked that it must almost have killed Lydia when she had to force her way into that huge crowd of strangers in the street. And that had led

Marcellus to interrupt himself long enough to describe those crowds; how the poor people had dropped their sickles and left their looms and followed for days, sleeping on the ground, going hungry and footsore—if only they might stay close to Jesus.

Diana listened with rapt attention, narrowed eyes, parted lips, as the Galilean story went on—and on—toward its close.

'And you honestly think he is alive—now?' she asked, earnestly.

Marcellus nodded his head, and after a moment continued with an account of the reappearances.

'And you really think Stephanos saw him?' asked Diana, in an awed voice.

'Do you find that so hard to believe, dear, after the other things I have told you?'

'I want to believe what you believe, Marcellus.'

He had drawn her into his arms and kissed her.

'It means much to me, my darling, to have shared this story with you,' he said, tenderly. 'Knowing how you felt about the supernatural, I hardly expected you to be so understanding.'

'Well—this is different!' Diana suddenly released herself and sat up to face him. 'What I feared was that it might somehow affect your life—and mine, too. It is a beautiful story, Marcellus, a beautiful mystery. Let it remain so. We don't have to understand it. And we don't have to do anything about it; do we? Let us plan to live—each for the other—just as if this hadn't happened.'

She waited a long time for his reply. His face was drawn, and his eyes were transfixed to the far horizon. Diana's slim fingers traced a light pattern on the back of his hand.

'But it *has* affected my life, darling!' said Marcellus, firmly. 'I *can't* go on as if it hadn't happened.'

'What had you thought of doing?' Diana's voice was unsteady.

'I don't know—yet,' he replied, half to himself. 'But I know I have a duty to perform. It is not clear—what I am to do. But I couldn't go back to living as I did—not even if I tried. I *couldn't!*'

Then, with a depth of earnestness that stilled her breathing, Marcellus poured out his pent-up convictions about this strange thing that had come to pass. It wasn't just a brief phenomenon that had mystified the country people of little Galilee. It was nothing less than a world-shaking event! For thousands of years, the common people of the whole earth had lived without hope of anything better than drudgery, slavery, and starvation. Always the rapacious rulers of some empire were murdering and pillaging the helpless.

'Look at our record!' he exclaimed, with mounting indignation. 'The Roman Empire has enslaved half the population of the world! And we have thought it brave to subdue these little, undefended states! Look at the heroic sculpture and the bronze tablets dedicated to Emperors and Princes, Knights and Prefects, Legates and Tribunes, who have butchered thousands whose only crime was their inability to protect themselves and their lands! This, we thought, was a great credit to the Empire; a gallant thing to do! "I sing of men and of arms!" chants old Publius Vergilius. Sounds brave; doesn't it?

'Diana, dear,' he went on, gravely, 'while on the ship coming home I fell to thinking about the Roman splendors, the monuments in the Forum, the marble palaces; and then I remembered that all of these beautiful and impressive things have either been stolen from other people of better talents than our own, or built with tribute money extorted from the ragged and hungry! And I hated these things! And I hated what we had called Heroism!'

'But you can't do anything about that, Marcellus,' protested Diana, weakly.

Marcellus' storm was subsiding to a mutter. With bitter irony he growled: 'Invincible old Rome—that lives in sloth and luxury—paid for by people up in Aquitania, Anglia, Hispania, Gaul—and down in Crete—and over in Cappadocia, Pontus, and Thrace—where little children cry for food! Ah, yes—our brave ones will sneer, no doubt, at the unarmed Jesus. They will revile him as a weakling, because the only blood he ever shed was his own! But the time will come, my dear, when this *Jesus will have his own way!*'

'So—then—what will you do?' Diana asked, with a weary sigh.

'For the present, I'm sure only of what I will *not* do!' declared Marcellus, passionately. 'I shall not be going back to lounge about in the Tribunes' Club, pretending to have forgotten I know a man who can save the world! I am done with this iniquity! I am free of this shame!'

'But—do you mean to cut yourself off from all your old friends—and—and go about with these poor slaves?' asked Diana.

'It is *we* who are the poor slaves, my dear,' deplored Marcellus. 'These ragged ones, who follow the divine Galilean, are on their way to freedom!'

'You mean—they will band together—and revolt?'

'They may still wear chains on their wrists, Diana, but not on their souls!'

'You're not thinking of joining them!' Diana's cheeks were pale.

'I *have* joined them!' muttered Marcellus.

Impetuously springing to her feet, Diana gave way to a surprising outburst of desperate disappointment.

'Then you can leave me out of it!' she cried. Burying her face in her arms, and weeping inconsolably, she went on, half-incoherently, 'If you're going to ruin yourself—and make an outcast of yourself—and become an object of ridicule—that's for you to decide—but—'

As impulsively as she had torn away from him, Diana slumped down dejectedly on the lectus, and threw her arms tightly around his neck.

'You are dreaming, Marcellus!' she sobbed. 'You are making a new world out of people and things that don't exist! And you know it! *If* men would stop fighting—*if* men would live as your Jesus wants them to—*if* men would be honest and merciful—then there would be a new world! Nobody would be killed! Little children would have enough to eat! Yes—but men are not made that way. Maybe there will come a time when people will stop mistreating one another—and weeds will stop growing—and lions will stop biting—but not in our time! Why shall we make ourselves wretched? Why not accept things as they are? Why throw your life away?' Diana pressed her wet face hard against his shoulder. 'Marcellus,' she moaned piteously, 'don't you know you are breaking my heart? Don't you care?'

'My darling,' said Marcellus, huskily, 'I care—so much—that I would rather die than see you in sorrow. I am not choosing—which way I shall go. I am not permitted a choice.'

There seemed nothing to say, after that. It was nearing noon and Marcellus would have to go to the Emperor. Diana raised her face and glanced at the sundial. Her eyes were heavy with weeping and the tight little curls on her forehead were damp. Marcellus' throat ached in pity as he looked down into her flushed face. She smiled pensively.

'I must be a dreadful sight,' she sighed.

Marcellus kissed her eyes.

'You must not keep him waiting,' she murmured, lifelessly. 'Come back to me—this afternoon—soon as you can—and tell me about it.'

He drew her tightly to him. Her lips trembled as he kissed her.

'Our happiness was too sweet to last, Marcellus. Go, now, dear, I shall try to understand. I know this has been as hard for you as for me. I shall always love you.' Her voice fell to a whisper, 'I hope your Jesus will take care of you.'

'Do you believe what I told you about him?' asked Marcellus, gently.

'Yes, dear—I believe it.'

'Then—I think he will take care of you, too.'

* * * * * *

The Chamberlain was waiting for him in the atrium and led him directly to the imperial suite. Opening the door, he stood aside deferentially, and when Marcellus had passed in, he noiselessly closed the door behind him.

Tiberius, propped up high in his pillows, regarded him with a penetrating scowl as he crossed the room and approached the massive bed. Marcellus, bowing deeply, came to attention and waited the Emperor's pleasure. For a long time the old man stared silently into his grave face.

'It is plain to see,' he said, soberly, 'that you have decided to cast your lot with your Jesus. We were sure you would take that course.'

Marcellus inclined his head—but made no audible reply.

There was another long, strained silence.

'That will be all, then,' growled Tiberius. 'You may go!'

Marcellus hesitated for a moment.

'Go!' shouted the Emperor. 'You are a fool!' The shrill old voice rose to a scream. 'You are a fool!'

Dazed and speechless in the face of the old man's clamorous anger, Marcellus retreated unsteadily toward the door, which had swung open.

'You are a fool!' shrieked Tiberius. 'You will die for your folly!' The cracked voice deepened to a hoarse bellow. '*You are a brave, brave fool!*'

* * * * * *

Stunned by the encounter, Marcellus walked slowly and indecisively into the atrium where the Chamberlain, bowing obsequiously, pointed him out toward the high-vaulted peristyle.

'If you are ready, sir,' he said, 'the chair is waiting to take you down to the wharf. Your luggage has preceded you, and is on the barge.'

'I am not ready to go,' declared Marcellus, crisply. 'I have another appointment here before I leave.'

The Chamberlain drew a frosty smile and shook his head.

'It is His Majesty's command, sir. You are to go—immediately.'

'May I not have a word with my slave?' protested Marcellus. 'Where is he?'

'Your Greek, sir, is temporarily in confinement. He objected so violently to seeing your effects packed and carried off that it was necessary to restrain him.'

'He fought?'

'One of the Nubians, sir, was slow about regaining consciousness. Your slave is rough—very rough. But—the Nubians will teach him better manners.' The Chamberlain bowed again, with exaggerated deference, and pointed toward the luxurious chair. Four brawny Thracians stood at attention beside it, waiting for their passenger. He hesitated. A file of palace guards quietly drew up behind him.

'Farewell, sir,' said the Chamberlain. 'A pleasant voyage to you.'

Chapter XXII

Apparently the word had been circulated on the spacious deck that as soon as this belated passenger arrived the barge would put off, for much interest was shown at the rail when the chair drew up beside the gangway. There was some annoyance, too, especially on the patrician faces of a group of Senators unaccustomed to waiting the convenience of a tardy Tribune.

The beautiful barge moved quietly away from the wharf, and the passengers—a score or more—disposed themselves in the luxurious chairs grouped under the gay awning. A light and lazy breeze ruffled the blue bay. The two banks of long oars swung rhythmically, gracefully, to the metallic beat of the boatswain's hammers. Click! Clack! A crimson sail slowly climbed the forward mast; and, after a few indecisive flutters, resolved to aid the slaves below.

Marcellus found a seat quite apart from the others and moodily surveyed the distant wharves of Puteoli, on the mainland. After a while, a dozen sleek and nearly naked Nubians came up from the hold, bearing silver trays high above their shaved brown heads, and spread fanwise among the passengers. The Emperor's midday hospitality was generous, but Marcellus was not hungry.

The Augusta, at her present speed, should be able to reach Rome by late afternoon of the day after tomorrow. For the first time in his life, Marcellus had no desire to go home. There would be endless explanations to make. His father would be disappointed, hurt, exasperated; his mother would resort to tears; Lucia would try to be sympathetic, but it would be sheer pity. He attempted to imagine a conversation with Tullus. They had been very close and confidential. What had they to talk about, were they to meet now? Tullus would inquire, rather gingerly, what all he had been up to, these past two years. Was there any conceivable answer to that question?

As the afternoon wore on, Marcellus' disinclination to return to Rome was crystallizing to a definite decision, and he began to consider alternatives. At sunset, he sauntered to the Captain's quarters and inquired casually whether *The Augusta* was calling at any of the coast ports before reaching Ostia, and was advised that she was making no stops; not even at Ostia.

He was hungry at dinner-time. A smart breeze had risen, as the twilight came on, and the deck was abandoned. Marcellus went to his cabin, opened his largest bag, and took out the Galilean Robe, folding it as compactly as possible. Wrapping it around his leather wallet, he secured it with a strap. The wallet was heavy.

On the evening he had left home, his father had sent Marcipor down to the galley with a parting gift. Distraught, Marcellus had not opened it until he and Demetrius were on board *The Cleo*. He was amazed. As if to make amends for his part in the estrangement, the Senator had provided him with a very large sum of money. It was all in gold pieces of high denomination. Marcellus had been touched by his father's lavish generosity; saddened, too, for it was almost as if the Senator had said that his son would now be free to go his own way.

Removing his toga, Marcellus rolled it up and stuffed it into the big bag to replace the Robe. Then, having refastened the bag, he stretched it out on his berth and waited for the time to pass. Most of his thoughts were about Diana, and his loss of her. Occasionally he glanced at the hourglass on his bedside table. Four times he reversed it. If his computation was correct, *The Augusta* would round the promontory off Capua about midnight.

There was only one sentry patrolling the afterdeck when Marcellus strolled aimlessly toward the stern with his package buckled to the back of his heavy tunic-sash. The sentry paid him but little attention as he stood at the rail. Doubtless the restless passenger had come out to look at the stars. Perhaps a gratuity might be forthcoming if a little service were offered.

A light blinked in the darkness a mile away.

'That is the lighthouse at Capua, sir,' volunteered the sentry.

'Yes,' said Marcellus, indifferently.

'May I bring you a chair, sir?'

'Yes.'

The water was not uncomfortably cold. Marcellus had let himself into it feet-first, without a splash. It was a gratifyingly long time before the sentry gave the alarm. Evidently he had made quite a business of finding a comfortable chair for the Tribune. Now there were other shouts. The boatswain had stopped beating on his anvil. *The Augusta* could not be more than two stadia away, but she was only a row of dim lights, her black hull already blended into the darkness.

Marcellus turned his face toward the shore and proceeded with long, overarm strokes to pull Capua nearer. After a while, flipping over on his back, he looked for *The Augusta.* Only the lamp at the masthead was visible. Doubtless the barge had resumed her journey.

It was the longest swim that Marcellus had ever undertaken. His clothing weighted him. The packet of gold was heavy. Once he thought seriously of tugging off the heavy silk tunic that dragged at his arms, but the threat of arriving at Capua clad only in trunks and a sheer subucula induced him to struggle on. He tried to unfasten his sandal-straps, but found it impossible. The beacon in the lighthouse seemed to be growing brighter. He hoped he was not imagining this, for he was getting very tired.

At length the choppy waves began to smooth out into long combers. Lower lights shone feebly along the shore. The surf grew rougher. Marcellus could hear it crash against the seawall. He shifted his course leftward to avoid the lighthouse escarpment and the huddle of docks. It was hard going, across the rip-tide. His lungs were beginning to hurt. A great wave carried him forward; and, retreating, left him a temporary footing. Bracing against the weight of its undertow, he held his ground until it had run out. All but spent, he staggered toward the beach and flung himself down in the lee of a fishing-dory, his teeth chattering with the cold. It occurred to him that he should feel immensely gratified over the success of his difficult adventure, but found himself indifferent.

Wringing the water out of his clothes, Marcellus vigorously swung his arms to warm himself, and plodded up wearily through the deepening sand until he found a dry spot that still retained something of its daytime heat. There he spent the rest of the night, sleeping lightly, and anxious for the dawn. When the sun rose, he spread out the Robe on the sand. It dried quickly and he put it on over his damp tunic, comforted by its warmth. He was in better spirits now, glad to be alive.

At a fisherman's hut he asked for something to eat, but he was eyed with suspicion by the surly old couple, who told him they had no food. Up farther in the town, at a sailor's inn, he was crudely served with black bread and a greasy pottage. Disheveled loungers gathered about him to ask questions which he made no effort to answer satisfactorily. When he opened his wallet to pay, they drew in closer about him, eyes wide with avaricious interest; but as he overtopped them all and appeared unalarmed by their curiosity, no one made a move to detain him.

Proceeding through the dirty little town, he turned eastward on a dusty, deserted highway. His sandals were drying now, and felt more comfortable, though they had begun to look quite disreputable. Marcellus was bareheaded, having lost his bandeau in the sea. Nobody could have mistaken him for a Tribune.

The expensive leather wallet was inappropriate, and he concealed it in the breast of his tunic. At the first village, three miles inland, he spent a few coppers for a well-worn goatskin bag, of considerable capacity, emptied his wallet into it; and, later, dropped the wallet into an abandoned cistern.

Before reaching the next village, he took off his tunic, wrapped it around the package of gold that had nearly drowned him last night, and bought another off the washline of a vintner's cottage, paying the owner ten sesterces, for which he was so well satisfied that he and his wife chuckled behind Marcellus' back as he moved away. The brown tunic was coarsely woven and had seen hard service, but it was clean.

The sun was high now, and Marcellus carried the Galilean Robe folded over his arm. He frequently paused to rest in the shade beside the descending stream that grew more and more active as the grade stiffened toward the foothills of the distant, snow-capped Apennines. He had no plans, but he was not depressed; nor was he lonesome. Indeed, he had a curious sense of well-being. The country was beautiful. The trees were in full leaf, the nesting birds were busy and happy, the wild-flowers along the bank of the lively stream were exquisite in their fragile beauty. Marcellus drew deep sighs of contentment, gratified but surprised that he could feel so free of any care. He regarded his own appearance with amusement. He had never looked like this before. He stroked his stubbly jaw and wondered whether a razor could be found in one of the villages. If not, no matter. That night, with the Robe for a cover, he slept in the open, remembering—as he drifted off—something Justus had said of Jesus' homelessness: 'The foxes had holes, the birds had nests; but Jesus had no bed, no pillow.' Marcellus drew the Robe closer about him. It was not heavy, but it was warm and comforting. He fell asleep thinking of Diana, but not hopelessly. In the morning he rose refreshed, bathed in the cold stream, and breakfasted on wild strawberries.

The stone mileposts had been announcing, with increasing optimism, that travelers on this uphill road were nearing Arpino. Marcellus cudgeled his memory. What did he know about Arpino? Delicious little melons! Arpino melons! And exactly the right time for them, too.

The road was wider now and showed better care. The fences were well-kept. On either side of the highway, vineyards—the plentiful grapes still green—were being cultivated and irrigated. The traffic on the road was increasing. Here were the melon fields; acres and acres of ripening melons; a procession of high-boxed carts laden with melons; dozens and scores of men, women, and children, scattered through the fields, all bent to the task of gathering melons.

Near a busy open gate, Marcellus sat down on the stone fence and viewed the scene. The little town at the top of the rise seemed to be built on a comparatively level terrain, sheltered on the east by a sheer wall of rock that based one of the loftiest peaks of the range. The village itself—or as much as could be seen of it—was composed of small square cottages crowded closely together. North of this cramped huddle of houses and on slightly higher ground the red-tile roofs of a quite imposing villa shone through the trees surrounding it, doubtless the home of the big man who owned the melon business.

After a while, Marcellus decided to move on up to the village. The swarthy overseer at the open gate, importantly checking the emerging carts on a slate held in the crook of his hand, hailed him. Was he looking for work?

'What kind of work?' Marcellus wanted to know.

The overseer jabbed a thumb toward the melon field.

'Two sesterces,' he said, gruffly—'and a cot—and food.'

'But the day is nearly half done, sir,' said Marcellus. 'Perhaps one sesterce would be sufficient. I have had no experience in picking melons.'

The bewildered overseer rested the heavy slate on his hip, spat thoughtfully, and stared at the newcomer, apparently lacking a formula for dealing with this unprecedented situation. While he deliberated, Marcellus picked up one of the big willow baskets from a heap piled beside the gate and was moving off toward his new occupation.

'Wait, fellow!' called the overseer. 'Can you read and write?'

Marcellus admitted that he could.

'And compute?'

Yes—Marcellus could compute.

'Kaeso has discharged his scrivener.'

'Who is Kaeso?' inquired Marcellus, so unimpressed that the overseer drew himself to full height before declaiming—with a sweep of his arm embracing the fields and the town—that Appius Kaeso owned everything in sight. He pointed toward the villa.

'Go up there,' he said, 'and ask for Kaeso. Tell him Vobiscus sent you. If he does not hire you, come back and work on the melons.'

'I'd much rather work on the melons,' said Marcellus.

The overseer blinked a few times, uncertainly.

'A scrivener is better paid and has better food,' he said, slightly nettled by the traveler's stupidity.

'I suppose so,' nodded Marcellus, adding, with cool obstinacy, 'I should prefer to pick melons.'

'Doesn't it make any difference to you, fellow,' snapped the overseer, 'whether you make two sesterces or ten?'

'Not much,' confessed Marcellus. 'I am not specially interested in money—and it's quite beautiful out here in the open, with that majestic mountain in sight.'

Vobiscus, shielding his eyes, gazed up at the towering peak beyond Arpino, frowned, looked up again, grinned a little, and rubbed his chin.

'You aren't crazy; are you?' he asked, soberly, and when Marcellus had said he didn't think so, the overseer told him to go on up to the villa.

* * * * * *

Kaeso had the traditional arrogance of a short-statured man of wealth and authority. He was of a pugnacious stockiness, fifty, smooth-shaven, expensively dressed, with carefully groomed, grizzled hair and amazingly well-preserved teeth. It was immediately evident that he was accustomed to barking impatient questions and drowning timorous replies in a deluge of belittling sarcasm.

Marcellus had stood quietly waiting while the restless, bumptious fellow marched heavily up and down the length of the cool atrium, shouting his unfavorable opinions of scriveners in general and his most recent one in particular. They were all alike; dishonest, lazy, incompetent. None of them was worth his salt. Every time Kaeso passed the applicant, he paused to glare at him belligerently.

At first, Marcellus had regarded this noisy exhibition with an impassive face, but as it continued, he found himself unable any longer to repress a broad grin. Kaeso stopped in his tracks and scowled. Marcellus chuckled good-humoredly.

'It is to laugh—is it?' snarled Kaeso, jutting his chin.

'Yes,' drawled Marcellus, 'it is to laugh. Maybe it wouldn't be funny if I were hungry—and in dire need of work. I suppose that's the way you talk to everybody who can't afford to talk back.'

Kaeso's mouth hung open and his eyes narrowed with unbelief.

'But—go right on.' Marcellus waved a hand negligently. 'Don't mind me; I'll listen. Do you care if I sit down? I've been walking all morning, and I'm tired.' He eased into a luxurious chair and sighed. Kaeso stalked toward him and stood with feet wide apart.

'Who are you, fellow?' he demanded.

'Well, sir,' replied Marcellus, with a smile, 'while your question, asked in that tone, deserves no answer at all, I am an unemployed wayfarer. Your man Vobiscus insisted that I offer my services as a scrivener. Realizing that this is your busiest season, I thought I might do you a good turn by helping out for a few days.'

Kaeso ran his stubby fingers through his graying hair and sat down on the edge of an adjacent lectus.

'And you, sir,' went on Marcellus, 'instead of giving me an opportunity to explain my call, began to pour forth.' His eyes drifted about through the well-appointed atrium. 'If I may venture to say so, you probably do not deserve to live in such a beautiful villa. Your manner of treating strangers doesn't seem to belong here. In these lovely surroundings, there should be nothing but quiet courtesy—and good will.'

Kaeso, stunned by the stranger's impudence, had listened with amazement. Now he came to his feet, his face contorted with anger.

'You can't say things like that to me!' he shouted. 'Who do you think you are? You insult me in my house—yet you look like a common vagrant—a beggar!'

'I am not a beggar, sir,' said Marcellus, quietly.

'Get out!' snapped Kaeso.

Marcellus rose, smiled, bowed, walked slowly toward the open peristyle, and down the broad marble steps, Kaeso following him as far as the portico. Sauntering through the village, he went back to the melon field, aware that he was being trailed at a little distance by a tall Macedonian. Vobiscus viewed his return with much interest.

'Kaeso didn't want you?' he inquired.

Marcellus shook his head, picked up a basket, and walked through the field until he came to the first little group of laborers. They glanced up with sour curiosity. One old man straightened, with a painful grimace, and looked him over with the utmost frankness.

It was a fine day, observed Marcellus, pleasantly. For a backache, retorted the old man. This drew a sullen chortle from the neighbors, one of whom—a scowling old woman of twenty—bitterly admonished him that he'd better work awhile, and then tell them how fine a day it was.

Conceding this point so cheerfully that the sulky girl gave him a reluctant but pathetically childish smile, Marcellus doffed his robe—folding it carefully and laying it on the ground beside the goat-skin bag—and fell to work with enthusiasm.

'Not so fast, not so fast,' cautioned the old man. 'Kaeso won't pay you any better for killing yourself.'

'And Vobiscus will be bawling at us for shirking,' added a cloddish fellow, up the line a little way.

'These are the finest melons in the world!' remarked Marcellus, stopping to wipe his dripping forehead. 'It's a pleasure to work with the finest—of something. Not many people have a chance to do that. Sunshine, blue sky, beautiful mountains—and the finest—'

'Oh—shut up!' yelled the clod.

'Shut up yourself!' put in the old woman of twenty. 'Let him talk! They *are* good melons!'

For some unknown reason everybody laughed at that, in various keys and tempers, and the mood of the sweating toilers brightened a little. Presently the overseer strolled over from the gate and the melon-pickers applied themselves with ostentatious diligence. He paused beside Marcellus, who looked up inquiringly. Vobiscus jerked his head toward the villa.

'He wants to see you,' he said, gruffly.

Marcellus nodded, picked up his laden basket in his arms, and poured out a few into the old man's basket. Then he gave some to the worn-out girl who raised her eyes in a smile that was almost pretty. On up the line of workers, he distributed his melons, emptying the last dozen of them into the basket of the oaf who had derided him. The sullen fellow pulled an embarrassed grin.

'Will you be coming back?' squeaked the old man.

'I hope so, sir,' said Marcellus. 'It is pleasant work—and good company.'

'Oh—it's *sir* you are now, old one?' teased the oaf. Much boisterous laughter rewarded this sally. The girl with the scowl did not join in the applause.

'What's paining you, Metella?' yelled the witty one.

She turned on him angrily.

'It's a pity that a stranger can't show us a little decent respect without being cackled at!'

As Marcellus turned to go, he gave her an approving wink that smoothed out the scowl and sent a flush through the tan. A dozen pairs of eyes followed him as he moved away at the side of Vobiscus, who had been an impatient spectator.

'They're not out here to joke—and play,' mumbled Vobiscus.

'You'd get more melons picked,' advised Marcellus. 'People work better when they're happy. Don't you think so?'

'I don't know,' said Vobiscus. 'I never saw anybody working who was happy.' He lengthened his steps. 'You'd better stretch your legs, fellow. Kaeso isn't good at waiting.'

'He's probably as good at waiting as I am at hurrying,' replied Marcellus, dryly.

'You don't know Kaeso,' muttered Vobiscus, with an ominous chuckle. 'He doesn't coddle people; only horses.'

'I can believe that,' said Marcellus. Throwing the old bag over his shoulder, he strolled out to the highway, tarried for another look at the mountain, and sauntered up the hill.

* * * * * *

Kaeso was at his desk when Marcellus was shown in. He was making a showy pretense of being busily engaged and did not glance up. After Marcellus had stood waiting before the desk for what seemed to him a long time, without receiving any attention, he turned away and walked over to a window that looked out upon a flower-garden.

'You say you are a scrivener?' called Kaeso, sharply.

'No, sir.' Marcellus slowly retraced his steps. 'Your man asked me if I could read, write, and compute. I can do that—but I am not a scrivener by profession.'

'Humph! How much do you want?'

'You will know, sir, how much my services are worth to you. I shall accept what you think is just.'

'I gave the last man ten sesterces—and his keep.'

'It seems a trifling wage,' observed Marcellus, 'but if you cannot afford to pay more—'

'It's not a question of what I can afford!' retorted Kaeso, pompously. 'It's a question of what you will take!'

'I shouldn't have thought that a proud and successful man like you, sir, would want a stranger to donate part of his time to serving you. You called me a beggar, an hour ago, in a tone indicating that you had no respect for beggars. Perhaps I misunderstood you.'

Kaeso pushed his folded arms halfway across the desk and glared up into Marcellus' complacent eyes. He appeared to be contemplating a savage rejoinder; but impulsively changed his tactics.

'I'll give you twenty,' he grumbled—'and let me tell you something!' His voice was rising to an angry pitch. 'There's to be no shirking—and no mistakes—and no—'

'Just a moment!' broke in Marcellus, coolly. 'Let me tell *you* something! You have a bad habit of screaming at people. I can't believe that you get any pleasure out of terrorizing others who can't help themselves. It's just a habit—but it's a hateful habit—and I don't like it—and you're not to indulge in it when you're addressing *me!*'

Kaeso rubbed his jaw with the back of his hand.

'Nobody ever dared to talk to me like that!' he smouldered. 'I don't know why I let you do it.'

'I'll gladly tell you.' Marcellus laid his hands flat on the desk and leaned far forward with a confidential smile. 'You have accumulated a great deal of property and power—but you are not contented. There is something you lack—something you would like to have. You are not sure what it is—but you think *I* know. That is why you sent for me to come back, Kaeso.'

'I sent for you, fellow'—Kaeso was wagging his head truculently—'because I need a scrivener!'

'Well—I'm not a scrivener,' drawled Marcellus, turning away, 'and you're shouting again. If you will excuse me, I'll go back to the melon field. I found some very companionable people out there.'

'What? Companionable? Those melon-pickers?' rasped Kaeso. 'They're a pack of dirty, lazy thieves!'

'Not naturally, I think,' said Marcellus, judicially. 'But for their extreme poverty and drudgery, they might be quite decent and industrious and honest—just as you, sir, might be a very charming person if you had no opportunity to be a bully.'

'See here, fellow!' snarled Kaeso. 'Are you going out there to gabble with these idlers—and try to make them believe they're unjustly treated?'

'No—any man who works from dawn to dusk at hard labor—for three sesterces—will not need to be told that he's getting bad treatment.'

'So!—they've been complaining; eh?'

'Not to me, sir. When I left them, I thought they were in quite a merry mood.'

'Humph! What have they got to be merry about?' Kaeso pushed back his chair, rose; and, opening a tall cabinet in the corner, drew out a large sheaf of papyrus sheets and an armful of scrolls. Dumping the correspondence on his desk, he pointed to it significantly.

'Sit down!' he commanded. 'Take up that stylus, and I'll tell you how to reply to these letters. They are orders from markets and great houses in Rome—for melons—and grapes—and pears. You will read them to me and I shall tell you what to say. And have a care! I do not read—but I will know what they are saying!'

Disinclined to argue, and alive with curiosity to see what might come of this unfamiliar business, Marcellus sat down and began to read the letters aloud. Kaeso seemed childishly pleased. He was selling melons! Cartloads and cartloads of choice Arpino melons! And getting a top price for them! And advance orders for grapes in August. Presently Marcellus came upon a letter written in Greek, and started to read it in that language.

'Ah—that Greek!' snorted Kaeso. 'I do not understand. What does it say?' And when Marcellus had translated it, he inquired, with something like respect, 'You write Greek, too? That is good.' He rubbed his hands with satisfaction. It would be pleasant to let these great ones know that he could afford to have a scholar for a scrivener. When the letter was ended, he remarked, irrelevantly, 'We will find you a better tunic.'

'I have a better tunic, thank you,' said Marcellus, without looking up.

'Is it that you like flowers?' asked Kaeso, after they had finished for the day; and when Marcellus had nodded, he said, condescendingly, 'The scrivener is permitted to walk in the gardens of the villa. If you like horses, you may visit my stables.'

'Very gracious of you, sir,' said Marcellus, absently.

* * * * * *

Antonia Kaeso was at least a dozen years younger than her husband. But for her tightly pursed mouth and unlighted eyes she might have been considered attractive, for her features were nicely moulded, her figure was shapely, and her tone was refined. Marcellus, encountering her among the roses with garden shears and a basket, had reasons for surmising that she was a victim of repression.

She greeted him casually, unsmilingly, remarking in a flat monotone that she supposed he must be her husband's new scrivener. Marcellus admitted this, adding that he was pleased to find employment in such a pleasant environment, which drew a sidelong, bitter smile from her eyes, a smile in which her lips had no share.

'You mean the flowers—and the mountain,' she said.

'Yes—they are beautiful.' He was for sauntering on, seeing that his permission to walk in the garden had not included the right to a leisurely chat with the mistress of the villa; but the enigmatic wife of Kaeso detained him.

'What is your name, scrivener? My husband did not say.'

'Marcellus Gallio.'

'There is a Senator of that name—Gallio.' She was cutting the half-opened roses with long stems and tossing them at random toward the basket. Marcellus stooped and began arranging them in orderly fashion.

'Yes—that is true,' he said.

'Are you related?' she asked, much occupied with her task.

Marcellus laughed, self-deprecatingly.

'Would a humble scrivener be related to a Senator?' he countered.

'Probably not,' she agreed, coolly. 'But you are not a humble scrivener. You are patrician.' She straightened up and faced him with level eyes. 'It's in your voice, in your face, in your carriage.' The short upper lip showed a row of pretty teeth, as she pointed with her shears. 'Look at your hands! They're not accustomed to work—of any kind! Don't be alarmed,' she went on, with a little shrug, 'I won't give you away, though that silk tunic may. Weren't you rather indiscreet to put it on? I saw you in the other one, this morning, from my window. Wherever did you find it?' She was stooping low, busy with her shears. 'How do you like masquerading as a scrivener, Marcellus Gallio? Are you sure you aren't related to the Senator?'

'He is my father,' said Marcellus.

'I believe that,' she replied, turning her face toward him with an honest smile. 'But why do you tell me?'

'Because you seem to like frankness—and because I prefer to tell you the truth. I have not tried to deceive your husband. He did not ask my name.'

'But I think you would be pleased if he did not know.'

'Yes—I should prefer that he does not know.'

'That is unfortunate,' she said, ironically. 'You are robbing Appius Kaeso of much pleasure. Were he able to say that he had the son of a Senator for his scrivener, he would be unbearably exalted.'

'Perhaps you don't understand Kaeso,' soothed Marcellus.

'*I* don't understand Kaeso!' she exclaimed. 'By all the gods! That is my occupation—understanding Kaeso!'

'He requires special handling, my friend,' declared Marcellus. 'Kaeso is immensely proud of his power over all these people in Arpino. They obey him because they fear him. He could have even more power over them if they obeyed because they liked him.'

'Imagine Kaeso doing anything to make them like him!' she scoffed.

'I can imagine it,' rejoined Marcellus, quietly. 'And if we can induce him to make the experiment, it will greatly improve the atmosphere of this place. Would you like to cooperate with me?'

'It's much too late,' she objected. 'Kaeso could never win their friendship—no matter what he might do for them. And you must remember that the common laborers of Arpino are a dirty, ignorant lot!'

'They *are* dirty!' agreed Marcellus. 'And you can't expect dirty people to be decent. They antagonize one another because each man despises himself—and no wonder. I was thinking about that, this morning. These people should have bathing facilities. There's not much temptation to get into this ice-cold mountain stream. It should not be much of a task to build a large swimming-pool, and let the hot sun warm the water. There is a quarry hard by. The people could construct the pool themselves in the idle interval between the melons and the grapes—if they had any encouragement.'

'Ah—you don't know the Arpinos!' protested the wife of Kaeso.

'If they are worse than other people, there must be a reason,' said Marcellus. 'I wonder what it is.'

'Why should you care, Marcellus Gallio?'

A handsome youth in his early teens was strolling toward them. There was no question about his identity. His resemblance to his mother was so striking as to bring a smile.

'Your son, I think,' said Marcellus.

'Antony,' she murmured, with an ecstatic little sigh. 'He is my life. He wants to be a sculptor. His father does not approve, and will not consent to his having instruction. He is such a lonely, unhappy child. . . . Come here, Antony, and meet the new scrivener, Marcellus Gallio.'

'Your mother tells me you are fond of modeling,' said Marcellus, when Antony had mumbled an indifferent greeting. 'Would you like to let me see what you are doing?'

Antony screwed up a sensitive mouth.

'Would you know anything about it?' he asked, with his mother's disconcerting candor.

'Enough to make a few suggestions, perhaps.'

* * * * * *

Antony couldn't wait until morning, but went to the scrivener's quarters after dinner, carrying the model he had been working on—two gladiators poised for action. He put it down on Marcellus' table and backed off from it shyly, murmuring that he knew it wasn't much.

'It's not at all bad, Antony,' commended Marcellus. 'The composition is good. The man on this side is a foolhardy fellow, though, to take that stance. What are their names?'

Suspecting that he was being teased, Antony grinned and said he hadn't named them.

'To do your best work on them,' said Marcellus, seriously, 'they must have personality. You should consider them as real people, and know all about them. Let us attend to that first; shall we?' He drew up a chair for Antony and they sat, facing the model.

'Now—the man on this side is Cyprius. The legionaries captured him down in Crete, burned his house down, drove off his cattle, murdered his wife and son—a boy about your age—and took him to Rome in a prison-ship. He was an excellent swordsman, so they gave him his choice of dueling in the arena or pulling an oar in a galley. So, he chose the arena, and now he is fighting for his life, hoping to kill this other man whom he never saw before.'

'Oh—you're just making that up,' accused Antony, glumly.

'Yes—but that's the way these duels are staged in the arena, Antony, between men who must kill or be killed. Now—your other man is a Thracian. His name is Galenzo. He had a little farm, and a vineyard, and some goats, and three small children. His wife tried to hide him in the hay when the legionaries came, but they struck her down before the children's eyes and dragged Galenzo away on a chain. He fought so hard that they sold him to a praetor who needed gladiators for the games at the Feast of Isis. Now Cyprius and Galenzo are fighting, so the people may have a chance to lay wagers on which one will kill the other. How were you betting, Antony? I shall risk a hundred sesterces on Galenzo. I don't like the way Cyprius stands.'

'I hadn't thought of betting,' said Antony, dispiritedly. He turned to Marcellus with pouting lips. 'You don't like fighting; do you?'

'Not that kind.'

'Maybe you never fought,' challenged Antony. 'Maybe you would be afraid to fight.'

'Maybe,' rejoined Marcellus, undisturbed by the boy's impudence.

'I'll take that back!' spluttered Antony. 'I don't think you'd be afraid to fight. I'll bet you could. Did you ever?'

'Not in the arena.'

'Did you ever kill anyone, sir?'

Marcellus postponed his reply so long that Antony knew his question could have but one answer. His eyes were bright with anticipation of an exciting story.

'Did he put up a good fight, sir?'

'It is not a pleasant recollection,' said Marcellus. There was an interval of silence. 'I wish you had chosen some other subject for your model, Antony. I'm not much interested in this one'—he suddenly invaded Antony's moody eyes—'nor are you, my boy! You're not the type that goes in for slaughter. You don't believe in it; you don't like it; and if you had it to do, it would turn your stomach. Isn't that so?'

Antony explored the inside of his cheek with a defenseless tongue and slowly nodded his head.

'It's worse than that,' he confessed. 'I would be afraid to fight. Maybe that's why I draw pictures of fighting—and make models of gladiators. Just trying to pretend.' He hung his head, morosely. 'I haven't a scrap of courage,' he went on. 'It makes me ashamed.'

'Well—I'm not so sure about that,' consoled Marcellus. 'There are many different kinds of courage, Antony. You've just come through with the best kind there is—the courage to tell the truth! It required much more bravery to say what you've just said than it takes to black another man's eye.'

Antony raised his head and brightened a little.

'Let's start another model,' he suggested.

'Very well—I shall try to think of something that we both might enjoy. Come back early in the morning. If you will lend me some clay, perhaps I may have a rough sketch to show you when you come.'

* * * * * *

Antony laughed merrily. Marcellus had made a rectangular swimming-pool. Seated on the stone ledges, at intervals, were figures of bathers—men, women, and children. One thin old man had an absurdly long beard tossed over his shoulder. A tiny baby on all fours was about to tumble in. Its mother was coming at full gallop. The large feet and bony legs of a diver protruded from the immobile water.

'You didn't do all that this morning!' said Antony.

'No—I worked on it most of the night. It's just a beginning, you see. We need many more people sitting around the pool, and diving and swimming. Would you like to complete it?'

'It would be fun, I think,' said Antony.

'You can give it a lot of detail. Move it to a much larger modeling-board and you will have room to do some landscaping. Remember that big white rock, down by the bridge, where there is a natural basin? You might put in the bridge and the rock and the acacia trees. Then everybody would know where the pool is.'

'I say, sir, it wouldn't be a bad idea to *have* a pool like that!'

* * * * * *

After a week's acquaintance with his new duties, Marcellus was able to complete his day's work by mid-afternoon. Antony would be loitering in the atrium, restlessly passing and repassing the open door to the library. Kaeso had observed this growing attachment, not without some satisfaction.

'They tell me you are helping to amuse my son,' he remarked. 'Don't feel that you must, if it's a burden. You have plenty of work to do.'

Marcellus had assured him that he enjoyed Antony's company; that the boy had artistic talent; that he needed encouragement; and when Kaeso had derided art as a profession, an argument arose.

'I can't think that a real man would want to waste his time playing with mud,' said Kaeso, scornfully.

'Clay,' corrected Marcellus, unruffled. 'Modeling-clay. There's as much difference between mud and clay as there is between Arpino melons and—ordinary melons. It is not unnatural, sir, a man's desire to create something beautiful. Antony may become an able sculptor.'

'Sculptor!' sneered Kaeso. 'And of what use is a sculptor?'

Marcellus had made no reply to that. He continued putting away his accounts and desk implements, with a private smile that stirred Kaeso's curiosity, and when queried, remarked that Antony probably came by it naturally.

'You, sir,' he explained, 'have created a successful business. Your son can hardly hope to improve upon it. It is complete. He, too, wants to create something. You have bequeathed him this ambition. And now you resent his having a desire that he inherited from you.'

Kaeso, purring with self-satisfaction, twirled his thumbs and grinned for more. Marcellus obliged him. Many sculptors starved to death before they were well enough known to earn a living by their art. Antony would not have to starve. His father was rich, and should take pride in his son's ability. Appius Kaeso had made his name important in commerce. Antony Kaeso might make his name mean as much in the field of art.

'You don't want Antony to be unhappy and unsuccessful when he might easily make you proud of him. Show him a little attention, sir, and you'll discover you have a loyal and affectionate son.'

'Ah—the boy has always been cold and disdainful,' complained Kaeso—'like his mother.'

'If I may venture to contradict you,' said Marcellus, 'Antony is a very warm-hearted youngster. You could have his love if you wanted it. Why not come along with me now, sir, and have a look at something he is making?'

Grumbling that he had no interest in such nonsense, Kaeso had accompanied him to Antony's room. They stood before the model in silence, Antony visibly nervous and expectant of derision.

Kaeso studied the elaborate scene, rubbed his jaw, chuckled a little, and shook his head. Antony, watching his father with pathetic wistfulness, sighed dejectedly.

'It's in the wrong place,' declared Kaeso. 'When the snow melts, the spring freshets come plunging through that hollow. It would tear your masonry out. You must build it on higher ground.'

With that, Marcellus said he had an errand, if they would excuse him, and left the room. He sauntered down the hall and out through the peristyle, wearing a smile of such dimensions that when he encountered Antonia she insisted on knowing what had happened. Her eyes widened with unbelief as he told her briefly that her husband and her son were conferring about the best place to build a swimming-pool.

'Shall I join them?' she asked, childishly.

'No—not this time,' said Marcellus.

* * * * * *

It was mid-July now. At sunset, every day, Marcellus went down to the melon field and sat by the gate where the workers from all the fields received their wages. For a while the people merely waved a hand and smiled as they passed him. Then some of them ventured to tarry and talk. The scrivener, they all agreed, was indeed a queer one, but there was something about him that inclined them to him. They had a feeling that he was on their side.

For one thing, there was this rumor that they were to have a swimming-pool. When the last of the melons were harvested, anyone who wished to work on the community pool could do so. Nobody knew how much would be paid for this labor, but they were to be paid. Everybody felt that the scrivener had been responsible for this project. Some of the bolder ones asked him about it, and he professed not to know much of the plan, which, he said, was Appius Kaeso's idea; and they would be told all about it, when the time came.

One afternoon, when fully a score of workers had gathered about him, Marcellus told them a story about a man he knew in a far-away country, who had important things to say to poor people with heavy burdens, and how he believed that a man's life did not consist of the things he owned, and how much unhappiness could be avoided if men did not covet other men's possessions. If you want to be happy, make other people happy. He paused—and found himself looking squarely into Metella's eyes, pleased to see them so softly responsive.

'And what did this Jesus do to make other people happy?' asked an old man.

Well—in the case of Jesus, Marcellus had explained, he wasn't just an ordinary man; for he performed remarkable deeds of healing. He could make blind men see. People had but to touch him, and they were cured of their diseases. It was dark that evening before the melon-workers trudged up the hill. Reproaching himself for having detained them so long, Marcellus had said, 'If you want to hear more stories about Jesus, let us meet tomorrow in the village, after you have your supper.'

And so it had become a daily event for Marcellus to meet the people of Arpino on the grassy knoll at the foot of the mountain. He told them of the great, surging crowds that had followed Jesus; told them, with much detail, about the miracles, about little Jonathan's foot—and the story of the donkey that the lad gave to his crippled friend. He told them about Miriam's voice, and the broken loom that Jesus had mended, and how the woman had woven him a robe.

They had sat motionless, hardly breathing, until darkness fell. All Arpino looked forward to these evening stories, and discussed them in the fields next day. Even Vobiscus came and listened. One evening, Antonio and Antony appeared at the edge of the crowd while Marcellus was telling them about the feeding of five thousand people from a small boy's lunch-basket. It was a story of many moods, and the Arpinos laughed and wept over it. And then there was the great storm that Jesus had stilled with a soothing word.

'I hear you've been entertaining the people with strange stories,' remarked Kaeso, next day.

'About a great teacher, sir,' explained Marcellus, 'and his deeds for the relief of the people in the provinces of Palestine.'

'What kind of deeds?' pursued Kaeso; and when Marcellus had told him a few of the miracle-stories he said, 'Did this Jesus deal only with the poor?'

'By no means!' said Marcellus. 'He had friends among the rich, and was frequently invited to their houses. You might be interested, sir, in something that happened at the home of a wealthy man named Zacchaeus.'

'Divided half of his money among the poor; eh?' remarked Kaeso, when the story was finished. 'Much thanks he got for that, I suppose.'

'I don't know,' said Marcellus. 'I daresay the only way you could find out how people would act, in such a case—'

'Divide your money with them—and see; eh?' grumbled Kaeso.

'Well—you might make a little experiment that wouldn't cost quite so much,' said Marcellus, soberly. 'For example, have Vobiscus pay everybody four sesterces, instead of three, from now to the end of the melon season.'

'Then they'd raise a row if we went back to the old wage!' protested Kaeso.

'Very likely,' agreed Marcellus. 'Maybe it isn't worth doing. It would probably just stir up trouble.'

'Vobiscus would think I had gone crazy!' exclaimed Kaeso.

'Not if you increased his wages, too. Vobiscus is a valuable man, sir, and very loyal. He isn't paid enough.'

'Did he say so?' snapped Kaeso.

'No—Vobiscus wouldn't complain to me.'

'He has never asked for more.'

'That does not mean he is getting enough.'

'Perhaps you will be wanting better wages, too.' Kaeso chuckled unpleasantly.

'Vobiscus gets six sesterces. Let us pay him ten, and I will be content with sixteen instead of twenty.'

'Very well,' said Kaeso. 'You're a fool—but if that's the way you want it—'

'With one stipulation, sir. Vobiscus is not to know how his raise in wages came about. Let him think you did it—and see what happens.'

* * * * * *

Kaeso took much pride in the pool, and admitted that he was glad the idea had occurred to him to build it. The people didn't know what had come over Kaeso, but they believed the same thing was happening to him that had happened to them. He even conceded to Marcellus that the sesterces he had added to the workers' wage might have had something to do with the gratifying fact there had been a surprisingly small loss lately on melons bruised by careless handling. Marcellus did not tell him that he had made them a speech, the next morning after their pay was increased, in which he had suggested that they show their appreciation by being more faithful to their employer's interests.

The grapes were ripening now, and Kaeso enjoyed strolling through the vineyards. Sometimes the older ones ventured to turn their heads in his direction, and smile, rather shyly. One afternoon, he heard them singing, as he came down the road. When he appeared at the gate, the song stopped. He asked Vobiscus.

'They thought it might annoy you, sir,' stammered Vobiscus.

'Let them sing! Let them sing!' shouted Kaeso, indignantly. 'What makes them think I don't want to hear them sing?'

Vobiscus was clean-shaven today, and carrying himself with an air. Yesterday the wife of Kaeso had called at his house to show his wife a tapestry pattern and ask her how she had dyed the shawl she wore last night.

Near the end of a day when Marcellus had said he was going to stroll down to the vineyards, Antony asked if he might go along. At the gate, Marcellus picked up a couple of baskets and handed one to Antony.

'Want to do me a little favor?' he asked. 'Come along—and we'll gather some grapes.'

'Why should we?' inquired Antony. 'What will they think of us?'

'They will think no less of us,' said Marcellus, 'and it will make them think better of themselves—and their work.'

Presently they came upon an old woman who was straining hard to lift her heavy basket up to the platform of a cart. The driver, lounging against the wheel, watched her lazily.

'Give her a hand, Antony,' said Marcellus, quietly.

Everybody in that vicinity stopped work for a moment to witness this strange sight. The elegant son of Kaeso, who, they all had thought, considered the people of Arpino as dirt under his dainty feet, had volunteered to share a laborer's burden. There was a spontaneous murmur of approval as Marcellus and Antony moved on.

'Thank you, Antony,' said Marcellus, in a low tone.

'I didn't mind giving her a lift,' said Antony, flushing as he noted the appreciative smiles of the workers.

'You gave *everybody* a lift,' said Marcellus, 'including yourself, I think.'

* * * * * *

When August was more than half gone and the orders for fruit had dwindled until the scrivener's duties for the season were of small importance, Marcellus told Kaeso that he would like to be on his way.

'How about staying on for a while to help Antony with his modeling?' suggested Kaeso.

'I have shown him almost everything I know,' said Marcellus.

'Nonsense!' scoffed Kaeso. 'He can learn much from you. Besides—you are good for him. Antony's a different boy. You're making a man of him.'

'That's your doing, Kaeso,' said Marcellus, gently. 'Can't you see the way Antony hangs on your words? He admires you greatly, sir. It should be your own privilege to make a man of him.'

'Will you come back to Arpino next summer?' asked Kaeso, almost entreatingly.

Marcellus expressed his gratitude for the invitation, but did not know where he might be, next summer. Finishing his work at the desk, he was more painstaking than usual in filing things away, Kaeso moodily watching him.

'When are you leaving?' he asked.

'Early in the morning, sir. I am going to Rome.'

Kaeso followed him out into the garden where they met Antonia. In her presence he invited Marcellus to dine with the family. Antonia smiled her approval.

'He is leaving us,' said Kaeso. 'Where is Antony? I shall tell him.' He turned back toward the house.

'Aren't you contented here, Marcellus?' asked Antonia, gently, after a little silence between them. 'Haven't we done everything you wished?'

'Yes—that's why I am going.'

She nodded understandingly and gave him a pensive smile.

'Marcellus—do you remember the story you told us about the people's belief—in Cana, was it?—that Jesus had changed water into wine?'

'You found that hard to believe, I think,' he said.

'No,' she murmured; 'I can believe that story. It's no more mysterious than the changes you have made—in Arpino.'

* * * * * *

That evening, according to their recent custom, all the villagers assembled on the knoll to wait for Marcellus to appear and tell them a story.

When he came, Kaeso and Antonia and Antony were with him. Sitting down in the open circle the people had left for him, Marcellus hesitated for a long moment before beginning to speak.

'You have all been very kind to me,' he said, 'and you will be much in my thoughts, wherever I may go.'

A disappointed little sigh went over the crowd.

'I have told you many stories about this strange man of Galilee, who befriended the poor and helpless. Tonight, I shall tell you one more story about him—the strangest story of them all. Let that be my parting gift to you.'

It was a sad story of a misunderstood man, forsaken at the last, even by his frightened friends; a dismaying story of an unfair trial and a cruel death, and Marcellus told it so impressively that most of his audience was in tears.

'Now, there was nothing so strange about that,' he went on, in a suddenly altered mood, 'for wise men have always been misunderstood and persecuted—and many of them have been slain—as Jesus was. But Jesus came to life again!'

'What? No!' shouted an old man, in a quavering voice. They hushed him down, and waited for Marcellus to go on.

In the tense silence, the amazing story proceeded. Jesus was in the world—alive—to remain until his kingdom of kindness should rule all men—everywhere.

'You need not weep for him!' declared Marcellus. 'He asks no pity! If you want to do something to aid him, be helpful to one another—and await his coming.'

'Where is he now, sir?' called the old man, shrilly.

'No one knows,' said Marcellus. 'He might appear—anywhere—any time. We must not be found doing anything that would grieve him if he should come upon us suddenly—at an hour when we were not expecting him. Will you keep that in your remembrance?'

The twilight was falling fast now and so was the dew. It was time they dispersed. Marcellus drew a folded, much-handled sheet of papyrus from the breast of his tunic, and held it up in the fading light.

'One day,' he said, 'when a great company of Galileans had assembled about him on a hilltop, Jesus talked to them quietly about what he called "the blessed life." My friend Justus remembered these words and recited them for me. I wrote them down. Let me read them to you—and then we will part.'

The Arpinos leaned forward to listen; all but Metella, who sat hugging her knees, with her face buried in her folded arms. A deep hush fell over them as Marcellus read:

'Blessed are the poor in spirit, for theirs is the kingdom of heaven. Blessed are they that mourn, for they shall be comforted. Blessed are the meek, for they shall inherit the earth. Blessed are they who hunger and thirst after righteousness, for they shall be filled. Blessed are the merciful, for they shall obtain mercy. Blessed are the pure in heart, for they shall see God. Blessed are the peace-makers, for they shall be called the children of God. Blessed are they who are persecuted for righteousness' sake, for theirs is the kingdom of heaven. Rejoice and be glad, for great will be your reward.'

* * * * * *

Rising before dawn, Marcellus slipped quietly out of the villa, meeting no one—except Metella, who startled him by stepping out of the shrubbery near the gate to say farewell in a tremulous little voice. Then she had started to scamper away. He spoke her name softly. Taking her toil-roughened hands, he said tenderly, 'Metella, you are indeed a faithful friend. I shall always remember you.'

'Please'—she sobbed—'take good care of yourself—Marcellus!' And then, abruptly tearing loose from him, she had disappeared in the dark.

It was with a strange sense of elation that he strode along the foothill road in the shadow of the mountain as a pink sunrise lighted the sky. Last night, after taking leave of the Kaeso family—who had made an earnest effort to dissuade him—he had gone to bed with misgivings. He was happy in Arpino. He knew he had been sent there on a mission. Lately, something kept telling him his work was done; telling him he must go to Rome. All night, with the entreaties of young Antony still sounding in his ears, he kept asking himself, 'Why *am* I going to Rome?'

This morning, his anxieties had been put aside. He did not know why he was headed toward Rome, but the reason would appear in due time. He had never been able to explain to himself why, when he had been washed up by the tide on the Capua beach, he had turned his face toward Arpino; or why, tarrying at Kaeso's melon field, he had accepted employment. It was almost as if he were being led about by an invisible hand.

By mid-afternoon, the winding road had angled away from the mountain range and was being joined and widened by many tributaries. It was becoming a busy highway now, drawing in all manner of laden carts and wagons from the gates and lanes of the fertile valley. The day was hot and the air was heavy with dust. Scowling drivers lashed their donkeys cruelly and yelled obscenities as they contended for the right of way. Every added mile increased the confusion and sharpened the ostentatious brutality of the men who pressed toward Rome.

It was as if the Imperial City had reached out her malevolent arms in all directions to clutch and pollute her victims as they moved into the orbit of her fetid breath; and they, ashamed of their rustic simplicities, had sought to appear urbane by cursing one another. Marcellus, making his way past this ill-tempered cavalcade, wondered whether many people could be found in Rome who would care to hear about the man of Galilee.

Arriving in the good-sized town of Alatri at sundown, Marcellus found the only tavern buzzing with excitement. An agitated crowd milled about in the stableyard. Inside, there was barely standing room. He made his way in and asked the tall man wedged beside him what was going on. The news had just come from Rome that Prince Gaius was dead.

At this juncture, the tavern-keeper stood up on a chair and announced importantly that all who did not wish to be served should get out and make way for his guests. Most of the shabby ones sullenly withdrew. In the center of the room, three flashily dressed wool-buyers from Rome sat at a table, laving the day's dust with a flagon of wine. Crowded about them was an attentive audience, eager for further details concerning the tragedy. Marcellus pressed close and listened.

Last night there had been a banquet at the palatial home of Tribune Quintus and his wife Celia, the niece of Sejanus, in honor of young Caligula, the son of Germanicus, who had just arrived from Gaul. Prince Gaius had been taken suddenly ill at dinner and had died within an hour.

The wool-merchants, conscious of their attentive auditors, and growing less discreet as they replenished their cups from the second flagon, continued to discuss the event with a knowledgeable air, almost as if they had been present at the fateful banquet. It was evident that they were well informed on court gossip, as indeed anyone in Rome could be if he made friends with servants.

There was little doubt, declared the wool-men, that the Prince had been poisoned. He had been in the best of health. The sickness had been swift and savage. Suspicion had not centered definitely on anyone. Tribune Tullus, who in the afternoon had married the young daughter of Senator Gallio—sister of Tribune Marcellus, the one who drowned himself in the sea, a few weeks ago—had spoken some hot words to the Prince, earlier in the evening; but they had both been so drunk that little importance had been attached to the argument.

Old Sejanus had sat opposite the Prince at dinner, and everybody knew that Sejanus had no use for Gaius. But it was agreed that if the crafty old man had wanted to assassinate the Prince he had too much sense to risk it in such circumstances.

'How does it happen that Quintus can live in a palace and give expensive dinners?' inquired the tavern-keeper, anxious to show that he knew a thing or two about the great ones. 'Old Tuscus, his father, is not rich. What did Quintus ever do to make a fortune? He has led no expeditions.'

The wool-merchants exchanged knowing glances and shrugged superiorly.

'Quintus and the Prince are great friends,' said the fat one who presided over the flagon.

'You mean the Prince and Quintus' wife are great friends,' recklessly chuckled the one with the silver trinkets on his bandeau.

'Oh, ho!' divined the tavern-keeper. 'Maybe that's how it happened!'

'Not so fast, wise man,' admonished the eldest of the three, thickly. 'Quintus was not present at the banquet. He had been sent, at the last minute, to Capri.'

'Who did it, then?' persisted the tavern-keeper.

'Well—that's what everybody wants to know,' said the fat one, holding up the empty flagon. 'Here! Fill that up—and don't ask so many questions.' He glanced about over the silent group, his eyes tarrying for a moment as they passed Marcellus. 'We're all talking too freely,' he muttered.

Marcellus turned away, followed by the tavern-keeper, and inquired for a bath and a room for the night. A servant showed him to his cramped and cheerless quarters, and he began tossing off his clothes. So—Diana need not be worried about Gaius' attentions any more. That was a great relief. Who would rule Rome now? Perhaps the Emperor would appoint tight-pursed old Sejanus to the regency for the present.

So—Gaius had been poisoned; eh? Perhaps Celia had done it. Maybe Gaius had mistreated her. He couldn't be loyal to anyone; not for very long. But, no—Celia wouldn't have done it. More likely that Quintus had left instructions with a servant, and had contrived some urgent business at Capri to provide an alibi. Quintus could dispose of the servant easily enough. Marcellus wondered if Quintus had encountered Demetrius at Capri. Well—if he had, Demetrius could take care of himself very nicely.

So—Lucia was married. That was good. She had always been in love with Tullus. Marcellus fell to speculating on the possibility that Lucia might have confided to her husband the story of Gaius' crude attempts to make love to her when she was little more than a child. If she had—and if Tullus were drunk enough to be foolhardy—but no, no—Tullus wouldn't get drunk enough to do a thing like that. Tullus would have used a dagger.

Marcellus reverted to Celia, trying to remember everything he could about her; the restless, sultry eyes; the sly, preoccupied smile that always made her manner seem older than her slim, girlish body. Yes—Celia might have done it. She was a deep one, like her Uncle Sejanus.

Well—whatever had caused the Prince's indigestion, the dangerous reptile was dead. That was a comfort. Perhaps Rome might now hope for a little better government. It was inconceivable that the Empire could acquire a worse ruler than Gaius Drusus Agrippa.

Chapter XXIII

When the hard-riding couriers brought the report to Capri that Gaius was dead, the Emperor—in the firm opinion of old Julia—was much too ill to be confronted with such shocking news. That, of course, was nonsense, as the Empress well knew; for her son had long been Tiberius' favorite aversion, and these tidings, far from doing the sick old man any damage, might have temporarily revived him.

But, assuming that the tragic death of a Prince Regent should be viewed as an event too calamitous to be announced at the bedside of a seriously ailing Emperor, everybody conceded that Julia was within her rights in commanding that no mention be made of it to her enfeebled husband, though it was something of an innovation for the Empress to display so much solicitude in his behalf.

With less mercy, Julia had immediately thrust a letter into the hands of the exhausted Centurion who had brought the bad news, bidding him return to Rome at top speed. The Centurion, resentful at being pushed off the island without so much as an hour's respite and a flagon of wine, had no compunctions about showing the address of the Empress' urgent message to his long-time friend the Chamberlain who had accompanied him and his aides to the wharf. The letter was going to Caligula.

'Little Boots,' growled the Centurion, contemptuously.

'Little brat!' muttered the Chamberlain, who had seen something of Germanicus' son when he was ten.

Old Julia, for whom Fate seemed always contriving fortuitous events, was feverish to see her grandson at this critical juncture. She had not felt so urgent a need of him, the day before yesterday, when Quintus had suddenly appeared with the suggestion—phrased as diplomatically as possible—that the Empress immediately invite the youngster to Capri. Julia had laughed almost merrily.

'He's a handful for Gaius; eh?' she snapped. 'Well—let Gaius bear his burden the best he can, for a month or two.'

'The Prince thought Your Majesty would be impatient to see Little Boots,' wheedled Quintus, 'and wanted me to say that he would not detain him in Rome if Your Majesty—'

'We can wait,' chuckled Julia.

But today the situation had changed. Julia wanted very much to see Little Boots. How lucky for him that he should have happened to be available at this important hour!

Bearing her bereavement with fortitude, as became a Roman and an Empress, Julia nervously counted the dragging hours; watched and waited at her northern windows; grew almost frantic at the sight of a large deputation of Senators being borne up the hill to the Villa Jovis; and strained her old eyes for a certain black-hulled ferry—her own ferry—plying across the bay from Puteoli.

Nobody on Capri thought, when young Caligula arrived, that his ambitious grandmother had anything larger in mind for the puny youth than a brief interim regency, probably under the guidance of Sejanus—as a little child might hold the dangling ends of the reins and pretend he was driving. Perhaps Julia herself had not ventured to dream of the amazing thing that came to pass.

Caligula, at sixteen, was wizened and frail. He jerked when he walked. His pasty-white, foxish face was perpetually in motion with involuntary grimaces and his restless fingers were always busily picking and scratching like a monkey. He was no fool, though. Back of the darting, close-set eyes a malicious imagination tirelessly invented ingenious pursuits to compensate for his infirmities.

Because of his child's defects, Germanicus had insisted on having him under his eye, even in the heat of military campaigns. The officers had petted and flattered him until he was abominably impudent and outrageously cruel. His bestial pranks were supposed to be amusing. Someone had made a pair of little boots for him, like those worn by the staff officers, and the legend spread that Germanicus' sick boy frequently waddled out in front of a legion on review and barked shrill orders. The whimsical nickname 'Caligula' ('Little Boots') stuck to him until nobody remembered that he had been named for his Uncle Gaius. As a lad, everything Caligula did was cute, including the most shocking vandalisms and brutalities. By the time he was sixteen, it wasn't thought so clever when 'Little Boots' would jerkily propel himself up to a Centurion and slap him in the face; and even Germanicus, noting that his heir was becoming an intolerable pest, thought it time he was given another change of scenery. So—he was sent back to Rome again to visit his Uncle Gaius, who, it was hoped, would make something of him. What manner of miracle the Prince might have wrought was to remain forever a matter of conjecture. It was rumored that Germanicus' staff officers, upon learning of the death of Gaius, agreed that he could hardly have timed his departure more opportunely.

Caligula arrived on Capri in the late afternoon and old Julia took him at once—duly instructed as to his behavior—into the deeply shadowed bedchamber of the Emperor, where a dozen or more Senators stood about in the gloom, obviously waiting for Tiberius to take notice of them.

The old man dazedly roused to find a weeping youth kneeling beside his pillow. In a grieving voice the Empress explained that poor Gaius was dead, and Caligula was inconsolable.

Tiberius pulled his scattered wits together, and feebly patted Caligula on the head.

'Germanicus' boy?' he mumbled, thickly.

Caligula nodded, wept noisily, and gently stroked the emaciated hand.

'Is there anything I can do for you, sire?' he asked, brokenly.

'Yes—my son.' Tiberius' tired old voice was barely audible.

'You mean—the Empire?' demanded Julia, in much agitation.

The attentive Senators moved in closer about the bed.

'Yes—the Empire,' breathed Tiberius, weakly.

'Have you heard that?' Julia's tone was shrill and challenging as she threw back her head to face the stunned group at the bedside. 'Caligula is to be the Emperor! Is it not so, Your Majesty?'

'Yes,' whispered Tiberius.

* * * * * *

It was late in the night. The Emperor lay dying. He had been close to it on several occasions. There was no doubt about it this time.

The learned physicians, having made all their motions, took turns holding the thin wrist. The priests, who had spent the day cooling their heels in the atrium, were admitted to do their solemn exercises. The Senators, who had been invited to withdraw after the incredible announcement had been made at sunset, were permitted to enter, now that it was reasonably sure the old man would have nothing more to say. They were still dazed by the blow he had delivered and were wondering how they would tell the Senate that Germanicus' deficient son was to rule the Empire. Of course the Senate, if it courageously took the bit in its teeth, could annul Tiberius' action; but it was unlikely that the solons would risk offending Germanicus and the army. No—their new Emperor—for good or ill—would be Little Boots.

Diana Gallus had not seen Tiberius for a fortnight. Old Julia had given orders that she was not to be admitted. Every morning and evening Diana had appeared at the door of the imperial bedchamber to inquire, and had been advised that the Emperor was too ill to be disturbed.

Shortly after Demetrius' arrival on Capri, he had been assigned to serve as Diana's bodyguard. Strangely enough, this had been done at the suggestion of Tiberius, who, perhaps with some premonition that he might not long be able to insist upon her adequate security, had felt that Marcellus' intrepid slave would protect her.

As the Emperor grew more frail, and the Empress' influence became more pressing throughout the island, Demetrius' anxiety about Diana's welfare increased; though he was careful not to let her know the full extent of his worry. He began making private plans for her rescue, in case her insecurity should become serious.

At the enforced departure of Marcellus, Diana had become restless, moody, and secluded. There was no one on the island in whom she could confide. Most of her daylight hours were spent in her pergola, reading without interest and indifferently toying with trifles of needlework. Sometimes she would bring one of her maids along for company. As often she came alone, with Demetrius trailing her at a respectful distance and always within call. Her admiration for the Greek had always been deep and sincere. Now she began to lean on him as a close and understanding friend.

When the rumor had drifted back to Capri that Marcellus had been drowned, Demetrius knew it wasn't true, and conforted Diana with his reasons. Marcellus had no cause to commit suicide. He had become aware of a new and serious obligation. The story that Marcellus had drowned himself as *The Augusta* was rounding the promontory off Capua, only a mile off shore, amused Demetrius, so confident was he that his master had taken that favorable occasion to disappear. Diana believed this, too, but Demetrius had to reassure her again and again when her loneliness was oppressive.

Their conversation became less formal as the days passed. Demetrius would sit on the side steps of the pergola answering Diana's persistent questions about their life in Athens, the House of Eupolis, Theodosia, and the escape after the affair with Quintus, for whom she had a bitter contempt.

'Why don't you go back to Theodosia when you are free?' she asked one day. 'Maybe she is waiting for you. Have you ever heard from her?'

Yes—Demetrius had written and he had heard from her, though not for a long time. One could never tell what might happen. Yes—if he were free, and Marcellus had no need of him, yes—he would go back to Athens.

The afternoons would pass quickly, Diana insatiable with her queries,

Demetrius telling his interminable stories of old Benyosef's shop, and Stephanos, and the Galileans who came to talk in low voices about the mysterious carpenter who had come alive to live evermore.

Diana would listen attentively as she bent over her small tapestries and lace medallions. Demetrius' hands would be busy, too, twisting and braiding short lengths of hemp that he had picked up on the wharves, and splicing them expertly into long, thick cords. Under the sea side of the pergola floor he had secreted his supplies, much to Diana's amusement.

'You are like a squirrel, Demetrius,' she had remarked, teasingly. 'Why do you hide your things, if they're worth nothing, as you say?' One day she bent over his shoulder and watched him deftly working the twisted hempen cords with his wooden awl. 'Why—you're making a rope!' she exclaimed. 'Whatever are you doing that for?' Following it around to the corner of the pergola, she was amazed to find a huge coil secreted. 'I think this is more than play!' she declared, soberly.

'It keeps my hands employed,' drawled Demetrius. 'You have your tapestry. I have my rope.'

After his daily duties had been discharged, and he had seen Diana safely to her suite, it was his custom to take long walks in the night. The sentries on the grounds became acquainted with his strange nocturnal habits, and attached no significance to them. Striding along the winding paths, pausing for a leisurely chat with lonesome guards, he would descend the long stairways to the wharves where the boatmen and dock employees came to know him. Sometimes he lent a hand for an hour or two, darning rents in a sailcloth, splicing ropes, and caulking leaks with pitch and tow. Not infrequently, having urged Diana to order more than she wanted for dinner, he would appear at the docks with confections and other delicacies.

'You seem immensely fond of those men down there,' Diana had remarked; and Demetrius had explained that they did not have many good things to eat; and, besides, he enjoyed their friendship.

Every night when he left the docks he would carry off as large a bundle of hemp as could be stowed under his tunic. Nobody cared. He was well liked and could do as he pleased. Sometimes he would take one of the idle dories and row up along the rocky rim of the island for an hour, explaining that he needed exercise. The lazy boatmen thought him peculiar, but were willing to humor him.

Early every morning, a freight barge went across to Puteoli to meet the farmers and fruit-growers and butchers who came with their products for the island. One night when Demetrius appeared at the wharf he found the dock hands especially interested in his arrival. A large consignment of Arpino melons had come over in the forenoon, and one of the melons—if he would believe it—had been sent expressly to Demetrius. They gave it to him, and stood about, wide-eyed with curiosity, as he opened the small, slatted box.

'Know somebody at Arpino?' they inquired.

'He's got a girl in Arpino!' guffawed a boatman.

Demetrius couldn't think of anyone who would be sending him a melon from Arpino—or anywhere else. He turned it over slowly in his hand. On one side, there had been lightly scratched with a knife-point a small, crude drawing.

'Somebody's name, is it?' one asked. They all crowded in close to contribute the flavor of garlic to this mystery.

'Probably just a joke,' muttered an old boatman, turning away. 'That silly Umbrian that skippers the barge has been playing a little trick on you.'

Demetrius chuckled and said he'd get even; but he could hardly conceal his excitement. It wasn't a bargeman's hoax. The scrawl on the melon was an irregular, almost unrecognizable outline of a fish! So—Marcellus was in the melon business!

Next morning, as they sat chatting in the pergola, Demetrius asked Diana if she had ever heard of Arpino melons, and she promptly remembered how much they had liked them at home.

'Yesterday,' said Demetrius, 'when the freight barge came over from the mainland with melons, there was one sent specially to me.' He rose and handed it to her. Diana inspected it with interest.

'How odd! Do you know anyone there? What is this device? It looks like a fish. Does it mean anything?'

'When the Christians in Judea and Galilee,' explained Demetrius, sauntering back to his seat on the steps, 'wanted to inform one another of their whereabouts, or the road they had taken, they drew a rough picture of a fish, in the sand by the roadside, on a rock at a crossing, or over a doorway. If two strangers met at a tavern table, and one of them wanted to know whether the other was a Christian, he idly traced the figure of a fish with his finger.'

'Why a fish?' inquired Diana.

'The Greek word for fish is made up of initials for the words which mean, "Jesus Christ Son of God Savior." '

'How interesting!' exclaimed Diana. 'But do you suppose there are any Christians at Arpino?'

Demetrius looked into her eyes and smiled mysteriously.

'There is at least one Christian in Arpino,' he said, 'and I think we both know who he is.'

'Marcellus!' whispered Diana, breathlessly.

* * * * * *

This afternoon, all Capri had been excited over the arrival of young Caligula. Demetrius had caught sight of him, kicking himself along at the side of the Empress as they entered the Villa Jovis. An hour later, the island had fairly rocked with the news that this repulsive youth would presently wear the crown. Coupled with this shocking rumor came the report that the Emperor had sunk into a deep coma from which his emergence was most unlikely.

Now that Tiberius was no longer to be reckoned with, and Julia's insufferable grandson was all but on the throne, the Empress would be capable of any atrocity that her caprice might suggest. She could even be vile enough, thought Demetrius, to insist on Diana's showing favors to Caligula.

By the time twilight fell, that evening, there was a confirmation of these forebodings. Diana had been invited to a quiet dinner with the Empress and her now eminent grandson. Despite the fact that the Emperor was snoring the tag end of his life away, young Caligula must have some pleasant diversion.

Reluctantly, Diana accepted the invitation, realizing that it was nothing less than a command, Demetrius accompanying her to the Villa Dionysus, where, for two anxious hours, he paced to and fro on the frescoed pavement, waiting for her to reappear. When, at length, she came out through the peristyle into the bright moonlight, it was evident from her manner that something had happened. In an agitated voice she confided that the loathsome Caligula had paid her such impudent attentions that even Julia had muttered a stern word of caution.

'That settles it!' declared Demetrius, firmly. 'You can't stay here! I am going to try to take you off the island—tonight!'

'But—it's impossible, Demetrius!' she protested.

'We shall see. It will be dangerous. But it is worth trying.' Briefly he instructed her what to do. Diana shuddered. 'You won't be afraid; will you?' he demanded, searching her eyes.

'Yes!' she confessed. 'Of course I'll be afraid! I don't see how I can do it! But—I'll try! I'd rather drown than have that slimy idiot put his hands on me again.'

'Slip out of the Jovis, then, and go alone to your pergola, an hour before midnight!'

Leaving Diana at her door, Demetrius set out on his usual nightly excursion, going first to the pergola, where he dragged the long rope from its hiding-place, secured one end to a small pine tree, and tossed the length of it down the almost perpendicular precipice. For a moment he stood there looking down over the face of the slightly slanting rock to the dashing surf far below, and winced as he pictured Diana's sensations when she confronted this hazardous adventure. Surely it would demand a great deal of courage. He wouldn't have wanted to do it himself.

Returning swiftly to his own quarters, he picked up the compact bundle of clothing he had assembled for Diana—a stonemason's coarse smock and heavy leggings, and a knitted cap such as the wharfmen wore.

Everywhere the inquisitive sentries detained him to chatter about the amazing events of the day, and he was obliged to tarry. Time was precious, but he must not arouse suspicion by an appearance of haste or stress. At the wharf he unchained the best dory available, shipped the oars, waved a hand to the boatmen, and made off slowly in the moonlight. As soon as it was discreet, he began to lengthen his strokes. It was a long, hard pull around the eastern point of the massive island. The waves grew suddenly rougher as he came out into the wind of the open sea.

Demetrius' heart pounded fiercely. It was not only the grueling exertion, but his fear that Diana might be overtaken. On an ordinary occasion it would have been next to impossible for her to go to her pergola so late at night without being questioned. But nothing was quite normal on Capri tonight. The Emperor was dying. Nobody's behavior would be scrutinized. People would be scurrying about on unfamiliar errands. Maybe Diana would have no trouble in keeping her engagement; but, even if she were lucky enough to do that, it was a perilous risk she still had to face.

At length he recognized, in the moonlight, the tall cliff and the overhanging eaves of the pergola. Maneuvering the heavy dory as close as he dared to the foot of the towering rock, Demetrius strained his eyes toward the summit. The boat was almost unmanageable in the insistent swells of a high tide. The agonizing minutes dragged along, as he scanned the ledge a full hundred and fifty feet above the waves.

Now his heart gave a great bound! A little way from the top, a gray-clad figure began slipping down. Diana seemed very small and insecure. Demetrius wished she would take it more slowly. He had cautioned her about that. She would burn her hands; perhaps lose her grip. When a little more than halfway down, she slipped several feet before checking herself by twining her legs more tightly about the rope.

Demetrius' eyes widened at the amazing thing that was happening. Diana's descent had slowed to a stop. Now she was actually moving up! He lifted his eyes to the top of the cliff. Two figures on the ledge above were toiling at the rope. Demetrius dropped the oars and funneled his hands about his mouth.

'Let go!' he shouted.

There was a tense moment of indecision in which Diana was tugged up another foot.

'Jump, Diana!' called Demetrius.

The uncontrolled dory was carried broadside on a wave that almost dashed it against the rock. Suddenly Diana leaped free of the rope and came hurtling down into a huge comber. Its retreat swept her far out. For a long moment, she was not to be seen. Bending to his oars, Demetrius tugged the dory away from the cliff, desperately searching the water. Now her head appeared on the curve of a great swell. Diana was swimming. Demetrius pulled alongside and threw an arm about her. She was badly frightened and her breath was coming in gasps and sobs. He bent far over the side of the boat. Diana put her arms around his neck, and he tugged her in over the rail. She crumpled up in a heap at his feet, drenched and exhausted.

Demetrius dragged the cumbersome dory about, and began the laborious trip around the curve of the island, keeping close in the shadow of the rock. It was hard going. Sometimes they seemed to be making no progress at all. Neither spoke until they were in the quiet water on the bay side. Thoroughly spent, Demetrius pulled the dory into the dark mouth of a grotto, and slumped over with his elbows on his knees and his head in his hands.

'You are a brave girl, Diana!' he said, huskily.

'I don't feel very brave,' she said, in a weak voice, 'but I am terribly cold.'

'There is some dry clothing for you in the locker at the bow.' He took her hand and steadied her as she climbed over his seat. 'Lift up the trap,' he said, 'and you will find it.'

'Is this supposed to be a disguise?' she inquired, presently.

'No—it's intended to keep you warm.'

'Why didn't Acteus and that other guard shoot at me?' asked Diana.

'Because they might have hit you,' said Demetrius. 'You need not be afraid of an arrow. Acteus was told to keep you on the island; not to harm you. Did you know he was following you?'

'Not until I was almost at the pergola. I heard them behind me, and recognized the voice of Acteus when he called. It was an awful feeling when I found myself being drawn up.' Diana shuddered. 'It was hard to let go of that rope.'

'I should think it might have been. Are you getting warm now?' Demetrius was taking up the oars. 'Did you find the cap?'

'Yes—it's dreadful. Where are we going now, Demetrius?'

'Over off the mainland—and up the coast to some open beach.'

'And then what—and where?'

'Hide for the day—and row all night tomorrow—and leave the boat somewhere near Formia. But—don't worry. You are off this dangerous island. Nothing else matters.'

Diana was quiet for a long time. Demetrius had settled to his heavy task. The oars swept steadily, powerfully, as the dory drove into a rapidly rising breeze. An occasional wave splashed against the rail and showered them with spray.

'Demetrius!' called Diana. 'How far is it from Formia to Arpino?'

'Fifty miles—northeast,' shouted Demetrius, between strokes.

'Were you ever there? You seem to be acquainted with that country.'

'No—never there—looked it up—on the map.'

'Are we going to Arpino?'

'Want to?'

Diana did not reply. The breeze was growing stronger and Demetrius was laboring hard. A wave broke over the side.

'You'll find—leather bailing bucket—up there," called Demetrius. 'You aren't frightened—are you?'

'No—not now,' she sang out cheerfully.

'Keep me headed for that row of lights at Puteoli.'

'A little to the right, then. Demetrius—it seems almost as if someone were looking after us tonight.'

'Yes, Diana.'

'Do you believe that—truly?'

'Yes.'

'Think he will take care of us—if a storm blows up?'

Demetrius tugged the unwieldly old tub out of the trough, and for an interval rowed hard. Then he replied, in detached phrases, measured by the sweep of the long oars.

'He has been known—to take care—of his friends—in a storm.'

* * * * * *

So impatient was Caligula to occupy his exalted office that the state funeral of Tiberius—which he did not attend because of some slight indisposition—was practically eclipsed by lavish preparations for the coronation; and, as for Uncle Gaius' obsequies, not many Princes had been put away with less pomp or at so modest an expense.

Perhaps, had Emperor Tiberius been a more popular hero, public sentiment might have demanded a better show of respect for the old man's departure, but so little had been heard of him for the past dozen years that nobody really cared whether he lived or died. Even in the Senate, where the most eloquent of the Romans were skilled in saying things they did not mean, the orations extolling Tiberius were of an appalling dullness.

There was no decent interval of perfunctory mourning. All night, workmen were busy tearing down the funereal trappings along the Corso and the Via Sacra through which the Emperor had taken his last ride that afternoon. The older patricians were shocked by this irreverence; not that they any longer cared a fig about Tiberius, who, for the Empire's sake, should have had the goodness to die years ago; but it boded ill for Rome, they felt, to be crowning a youth so impudently defiant of the proprieties. But the traditions meant as little to Caligula as the counsel of his dismayed ministers. The stories of his insane egotism, his fits and rages, and his utter irresponsibility swept through the city like a fire.

The coronation festivities lasted for a week and were conducted with an extravagance that knew no precedent in the experience of any nation's capital. Hundreds of thousands were fed and wined and welcomed to the games, which for wanton brutality and reckless bloodshed quite surpassed anything that Rome had ever seen. The substantial citizenship of the Empire stood aghast, stunned to silence. As for the habitually empty-bellied rabble, Little Boots was their man. So long as he dished out bread and circuses it was no concern of theirs how or whether the bill was settled. Indeed, Little Boots led them to believe that it was by his personal generosity that they were fed and entertained, and was forthright in his denunciation of the wealthy, who, he shouted, were responsible for the people's poverty.

Old Sejanus, frightened and desperate, came before the Senate to remonstrate and plead for immediate action; but nothing was done, and that night Sejanus was assassinated. Crafty old Julia, who had come to Rome expecting to be glorified as the Empress dowager, was hustled onto the imperial barge without ceremony and shipped back to Capri.

The palace reeked of dissolute parties that continued for days and nights and days. All the common decencies were abandoned. Uninvited hundreds crowded into the banquets. Priceless art objects were overturned and broken on the mosaic floors. Riotous guests slipped and rolled down the slimy marble stairways. Never had so many been so drunk.

Triumphal processions, hastily improvised in celebration of some half-forgotten holiday, would move out unannounced into the avenue, bearing in the foremost golden chariot the garishly arrayed, drunken, disheveled, grimacing, twitching Emperor, sowing handfuls of sesterces into the hysterical street-crowds from a grain-bag that Quintus held in his arms, while the greedy rabble fought in the filthy gutters like dogs, and the pompous

Quintus—Little Boots' favorite—laughed merrily at the sport, his lips still cut and swollen from the brutal slapping he had received from the bejeweled hands of old Julia's whimsical grandson.

The patricians kept to their villas, inarticulate and numb with cold anger and despair. There was nothing they could do. They did not protest when Caligula ordered the heads knocked off the venerated busts of the great in the Forum, and marble models of his own installed with impressive ceremonies. They did not protest when he fitted up a gold-and-ivory stall in the palace for his horse Incitatus, nor did they protest when he elevated Incitatus to the rank of Consul.

The populace laughed inopportunely when Little Boots announced that Incitatus was divine; and, annoyed that this declaration should have been taken lightly, he brought forth an edict demanding that his distinguished horse must henceforth be worshiped in the temples, to the considerable embarrassment of the priests, whose dignity—by reason of other eccentric orders from the throne—was already somewhat in need of repair.

Almost every day the Emperor savagely inquired of Quintus whether any progress had been made in his search for the haughty and beautiful daughter of Gallus, and would be freshly enraged to learn that no trace of her had been discovered. A guard had been set about the absent Legate Gallus' villa. Paula's movements—if the unhappy woman could be said to move at all—were carefully watched. Her servants were questioned, threatened, tortured. On Capri, the guard Acteus and three wharf attendants had been put to death. And Quintus had been advised that he had better contrive some more favorable news of his far-flung investigation if he knew what was good for him.

But Quintus' failure to find Diana was for no lack of personal interest in this quest. For one thing, when they found Diana they would probably find Demetrius, too. He had a score to settle there. It fretted him that he had not been told of the Greek's presence on the island when he had visited the Empress, at Gaius' behest, to implore her to take Caligula off his hands.

Of course it was possible that Diana and Demetrius might have been drowned. Their dory had been found adrift. The weather had been stormy. Nobody along the coast, all the way up from Formia to Capua, had seen anything of the fugitives.

Little Boots fumed and shouted. Diana was the only person he knew who had regarded him with undisguised contempt. Moreover, according to the story of her escape from Capri, she had plenty of courage. It would be a pleasure to break her, he muttered. Quintus' mobile lips still smiled obsequiously, but his brows contracted in a cautioning frown.

'The slave Demetrius, Your Majesty, who contrived her flight, should be disposed of before the daughter of Gallus is taken.'

'Why?' barked Caligula. 'Is the slave in love with her? You said she was in love with that mad Tribune who crucified the Jew, and lost his head over thinking he had killed a god.'

Quintus' eyes had lighted with surprise that Little Boots remembered what he had told him about the Galilean, and the large following he had attracted. Caligula had been so very drunk, and had seemed to pay no attention. Apparently the story had impressed him.

'True, Your Majesty,' said Quintus. 'This Demetrius was the slave of Marcellus, the son of old Gallio. Doubtless he has sworn to protect Diana.'

'If he can!' sneered Caligula.

'If he cannot, sire—and Diana is captured—this Greek would not hesitate to risk his life in avenging her.'

'Pouf! What could he do? You are a timid fool, Quintus! Do you think this slave would force a violent entrance into our presence?'

'The Greek is a dangerous man, Your Majesty,' warned Quintus. 'He was once reckless enough to attack a Tribune with his bare hands!'

'And lived?' shouted Caligula.

'Quite openly! And became a member of the Emperor's guard at the Villa Jovis!'

'Did Tiberius know of the slave's crime?'

'Doubtless. The Empress knew—for I told her.'

'Who was the Tribune that the Greek attacked?'

Quintus fidgeted, and Caligula—eyeing him sharply—burst into laughter. Quintus flushed, and grinned sheepishly.

'Emperor Tiberius never liked me, sire,' he mumbled.

'Perhaps the old man appointed the slave a member of his guard to reward him,' chuckled Caligula. 'Well—here is your chance to settle with this savage. Find him—and run him through!' he advised, with an appropriate gesture.

Quintus pursed his lips and slowly elevated a prudent shoulder.

'I should not enjoy fighting a duel with a slave, Your Majesty.'

Little Boots rocked with laughter.

'Not with this one—in any case!' He suddenly sobered and scowled. 'You make haste to find that Greek! If you are afraid to meet him, let a braver man attend to it! We do not like the idea of his being at large. But—tell me more of this Marcellus, who threw himself into the sea. He became a follower of the Jew; eh? Does the daughter of Gallus entertain such notions?'

Quintus said he didn't know, but that he had reasons to believe the Greek slave was a Christian, as he had consorted with these people in Jerusalem.

'But he fights; eh?' commented Caligula. 'It was our understanding that this crazy Jesus-cult does not permit fighting.'

'Well—that may be so, Your Majesty,' conceded Quintus, 'but if this Greek is enraged, he will not ask anybody's permission to fight. He is a wild animal!'

Little Boots nervously picked at his pimples.

'What do you think of the strength of our palace guard, Quintus?'

'They are awake, sire, and loyal.'

'It would be quite impossible for an assassin to enter our bedchamber; eh?'

'From without, yes, Your Majesty. But if the Greek decided to kill the Emperor, he might not try to enter the palace. He would probably leap up over the Emperor's chariot-wheel with a dagger.'

'And be instantly bludgeoned to death by the people,' declared Caligula, his chin working convulsively.

'Of course, Your Majesty,' assented Quintus, not displeased to note Little Boots' agitation. 'But the bludgeoning might come too late to be of service to the Emperor. As for the Greek, if he decided to get revenge, he would not haggle at the price.'

Caligula held up a shaky goblet and Quintus made haste to replenish it.

'Hereafter, there must be better protection of our person when we are before the people. There must be a strong double guard marching on either side of the imperial chariot, Quintus. You shall see to it!'

'Your Majesty's order will be obeyed. But if I may venture to say so, this danger could be avoided, sire. Let the daughter of Gallus—if she still lives—go her way unmolested. The Emperor would have no comfort with her; and to keep her in chains might provoke much unrest in the army where Legate Gallus is held in high esteem.'

Little Boots drank deeply, hiccoughed, and drew a surly grin.

'When we need your advice, Quintus, we will ask for it. The Emperor of the Roman Empire does not inquire whether his decisions are approved by every legionary in the army.' Little Boots' voice rose shrilly. 'Nor are we concerned over the mutterings of the fat old men in the Senate! We have the people with us!'

Quintus smiled obediently, but offered no comment.

'Speak up, fool!' screamed Little Boots. 'The people are with us!'

'As long as they are fed, Your Majesty,' ventured Quintus.

'We shall feed them when we like,' snarled Little Boots, thickly.

Quintus did not reply to that. Observing that the large silver goblet was empty again, he refilled it.

'And when we stop feeding them—then what?' challenged Little Boots, truculently. 'Is there to be disorder—and do we have to lash them back to their kennels?'

'Hungry people, sire,' said Quintus, quietly, 'can make themselves very annoying.'

'By petty pillaging? Let them steal! The owners of the markets are rich. Why should we concern ourself about that? But we will tolerate no mobs, no meetings!'

'It is not difficult, Your Majesty, to deal with mobs,' remarked Quintus. 'They can be quickly dispersed after the spokesmen are apprehended. It is not so easy to break up the secret meetings.'

Caligula set down his goblet—and scowled darkly.

'What kind of people are they who dare to hold secret meetings?'

Quintus deliberated a reply, frowning thoughtfully.

'I have not mentioned this to Your Majesty, because the Emperor is already burdened with cares; but it is believed that there are many followers of this new Galilean cult.'

'Ah—the people who are forbidden to fight. Let them meet! Let them whisper! How many are there?'

'Nobody knows, sire. But we have word that the party is growing. Several houses, where numbers of men were seen to enter nightly, have been watched. In a few cases the patrol has entered, finding no disorder, no arms, and apparently no heated talk. In each instance, no more meetings were held in the house that had been investigated. That probably means they resolved to meet elsewhere. Prince Gaius had been investigating them for months, but without much success.'

'It's a small matter,' mumbled Caligula, drowsily. 'Let them meet and prattle. If they want to think their dead Jew is divine, what of it? Incitatus is divine'—he giggled, drunkenly—'but nobody cares much.'

'But these Christians claim that the Galilean is not dead, sire,' rejoined Quintus. 'According to their belief, he has been seen on many occasions since his crucifixion. They consider him their King.'

'King!' Little Boots suddenly stirred from his torpor. 'We will see to that! Let them believe what else they please about this Jew—but we will have no nonsense about this kingship! Arrest these fools, wherever you find them, and we will break this thing up before it starts!'

'It has started, Your Majesty,' said Quintus, soberly. 'All Palestine is full of it. Recently the party has become strong enough to come out openly in Corinth, Athens, and other Grecian cities.'

'Where are the authorities?' demanded Caligula. 'Are they asleep?'

'No, Your Majesty. The leaders have been imprisoned and some have been put to death; but these people are fanatically brave. They think that if they die for this cause they shall live again.'

'Bah!' shouted Caligula. 'Not many will be found believing in such rubbish! And the few who do believe it will be helpless nobodies!'

Quintus sat silently for a while with his eyes averted.

'Cornelius Capito is anxious about it, sire. He estimates that there are more than four thousand of these Christians in Rome at the present hour.'

'And what is he doing about this treason?' demanded Caligula.

Quintus shook his head.

'It is a strange movement, sire. It has only one weapon; its belief that there is no death. Cornelius Capito is not equipped to crush something that refuses to die when it is killed.'

'You are talking like a fool, Quintus!' mumbled Caligula. 'Command this cowardly old dotard to come here tomorrow, and give an account of himself! And—see you to it that the Greek slave is arrested before many days have passed. Bring him here alive, if possible.' The imperial voice was becoming incoherent. 'Call the Chamberlain. We would retire.'

* * * * * *

If, on his faraway travels, some chance acquaintance had asked Marcellus Gallio whether he knew his way about in Rome, he would have replied that he surely ought to know Rome, seeing he had lived there all his life.

He was now discovering that it was one thing to know Rome from the comfortable altitude of a wealthy young Tribune, son of an influential Senator, and quite another thing to form one's estimates of Rome from the viewpoint of an unemployed, humbly dressed wayfarer with temporary lodging at a drovers' tavern hard by the public markets that crawled up the bank of the busy Tiber to front a cobbled, crowded, littered street, a street that clamored and quarreled and stank—all day and all night.

It had not yet been disclosed to Marcellus why he had felt impelled to return to Rome. He had been here ten days now, jostled by the street crowds, amazed and disgusted by the shameless greed, filth, and downright indecency of the unprivileged thousands who lived no better than the rats that overran the wharf district. The Arpinos had been poor and dirty, too, and ragged and rude; but they were promptly responsive to opportunities for improvement. Surely these underdogs of Rome were not of a different species. Marcellus tried to analyze the problem. Perhaps this general degradation was the result of too much crowding, too little privacy, too much noise. You couldn't be decent if you weren't intelligent; you couldn't be intelligent if you couldn't think—and who could think in all this racket? Add the stench to the confusion of cramped quarters, and who could be self-respecting? Marcellus felt himself deteriorating; hadn't shaved for three days. He had a good excuse. The facilities at Apuleius' tavern were not conducive to keeping oneself fit. Nobody shaved; nobody was clean; nobody cared.

On the day of the Emperor's funeral, Marcellus was in the sweating, highly flavored throng that packed the plaza in front of the Forum Julium as the solemn procession arrived for the ceremonies. He was shocked to see how his father had aged in these recent weeks. Of course he had had much to worry about. There was a haunted expression on the faces of all these eminent men, and no wonder; for the Empire was in a shameful plight indeed! Marcellus winced at the sight of Senator Gallio, who had ever borne himself with such stately dignity, and had now surrendered to despair. It made his heart ache.

Day after day, for another fortnight, he wandered about the streets, pausing now and then to listen to a hot dispute, or ask a friendly question of a neighbor; but usually men turned away when he tried to engage them in conversation. By his tone and manner, he was not their sort, and they distrusted him. And always the memory of his father's melancholy face and feeble step haunted him.

One evening, intolerably depressed, he dispatched a message to Marcipor, stating briefly where he was living, and requesting a private interview at such a time and place as Marcipor might suggest; preferably not at the tavern of Apuleius. Two hours later the messenger returned with a letter directing Marcellus to go out, the next day, along the Via Appia, until he came to the old Jewish cemetery. Marcipor would meet him there about mid-afternoon.

Marcellus remembered the place. There was an interesting story about it. Two centuries ago, when Antiochus had conquered Palestine, life had been made so wretched for the Jews that thousands of them had migrated, and Rome had got more than her share.

Alarmed by the volume of this immigration, laws were passed to restrict the liberties of these refugees. They were banished to the wrong side of the Tiber, limited as to the occupations they might pursue, denied Roman citizenship, and—as the animosity against them increased—ruthlessly persecuted.

Traditionally respectful to their dead, the Jews were greatly distressed when Rome assigned them a burial ground far south of the city where only a shallow deposit of soil covered a massive tufa rock fully a hundred feet deep. Passionate patriots made it a practice to go out there by night and desecrate the graves.

At a prodigious cost of labor, the afflicted Jews proceeded to carve an oblique tunnel into the solid stone. On the lower level, they made long, labyrinthine corridors in the walls of which they dug crypts for their dead, and rooms where hard-pressed fugitives might hide.

As time passed, the persecutions eased. Many wealthy Jews, having contributed generously to the erection of state buildings and monuments, were admitted to citizenship; and by their influence the burdens laid upon their less lucky kindred were lightened. The old burial ground fell into disuse. Few persons visited 'The Catacombs' now except students of antiquities. Marcellus wondered why Marcipor, who was getting to be an old man, had selected this place for their meeting. It was a long walk.

He arrived somewhat earlier than the appointed time, but Marcipor was already there, waiting for him in the cypress grove that extended from the busy highway a full quarter-mile to the abandoned subterranean tombs.

Marcipor, who had been sitting on the ground, scrambled to his feet and hurried forward with outstretched hands, his deep-lined face contorted with emotion. Deeply moved by the old servitor's attitude, Marcellus grasped his hands hungrily. He was not a Tribune now. Time swung backward for both of them. The little boy, who had so often come running to the calm and resourceful Corinthian when there was a cut finger or a broken toy, now put his arms around the old man, and held him close.

'We feared you were dead,' said Marcipor, brokenly. 'The family has mourned for you. Tell me'—he held Marcellus at arm's length and studied his face—'why did you afflict them so? It was not like you to do that, my son. . . . Come—let us sit down. I am very weary.'

'Good Marcipor, I was forced to an unhappy choice of afflictions for my family. If they thought me dead, they would grieve; but they would remember me with affection. Had I come home, sworn to spend my life in the service of a cause which demands the complete breaking away from the manner of life expected of Senator Gallio's son, I should have caused them all a greater sorrow. As it stands, they are bereaved; but not humiliated.'

'And why have you told *me?*' asked Marcipor. 'This is indeed a weighty secret to confide to one who would be loyal to his master.'

'I saw my father on the day of the Emperor's funeral, Marcipor. His handsome face was haggard, his eyes were dulled with despair, his shoulders slumped, the proud, statesmanly bearing was gone. The light was out.

I tried to forget that harrowing glimpse of my father, but it tortured me. That is why I have sought your counsel. Shall I return? Is there anything I can do?'

With bowed head and downcast eyes, Marcipor meditated a reply.

'Of course you will say,' continued Marcellus, 'that I should renounce the work I have undertaken and resume my former place in my father's house. I cannot expect you to understand the obligation that is laid on me, for you have had no opportunity to—'

'No—my son!' broke in Marcipor. 'You could not renounce your new calling; not even if you tried! I am not as ignorant of this matter as you think. Once a man has become convinced that Jesus is the living Son of God, who is here to set up a kingdom of justice and good will for all people, he does not surrender that faith! If—for any reason—he turns away from it, that means he never had it!'

Marcellus leaned forward to listen, with widening eyes.

'Marcipor!' he exclaimed. 'You are a Christian?'

'When you were at home, the last time, Demetrius thought I should tell you of my belief, and my association with the other Christians in Rome—'

'Other Christians?' repeated Marcellus, amazed.

'Yes, my son—and they are in grave danger. I knew that if you were told of a growing Christian party in Rome, you would join it. These men—for the most part obscure—can assemble secretly, in small groups, without attracting much attention. A Tribune could not do that. I thought it more prudent that you keep away from these meetings. Now—in the past few days—the new Emperor has published an edict threatening death to anyone found in an assembly of Christians. What will happen to our cause in Rome remains to be seen. Young Caligula is cruel and headstrong, they say.'

'Young Caligula is insane!' muttered Marcellus.

'It would seem so,' went on Marcipor, calmly, 'but he is bright enough to carry out his design for slaughter. I knew, when you wrote me you were here, that you would presently locate some Christians and associate with them. You should think twice before you take that risk. We who are unimportant can hide. You cannot; not for long. The Emperor would welcome the opportunity to make an example of you!'

'But you would not counsel me to run away!' challenged Marcellus.

'No one who knows you as well as I do, my son, would use those words. But—your life is valuable. While this threat is active, there is little you can do for frightened people in hiding. If you leave the city, until the Emperor's diseased mind turns toward some other cruel pastime, you could return—and be of service. There's no use throwing your life away!'

Marcellus reached out a hand and affectionately patted the old man's knee.

'Marcipor,' he said, gently, 'you have been speaking as my father's trusted servant, concerned for the welfare of his son. For that I am grateful. But this is not the kind of advice that one Christian gives another. Has Demetrius—or anyone—told you of Jesus' last journey to Jerusalem, when his disciples—knowing how dangerous it would be for him to appear there during the Passover—tried to dissuade him from going? They pointed out that his life was precious; that it mustn't be wasted; that he must be saved for service to the people.'

'What did he say?' wondered Marcipor.

'He told them it was poor advice; told them that no man should caution his friend against going into danger for duty's sake; told them that sometimes a man had to lose his life to save it, and that those who tried to save themselves would surely lose themselves. No—you mean it well enough, Marcipor; but I'm remaining in Rome! Can't you realize that our cause might be lost if we who believe in it are frugal of our blood?'

Marcipor slowly nodded his head, and laboriously came to his feet.

'Come, then,' he said. 'Let us go—and join them.'

'Where?' asked Marcellus.

'In the tombs,' said Marcipor, pointing through the trees. 'About thirty men are meeting there to seek counsel about future plans.'

'Are there so many as thirty Christians in Rome?' Marcellus was surprised and pleased.

'My son,' said Marcipor, 'there are nearly four thousand Christians in Rome! These men are their appointed leaders.'

Marcellus stood speechless for a long moment, pondering this almost incredible announcement. At length he found his voice.

'His kingdom is coming, Marcipor! It is gaining strength, faster than I had thought!'

'Patience, my son!' murmured Marcipor, as he led the way toward the tombs. 'It has still a long, hard road to travel.'

The narrow, uneven steps down into the tunnel were dark as night. As they reached the lower level, a feeble glow outlined the entrance to a corridor at the left. Marcipor proceeded into it with the confidence of one who knew his way. A tall man, in a laborer's tunic, stepped forward; and, holding a dim lantern high above his head, peered into Marcellus' face.

'Who is this, Marcipor?' he demanded.

'Tribune Marcellus Gallio. He is one of us, Laeto.'

'And what have we to do with Tribunes?' asked Laeto, gruffly.

'Marcellus has given up much for his faith, Laeto,' said Marcipor, gently. 'He knows more about the Galilean than any of us—save one.'

'Very well,' consented Laeto, reluctantly—'if you vouch for him.'

They proceeded through the long corridor, groping their way, Marcellus wondering at its vast extent. Marcipor lagged and took his arm.

'Laeto views our new cause as a banding together of the poor,' he confided, softly. 'You will find a good deal of that sentiment among the Christians. They can't be blamed much, for they have been long oppressed. But it would be unfortunate if Jesus' kingdom turned out to be a poor man's exclusive haven.'

'Perhaps it would have been better if my identity had remained a secret,' said Marcellus.

'No—it will be good for the Christians in Rome to know that a man with a few coins in his purse can be a worthy follower. We have been hearing too much about the virtues of poverty.'

They turned an abrupt corner to the right and faced another narrower passage that continued on and on, the walls studded with stone slabs bearing names and dates of Jews long dead. A small light flickered, revealing a heavy wooden door at the end of the corridor. Another sentinel moved out of the shadows and confronted them. Marcipor again explained Marcellus. The sentinel pointed with his torch to a small drawing on the lintel.

'Do you know what that sign means?' he inquired.

'It is the Christian's secret symbol, sir,' replied Marcellus.

'Did someone tell you that—or have you seen it before?'

'I have seen it in many places—in Galilee—and Jerusalem.'

'Let me ask you then,' said the sentinel, 'why is the symbol a fish? Is there anything sacred about a fish?'

Marcellus explained respectfully. The sentinel listened with keen attention.

'You may enter,' he said, stepping aside.

It was a large rectangular room with accommodations for many more people than sat in the semicircular rows in the far corner, huddled closely about a huge, bearded man who was talking to them in a deep guttural tone.

They moved quietly forward, in the dim light, Marcipor leading, until the speaker's earnest voice became plainly audible. Marcellus recognized it, and plucked at the good old Corinthian's sleeve.

'Know him?' whispered Marcipor, with a pleased smile.

'Of course!' said Marcellus, excitedly.

It was the Big Fisherman!

Marcellus [illegible] up [illegible] his faith [illegible]
He knew nothing about the Cause, [illegible]
[illegible] he [illegible] [illegible]
They proceeded through the long, [illegible]
[illegible] this [illegible]. [illegible]
[illegible] now comes [illegible]
[illegible] safety. [illegible] you will find [illegible] of [illegible]
[illegible] the [illegible]
But [illegible] the [illegible] Kingdom [illegible]
[illegible]

[illegible] it would have been [illegible]
[illegible]

[illegible] the [illegible]
[illegible] in his [illegible]
[illegible] about the virtues of poverty.
[illegible]
[illegible]
[illegible]
[illegible]
[illegible]
[illegible]
[illegible]

[illegible]
[illegible] the Christ [illegible]
[illegible]
[illegible]
[illegible]
[illegible]
[illegible]

[illegible]
[illegible]
[illegible]
[illegible]

[illegible]
[illegible]
[illegible]
[illegible] Marcellus [illegible]
[illegible]
[illegible]

Chapter XXIV

IT WAS early morning but already promising to be another hot day. The swarthy overseer of the vineyard, temporarily at ease, lounged against the gatepost and yawningly watched the laborers—four score or more of men, women, and grown-up children—as they cut the huge purple clusters; carefully, for this fruit was going to a select market.

Some distance down the highway a little wisp of dust was riding from the lazy feet of a shaggy gray donkey attached to a decrepit high-wheeled cart filled with hay. A slim youth walked ahead, impatiently tugging at a long lead-strap. At intervals the donkey stopped and the tall boy in the knitted cap would brace his feet and pull with all his weight, his manner suggesting complete exasperation.

Vobiscus, the overseer, watched and grinned. The young fellow didn't know much about donkeys or he would walk alongside with a stout thornbush in hand. Who was he? Vobiscus was acquainted with all the donkeys, carts, and farmer-boys likely to be plodding along the road in the vicinity of Arpino, but this forlorn outfit lacked identification. He studied it with increasing interest as it crept forward. Nobody would be hauling hay to market in such a cart, and this youngster hadn't come from a hayfield. He wore a long, coarse tunic and the sort of leggings that quarrymen used for protection against flying chips of stone. The bulging old cap might have belonged to a boatman. It was much too heavy for this weather. Vobiscus wondered why he didn't take it off.

Directly in front of the open gate, the donkey took root again, and the slim youth—without a glance at Vobiscus, who was sauntering out into the road—jerked so furiously at the lead-strap that the old bridle broke. Finding himself at liberty, the donkey ambled off to the roadside and began nibbling at the grass, while the angry boy trailed along, pausing to pick up the dragging bridle which he examined with distaste. Then he threw it down and scrubbed his dusty hands up and down on the skirt of his ill-fitting tunic. They were delicate hands, with long, tapering fingers. He glanced about now, gave the overseer a brief and not very cordial inspection, and walked with short, clipped steps to the donkey's head.

Vobiscus, thoughtfully stroking his jaw, made a thorough, item by item, head to foot appraisal of the unhappy young stranger. Then his cheek began to bulge with a surmising tongue and an informed smile wrinkled his face. He picked up the brittle old harness and unbuckled the broken straps.

'I thought you were a boy,' he said, kindly. 'I'll fix the bridle for you, daughter. Go over there and sit down in the shade—and help yourself to some grapes from that basket. You look worn out.'

The tall girl gave him a long, cool stare. Then her lips parted in a smile that made Vobiscus' heart skip a beat. She rubbed her forehead wearily, and tugged off the outlandish old woolen cap, releasing a cascade of blue-black hair that came tumbling down over her shoulders. Vobiscus laughed discreetly, appreciatively. The girl laughed, too, a tired little whimpering laugh that was almost crying.

'You are kind,' she murmured. 'I will do that. I am so warm—and thirsty.'

The intolerable donkey had now jammed a wheel against the stone fence and was straining to free himself. Vobiscus went around to the tail of the cart for an armful of hay to entertain him until the bridle was put in order.

'Oh, no, please!' called the girl, sharply. 'He mustn't have any of the hay. It—it isn't good for him!' Her eyes were frightened.

Vobiscus turned his head toward her and scowled.

'What have you in this cart, young woman?' he demanded, roughly, thrusting his arm deep into the hay.

'Please!—it's my brother! He is ill! Don't disturb him!'

'Your brother is ill; eh?' scoffed Vobiscus. 'So—you load him into a cart and cover him up with hay! A likely tale!' He began tossing the hay out onto the road. 'Ah—so you're the sick brother!'

The girl came swiftly to Vobiscus' side and laid her hand on his arm as Demetrius sat up, frowning darkly.

'We are in trouble,' she confided. 'We came here hoping to find a man named Marcellus Gallio, knowing he would aid us.'

'Marcellus has been gone for a week.' The scowl on Vobiscus' face relaxed a little. 'Are you friends of his?'

They both nodded. Vobiscus looked from one to the other, suspiciously.

'You are a slave, fellow!' he said, pointing at Demetrius' ear. A sudden illumination widened his eyes. 'Ah-ha!' he exclaimed. 'I have it! You're wanted! Both of you! Only yesterday legionaries from Capri were at the villa searching for the daughter of Gallus and a Greek slave who were thought to be on the way to Rome.'

'You are right, sir,' confessed Demetrius. 'This young woman is the daughter of Legate Gallus, and engaged to marry Marcellus Gallio, who is my master. My name is Demetrius.' Vobiscus started.

'That sounds like the name,' he mumbled to himself. 'Tell me—did Marcellus send you a message, some weeks ago?'

'Yes, sir—a small melon, in a box.'

'Any writing?'

'A picture—of a fish.'

Demetrius gazed anxiously up and down the road and stepped out of the cart. Deep in the vineyard a lumbering load of fruit was slowly moving toward the gate.

'Before this fellow sees you,' cautioned Vobiscus, 'busy yourself with that donkey, and keep out of sight. You had better stay here for the present.' He turned to Diana. 'You will be safe, I think, to go up to the villa. Don't hurry. Inquire for Antonia, the wife of Appius Kaeso. Tell her who you are. You two must not be seen together. Everybody in Arpino knows about the search for you.'

'Perhaps they will be afraid to give me shelter,' said Diana.

'Well—they will tell you—if they are,' replied Vobiscus. 'You can't stay here! That's sure!'

* * * * * *

The tall Macedonian by the villa gate gave her a disapproving look.

'And why do you want to see the wife of Kaeso?' he demanded, sharply. 'Perhaps you had better talk to Appius Kaeso, young fellow.'

'No—his wife,' insisted Diana. 'But I am not a beggar,' she added.

The Macedonian cocked his head thoughtfully and grinned.

'Come with me,' he said, in the soft voice of a conspirator. Leading the way to the garden, and sighting his mistress, he signed to the newcomer to proceed, and turned back toward the gate.

Antonia, girlishly pretty in gay colors and a broad-brimmed reed hat, was supervising a slave as he wielded a pruning-knife in the rose arbor. Hearing footsteps, she glanced about and studied the approaching stranger.

'You may go!' she said to the slave. He turned to stare at the visitor. 'At once!' commanded Antonia.

'Please forgive my intrusion,' began Diana—'and my dreadful appearance. It has been necessary for me to look like a boy.'

Antonia showed a row of pretty teeth.

'Well—maybe it has been necessary,' she laughed—'but you don't look like a boy.'

'I've tried to,' insisted Diana. 'What is it that gives me away?'

'Everything,' murmured Antonia. She drifted to the stone lectus beside the path. 'Come—sit down—and tell me what this is all about. They are hunting for you: is that not so?'

Briefly but clearly, the words tumbling over one another, Diana poured out her story with a feeling of confidence that she would not be betrayed.

'I mustn't get you into trouble,' she went on—'but—oh—if I might bathe—if you would hide me away until I had a night's sleep—I could go on.' Diana's weary eyes were swimming.

'We can take some chances for anyone who loves Marcellus,' said Antonia. 'Come—let us go into the house.' She led the way to the atrium where they encountered Kaeso emerging from his library. He stopped and blinked a few times, incredulously. Antonia said, 'Appius, this is the daughter of Legate Gallus whom the soldiers were inquiring about. . . . Diana, this is my husband.'

'I shall go away, sir, if you wish.' Diana's voice was plaintive.

'What have you done, that they want to arrest you?' inquired Kaeso, facing her soberly.

'She ran away from Capri,' volunteered Antonia, 'because she was afraid of the boy Emperor. Now he is determined to find her.'

'Ugh!' growled Kaeso. 'Little Boots! *Little skunk!*'

'Hush!' warned Antonia. 'You'll have us all in prison yet! Now—what shall we do with Diana? Appius, she is engaged to marry Marcellus!'

Kaeso exclaimed joyfully and grasped her hands.

'You're going to stay here with us,' he declared. 'Whoever takes you away will have to fight! Are you alone? The legionaries said they were looking also for a Greek slave who had escaped with you.'

'He is down at the vineyard with Vobiscus,' said Antonia. 'And you'd better do something about it, Appius.'

'How about the servants? How much do they know?'

'Let us not try to make a secret of it,' suggested Antonia. 'We will tell them the truth. When they know that Diana is to marry Marcellus—and that the Greek is his slave—there is no one in Arpino who would—'

'Don't be too sure of that!' said Kaeso. 'There's a reward posted, you know.' He pointed toward the peristyle. 'That Macedonian out there could have quite a merry fling with a thousand sesterces. I shall tell him—and all of them—that if anyone gives out information he will be flogged! Or worse!'

'Do as you think best, dear,' consented Antonia, gently. 'But I believe that trusting them will be safer than threatening them. I think that would be Marcellus' advice if he were here.'

'Marcellus is always giving people credit for being bigger than they are,' remembered Kaeso. He gave Diana an inquiring smile. 'Are you one of these Christians, too?'

'I'm afraid not,' sighed Diana. 'It's too hard for me to understand. . . . Did he'—she glanced toward Antonia—'did he talk much about it while he was here?'

'Turned the village upside-down with it!' chuckled Kaeso. 'Antonia will tell you. She has gone Christian, too!'

'Marcellus was good for us all,' murmured Antonia. She gave Appius a sidelong smile, and added, 'including the master of Arpino.'

* * * * * *

Young Antony had been so absorbed in his modeling that he had remained in his studio all day, unaware that they were housing a fugitive. Breezing into the dining-room, that evening, spluttering apologies for his tardiness, he stopped suddenly just inside the doorway and looked into the smiling eyes of the most beautiful creature he had ever seen, wearing the most beautiful pink silk stola he had ever seen, failing to recognize it as his mother's.

On three different occasions, Anthony had gone with his parents to Rome for a few days' attendance at great national festivals. There had been fleeting glimpses of lovely patrician girls in their gay litters and— at a distance—in their boxes at the circus; but never before had he been this close to a young woman of Diana's social caste. He faced her now with such spontaneous and unreserved admiration that Kaeso, glancing up over his shoulder, chuckled softly.

'Our son, Antony,' said his mother, tenderly. 'Our guest is Diana, dear, the daughter of Legate Gallus.'

'Oh!' Antony swallowed hard. 'They are after you!' He eased into his seat across from her, still gazing intently into her face. 'How did you get here?'

'Diana hoped to find Marcellus,' explained Antonia.

'Do you know Marcellus?' asked Antony, happily.

'She is his girl,' announced the elder Kaeso, adding, in the little silence that followed, 'And he is a lucky fellow!'

'Y-e-s,' agreed Antony, so fervently that his parents laughed.

Diana smiled appreciatively into Antony's enraptured eyes, but refused to be merry over his honest adoration. It was no joke.

'I am glad you all liked Marcellus so well,' she said, softly. 'He must have had a good time here. You are a sculptor; aren't you? Your mother told me.' And when Antony had hitched about, protesting that he hadn't done anything very important, she said, 'Perhaps you will let me see.' Her voice was unusually deep-toned for a girl, he thought. Girls were always screaming what they had to say. Diana's throaty voice made you feel you had known her a long time. Antony nodded, with a defensive smile and a little shrug that hoped she wouldn't be expecting to see something really good.

'Marcellus taught him about all he knows,' Antonia remarked, gratefully, as if Diana should be thanked too for this favor.

'He should have been a sculptor,' said Diana, 'instead of a soldier.'

'Right!' declared Antony. 'He detests fighting!'

'But not because he doesn't know how to fight,' Diana hastened to say. 'Marcellus is known to be one of the most expert swordsmen in Rome.'

'Indeed!' exclaimed Kaeso. 'I wouldn't have thought he had any interest in dangerous sports. He never discussed such things with us.'

'Once I asked him if he had ever killed anybody,' put in Antony, 'and it made him awfully unhappy. He said he didn't want to talk about it.'

Diana's face had suddenly lost its animation, and Antony knew he had blundered upon a painful subject. His embarrassment increased when his father said to her, 'Perhaps you know.'

Without raising her eyes, Diana nodded and gave a little sigh.

'Do you like horses?' asked Kaeso, sensing the need of a new topic.

'Yes, sir,' replied Diana, obviously preoccupied. Glancing from one to another, she went on: 'Perhaps we should not leave it—just that way. It wouldn't be quite fair to Marcellus. A couple of years ago he was ordered to put a man to death—and it turned out that the man was innocent of any crime, and had been held in high esteem by many people. He has grieved over it.'

'He would!' sympathized Antonia. 'There never was a more gentle or generous person; always trying to do things for other people.'

Appius Kaeso, eager to lift Diana's depression, seemed anxious to talk about Marcellus' popularity in Arpino. Soon he was pleased to observe that she was listening attentively, her eyes misty as he elaborated on the many kindnesses Marcellus had done, even giving him full credit for the new swimming-pool.

'He was a crafty fellow,' chuckled Kaeso. 'He would trap you into doing things like that, and then pretend it was your own idea. Of course—that was to make you feel good, so you would want to do something else for the people—on your own hook.'

Antony, amazed by his father's admissions, covertly sought the surprised eyes of his pretty mother, and gave her a slow wink that tightened her lips in a warning not to risk a comment.

'Marcellus certainly was an unusual fellow,' continued Kaeso. 'It was easy to see that he had had every advantage and had lived well, but he used to go down into the melon fields and work alongside those people as if they were his own sort: and how they loved it! Every evening, out here on the green, they would gather about him and he would tell them stories about this man Jesus—from up in the Jews' country somewhere—who went about performing all manner of strange miracles. But he must have told you about this man, Diana.'

'Yes,' she nodded, soberly. 'He told me.'

'They put him to death,' said Antonia.

'And Marcellus insists he came to life again,' said Kaeso, 'though I'm sure there was some mistake about that.'

Antony, who had dropped out of the conversation, and apparently wasn't hearing a word of it—to judge from his wide-eyed, vacant stare—had attracted his mother's attention. Kaeso and Diana instinctively followed her perplexed eyes.

'What are you thinking about, boy?' Kaeso wanted his question to sound playful.

Ignoring his father's inquiry, Antony turned to Diana.

'Do you know who crucified that Galilean?' he asked, earnestly.

'Yes,' admitted Diana.

'Do I know?'

Diana nodded, and Antony brought his first down hard on the table.

'Now it all makes sense!' he declared. 'Marcellus killed this man who had spent his life doing kind things for needy people—and the only way he can square up for it is to spend *his* life that way!' Antony's voice was unsteady. 'He can't help himself! He has to make things right with this Jesus!'

Appius and Antonia speechlessly regarded their son with a new interest.

'Yes—but that isn't quite all, Antony,' said Diana. 'Marcellus thinks this man is in the world to remain forever; believes there is to be a new government ruled by men of good will; no more fighting; no more stealing—'

'That's a noble thought, Diana,' interposed Kaeso. 'Who doesn't long for peace? Who wouldn't be glad to see good men rule? Nothing new about that wish. Indeed—any kind of government would be better than ours! But it's absurd to hope for such a thing, and a man as bright as Marcellus ought to know it! He is throwing his life away!'

'Maybe not!' protested Antony. 'Maybe this Jesus didn't throw his life away! If we're ever to have a better world—well—it has to begin *sometime—somewhere*—hasn't it? Maybe it has begun now! What do you think, Diana?'

'I—don't—know, Antony.' Diana put both hands over her eyes and shook her head. 'All I know is—I wish it hadn't happened.'

* * * * * *

When three weeks had passed uneventfully, Diana began to wonder whether it might not now be safe for her to proceed to Rome. Perhaps the young Emperor had forgotten his grievance and had given up searching for her. Kaeso was not so optimistic.

'Little Boots has been much occupied,' he said. 'What with the funeral of old Tiberius, his own coronation, and the festal week, he hasn't had much time to think about anything else. Moreover, his legionaries have all been on duty in the processions and at the games. But he will not forget you. Better wait a little while longer.'

Antonia had slipped an arm around Diana affectionately.

'You can see that Appius wants to keep you here, dear, as long as possible—and so do Antony and I.'

Diana knew that. Their hospitality had been boundless. She had come to love Antonia, and young Antony's attitude toward her had been but little short of worship.

'You have all been so kind,' she said. 'But my mother will be dreadfully worried. Naturally they would go first to her seeking information about me. All she knows is that I escaped from Capri in a little boat. I can't even send her a message, for the guards would trace it back to Arpino.'

Sometimes in the evening Demetrius, who was working in the vineyard and lodging with Vobiscus, would come to inquire. Diana would tell him to be patient, but she knew he was consumed with restlessness and anxious to rejoin Marcellus.

One night at dinner, Kaeso had seemed so preoccupied that Diana felt something had happened. When they returned to the atrium, Vobiscus was found waiting with a note for her. It had been hastily written—in Greek. Demetrius was just leaving for Rome, hoping to find his master.

'My presence here only adds to your danger,' he wrote. 'Kaeso approves my going. He has been most generous. Follow his advice. Do not try to communicate with your home. I shall see your mother if possible.'

Vobiscus had tarried near the open doorway to the peristyle, and Diana went to him. Had Demetrius left on foot—or was he driving the donkey?

'He rode one of the master's fast horses,' said Vobiscus, 'and wore an outfit of the master's clothing.'

Diana rejoined the family seated about the fountain. Their voices were low. She felt they had been discussing her problem.

'You were very kind to Demetrius,' she said, softly. 'I hope you know how deeply I appreciate what you have done for him—and for me—and Marcellus.'

Kaeso flipped a negligent gesture, but his eyes were troubled.

'The Greek was not safe here,' he said, soberly. 'Indeed, nobody is any longer safe anywhere! Two of our carters returned this afternoon from Rome. The city is in disorder. Drunken mobs of vandals have been looting the shops and assaulting respectable citizens. The Emperor pretends to believe that the Christians have a hand in it, and they are being thrown into prison and whipped.'

The color left Diana's cheeks.

'I wonder how Marcellus is faring,' she said. 'He would do so little to protect himself.'

'Our men say that the search for your Greek has become active again,' said Kaeso—'and for you, too, Diana. It appears that Demetrius is wanted on an old charge of having assaulted a Tribune. He is to be taken, dead or alive. As for you, the Emperor pretends to be concerned about your safety. The rumor is that the Greek slave made off with you, and Caligula wants you to be found.'

'Poor Demetrius!' murmured Diana. 'What chance will he have, with so many looking for him?'

'Well—he knows his life is worth nothing if they catch him,' said Kaeso, grimly. 'He will make them earn their reward: you may be sure of that!'

'Was he armed?' wondered Diana.

'Nothing but a dagger,' said Kaeso.

'Appius is posting sentries at elevated points on our two highways,' said Antonia. 'The sight of legionaries approaching will be their signal to speed back here and report.'

'When they were here before,' said Kaeso, 'they searched the villa thoroughly, but never so much as turned their heads to inquire among the laborers. They would not expect to find the daughter of Legate Gallus working in a vineyard.'

'Why—that is just the place for me, then!' exclaimed Diana.

Antonia and Appius exchanged glances.

'Appius hesitated to suggest it,' said Antonia.

'It might be fun,' said Diana.

'Early in the morning, then,' said Kaeso, relieved. 'Antonia will find you suitable clothing. I wish there were some other way to hide you, Diana—but you are not safe here in the villa. It is possible that if they found you they might treat you with every consideration; but it's the Emperor's doings—and everything he does is evil!'

* * * * * *

About two hours after midnight, old Lentius—dead asleep on his pallet of straw in the corner of a vacant box-stall—came suddenly awake and rose up on both elbows to listen. Bambo, who always slept beside him, was listening sharply, too—and growling ominously.

From outside in the stable-yard came the sound of sandals and hoofs. Someone was leading a horse. Lentius took down his dim lantern from its peg and unfastened the door. Bambo scurried out with savage threats, but in an instant was barking joyfully. Lentius trudged after him, holding the lantern high.

'No, no—Bambo!' came a weary voice. 'Make him shut up, Lentius. He'll rouse the house.'

'Demetrius!' The bent old man peered up into a haggard face.

'Rub this horse down, Lentius. I've abused him. Careful about the water. He's very hot.' Demetrius patted the sagging head sympathetically.

'Bring him in here.' Lentius led the way into his bedchamber. 'They've been hunting you!' he said, in a husky whisper, as he closed the door. 'See here! This horse has been hurt! There's blood all over his shoulder and down his leg!'

'That's mine,' mumbled Demetrius, stripping his shoulder bare. 'I was being pursued by three cavalrymen—out on the Via Appia—about five miles. I outdistanced two of them, but one overtook me, and nicked me with his sword while I was dragging him out of his saddle. Find me some water, Lentius, and a bandage.'

The old slave examined the deep cut and drew a hissing breath through his lips.

'That's a bad one!' he muttered. 'You've lost a lot of blood. Your tunic is soaked. Look at your sandal! You'd better lie down over there!'

'I believe I will,' said Demetrius, weakly, tumbling down on the pallet. Lentius was hovering over him with a basin of water and a sponge. Bambo sniffed inquisitively and turned away to lick the horse's foreleg. 'Lentius—has Tribune Marcellus been here lately?'

Lentius stopped laving the wound—and stared.

'The Tribune! Hadn't you heard? He's been dead—these three months or more! Drowned himself in the sea—poor young master!'

'Lentius, you were fond of the young master, and he liked you. 'I'm going to trust you with a secret. Now—you're not to repeat this to anybody! Understand? The Tribune is alive—here in Rome.'

'No!' exulted the old man. 'Why doesn't he come home?'

'He will—some day. Lentius—I wonder if you could wake up Marcipor without tearing the house down.'

'It would be easier to awaken Decimus. He is on the first floor.'

'I don't want Decimus. Here—let me up. I'll go myself.' Demetrius made an effort to rise, but slumped down again. 'I'm weaker than I thought,' he admitted. 'See if you can get Marcipor. Throw something into his room, and when he comes to the window tell him you want him. Don't speak my name. And ask him to bring some bandages. This isn't going to do any good. Give that horse another drink of water now. Go away—Bambo!'

Marcipor arrived presently, much excited and out of breath, trailed by old Lentius.

'You're badly hurt, my son!' he murmured. 'We must send for the physician.'

'No, Marcipor,' objected Demetrius. 'I'd rather take my chances with this sword-wound than risk having my head cut off. . . . Lentius, if you have another vacant stall, take this friendly horse away and clean him up. And you might take the dog, too. Marcipor will look after me.'

Reluctantly, old Lentius led out the tired horse, Bambo following dutifully. Marcipor fastened the door and knelt down in the straw close to Demetrius. He began bandaging the cut.

'You're in danger!' he said, in a trembling voice.

'Not for the moment. Tell me, Marcipor—what's the news? Have you seen anything of Marcellus?'

'He is in the Catacombs.'

'Weird place to hide!'

'Not so bad as you'd think. The Christians have been stocking it with provisions for months. More than a hundred men down there now; the ones who have been identified and are being hunted.'

'They'll be caught like hares in a trap—when the patrols discover where they are.'

'No—it won't be so easy as that,' said Marcipor. 'There are miles of confusing tunnels in that old hideout. The legionaries will not be anxious to go down single-file into that dark hole. They know the old stories about searching parties who went into the Catacombs to hunt fugitive Jews—and never found their way out. . . . How does it feel, Demetrius? Is that too tight?'

There was no answer. Marcipor laid his ear against Demetrius' bared chest, listened, shook him gently, called him in a frightened voice, splashed water in his face; but without response. For an instant he stood irresolute, desperate; then ran panting toward the house, wondering whom he should call for help. Gallio, in his nightclothes, was descending the stairs as Marcipor rushed through the atrium.

'What is the commotion about, Marcipor?' he demanded.

'It's Demetrius, sir!' cried Marcipor. 'He is wounded—dying—out here in the stable!'

'Have you sent for the physician?' asked Gallio, leading the way with long strides.

'No, sir—he did not want a physician. He is in hiding.'

'Put one of the servants on a horse—instantly—and summon Sarpedon. And find help to carry Demetrius into the house. He shall not die in a stable—like a dog!'

Lentius was holding up the lantern for him as Gallio hurried into the stall. 'Demetrius!' he called. 'Demetrius!'

The sunken eyes slowly opened and Demetrius drew a painful sigh.

'At—your—service, sir.' His white lips moved clumsily.

'Attention!' barked Gallio, surveying the wide-eyed group that had crowded about the door. 'Take him up carefully and bring him to the house. Put him in Marcellus' room, Marcipor. Get him out of these soiled garments and wrap him in heated blankets.'

There was a little excitement in the stable-yard as one of the younger slaves made off at a gallop for Sarpedon. A half-dozen grooms and gardeners gathered about the straw pallet and raised it gently.

'You should have called me at once, Marcipor!' said Gallio, sternly, as they followed toward the house. 'Am I then known among you to be so heartless I must not be told when a loyal servant is sick unto death?'

'It was difficult to know what to do,' stammered Marcipor. 'He is being hunted down. He would not have come here, sir, but he wanted to inquire about his master.'

'Meaning me?' Gallio halted abruptly in Marcipor's path.

'Meaning Marcellus, sir.'

'But—had he not heard?'

'He thinks Marcellus is still alive, sir.' Marcipor's voice was weak. 'Demetrius believes that his master is here—in Rome.' They moved past the slaves, shuffling along with their burden, and mounted the steps.

'You told him the truth?' asked Gallio, dejectedly.

'That is the truth, sir,' confessed Marcipor. He put out a hand to steady Gallio, whose face was working convulsively.

'Why have I not been told this?' he demanded, hoarsely.

The Trial

'Your Majesty,' she said, calmly, 'I, too, am a Christian. Marcellus is my husband. May I go with him?'

From page 507 of text

DEAN
CORNWELL

'Marcellus is a Christian, sir. They are being closely watched. He did not want to endanger the family by coming home.'

'Where is he, Marcipor?' Gallio was climbing the stairs, slowly, a very old man clutching at the balustrade.

'In the Catacombs, sir,' whispered Marcipor.

'What? My son? Down in those old caves with a rabble of brawlers and looters?'

'Not rabble, sir!' disputed Marcipor, recklessly. 'Not brawlers! Not looters! They are honest men of peace—hiding from a cruel idiot who calls himself an Emperor!'

'Quiet, Marcipor!' commanded Gallio, in a husky whisper, as they passed the apartment of Lucia—at home for a few days while Tullus was on special duty. 'How can we get word to my son?'

'It will jeopardize the household, sir, if Marcellus is trailed here.'

'Never mind that! Send for him!'

The slaves had deposited Demetrius on his bed now and were filing out of the room.

'Hold your tongues—about this!' warned Marcipor. He was closing the door on them when Tertia appeared, much frightened.

'What has happened, Marcipor?' She glanced into the room, gave a smothered cry, and dashed through the doorway, throwing herself down on her knees beside the bed. 'Oh—what have they done to you?' she moaned. 'Demetrius!'

Marcipor laid his hand on her shoulder.

'Come,' he said, gently. 'You must help. Go and find more blankets—and heat them.'

'I cannot send for Marcellus, sir.' Marcipor was tugging off his friend's blood-soaked tunic. 'There is no one in this house—except myself—who would be admitted to the Catacombs.'

'And why should they admit *you*?' challenged Gallio sharply. 'You are not one of them; are you?'

Marcipor nodded gravely and busied himself unstrapping Demetrius' sandals.

'Then—saddle a couple of horses—and go!' commanded Gallio. 'Here!—let me do that!' He turned back his sleeves and attacked the stiffened sandal-straps.

Presently Tertia returned with additional blankets, followed by Lucia with a cup of mulled wine. Gallio took the spoon from her hand and poured a few drops of the hot stimulant between Demetrius' parted lips. He swallowed unconsciously. Gallio raised him up a little and put the cup to his mouth, but he did not respond to it. Tertia was sobbing. Lucia gave her a gentle push and pointed to the door.

'Your brother is alive!' said Gallio, when they were alone.

Lucia started, put both hands to her face, and opened her mouth in amazement—but no words came. She clutched at her father's sleeve.

'Marcipor has gone for him,' murmured Gallio, continuing to administer the hot wine with the spoon. 'I hope he gets here—in time.'

'Marcellus—alive!' whispered Lucia, incredulously. 'Where is he?'

Gallio frowned darkly.

'In the Catacombs!' he muttered.

'Oh—but he can't!' exclaimed Lucia. 'He mustn't! Those people are all to be killed! Father!' she moaned. 'That's where Tullus is! He has been ordered to raid the Catacombs!'

Gallio passed his hand over his forehead as to rub away the stunning blow. Tertia pushed the door open to admit Sarpedon, who walked to the bed without speaking, and pushed up Demetrius' eyelids with a practiced thumb. He pressed the back of his hand against the feeble beating in the throat, shook his head, laid his palm against his patient's heart.

'Hot water,' he ordered. 'Fomentations. It may be useless—but—we can try.'

* * * * * *

No explanations were needed to account for Diana's employment in the vineyard. Everybody in Arpino knew her story; had known it and discussed it for nearly three weeks. The villa had not tried to make a secret of her presence there; and the villagers, pleased at being trusted, had felt a partnership in her protection.

Kaeso was proud of his town. It was no small thing, he thought, for all Arpino to hold its tongue in the face of the reward offered for information leading to Diana's discovery. There were, however, a couple of good reasons for this unanimous fidelity.

In the first place, a reward promised by the Emperor was a doubtful claim, even if you had earned it honorably. When had the officials ever kept their promises to the people? In the opinion of Arpino, the fewer dealings you had with the Government, the better you were off. It was crammed with deceit and subterfuge, all the way from the Emperor and the other great ones on down to the lazy drunkard who rode over from Alatri once a year to collect the poll-tax. The Arpinos hadn't a scrap of respect for the Government, either local or national, believing it to be operated by fools and rascals. Even if you were mean enough to disclose the whereabouts of Marcellus' girl, you could be sure that whoever got the reward it wouldn't be you. So reasoned the younger men, lounging of an evening on the green, after arguing idly for an hour on what one might do with a thousand sesterces.

But—according to Antonia—there was a better reason than that why Arpino had kept its secret. Marcellus was gratefully remembered for the many benefits he had contrived. He was already in a fair way to become a legendary character. They had never known anyone like him. It was generally believed—for Arpino was amenable to superstitions—that Marcellus was under the special protectorate of this new Galilean god who, albeit devoted to peace and good will, had been known to enter people's houses without knocking; and you didn't care to risk having him appear at your bedside, some dark night, to shake you awake, and inquire why you had sold his friend Marcellus' promised bride to Caligula.

Early in the morning of Diana's first day in the vineyard, Vobiscus halted a few of the older men and women as they entered, informing them that she would presently arrive for work—and why. They were to spread the word among the others that the daughter of Legate Gallus was to be treated as they treated one another. She was not to be favored or queried or stared at; nor was she to be shunned. If the legionaries should appear in the vineyard, everyone was to attend to his own business and make no effort to protect Diana, which might only draw attention to her.

When Metella came in, Vobiscus detained her at the gate, explaining that she was to wait until Diana arrived. Then she was to conduct her to a section of the vineyard farthest from the highway, and show her what to do.

'She needn't really work, you know,' grinned Vobiscus, 'but she ought to know how, in case—'

'I don't see why you picked on me,' complained Metella. 'Will I be expected to carry her basket, so she won't soil her lily-white hands?'

'She will not impose on you,' said Vobiscus. 'I should think you would like to get acquainted with someone of her sort. You liked Marcellus; didn't you?'

'Get acquainted; eh?' sniffed Metella. 'I can just see her getting acquainted with anybody like me!'

'Don't be so touchy!' said Vobiscus. 'Here she comes now. Take her with you. Don't be embarrassed. Treat her as if she was—a nobody.'

'A nobody—like me; eh?' commented Metella, bitterly.

'Here I am, Vobiscus,' announced Diana. 'Tell me where I am to go, please.'

'Metella will look after you.' Vobiscus pointed his thumb at the girl, who stood by, scowling. She handed Diana a basket and stiffly led the way, Diana quickly coming abreast of her.

'I hope I'm not going to be a nuisance, Metella. Maybe—if you show me how you do it—'

'You won't need any showing,' said Metella, crisply, staring straight ahead as they passed between rows of curious eyes. 'You'll be just pretending to work.'

'Oh—I shall want to do better than that,' protested Diana, in the low voice that made everything she said sound like a secret.

'It will spoil your hands,' said Metella, sourly—after a long delay.

'Come, now!' coaxed Diana. 'If you'll tell me what I'm doing or saying that makes me seem a snob, I'll try to stop it.'

Metella drew a slow, reluctant smile that lighted her face a little. Then the scowl returned, as she plodded along doggedly.

'You had decided you weren't going to like me,' said Diana, 'and I don't think that's fair. That isn't the way one girl should treat another.'

'But we aren't just two girls together,' objected Metella. 'You're somebody—and I'm nobody.'

'That's partly true,' agreed Diana, soberly. 'I *am* somebody—and I thought you were, too. You certainly don't look like a nobody, but you ought to know.'

Metella gave her a quick glance out of the tail of her eye, shrugged and grinned.

'You're funny,' she said, half to herself.

'I don't feel very funny,' confided Diana. 'I'm frightened, and I want to go home to my mother.'

Metella's steps slowed, and she regarded Diana with an almost sympathetic interest.

'They will not look for you in the vineyard,' she said. 'But they might find you in the night, at the villa.'

'I have thought of that,' said Diana, 'but there's no place else for me to sleep.'

Metella mumbled, 'That's so,' and put down her basket. She handed Diana a pair of short, heavy shears. 'All you have to do,' she demonstrated, 'is to clip off the bunch close to the branch, and be careful not to bruise it.' For some time they worked side by side in silence.

'Have you any room to spare in your house, Metella?' asked Diana.

'I'm sorry,' said Metella. 'It's only a little house, with two small bedrooms. One for my father and mother.' There was a long pause. 'You wouldn't want to share my kennel.'

'Why not?' said Diana. 'Would you let me?'

'It would make me very happy,' said Metella, wistfully.

'I would pay you, of course.'

'Please!' murmured Metella. 'Don't spoil it.'

Diana laid her hand gently on the girl's thin shoulder, and looked squarely into her face.

'You told me you were a nobody,' she murmured. 'Aren't you ashamed?'

Metella gave an embarrassed little chuckle and rubbed the corner of her eye with a tanned finger.

'You're funny, Diana,' she whispered.

* * * * * *

Marcipor rode swiftly, for his errand was urgent. The night air was chilly. The horses were lively, especially the Senator's black gelding, capering alongside. Old Marcipor, who in recent years was not often in the saddle, wished he had chosen to ride Gallio's mount. He could have controlled him better.

Crossing the river on the imposing stone bridge that Julius had built to serve the Via Appia, Marcipor left the celebrated highway and turned off to the right on a rutted road that angled southerly toward the extensive tufa quarries.

It was quite too hazardous an adventure, he felt, to approach the Catacombs by the usual entrance. If the tunnel in the cypress grove were being watched, even from a distance, a man with two horses in charge would most certainly be challenged.

He had never used the secret entrance when alone, and was far from sure that he would be able to find it, for it was skillfully concealed in one of the long-abandoned quarries. He knew he would recognize the quarry, when he came to it, for it was the next one beyond an old toolhouse beside the road. Arriving there, he tied the horses and made his way slowly down the precipitous grade to the floor of the quarry. Feeling his way carefully along the wall in the feeble light of a quarter-moon, the old man came upon a shallow pool—and remembered having waded through it. Beyond the pool there was a cleft in the jutting rock. He entered the narrow aperture and was moving cautiously into its deeper darkness when a gruff voice halted him. Marcipor gave his name, and the sentry—whom he recognized—told him to proceed.

'I came for Marcellus Gallio,' he said. 'His Greek slave, also one of us, lies dying of wounds. It is a hard trip for an old man, Thrason. Will you go and find Marcellus, giving him this message?'

'If you will stand guard, Marcipor.'

It seemed a long time, waiting in the stifling darkness, hearing no sound but the dull thump of his own aging heart. He strained to listen for the scrape of sandals on the rough tufa. At length he saw the frail glow of a taper, far down the slanting tunnel. As it approached, Marcipor saw that two men were following Thrason; Marcellus first, and—the Big Fisherman!

There was a brief, low-voiced colloquy. It was agreed that Marcellus and Peter were to take the horses. Marcipor would spend the night in the Catacombs.

'You told my father I was out here?' asked Marcellus.

'Yes—but he is so rejoiced to know you are alive, sir, that he was not disturbed by your being with the Christians. You may be sure he will keep your secret. Go now, sir. Demetrius had not long to live!'

* * * * * *

Lentius led the hot horses away. Lucia, waiting on the portico, ran down the steps and threw herself into her brother's arms, weeping softly and clutching his sleeves in her trembling fingers.

'Is Demetrius still alive?' asked Marcellus, urgently.

'He is still breathing,' said Lucia—'but Sarpedon says he is losing ground very fast and can't live more than another hour.'

Marcellus turned and beckoned to his companion.

'This is Simon Peter, Lucia. He is lately come from Galilee. He, too, knows Demetrius.'

The huge, heavily bearded outlander bowed to her.

'Your servant, my sister!' he said, in a rich, deep voice.

'Welcome,' said Lucia, tearfully. 'Come—let us lose no time.'

Gallio, aged and weary, met them at the top of the stairs, embracing his son in silence. Cornelia, much shaken by the night's events, swayed weakly into his arms, whimpering incoherent endearments. Peter stood waiting on the stairway. The Senator turned toward him with a challenging stare. Lucia indifferently supplied the introduction.

'A friend of Marcellus,' she said. 'What is your name, please?'

'Peter,' he said, in his deep guttural voice.

The Senator nodded coolly, his attitude signifying that the ungroomed stranger was out of his proper environment. But now Peter, who had grown impatient over the delay, had a surprise for Senator Gallio. Advancing, the huge Galilean confronted his haughty Roman host with the authoritative air of one accustomed to giving commands.

'Take me to Demetrius!' he demanded.

At the sound of this strange, insistent voice, Cornelia released Marcellus and gazed at the big foreigner with open-mouthed curiosity. Gallio, dwarfed by the towering figure, obediently led the way to Demetrius' room. They all followed, and ranged themselves about the bedside, Marcellus laying his hand gently on the tousled head. At a sign from Gallio, who was obviously impressed by the determined manner of their mysterious guest, Sarpedon rose from his chair by the bed and made way for the newcomer.

With calm self-assurance, Peter took up Demetrius' limp hands in his great, brown fists and shook him.

'Demetrius!' he called, as if he were shouting to him at a vast distance; as if the dying Greek were miles and leagues away. There was no response; not so much as the flicker of an eyelid. Peter called again—in a booming voice that could easily have been heard over on the avenue. *'Demetrius! Return!'*

Nobody breathed. The company about the bed stood statuesque, waiting. Suddenly Peter straightened to his full height and faced them with extended arms and dismissing hands.

'Go!' he commanded. 'Leave us—alone—together!'

They silently obeyed, filing out into the corridor; all but Marcellus, who lagged to ask if he should go, too. Peter nodded. He was stripping off his homespun robe as Marcellus closed the door. They all drifted along the corridor to the head of the stairway where, for some time, they stood silently listening for further loud calls from the big Galilean who had taken possession of their house. Marcellus expected to hear some whispers of protest, but no one spoke. A tense silence prevailed. No sound came from Demetrius' room.

After a while the Senator broke the tension by turning toward the stairs. With the cautious tread of a frail old man he slowly descended. Sarpedon sullenly followed, and eased himself into a chair in the atrium. Cornelia took Marcellus by the arm and led him into her bedchamber, Lucia following. No one was left in the corridor now but Tertia, who tiptoed back to Demetrius' door. Crouching down beside it, she waited and listened, hearing nothing but her own stifled sobs.

A half-hour later, Marcellus came out of his mother's room, and queried Tertia with a whisper. She shook her head sadly. He went down to the library and found his father seated at his desk, with no occupation. The haggard old Senator pointed to a chair. After a long moment, he cleared his throat and drew a cynical smile.

'Does your unkempt friend think he is a miracle-worker?'

'Peter is strangely gifted, sir,' said Marcellus, feeling himself at a serious disadvantage.

'Very unusual procedure, I must say! He takes command of the case, discharges our physician, dismisses us from the room. Do you expect him to perform some supernatural feat up there?'

'It would not surprise me,' said Marcellus. 'I admit, sir, Peter has no polish, but he is thoroughly honest. Perhaps we should withhold judgment until we see what happens.'

'Well—the thing that will happen is the death of Demetrius,' said Gallio. 'However—it would have happened, in any event. I should have protested against this nonsense, if there had been the shadow of a hope that Demetrius might recover with proper treatment. I wonder how long we will have to wait for this Jew to finish his incantations—or whatever he is doing.'

'I don't know, sir,' confessed Marcellus. After a considerable pause, he asked, 'Have you learned any of the particulars about Demetrius' injuries?'

Gallio shook his head.

'You will have heard, of course, that he helped Diana escape from Capri? It is said that he is wanted on an old charge of assaulting a Tribune.'

Marcellus came to his feet and leaned over his father's desk.

'She escaped! I haven't heard a word of it. Where is she now?'

'No one seems to know. She is not at home. The Emperor pretends to be much concerned about her welfare, and has had searching parties looking for her.'

'And why is *he* so interested?' asked Marcellus, indignantly; and when his father made no reply, he added, 'Perhaps Demetrius knows where she is. Maybe he got into trouble on her account.'

Gallio made a weary, hopeless gesture.

'If Demetrius knows,' he said, 'he will take his secret along with him, my son.'

Restless and distraught, Marcellus returned to his mother's room and found her sleeping. Lucia was curled up on a couch. He sat down beside her and held her hand. The gray-blue light of dawn had begun to invade the dark corners.

'Is that man still in there?' whispered Lucia.

Marcellus nodded dejectedly, walked to the door, opened it and looked down the corridor. Tertia had left her post. He closed the door, and resumed his seat on the couch beside his sister.

* * * * * *

Tertia started at the sound of the door-latch. The bearded face of the massive Galilean peered out into the corridor.

'Go—quietly,' whispered Peter—'and prepare some hot broth.'

'Oh—is he going to live?' breathed Tertia.

Peter closed the door softly, without replying. Sensing that the family was not yet to be summoned, Tertia slipped down the rear stairway. When she returned, she tapped gently on the door and Peter opened it only far enough to admit her, and closed it again. Demetrius, very white, was propped up in the pillows, awake, but seemingly dazed. He regarded her with a listless glance.

'Do not talk to him yet,' advised Peter, kindly. 'He has come a long way, and is still bewildered.' He took up his robe and put it on. 'You may feed him the broth, as much or as little as he wants. You remain with him. Do not call his master until he asks for him. Admit no others until he is stronger. I am going now.'

'But, sir,' protested Tertia, 'are you leaving without seeing the family? They will want to thank you.'

'I do not want to answer questions,' said Peter, huskily; and Tertia could see that the big man was fatigued. 'I do not want to talk. I am spent.'

At the door, he turned to look again at Demetrius.

'Courage!' he said, in a low tone of command. 'Remember the promise I have made—for you to keep! You are to return to your own countrymen—and testify for our Christos who has made you whole!'

Demetrius' white forehead wrinkled a little, but he made no reply.

After the door had closed, Tertia held a spoonful of the hot broth to his lips. He took it apathetically, studying her face for recognition. She gave him more broth and smiled into his perplexed eyes.

'Know me now?' she whispered, wistfully.

'Tertia,' he answered, with an effort; then, 'Call Marcellus.'

She put down the cup and hastened to find the Tribune. The others crowded about her, asking insistent questions, but she was resolute that only his master might see him now. Marcellus went swiftly, his heart beating hard. He took Demetrius' hands.

'Peter has brought you back!' he said, in an awed voice.

Demetrius moistened his lips with a sluggish tongue.

'A long journey,' he mumbled.

'Do you remember anything?'

'A little.'

'See anyone?'

'Not clearly—but there were many voices.'

'Did you want to return?'

Demetrius sighed and shook his head.

'Where is Peter?' asked Marcellus.

'Gone,' said Demetrius.

Tertia, suspecting that his laconic replies meant he wished to talk to Marcellus privately, slipped out of the room. Demetrius brightened perceptibly.

'Diana is at Arpino—at the villa of Kaeso—in good hands—but—you had better go to her. The Emperor wants her. She is in danger.'

'Are you well enough, Demetrius,' asked Marcellus, nervously—'to let me go—at once?'

'Yes, sir. I shall be leaving, too. Peter made a vow. I am to return to Greece.'

'For the new Kingdom!' Marcellus regarded him with an expression of deference. 'You have been given a great responsibility—full of danger. I shall make out your certificate of manumission—today.'

'I shall be sorry to leave you, sir,' sighed Demetrius.

'Nor do I want you to go,' declared Marcellus. 'But if your life has been saved with a vow, you must fulfill it—at any cost!'

Tertia had opened the door a little way, her anxious frown hinting that there had been enough talk. Marcellus nodded for her to come in. She brought the bowl of broth to the bedside. Demetrius took it hungrily.

'That's good!' said Marcellus. 'You're gaining fast.'

Feeling that the other members of the family should be notified without further delay, he went to his mother's room, finding them all there. He blurted out the news that Demetrius had recovered and was having his breakfast.

'Impossible!' said Gallio, starting toward the door.

Marcellus intercepted him.

'Wait a little, sir,' he advised. 'He's not very strong yet. It is an effort for him to talk.'

'But I want to speak to this Galilean!' said Gallio. 'This is no small thing that has happened. Demetrius was dying! Sarpedon said so!'

'Peter has left, sir. Tertia says he was very weary and didn't want to see anyone.'

'How do you think he did all this?' inquired Cornelia.

'He is a Christian,' replied Marcellus. 'Some of these men who lived close to Jesus have developed peculiar powers. It was no great surprise to me, mother, that Demetrius recovered. He, too, is a Christian. He says that Peter made a vow for him to keep. He is to go back to Greece and work among his own countrymen—'

'What kind of work?' Lucia wanted to know.

'Enlisting people to support the new Kingdom,' said her brother.

'Won't he get into trouble—talking about a new Kingdom?' she asked.

'Doubtless,' agreed Marcellus. 'But Demetrius will not let that detain him.'

'Perhaps he may be glad to return to Greece,' said Lucia. 'Didn't you tell me he was fond of a girl in Athens? What was her name—Theodosia?'

The Senator said he was going down to have his breakfast in the library, and asked Marcellus to join him. Cornelia said she was going back to sleep.

Lucia went to her suite; and, a few minutes later, tapped softly on Demetrius' door. Tertia admitted her, and left the room.

'We are so glad you are better,' said Lucia. 'Marcellus says you are going home to Greece.' She laid a ring in his hand. 'I have kept it safely for you. Now you should have it back.'

Demetrius regarded the ring with brooding eyes, and rubbed it caressingly between his palms. Lucia gave him a sly smile.

'Perhaps you will give it to Theodosia,' she said.

He smiled—but sobered instantly.

'She may find it a costly gift,' he said. 'It might not be fair—to ask Theodosia to share my dangers.'

Sarpedon came in now and stood at the foot of the bed, silently viewing his patient with baffled eyes. It was plain to see that Demetrius was surprised to see him.

'The physician,' said Lucia. 'Do you remember his being here in the night?'

'No,' said Demetrius. 'I don't remember.'

'What did he do—that big fellow from Galilee?' queried Sarpedon, moving around to the other side of the bed.

'He prayed,' said Demetrius.

'What god does he pray to?' asked Sarpedon.

'There is only one,' replied Demetrius.

'A Jewish god?'

'No—not Jewish. God is the father of all men—everywhere. Anyone may pray to him in the name of Jesus who has come to establish a Kingdom in justice and peace.'

'Ah—this new Christian heresy!' said Sarpedon. 'Is your friend from Palestine aware that he can be arrested for pretending to heal diseases by such practices?'

'Pretending?' exclaimed Lucia. 'He wasn't pretending when he healed Demetrius!'

'He should be reported to the authorities,' said Sarpedon, walking stiffly toward the door.

'One would think that a physician would rejoice to see his patient get well,' remarked Lucia, 'no matter how he was healed.'

Sarpedon made no comment. Closing the door emphatically, he proceeded downstairs and entered the library where the Senator and Marcellus were at breakfast. Abandoning his customary suavity, he voiced an indignant protest.

'Come, Sarpedon, sit down,' said the Senator, amiably, 'and have breakfast with us. We do not blame you for feeling as you do. But this is an unusual occurrence. You did the best you could. Doubtless you are pleased that the Greek is recovering, even if the treatment was—what shall we say?—irregular?'

Sarpedon refused the fruit that Decimus obsequiously offered him, and remained standing, flushed with anger.

'It might be unfortunate,' he said, frostily, 'if it were known that Senator Gallio had called in one of the Christian seditionists to treat an illness in his household.'

Marcellus leaped from his chair and confronted Sarpedon, face to face.

'You—and your Hippocratic oath!' he shouted. 'You are supposed to be interested in healing! Has it come to pass that your profession is so jealous—and wretched of heart—that it is enraged when a man's life is restored by some other means than your futile remedies?'

Sarpedon backed toward the door.

'You will regret that speech, Tribune Marcellus!' he declared, as he stamped out of the room.

For a few minutes, neither the Senator nor Marcellus spoke, as they resumed their places at the table.

'I had hoped we might conciliate him,' said Gallio. 'His pride has been wounded. He can cause us much trouble. If he lets it be known that we are harboring Demetrius—'

'True—we must get Demetrius out of here!'

'Will he be able to travel—today?'

'He must! I am riding to Arpino. He shall go with me.'

'Nonsense!' scoffed the Senator. 'He cannot sit a horse today! I have it! We will send him in a carriage to Pescara. They will hardly be looking for him at an Adrian port.' He rose and paced the room. 'I shall go with him. My presence in the carriage may help him to evade too close scrutiny. Besides—I may be of some service in securing his passage. If there is no ship sailing at once, I may be able to charter one that would see him as far as Brundisium. He should have no difficulty finding a ship there, bound for Corinth.'

'This is most generous of you, sir,' declared Marcellus. 'If every man treated his slaves—'

'Well—as for that'—the Senator chuckled a little—'it has not been my custom to turn out my carriage and personally escort my slaves when they embark for foreign lands. Demetrius' case is different. He has had his life handed back to him in an extraordinary manner and he must keep the pledge that was made for him. Otherwise—he has no right to live!'

'You would make a good Christian, sir,' said Marcellus, realizing at once—by his father's sudden scowl—that the remark was untimely.

'Honorable men were keeping their word, my son, long before this Christian religion was proposed. . . . Come—let us arrange to be on our way. This is not a bad day for it. Rome will not be looking for fugitives this morning. The Ludi Romani will be the city's only concern. Tell Lentius to get out the carriage.'

Chapter XXV

Skirting the rim of the city by a circuitous route, and avoiding the congested highways until they were a dozen miles to the east, the carriage, and the horsemen who followed at a little distance, had proceeded without being challenged. Sometimes they had been detained at intersections by the heavy traffic pouring in from the country, but no one had questioned them.

The Senator's belief that this might be safely accomplished had proved correct. If a man wished to leave Rome inconspicuously, this was the day for it. The Ludi Romani—most venerable and popular of all the festivals—was at hand. Though still three days in the offing, the annual celebration in honor of Jupiter was casting a pleasant shadow before it.

Already the populace was in a carnival mood, the streets crowded with riotous merrymakers. Residents were decorating their houses with gay banners and bunting. Their guests were arriving from afar. The noise and confusion increased hourly as every avenue of approach to the capital was jammed with tourists, homecomers, minstrels, magicians, hawkers, dancers, acrobats, pickpockets, and traveling menageries of screeching monkeys and trained bears.

Everyone had caught the contagion of hilarity. All serious work had been abandoned; all discipline relaxed. The word had spread that this year's Ludi Romani would be notable for its gaiety. The new Emperor was not stingy. Glum old Tiberius, who frowned on amusements, was dead and buried. Tight-pursed old Sejanus, who had doled out the sesterces—a few at a time—to Prince Gaius, was also dead. So was Gaius—and good riddance it was, too. This season's Ludi Romani would be worth attending! Little Boots would see to it that everybody had a good time. Even the harried Christians could count upon a ten-day respite from persecution, for the authorities would be too drunk to bother with them.

At Avezzano, the Senator's carriage halted in the shade near a fork in the road. Marcellus, reining up alongside, dismounted to bid farewell to the occupants, for their ways parted here. Thrusting his arm through the open window, he shook hands with his father, assuring him that they would meet soon; and then with Demetrius, who, still weak, was much moved by their parting. Marcellus tried bravely to keep his own voice under control.

'Safe journey, Demetrius!' he said. 'And success to all your undertakings! It may be a long time before we meet—'

'Perhaps not, sir,' murmured Demetrius, smiling wanly.

'Well—be the time long or short, my friend, we shall meet! You believe that; don't you?'

'With all my heart!'

Remounting the mettlesome Ishtar, Marcellus galloped away, waving a hand as he turned south on the road to Arpino. Here the traffic was lighter and better time could be made. As the grade stiffened, Ishtar's enthusiasm cooled somewhat, and she settled to an easy canter.

Now that he had seen Demetrius safely started on his journey, Marcellus found his spirits reviving. He was on the way to Diana! Nothing else mattered now. At Alatri, he fed Ishtar in the stable-yard of the inn, while a slave—to whom he had tossed a few coppers—rubbed her down. Leaving the town, Marcellus led the mare for a mile; then, remounting, pressed on. The peaks of the Apennines glistened in the afternoon sunshine.

It was deep in the night when he reached Arpino and was recognized by the guard at the villa gate.

'Do not rouse anyone,' he said. 'I shall stable the mare and find some place to sleep.'

Not content to trust even Kaeso's competent hostlers with the care of Ishtar, Marcellus supervised her drinking, talking to her all the while in a fraternal tone that made the stable-boys laugh. Learning that his former quarters were unoccupied, he went to bed utterly exhausted by his experiences during the past twenty-four hours.

* * * * * *

Appius Kaeso had felt it an unnecessary precaution for Diana to work in the vineyard through these days immediately preceding and during the Ludi Romani which, he knew, would be occupying the full attention of all who were interested in taking her to the Emperor.

Last night they had brought her back to the villa; and as this was the first morning, for some time, that Diana could feel comparatively safe and at leisure, Antonia had insisted upon her sleeping undisturbed until she was thoroughly rested.

Coming out to the stables shortly after dawn, Kaeso learned of Marcellus' arrival and went to his room, finding him awake. In the ensuing half-hour of serious talk, they informed each other of everything that had occurred since they parted. Kaeso, Marcellus observed, had lost much of his impetuous bluster, but could still be identified by his willingness to offer prompt advice.

'Why don't you marry Diana at once?' queried Kaeso. 'As you are supposed to be dead, Caligula thinks he has a right to pretend an interest in her welfare. When she becomes your wife, he has no further justification for concerning himself about her.'

Marcellus, sitting half-dressed on the edge of his bed, spent so long a moment of meditation that Kaeso added, impatiently, 'You two are in love with each other: aren't you?'

'Yes—but the fact is, Kaeso,' said Marcellus, disconsolately, 'Diana is not at all sure that she wants to marry me.'

'Isn't sure?' retorted Kaeso. 'Of course she's sure! Why else would she say she was engaged to you?'

'Did she say that?' Marcellus sat up attentively.

'Nothing less! Isn't it true?'

'Last time I saw her, Kaeso, she insisted that our marriage would be a mistake, because of my being a Christian.'

'Pouff! Diana is as good a Christian as you are! If being a Christian means showing sympathy and friendliness for people who are beneath you, Diana is entitled to a prize! You should have seen her in the vineyard! For a week or more she has been living in a small cottage, rooming with the girl Metella, to whom she has become much attached; and, as for Metella, it has made her over into another kind of person! You wouldn't know her!'

'I'm glad,' said Marcellus. 'I'm glad Diana has had this experience.' His eyes clouded. 'But there is a great deal of difference between Diana's willingness to practice Christian principles and my own obligation to associate myself with a movement that the Government has outlawed—and spend my time with men whose lives are in constant danger. That is what Diana objects to.'

'Well—you can't blame her for that!' snorted Kaeso.

'Nor me,' declared Marcellus. 'I have no choice in this matter.'

* * * * * *

They met alone in the cool atrium. Antonia, who had been seated beside him, suddenly broke off in the midst of what she was saying, and sped away. Diana was slowly descending the marble stairway. Coming quickly to his feet, Marcellus crossed the room to meet her. She hesitated for a moment at first sight of him; then, with an ecstatic smile, came swiftly into his arms.

'My beloved!' murmured Marcellus, holding her tightly to him. For a long moment they stood locked in their embrace, hungrily sharing the kiss she had offered him. With closed eyes, and tiny breaths like a child's sobs, Diana relaxed in his arms.

'You came for me,' she whispered.

'I wish I could have you—always—darling.'

She nodded slowly, without opening her eyes.

'It was meant to be,' she breathed, softly.

'Diana!' He laid his cheek against hers, gently. 'Do you mean that? Are you mine—in spite of everything?'

Reaching up both arms, she wrapped them tightly around his neck and gave him her lips passionately.

'Today?' whispered Marcellus, deeply stirred.

She drew back to face him with wide eyes, bright with tears.

'Why not?' she murmured. Slipping out of his arms, she took him by the hand. 'Come!' she said, happily. 'Let us tell them!' Her voice was tender. 'Marcellus—they have been so very good to me. This will please them.'

Antonia had joined Appius in the garden. Their faces beamed as Marcellus and Diana came down the path, arm in arm, and they rose to meet them. Antonia surprised Marcellus with a kiss that was by no means a mere performance of a social duty, and Diana kissed Appius, to his immense gratification. Then she hugged Antonia, joyfully.

'Appius,' she said, 'as the master of Arpino, you can marry us. Is that not so?'

'It's the very best thing I do!' boasted Appius, thumping his chest.

'Today?' asked Marcellus.

'Of course!' assured Appius.

'Let us sit down,' suggested Antonia, 'and make some plans. Now—we can have a quiet little wedding in the atrium, with nobody but the family—By the way—where is Antony?'

'Not up yet,' said Marcellus. 'I've inquired for him.'

'Or'—went on Antonia—'we can invite everybody! These people in Arpino love you both. It would be wonderful for them if—'

'Let's have it out on the green,' urged Diana.

'Where Marcellus used to talk to them,' said Appius.

'At sunset,' said Antonia.

'If we are agreed on that,' said Appius, 'I shall send word to Vobiscus that they are to have a holiday. It will give them a chance to clean up, and be presentable.'

'That's very kind,' said Marcellus.

'Here comes Antony now—the sluggard,' said his mother, tenderly. Antony was sauntering along with his head bent, apparently in a profound study. Presently he glanced up, paused momentarily, and then came running. Marcellus embraced him affectionately.

'Why hasn't someone called me?' complained Antony. 'How long can you stay with us, Marcellus?'

'We are going to keep them as long as we can, dear,' said his mother. 'Diana and Marcellus are to be married—tonight.'

Antony, stunned a little by the announcement, solemnly offered Marcellus his hand. Then he turned to Diana, hardly knowing how to felicitate her.

'She's supposed to be kissed,' advised his father.

Antony flushed and appeared at a great disadvantage until Diana came to his rescue with a kiss so frankly given that his composure was restored.

Saying that he must dispatch a servant to the vineyard, Kaeso turned away. Antonia announced that if they were to have a party tonight, she would have to do something about it without delay. Antony, surmising that he, too, was expected to contrive an errand, remembered that he hadn't had his breakfast. Marcellus and Diana sat down on the lectus, their fingers intertwined.

'Now you must tell me how Demetrius found you,' said Diana.

It was a long story, a moving story that brought the tears to her eyes. Poor Demetrius—so loyal and so brave! And his restoration—so mysterious! How happy to be free—and going home! And back to Theodosia!

'He hasn't much to offer her,' said Marcellus. 'The life of an active Christian, my dear, is lightly held. Demetrius is not a man to shun danger. However—Theodosia will love him no less on that account. If he goes to her, she will take him—for good or ill.'

'I think you meant a little of that for me,' murmured Diana. 'Very well, Marcellus—I shall accept you that way.'

He drew her close and kissed her.

'Kaeso believes,' he said, after a long silence, 'and I agree with him, that it may be fairly safe now for me to take you home to your mother. There is no charge against you. There will be no point to Caligula's pretense of rescuing you, after we are married.'

'But how about *you*, dear?' asked Diana, anxiously. 'There will be much talk about your return, after you were thought to be drowned. Will it come to the Emperor's ears that you are a Christian?'

'Very likely—but we must take that risk. Caligula is erratic. His attention may be diverted from the Christians. The fact that my father is an influential Senator might make the youngster think twice before arresting me. In any case—you can't remain in seclusion indefinitely. Let's have it done with—and see what comes of it.'

'When shall we go?'

'The Kaesos will be hurt if we rush away. Let us wait until the day after tomorrow. The Ludi Romani will have begun. Perhaps we can make the trip safely.'

'Without any attempt to avoid the patrols?'

'Yes, darling. If we were to disguise ourselves—and be apprehended—we would have thrown our case away.'

Diana snuggled into his arms.

'I shall not be afraid,' she murmured, 'if you are with me.'

* * * * * *

All afternoon the men of Arpino raked the grass on the village green. Vobiscus superintended the building of a little arbor which the girls decorated with ferns and flowers. All day long, the kitchens of the villa were busy. The ovens turned out honey cakes. The air was heavy with the appetizing aroma of lambs and ducks roasting on spits before hot charcoal fires. Kaeso's vintner thought his master had gone mad when he learned that wine was to be served to all Arpino!

The hum of voices on the green was hushed when the wedding-party appeared at the villa gate. Then there arose a concerted shout! Cheers for Diana! Cheers for Marcellus! Cheers, too, for the Kaesos!

They took their places under the little, impromptu portico, and a silence fell as Kaeso—never so dignified—joined their hands and demanded them to say that they wished to be husband and wife. In orotund tones, he announced their marriage.

The wedded pair turned about to face the Arpinos. Another happy shout went up! The Kaeso family offered affectionate wishes and caresses. For a moment, the village wasn't sure what to do. An old man ventured to come forward and take their hands, bobbing his head violently. Vobiscus came strutting a little, as became the overseer, followed by his wife, who wore the gayest shawl present. More women came up, trailed by their husbands who shouldered themselves along, grinning awkwardly and scratching an ear. Marcellus knew most of them by name. Diana hugged Metella, and Metella cried. She was going to put Marcellus off with a stiff little curtsy, but he caught her to him and kissed her, which was by far the most noteworthy incident of the occasion. There were cheers for Metella—who was so embarrassed she didn't know where to go or what to do when she got there. Presently Appius Kaeso signaled Vobiscus that he wanted to make an announcement, and Vobiscus gave a stentorian growl that produced a profound silence. The master, he declaimed, had something to say. Kaeso bade them to the feast. Already the villa slaves were coming out through the gate in an imposing procession, weighted by their pleasant burdens.

'Well'—said Kaeso—'shall we return to the villa?'

'Oh, please, no!' said Diana. 'Let us have our dinner here—with them.'

'You surely are a precious darling!' murmured Marcellus.

'But we have ices!' protested Kaeso.

Diana slipped her arm through his, affectionately.

'They can wait,' she whispered.

Kaeso smiled down into her eyes, and nodded indulgently.

'Will you look at Antony?' laughed his mother. Antony, behind a table, wearing an apron, was slicing lamb for the common people of Arpino.

* * * * * *

Sarpedon told. With his professional pride deeply wounded, and nothing left to lose in the regard of the Gallio household, he decided to make good his threat to Marcellus.

But it was something more than an impulsive desire to avenge his humiliation that led the physician to betray the family whose lucrative patronage he had inherited from his noted father.

Had the unhappy incident occurred a few weeks earlier, Sarpedon would have pocketed his indignation; but times had changed. Nothing was now to be had by currying favor with the conservatives. Indeed, under the present dynasty one had far better cut loose from such dead weight and not risk going down with it. Young Caligula had no patience with the elder statesmen who believe in national economy and viewed his reckless extravagances with stern disapproval. It was common knowledge that Little Boots intended to break the gray-haired obstructionists at the earliest opportunity.

Sarpedon knew Quintus, though he had seen nothing of him since his sudden elevation to a place of prominence in Caligula's court. Fortunately for himself, old Tuscus had died in the spring; and Sarpedon, who had ministered to the aged poet-statesman's infirmities, had had no occasion to see anything more of their household. He did not know whether he was to be retained as the family physician, now that the old man was gone.

Doubtless it would be greatly to his advantage if he could show Quintus which side he was on in the struggle between Little Boots and the Senate.

Hot and eager though he was, Sarpedon had too much sense to go plunging into Quintus' august presence with his betrayal of the Gallios. He dignifiedly asked for an appointment, and restlessly waited the three days which elapsed before the high and mighty Quintus could give him an audience. This delay, however, had enabled Sarpedon to improve his story; for, in the meantime, his butler had learned from Decimus that the Senator and Marcellus had made off with the convalescent Greek on some secret journey.

Having fought his way through the swirling crowds, and arriving at the Imperial Palace disheveled and perspiring, Sarpedon was left standing—for there was no place to sit down—in the great gold and marble and ivory foyer swarming with provincial potentates waiting their turn for favors. Though it was still early in the forenoon, the garishly arrayed dignitaries represented every known state of intoxication, ranging from rude clownishness on through to repulsively noisy nausea.

At length the physician was permitted a brief interview with Quintus, who was prepared to make short work of him until he said he had information about Gallio's Greek slave Demetrius. At that, Quintus gave attention. A Jewish Christian had been invited into the Gallio villa to perform mummeries over the Greek, who had been slightly wounded. Tribune Marcellus—far from dead—had brought the Christian quack to the villa, and had made it plain enough that he, too, was thoroughly in sympathy with these Christian revolutionists. The Senator and Marcellus had spirited the Greek out of the house and set off with him, doubtless to hide him somewhere.

Quintus was deeply interested, but all the thanks Sarpedon received was a savage denunciation for waiting so long before bringing the news.

'You always were a bungler, Sarpedon!' yelled Quintus. 'Had you not been the son of your wise father, no one would trust you to purge a dog of his worms!'

Having thus learned where he stood in the esteem of the Emperor's favorite, Sarpedon bowed deeply and backed himself out of the room and into the stinking foyer. One hardly knew, these days, how to conduct oneself with any hope of favor at Caligula's hands. One thing was sure, the Empire was on the way toward ruin; but, long before Caligula crashed, he would have seen to it that everybody who believed in any decencies at all was battered into silent submission.

Quintus did not immediately notify Little Boots of Sarpedon's disclosures, thinking it better to capture his quarry. Perhaps he might learn something that would please the Emperor. Marcellus was alive. Without question, he would know the whereabouts of Diana.

A small contingent of seasoned Palace Guards was detailed to put the Gallio villa under surveillance and report all movements there.

Next day they brought back word that the Senator had returned alone in his carriage; but so great was the confusion at the Palace that Quintus decided to wait a more convenient season for action. The court festivities were at such a pitch that there was no room for anything more. The Senator's case would have to wait. Meantime—he told the guards—they should continue their watch at the villa. If Tribune Marcellus showed up they were to place him under arrest.

This affair was likely to cause the haughty Tullus some embarrassment before they had done with it; but—Quintus shrugged—let Tullus take his medicine and like it. He had no more use for Tullus than he had for Marcellus. It pleased him now to reflect that he had suggested Tullus for the dirty job of cleaning the Christians out of the Catacombs. Quintus chuckled. It would be droll, indeed, if Tullus found himself obliged to arrest his long-time friend: his brother-in-law, too! Very well—let them take it!

* * * * * *

Late in the night of the third day of the Ludi Romani, the news was brought to Quintus that Diana had just arrived at her mother's home, accompanied by Marcellus.

Little Boots, who had been drinking heavily all day, was in a truculent mood, cursing and slapping his attendants as they tried to get him to bed. Ordinarily, after a whole day's drunkenness, His Majesty could be put away quietly; but such was the infernal din of the streets below and throughout the Palace that the Emperor was wide awake with a bursting head.

Even Quintus was coming in for his share of abuse. He found himself responsible for the noise of the celebrants and the shocking condition of the palace. Furthermore, declared the thick-tongued Emperor, the ceremonies today in the Forum Julium had been a disgrace; and whose fault was that, if not Quintus'? Never had there been anything so tiresome as that interminable Ode to Jupiter! Never had there been anything so dull as those solemn choruses!

'Yes—but—Your Majesty, were we not obliged to follow the ancient ritual?' Quintus had asked in honeyed tones. Immediately he repented of having tried to defend himself. It was the wrong time to answer Little Boots with a 'yes—but—,' no matter what justification warranted it. His

Majesty went into a shrieking, slobbering rage! He was aweary of being served by fools. High time, he felt, to give some better man a chance to do his bidding. In nothing—in *nothing* had Quintus proved himself an able minister!

At that point, Quintus, needing to improve his standing in the Emperor's regard, had motioned them all out of the imperial bedchamber.

'The daughter of Gallus has been found, Your Majesty,' he announced.

'Ha!' shouted Little Boots. 'So—at last—your snails caught up with her; eh? And where did they find this beautiful icicle?'

'At home, sire. She arrived there but an hour ago.'

'Did your favorite Greek bring her back?'

'No, sire—the Greek has been hidden by Senator Gallio. Diana was brought back by Tribune Marcellus, who was thought to have drowned himself.'

'Oh?—so he turned up; eh? The lover! And what has he been doing since he was supposed to have drowned?'

'In seclusion somewhere, sire. It is reported that he is a Christian.'

'What?' screamed Little Boots. 'A Christian! And why should a Tribune consort with such rabble? Does the fool think he can lead a revolution? Let him be arrested for sedition! Bring him here at once! Now!'

'It is very late, Your Majesty, and tomorrow is a crowded day.'

'We are weary unto death, Quintus, with these tiresome ceremonies. What manner of torture does old Jupiter inflict on us tomorrow?'

'Your Majesty attends the games in the forenoon. Then there is the reception to the Praetorian Guard and the Senate, followed by the banquet for them—and their women.'

'Speeches—no doubt,' groaned Little Boots.

'It is the custom, sire, and after the banquet there is a procession to the Temple of Jupiter where the Senate does its homage at twilight.'

'A dull occasion, Quintus. Has it occurred to you that this banquet for the sullen old dotards might be enlivened with something besides oratory?'

'Your Majesty will have diverting company at table—the daughter of Herod Antipas, sire, who is the Tetrarch of Galilee and Peraea.'

'That scrawny, jingling wench—Salome?' yelled Little Boots. 'We have seen quite enough of her!'

'But I thought Your Majesty had found her very entertaining,' said Quintus, risking a sly smile. 'Was she not eager to please Your Majesty?'

Little Boots made a wry face. Suddenly his heavy eyes lighted.

'Invite the daughter of Gallus! Let her be seated at our right, and Salome at our left. We will encourage Salome to repeat some of her best stories.' He laughed painfully, holding his head.

'Would not Legate Gallus consider that a grave offense to his daughter, sire?'

'It will serve her right,' mumbled Little Boots, 'for bestowing her precious smiles upon a Tribune who hopes to see another government. Send for him without delay, and let him be confined in the Palace prison!'

Quintus made a fluttering gesture of protest.

'Imprisoned—as a Tribune—of course,' Little Boots hastened to add. 'Make him comfortable. And let Diana be bidden to this banquet. You, personally, may extend the invitation, Quintus, early tomorrow. If she is reluctant to accept, suggest that the Emperor might be more disposed to deal leniently with her Christian friend should she be pleased to honor this occasion with her presence.'

'But I thought Your Majesty had been attracted to Diana, and had hoped to win her favor. Would it serve Your Majesty best to threaten her? Perhaps—if she were made much of by the Emperor, the daughter of Gallus might forget her fondness for Marcellus.'

'No!' barked Little Boots. 'What that haughty creature needs is not flattery, but a flick of the whip! And as for her lover'—he cocked his head and grinned bitterly—'we have other plans for him.'

'He is the son of Senator Gallio, sire!' said Quintus.

'All the worse for him!' shouted Little Boots. 'We'll give the old man a lesson, too—and the Senate can draw its own conclusions!'

* * * * * *

No less a personage than Quintus himself, attended by a handsomely uniformed contingent of Equestrian Knights, delivered the banquet invitation to Diana. Summoned early from her rooms, she met him in the atrium. She was pale and her eyes were swollen with weeping, but she bore herself proudly. Paula, dazed and frightened, stood by her side.

Quintus deferentially handed her the ornate scroll; and while Diana helplessly fumbled with the gaudy seals, he thought to save a little precious time—for the forenoon was well advanced and the day was loaded with duties. He explained the message. Diana gasped involuntarily.

'Will you say to His Majesty,' spoke up Paula, trying to steady her trembling voice, 'that the daughter of Legate Gallus is far too heartsick to be a suitable dinner companion for the Emperor?'

'Madame'—Quintus bowed stiffly—'this imperial summons is not addressed to the wife of the Legate Gallus, but to his daughter. As she is present, she shall answer for herself.'

'My mother has spoken the truth, sir,' said Diana, weakly. 'Please tell the Emperor that I must be excused. I am too ill.'

'Perhaps you should be told,' said Quintus, coldly, 'that your friend Tribune Marcellus, now resting in a dungeon at the Palace, will be arraigned tomorrow on a charge of sedition. The Emperor's judgment in this case may be tempered somewhat if the daughter of the Legate Gallus is disposed to be gracious to His Majesty.'

'Very well.' Diana's voice was barely audible. 'I shall come.'

'If my husband were here," announced Paula, throwing all prudence aside, 'some blood would flow before this cruel thing came to pass!'

'Madame—you are overwrought,' observed Quintus. 'May I suggest that it is not to your advantage to make such statements? I shall not report this to His Majesty—but I advise you to be more discreet.' Bowing deeply, he turned and marched out through the peristyle, followed stiffly by his retinue.

* * * * * *

Marcellus was surprised at the consideration he was shown by the Palace Guards who arrested him and by the officials at the prison. Perhaps it was due to his rank. Roused from a deep sleep, at the Gallus villa, he had gone down to the atrium to face a Centurion attended by a deputation of twenty legionaries.

Aware that it was useless to resist so formidable a party, he had asked permission to return to his room for his personal belongings, and the request was courteously granted. It was a sorry parting. Diana clung to him, weeping piteously.

'Be brave, darling,' he had entreated. 'Perhaps this is only to humiliate me. The Emperor will probably rebuke me—and set me free—with an admonition. Let us not despair.'

Tearing himself away, he had obediently followed the Centurion. They had offered him a horse; had put him in the midst of them; no one of the drunken merrymakers on the streets could have suspected that he was under arrest.

At the Palace he was taken to the prison. It was subterranean, but well lighted and ventilated, and the room they gave him was comfortably furnished. The Centurion informed him that he was free to notify his friends of his whereabouts: his messages would be dispatched forthwith, and any visitors would be admitted.

Marcellus sat down at once before the desk and wrote a letter.

Marcipor: I am in the Palace prison, held on a charge of treason. Inform my family. You will be permitted to visit me, but perhaps it would be better if the Senator does not subject himself to such a painful errand. I am well treated. Bring me the Robe.—Marcellus.

Shortly after dawn, Marcipor appeared. He bore himself with the gravity and weariness of a very old man. The guards retired after admitting him, their demeanor indicating that no effort would be made to listen to their conversation. Marcipor's hands were cold and shaky. His eyes were full of trouble.

'I would rather die, my son,' he quavered, 'than see you subjected to this grievous persecution.'

'Marcipor—it has sometimes been found necessary for a man to give up his life in defense of a great cause. I am sorely troubled, but not for myself. I sorrow for those who love me.'

'Let me send for Peter!' entreated Marcipor. 'He has great power. He might even be able to deliver you from prison.'

Marcellus shook his head.

'No—Marcipor; Peter's life is too valuable to be put in jeopardy.'

'But the Christos! Might he not come to your rescue—and Peter's?' asked the old man, tearfully.

'It is not right to put the Christos to a test, Marcipor.'

'Here is the Robe, sir.' Marcipor unlaced his tunic and drew out the seamless garment.

Marcellus held it in his arms.

'Let not your heart be troubled, Marcipor,' he said, gently, laying his hand on the old slave's bowed shoulder. 'Come again, tomorrow. There may be better tidings.'

* * * * * *

What hurt Diana most, as she sat at the high table beside the drunken Emperor, was the baffled look of disappointment in Senator Gallio's eyes. He had come alone to the banquet, and only because he must. They had seated him at a distant table, but he and Diana had exchanged glances, and it was plain to see that he believed she had forsaken his son in his hour of peril. She longed to go to him and explain her predicament, but it was quite impossible. Their situation was already much too precarious.

Caligula was giving most of his attention to Salome. He had tried, without success, to have her repeat some of her ribald stories; but Salome, suspecting that she was being used as a catspaw, had assumed an air of virtue. Little Boots, not having seen her in this rôle, was at a loss to know what to do with her. His plan for his entertainment at this boresome banquet was getting quite out of hand. With Diana on his right, coldly dignified and taciturn, and Salome on his left, refusing to conspire with him for Diana's discomfiture, the Emperor—who had arrived at the surly stage of his drunkenness—decided to better his position.

Turning to Salome, he remarked, with intention that Diana should overhear:

'We have captured one of these Christians who seem bent on overturning the government. His case is of special interest because he is a Tribune. Would it amuse you, sweet Salome, to see a Christian Tribune recant—in the presence of the Praetorian Guard and the Senate?'

Salome gave him an enigmatic smile, over her shoulder.

'Unless the Emperor means to see it through,' she drawled, 'it is risky. These Christians do not recant, Your Majesty. My father once undertook to humiliate a Christian before our court; and the fellow—instead of recanting—delivered an address that practically ruined the reputation of the whole family! Me—especially! You should have heard the things he said about me! It was intolerable! We had to punish him.'

Caligula's malicious little, close-set eyes sparkled.

'Whip him?' he asked—making sure Diana heard.

'We beheaded him!' rasped Salome.

'Well—' responded Caligula. 'You *did* punish him; didn't you? What do you do to people, up there in Galilee, when they say something *false* about you?' He laughed loudly, punching Salome in the ribs with his elbow. Then he turned about to see how Diana was liking the conversation. She was deathly white.

Quintus, acting as Praetor, arose to announce Cornelius Capito, who proceeded to make the worst speech of his life; for it was inevitable that it should be a eulogy of Caligula, and old Capito was an honest man. A chorus choir filed in and sang an ode. An Egyptian Prince delivered an address which all but put Caligula to sleep. He beckoned to Quintus, and Quintus whispered to an aide.

'Now,' said Little Boots to Salome, 'we will look into the loyalty of our Christian Tribune. They have gone to fetch him.'

'Remember what I said, sire! These people have no fear.'

'Would you like to lay a little wager?'

'Anything you say, Your Majesty,' she shrugged.

Caligula unclasped an emerald bracelet from his wrist and laid it on the table.

Salome unfastened a gold locket from the chain about her neck and opened it.

'Humph!' grunted Caligula. 'What is it—a lock of hair; eh?'

'From the head of the only honest man I ever met,' declared Salome. 'He was also the bravest.'

Caligula struggled to his feet and the entire assembly of Roman dignitaries rose and bowed. With a benevolent sweep of his arm, he bade them resume their seats. He was moved, he said, by the many expressions of fidelity to the Crown. It was apparent, he went on, thickly, that the Praetorian Guard and the Senate appreciated the value of a united loyalty to the Emperor and the Empire. They cheered him, briefly.

It had lately come to the Emperor's notice, he said, that a secret party of seditionists, calling themselves Christians, had been giving themselves to vain talk about a King—one Jesus, a Jewish brawler—who for treason and disturbance of the peace had been put to death in Jerusalem. His disciples—a small company of ignorant and superstitious fishermen—had spread the word that their dead chieftain had come alive and intended to set up a Kingdom.

'This foolishness,' continued Caligula, 'would hardly deserve our recognition were it confined to the feeble-minded fanatics and the brawlers who fan the flame of such superstitions in hope of gain. But it now comes to our attention that one of our Tribunes—Marcellus Gallio—'

Slowly the eyes of the banquet guests moved toward Senator Gallio. He did not change countenance; sat staring, gray-faced, at Caligula; his mouth firm-set, his deep eyes steady.

'We are reluctant to believe,' went on Caligula, 'that these reports concerning Tribune Marcellus are true. It is his right, under our law, to stand up before you—and make his defense!'

* * * * * *

Diana was so very proud of him; so very, very proud of him as he marched, head erect, in the hollow square of Palace Guards as they stalked into the banquet hall and came to a halt before the Emperor's high table. The guards were all fine specimens of manhood, in their late twenties and early thirties; athletes, square-jawed, broad-shouldered, bronzed; yet—in every way—Marcellus, thought Diana, was the fittest of them all; and if ever this Jesus, whose own heroism had inspired her beloved Marcellus to endure this trial—if ever this Jesus was to have a champion worthy of him—surely he could ask for none more perfect than her Marcellus!

She had been so, so afraid he might not understand her being here beside this sick and drunk and loathsome little wretch, with the pasty skin and beady eyes and cruel mouth. But no—but no!—Marcellus understood. Their eyes met, his lighting in an endearing smile. His lips pantomimed a kiss! Diana's heart beat hard—and her eyes were swimming.

Marcellus was asked to stand forth—and he stepped forward to face the Emperor. Everybody stood. The silence in the hall was oppressive. Outside in the Palace plaza the procession was forming that would convey Rome's lawgivers to the Temple of Jupiter. The triumphal music was blaring discordantly from a dozen gaudily decorated equipages in the waiting cavalcade, and the sweating crowds that had massed in the avenue were shouting drunkenly; but, within the spacious banquet-hall, the silence was tense.

'Tribune Marcellus Gallio,' began Caligula, with attempted dignity, 'you have been accused of consorting with a party of revolutionists known as Christians. It is said that these promoters of sedition—for the most part slaves and vandals—have proclaimed the kingship of one Jesus, a Palestinian Jew, who was put to death for treason, blasphemy, and disturbances of the public peace. What have you to say?'

Diana searched her beloved's impassive face. There was not a trace of fear. Indeed, to judge by his demeanor, the Emperor might have been bestowing an honor. How handsome he was in his Tribune's uniform! What was that brown garment that he held tightly in his folded arms? Diana's throat tightened as she identified the Robe. A hot tear rolled down her cheek. Oh—please—Christos! Marcellus is carrying your Robe! Please—Christos—Marcellus loves you so! He has given up so much for you! He is trying so hard to atone for what he did to you! Please—Christos! Do something for my Marcellus!

'It is true, Your Majesty,' Marcellus was replying, in a steady voice that could be heard through the banquet-hall, 'I am a Christian. But I am not a seditionist. I am not engaged in a plot to overthrow the Government. This Jesus, whom *I* put to death on a cross, is indeed a King; but his Kingdom is not of this world. He does not seek an earthly throne. His Kingdom is a state of mind and heart that strives for peace and justice and good will among all men.'

'You say *you* put this Jew to death?' barked Caligula. 'Why, then, are you risking your life to serve as his ambassador?'

'It is a fair question, sire. This Jesus was innocent of any crime. At his trial, the Procurator, who sat in judgment, entreated the prosecutors to release him. He had gone about among the country people advising them to be kind to one another, to be honest and truthful, merciful and forbearing. He had healed their sick, opened the eyes of the blind, and had spoken simple words of consolation to the distressed. They followed him—thousands of them—from place to place—day by day—hanging on his words and crowding close to him for comfort. They forsook their synagogues, where their priests had been interested in them only for their tithes and lambs, and banded themselves together to barter only with men who weighed with honest scales.' Marcellus paused, in his lengthy speech.

'Proceed!' commanded the Emperor. 'You are an able advocate!' He smiled contemptuously. 'You are almost persuading us to be a Christian.'

'Your Majesty,' went on Marcellus, in a remorseful tone, 'I was ordered to conduct the execution. The trial had been held in a language I did not understand; and not until my crime had been committed did I realize the enormity of it.'

'Crime—you say?' shouted Caligula, truculently. 'And was it a crime, then, to obey the command of the Empire?'

'The Empire, Your Majesty, is composed of fallible men who sometimes make mistakes. And this, sire, was the greatest mistake that was ever made!'

'So!—the Empire makes mistakes, then!' growled Caligula. 'Perhaps you will be foolhardy enough to say that the Emperor himself might make a mistake!'

'It is I, Your Majesty, who am on trial; not the Emperor,' said Marcellus, bowing.

Caligula was not quite prepared to deal with that comment. He flushed darkly. A throaty little chuckle came up from Salome's direction, spurring his anger.

'What is that brown thing you have clutched in your arms?' he demanded, pointing his finger.

'It is his Robe, Your Majesty.' Marcellus held it up for inspection. 'He wore it to the cross.'

'And you have the impudence to bring it along to your trial; eh? Hand it to the Commander of the Guard.'

Marcellus obeyed. The Centurion reached out a hand, rather reluctantly, and in effecting the transfer, the Robe fell to the floor. The Centurion haughtily waited for the prisoner to pick it up, but Marcellus made no move to do so.

'Hand that garment to the Commander!' ordered Caligula.

Marcellus stooped, picked up the Robe, and offered it to the Commander who motioned to the guard beside him to receive it. The guard took it—and dropped it. All breathing was suspended in the banquet-hall.

'Bring that thing here!' shouted Caligula, bravely. He extended his hand with fingers outspread. Marcellus moved to obey. Salome glanced up suddenly, caught Caligula's eye, and ventured a warning frown. 'Hand it to the daughter of Legate Gallus,' he commanded. 'She will keep it for you—as a memento.'

It was a most impressive moment. Marcellus reached up and handed the Robe to Diana, who leaned forward eagerly to receive it. They exchanged an intimate, lingering smile quite as if they were alone together. Marcellus stepped back to his place beside the Commander, and all eyes were fixed on Diana's enraptured face as she gathered the Robe to her bosom, regarding it with a tenderness that was almost maternal.

Little Boots was not easily embarrassed, but it was plain to see that the situation was becoming somewhat complicated. He had intended it as a drama to impress the Senate. These great ones needed to learn that their new Emperor expected unqualified loyalty and obedience, and plenty of it, whether the subject be a penniless nobody or a person of high rank. The play hadn't gone well. The other actors were neglecting to furnish cues for the imperial speeches. His face was twisted with a mounting rage. He glared at Marcellus.

'You seem to attach a great deal of significance to this old coat!'

'Yes, Your Majesty,' replied Marcellus, quietly.

'Are you fool enough to believe that there is some magic in it?'

'It does possess a peculiar power, Your Majesty, for those who believe that it was worn by the Son of God.'

There was a concerted stir throughout the great room; sound of a quick, involuntary intake of breath; throaty sound of incredulous murmurs; metallic sound of sidearms suddenly jostled in their scabbards as men turned about to dart inquiring glances at their neighbors.

'Blasphemer!' bellowed Caligula. 'Have you the effrontery to stand there—at this sacred feast in honor of Jupiter—and calmly announce that your crucified Jew is divine?'

'It is not in disrespect to Jupiter, Your Majesty. Many generations of our people have said their prayers to Jupiter, and my King is not jealous of that homage. He has compassion upon every man's longing to abide under the shadow of some sheltering wing. Jesus did not come into the world to denounce that aspiration, but to invite all who love truth and mercy to listen to his voice—and walk in his way.'

Diana was so proud; so very proud of Marcellus! Really—it wasn't Marcellus who was on trial! Everybody in the great room was on trial—all but Marcellus! Caligula was storming—but he had no case! Oh—she thought—what an Emperor Marcellus would have made! She wanted to shout, "Senators! Give Marcellus the crown! Let him make our Empire great!'

The stirring music from the plaza was growing in volume. The shouts of the multitude were strident, impatient. It was time for the procession to start.

'Tribune Marcellus Gallio'—said Caligula, sternly—'it is not our wish to condemn you to death in the presence of your aged father and the honorable men who, with him, serve the Empire in the Senate. Deliberate well, therefore, when you reply to this final question, Do you now recant—and forever renounce—your misguided allegiance to this Galilean Jew—who called himself a King?'

Again a portentous hush fell over the banquet-hall. Salome was observed to glance up with an arch smile and a little shrug, as she picked up the Emperor's emerald bracelet and clasped it on her arm.

'Your Majesty,' replied Marcellus, 'if the Empire desires peace and justice and good will among all men, my King will be on the side of the Empire and her Emperor. If the Empire and the Emperor desire to pursue the slavery and slaughter that have brought agony and terror and despair to the world'—Marcellus' voice had risen to a clarion tone—'if there is then nothing further for men to hope for but chains and hunger at the hands of our Empire—my King will march forward to right this wrong! Not tomorrow, sire! Your Majesty may not be so fortunate as to witness the establishment of this Kingdom—but it is coming!'

'And that is your final word?' asked Caligula.

'Yes, Your Majesty,' said Marcellus.

Caligula drew himself up erectly.

'Tribune Marcellus Gallio,' he announced, 'it is our decree that you be taken immediately to the Palace Archery Field—and put to death—for high treason.'

Even while the sentence was being passed, a fresh sensation stirred the audience. Diana had left her place at the Emperor's table and was walking proudly, confidently, down the steps of the dais, to take her stand beside Marcellus. He slipped his arm about her, tenderly.

'No, darling—no!' he entreated, as if no one heard. 'Listen to me, my sweetheart! You mustn't do this! I am willing to die—but there is no reason why you should risk your life! Bid me farewell—and leave me!'

Diana smiled into his eyes, and faced the Emperor. When she spoke, her voice was uncommonly deep, for a girl, but clearly audible to the silent spectators of this strange drama.

'Your Majesty,' she said, calmly, 'I, too, am a Christian. Marcellus is my husband. May I go with him?'

There was an inarticulate murmur of protest through the banquet-hall. Caligula nervously fumbled with his fingers and shook his head.

'The daughter of Gallus is brave,' he said, patronizingly. 'But we have no charge against her. Nor have we any wish to punish her. You love your husband—but your love will do him no good—when he is dead.'

'It will, sire, if I go with him,' persisted Diana, 'for then we will never part. And we will live together—always—in a Kingdom of love—and peace.'

'In a Kingdom; eh?' chuckled Caligula, bitterly. 'So—you, too, believe in this nonsense about a Kingdom. Well'—he flicked a negligent gesture—'you may stand aside. You are not being tried. There is no indictment.'

'If it please Your Majesty,' said Diana, boldly, 'may I then provide evidence to warrant a conviction? I have no wish to live another hour in an

Empire so far along on the road to ruin that it would consent to be governed by one who has no interest in the welfare of his people.'

There was a spontaneous gasp from the audience. Caligula, stunned to speechlessness, listened with his mouth open.

'I think I speak the thoughts of everyone present, sire,' went on Diana, firmly. 'These wise men all know that the Empire is headed for destruction—and they know why! As for me—I have another King—and I desire to go with my husband—into that Kingdom!'

Little Boots' face was livid.

'By the gods—you shall!' he screamed. 'Go—both of you—into your Kingdom!'

He jerked a gesture toward the Commander of the Guards. There was an order barked. A bugle sounded a strident blast. The drums rattled a prolonged roll. The tall soldiers, marking time, waited the crisp command. The word was given. Marcellus and Diana, hand in hand, marched in the hollow square, as it moved down the broad aisle toward the imposing archway. Old Gallio, trembling, pushed forward through the crowd, but was detained by friendly hands and warning murmurs.

As the procession of guards, and the condemned, disappeared through the great marble arch, the audience was startled by the harsh, drunken laughter of Little Boots.

Amid loud, hysterical guffaws, he shrieked, 'They are going into a better Kingdom! Ha! Ha! They are going now to meet their King!'

But nobody—except Little Boots—thought it was an occasion for derisive laughter. There was not a smile on any face. They all stood there, grim and silent. And when Little Boots observed that his merriment was not shared, he suddenly grew surly, and without a dismissing word, stumbled toward the steps of the dais where Quintus took his arm. Outside—the metal music blared for Jupiter.

Hand in hand, Diana and Marcellus kept step with the Guards. They were both pale—but smiling. With measured tread the procession marched briskly the length of the corridor, and down the marble steps into the congested plaza. The massed multitude, not knowing what was afoot, but assuming that this was the first contingent of the notables who would join the gaudy parade to the Temple of Jupiter, raised a mighty shout.

Old Marcipor strode forward from the edge of the crowd, tears streaming down his face. Marcellus whispered something into Diana's ear. She smiled—and nodded.

Slipping between two of the guards, she tossed the Robe into the old man's arms.

'For the Big Fisherman!' she said.

THE END